NEW PERSPECTIVES ON

HTML, CSS, and XML

4th Edition

COMPREHENSIVE

NEW PERSPECTIVES ON

HTML, CSS, and XML

4th Edition

COMPREHENSIVE

Patrick Carey
Sasha Vodnik

CENGAGE
Learning®

Australia • Brazil • Japan • Korea • Mexico • Singapore • Spain • United Kingdom • United States

CENGAGE
Learning·

New Perspectives on HTML, CSS, and XML
4th Edition, Comprehensive

Director of Development: Marah Bellegarde

Executive Editor: Donna Gridley

Associate Acquisitions Editor: Amanda Lyons

Product Development Manager: Leigh Hefferon

Senior Product Manager: Kathy Finnegan

Product Manager: Julia Leroux-Lindsey

Editorial Assistant: Melissa Stehler

Brand Manager: Elinor Gregory

Market Development Managers: Kristie Clark,
    Gretchen Swann

Developmental Editor: Pam Conrad

Senior Content Project Manager:
    Jennifer Goguen McGrail

Composition: GEX Publishing Services

Art Director: Marissa Falco

Text Designer: Althea Chen

Cover Designer: GEX Publishing Services

Cover Art: ©altrendo nature/Stockbyte/Getty
    Images

Copyeditor: Suzanne Huizenga

Proofreader: Kathy Orrino

Indexer: Alexandra Nickerson

© 2014 Cengage Learning

ALL RIGHTS RESERVED. No part of this work covered by the copyright herein may be reproduced, transmitted, stored or used in any form or by any means graphic, electronic, or mechanical, including but not limited to photocopying, recording, scanning, digitizing, taping, Web distribution, information networks, or information storage and retrieval systems, except as permitted under Section 107 or 108 of the 1976 United States Copyright Act, without the prior written permission of the publisher.

For product information and technology assistance, contact us at
Cengage Learning Customer & Sales Support, 1-800-354-9706
For permission to use material from this text or product, submit all
requests online at **www.cengage.com/permissions**
Further permissions questions can be emailed to
permissionrequest@cengage.com

Some of the product names and company names used in this book have been used for identification purposes only and may be trademarks or registered trademarks of their respective manufacturers and sellers.

Microsoft and the Office logo are either registered trademarks or trademarks of Microsoft Corporation in the United States and/or other countries. Cengage Learning is an independent entity from the Microsoft Corporation, and not affiliated with Microsoft in any manner.

Disclaimer: Any fictional data related to persons or companies or URLs used throughout this book is intended for instructional purposes only. At the time this book was printed, any such data was fictional and not belonging to any real persons or companies.

Library of Congress Control Number: 2013942735

ISBN-13: 978-1-285-05909-9

ISBN-10: 1-285-05909-3

Cengage Learning
200 First Stamford Place, 4th Floor
Stamford, CT 06902
USA

Cengage Learning is a leading provider of customized learning solutions with office locations around the globe, including Singapore, the United Kingdom, Australia, Mexico, Brazil, and Japan. Locate your local office at:
www.cengage.com/global

Cengage Learning products are represented in Canada by Nelson Education, Ltd.

For your course and learning solutions, visit **www.cengage.com**

Purchase any of our products at your local college store or at our preferred online store **www.cengagebrain.com**

ProSkills Icons © 2014 Cengage Learning.

Printed in the United States of America
1 2 3 4 5 6 7 19 18 17 16 15 14 13

Preface

The New Perspectives Series' critical-thinking, problem-solving approach is the ideal way to prepare students to transcend point-and-click skills and take advantage of all that HTML, CSS, and XML have to offer.

In developing the New Perspectives Series, our goal was to create books that give students the software concepts and practical skills they need to succeed beyond the classroom. We've updated our proven case-based pedagogy with more practical content to make learning skills more meaningful to students. With the New Perspectives Series, students understand *why* they are learning *what* they are learning, and are fully prepared to apply their skills to real-life situations.

About This Book

This book provides complete coverage of HTML, CSS, and XML and includes the following:
- Up-to-date coverage of using HTML5 and CSS3 to create Web sites
- Instruction on creating multimedia Web pages, interactive Web forms, and mobile Web sites
- Creating XML documents and validating them against DTDs or schemas

New for this edition!
- Each session begins with a Visual Overview, which includes colorful, enlarged figures with numerous callouts and key term definitions, giving students a comprehensive preview of the topics covered in the session, as well as a handy study guide.
- New ProSkills boxes provide guidance for how to use the software in real-world, professional situations, and related ProSkills exercises integrate the technology skills students learn with one or more of the following soft skills: decision making, problem solving, teamwork, verbal communication, and written communication.
- Important steps are highlighted in yellow with attached margin notes to help students pay close attention to completing the steps correctly and avoid time-consuming rework.

System Requirements

This book assumes that students have an Internet connection, a text editor, and a current browser that supports HTML5 and CSS3. The following is a list of the most recent versions of the major browsers at the time this text was published: Internet Explorer 10, Firefox 21, Safari 6.0.5, Opera 12.15, and Chrome 27. More recent versions may have come out since the publication of this book. Students should go to the Web browser home page to download the most current version. All browsers interpret HTML and CSS code in slightly different ways. It is highly recommended that students have several different browsers installed on their systems for comparison. Students might also want to run older versions of these browsers to highlight compatibility issues. Students who intend to validate their XML documents in Tutorials 12-14 should have access to an XML validating parser such as Exchanger XML Editor or to an online validation service. The screenshots in this book were produced using Internet Explorer 9.0 (Tutorials 1-10) or Internet Explorer 10.0 (Tutorials 11-14) running on Windows 7 Professional (64-bit), unless otherwise noted. If students are using different browsers or operating systems, their screens will vary slightly from those shown in the book; this should not present any problems in completing the tutorials.

www.cengage.com/series/newperspectives

> "I love this text because it provides detailed instructions and real-world application examples. It is ideal for classroom and online instruction. At the end of the term my students comment on how much they've learned and put to use outside the classroom."
>
> —Bernice Howard
> St. Johns River Community
> College

> *"New Perspectives texts provide up-to-date, real-world application of content, making book selection easy. The step-by-step, hands-on approach teaches students concepts they can apply immediately."*
>
> —John Taylor
> Southeastern Technical
> College

VISUAL OVERVIEW

PROSKILLS

KEY STEP

INSIGHT

TIP

REVIEW

APPLY

REFERENCE

GLOSSARY/INDEX

The New Perspectives Approach

Context

Each tutorial begins with a problem presented in a "real-world" case that is meaningful to students. The case sets the scene to help students understand what they will do in the tutorial.

Hands-on Approach

Each tutorial is divided into manageable sessions that combine reading and hands-on, step-by-step work. Colorful screenshots help guide students through the steps. **Trouble?** tips anticipate common mistakes or problems to help students stay on track and continue with the tutorial.

Visual Overviews

New for this edition! Each session begins with a Visual Overview, a new two-page spread that includes colorful, enlarged figures with numerous callouts and key term definitions, giving students a comprehensive preview of the topics covered in the session, as well as a handy study guide.

ProSkills Boxes and Exercises

New for this edition! ProSkills boxes provide guidance for how to use the software in real-world, professional situations, and related ProSkills exercises integrate the technology skills students learn with one or more of the following soft skills: decision making, problem solving, teamwork, verbal communication, and written communication.

Key Steps

New for this edition! Important steps are highlighted in yellow with attached margin notes to help students pay close attention to completing the steps correctly and avoid time-consuming rework.

InSight Boxes

InSight boxes offer expert advice and best practices to help students achieve a deeper understanding of the concepts behind the software features and skills.

Margin Tips

Margin Tips provide helpful hints and shortcuts for more efficient use of the software. The Tips appear in the margin at key points throughout each tutorial, giving students extra information when and where they need it.

Assessment

Retention is a key component to learning. At the end of each session, a series of Quick Check questions helps students test their understanding of the material before moving on. Engaging end-of-tutorial Review Assignments and Case Problems have always been a hallmark feature of the New Perspectives Series. Colorful bars and brief descriptions accompany the exercises, making it easy to understand both the goal and level of challenge a particular assignment holds.

Reference

Within each tutorial, Reference boxes appear before a set of steps to provide a succinct summary and preview of how to perform a task. In addition, each book includes a combination Glossary/Index to promote easy reference of material.

www.cengage.com/series/newperspectives

Our Complete System of Instruction

Coverage To Meet Your Needs

Whether you're looking for just a small amount of coverage or enough to fill a semester-long class, we can provide you with a textbook that meets your needs.

- Brief books typically cover the essential skills in just 2 to 4 tutorials.
- Introductory books build and expand on those skills and contain an average of 5 to 8 tutorials.
- Comprehensive books are great for a full-semester class, and contain 9 to 12+ tutorials.

So if the book you're holding does not provide the right amount of coverage for you, there's probably another offering available. Go to our Web site or contact your Cengage Learning sales representative to find out what else we offer.

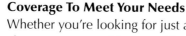

CourseCasts – Learning on the Go. Always available…always relevant.

Want to keep up with the latest technology trends relevant to you? Visit http://coursecasts.course.com to find a library of weekly updated podcasts, CourseCasts, and download them to your mp3 player.

Ken Baldauf, host of CourseCasts, is a faculty member of the Florida State University Computer Science Department where he is responsible for teaching technology classes to thousands of FSU students each year. Ken is an expert in the latest technology trends; he gathers and sorts through the most pertinent news and information for CourseCasts so your students can spend their time enjoying technology, rather than trying to figure it out. Open or close your lecture with a discussion based on the latest CourseCast.

Visit us at http://coursecasts.course.com to learn on the go!

Instructor Resources

We offer more than just a book. We have all the tools you need to enhance your lectures, check students' work, and generate exams in a new, easier-to-use and completely revised package. This book's Instructor's Manual, ExamView testbank, PowerPoint presentations, data files, solution files, figure files, and a sample syllabus are all available on a single CD-ROM or for downloading at http://www.cengage.com.

SAM: Skills Assessment Manager

Get your students workplace-ready with SAM, the premier proficiency-based assessment and training solution for Microsoft Office! SAM's active, hands-on environment helps students master computer skills and concepts that are essential to academic and career success.

Skill-based assessments, interactive trainings, business-centric projects, and comprehensive remediation engage students in mastering the latest Microsoft Office programs on their own, allowing instructors to spend class time teaching. SAM's efficient course setup and robust grading features provide faculty with consistency across sections. Fully interactive MindTap Readers integrate market-leading Cengage Learning content with SAM, creating a comprehensive online student learning environment.

Acknowledgments

I would like to thank the people who worked so hard to make this book possible. Special thanks to my developmental editor, Sasha Vodnik, for his hard work and valuable insights, and to my Product Manager, Kathy Finnegan, who has worked tirelessly in overseeing this project and made my task so much easier with her enthusiasm and good humor. Other people at Course Technology who deserve credit are Marie Lee, Executive Editor; Julia Leroux-Lindsey, Associate Product Manager; Jacqueline Lacaire, Editorial Assistant; Jennifer Goguen McGrail, Senior Content Project Manager; Christian Kunciw, Manuscript Quality Assurance (MQA) Supervisor; and John Freitas, Serge Palladino, Susan Pedicini, Danielle Shaw, Marianne Snow, Ashlee Welz Smith, and Susan Whalen, MQA testers.

Feedback is an important part of writing any book, and thanks go to the following reviewers for their helpful ideas and comments: Bernice Howard, St. Johns River Community College; Lisa Macon, Valencia Community College; Sharon Scollard, Mohawk College; Luke Sui, Daytona State College; and John Taylor, Southeastern Technical College.

I want to thank my wife Joan and my six children for their love, encouragement and patience in putting up with a sometimes distracted husband and father. This book is dedicated to the memory of Mac Mendelsohn, who generously gave me my chance in this business and whose constant encouragement in the early years inspired me and taught me so much.
– Patrick Carey

Many thanks to everyone who helped in this revision. Pam Conrad, my sharp-eyed developmental editor, suggested improvements and asked a lot of important questions that helped me immeasurably in tightening up the material. The good advice of Kathy Finnegan, my product manager, kept me focused on the important aspects of the revision process, and she sweated a lot of the small stuff so I didn't have to. I'm also grateful to Donna Gridley, the series executive editor, for keeping the faith during the evolution of this revision. Jen Goguen McGrail, Kelly Morrison, and the staff at GEX Publishing Services made it all look amazing. And MQA testers Serge Palladino, Danielle Shaw, and Susan Whalen read everything through, completed all the steps, and gave smart feedback that removed many roadblocks for future users. Finally, thanks to my husband, Jason Bucy, for encouraging me to balance diving deep into XML with stepping away from the computer, getting outside, and enjoying the world with him.
– Sasha Vodnik

BRIEF CONTENTS

TABLE OF CONTENTS

HTML LEVEL II TUTORIALS

HTML LEVEL III TUTORIALS

XML LEVEL IV TUTORIALS

HTML

OBJECTIVES

Session 1.1
- Explore the history of the Internet, the Web, and HTML
- Compare the different versions of HTML
- Study the syntax of HTML tags and attributes
- Define a Web page head, body, and title
- Work with the HTML5 structural elements

Session 1.2
- Mark page headings, paragraphs, block quotes, and addresses
- Create unordered and ordered lists
- Apply an external style sheet to a Web page
- Run a JavaScript program
- Mark text-level elements including strong and emphasized text
- Insert inline images and line breaks
- Insert special characters from extended character sets

Getting Started with HTML5

Creating a Product Page for a Small Business

Case | *The J-Prop Shop*

Dave Vinet owns a small business called the J-Prop Shop that builds and sells circus props and equipment. Dave is looking to expand his business and his visibility by upgrading his Web site. Dave has already written the text for the Web site's home page and has generated some of the graphic images for it. He has come to you for help in designing a Web page and writing the code. Dave hopes to build on his Web page in the future as his business expands, so he would like you to write code that takes advantage of the latest Web standards, including HTML5. Your job will be to create a sample home page that Dave can use as a foundation for his new Web site.

STARTING DATA FILES

tutorial.01 →

tutorial
jpslogo.png
jpsstyles.css
modernizr-1.5.js

review
basiclogo.png
basicstick.png
basicstyles.css
stick.txt
modernizr-1.5.js

case1
mhlogo.jpg
mhstyles.css
mhtxt.htm
modernizr-1.5.js

case2
macbeth.jpg
macbethtxt.htm
macstyles.css
modernizr-1.5.js

case3
dessertstyles.css
dessertweb.jpg
modernizr-1.5.js
torte.jpg
tortetxt.htm

case4
logo.jpg
smith.jpg
smith.txt

demo
cengage.jpg
demo.gif
demo_characters.htm
demo_html.htm
demo2.gif
modernizr-1.5.js

SESSION 1.1 VISUAL OVERVIEW

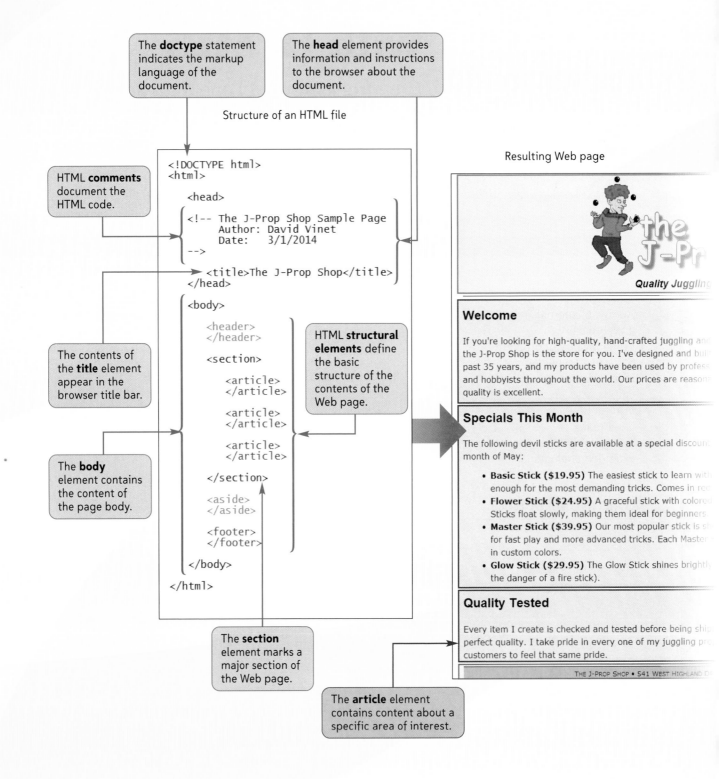

The **doctype** statement indicates the markup language of the document.

The **head** element provides information and instructions to the browser about the document.

Structure of an HTML file

Resulting Web page

HTML **comments** document the HTML code.

The contents of the **title** element appear in the browser title bar.

The **body** element contains the content of the page body.

HTML **structural elements** define the basic structure of the contents of the Web page.

The **section** element marks a major section of the Web page.

The **article** element contains content about a specific area of interest.

THE STRUCTURE OF AN HTML5 DOCUMENT

The **head**er element contains an introduction to the page.

Markup Tags

Document elements are marked using **tags**.

```
<h2>Welcome</h2>
<p>If you're looking for high-
   juggling and circus product
   the store for you. I've des
   for the past 35 years, and
   used by professional entert
   throughout the world. Our p
   our quality is excellent.
</p>
```

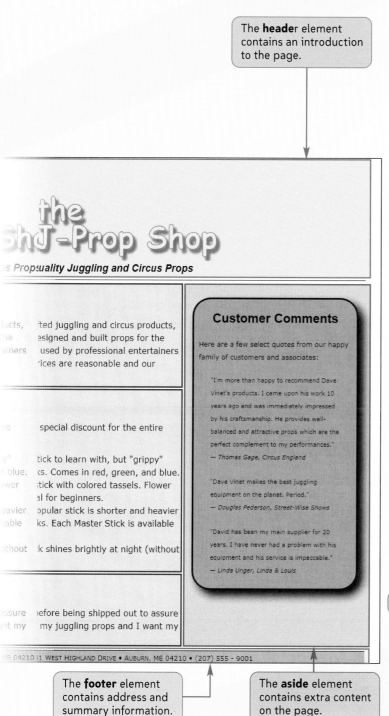

Resulting Web page

Welcome

If you're looking for high-quali
the J-Prop Shop is the store fo
past 35 years, and my produc
and hobbyists throughout the
quality is excellent.

Two-sided tags mark elements that contain textual content or other elements

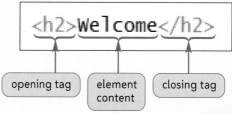

opening tag   element content   closing tag

One-sided tags mark elements that contain no textual content

```
<br />
```

The **footer** element contains address and summary information.

The **aside** element contains extra content on the page.

Exploring the History of the World Wide Web

Before you start creating a Web page for Dave, it will be helpful to first look at the history of the Web and the development of HTML. You'll start by reviewing networks and learn how they led to the creation of the World Wide Web.

Networks

A **network** is a structure that allows devices known as **nodes** or **hosts** to be linked together to share information and services. Hosts can include devices such as computers, printers, and scanners because they are all capable of sending and receiving data electronically over a network.

A host that provides information or a service is called a **server**. For example, a **print server** is a network host that provides printing services to the network; a **file server** is a host that provides storage space for saving and retrieving files. A computer or other device that receives a service is called a **client**. Networks can follow several different designs based on the relationship between the servers and the clients. One of the most commonly used designs is the **client-server network** in which several clients access information provided by one or more servers. You might be using such a network to access your data files for this tutorial.

Networks can also be classified based on the range they cover. A network confined to a small geographic area, such as within a building or department, is referred to as a **local area network** or **LAN**. A network that covers a wider area, such as several buildings or cities, is called a **wide area network** or **WAN**. Wide area networks typically consist of two or more interconnected local area networks.

The largest WAN in existence is the **Internet**, which incorporates an almost uncountable number of networks and hosts involving computers, mobile phones, PDAs, MP3 players, gaming systems, and television stations. Like many business owners, Dave uses the Internet to advertise his business to potential customers.

Locating Information on a Network

One of the biggest obstacles to effectively using the Internet is the network's sheer scope and size. Most of the early Internet tools required users to master a bewildering array of terms, acronyms, and commands. Because network users had to be well versed in computers and network technology, Internet use was limited to universities and the government. To make the Internet accessible to the general public, it needed to be easier to use. The solution turned out to be the World Wide Web.

The foundations for the **World Wide Web**, or the **Web** for short, were laid in 1989 by Timothy Berners-Lee and other researchers at the CERN nuclear research facility near Geneva, Switzerland. They needed an information system that would make it easy for their researchers to locate and share data on the CERN network with minimal training and support. To meet this need, they developed a system of hypertext documents that enabled users to easily navigate from one topic to another. **Hypertext** is a method of organization in which data sources are interconnected through a series of **links** or hyperlinks that users can activate to jump from one piece of information to another. Hypertext is ideally suited for the Internet because end users do not need to know where a particular document, information source, or service is located—they need to know only how to activate the link. The fact that the Internet and the World Wide Web are synonymous in many users' minds is a testament to the success of the hypertext approach.

Web Pages and Web Servers

Each document on the World Wide Web is referred to as a **Web page** and is stored on a **Web server**. When you access a Web page, a **Web browser** retrieves the page from its Web server and renders it on your computer or other device.

The earliest browsers, known as **text-based browsers**, were limited to displaying only text. Today's browsers are capable of handling text, images, audio, video, and interactive programs. In the early days of the Internet, Web browsing was limited to computers. Now browsers are installed on devices such as mobile phones, cars, handheld media devices, and gaming systems, to name only a few. How does a Web page work with so many combinations of browsers and devices? To understand, you need to look at how Web pages are created.

Introducing HTML

Web pages are text files written in **Hypertext Markup Language** (**HTML**). We've already discussed hypertext, but what is a markup language? A **markup language** is a language that describes the content and structure of a document by identifying, or **tagging**, different elements in the document. For example, this tutorial contains paragraphs, figure captions, page headings, and so forth; each of these items could be tagged as a distinct element using a markup language. Thus, HTML is a markup language that supports both hypertext and the tagging of distinct document elements.

The History of HTML

HTML evolved as the Web itself evolved. Thus, in order to fully appreciate the nuances of HTML, it's a good idea to review the language's history. The first popular markup language was the **Standard Generalized Markup Language** (**SGML**). Introduced in the 1980s, SGML is device- and system-independent, meaning that it can be applied to almost any type of document stored in almost any format. While powerful, SGML is also quite complex; for this reason, SGML is limited to those organizations that can afford the cost and overhead of maintaining complex SGML environments. However, SGML can also be used to create other markup languages that are tailored to specific tasks and are simpler to use and maintain. HTML is one of the languages created with SGML.

In the early years after HTML was created, no single organization was responsible for the language. Web developers were free to define and modify HTML in whatever ways they thought best. This led to incompatibilities between the various browsers and, as a result, Web page authors faced the challenge of writing HTML code that would satisfy different browsers and browser versions.

Ultimately, a group of Web designers and programmers called the **World Wide Web Consortium**, or the **W3C**, created a set of standards or specifications for all browser manufacturers to follow. The W3C has no enforcement power; but because using a uniform language is in everyone's best interest, the W3C's recommendations are usually followed, though not always immediately. For more information on the W3C and the services it offers, see its Web site at *www.w3.org*.

As HTML evolves, earlier features of the language are often **deprecated**, or phased out. While deprecated features might not be part of the current specification for HTML, that doesn't mean that you won't encounter them in your work—indeed, if you are maintaining older Web sites, you will often need to be able to interpret code from earlier versions of HTML.

XHTML and the Development of HTML5

Near the end of the 1990s, the W3C released the final specifications for the 4th version of HTML, called HTML 4, and began charting a course for the next version. The path chosen by the W3C was to reformulate HTML in terms of XML. **XML (Extensible Markup Language)** is a compact offshoot of SGML and is used to define new markup languages, known as **XML vocabularies**. A document based on an XML vocabulary is forced to obey specific rules for content and structure to avoid being rejected as invalid. By contrast, HTML allows for a wide variety in syntax between one HTML document and another. Another important aspect of XML is that several XML vocabularies can be combined within a single document, making it easier to extend XML into different areas of application.

The W3C developed an XML vocabulary that was a stricter version of HTML4, known as **XHTML (Extensible Hypertext Markup Language)**. XHTML was designed to confront some of the problems associated with the various competing versions of HTML and to better integrate HTML with other markup languages. Because XHTML was an XML version of HTML, most of what Web designers used with HTML could be applied to XHTML with only a few modifications, and many tools and features associated with XML could be easily applied to XHTML.

By 2002, the W3C had released the specifications for XHTML 1.1. This version was intended to be only a minor upgrade on the way to **XHTML 2.0**, which would contain a set of XML vocabularies moving HTML into the future with robust support for multimedia, social networking, interactive Web forms, and other features needed by Web designers. One problem was that XHTML 2.0 would not be backward compatible with earlier versions of HTML and thus older Web sites could not be easily integrated with the proposed new standard.

Web designers rebelled at this development. In 2004, Ian Hickson, who was working for Opera Software at the time, proposed a different path. Hickson's proposal would have allowed for the creation of new Web applications while still maintaining backward compatibility with HTML 4. He argued that HTML was whatever the browser market determined it to be, and that trying to enforce a new specification that did not accommodate the needs and limitations of the market was a fruitless exercise.

Hickson's proposal was rejected by the W3C and, in response, a new group of Web designers and browser manufacturers formed the **Web Hypertext Application Technology Working Group (WHATWG)** with the mission to develop a rival version to XHTML 2.0, called **HTML5**. For several years, it was unclear which specification would represent the future of the Web; but by 2006, work on XHTML 2.0 had completely stalled. The W3C issued a new charter for an HTML Working Group to develop HTML5 as the next HTML specification. Work on XHTML 2.0 was halted in 2009, leaving HTML5 as the de facto standard for the next generation of HTML.

Figure 1-1   **Versions of HTML**

Version	Date	Description
HTML1.0	1989	The first public version of HTML.
HTML 2.0	1995	Added interactive elements including Web forms.
HTML 3.0	1996	A proposed replacement for HTML 2.0 that was never widely adopted.
HTML 3.2	1997	Included additional support for Web tables and expanded the options for interactive form elements and a scripting language.
HTML 4.01	1999	Added support for style sheets to give Web designers greater control over page layout and appearance, and provided support for multi-media elements such as audio and video. Current browsers support almost all of HTML 4.01.
XHTML 1.0	2001	A reformulation of HTML 4.01 in the XML language in order to provide enforceable standards for HTML content and to allow HTML to interact with other XML languages.
XHTML 1.1	2002	A minor update to XHTML 1.0 that allows for modularity and simplifies writing extensions to the language.
XHTML 2.0	discontinued	The follow-up version to XHTML 1.1 designed to fix some of the problems inherent in HTML 4.01 syntax. Work on this version was discontinued in 2009 due to lack of browser support.
HTML 5.0	In development	An update to HTML 4.01 that provides support for a variety of new features including semantic page elements, column layout, form validation, offline storage, and enhanced multimedia.
XHTML 5.0	In development	A version of HTML 5.0 written under the XML language; unlike XHTML 2.0, XHTML 5.0 will be backward compatible with XHTML 1.1.

Figure 1-1 summarizes the various versions of HTML that have been developed over the past 20 years. You may be wondering how on Earth anything can be written with so many versions of HTML to consider. At the time of this writing, you can write your code following the standards of HTML 4.01 or XHTML 1.1 and be assured that it will be supported by all major browsers. Many features of HTML5 are also being rapidly adopted by the market even as work continues on developing the language. HTML5 is the future, but the challenges for Web designers today lie in knowing which parts of HTML5 are supported by which browsers, and in developing strategies for supporting older browsers even as HTML5 is being implemented.

In this book you'll use HTML5 code for those features that have already achieved support among current browsers, but you'll also learn the standards used for HTML 4.01 and XHTML 1.1 and practice writing code that will support both current and older browsers.

HTML and Style Sheets

HTML marks the different parts of a document, but it does not indicate how document content should be displayed by browsers. This is a necessary facet of HTML because a Web page author has no control over what device will actually view his or her document. An end user might be using a large-screen television monitor, a mobile phone, or even a device that renders Web pages in Braille or in aural speech.

For this reason, the exact appearance of each page element is described in a separate document known as a **style sheet**. Each browser has its own **internal style sheet** that specifies the appearance of different HTML elements. For example, content that is marked as containing the text of an address is rendered by most Web browsers in italic, while major headings usually appear in large bold-faced fonts.

A Web page author can also create a style sheet that takes precedence over the internal style sheets of browsers. In addition, an author can create multiple style sheets for different output devices: one for rendering a page on a computer screen, another for printed output, and another for rendering the page aurally. In each case, the markup of the document content is the same, but the presentation is determined by the style sheet.

Tools for Creating HTML Documents

Because HTML documents are simple text files, you can create them using nothing more than a basic text editor such as Windows Notepad. Other software programs that enable you to create documents in different formats, such as Microsoft Word or Adobe Acrobat, include tools to convert their documents into HTML for quick and easy publishing on the Web.

If you intend to create a large Web site incorporating dozens of Web pages, you should invest in specialized Web publishing software to manage all of the code and extended features of your site. Programs such as Adobe Dreamweaver and Microsoft Expression Web are among the leaders in this field.

Since this book is focused on the HTML language itself and not how to work with different software programs, you'll need nothing more than a text editor and a Web browser to complete the assignments that follow.

Entering Elements and Attributes

Now that you've had a chance to review a brief history of the Web and the role of HTML in its development, you are ready to write your first HTML document for the J-Prop Shop. You'll start by studying the rules for entering HTML code.

Introducing HTML Tags

An HTML document is composed of **elements** that represent distinct items in the Web page, such as a paragraph, the page heading, or even the entire body of the page itself. Each element is marked within the HTML file by one or more **tags**. If an element contains text or another element, it is marked using a **two-sided tag set** in which an **opening tag** and a **closing tag** enclose the element content. The syntax of a two-sided tag set is

```
<element>content</element>
```

where *element* is the name of the element and *content* is the content of the element. For example, the following code marks a paragraph using a two-sided tag set:

```
<p>Welcome to the J-Prop Shop.</p>
```

In this example, the `<p>` tag marks the beginning of the paragraph, the text *Welcome to the J-Prop Shop.* is the content of the paragraph element, and the `</p>` tag marks the end of the paragraph. Elements can also contain other elements. For example, in the code

```
<p>Welcome to <em>Dave's Devil Sticks</em>.</p>
```

the paragraph tags enclose both the text of the paragraph and the tag set `<em> ... </em>`, which is used to mark content that should be treated by the browser as emphasized text. Note that the `<em>` tag set must be completely enclosed, or **nested**, within the `<p>` tags. It's improper to have tags overlap as in the following code sample:

```
<p>Welcome to <em>Dave's Devil Sticks.</p></em>
```

In this example, the closing `</em>` tag is placed *after* the closing `</p>` tag, which is improper because one element must be completely contained within another.

An element that does not enclose content is an **empty element** and it is marked with a **one-sided tag** using the syntax

```
<element />
```

where `element` is the name of the element. For example, you can mark a line break using the `br` element, which has the following syntax:

```
<br />
```

Since empty elements don't contain content, they're often employed to send directives to browsers regarding how a page should be rendered. A browser encountering the `br` element would insert a line break, causing the text of the next element in the document to be placed on a new line.

Specifying an Element Attribute

In addition to content, elements also support **attributes** that specify the use, the behavior, and in some cases the appearance of an element. Attribute values don't appear in the rendered Web page; rather, they provide information to the browser about the properties of the element.

To add an attribute to an element, you insert the attribute within the element's opening tag. For a two-sided tag, the syntax is:

```
<element attribute1="value1" attribute2="value2" ...>
   content
</element>
```

Attributes are added to one-sided tags in the same way:

```
<element attribute1="value1" attribute2="value2" ... />
```

In these examples, `attribute1`, `attribute2`, etc. are the names of attributes associated with the element, and `value1`, `value2`, etc. are the values of those attributes. For instance, the following code adds the `id` attribute to a paragraph marked with the `p` element:

```
<p id="opening">Welcome to the J-Prop Shop.</p>
```

A browser interpreting this code would recognize that the text *Welcome to the J-Prop Shop.* should be treated as a paragraph and given the id value *opening*.

> **TIP**
>
> Attributes can be listed in any order, but they must be separated from one another by a blank space and enclosed within single or double quotation marks.

REFERENCE

Adding an Attribute to an Element

• To add an element attribute, use the format

```
<element attribute1="value1"
        attribute2="value2" ...>content</element>
```

where `attribute1`, `attribute2`, etc. are the names of attributes associated with the element, and `value1`, `value2`, etc. are the values of those attributes.

White Space and HTML

Since an HTML file is a text file, it's composed of text characters and white space. **White space** includes the blank spaces, tabs, and line breaks found within the file. As far as a browser is concerned, there is no difference between a blank space, a tab, or a line break. Browsers also ignore consecutive occurrences of white space, collapsing extra white space characters into a single blank space. Thus, browsers treat the following paragraph elements in the same way:

```
<p>Welcome to the J-Prop Shop.</p>


<p>
    Welcome to the J-Prop Shop.
</p>


<p>Welcome
to the J-Prop Shop.</p>


<p>Welcome    to    the    J-Prop    Shop.</p>
```

Because HTML handles white space in this way, you can make your code easier for others to read by indenting lines and adding extra blank lines to separate one tag from another in the file.

Exploring the Structure of an HTML Document

The structure of an HTML document consists of different elements nested within each other in a hierarchy of elements. The top element in that hierarchy is the **html element**, which contains all of the other elements within an HTML file. Directly below the **html** element in the hierarchy are the **head** and **body** elements. The **head element** contains general information about the document—for example, the document's title, or a list of keywords that would aid search engines in directing interested users to the page. The **body element** contains all of the content that appears in the rendered Web page. Thus, the general structure of an HTML file is

```
<html>
    <head>
        head content
    </head>
    <body>
        body content
    </body>
</html>
```

where *head content* and *body content* are the content you want to place within the document's head and body. Note that the `body` element is always placed after the `head` element.

The Document Type Declaration

Prior to the opening `<html>` tag, many HTML files also include a **Document Type Declaration**, or **doctype**, to indicate the type of markup language used in the document. The doctype is used by **validators**, which are programs that examine document code to ensure that it meets all the syntax requirements of the specified language. All XHTML files require a doctype because those documents must be validated against a set of standards.

Most current browsers also use the presence or absence of a doctype to decide which mode they should use to render a document in a process known as **doctype switching**. If a doctype is included, such browsers render the Web page in **standards mode**, in accordance with the most current specifications of the language. If no doctype is provided, these browsers render the document in **quirks mode** based on practices followed in the 1990s. The differences can be striking. Figure 1-2 shows an example of two documents rendered by Internet Explorer under standards mode and quirks mode. The only difference in the code between these two documents is the presence or absence of a doctype, but the browser renders the two documents very differently.

Figure 1-2   A Web page rendered in standards mode and quirks mode

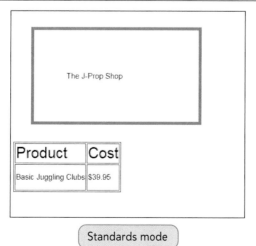

Standards mode

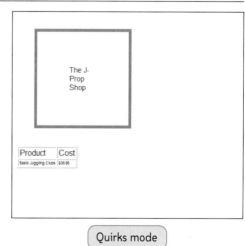

Quirks mode

Different HTML versions have different doctypes. The doctype for HTML 4.01 is:

```
<!DOCTYPE HTML PUBLIC "-//W3C//DTD HTML 4.01/EN"
    "http://www.w3.org/TR/html4/strict.dtd">
```

The doctype for XHTML is:

```
<!DOCTYPE html PUBLIC "-//W3C//DTD XHTML 1.0 Strict//EN"
  "http://www.w3.org/TR/xhtml1/DTD/xhtml1-strict.dtd">
```

Finally, the doctype for HTML5 is much simpler than what was required for HTML 4.01 or XHTML:

```
<!DOCTYPE html>
```

HTML5 documents should always be opened in standards mode because they are based on the latest specifications for the HTML language.

You can learn more about standards mode and quirks mode by searching the Web for examples of the differences between the two modes.

Creating the Initial Document

Now that you've seen the basic structure of an HTML document, you are ready to begin creating the sample Web page for Dave's Web site.

TIP

Unless you are working with a legacy page that absolutely needs to be compatible with old browsers from the 1990s, you should always include a doctype and put your browser in standards mode.

REFERENCE

Creating the Basic Structure of an HTML Document

Enter the HTML tags

```
doctype
<html>
    <head>
        head content
    </head>
    <body>
        body content
    </body>
</html>
```

where *doctype* is the Document Type Declaration, and *head content* and *body content* are the content of the document's head and body.

You can start creating Dave's Web page using a basic editor such as Windows Notepad. Since Dave wants his document to be based on HTML5, you'll use the HTML5 doctype in your file.

To create the basic structure of an HTML document:

▸ **1.** Start your text editor, opening a blank text document.

Trouble? If you don't know how to start or use your text editor, ask your instructor or technical support person for help. Note that some editors do not save files in text file format by default, so check your editor's documentation to ensure that you are creating a basic text document.

Make sure you include the exclamation point (!) within the doctype; otherwise, browsers will not recognize the doctype.

2. Type the following lines of code in your document. Press the **Enter** key after each line. Press the **Enter** key twice for a blank line between lines of code. See Figure 1-3.

```
<!DOCTYPE html>
<html>

    <head>
    </head>

    <body>
    </body>

</html>
```

Figure 1-3	Basic structure of an HTML file

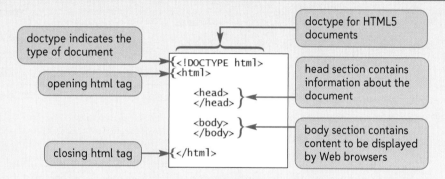

doctype indicates the type of document

opening html tag

closing html tag

```
<!DOCTYPE html>
<html>

    <head>
    </head>

    <body>
    </body>

</html>
```

doctype for HTML5 documents

head section contains information about the document

body section contains content to be displayed by Web browsers

TIP

To make it easier to link to your Web pages, follow the Internet convention of naming HTML files and folders using only lowercase letters with no spaces.

3. Save the file as **jprop.htm** in the tutorial.01\tutorial folder included with your Data Files.

Trouble? If you are using the Windows Notepad text editor to create your HTML file, make sure you don't save the file with the extension *.txt*, which is the default file extension for Notepad. Instead, save the file with the file extension *.htm* or *.html*. Using the incorrect file extension might make the file unreadable to Web browsers, which require file extensions of *.htm* or *.html*.

Now that you've entered the basic structure of your HTML file, you can start entering the content of the head element.

Marking the Head Element

In general, the head element is where you provide browsers with information about your document. This can include the page's title, the location of any style sheets used with the document, the location of any programs that browsers should run when they load the page, and information for use by search engines to aid users in locating the Web site.

Defining the Page Title

The first element you'll add to the head of Dave's document is the title element, which has the syntax

```
<title>document title</title>
```

where *document title* is the text of the document title. The document title is not displayed within the page, but is usually displayed in a browser's title bar or on a browser tab. The document title is also used by search engines like Google or Yahoo! when compiling an index of search results.

To add a title to your Web page:

1. Click at the end of the opening `<head>` tag, and then press the **Enter** key to insert a new line in your text editor.

2. Press the **Spacebar** several times to indent the new line of code, and then type `<title>The J-Prop Shop</title>` as shown in Figure 1-4.

Figure 1-4 | Specifying the page title

```
<!DOCTYPE html>
<html>

    <head>
        <title>The J-Prop Shop</title>
    </head>

    <body>
    </body>

</html>
```

text will appear in browser title bar or on browser tab

Adding Comments

As you write your HTML file, you can add notes or comments about your code. These comments might include the name of the document's author and the date the document was created. Such notes are not intended to be displayed by browsers, but are instead used to help explain your code to yourself and others. To add notes or comments, insert a **comment tag** using the syntax

```
<!-- comment -->
```

where *comment* is the text of the comment or note. For example, the following code inserts a comment describing the page you'll create for Dave's business:

```
<!-- Sample page for the J-Prop Shop -->
```

A comment can also be spread out over several lines as follows:

```
<!-- Sample page for the J-Prop Shop.
    Created by Dave Vinet -->
```

Because they are ignored by the browser, comments can be added anywhere within the `html` element.

REFERENCE

Adding an HTML Comment

To insert an HTML comment anywhere within your document, enter

```
<!-- comment -->
```

where *comment* is the text of the HTML comment.

You'll add a comment to the *jprop.htm* file, identifying the author and purpose of this document.

To add a comment to the document head:

▶ **1.** Click at the end of the opening `<head>` tag, and then press the **Enter** key to insert a new line in your text editor directly above the opening `<title>` tag.

▶ **2.** Type the following lines of code as shown in Figure 1-5:

```
<!-- The J-Prop Shop Sample Page
     Author: your name
     Date:   the date
-->
```

where *your name* is your name and *the date* is the current date.

Figure 1-5   Adding comments to the HTML file

```
<!DOCTYPE html>
<html>

    <head>
        <!-- The J-Prop Shop Sample Page
             Author: David Vinet
             Date:   3/1/2014
        -->
        <title>The J-Prop Shop</title>
    </head>

    <body>
    </body>

</html>
```

multi-line comment describing the document

Displaying an HTML File

As you continue modifying the HTML code, you should occasionally view the page with your Web browser to verify that you have not introduced any errors. You might even want to view the results using different browsers to check for compatibility. In this book, Web pages are displayed using the Windows Internet Explorer 9 browser. Be aware that if you are using a different browser or a different operating system, you might see slight differences in the layout and appearance of the page.

To view Dave's Web page:

▶ **1.** Save your changes to the **jprop.htm** file.

▶ **2.** Start your Web browser. You do not need to be connected to the Internet to view local files stored on your computer.

Trouble? If you start your browser and are not connected to the Internet, you might get a warning message. Click the OK button to ignore the message and continue.

▶ **3.** After your browser loads its home page, open the **jprop.htm** file from the tutorial.01\tutorial folder.

Trouble? If you're not sure how to open a local file with your browser, check for an Open or Open File command under the browser's File menu. If you are still having problems accessing the *jprop.htm* file, talk to your instructor or technical resource person.

Your browser displays the Web page shown in Figure 1-6. Note that in this case, the page title appears in the browser tab; in other cases, it will appear in the browser's title bar. The page itself is empty because you have not yet added any content to the body element.

Figure 1-6 **Viewing the initial HTML file in a Web browser**

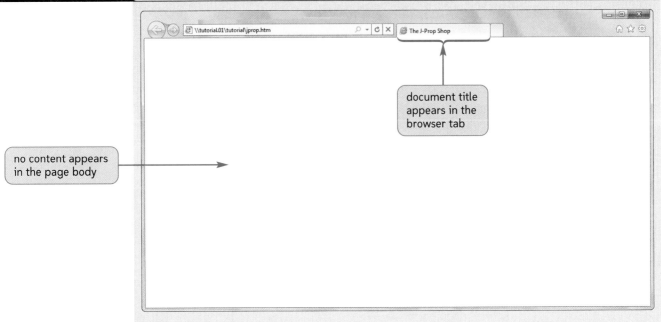

document title appears in the browser tab

no content appears in the page body

INSIGHT

Converting an HTML Document into XHTML

There is considerable overlap between HTML and XHTML. You can quickly change an HTML document into an XHTML document just by altering the first three lines of code. To convert an HTML file into an XHTML file, replace the doctype and the opening `<html>` tag with the following:

```
<?xml version="1.0" encoding="UTF-8" standalone="no" ?>
<!DOCTYPE html PUBLIC "-//W3C//DTD XHTML 1.0 Strict//EN"
    "http://www.w3.org/TR/xhtml1/DTD/xhtml1-strict.dtd">
<html xmlns="http://www.w3.org/1999/xhtml">
```

Since XHTML is an XML vocabulary, the first line notifies browsers that the document is an XML file. The version number—1.0—tells the browser that the file is written in XML 1.0. The second line provides the doctype for an XHTML document written under a strict interpretation of XHTML syntax. The third line of the file contains the opening `<html>` tag. In XHTML, the `<html>` tag must include what is known as a **namespace declaration** indicating that any markup tags in the document should, by default, be considered part of the XHTML language. Because XML documents can contain a mixture of several different vocabularies, the namespace declaration is necessary to specify the default language of the document. With these three lines in place, browsers will recognize the file as an XHTML document.

Defining the Structure of the Page Body

Now that you've marked the document head and inserted a page title, you'll turn to the contents of the body of the Web page. It's always a good idea to plan your Web page before you start coding it. You can do this by drawing a sketch or by creating a sample document within a word processor. Your preparatory work can weed out textual errors or point to potential problems in your page layout. In this case, Dave has already drawn up a flyer that he's passed out at juggling and circus conventions. Figure 1-7 shows the handout, which provides information about Dave's company and his products.

Figure 1-7 Dave's flyer

Quality Juggling and Circus Props

Welcome

If you're looking for high-quality, hand-crafted juggling and circus products, the J-Prop Shop is the store for you. I've designed and built props for the past 35 years, and my products have been used by professional entertainers and hobbyists throughout the world. Our prices are reasonable and our quality is excellent.

Specials This Month

The following devil sticks are available at a special discount for the entire month of May:

- **Basic Stick ($19.95)** The easiest stick to learn with, but "grippy" enough for the most demanding tricks. Comes in red, green, and blue.
- **Flower Stick ($24.95)** A graceful stick with colored tassels. Flower Sticks float slowly, making them ideal for beginners.
- **Master Stick ($39.95)** Our most popular stick is shorter and heavier for fast play and more advanced tricks. Each Master Stick is available in custom colors.
- **Glow Stick ($29.95)** The Glow Stick shines brightly at night (without the danger of a fire stick).

Quality Tested

Every item I create is checked and tested before being shipped out to assure perfect quality. I take pride in every one of my juggling props and I want my customers to feel that same pride.

Customer Comments

Here are a few select quotes from our happy family of customers and associates:

"I'm more than happy to recommend Dave Vinet's products. I came upon his work 10 years ago and was immediately impressed by his craftsmanship. He provides well-balanced and attractive props which are the perfect complement to my performances."
— *Thomas Gage, Circus England*

"Dave Vinet makes the best juggling equipment on the planet. Period."
— *Douglas Pederson, Street-Wise Shows*

"David has been my main supplier for 20 years. I have never had a problem with his equipment and his service is impeccable."
— *Linda Unger, Linda & Louis*

THE J-PROP SHOP • 541 WEST HIGHLAND DRIVE • AUBURN, ME 04210 • (207) 555 - 9001

Dave's flyer contains several elements that are common to many Web pages, as shown in Figure 1-8. A header displays the company's logo and a footer displays contact information for the J-Prop Shop. The main section, which describes Dave's business, includes several subsections, also known as articles. A second section that appears as a sidebar displays quotes from some J-Prop customers.

Figure 1-8 Structure of Dave's Web page

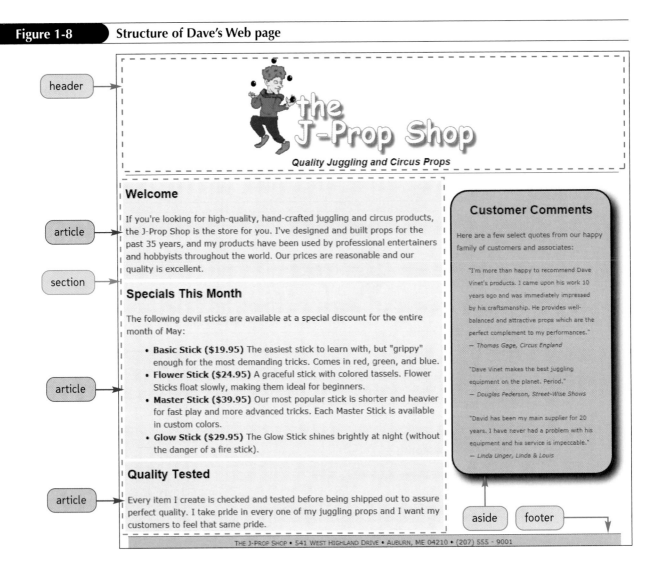

Working with HTML5 Structural Elements

Each of these parts of Dave's document can be marked using HTML5 **structural elements**, which are the elements that define the major sections of a Web page. Figure 1-9 describes some of these elements.

Figure 1-9 HTML5 structural elements

Structural Element	Description
article	A subsection covering a single topic
aside	Content containing tangential or side issues to the main topic of the page
footer	Content placed at the bottom of the page
header	Content placed at the top of the page
nav	A navigation list of hypertext links
section	A major topical area in the page

For example, to mark the header of your Web page, you would enter a `header` element within the page body, using the syntax

```
<header>
   header content
</header>
```

where *header content* is the page content that you want displayed within the page header. One of the reasons we want to define these structural elements is that we can write styles for them and define the layout of the Web page content.

REFERENCE

Marking Structural Elements in HTML5

- To mark the page header, use the `header` element.
- To mark the page footer, use the `footer` element.
- To mark a main section of page content, use the `section` element.
- To mark a sidebar, use the `aside` element.
- To mark an article, use the `article` element.

Based on Dave's sample document shown in Figure 1-8, you'll add the `header`, `section`, `aside`, and `footer` structural elements to your HTML file.

To insert the HTML5 structural elements:

1. Return to the **jprop.htm** file in your text editor.

2. Within the `body` element, insert the following tags as shown in Figure 1-10:

```
<header>
</header>

<section>
</section>

<aside>
</aside>

<footer>
</footer>
```

Figure 1-10   **Inserting structural elements**

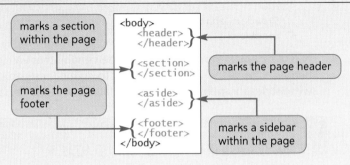

▶ **3.** Save your changes to the file.

Structural elements can also be nested within one another. In the structure of Dave's page from Figure 1-8, notice that the section element contains three article elements. Add this content to your HTML file by nesting three `article` elements within the `section` element.

To add three article elements:

▶ **1.** Within the `section` element, insert the following code as shown in Figure 1-11:

```
<article>
</article>

<article>
</article>

<article>
</article>
```

Figure 1-11   **Inserting nested elements**

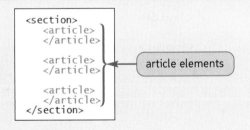

▶ **2.** Save your changes to the file.

Marking a Section with the `div` Element

The structural elements are part of the current specifications for HTML5, but they are not part of HTML 4.01 or XHTML. Pages written to those languages instead use the **div element** to identify different page divisions. The syntax of the `div` element is

```
<div id="id">
    content
</div>
```

where *id* is a unique name assigned to the division and *content* is page content contained within the division. While not required, the id attribute is useful to distinguish one `div` element from another. This becomes particularly important if you apply different styles to different page divisions.

Figure 1-12 shows how the same page layout marked up using structural elements under HTML5 would be marked up in HTML 4.01 using the `div` element.

Figure 1-12	Structural elements in HTML5 and HTML 4.01

HTML5

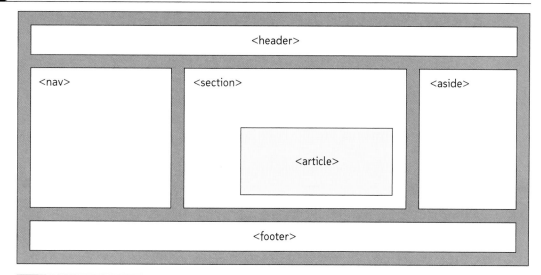

HTML 4.01

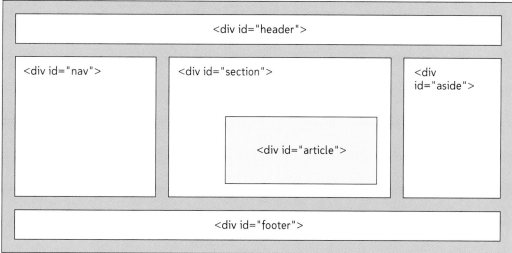

You can use either HTML5's structural elements or HTML 4.01's `div` elements to identify the major sections of your document. The HTML5 approach is preferred because it represents the future standard of the Web, and structural elements are more descriptive than the generic `div` element. One problem with the `div` element is that there are no rules for id names. One Web designer might identify the page heading with the id name *header* while another designer might use *heading* or *top*. This makes it harder for Web search engines to identify the main topics of interest in each Web page.

PROSKILLS

Written Communication: Writing Effective HTML Code

Part of writing good HTML code is being aware of the requirements of various browsers and devices, as well as understanding the different versions of the language. Here are a few guidelines for writing good HTML code:

- *Become well versed in the history of HTML and the various versions of HTML and XHTML.* Unlike other languages, HTML's history does impact how you write your code.
- *Know your market.* Do you have to support older browsers, or have your clients standardized on one particular browser or browser version? Will your Web pages be viewed on a single device such as a computer, or do you have to support a variety of devices?
- *Test your code on several different browsers and browser versions.* Don't assume that if your page works in one browser it will work in other browsers, or even in earlier versions of the same browser. Also check on the speed of the connection. A large file that performs well with a high-speed connection might be unusable with a dial-up connection.
- *Read the documentation on the different versions of HTML and XHTML at the W3C Web site and keep up to date with the latest developments in the language.*

In general, any HTML code that you write should be compatible with the current versions of the following browsers: Internet Explorer (Windows), Firefox (Windows and Macintosh), Safari (Windows and Macintosh), Chrome (Windows and Macintosh), and Opera (Windows and Macintosh). In addition, you should also view your pages on a variety of devices including laptops, mobile phones, and tablets. To effectively communicate with customers and users, you need to make sure your Web site is always readable.

At this point, you've created the basic framework of Dave's Web page. In the next session, you'll insert the page content and learn how to apply a visual style to that content to create a nicely formatted Web page. If you want to take a break before starting the next session, you can close any open files or applications.

REVIEW

Session 1.1 Quick Check

1. What is a markup language?
2. What is XHTML? How does XHTML differ from HTML?
3. What is the W3C? What is the WHATWG?
4. What is a doctype? What are two uses of the doctype?
5. What is incorrect about the syntax of the following code?

```
<p>Welcome to the <em>J-Prop Shop</p></em>
```

6. What is white space? How does HTML treat consecutive occurrences of white space?
7. What structural element would you use to mark a sidebar?
8. What structural element would you use to mark the page footer?

SESSION 1.2 VISUAL OVERVIEW

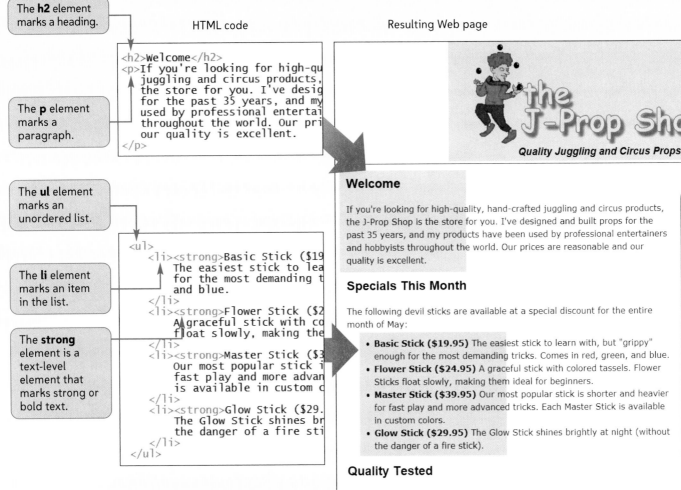

The **h2** element marks a heading.

HTML code

Resulting Web page

```
<h2>Welcome</h2>
<p>If you're looking for high-qu
   juggling and circus products,
   the store for you. I've desig
   for the past 35 years, and my
   used by professional entertai
   throughout the world. Our pri
   our quality is excellent.
</p>
```

The **p** element marks a paragraph.

The **ul** element marks an unordered list.

```
<ul>
   <li><strong>Basic Stick ($19
      The easiest stick to lea
      for the most demanding t
      and blue.
   </li>
   <li><strong>Flower Stick ($2
      A graceful stick with co
      float slowly, making the
   </li>
   <li><strong>Master Stick ($3
      Our most popular stick i
      fast play and more advan
      is available in custom c
   </li>
   <li><strong>Glow Stick ($29.
      The Glow Stick shines br
      the danger of a fire sti
   </li>
</ul>
```

The **li** element marks an item in the list.

The **strong** element is a text-level element that marks strong or bold text.

the J-Prop Shop
Quality Juggling and Circus Props

Welcome

If you're looking for high-quality, hand-crafted juggling and circus products, the J-Prop Shop is the store for you. I've designed and built props for the past 35 years, and my products have been used by professional entertainers and hobbyists throughout the world. Our prices are reasonable and our quality is excellent.

Specials This Month

The following devil sticks are available at a special discount for the entire month of May:

- **Basic Stick ($19.95)** The easiest stick to learn with, but "grippy" enough for the most demanding tricks. Comes in red, green, and blue.
- **Flower Stick ($24.95)** A graceful stick with colored tassels. Flower Sticks float slowly, making them ideal for beginners.
- **Master Stick ($39.95)** Our most popular stick is shorter and heavier for fast play and more advanced tricks. Each Master Stick is available in custom colors.
- **Glow Stick ($29.95)** The Glow Stick shines brightly at night (without the danger of a fire stick).

Quality Tested

Every item I create is checked and tested before being shipped out to assure perfect quality. I take pride in every one of my juggling props and I want my customers to feel that same pride.

THE J-PROP SHOP • 541 WEST HIGHLAND DRIVE • AUBURN, ME 04210 • (207) 555 - 9

The **address** element marks an address or contact info.

```
<address>The J-Prop Shop &bull;
         541 West Highland Drive &bull;
         Auburn, ME 04210 &bull;
         (207) 555 - 9001
</address>
```

The **•** entity represents the bullet character.

PAGE CONTENT ELEMENTS

HTML code

The **hgroup** element groups main headings and subheadings.

The **img** element is used to insert images into the Web page.

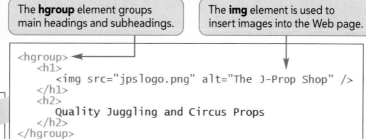

```
<hgroup>
    <h1>
        <img src="jpslogo.png" alt="The J-Prop Shop" />
    </h1>
    <h2>
        Quality Juggling and Circus Props
    </h2>
</hgroup>
```

```
<blockquote>
    <p>"I'm more than happy to reco
        products. I came upon his wo
        was immediately impressed by
        He provides well-balanced an
        props which are the perfect
        performances."
    <br />
    &#8212; <cite>Thomas Gage, C
    </p>
```

The **blockquote** element marks large blocks of quoted material.

The **cite** element marks a citation.

The **—** entity represents the em-dash character.

A page rendered with the default browser style sheet

The same page rendered with a user-defined style sheet

```
<link href="jpsstyles.css" rel="stylesheet" type="text/css" />
```

The **link** element connects the Web page to the style sheet.

The href attribute indicates the name of the style sheet file.

The type attribute indicates the language of the style sheet.

Working with Grouping Elements

You're now ready to begin entering content into the body of Dave's Web page. The first elements you'll add are **grouping elements**, which are elements that contain content that is viewed as a distinct block within the Web page. Paragraphs, which were presented in the last session, are one example of a grouping element, as are page divisions marked using the div element. Figure 1-13 lists some of the commonly used grouping elements.

Figure 1-13   Grouping elements

Grouping Element	Description
address	Contact information (usually rendered as *italicized* text)
blockquote	An extended quotation (usually indented from the left and right margins)
dd	A definition from a description list
div	A generic grouping element
dl	A description list
dt	A definition term from a description list
figure	A figure or illustration (HTML5 only)
figcaption	The caption of a figure, which must be nested within the figure element (HTML5 only)
h*n*	A heading, where *n* is a value from 1 to 6, with h1 as the most prominent heading and h6 the least prominent (usually displayed in **bold** text)
li	A list item from an ordered or unordered list
ol	An ordered list
p	A paragraph
pre	Preformatted text, retaining all white space and special characters (usually displayed in a fixed width font)
ul	An unordered list

To explore how grouping elements are typically rendered by your Web browser, a demo page has been prepared for you.

To open the HTML Tags demo page:

▶ **1.** Use your browser to open the **demo_html.htm** file from the tutorial.01\demo folder.

▶ **2.** If your browser prompts you to allow code from the Web page to be run, click the **Allow blocked content** button.

Marking Content Headings

The first grouping elements you'll explore are **heading elements**, which contain the text of main headings on a Web page. They're often used for introducing new topics or for dividing the page into topical sections. The syntax to mark a heading element is

```
<hn>content</hn>
```

where *n* is an integer from 1 to 6. Content marked with <h1> tags is considered a major heading, and is usually displayed in large bold text. Content marked with <h2> through <h6> tags is used for subheadings, and is usually displayed in progressively smaller bold text.

REFERENCE

Marking Grouping Content

- To mark a heading, enter
  `<hn>`*content*`</hn>`
  where *n* is an integer from 1 to 6 and *content* is the text of the heading.
- To mark a paragraph, enter
  `<p>`*content*`</p>`
- To mark a block quote, enter
  `<blockquote>`*content*`</blockquote>`

To see how these headings appear on your computer, use the demo page.

To view heading elements:

1. Click in the blue box in the lower-left corner of the demo page, type `<h1>The J-Prop Shop</h1>` and then press the **Enter** key to go to a new line.

2. Type `<h2>Quality Juggling and Circus Props</h2>`.

3. Click the **Preview Code** button located below the blue code window. Your browser displays a preview of how this code would appear in your Web browser (see Figure 1-14).

Figure 1-14	Previewing h1 and h2 headings

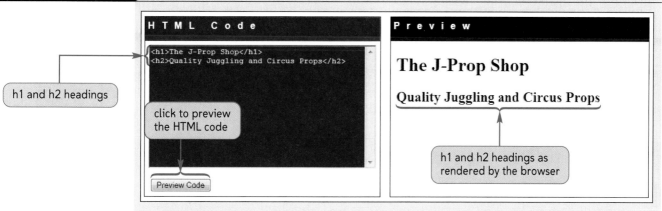

h1 and h2 headings

click to preview the HTML code

h1 and h2 headings as rendered by the browser

Trouble? If you are using a browser other than Internet Explorer 9 running on Windows 7, your screen might look slightly different from that shown in Figure 1-14.

4. To see how an h3 heading would look, change the opening tag for the store description from `<h2>` to `<h3>` and change the closing tag from `</h2>` to `</h3>`. Click the **Preview Code** button again.

Your browser renders the code again, this time with the store information displayed in a smaller font. If you continued to change the heading element from h3 to each of the elements down to h6, you would see the second line in the Preview box get progressively smaller.

It's important not to treat markup tags as simply a way of formatting the Web page. The h1 through h6 elements are used to identify headings, but the exact appearance of these headings depends on the browser and the device being used. While most browsers display an h1 heading in a larger font than an h2 heading, remember that the headings might not even be displayed at all. A screen reader, for example, doesn't display text, but rather conveys the presence of an h1 heading with increased volume or with special emphasis preceded by an extended pause.

Now that you've seen how to mark page headings, you can add them to Dave's Web page. The first heading Dave wants to add is an h1 heading containing the company's name. He also wants you to insert h2 headings in several places—as titles for the three articles on the page, as a title for the sidebar containing the customer comments, and as a subheading to the main heading on the page.

To add headings to Dave's document:

1. Return to the **jprop.htm** file in your text editor.

   Trouble? If you are using the Macintosh TextEdit program, you must select the *Ignore rich text commands* check box when reopening the file.

2. Within the header element, insert the following tags:

   ```
   <h1>The J-Prop Shop</h1>
   <h2>Quality Juggling and Circus Props</h2>
   ```

3. Within the first article element, insert the following h2 heading:

   ```
   <h2>Welcome</h2>
   ```

4. Within the second article element, insert

   ```
   <h2>Specials This Month</h2>
   ```

5. Within the third and final article element, insert

   ```
   <h2>Quality Tested</h2>
   ```

6. Finally, within the aside element, insert

   ```
   <h2>Customer Comments</h2>
   ```

   Figure 1-15 highlights the revised code in the file.

Figure 1-15	Inserting h1 and h2 headings

```
<body>
    <header>
        <h1>The J-Prop Shop</h1>
        <h2>Quality Juggling and Circus Props</h2>
    </header>

    <section>
        <article>
            <h2>Welcome</h2>
        </article>

        <article>
            <h2>Specials This Month</h2>
        </article>

        <article>
            <h2>Quality Tested</h2>
        </article>
    </section>

    <aside>
        <h2>Customer Comments</h2>
    </aside>

    <footer>
    </footer>
</body>
```

▶ **7.** Save your changes to the file and then reload or refresh the **jprop.htm** file in your Web browser. Figure 1-16 shows the initial view of the page body content.

Figure 1-16	Viewing h1 and h2 headings in Dave's document

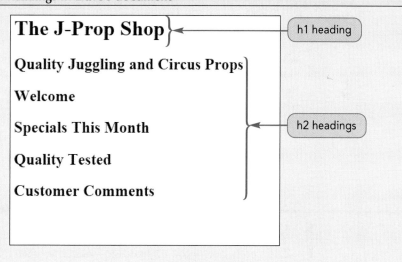

Grouping Headings

The interpretation of a particular heading depends on how it's used. For example, the h2 headings you just entered were used either to provide a title for articles or sections in the Web page or as a subtitle to the main title of the page. You can indicate that an h2 heading acts as a subtitle by grouping it with a main title heading using the **hgroup element**. The hgroup element uses the syntax

```
<hgroup>
    heading elements
</hgroup>
```

> **TIP**
>
> The hgroup element can contain only h1 through h6 elements or other hgroup elements.

where *heading elements* are elements marked with the <h1> through <h6> heading tags. The hgroup element was introduced in HTML5 and is not part of older HTML or XHTML specifications.

Group the first two headings in Dave's document to indicate that they should be interpreted as a main title and a subtitle.

To group the first two headings in the document:

▶ **1.** Return to the **jprop.htm** file in your text editor.

▶ **2.** Indent the first two headings in the document and then enclose them within <hgroup> tags as shown in Figure 1-17.

Figure 1-17 ▶ **Grouping the h1 and h2 headings**

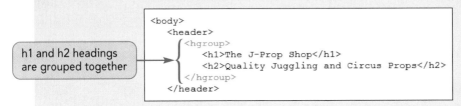

h1 and h2 headings are grouped together

```
<body>
   <header>
      <hgroup>
         <h1>The J-Prop Shop</h1>
         <h2>Quality Juggling and Circus Props</h2>
      </hgroup>
   </header>
```

▶ **3.** Save your changes to the file.

Marking Paragraph Elements

As you saw earlier, you can mark a paragraph element using the <p> tag, which has the syntax

```
<p>content</p>
```

where *content* is the content of the paragraph. In older HTML code, you might occasionally see paragraphs marked with only the opening <p> tags, omitting closing tags. In those situations, a <p> tag marks the start of each new paragraph. While this convention is still accepted by many browsers, it violates HTML's syntax rules. In addition, if you want XHTML-compliant code, you must always include closing tags.

Many articles on the J-Prop Shop page are enclosed within paragraphs. You'll add these paragraphs now.

To add four paragraphs to Dave's Web page:

▶ **1.** Return to the **jprop.htm** file in your text editor.

▶ **2.** Directly below the h2 heading *Welcome*, insert the following paragraph code, indented as shown in Figure 1-18:

```
<p>If you're looking for high-quality, hand-crafted
   juggling and circus products, the J-Prop Shop is
   the store for you. I've designed and built props
   for the past 35 years, and my products have been
   used by professional entertainers and hobbyists
   throughout the world. Our prices are reasonable and
   our quality is excellent.
</p>
```

3. Directly below the h2 heading *Specials This Month*, insert the following:

```
<p>The following devil sticks are available at a
   special discount for the entire month of May:
</p>
```

4. Directly below the h2 heading *Quality Tested*, insert the following:

```
<p>Every item I create is checked and tested before
   being shipped out to assure perfect quality. I take
   pride in every one of my juggling props and I want
   my customers to feel that same pride.
</p>
```

5. Finally, below the h2 heading *Customer Comments*, insert the following:

```
<p>Here are a few select quotes from our happy family
   of customers and associates:
</p>
```

Figure 1-18 highlights the newly added paragraphs in the document.

Figure 1-18   **Adding paragraph elements**

```
<section>
    <article>
        <h2>Welcome</h2>
        <p>If you're looking for high-quality, hand-crafted
           juggling and circus products, the J-Prop Shop is
           the store for you. I've designed and built props
           for the past 35 years, and my products have been
           used by professional entertainers and hobbyists
           throughout the world. Our prices are reasonable and
           our quality is excellent.
        </p>
    </article>

    <article>
        <h2>Specials This Month</h2>
        <p>The following devil sticks are available at a
           special discount for the entire month of May:
        </p>
    </article>

    <article>
        <h2>Quality Tested</h2>
        <p>Every item I create is checked and tested before
           being shipped out to assure perfect quality. I take
           pride in every one of my juggling props and I want
           my customers to feel that same pride.
        </p>
    </article>
</section>

<aside>
    <h2>Customer Comments</h2>
    <p>Here are a few select quotes from our happy family
       of customers and associates:
    </p>
</aside>
```

Trouble? Don't worry if your lines do not wrap at the same locations shown in Figure 1-18. Where the line wraps in the HTML code does not affect how the page is rendered by the browser.

6. Save your changes to the file and then refresh the **jprop.htm** file in your Web browser. Figure 1-19 shows the new paragraphs added to the Web page.

Figure 1-19   Paragraphs in the Web page

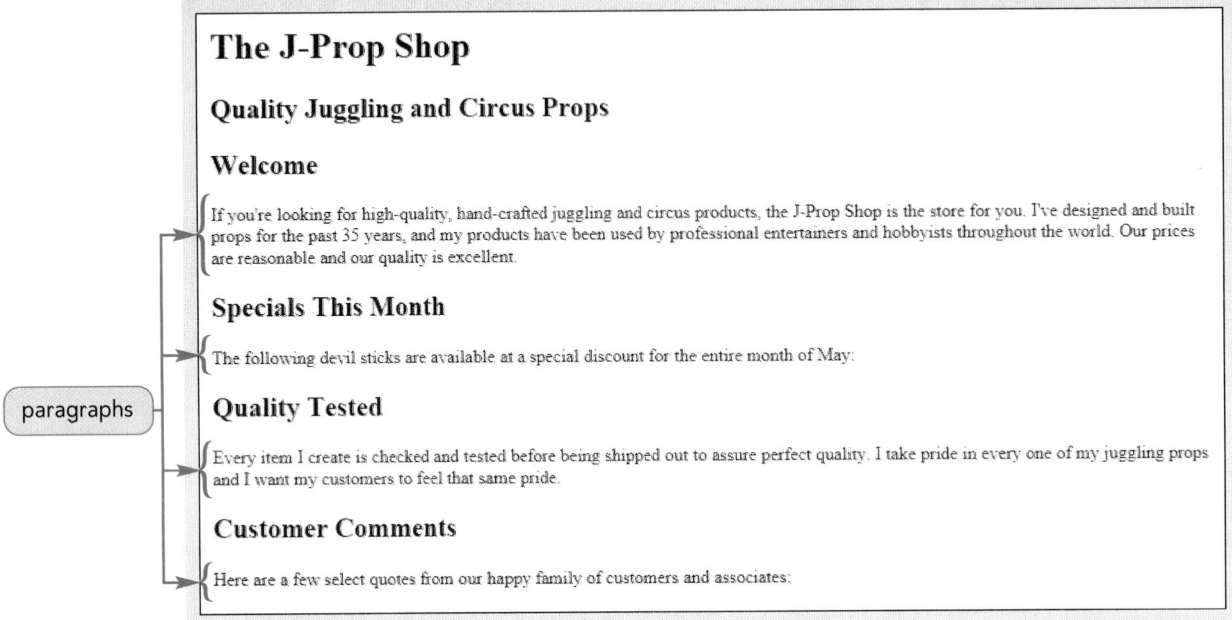

The J-Prop Shop

Quality Juggling and Circus Props

Welcome

paragraphs

If you're looking for high-quality, hand-crafted juggling and circus products, the J-Prop Shop is the store for you. I've designed and built props for the past 35 years, and my products have been used by professional entertainers and hobbyists throughout the world. Our prices are reasonable and our quality is excellent.

Specials This Month

The following devil sticks are available at a special discount for the entire month of May:

Quality Tested

Every item I create is checked and tested before being shipped out to assure perfect quality. I take pride in every one of my juggling props and I want my customers to feel that same pride.

Customer Comments

Here are a few select quotes from our happy family of customers and associates:

Marking a Block Quote

Next, Dave wants you to enter a few select quotes from his satisfied customers. You mark extended quotes with the HTML `blockquote` element, which uses the syntax

```
<blockquote>content</blockquote>
```

where `content` is the text of the quote. Most browsers render block quotes by indenting them to make it easier for readers to separate quoted material from the author's own words. You'll add the customer comments as block quotes.

To create the customer comment block quotes:

1. Return to the **jprop.htm** file in your text editor.

2. Scroll down to the `aside` element, and after the paragraph within that element, insert the following block quote, as shown in Figure 1-20:

```
<blockquote>
   <p>"I'm more than happy to recommend Dave Vinet's
      products. I came upon his work 10 years ago and
      was immediately impressed by his craftsmanship.
      He provides well-balanced and attractive
      props which are the perfect complement to my
      performances."
   </p>
   <p>"Dave Vinet makes the best juggling equipment on
      the planet. Period."
   </p>
   <p>"David has been my main supplier for 20 years. I
      have never had a problem with his equipment and
      his service is impeccable."
   </p>
</blockquote>
```

Figure 1-20	Adding a block quote

```
<aside>
   <h2>Customer Comments</h2>
   <p>Here are a few select quotes from our happy family
      of customers and associates:
   </p>
   <blockquote>
      <p>"I'm more than happy to recommend Dave Vinet's
         products. I came upon his work 10 years ago and
         was immediately impressed by his craftsmanship.
         He provides well-balanced and attractive
         props which are the perfect complement to my
         performances."
      </p>
      <p>"Dave Vinet makes the best juggling equipment on
         the planet. Period."
      </p>
      <p>"David has been my main supplier for 20 years. I
         have never had a problem with his equipment and
         his service is impeccable."
      </p>
   </blockquote>
</aside>
```

▶ **3.** Save your changes to the file, and then reload **jprop.htm** in your Web browser. Figure 1-21 shows the revised page with the quoted material.

Figure 1-21	Block quote in the Web page

Customer Comments

Here are a few select quotes from our happy family of customers and associates:

> "I'm more than happy to recommend Dave Vinet's products. I came upon his work 10 years ago and was immediately impressed by his craftsmanship. He provides well-balanced and attractive props which are the perfect complement to my performances."
>
> "Dave Vinet makes the best juggling equipment on the planet. Period."
>
> "David has been my main supplier for 20 years. I have never had a problem with his equipment and his service is impeccable."

quoted paragraphs are indented in the page

Note that the customer quote also included three paragraph elements nested within the `blockquote` element. The indentation applied by the browser to the block quote was also applied to any content within that element, so those paragraphs were indented even though browsers do not indent paragraphs by default.

Marking an Address

Dave wants to display the company's address at the bottom of the body of his page. Contact information such as addresses can be marked using the `address` element, which uses the syntax

```
<address>content</address>
```

where *content* is the contact information. Most browsers render addresses in italic. You'll use the `address` element to display the address of the J-Prop Shop.

To add the J-Prop Shop address:

▶ **1.** Return to the **jprop.htm** file in your text editor.

▶ **2.** Scroll down to the bottom of the file, and then within the `footer` element insert the following code, as shown in Figure 1-22:

```
<address>The J-Prop Shop
         541 West Highland Drive
         Auburn, ME 04210
         (207) 555 - 9001
</address>
```

Figure 1-22	Adding an address

```
<footer>
    <address>The J-Prop Shop
             541 West Highland Drive
             Auburn, ME 04210
             (207) 555 - 9001
    </address>
</footer>
</body>
```

▶ **3.** Save your changes to the file, and then refresh **jprop.htm** in your Web browser. Figure 1-23 shows the revised page with the address text.

Figure 1-23	Address as rendered in the Web page

Customer Comments

Here are a few select quotes from our happy family of customers and associates:

"I'm more than happy to recommend Dave Vinet's products. I came upon his work 10 years ago and was immediately impressed by his craftsmanship. He provides well-balanced and attractive props which are the perfect complement to my performances."

"Dave Vinet makes the best juggling equipment on the planet. Period."

"David has been my main supplier for 20 years. I have never had a problem with his equipment and his service is impeccable."

The J-Prop Shop 541 West Highland Drive Auburn, ME 04210 (207) 555 - 9001

> address text is displayed in italic by default

The address text appears in italic at the bottom of the page. Note that even though you entered the company name, street address, city, state, and phone number on multiple lines, in the browser they all appear to run together on a single line. Remember that the browser ignores the occurrence of line breaks, tabs, and other white space in your text document. Shortly, you'll learn how to make this text more readable by adding a character symbol to separate the different parts of the address. For now, you'll leave the address text as it is.

Marking a List

Dave wants to display a list of products on this sample page. This information is presented on his flyer as a bulleted list. He wants something similar on the Web site. HTML supports three kinds of lists: ordered, unordered, and description.

REFERENCE

Marking Lists

- To mark an ordered list, enter

```
<ol>
    <li>item1</li>
    <li>item2</li>
...
</ol>
```
where *item1*, *item2*, and so forth are the items in the list.
- To mark an unordered list, enter

```
<ul>
    <li>item1</li>
    <li>item2</li>
...
</ul>
```
- To mark a description list, enter

```
<dl>
    <dt>term1</dt>
    <dd>description1</dd>
    <dt>term2</dt>
    <dd>description2a</dd>
    <dd>description2b</dd>
...
</dl>
```
where *term1*, *term2*, etc. are the terms in the list and *description1*, *description2a*, *description2b*, etc. are descriptions associated with the preceding terms.

Ordered Lists

Ordered lists are used for items that follow some defined sequential order, such as lists ordered from smallest to greatest or from oldest to youngest. The beginning of an ordered list is marked by the <ol> (ordered list) tag. Each item within an ordered list is marked using the <li> (list item) tag. The structure of an ordered list is therefore

```
<ol>
    <li>item1</li>
    <li>item2</li>
...
</ol>
```

where *item1*, *item2*, and so forth are the items in the list. To explore creating an ordered list, you'll return to the HTML demo page.

To create an ordered list:

1. Return to the **demo_html.htm** file in your Web browser.
2. Delete the HTML code in the left box and replace it with the following:

```
<ol>
    <li>First Item</li>
    <li>Second Item</li>
    <li>Third Item</li>
</ol>
```

3. Click the **Preview Code** button. Figure 1-24 shows how the browser renders the ordered list contents.

Figure 1-24 **Viewing an ordered list**

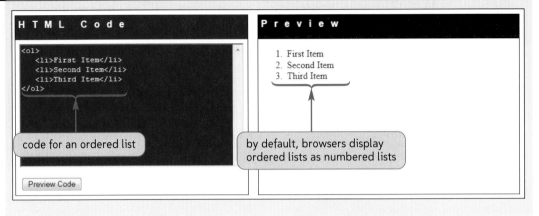

By default, entries in an ordered list are numbered, with the numbers added automatically by the browser.

Unordered Lists

To mark a list in which the items are not expected to occur in any specific order, you create an **unordered list**. The structure of ordered and unordered lists is the same, except that the list items for an unordered list are nested within the ul element, as follows:

```
<ul>
   <li>item1</li>
   <li>item2</li>
...
</ul>
```

You'll practice creating an unordered list with the demo page.

To create an unordered list:

1. Delete the HTML code in the left box and replace it with the following:

```
<ul>
   <li>Basic Stick</li>
   <li>Flower Stick</li>
   <li>Master Stick</li>
   <li>Glow Stick</li>
</ul>
```

2. Click the **Preview Code** button. Figure 1-25 shows how the browser renders the unordered list.

Figure 1-25   **Viewing an unordered list**

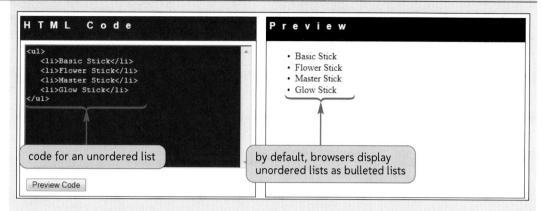

Trouble? In some browsers, the list appears with diamond shapes rather than circular bullets.

By default, most browsers display unordered lists using a bullet symbol. The exact bullet symbol depends on the browser, but most browsers use a filled-in circle.

Nesting Lists

You can place one list inside of another to create several levels of list items. The top level of a nested list contains the major items, with each sublevel containing items of lesser importance. Most browsers differentiate the various levels by increasing the indentation and using a different list symbol at each level. You'll use the demo page to see how this works with unordered lists.

To create a nested list:

1. Click after the word *Stick* in the `<li>Basic Stick</li>` line, and then press the **Enter** key to insert a new blank line.

2. Indent the following code between the code `<li>Basic Stick` and the closing `</li>` tag:

```
<ul>
    <li>Red</li>
    <li>Blue</li>
    <li>Green</li>
</ul>
```

3. Click the **Preview Code** button. Figure 1-26 shows the resulting nested list in the browser.

Figure 1-26   Viewing a nested list

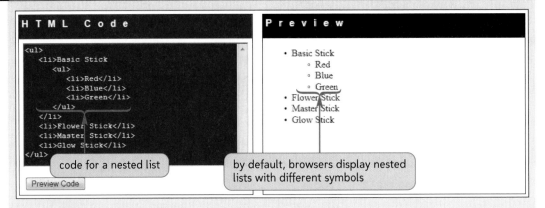

Trouble? Depending on your browser, the nested list of basic stick colors might appear with solid bullets rather than open circles.

The lower level of items is displayed using an open circle as the list bullet and additional indentation on the page. Once again, the exact format applied to these lists is determined by each browser's internal style sheet.

Description Lists

A third type of list is the **description list**, which contains a list of terms, each followed by its description. The structure of a description list is

```
<dl>
    <dt>term1</dt>
    <dd>description1</dd>
    <dt>term2</dt>
    <dd>description2a</dd>
    <dd>description2b</dd>
...
</dl>
```

where *term1*, *term2*, etc. are the terms in the list and *description1*, *description2a*, *description2b*, etc. are the descriptions associated with the terms. Note that description lists must follow a specified order, with each dt (definition term) element followed by one or more dd (definition description) elements.

You'll study how to work with description lists by returning to the demo page.

To create a description list:

1. Replace the code in the left box of the HTML demo page with

```
<dl>
    <dt>Basic Stick</dt>
    <dd>Easiest stick to learn</dd>
    <dt>Flower Stick</dt>
    <dd>A graceful stick with tassels</dd>
    <dt>Master Stick</dt>
    <dd>Our most popular stick</dd>
</dl>
```

2. Click the **Preview Code** button. Figure 1-27 shows the appearance of the description list in the browser.

Figure 1-27	Viewing a description list

TIP

Description lists can also mark dialog, with each dt element naming a speaker, and each dd element containing the speaker's words.

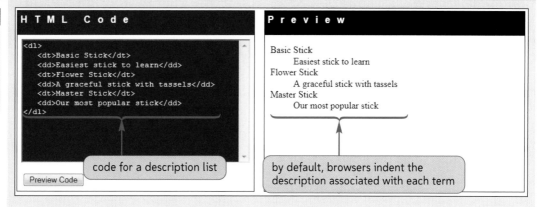

The demo page shows each term followed by its description, which is placed in a new block below the term and indented on the page. If you had included multiple dd elements for a single dt element, each description would have been contained within its own block and indented.

Now that you've experimented with the three types of HTML lists, you'll add an unordered list of products to Dave's Web page. By default, the product names will appear as a bulleted list.

To add an unordered list to Dave's Web page:

1. Return to the **jprop.htm** file in your text editor.

2. Within the Specials This Month article, directly below the p element, insert the following code, as shown in Figure 1-28:

```
<ul>
    <li>Basic Stick ($19.95)
        The easiest stick to learn with, but "grippy" enough
        for the most demanding tricks. Comes in red, green,
        and blue.
    </li>
    <li>Flower Stick ($24.95)
        A graceful stick with colored tassels. Flower Sticks
        float slowly, making them ideal for beginners.
    </li>
    <li>Master Stick ($39.95)
        Our most popular stick is shorter and heavier for
        fast play and more advanced tricks. Each Master Stick
        is available in custom colors.
    </li>
    <li>Glow Stick ($29.95)
        The Glow Stick shines brightly at night (without
        the danger of a fire stick).
    </li>
</ul>
```

Figure 1-28 Adding an unordered list

```
<article>
   <h2>Specials This Month</h2>
   <p>The following devil sticks are available at a
      special discount for the entire month of May:
   </p>
   <ul>
      <li>Basic Stick ($19.95)
         The easiest stick to learn with, but "grippy" enough
         for the most demanding tricks. Comes in red, green,
         and blue.
      </li>
      <li>Flower Stick ($24.95)
         A graceful stick with colored tassels. Flower Sticks
         float slowly, making them ideal for beginners.
      </li>
      <li>Master Stick ($39.95)
         Our most popular stick is shorter and heavier for
         fast play and more advanced tricks. Each Master Stick
         is available in custom colors.
      </li>
      <li>Glow Stick ($29.95)
         The Glow Stick shines brightly at night (without
         the danger of a fire stick).
      </li>
   </ul>

</article>
```

unordered list element → `<ul>`

list item → `<li>`

3. Save your changes to the file, and then refresh the **jprop.htm** file in your Web browser. As shown in Figure 1-29, the list of products appears as a bulleted list in the middle of the page.

Figure 1-29 Unordered list as rendered in the Web page

Specials This Month

The following devil sticks are available at a special discount for the entire month of May:

unordered list items are displayed with bullet markers

- Basic Stick ($19.95) The easiest stick to learn with, but "grippy" enough for the most demanding tricks. Comes in red, green, and blue.
- Flower Stick ($24.95) A graceful stick with colored tassels. Flower Sticks float slowly, making them ideal for beginners.
- Master Stick ($39.95) Our most popular stick is shorter and heavier for fast play and more advanced tricks. Each Master Stick is available in custom colors.
- Glow Stick ($29.95) The Glow Stick shines brightly at night (without the danger of a fire stick).

Although you've added much of the text content to Dave's sample page, the page as rendered by the browser still looks nothing like the flyer shown in Figure 1-7. That's because all of the page elements have been rendered using your browser's internal style sheet. To change the page's appearance, you need to substitute your own style sheet for the browser's internal one.

Applying an External Style Sheet

Style sheets are written in the **Cascading Style Sheet (CSS)** language. Like HTML files, CSS files are text files and can be created and edited using a simple text editor. A style sheet file has the file extension *.css*, which distinguishes it from an HTML file. Dave already has a style sheet for his Web page stored in the file *jpsstyles.css*.

Linking to an External Style Sheet

To apply an external style sheet to a Web page, you create a link within the document head to the style sheet file using the `link` element

```
<link href="file" rel="stylesheet" type="text/css" />
```

where *file* is the filename and location of the style sheet file. When a browser loads the page, it substitutes the style from the external style sheet file for its own internal style sheet.

See how the format and layout of Dave's sample page change when the page is linked to the *jpsstyles.css* file.

To apply Dave's external style sheet:

1. Return to the **jprop.htm** file in your text editor.

2. Within the head element at the top of the file, insert the following link element, as shown in Figure 1-30:

```
<link href="jpsstyles.css" rel="stylesheet" type="text/css" />
```

Figure 1-30 ▶ **Linking to the jpsstyles.css style sheet**

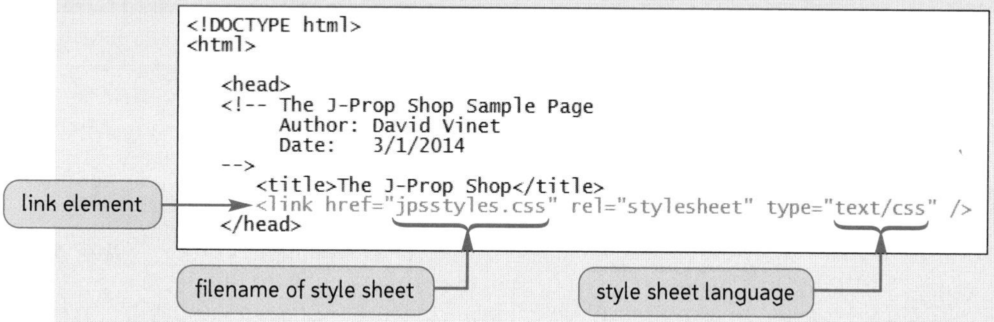

```
<!DOCTYPE html>
<html>

   <head>
   <!-- The J-Prop Shop Sample Page
        Author: David Vinet
        Date:   3/1/2014
   -->
      <title>The J-Prop Shop</title>
      <link href="jpsstyles.css" rel="stylesheet" type="text/css" />
   </head>
```

link element → · filename of style sheet · style sheet language

3. Save your changes to the file.

4. Reload the **jprop.htm** file in your Web browser. As shown in Figure 1-31, the format and the layout change to reflect the styles in Dave's style sheet.

Figure 1-31   **Web page rendered with the jpsstyles.css style sheet**

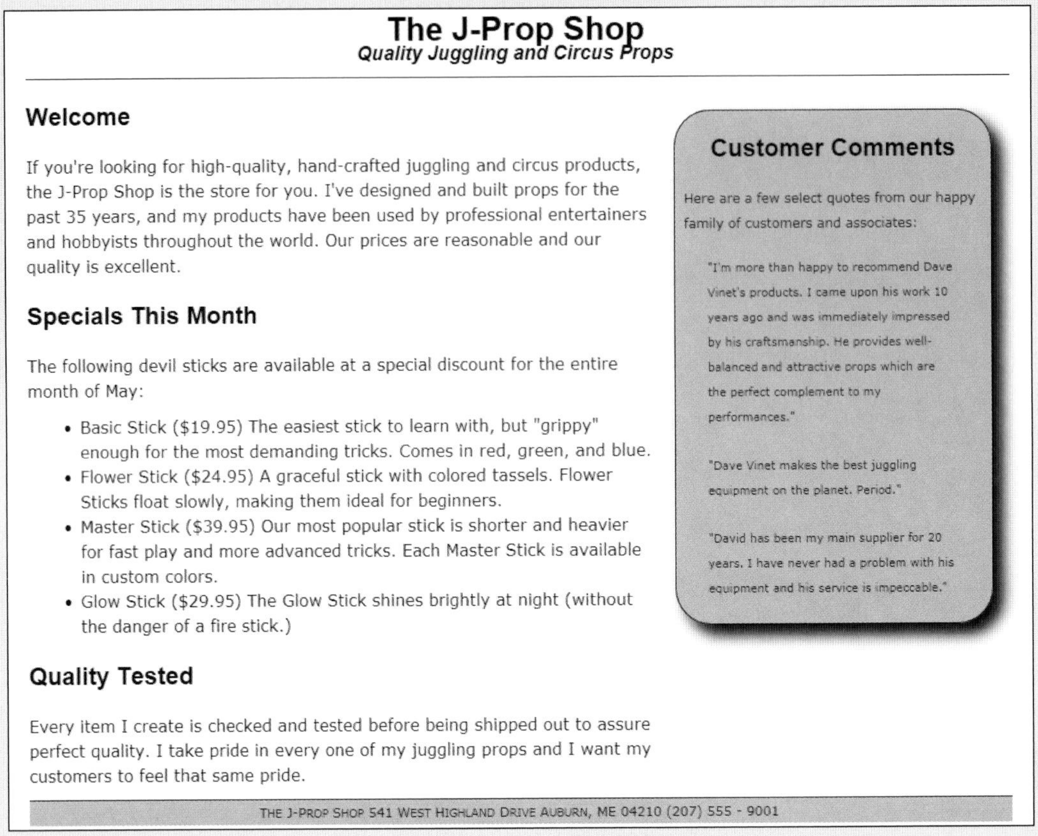

The J-Prop Shop
Quality Juggling and Circus Props

Welcome

If you're looking for high-quality, hand-crafted juggling and circus products, the J-Prop Shop is the store for you. I've designed and built props for the past 35 years, and my products have been used by professional entertainers and hobbyists throughout the world. Our prices are reasonable and our quality is excellent.

Specials This Month

The following devil sticks are available at a special discount for the entire month of May:

- Basic Stick ($19.95) The easiest stick to learn with, but "grippy" enough for the most demanding tricks. Comes in red, green, and blue.
- Flower Stick ($24.95) A graceful stick with colored tassels. Flower Sticks float slowly, making them ideal for beginners.
- Master Stick ($39.95) Our most popular stick is shorter and heavier for fast play and more advanced tricks. Each Master Stick is available in custom colors.
- Glow Stick ($29.95) The Glow Stick shines brightly at night (without the danger of a fire stick.)

Quality Tested

Every item I create is checked and tested before being shipped out to assure perfect quality. I take pride in every one of my juggling props and I want my customers to feel that same pride.

Customer Comments

Here are a few select quotes from our happy family of customers and associates:

"I'm more than happy to recommend Dave Vinet's products. I came upon his work 10 years ago and was immediately impressed by his craftsmanship. He provides well-balanced and attractive props which are the perfect complement to my performances."

"Dave Vinet makes the best juggling equipment on the planet. Period."

"David has been my main supplier for 20 years. I have never had a problem with his equipment and his service is impeccable."

THE J-PROP SHOP 541 WEST HIGHLAND DRIVE AUBURN, ME 04210 (207) 555 - 9001

Trouble? Many elements in HTML5 are still not completely supported in current browsers, so the appearance of your Web page might differ slightly from that shown in Figure 1-31. If you are running Internet Explorer 8 or earlier, you'll see a significant difference. You'll learn how to correct this problem shortly.

Using the new style sheet, Dave's Web page is much more readable. The page is displayed in a two-column layout with the main content of the section element displayed in the left column. The content of the aside element is shown as a sidebar in the right column with a light purple background, rounded corners, and a drop shadow. The content of the footer element is styled with a smaller font, a top border line, and a light purple background.

Styles for HTML5 Elements

The section, aside, and footer elements used in the code of the *jprop.htm* file are new HTML5 elements that were not part of earlier HTML specifications. For most browsers this is not a problem, and the Web page should be rendered with a format and layout close to what Dave requested. An important exception, though, is the Internet Explorer browser. Internet Explorer version 8 and earlier versions provide almost no support for HTML5 and do not recognize styles applied to HTML5 elements. For example, as Figure 1-32 shows, even with the new style sheet, Internet Explorer 8 displays Dave's Web page with a few of the styles shown in Figure 1-31.

Figure 1-32   Web page as it appears in Internet Explorer 8

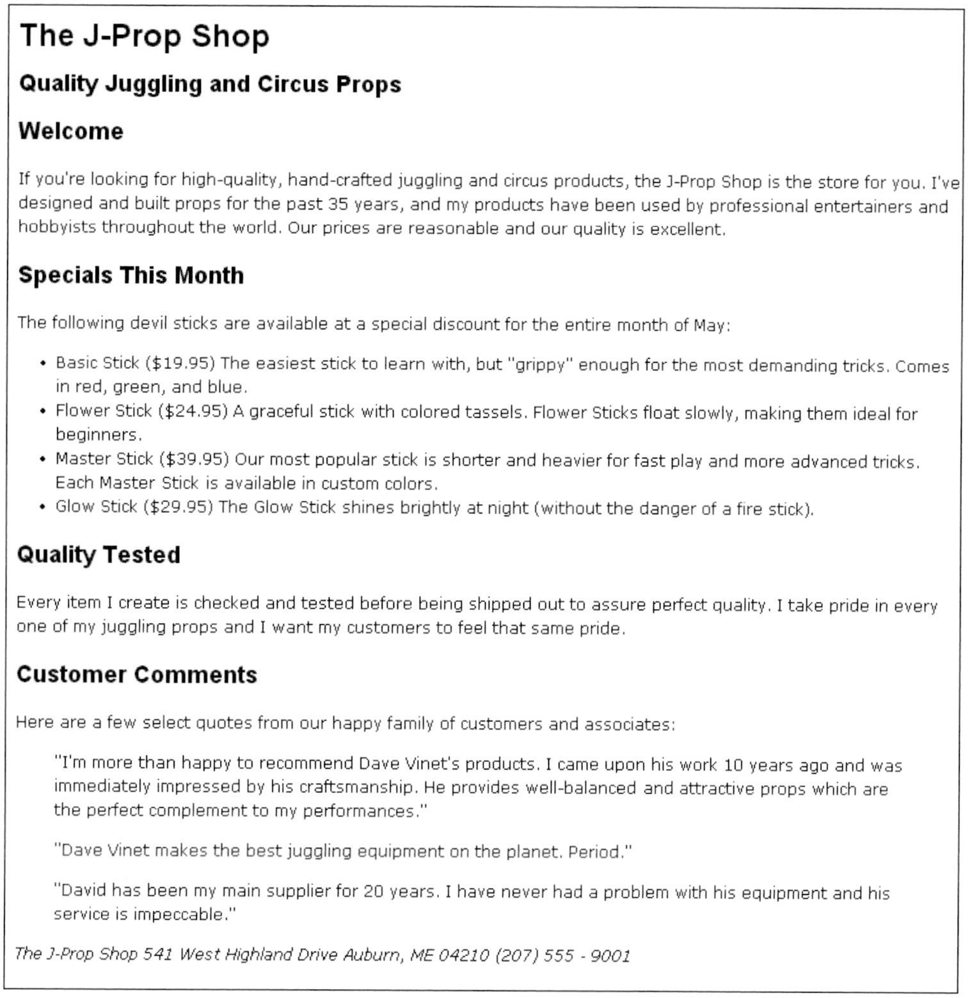

The J-Prop Shop

Quality Juggling and Circus Props

Welcome

If you're looking for high-quality, hand-crafted juggling and circus products, the J-Prop Shop is the store for you. I've designed and built props for the past 35 years, and my products have been used by professional entertainers and hobbyists throughout the world. Our prices are reasonable and our quality is excellent.

Specials This Month

The following devil sticks are available at a special discount for the entire month of May:

- Basic Stick ($19.95) The easiest stick to learn with, but "grippy" enough for the most demanding tricks. Comes in red, green, and blue.
- Flower Stick ($24.95) A graceful stick with colored tassels. Flower Sticks float slowly, making them ideal for beginners.
- Master Stick ($39.95) Our most popular stick is shorter and heavier for fast play and more advanced tricks. Each Master Stick is available in custom colors.
- Glow Stick ($29.95) The Glow Stick shines brightly at night (without the danger of a fire stick).

Quality Tested

Every item I create is checked and tested before being shipped out to assure perfect quality. I take pride in every one of my juggling props and I want my customers to feel that same pride.

Customer Comments

Here are a few select quotes from our happy family of customers and associates:

"I'm more than happy to recommend Dave Vinet's products. I came upon his work 10 years ago and was immediately impressed by his craftsmanship. He provides well-balanced and attractive props which are the perfect complement to my performances."

"Dave Vinet makes the best juggling equipment on the planet. Period."

"David has been my main supplier for 20 years. I have never had a problem with his equipment and his service is impeccable."

The J-Prop Shop 541 West Highland Drive Auburn, ME 04210 (207) 555 - 9001

Dave needs this problem fixed because he can't assume that users will always be running the latest version of Internet Explorer. Workarounds for this problem involve running an external program known as a **script**. The most often used program language for the Web is **JavaScript**. Like HTML and CSS files, JavaScript files are text files that require no special software other than a Web browser to run. At this point, you don't need to know how to write a JavaScript program to correct Internet Explorer's problem with HTML5 elements; someone else has already done that. You just need to know how to access and run their program.

One of the most useful programs to enable HTML5 support in older browsers is Modernizr. **Modernizr** is a free, open-source, MIT-licensed JavaScript library of functions that provides support for many HTML5 elements and for the newest CSS styles. One of the many uses of Modernizr is to enable support for HTML5 in older browsers. Modernizr is distributed in a single JavaScript file that you can download from *www.modernizr.com* and add to your Web site. To link a Web page to a JavaScript file, you add the `script` element

```
<script src="file"></script>
```

to the document head, where *file* is the name of the JavaScript file. The current version of Modernizr at the time of this writing is stored in the file *modernizr-1.5.js*. To link to this file, you add the following to the document head:

```
<script src="modernizr-1.5.js"></script>
```

The *modernizr-1.5.js* file has already been added to your data folder. Link to this file now to apply it to Dave's Web page.

To link to the Modernizr file:

▶ **1.** Return to the **jprop.htm** file in your text editor.

▶ **2.** Scroll to the top of the file and add the following tag pair above the `link` element, as shown in Figure 1-33:

```
<script src="modernizr-1.5.js"></script>
```

Figure 1-33 Linking to the Modernizr script

```
<!DOCTYPE html>
<html>

   <head>
   <!-- The J-Prop Shop Sample Page
        Author: David Vinet                    Modernizr script file
        Date:    3/1/2014
   -->
      <title>The J-Prop Shop</title>
      <script src="modernizr-1.5.js"></script>
      <link href="jpsstyles.css" rel="stylesheet" type="text/css" />
   </head>
```

▶ **3.** Save your changes to the file.

▶ **4.** If you have access to Internet Explorer 8, use that browser to open the **jprop.htm** file. As shown in Figure 1-34, the browser renders the Web page employing the page layout and many of the formats shown earlier in Figure 1-29.

Figure 1-34 Web page as it appears in Internet Explorer 8 with Modernizr

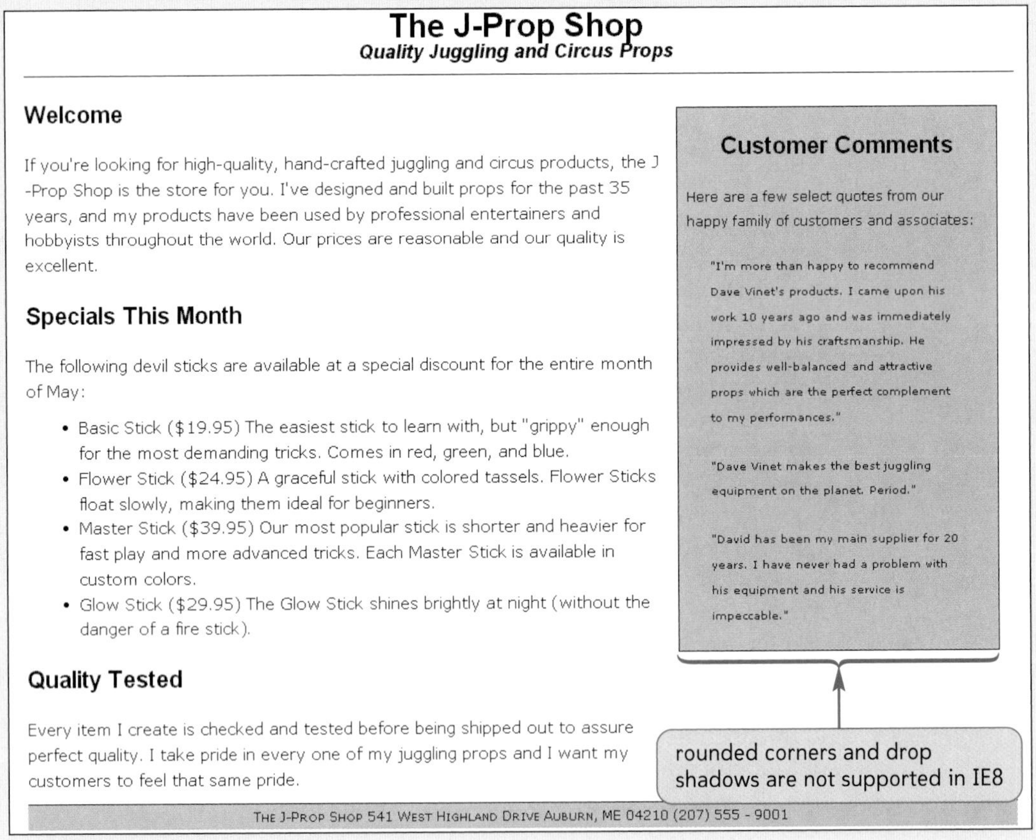

The J-Prop Shop
Quality Juggling and Circus Props

Welcome

If you're looking for high-quality, hand-crafted juggling and circus products, the J-Prop Shop is the store for you. I've designed and built props for the past 35 years, and my products have been used by professional entertainers and hobbyists throughout the world. Our prices are reasonable and our quality is excellent.

Specials This Month

The following devil sticks are available at a special discount for the entire month of May:

- Basic Stick ($19.95) The easiest stick to learn with, but "grippy" enough for the most demanding tricks. Comes in red, green, and blue.
- Flower Stick ($24.95) A graceful stick with colored tassels. Flower Sticks float slowly, making them ideal for beginners.
- Master Stick ($39.95) Our most popular stick is shorter and heavier for fast play and more advanced tricks. Each Master Stick is available in custom colors.
- Glow Stick ($29.95) The Glow Stick shines brightly at night (without the danger of a fire stick).

Quality Tested

Every item I create is checked and tested before being shipped out to assure perfect quality. I take pride in every one of my juggling props and I want my customers to feel that same pride.

Customer Comments

Here are a few select quotes from our happy family of customers and associates:

"I'm more than happy to recommend Dave Vinet's products. I came upon his work 10 years ago and was immediately impressed by his craftsmanship. He provides well-balanced and attractive props which are the perfect complement to my performances."

"Dave Vinet makes the best juggling equipment on the planet. Period."

"David has been my main supplier for 20 years. I have never had a problem with his equipment and his service is impeccable."

rounded corners and drop shadows are not supported in IE8

THE J-PROP SHOP 541 WEST HIGHLAND DRIVE AUBURN, ME 04210 (207) 555 - 9001

The rendering done by Internet Explorer 8 does not completely match what was shown under Internet Explorer 9 or many of the other competing browsers such as Firefox, Safari, or Google Chrome. For example, Internet Explorer 8 doesn't support styles for rounded corners and drop shadows. All of this underscores an important point: You may find variations between one browser and another in how your page is rendered, especially when using the newest HTML5 elements and CSS styles. This means you have to test your page under multiple browsers and devices, and make sure that any differences in format or layout do not impact your users' ability to read and understand your page.

Marking Text-Level Elements

Grouping elements like paragraphs and headings start their content on a new line. Another type of element is a **text-level element**, which marks content within a grouping element. A text-level element is like a phrase or a collection of characters within a paragraph or heading. Text-level elements do not start out on a new line, but instead flow alongside of, or **inline** with, the rest of the characters in the grouping element. Figure 1-35 lists some of the text-level elements in HTML.

Figure 1-35	Text-level elements

Text-Level Element	Description
a	A hypertext link
abbr	An abbreviation
b	Text offset from the surrounding content (usually displayed in **boldface** text)
cite	A citation (usually displayed in *italics*)
code	Program code (usually displayed in a `fixed width` font)
del	Deleted text (usually displayed with a ~~strikethrough~~ line)
dfn	A definition term (usually displayed in *italics*)
em	Emphasized content (usually displayed in *italics*)
i	Text representing an alternate voice or mood (usually displayed in *italics*)
ins	Inserted text (usually displayed with an <u>underline</u>)
kbd	Keyboard text (usually displayed in a `fixed width` font)
mark	Highlighted or marked text (usually displayed with a highlight. HTML5 only)
q	Quoted text (occasionally enclosed in "quotes")
samp	Sample computer code (usually displayed in a `fixed width` font)
small	Text displayed in a smaller font than surrounding content
span	A span of generic text
strong	Strongly emphasized content (usually displayed in **boldface** text)
sub	Subscripted text
sup	Superscripted text
time	A date and time value (HTML5 only)
var	Programming variables (usually displayed in *italic*)

TIP

Text-level elements should always be nested within grouping elements such as paragraphs or headings.

To practice using text-level elements in conjunction with grouping elements, you'll return to the HTML demo page.

To explore the use of inline elements:

▶ **1.** Return to the **demo_html.htm** file in your Web browser.

▶ **2.** Replace the code in the HTML Code box with the following:

```
<p>Welcome to the J-Prop Shop, owned and operated by David
Vinet</p>
```

▶ **3.** Click the **Preview Code** button to display this paragraph in the Preview box.

To mark *J-Prop Shop* as strongly emphasized text, you can enclose that phrase within a set of <strong> tags.

▶ **4.** Insert the <strong> opening tag directly before the word *J-Prop* in the box on the left. Insert the closing </strong> tag directly after the word *Shop*. Click the **Preview Code** button to confirm that *J-Prop Shop* is now displayed in a bold-faced font.

Another text-level element is the cite element used to make citations. Explore how citations are rendered by your browser by enclosing *David Vinet* within a set of <cite> tags.

▶ **5.** Insert an opening <cite> tag directly before the word *David* and insert the closing </cite> tag directly after *Vinet*. Click the **Preview Code** button to view the revised code. Figure 1-36 shows the result of applying the <strong> and <cite> tags to the paragraph text.

Figure 1-36 Applying the strong and cite text-level elements

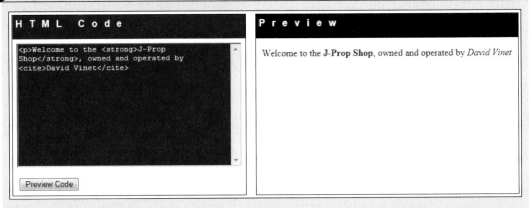

▶ **6.** Continue exploring other HTML elements listed in Figure 1-35 to see their effects on the rendered text. Close the demo file when you're done.

You can nest text-level tags to mark a single text string with more than one element. For example, the HTML code

```
<p>Welcome to the <strong><em>J-Prop Shop</em></strong>.</p>
```

marks the text string *J-Prop Shop* as both strong and emphasized text. In most browsers it appears in a ***bold italic*** font.

Dave wants the names of all of the items in his product list to be marked as strong text. Revise the code for the product names now.

To mark strong text:

▶ **1.** Return to the **jprop.htm** file in your text editor.

▶ **2.** Scroll down to the unordered list and enclose the name and price of each product within a set of **<strong>** tags as shown in Figure 1-37.

Figure 1-37 ▶ Marking product names using the strong element

```
<article>
    <h2>Specials This Month</h2>
    <p>The following devil sticks are available at a
        special discount for the entire month of May:
    </p>

    <ul>
        <li><strong>Basic Stick ($19.95)</strong>
            The easiest stick to learn with, but "grippy" enough
            for the most demanding tricks. Comes in red, green,
            and blue.
        </li>
        <li><strong>Flower Stick ($24.95)</strong>
            A graceful stick with colored tassels. Flower Sticks
            float slowly, making them ideal for beginners.
        </li>
        <li><strong>Master Stick ($39.95)</strong>
            Our most popular stick is shorter and heavier for
            fast play and more advanced tricks. Each Master Stick
            is available in custom colors.
        </li>
        <li><strong>Glow Stick ($29.95)</strong>
            The Glow Stick shines brightly at night (without
            the danger of a fire stick).
        </li>
    </ul>

</article>
```

▶ **3.** Save your changes to the file and then reload the **jprop.htm** file in your Web browser. Figure 1-38 shows the revised appearance of the bulleted list of products.

Figure 1-38 ▶ Product names rendered in a boldfaced font

Specials This Month

The following devil sticks are available at a special discount for the entire month of May:

- **Basic Stick ($19.95)** The easiest stick to learn with, but "grippy" enough for the most demanding tricks. Comes in red, green, and blue.
- **Flower Stick ($24.95)** A graceful stick with colored tassels. Flower Sticks float slowly, making them ideal for beginners.
- **Master Stick ($39.95)** Our most popular stick is shorter and heavier for fast play and more advanced tricks. Each Master Stick is available in custom colors.
- **Glow Stick ($29.95)** The Glow Stick shines brightly at night (without the danger of a fire stick).

PROSKILLS

Written Communication: Logical and Physical Interpretation of Elements

As you learn more HTML, you'll notice some overlap in how browsers display certain elements. To display italicized text, you could use the <dfn>, <em>, <i>, or <var> tags; or if you wanted to italicize an entire block of text, you could use the <address> tag. However, browsers differ in how they display elements, so you should not rely on the way any browser or group of browsers commonly displays an element.

In addition, it's important to distinguish between the way a browser displays an element, and the purpose of the element in the document. Although it can be tempting to ignore this difference, your HTML code benefits when you respect that distinction because search engines often look within specific elements for information. For example, a search engine may look for the address element to find contact information for a particular Web site. It would be confusing to end users if you used the address element to simply italicize a block of text. Web programmers can also use elements to extract information from a page. For example, a JavaScript program could automatically generate a bibliography from all of the citations listed within a Web site by looking for occurrences of the cite element.

The best practice for communicating the purpose of your document is to use HTML to mark content but not to rely on HTML to format that content. Formatting should be done solely through style sheets, using either the internal style sheets built into browsers or through your own customized styles.

Using the Generic Elements div and span

Most of the page elements you've examined have a specific meaning. However, sometimes you want to add an element that represents a text block or a string of inline text without it having any other meaning. HTML supports two such generic elements: div and span. The div element is used to mark general grouping content and has the following syntax:

```
<div>content</div>
```

The span element, which is used to mark general text-level content, has the following syntax:

```
<span>content</span>
```

Browsers recognize both elements but do not assign any default format to content marked with these elements. This frees Web authors to develop styles for these elements without worrying about overriding any styles imposed by browsers. Note that the main use of the div element to mark sections of the page has been superseded in HTML5 by the sectional elements such as header and article; however, you will still encounter the div element in many current and older Web sites.

Presentational Attributes

Early versions of HTML were used mostly by scientists and researchers who, for the most part, didn't need flashy graphics, decorative text fonts, or even much color on a page. The earliest Web pages weren't fancy and didn't require much from the browsers that displayed them. This changed as the Web became more popular and attracted the attention of commercial businesses, graphic designers, and artists.

One way that HTML changed to accommodate this new class of users was to introduce **presentational elements** and **presentational attributes** designed to describe how each element should be rendered by Web browsers. For example, to align text on a page, Web authors would use the `align` attribute

```
<element align="alignment">content</element>
```

where *alignment* is either *left, right, center,* or *justify.* Thus, to center an `h1` heading on a page, you could apply the following `align` attribute to the `<h1>` tag:

```
<h1 align="center">The J-Prop Shop</h1>
```

Almost all presentational elements and attributes are now deprecated in favor of style sheets, but you may still see them used in older Web sites. Using a deprecated attribute like `align` would probably not cause a Web page to fail, but it's still best to focus your HTML code on describing the content of a document and not its appearance.

Marking a Line Break

After examining your work, Dave notices that the list of customer comments lacks the names of the customers who made them. He asks you to add this information to the Web page, marking the customer information as citations.

To append customer names to the Customer Comments section:

1. Return to the **jprop.htm** file in your text editor.

2. Locate the first customer comment and then add the following code at the end of the paragraph, directly before the closing `</p>` tag:

   ```
   <cite>Thomas Gage, Circus England</cite>
   ```

3. At the end of the paragraph for the second customer comment, insert

   ```
   <cite>Douglas Pederson, Street-Wise Shows</cite>
   ```

4. Finally, at the end of the paragraph for the third customer comment, insert

   ```
   <cite>Linda Unger, Linda & Louis</cite>
   ```

   Figure 1-39 shows the revised code in the file.

Figure 1-39   Providing citations for the customer quotes

```
<aside>
   <h2>Customer Comments</h2>
   <p>Here are a few select quotes from our happy family
      of customers and associates:
   </p>
   <blockquote>
      <p>"I'm more than happy to recommend Dave Vinet's
         products. I came upon his work 10 years ago and
         was immediately impressed by his craftsmanship.
         He provides well-balanced and attractive
         props which are the perfect complement to my
         performances."
         <cite>Thomas Gage, Circus England</cite>
      </p>
      <p>"Dave Vinet makes the best juggling equipment on
         the planet. Period."
         <cite>Douglas Pederson, Street-Wise Shows</cite>
      </p>
      <p>"David has been my main supplier for 20 years. I
         have never had a problem with his equipment and
         his service is impeccable."
         <cite>Linda Unger, Linda & Louis</cite>
      </p>
   </blockquote>
</aside>
```

▶ **5.** Save your changes to the file and then refresh the **jprop.htm** file in your Web browser. Figure 1-40 shows the revised text of the Customer Comments sidebar.

Figure 1-40   Revised Customer Comments sidebar

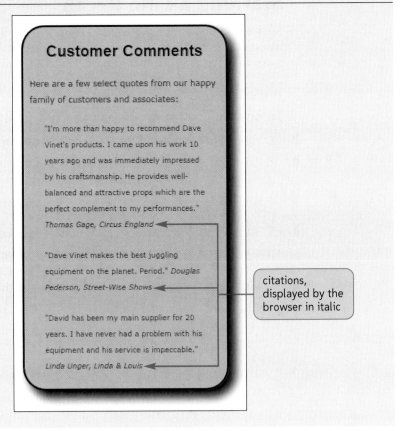

Dave thinks the comments are difficult to read when the text of a comment runs into the citation. He suggests that you start each citation on a new line. To do this, you can insert a line break into the Web page using the following empty element tag:

```
<br />
```

Line breaks must be placed within grouping elements such as paragraphs or headings. Some browsers accept line breaks placed anywhere within the body of a Web page; however, this is not good coding technique. A browser displaying an XHTML document will reject code in which a text-level element such as br is placed outside of any grouping element.

You'll use the br element to mark a line break between each customer comment and its associated citation in Dave's Web page.

To insert line breaks in the comments:

1. Return to the **jprop.htm** file in your text editor.

2. Insert the tag `<br />` between the comment and the citation for each of the three customer comments in the file. See Figure 1-41.

Figure 1-41   **Inserting line breaks**

```
<blockquote>
    <p>"I'm more than happy to recommend Dave Vinet's
       products. I came upon his work 10 years ago and
       was immediately impressed by his craftsmanship.
       He provides well-balanced and attractive
       props which are the perfect complement to my
       performances."
       <br />
       <cite>Thomas Gage, Circus England</cite>
    </p>
    <p>"Dave Vinet makes the best juggling equipment on
       the planet. Period."
       <br />
       <cite>Douglas Pederson, Street-Wise Shows</cite>
    </p>
    <p>"David has been my main supplier for 20 years. I
       have never had a problem with his equipment and
       his service is impeccable."
       <br />
       <cite>Linda Unger, Linda & Louis</cite>
    </p>
</blockquote>
```

line break element

3. Save your changes to the file and then refresh the **jprop.htm** file in your Web browser. Verify that each citation starts on a new line below the associated customer comment.

INSIGHT

Marking a Horizontal Rule

Another empty element is hr, the horizontal rule element, which marks a major topic change within a section. The syntax of the hr element is as follows:

```
<hr />
```

The exact appearance of the hr element is left to the browser. Most browsers display a gray-shaded horizontal line a few pixels in height. The hr element was originally used as a quick way of inserting horizontal lines within a Web page. Although that task now should be left to style sheets, you will still see the hr element in older Web pages.

Inserting an Inline Image

Dave wants you to replace the name of the company at the top of his Web page with an image of the company logo. Because HTML files are simple text files, non-textual content such as graphics must be stored in separate files, which are then loaded by browsers as they render pages. To add a graphic image to a Web page, you have to insert an inline image into your code.

The `img` Element

Inline images are inserted into a Web page using the one-sided `img` element with the syntax

```
<img src="file" alt="text" />
```

where *file* is the name of the graphic image file and *text* is text displayed by browsers in place of the graphic image. In this tutorial, you'll assume that the graphic image file is located in the same folder as the Web page, so you don't have to specify the location of the file. In the next tutorial, you'll learn how to reference files placed in other folders or locations on the Web.

Browsers retrieve the specified image file and display the image alongside the rest of the Web page content. The size of the image is based on the dimensions of the image itself; however, you can specify a different size using the `width` and `height` attributes

```
width="value" height="value"
```

where the width and height values are expressed in pixels. If you specify only the width, browsers automatically set the height to maintain the proportions of the image; similarly, if you define the height, browsers automatically set the width to maintain the image proportions. Thus, by setting the width and height values yourself, you can enlarge or reduce the size of the rendered image.

Inline images are considered text-level elements and thus must be placed within a grouping element such as a heading or a paragraph. An inline image is most commonly stored in one of three formats: GIF (Graphics Interchange Format), JPEG (Joint Photographic Experts Group), or PNG (Portable Network Graphics). Dave has already created his graphic image in PNG format and stored it with his other files using the filename *jpslogo.png*. You'll replace the text of the `h1` heading with this inline image.

To insert the company logo at the top of the page:

1. Return to the **jprop.htm** file in your text editor.

2. Go to the `h1` heading element at the top of the body section, delete the text *The J-Prop Shop* from between the opening and closing <h1> tags, and then replace it with

   ```
   <img src="jpslogo.png" alt="The J-Prop Shop" />
   ```

   Figure 1-42 highlights the revised code in the **jprop.htm** file.

Figure 1-42   Adding an inline image

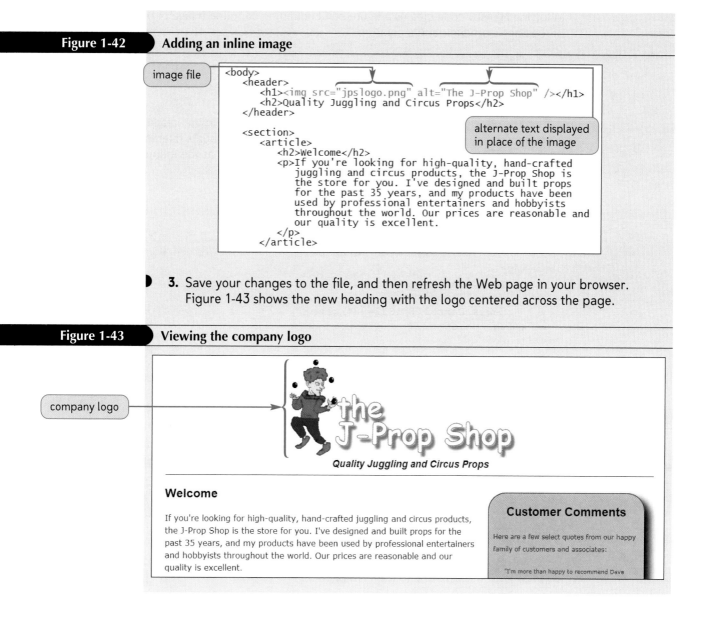

image file

```
<body>
    <header>
        <h1><img src="jpslogo.png" alt="The J-Prop Shop" /></h1>
        <h2>Quality Juggling and Circus Props</h2>
    </header>

    <section>
        <article>
            <h2>Welcome</h2>
            <p>If you're looking for high-quality, hand-crafted
               juggling and circus products, the J-Prop Shop is
               the store for you. I've designed and built props
               for the past 35 years, and my products have been
               used by professional entertainers and hobbyists
               throughout the world. Our prices are reasonable and
               our quality is excellent.
            </p>
        </article>
```

alternate text displayed in place of the image

3. Save your changes to the file, and then refresh the Web page in your browser. Figure 1-43 shows the new heading with the logo centered across the page.

Figure 1-43   Viewing the company logo

company logo

Quality Juggling and Circus Props

Welcome

If you're looking for high-quality, hand-crafted juggling and circus products, the J-Prop Shop is the store for you. I've designed and built props for the past 35 years, and my products have been used by professional entertainers and hobbyists throughout the world. Our prices are reasonable and our quality is excellent.

Customer Comments

Here are a few select quotes from our happy family of customers and associates:

"I'm more than happy to recommend Dave

Figures and Figure Captions

In books and magazines, figures and figure captions are often placed within boxes that stand aside from the main content of an article. HTML5 introduced this type of object to Web page markup with the figure and figcaption elements

```
<figure>
    content
    <figcaption>caption</figcaption>
</figure>
```

where *content* is the content that will appear in the figure box and *caption* is the text of the figure caption. The figcaption element is optional; but if the figcaption element is used, it must be nested within a set of <figure> tags either directly after the opening <figure> tag or directly before the closing </figure> tag. For example, the following HTML5 code creates a figure box containing an inline image of one of the J-Prop Shop's products and a caption:

```
<figure>
    <img src="stick03.png" alt="Master Stick" />
    <figcaption>Master Stick ($39.95)</figcaption>
</figure>
```

The `figure` element doesn't necessarily need to contain an inline image. It can be used to mark any content that stands aside from a main article but is referenced by it. For instance, it could be used to contain an excerpt of a poem, as the following code demonstrates:

```
<figure>
    <p>'Twas brillig, and the slithy toves<br />
        Did gyre and gimble in the wabe;<br />
        All mimsy were the borogoves,<br />
        And the mome raths outgrabe.
    </p>
    <figcaption>
        <cite>Jabberwocky,
        Lewis Carroll, 1832-98</cite>
    </figcaption>
</figure>
```

As with other HTML elements, the exact appearance of a figure box is determined by a style sheet. At this time, Dave does not need to create a figure box for his company's home page.

Working with Character Sets and Special Characters

Dave likes the work you've done so far on the Web page. He has only one remaining concern: The company's address in the page footer is difficult to read because the street address, city name, zip code, and phone number all run together on one line. Dave would like to have the different parts of the address separated by a solid circular marker (•). However, this marker is not represented by any keys on your keyboard. How, then, do you insert this symbol into the Web page?

Character Sets

Every character that your browser is capable of rendering belongs to a collection of characters and symbols called a **character set**. Character sets come in a wide variety of sizes. For English, no more than about 127 characters are needed to represent all of the upper- and lowercase letters, numbers, punctuation marks, spaces, and special typing symbols in the language. Other languages, such as Japanese or Chinese, require character sets containing thousands of symbols. Beyond the basic characters used by a language are special characters such as ©, ½, π, and ®. Thus, a complete character set that includes all possible printable characters is made up of hundreds of symbols.

The character set used for the alphabet of English characters is called **ASCII (American Standard Code for Information Interchange)**. A more extended character set, called **Latin-1** or the **ISO 8859-1** character set, supports 255 characters and can be used by most languages that employ the Latin alphabet, including English, French, Spanish, and Italian. **Unicode**, the most extended character set, supports up to 65,536 symbols and can be used for any of the world's languages. The most commonly used character set on the Web is **UTF-8**, which is a compressed version of Unicode and is probably the default character set assumed by your browser. You can learn more about character sets by visiting the W3C Web site and the Web site for the Internet Assigned Numbers Authority at *www.iana.org*.

Character Encoding

Character encoding associates each symbol from a character set with a numeric value called the **numeric character reference**. For example, the copyright symbol © from the UTF-8 character set is encoded with the number 169. If you know the character encoding number, you can insert the corresponding character directly into your Web page using the entity

    &#code;

where *code* is the encoding number. Thus, to display the © symbol in your Web page, you would enter

    ©

into your HTML file.

Character Entity References

Another way to insert a special symbol is to use a **character entity reference**, which is a short memorable name used in place of the encoding number. Character entity references are inserted using the syntax

    &char;

where *char* is the character's entity reference. The character entity reference for the copyright symbol is *copy*. So to display the © symbol in your Web page, you could insert

    ©

into your HTML code.

REFERENCE

Inserting Symbols from a Character Set

- To insert a symbol based on the encoding number, use the entity
  &#code;
  where *code* is the encoding number.
- To insert a symbol based on a character entity reference, use the entity
  &char;
  where *char* is the name assigned to the character.
- To insert a nonbreaking space, use the following entity:

- To insert the < symbol, use the following entity:
  <
- To insert the > symbol, use the following entity:
  >

You can explore various encoding numbers and character entity references by opening the demo page supplied with your Data Files.

To view the demo page:

1. Use your Web browser to open the **demo_characters.htm** file from the tutorial.01\demo data folder.

2. Type £ in the input box and then click the **Show** button. The Web browser displays the £ symbol in the ivory-colored box below.

3. Replace the value in the input box with `&reg;` and then click the **Show** button. The browser now displays the ® symbol, the symbol for registered trademarks, which you specified using a character entity reference.

   You can also view a collection of numeric character references and character entity references by selecting a table from the list box on the page.

4. Verify that General Symbols is displayed in the selection list box, and then click the **Show Table** button. As shown in Figure 1-44, the browser displays a list of 35 symbols with the character entity reference and the numeric character reference displayed beneath each symbol.

Figure 1-44   HTML characters demo page

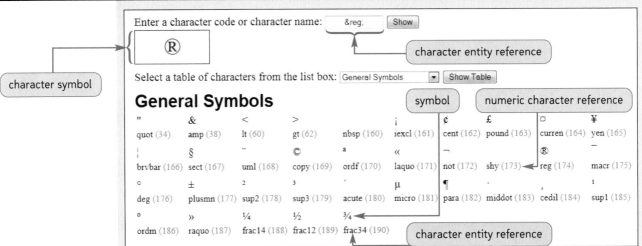

5. Take some time to explore the variety of numeric character references and character entity references supported by your browser. Close the demo page when you're finished, but leave your browser open.

Special Characters

One use of character codes is to insert text about HTML itself. For example, if you want your Web page to describe the use of the `<h1>` tag, you cannot simply type

    The <h1> tag is used to mark h1 headings.

because browsers would interpret the `<h1>` text as marking the beginning of an `h1` heading! Instead, you have to use the `&lt;` and `&gt;` entity references to insert the < and > symbols. The text would then be:

    The <h1> tag is used to mark h1 headings.

Another use of character codes is to add extra spaces to your Web page. Remember that browsers ignore extra blank spaces in an HTML file. To insert an additional space, use the ` ` entity reference (*nbsp* stands for *nonbreaking space*), which forces browsers to insert an extra space.

On Dave's Web page, you decide to use the bullet symbol (•) to break up the address text into sections. The symbol has a character encoding number of 8226 and the character entity reference name *bull*. Dave suggests that you also add a long horizontal line known as an em-dash (—) to mark the customer names in the customer comments section. The character encoding number for an em-dash is 8212 and the entity reference is *mdash*.

To add bullets and an em-dash to Dave's Web page:

1. Return to the **jprop.htm** file in your text editor.

2. Locate the customer comment from Thomas Gage, and then directly before the opening <cite> tag insert the character code — followed by a space.

3. Repeat Step 2 for the two remaining customer comments.

> Always include a semi-colon so that browsers recognize the entry as a character code.

4. Scroll down to the address element within the page footer. At the end of each line within the address (except the last line), insert a space followed by the • character entity. Figure 1-45 highlights the revised code in the Web page.

Figure 1-45	Adding symbols from a character set

```
<aside>
    <h2>Customer Comments</h2>
    <p>Here are a few select quotes from our happy family
        of customers and associates:
    </p>
    <blockquote>
        <p>"I'm more than happy to recommend Dave Vinet's
            products. I came upon his work 10 years ago and
            was immediately impressed by his craftsmanship.
            He provides well-balanced and attractive
            props which are the perfect complement to my
            performances."
            <br />
            &#8212; <cite>Thomas Gage, Circus England</cite>
        </p>
        <p>"Dave Vinet makes the best juggling equipment on
            the planet. Period."
            <br />
            &#8212; <cite>Douglas Pederson, Street-Wise Shows</cite>
        </p>
        <p>"David has been my main supplier for 20 years. I
            have never had a problem with his equipment and
            his service is impeccable."
            <br />
            &#8212; <cite>Linda Unger, Linda & Louis</cite>
        </p>
    </blockquote>
</aside>

<footer>
    <address>The J-Prop Shop &bull;
            541 West Highland Drive &bull;
            Auburn, ME 04210 &bull;
            (207) 555 - 9001
    </address>
</footer>
</body>
```

character encoding number →

character entity reference

5. Save your changes to the file.

6. Refresh the **jprop.htm** file in your Web browser. Figure 1-46 shows the final content of Dave's Web page.

Figure 1-46 **Completed Web page**

Welcome

If you're looking for high-quality, hand-crafted juggling and circus products, the J-Prop Shop is the store for you. I've designed and built props for the past 35 years, and my products have been used by professional entertainers and hobbyists throughout the world. Our prices are reasonable and our quality is excellent.

Specials This Month

The following devil sticks are available at a special discount for the entire month of May:

- **Basic Stick ($19.95)** The easiest stick to learn with, but "grippy" enough for the most demanding tricks. Comes in red, green, and blue.
- **Flower Stick ($24.95)** A graceful stick with colored tassels. Flower Sticks float slowly, making them ideal for beginners.
- **Master Stick ($39.95)** Our most popular stick is shorter and heavier for fast play and more advanced tricks. Each Master Stick is available in custom colors.
- **Glow Stick ($29.95)** The Glow Stick shines brightly at night (without the danger of a fire stick).

Quality Tested

Every item I create is checked and tested before being shipped out to assure perfect quality. I take pride in every one of my juggling props and I want my customers to feel that same pride.

Customer Comments

Here are a few select quotes from our happy family of customers and associates:

"I'm more than happy to recommend Dave Vinet's products. I came upon his work 10 years ago and was immediately impressed by his craftsmanship. He provides well-balanced and attractive props which are the perfect complement to my performances."
— *Thomas Gage, Circus England*

"Dave Vinet makes the best juggling equipment on the planet. Period."
— *Douglas Pederson, Street-Wise Shows*

"David has been my main supplier for 20 years. I have never had a problem with his equipment and his service is impeccable."
— *Linda Unger, Linda & Louis*

THE J-PROP SHOP • 541 WEST HIGHLAND DRIVE • AUBURN, ME 04210 • (207) 555 - 9001

Specifying the Character Set

To render a numeric character reference correctly, a browser must apply the correct character set to a Web page. This information is typically sent by the Web server as it transfers an HTML page to a browser. However, to be doubly certain that browsers employ the correct character set, you can specify the character set within the `head` element of your HTML document. For HTML 4.01 and XHTML, you add the `meta` element

```
<meta http-equiv="Content-Type"
      content="text/html; charset=character_set" />
```

to the document head, where *character_set* is the name of the character set you want the browser to employ when interpreting your HTML code. Under HTML5, the meta element is simply:

```
<meta charset="character_set" />
```

HTML5 also supports the syntax of the HTML 4.01 and XHTML meta element. You should always specify the character encoding in your document, even if you are not using any special symbols. It relieves the browser from having to guess about the correct encoding; and in certain situations, not specifying the encoding can lead to a security hole in the transfer of a page from the Web server to the client.

You'll add the meta element to Dave's document to specify that his file has been encoded using the UTF-8 character set.

To specify the character encoding for Dave's document:

▶ **1.** Return to the **jprop.htm** file in your text editor.

▶ **2.** Scroll to the top of the file. Directly below the comment in the head section, insert the following meta element as shown in Figure 1-47:

```
<meta charset="UTF-8" />
```

Figure 1-47	Specifying the character encoding

```
<!DOCTYPE html>
<html>

    <head>
        <!-- The J-Prop Shop Sample Page
             Author: David Vinet
             Date:    3/1/2014                          character set
        -->
        <meta charset="UTF-8" />
        <title>The J-Prop Shop</title>
        <script src="modernizr-1.5.js"></script>
        <link href="jpsstyles.css" rel="stylesheet" type="text/css" />
    </head>
```

▶ **3.** Close the **jprop.htm** file, saving your changes.

▶ **4.** Refresh the **jprop.htm** file in your browser and verify that the browser renders the page with no errors.

Written Communication: Publishing Your Web Page

Once you've completed your Web page, your next step is to get it on the Web. You first need to find a Web server to host the page. In choosing a Web server, you'll need to consider how much you want to pay, how much space you need, and how much traffic you expect at your Web site. If you'd prefer a free or low-cost option and don't need much space, you might first look toward the company that provides your Internet access. Most **Internet service providers** (ISPs) offer space on their Web servers as part of their regular service or for a small fee. However, they usually limit the amount of space available to you, unless you pay an extra fee to host a larger site. There are also free Web hosts, which provide space on servers for personal or noncommercial use. Once again, the amount of space you get is limited. Free Web hosting services make their money from selling advertising space on your site, so you should be prepared to act as a billboard in return for space on their servers. Finally, you can pay a monthly fee to an ISP to host your Web site to get more space and bandwidth.

Once you identify a Web host, you next need to consider the domain name that identifies your site. If you're planning to create a commercial site to advertise a product or service, you'll want the domain name to reflect your business. Free Web hosts usually include their names in your Web address. Thus, instead of having a Web address like

thejpropshop.com

you might have something like

freewebhosting.net/members/thejpropshop.html

If you're running a site for personal use, this might not be a problem—but it would look unprofessional on a commercial site. If you are planning a commercial site and simply want to advertise your product by publishing an online brochure, you can usually find an inexpensive host and pay a nominal yearly fee to reserve a Web address that reflects your company's name.

Session 1.2 Quick Check

1. Specify the code you would enter to mark the text *The J-Prop Shop* as an `h1` heading and the text *Product List* as an `h2` heading. Add code to group these two headings so browsers recognize them as a heading and subheading, respectively.

2. Specify the code you would enter to mark the text *Hamlet by William Shakespeare* as an `h1` heading, with a line break after the word *Hamlet*.

3. Create an ordered list of the following items: Packers, Bears, Lions, Vikings.

4. Specify the code to access the CSS style sheet file *uwstyles.css*. Where should you place this code within an HTML file?

5. Mark the graphic file *portrait.gif* as an inline image, setting the dimensions to 250 pixels wide by 300 pixels high. Specify the text *David Vinet* as alternate text to be displayed in place of the image for non-graphical browsers.

6. Specify the code to place the *portrait.gif* image from the previous question within a figure box with the caption *David Vinet, owner of the J-Prop Shop*.

7. The trademark symbol (™) has the character encoding number 8482. Provide the HTML code to enter this symbol into your Web page.

8. The Greek letter ß has the character entity name *beta*. How would you enter this symbol into your Web page?

PRACTICE

Review Assignments

Data Files needed for the Review Assignments: basiclogo.png, basicstick.png, basicstyles.css, modernizr-1.5.js, stick.txt

Dave has found a host for his Web page and has published the document you helped him create on the Internet. Now he wants to start adding more pages to his Web site. He's come to you for help in creating a page describing his basic stick. He's already written the text for the Web page; he needs you to mark up that text with HTML code. Figure 1-48 shows a preview of the page you'll create for Dave.

Figure 1-48   **The Basic Stick product page**

Specials This Month

The Basic Stick

The Basic Stick is the perfect stick for beginners. The stick rotates slowly to provide extra time for performing stick tricks, but is flashy enough to impress your friends. Enjoy the following:

Our Basic Stick

Patented Dura-Coat® finish ensures sticks can withstand all weather conditions. More durable than other sticks, these props will keep looking like new for as long as you own them.

Enhanced stick flexibility provides more bounce, allowing for better tricks. A soft rubber core adds a whole new element to the sticking experience that you have to feel to believe!

Full customization will give you the chance to own a pair of sticks unlike any others out there. I make exactly what you want, with your colors and your designs.

A personal touch through both my customization options and hand-crafted designs.

Specifications

- Main Stick
  - Weight: 7 oz.
  - Length: 24 inches
  - Tape: Dura-Coat® finish with laser-style color choices
- Handle Sticks (one pair)
  - Weight: 2 oz.
  - Length: 18 inches
  - Tape: Soft ivory tape with rubber core

THE J-PROP SHOP ♦ 541 WEST HIGHLAND DRIVE ♦ AUBURN, ME 04210 ♦ (207) 555 - 9001

Complete the following:

1. Use your text editor to create a new file named **basic.htm**, and then save it in the tutorial.01\review folder included with your Data Files.
2. Add the doctype for an HTML5 document.
3. Create the root `html` element and nest the `head` and `body` elements within it.

4. Within the `head` element, insert the comment

   ```
   The J-Prop Shop
   Sample Page for the Basic Stick
   Author: your name
   Date:   the date
   ```

   where *your name* is your name and *the date* is the current date.

5. Add code to specify that the page uses the UTF-8 character set.

6. Set the page title as **Basic Sticks**.

7. Link the file to the **modernizr-1.5.js** script file to enable HTML5 support for older browsers.

8. Link the file to the **basicstyles.css** style sheet file.

9. Within the `body` element, create structural elements for the page header, main section, and footer.

10. Within the page header, insert an `h1` heading containing the inline image file **basiclogo.png**. Specify the following alternate text for the image: **The J-Prop Shop**. Below the `h1` heading, insert an `h2` heading containing the text **Specials This Month**. Group the `h1` and `h2` headings using the `hgroup` element.

11. Within the `section` element, insert an `aside` element. The `aside` element should contain an inline image pointing to the *basicstick.png* file and having the text string **photo** as the alternate text. Below the inline image within the `aside` element, insert a paragraph containing the text string **Our Basic Stick**.

12. Add two `article` elements to the `section` element.

13. Within the first article, insert an `h2` heading containing the text **The Basic Stick**. Add a paragraph containing the following text:

    The Basic Stick is the perfect stick for beginners. The stick rotates slowly to provide extra time for performing stick tricks, but is flashy enough to impress your friends. Enjoy the following:

14. Add a block quote containing the following four paragraphs (you can copy this text from the *stick.txt* file):

    Patented Dura-Coat finish ensures sticks can withstand all weather conditions. More durable than other sticks, these props will keep looking like new for as long as you own them.

    Enhanced stick flexibility provides more bounce, allowing for better tricks. A soft rubber core adds a whole new element to the sticking experience that you have to feel to believe!

    Full customization will give you the chance to own a pair of sticks unlike any others out there. I make exactly what you want, with your colors and your designs.

    A personal touch through both my customization options and hand-crafted designs.

15. Mark the first few words of each of the four paragraphs as strong text, as shown in Figure 1-48.

16. Within the second article element, insert an `h2` heading with the title **Specifications**.

17. Directly below the `h2` heading, insert an unordered list. The list should contain two items: **Main Stick** and **Handle Sticks (one pair)**.

18. Within the *Main Stick* list item, insert a nested unordered list containing the following items:
    - **Weight: 7 oz.**
    - **Length: 24 inches**
    - **Tape: Dura-Coat finish with laser-style color choices**

19. Within the *Handle Sticks (one pair)* list item, insert a nested unordered list containing the following items:
    - **Weight: 2 oz.**
    - **Length: 18 inches**
    - **Tape: Soft ivory tape with rubber core**

20. Locate the two occurrences of *Dura-Coat* in the document. Directly after the word *Dura-Coat*, insert the registered trademark symbol ®. The character entity name of the ® symbol is *reg*. Display the ® symbol as a superscript by placing the character within the sup element.

21. Within the page footer, insert the company's address:
    The J-Prop Shop
    541 West Highland Drive
    Auburn, ME 04210
    (207) 555 - 9001

22. Separate the different sections of the address using a solid diamond (character code 9830).

23. Save your changes to the file, open it in your Web browser, and then compare your Web page to Figure 1-48 to verify that it was rendered correctly. Older browsers may display some slight differences in the design.

24. Submit your completed files to your instructor, in either printed or electronic form, as requested.

Apply your knowledge of HTML5 to create a Web page for a mathematics Web site.

APPLY

Case Problem 1

Data Files needed for the Case Problem: mhlogo.jpg, mhstyles.css, mhtxt.htm, modernizr-1.5.js

Math High   Professor Lauren Coe of the Mathematics Department of Coastal University in Anderson, South Carolina, is one of the founders of *Math High*, a Web site containing articles and course materials for high school and college math instructors. She has written a series of biographies of famous mathematicians for the Web site and would like you to transfer content she's already written to an HTML5 file. You'll create the first one in this exercise. Figure 1-49 shows a preview of the page you'll create, which profiles the mathematician Leonhard Euler.

Figure 1-49 Math High Web page

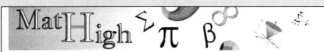

Leonhard Euler (1707-1783)

The greatest mathematician of the eighteenth century, **Leonhard Euler** was born in Basel, Switzerland. There, he studied under another giant of mathematics, **Jean Bernoulli**. In 1731 Euler became a professor of physics and mathematics at St. Petersburg Academy of Sciences. Euler was the most prolific mathematician of all time, publishing over *800 different books and papers.* His influence was felt in physics and astronomy as well.

He is perhaps best known for his research into mathematical analysis. Euler's work, *Introductio in analysin infinitorum (1748)*, remained a standard textbook in the field for well over a century. For the princess of Anhalt-Dessau he wrote *Lettres à une princesse d'Allemagne (1768-1772)*, giving a clear non-technical outline of the main physical theories of the time.

One can hardly write a mathematical equation without copying Euler. Notations still in use today, such as *e* and π, were introduced in Euler's writings. Leonhard Euler died in 1783, leaving behind a legacy perhaps unmatched, and certainly unsurpassed, in the annals of mathematics.

The Most Beautiful Theorem?

Euler's Equation:

$$\cos(x) + i\sin(x) = e^{(ix)}$$

demonstrates the relationship between algebra, complex analysis, and trigonometry. From this equation, it's easy to derive the identity:

$$e^{(\pi i)} + 1 = 0$$

which relates the fundamental constants: 0, 1, π, *e*, and *i* in a single beautiful and elegant statement. A poll of readers conducted by *The Mathematical Intelligencer* magazine named Euler's Identity as the most beautiful theorem in the history of mathematics.

MATH HIGH: A SITE FOR EDUCATORS AND RESEARCHERS

Complete the following:

1. In your text editor, open the **mhtxt.htm** file from the tutorial.01\case1 folder included with your Data Files. Save the file as **mathhigh.htm** in the same folder.

2. Enclose the contents of the file within a set of opening and closing `<html>` tags. Set the doctype of the file to indicate that this is an HTML5 document.

3. Add `head` and `body` elements to the file, enclosing the page contents within the body element.

4. Within the document head, insert the comment

   Math High: Leonhard Euler

   Author: *your name*

   Date: *the date*

   where *your name* is your name and *the date* is the current date.

5. Set the character set of the document to **UTF-8**.

6. Add the page title **Math High: Leonhard Euler** to the document head.

7. Link to the **modernizr-1.5.js** script file.

8. Link to the **mhstyles.css** style sheet.

9. Within the page body, create a `header` element. Within this element, insert an inline image using the **mhlogo.jpg** file as the source and **Math High** as the alternate text.

10. Mark the page text from the line *Leonhard Euler (1707 - 1783)* up to (but not including) the line *The Most Beautiful Theorem?* as an article.

11. Mark the first line in the article element, containing *Leonhard Euler (1707 - 1783)*, as an `h1` heading.

12. Mark the next three blocks of text describing Euler's life as paragraphs.

13. Within the first paragraph, mark the names *Leonhard Euler* and *Jean Bernoulli* using the `strong` element. Mark the phrase *800 different books and papers* as emphasized text using the `em` element.

14. In the second paragraph, mark the phrase *Introductio in analysin infinitorum (1748)* as a citation.

15. In the phrase *Lettres a une princesse d'Allemagne*, replace the one-letter word *a* with **à** (the character entity name is *agrave*). Mark the entire publication name as a citation.

16. In the third paragraph, mark the notation for *e* as a `var` element and replace *pi* with the character **π** (the character reference name is *pi*).

17. Enclose the next section of text from the line *The Most Beautiful Theorem?* up to (but not including) the line *Math High: A Site for Educators and Researchers* as an aside.

18. Mark the text *The Most Beautiful Theorem?* as an `h1` heading.

19. Mark the next five blocks of text as individual paragraphs.

20. In the first equation, mark the letters *e*, *i*, and *x* using the `var` element (but do not italicize the *i* in *sin*). Mark the term (ix) as a superscript.

21. In the second equation, replace *pi* with the character **π**. Mark the letters *e* and *i* using the `var` element. Mark (πi) as a superscript.

22. In the last paragraph, mark the notations for *e* and *i* with the `var` element and replace *pi* with **π**.

23. Mark the journal name *The Mathematical Intelligencer* as a citation.

24. Mark the final line in the file as a footer.

25. Save your changes to the file, and then verify that the page appears correctly in your Web browser.

26. Submit your completed files to your instructor, in either printed or electronic form, as requested.

Apply your knowledge of HTML to create a page showing text from a scene of a Shakespeare play.

APPLY

Case Problem 2

Data Files needed for the Case Problem: macbeth.jpg, macbethtxt.htm, macstyles.css, modernizr-1.5.js

Mansfield Classical Theatre   Steve Karls is the director of Mansfield Classical Theatre, a theatre company for young people located in Mansfield, Ohio. This summer the company is planning to perform the Shakespeare play *Macbeth*. Steve wants to put the text of the play on the company's Web site and has asked for your help in designing and completing the Web page. Steve wants a separate page for each scene from the play. A preview of the page you'll create for Act I, Scene 1 is shown in Figure 1-50. Steve has already typed the text of the scene. He needs you to supply the HTML code.

Figure 1-50 Macbeth Act I, Scene 1 Web page

Presented by: Mansfield Classical Theatre

ACT I

SCENE 1

Summary A thunderstorm approaches and three witches convene. They agree to confront the great Scot general Macbeth upon his victorious return from a war between Scotland and Norway. Soon, heroic Macbeth will receive the title of Thane of Cawdor from King Duncan. However, Macbeth learns from the witches that he is fated for greater things and he will be led down the path of destruction by his unquenchable ambition.

A desert place.

Thunder and lightning. Enter three Witches.

First Witch
> When shall we three meet again
> In thunder, lightning, or in rain?

Second Witch
> When the hurlyburly's done,
> When the battle's lost and won.

Third Witch
> That will be ere the set of sun.

First Witch
> Where the place?

Second Witch
> Upon the heath.

Third Witch
> There to meet with Macbeth.

First Witch
> I come, Graymalkin!

Second Witch
> Paddock calls.

Third Witch
> Anon.

ALL
> Fair is foul, and foul is fair:
> Hover through the fog and filthy air.

Exeunt

Go to Scene 2 ⇒

TEXT PROVIDED BY ONLINE SHAKESPEARE

Complete the following:

1. Open the **macbethtxt.htm** file from the tutorial.01\case2 folder included with your Data Files. Save the file as **macbeth.htm** in the same folder.

2. Enclose the entire Macbeth text within the structure of an HTML document including the `html`, `head`, and `body` elements. Add a doctype to the document head to indicate that the page is written in HTML5.

3. Within the head section, insert a comment containing the following text:

   Macbeth: Act I, Scene 1

   Author: *your name*

   Date: *the date*

4. Add the page title **Macbeth: Act I, Scene 1**.

5. Link the file to the **modernizr-1.5.js** script file and to the **macstyles.css** style sheet. Set the character set to **UTF-8**.

6. Within the `body` element, insert a heading group consisting of an `h1` heading and an `h2` heading. Within the `h1` heading, insert an inline image containing the *macbeth.jpg* image file. Specify **Macbeth** as the alternate text. Within the `h2` heading, enter the text **Presented by: Mansfield Classical Theatre**.

7. Enclose the text of the play within a `section` element.

8. Mark the text *ACT I* as an `h2` heading. Mark *SCENE 1* as an `h3` heading. Group the two headings within an `hgroup` element.

9. Mark the summary of the scene as a paragraph. Mark the word *Summary* using the strong element.

10. In the text of the play, mark the descriptions of setting, scene, and exits as separate paragraphs and italicize the text using the `i` element, as shown in Figure 1-50.

⊕ EXPLORE 11. Mark the dialog as a description list, with each character's name marked as a description term and each speech marked as a description. When a speech includes two lines, add a line break at the end of the first line to keep the speech on separate lines, as shown in the figure.

⊕ EXPLORE 12. Directly below the paragraph containing the text *Exeunt*, insert the line **Go to Scene 2**. Mark this line as a `div` element with the id value *direction*. At the end of this line, insert a **right arrow character** using the 8658 character number. Add horizontal rules directly above and below this statement.

13. Mark the line *Text provided by Online Shakespeare* as a footer. Make sure the `footer` element is below the `section` element.

14. Save your changes to the file, and then confirm the layout and content of the page in your Web browser.

15. Submit the completed files to your instructor, in either printed or electronic form, as requested.

Explore how to use HTML to create a recipe page.

CHALLENGE

Case Problem 3

Data Files needed for the Case Problem: dessertstyles.css, dessertweb.jpg, modernizr-1.5.js, torte.jpg, tortetxt.htm

dessertWEB Amy Wu wants to take her enjoyment of cooking and her love of sharing recipes to the World Wide Web. She's interested in creating a new Web site called *dessertWEB* where other cooks can submit and review dessert recipes. Each page within her site will contain a photo and description of a dessert, along with a list of ingredients, cooking directions, and a list of reviews. Each recipe will be rated on a five-star scale. She already has information on one recipe: Apple Bavarian Torte. She's asked for your help in creating a Web page from the data she's collected. A preview of the completed page is shown in Figure 1-51.

Figure 1-51   dessertWeb menu page

dessertWEB

Apple Bavarian Torte (★★★★)

A classic European torte baked in a springform pan. Cream cheese, sliced almonds, and apples make this the perfect holiday treat (12 servings).

INGREDIENTS
- ½ cup butter
- ⅓ cup white sugar
- ¼ teaspoon vanilla extract
- 1 cup all-purpose flour
- 1 (8 ounce) package cream cheese
- ¼ cup white sugar
- 1 egg
- ½ teaspoon vanilla extract
- 6 apples - peeled, cored, and sliced
- ⅓ cup white sugar
- ½ teaspoon ground cinnamon
- ¼ cup sliced almonds

DIRECTIONS
1. Preheat oven to 450° F (230° C).
2. Cream together butter, sugar, vanilla, and flour.
3. Press crust mixture into the flat bottom of a 9-inch springform pan. Set aside.
4. In a medium bowl, blend cream cheese and sugar. Beat in egg and vanilla. Pour cheese mixture over crust.
5. Toss apples with sugar and cinnamon. Spread apple mixture over all.
6. Bake for 10 minutes. Reduce heat to 400° F (200° C) and continue baking for 25 minutes.
7. Sprinkle almonds over top of torte. Continue baking until lightly browned. Cool before removing from pan.

REVIEWS

★★★★
I loved the buttery taste of the crust which complements the apples very nicely.
— Reviewed on Sep. 22, 2014 by MMASON.

★★
Nothing special. I like the crust, but there was a little too much of it for my taste, and I liked the filling but there was too little of it. I thought the crunchy apples combined with the sliced almonds detracted from the overall flavor.
— Reviewed on Sep. 1, 2014 by GLENDACHEF.

★★★★★
Delicious!! I recommend microwaving the apples for 3 minutes before baking, to soften them. Great dessert - I'll be making it again for the holidays.
— Reviewed on August 28, 2014 by BBABS.

Complete the following:

1. Open the **tortetxt.htm** file from the tutorial.01\case3 folder included with your Data Files. Save the file as **torte.htm** in the same folder.

2. Add the structure of an HTML5 document around the recipe text. Within the `head` element, insert a comment containing the following text:
   Apple Bavarian Torte
   Author: *your name*
   Date: *the date*

3. Set the character set of the document to **ISO-8859-1**.

4. Link the document to the **modernizr-1.5.js** script file and the **dessertstyles.css** style sheet file.

5. Specify **Apple Bavarian Torte Recipe** as the page title.

6. Within the `body` element, add a `header` element. Within the `header` element, insert an `h1` heading containing the inline image **dessertweb.jpg** with the alternate text **dessertWEB**.

7. Enclose the recipe description, ingredients list, and directions within a `section` element. Enclose the recipe reviews within an `aside` element.

8. Mark the text *Apple Bavarian Torte* as an `h1` heading.

⊕ EXPLORE 9. Replace the text *(4 stars)* in the `h1` heading with a set of four **star symbols** (character number 9733).

⊕ EXPLORE 10. Directly below the `h1` heading, insert the inline image **torte.jpg**. Specify the alternate text **Torte image**. Set the width of the image to **250** pixels.

11. Mark the description of the dessert as a paragraph.

12. Mark *INGREDIENTS* and *DIRECTIONS* as `h2` headings.

13. Mark the list of ingredients as an unordered list. Mark the list of directions as an ordered list.

⊕ EXPLORE 14. Within the ingredients, replace the occurrences of 1/2 with the character symbol ½ (reference number 189), the occurrences of 1/4 with the symbol ¼ (reference number 188), and the occurrences of 1/3 with the symbol ⅓ (reference number 8531.)

⊕ EXPLORE 15. Replace each occurrence of the word *degrees* in the directions with the degree symbol (°) (character name *deg*).

16. Mark *REVIEWS* within the `aside` element as an `h1` heading.

17. Change the text of each customer star rating to a set of **star symbols** using character number 9733 placed within a paragraph.

⊕ EXPLORE 18. Enclose the text of each customer review in a paragraph nested within a `blockquote` element. Place the name of the reviewer and the date on a new line within that paragraph. Insert an **em-dash** (character name *mdash*) before the word *Reviewed* in each of the reviews. Enclose the date of each review within a `time` element and enclose by *reviewer* within a `cite` element where *reviewer* is the name of the reviewer.

19. Save your changes to the file, and then verify the layout and content of the page in your Web browser.

20. Submit the completed files to your instructor, in either printed or electronic form, as requested.

Test your knowledge of HTML and use your creativity to design a Web page for an exercise equipment company.

RESEARCH

Case Problem 4

Data Files needed for the Case Problem: logo.jpg, smith.jpg, and smith.txt

Body Systems   Body Systems is a leading manufacturer of home gyms. The company recently hired you to assist in developing its Web site. Your first task is to create a Web page for the LSM400, a popular weight machine sold by the company. You've been given a text file describing the features of the LSM400. You've also received two image files: one of the company's logo and one of the LSM400. You are free to supplement these files with any other resources available to you. You are responsible for the page's content and appearance.

Complete the following:

1. Create a new HTML5 file named **smith.htm** and save it in the tutorial.01\case4 folder included with your Data Files.

2. Add the appropriate doctype for HTML5 to the beginning of the file.

3. Add a comment to the document head describing the document's content and containing your name and the date.

4. Add an appropriate page title to the document head.

5. Set the character set of the file to **UTF-8**.

6. Use the contents of the **smith.txt** document (located in the tutorial.01\case4 folder) as the basis of the document body. Include at least one example of each of the following:

   - structural elements such as the `header`, `footer`, `section`, and `aside` elements
   - grouping elements including a heading and a paragraph
   - an ordered or unordered list
   - a text-level element
   - an inline image
   - a character entity reference or a character encoding number

7. Structure your HTML5 code so that it's easy for others to read and understand.

8. Save your changes to the file, and then open it in your Web browser to verify that it is readable.

9. Submit your completed files to your instructor, in either printed or electronic form, as requested.

ENDING SOLUTION FILES

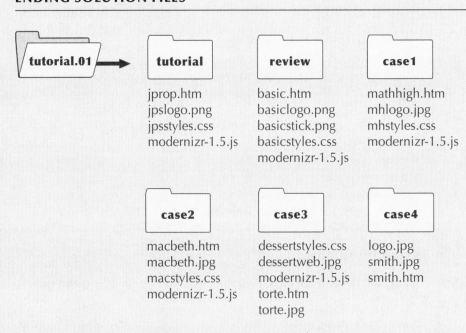

tutorial.01

tutorial
jprop.htm
jpslogo.png
jpsstyles.css
modernizr-1.5.js

review
basic.htm
basiclogo.png
basicstick.png
basicstyles.css
modernizr-1.5.js

case1
mathhigh.htm
mhlogo.jpg
mhstyles.css
modernizr-1.5.js

case2
macbeth.htm
macbeth.jpg
macstyles.css
modernizr-1.5.js

case3
dessertstyles.css
dessertweb.jpg
modernizr-1.5.js
torte.htm
torte.jpg

case4
logo.jpg
smith.jpg
smith.htm

TUTORIAL **2**

OBJECTIVES

Session 2.1
- Explore how to storyboard a Web site
- Create navigation lists
- Create links between documents in a Web site
- Understand absolute and relative folder paths
- Set a base path
- Mark a location with the id attribute
- Create a link to an id

Session 2.2
- Mark an image as a link
- Create an image map
- Understand URLs
- Link to a resource on the Web
- Link to an e-mail address
- Work with hypertext attributes
- Work with metadata

Developing a Web Site

Creating a Web Site for Amateur Photographers

Case | *CAMshots*

Gerry Hayward is an amateur photographer and digital camera enthusiast. He's creating a Web site named *CAMshots*, where he can offer advice and information to people who are just getting started with digital photography, or who are long-time hobbyists like himself and are looking to share tips and ideas. Gerry's Web site will contain several pages, with each page dedicated to a particular topic. He has created a few sample pages for the Web site, but he hasn't linked them together. He has asked for your help in designing his site and creating links between the pages.

STARTING DATA FILES

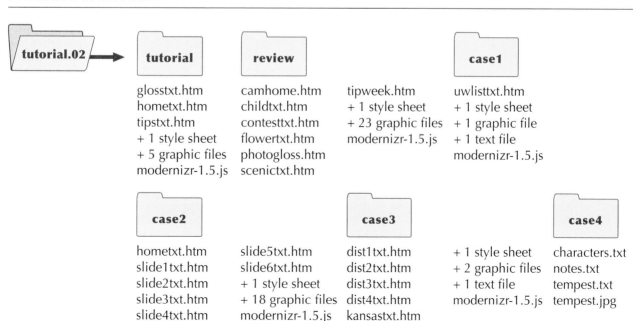

tutorial.02 → **tutorial**
glosstxt.htm
hometxt.htm
tipstxt.htm
+ 1 style sheet
+ 5 graphic files
modernizr-1.5.js

review
camhome.htm
childtxt.htm
contesttxt.htm
flowertxt.htm
photogloss.htm
scenictxt.htm

tipweek.htm
+ 1 style sheet
+ 23 graphic files
modernizr-1.5.js

case1
uwlisttxt.htm
+ 1 style sheet
+ 1 graphic file
+ 1 text file
modernizr-1.5.js

case2
hometxt.htm
slide1txt.htm
slide2txt.htm
slide3txt.htm
slide4txt.htm

slide5txt.htm
slide6txt.htm
+ 1 style sheet
+ 18 graphic files
modernizr-1.5.js

case3
dist1txt.htm
dist2txt.htm
dist3txt.htm
dist4txt.htm
kansastxt.htm

+ 1 style sheet
+ 2 graphic files
+ 1 text file
modernizr-1.5.js

case4
characters.txt
notes.txt
tempest.txt
tempest.jpg

SESSION 2.1 VISUAL OVERVIEW

The nav element marks a list of hypertext links used to navigate through the pages in the Web site.

The **<a> tag** is used to mark hyperlinks to external documents or to locations within the current document. The **href** attribute indicates the reference or address of the linked resource.

By default, browsers underline hypertext links.

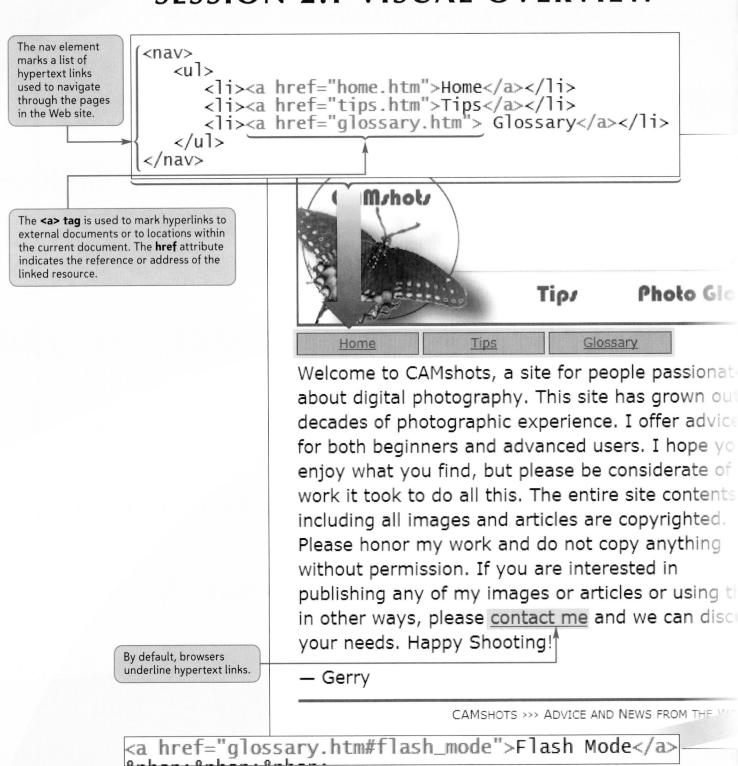

```
<nav>
    <ul>
        <li><a href="home.htm">Home</a></li>
        <li><a href="tips.htm">Tips</a></li>
        <li><a href="glossary.htm"> Glossary</a></li>
    </ul>
</nav>
```

Home   Tips   Glossary

Welcome to CAMshots, a site for people passionate about digital photography. This site has grown out of decades of photographic experience. I offer advice for both beginners and advanced users. I hope you enjoy what you find, but please be considerate of work it took to do all this. The entire site contents including all images and articles are copyrighted. Please honor my work and do not copy anything without permission. If you are interested in publishing any of my images or articles or using them in other ways, please contact me and we can discuss your needs. Happy Shooting!

— Gerry

CAMSHOTS >>> ADVICE AND NEWS FROM THE WO

```
<a href="glossary.htm#flash_mode">Flash Mode</a>
```

Links to locations within a document are referenced using the form *file#id*, where file is the name of the file and id is the id marking the location within the file.

CREATING HYPERLINKS

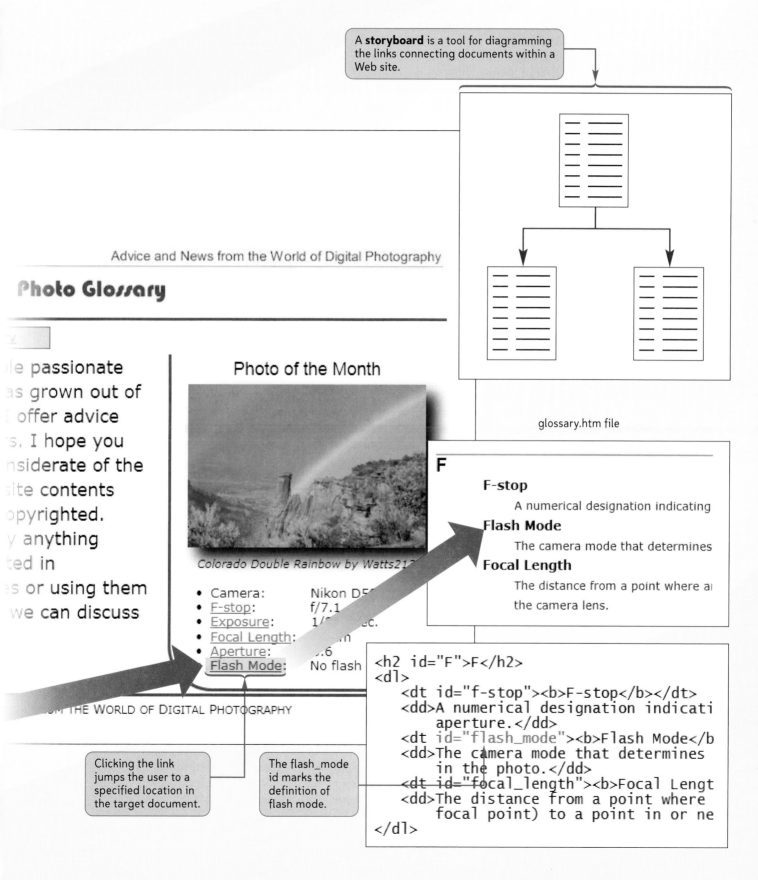

A **storyboard** is a tool for diagramming the links connecting documents within a Web site.

glossary.htm file

Advice and News from the World of Digital Photography

Photo Glossary

le passionate
as grown out of
offer advice
s. I hope you
nsiderate of the
site contents
opyrighted.
y anything
ted in
s or using them
we can discuss

Photo of the Month

Colorado Double Rainbow by Watts21

- Camera: Nikon D5
- F-stop: f/7.1
- Exposure: 1/   ec.
- Focal Length:
- Aperture: .6
- Flash Mode: No flash

M THE WORLD OF DIGITAL PHOTOGRAPHY

F

F-stop
   A numerical designation indicating

Flash Mode
   The camera mode that determines

Focal Length
   The distance from a point where a
   the camera lens.

```
<h2 id="F">F</h2>
<dl>
   <dt id="f-stop"><b>F-stop</b></dt>
   <dd>A numerical designation indicati
      aperture.</dd>
   <dt id="flash_mode"><b>Flash Mode</b
   <dd>The camera mode that determines
      in the photo.</dd>
   <dt id="focal_length"><b>Focal Lengt
   <dd>The distance from a point where
      focal point) to a point in or ne
</dl>
```

Clicking the link jumps the user to a specified location in the target document.

The flash_mode id marks the definition of flash mode.

Exploring Web Site Structures

You meet with Gerry to discuss his plans for the CAMshots Web site. Gerry has already created a prototype for the Web site containing three pages written in HTML5: One page is the site's home page and contains general information about CAMshots; the second page contains tips about digital photography; and the third page contains a partial glossary of photographic terms. The pages are not complete, nor are they linked to one another. You'll begin your work for Gerry by viewing these files in your text editor and browser.

To view Gerry's Web pages:

▶ 1. Start your text editor, and then open the **hometxt.htm**, **tipstxt.htm**, and **glosstxt.htm** files, located in the tutorial.02\tutorial folder included with your Data Files.

▶ 2. Within each file, go to the comment section at the top of the file and add *your name* and *the date* in the space provided.

▶ 3. Save the files as **home.htm**, **tips.htm**, and **glossary.htm**, respectively, in the tutorial.02\tutorial folder.

▶ 4. Take some time to review the HTML code within each document so that you understand the structure and content of the files.

▶ 5. Start your Web browser and open the **home.htm**, **tips.htm**, and **glossary.htm** files. Figure 2-1 shows the current layout and appearance of Gerry's three Web pages.

| Figure 2-1 | Versions of HTML |

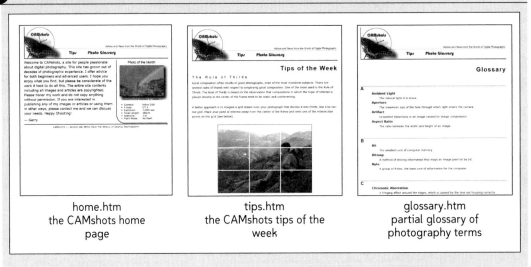

home.htm
the CAMshots home
page

tips.htm
the CAMshots tips of the
week

glossary.htm
partial glossary of
photography terms

Gerry wants to create links among the three pages so that users can easily navigate from one page to another. Before you write code for the links, it's worthwhile to use a technique known as storyboarding to map out exactly how you want the pages to relate to each other. A storyboard is a diagram of a Web site's structure, showing all the pages in the site and indicating how they are linked together. Because Web sites use a variety of structures, it's important to storyboard your Web site before you start creating your pages. This helps you determine which structure works best for the type of information your site contains. A well-designed structure ensures that users will be able to navigate the site without getting lost or missing important information.

Every Web site should begin with a single **home page** that acts as a focal point for the Web site. It is usually the first page that users see. From that home page, you add links to other pages in the site, defining the site's overall structure. The Web sites you commonly encounter as you navigate the Web employ several different Web structures. You'll examine some of these structures to help you decide how to design your own sites.

Linear Structures

If you wanted to create an online version of a famous play, like Shakespeare's *Hamlet*, one method would be to link the individual scenes of the play in a long chain. Figure 2-2 shows the storyboard for this **linear structure**, in which each page is linked with the pages that follow and precede it. Readers navigate this structure by moving forward and backward through the pages, much as they might move forward and backward through the pages of a book.

Figure 2-2   **A linear structure**

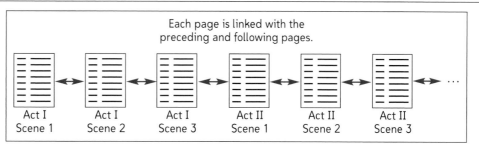

Linear structures work for Web sites that are small in size and have a clearly defined order of pages. However, they can be difficult to work with as the chain of pages increases in length. An additional problem is that in a linear structure, you move farther and farther away from the home page as you progress through the site. Because home pages often contain important general information about a site and its author, this is usually not the best design technique.

You can modify this structure to make it easier for users to return immediately to the home page or other main pages. Figure 2-3 shows this online play with an **augmented linear structure**, in which each page contains an additional link back to the opening page of each act.

Figure 2-3   **An augmented linear structure**

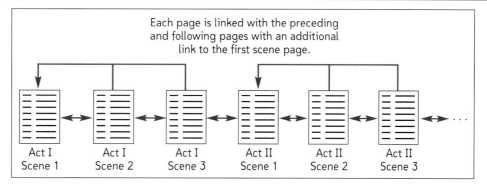

Hierarchical Structures

Another popular structure is the **hierarchical structure**, in which the home page links to pages dedicated to specific topics. Those pages, in turn, can be linked to even more specific topics. A hierarchical structure allows users to easily move from general to specific and back again. In the case of the online play, you could link an introductory page containing general information about the play to pages that describe each of the play's acts, and within each act you could include links to individual scenes. See Figure 2-4. Within this structure, a user could move quickly to a specific scene within the play, bypassing the need to move through each scene that precedes it.

Figure 2-4 **A hierarchical structure**

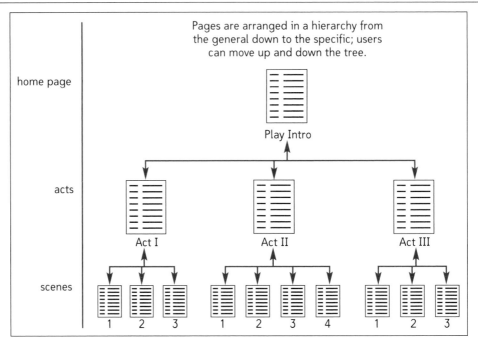

Pages are arranged in a hierarchy from the general down to the specific; users can move up and down the tree.

Mixed Structures

With larger and more complex Web sites, you often need to use a combination of structures. Figure 2-5 shows the online play using a mixture of hierarchical and linear structures. The overall form is hierarchical, as users can move from a general introduction down to individual scenes; however, users can also move through the site in a linear fashion, going from act to act and scene to scene. Finally, each individual scene contains a link to the home page, allowing users to jump to the top of the hierarchy without moving through the different levels.

| Figure 2-5 | A mixed structure |

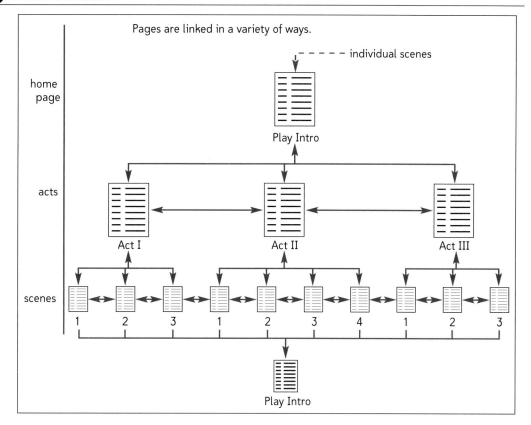

As these examples show, a little foresight can go a long way toward making your Web site easier to use. Also keep in mind that search results from a Web search engine such as Google or Yahoo! can point users to any page in your Web site—not just your home page—so they will need to be able to quickly understand what your site contains and how to navigate it. At a minimum, each page should contain a link to the site's home page or to the relevant main topic page. In some cases, you might want to supply your users with a **site index**, which is a page containing an outline of the entire site and its contents. Unstructured Web sites can be difficult and frustrating to use. Consider the storyboard of the site displayed in Figure 2-6.

Figure 2-6 Web site with no coherent structure

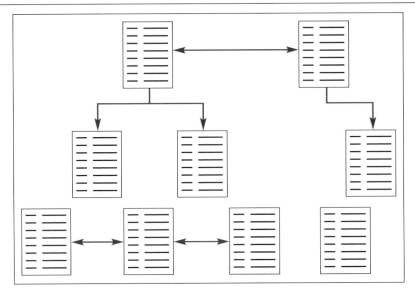

This confusing structure makes it difficult for users to grasp the site's contents and scope. The user might not even be aware of the presence of some pages because there are no connecting links, and some of the links point in only one direction. The Web is a competitive place; studies have shown that users who don't see how to get what they want within the first few seconds often leave a Web site. How long would a user spend on a site like the one shown in Figure 2-6?

Protected Structures

Sections of most commercial Web sites are off-limits except to subscribers and registered customers. As shown in Figure 2-7, these sites have a password-protected Web page that users must go through to get to the off-limits areas. The same Web site design principles apply to the protected section as the regular, open section of the site.

Figure 2-7 A protected structure

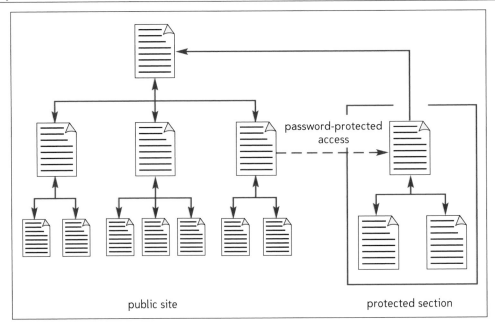

Storyboarding a protected structure is particularly important to ensure that no unauthorized access to the protected area is allowed in the site design.

Creating a Navigation List

Every Web site should include a **navigation list**, which is a list containing links to the main topic areas of the site. Ideally, this same list should appear prominently on every page, usually near the top of the page as part of the header or as a sidebar to the main content.

HTML5 introduced the `nav` structural element to make it easier to mark up navigation lists. The syntax of the element is

```
<nav>
   list of navigation links
</nav>
```

where `list of navigation links` is a list of elements that are linked to other pages on the Web site. Prior to HTML5, such lists would often be inserted within the generic `div` element as

```
<div id="id">
   list of navigation links
</div>
```

where `id` is whatever id the page author would supply to identify the navigation list.

Gerry suggests you add the topics for his three sample pages as an unordered list within the `nav` element as follows:

```
<nav>
   <ul>
       <li>Home</li>
       <li>Tips</li>
       <li>Glossary</li>
   </ul>
</nav>
```

Gerry has already designed styles for these new elements and placed them within the camstyles.css style sheet. The style sheet will format the elements so that the list appears as a horizontally aligned set of boxes. As Gerry adds more sample pages, he can easily extend this list to include the new topics, but for now he needs only these three.

Add this navigation list to each of the three sample pages that Gerry has given you.

To create the navigation list:

1. Return to the **home.htm** file in your text editor.

2. At the top of the file directly below the header element, insert the following code as shown in Figure 2-8:

```
<nav>
   <ul>
       <li>Home</li>
       <li>Tips</li>
       <li>Glossary</li>
   </ul>
</nav>
```

Figure 2-8   Marking a navigation list

navigation list marked with the nav element

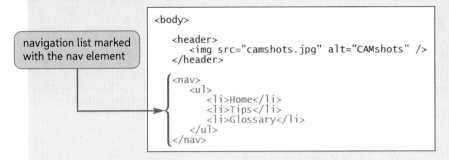

```
<body>

    <header>
        <img src="camshots.jpg" alt="CAMshots" />
    </header>

    <nav>
        <ul>
            <li>Home</li>
            <li>Tips</li>
            <li>Glossary</li>
        </ul>
    </nav>
```

> **3.** Save your changes to the file.

> **4.** Go to the **tips.htm** file in your text editor and then repeat Steps 2 and 3, placing the navigation list in the same place as you did in the home.htm file and saving your changes.

> **5.** Go to the **glossary.htm** file in your text editor and then repeat Steps 2 and 3 to add a navigation list to that file.

> **6.** Open or refresh the **home.htm** file in your Web browser. Verify that the navigation list appears directly below the page header as shown in Figure 2-9.

Figure 2-9   Navigation list in the CAMshots home page

navigation list formatted as a horizontal set of boxes

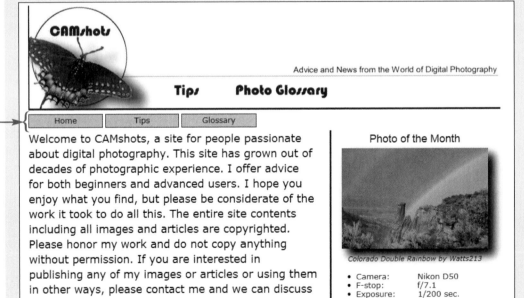

> **7.** Open or refresh the **tips.htm** and **glossary.htm** files in your Web browser and verify that a similar navigation list appears at the top of those pages.

Navigation Lists and Web Accessibility

One challenge of Web design is creating Web documents that are accessible to users with disabilities. Studies indicate that about 20% of the population has some type of disability. Many of these disabilities don't affect users' capacity to interact with the Web. But in some cases, users may need specialized Web browsers, such as screen readers that provide Web content aurally for visually impaired users.

To accommodate these users, Web page authors can take advantage of the structural elements provided by HTML5. For example, the nav element can allow users to either quickly jump to a list of links or bypass such a list if they are more interested in the content of the current document. Prior to HTML5 and the nav element, there was no way of differentiating one list from another, and thus disabled users would be forced to wait through a rendering of the same navigation list for each page they visited.

Because support for HTML5 is still in its infancy at the time of this writing, most specialized browsers have not incorporated features that enable users to quickly access the structural elements of most interest to them. However, as the specifications for HTML5 are finalized and fully supported by the browser market, this ability will become more commonly supported. Thus you should use the nav element and other structural elements from HTML5 to provide more information to browsers about the content and structure of your Web documents.

Working with Hypertext Links

Now that you've added a navigation list to each of the three sample pages, you will change each item in those lists into a hypertext link so that users can easily move between the three sample pages. Figure 2-10 shows the storyboard for the simple structure you have in mind.

Figure 2-10 Storyboard for the CAMshots sample Web site

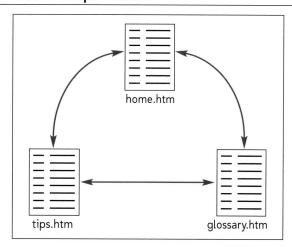

Hypertext links are created by enclosing some document content within a set of opening and closing <a> tags. The general syntax to create a hypertext link is

```
<a href="reference">content</a>
```

where *reference* is the location being linked to and *content* is the document content that is being marked as a link. The *reference* value can be a page on the World Wide

Web, a local file, an e-mail address, or a network server. For example, to create a hypertext link to the tips.htm file, you could enter the following code:

```
<a href="tips.htm">Photography Tips</a>
```

This code marks the text *Photography Tips* as a hypertext link. If a user clicks the text, the browser will load the linked resource (tips.htm). Note that filenames are case sensitive on some operating systems, such as the UNIX operating system. Web servers running on those systems differentiate between files named tips.htm and Tips.htm. For this reason, you might find that links you create on your computer do not work when you transfer your files to a Web server. To avoid this problem, the current standard is to always use lowercase filenames for all Web site files and to avoid using special characters and blank spaces.

Most browsers underline hypertext links unless a different style is specified in a user-defined style sheet. The font color of a link also changes based on whether or not the user has also visited the linked resource. By default, most browsers display hypertext links as follows:

• An unvisited link is underlined and blue.
• A previously visited link is underlined and purple.
• A link currently being clicked or activated is underlined and red.

However, Web page authors can use CSS to override these default settings.

TIP

Keep your filenames short and descriptive so that users are less apt to make a typing error when accessing your Web site.

REFERENCE

Marking a Hypertext Link

• To mark content as a hypertext link, use

```
<a href="reference">content</a>
```

where *reference* is the location being linked to and *content* is the document content that is being marked as a link.

You'll mark the names of the three sample pages in the navigation list you just created as hypertext links.

To create a hypertext link to a document:

1. Return to the **home.htm** file in your text editor and go to the navigation list at the top of the page.

2. Mark the text *Home* as a hypertext link using a set of <a> tags as follows:

```
<a href="home.htm">Home</a>
```

3. Mark the text *Tips* as a hypertext link using the following code:

```
<a href="tips.htm">Tips</a>
```

4. Mark the text *Glossary* as a hypertext link as follows:

```
<a href="glossary.htm">Glossary</a>
```

Figure 2-11 highlights the revised text in the home.htm file.

Figure 2-11   **Marking hypertext links in the navigation list**

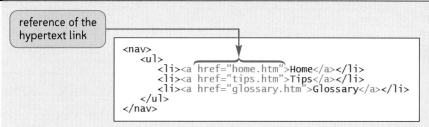

reference of the hypertext link

```
<nav>
    <ul>
        <li><a href="home.htm">Home</a></li>
        <li><a href="tips.htm">Tips</a></li>
        <li><a href="glossary.htm">Glossary</a></li>
    </ul>
</nav>
```

▶ **5.** Save your changes to the file.

▶ **6.** Go to the **tips.htm** file in your text editor and then repeat Steps 2 through 5 to change the text of the navigation list to hypertext links, saving your changes.

▶ **7.** Go to the **glossary.htm** file in your text editor and then repeat Steps 2 through 5, saving your changes.

Now that you've added hypertext links to each of the three documents, you'll test those links in your browser.

▶ **8.** Reload or refresh the **home.htm** file in your Web browser. As shown in Figure 2-12, the entries in the navigation list are underlined, providing a visual clue to the user that they are hypertext links.

Figure 2-12   **Viewing hypertext links in the navigation list**

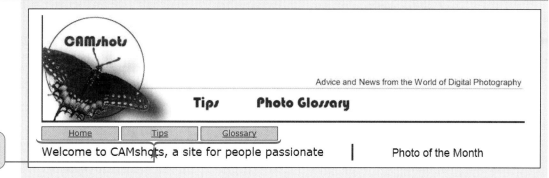

hypertext links underlined by default

▶ **9.** Click the **Tips** link in the navigation list. The Tips page should open in your browser.

▶ **10.** Within the Tips page, click the **Glossary** link in the navigation list and then verify that the Glossary page opens.

▶ **11.** Within the Glossary page, click the **Home** link in the navigation list to return to the CAMshots home page.

Trouble? If the links do not work, check the spelling of the filenames in the href attributes of the <a> tags. Because some Web servers require you to match capitalization in a filename, you should verify this in your attributes as well.

Interpreting the <a> Tag in Different Versions of HTML

The <a> tag is treated slightly differently in versions of HTML prior to HTML5. In HTML 4.01 and XHTML, the <a> tag can be used to enclose only text-level elements and should not be used to group content or structural elements. This means that the code

```
<a href="home.htm">
   <p>Go to the home page</p>
</a>
```

would not be allowed because the hyperlink is applied to an entire paragraph. HTML5 does not make this distinction, allowing the <a> tag to enclose text-level, grouping, and structural elements.

A second important difference is that in HTML 4.01 and XHTML, the <a> tag can also be used as an anchor to mark specific locations within the document. For that reason, the <a> tag is commonly referred to as the tag for the anchor element. HTML5 does not support this interpretation; the <a> tag can be used only to mark hypertext links.

Attributes of the a Element

The a element supports several attributes in addition to the href attribute. Some of these attributes are listed in Figure 2-13.

Figure 2-13   Attributes of the anchor (a) element

Attribute	Description
charset="*encoding*"	Specifies the character encoding used in the linked resource (*not supported in HTML5*)
href="*url*"	Indicates the resource targeted by the hypertext link
media="*media type*"	Indicates the media device in which the linked resource should be viewed (*HTML5*)
name="*name*"	Assigns a name for the section anchored by the <a> tag (*not supported in HTML5*)
rel="*relationship*"	Specifies the relationship between the current document and the linked resource
ping="*url*"	A space-separated list of resources that get notified when the user follows the hyperlink (*HTML5*)
target="*target_type*"	Specifies where to open the linked resource
type="*mime-type*"	Specifies the content (the mime-type) of the linked resource

For example, the following code uses the media attribute to indicate to browsers that the linked resource is suitable for printing:

```
<a href="orderform.htm" media="print">
   View an Order Form
</a>
```

The media attribute doesn't instruct the browser to print the linked file; it just tells the browser for what kind of output media the file has been designed. On the other hand, the following code uses the type attribute to indicate the file format of the linked file:

```
<a href="photo.png" mime-type="image/png">
   View the photo of the month
</a>
```

In this case, the browser is forewarned that the linked file is a graphic image file in the PNG format. Some browsers can use the mime-type attribute to load applications and programs to view the linked document. But in most cases, the browser determines the file format as it receives the document from the Web server, and thus no mime-type attribute is required.

Specifying a Folder Path

In the links you just created, you specified the filename but not the location of the file. When you specify only the filename, the browser assumes that the file is in the same folder as the document containing the hypertext link. However, large Web sites containing hundreds of documents often place documents in separate folders to make them easier to manage.

As Gerry adds more files to his Web site, he will probably want to use folders to organize the files. Figure 2-14 shows a preview of how Gerry might employ those folders. In this case, the top folder containing all of the content of the Web site is named *camshots*. Gerry might place some of his HTML files within the *pages* folder, which he would then divide into three subfolders, named *tips*, *glossary*, and *articles*. He could also create separate folders for the images and video clips used on his Web site.

Figure 2-14 A sample folder structure

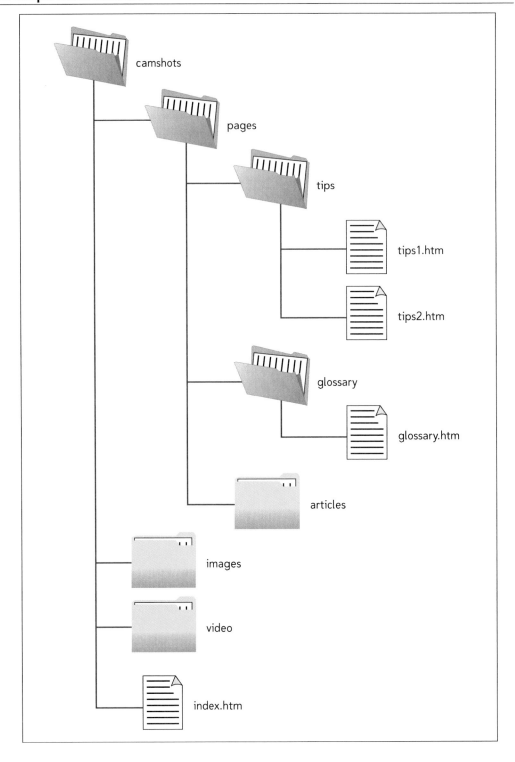

TIP

To make your Web site easier to maintain, organize your folders to match the organization of the pages on the Web site, and group images and other media files within folders separate from your HTML files.

To create a link to a file located in a folder other than the current document's folder, you must specify that file's location, or **path**. HTML supports two kinds of paths: absolute and relative.

Absolute Paths

An **absolute path** specifies a file's precise location within the entire folder structure of a computer. Absolute paths employ the syntax

```
/folder1/folder2/folder3/file
```

where *folder1* is the top folder in the hierarchy, followed by *folder2*, *folder3*, and so forth, down to the file you want to link to. Figure 2-15 shows how you would express absolute paths to the four files listed in Figure 2-14.

Figure 2-15	Absolute paths

Absolute Path	Interpretation
/camshots/pages/tips/tips1.htm	The tips1.htm file located in the pages/tips subfolder
/camshots/pages/tips/tips2.htm	The tips2.htm file located in the pages/tips subfolder
/camshots/pages/glossary/glossary.htm	The glossary.htm file located in the pages/glossary subfolder
/camshots/index.htm	The index.htm file located in the camshots folder

If files are located on different drives as well as in different folders, you must include the drive letter in the path

```
/drive|/folder1/folder2/folder3/file
```

where *drive* is the letter assigned to the drive. For example, the tips1.htm file located on drive C in the */camshots/pages/tips* folder would have the absolute path

```
/C|/camshots/pages/tips/tips1.htm
```

Note that you don't have to include a drive letter if the linked document is located on the same drive as the current file.

TIP

Because hypertext links cannot contain blank spaces, avoid blank spaces in the names you give to your Web site folders and files.

Relative Paths

When many folders and subfolders are involved, absolute paths can be cumbersome and confusing to use. For this reason, most Web designers prefer to use relative paths. A **relative path** specifies a file's location in relation to the location of the current document. If the file is in the same location as the current document, the relative path is simply the filename. If the file is in a subfolder of the current document, include the name of the subfolder without the forward slash, as follows

```
folder/file
```

where *folder* is the name of the subfolder, which is also known as a **child folder**. Note that folders used in relative paths are often referenced using relative names, such as parent, child, sibling, and so forth. For example, to go farther down the folder tree to other subfolders, include those folder names in the relative path separated by forward slashes, as in

```
folder1/folder2/folder3/file
```

where *folder1*, *folder2*, *folder3*, and so forth are subfolders, or **descendent folders**, of the current folder. Going in the opposite direction, a relative path moving up the folder tree to a **parent folder** is indicated by starting the path with a double period (..) followed by a forward slash and the name of the file. Thus, the relative path

    ../file

TIP

You can reference the current folder using a single period (.) character.

references the *file* document located in the parent folder. Finally, to reference a different folder on the same level as the current folder, known as a **sibling folder**, you move up the folder tree using the double period (..) to the parent and then back down to a different folder. The general syntax is

    ../folder/file

where *folder* is the name of the sibling folder. Figure 2-16 shows the relative paths to the six files in the tree from Figure 2-14, starting from the *camshots/pages/tips* subfolder.

Figure 2-16   Relative paths

Relative Path from the /camshots/pages/tips Subfolder	Interpretation
tips1.htm	The tips1.htm file located in the current folder
tips2.htm	The tips2.htm file located in the current folder
../glossary/glossary.htm	The glossary.htm file located in the sibling glossary folder
../../index.htm	The index.htm file located in the parent camshots folder

You should almost always use relative paths in your links. If you have to move your files to a different computer or server, you can move the entire folder structure without having to edit the relative paths you've created. If you use absolute paths, you will probably have to revise each link to reflect the new location of the folder tree on the computer.

Setting the Base Path

As you've just seen, a browser resolves relative paths based on the location of the current document. You can change this behavior by using the base element to specify a different starting location for all relative paths. The base element has the syntax

    <base href="path" />

where *path* is the folder location that you want the browser to use when resolving relative paths in the current document. The base element must be nested within the head element of the HTML file so it can be applied to all hypertext links found within the document.

REFERENCE

Using the base Element

• To set the default location for a relative path, add the element

    <base href="path" />

to the document head, where *path* is the folder location that you want browsers to use when resolving relative paths in the current document.

The base element is useful when a single document is moved to a new folder. Rather than rewriting all of the relative paths to reflect the document's new location, the base element redirects browsers to the document's old location, allowing any relative paths to be resolved as they were before.

Problem Solving: Managing Your Web Site

Web sites can quickly grow from a couple of pages to dozens or hundreds of pages. As the size of a site increases, it becomes more difficult to get a clear picture of the site's structure and content. Imagine deleting or moving a file in a Web site that contains dozens of folders and hundreds of files. Could you easily project the effect of this change? Would all of your hypertext links still work after you moved or deleted the file?

To effectively manage a Web site, you should follow a few important rules. The first is to be consistent in how you structure the site. If you decide to collect all image files in one folder, you should continue that practice as you add more pages and images. Web sites are more likely to break down if files and folders are scattered throughout the server without a consistent rule or pattern. Decide on a structure early and stick with it.

The second rule is to create a folder structure that matches the structure of the Web site itself. If the pages can be easily categorized into different groups, those groupings should also be reflected in the groupings of the subfolders. The names you assign to your files and folders should also reflect their uses on the Web site. This makes it easier for you to predict how modifying a file or folder might impact other pages on the site.

Finally, you should document your work by adding comments to each new Web page. Comments are useful not only for colleagues who may be working on the site, but also for the author who must revisit those files months or even years after creating them. The comments should include:

- The page's filename and location
- The page's author and the date the page was initially created
- A list of any supporting files used in the document, such as image and audio files
- A list of the files that link to the page, and their locations
- A list of the files that the page links to, and their locations

By following these rules, you can reduce a lot of the headaches associated with maintaining a large and complicated Web site.

Linking to Locations within a Document

Gerry has studied the navigation lists you created and would like you to add another navigation list to the Glossary page. Recall that the Glossary page contains a list of digital photography terms. The page is very long, requiring users to scroll through the document to find a term of interest. Gerry would like you to create a navigation list containing the letters A through Z. From this list, Gerry wants to give users the ability to jump to a specific section in the glossary matching the clicked letter.

See Figure 2-17.

Figure 2-17	Jumping to a location within a document

TIP

In general, Web pages should not span more than one or two screen heights. Studies show that busy users often skip long Web pages.

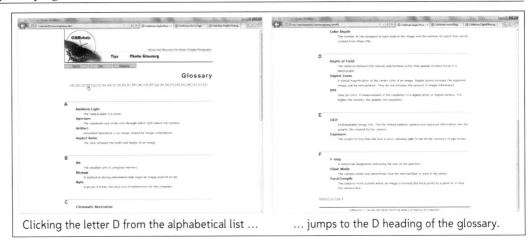

Clicking the letter D from the alphabetical list ...   ... jumps to the D heading of the glossary.

Add the navigation list to the glossary page now.

To create the navigation list:

1. Return to the **glossary.htm** file in your text editor.

2. Scroll down to the section element. Directly below the h1 *Glossary* heading, insert the following navigation list (see Figure 2-18):

```
<nav>
    [A] [B] [C]
    [D] [E] [F]
    [G] [H] [I]
    [J] [K] [L]
    [M] [N] [O]
    [P] [Q] [R]
    [S] [T] [U]
    [V] [W] [X]
    [Y] [Z]
</nav>
```

Figure 2-18	Adding a navigation element to the glossary

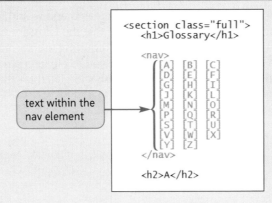

```
<section class="full">
    <h1>Glossary</h1>

    <nav>
        [A]  [B]  [C]
        [D]  [E]  [F]
        [G]  [H]  [I]
        [J]  [K]  [L]
        [M]  [N]  [O]
        [P]  [Q]  [R]
        [S]  [T]  [U]
        [V]  [W]  [X]
        [Y]  [Z]
    </nav>

    <h2>A</h2>
```

text within the nav element

3. Save your changes to the file.

Marking Locations with the `id` Attribute

To enable users to jump to a specific location within a document, you first need to mark that location. One way of doing this is to add the `id` attribute to an element at that location in the document. Recall that the syntax of the `id` attribute is

```
id="text"
```

where *text* is the name you want to assign to the id. For example, the following code marks an `h2` element with an id of `H`:

```
<h2 id="H">H</h2>
```

Note that id names must be unique. If you assign the same id name to more than one element on a Web page, browsers use the first occurrence of the id name. XHTML documents are rejected if they contain elements with duplicate ids. Id names are also case sensitive and most browsers other than Internet Explorer differentiate between ids named, for example, *top* and *TOP*.

REFERENCE

Defining an Element id

- To define the id of a specific element in a Web document, use the attribute

  ```
  id="text"
  ```

  where *text* is the value of the element id.

The Glossary page contains only a partial list of the photography terms that Gerry will eventually add to his Web site. For now, you'll mark only sections in the glossary corresponding to the letters A through F.

To add the `id` attribute to `h2` headings:

▶ 1. Scroll down the file and locate the `h2` heading for the letter A. Within the opening `<h2>` tag, insert the following attribute:

```
id="A"
```

▶ 2. Locate the `h2` heading for the letter B and insert the following attribute in the opening `<h2>` tag:

```
id="B"
```

Figure 2-19 highlights the revised code.

Figure 2-19 Adding the id attribute to h2 headings

h2 heading marked
with an id value of "A"

h2 heading marked
with an id value of "B"

```
<h2 id="A">A</h2>
<dl>
    <dt><b>Ambient Light</b></dt>
    <dd>The natural light in a scene.</dd>
    <dt><b>Aperture</b></dt>
    <dd>The maximum size of the hole through which light
        enters the camera.</dd>
    <dt><b>Artifact</b></dt>
    <dd>Unwanted distortions in an image caused by image
        compression.</dd>
    <dt><b>Aspect Ratio</b></dt>
    <dd>The ratio between the width and height of an
        image.</dd>
</dl>

<h2 id="B">B</h2>
<dl>
    <dt><b>Bit</b></dt>
    <dd>The smallest unit of computer memory.</dd>
    <dt><b>Bitmap</b></dt>
    <dd>A method of storing information that maps an image
        pixel bit by bit.</dd>
    <dt><b>Byte</b></dt>
    <dd>A group of 8 bits, the basic unit of information
        for the computer.</dd>
</dl>
```

▶ **3.** Continue going down the file, adding `id` attributes to the opening `<h2>` heading tags for C, D, E, and F corresponding to the letters of those headings.

For longer documents like the Glossary page, it's also helpful for users to be able to jump directly from the bottom to the top of the page, rather than having to scroll back up. With that in mind, you'll also add an id attribute marking the element at the top of the page.

To mark the top of the page:

▶ **1.** Scroll up the **glossary.htm** file in your text editor and locate the `header` element directly below the opening `<body>` tag.

▶ **2.** Insert the following attribute within the opening `<header>` tag, as shown in Figure 2-20:

```
id="top"
```

Figure 2-20 Adding the id attribute to the page header

header marked with
an id value of "top"

```
<body>
    <header id="top">
        <img src="camshots.jpg" alt="CAMshots" />
    </header>
```

▶ **3.** Save your changes to the file.

Linking to an id

Once you've marked an element using the id attribute, you can create a hypertext link to that element using the a element

```
<a href="#id">content</a>
```

where *id* is the value of the id attribute of the element. For example, to create a link to the h2 heading for the letter A in the glossary document, you would enter the following code:

```
<a href="#A">A</a>
```

You'll change each entry on the Glossary page to a hypertext link pointing to the section of the glossary corresponding to the selected letter.

To change the list of letters to hypertext links:

1. Locate the letter A in the list of letters at the top of the **glossary.htm** file.

2. After the [character, insert the following opening tag:

```
<a href="#A">
```

3. Between the letter A and the] character, insert the closing </a> tag. Figure 2-21 shows the revised code.

Figure 2-21   Marking a hypertext link for "A"

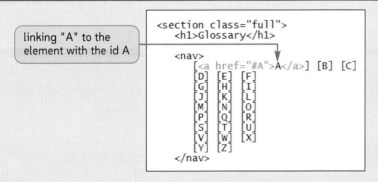

Make sure you include the pound symbol (#) in the hypertext link, and ensure that the id text matches both upper- and lowercase letters in the linked id.

4. Mark the letters B through F in the list as hypertext links pointing to the appropriate h2 headings in the document. Figure 2-22 shows the revised code for the list of letters.

Figure 2-22   Hypertext links for the list of letters

```
<nav>
   [<a href="#A">A</a>] [<a href="#B">B</a>] [<a href="#C">C</a>]
   [<a href="#D">D</a>] [<a href="#E">E</a>] [<a href="#F">F</a>]
   [G] [H] [I]
   [J] [K] [L]
   [M] [N] [O]
   [P] [Q] [R]
   [S] [T] [U]
   [V] [W] [X]
   [Y] [Z]
</nav>
```

Gerry also wants you to create a hypertext link at the bottom of the file that points to the top. You'll use the id attribute you created in the last set of steps.

5. Scroll to the bottom of the file and locate the text *Return to Top*.

6. Mark the text as a hyperlink, pointing to the element with an id value of *top*. See Figure 2-23.

Figure 2-23   **Hypertext link to jump to the top**

link to the element with the id *top*

```
    <div><a href="#top">Return to Top</a> &#8657;</div>
</section>

<footer>
    <address>
        CAMshots &#8250;&#8250;&#8250; Advice and News from
        the World of Digital Photography
    </address>
</foooter>
```

7. Save your changes to the file and then reload or refresh the **glossary.htm** file in your Web browser. As shown in Figure 2-24, the letters A through F in the alphabetical list are displayed as hypertext links.

8. Click the link for **F** and verify that you jump down to the end of the document, where the photographic terms starting with the letter F are listed.

Figure 2-24   **Hypertext links in the glossary page**

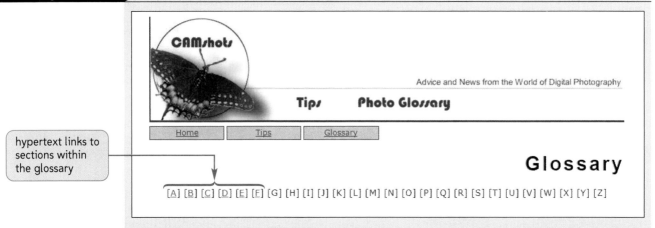

hypertext links to sections within the glossary

9. Click the **Return to Top** hypertext link and verify that you jump back to the top of the document.

10. Click the other links within the document and verify that you jump to the correct sections of the glossary.

Trouble? The browser cannot scroll farther than the end of the page. As a result, you might not see any difference between jumping to the E section of the glossary and jumping to the F section.

INSIGHT

Anchors and the name *Attribute*

Early Web pages did not support the use of the id attribute as a way of marking locations within a document. Instead, they used the <a> tag as an **anchor** or bookmark using the name attribute

```
<a name="anchor">content</a>
```

where *anchor* is the name of the anchor that marks the location of the document content. For example, to add an anchor to an h2 heading, you would enter the following code:

```
<h2><a name="A">A</a></h2>
```

Marking a location with an anchor does not change your document's appearance in any way; it merely creates a destination within your document. You use the same syntax to link to locations marked with an anchor as you would with locations marked with id attributes. To link to the above anchor, you could use the following code:

```
<a href="#A">A</a>
```

The use of anchors is a deprecated feature of HTML and is not supported in strict applications of XHTML. The name attribute is not part of HTML5, but you will still see anchors used in older code and in code generated by HTML editors and converters.

Creating Links to ids in Other Documents

Gerry knows that the glossary will be one of the most useful parts of his Web site, especially for novice photographers. However, he's also aware that most people do not read through glossaries. He would like to create links from the words he uses in his articles to glossary entries so that readers of his articles can quickly access definitions for terms they don't understand. His articles are not on the same page as his Glossary page, so he'll have to create a link between those pages and specific glossary entries.

To create a link to a specific location within a document, mark the hypertext link as follows

```
<a href="reference#id">content</a>
```

where *reference* is a reference to an HTML or XHTML file and *id* is the id of an element marked with the *id* attribute within that file. For example, the HTML code

```
<a href="glossary.htm#D">"D" terms in the Glossary</a>
```

creates a hypertext link to the D entries in the glossary.htm file. Note that this assumes that the glossary.htm file is located in the same folder as the document containing the hypertext link. If not, you have to include either the absolute or relative path information along with the filename, as described earlier.

Linking to an id

- To link to a specific location within the current file, use

  `<a href="#id">content</a>`

  where *id* is the id value of an element within the document.
- To link to a specific location in another file, use

  `<a href="reference#id">content</a>`

  where *reference* is a reference to an external file and *id* is the id value of an element in that file.

On Gerry's home page, he wants to showcase a Photo of the Month, displaying a photo that his readers might find interesting or useful in their own work. Along with the photo, he has included the digital camera settings used in taking the photo. Many of the camera settings are described on the Glossary page. Gerry suggests that you create a link between the setting name and the glossary entry. The five entries he wants to link to are F-stop, Exposure, Focal Length, Aperture, and Flash Mode. Your first step is to mark these entries in the glossary using the id attribute.

To mark the glossary entries:

1. Return to the **glossary.htm** file in your text editor.

2. Scroll through the file and locate the *Aperture* definition term.

3. As shown in Figure 2-25, within the opening `<dt>` tag, insert the following attribute:

   `id="aperture"`

Figure 2-25 **Adding the id attribute to the aperture definition**

```
<h2 id="A">A</h2>
<dl>
    <dt><b>Ambient Light</b></dt>
    <dd>The natural light in a scene.</dd>
    <dt id="aperture"><b>Aperture</b></dt>
    <dd>The maximum size of the hole through which light
        enters the camera.</dd>
    <dt><b>Artifact</b></dt>
    <dd>Unwanted distortions in an image caused by image
        compression.</dd>
    <dt><b>Aspect Ratio</b></dt>
    <dd>The ratio between the width and height of an
        image.</dd>
</dl>
```

4. Scroll down the file and locate the *Exposure* definition term.

5. Within the opening `<dt>` tag, insert the following attribute:

   `id="exposure"`

6. Go to the F section of the glossary and mark the terms with the following ids (see Figure 2-26):

   F-stop with the id `f-stop`

   Flash Mode with the id `flash_mode`

   Focal Length with the id `focal_length`

Figure 2-26   Adding ids to the other photographic definitions

```
<h2 id="E">E</h2>
<dl>
    <dt><b>EXIF</b></dt>
    <dd>Exchangeable Image File. This file format embeds camera
        and exposure information into the graphic file created
        by the camera.</dd>
    <dt id="exposure"><b>Exposure</b></dt>
    <dd>The length of time that the lens is open, allowing light
        to fall on the camera's image sensor.</dd>
</dl>

<h2 id="F">F</h2>
<dl>
    <dt id="f-stop"><b>F-stop</b></dt>
    <dd>A numerical designation indicating the size of the
        aperture.</dd>
    <dt id="flash_mode"><b>Flash Mode</b></dt>
    <dd>The camera mode that determines how the internal flash is used
        in the photo.</dd>
    <dt id="focal_length"><b>Focal Length</b></dt>
    <dd>The distance from a point where an image is formed (the
        focal point) to a point in or near the camera lens.</dd>
</dl>
```

▶ **7.** Save your changes to the **glossary.htm** file.

Next you'll go to the Home page and create links from these terms in the Photo of the Month description to their entries on the Glossary page.

To create links to the glossary entries:

▶ **1.** Open the **home.htm** file in your text editor.

▶ **2.** Scroll down the file and locate the *F-stop* term in the unordered list.

▶ **3.** Mark *F-stop* as a hypertext link using the following code:

```
<a href="glossary.htm#f-stop">F-stop</a>
```

▶ **4.** Mark *Exposure* as a hypertext link using the following code:

```
<a href="glossary.htm#exposure">Exposure</a>
```

▶ **5.** Mark the remaining three entries in the unordered list as hypertext pointing to their corresponding entries on the Glossary page. Figure 2-27 highlights the revised code in the file.

Figure 2-27   **Linking to a location within another document**

```
<aside>
   <h1>Photo of the Month</h1>

   <figure>
      <img src="rainbow.png" alt="Photo" />
      <figcaption>Colorado Double Rainbow by Watts213</i></figcaption>
   </figure>

   <ul>
      <li>Camera:
                 
         Nikon D50
      </li>
      <li><a href="glossary.htm#f-stop">F-stop</a>:
                  
         f/7.1
      </li>
      <li><a href="glossary.htm#exposure">Exposure</a>:
               
         1/200 sec.
      </li>
      <li><a href="glossary.htm#focal_length">Focal Length</a>:
          
         18mm
      </li>
      <li><a href="glossary.htm#aperture">Aperture</a>:
                
         3.6
      </li>
      <li><a href="glossary.htm#flash_mode">Flash Mode</a>:
            
         No flash
      </li>
   </ul>
</aside>
```

document   element id

▶ **6.** Save your changes to the file.

▶ **7.** Refresh the **home.htm** file in your Web browser. As shown in Figure 2-28, the settings from the Photo of the Month description are now displayed as hypertext links.

Figure 2-28   **Linked photography terms**

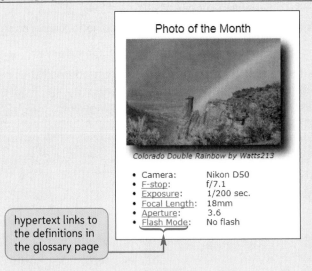

hypertext links to the definitions in the glossary page

▶ **8.** Click the **F-stop** hypertext link and verify that you jump to the Glossary page with the F-stop entry displayed in the browser window.

▶ **9.** Return to the CAMshots home page and click the hypertext links for the other terms in the list of photo settings, verifying that you jump to the section of the glossary that displays each term's definition.

PROSKILLS

Written Communication: Creating Effective Hypertext Links

To make it easier for users to navigate your Web site, the text of your hypertext links should tell readers exactly what type of document the link points to. For example, the link text

Click here for more information.

doesn't tell the user what type of document will appear when *here* is clicked. In place of phrases like *click here*, use descriptive link text such as

For more information, view our list of frequently asked questions.

If the link points to a non-HTML file, such as a PDF document, include that information in the link text. If the linked document is extremely large and will take a while to download to the user's computer, include that information in your link text so that users can decide whether or not to initiate the transfer. For example, the following link text informs users of both the type of document and its size before they initiate the link:

Download our complete manual (PDF 2 MB).

Finally, when designing the style of your Web site, make your links easy to recognize. Because most browsers underline hypertext links, don't use underlining for other text elements; use italic or boldface fonts instead. Users should never be confused about what is a link and what is not. Also, if you apply a color to your text, do not choose colors that make your hyperlinks harder to pick out against the Web page background.

You've completed your initial work linking the three files in Gerry's Web site. In the next session, you'll learn how to work with linked images and how to create links to external Web sites and Internet resources. If you want to take a break before starting the next session, you can close your files and your Web browser now.

Session 2.1 Quick Check

REVIEW

1. What is a navigation list? How would you mark up a navigation list in HTML5? How would you mark up a navigation list prior to HTML5?
2. What is a linear structure? What is a hierarchical structure?
3. What code would you enter to link the text *Sports Info* to the sports.htm file? Assume that the current document and sports.htm are in the same folder.
4. What's the difference between an absolute path and a relative path?
5. What is the purpose of the `base` element?
6. Specify the code for marking the text *CAMshots FAQ* as an `h2` heading with the id *faq*.
7. Specify the code for marking the text *Read our FAQ* as a hypertext link to an element in the current document with the id *faq*.
8. Specify the code for marking the text *Read our FAQ* as a hypertext link pointing to an element with the id *faq* in the help.htm file. Assume that help.htm lies in the same folder as the current document.

SESSION 2.2 VISUAL OVERVIEW

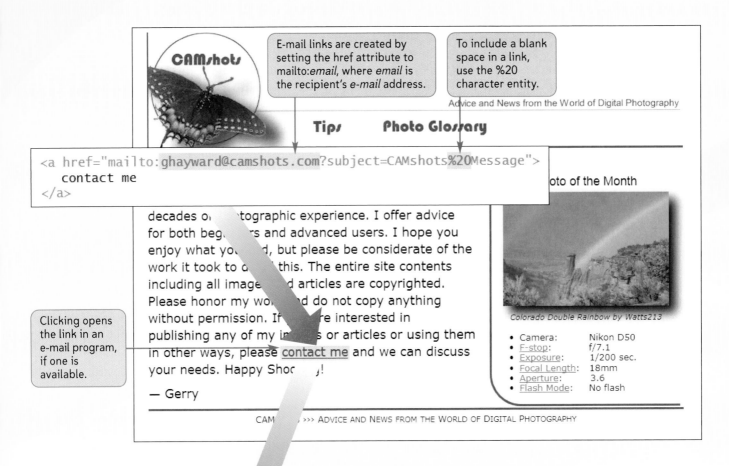

E-mail links are created by setting the href attribute to mailto:*email*, where *email* is the recipient's e-mail address.

To include a blank space in a link, use the %20 character entity.

```
<a href="mailto:ghayward@camshots.com?subject=CAMshots%20Message">
   contact me
</a>
```

Clicking opens the link in an e-mail program, if one is available.

decades o... ...tographic experience. I offer advice for both beg..... ...rs and advanced users. I hope you enjoy what yo... ...d, but please be considerate of the work it took to ...... this. The entire site contents including all image.... ...d articles are copyrighted. Please honor my wo..... ...d do not copy anything without permission. If ...... re interested in publishing any of my im..... s or articles or using them in other ways, please contact me and we can discuss your needs. Happy Sho..... ..y!

— Gerry

...oto of the Month

Colorado Double Rainbow by Watts213

- Camera: Nikon D50
- F-stop: f/7.1
- Exposure: 1/200 sec.
- Focal Length: 18mm
- Aperture: 3.6
- Flash Mode: No flash

CAM..... >>> ADVICE AND NEWS FROM THE WORLD OF DIGITAL PHOTOGRAPHY

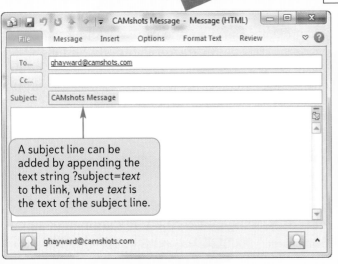

A subject line can be added by appending the text string ?subject=*text* to the link, where *text* is the text of the subject line.

```
<a href="glossary.htm#flash_mode"
   title="View Definition">
Flash Mode
</a>:
```

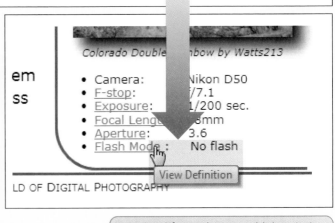

Use the **title** attribute to add descriptive **tooltips** to hypertext links.

IMAGE MAPS AND EXTERNAL LINKS

```
<img src="camshots.jpg" alt="CAMshots" usemap="#logomap" />

<map name="logomap">
    <area shape="circle" coords="82, 78,80"
     href="home.htm" alt="Home Page" />
    <area shape="rect" coords="235, 120, 310, 150"
     href="tips.htm" alt="Tips" />
    <area shape="rect" coords="340, 120, 510, 150"
     href="glossary.htm" alt="Glossary" />
</map>
```

An inline image is attached to an image map with the usemap attribute.

An **image map** maps areas called **hotspots** within an image to different linked documents.

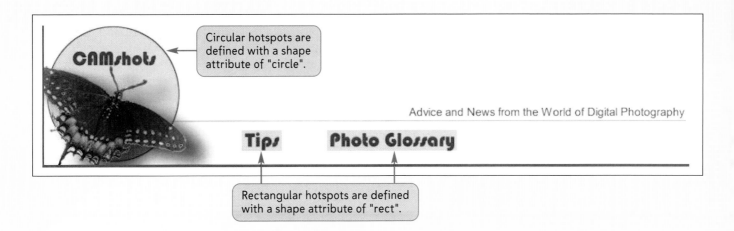

Circular hotspots are defined with a shape attribute of "circle".

Rectangular hotspots are defined with a shape attribute of "rect".

Sample URLs to link to Internet resources

URL	Description
file:///C\server\camshots.htm	Links to the camshots.htm file in the server folder on the C drive
ftp://ftp.microsoft.com	Links to the FTP server at ftp.microsoft.com
http://www.camshots.com	Links to the Web site www.camshots.com
https://www.camshots.com	Links to the Web site www.camshots.com over a secure connection

Working with Linked Images and Image Maps

Inline images can be marked as hyperlinks using the same techniques you employed in the last session. For example, a standard practice on the Web is to turn a Web site's logo into a hyperlink pointing to the home page. This gives users quick access to the home page rather than spending time searching for a link. To mark an inline image as a hyperlink, you enclose the `<img>` tag within a set of `<a>` tags as follows:

```
<a href="reference"><img src="file" alt="text" /></a>
```

Once the image has been marked as hypertext, clicking anywhere within the image jumps the user to the linked file.

The target of the link need not be a Web page; it can also be another image file. This is commonly done for **thumbnail images** that are small representations of larger image files. Gerry has done this for his image of the photo of the month. The image on the site's home page is a thumbnail of the larger photo. Gerry wants users to be able to view the larger image file by clicking the thumbnail.

You'll turn the Photo of the Month image into a hyperlink pointing to the larger image file.

> **TIP**
>
> Always include alternate text for your linked images to allow non-graphical browsers to display a text link in place of the linked image.

To link the Photo of the Month image:

1. Return to the **home.htm** file in your text editor.

2. Scroll down to the `img` element for the Photo of the Month and then enclose the inline image within a set of `<a>` tags as follows (see Figure 2-29):

```
<a href="rainbow_lg.png">
    <img src="rainbow.png" alt="Photo" />
</a>
```

Figure 2-29 | Linking an inline image

```
<aside>
    <h1>Photo of the Month</h1>

    <figure>
        <a href="rainbow_lg.png">
            <img src="rainbow.png" alt="Photo" />
        </a>
        <figcaption>Colorado Double Rainbow by Watts213</i></figcaption>
    </figure>
```

link to a large image of the photo

3. Save your changes to the file.

4. Reload the **home.htm** file in your Web browser. Click the Photo of the Month image and verify that the browser displays a larger, more detailed version of the image.

INSIGHT

Removing Image Borders

By default, Web browsers underline hypertext links. If an image is linked, browsers usually display the image with a colored border. To remove the border, you can add the following `style` attribute to the `img` element:

```
<img src="file" alt="text" style="border-width: 0px" />
```

This attribute sets the width of the border to 0 pixels, effectively removing it from the rendered Web page. You can also set the border width to 0 by using the following `border` attribute:

```
<img src="file" alt="text" border="0" />
```

Note that the `border` attribute is not supported in HTML5 but you will still see it used in many Web sites. Despite the fact that many browsers still support the use of the `border` attribute, you should not use it, relying instead on either the style attribute or styles set within an external style sheet.

Introducing Image Maps

When you mark an inline image as a hyperlink, the entire image is linked to the same destination file. However, HTML also allows you to divide an image into different zones, or **hotspots,** each linked to a different destination. Gerry is interested in doing this with the current image in the CAMshots header. He would like you to create hotspots for the logo so that if a user clicks anywhere within the CAMshots circle on the left side of the logo, the user jumps to the Home page; and if the user clicks either Tips or Photo Glossary in the logo, the user jumps to the Tips page or to the Glossary page, respectively. See Figure 2-30.

Figure 2-30   **Hotspots within the CAMshots header image**

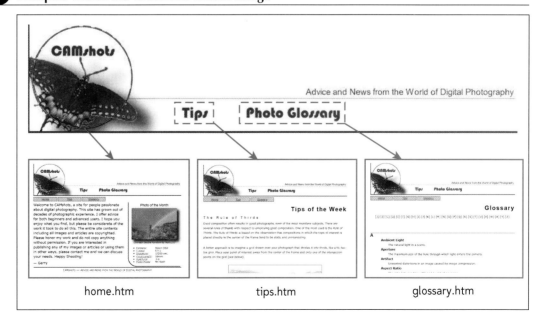

To define these hotspots, you create an **image map** that links a specified region of the inline image to a specific document. HTML supports two kinds of image maps: client-side image maps and server-side image maps. A **client-side image map** is an image map that is defined within the Web page and handled entirely by the Web browser running on a user's computer, while a **server-side image map** relies on a program running on the Web server to create and administer the map. For the CAMshots Web site, you'll create a client-side image map.

Client-Side Image Maps

Client-side image maps are defined with the map element

```
<map name="text">
   hotspots
</map>
```

where *text* is the name of the image map and *hotspots* are the locations of the hot-spots within the image. For example, the following map element creates a client-side image map named *logomap*:

```
<map name="logomap">
   ...
</map>
```

TIP

For XHTML documents, use the id attribute in place of the name attribute to identify an image map.

Client-side image maps can be placed anywhere within the body of a Web page because they are not actually displayed by browsers, but simply used as references for mapping hotspots to inline images. The most common practice is to place a map element below the corresponding inline image.

Defining Hotspots

An individual hotspot is defined using the area element

```
<area shape="shape" coords="coordinates" href="reference"
   alt="text" />
```

where *shape* is the shape of the hotspot region, *coordinates* are the list of points that define the boundaries of the region, *reference* is the file or location that the hotspot is linked to, and *text* is alternate text displayed for non-graphical browsers. Hotspots can be created in the shapes of rectangles, circles, or polygons (multisided figures). You use a shape value of rect for rectangular hotspots, circle for circular hotspots, and poly for polygonal or multisided hotspots. A fourth possible value for the shape attribute, default, represents the remaining area of the inline image not covered by any hotspots. There is no limit to the number of hotspots you can add to an image map. Hotspots can also overlap. If they do and the user clicks an overlapping area, the browser opens the link of the first hotspot listed in the map.

Hotspot coordinates are measured in **pixels**, which are the smallest unit or dot in a digital image or display. Your computer monitor might have a size of 1024 x 768 pixels, which means that the display is 1024 dots wide by 768 dots tall. For example, the header image that Gerry uses in his Web site has dimensions of 780 pixels wide by 167 pixels tall. When used with the coords attribute of the area element, pixel values exactly define the location and size of a hotspot region.

Each hotspot shape has a different set of coordinates that define it. To define a rectan-gular hotspot, apply the area element

```
<area shape="rect" coords="x1, y1, x2, y2" ... />
```

where *x1*, *y1* are the coordinates of the upper-left corner of the rectangle and *x2*, *y2* are the coordinates of the rectangle's lower-right corner. Figure 2-31 shows the coordinates of the rectangular region surrounding the Photo Glossary hotspot.

Figure 2-31   Defining a rectangular hotspot

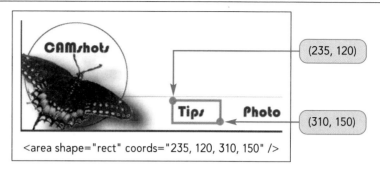

The upper-left corner of the rectangle has the image coordinates (235, 120), indicating that it is 235 pixels to the right and 120 pixels down from the upper-left corner of the image. The lower-right corner is found at the image coordinates (310, 150), placing it 310 pixels to the right and 150 pixels down from the upper-left corner of the image. Note that coordinates are always expressed relative to the upper-left corner of the image, regardless of the position of the image on the page.

Circular hotspots are defined using the coordinates

```
<area shape="circle" coords="x, y, r" ... />
```

where *x* and *y* are the coordinates of the center of the circle and *r* is the circle's radius. Figure 2-32 shows the coordinates for a circular hotspot around the CAMshots image from the Web site logo. The center of the circle is located at the coordinates (92, 82) and the circle has a radius of 80 pixels.

Figure 2-32   Defining a circular hotspot

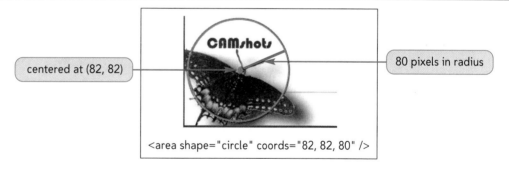

Polygonal hotspots are defined with

```
<area shape="poly" coords="x1, y1, x2, y2, x3, y3, ..." ... />
```

where (*x1*, *y1*), (*x2*, *y2*), (*x3*, *y3*) and so forth define the coordinates of each corner in the multisided shape. Figure 2-33 shows the coordinates for a polygonal region that covers the CAMshots logo, including the butterfly wings.

Figure 2-33   Defining a polygonal hotspot

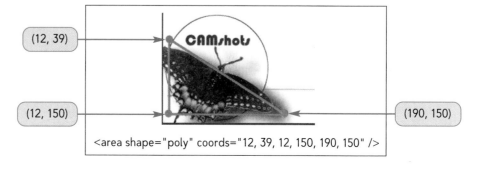

Finally, to define the default hotspot for an image, use

```
<area shape="default" coords="0, 0, x, y" ... />
```

where *x* is the width of the inline image in pixels and *y* is the height of the image. Any spot in an inline image that is not covered by another hotspot activates the default hotspot link.

REFERENCE

Creating a Client-Side Image Map

- To create a client-side image map, insert the map element

```
<map name="text">
   hotspots
</map>
```

anywhere within the Web page body, where *text* is the name of the image map and *hotspots* is a list of hotspot areas defined within the image map. (Note: For XHTML, use the id attribute in place of the name attribute.)
- To add a hotspot to the image map, place the area element

```
<area shape="shape" coords="coordinates" href="reference"
 alt="text" />
```

within the map element, where *shape* is the shape of the hotspot region, *coordinates* is the list of points that defines the boundaries of the region, *reference* is the file or location that the hotspot is linked to, and *text* is alternate text displayed for non-graphical browsers.
- To define a rectangular-shaped hotspot, use

```
<area shape="rect" coords="x1, y1, x2, y2" ... />
```

where *x1, y1* are the coordinates of the upper-left corner of the rectangle and *x2, y2* are the coordinates of the lower-right corner of the rectangle.
- To define a circular hotspot, use

```
<area shape="circle" coords="x, y, r" ... />
```

where *x* and *y* are the coordinates of the center of the circle and *r* is the radius of the circle.
- To define a polygonal hotspot, use

```
<area shape="poly" coords="x1, y1, x2, y2, x3, y3, ..." ... />
```

where (*x1, y1*), (*x2, y2*), (*x3, y3*), and so forth define the coordinates of each corner in the multisided shape.
- To define the default hotspot, use

```
<area shape="default" coords="0, 0, x, y" ... />
```

where *x* is the width of the inline image in pixels and *y* is the height in pixels.
- To apply an image map to an inline image, add the usemap attribute

```
<img src="file" alt="text" usemap="#map" />
```

to the inline image, where *map* is the name assigned to the image map.

To determine the coordinates of a hotspot, you can use either a graphics program such as Adobe Photoshop or image map software that automatically generates the HTML code for the hotspots you define.

In this case, assume that Gerry has already determined the coordinates for the hot-spots in his image map and provided them for you. He wants you to create three hot-spots, which are shown earlier in Figure 2-30. The first is a circular hotspot linked to the home.htm file, centered at the point (92, 82) and with a radius of 80 pixels. The second is a rectangular hotspot linked to the tips.htm file, with corners at (235, 120) and (310, 150). The third is also rectangular, linked to the glossary.htm file, with corners at (340, 120) and (510, 150). You do not have to create a polygonal hotspot.

You'll name the image map containing these hotspots *logomap*.

To create an image map:

▶ **1.** Return to the **home.htm** file in your text editor.

▶ **2.** Directly below the `<img>` tag for the CAMshots header image, insert the following `map` element:

```
<map name="logomap">
</map>
```

▶ **3.** Within the `map` element, insert a circular hotspot that points to the home.htm file using the following `area` element:

```
<area shape="circle" coords="82, 82, 80"
 href="home.htm" alt="Home Page" />
```

▶ **4.** Directly below the `<area>` tag for the circular hotspot, insert the following two rectangular hotspots pointing to the tips.htm and glossary.htm files:

```
<area shape="rect" coords="235, 120, 310, 150"
 href="tips.htm" alt="Tips" />
```

```
<area shape="rect" coords="340, 120, 510, 150"
 href="glossary.htm" alt="Glossary" />
```

Figure 2-34 highlights the new code in the file.

Figure 2-34	Creating the logomap image map

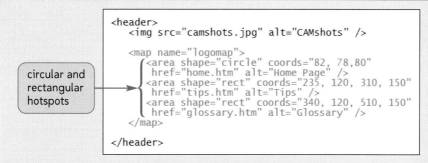

```
<header>
    <img src="camshots.jpg" alt="CAMshots" />

    <map name="logomap">
        <area shape="circle" coords="82, 78,80"
         href="home.htm" alt="Home Page" />
        <area shape="rect" coords="235, 120, 310, 150"
         href="tips.htm" alt="Tips" />
        <area shape="rect" coords="340, 120, 510, 150"
         href="glossary.htm" alt="Glossary" />
    </map>

</header>
```

circular and rectangular hotspots

▶ **5.** Save your changes to the file.

With the image map defined, your next task is to apply that map to the CAMshots header.

Applying an Image Map

To apply an image map to an image, you add the `usemap` attribute

```
<img src="file" alt="text" usemap="#map" />
```

to the inline image, where *map* is the name assigned to the image map.

Apply the *logomap* image map to the CAMshots logo and then test it in your Web browser.

To apply the *logomap* image map:

▶ 1. Add the following attribute to the `<img>` tag for the CAMshots logo, as shown in Figure 2-35:

```
usemap="#logomap"
```

Figure 2-35 **Applying the logomap image map**

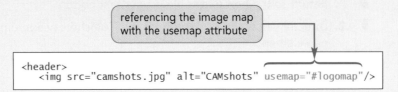

▶ 2. Save your changes to the file and then reload or refresh the **home.htm** file in your Web browser.

▶ 3. Click anywhere within the word **Tips** in the header image and verify that the browser opens the Tips page.

▶ 4. Return to the home page and click anywhere within the words **Photo Glossary** in the header image to verify that the browser opens the Glossary page.

Now that you've created an image map for the logo on the home page, you can create similar image maps for the logos on the Tips and Glossary pages.

To add image maps to the other Web pages:

▶ 1. Return to the **tips.htm** file in your text editor.

▶ 2. Replace the code within the header element with the code shown earlier in Figure 2-34. (Hint: You can use the copy and paste feature of your text editor to copy the code from the home.htm file into the tips.htm file.)

▶ 3. Save your changes to the file.

▶ 4. Go to the **glossary.htm** file in your text editor.

▶ 5. As you did for the tips.htm file, replace the code within the header element for the inline image with the code from the home.htm file. Save your changes to the file.

▶ 6. Reload the **home.htm** file in your Web browser and verify that you can switch among the three Web pages by clicking the hotspots in the CAMshots header image.

Server-Side Image Maps

The other type of image map you might encounter on the Web is a server-side image map, in which information about the hotspots is stored on the Web server rather than entered into the HTML code of a Web page. When you click a hotspot on a server-side image map, the coordinates of the mouse click are sent to the server, which activates the corresponding link, sending the linked page to your Web browser.

The server-side image map was the original HTML standard and is still supported on the Web. However, server-side maps have some limitations compared to client-side image maps. Because the map is located on the server, you need server access to test your image map code. Also, server-side image maps might be slower because information must be sent to the server with each mouse click. Finally, unlike client-side image maps, server-side image maps require the use of a mouse to send the information to the server. This makes them unsuitable for users with disabilities or users running non-graphical browsers.

To create a server-side image map, you enclose an inline image within a hypertext link such as

```
<a href="map">
    <img src="file" alt="text" ismap="ismap" />
</a>
```

where `map` is the name of a program or file running on the Web server that handles the image map. The `ismap` attribute tells the Web browser to treat the inline image as an image map.

Linking to Resources on the Internet

In the tips.htm file, Gerry has listed some of the Web sites he finds useful in his study of photography. He would like to change the entries in this list to hypertext links that his readers can click to quickly access the sites.

Introducing URLs

To create a link to a resource on the Internet, you need to know its URL. A **Uniform Resource Locator** (**URL**) specifies the location and type of a resource on the Internet. Examples of URLs include *www.whitehouse.gov*, the home page of the President of the United States, and *www.w3.org*, the home page of the World Wide Web consortium. All URLs share the general structure

   `scheme:location`

where `scheme` indicates the type of resource referenced by the URL and `location` is the location of that resource. For Web pages, the location refers to the location of the HTML file; but for other resources, the location might simply be the name of the resource. For example, a link to an e-mail account has the recipient's e-mail address as the location.

The name of the scheme is taken from the network protocol used to access the resource. A **protocol** is a set of rules defining how information is passed between two devices. Your Web browser communicates with Web servers using the **Hypertext Transfer Protocol** (**HTTP**). Therefore, the URLs for all Web pages must start with the http scheme. Other Internet resources, described in Figure 2-36, use different communication protocols and thus have different scheme names.

Figure 2-36	Internet protocols

Protocol	Used To
file	Access documents stored locally on a user's computer
ftp	Access documents stored on an FTP server
http	Access Web pages
https	Access Web pages over a secure encrypted connection
mailto	Open a user's e-mail client and address a new message

Linking to a Web Site

The URL for a Web page has the general form

```
http://server/path/filename#id
```

where *server* is the name of the Web server, *path* is the path to the file on that server, *filename* is the name of the file, and if necessary, *id* is the name of an id or anchor within the file. A Web page URL can also contain specific programming instructions for a browser to send to the Web server (a topic beyond the scope of this tutorial). Figure 2-37 identifies the different parts of a sample URL for a sample Web page.

Figure 2-37	Parts of a URL

You might have noticed that a URL like *http://www.camshots.com* doesn't include any pathname or filename. If a URL doesn't specify a path, then it indicates the top folder in the server's directory tree. If a URL doesn't specify a filename, the server returns the default home page. Many servers use index.html as the filename for the default home page, so the URL *http://www.camshots.com/index.html* would be equivalent to *http://www.camshots.com*.

Understanding Domain Names

The server name portion of a URL is also called the **domain name**. By studying a domain name, you learn about the server hosting the Web site. Each domain name contains a hierarchy of names separated by periods (.), with the top level appearing at the end. The top level, called an **extension**, indicates the general audience supported by the Web server. For example, *.edu* is the extension reserved for educational institutions, *.gov* is used for agencies of the United States government, and *.com* is used for commercial sites or general-use sites.

The next lower level appearing before the extension displays the name of the individual or organization hosting the site. The domain name *camshots.com* indicates a commercial or general-use site owned by CAMshots. To avoid duplicating domain names, the top two levels of the domain must be registered with the IANA (Internet Assigned Numbers Authority) before they can be used. You can usually register your domain name through your Web host. Be aware that you must pay an annual fee to keep a domain name.

The lowest levels of the domain, which appear farthest to the left in the domain name, are assigned by the individual or company hosting the site. Large Web sites involving hundreds of pages typically divide their domain names into several levels. For example, a large company like Microsoft might have one domain name for file downloads—*downloads.microsoft.com*—and another for customer service—*service.microsoft.com*. Finally, the first part of the domain name displays the name of the hard drive or resource storing the Web site files. Many companies have standardized on *www* as the initial part of their domain names.

Gerry has listed four Web pages that he wants his readers to be able to access. He's also provided you with the URLs for these pages, which are shown in Figure 2-38.

Figure 2-38   **Photography URLs**

Web Site	URL
Apogee Photo	http://www.apogeephoto.com
Outdoor Photographer	http://www.outdoorphotographer.com
Digital Photo	http://www.dpmag.com
Popular Photography and Imaging	http://www.popphoto.com

You'll link the names of the Web sites that Gerry has listed in the Tips page to the URLs listed in Figure 2-38. For example, to link the text *Apogee Photo* to the Apogee Photo Web site, you would use the following <a> tag:

```
<a href="http://www.apogeephoto.com">Apogee Photo</a>
```

REFERENCE

Linking to Internet Resources

- The URL for a Web page is

  ```
  http://server/path/filename#id
  ```

  where *server* is the name of the Web server, *path* is the path to a file on that server, *filename* is the name of the file, and if necessary, *id* is the name of an id or anchor within the file.
- The URL for an FTP site is

  ```
  ftp://server/path/filename
  ```

  where *server* is the name of the FTP server, *path* is the folder path, and *filename* is the name of the file.
- The URL for an e-mail address is

  ```
  mailto:address?header1=value1&header2=value2&...
  ```

  where *address* is the e-mail address; *header1*, *header2*, etc. are different e-mail headers; and *value1*, *value2*, and so on are the values of the headers.
- The URL to reference a local file is

  ```
  file://server/path/filename
  ```

  where *server* is the name of the local server or computer, *path* is the path to the file on that server, and *filename* is the name of the file. If you are accessing a file on your own computer, the server name is replaced by a third slash (/).

You'll use the information that Gerry has given you to create links to all four of the Web sites listed on his Tips page.

To create links to sites on the Web:

1. Return to the **tips.htm** file in your text editor.
2. Scroll to the bottom of the file and locate the definition list containing the list of Web sites.
3. Mark the entry for Apogee Photo as a hypertext link using the following code:

   ```
   <a href="http://www.apogeephoto.com">Apogee Photo</a>
   ```

4. Mark the remaining three entries in the list as hypertext links pointing to each company's Web site. Figure 2-39 highlights the revised code in the file.

Figure 2-39	Linking to sites on the Web

```
<article>
   <h1>Photography Sites on the Web</h1>
   <p>The Web is an excellent resource for articles on photography and
      digital cameras. Here are a few of my favorites.
   </p>

   <dl>
      <dt>&#9758; <a href="http://www.apogeephoto.com">Apogee Photo</a></dt>
      <dd>An established online photography magazine with articles by
         top pros, discussion forums, workshops, and more.
      </dd>
      <dt>&#9758; <a href="http://www.outdoorphotographer.com">Outdoor Photographer</a></dt>
      <dd>The premier magazine for outdoor photography. The site
         includes extensive tips on photographing wildlife, action
         sports, scenic vistas, and travel sites.
      </dd>
      <dt>&#9758; <a href="http://www.dpmag.com">Digital Photo</a></dt>
      <dd>An excellent site for novices and professionals with
         informative reviews and buying guides for the latest equipment
         and software.
      </dd>
      <dt>&#9758; <a href="http://www.popphoto.com">Popular Photography and Imaging</a></dt>
      <dd>A useful and informative site with articles from the
         long-established magazine of professional and amateur
         photographers.
      </dd>
   </dl>
</article>
```

▶ **5.** Save your changes to the file.

▶ **6.** Reload or refresh the **tips.htm** file in your Web browser. Figure 2-40 shows the revised list with each entry appearing as a hypertext link.

Figure 2-40	Links on the Tips page

Photography Sites on the Web

The Web is an excellent resource for articles on photography and digital cameras. Here are a few of my favorites.

☞ Apogee Photo
   An established online photography magazine with articles by top pros, discussion forums, workshops, and more.
☞ Outdoor Photographer
   The premier magazine for outdoor photography. The site includes extensive tips on photographing wildlife, action sports, scenic vistas, and travel sites.
☞ Digital Photo
   An excellent site for novices and professionals with informative reviews and buying guides for the latest equipment and software.
☞ Popular Photography and Imaging
   A useful and informative site with articles from the long-established magazine of professional and amateur photographers.

▶ **7.** Click each link on the page and verify that the appropriate Web site opens.

Trouble? To open these sites, you must be connected to the Internet. If you are still having problems after connecting to the Internet, compare your code to the URLs listed in Figure 2-38 to confirm that you have not made a typing error. Also keep in mind that because the Web is constantly changing, the Web sites for some of these links might have changed, or a site might have been removed since this book was published.

Web pages are only one type of resource that you can link to. Before continuing work on the CAMshots Web site, you'll explore how to access some of these other resources.

Linking to FTP Servers

Another method of storing and sharing files on the Internet is through FTP servers. **FTP servers** are file servers that act like virtual file cabinets in which users can store and retrieve data files, much as they store files on and retrieve files from their own computers. FTP servers transfer information using a communication protocol called **File Transfer Protocol** (**FTP**). The URL to access an FTP server follows the general format

```
ftp://server/path/
```

where *server* is the name of the FTP server and *path* is the folder path on the server that contains the files you want to access. When you access an FTP site, you can navigate through its folder tree as you would navigate the folders on your own hard disk. Figure 2-41 shows an example of an FTP site viewed as a directory listing within the Internet Explorer browser, and viewed as a collection of folders that can be navigated as if they were on the user's local machine.

Figure 2-41	Accessing an FTP site over the Web

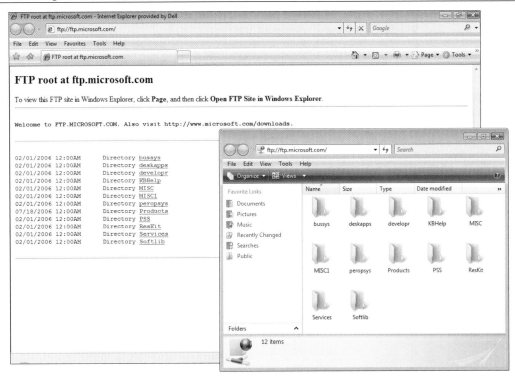

FTP servers require each user to enter a password and a username to gain access to the server's files. The standard username is *anonymous* and requires no password. Your browser supplies this information automatically, so in most situations you don't have to worry about passwords and usernames. However, some FTP servers do not allow anonymous access. In these cases, either your browser prompts you for the username and password, or you can supply a username and password within the URL using the format

```
ftp://username:password@server/path
```

where *username* and *password* are a username and password that the FTP server recognizes. It is generally *not* a good idea, however, to include usernames and passwords in URLs, as it can allow others to view your sensitive login information. It's better to let the browser send this information or to use a special program called an **FTP client**, which can encrypt or hide this information during transmission.

Linking to a Local File

HTML is a very useful language for creating collections of linked documents. Many software developers have chosen to distribute their online help in the form of HTML files. The Web sites for these help files then exist locally on a user's computer or network. If a Web site needs to reference local files (as opposed to files on the Internet or another wide area network), the URLs need to reflect this fact. The URL for a local file has the general form

```
file://server/path/filename
```

where `server` is the name of the local network server, `path` is the path on that server to the file, and `filename` is the name of the file. If you're accessing a file from your own computer, the server name can be omitted and replaced by an extra slash (/). Thus, a file from the *documents/articles* folder might have the following URL:

```
file:///documents/articles/tips.htm
```

If the file is on a different disk within your computer, the hard drive letter would be included in the URL as follows:

```
file://D:/documents/articles/tips.htm
```

Unlike the other URLs you've examined, the `file` scheme in this URL does not imply any particular communication protocol; instead, browsers retrieve the document using whatever method is the local standard for the type of file specified in the URL.

Linking to an E-Mail Address

Many Web sites use e-mail to allow users to communicate with a site's owner, sales representative, or technical support staff. You can turn an e-mail address into a hypertext link; when a user clicks the link, the user's e-mail program opens and automatically inserts the e-mail address into the *To* field of a new outgoing message. The URL for an e-mail address follows the form

```
mailto:address
```

where `address` is the e-mail address. To create a hypertext link to the e-mail address *ghayward@camshots.com*, you could use the following URL:

```
mailto:ghayward@camshots.com
```

TIP

To link to more than one e-mail address, add the addresses to the mailto link in a comma-separated list.

The mailto protocol also allows you to add information to the e-mail, including the subject line and the text of the message body. To add this information to the link, you use the form

```
mailto:address?header1=value1&header2=value2&...
```

where `header1`, `header2`, etc. are different e-mail headers and `value1`, `value2`, and so on are the values of the headers. Thus, to create a link containing the e-mail message

```
TO: ghayward@camshots.com
SUBJECT: Test
BODY: This is a test message
```

you would use the following URL:

```
mailto:ghayward@camshots.com?subject=Test&Body=This%20is%20a%
20test%20message
```

Notice that the spaces in the message body *This is a test message* have been replaced with the %20 character code. This is necessary because URLs cannot contain blank spaces.

Although the mailto protocol is not technically an approved communication protocol, it is supported by almost every Web browser. However, note that a user's browser may not automatically access Web-based mail clients, such as Hotmail or Gmail, when the user clicks an e-mail link. End users accessing their mail from a Web-based mail client must configure their browsers to automatically open those Web sites in response to a mailto link.

Gerry wants you to add a link to his e-mail address on the CAMshots home page. This will give people who view his site the ability to contact him with additional questions or ideas.

To link to an e-mail address on Gerry's home page:

▶ **1.** Return to the **home.htm** file in your text editor.

▶ **2.** Go to the first paragraph and locate the text *contact me*.

▶ **3.** Mark *contact me* as a hypertext link using the following code, as shown in Figure 2-42:

```
<a href="mailto:ghayward@camshots.com?subject=CAMshots%20Message">
   contact me
</a>
```

Figure 2-42	Linking to an e-mail address

```
<p>Welcome to CAMshots, a site for people passionate about
   digital photography. This site has grown out of decades
   of photographic experience. I offer advice for both
   beginners and advanced users. I hope you enjoy what you find,
   but please be considerate of the work it took to do all this.
   The entire site contents including all images and articles
   are copyrighted. Please honor my work and do not copy anything
   without permission. If you are interested in publishing any
   of my images or articles or using them in other ways,
   please <a href="mailto:ghayward@camshots.com?subject=CAMshots%20Message">contact me</a>
   and we can discuss your needs. Happy Shooting!</p>
<p>&mdash; Gerry</p>
```

e-mail address   e-mail subject heading

▶ **4.** Save your changes to the file.

▶ **5.** Refresh the **home.htm** file in your browser. Verify that the text *contact me* in the opening paragraph now appears as a hypertext link.

▶ **6.** Click **contact me** and verify that your e-mail program displays a message with *ghayward@camshots.com* as the recipient and *CAMshots Message* as the subject.

   Trouble? If you are using a Web-based e-mail client such as Gmail or Hotmail, the browser will not open your e-mail client. You can view online documentation for your browser to determine whether it supports linking to Web-based e-mail clients.

▶ **7.** Close your message window without saving the message.

Problem Solving: E-Mail Links and Spam

Use caution when adding e-mail links to your Web site. While it may make it more convenient for users to contact you, it also might make you more vulnerable to spam. **Spam** is unsolicited e-mail sent to large numbers of people, promoting products, services, and in some cases inappropriate Web sites. Spammers create their e-mail lists by scanning discussion groups, stealing Internet mailing lists, and using programs called **e-mail harvesters** to scan HTML code for the e-mail addresses contained in mailto URLs. Many Web developers have removed e-mail links from their Web sites in order to foil these harvesters, replacing the links with Web forms that submit e-mail requests to a secure server. If you need to include an e-mail address as a link on your Web page, you can take a few steps to reduce your exposure to spammers:

- Replace the text of the e-mail addresses with inline images that are more difficult for e-mail harvesters to read.
- Write a program to scramble any e-mail addresses in the HTML code, unscrambling the e-mail address only when a user clicks it.
- Replace the characters of the e-mail address with escape characters. For example, you can replace the @ symbol with the escape sequence %40.

There is no quick and easy solution to this problem. Fighting spammers is an ongoing battle, and they have proved very resourceful in overcoming some of the defenses people have created. As you develop your Web site, you should carefully consider how to handle e-mail addresses and review the most current methods for safeguarding that information.

Working with Hypertext Attributes

HTML provides several attributes to control the behavior and appearance of your links. Gerry suggests that you study a few of these to see whether they would be effective in his Web site.

Opening a Secondary Window or Tab

By default, each page you open replaces the contents of the current page in the browser window. This means that when Gerry's readers click on one of the four external links listed on the Tips page, they leave the CAMshots Web site. To return to the Web site, a user would have to click the browser's Back button.

Gerry wants his Web site to stay open when a user clicks one of the links to the external Web sites. Most browsers allow users to open multiple browser windows or multiple tabs within the same browser window. Gerry suggests that links to external sites be opened in a second browser window or tab. This arrangement allows continual access to his Web site, even as users are browsing other sites.

To force a document to appear in a new window or tab, you add the `target` attribute to the <a> tag. The general syntax is

```
<a href="url" target="window">content</a>
```

where `window` is a name assigned to the new browser window or browser tab. The value you use for the `target` attribute doesn't affect the appearance or content of the page being opened; the target simply identifies the different windows or tabs that are currently open. You can choose any name you wish for the target. If several links have the same target name, they all open in the same location, replacing the previous content in the browser window or tab. HTML also supports the special target names described in Figure 2-43.

Figure 2-43   **Target names for browser windows and tabs**

Target Name	Description
target	Opens the link in a new window or tab named *target*
_blank	Opens the link in a new, unnamed window or tab
_self	Opens the link in the current browser window or tab

Whether the new page is opened in a tab or in a browser window is determined by the browser settings. It cannot be set by the HTML code.

REFERENCE

Opening a Link in a New Window or Tab

• To open a link in a new browser window or browser tab, add the attribute

```
target="window"
```

to the <a> tag, where `window` is a name assigned to the new browser window or tab. The target attribute can also be set to `_blank` for a new, unnamed browser window or tab, or to `_self` for the current browser window or tab.

Gerry suggests that all of the external links from his page be opened in a browser window or tab identified with the target name *new*.

To specify a link target:

1. Return to the **tips.htm** file in your text editor.

2. Scroll to the bottom of the file and locate the four links to the external Web sites.

3. Within each of the opening <a> tags, insert the following attribute, as shown in Figure 2-44:

```
target="new"
```

Figure 2-44   **Setting a target for hyperlinks**

```
<dl>
    <dt>&#9758; <a href="http://www.apogeephoto.com" target="new">Apogee Photo</a></dt>
    <dd>An established online photography magazine with articles by
        top pros, discussion forums, workshops, and more.
    </dd>
    <dt>&#9758; <a href="http://www.outdoorphotographer.com" target="new">Outdoor Photographer</a></dt>
    <dd>The premier magazine for outdoor photography. The site
        includes extensive tips on photographing wildlife, action
        sports, scenic vistas, and travel sites.
    </dd>
    <dt>&#9758; <a href="http://www.dpmag.com" target="new">Digital Photo</a></dt>
    <dd>An excellent site for novices and professionals with
        informative reviews and buying guides for the latest equipment
        and software.
    </dd>
    <dt>&#9758; <a href="http://www.popphoto.com" target="new">Popular Photography and Imaging</a></dt>
    <dd>A useful and informative site with articles from the
        long-established magazine of professional and amateur
        photographers.
    </dd>
</dl>
</article>
```

4. Save your changes to the file.

5. Refresh the **tips.htm** file in your browser. Click each of the four links to external Web sites and verify that each opens in the same new browser window or tab.

6. Close the secondary browser window or tab.

TIP

To force all hypertext links in your page to open in the same target, add the `target` attribute to a base element located in the document's header.

You should use the `target` attribute sparingly in your Web site. Creating secondary windows can clutter up a user's desktop. Also, because the page is placed in a new window, users cannot use the Back button to return to the previous page in that window; they must click the browser's program button or the tab for the original Web site. This confuses some users and annoys others. Many Web designers now advocate not using the target attribute at all, leaving the choice of opening a link in a new tab or window to users. Note that the target attribute is not supported in strict XHTML-compliant code.

Creating a Tooltip

If you want to provide additional information about a link on your Web page, you can add a tooltip to the link. A **tooltip** is descriptive text that appears when a user positions the mouse pointer over a link. Figure 2-45 shows an example of a tooltip applied to one of Gerry's links.

Figure 2-45   Viewing a tooltip

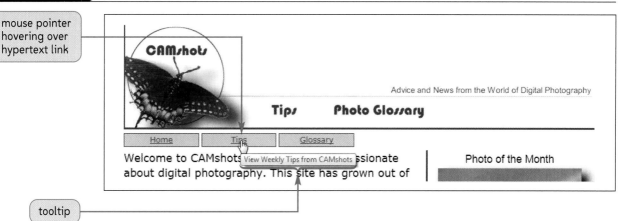

mouse pointer hovering over hypertext link

tooltip

To create the tooltip, add the title attribute to the opening `<a>` tag in the form

```
<a href="url" title="text">content</a>
```

where *text* is the text that appears in the tooltip. To create the tooltip shown in Figure 2-45, you would enter the following HTML code:

```
<a href="tips.htm"
   title="View Weekly Tips from CAMshots">
   Tips
</a>
```

Tooltips can also be added to image map hotspots to provide more useful feedback to the user.

Creating a Semantic Link

The text of a hypertext link should always describe to users the type of document that the link opens. You can also use the `rel` attribute to indicate the type of document that a link calls. For example, in the links to the site's home page, Gerry could insert the following `rel` attribute, setting its value to *first* to indicate that the home page is the first document in the CAMshots Web site:

```
<a href="home.htm" rel="first">Home Page</a>
```

A hypertext link containing the `rel` attribute is called a **semantic link** because the tag contains information about the relationship between the link and its destination. This information is not intended for the user, but for the browser. For example, a browser could be set up to mark the first Web page in a site with a special icon or to provide scripts that allow quick access to a site's first page.

Although the `rel` attribute is not limited to a fixed set of values, the specifications for HTML and XHTML include a proposed list of special values. Figure 2-46 shows some of these proposed relationship values.

Figure 2-46 **Proposed values for the rel attribute**

rel Attribute	Link To ...
alternate	An alternate version of the document
archives	A collection of historical documents
author	Information about the author of the document
external	An external document
first	The first document in a selection
help	A help document
index	An index for the document
last	The last document in a selection
license	Copyright information for the document
next	The next document in a selection
prev	The previous document in a selection
search	A search tool for the selection
sidebar	A document that should be shown in the browser's sidebar
stylesheet	An external style sheet

HTML 4.01 and XHTML also support the `rev` attribute to describe the reverse relationship: how a linked document views the current document. For example, if you're linking to the Glossary page from the home page, the reverse relation is *first* (because that is how the Glossary page views the home page). The HTML code would be

```
<a href="glossary.htm" rel="glossary" rev="first">Glossary</a>
```

The `rev` attribute is not supported in HTML5.

At this point, Gerry decides against using the `rel` and `rev` attributes on his Web site. However, he'll keep them in mind as an option as his Web site expands in size and complexity.

Using the `link` Element

Another way to add a hypertext link to your document is to add a `link` element to the document's head with the syntax

```
<link href="url" rel="text" rev="text" target="window" />
```

where the *href*, *rel*, *rev*, and *target* attributes serve the same purpose as in the `<a>` tag. You've already used the `link` element to link your Web pages to external style sheets, but you can use it to link to other types of documents as well. For example, to use the `link` element to create semantic links to the three pages of Gerry's Web site, you could add the following link elements to the `head` element of each document:

```
<link rel="first" href="home.htm" />
<link rel="help" href="tips.htm" />
<link rel="index" href="glossary.htm" />
```

Because they are placed within a document's head, `link` elements do not appear as part of the Web page. Instead, if a browser supports it, the links can be displayed in a browser toolbar. The advantage of the `link` element used in this way is that it places the list of links outside of the Web page, freeing up page space for other content. Also, because the links appear in a browser toolbar, they are always easily accessible to users. Currently, Opera is one of the few browsers with built-in support for the `link` element. Third-party software exists to provide this support for Internet Explorer and Firefox. Because no single list of relationship names is widely accepted, you must check with each browser's documentation to find out what relationship names it supports. Until semantic links are embraced by more browsers, you should use them only if you duplicate that information elsewhere on the page.

Working with Metadata

Gerry is happy with the work you've done on the design for his CAMshots Web site. Now he wants to start working on getting the site noticed. When someone searches for "digital photography tips" or "camera buying guide," will they find Gerry's Web site? There are thousands of photography sites on the Web. Gerry knows he needs to add a few extra touches to his home page to make it more likely that the site will be picked up by major search engines such as Yahoo! and Google.

Optimizing a Web site for search engines can be a long and involved process. For the best results, Web authors often turn to **search engine optimization** (**SEO**) tools to make their sites appear more prominently in search engines. Because CAMshots is a hobby site, Gerry does not want to invest any money in improving the site's visibility; but he would like to do a few simple things that would help.

Using the `meta` Element

To be noticed on the Web, a site needs to include information about itself for search engines to read and add to their search indices. Information about a site is called **metadata**. You can add metadata to your Web pages by adding a `meta` element to the document head. In the last tutorial, you saw how to use the `meta` element to store information about the character set used by the page; but you can also use it to store other information about the document. The syntax of the `meta` element is

```
<meta name="text" content="text" scheme="text" http-equiv="text" />
```

where the `name` attribute specifies the type of metadata, the `content` attribute stores the metadata value, the `scheme` attribute defines the metadata format, and the `http-equiv` attribute is used to attach metadata or commands to the communication stream between the Web server and the browser. Note that the `scheme` attribute is not supported under HTML5, while the `charset` attribute (not listed above) is supported only under HTML5.

There are three uses of the `meta` element:

- To store information about a document that can be read by the author, other users, and Web browsers
- To control how browsers handle a document, including forcing browsers to automatically refresh the page at timed intervals
- To assist Web search engines in adding a document to their search index

For example, the following `meta` element stores the name of the Web page's author:

```
<meta name="author" content="Gerry Hayward" />
```

For search engines, you should include metadata describing the site and the topics it covers. This is done by adding a `meta` element containing the site description and another meta element with a list of keywords. The following two elements would summarize the CAMshots Web site for search engines:

```
<meta name="description" content="CAMshots provides advice on
digital cameras and photography" />

<meta name="keywords" content="photography, cameras, digital
imaging" />
```

Figure 2-47 lists some other examples of metadata that you can use to describe your documents.

Figure 2-47   **Examples of the uses of the meta element**

Meta Name	Example	Description
author	`<meta name="author" content="Gerry Hayward" />`	Supplies the name of the document author
classification	`<meta name="classification" content="photography" />`	Classifies the document category
copyright	`<meta name="copyright" content="&copy; 2014 CAMshots" />`	Provides a copyright statement
description	`<meta name="description" content="Digital photography and advice" />`	Provides a description of the document
generator	`<meta name="generator" content="Dreamweaver" />`	Indicates the name of the program that created the HTML code for the document
keywords	`<meta name="keywords" content="photography, cameras, digital imaging" />`	Provides a list of keywords describing the document
owner	`<meta name="owner" content="CAMshots" />`	Indicates the owner of the document
rating	`<meta name="rating" content="general" />`	Provides a rating of the document in terms of its suitability for minors
reply-to	`<meta name="reply-to" content="ghayward@camshots.com (G. Hayward)" />`	Supplies a contact e-mail address and name for the document

In recent years, search engines have become more sophisticated in evaluating Web sites. In the process, the meta element has decreased in importance. However, it is still used by search engines when adding a site to their indices. Because adding metadata requires very little effort, you should still include meta elements in your Web documents.

REFERENCE

Working with Metadata

- To document the contents of a Web page, use the meta element

  ```
  <meta name="text" content="text" />
  ```

  where the name attribute specifies the type of metadata and the content attribute stores the metadata value.
- To add metadata or a command to the communication stream between the Web server and Web browsers, use

  ```
  <meta http-equiv="text" content="text" />
  ```

  where the http-equiv attribute specifies the type of data or command attached to the communication stream and the content attribute specifies the data value or command.

Having discussed metadata issues with you, Gerry asks that you include a few meta elements to describe his new site.

To add metadata to Gerry's document:

▶ **1.** Return to the **home.htm** file in your text editor.

▶ **2.** Directly below the meta element that defines the document's character set, insert the following meta elements, as shown in Figure 2-48:

```
<meta name="author" content="your name" />
<meta name="description" content="A site for sharing information on
digital photography and cameras" />
<meta name="keywords" content="photography, cameras, digital
imaging" />
```

| Figure 2-48 | Adding meta elements to the CAMshots home page |

```
<meta charset="UTF-8" />
<meta name="author" content="Gerry Hayward" />
<meta name="description" content="A site for sharing information on
               digital photography and cameras" />
<meta name="keywords" content="photography, cameras, digital imaging" />

<title>CAMshots Home Page</title>
<script src="modernizr-1.5.js"></script>
<link href="camstyles.css" rel="stylesheet" type="text/css" />
</head>
```

metadata category

metadata value

▶ **3.** Close the file, saving your changes.

▶ **4.** Close any open files or applications.

Using the `meta` Element to Reload a Web Page

Describing your document is not the only use of the `meta` element. As you learned earlier, servers transmit Web pages using a communication protocol called HTTP. You can add information and commands to this communication stream with the `http-equiv` attribute of the `meta` element. One common use of the `http-equiv` attribute is to force browsers to refresh a Web page at timed intervals, which is useful for Web sites that publish scoreboards or stock tickers. For example, to automatically refresh a Web page every 60 seconds, you would apply the following `meta` element:

```
<meta http-equiv="refresh" content="60" />
```

Another use of the `meta` element is to redirect the browser from the current document to a new document. This might prove useful to Gerry someday if he changes the URL of his site's home page. As his readers get accustomed to the new Web address, he can keep the old address online, automatically redirecting readers to the new site. The `meta` element to perform an automatic redirect has the general form

```
<meta http-equiv="refresh" content="sec;url=url" />
```

> **TIP**
>
> When redirecting a Web site to a new URL, avoid confusion by always including text notifying users that the page is being redirected, and provide users several seconds to read the text.

where *sec* is the time in seconds before the browser redirects the user and *url* is the URL of the new site. To redirect users after five seconds to the Web page at *http://www.camshots.com*, you could enter the following meta element:

```
<meta http-equiv="refresh" content="5;url=http://www.camshots.com" />
```

At this point, Gerry does not need to use the `meta` element to send data or commands through the HTTP communication protocol. However, he will keep this option in mind if he moves the site to a new address.

Gerry is happy with the Web site you've started. He'll continue to work on the site and will come back to you for more assistance as he adds new pages and elements.

Session 2.2 Quick Check

REVIEW

1. The CAMmap image map has a circular hotspot centered at the point (50, 75) with a radius of 40 pixels pointing to the faq.htm file. Specify the code to create a map element containing this circular hotspot.
2. An inline image based on the logo.jpg file with the alternate text *CAMshots* needs to use the CAMmap image map. Specify the code to apply the image map to the image.
3. What are the five parts of a URL?
4. Specify the code to link the text *White House* to the URL *http://www. whitehouse.gov*, with the destination document displayed in a new unnamed browser window.
5. Specify the code to link the text *University of Washington* to the FTP server at *ftp.uwash.edu*.
6. Specify the code to link the text *President of the United States* to the e-mail address *president@whitehouse.gov*.
7. What attribute would you add to a hypertext link to display the tooltip *Tour the White House*?
8. Specify the code to add the description *United States Office of the President* as metadata to a document.
9. Specify the code to automatically refresh your Web document every 5 minutes.

Review Assignments

Data Files needed for the Review Assignments: camhome.htm, child1.jpg– child3.jpg, childtxt.htm, conlogo.jpg, constyles.css, contest1.png–contest3. png, contesttxt.htm, flower1.jpg–flower3.jpg, flowertxt.htm, modernizr-1.5.js, photogloss.htm, scenic1.jpg–scenic3.jpg, scenictxt.htm, thirdstip.jpg, thumb1.jpg– thumb9.jpg, tipweek.htm

Gerry has been working on the CAMshots Web site for a while. During that time, the site has grown in popularity with amateur photographers. Now he wants to host a monthly photo contest to highlight the work of his colleagues. Each month Gerry will pick the three best photos from different photo categories. He's asked for your help in creating the collection of Web pages highlighting the winning entries. Gerry has already created four pages. The first page contains information about the photo contest; the remaining three pages contain the winning entries for child photos, scenic photos, and flower photos. Although Gerry has already entered much of the page content, he needs you to work on creating the links between and within each page. Figure 2-49 shows a preview of the photo contest's home page.

Figure 2-49   CAMshots Contest Winners page

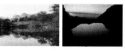

Complete the following:

1. Use your text editor to open the **contesttxt.htm**, **childtxt.htm**, **scenictxt.htm**, and **flowertxt.htm** files from the tutorial.02\review folder included with your Data Files. Enter *your name* and *the date* within each file, and then save them as **contest.htm**, **child.htm**, **scenic.htm**, and **flower.htm**, respectively, in the same folder.

2. Go to the **child.htm** file in your text editor. Directly below the `header` element, create a navigation list containing an unordered list with the following list items as hyperlinks:

   a. **Home** linked to the camhome.htm file

   b. **Tips** linked to the tipweek.htm file

   c. **Contest** linked to the contest.htm file

   d. **Glossary** linked to the photogloss.htm file

3. Go to the `section` element and locate the contest1.png inline image. Directly below the inline image, insert an image map with the following properties:

   a. Set the name of the image map as **contestmap**.

   b. Add a polygonal hotspot pointing to the child.htm file containing the points (427, 5), (535, 20), (530, 59), and (421, 43). Enter **Child Photos** as the alternate text for the hotspot.

   c. Add a polygonal hotspot pointing to the flower.htm file containing the points (539, 57), (641, 84), (651, 46), and (547, 26). Enter **Flower Photos** as the alternate text for the hotspot.

   d. Add a polygonal hotspot pointing to the scenic.htm file containing the points (650, 86), (753, 125), (766, 78), and (662, 49). Enter **Scenic Photos** as the alternate text for the hotspot.

4. Apply the contestmap image map to the contest1 inline image.

5. Locate the three `h2` elements naming the three child photo winners. Assign the `h2` elements the ids **photo1**, **photo2**, and **photo3**, respectively.

6. Save your changes to the file.

7. Go to the **flower.htm** file in your text editor. Repeat Steps 2 through 6, applying the image map to the contest2.png image at the top of the `section` element.

8. Go to the **scenic.htm** file in your text editor. Repeat Steps 2 through 6 applying the image map to the contest3.png image at the top of the `section` element.

9. Go to the **contest.htm** file in your text editor. Repeat Step 2 to insert a navigation list at the top of the page.

10. Scroll down to the second article. Link the text *Child Photos* to the child.htm file. Link *Flower Photos* to the flower.htm file. Link *Scenic Photos* to the scenic.htm file.

11. Scroll down to the nine thumbnail images (named *thumb1.jpg* through *thumb9.jpg*). Link each inline image to the corresponding `h2` heading in the child.htm, flower.htm, or scenic.htm file you identified in Step 5.

12. Scroll down to the aside element. Mark the text *Gerry Hayward* as a hypertext link to an e-mail address with **ghayward@camshots.com** as the e-mail address and **Photo Contest** as the subject line.

13. Mark the text *BetterPhoto.com* as a hypertext link pointing to the URL **http://www.betterphoto.com**. Set the attribute of the link so that it opens in a new browser window or tab.

14. Save your changes to the file.

15. Open **contest.htm** in your Web browser. Verify that the e-mail link opens a new mail message window with the subject line *Photo Contest*. Verify that the link to BetterPhoto.com opens that Web site in a new browser window or tab. Verify that you can navigate through the Web site using the hypertext links in the navigation list. Finally, click each of the nine thumbnail images at the bottom of the page and verify that each connects to the larger image of the photo on the appropriate photo contest page.

16. Go to the **child.htm** file in your Web browser. Verify that you can navigate forward and backward through the three photo contest pages by clicking the hotspots in the image map.

17. Submit your completed files to your instructor, in either printed or electronic form, as requested.

Apply your knowledge of hypertext links to create a directory of universities and colleges.

APPLY

Case Problem 1

Data Files needed for this Case Problem: colleges.txt, hestyles.css, highered.jpg, modernizr-1.5.js, uwlisttxt.htm

HigherEd   Adella Coronel is a guidance counselor for Eagle High School in Waunakee, Wisconsin. She wants to take her interest in helping students choose colleges to the Web by starting a Web site called HigherEd. She's come to you for help in creating the site. The first page she wants to create is a simple directory of Wisconsin colleges and universities. She's created the list of schools, but has not yet marked the entries in the list as hypertext links. The list is very long, so she has broken it down into three categories: private colleges and universities, technical colleges, and public universities. Because of the length of the page, she wants to include hypertext links that allow students to jump down to a specific college category. Figure 2-50 shows a preview of the page you'll create for Adella.

Figure 2-50	**HigherEd Web site**

Higher ◆ Ed

The Directory of Higher Education Opportunities

Wisconsin Colleges and Universities

Private Colleges and Universities	Technical College System	University of Wisconsin System

Private Colleges and Universities

Alverno College
Beloit College
Cardinal Stritch University
Carroll College
Concordia University Wisconsin
Edgewood College
Lakeland College
Lawrence University
Marian University
Medical College of Wisconsin
Milwaukee Institute of Art and Design
Milwaukee School of Engineering

Complete the following:

1. In your text editor, open the **uwlisttxt.htm** file from the tutorial.02\case1 folder included with your Data Files. Enter *your name* and *the date* in the file comments. Save the file as **uwlist.htm** in the same folder.

2. Directly below the `h1` heading, insert a navigation list containing an unordered list with following list items: **Private Colleges and Universities**, **Technical College System**, and **University of Wisconsin System**.

3. Add the ids **private**, **technical**, and **public** to the three `h2` headings that categorize the list of schools.

4. Mark each of the school entries on the page as a hypertext link. Use the URLs provided in the colleges.txt file. (Hint: Use the copy and paste feature of your text editor to efficiently copy and paste the URL text.)

⊕ EXPLORE
5. Adella wants the links to the school Web sites to appear in a new tab or window. Because there are so many links on the page, add a `base` element to the document head specifying that all links open by default in a new browser window or tab named **collegeWin**.

6. Link the three items in your navigation list to the corresponding `h2` headings.

⊕ EXPLORE
7. For each of the hypertext links you marked in Step 6, set the link to open in the current browser window and not in a new browser window or tab.

8. Save your changes to the file.

9. Open **uwlist.htm** in your Web browser and verify that the school links all open in the same browser window or tab, and that the links within the document to the different school categories bring the user to those locations on the page but not in a new window or tab.

10. Submit your completed files to your instructor, in either printed or electronic form, as requested.

Apply your knowledge of HTML to create a slide show Web site.

APPLY

Case Problem 2

Data Files needed for this Case Problem: fiddler.jpg, fidstyles.css, first.png, home.png, hometxt.htm, last.png, modernizr-1.5.js, next.png, prev.png, slide1.jpg–slide6.jpg, slide1txt.htm–slide6txt.htm, thumb1.jpg–thumb6.jpg

Lakewood School Tasha Juroszek is a forensics teacher at Lakewood School, a small private school in Moultrie, Georgia. Tasha has just finished directing her students in *Fiddler on the Roof, Jr.* and wants to place a slide show of the performances on the Web. She has already designed the layout and content of the pages, but needs help to finish the slide show. She has asked you to add hypertext links between the slide pages and the site's home page. Figure 2-51 shows a preview of one of the slide pages on the Web site.

Figure 2-51   Fiddler on the Roof, Jr. slide page

If I Were a Rich Man sung by T. Gates

Complete the following:

1. Use your text editor to open the **hometxt.htm** file and the **slide1txt.htm** through **slide6txt.htm** files from the tutorial.02\case2 folder included with your Data Files. Enter *your name* and *the date* in the comment section of each file. Save the files as **home.htm** and **slide1.htm** through **slide6.htm**, respectively.

2. Return to the **slide1.htm** file in your text editor. At the top of the page are five buttons used to navigate through the slide show. Locate the inline image for the home button (home.png) and mark it as a hypertext link pointing to the home.htm file. Add the tooltip **Home Page** to the hyperlink.

3. There are six slides in Tasha's slide show. Mark the First Slide button as a hypertext link pointing to the slide1.htm file. Mark the Last Slide button as a link to the slide6.htm file. Link the Previous Slide button to slide1.htm, the first slide in the show. Link the Next Slide button to the slide2.htm file. Add an appropriate tooltip to each hyperlink.

4. Directly below the slide show buttons are thumbnail images of the six slides. Link each thumbnail image to its slide page.

5. Save your changes to the file.

6. Repeat Steps 2 through 5 for the five remaining slide pages. Within each page, set the navigation buttons to go back and forth through the slide show. For the slide6.htm file, the Next Slide button should point to the slide6.htm file because it is the last slide in the show.

7. Go to the **home.htm** file in your text editor. Go to the first paragraph in the article and mark the text string *slide show* as a hypertext link pointing to the slide1.htm file.

8. Go to the end of the second paragraph and mark the phrase *contact me* as a hypertext link pointing to the e-mail address **tashajur@lakewood.edu**, with the subject heading **Digital Photo**.

9. Save your changes to the file.

10. Load the **home.htm** file in your Web browser. Test the links in the Web site and verify that they allow the user to easily move back and forth through the slide show.

11. Submit your completed files to your instructor, in either printed or electronic form, as requested.

Explore how to use HTML to create an election results Web site.

CHALLENGE

Case Problem 3

Data Files needed for this Case Problem: dcoords.txt, dist1txt.htm–dist4txt.htm, ewlogo.png, ewstyles.css, kansasmap.png, kansastxt.htm, modernizr-1.5.js

ElectionWeb Allison Hawks is a political science student at the University of Kansas. As part of a project for one of her courses, she is setting up a Web site to report results from the upcoming elections. She's asked for your help in designing and writing the hypertext links and image maps to be used throughout her site. She has created a set of sample files detailing hypothetical results for the races for governor, senator, and the four Kansas congressional districts. A preview of the site's home page is shown in Figure 2-52.

Figure 2-52	Kansas results from ElectionWeb

News Sources

- Yahoo! News
- FOX News
- CNN
- MSNBC
- Google News
- New York Times
- digg
- Washington Post
- LATimes
- Reuters
- ABCNews
- USA Today

Kansas Statewide Races

The Kansas Election polls have officially been closed now for two hours and results are being constantly updated. As of 10pm with 65% of the ballots counted, leaders in the state-wide races for governor and senator are as follows:

Governor (65% reporting)

Charles Young (R) - 371,885 (47%)
Karen Drew (D) - 356,060 (45%)
Barry Davis (I) - 39,562 (5%)

U.S. Senate (65% reporting)

✔ Helen Sanchez (D) - 387,710 (49%)
Linda Epstein (R) - 348,147 (44%)
Hunter Ryan (I) - 47,474 (6%)

Get up-to-the-minute election results from the Kansas Secretary of State.

Click to view congressional district results

ElectionWeb: *Your Source for Online Election Results*

Complete the following:

1. Use your text editor to open the **kansastxt.htm** file and the **dist1txt.htm** through **dist4txt.htm** files from the tutorial.02\case3 folder included with your Data Files. Enter *your name* and *the date* in the comment section of each file. Save the files as **kansas.htm** and **district1.htm** through **district4.htm,** respectively.

EXPLORE 2. Go to the **kansas.htm** file in your text editor. Use the meta element to specify *your name* as the document author, and **Kansas** and **elections** as keywords for Web search engines.

EXPLORE 3. Create a semantic link in the document head linking this document to the Office of the Kansas Secretary of State at the following address:
http://www.kssos.org/elections/elections_statistics.html
Use a rel attribute value of **external** for the link.

4. Set the base target of the Web page to **new** so that links on the page open, by default, in a new browser window or tab.

5. Go to the page body, and then directly below the header element insert a navigation list with the following content:

   a. An h2 heading with the text **News Sources**

   b. An unordered list containing the following entries: **Yahoo! News, FOX News, CNN, MSNBC, Google News, New York Times, digg, Washington Post, LATimes, Reuters, ABCNews,** and **USA Today**.

   c. Look up the Web addresses of the 12 news sources and link your list entries to the appropriate Web sites. Set the rel attribute of each link to **external**.

6. Scroll down to the last paragraph before the figure box and link the text *Secretary of State* to the Office of the Kansas Secretary of State Web site.

7. Directly below the figure box, create an image map named **kansasdistricts** containing four polygonal hotspots for each of the four Kansas congressional districts. Use the coordinates found in the dcoords.txt file as the coordinates of the hotspots.

⊕EXPLORE

8. Set the hotspots in your image map to access the district1.htm, district2.htm, district3.htm, and district4.htm files, using the target attribute value of **_self** so that those Web pages open within the current browser window or tab.

9. Apply the kansasdistricts image map to the kansasmap.png inline image.

10. Save your changes to the file.

11. Go to the **district1.htm** file in your text editor.

12. Directly below the opening <section> tag, insert a navigation list containing an unordered list with the items **District 1, District 2, District 3,** and **District 4**. Link each entry to its corresponding Web page in the ElectionWeb Web site.

13. Scroll down to the last paragraph before the figure box and link the text *statewide races* to the kansas.htm file.

14. Apply the same image map you created in Step 7 for the kansas.htm file to the kansasmap.png inline image.

15. Save your changes to the file.

16. Open the **district2.htm, district3.htm,** and **district4.htm** files in your text editor and repeat Steps 12 through 15 for each file.

17. Open the **kansas.htm** file in your Web browser and verify that you can navigate through Allison's sample pages by clicking the hypertext links within the page body and within the image maps. Verify that you can access the external Web sites listed in the news sources and the Office of the Kansas Secretary of State.

18. Submit your completed project to your instructor, in either printed or electronic form, as requested.

Test your knowledge of HTML and use your creativity to design a Web site documenting a Shakespeare play.

RESEARCH

Case Problem 4

Data Files needed for this Case Problem: characters.txt, notes.txt, tempest.jpg, tempest.txt

Mansfield Classical Theatre   Steve Karls continues to work as the director of Mansfield Classical Theatre in Mansfield, Ohio. The next production he plans to direct is *The Tempest*. Steve wants to put the text of this play on the Web, but he also wants to augment the dialog of the play with notes and commentary. However, he doesn't want his commentary to get in the way of a straight-through reading of the text, so he has hit on the idea of linking his commentary to key phrases in the dialog. Steve has created text files containing an excerpt from *The Tempest* as well as his commentary and other supporting documents. He would like you to take his raw material and create a collection of linked pages.

Complete the following:

1. Create HTML files named **tempest.htm**, **commentary.htm**, and **cast.htm**, saving them in the tutorial.02\case4 folder included with your Data Files. Add comment tags to the head section of each document containing your name and the date. Add an appropriate page title to each document.

2. Using the contents of the tempest.txt, notes.txt, and characters.txt text files, create the body of the three Web pages in Steve's Web site. You can supplement the material on the page with appropriate material you find on your own.

3. Use the tempest.jpg file as a logo for the page. Create an image map from the logo pointing to the tempest.htm, commentary.htm, and cast.htm files. The three rectangular boxes on the logo have the following coordinates for their upper-left and lower-right corners:
   The Play: (228, 139) (345, 173)
   Commentary: (359, 139) (508, 173)
   The Cast: (520, 139) (638, 173)

4. Use this image map in all three of the Web pages for this Web site.

5. Create links between the dialog on the play page and the notes on the commentary page. The notes contain line numbers to aid you in linking each line of dialog to the appropriate note.

6. Create a link between the first appearance of each character's name in the tempest.htm page and the character's description on the cast.htm page.

7. Include a link to Steve Karls' e-mail address on the tempest.htm page. Steve's e-mail address is **stevekarls@mansfieldct.com**. E-mail sent to Steve's account from this Web page should have the subject line **Comments on the Tempest**.

8. Add appropriate `meta` elements to each of the three pages documenting the page's contents and purpose.

9. Search the Web for sites that would provide additional material about the play. Add links to these pages on the tempest.htm page. The links should open in a new browser window or tab.

10. Submit your completed files to your instructor, in either printed or electronic form, as requested.

ENDING DATA FILES

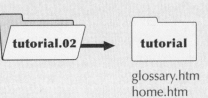

tutorial

glossary.htm
home.htm
tips.htm
+ 1 style sheet
+ 5 graphic files
modernizr-1.5.js

review

camhome.htm
child.htm
contest.htm
flower.htm
photogloss.htm
scenic.htm
tipweek.htm
+ 1 style sheet
+ 23 graphic files
modernizr-1.5.js

case1

uwlist.htm
+ 1 style sheet
+ 1 graphic file
modernizr-1.5.js

case2

home.htm
slide1.htm
slide2.htm
slide3.htm
slide4.htm
slide5.htm
slide6.htm
+ 1 style sheet
+ 18 graphic files
modernizr-1.5.js

case3

district1.htm
district2.htm
district3.htm
district4.htm
kansas.htm
+ 1 style sheet
+ 2 graphic files
modernizr-1.5.js

case4

cast.htm
commentary.htm
tempest.htm
+ 1 graphic file

Written Communication

Avoiding Common Mistakes in Written Communication

Most written communication errors can be easily avoided, yet are often overlooked. It's particularly important to catch writing errors on a personal Web site or online resume, which often help determing the first impression that a colleague or potential employer forms of you. Whether you are pressed for time, don't pay attention to detail, or have never learned the basics of good writing in the first place, these guidelines should help turn your writing into works you can be proud to claim.

Plan and Focus Your Writing

- Think about your audience. Who will read what you write? What knowledge do they already possess, and what attitudes might they have about your subject? Who will be viewing your Web documents, and what will they expect to see?

- Be clear about why you are writing in the first place. Are you writing to inform, or do you want action to be taken? Do you hope to change a belief or simply state your position? For a personal Web site or resume, make sure you understand what information potential employers and professional contacts will mostly likely be looking for.

- Research your topic. Provide all the necessary information the reader will need to make a decision or take action, if needed. If facts are included, be sure you can substantiate them. For a resume, ensure all your dates are accurate, and look up the exact names of organizations, institutions, and endorsements.

- Don't be afraid to rewrite or revise. If it's an important document, consider having someone else read it so you can determine whether your meaning is clear. At a minimum, read what you have written out loud to determine whether the message and impact come across as you intended. For online documents, continue the revision process on a regular basis so your documents do not become inaccurate or outdated.

Check Grammar and Spelling

Text editing programs remove all excuses for not checking your spelling and grammar in written communications. Keep in mind that spellchecking doesn't catch every error, so be sure to review your work carefully. Hiring managers are often inundated with resumes for a job opening, and an error in spelling or grammar is sometimes all it takes for an otherwise promising application to be rejected.

Set the Right Tone

When you write informal communications, you may use abbreviated or incomplete sentences and phrases or slang. In the workplace, however, you must carefully consider the tone of your written communication so you don't unintentionally offend your readers. Using contractions is considered friendly and is usually all right, but it is never acceptable to use offensive language. Anything you post about yourself online may be viewed by colleagues or a prospective employer, no matter how informal the context, so be sure that anything you write reflects well on you.

ProSkills

Write Clearly and Accessibly

When you write, your language should be free of buzzwords and jargon that will weaken your message, or make it difficult for your reader to understand your meaning.

Create Your Own Web Site

The Web has become an important medium for advertising yourself. By making your resume available online, you can quickly get prospective employers the information they need to make a hiring decision. There are many sites that will assist you in writing and posting your resume. They will also, for a fee, present your online resume to employers in your chosen field. Assuming you don't want to pay to use such a site, you can also create your own Web site containing your employment history and talents. In this exercise, you'll use the skills you learned in Tutorials 1 and 2 to design your own Web site and create an online resume.

Note: Please be sure *not* to include any personal information of a sensitive nature in the documents you create to be submitted to your instructor for this exercise. Later on, you can update the documents with such information for your own personal use.

1. Collect material about yourself that would be useful in an online resume. You should include material for a page on your employment history, talents and special interests, a general biography, and a summary of the main points of your resume.
2. Create a storyboard outlining the pages on your Web site. Clearly indicate the links between the pages. Make sure that your site is easy to navigate no matter which page users start on.
3. Collect or create graphical image files to make your site interesting to viewers. If you obtain graphics from the Web, be sure to follow all copyright restrictions on the material.
4. Start designing your site's home page. It should include an interesting and helpful logo. The home page should be brief and to the point, summarizing the main features of your resume. Its height should not be greater than two screens.
5. Add other pages containing more detailed information. Each page should have a basic theme and topic. The pages should follow a unified theme and design.
6. Use the `em` and `strong` elements to highlight important ideas. Do not overuse these page elements; doing so can detract from your page's readability rather than enhancing it.
7. Use numbered and bulleted lists to list the main points in your resume.
8. Use block quotes to highlight recommendations from colleagues and former employers.
9. Use the `hr` element to divide longer pages into topical sections.
10. If sites on the Web would be relevant to your online resume (such as the Web sites of former or current employers), include links to those sites.
11. Include a link to your e-mail address. Write the e-mail address link so that it automatically adds an appropriate subject line to the e-mail message it creates.
12. Save your completed Web site and present it to your instructor.

TUTORIAL 3

HTML

OBJECTIVES

Session 3.1
- Explore the history and theory of CSS
- Define a style rule
- Study style precedence and inheritance
- Apply color using CSS
- Explore CSS3 color extensions

Session 3.2
- Use contextual selectors
- Work with attribute selectors
- Apply text and font styles
- Install a Web font

Session 3.3
- Define list styles
- Use pseudo-classes and pseudo-elements
- Create a rollover effect

Designing a Web Page with CSS

Creating a Web Site for a Rural Farm

Case | *Sunny Acres*

Tammy Nielsen and her husband, Brent, live and work at Sunny Acres, a 200-acre farm near Council Bluffs, Iowa. Over the past 25 years, the Nielsen family has expanded the farm's operations to include a farm shop, which sells fresh produce, baked goods, jams, jellies, and gifts; a pick-your-own garden, which operates from May through October and offers great produce at discounted prices; a petting barn with over 100 animals and the opportunity to bottle-feed the baby animals; a corn maze with over 4 miles of twisting trails through harvested corn fields; and a Halloween Festival featuring the corn maze haunted with dozens of spooky effects and tricks. The farm also hosts special holiday events during the winter.

Tammy created a Web site for Sunny Acres several years ago to make information about the farm easily accessible to her customers. The Web site has become outdated, so Tammy would like to enliven it with a new design based on the latest elements and styles from HTML and CSS. Tammy's knowledge of HTML and Web styles is limited, so she's come to you for help in creating a new look for the Sunny Acres Web site.

STARTING DATA FILES

tutorial
haunttxt.htm
hometxt.htm
mazetxt.htm
pettingtxt.htm
producetxt.htm
sa_stylestxt.css

+ 1 style sheet
+ 7 graphic files
+ 4 Web fonts
+ 1 text file
modernizr-1.5.js

review
holidaytxt.htm
hs_stylestxt.css
+ 1 style sheet
+ 3 graphic files
+ 4 Web fonts
+ 1 text file
modernizr-1.5.js

case1
crypttxt.htm
c_stylestxt.css
+ 5 HTML files
+ 1 style sheet
+ 3 graphic files
modernizr-1.5.js

case2
bmtourtxt.htm
mw_stylestxt.css
+ 1 style sheet
+ 2 graphic files
modernizr-1.5.js

case3
civilwartxt.htm
cw_stylestxt.css
+ 1 style sheet
+ 3 graphic files
modernizr-1.5.js

case4
choirtxt.htm
gcc_stylestxt.css
+ 1 style sheet
+ 2 graphic files
+ 4 Web fonts
+ 1 text file
modernizr-1.5.js

demo
demo_color_names.htm
demo_css.htm
+ 3 graphic files

SESSION 3.1 VISUAL OVERVIEW

Style comments provide information about the style sheet.

```
/*
    Sunny Acres Style Sheet

    Author: Tammy Nielsen
    Date:    3/1/2014
*/


/* Body styles */

body {
    background-color: white;
    font-family: Verdana, Geneva, sans-serif;
    line-height: 1.4em;
}
```

The appearance of the Web page is determined by the styles in a style sheet.

```
h2 {
    background-color: rgb(0, 165, 0);
    color: rgba(255, 255, 255, 0.8);
}
```

The color is 80% opaque.

Color values using the rgba or hsla properties can include opacity to create semi-transparent colors.

Sunny
Acres

HOME

Autumn Fun

Scary Good

Meet the Animals

For your Tastebuds

The Farm Sh

The Sunny Acres Farm Shop aims to o
highest quality fresh produce. You can
your own or buy it in our shop. Set am
acres of outstanding natural beauty o
beautiful rolling hills northeast of Cou
Bluffs, the Farm Shop is easily reached
Highway G, with easy access from Inte
80.

The Farm Shop was established over 2
ago with great success. Our products h
won numerous awards at local festiva
fairs. We also cater to local supermark
the Council Bluffs/Omaha area. Look f
products every Saturday morning fron
to October at the Council Bluffs Farme

Hours

Hou

> Monday - Friday: 9 am - 5 pm
> Saturday: 9 am - 3 pm
> Pick Your Own Produce is availab
> The Farm Shop is open year-roun

Products

> Freshly baked breads and quiche
> High quality meats
> Cheese and other dairy products
> Freshly-picked fruits and vegetab
> Canned goods and preserves

SUNNY ACRES ✳ TAMMY & BRENT NIELSEN ✳ 1977 HIGHWAY G

STYLE SHEETS AND COLOR

Tammy and Brent Nielsen
1973 Hwy G
Council Bluffs, IA 51503

Every style rule needs to be enclosed in curly braces, with the style property values separated by semicolons.

The **selector** defines what element or elements are affected by a rule.

```
h1 {
    color: white;
    background-color: rgb(50, 69, 99);
}
```

The background-color style property sets the background color.

The color style property sets the text color.

CSS supports **color names** for a select group of commonly used colors.

The **HSL model** selects color from a color wheel at varying levels of saturation and lightness.

rm Shop

n Shop aims to offer the
produce. You can pick
our shop. Set amidst
natural beauty on the
northeast of Council
is easily reached on
access from Interstate

stablished over 25 years
s. Our products have
s at local festivals and
local supermarkets in
naha area. Look for our
day morning from May
ncil Bluffs Farmers' Market.

: 9 am - 5 pm
- 3 pm
roduce is available from May 15 - October 22
s open year-round

t s

eads and quiches
ats
r dairy products
ruits and vegetables (in season)
nd preserves

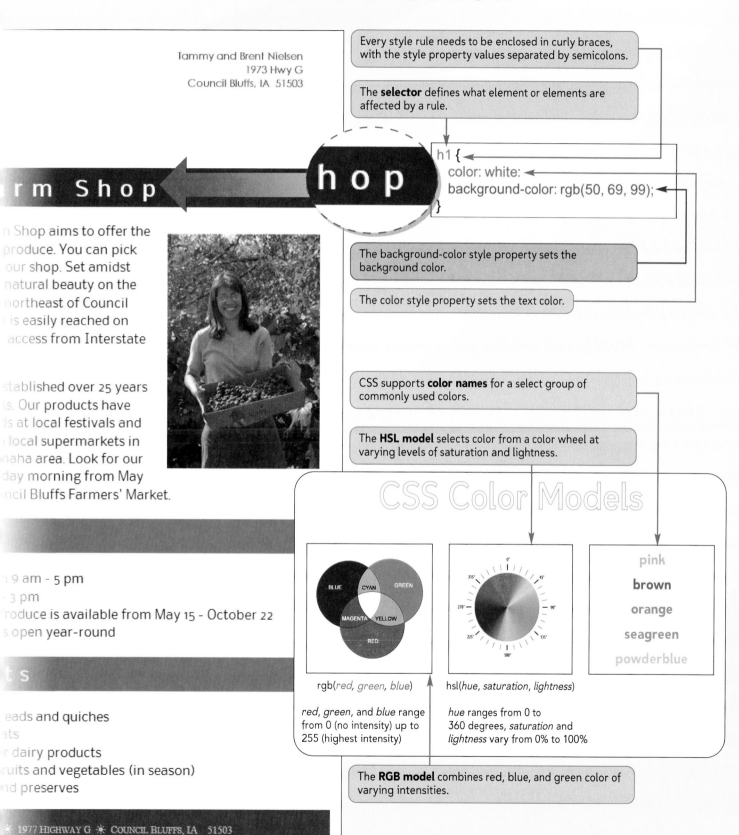

CSS Color Models

rgb(*red, green, blue*)

red, *green*, and *blue* range from 0 (no intensity) up to 255 (highest intensity)

hsl(*hue, saturation, lightness*)

hue ranges from 0 to 360 degrees, *saturation* and *lightness* vary from 0% to 100%

pink
brown
orange
seagreen
powderblue

The **RGB model** combines red, blue, and green color of varying intensities.

Introducing CSS

You and Tammy met to discuss her ideas for upgrading the design of the Sunny Acres Web site. She's created a few sample pages that she wants you to work with:

- *home.htm*—the home page, describing the operations and events sponsored by the farm
- *maze.htm*—a page describing the farm's corn maze
- *haunted.htm*—a page describing the farm's annual Halloween Festival and haunted maze
- *petting.htm*—a page describing the farm's petting barn
- *produce.htm*—a page describing the Sunny Acres farm shop and the pick-your-own produce garden

Figure 3-1 shows the links among these sites in the Sunny Acres storyboard.

Figure 3-1	Storyboard of the Sunny Acres Web site

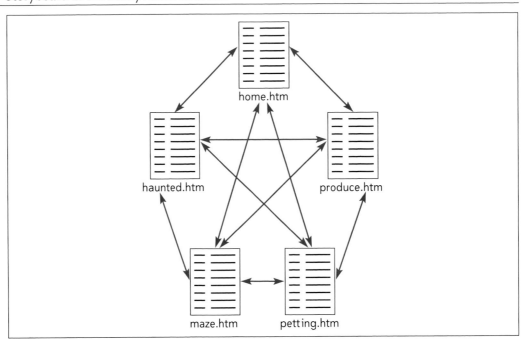

You'll start by opening these files in your text editor and browser.

To view the Sunny Acres Web pages:

1. Use your text editor to open the **haunttxt.htm, hometxt.htm, mazetxt.htm, pettingtxt.htm,** and **producetxt.htm** files, located in the tutorial.03\tutorial folder included with your Data Files. Within each file, go to the comment section at the top of the file and add *your name* and *the date* in the space provided. Save the files as **haunted.htm, home.htm, maze.htm, petting.htm,** and **produce.htm**, respectively, in the same folder.

2. Take some time to review the HTML code within each document so that you understand the structure and content of the files.

3. Open the **home.htm** file in your Web browser, and then click the links at the top of the page to view the current appearance of the *haunted.htm, maze.htm, petting.htm,* and *produce.htm* files. Figure 3-2 shows the current layout and appearance of the Sunny Acres home page.

Figure 3-2	Initial Sunny Acres home page

Sunny
Acres

Tammy and Brent Nielsen
1973 Hwy G
Council Bluffs, IA 51503

- Home
- Autumn Fun
- Scary Good
- Meet the Animals
- For your Tastebuds

Welcome

There's always something happening at Sunny Acres. With the coming of fall, we're gearing up for our big AutumnFest and Farm Show. If you haven't visited our famous Corn Maze, be sure to do so before it gets torn down on November 5. This year's maze is bigger and better than ever.

Farms can be educational and Sunny Acres is no exception. Schools and home-schooling parents, spend an afternoon with us at our Petting Barn. We have over 100 friendly farm animals in a clean environment. Kids can bottle feed the baby goats, lambs, and calves while they learn about nature and the farming life. Please call ahead for large school groups.

When the sun goes down this time of year, we're all looking for a good fright. Sunny Acres provides that too with another year of the Haunted Maze. Please plan on joining us during weekends in October or on Halloween for our big Halloween Festival.

Of course, Sunny Acres is, above all, a *farm*. Our Farm Shop is always open with reasonable prices on great produce. Save even more money by picking your own fruits and vegetables from our orchards and gardens.

We all hope to see you soon, down on the farm.
— Tammy & Brent Nielsen

Hours

- Farm Shop: 9 am - 5 pm Mon - Fri; 9 am - 3 pm Sat
- The Corn Maze: 11 am - 9 pm Sat; 11 am - 5 pm Sun
- The Haunted Maze: 5 pm - 9 pm Fri & Sat
- Petting Barn: 9 am - 4 pm Mon - Fri; 11 am - 3 pm Sat & Sun

Directions

- From Council Bluffs, proceed east on I-80
- Take Exit 38 North to the Drake Frontage Road
- Turn right on Highway G
- Proceed east for 2.5 miles
- Sunny Acres is on your left; watch for the green sign

Sunny Acres ☀ Tammy & Brent Nielsen ☀ 1977 Highway G ☀ Council Bluffs, IA 51503

Tammy already has created most of the content for the new and revised pages, but she has not upgraded the Web site design. She needs your help with that. In Figure 3-3, she sketches the basic design she has in mind for her pages.

Figure 3-3   **Proposed design for the Sunny Acres home page**

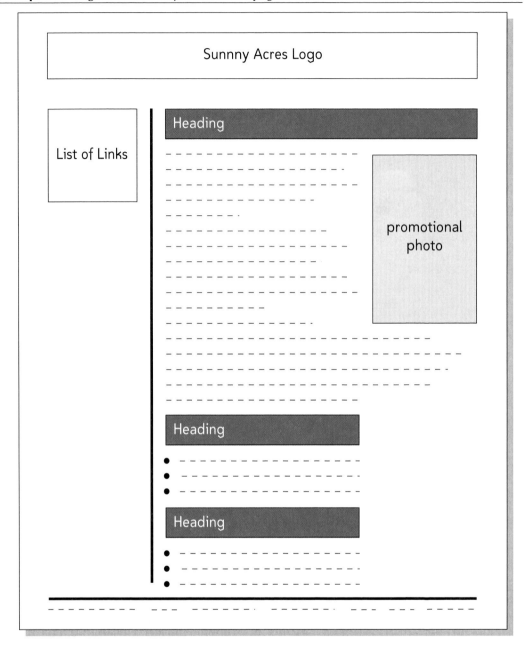

To apply this page format, Tammy wants you to use the design features available with CSS. Before starting, you'll review the history and concepts behind CSS.

The History of CSS

You learned in Tutorial 1 that HTML specifies a document's content and structure, but not how that document should be rendered. To render a document, the device displaying the page needs a style sheet that specifies the appearance of each page element. The style sheet language used on the Web is the Cascading Style Sheets language, also known as CSS.

The specifications for CSS are maintained by the World Wide Web Consortium (W3C); and as with HTML and XHTML, several versions of CSS exist with varying levels of browser support. The first version of CSS, called **CSS1**, was introduced in 1996 and enabled Web designers to create styles to:

- Set the font size, type, and other properties of Web page text
- Control text alignment and apply decorative elements such as underlining, italic, and capitalization
- Specify background and foreground colors of different page elements
- Apply a background image to any element
- Set the margins, internal space, and borders of grouping elements such as paragraphs and headings

CSS1 made it possible to create Web pages that had visually interesting and attractive designs and layouts. The second version of CSS, **CSS2**, was introduced in 1998, expanding the language to provide styles to:

- Position elements at specific locations on a page
- Clip and hide element content
- Design styles for different output devices, including printed media and aural devices
- Control the appearance and behavior of browser features such as scroll bars and mouse cursors

An update to CSS2, **CSS 2.1**, was introduced by the W3C in April 2002. Although the update did not add any new features to the language, it cleaned up minor errors that were introduced in the original specification. At the time of this writing, almost all aspects of CSS2 are supported by current browsers.

As browsers were implementing all of the features of CSS2, in December 2005 the W3C pressed forward to the next version, **CSS3**, which further expanded the design tools available to Web page authors. Currently still in a working draft, CSS3 adds styles for:

- Enhanced text effects, including drop shadows and Web fonts
- Semi-transparent colors and overlays
- Column-based layout
- Rounded borders, drop shadows, and box outlines
- Transformations of page elements, including scaling, skewing, and rotation

With CSS, as with HTML, Web page designers need to be aware of compatibility issues that arise not just among different versions of the language, but also among different versions of the same browser. Although it's tempting to always apply the latest and most exciting features of CSS, you should not create a situation where users of older browsers will not be able to view your Web pages.

Browser Extensions

Not content to wait for the W3C's final specifications, several browser manufacturers are creating their own extensions to the CSS language. Many of these extensions have been incorporated in the CSS3 specification. By putting forward their own extensions, these vendors are able to test and debug new styles that are still in the development stage with CSS3. You can use these browser extensions as long as you realize that they might not be supported by other browsers and you do not make their use crucial to your page's readability.

Defining a Style Rule

In every version of CSS, you apply a **style rule** containing a list of style properties to an element or a group of elements known as a selector. The general syntax of a CSS style rule is

```
selector {
    property1: value1;
    property2: value2;
    property3: value3;
    ...
}
```

where `selector` identifies an element or a group of elements within the document and the `property: value` pairs specify the style properties and their values. For example, to display the text of all `h1` headings in blue and centered horizontally on the page, you could use the following style rule:

```
h1 {
    color: blue;
    text-align: center;
}
```

To apply these style properties to more than one element, you specify the elements in a comma-separated list. The following style rule causes all `h1` through `h6` headings to be displayed in blue and centered on the page:

```
h1, h2, h3, h4, h5, h6 {
    color: blue;
    text-align: center;
}
```

Like HTML, CSS ignores the use of white space, so you can also enter your styles on a single line, as in the following example:

```
h1 {color: blue; text-align: center;}
```

Writing a style rule on a single line saves space, but entering each style property on a separate line often makes your code easier to read and edit. You will see both approaches used in the CSS files you encounter on the Web.

Applying a Style Sheet

TIP

You can make your style sheets easier to manage by entering the style names in alphabetical order.

The design you apply to a Web site is usually a combination of several style sheets. In general, the style sheet that is loaded last has precedence over style sheets loaded earlier. Figure 3-4 summarizes the different types of style sheets in the order they are usually installed and processed by browsers.

Figure 3-4	Order in which style sheets are interpreted

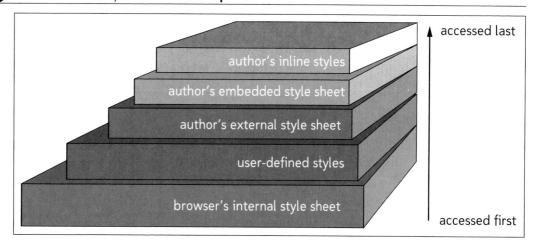

The first style sheet interpreted by the browser is the one built into the browser itself. The current appearance of the Sunny Acres Web page displayed in Figure 3-2 is based on styles applied by the browser itself that are contained within its own style rules about how headings, paragraphs, inline images and so forth, should be rendered. Browsers use similar default styles. So if you rely only on the browser's internal style sheet, your Web sites should appear alike across most browsers.

User-Defined Styles

Almost all browsers allow users to modify the default settings of the internal style sheet. For example, a user could change the font size assigned to paragraph and heading text, set foreground and background colors, and specify whether or not to display inline images. Browsers such as Internet Explorer and Safari also allow users to substitute their own style sheets for the browser's internal sheet, providing more control over how the browser renders the pages it encounters. One advantage of user-defined style sheets is that they make the Web more accessible to visually impaired users who may require larger fonts or the absence of clashing color schemes. Figure 3-5 shows the Advanced dialog box from Safari, in which users can replace the browser's internal style sheet with their own.

Figure 3-5	Choosing a user-defined style sheet in Safari

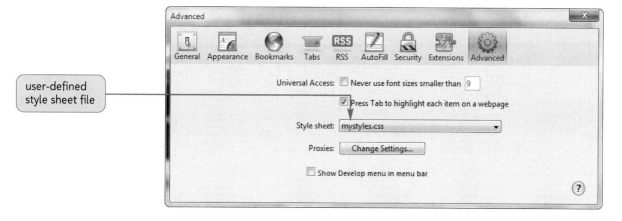

user-defined style sheet file

External Style Sheets

Styles set by the author of a Web page and stored in an external style sheet are loaded after internal and user-defined style sheets. You've already worked with external style sheets in the first two tutorials using CSS files created for you. Recall that an external style sheet is included by adding the `link` element

```
<link href="url" rel="stylesheet" type="text/css" />
```

to the document head, where *url* is the URL of the external style sheet file. The style sheet rules in an external style sheet take precedence over any rules set in the browser's internal style sheet or in a user-defined style sheet.

Tammy already has created a style sheet for her sample pages to define how the elements should be laid out on the page. You'll apply the style rules from her *sa_layout.css* file to the Sunny Acres home page now.

To link to the layout style sheet:

▶ **1.** Return to the **home.htm** file in your text editor.

▶ **2.** Directly above the closing `</head>` tag, insert the following `link` element (see Figure 3-6):

```
<link href="sa_layout.css" rel="stylesheet" type="text/css" />
```

Figure 3-6 Linking to an external style sheet

```
<meta charset="UTF-8" />
<title>Sunny Acres</title>
<script src="modernizr-1.5.js"></script>
<link href="sa_layout.css" rel="stylesheet" type="text/css" />
</head>
```

style sheet file

▶ **3.** Save your changes to the file.

▶ **4.** Reopen the **home.htm** file in your browser. As shown in Figure 3-7, the layout of the page has been altered using the design styles present in the *sa_layout.css* file.

Figure 3-7   **Sunny Acres home page using the sa_layout.css style sheet**

Sunny
Acres

Tammy and Brent Nielsen
1973 Hwy G
Council Bluffs, IA 51503

- Home
- Autumn Fun
- Scary Good
- Meet the Animals
- For your Tastebuds

Welcome

There's always something happening at Sunny Acres. With the coming of fall, we're gearing up for our big AutumnFest and Farm Show. If you haven't visited our famous Corn Maze, be sure to do so before it gets torn down on November 5. This year's maze is bigger and better than ever.

Farms can be educational and Sunny Acres is no exception. Schools and home-schooling parents, spend an afternoon with us at our Petting Barn. We have over 100 friendly farm animals in a clean environment. Kids can bottle feed the baby goats, lambs, and calves while they learn about nature and the farming life. Please call ahead for large school groups.

When the sun goes down this time of year, we're all looking for a good fright. Sunny Acres provides that too with another year of the Haunted Maze. Please plan on joining us during weekends in October or on Halloween for our big Halloween Festival.

Of course, Sunny Acres is, above all, a *farm*. Our Farm Shop is always open with reasonable prices on great produce. Save even more money by picking your own fruits and vegetables from our orchards and gardens.

We all hope to see you soon, down on the farm.
— Tammy & Brent Nielsen

Hours

- Farm Shop: 9 am - 5 pm Mon - Fri; 9 am - 3 pm Sat
- The Corn Maze: 11 am - 9 pm Sat; 11 am - 5 pm Sun
- The Haunted Maze: 5 pm - 9 pm Fri & Sat
- Petting Barn: 9 am - 4 pm Mon - Fri; 11 am - 3 pm Sat & Sun

Directions

- From Council Bluffs, proceed east on I-80
- Take Exit 38 North to the Drake Frontage Road
- Turn right on Highway G
- Proceed east for 2.5 miles
- Sunny Acres is on your left; watch for the green sign

Sunny Acres ☀ Tammy & Brent Nielsen ☀ 1977 Highway G ☀ Council Bluffs, IA   51503

The *sa_layout.css* style sheet changes the layout of the page, displaying the navigation links in a column on the left and the main page content in a column on the right. The width of the page also has been reduced to make the content easier to read.

Importing Style Sheets

On large Web sites that involve hundreds of pages, you might decide to use different styles for different groups of pages to give a visual cue to users about where they are on the site. One way of organizing these different styles is to break them into smaller, more manageable units. The different style sheets then can be imported into a single sheet. To import a style sheet, add the command

```
@import url(url);
```

to the style sheet file, where *url* is the URL of an external style sheet file. For example, a company might have one style sheet named *company.css* that contains basic styles used in all Web pages, and another style sheet named *support.css* that only applies to Web pages containing technical support information. The following code added to a style sheet imports both files:

```
@import url(company.css);
@import url(support.css);
```

The @import statement must always come before any other style rules in the style sheet. When a browser encounters the @import statement, it imports the content of the style sheet file directly into the current style sheet, much as if you had typed the style declarations yourself.

The @import rule has the same impact as adding multiple link elements to the HTML file. An advantage of the @import rule is that it simplifies your HTML file (since you only need to access one style sheet file), and it places all style rules and decisions about which style sheets to include and exclude in an external file. This is an important distinction if you want to put all of your design choices in the external style sheet file, which you can then easily edit and modify without having to touch the HTML document.

Embedded Style Sheets

Another type of style sheet created by a Web page author is an embedded style sheet, in which the styles are inserted directly within the head element of an HTML document using the style element

```
<style type="text/css">
    styles
</style>
```

where *styles* are the rules of the style sheet. For example, the following embedded style sheet applies a rule to display the text of all h1 headings from the current document centered horizontally and in red:

```
<style type="text/css">
   h1 {
   color: red;
   text-align: center;
   }
</style>
```

The exact order in which external style sheets and embedded style sheets are processed by the browser depends on the order in which they are listed within the HTML file. The HTML code

```
<link href="sa_layout.css" rel="stylesheet" type="text/css" />
<style type="text/css">
   h1 {color: red; }
</style>
```

loads the external style sheet first and then the embedded sheet. However, if that order is switched as in the code

```
<style type="text/css">
   h1 {color: red; }
</style>
<link href="sa_layout.css" rel="stylesheet" type="text/css" />
```

then the external style sheet is processed after the embedded sheet.

Unlike an external style sheet, an embedded style sheet is applied only to the Web page in which it is placed. Thus, if you want to apply the same style to all of the headings on your Web site, it is more efficient and easier to manage if you define your styles only once within an external style sheet and link all of the pages to that file. If you later need to change the site design, you'll have to edit only one file, rather than dozens.

TIP

Always place embedded styles after external style sheets to avoid confusion about which style sheet is loaded last.

Inline Styles

The very last styles to be interpreted by the browser are inline styles, which are styles applied directly to specific elements using the `style` attribute

```
<element style="style rules"> … </element>
```

where `element` is the HTML element and `style rules` are CSS styles applied to that element. For example, the following `style` attribute is used to display the text of a specific `h1` heading in green and centered on the page:

```
<h1 style="color: green; text-align: center;">
   Sunny Acres
</h1>
```

The advantage in using inline styles is that it is clear exactly what page element is being formatted; however, inline styles are not recommended in most cases because they make changing styles tedious and inefficient. For example, if you wanted to use inline styles to format all of your headings, you would have to locate all of the `h1` through `h6` elements in all of the Web pages within the entire Web site and add `style` attributes to each tag. This would be no small task on a large Web site containing hundreds of headings spread out among dozens of Web pages, and it would be a nightmare if you had to modify the design of a large Web site that was created using inline styles.

TIP

View your Web site with and without your style sheet. It should be readable even if a user is limited to the default styles supplied by a Web browser.

However, the primary reason to not use inline styles is that you want to, as much as possible, separate document content from document design. Ideally, the HTML code and CSS styles should be so separate that one group of employees could define the page content using HTML and another group could define the page design using CSS. This isn't possible with inline styles because the code for the page design is intermingled with the code for the page content.

Exploring the Style Cascade

With the potential for many different style sheets to be applied to the same Web page, there has to be an orderly method by which conflicts between those different style sheets are resolved. CSS does this by assigning a level of importance to each style, with the most important style rule taking precedence over other competing rules.

Style Precedence and Specificity

Many factors determine how the importance of each style is calculated. But as a general rule of thumb, *all other things being equal, the more specific style is applied instead of the more general.* Thus, a style applied to a specific paragraph is given more importance than a general style applied to an entire Web page, and a style applied to a section of text within that paragraph has more importance than the style for the entire paragraph. For example, the following set of style rules would set the text color of the Web page to black, except for text within the `header` element:

```
body {color: black;}
header {color: red;}
```

Specificity is only a concern when two or more styles conflict. If the style rules involve different properties, there is no conflict and both rules are applied. If two style rules have equal specificity, and thus equal importance, then the one that is defined last in the style sheet is the one used.

Style Inheritance

An additional factor in applying a style sheet is that properties are passed from a parent element to its children in a process known as **style inheritance**. For example, to set the text color of a page to blue, you could apply the style

```
body {color: blue;}
```

and every element nested within the `body` element (which is every element on the Web page) would inherit this style. This means that the text of every heading, every paragraph, every numbered list, and so forth would be displayed in blue unless a different text color were defined for those specific elements. Thus, the style rules

```
body {color: blue;}
h1 {text-align: center;}
```

would result in the `h1` heading text appearing in blue and centered even though only the text alignment is specifically set within the style rule for the `h1` element.

Not all properties are inherited. For example, the style property above that defines the text color for the page body has no meaning if applied to an inline image.

The final rendering of any page element thus becomes the result of multiple style sheets and multiple style rules. You may have to track a set of styles as they are passed from one style sheet to another. For example, browsers typically display all `h1` headings in a large bold black font and left-aligned on the page. The following rule applied within an external style sheet modifies the color of `h1` headings on the Web site, but does nothing to change the default settings for size, weight, or alignment:

```
h1 {color: red;}
```

The combination of the internal and external style sheets results in all `h1` headings being displayed in a large bold red font and left-aligned on the page. However, if a particular heading is formatted with the inline style

```
<h1 style="text-align: center;">Sunny Acres</h1>
```

then that `h1` heading will be centered, displayed in red (defined in the external style sheet), and rendered in a large bold font (defined in the browser's default style sheet). The final appearance is thus a result of a combination of several styles drawn from multiple sources. Many Web browsers now include developer tools to allow page designers to track each style back to its source.

Defining Important Styles

If you need browsers to enforce a style, you can append the `!important` keyword to the style property, using the syntax

```
property: value !important;
```

where *property* is the style property and *value* is the property value. The following style rule sets the color of all `h1` headings to orange; and because this property is marked as important, it takes precedence over any other style that may be defined in the style sheet:

```
h1 {color: orange !important;}
```

<table><tr><td>

TIP

Make sure that the `!important` keyword is placed between the style property value and the closing semicolon; it is invalid if placed elsewhere.

</td><td>

The `!important` keyword is often necessary for visually impaired users who require their pages rendered with large, clear text and highly contrasting colors. Such a user could set the text size in a user-defined style sheet and override any styles specified by the page author through the use of the `!important` keyword. In general, Web page authors should not use the `!important` keyword and should instead write style sheets that are based on the content of the Web documents. This practice makes the style sheets easier to edit and maintain if the content or design of the Web site changes.

</td></tr></table>

Writing Style Comments

Now that you've reviewed some principles of style sheet design and application, you can begin creating your own style sheets. You'll start by creating an external style sheet that will be used to format the appearance of text on the Sunny Acres Web site. Because style sheets are text files, you can create your style sheets with the same text editor you used for creating and editing your HTML files.

To start creating the sa_styles.css style sheet:

1. Use your text editor to open the blank text file **sa_stylestxt.css** from the tutorial.03/tutorial folder.

2. Save the file as **sa_styles.css**.

TIP

Style comments can also be added to embedded style sheets as long as they are placed between the opening and closing `<style>` tags.

Style sheets can be as long and complicated as HTML files. To help others read your style sheet code, you should document the content and purpose of the style sheet using style sheet comments. Style sheet comments are entered as follows

```
/* comment */
```

where *comment* is the text of the comment. Like HTML, CSS ignores the presence of white space, so you can place style comments on several lines to make them easier to read. For example, the following style comment extends over four lines in the style sheet:

```
/*
   Sunny Acres
   Style Sheet
*/
```

Add style comments to the *sa_styles.css* file now to document the purpose and authorship of the style sheet.

To document the style sheet:

▶ **1.** At the top of the file, insert the following style comments, as shown in Figure 3-8:

```
/*
    Sunny Acres Style Sheet

    Author: your name
    Date:   the date
*/
```

Figure 3-8	Entering style sheet comments

```
/*
    Sunny Acres Style Sheet

    Author: Tammy Nielsen
    Date:   3/1/2014
*/
```

▶ **2.** Save your changes to the file.

Next, you'll link the Sunny Acres home page to this new style sheet.

To link to the sa_styles.css file:

▶ **1.** Return to the **home.htm** file in your text editor.

▶ **2.** Directly below the link element for the *sa_layout.css* file, insert the following:

```
<link href="sa_styles.css" rel="stylesheet" type="text/css" />
```

▶ **3.** Save your changes to the file.

Defining Color in CSS

The first part of your style sheet will focus on color. If you've worked with graphics software, you've probably made your color selections using a graphical interface where you can see your color options. Specifying color with CSS is somewhat less intuitive because CSS is a text-based language and requires colors to be defined in textual terms. This is done through either a color value or a color name.

RGB Color Values

A **color value** is a numerical expression that describes the properties of a color. To better understand how numbers can represent colors, it can help to review some of the basic principles of color theory and how they relate to the way colors are rendered in a browser.

In classical color theory, all colors are based on adding three primary colors—red, green, and blue—at different levels of intensity. For example, adding all three primary colors at maximum intensity produces the color white, while adding any two of the three primary colors at maximum intensity produces the trio of complementary colors—yellow, magenta, and cyan (see Figure 3-9).

| **Figure 3-9** | **Color addition in the RGB color model** |

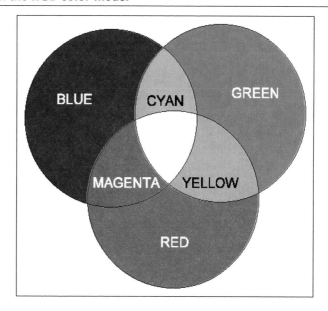

Varying the intensity of the three primary colors creates other colors. Orange, for example, is created from a high intensity of red, a moderate intensity of green, and a total absence of blue. CSS represents these intensities mathematically as a set of numbers called an **RGB triplet**, which has the format

`rgb(red, green, blue)`

where `red`, `green`, and `blue` are the intensities of the red, green, and blue components of the color. Intensity values range from 0 (absence of color) to 255 (maximum intensity); thus, the color white has the color value `rgb(255, 255, 255)`, indicating that red, green, and blue are mixed equally at the highest intensity, and orange is represented by `rgb(255, 165, 0)`. RGB triplets can describe 256^3 (16.7 million) possible colors, which is a greater number of colors than the human eye can distinguish. You can also enter each component value as a percentage, with 100% representing the highest intensity. In this form, you would specify the color orange with the following values:

`rgb(100%, 65%, 0%)`

The percentage form is less commonly used than RGB values, but many page designers find it easier to work with.

CSS also allows RGB values to be entered as hexadecimal numbers. A **hexadecimal** number is a number expressed in the base 16 numbering system rather than in the commonly used base 10 system. In base 10 counting, numeric values are expressed using combinations of 10 characters (0 through 9); hexadecimal numbering includes six extra characters: A (for 10), B (for 11), C (for 12), D (for 13), E (for 14), and F (for 15). For values above 15, you use a combination of those 16 characters. For example, 16 has a hexadecimal representation of 10, and a value of 255 is represented as FF in hexadecimal numbering. The style value for color represented as a hexadecimal number has the form

`#redgreenblue`

where `red`, `green`, and `blue` are the hexadecimal values of the red, green, and blue components. Therefore, the color yellow could be represented either by the RGB triplet

`rgb(255,255,0)`

or by the hexadecimal

`#FFFF00`

One advantage of using the compact hexadecimal format is that it results in smaller style sheet files; the disadvantage is that hexadecimals are more difficult to read and interpret. Most graphics programs provide color values in either a decimal or a hexadecimal format that you can easily copy into a style sheet. So a common practice is to use graphics software to choose your colors, and then copy the color values from your graphics package.

REFERENCE

Defining Color Values

- To define a color value using the RGB color model, use the property value

  rgb(red, green, blue)

  where red, green, and blue are the intensities of red, green, and blue ranging in value from 0 up to 255.
- To define a color value using the HSL color mode, use

  hsl(hue, saturation, lightness)

  where hue is the tint of the color on the color wheel measured in degrees, saturation is the intensity of the color in percent, and lightness is the brightness of the color in percent.
- To create a semi-transparent color, use either

  rgba(red, green, blue, opacity)

  or

  hsla(hue, saturation, lightness, opacity)

  where opacity ranges from 0 (transparent) up to 1 (opaque).

Using Color Names

If you don't want to use color values, you can also specify colors by name. CSS supports the 16 basic color names shown in Figure 3-10.

Figure 3-10   **The 16 basic CSS2 color names**

Color Name	RGB Triplet	Hexadecimal	Color Name	RGB Triplet	Hexadecimal
Aqua	(0, 255, 255)	00FFFF	Navy	(0, 0, 128)	000080
Black	(0, 0, 0)	000000	Olive	(128, 128, 0)	808000
Blue	(0, 0, 255)	0000FF	Purple	(128, 0, 128)	FF0000
Fuchsia	(255, 0, 255)	FF00FF	Red	(255, 0, 0)	C0C0C0
Gray	(128, 128, 128)	808080	Silver	(192, 192, 192)	008080
Green	(0, 128, 0)	008000	Teal	(0, 128, 128)	FFFFFF
Lime	(0, 255, 0)	00FF00	White	(255, 255, 255)	FFFF00
Maroon	(128, 0, 0)	800000	Yellow	(255, 255, 0)	

Sixteen colors are not a lot, so most browsers support an extended list of 140 color names, including such colors as orange, crimson, khaki, and brown. Although this extended color list was not part of the CSS specification until CSS3, most browsers support it. You can view these color names in the appendix and in a demo page.

To view the extended list of color names:

▶ **1.** Use your browser to open the **demo_color_names.htm** file from the tutorial.03\demo folder included with your Data Files.

▶ **2.** As shown in Figure 3-11, the demo page displays the list of 140 color names along with their color values expressed both as RGB triplets and in hexadecimal form.

Figure 3-11   A partial list of extended color names

Sample	Name	RGB	Hexadecimal
	aliceblue	(240,248,255)	#F0F8FF
	antiquewhite	(250,235,215)	#FAEBD7
	aqua	(0,255,255)	#00FFFF
	aquamarine	(127,255,212)	#7FFFD4
	azure	(240,255,255)	#F0FFFF
	beige	(245,245,220)	#F5F5DC
	bisque	(255,228,196)	#FFE4C4
	black	(0,0,0)	#000000
	blanchedalmond	(255,235,205)	#FFEBCD
	blue	(0,0,255)	#0000FF
	blueviolet	(138,43,226)	#8A2BE2
	brown	(165,42,42)	#A52A2A
	burlywood	(222,184,135)	#DEB887

▶ **3.** Close the page when you are finished reviewing the extended color names list.

Written Communication: Communicating in Color

Humans are born to respond to color. Studies have shown that infants as young as two months prefer colorful objects to non-colored objects, and that memory is often associated with color. While marketing products such as clothes, companies rely on knowing what colors are "in" and what colors are passé. Your color choices can also impact the way your Web pages are received. You want to choose a color scheme that is tailored to the personality and interests of your target audience.

Color also evokes an emotional response, in which certain colors are associated with particular feelings or concepts, such as:

- *red*—assertive, powerful, sexy, dangerous
- *pink*—innocent, romantic, feminine
- *black*—strong, classic, stylish
- *gray*—business-like, detached
- *yellow*—warm, cheerful, optimistic
- *blue*—consoling, serene, quiet
- *orange*—friendly, vigorous, inviting
- *white*—clean, pure, straightforward, innocent

International businesses need to understand how cultural differences can affect people's responses to color. For instance, white, which is associated with innocence in Western cultures, is the color of mourning in China; yellow is considered a bright, cheerful color in the West, while in Buddhist countries it represents spirituality.

When you develop a Web site design, you should test it out before a group of potential customers. In addition to evaluating responses to the content of your Web site, pay attention to reactions to its presentation and appearance, including your color choices.

Defining Text and Background Colors

Now that you've studied how CSS works with colors, you can start applying color to some of the elements of the Sunny Acres Web site. CSS supports styles to define both the text and background color for each element on your page. You've already seen examples of how to set the text color of a page element using the `color` property, which has the form

```
color: color;
```

where *color* is either a color value or a color name. Background colors are defined using the property

```
background-color: color;
```

where once again *color* is either a color name or value. Tammy wants the body of each page on her Web site to have a white background. Although most browsers by default will apply a white background, it's a good idea to make this explicit. Also, she wants the text of the `h2` headings to be displayed in white on a green background. The style rules to apply these two design choices are:

```
body {
    background-color: white;
}

h2 {
    background-color: rgb(0, 154, 0);
    color: white;
}
```

Whether to use a color value in place of a color name is often a matter of personal preference. This code does both, with the RGB triplet (0, 154, 0) representing the color green, and the color name *white* used for the text color of the `h2` headings and the background color of the page body. You'll add these style rules to the *sa_styles.css* style sheet.

REFERENCE

Setting Foreground and Background Color

- To set the background color of an element, use the property

  ```
  background-color: color;
  ```

  where *color* is a color name or a color value.
- To set the foreground or text color of an element, use the following property:

  ```
  color: color;
  ```

To format the text and background colors:

▶ **1.** Return to the **sa_styles.css** file in your text editor.

▶ **2.** Directly below the style comments, insert the following style rules, as shown in Figure 3-12:

```
/* Body styles */

body {
   background-color: white;
}


/* Heading styles */

h2 {
   background-color: rgb(0, 165, 0);
   color: white;
}
```

Make sure you end every style property value with a semicolon to separate it from other style properties.

TIP

About 8% of all men and 0.5% of all women have some form of color blindness. Because red-green color blindness is the most common form of color impairment, you should avoid using red text on a green background or vice versa.

Figure 3-12   **Setting the foreground and background colors**

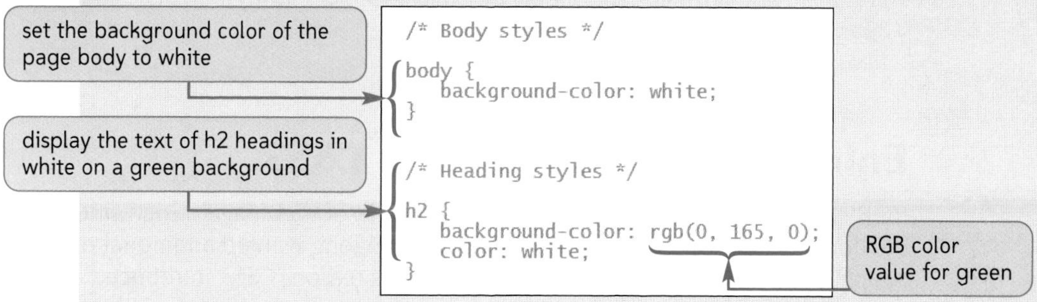

set the background color of the page body to white

display the text of h2 headings in white on a green background

```
/* Body styles */

body {
   background-color: white;
}

/* Heading styles */

h2 {
   background-color: rgb(0, 165, 0);
   color: white;
}
```

RGB color value for green

▶ **3.** Save your changes to the file and then reload the **home.htm** file in your Web browser. As shown in Figure 3-13, the h2 heading text appears in white on a green background.

Figure 3-13   **Formatted h2 headings**

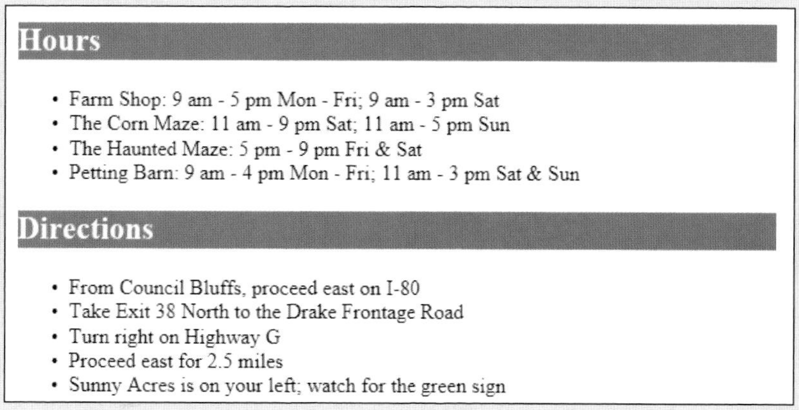

Hours

- Farm Shop: 9 am - 5 pm Mon - Fri; 9 am - 3 pm Sat
- The Corn Maze: 11 am - 9 pm Sat; 11 am - 5 pm Sun
- The Haunted Maze: 5 pm - 9 pm Fri & Sat
- Petting Barn: 9 am - 4 pm Mon - Fri; 11 am - 3 pm Sat & Sun

Directions

- From Council Bluffs, proceed east on I-80
- Take Exit 38 North to the Drake Frontage Road
- Turn right on Highway G
- Proceed east for 2.5 miles
- Sunny Acres is on your left; watch for the green sign

Deprecated Approaches to Color

Because CSS was not part of the original HTML specifications, older HTML code used HTML attributes to define page colors. If you work with older Web pages, you may encounter some of these deprecated attributes. For example, the bgcolor attribute in the <body> tag was used to define the background color for an entire page. To define the text color for the entire page, the text attribute was used. Both attributes required the page author to enter either a hexadecimal color value or a recognized color name. Thus, the following code set the page background to yellow and the page text color to sky blue with the hexadecimal color value 99CCFF:

```
<body bgcolor="yellow" text="#99CCFF">
```

To color a section of text, page authors enclosed the text within a two-sided <font> tag, which supported several design attributes. One of these, color, defined the font color of the enclosed text. For example, the following deprecated code sets the text color of an h1 heading to green:

```
<h1><font color="green">Sunny Acres</font></h1>
```

These attributes, as well as the <font> tag, have been deprecated due to the desire to completely separate page content from page design. Although you may still encounter them and browsers still support them, you should always use style sheets to set your page design.

Enhancements to Color in CSS3

RGB color values and color names have been part of Web page design since the introduction of CSS. However, graphic designers have long wanted additional options for creating and working with colors in CSS. For this reason, CSS3 introduced additional tools to allow Web page designers to create more interesting and flexible designs based on color.

HSL Color Values

The RGB color model is only one way of describing colors. CSS3 also supports the Hue Saturation Lightness (HSL) model that describes colors based on hue, saturation, and lightness. **Hue** is the tint of the color and is based on the color's location on the color wheel. Hue values range from 0° up to 360°, where 0° matches the location of red on the color wheel, 120° matches green, and 240° matches blue. **Saturation** measures the intensity of the chosen color and ranges from 0% (no color) up to 100% (full color). Finally, **lightness** measures the brightness of the color and ranges from 0% (black) up to 100% (white). Color values using the HSL model are described in CSS3 using

```
hsl(hue, saturation, lightness)
```

where *hue* is the tint of the color in degrees, *saturation* is the intensity of the color in percent, and *lightness* is the brightness of the color in percent. Figure 3-14 shows how setting the hue to 38°, the saturation to 90%, and the lightness to 60% results in a medium shade of orange.

Figure 3-14 HSL color saturation model

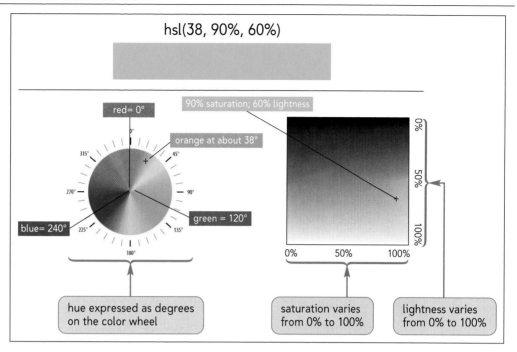

Graphic designers consider HSL easier to use because it allows you to guess at an initial color based on hue and then tweak the saturation and lightness values to fine-tune the final color. This is more difficult in the RGB model because you have to balance three completely different colors to achieve the right mix. For example, the RGB equivalent to the color in Figure 3-14 would be the color value rgb(245, 177, 61); however, it's not immediately apparent why that mixture of red, green, and blue would result in that particular shade of orange.

Opacity Values in CSS3

CSS3 also allows page designers to augment RGB and HSL color values by specifying a color's opacity. Opacity defines how much of the colors below the surface of the current object show through to affect its appearance. The opacity of a color can be specified using either of the following rgba and hsla color values

```
rgba(red, green, blue, opacity)
hsla(hue, saturation, lightness, opacity)
```

where *opacity* sets the transparency of the color as a decimal ranging from 0 (completely transparent) up to 1.0 (completely opaque). For example, the following style displays the text of h1 headings in a medium shade of orange at 70% opacity:

```
hsla(38, 90%, 60%, 0.7)
```

With semi-transparent colors, the final color rendered by a browser depends on the background color of the parent element. Displayed against a white background, this medium orange color would appear in a lighter shade of orange, while displayed against a black background it would appear as very dark orange. The advantage of using semi-transparent colors is that it makes it easier to create a color theme in which similarly tinted colors are used throughout the page.

TIP

The *a* in rgba and hsla stands for *alpha* and refers to the alpha channel, a color concept developed in the 1970s to add transparency to the color model.

Styles Using Progressive Enhancement

Tammy suggests that you modify the style of the h2 headings to make the text appear as a semi-transparent white against a green background. To create this effect, you can employ the following style rule:

```
h2 {
    background-color: rgb(0, 154, 0);
    color: white;
    color: rgba(255, 255, 255, 0.8);
}
```

Notice that this code doesn't remove the initial `color` property that set the text color to white, but simply adds another `color` property to the style rule. This is an example of a technique known as **progressive enhancement**, which places code conforming to older standards before newer properties. Older browsers that do not support CSS3 will ignore the RGBA color value and display the text in white, while newer browsers that do support CSS3 will apply the RGBA color value because that color value, being declared last, has precedence. Thus, both older and newer browsers are served by this style rule.

To make the heading text semi-transparent:

1. Return to the **sa_styles.css** file in your text editor.

2. Within the style rule for the h2 selector, insert the following `color` property, as shown in Figure 3-15:

   ```
   color: rgba(255, 255, 255, 0.8);
   ```

Figure 3-15 Setting a semi-transparent color

```
h2 {
    background-color: rgb(0, 165, 0);
    color: white;
    color: rgba(255, 255, 255, 0.8);
}
```

older browsers will display h2 text in white

white color with 80% opacity

3. Save your changes and then reload the **home.htm** file in your Web browser. If you're using a current browser that supports CSS3, the h2 heading text should appear as light green (see Figure 3-16). Under older browsers, the text should retain the white color shown earlier in Figure 3-13.

Figure 3-16 Heading text in semi-transparent white

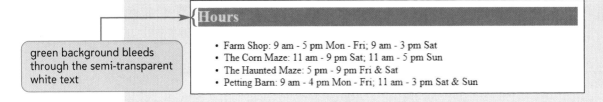

green background bleeds through the semi-transparent white text

Hours

- Farm Shop: 9 am - 5 pm Mon - Fri; 9 am - 3 pm Sat
- The Corn Maze: 11 am - 9 pm Sat; 11 am - 5 pm Sun
- The Haunted Maze: 5 pm - 9 pm Fri & Sat
- Petting Barn: 9 am - 4 pm Mon - Fri; 11 am - 3 pm Sat & Sun

PROSKILLS

Problem Solving: Choosing a Color Scheme

One of the worst things you can do to your Web site is to associate interesting and useful content with jarring and disagreeable color. Many designers prefer the HSL color system because it makes it easier to select visually pleasing color schemes. The following are some basic color schemes you may want to apply to your own Web sites:

- *monochrome*—a single hue with varying values for saturation and lightness; this color scheme is easy to manage but is not as vibrant as other designs
- *complementary*—two hues separated by 180° on the color wheel; this color scheme is the most vibrant and offers the highest contrast and visual interest, but can be misused and might distract users from the page content
- *triad*—three hues separated by 120° on the color wheel; this color scheme provides the same opportunity for pleasing color contrasts as a complementary design, but might not be visibly striking
- *tetrad*—four hues separated by 90° on the color wheel; perhaps the richest of all color schemes, it is also the hardest one in which to achieve color balance
- *analogic*—two hues close to one another on the color wheel in which one color is the dominant color and the other is a supporting color used only for highlights and nuance; this scheme lacks color contrasts and is not as vibrant as other color schemes

Once you have selected a color design and the main hues, you then vary those colors by altering the saturation and lightness. One of the great advantages of style sheets is that you can quickly modify your color design choices and view the impact of those changes on your Web page content.

You show Tammy the work you've done on colors. She's pleased with the ease of using CSS to modify the design and appearance of elements on the Sunny Acres Web site. In the next session, you'll continue to explore CSS styles, focusing on text and image styles.

REVIEW

Session 3.1 Quick Check

1. What are inline styles, embedded styles, and external style sheets? Which would you use to define a design for an entire Web site?
2. What keyword do you add to a style property to override style precedence and style inheritance?
3. Specify the code to enter the comment *Sunny Acres Color Styles* in a style sheet.
4. Provide the style rule to display blockquote text in red using an RGB triplet.
5. The color chartreuse is located at 90° on the color wheel with 100% saturation and 50% lightness. Provide a style rule to display address text with chartreuse as the background color.
6. What is progressive enhancement?
7. Based on the following style rule for paragraph text, which style property will be used by an older browser that supports only CSS2?

```
p {
   color: rgb(232, 121, 50);
   color: hsla(23, 80%, 55%, 0.75);
}
```

8. Provide a style rule to display h1 and h2 headings with a background color of yellow (an equal mixture of red and green at highest intensity with no blue) at 70% opacity.

SESSION 3.2 VISUAL OVERVIEW

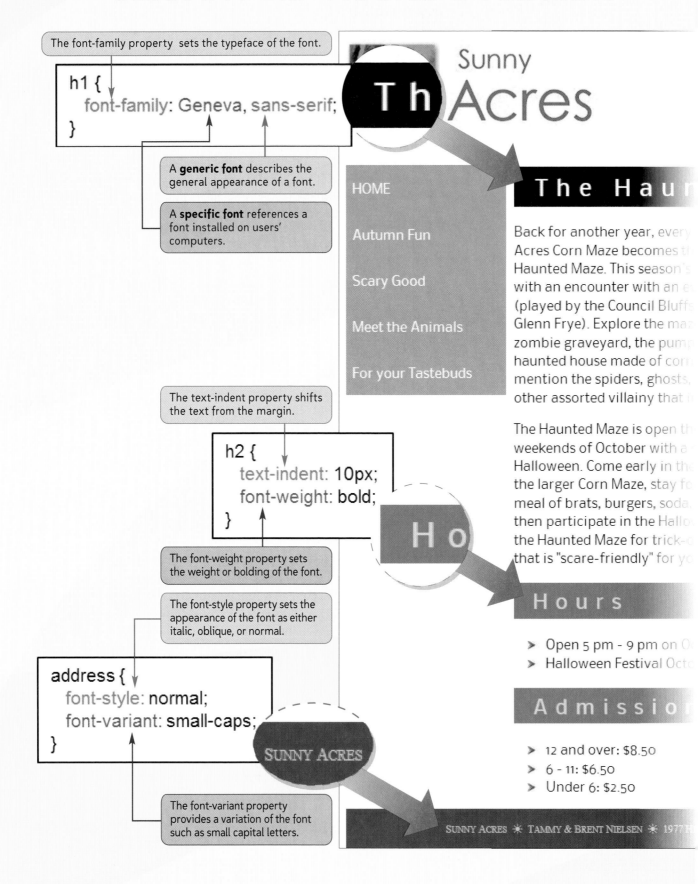

The font-family property sets the typeface of the font.

```
h1 {
    font-family: Geneva, sans-serif;
}
```

A **generic font** describes the general appearance of a font.

A **specific font** references a font installed on users' computers.

The text-indent property shifts the text from the margin.

```
h2 {
    text-indent: 10px;
    font-weight: bold;
}
```

The font-weight property sets the weight or bolding of the font.

The font-style property sets the appearance of the font as either italic, oblique, or normal.

```
address {
    font-style: normal;
    font-variant: small-caps;
}
```

The font-variant property provides a variation of the font such as small capital letters.

Sunny
Acres

HOME

Autumn Fun

Scary Good

Meet the Animals

For your Tastebuds

The Haur

Back for another year, every
Acres Corn Maze becomes t
Haunted Maze. This season's
with an encounter with an e
(played by the Council Bluff
Glenn Frye). Explore the ma
zombie graveyard, the pump
haunted house made of cor
mention the spiders, ghosts,
other assorted villainy that

The Haunted Maze is open t
weekends of October with a
Halloween. Come early in th
the larger Corn Maze, stay f
meal of brats, burgers, soda
then participate in the Hallo
the Haunted Maze for trick-
that is "scare-friendly" for y

Hours

> Open 5 pm - 9 pm on O
> Halloween Festival Oct

Admissio

> 12 and over: $8.50
> 6 - 11: $6.50
> Under 6: $2.50

SUNNY ACRES ✹ TAMMY & BRENT NIELSEN ✹ 1977

SELECTORS AND TEXT STYLES

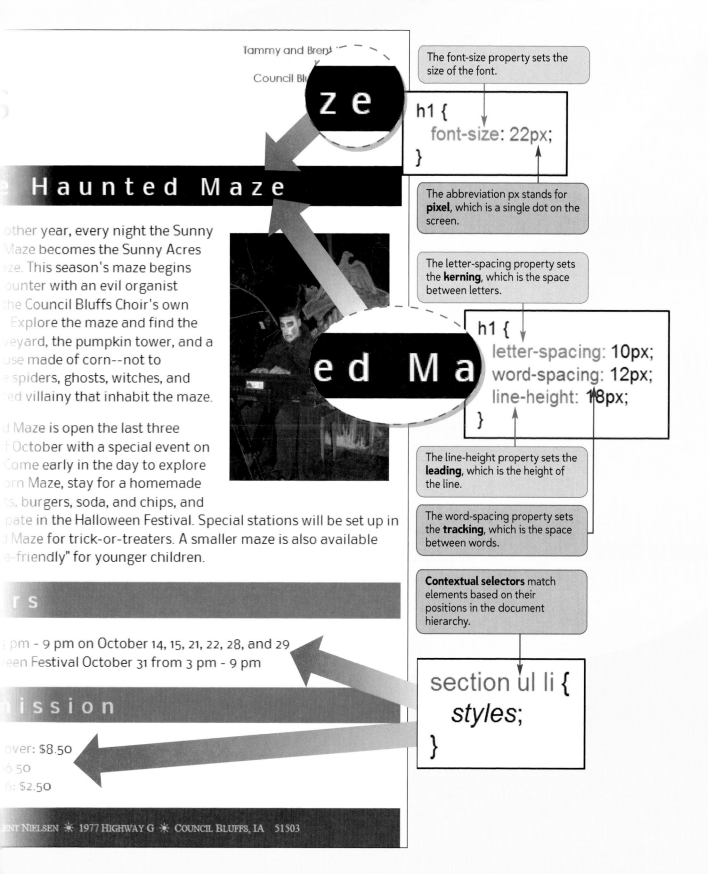

Tammy and Bren~
Council Bl~

z e

The font-size property sets the size of the font.

h1 {
    font-size: 22px;
}

The abbreviation px stands for **pixel**, which is a single dot on the screen.

e H a u n t e d   M a z e

other year, every night the Sunny
Maze becomes the Sunny Acres
-ze. This season's maze begins
ounter with an evil organist
the Council Bluffs Choir's own
 Explore the maze and find the
veyard, the pumpkin tower, and a
use made of corn--not to
 spiders, ghosts, witches, and
ed villainy that inhabit the maze.

The letter-spacing property sets the **kerning**, which is the space between letters.

e d   M a

h1 {
    letter-spacing: 10px;
    word-spacing: 12px;
    line-height: 18px;
}

d Maze is open the last three
 October with a special event on
Come early in the day to explore
rn Maze, stay for a homemade
s, burgers, soda, and chips, and
pate in the Halloween Festival. Special stations will be set up in
 Maze for trick-or-treaters. A smaller maze is also available
e-friendly" for younger children.

The line-height property sets the **leading**, which is the height of the line.

The word-spacing property sets the **tracking**, which is the space between words.

r s

Contextual selectors match elements based on their positions in the document hierarchy.

 pm - 9 pm on October 14, 15, 21, 22, 28, and 29
een Festival October 31 from 3 pm - 9 pm

i s s i o n

over: $8.50
 50
: $2.50

section ul li {
    styles;
}

ENT NIELSEN ☀ 1977 HIGHWAY G ☀ COUNCIL BLUFFS, IA   51503

Exploring Selector Patterns

Tammy has examined your work on color styles from the last session and asks that you create another color style for h1 headings. She suggests that you display the text of your h1 headings in white on a sky blue background.

To format h1 headings:

▶ **1.** Return to the **sa_styles.css** file in your text editor.

▶ **2.** Directly above the style rule for h2 headings, insert the following style rule, as shown in Figure 3-17:

```
h1 {
    background-color: rgb(125, 186, 240);
    color: white;
}
```

Figure 3-17   **Creating a style for h1 headings**

display h1 headings in white on a sky blue background		`/* Heading styles */`
		
		`h1 {`
		`    background-color: rgb(125, 186, 240);`
		`    color: white;`
		`}`

▶ **3.** Save your changes to the file and then reload the **home.htm** file in your Web browser. Figure 3-18 shows the revised appearance of the page.

Figure 3-18   **Effect of the h1 style rule**

sky blue background added to the company logo

formatted h1 heading

Tammy notices that the sky blue background has been added to the Welcome text in the h1 heading, but it also has been added to the company logo. A quick investigation of the HTML code reveals that the logo itself is also within an h1 heading:

```
<header>
    <h1>
        <img src="salogo.png" alt="Sunny Acres" />
    </h1>
</header>
```

Tammy doesn't want all h1 headings formatted the same way. To specify which h1 headings receive a sky blue background and which ones don't, you have to modify the selector in the style rule you just entered.

Contextual Selectors

So far, the only selectors you've studied involve either single elements or groups of elements in a comma-separated list. However, this approach doesn't take into account that Web pages are structured documents in which elements are nested within other elements, forming a hierarchy of elements. Figure 3-19 shows an example of such a tree structure for a Web page consisting of a few headings, a couple of paragraphs, and a few text-level elements, all descending from the body element.

Figure 3-19   **A sample hierarchy of page elements**

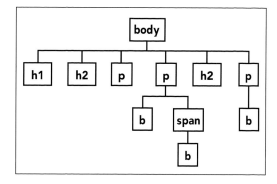

To create styles that take advantage of this tree structure, CSS allows you to create contextual selectors whose values represent the locations of elements within the hierarchy. As with the folder structure discussed in Tutorial 2, elements in a Web page are often referenced using their familial relationships. A **parent element** is an element that contains one or more other elements, which are **child elements** of the parent. Two child elements that share the same parent are referred to as **sibling elements**. Each child element may contain children of its own and so forth down the hierarchy, creating a set of **descendant elements** that are all descended from a common parent. The ultimate parent element for the HTML file is the html element itself, and the parent element for all elements within the page body is the body element.

One commonly used selector that takes advantage of these familial relationships has the form

```
parent descendant {styles}
```

where *parent* is the parent element, *descendant* is a descendant of the parent, and *styles* are the style properties applied to the descendant element. For example, to display the text of all h1 headings found within a page header in blue, you could apply the following style rule:

```
header h1 {color: blue;}
```

In this case, header is the parent element and h1 is the descendant element (because it is contained within the header element). Any h1 heading that is not placed within a page header is not affected by this style. Note that the descendant element does not have to be a direct child of the parent; it can appear several levels below the parent in the hierarchy. This style applies equally to the following HTML code:

```
<header>
   <hgroup>
      <h1>Sunny Acres</h1>
   </hgroup>
</header>
```

Here, the h1 element is a direct child only of the hgroup element; but because it is still a descendant of the header element, it would still appear in blue.

Contextual selectors take advantage of the general rule that the more specific style is applied in preference to the more general. For instance, the styles

```
section h1 {color: red;}
h1          {color: blue;}
```

would result in any `h1` heading text nested within a `section` element appearing in red, even though the last style sets the text color to blue. The more specific style using the contextual selector takes precedence over the general style in which no context has been given.

Contextual selectors also can be listed with other selectors. The following style rule is applied both to `strong` elements nested within list items and to `h2` headings:

```
li strong, h2 {color: blue;}
```

The parent/descendant form is only one example of a contextual selector. Figure 3-20 describes some of the other contextual forms supported by CSS.

Figure 3-20   **Contextual selectors**

Selector	Description
*	Matches any element in the hierarchy
e	Matches any element, e, in the hierarchy
e1, e2, e3, ...	Matches the group of elements e1, e2, e3, ...
e f	Matches any element, f, that is a descendant of an element, e
e>f	Matches any element, f, that is a direct child of an element, e
e+f	Matches any element, f, that is immediately preceded by a sibling element, e
e~f	Matches any element, f, that is a sibling to an element, e

For example, the style rule

```
* {color: blue;}
```

uses the asterisk (*) selector—also known as the **wildcard selector**—to select all elements in the document. The result is that the text of all elements in the document appears in blue. On the other hand, the rule

```
p > em {color: blue;}
```

applies the blue text color only to emphasized text placed as a direct child of a paragraph. Figure 3-21 provides additional examples of selectors applied to a document tree. Selected elements are highlighted in red for each pattern. Remember that because of style inheritance, any style applied to an element is passed down the document tree. Thus, a style applied to a paragraph element is automatically passed down to elements contained within that paragraph unless that style conflicts with a more specific style.

Figure 3-21   Examples of contextual selectors

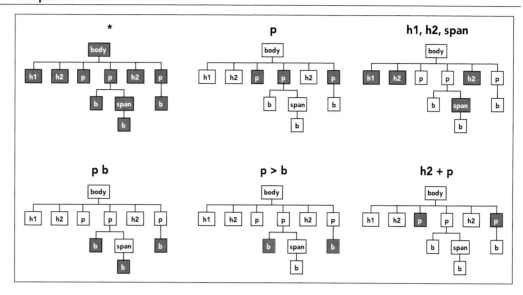

REFERENCE

Using Contextual Selectors

- To apply a style to all elements in a document, use the * selector.
- To apply a style to a single element, use the *e* selector, where *e* is the name of the element.
- To apply a selector to a descendant element, *f*, use the *e f* selector, where *e* is the name of the parent element and *f* is an element nested within the parent.
- To apply a selector to a child element, *f*, use the *e > f* selector, where *e* is the name of a parent element and *f* is an element that is a direct child of the parent.
- To apply a selector to a sibling element, use the *e + f* selector, where *e* and *f* are siblings and *f* immediately follows *e* in the document tree.
- To apply a selector to any sibling element, use the *e ~ f* selector, where *e* and *f* are siblings.

Now that you've seen how to create contextual selectors, you can fix the style rule you created earlier. Rather than applying white text and a sky blue background to every h1 heading, you'll apply those properties only to h1 headings that are descendants of the section element. The style rule thus becomes

```
section h1 {
    background-color: rgb(125, 186, 240);
    color: white;
}
```

with the section h1 selector replacing simply h1. You'll revise the style sheet accordingly.

To revise the style sheet:

1. Return to the **sa_styles.css** file in your text editor.

2. Change the selector for the h1 heading rule to **section h1** (see Figure 3-22).

Figure 3-22   **Applying a contextual selector**

style rule applied only to h1 headings
nested within section elements

```
section h1 {
    background-color: rgb(125, 186, 240);
    color: white;
}
```

> **3.** Save your changes to the style sheet and then reload the **home.htm** file in your
> Web browser. Verify that the sky blue background is applied only to the Welcome
> heading.

Attribute Selectors

Selectors also can be defined based on attributes and attribute values associated with
elements. Two attributes, `id` and `class`, are often key in targeting styles to a specific
element or group of elements. Recall that the `id` attribute is used to identify specific elements within the Web document. To apply a style to an element based on its id, you use
the selector

`#id`

where `id` is the value of the `id` attribute. Thus, to format the text of the `h1` heading

`<h1 id="main">Sunny Acres</h1>`

to appear in red, you could apply the following style rule:

`#main {color: red;}`

TIP

A style rule involving an
id selector has prece-
dence over any rule except
those defined within an
inline style.

Because no two elements can share the same id value, HTML uses the `class` attribute
to identify groups of elements that share a similar characteristic or property. The attribute
has the syntax

`<elem class="className"> … </elem>`

where `className` is the name of the element class. For example, the following `h1` heading and paragraph both belong to the *intro* class of elements.

```
<h1 class="intro">Sunny Acres</h1>
<p class="intro">
    Welcome to Sunny Acres, where there's always
    something happening on the farm.
</p>
```

TIP

You can associate a single
element with several
classes by listing each
class name, separated
by a space, as part of the
class attribute value.

One reason to use the `class` attribute is to assign the same style to multiple elements
that belong to the same class. A selector based on a class has the form

`.class {styles}`

where `class` is the name of the class and `styles` are styles associated with that class of
element. Thus, to display the text of all elements belonging to the *intro* class in blue, you
could apply the following style:

`.intro {color: blue;}`

Because different types of elements can belong to the same class, you can also specify
exactly which kinds of elements within that class receive the style rule by using the
selector

`elem.class {styles}`

where *elem* is the name of the element. Thus, the style rule

```
h1.intro {color: blue;}
```

causes the text of all `h1` headings that belong to the intro class to appear in blue.

While `id` and `class` are the most common attributes to use with selectors, any attribute or attribute value can be the basis for a selector. Figure 3-23 lists the selector patterns that are based on attributes and their values.

Figure 3-23   **Attribute selectors**

Selector	Description	Example	Matches
#id	The element with the id value, *id*	#intro	The element with the id *intro*
.class	All elements with the class value, *class*	.main	All elements belonging to the *main* class
elem.class	All *elem* elements with the class value *class*	p.main	All paragraphs belonging to the *main* class
elem[att]	All *elem* elements containing the *att* attribute	a[href]	All hypertext elements containing the `href` attribute
elem[att="text"]	All *elem* elements whose *att* attribute equals *text*	a[href="gloss.htm"]	All hypertext elements whose `href` attribute equals *gloss.htm*
elem[att~="text"]	All *elem* elements whose *att* attribute contains the word *text*	a[rel-="glossary"]	All hypertext elements whose `rel` attribute contains the word *glossary*
elem[att|="text"]	All *elem* elements whose *att* attribute value is a hyphen-separated list of words beginning with *text*	p[id|="first"]	All paragraphs whose id attribute starts with the word *first* in a hyphen-separated list of words
elem[att^="text"]	All *elem* elements whose *att* attribute begins with *text* (CSS3)	a[rel^="prev"]	All hypertext elements whose `rel` attribute begins with *prev*
elem[att$="text"]	All *elem* elements whose *att* attribute ends with *text* (CSS3)	a[href$="org"]	All hypertext elements whose `href` attribute ends with *org*
elem[att*="text"]	All *elem* elements whose *att* attribute contains the value *text* (CSS3)	a[href*="faq"]	All hypertext elements whose `href` attribute contains the text string *faq*

All current browsers support the attribute selector patterns listed in Figure 3-23; be aware, however, that some older browsers—primarily IE6—may not support these selectors in your style sheets.

Using Attribute Selectors

- To apply a style based on the id value of an element, use the #*id* selector, where *id* is the value of the id attribute.
- To apply a style based on the class value of elements, use either the .*class* or the *elem*.*class* selectors, where *class* is the value of the class attribute and *elem* is the element name.
- To apply a style based on whether an element contains an attribute, use the *elem*[*att*] selector, where *class* is the class name and *att* is the attribute name.
- To apply a style based on whether the attribute value for elements equals a specified value, use the *elem*[*att*="*val*"] where *val* is the specified value.

In the Sunny Acres home page, Tammy has added the following class attribute to the last paragraph that introduces the Web site:

```
<p class="closing">We all hope to see you soon,
   down on the farm.<br />
   &mdash; <span>Tammy &amp; Brent Nielsen</span>
</p>
```

She suggests that you format this paragraph so that it appears in green and is right-aligned on the page. To do this, you'll add the following style to the *sa_styles.css* style sheet:

```
section p.closing {
   color: rgb(0, 165, 0);
   text-align: right;
}
```

Note that this style rule applies to paragraphs belonging to the closing class and nested within the section element. You could have simply used the .closing selector, but then the style rule would apply to any element belonging to the *closing* class. Usually, you want to be as specific as possible in your style sheet so that you are always targeting exactly the elements that you want to target.

To create a style based on the class attribute:

1. Return to the **sa_styles.css** file in your text editor.

2. Add the following style rule at the bottom of style sheet (see Figure 3-24):

```
/* Section styles */

section p.closing {
   color: rgb(0, 165, 0);
   text-align: right;
}
```

Figure 3-24 Applying a selector based on class

```
/* Section styles */

section p.closing {
   color: rgb(0, 165, 0);
   text-align: right;
}
```

style rule for paragraphs in the closing class nested within a section element

display the text in green and right-aligned

> **3.** Save your changes to the style sheet and then reload the **home.htm** file in your Web browser. Verify that the text of the last paragraph appears in green and is right-aligned on the page (see Figure 3-25).

Figure 3-25 **Closing paragraph of the home page**

Of course, Sunny Acres is, above all, a *farm*. Our Farm Shop is always open with reasonable prices on great produce. Save even more money by picking your own fruits and vegetables from our orchards and gardens.

We all hope to see you soon, down on the farm.
— Tammy & Brent Nielsen

Styling Web Page Text

The `text-align` property you used in your style rule to right-align the contents of the closing paragraph is an example of a text style. In this section, you'll explore other CSS styles used to format the appearance of Web page text.

Choosing the Text Font

Tammy has noticed that all of the text in her sample pages is displayed in the same type-face, or **font**. She'd like to see more variety in how the Web page text is rendered. The default font used by most browsers is Times New Roman, but you can specify a different font for any page element using the property

```
font-family: fonts;
```

where `fonts` is a comma-separated list of specific or generic font names. A specific font is a font that is identified by name, such as Times New Roman or Helvetica. When referenced by the `font-family` property, a specific font refers to a font definition that is stored on a user's computer. A generic font describes the general appearance of a type-face, but does not rely on a specific font definition. CSS supports the following generic font groups:

- *serif*—a typeface in which a small ornamentation appears at the tail end of each character
- *sans-serif*—a non-serif font without any ornamentation
- *monospace*—a typeface in which each character has the same width; often used to display programming code
- *cursive*—a typeface that mimics handwriting with highly stylized elements and flour-ishes; best used in small doses for decorative page elements
- *fantasy*—a highly ornamental typeface used for page decoration; should never be used with body text

When you use generic fonts, you have no control over which font a user's browser will choose for your Web page. Therefore, the common practice is to list specific fonts first, in order of preference, and end the list with a generic font. If a user's browser can-not find any of the specific fonts listed, it uses a generic font of its own choosing. For example, the style

```
font-family: 'Arial Black', Gadget, sans-serif;
```

tells a browser to use the Arial Black font if available; if not, to look for the Gadget font; and if neither are available, to use a generic sans-serif font of its own selection. Note that font names containing one or more blank spaces (such as Arial Black) must be enclosed within single or double quotes.

Because the available fonts vary with each user's operating system, the challenge is to choose a list of fonts known as **Web safe fonts**, which will be displayed in mostly the same way in all browsers and on all devices. Figure 3-26 shows several commonly used fonts.

Figure 3-26   Web safe fonts

Arial
abcdefghijklmnopqrstuvwxyz/1234567890
font-family: Arial, Helvetica, sans-serif;

Arial Black
abcdefghijklmnopqrstuvwxyz/1234567890
font-family: 'Arial Black', Gadget, sans-serif;

Century Gothic
abcdefghijklmnopqrstuvwxyz/1234567890
font-family: 'Century Gothic', sans-serif;

Comic Sans MS
abcdefghijklmnopqrstuvwxyz/1234567890
font-family: 'Comic Sans MS', cursive;

Courier New
abcdefghijklmnopqrstuvwxyz/1234567890
font-family: 'Courier New', Courier, monospace;

Georgia
abcdefghijklmnopqrstuvwxyz/1234567890
font-family: Georgia, serif;

Impact
abcdefghijklmnopqrstuvwxyz/1234567890
font-family: Impact, Charcoal, sans-serif;

Lucida Console
abcdefghijklmnopqrstuvwxyz/1234567890
font-family: 'Lucida Console', Monaco, monospace;

Lucida Sans Unicode
abcdefghijklmnopqrstuvwxyz/1234567890
font-family: 'Lucida Sans Unicode', 'Lucida Grande', sans-serif;

Palatino Linotype
abcdefghijklmnopqrstuvwxyz/1234567890
font-family: 'Palatino Linotype', 'Book Antiqua', Palatino, serif;

Tahoma
abcdefghijklmnopqrstuvwxyz/1234567890
font-family: Tahoma, Geneva, sans-serif;

Times New Roman
abcdefghijklmnopqrstuvwxyz/1234567890
font-family: 'Times New Roman', Times, serif;

Trebuchet MS
abcdefghijklmnopqrstuvwxyz/1234567890
font-family: 'Trebuchet MS', Helvetica, sans-serif;

Verdana
abcdefghijklmnopqrstuvwxyz/1234567890
font-family: Verdana, Geneva, sans-serif;

A general rule for printing is to use sans-serif fonts for headlines and serif fonts for body text. For computer monitors, which have lower resolutions than printed material, the general rule is to use sans-serif fonts for headlines and body text, leaving serif fonts for special effects and large text.

REFERENCE

Setting Font Face and Sizes

- To define a font face, use the style property

  font-family: *fonts*;

  where *fonts* is a comma-separated list of fonts that the browser can use with the element. List specific fonts first and complete the list with a generic font.
- To set a font size, use the style property

  font-size: *size*;

  where *size* is a CSS unit of length in either relative or absolute units.
- To set kerning (the space between letters), use the following style property:

  letter-spacing: *size*;

- To set tracking (the space between words), use the following style property:

  word-spacing: *size*;

Tammy expects that her Web page will be viewed only on computer monitors, so you'll use a sans-serif font for all of the body text by adding the style

```
font-family: Verdana, Geneva, sans-serif;
```

to the body selector. Browsers will first try to load the Verdana font, followed by the Geneva font. If both are unavailable, browsers will load a generic sans-serif font.

To apply a sans-serif font to the body text:

1. Return to the **sa_styles.css** file in your text editor.

2. Add the following style to the body style rule at the top of the style sheet, as shown in Figure 3-27:

```
font-family: Verdana, Geneva, sans-serif;
```

Figure 3-27   Specify the default font for the Web page body

```
body {
    background-color: white;
    font-family: Verdana, Geneva, sans-serif;
}
```

3. Save your changes to the style sheet and then reload the **home.htm** file in your Web browser. As shown in Figure 3-28, the text of the entire page is displayed in a sans-serif font.

Figure 3-28   Displaying the page text in a sans-serif font

Sunny
Acres

Tammy and Brent Nielsen
1973 Hwy G
Council Bluffs, IA 51503

- Home
- Autumn Fun
- Scary Good
- Meet the Animals
- For your Tastebuds

Welcome

There's always something happening at Sunny Acres. With the coming of fall, we're gearing up for our big AutumnFest and Farm Show. If you haven't visited our famous Corn Maze, be sure to do so before it gets torn down on November 5. This year's maze is bigger and better than ever.

Farms can be educational and Sunny Acres is no exception. Schools and home-schooling parents, take an afternoon with us at our Petting Barn. We have over 100 friendly farm animals in a clean environment. Kids can bottle feed the baby goats, lambs, and calves while they learn about nature and the farming life. Please call ahead for large school groups.

Setting the Font Size

Tammy would like the Welcome heading on her home page to be displayed in slightly smaller text than is generally set by a browser's internal style sheet. The style to change the font size is

```
font-size: size;
```

where $size$ is a length measurement. Lengths can be specified in four different ways:

- with a unit of measurement
- as a percentage of the size of the containing element
- with a keyword description
- with a keyword expressing the size relative to the size of the containing element

If you choose to specify lengths using measurement units, you can use absolute units or relative units. **Absolute units** are units that are fixed in size regardless of the device rendering the Web page. They are specified in one of five standard units of measurement: mm (millimeters), cm (centimeters), in (inches), pt (points), and pc (picas). Points and picas might not be as familiar to you as inches, millimeters, and centimeters. For comparison, there are 72 points in an inch, 12 points in a pica, and 6 picas in an inch. Size values for any of these measurements can be whole numbers (0, 1, 2 ...) or decimals (0.5, 1.6, 3.9 ...). For example, if you want your text to be 1/2 inch in size, you can use any of the following styles:

```
font-size: 0.5in
font-size: 36pt
font-size: 3pc
```

Note that you should not insert a space between the size value and the unit abbreviation.

Absolute measurements are appropriate when you know the physical properties of an output device and want to fix a size to a specific value. Of course, this is not often the case with Web pages that can be displayed on a variety of devices and under several possible screen or page resolutions. To cope with the uncertainty about how their pages will be viewed, many Web page designers opt to use **relative units**, which are expressed relative to the size of other objects within the Web page. One commonly used relative unit is the **em unit**. The exact meaning of the em unit depends on its use in the style sheet. If the em unit is used for setting font size, it expresses the size relative to the font size of the parent element. For an h1 heading, the parent element is the Web page body. Thus, the style rule

```
h1 {font-size: 2em;}
```

sets the font size of h1 headings to twice the font size of body text. If body text is displayed in a 12-point font, this style will cause h1 headings to be displayed in a 24-point font. On the other hand, if the h1 heading is nested within another element, such as a section element, the size of the h1 heading will be twice the size of text in that parent element. Context is important when interpreting the effect of the em unit.

One of the great advantages of relative units like the em unit is that they can make your page **scalable**, allowing the page to be rendered the same way no matter what font size is used by the browser. Setting the font size of h1 headings to 1.5em ensures the heading will be 50% larger than the body text for all users.

Another way to create relative font sizes is to express the font size as a percentage. Like the em unit, percentages are based on the font size of the parent element. The style

```
h1 {font-size: 200%;}
```

sets the font size of h1 headings to 200%, or twice the font size of body text.

Another unit of measurement widely used on the Web is the **pixel**, which represents a single dot on the output device. The size or **resolution** of most output devices is typically expressed in terms of pixels. Thus a 1280 × 720 screen resolution on a computer monitor is 1280 pixels wide by 720 pixels tall, for a total of 921,600 pixels or 0.92 megapixels. A pixel is a relative unit because the actual rendered size depends on the **density** of the output device. A Windows PC, for example, has a density of 96 dpi (dots per inch), while a Macintosh computer has a density of 72 dpi. Some mobile phones have densities as high as 200 or 300 dpi. The pixel measure is the most precise unit of measure and gives designers the most control over the appearance of a page; however, pixels are not scalable. This can pose a problem for visually impaired users who need larger fonts, or for users of mobile devices with very dense screens.

Finally, you also can express font sizes using one of the following keywords: `xx-small`, `x-small`, `small`, `medium`, `large`, `x-large`, `xx-large`, `larger`, or `smaller`. The size corresponding to each of these keywords is determined by the browser. Note that the `larger` and `smaller` keywords are relative sizes, making the font size of the element one size larger or smaller than the surrounding text. For example, the following set of styles causes the `body` text to be displayed in a small font, while `h2` text is displayed in a font one size larger (medium):

```
body {font-size: small;}
h2   {font-size: larger;}
```

Tammy suggests that you set the size of the `h1` headings to 1.7em, making the headings 70% larger than the default size of the body text in the document.

To set the font size of the `h1` headings:

1. Return to the **sa_styles.css** file in your text editor.

2. Add the following style to the style rule for `h1` headings in the `section` element (see Figure 3-29):

   ```
   font-size: 1.7em;
   ```

Figure 3-29	Setting the font size of h1 headings

```
section h1 {
    background-color: rgb(125, 186, 240);
    color: white;
    font-size: 1.7em;
}
```

3. Save your changes to the file and then reload the **home.htm** file in your Web browser. Verify that the font size of the `h1` heading appears slightly smaller under the revised style sheet.

Decision Making: Selecting a Text Font

The challenge with designing Web text is that you don't have the same control over the output device as you do when choosing a font style for printed output. A user may not have that beautiful font you selected, and may have installed a font that will render your page unreadable. If you absolutely must have a section of text rendered in a specific font at a specific size, then your best choice may be to use an inline image in place of text.

Of course, you can't make your entire page an inline image, so you *always* should provide options for your customers in the form of extensive font lists. Other important things to consider when designing your text include the following:

- *Keep it plain*—Avoid large blocks of italicized text and boldfaced text. Those styles are designed for emphasis, not readability.
- *Sans-serif vs. serif*—Because they are more easily read on a computer monitor, use sans-serif fonts for your body text. Reserve the use of serif, cursive, and fantasy fonts for page headings and special decorative elements.
- *Relative vs. absolute*—Font sizes can be expressed in relative or absolute units. A relative unit like the em unit is more flexible and will be sized to match the screen resolution of the user's device; but you have more control over your page's appearance with an absolute unit. Generally, you want to use an absolute unit only when you know the configuration of the device the reader is using to view your page.
- *Size matters*—Almost all fonts are readable at a size of 14 pixels or greater; however, for smaller sizes you should choose fonts that were designed for screen display, such as Verdana and Georgia. On the other hand, Times and Arial often do not render well at smaller sizes. If you have to go really small (at a size of only a few pixels), you should either use a Web font that is specially designed for that purpose or replace the text with an inline image.
- *Avoid long lines*—With more users accessing the Web with widescreen monitors, you run the risk of presenting users with long lines of text. In general, try to keep the length of your lines to 60 characters or less. Anything longer is difficult to read.

When choosing any typeface and font style, the key is to test your selection on a variety of browsers, devices, screen resolutions, and densities. Don't assume that text that is readable and pleasing to the eye on your computer screen will work as well on another screen.

Controlling Spacing and Indentation

Tammy thinks that the text for the Welcome heading looks too crowded. She's wondering if you can further spread it out across the width of the page. She also would like to see more space between the first letter, W, and the left edge of the sky blue background.

CSS supports styles that allow you to control some basic typographic attributes, such as kerning and tracking. **Kerning** refers to the amount of space between characters, while **tracking** refers to the amount of space between words. The styles to control an element's kerning and tracking are

```
letter-spacing: value;
word-spacing:   value;
```

where *value* is the size of space between individual letters or words. You specify these sizes with the same units that you use for font sizing. The default value for both kerning and tracking is 0 pixels. A positive value increases the letter and word spacing, while a negative value reduces the space between letters and words. If you choose to make your pages scalable for a variety of devices and resolutions, you will want to express kerning and tracking values as percentages or in em units.

To see how modifying these values can affect the appearance of text, a demo page has been created for you.

To use the demo to explore kerning and tracking styles:

1. Open the **demo_css.htm** file from the tutorial.03/demo folder in your Web browser.

   The demo page contains a collection of CSS text styles. You can specify text style values using the boxes on the left side of the demo. In the top-right box, you can enter text to be displayed using the selected styles. The style as applied to the sample text appears in the middle box. The CSS code for the style appears in the bottom-right box. You press the Tab key to apply the style and view the results.

2. Click the top-right box, select and delete the text *Enter sample text here*, type **Sunny Acres**, press the **Enter** key, and then type **Corn Maze** on the second line. Press the **Tab** key to display this text in the Preview box.

3. Select **sans-serif** from the font-family box.

4. In the font-size box, replace the default text with **2**, and then select **em** in the corresponding unit box.

5. Enter **0.3** in the letter-spacing box, and then select **em** in the corresponding unit box. Press the **Tab** key.

6. Enter **0.8** in the word-spacing box and then select **em** in the corresponding unit box. Press the **Tab** key. Figure 3-30 shows the revised appearance of the text after applying the letter-spacing and word-spacing styles.

| Figure 3-30 | Using the demo page to explore letter-spacing and word-spacing |

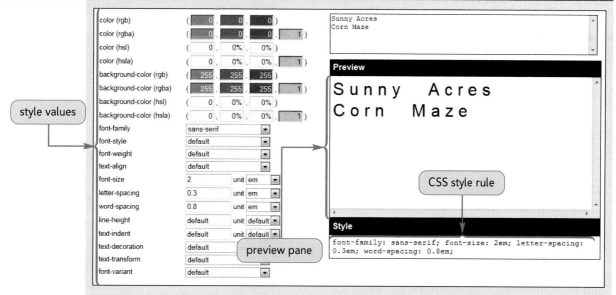

7. Experiment with other letter-spacing and word-spacing style values to see their effects on kerning and tracking.

Another typographic feature that you can set is **leading**, which is the space between lines of text. The style to set the leading value is

```
line-height: size;
```

where *size* is a specific length or a percentage of the font size of the text on the affected lines. If no unit is specified, most browsers interpret the number to represent the ratio of the line height to the font size. The standard ratio is 1.2:1, which means that the line height is usually 1.2 times the font size. By contrast, the style rule

```
p {line-height: 2em;}
```

makes all paragraphs double-spaced. A common technique for multi-line titles is to give title text more impact using large fonts and small line heights. Use the demo page to see how this works.

To use the demo to explore leading styles:

 1. If necessary, return to the **demo_css.htm** page in your Web browser.

 2. Enter **0.75** in the line-height box, and then select **em** from the corresponding unit box.

 3. Press the **Tab** key to apply the line-height style. Figure 3-31 shows the revised appearance of the text.

Figure 3-31 **Setting the line height**

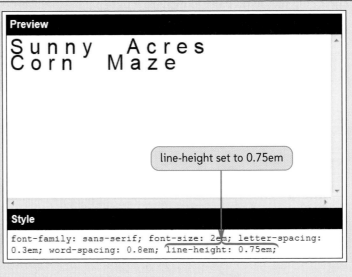

An additional way to control text spacing is to set the indentation for the first line of a block of text. The style is

```
text-indent: size;
```

where *size* is a length expressed in absolute or relative units, or as a percentage of the width of the text block. For example, an indentation value of 5% indents the first line by 5% of the width of the block. The indentation value also can be negative, extending the first line to the left of the text block to create a **hanging indent**.

Now you can use what you've learned about spacing to make the changes that Tammy has suggested. To spread out her heading text, you'll set the kerning of the h1 heading to 0.4em. You'll also set the indentation to 1em, moving the text of both h1 and h2 headings to the left.

To change the spacing of the headings on the Web site:

▸ **1.** Return to the **sa_styles.css** file in your text editor.

▸ **2.** Within the style rules for the section h1 selector and the h2 selector, insert the following style values (see Figure 3-32):

```
letter-spacing: 0.4em;
text-indent: 1em;
```

Figure 3-32 **Defining letter-spacing and text-indent**

```
section h1 {
    background-color: rgb(125, 186, 240);
    color: white;
    font-size: 1.7em;
    letter-spacing: 0.4em;
    text-indent: 1em;
}

h2 {
    background-color: rgb(0, 165, 0);
    color: white;
    color: rgba(255, 255, 255, 0.8);
    letter-spacing: 0.4em;
    text-indent: 1em;
}
```

▸ **3.** Save your changes to the file and then reload the **home.htm** file in your browser. As shown in Figure 3-33, the indent and the spacing between the letters have increased.

Figure 3-33   **Revised spacing in h1 and h2 headings**

- Home
- Autumn Fun
- Scary Good
- Meet the Animals
- For your Tastebuds

text is indented with increased kerning

Welcome

There's always something happening at Sunny Acres. With the coming of fall, we're gearing up for our big AutumnFest and Farm Show. If you haven't visited our famous Corn Maze, be sure to do so before it gets torn down on November 5. This year's maze is bigger and better than ever.

Farms can be educational and Sunny Acres is no exception. Schools and home-schooling parents, spend an afternoon with us at our Petting Barn. We have over 100 friendly farm animals in a clean environment. Kids can bottle feed the baby goats, lambs, and calves while they learn about nature and the farming life. Please call ahead for large school groups.

When the sun goes down this time of year, we're all looking for a good fright. Sunny Acres provides that too with another year of the Haunted Maze. Please plan on joining us during weekends in October or on Halloween for our big Halloween Festival.

Of course, Sunny Acres is, above all, a *farm*. Our Farm Shop is always open with reasonable prices on great produce. Save even more money by picking your own fruits and vegetables from our orchards and gardens.

We all hope to see you soon, down on the farm.
— Tammy & Brent Nielsen

Hours

- Farm Shop: 9 am - 5 pm Mon - Fri; 9 am - 3 pm Sat
- The Corn Maze: 11 am - 9 pm Sat; 11 am - 5 pm Sun
- The Haunted Maze: 5 pm - 9 pm Fri & Sat
- Petting Barn: 9 am - 4 pm Mon - Fri; 11 am - 3 pm Sat & Sun

By increasing the kerning in the headings, you've made the text appear less crowded, making it easier to read.

Working with Font Styles

Browsers often apply default font styles to particular types of elements; for instance, `address` elements are usually displayed in italic. You also can specify a different font style using the style

```
font-style: type;
```

where `type` is normal, italic, or oblique. The italic and oblique styles are similar in appearance, but might differ subtly depending on the font in use.

You also have seen that browsers render certain elements in heavier fonts. For example, most browsers render headings in a boldfaced font. You can specify the font weight for any page element using the style

```
font-weight: weight;
```

where `weight` is the level of bold formatting applied to the text. The `weight` value ranges from 100 to 900 in increments of 100. In practice, however, most browsers cannot

TIP

To prevent your browser from displaying address text in italic, you can set the `font-style` property to normal.

distinguish between nine different font weights. For practical purposes, you can assume that 400 represents normal (not bold) text, 700 is bold text, and 900 represents heavy bold text. You also can use the keywords `normal` or `bold` in place of a weight value, or you can express the font weight relative to the text of the containing element, using the keywords `bolder` or `lighter`.

Another style you can use to change the appearance of your text is

```
text-decoration: type;
```

where the *type* values include `none` (for no decoration), `underline`, `overline`, and `line-through`. You can apply several decorative features to the same element by listing them as part of the text-decoration style. For example, the style

```
text-decoration: underline overline;
```

places a line under and over the text in the element. Note that the text-decoration style has no effect on nontextual elements, such as inline images.

To control the case of the text within an element, use the style

```
text-transform: type;
```

where *type* is `capitalize`, `uppercase`, `lowercase`, or `none` (to make no changes to the text case). For example, if you want to capitalize the first letter of each word in an element, you could use the following style:

```
text-transform: capitalize;
```

Finally, you can display text in uppercase letters and a small font using the style

```
font-variant: type;
```

where *type* is `normal` (the default) or `small-caps` (small capital letters). Small caps are often used in legal documents, such as software agreements, in which the capital letters indicate the importance of a phrase or point, but the text is made small so as to not detract from other elements in the document.

REFERENCE

Setting Font and Text Appearance

- To specify the font style, use

  ```
  font-style: type;
  ```

  where *type* is `normal`, `italic`, or `oblique`.
- To specify the font weight, use

  ```
  font-weight: type;
  ```

  where *type* is `normal`, `bold`, `bolder`, `light`, `lighter`, or a font weight value.
- To specify a text decoration, use

  ```
  text-decoration: type;
  ```

  where *type* is `none`, `underline`, `overline`, or `line-through`.
- To transform text, use

  ```
  text-transform: type;
  ```

  where *type* is `capitalize`, `uppercase`, `lowercase`, or `none`.
- To display a font variant of text, use

  ```
  font-variant: type;
  ```

  where *type* is `normal` or `small-caps`.

To see the impact of these styles, you'll return to the demo page.

To use the demo to view the various font styles:

1. Return to the **demo_css.htm** page in your Web browser.

2. Select **bold** in the font-weight box.

3. Select **small-caps** in the font-variant box. Figure 3-34 shows the impact of applying the font-weight and font-variant styles.

Figure 3-34   **Applying the font-weight and font-variant styles**

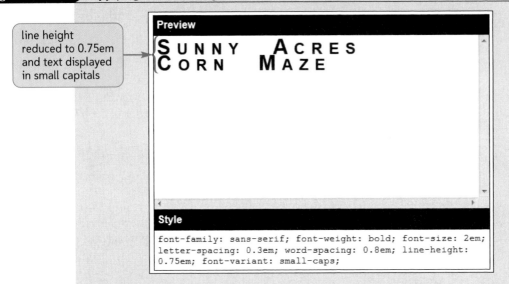

line height reduced to 0.75em and text displayed in small capitals

Preview

SUNNY ACRES
CORN MAZE

Style

```
font-family: sans-serif; font-weight: bold; font-size: 2em;
letter-spacing: 0.3em; word-spacing: 0.8em; line-height:
0.75em; font-variant: small-caps;
```

4. You've completed your work with the CSS demo page. If you wish, continue to explore different CSS font and text styles. When you're finished, close the demo Web page.

Aligning Text Horizontally and Vertically

In earlier examples from this tutorial, you saw how the text-align style could be used to align text horizontally. The specific style is

```
text-align: alignment;
```

where *alignment* is left, right, center, or justify (align the text with both the left and the right margins). To vertically align the text, use the style

```
vertical-align: alignment;
```

where *alignment* is one of the keywords described in Figure 3-35.

Figure 3-35	Values of the vertical-align style

Value	Description
baseline	Aligns the element with the bottom of lowercase letters in surrounding text (the default)
bottom	Aligns the bottom of the element with the bottom of the lowest element in surrounding content
middle	Aligns the middle of the element with the middle of the surrounding content
sub	Subscripts the element
super	Superscripts the element
text-bottom	Aligns the bottom of the element with the bottom of the font of the surrounding content
text-top	Aligns the top of the element with the top of the font of the surrounding content
top	Aligns the top of the element with the top of the tallest object in the surrounding content

TIP

The subscript and super-script styles lower or raise text vertically, but do not resize it. To create true subscripts and super-scripts, you also must reduce the font size.

Instead of using keywords, you can specify a length or a percentage for an element to be aligned relative to the surrounding content. A positive value moves the element up and a negative value lowers the element. For example, the style

```
vertical-align: 50%;
```

raises the element by half of the line height of the surrounding content, while the style

```
vertical-align: -100%;
```

drops the element an entire line height below the baseline of the current line.

Combining All Text Formatting in a Single Style

You've seen a lot of different text and font styles. You can combine most of them into a single property using the shortcut `font` property

```
font: font-style font-variant font-weight font-size/line-height
font-family;
```

where `font-style` is the font's style, `font-variant` is the font variant, `font-weight` is the weight of the font, `font-size` is the size of the font, `line-height` is the height of each line, and `font-family` is the font face. For example, the style

```
font: italic small-caps bold 18px/24px Arial, sans-serif;
```

displays the text of the element in italic, bold, and small capital letters in Arial or another sans-serif font, with a font size of 18 pixels and spacing between the lines of 24 pixels. You do not have to include all of the values in the `font` property; the only required values are `font-size` and `font-family`. A browser assumes the default value for any omitted property. However, you must place any properties that you do include in the order indicated above.

Tammy would like the address in the page footer formatted differently from the default style imposed by the browser's internal style sheet. She suggests that you display the text in a semi-transparent white Times New Roman font on a dark green background and centered on the page. She also suggests that you use the small-cap font variant to add visual interest, and increase the height of the address line to 4em. To make your CSS code more compact, you'll add all of the font values within a single line using the `font` property.

To change the style of the `address` element:

1. Return to the **sa_styles.css** file in your text editor.

2. At the bottom of the style sheet, add the following style rule for the `address` element nested within the `footer` element (see Figure 3-36):

```
/* Footer styles */

footer address {
    background-color: rgb(55, 102, 55);
    color: white;
    color: rgba(255, 255, 255, 0.8);
    font: normal small-caps 0.8em/4em 'Times New Roman', Times, serif;
    text-align: center;
}
```

Figure 3-36 ▶ Designing the footer address

set the background color to dark and the text color to white or semi-transparent white

shortcut font property

center the text horizontally

```
/* Footer styles */
footer address {
    background-color: rgb(55, 102, 55);
    color: white;
    color: rgba(255, 255, 255, 0.8);
    font: normal small-caps 0.8em/4em 'Times New Roman', Times, serif;
    text-align: center;
}
```

3. Save your changes to the file and then reload the **home.htm** file in your Web browser. Scroll to the bottom of the page and verify that the style of the `address` element has been changed as shown in Figure 3-37.

Figure 3-37 ▶ Reformatted address text

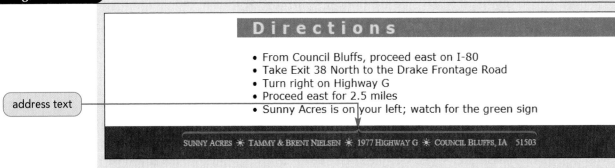

address text

Tammy likes the way the fonts appear on her Web site. She especially likes the fact that because these changes were made in a CSS style sheet, the styles automatically apply to the other Web pages on the site, as well as any Web page she adds to the site in the future.

Setting up Alternative Style Sheets

Many browsers recognize alternative style sheets. This is particularly useful in situations when you are supporting users who have special needs, such as a need for large text with highly contrasting colors. To support these users, you can make an alternative style sheet with the link element, using the code

```
<link href="url1" rel="alternate stylesheet"
      type="text/css" title="title1" />
```

```
<link href="url2" rel="alternate stylesheet"
      type="text/css" title="title2" />
```

where *url1*, *url2*, and so forth are the URLs of the style sheet files, and *title1*, *title2*, etc. are the titles of the alternate style sheets. For example, the following HTML code creates links to two style sheets, named *Large Text* and *Regular Text*:

```
<link href="large.css" rel="alternate stylesheet"
 type="text/css" title="Large Text" />
```

```
<link href="regular.css" rel="alternate stylesheet"
 type="text/css" title="Regular Text" />
```

Browsers that support alternative style sheets provide a menu option or toolbar that enables users to select which style sheet to apply. Among current browsers, Firefox, Opera, and Safari support alternate style sheets.

Working with Web Fonts

Text design on the Web largely has been limited to a few Web safe fonts that are supported by all major browsers. It would be better if a browser would automatically download whatever fonts are required for a Web page in the same way it downloads images. Specifications for downloadable fonts, or **Web fonts**, have been around for several years, but most browsers have begun to support this technology only in recent years. However, different browsers support different font file formats. Figure 3-38 describes these different formats and their current levels of browser support.

Figure 3-38   **Web font formats**

Format	Description	Browser
TrueType/OpenType	The most common font format, freely available on most computers; no support for licensing.	Chrome, Firefox, Opera, Safari
Embedded OpenType	Proprietary format developed by Microsoft for Internet Explorer; supports licensing and security against unauthorized use.	Internet Explorer
Scalable Vector Graphics	An XML vocabulary designed to describe resizable graphics and primarily supported by mobile browsers.	Chrome, Opera, Safari
Web Open Font Format	A new standard for Web fonts that is quickly gaining support; provides support for font licensing.	Firefox, other browsers in development

Web font files are available on several sites on the Web. In many cases, these are not free fonts and you must pay for their use. Other fonts are free but are licensed only for non-commercial use. You always should check the EULA (End User License Agreement) before downloading and using a Web font to make sure you are in compliance with the license. Finally, many Web fonts are available through **Web Font Service Bureaus**, which supply Web fonts on their servers that page designers can link to for a fee.

The great advantage of a Web font is that it gives a designer control over the typeface used in a document. The disadvantage is that it becomes another file for the browser to download and install, adding to the time required to render the page.

The @font-face Rule

To access and load a Web font, you add the rule

```
@font-face {
    font-family: name;
    src: url(url) format(text);
    descriptor:value;
    descriptor:value;
    ...
}
```

to the style sheet, where *name* is the name assigned to the Web font, *url* is the location of the font definition file, *text* is an optional text description of the font format, and the *descriptor*:*value* pairs are optional style properties that describe how and when the font should be used. For example, the following @font-face rule defines a font face named *GentiumBold*:

```
@font-face {
    font-family: GentiumBold;
    src: url(GentiumB.ttf) format('truetype');
    font-weight: bold;
}
```

The GentiumBold font in this code is a TrueType font based on a description stored in the *GentiumB.ttf* file. The font-weight properties tell browsers to apply this font only for bold text. Note that at the time of this writing, you should avoid including the font-weight and font-style properties in the @font-face rule because those features are not well supported by most browsers and can produce unexpected results.

Once you've defined a font using the @font-face rule, you can use the font elsewhere in your style sheets by including the font name in your font lists. For example, the style

```
font-family: GentiumBold, 'Arial Black', Gadget, sans-serif;
```

attempts to load the GentiumBold font defined above, followed by Arial Black, Gadget, and then a sans-serif font of the browser's choosing.

Installing a Cross-Browser Web Font

To support all of the font formats described in Figure 3-38, you can add additional source files to the @font-face rule. A browser then will go through the list, loading the last font file format from the list that it supports. Part of the challenge is that at the time of this writing, Internet Explorer does not support all of the features of the @font-face rule and returns an error if it attempts to load another font file. Thus, to define a font that works across different browsers, you should design the @font-face rule as follows

```
@font-face {
    font-family: name;
    src: url(eot);
    src: local('☺'),
         url(woff) format(text),
         url(ttf) format(text),
         url(svg) format(text);
    descriptor:value;
    …
}
```

where *eot* is the font defined in an Embedded OpenType file (the only format supported by Internet Explorer at the time of this writing), *woff* is the font defined in a Web Open Font file, *ttf* is the font defined in a TrueType or an OpenType file, and *svg* is the font defined in a Scalable Vector Graphics file. The local('☺') part of this code is a programming hack developed by Paul Irish (*www.paulirish.com*) to prevent Internet Explorer from attempting to load the other font files, causing an error. Note that to enter this symbol, your text must be stored using Unicode encoding rather than ASCII or ANSI. The sa_styles.css file already has been created for you using that text encoding.

Tammy is not completely pleased with the Verdana font you've used for the home page and would like a typeface with thinner lines. She has located a Web font named *NobileRegular* that she is free to use under the End User License Agreement and thinks would work better. In acquiring this font, she also obtained the following @font-face rule that can be used to load the font into a CSS style sheet:

```
@font-face {
    font-family: 'NobileRegular';
    src: url('nobile-webfont.eot');
    src: local('☺'),
         url('nobile-webfont.woff') format('woff'),
         url('nobile-webfont.ttf') format('truetype'),
         url('nobile-webfont.svg#webfontsKo9tqe9') format('svg');
}
```

Rather than retype this code, you'll copy it from her text file and paste it into your style sheet. Add this font definition now.

To insert and apply the NobileRegular font:

▶ **1.** Using your text editor, open the **nobile.txt** text file located in the tutorial.03/tutorial folder.

▶ **2.** Copy the `@font-face` rule located at the top of the file.

▶ **3.** Return to the **sa_styles.css** file in your text editor.

▶ **4.** Paste the copied text of the `@font-face` rule into your style sheet directly above the style rule for the `body` element.

Next, you'll revise the style rule for the `body` element so that it uses the NobileRegular font as the first option, if available and supported by the browser. You'll also set the line height of body text to 1.4 em and the line height of the page headings to 1.8 em to accommodate the metrics of this new font.

▶ **5.** Within the `font-family` property for the `body` element, insert **NobileRegular** followed by a comma and a space, at the beginning of the font list.

▶ **6.** Add the property `line-height: 1.4em;` to the style rule for the `body` element and `line-height: 1.8em;` to the style rules for the `h1` and `h2` elements.

Figure 3-39 highlights the newly inserted text in the style sheet.

| Figure 3-39 | Inserting a Web font |

Embedded OpenType font (Internet Explorer)
Web Open Font Format font
TrueType font

```
@font-face {
    font-family: 'NobileRegular';
    src: url('nobile-webfont.eot');
    src: local('☺'),
        url('nobile-webfont.woff') format('woff'),
        url('nobile-webfont.ttf') format('truetype'),
        url('nobile-webfont.svg#webfontsKo9tqe9') format('svg');
}

/* Body styles */

body {
    background-color: white;
    font-family: NobileRegular, Verdana, Geneva, sans-serif;
    line-height: 1.4em;
}

/* Heading styles */

section h1 {
    background-color: rgb(125, 186, 240);
    color: white;
    font-size: 1.7em;
    letter-spacing: 0.4em;
    line-height: 1.8em;
    text-indent: 1em;
}

h2 {
    background-color: rgb(0, 165, 0);
    color: white;
    color: rgba(255, 255, 255, 0.8);
    letter-spacing: 0.4em;
    line-height: 1.8em;
    text-indent: 1em;
}
```

Scalable Vector Graphics font

instructs browsers to use the Web font first, if available, as the default for all body text

set the line height to accommodate the new font

7. Save your changes to the file and then reload **home.htm** in your Web browser. As shown in Figure 3-40, the body text of the Web page has changed, using the NobileRegular font in place of the previous font.

Figure 3-40   **Text rendered in the NobileRegular font**

- Home
- Autumn Fun
- Scary Good
- Meet the Animals
- For your Tastebuds

Welcome

There's always something happening at Sunny Acres. With the coming of fall, we're gearing up for our big AutumnFest and Farm Show. If you haven't visited our famous Corn Maze, be sure to do so before it gets torn down on November 5. This year's maze is bigger and better than ever.

Understanding the CSS @rules

The `@font-face` rule is one example of a **CSS @rule**, which specifies a command or directive that controls how browsers interpret and run the contents of a CSS style sheet. Figure 3-41 lists the @rules and describes how they are used.

Figure 3-41   **CSS @rules**

@rule	Description
`@charset "encoding";`	Defines the character encoding used in an external style sheet where *encoding* is the name of the character set
`@import url(url) media`	Imports an external style sheet file located at *url*. The optional *media* attribute provides a comma-separated list of media devices to be used with the style sheet

`@media media {`
    `styles`
`}`
	Targets the style rules in *styles* to devices that match the media types specified in *media*

`@page location {`
    `margins`
`}`
	Defines the page margins for printed output where *location* is either `left`, `right`, or `first` for left page, right page, or first page, and *margins* set the margin widths

`@font-face {`
    `font_description`
`}`
	Defines the properties of a custom Web font where *font_description* indicates the source and features of the font

`@namespace prefix uri`	Defines an XML namespace where *prefix* is the namespace prefix and *uri* is the location of the namespace

In general, all of the CSS @rules should be placed at the top of the style sheet before the style properties that may use them.

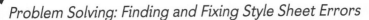

PROSKILLS

Problem Solving: Finding and Fixing Style Sheet Errors

As a style sheet increases in size and complexity, you will likely encounter a major headache: a Web page whose appearance in a browser does not match the style you planned for it. Once you recognize that a syntax error in your style sheet likely caused the browser to ignore some of your style rules, you need to figure out where the error is. The following are some errors that can cause your style sheets to fail:

- *Missing semicolons*—All style properties need to be separated by a semicolon. If you omit a semicolon, all subsequent properties within the affected style rule will be ignored.
- *Missing curly braces*—Every style rule must be enclosed within a set of curly braces. Failure to close off the style rule will cause that style rule and all subsequent rules to be ignored.
- *Missing closing quotes*—If you use quotes within typeface names or other text strings, you need to enclose the entire text within either double or single quotation marks. Omitting a closing quotation mark will cause the rest of the style sheet to fail.
- *Typos*—All selector names, style properties, and style values need to be typed correctly.
- *Improper application of a style*—Some styles are associated with all elements, but some are not. For instance, you can't change the color of an inline image using the background-color style, no matter how much you might want to.
- *Conflicting properties*—Remember the general principle that *the more specific style outweighs the less specific*. A style rule in one part of a style sheet might be superseded by a rule somewhere else in the file.
- *Inherited properties*—Properties are also inherited down the document tree. A style property applied to a `section` element affects all nested elements unless you override it with another rule.

If a problem persists after finding and fixing these common errors, try other techniques to locate the source of the trouble, such as removing style rules one by one until you locate the source of the trouble. Also consider using the `!important` keyword to temporarily force the browser to apply a rule regardless of specificity. Finally, many browsers now include debugging tools to assist you in writing your CSS code. Use these tools whenever you encounter an error that you can't easily find and fix.

You've completed your work on creating and editing the text styles used in the Sunny Acres home page. In the next session, you'll explore how to design styles for hypertext links and lists, and you'll learn how to use CSS to add special visual effects to your Web pages.

REVIEW

Session 3.2 Quick Check

1. Provide a style rule to display the text of all `address` elements nested within a `footer` element in red.

2. The initial `h1` heading in a document has the id *top*. Provide a style rule to display the text of this `h1` heading in Arial, Helvetica, or a sans-serif font.

3. Provide a style rule to display all `blockquote` elements belonging to the *reviews* class in italic and indented 3em.

4. Provide a style rule to center all `h1` through `h6` headings, and to display the text with normal weight.

5. What is the difference between an absolute unit and a relative unit?

6. Provide a style rule to double space the text of all paragraphs in the document.

7. Provide a style rule to remove underlining from the hypertext links for all elements marked with the <a> tag and nested within a navigation list.

8. If you want to use Web fonts with Internet Explorer, what font file format should you use?

9. Provide the `@font-face` rule to create a Web font named *Cantarell* based on the font file *cantarell.ttf*. Which browsers will be able to work with this font file?

SESSION 3.3 VISUAL OVERVIEW

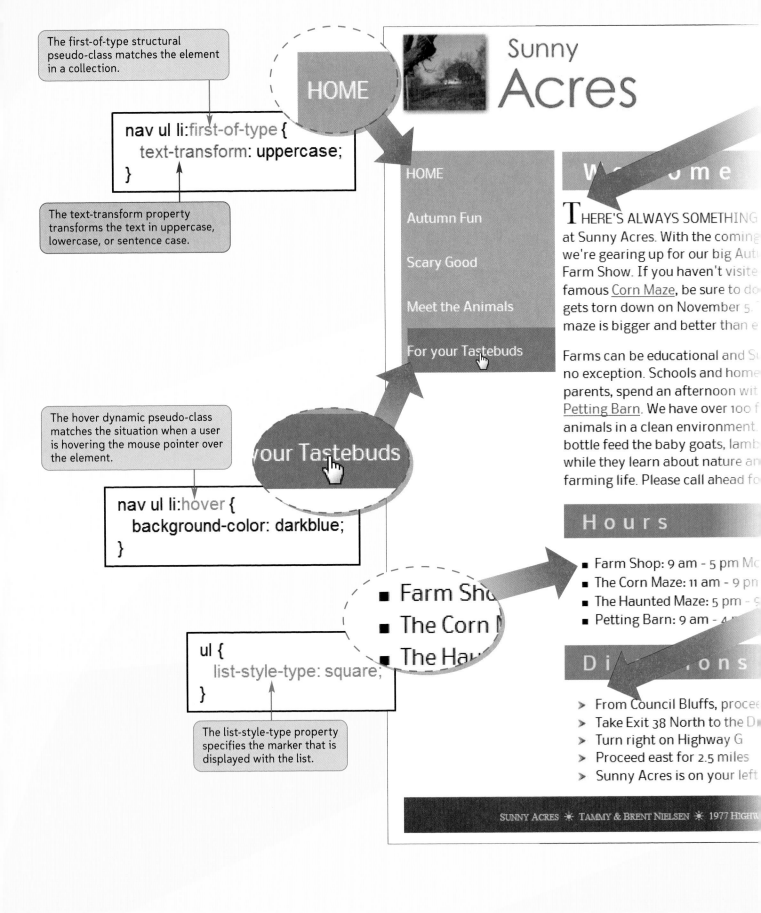

The first-of-type structural pseudo-class matches the element in a collection.

```
nav ul li:first-of-type {
    text-transform: uppercase;
}
```

The text-transform property transforms the text in uppercase, lowercase, or sentence case.

The hover dynamic pseudo-class matches the situation when a user is hovering the mouse pointer over the element.

```
nav ul li:hover {
    background-color: darkblue;
}
```

```
ul {
    list-style-type: square;
}
```

The list-style-type property specifies the marker that is displayed with the list.

Sunny Acres

HOME

Autumn Fun

Scary Good

Meet the Animals

For your Tastebuds

W   o m e

THERE'S ALWAYS SOMETHING
at Sunny Acres. With the coming
we're gearing up for our big Au
Farm Show. If you haven't visite
famous Corn Maze, be sure to do
gets torn down on November 5.
maze is bigger and better than e

Farms can be educational and S
no exception. Schools and home
parents, spend an afternoon wit
Petting Barn. We have over 100 f
animals in a clean environment.
bottle feed the baby goats, lamb
while they learn about nature an
farming life. Please call ahead fo

Hours

- Farm Shop: 9 am - 5 pm Mo
- The Corn Maze: 11 am - 9 pn
- The Haunted Maze: 5 pm -
- Petting Barn: 9 am -

D i   **o** n s

- From Council Bluffs, procee
- Take Exit 38 North to the D
- Turn right on Highway G
- Proceed east for 2.5 miles
- Sunny Acres is on your left

SUNNY ACRES ✳ TAMMY & BRENT NIELSEN ✳ 1977 HIGHW

LISTS AND PSEUDO-ITEMS

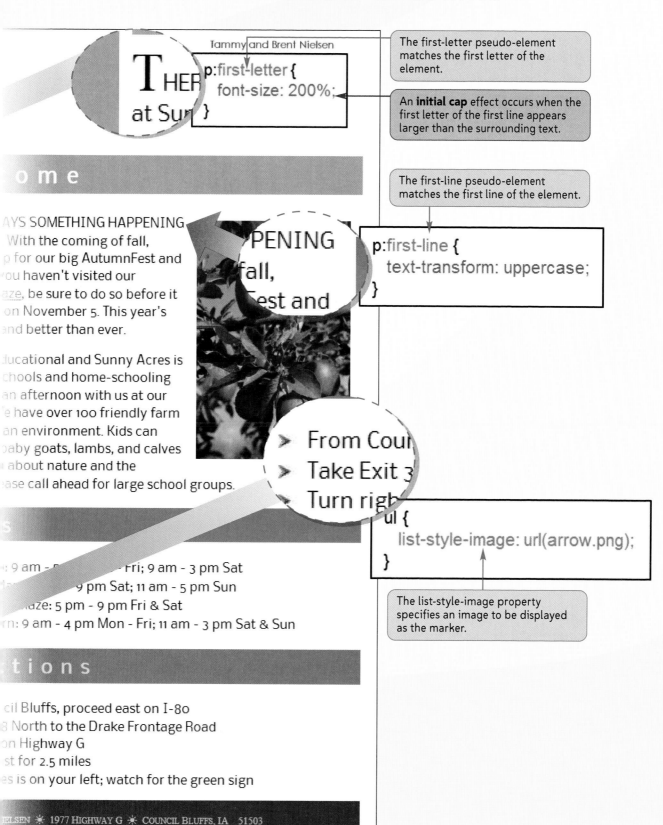

Tammy and Brent Nielsen

T HER
at Sur

```
p:first-letter {
    font-size: 200%;
}
```

The first-letter pseudo-element matches the first letter of the element.

An **initial cap** effect occurs when the first letter of the first line appears larger than the surrounding text.

The first-line pseudo-element matches the first line of the element.

AYS SOMETHING HAPPENING
With the coming of fall,
p for our big AutumnFest and
ou haven't visited our
aze, be sure to do so before it
on November 5. This year's
nd better than ever.

ducational and Sunny Acres is
chools and home-schooling
an afternoon with us at our
e have over 100 friendly farm
an environment. Kids can
baby goats, lambs, and calves
about nature and the
ase call ahead for large school groups.

PENING
fall,
est and

```
p:first-line {
    text-transform: uppercase;
}
```

> From Cour
> Take Exit 3
> Turn righ

```
ul {
    list-style-image: url(arrow.png);
}
```

The list-style-image property specifies an image to be displayed as the marker.

: 9 am - 5   Fri; 9 am - 3 pm Sat
9 pm Sat; 11 am - 5 pm Sun
aze: 5 pm - 9 pm Fri & Sat
n: 9 am - 4 pm Mon - Fri; 11 am - 3 pm Sat & Sun

t i o n s

cil Bluffs, proceed east on I-80
North to the Drake Frontage Road
n Highway G
st for 2.5 miles
es is on your left; watch for the green sign

ELSEN ☀ 1977 HIGHWAY G ☀ COUNCIL BLUFFS, IA   51503

Designing Styles for Lists

Tammy has placed her navigation links in an unordered list set on the left page margin. As with all unordered lists, browsers display the list contents with bullet markers. Tammy would like the bullets removed. To alter the appearance of this navigation list, you change the default style applied by browsers.

Choosing a List Style Type

To change the marker displayed in ordered or unordered lists, you apply the style

```
list-style-type: type;
```

where `type` is one of the markers discussed in Figure 3-42.

Figure 3-42   **List style types**

list-style-type	Marker (s)
disc	●
circle	○
square	■
decimal	1, 2, 3, 4, …
decimal-leading-zero	01, 02, 03, 04, …
lower-roman	i, ii, iii, iv, …
upper-roman	I, II, III, IV, …
lower-alpha	a, b, c, d, …
upper-alpha	A, B, C, D, …
lower-greek	α, β, γ, δ, …
upper-greek	A, B, Γ, Δ, …
none	no marker displayed

For example, to display an ordered list with alphabetical markers such as

```
A. Home
B. Getting Started
C. Scrapbooking Tips
D. Supply List
```

you would apply the following list style to the `ol` element:

```
ol {list-style-type: upper-alpha;}
```

Designing a List

- To define the appearance of the list marker, use the style

  ```
  list-style-type: type;
  ```

  where *type* is disc, circle, square, decimal, decimal-leading-zero, lower-roman, upper-roman, lower-alpha, upper-alpha, lower-greek, upper-greek, or none.
- To insert a graphic image as a list marker, use the style

  ```
  list-style-image: url(url);
  ```

  where *url* is the URL of the graphic image file.
- To set the position of list markers, use the style

  ```
  list-style-position: position;
  ```

  where *position* is inside or outside.
- To define all of the list style properties in a single style, use the following style:

  ```
  list-style: type url(url) position;
  ```

- To set the indentation of a list, apply the style

  ```
  padding-left: size;
  ```

  where *size* is the length that the list should be indented.

List style types can be used with contextual selectors to create an outline style based on nested lists. Figure 3-43 shows an example in which several levels of list style markers are used in formatting an outline. Note that each marker style is determined by the location of the ordered list within the outline hierarchy. The top level is displayed with uppercase Roman numerals; the bottom level, which is nested within three other ordered lists, uses lowercase letters for markers.

Figure 3-43   **Creating an outline style**

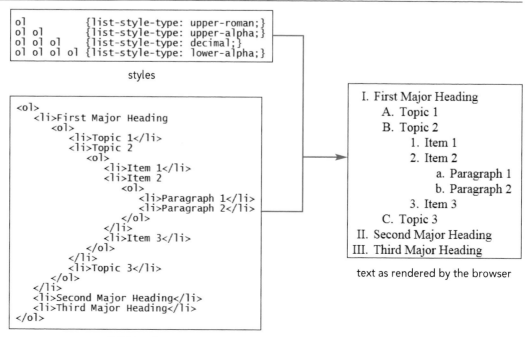

```
ol           {list-style-type: upper-roman;}
ol ol        {list-style-type: upper-alpha;}
ol ol ol     {list-style-type: decimal;}
ol ol ol ol  {list-style-type: lower-alpha;}
```

styles

```
<ol>
    <li>First Major Heading
        <ol>
            <li>Topic 1</li>
            <li>Topic 2
                <ol>
                    <li>Item 1</li>
                    <li>Item 2
                        <ol>
                            <li>Paragraph 1</li>
                            <li>Paragraph 2</li>
                        </ol>
                    </li>
                    <li>Item 3</li>
                </ol>
            </li>
            <li>Topic 3</li>
        </ol>
    </li>
    <li>Second Major Heading</li>
    <li>Third Major Heading</li>
</ol>
```

HTML code

```
I. First Major Heading
    A. Topic 1
    B. Topic 2
        1. Item 1
        2. Item 2
            a. Paragraph 1
            b. Paragraph 2
        3. Item 3
    C. Topic 3
II. Second Major Heading
III. Third Major Heading
```

text as rendered by the browser

Because Tammy wants to remove the markers from the navigation list, you'll set the `list-style-type` value of that list to `none`. Because you don't want to remove the bullet markers from all lists on the Web site, you'll use a contextual selector that targets only unordered lists nested within a `nav` element.

To remove the bullets from the navigation links:

▶ 1. Return to the **sa_styles.css** file in your text editor.

▶ 2. Directly below the style rule for the `h2` element, insert the following (see Figure 3-44):

```
/* Navigation list styles */

nav ul {
    list-style-type: none;
}
```

Figure 3-44 **Removing bullet markers from navigation list items**

```
            letter-spacing: 0.4em;
            line-height: 1.8em;
            text-indent: 1em;
    }

    /* Navigation list styles */

    nav ul {
        list-style-type: none;
    }
```

▶ 3. Save your changes to the file and then reload the **home.htm** file in your Web browser. Verify that the bullet markers have been removed from the items in the navigation list.

Using Images for List Markers

You can supply your own graphic image for the list marker using the style

```
list-style-image: url(url);
```

where *url* is the URL of a graphic file containing the marker image. This is only done for unordered lists, in which the marker is the same for every list item. For example, the style rule

```
ul {list-style-image: url(redball.gif);}
```

displays items from unordered lists marked with the graphic image in the *redball.gif* file. Tammy suggests that you display the list of hours and driving directions using a green arrow graphic she created. Both of these unordered lists are immediately preceded by an `h2` element and nested within a `section` element, so the style rule to change the list marker is:

```
section h2+ul {
    list-style-image: url(arrow.png);
}
```

You'll add this style rule to your style sheet.

To use an image for a list bullet:

1. Return to the **sa_styles.css** file in your text editor.

2. Directly below the style rule for the closing paragraph, insert the following as shown in Figure 3-45:

```
section h2+ul {
    list-style-image: url(arrow.png);
}
```

Figure 3-45	Displaying an image in place of a marker

```
section p.closing {
    color: rgb(0, 165, 0);
    text-align: right;
}

section h2+ul {
    list-style-image: url(arrow.png);
}
```

marker image

3. Save your changes to the file and then reload the **home.htm** file in your Web browser. As shown in Figure 3-46, the items for farm hours and driving directions are now displayed with green arrow markers.

Figure 3-46	Green arrow markers

Hours

bullets replaced with graphic markers

- Farm Shop: 9 am - 5 pm Mon - Fri; 9 am - 3 pm Sat
- The Corn Maze: 11 am - 9 pm Sat; 11 am - 5 pm Sun
- The Haunted Maze: 5 pm - 9 pm Fri & Sat
- Petting Barn: 9 am - 4 pm Mon - Fri; 11 am - 3 pm Sat & Sun

Directions

- From Council Bluffs, proceed east on I-80
- Take Exit 38 North to the Drake Frontage Road
- Turn right on Highway G
- Proceed east for 2.5 miles
- Sunny Acres is on your left; watch for the green sign

Changing the List Layout

Tammy likes the revised markers, but she thinks there's too much empty space to the left of the entries in the navigation list. She would like you to modify the layout to remove the extra space. Each list item is treated as a group-level element and placed within its own box. By default, most browsers place the list marker to the left of this box, lining up each marker with its list item. You can change this default behavior using the property

```
list-style-position: position;
```

where *position* is either outside (the default) or inside. Placing the marker inside of the block causes the list text to flow around the marker. Figure 3-47 shows how the list-style-position property affects the appearance of a bulleted list.

Figure 3-47 **Marker positions**

- Farm Shop: 9 am - 5 pm Mon - Fri; 9 am - 3 pm Sat
- The Corn Maze: 11 am - 9 pm Sat; 11 am - 5 pm Sun
- The Haunted Maze: 5 pm - 9 pm Fri & Sat
- Petting Barn: 9 am - 4 pm Mon - Fri; 11 am - 3 pm Sat & Sun

list-style-position: outside;

- Farm Shop: 9 am - 5 pm Mon - Fri; 9 am - 3 pm Sat
- The Corn Maze: 11 am - 9 pm Sat; 11 am - 5 pm Sun
- The Haunted Maze: 5 pm - 9 pm Fri & Sat
- Petting Barn: 9 am - 4 pm Mon - Fri; 11 am - 3 pm Sat & Sun

list-style-position: inside;

All three of the list styles can be combined within the property

```
list-style: type image position;
```

where *type* is the marker type, *image* is an image to be displayed in place of the marker, and *position* is the location of the marker. For example, the style rule

```
ul {list-style: circle url(bullet.jpg) inside;}
```

displays all ordered lists with the marker found in the *bullet.jpg* image placed inside the containing block. If a browser is unable to display the bullet image, it uses a circle marker instead. You do not need to include all three style properties with the list style. Browsers will set any property you omit to the default value.

By default, browsers offset ordered and unordered lists from the surrounding text. Tammy has noticed this and worries that the entries in the navigation list are crowding the text in the Welcome paragraph by being shifted too far to the right. She would like you to move the navigation list to the left, aligning it more toward the left edge of the Sunny Acres logo. To reduce the space that the browser inserts, you use the style property

TIP

Any page element can be turned into a list item by applying the display: list-item style.

```
padding-left: size;
```

where *size* is the length that the list should be shifted to the right. The padding-left style is one of the styles you'll study in more detail in the next tutorial on page layout. For now, you'll limit your use of this style to reduce the extra space inserted by the browser in the navigation list. After some experimenting, you settle on the following value for the style:

```
padding-left: 0.5em;
```

You'll add this style to the style rule for the navigation list.

To move the navigation list to the left:

▶ **1.** Return to the **sa_styles.css** file in your text editor.

▶ **2.** Within the style rule for the navigation list, insert the following style value, as shown in Figure 3-48:

```
padding-left: 0.5em;
```

Figure 3-48 ▶ Setting the padding space within a list

adds space to the
left of the list items

```
nav ul {
    list-style-type: none;
    padding-left: 0.5em;
}
```

▶ **3.** Save your changes to the file and then reload the **home.htm** file in your Web browser. Verify that the entries in the navigation list have been shifted to the left, aligned roughly with the left edge of the Sunny Acres logo.

To complete the design style for the navigation list, Tammy wants to change the background color of the list to sky blue, and to increase the space between the items by increasing the line height to 3.5em. Also, while browsers underline hypertext by default, the current Web design standard is to not underline the links in a navigation list; thus, Tammy also wants to change the text color of the navigation links to white and remove the underlining. You'll add these styles to the style sheet now.

To reformat the navigation list:

▶ **1.** Return to the **sa_styles.css** file in your text editor.

▶ **2.** Add the following style properties to the `nav ul` style rule

```
background-color: rgb(125, 186, 240);
line-height: 3.5em;
```

▶ **3.** Directly below the `nav ul` style rule, add the following rule for navigation hypertext links (see Figure 3-49):

```
nav ul li a {
    color: white;
    text-decoration: none;
}
```

Figure 3-49 ▶ Formatting the navigation list

```
nav ul {
    background-color: rgb(125, 186, 240);
    line-height: 3.5em;
    list-style-type: none;
    padding-left: 0.5em;
}

nav ul li a {
    color: white;
    text-decoration: none;
}
```

displays hypertext in
the navigation list in
white with no
underlining

displays the unordered
list with a sky blue
background and a line
height of 3.5em

▶ **4.** Save your changes to the file and then reload the **home.htm** file in your Web browser. Figure 3-50 shows the revised appearance of the navigation sidebar.

Figure 3-50   Revised navigation list

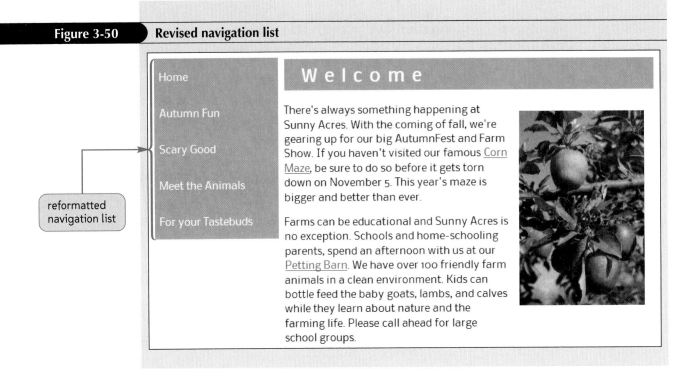

Using Pseudo-Classes and Pseudo-Elements

Without underlines, there is no visual clue that the links in the navigation list act as hypertext. Tammy has seen Web sites in which links are underlined or highlighted only when the mouse pointer hovers over the linked text. This type of effect is called a rollover effect because it is applied only when a user "rolls" the mouse pointer over an element. Tammy would like you to add a rollover effect to the navigation list.

Pseudo-Classes

Rollover effects can be created using pseudo-classes. A pseudo-class is a classification of an element based on its current status, position, or use in the document. Styles for pseudo-classes are created using the syntax

```
selector:pseudo-class {styles;}
```

where *selector* is an element or a group of elements within a document, *pseudo-class* is the name of a pseudo-class, and *styles* are the style properties applied to that selector pseudo-class. Pseudo-classes are organized into dynamic and structural classes. A dynamic pseudo-class changes with a user's actions. For example, the visited pseudo-class indicates whether a hypertext link previously has been visited by the user. To display the text of all such links in red, you would apply the following style rule to the a element:

```
a:visited {color: red;}
```

To change the text color to blue when users hover the mouse pointer over the link, you would add the following style rule:

```
a:hover {color: blue;}
```

Figure 3-51 lists the other dynamic pseudo-classes supported by CSS.

Figure 3-51	Dynamic pseudo-classes

Pseudo-Class	Description	Example
link	The link has not yet been visited by the user.	`a:link {color: red;}`
visited	The link has been visited by the user.	`a:visited {color: green;}`
active	The element is in the process of being activiated or clicked by the user.	`a:active {color: yellow;}`
hover	The mouse pointer is hovering over the element.	`a:hover {color: blue;}`
focus	The element has received the focus of the keyboard or mouse pointer.	`input:focus {background-color: yellow;}`

In some cases, two or more pseudo-classes can apply to the same element. For example, a hypertext link can be both previously visited and hovered over. In such situations, the standard cascading rules apply—the pseudo-class that is listed last is applied to the element. You should enter the hypertext pseudo-classes in the following order in your style sheets—`link`, `visited`, `hover`, and `active`. The `link` pseudo-class comes first because it represents a hypertext link that has not yet been visited or even clicked by the user. The `visited` pseudo-class comes next, for links that previously have been visited or clicked. The `hover` pseudo-class follows, for the situation in which a user has once again moved the mouse pointer over a hypertext link before clicking the link. The `active` pseudo-class is last, representing the exact instant in which a link is clicked by a user. Any styles set with the `link` pseudo-class are inherited by the `visited`, `hover`, and `active` pseudo-classes.

REFERENCE

Creating a Hypertext Rollover

- To create a rollover for a hypertext link, apply the styles

      a:link   {styles;}
      a:visited {styles;}
      a:hover   {styles;}
      a:active   {styles;}

  to the a element, where *styles* are the CSS styles applied to hypertext links that have not been visited (`link`), have already been visited (`visited`), have the mouse pointer over them (`hover`), or are actively being clicked (`active`).

The `hover`, `active`, and `focus` dynamic pseudo-classes also can be applied to non-hypertext elements. For example, the following style rule causes the background color of each entry in a navigation list to change to medium blue whenever a user hovers the mouse pointer over it:

```
nav ul li:hover {
   background-color: rgb(83, 142, 213);
}
```

Tammy suggests that you add this style rule to provide users with the visual feedback that is missing from the navigation links as a result of removing the underlining.

To apply the hover pseudo-class:

▸ **1.** Return to the **sa_styles.css** file in your text editor.

▸ **2.** Add the following style rule, as shown in Figure 3-52:

```
nav ul li:hover {
    background-color: rgb(83, 142, 213);
}
```

Figure 3-52 Applying the hover pseudo-class

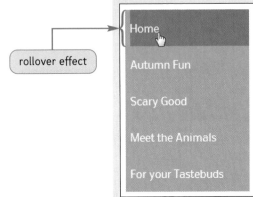

change the background color to medium blue when the user hovers the mouse pointer over the list items

```
nav ul {
    background-color: rgb(125, 186, 240);
    line-height: 3.5em;
    list-style-type: none;
    padding-left: 0.5em;
}

nav ul li:hover {
    background-color: rgb(83, 142, 213);
}
```

▸ **3.** Save your changes to the file and then reload **home.htm** in your Web browser. Move your mouse pointer over the navigation list items. As shown in Figure 3-53, the background color of the navigation list items changes to medium blue in response to the hover event.

Figure 3-53 Viewing the rollover effect

rollover effect

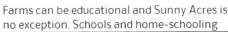

Welcome

Home

Autumn Fun

Scary Good

Meet the Animals

For your Tastebuds

There's always something happening at Sunny Acres. With the coming of fall, we're gearing up for our big AutumnFest and Farm Show. If you haven't visited our famous Corn Maze, be sure to do so before it gets torn down on November 5. This year's maze is bigger and better than ever.

Farms can be educational and Sunny Acres is no exception. Schools and home-schooling

INSIGHT

Deprecated Attributes for Hypertext Links

Earlier versions of HTML did not support CSS and the link, visited, hover, and active pseudo-classes. If a Web page author wanted to change the color of a hypertext link, he or she would have to add the attributes

```
<body link="color" vlink="color" alink="color">
```

to the <body> tag, where the link attribute specifies the color of unvisited links, the vlink attribute specifies the color of visited links, and the alink attribute specifies the color of active links. Colors had to be entered either as a supported color name or as a hexadecimal color value. The link, vlink, and alink attributes have been deprecated and their use is discouraged, but you still might see them in the code of older Web pages.

Structural pseudo-classes are used to classify items based on their locations within the hierarchy of page elements. For example, the style rule

```
body:first-child {background-color: yellow;}
```

changes the background color to yellow in the first child of the body element within the document. Notice that the selector does not specify the element. It could be an h1 heading, a section element, or anything else, as long as it is the first child of the body element. Figure 3-54 describes the structural pseudo-classes.

Figure 3-54   Structural pseudo-classes

Pseudo-Class	Matches
root	The top element in the document hierarchy (the html element)
empty	An element with no children
only-child	An element with no siblings
first-child	The first child of the parent element
last-child	The last child of the parent element
first-of-type	The first element of the parent that matches the specified type
last-of-type	The last element of the parent that matches the specified type
nth-of-type(n)	The nth element of the parent of the specified type
nth-last-of-type(n)	The nth from the last element of the parent of the specified type
only-of-type	An element that has no siblings of the same type
lang(code)	The element that has the specified language indicated by code
not(s)	An element not matching the specified selector, s

The first entry in a navigation list is often the most prominent or important. On the Sunny Acres Web site, the first entry is linked to the site's home page. Tammy would like this link to always be displayed in capital letters. Although you could edit the HTML code to make this happen, you decide to make this change to the style sheet using the following style rule because you want to separate content from design:

```
nav ul li:first-of-type {
    text-transform: uppercase;
}
```

The style rule uses the first-of-type pseudo-class to apply the uppercase transformation to the first li element found nested within the navigation list. You'll add this rule now to your style sheet.

To transform the text of the first navigation list element:

1. Return to the **sa_styles.css** file in your text editor.

2. Add the following style rule as shown in Figure 3-55:

```
nav ul li:first-of-type {
    text-transform: uppercase;
}
```

TIP

For browsers that don't support the first-of-type pseudo-class, you can use the id attribute to mark the first list item and write the style based on that id.

Figure 3-55	Applying a structural pseudo-class

```
nav ul li:hover {
    background-color: rgb(83, 142, 213);
}
nav ul li:first-of-type {
    text-transform: uppercase;
}
```

displays the text of the first li element in the navigation list in uppercase

3. Save your changes to the file and then reload **home.htm** in your Web browser. Verify that the first entry in the navigation list, Home, is displayed in uppercase letters.

Trouble? If you are running a version of Internet Explorer earlier than 9, the first list item will not be displayed in uppercase letters.

Pseudo-Elements

Tammy has a few more changes she wants you to make to the Sunny Acres home page. In the first paragraph of the home page, she would like the following styling:

- The first line displayed in all uppercase letters
- The first letter increased in size and displayed as an initial cap

So far, all of your selectors have been based on elements that exist somewhere within the document hierarchy and are tagged in the HTML file. You also can define selectors based on pseudo-elements, which are not elements that exist in the document hierarchy but rather are based on objects that exist in the rendered Web page. For example, a paragraph is an element in the document hierarchy, but the first line of the paragraph is not. It only exists as an object once the paragraph has been rendered by the browser. Similarly, the first letter of that paragraph is also not a document element, but it certainly can be identified as an object in the Web page. Both the first line and the first letter are pseudo-elements, and you can create a style rule to format their appearance. A selector based on a pseudo-element is similar to one that is based on a pseudo-class, such as

```
selector:pseudo-element {styles;}
```

where *pseudo-element* is an abstract element from the rendered Web page. Figure 3-56 lists some of the pseudo-elements supported by CSS.

Figure 3-56	Pseudo-elements

Pseudo-Element	Description	Example
first-letter	The first letter of the element text	p:first-letter {font-size:200%}
first-line	The first line of the element text	p:first-line {text-transform: uppercase}
before	Content inserted directly before the element	p:before {content:"Special! "}
after	Content inserted directly after the element	p:after {content:"eof"}

In order to differentiate between pseudo-elements and pseudo-classes, CSS3 changes the syntax of pseudo-elements by adding an extra colon to the selector:

```
selector::pseudo-element {styles;}
```

To maintain backward compatibility with older browsers, however, you still should use the single colon syntax.

The style rules to format the first line and first letter of the opening paragraph are:

```
section > p:first-of-type:first-letter {
   font-size: 250%;
   font-family: 'Times New Roman', Times, serif;
}
section > p:first-of-type:first-line {
   text-transform: uppercase;
}
```

Notice that the selector uses the `first-of-type` pseudo-class combined with the `first-letter` and `first-line` pseudo-elements so that the styles are applied only to the first paragraph of the `section` element and then to the first letter and first lines within that paragraph. After you apply the rule, the first letter will appear 250% larger than the surrounding text, and in a Times New Roman or other serif font. In addition, all of the text on the first line will appear in uppercase.

TIP

Only one pseudo-element may be used per selector.

REFERENCE

Working with Pseudo-Elements

- To apply a style to the first line of an element, use the pseudo-element selector

  `selector:first-line`

  where `selector` is the name of the element or elements in the document.
- To apply a style to the first letter of an element, use the following pseudo-element selector:

  `selector:first-letter`

- To insert a text string before an element, use the style rule

  `selector:before {content: text;}`

  where `text` is the content of the text string.
- To insert a text string after an element, use the following style rule:

  `selector:after {content: text;}`

Since Tammy wants to apply this style rule only to the home page and not to every page on her Web site, you'll add the rule to an embedded style sheet placed within the *home.htm* file.

To create the initial cap and first line styles:

▶ **1.** Go to the **home.htm** file in your text editor.

▶ **2.** Directly above the closing `</head>` tag, insert the following code, as shown in Figure 3-57:

```
<style type="text/css">
    section > p:first-of-type:first-line {
        text-transform: uppercase;
    }

    section > p:first-of-type:first-letter {
        font-size: 250%;
        font-family: 'Times New Roman', Times, serif;
    }

</style>
```

Figure 3-57 ▶ Styling pseudo-elements

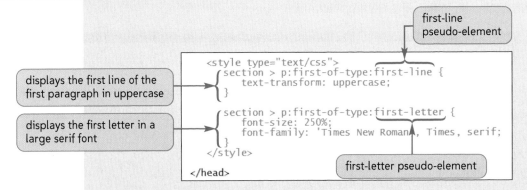

▶ **3.** Save your changes to the file and then reload **home.htm** in your Web browser. As shown in Figure 3-58, the first line of the opening paragraph is displayed in uppercase letters, and the first letter of that line is larger than the surrounding text.

Figure 3-58 ▶ First letter and first line styles

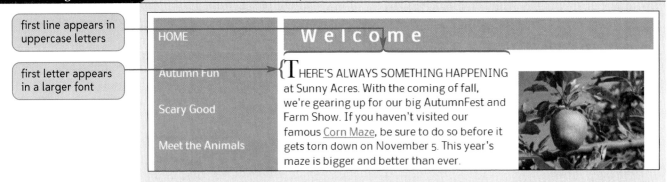

Trouble? At the time of this writing, neither Safari nor Chrome is able to apply the `text-transform` style property with the `first-line` pseudo-element.

INSIGHT

Generating Content with CSS

You can generate page content using the following `before` and `after` pseudo-elements along with the `content` property

```
selector:before {content: text;}
selector:after {content: text;}
```

where `text` is the text you want to add to the element. For example, the style rule

```
em:after {content: " !";}
```

appends a space and an exclamation point to the end of every em element. You also can use the `before` and `after` pseudo-elements in conjunction with pseudo-classes. The style rules

```
a:hover:before {content: "<";}
a:hover:after {content: ">";}
```

create a rollover effect in which the < and > characters are placed around a hypertext link when a mouse pointer hovers over the link.

Another way to insert content using CSS is to retrieve information from an element attribute using the `attr` property, which has the syntax

```
content: attr(attribute)
```

where `attribute` is an attribute of the element. For example, the following style appends every hypertext link with the text of the link's URL as stored in the `href` attribute:

```
a:after {
    content: attr(" [" attr(href) "] ");
}
```

When applied to the hypertext link

```
<a href="home.htm">Sunny Acres</a>
```

this style will be rendered by the browser as follows:

Sunny Acres [home.htm]

Finally, you can insert an image by specifying the URL of the image file for the value of the `content` property, as the following code demonstrates:

```
a[href^="http"]:after {
    content: url(uparrow.png);
}
```

In this example, the *uparrow.png* file is appended to any hypertext link that contains the text string *http* within its `href` attribute. This technique is sometimes used to visually identify hypertext links that point to external Web sites.

By generating content through your CSS style sheets, you can create interesting dynamic effects for your Web site that are easy to develop and maintain. Note, however, that the `content` pseudo-class is not supported in older browsers, and so you should not rely on it to create text critical to the understanding of your Web site.

Tammy is pleased with your work on the style sheet for the Sunny Acres home page. Your only remaining task is to apply your style sheet to the other pages to confirm that your design choices work properly for every page. Tammy also would like a different background color for the h1 headings on each page. You'll set the background colors using embedded style sheets in the other pages on the Web site.

To apply the style sheet to the other pages on the site:

▶ **1.** Go to the **maze.htm** file in your text editor.

▶ **2.** Directly above the closing </head> tag, insert the following link elements and embedded style sheet (see Figure 3-59):

```
<link href="sa_layout.css" rel="stylesheet" type="text/css" />
<link href="sa_styles.css" rel="stylesheet" type="text/css" />
<style type="text/css">
   section h1 {
      background-color: rgb(191, 141, 101);
   }
</style>
```

Figure 3-59   Style sheets for the maze.htm file

```
<link href="sa_layout.css" rel="stylesheet" type="text/css" />
<link href="sa_styles.css" rel="stylesheet" type="text/css" />
<style type="text/css">
   section h1 {
      background-color: rgb(191, 141, 101);
   }
</style>
</head>
```

▶ **3.** Save your changes to the file.

▶ **4.** Repeat Steps 2 and 3 for the **haunted.htm**, **petting.htm**, and **produce.htm** files. Set the h1 background colors for these three files to **rgb(0, 0, 0)**, **rgb(133, 109, 85)**, and **rgb(50, 69, 99)**, respectively.

▶ **5.** Reopen the **home.htm** file in your Web browser and navigate through Tammy's Web site. Verify that the layout and color scheme have been applied to every sample page that Tammy has developed. Figure 3-60 shows the completed Web page for the Farm Shop.

▶ **6.** Submit your completed files to your instructor, in either printed or electronic form, as requested.

Figure 3-60   Farm Shop Web page

Sunny
Acres

Tammy and Brent Nielsen
1973 Hwy G
Council Bluffs, IA 51503

HOME

Autumn Fun

Scary Good

Meet the Animals

For your Tastebuds

The Farm Shop

The Sunny Acres Farm Shop aims to offer the highest quality fresh produce. You can pick your own or buy it in our shop. Set amidst acres of outstanding natural beauty on the beautiful rolling hills northeast of Council Bluffs, the Farm Shop is easily reached on Highway G, with easy access from Interstate 80.

The Farm Shop was established over 25 years ago with great success. Our products have won numerous awards at local festivals and fairs. We also cater to local supermarkets in the Council Bluffs/Omaha area. Look for our products every Saturday morning from May to October at the Council Bluffs Farmers' Market.

Hours

> Monday - Friday: 9 am - 5 pm
> Saturday: 9 am - 3 pm
> Pick Your Own Produce is available from May 15 - October 22
> The Farm Shop is open year-round

Products

> Freshly baked breads and quiches
> High quality meats
> Cheese and other dairy products
> Freshly-picked fruits and vegetables (in season)
> Canned goods and preserves

SUNNY ACRES ✳ TAMMY & BRENT NIELSEN ✳ 1977 HIGHWAY G ✳ COUNCIL BLUFFS, IA 51503

Teamwork: Managing a Style Sheet

Your style sheets often will be as long and as complex as your Web site content. As the size of a style sheet increases, you might find yourself overwhelmed by multiple style rules and definitions. This can be an especially critical problem in a workplace where several people need to interpret and sometimes edit the same style sheet. Good management skills are as crucial to good Web design as a well-chosen color or typeface. As you create your own style sheets, here are some techniques to help you manage your creations:

- Use style comments throughout, especially at the top of the file. Clearly describe the purpose of the style sheet, where it's used, and who created it and when.
- Because color values are not always immediately obvious, include comments that describe your colors. For example, annotate a color value with a comment such as "body text is tan".
- Divide your style sheet into sections, with comments marking the section headings.
- Choose an organizing scheme and stick with it. You may want to organize style rules by the order in which they appear in your documents, or you may want to insert them alphabetically. Whichever you choose, be consistent and document the organizing scheme in your style comments.
- Keep your style sheets as small as possible, and break them into separate files if necessary. Use one style sheet for layout, another for text design, and perhaps another for color and graphics. Combine the style sheets using the `@import` rule, or combine them within each Web page. Also consider creating one style sheet for basic pages on your Web site, and another for pages that deal with special content. For example, an online store could use one style sheet (or set of sheets) for product information and another for customer information.

By following some of these basic techniques, you'll find your style sheets easier to manage and develop, and it will be easier for your colleagues to collaborate with you to create an eye-catching Web site.

You've completed your work on designing a style sheet to format the text and backgrounds on the Sunny Acres Web site. Tammy will continue to examine your work and get back to you with future projects or design changes.

Session 3.3 Quick Check

1. Provide a style rule to display all ordered lists with lowercase letters as the marker.
2. Provide a style rule to display all unordered lists using the *star.png* image file, placed inside of the containing box.
3. By default, most browsers indent lists from the surrounding text. Provide a style rule to remove the indentation from every unordered list nested within a `section` element.
4. Provide a style rule to display the text of all previously visited hypertext links in gray.
5. Describe the item selected by the following selector:

   `#top > p:first-of-type:first-line`

6. Describe the items selected by the following selector:

   `div.links img[usemap]`

7. Provide a style rule to insert the text string "*** " before every paragraph belonging to the *review* class.

Review Assignments

Data Files needed for the Review Assignments: CloisterBlack.eot, CloisterBlack.svg, CloisterBlack.ttf, CloisterBlack.txt, CloisterBlack.woff, flake.png, holiday.jpg, holidaytxt.htm, hs_layout.css, hs_stylestxt.css, modernizr-1.5.js, salogo.png

Tammy has been working with the Web site you designed. She's returned to you for help with another Web page. The Sunny Acres farm is planning a festival called *Holidays on the Farm* to bring people to Sunny Acres during the months of November and December. The farm is planning to offer sleigh rides, sledding (weather permitting), and visits with Santa Claus. Tammy already has created the content for this page and located a few graphics she wants you to use. She needs you to complete the Web page by creating a style sheet for the text and colors in the page. A preview of the page you'll create for Tammy is shown in Figure 3-61.

Figure 3-61   Holidays on the Farm page

Sunny
Acres

Tammy and Brent Nielsen
1973 Hwy G
Council Bluffs, IA 51503

HOME

The Corn Maze

The Haunted Barn

Petting Barn

The Farm Shop

Holidays on the Farm

Holidays on the Farm

This year Sunny Acres becomes Wintery Acres as we institute our first Holidays on the Farm. Join us on weekends from November 23 through January 5 for holiday cheer and festivities.

Saint Nick visits Sunny Acres

The Sunny Acres Farm Shop will be decked out in bright and colorful holiday decorations with special prices on garlands, tinsel, ornaments, and wreaths. Be sure to sample our homemade egg nog and bring some home for your family.

The trails and hills around Sunny Acres will be alive with fun and games. Come join us for sleigh rides or zoom down our awesome sledding hill (weather permitting). Sunny Acres is adjacent to Dawson Park, which has a vast network of cross country ski trails for every level of skier.

We've even decorated our barn for the holidays. Come visit Santa's stables, where you might even see a few reindeer--perhaps even one with a red nose!

Hours

✻ Saturdays: 10 am - 5 pm
✻ Sundays: 11 am - 3 pm
✻ Closed: December 25, 31, January 1

Directions

✻ From Council Bluffs, proceed east on I-80
✻ Take Exit 38 North to the Drake Frontage Road
✻ Turn right on Highway G
✻ Proceed east for 2.5 miles
✻ Sunny Acres is on your left; watch for the green sign

SUNNY ACRES ✻ TAMMY & BRENT NIELSEN ✻ 1977 HIGHWAY G ✻ COUNCIL BLUFFS, IA 51503

Complete the following:

1. Use your text editor to open the **holidaytxt.htm** and **hs_stylestxt.css** files from the tutorial.03\review folder included with your Data Files. Enter *your name* and *the date* within the comment section of each file, and then save them as **holiday.htm** and **hs_styles.css**, respectively.

2. Go to the **holiday.htm** file in your text editor and take some time to review the contents and structure of the document. Link the file to the **hs_layout.css** style sheet file. Open the Web page in your browser to study its current layout.

3. Tammy wants to use a Web font for the heading on the page. She has stored the CSS code for the font definition in the **CloisterBlack.txt** file. Open this file, copy the CSS code, and then go to the **hs_styles.css** style sheet file. Paste the copied CSS code into the file below the comment header.

4. Create a style rule for the page body, set the background color to **white**, and set the default font list to **Trebuchet MS**, **Helvetica**, and **sans-serif**.

5. Create a style rule for unordered lists within the `nav` element that: a) sets the background color to the value (**248, 175, 175**); b) sets the line height to **3.5em**; c) removes the bullet marker; d) sets the width of the `padding-left` property to **0** pixels; and e) indents the text **5** pixels. For the first list item, create a style rule to: a) increase the font size to **150%**; b) display the text in small caps; and c) display the text in **bold**. For every hypertext link within the navigation list, create a style that removes the underlining and sets the font color to **white**.

6. When the user hovers the mouse pointer over list items in the navigation list, change the background color to the value (**148, 51, 62**). When the user hovers the mouse pointer over a hypertext link in the navigation list, change the font color to **yellow**.

7. Tammy has placed a promotional photo in a figure box. Set the background color of figure boxes to the color value (**248, 175, 175**) and **center** the contents of figure boxes. For the caption within the figure box, add styles to: a) set the font size to **14** pixels; b) display the text in **italic**; and c) **center** the caption text.

8. For `h1` headings nested within the `section` element, create a style rule to: a) set the background color to the value (**148, 51, 62**); b) set the font color to **white**; c) use the font list containing the **CloisterBlack** and **fantasy** fonts; d) set the font size to **2.5em**; e) remove boldface from the text; f) set the kerning to **0.3em**; g) set the line height to **2em**; and h) indent the text **5** pixels.

9. For `h2` headings nested within the `section` element, create a style rule to: a) set the background color to the value (**182, 134, 52**); b) set the font color to **white** for older browsers and to the color value (**255, 255, 255**) with an opacity of **0.8** for newer browsers; c) set the font weight to **normal**; d) set the kerning to **0.7em**; and e) indent the text **1em**.

10. For unordered lists directly after `h2` headings nested within the `section` element, create a style rule that displays the image file **flake.png** as the bullet marker.

11. For `address` elements nested within the `footer` element, create a style rule to: a) set the background to the color (**148, 51, 62**); b) set the font color to **white** for older browsers and to the value (**255, 255, 255**) with 80% opacity for newer browsers; c) change the font style to **normal** weight in small caps, **0.8em** in size with a line height of **4em**, and use fonts from the list **Palatino Linotype**, **Book Antiqua**, **Palatino**, and **serif**; and d) **center** the address text.

12. Add comments to the style sheet to document what you've done.

13. Save your changes to the **hs_styles.css** style sheet.

14. Return to the **holiday.htm** file in your text editor and link to the **hs_styles.css** file.

15. Open the **holiday.htm** file in your Web browser and verify that the page matches the page shown in Figure 3-61.

16. Submit your completed files to your instructor, in either printed or electronic form, as requested.

Apply your knowledge of CSS text and color styles to format a Web page for a cryptographic institution.

APPLY

Case Problem 1

Data Files needed for this Case Problem: algo.htm, c_layout.css, c_stylestxt.css, crypttxt.htm, enigma.htm, history.htm, locks.jpg, logo.gif, modernizr-1.5.js, public.htm, scytale.gif, single.htm

International Cryptographic Institute Sela Dawes is the media representative for the ICI, the International Cryptographic Institute. The ICI is an organization of cryptographers who study the science and mathematics of secret codes, encrypted messages, and code breaking. Part of the ICI's mission is to inform the public about cryptography and data security. Sela has asked you to work on a Web site containing information about cryptography for use by high school science and math teachers. She wants the design to be visually interesting in order to help draw students into the material. Figure 3-62 shows a preview of your design.

Figure 3-62	Cryptography home page

Complete the following:

1. In your text editor, open the **crypttxt.htm** and **c_stylestxt.css** files from the tutorial.03\case1 folder included with your Data Files. Enter *your name* and *the date* in the comment section of each file. Save the files as **crypt.htm** and **c_styles.css** respectively.

2. Go to the **crypt.htm** file in your text editor, and review the contents and structure of the document. Link the file to the **c_layout.css** style sheet.

3. Locate the three `strong` elements in the two paragraphs and add the `class` attribute to each element with the class value set to **keyword**.

4. Locate the *locks.jpg* inline image, and below the image create an image map with the name **locks**. Add the following hotspots to the image map:

   a. A circular hotspot linked to the **history.htm** file, centered at the coordinates (**52, 52**) with a radius of **43** pixels; the alternate text should be **History**.

   b. A circular hotspot with a radius of **43** pixels located at the coordinates (**155, 52**); link the hotspot to the **enigma.htm** file, and with the alternate text set to **Enigma**.

   c. A circular hotspot with a radius of **43** pixels located at the coordinates (**255, 52**); link the hotspot to the **algo.htm** file and set the alternate text to **Algorithms**.

   d. A circular hotspot with a radius of **43** pixels located at the coordinates (**355, 52**); link the hotspot to the **single.htm** file and set the alternate text to **Single Key**.

   e. A circular hotspot with a radius of **43** pixels located at the coordinates (**455, 52**); link the hotspot to the **public.htm** file and set the alternate text to **Public Key**.

5. Apply the **locks** image map to the *locks.jpg* inline image.

6. Save your changes to the **crypt.htm** file.

7. Go to the **c_styles.css** style sheet file in your text editor. Set the color of the page body background and text to **black** and **white**, respectively. Set the default font to a list consisting of **Century Gothic** followed by a generic **sans-serif** font.

8. Add a style rule for `h1` headings nested within a `header` element to: a) display the text in **yellow**; b) use **Courier New**, **Courier**, or another **monospace** font; c) set the font size to **28** pixels with a kerning of **20** pixels; and d) **center** the text.

9. Add a style rule for `h2` headings nested within an `article` element to: a) set the font size to **24** pixels; b) display the text without boldface; and c) set the kerning to **5** pixels.

10. Align paragraph text within the `article` element using full justification.

11. For `strong` elements belonging to the `keyword` class, create a style rule that displays the text in a **yellow**, non-bold font.

12. Center the contents of paragraphs nested within the `footer` element.

⊕ **EXPLORE**   13. You don't want image maps to appear with a colored border. To remove the border, create a style rule for inline images that contain the `usemap` attribute and set the border width to **0** pixels.

14. Document your work with style comments and then save your changes to the file.

15. Return to the **crypt.htm** file in your text editor and link the file to the **c_styles.css** style sheet.

16. Open **crypt.htm** in your Web browser and confirm that it matches the design shown in Figure 3-62.

17. Submit your completed files to your instructor, in either printed or electronic form, as requested.

Apply your knowledge of CSS to design a Web page for a bike touring company.

APPLY

Case Problem 2

Data Files needed for this Case Problem: bmtourtxt.htm, modernizr-1.5.js, mw_layout.css, mw_stylestxt.css, mwlogo.png, wheelmarker.png

Mountain Wheels   Adriana and Ivan Turchenko are the co-owners of Mountain Wheels, a bike shop and touring agency in Littleton, Colorado. One of their most popular tours is the Bike the Mountains Tour, a six-day excursion over some of the highest roads in Colorado. Adriana wants to update the company's Web site to provide more informa-tion about the Bike the Mountains Tour. She already has had a colleague design a three-column layout with a list of links in the first column and descriptive text in the second and third columns. She has asked for your help in completing the design by formatting the text and colors in the page. Figure 3-63 shows a preview of the Web page you'll create.

Figure 3-63   **Bike the Mountains page**

Bike the Mountains Tour

Home

⊙ Learn More

Testimonials

Route Maps

Register

Lodging

Meals

Training

Equipment

Forums

FAQs

Contact Us

THE BIKE THE MOUNTAINS TOUR RISES from the town of Littleton, Colorado and explores the Colorado Front Range. Our tour crosses the Continental Divide twice, giving you the opportunity to bike the highest paved roads in the United States. This tour is a classic showcase of Colorado's Rocky Mountain scenery.

Not designed for the weekend cyclist, this tour is offered only for those fit enough to ride high mountain passes. We provide sag wagons and support. Your lodging and meals are also part of the registration fee. We guarantee tough climbs, amazing sights, sweaty jerseys, and lots of fun.

This is the seventh year we've offered the Bike the Mountains Tour. It is our most popular tour and riders are returning again and again. Our experienced tour leaders will be there to guide, help, encourage, draft, and lead you every stroke of the way. Come join us!

"The Bike the Mountains Tour is amazing. I highly recommend it and would gladly return."

— Steve H.

Itinerary

Day 1
We start from the foothills above Littleton, Colorado, promptly at 9am. The first day is a chance to get your legs in shape, test your gearing, and prepare for what's to come.

Day 2
Day 2 starts with a climb up Bear Creek Canyon to Lookout Mountain, followed by a swift and winding descent into the town of Golden. Refresh yourself at the famous Coors Brewery.

Day 3
Day 3 takes you along the Peak to Peak Highway. This 55-mile route showcases the mountains of the Front Range, providing amazing vistas from Golden Gate Canyon State Park to Rocky Mountain National Park.

Day 4
Now for the supreme challenge: Day 4 brings some real high-altitude cycling through Rocky Mountain National Park and up Trail Ridge Road. It's an amazing ride, high above timberline, topping out at over 11,000 feet.

Day 5
We start Day 5 on the west side of the Continental Divide. From Grand Lake, you'll bike to Winter Park and then over Berthoud Pass, and back to the eastern side of the Continental Divide.

Day 6
On Day 6 we ride back to Littleton over Squaw Pass and Bear Creek and then enjoy a celebratory dinner as we share memories of a great tour.

Mountain Wheels • Littleton, CO 80123 • (303) 555 - 5499

Complete the following:

1. Open the **bmtourtxt.htm** and **mw_stylestxt.css** files from the tutorial.03\case2 folder. Enter *your name* and *the date* in the comment section of each file. Save the files as **bmtour.htm** and **mw_styles.css** in the same folder.

2. Return to the **bmtour.htm** file in your text editor. Link the file to the **mw_layout.css** style sheet. Take some time to review the contents and structure of the document.

3. You need to name different elements within the document using the id attribute. Add the following ids to the document: a) name the first header element **pageheader** and the second header element **articleheader**; and b) name the first section element **leftsection** and the second section element **rightsection**.

4. Save your changes to the file and then go to the **mw_styles.css** style sheet in your text editor.

5. Set the default font for the page body to a font list containing **Tahoma**, **Geneva**, and **sans-serif**.

6. For the articleheader id, apply a style rule that: a) sets the font size to **18** pixels and removes boldface; b) sets the kerning to **7** pixels; and c) centers the text.

7. Set the background color of the navigation list to the value (**125, 120, 89**) and set the line height to **3em**. Remove the bullet markers from the navigation list.

8. For hypertext links within the navigation list, create a style rule that: a) sets the font color to **white** for older browsers, and to **white** with 50% opacity for newer browsers; and b) removes the underlining from the link text.

EXPLORE 9. When a user hovers the mouse pointer over list items in the navigation list, change the background color to the value (**131, 121, 36**) and display the image file *wheelmarker.png* as the bullet image. When a user hovers the mouse pointer over a hypertext link in the navigation list, change the font color to **yellow** for older browsers, and to **white** with 100% opacity for newer browsers.

10. For paragraphs that are direct children of the leftsection id, set the font size to **22** pixels. Also, for the first paragraph that is also a direct child of the leftsection id, display the first line of the paragraph in uppercase.

11. For the blockquote element, create a style rule to set: a) the background color to (**131, 121, 36**); b) the font color to **white**; c) the font size to **16** pixels; and d) the font family to **Comic Sans MS**, **Times**, and cursive.

EXPLORE 12. For paragraphs within the blockquote element, create styles to insert a **double quotation mark** directly before and after the text of the paragraph.

13. For h1 headings within the rightsection id, create a style rule to: a) set the font size to **22** pixels and the kerning to **3** pixels; b) remove the boldface from the text; and c) **center** the text. For h2 headings within the rightsection id, create a style rule to: a) set the font size to **18** pixels; b) right-align the text; and c) remove the boldface from the text. Finally, for paragraphs within the rightsection id, create a style rule to: a) set the font color to **gray**; b) set the font size to **14** pixels; and c) **justify** the text.

14. For address elements within the page footer, create a style rule to: a) set the font size to **16** pixels; b) remove the italic style from the address; and c) **center** the text.

15. Add style comments to document your work and then save your changes to the file.

16. Return to the **bmtour.htm** file in your text editor and link that file to the **mw_styles.css** style sheet.

17. Open the **bmtour.htm** file in your Web browser and confirm that it matches the design and layout shown in Figure 3-63.

18. Submit your completed files to your instructor, in either printed or electronic form, as requested.

CHALLENGE

Explore how to use CSS to design a Web page for an online Civil War History course.

Case Problem 3

Data Files needed for this Case Problem: civilwartxt.htm, cw_layout.css, cw_stylestxt.css, cwphoto.png, modernizr-1.5.js, mwulogo.png, pcphoto.png

The Civil War and Reconstruction   Peter Craft is a professor of military history at Midwest University. The college is offering a series of online courses, one of which is *The Civil War and Reconstruction* taught by Professor Craft. He has developed the online content and has had a colleague help with the page layout. You've been asked to complete the project by creating text and color styles. A preview of the sample page is shown in Figure 3-64.

Figure 3-64   Civil War and Reconstruction page

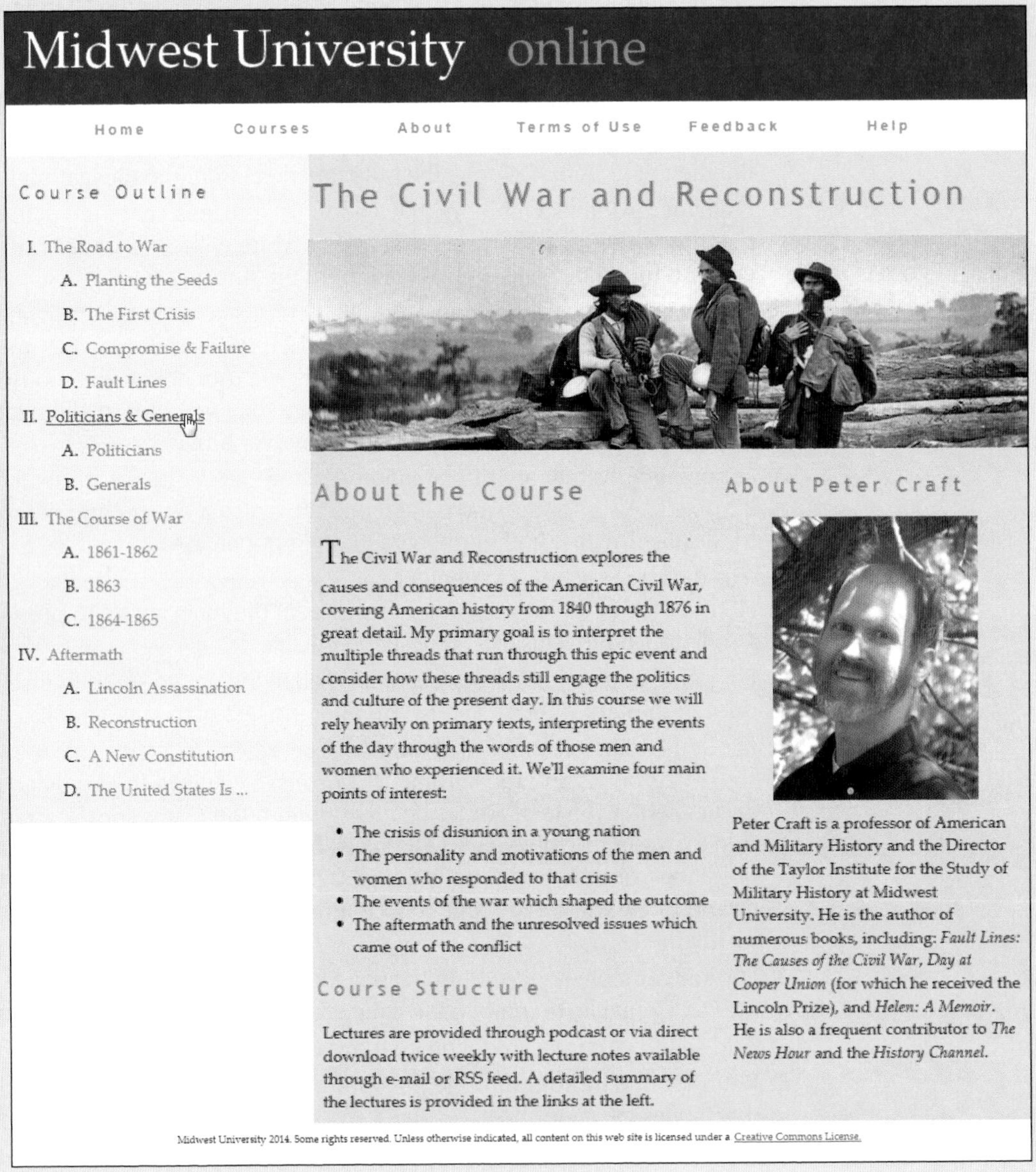

Complete the following:

1. Open the **civilwartxt.htm** and **cw_stylestxt.css** files in your text editor. Add ***your name*** and ***the date*** to the comment section of each file, and then save the files as **civilwar.htm** and **cw_styles.css**, respectively.

2. Go to the **civilwar.htm** file in your text editor. Take some time to review the content and structure of the Web page. There are two navigation lists in the document. Peter wants the first navigation list to be displayed horizontally and the second navigation list to be displayed vertically. Add the `class` attribute to each `nav` element, setting the class values to **horizontal** and **vertical** respectively.

3. Save your changes to the file, and then go to the **cw_styles.css** file in your text editor.

EXPLORE

4. Peter already has stored the layout styles in the *cw_layout.css* file. Directly after the opening comments, use the `@import` rule to import this style sheet. Add a comment describing the purpose of the `@import` rule.

5. Set the typeface of the page body to the font list **Palatino Linotype**, **Book Antiqua**, **Palatino**, and **serif**.

EXPLORE

6. For every `h1` through `h6` heading, apply styles to: a) set the color to the HSL value of (**212, 0%, 0%**) with an opacity of **0.4**; b) set the font family to **Trebuchet MS**, **Helvetica**, and **sans-serif**; c) remove the boldface; and d) set the kerning and text indent to **5** pixels.

7. For h1 headings that are direct children of a `header` element that is a direct child of the `body` element, set the background color to the HSL value (**212, 100%, 29%**).

8. For an unordered list within the horizontal navigation list, apply styles to: a) display the text in **Century Gothic MS** or another **sans-serif** font; b) set the font size to **14** pixels; c) display the text in **bold**; d) set the kerning to **3** pixels and the line height to **20** pixels; and e) remove the markers from the list.

9. For hypertext links within the horizontal navigation list, set the text to the HSL value (**212, 100%, 70%**) and remove the underlining. When the mouse hovers over a hypertext link in this list, change the font color to the HSL value (**212, 100%, 29%**).

10. Set the background color of the vertical navigation list to the HSL value (**32, 100%, 95%**).

11. For the `h4` element within the vertical navigation list, create a style rule to: a) set the color to the HSL value (**32, 0%, 0%**) with an opacity of **0.5**; and b) set the font size to **18** pixels and the text indent to **15** pixels.

12. Display the ordered list items in the vertical navigation list in an outline style with uppercase Roman numerals for the top level, and uppercase alphabetic letters for the second level. Set the line height of the lists to **2em**.

EXPLORE

13. Set the color of the hypertext links in the vertical navigation list to the HSL value (**212, 100%, 29%**) with an opacity of **0.6**. Remove the underlining from the hypertext links. If the user hovers the mouse pointer over a link in the list, increase the opacity to **1.0** and display the underline.

14. Set the background color of the `section` element to the HSL value (**212, 95%, 90%**).

15. For the first paragraph after the `h2` heading within the `article` element, create a style rule to display the first letter with a font size of **32** pixels.

16. For the paragraph within the page footer, create a style rule that sets the font size to **10** pixels and the line height to **30** pixels and centers the text.

17. Save your changes to the style sheet.

18. Return to the **civilwar.htm** file in your text editor and link the file to the **cw_styles.css** style sheet.

19. Add style comments to document your work and then save your changes to the style sheet.

20. Open the **civilwar.htm** file in your Web browser. Verify that the style layout and design match that of the Web page shown in Figure 3-64. Verify that when you hover the mouse pointer over the links in the horizontal navigation list, the text changes color. Verify that when you hover the mouse pointer over the links in the vertical navigation list, the text color changes and the text is underlined.

21. Submit your completed project to your instructor, in either printed or electronic form, as requested.

Test your knowledge of CSS to design text and color styles for a children's choir Web site.

APPLY

Case Problem 4

Data Files needed for this Case Problem: chen.png, choirtxt.htm, gcc_layout.css, gcc_stylestxt.css, gcclogo.png, modernizr-1.5.js, nobile.txt, nobile-webfont.eot, nobile-webfont.svg, nobile-webfont.ttf, nobile-webfont.woff

Gresham Children's Choir Faye Dawson is the program director for Gresham Children's Choir in Mentor, Ohio. The choir offers a chance for talented youth to perform and to learn about music history. Faye is working on redesigning the choir's Web site and has asked for your help. She already has created a sample Web page for you to work on and has developed a page layout. She wants you to complete the design by creating styles for the text and colors in the page.

Complete the following:

1. Use your text editor to open the **choirtxt.htm** and **gcc_stylestxt.css** files from the tutorial.03\case4 folder. Add *your name* and *the date* in the comment section of each file. Save the files as **choir.htm** and **gcc_styles.css**, respectively.

2. Go to the **choir.htm** file in your text editor and link the file to the **gcc_layout.css** file. Take some time to study the content and structure of the document. Save your changes to the file and then view the current layout in your Web browser.

3. Go to the **gcc_styles.css** file and create a style sheet with style rules that:
   - modify the typeface, font weight, font size, kerning, and line height
   - employ a Web font
   - modify the appearance of list items
   - change the text and background color, including at least one example of a semi-transparent color
   - employ contextual selectors, pseudo-elements, and pseudo-classes
   - create rollover effects
   - employ progressive enhancement

   Document all of your work with informative style comments.

4. Add an embedded style sheet to the **choir.htm** file to apply a style rule of your own choosing to that page only.

5. Test your Web site in a variety of browsers to ensure your design works under different conditions.

6. Submit your completed files to your instructor, in either printed or electronic form, as requested.

ENDING DATA FILES

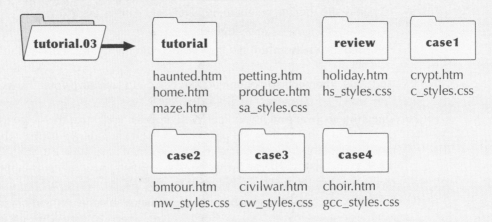

tutorial.03 → tutorial

haunted.htm   petting.htm
home.htm   produce.htm
maze.htm   sa_styles.css

review
holiday.htm
hs_styles.css

case1
crypt.htm
c_styles.css

case2
bmtour.htm
mw_styles.css

case3
civilwar.htm
cw_styles.css

case4
choir.htm
gcc_styles.css

TUTORIAL 4

Creating Page Layouts with CSS

Designing a Web Site for a Cycling Club

OBJECTIVES

Session 4.1
- Set display properties
- Create a reset style sheet
- Define a background image
- Set background image properties
- Use browser extension styles
- Explore fixed, fluid, and elastic layouts
- Float elements in a Web page

Session 4.2
- Set margin and padding spaces
- Format an element border
- Create rounded corners
- Display an element outline

Session 4.3
- Explore absolute and relative positioning
- Work with overflow content
- Explore clipped objects
- Stack objects in a page

Case | *Cycle Pathology*

Dan Atwood is a cyclist who lives and works in Grand Junction, Colorado. About 30 years ago, he and a few friends started a cycling group called *Cycle Pathology*. At the beginning, the group's activities consisted of weekend rides through the western Colorado countryside. However, with the growth in the popularity of cycling, the group has expanded to several hundred active members and now organizes rides and tours for much of western Colorado.

To keep current and potential members informed about future rides and events, Dan created the Cycle Pathology Web site in the late 1990s. With the growth of the group, he has decided to redesign the site and has asked you for help in planning a new layout and design.

STARTING DATA FILES

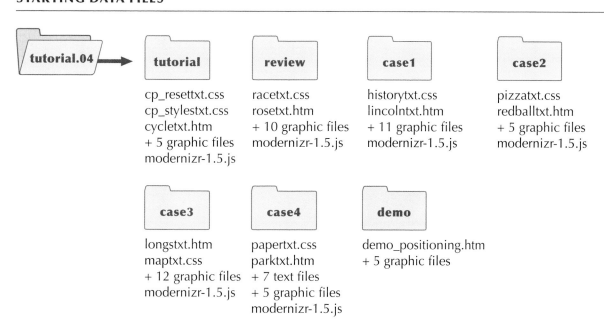

tutorial.04 →

tutorial
cp_resettxt.css
cp_stylestxt.css
cycletxt.htm
+ 5 graphic files
modernizr-1.5.js

review
racetxt.css
rosetxt.htm
+ 10 graphic files
modernizr-1.5.js

case1
historytxt.css
lincolntxt.htm
+ 11 graphic files
modernizr-1.5.js

case2
pizzatxt.css
redballtxt.htm
+ 5 graphic files
modernizr-1.5.js

case3
longstxt.htm
maptxt.css
+ 12 graphic files
modernizr-1.5.js

case4
papertxt.css
parktxt.htm
+ 7 text files
+ 5 graphic files
modernizr-1.5.js

demo
demo_positioning.htm
+ 5 graphic files

SESSION 4.1 VISUAL OVERVIEW

The **border box** contains the content and padding as well as the box border.

The **padding box** contains the space directly around the content but within the element box.

In the CSS box model, the **content box** contains the content of the element.

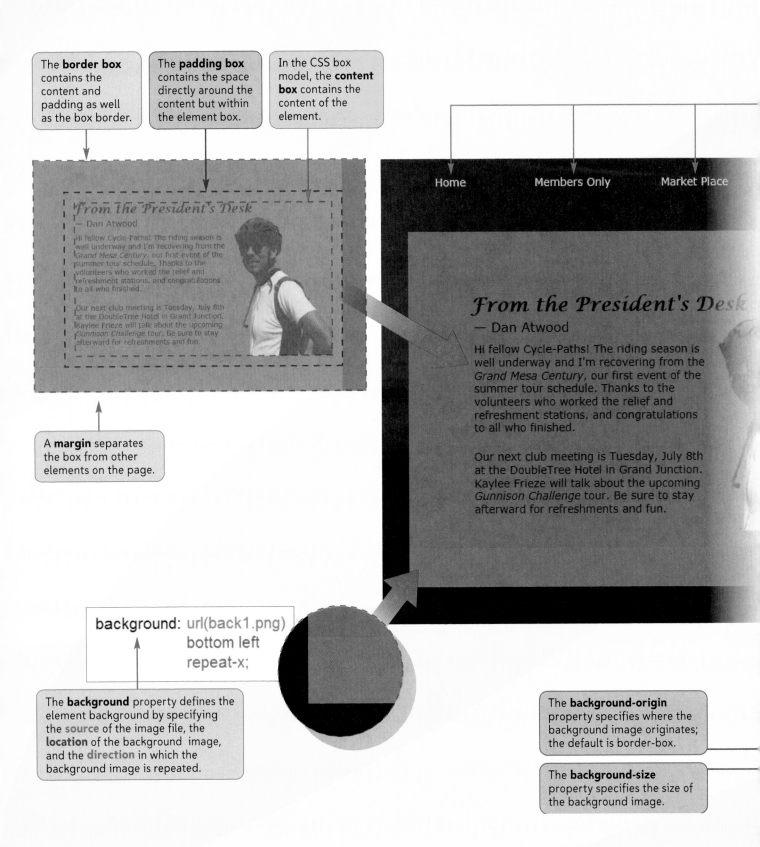

A **margin** separates the box from other elements on the page.

```
background: url(back1.png)
            bottom left
            repeat-x;
```

The **background** property defines the element background by specifying the **source** of the image file, the **location** of the background image, and the **direction** in which the background image is repeated.

The **background-origin** property specifies where the background image originates; the default is border-box.

The **background-size** property specifies the size of the background image.

Home   Members Only   Market Place

From the President's Desk
— Dan Atwood

Hi fellow Cycle-Paths! The riding season is well underway and I'm recovering from the *Grand Mesa Century*, our first event of the summer tour schedule. Thanks to the volunteers who worked the relief and refreshment stations, and congratulations to all who finished.

Our next club meeting is Tuesday, July 8th at the DoubleTree Hotel in Grand Junction. Kaylee Frieze will talk about the upcoming *Gunnison Challenge* tour. Be sure to stay afterward for refreshments and fun.

BACKGROUNDS AND FLOATING OBJECTS

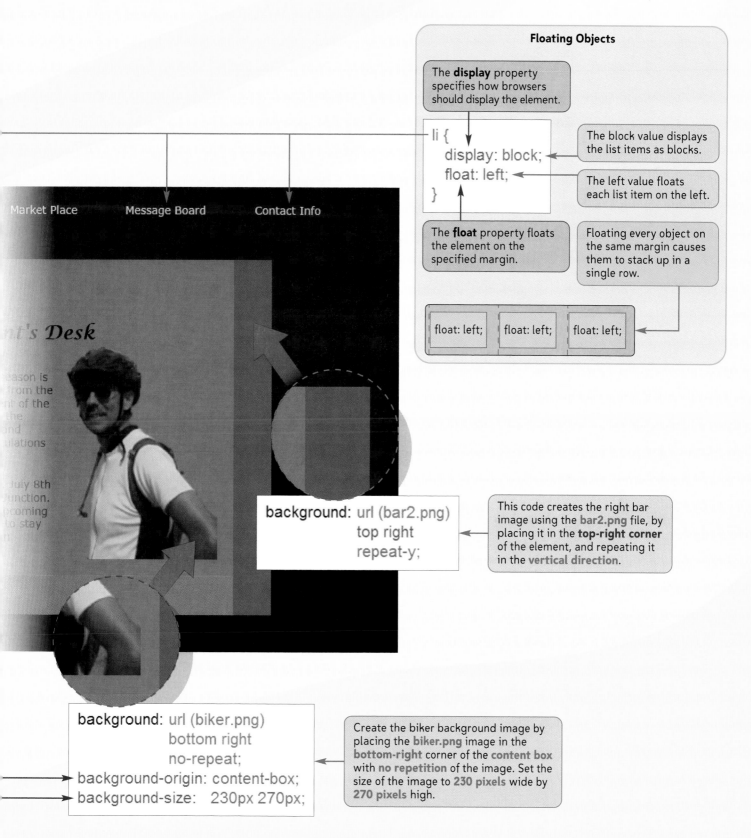

Floating Objects

The **display** property specifies how browsers should display the element.

```
li {
    display: block;
    float: left;
}
```

The block value displays the list items as blocks.

The left value floats each list item on the left.

The **float** property floats the element on the specified margin.

Floating every object on the same margin causes them to stack up in a single row.

| float: left; | float: left; | float: left; |

Market Place   Message Board   Contact Info

nt's Desk

background: url (bar2.png)
top right
repeat-y;

This code creates the right bar image using the **bar2.png** file, by placing it in the **top-right corner** of the element, and repeating it in the **vertical direction**.

background: url (biker.png)
bottom right
no-repeat;
background-origin: content-box;
background-size: 230px 270px;

Create the biker background image by placing the **biker.png** image in the **bottom-right** corner of the **content box** with **no repetition** of the image. Set the size of the image to **230 pixels** wide by **270 pixels** high.

Exploring Display Styles

You and Dan meet to discuss the redesign of the Cycle Pathology Web site. Dan already has created a sample Web page for you to work on. He's written all of the content for the sample page but has not done any design work, so the current appearance of the page relies on the default styles of whatever Web browser opens it. View Dan's sample page now.

To open the Cycle Pathology Web page:

1. Use your text editor to open the **cycletxt.htm** file from the tutorial.04/tutorial folder. Enter **your name** and **the date** in the comment section of the file, and then save it as **cycle.htm**.

2. Take some time to review the content and structure of the *cycle.htm* file in your text editor.

3. Open the **cycle.htm** file in your Web browser. Figure 4-1 shows the current appearance of part of the page using one browser's internal style sheet.

Figure 4-1	Part of the initial Cycle Pathology home page

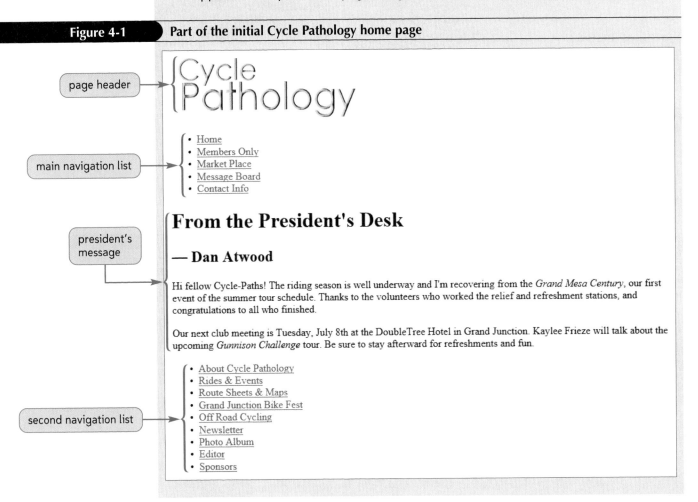

The Cycle Pathology Web page has the following main parts:

- the page header, including the Cycle Pathology logo
- a navigation list pointing to main topical areas on the site
- a section containing a message from the club president, Dan Atwood
- a second navigation list containing links to the club's newsletter, sponsored events, and other information
- a section containing an article by Kathy Rawlings about cycling in the Colorado National Monument and a figure box of a cyclist on Rim Rock Drive
- an aside describing upcoming tours and events
- a footer containing the Cycle Pathology address

Dan has sketched out how he would like each of these sections arranged in the page. His sketch is shown in Figure 4-2.

Figure 4-2   Cycle Pathology layout design

Dan wants the first navigation list placed in a horizontal bar at the top of the page, and the second list moved to a vertical column at the page's right margin. The president's message should appear in a rounded box at the top of the page, with Kathy Rawlings' article set below it and the image of Rim Rock Drive placed to the right. The sidebar describing upcoming club events should be moved to the page's lower-left corner, and the footer should be placed at the bottom of the page. Dan also wants to add images of himself, Kathy Rawlings, and another cyclist in the background of different sections of the page.

To create this type of layout, you'll need to work with the display properties of the different page elements. You'll start by learning how browsers arrange different types of elements, and how you can use CSS to change those default display styles.

The `display` style

Most page elements are displayed in one of two ways. **Blocks**, such as paragraphs or block quotes, occupy a defined rectangular area within a page. **Inline elements**, on the other hand, such as a sentence within a paragraph or a citation within a block quote, flow within a block. The browser market is pretty consistent in what is treated as a block and what is treated as an inline element. But if you need to, you can specify the display type using the style property

```
display: type;
```

where *type* is a display type like those shown in Figure 4-3.

Figure 4-3   **Values of the display property**

Display Value	Effect On Element
block	Displayed as a block
inline	Displayed in line within a block
inline-block	Treated as a block placed in line within another block
run-in	Displayed as a block unless its next sibling is also a block, in which it is displayed in line, essentially combining the two blocks into one
inherit	Inherits the display property of the parent element
list-item	Displayed as a list item along with a bullet marker
none	Prevented from displaying, removing it from the page structure

For example, most browsers display a citation in line within a block. But you can place a citation in its own block using the following style rule:

```
cite {
    display: block;
}
```

On the other hand, the style rule

```
blockquote {
    display: list-item;
}
```

would cause a browser to display all block quotes as items from a list, complete with bullet markers. You even can prevent browsers from displaying an element by setting its `display` property to `none`. In that case, the element is still part of the document structure but is not shown to users. This is useful for elements that include content that users shouldn't see or have no need to see.

The Box Model

Elements also are laid out in a Web page following the structure of the **box model**, shown in Figure 4-4, which is composed of the following series of concentric boxes:

- the content of the element itself
- the padding extending between the element's content and the border
- the border of the box surrounding the padding space
- the margin containing the space between the border and the next page element

Figure 4-4 The CSS box model

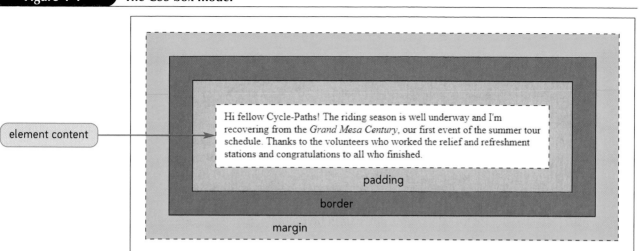

The size and appearance of these four sections control how an element is displayed by browsers and play an important role in determining page layout. Each browser's internal style sheet sets the size of the margin, border, and padding spaces, and those sizes differ between one page element and another. You already may have noticed that major headings, such as `h1` headings, often are offset from their surrounding content by a large external margin. As you'll learn later, CSS supports styles for modifying the margin, border, and padding space, allowing you to override the browser defaults.

Creating a Reset Style Sheet

Because the internal style sheets of various browsers have small—and sometimes not-so-small—differences, many designers create a **reset style sheet** to define their own default styles. Resetting the styles allows the designer to start from a known baseline, confident that no unwanted styles will creep in from any browser's internal style sheet.

You'll create a reset style sheet for the Cycle Pathology Web site. You'll start by adding a style rule that defines all HTML5 structural elements as block elements. This is necessary because currently Internet Explorer, unlike the other major browsers, does not define structural elements as block elements. Without a rule setting the `display` properties of all these elements to `block`, your choices for formatting those elements under Internet Explorer would be more limited.

To create the reset style sheet:

1. Use your text editor to open the **cp_resettxt.css** file from the tutorial.04/tutorial folder. Enter *your name* and *the date* in the comment section of the file and then save it as **cp_reset.css**.

2. Below the comment section, add the following comment and style rule:

```
/* Display HTML5 structural elements as blocks */

article, aside, figure, figcaption, footer, hgroup, header,
section, nav {
   display: block;
}
```

3. Save your changes to the file.

Next, you'll define some default styles for all of your page body elements. Your initial style rule will be as follows:

```
body * {
    font-family: Verdana, Geneva, sans-serif;
    font-size: 100%;
    font-weight: inherit;
    line-height: 1.2em;
    list-style: none;
    vertical-align: baseline;
}
```

Note that this style rule uses an asterisk selector (*) to apply the styles to every element nested within the `body` element. Thus, the text of every element will be displayed by default in a Verdana, Geneva, or sans-serif font at the default font size of 100%. The weight of each element will be inherited from its parent. Finally, the default line height will be set to 1.2 em units, there will be no bullet markers, and each element's text will be vertically aligned with the baseline. When you start formatting individual elements, you will override some of these default styles; but for now they'll establish a foundation for your future work.

To set the default styles for the Web site:

▶ **1.** Below the style rule you just created in the **cp_reset.css** file, enter the following rule:

```
/* Set the default page element styles */

body * {
    font-family: Verdana, Geneva, sans-serif;
    font-size: 100%;
    font-weight: inherit;
    line-height: 1.2em;
    list-style: none;
    vertical-align: baseline;
}
```

▶ **2.** Save your changes to the file.

Finally, as you lay out the Cycle Pathology home page, you'll format the main sections of the page one at a time. Rather than the page being cluttered with those sections that you haven't formatted yet, you'll temporarily hide each section. You'll do this by setting the initial `display` property for each section to `none`, and then re-displaying only the sections that you're ready to work on. Recall that the sections in the Cycle Pathology home page are the navigation lists (with class names of *horizontalNAV* and *verticalNAV*), the president's message (with an id value of *president*), another section containing an article and a figure about cycling on Rim Rock Drive (with the id value of *story*), a page header, a sidebar note about upcoming events, and finally the page footer. You'll add a style rule to the reset style sheet to initially hide all of these sections.

To hide the different sections of the page:

1. At the bottom of the **cp_reset.css** style sheet, enter the following style rule:

```
/* Temporarily hide the page sections */

nav.horizontalNAV, #president, nav.verticalNAV,
#story, header, aside, footer {
    display: none;
}
```

Figure 4-5 shows the complete *cp_reset.css* style sheet.

Figure 4-5   Initial reset style sheet

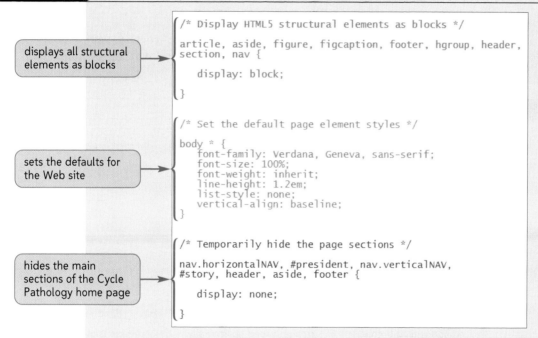

displays all structural elements as blocks

sets the defaults for the Web site

hides the main sections of the Cycle Pathology home page

```
/* Display HTML5 structural elements as blocks */
article, aside, figure, figcaption, footer, hgroup, header,
section, nav {
    display: block;
}

/* Set the default page element styles */
body * {
    font-family: Verdana, Geneva, sans-serif;
    font-size: 100%;
    font-weight: inherit;
    line-height: 1.2em;
    list-style: none;
    vertical-align: baseline;
}

/* Temporarily hide the page sections */
nav.horizontalNAV, #president, nav.verticalNAV,
#story, header, aside, footer {
    display: none;
}
```

2. Save your changes to the file and then return to the **cycle.htm** file in your text editor.

3. Directly above the closing `</head>` tag, insert the following link to the reset style sheet:

```
<link href="cp_reset.css" rel="stylesheet" />
```

4. Save your changes to the file and then reload the **cycle.htm** file in your Web browser. Verify that no content is displayed in the browser window.

With the browser window now clear, you are ready to design. You'll start by working on the background for the page.

TIP

You also can hide objects using the `visibility: hidden;` property, which hides the element content but leaves the element still occupying the same space in the page.

Designing the Background

In the last tutorial, you learned how to set the background color using the `background-color` property. CSS also supports background images using

```
background-image: url(url);
```

where *url* defines the name and location of the background image file. Background images can be added to almost any page element. For example, the style rule

```
body {
    background-image: url(cyclist.png);
}
```

displays the image file *cyclist.png* in the background of the Web page body.

Background Image Options

When a browser loads a background image, it repeats the image in both the vertical and horizontal directions until the entire background is filled. This process is known as **tiling** because of its similarity to the process of filling up a floor or other surface with tiles. You can specify the direction of tiling using the style

```
background-repeat: type;
```

where *type* is repeat (the default), repeat-x, repeat-y, no-repeat, round, or space. Figure 4-6 describes each of the repeat types. At the time of this writing, the round and space options are not well supported by current browsers.

Figure 4-6 **background-repeat property**

background-repeat: repeat;
image is tiled both horizontally and vertically

background-repeat: repeat-x;
image is tiled horizontally

background-repeat: repeat-y;
image is tiled vertically

background-repeat: no-repeat;
image is not tiled

background-repeat: round;
background image is tiled and resized to fit in the container a whole number of times

background-repeat: space;
background image is tiled and spaces added to fit in the container a whole number of times

TIP

You can use negative distances to move an image to the left or up from the top-left corner of an element.

By default, browsers place the background image in the element's upper-left corner; and then if the code specifies tiling, the image is repeated from there. You can change the initial position of a background image using the property

```
background-position: horizontal vertical;
```

where *horizontal* is the horizontal position of the image and *vertical* is its vertical position. The image's position is defined by: a) the distance from the top-left corner of the element using one of the CSS units of length, b) the distance from the top-left corner using a percentage of the element's width or height, or c) a keyword. Keyword options are `top`, `center`, or `bottom` for vertical position, and `left`, `center`, or `right` for horizontal placement. For example,

```
background-position: 10% 20%;
```

sets the initial position of the image 10% of the width to the right and 20% of the length down from the upper-left corner of the element, while

```
background-position: right bottom;
```

places the background image at the lower-right corner of the element. If you include only one position value, browsers apply that value to the horizontal position and vertically center the image. Thus, the style

```
background-position: 30px;
```

places the background image 30 pixels to the right of the element's left border and centers it vertically.

By default, a background image moves along with the element content as a user scrolls through the page. You can change this using the property

```
background-attachment: type;
```

where *type* is `scroll`, `fixed`, or `local`. The default, `scroll`, scrolls the background along with the document, while the `fixed` keyword fixes the background in the browser window, even as the user scrolls through the document. A fixed background image can be used to create a **watermark** effect, in which a subtle, often translucent graphic is displayed behind elements to mimic the watermarks found on some specialized stationery. Finally, the `local` keyword is similar to `scroll` but is used for elements such as scroll boxes to allow the element background to scroll along with the element content.

CSS3 Background Styles

CSS3 introduces several style properties for background images, most of which have now gained popular acceptance among current browsers. The first is the `background-size` property, which sets the size of an element's background image. This property has the syntax

```
background-size: width height;
```

where *width* and *height* are the width and height of the image in one of the CSS units of length or as a percentage of the element's width and height, or the keywords `auto`, `cover`, or `contain`. For example, the following style sets the size of the background image to 300 pixels wide by 200 pixels high:

```
background-size: 300px 200px;
```

The `auto` keyword allows the browser to set the background image automatically based on the size of the image in the image file. The style

```
background-size: auto 200px;
```

sets the height of the background image to 200 pixels and automatically sets the width to retain the image proportions.

The `cover` keyword tells browsers to scale the image in order to cover all of the background while still retaining the proportions of the image, even if that means cropping the image. The `contain` keyword, on the other hand, tells browsers to scale the image so that all of the image is completely contained within the element, even if that means that not all of the element is covered by the image. Figure 4-7 provides examples of a background image scaled to a specific size, and scaled using the `cover` and `contain` keywords.

Figure 4-7   **background-size property**

background-size: 300px 200px;

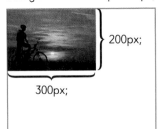

200px;

300px;

the image is displayed at a specific size

background-size: cover;

the image is scaled until it covers the entire element, but part of the image is cropped

background-size: contain;

the image is scaled so that the entire image is contained within the element, but part of the element remains uncovered

Vaclav Volrab/Shutterstock.com

Thus, to create a background image that is half the width and height of the containing element, centered vertically and horizontally, and not tiled, you could apply the following styles:

```
background-position: center center;
background-repeat: no-repeat;
background-size: 50% 50%;
```

In the box model discussed earlier, every element contains a content box, a padding box, and a border box. You can define the extent of a background image or color using the style

```
background-clip: box;
```

where *box* is `content-box`, `padding-box`, or `border-box` (the default). As shown in Figure 4-8, the keyword you choose controls whether the background image or color is clipped at the edge of the content or the edge of the padding, or runs all the way to the edge of the element border.

Figure 4-8 **background-clip property**

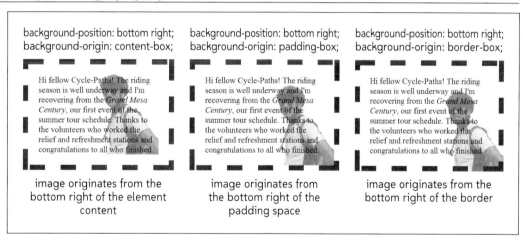

background-clip: content-box;   background-clip: padding-box;   background-clip: border-box;

Hi fellow Cycle-Paths! The riding season is well underway and I'm recovering from the *Grand Mesa Century*, our first event of the summer tour schedule. Thanks to the volunteers who worked the relief and refreshment stations and congratulations to all who finished.

background is clipped at the edge of the content   background is clipped at the edge of the padding space   background is clipped at the edge of the border

Finally, you can specify the context of the `background-position` property using

`background-origin: box;`

where *box* is once again `content-box`, `padding-box` (the default), or `border-box`. The `background-origin` property defines whether `background-position` values refer to the content box, the padding box, or the border box. Figure 4-9 shows the effect of different `background-origin` values on the location of the bottom-right position.

Figure 4-9 **background-origin property**

background-position: bottom right;   background-position: bottom right;   background-position: bottom right;
background-origin: content-box;   background-origin: padding-box;   background-origin: border-box;

Hi fellow Cycle-Paths! The riding season is well underway and I'm recovering from the *Grand Mesa Century*, our first event of the summer tour schedule. Thanks to the volunteers who worked the relief and refreshment stations and congratulations to all who finished.

image originates from the bottom right of the element content   image originates from the bottom right of the padding space   image originates from the bottom right of the border

The `background` Shorthand Property

Like the `font` property discussed in the last tutorial, you can combine the various `background` properties into the shorthand property

`background: color url(url) attachment position repeat;`

where *color*, *url*, *attachment*, *position*, and *repeat* are values corresponding to the `background-color`, `background-image`, `background-attachment`, `background-position`, and `background-repeat` style properties, respectively. If you don't specify all of the values in the shorthand property, browsers assume default values for the missing properties. The style

`background: yellow url(logo.png) fixed center center no-repeat;`

creates a yellow background on which the image file *logo.png* is displayed. The image file is not tiled across the background, but is instead fixed in the horizontal and vertical center.

CSS3 provides an expanded form of the `background` property that includes values for image size, origin, and the location of the clipping box

```
background: color url(url) position / size repeat attachment box box;
```

where *size* and *box box* are values corresponding to `background-size`, `background-origin`, and `background-clip` properties, respectively. If only one *box* value is present, browsers set both the `background-origin` and `background-clip` properties to that value. At the moment, few browsers support the expanded form; therefore, you only should use the brief form and set the size, origin, and clipping box values separately.

Multiple Image Backgrounds

There is no reason to limit your background to a single image. CSS allows you to specify multiple images and their properties in a comma-separated list. The general syntax is

```
background-property: value1, value2, … ;
```

where `background-property` is one of the CSS background image properties and `value1`, `value2`, etc. are values for each image associated with that property. For example, the following style rule creates two background images for the `header` element; one is located in the top-left corner, the other is located in the bottom-right corner, and both are superimposed on a yellow background:

```
header {
    background-color: yellow;
    background-image: url(logo.png), url(logo2.png);
    background-position: top left, bottom right;
    background-repeat: no-repeat;
}
```

Notice that if a value is listed just once, it is applied to all images in the list. Thus, neither the *logo.png* image nor the *logo2.png* image is tiled in the example above. Multiple backgrounds also can be applied using the `background` shorthand property as follows:

```
header {
    background: url(logo.png) top left no-repeat,
                url(logo2.png) bottom right no-repeat yellow;
}
```

When browsers render an element with multiple backgrounds, the images that are listed last are the first ones loaded. If images overlap, the first images listed appear on top of subsequent images.

REFERENCE

Formatting the Background

- To display a background image, use

  ```
  background-image: url(url);
  ```

  where *url* is the filename and location of the image file.
- To set how a background image repeats, use

  ```
  background-repeat: type;
  ```

  where *type* is repeat, no-repeat, repeat-x, repeat-y, round, or space.
- To set the position of a background image, use

  ```
  background-position: horizontal vertical;
  ```

  where *horizontal* is the horizontal position of the image and *vertical* is its vertical position.
- To set the attachment of an image to the background, use

  ```
  background-attachment: type;
  ```

  where *type* is scroll, fixed, or local.
- To set the size of a background image, use

  ```
  background-size: width height;
  ```

  where width and height are the width and height of the image in one of the CSS units of length or as a percentage of the element's width and height, or the keywords auto, cover, or contain.
- To clip a background, use

  ```
  background-clip: box;
  ```

  where *box* is content-box, padding-box, or border-box (the default).
- To specify the origin of a background image, use

  ```
  background-origin: box;
  ```

  where *box* is content-box, padding-box (the default), or border-box.

Adding a Page Background

You're now ready to create a background for the Cycle Pathology home page. Dan has a graphic image of a cyclist standing before a sunset. He wants you to place this image in the top-left corner of the page body against a black background. He does not want you to tile the image.

You'll place a style rule for the page background in a new style sheet file that you'll create now.

To format the page background:

1. Open the **cp_stylestxt.css** file in your text editor. Type **your name** and **the date** in the comment section at the top of the file, and then save the file as **cp_styles.css**.

2. Below the comment section, insert the following style rule (see Figure 4-10):

   ```
   /* Styles for the Page Body */
   body {
       background: black url(bike_bg.png) top left no-repeat;
   }
   ```

Figure 4-10   Defining the background for the Cycle Pathology home page

```
/* Styles for the Page Body */

body {
    background: black url(bike_bg.png) top left no-repeat;
}
```

3. Save your changes to the file and then return to the **cycle.htm** file in your text editor.

4. Directly below the `link` element for the *cp_reset.css* style sheet, insert the following:

   ```
   <link href="cp_styles.css" rel="stylesheet" />
   ```

5. Save your changes to the file and then reload the **cycle.htm** file in your Web browser. As shown in Figure 4-11, the page now displays the image of a cyclist silhouetted against the sunset on a black background.

Figure 4-11   Cycle Pathology home page background

Vaclav Volrab/Shutterstock.com

Exploring Browser Extensions

Some of the background styles you just examined were added to the CSS3 specifications in the last few years. Before that, many of them were extensions to CSS developed and supported by a few browser vendors. Browser extensions that are not part of the official CSS specifications can be identified through the use of a **vendor prefix** that indicates the browser vendor that created and supports the property. Figure 4-12 lists the browser extensions you'll encounter in your work on Web design.

Figure 4-12   **Browser-specific extensions to CSS**

Vendor Prefix	Rendering Engine	Browsers
-khtml-	KHTML	Konqueror
-moz-	Mozilla	Firefox, Camino
-ms-	Trident	Internet Explorer
-o-	Presto	Opera, Nintendo Wii browser
-webkit-	WebKit	Android browser, Chrome, Safari

Older browser versions might not support the current CSS specifications, but might support one of the browser extensions. In order to support the widest range of browsers and browser versions, you should employ progressive enhancement with the most widely supported CSS2 property—if one exists—listed first, followed by the browser extensions, and then the latest CSS3 property. As you encounter this situation in this and future tutorials, you'll use the following structure:

```
selector {
    css2_property: value;
    -khtml-property: value;
    -o-property: value;
    -moz-property: value;
    -webkit-property: value;
    -ms-property: value;
    css3_property: value;
}
```

As always, the last property listed and recognized by the browser will be the one applied to the Web page; thus, you always should start with the oldest and most basic standard and finish with the most current. For example, several browsers have their own extensions to specify the origin of a background image and to ensure the widest possible support for this feature, you would apply the following style properties to the selector:

```
-o-background-origin: padding-box;
-moz-background-origin: padding;
-webkit-background-origin: padding-box;
background-origin: padding-box;
```

Notice that the background origin values differ among browser extensions. With the Mozilla rendering engine, you set the origin of the background image to the padding box by using the keyword `padding`; while the Presto and WebKit extensions employ the same `padding-box` keyword that was later adopted into the CSS3 specifications.

WebKit, Mozilla, and Presto support similar extensions that mirror the CSS3 `background-size` and `background-clip` properties. At this point you don't have a need for these browser extensions, but you will use them later in the tutorial.

Exploring Layout Designs

One challenge of Web page layout is that your document will be viewed on many different devices with different screen resolutions. As shown in Figure 4-13, the most common screen resolution at the time of this writing is 1024 × 768, though the majority of user devices are displaying the Web at even higher resolutions than that.

Figure 4-13 **Screen resolutions on the Web**

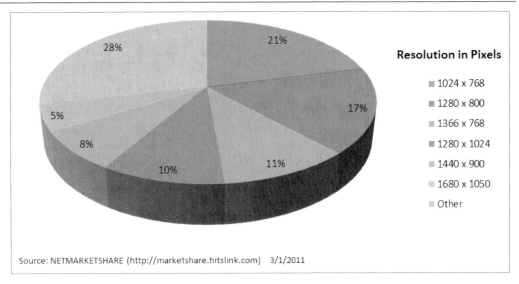

Source: NETMARKETSHARE (http://marketshare.hitslink.com)   3/1/2011

In page design, you're usually more concerned about the available page width than the total screen resolution. Users can scroll vertically down the length of a Web page, but it's considered bad design to make them scroll horizontally. Figure 4-14 breaks down current data on screen resolution in terms of page width.

Figure 4-14 **Screen widths on the Web**

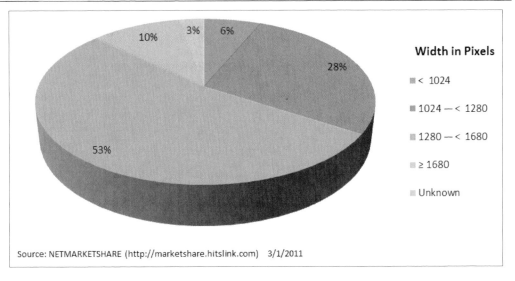

Source: NETMARKETSHARE (http://marketshare.hitslink.com)   3/1/2011

Roughly 63% of users view the Web at a screen width of 1280 pixels or more. On the other end of the scale, about 6% of users have their screens set at less than 1024 pixels. Complicating matters is that as more users access the Web through small mobile devices, some users will require page layouts that work with smaller screen widths. Finally, while screen widths represent the maximum space available to users, some space is also taken up with toolbars, sidebar panes, and other browser features. In addition, a user might not even have his or her browser window maximized to fill up the entire screen. Thus, you need a layout strategy to accommodate all of these possible screen and browser window configurations.

Fixed, Fluid, and Elastic Layouts

Web page layouts fall into three general categories: fixed, fluid, and elastic. A **fixed layout** is one in which the size of the Web page and the size of the elements within it are set without regard to the screen resolution. A **fluid** or **liquid layout** defines the size of the page and its elements as a percentage of the screen width, meaning that a Web page and its elements are wider on a wider screen (see Figure 4-15).

Figure 4-15   **Fixed and fluid layouts**

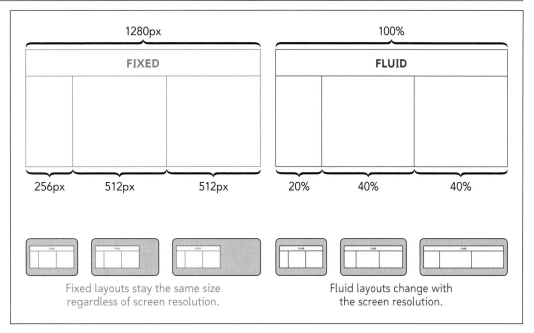

The advantages and disadvantages of the fixed and fluid approaches are laid out in Figure 4-16. In general, fixed layouts are easier to set up and maintain, but they're less pleasing to the eye when viewed on wider screens. A fluid layout may be more difficult to set up initially, but it's more adaptable to a market in which users access the Web from a variety of devices and screen resolutions.

| Figure 4-16 | Comparing fixed and fluid layouts |

Fixed Layout	Fluid Layout
Pros	Pros
✓ Easier to use and maintain	✓ Easier for the user since it adapts to his or her screen resolution
✓ Works better with fixed-size objects such as images and embedded video clips	✓ All available screen space is used, allowing for more content on larger monitors
✓ Unless the user's screen is extremely wide, the page will still be readable	✓ Responds well to user-defined font sizes
✓ Can be used with more complicated page layouts	✓ Maintains a consistent look across different screen resolutions
Cons	Cons
✗ Can create excessive white space under higher resolutions	✗ Testing is more involved as the designer must confirm the layout works under a variety of resolutions
✗ Doesn't react well to user-defined font sizes	✗ May result in overly wide lines of text, making the page difficult to read
✗ Users with small screens may be forced to scroll horizontally to view all page content	✗ Less adaptable to more complicated page layouts
✗ Layout is less pleasing to the eye under higher screen resolutions	✗ Difficult to work with fixed-size objects such as images and video clips

TIP

If you're new to Web page design, try formatting the initial draft of your page using a fixed layout. Then, once you have a workable page design, you can change it to a fluid or an elastic design.

Many designers use a combination of fixed and fluid page elements, enabling them to have the best of both worlds. Another approach is to use a script that queries each browser about its screen resolution and then adapts the page to that resolution. Finally, some designers propose the use of **elastic layouts**, in which all measurements are expressed relative to the default font size using the em unit. If a user or the designer increases the font size, the width, height, and location of all of the other page elements, including images, change to match. Thus, images and text are always sized in proportion with each other. The disadvantage to this approach is that since sizing is based on the font size and not on the screen resolution, there is a danger that if a user sets the default font size large enough, the page will extend beyond the boundaries of the browser window.

Setting the Page Width and Height

Element widths and heights are set using the style properties

```
width: value;
height: value;
```

where `value` is the width or height using one of the CSS units of measurement or as a percentage of the width or height of the containing element. The width and height measures only apply to the element content, not to the padding space, borders, or margins around the element. Usually you do not set the height value because browsers automatically increase the height of an element to match its content.

Although you don't specify an exact width for fluid or elastic layouts, you might want to provide limits on how narrow or wide an element can extend. If an element is very wide, its lines of text might become too long to be easily readable; likewise, if it is too narrow, its text also can be difficult to read. Rather than allowing these problems to occur, you can specify a minimum or maximum height or width for an element using the style properties

```
min-width: value;
min-height: value;
max-width: value;
max-height: value;
```

where *value* is once again a length expressed in one of the CSS units of measure. For example, the style rule

```
body {
    width: 95%;
    min-width: 1000px;
    max-width: 1400px;
}
```

sets the width of the page body to 95% of the width of the browser window, and also limits the width to a range of 1000 to 1400 pixels. No matter the screen resolution, the page body width will never go below 1000 pixels or above 1400 pixels. After discussing the page layout issue with Dan, you both agree to develop the Cycle Pathology home page as a fluid layout starting with this particular style rule. You'll add it now to the *cp_styles.css* style sheet file.

To set the page width:

1. Return to the **cp_styles.css** style sheet in your text editor.

2. Within the style rule for the body element, insert the following properties, as shown in Figure 4-17:

```
width: 95%;
min-width: 1000px;
max-width: 1400px;
```

TIP

Keep your style sheets organized by placing style rules that relate to the same section near one another in the document.

Figure 4-17 **Setting the page width**

width of Web page body is 95% of the width of the browser window

width is constrained to the range 1000 pixels to 1400 pixels

```
body {
    background: black url(bike_bg.png) top left no-repeat;
    width: 95%;
    min-width: 1000px;
    max-width: 1400px;
}
```

3. Save your changes to the file.

PROSKILLS

Written Communication: Getting to the Point with Layout

Page layout is one of the most important aspects of Web design. A well-constructed page layout naturally guides a reader's eyes to the most important information in the page. Use the following principles to help your readers quickly get to the point:

- *Guide the eye.* Usability studies have shown that a reader's eye first lands in the top center of the page, then scans to the left, and then to the right and down. Arrange your page content so that the most important items are the first items a user sees.
- *Avoid clutter.* If a graphic or an icon is not conveying information or making the content easier to read, remove it.
- *Avoid overcrowding.* Focus on a few key items that will be easy for readers to locate while scanning the page, and separate these key areas from one another with ample white space. Don't be afraid to move a topic to a different page if it makes the current page easier to scan.
- *Make your information manageable.* It's easier for the brain to process information when it's presented in smaller chunks. Break up long extended paragraphs into smaller paragraphs or bulleted lists.
- *Use a grid.* Users find it easier to scan content when page elements are aligned vertically and horizontally. Use a grid to help you line up your elements in a clear and consistent way.
- *Cut down on the noise.* If you're thinking about using blinking text or a cute animated icon, *don't*. The novelty of such features wears off very quickly and distracts users from the valuable content in your page.

Always remember that your goal is to convey information to readers, and that an important tool in achieving that is to make it as easy as possible for readers to find that information. A thoughtfully constructed layout is a great aid to effective communication.

Floating Elements

The first content you'll display in the Cycle Pathology home page is the navigation list for the main topical areas of the site. Lists are displayed vertically by default, but Dan wants this one displayed horizontally. One way to accomplish this is by floating each list item.

Setting a Float

Floating an element takes that element out of the normal flow of the document and positions it along the left or right edge of its containing element. Subsequent elements that are not floated are then moved up to occupy the position previously occupied by the floating element. Figure 4-18 shows a diagram of an element that is floated along the right margin of the page body.

Figure 4-18   **Floating an element**

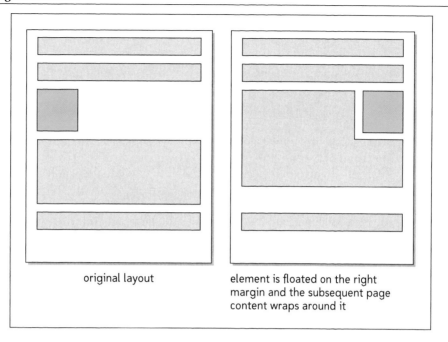

original layout

element is floated on the right margin and the subsequent page content wraps around it

To float an element, you apply the style property

```
float: position;
```

where *position* is none (the default), left, or right. If sibling elements are floated in the same direction, they stack up, creating a row of elements each aligned with the margin of the previous element (see Figure 4-19).

Figure 4-19   **Floating multiple elements in a row**

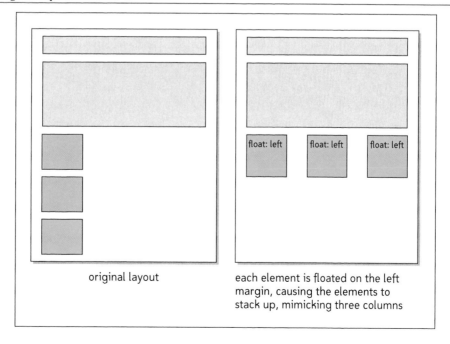

original layout

each element is floated on the left margin, causing the elements to stack up, mimicking three columns

This is the effect you want for your navigation list. To float the items in that list, you'll apply the following style rule:

```
nav.horizontalNAV li {
    font-size: 87.5%;
    float: left;
    text-align: center;
    width: 20%;
}
```

TIP

If there is not enough room in a container for all of the floating elements, they automatically wrap to the next line in the page.

Besides floating each list item, this style rule also reduces the text to 87.5% of the default size, centers the text of the hyperlinks within each item, and sets the width of each of the five list items to 20% of the total width of the nav element. Because by default the width of the nav element is equal to the width of the page body, the five links will be equally spaced across the browser window.

You'll also need to format the text of the hypertext links so that they are visible against the black background. To do this, you'll use the following style rules:

```
nav a {
    text-decoration: none;
}
nav.horizontalNAV a {
    color: rgb(255, 255, 99);
}
nav.horizontalNAV a:hover {
    color: white;
}
```

The first rule removes underlining from all hypertext links within any navigation list. The next two rules set the color of the links in navigation lists that are part of the horizontalNAV class to yellow except when a user hovers the mouse pointer over a link, in which case the link color turns to white. You'll add these style rules to your style sheet with the appropriate comments.

To format the navigation list:

▶ 1. Return to the **cp_styles.css** style sheet in your text editor.

▶ 2. Below the style rule for the body selector, add the following code, as shown in Figure 4-20:

```
/* General Navigation List Style */

nav a {
    text-decoration: none;
}

/* Horizontal Navigation List */

nav.horizontalNAV li {
    font-size: 87.5%;
    float: left;
    text-align: center;
    width: 20%;
}
```

```
nav.horizontalNAV li a {
    color: rgb(255, 255, 99);
}

nav.horizontalNAV li a:hover {
    color: white;
}
```

Figure 4-20	Styling the horizontal navigation list

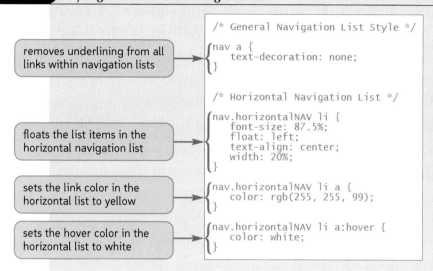

removes underlining from all links within navigation lists →

```
/* General Navigation List Style */

nav a {
    text-decoration: none;
}

/* Horizontal Navigation List */

nav.horizontalNAV li {
    font-size: 87.5%;
    float: left;
    text-align: center;
    width: 20%;
}

nav.horizontalNAV li a {
    color: rgb(255, 255, 99);
}

nav.horizontalNAV li a:hover {
    color: white;
}
```

floats the list items in the horizontal navigation list →

sets the link color in the horizontal list to yellow →

sets the hover color in the horizontal list to white →

3. Save your changes to the file.

Next, you'll change the reset style sheet rules so that the horizontal navigation list is once again displayed.

4. Return to the **cp_reset.css** style sheet in your text editor and then scroll down to the style rule at the bottom of the page. Remove the selector `nav.horizontalNAV` along with the comma separator that follows it from the start of the selector list.

5. Save your changes to the reset style sheet and then reload **cycle.htm** in your Web browser. As shown in Figure 4-21, the hypertext links are now rendered in a single row across the top of the page.

6. Verify that the color of each link changes to white in response to the hover event.

Figure 4-21	Horizontal navigation list

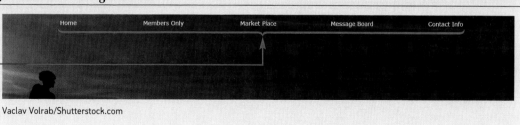

each list item is floated left, creating a row of items

Vaclav Volrab/Shutterstock.com

Floating Elements and the Great Collapse

By default, elements are rendered in the page based on the element hierarchy in the HTML file. For example, a child element is positioned within its parent element in the Web page. However, this does not happen when you float an object; instead, the floated element is untethered from its parent element.

This can lead to some surprising results. For example, a parent element with all of its child elements floated has no content in the rendered page and collapses down to an empty element with zero height. If you're counting on using a parent element to set the background color for all of its floating children, you're out of luck unless you explicitly define a height for the parent that's large enough to provide a background for all of its child elements.

Clearing a Float

Sometimes you'll want to prevent an object from wrapping around a floating element; or in the case of a row of floats, you'll want to ensure that the following element appears after the row is completed. To place an element below a float, you use the style

```
clear: position;
```

where *position* is none (the default), left, right, or both (to ensure that both margins are clear of floating elements). For example, the style

```
clear: right;
```

causes an element not to be displayed until the right margin is clear of floating objects. See Figure 4-22.

Figure 4-22   **Clearing a float**

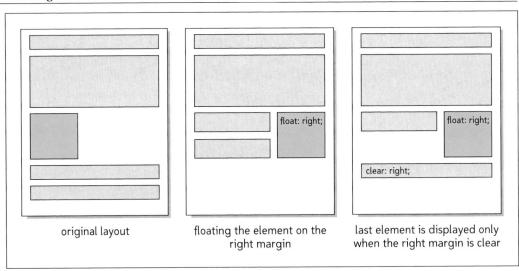

| original layout | floating the element on the right margin | last element is displayed only when the right margin is clear |

REFERENCE

Floating an Element

- To float an element, use the style property

```
float: position;
```

where *position* is none (the default), left, or right.
- To display an element clear of floating elements, use

```
clear: position;
```

where *position* is none (the default), left, right, or both.

The next item you want to add to Dan's Web page is the president's message article. Because that article appears below the horizontal navigation list, you'll use the clear property to ensure that it's displayed only when the left margin is clear of floated objects. Dan also wants to stack this item alongside the second navigation list, so you'll float the president's message article on the left margin even as you clear it from the first navigation list. You'll add the following rule to your style sheet:

```
#president {
    background-color: rgb(105, 96, 87);
    background-color: rgba(255, 255, 255, 0.3);
    clear: left;
    float: left;
    width: 40%;
}
```

The style rule uses progressive enhancement to set the background color either to medium gray or to white with 30% opacity. The rule also sets the width of the article to 40% of the width of the page body.

To format the navigation list:

1. Return to the **cp_styles.css** style sheet in your text editor, and then at the bottom of the style sheet, insert the following rule (see Figure 4-23):

```
/* President's message */

#president {
    background-color: rgb(105, 96, 87);
    background-color: rgba(255, 255, 255, 0.3);
    clear: left;
    float: left;
    width: 40%;
}
```

Figure 4-23 ▸ **Styling the president's message**

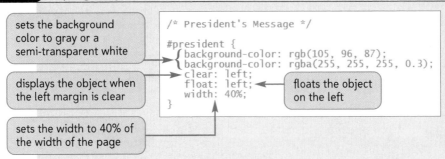

sets the background color to gray or a semi-transparent white

```
/* President's Message */

#president {
    background-color: rgb(105, 96, 87);
    background-color: rgba(255, 255, 255, 0.3);
    clear: left;
    float: left;
    width: 40%;
}
```

displays the object when the left margin is clear

floats the object on the left

sets the width to 40% of the width of the page

TIP

A width percentage refers to the percentage of the width of the containing element.

▸ **2.** Save your changes to the file.

Now re-display the president's message.

▸ **3.** Return to the **cp_reset.css** style sheet in your text editor. Remove the selector *#president* and the comma that follows it from the start of the selector list in the style rule at the bottom of the file. Save your changes.

▸ **4.** Reload the **cycle.htm** file in your Web browser. As shown in Figure 4-24, the article appears in the page below the horizontal navigation list.

Figure 4-24 ▸ **Re-displaying the president's message**

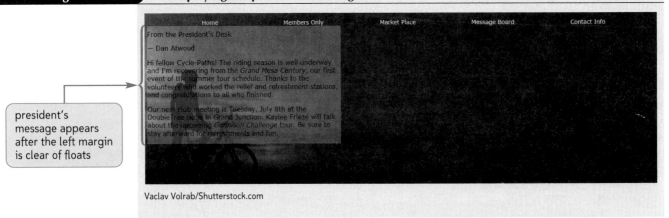

president's message appears after the left margin is clear of floats

Vaclav Volrab/Shutterstock.com

Dan stops by to see your progress on the Web page. He likes the page background and the navigation list. However, he wants you to move the president's message article farther to the right. You'll learn how to relocate page objects and work with margins, padding space, and borders in the next session.

Session 4.1 Quick Check

REVIEW

1. Provide a style rule to display all inline images as blocks.
2. Provide a style rule to add the file *author.jpg* as a background image to the `header` element, display the image on the bottom-right corner of the element without tiling, and set the background color to yellow.
3. What style rule would you use to tile the background image file *bar.png* horizontally in the background of the page body, starting from the top-left corner of the page?
4. Provide a style rule to display the *logo.png* and *side.png* image files in the page body background. Place *logo.png* in the top-left corner of the background and *side.png* in the top-right corner. Do not tile the *logo.png* image, and tile the *side.png* image only vertically. Set up your style so that *logo.png* is loaded last by the browser.
5. Provide a style rule for the first `section` element within the page body to set the size of the section's background image file, *author.png*, to 300 pixels wide by 200 pixels high. Use progressive enhancement to support the Presto, Mozilla, and WebKit rendering engines as well as browsers that support the CSS3 specifications.
6. What type of layout design should you use to set the width of the page to 1200 pixels, regardless of the rendering device?
7. Provide a style rule to float all figure boxes on the right margin when nested within an `article` element.
8. Provide a style rule to display the `footer` element only when both left and right margins are free of floating elements.

SESSION 4.2 VISUAL OVERVIEW

The **border** property creates a border around an element. These values create a **10-pixel-wide double line** with a color value of **(219, 152, 96)**.

```
border: 10px
        double;
        rgb(219, 152, 96) ;
```

The **outline** property creates an outline around an element. These values create a **1-pixel-wide, red single line**.

```
outline: 1px
         red
         single;
```

```
margin: 10px 5px 10px 20px;
```

The **margin** property sets the margin space around an element. These values create a margin that is **10 pixels** on top, **5 pixels** on the right, **10 pixels** on the bottom, and **20 pixels** on the left.

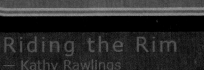

Home   Members Only   Market Place

From the President's Desk
— Dan Atwood

Hi fellow Cycle-Paths! The riding season is well underway and I'm recovering from the *Grand Mesa Century*, our first event of the summer tour schedule. Thanks to the volunteers who worked the relief and refreshment stations, and congratulations to all who finished.

Our next club meeting is Tuesday, July 8th at the DoubleTree Hotel in Grand Junction. Kaylee Frieze will talk about the upcoming *Gunnison Challenge* tour. Be sure to stay afterward for refreshments and fun.

Riding the Rim
— Kathy Rawlings

Rim Rock Drive in Colorado National Monument has tested many of the world's strongest riders, but is still accessible to the weekend cyclist. If you decide to *Tour the Moon*, here are some tips to help you have a great ride:

Keep Hydrated The canyon sun can quickly sap your energy. Make sure you carry plenty of water; there are no watering holes along the Rim.

Bring Lights All bikes must be equipped with front and rear lights for safe passage through the Rim's tunnels. Cyclists must use a white light visible at least 500 feet in front and a red light visible at least 200 feet from the rear.

Ride Single File Rim Rock Drive is narrow, with sheer drop-offs to the canyon valley. Leave plenty of room for drivers to pass you and your group.

MARGINS, PADDING, AND BORDERS

```
-moz-border-radius:      40px;
-webkit-border-radius:   40px;
border-radius:           40px;
```

The **border-radius** property creates a round corner for page elements. These values base corners on a circle that is **40 pixels** in radius. The **Mozilla browser extension** defines this property for Mozilla-based browsers, while the **WebKit extension** defines the property for Safari browsers.

Market Place   Message Board   Contact Info

About Cycle Pathology

Rides & Events

Route Sheets & Maps

Grand Junction Bike Fest

Off Road Cycling

Newsletter

Photo Album

Editor

Sponsors

```
border-bottom: 1px
               solid
               rgb(182, 182, 92);
```

The **border-bottom** property defines the appearance of an element's bottom border. These values create a **1-pixel** border in a **solid** style with the color value **(182, 182, 92)**.

```
border: 5px
        inset
        rgb(227, 168, 145);
```

These values create a **5-pixel** border in the **inset** style with the color value **(227, 168, 145)**.

```
padding: 10px auto 5px auto;
```

The **padding** property sets the padding space around element content. These values create padding space that is **10 pixels** above the content, **5 pixels** below the content, and **automatic** to the left and right of the content.

Cycling in Colorado National Monument

has tested
accessible
Moon,

sap your
there

front
Rim's
at least
200

with
enty of

Setting Margins and Padding

You and Dan are continuing to work on the page layout for the Cycle Pathology home page. One layout principle suggests that the page should be divided into thirds with different page content placed in each of the three sections. You'll apply this general principle to the Cycle Pathology page (see Figure 4-25).

Figure 4-25   **Page layout percentages**

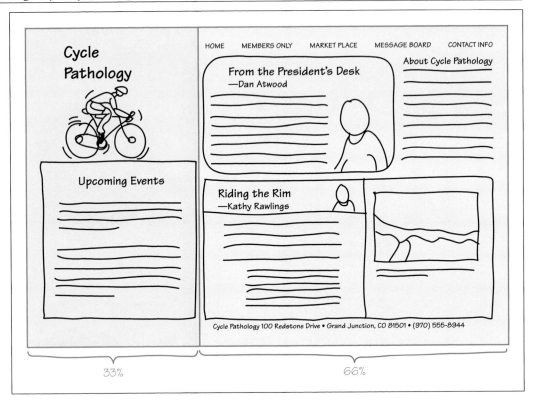

Based on the proposed layout for the page, you'll shift the horizontal navigation list and the president's message at the top of the page to the right, into the middle page section. One way to shift these two items is to change the margin space around those elements.

Margin Styles

Recall from Figure 4-4 in the last session that CSS uses the box model to format the space around element content. On the very outside of the box is the margin, separating one element from another. CSS supports several styles to set the size of this margin, including the properties

```
margin-top: length;
margin-right: length;
margin-bottom: length;
margin-left: length;
```

which set the sizes of the top, right, bottom, and left margins, respectively. Here, *length* is a length expressed in one of the CSS units of measure or a percentage of the containing element's width or height, or the keyword `auto` to allow browsers to automatically set the margin size for you. For example, the style rule

```
h1 {
    margin-top: 10px;
    margin-right: 20px;
    margin-bottom: 10px;
    margin-left: 20px;
}
```

creates margins of 10 pixels above and below every `h1` element, and margins of 20 pixels to the left and right of the heading.

These four margin styles can be combined into the single style

```
margin: top right bottom left;
```

where *top*, *right*, *bottom*, and *left* are the sizes of the top, right, bottom, and left margins, respectively. To help remember this order, think of moving clockwise around the element, starting with the top margin. The style rule

```
h1 {margin: 10px 20px 10px 20px;}
```

applies the same set of margins as in the previous code sample.

You don't have to supply values for all of the margins. If you specify a single value, it's applied to all four sides equally. Likewise, two values set the top/bottom margins and the right/left margins, respectively. Finally, three values set the margins for the top, right/left, and bottom, respectively. For example, the style rule

```
h1 {margin: 10px 20px;}
```

applies a 10-pixel margin above and below every `h1` element, and a 20-pixel margin to the left and right. The style rule

```
h1 {margin: 10px;}
```

creates a 10-pixel margin around the entire heading.

TIP

You can overlap page elements by specifying negative values for the margins.

REFERENCE

Setting Margin and Padding Space in the Box Model

- To set the margin space around an element, use

  ```
  margin: length;
  ```

  where *length* is the size of the margin using one of the CSS units of measure.
- To set the padding space within an element, use the following:

  ```
  padding: length;
  ```

- To set a margin or padding for one side of the box model only, specify the direction (top, right, bottom, or left). For example, use

  ```
  margin-right: length;
  ```

  to set the length of the right margin.
- To set multiple margin or padding spaces, specify the values in a space-separated list starting from the top and moving clockwise around the element. For example, the style

  ```
  margin: top right bottom left;
  ```

  sets margins for the top, right, bottom, and left sides of the element, respectively.
- To set matching top and bottom values and matching right and left values for margins and padding, enter only two values. For example, the style

  ```
  margin: vertical horizontal;
  ```

  sets margins for the top and bottom sides of the element to the value specified by *vertical*, and sets margins for the right and left sides of the element to the value specified by *horizontal*.

Each browser's internal style sheet sets the margins around block elements such as paragraphs and headings. One part of most reset style sheets is a style rule that sets the default margin size to 0 pixels so the page designer explicitly can define the margins for all elements.

To define the default margin size:

▶ **1.** Return to the **cp_reset.css** style sheet file in your text editor.

▶ **2.** Locate the style rule that defines the default page element styles and add the following style property (see Figure 4-26):

```
margin: 0px;
```

Figure 4-26   Setting the default margin size for every element

```
body * {
    font-family: Verdana, Geneva, sans-serif;
    font-size: 14px;
    font-weight: normal;
    line-height: 1.2em;
    list-style: none;
    margin: 0px;
    vertical-align: baseline;
}
```

by default, every element has no margin

▶ **3.** Save your changes to the file.

Next, you'll change the left margins for the horizontal navigation list and the president's message so they are offset from the page's left edge by 33% of the page body width. You'll also resize the width of the navigation list to 66% of the total page width.

To change the margin spaces in the page:

▶ 1. Return to the **cp_styles.css** style sheet file in your text editor, and then directly below the comment *Horizontal Navigation List* add the following style rule:

```
nav.horizontalNAV {
    margin-left: 33%;
    width: 66%;
}
```

▶ 2. Scroll down to the style rule for the president's message and add the following style:

```
margin-left: 33%;
```

Figure 4-27 highlights the new and revised styles in the style sheet.

Figure 4-27 Setting left margins

sets the width of the navigation list to 66% of the page width and the left margin to 33% of the page width

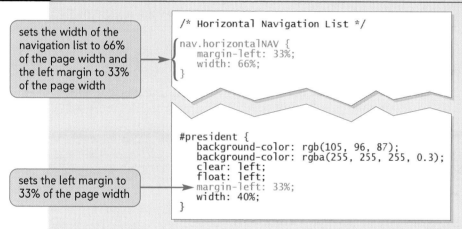

sets the left margin to 33% of the page width

▶ 3. Save your changes to the file and then reload **cycle.htm** in your Web browser. Figure 4-28 shows the revised layout of the page.

Figure 4-28 Revised page layout

33% left margin

page content in the remaining 66% of the page width

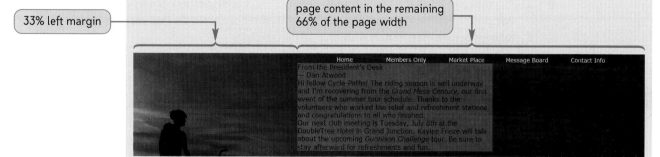

Vaclav Volrab/Shutterstock.com

Margin styles also can be applied to the body element. For example, by setting the margin around the page body to 0 pixels, you can remove the extra space many browsers insert by default between the page content and the edge of the browser window.

Padding Styles

While setting the default margin size to 0 pixels has made the appearance of page elements more predictable, it also has resulted in the navigation list crowding the president's message. You can increase the gap between them by increasing the padding around the text of the navigation links. Setting padding is similar to setting margins, with these separate styles available for specifying the padding space around element content

```
padding-top: length;
padding-right: length;
padding-bottom: length;
padding-left: length;
```

and the following style to set all of the padding spaces within one property:

```
padding: top right bottom left;
```

As with the `margin` property, you can specify any or all of the four padding values. When you specify a single value, it is applied to all four padding values. The style

```
h1 {padding: 5px;}
```

sets the padding space around the `h1` heading content to 5 pixels in each direction.

You'll use the reset style sheet to set the default padding for all elements to 0 pixels, and then you'll set the padding space above and below the navigation list to 15 pixels.

To modify the padding size:

▶ 1. Return to the **cp_reset.css** style sheet file in your text editor. Within the style rule for default page styles, add the following property (see Figure 4-29):

```
padding: 0px;
```

Figure 4-29	Setting the default padding size for every element

```
body * {
    font-family: Verdana, Geneva, sans-serif;
    font-size: 14px;
    font-weight: normal;
    line-height: 1.2em;
    list-style: none;
    margin: 0px;
    padding: 0px;
    vertical-align: baseline;
}
```

by default, every element has no padding

▶ 2. Save your changes to the file and return to the **cp_styles.css** file in your text editor. Within the style rule for list items in the horizontal navigation list, add the following style (see Figure 4-30):

```
padding: 15px 0px;
```

Figure 4-30	Setting the padding of the navigation list items

each list item has 15 pixels of padding above and below the content

```
nav.horizontalNAV li {
    font-size: 87.5%;
    float: left;
    padding: 15px 0px;
    text-align: center;
    width: 20%;
}
```

This style sets the top and bottom padding space to 15 pixels, and the right and left padding space to 0 pixels.

3. Save your changes to the file and then reload **cycle.htm** in your Web browser. Verify that additional space has been added above and below the horizontal navigation list.

Dan has several style rules he wants you to apply to the elements within the president's message. Complete the formatting of this page object by revising the *cp_styles.css* style sheet file.

To format the headings in the president's message:

1. Return to the **cp_styles.css** style sheet file in your text editor.

2. Add the following style rule at the bottom of the file to display the h1 heading in the president's message in a bold cursive-style font that is 158% of the size of the default text, with 10-pixel margins above and to the left of the text content:

```
#president h1 {
    font-family: 'Lucida Calligraphy', 'Apple Chancery', cursive;
    font-size: 158%;
    font-weight: bold;
    margin: 10px 0px 0px 10px;
}
```

3. Below that style rule, add the following style rule to display the h2 heading in the president's message in a font size that is 105% of the size of the default text, with a 10-pixel margin below the text and a 15-pixel margin to the left of the text:

```
#president h2 {
    font-size: 105%;
    margin: 0px 0px 10px 15px;
}
```

Figure 4-31 shows the new style rules.

Figure 4-31   **Styling the h1 and h2 headings**

sets the h1 heading to be displayed in a bold cursive font 158% of the size of the default text with top and left margins of 10 pixels

```
#president h1 {
    font-family: 'Lucida Calligraphy', 'Apple Chancery', cursive;
    font-size: 158%;
    font-weight: bold;
    margin: 10px 0px 0px 10px;
}
```

sets the h2 heading to be displayed at 105% of the size of the default text with a bottom margin of 10 pixels and a left margin of 15 pixels

```
#president h2 {
    font-size: 105%;
    margin: 0px 0px 10px 15px;
}
```

4. Save your changes to the file.

PROSKILLS

Problem Solving: The Virtue of Being Negative

It's common to think of layout in terms of placing content, but good layout also must be concerned with placing emptiness. In art and page design, this is known as working with positive and negative space. Positive space is the part of the page occupied by text, graphics, borders, icons, and other page elements. Negative space, or white space, is the unoccupied area, and provides balance and contrast to elements contained in positive space.

A page that is packed with content leaves the eye with no place to rest; this also can mean that the eye has no place to focus and maybe even no clear indication about where to start reading. Instead, it's important to use negative space to direct users to resting stops before moving on to the next piece of page content. This can be done by providing a generous margin between page elements and by increasing the padding within an element. Even increasing the spacing between letters within an article heading can alleviate eye strain and make the text easier to read.

White space also has an emotional aspect. In the early days of print advertising, white space was seen as wasted space, and thus smaller magazines and direct mail advertisements would tend to crowd content together in order to reduce waste. By contrast, upscale magazines and papers could distinguish themselves from those publications with an excess of empty space. This difference carries over to the Web, where a page with less content and more white space often feels more classy and polished, while a page crammed with a lot of content feels more commercial. Both can be effective; you should decide which approach to use based on your customer profile.

The increase in screen sizes has reduced the need for designers to cram content into small spaces. The result has been a greater emphasis on designs that provide generous amounts of white space, which has improved the readability and visual appeal of Web pages.

Next, Dan wants to add a graphic image of himself in the background of the president's message box. He wants the image to be placed in the bottom-right corner of the box and sized to 40% of the width of the box. To make room for this image, you'll set the font size of the paragraph text to 87.5% of the default font size, and the right margins of the paragraphs to 40%. Note that in this context, a value of 40% refers not to the width of the page, but only to the width of the president's message box that contains the paragraphs.

To add the background image:

1. At the bottom of the **cp_styles.css** file, insert the following style rule to set the paragraph font size and margins (see Figure 4-32):

```
#president p {
    font-size: 87.5%;
    margin: 0px 40% 20px 15px;
}
```

Figure 4-32 — Setting the margin around the paragraph

```
#president h2 {
    font-size: 105%;
    margin: 0px 0px 10px 15px;
}

#president p {
    font-size: 87.5%;
    margin: 0px 40% 20px 15px;
}
```

sets the paragraph margin to 20 pixels below, 15 pixels to the left, and 40% of the width of the president's message to the right

In this case, the margins are a mixture of absolute and relative lengths. The top, bottom, and left margins are set to 0 pixels, 20 pixels, and 15 pixels, respectively. The size of the right margin will depend on the size of the president's box, which in turn will vary depending on the width of the Web page.

Make sure you start every browser extension style with the - (hyphen) character.

2. Add the following properties to the #president selector style rule to define the source, position, tiling, and size of the background image (see Figure 4-33):

```
background-image: url(atwood.png);
background-position: bottom right;
background-repeat: no-repeat;

-o-background-size: 40%;
-moz-background-size: 40%;
-webkit-background-size: 40%;
background-size: 40%;
```

Figure 4-33 — Setting the padding of the navigation list items

```
#president {
    background-color: rgb(105, 96, 87);
    background-color: rgba(255, 255, 255, 0.3);
    background-image: url(atwood.png);
    background-position: bottom right;
    background-repeat: no-repeat;

    -o-background-size: 40%;
    -moz-background-size: 40%;
    -webkit-background-size: 40%;
    background-size: 40%;

    clear: left;
    float: left;
    margin-left: 33%;
    width: 40%;
}
```

displays the atwood.png file as the background image in the bottom-right corner of the president's message

sets the width of the background image to 40% of the width of the president's message

progressive enhancement using browser extensions

Notice that the style rule uses progressive enhancement and vendor prefixes in order to provide support for the widest range of browsers and browser versions.

3. Save your changes to the file and then reload **cycle.htm** in your Web browser. Figure 4-34 shows the revised appearance of the president's message box.

Figure 4-34 Formatted president's message

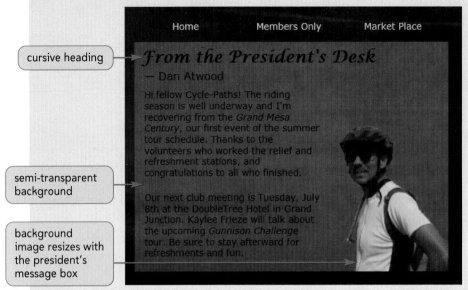

cursive heading

semi-transparent background

background image resizes with the president's message box

Vaclav Volrab/Shutterstock.com

4. If you have a widescreen monitor in which you can change the width of the browser window from 1000 to 1400 pixels, resize the browser window and verify that the placement of the page elements and the size of the *atwood.png* background image change in response.

The next item on the Cycle Pathology home page is the vertical navigation list. Dan wants this list floated alongside the president's message. You'll redisplay that item and float it now.

To redisplay the vertical navigation list:

1. Return to the **cp_reset.css** style sheet in your text editor and remove the selector *nav.verticalNAV* and the comma that follows it from the last style rule. Save your changes to the file.

2. Go to the **cp_styles.css** style sheet in your text editor. At the bottom of the file, insert the following style rules to format the vertical navigation list (see Figure 4-35):

```
/* Vertical Navigation List */

nav.verticalNAV {
    float: left;
    margin-left: 3%;
    width: 23%;
}
nav.verticalNAV a {
    color: rgb(182, 182, 92);
    line-height: 2.2em;
}
```

Figure 4-35	Redisplaying the vertical navigation list

sets the width of the vertical navigation list to 23% of the page width, floated on the left, with a left margin of 3%

sets the color of the hyperlinks to a light yellow and the line height to 2.2 em units

```
/* Vertical Navigation List */

nav.verticalNAV {
    float: left;
    margin-left: 3%;
    width: 23%;
}

nav.verticalNAV a {
    color: rgb(182, 182, 92);
    line-height: 2.2em;
}
```

3. Save your changes to the file and then reload **cycle.htm** in your browser. Figure 4-36 shows the revised appearance of the page.

Figure 4-36	Vertical navigation list

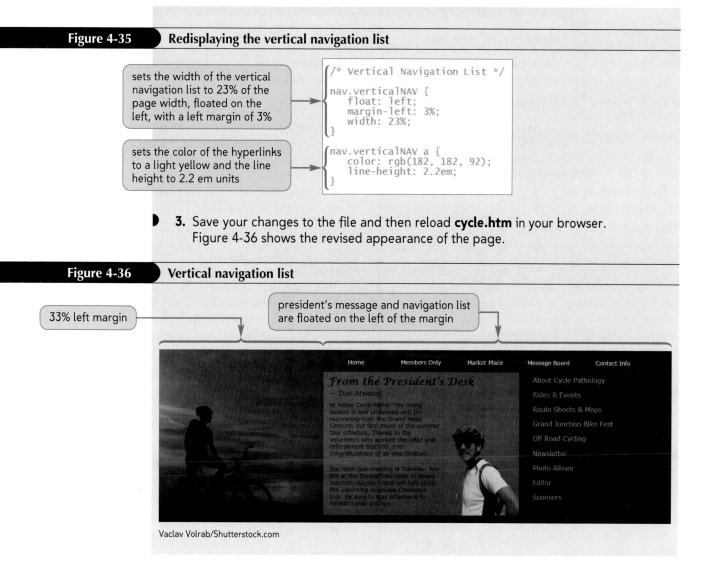

33% left margin

president's message and navigation list are floated on the left of the margin

Vaclav Volrab/Shutterstock.com

INSIGHT

Keeping It Centered

Many page layouts are based on centering objects either horizontally or vertically. You've already learned how to horizontally center inline elements using the following style:

```
text-align: center;
```

However, while this will center a block's contents, it won't center the entire block itself. To do that, you set the left and right margin values to `auto`. For example, the following style rule horizontally centers every paragraph in a Web page while also setting the top and bottom margins to 10 pixels:

```
p {
    margin: 10px auto;
    width: 600px;
}
```

Note that you must define the width of the block element or else the block will assume the entire width of its container, making centering irrelevant.

There is no CSS style to vertically center a block element, but you can find several workarounds on the Web to accomplish the trick. One approach is to create a container element for the block and display that container as a table cell with the `vertical-align` property set to `middle`. For example, to vertically center an `h1` heading, you could place it within a `div` container, as in the code

```
<div>
    <h1>Cycle Pathology</h1>
</div>
```

and apply the style rule

```
div {
    display: table-cell;
    vertical-align: middle;
}
```

Note that this approach does not work with Internet Explorer versions before IE8 because those versions do not support the `table-cell` value for the `display` property. You'll learn more about tables and table cells in the next tutorial.

Another trick for vertically centering a block element is to use the `display` property to make the element into an inline element. You then can vertically center it by setting the line height equal to the height of the container box itself. This approach has the added benefit of enabling you to use the `text-align` property to horizontally center it at the same time. The disadvantage is that the element is no longer a block and thus may not be suitable as a container for other elements.

You'll examine one additional vertical centering technique in the next session on absolute and relative positioning.

Working with Borders

Dan wants you to format the vertical navigation list so that each list item has a bottom border; and when a user hovers the mouse pointer over the hypertext link, the background color of the entire length of the list item is highlighted (see Figure 4-37).

Figure 4-37	Hover style for the vertical navigation list

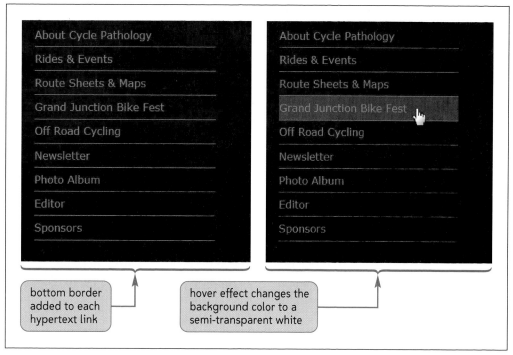

Vaclav Volrab/Shutterstock.com

To create this effect, you'll work with the CSS border styles.

Setting Border Width and Color

CSS supports several style properties to format the border around each element. As with the margin and padding styles, you can apply a style to the top, right, bottom, or left border, or to all borders at once. To define the thickness of a border, use the style properties

```
border-top-width: width;
border-right-width: width;
border-bottom-width: width;
border-left-width: width;
```

where *width* is defined as a percentage or as one of the CSS units of measure. Border widths also can be expressed using the keywords `thin`, `medium`, or `thick`; the exact application of these keywords depends on the browser. You also can define the border thickness using the following single style property:

```
border-width: top right bottom left;
```

As with the `margin` and `padding` properties, if you enter one value, it's applied to all four borders; two values set the width of the top/bottom and left/right borders, respectively; and three values are applied to the top, left/right, and bottom borders, in that order.

You set the border color with the style properties

```
border-top-color: color;
border-right-color: color;
border-bottom-color: color;
border-left-color: color;

border-color: top right bottom left;
```

TIP

If you don't specify a color, browsers use the text color of the element content.

where *color* is a color name, color value, or the keyword `transparent` to create an invisible border. For example, the following style rule adds a 4-pixel red border directly above the `address` element:

```
address {
    border-top-width: 4px;
    border-top-color: red;
}
```

Setting the Border Design

CSS allows you to further define the appearance of borders using the border styles

```
border-top-style: style;
border-right-style: style;
border-bottom-style: style;
border-left-style: style;

border-style: top right bottom left;
```

where *style* is one of the nine border styles displayed in Figure 4-38. The CSS3 specifications also include the `wavy`, `dot-dash`, and `dot-dot-dash` styles, but they have little browser support at the time of this writing.

Figure 4-38	Border style designs

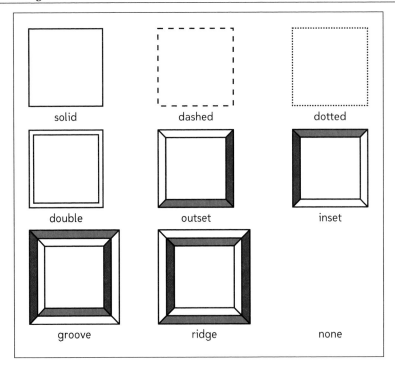

You specify styles for different sides in the same way you do for padding or margins. For example, the style

```
border-style-bottom: double single;
```

places a double border above and below the element, and a single border on the element's left and right edges.

TIP

Browsers will render a border correctly no matter the order in which you specify the *width*, *style*, and *color* values.

All of the border styles discussed above can be combined into a single style that defines each or all of the borders around the element. The syntax of these border styles is

```
border-top: width style color;
border-right: width style color;
border-bottom: width style color;
border-left: width style color;

border: width style color;
```

where *width* is the thickness of the border, *style* is the style of the border, and *color* is the border color. Thus, the style rule

```
h1 {border: 2px solid blue;}
```

adds a 2-pixel-wide solid blue border around every `h1` heading.

REFERENCE

Setting Border Styles in the Box Model

- To set the border width, use the property

  `border-width: width;`

  where *width* is the thickness of the border using one of the CSS units of measure.
- To set the border color, use

  `border-color: color;`

  where *color* is a color name or value.
- To set the border design, use

  `border-style: style;`

  where *style* is none, solid, dashed, dotted, double, outset, inset, groove, or ridge.
- To set all of the border options in one style, use the following:

  `border: width color style;`

You'll use the CSS border styles to add a bottom border to each hypertext link in the vertical navigation list. To extend the bottom border across the complete width of the list, you'll also change the `display` property of each hyperlink to block. By default, block-level elements have a width equal to the width of their containing element unless a different width is set by the page design.

To add a bottom border to the hypertext links:

1. Return to the **cp_styles.css** file in your text editor.

2. Within the style rule for the `nav.verticalNAV a` selector, add the following styles in alphabetical order within the curly braces as indicated in Figure 4-39:

```
border-bottom: 1px solid rgb(182, 182, 92);
display: block;
```

▶ **3.** At the bottom of the file, add the following style rule to change the background color of the hyperlinks in the vertical navigation list in response to the hover event:

```
nav.verticalNAV a:hover {
   background-color: rgb(105, 96, 87);
   background-color: rgba(255, 255, 255, 0.3);
}
```

Figure 4-39 highlights the new code in the file.

Figure 4-39　　**Adding a border to the hyperlinks**

displays each hyperlink as a block element with a light yellow bottom border

changes the background color to medium gray or a semi-transparent white during the hover event

```
nav.verticalNAV a {
   border-bottom: 1px solid rgb(182, 182, 92);
   color: rgb(182, 182, 92);
   display: block;
   line-height: 2.2em;
}

nav.verticalNAV a:hover {
   background-color: rgb(105, 96, 87);
   background-color: rgba(255, 255, 255, 0.3);
}
```

▶ **4.** Save your changes to the file and reload **cycle.htm** in your Web browser. Verify that the hyperlinks now display a bottom border with the hover effect shown earlier in Figure 4-37.

Creating Rounded Corners

Dan thinks the current layout is too boxy and would like to soften the design by adding curves to some of the page elements. Specifically, he would like you to add rounded corners to the president's message box. Rounded corners can be applied to any of the four corners of a block element using the styles

```
border-top-left-radius: radius;
border-top-right-radius: radius;
border-bottom-right-radius: radius;
border-bottom-left-radius: radius;

border-radius: top-left top-right bottom-right bottom-left;
```

where *radius* is the radius of the rounded corner in one of the CSS units of measurement and *top-left*, *top-right*, *bottom-right*, and *bottom-left* are the radii of the individual corners. The radii are equal to the radii of hypothetical circles placed at the corners of the box with the arcs of the circles defining the rounded corners (see Figure 4-40).

| Figure 4-40 | Setting the corner radii |

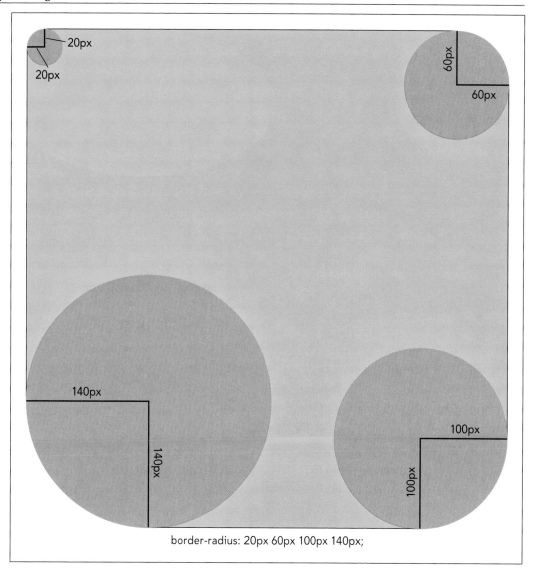

border-radius: 20px 60px 100px 140px;

If you enter only one value for the `border-radius` property, that radius is applied to all four corners; if you enter two values, the first is applied to the top-left and bottom-right corners, and the second is applied to the top-right and bottom-left corners. If you specify three radii, they are applied to the top-left, top-right/bottom-left, and bottom-right corners, in that order.

Elongated Corners

The CSS rounded-corner model also allows designers to create elongated or elliptical corners by specifying two values for the radius separated by a slash

```
horizontal/vertical
```

where `horizontal` is the horizontal radius and `vertical` is the vertical radius (see Figure 4-41).

Figure 4-41	Creating an elongated corner

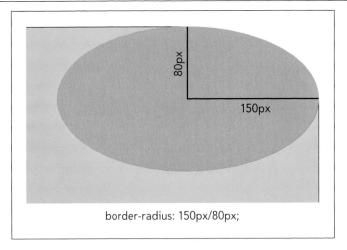

border-radius: 150px/80px;

To apply an elongated corner to a single corner, you do *not* include the slash between the horizontal and vertical radii. For example, to create an elongated bottom-left corner, you could apply the style

```
border-bottom-left-radius: 150px 80px;
```

which would set the horizontal radius of the bottom-left corner to 150 pixels and the vertical radius to 80 pixels.

Rounded and elongated corners do not clip element content. If the content of the element extends into the corner, it still will be displayed as part of the background. Because this is often unsightly, you should avoid heavily rounded or elongated corners unless you can be sure they will not obscure or distract from the element content.

Browser Extensions to Rounded Corners

Rounded corners were first introduced in both the WebKit and Mozilla browser extensions. The syntax is largely the same as that adopted by CSS3 except when applied to individual corners. Figure 4-42 compares the syntax of three versions of the rounded corner style.

Figure 4-42	Browser extensions to the rounded corner styles

CSS3	Mozilla	WebKit
border-radius	-moz-border-radius	-webkit-border-radius
border-top-right-radius	-moz-border-radius-topright	-webkit-border-top-right-radius
border-bottom-right-radius	-moz-border-radius-bottomright	-webkit-border-bottom-right-radius
border-bottom-left-radius	-moz-border-radius-bottomleft	-webkit-border-bottom-left-radius
border-top-left-radius	-moz-border-radius-topleft	-webkit-border-top-left-radius

For example, you would use progressive enhancement to set the radius of the top-right corner to 15 pixels with the following style values:

```
-moz-border-radius-topright: 15px;
-webkit-border-top-right-radius: 15px;
border-top-right-radius: 15px;
```

The other important difference is that the WebKit extension separates horizontal and vertical radii with a space rather than with a slash. Thus, to create elongated corners of 45 pixels wide and 15 pixels high, you would enter the following style values:

```
-moz-border-radius: 45px/15px;
-webkit-border-radius: 45px 15px;
border-radius: 45px/15px;
```

The current versions of both Firefox and Safari have adopted the CSS3 standard. You need to use the browser extension only if you have to support earlier versions of those browsers. Internet Explorer does not support rounded corners until IE9. There are work-arounds for Internet Explorer users involving nested div elements with background images displaying rounded corners, but they are difficult and cumbersome to create. As long as the rounded corners are used only to enhance your page's appearance and are not an essential part of understanding your page's content, you should feel free to use the CSS3 styles even with browsers that don't support them.

Modify your style sheet now to add 30-pixel rounded corners to the president's message box.

To create rounded corners:

▶ **1.** Return to the **cp_styles.css** file in your text editor.

▶ **2.** Within the style rule for the #president selector, add the following style properties as shown in Figure 4-43:

```
-moz-border-radius: 30px;
-webkit-border-radius: 30px;
border-radius: 30px;
```

Figure 4-43   **Specifying the border radius**

```
-o-background-size: 40%;
-moz-background-size: 40%;
-webkit-background-size: 40%;
background-size: 40%;
```

sets rounded corners with a radius of 30 pixels →
```
-moz-border-radius: 30px;
-webkit-border-radius: 30px;
border-radius: 30px;
```

▶ **3.** Save your changes to the file and then reload **cycle.htm** in your Web browser. As shown in Figure 4-44, the president's message should now display rounded corners.

Figure 4-44   Rounded corners for the president's message

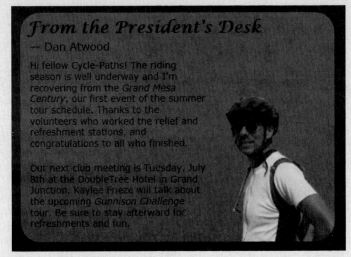

Vaclav Volrab/Shutterstock.com

INSIGHT

Creating an Irregular Line Wrap

Many desktop publishing and word-processing programs allow designers to create irregular line wraps in which the text appears to flow tightly around an image. This is not easily done in Web page design because all inline images appear as rectangles rather than as irregularly shaped objects. However, with the aid of a graphics package, you can simulate an irregularly shaped image.

The trick is to use your graphics package to slice the image horizontally into several pieces and then crop the individual slices to match the edge of the image you want to display. Once you've edited all of the slices, you can use CSS to stack the separate slices by floating them on the left or right margin, displaying each slice only after the previous slice has been cleared. For example, the following style rule stacks inline images on the right margin:

```
img {
    clear: right;
    float: right;
    margin-top: 0px;
    margin-bottom: 0px;
}
```

Always set the top and bottom margins to 0 pixels so that the slices join together seamlessly. You can see an example of this technique in Figure 4-78 as part of Case Problem 1 at the end of this tutorial.

Managing Your Layout

In layout design, you must be very aware of the width taken up by your page elements. If the total width allotted to an element extends beyond its container, the element will wrap to a new line, ruining your layout. The width taken up by an element is calculated as follows:

```
total width = content width + padding + border width
```

Thus, the style rule

```
div {
   border: 5px solid black;
   padding: 10px;
   width: 600px;
}
```

sets the total width allotted to the div element to 600 + 2(10) + 2(5) = 630 pixels. Note that this calculation must include the widths of both the left and right borders and padding space. In addition to knowing each element's total width, you also must keep track of the margin spaces around your elements if you want to ensure that your content will fit nicely within the width of your Web page.

Older versions of Internet Explorer calculated widths differently from the CSS standard. In those versions, the width property set the total width of an element including the content, padding, and border. Thus, a div element with the above style rule would measure 600 pixels wide, not 630, as Internet Explorer would assign only 570 pixels to the element content, leaving 20 pixels for the left and right padding and 10 pixels for the left and right borders. To avoid confusion—and to avoid ruining your layouts—always include a DOCTYPE declaration in your HTML file to put Internet Explorer and other browsers into Standards mode rather than Quirks mode. For a discussion of Standards vs. Quirks mode, see Tutorial 1.

Using the Outline Style

One way of simplifying your layout width calculations is to avoid using left and right padding. Instead, you can set the left and right padding to 0 pixels and separate your elements using only the left and right margins. In some cases, you also can replace your borders with outlines. An outline is a line drawn around an element; but unlike borders, an outline does not add to the total space allotted to an element, nor does it affect the position of the element in the page. Unlike borders, outlines also can be non-rectangular in shape (see Figure 4-45).

Figure 4-45   **Applying an irregularly shaped outline**

An outline width is defined using the style property

```
outline-width: value;
```

where value is expressed in one of the CSS units of length, or with the keywords thin, medium, or thick. Outline colors are defined using the property

```
outline-color: color;
```

where color is a CSS color name or value. Finally, the outline design is defined using the style property

```
outline-style: style;
```

where style is one of the design styles listed in Figure 4-46.

Figure 4-46   Outline design styles

Value	Description
none	No outline is displayed
dotted	Outline is dotted
dashed	Outline is dashed
solid	Outline is a single solid line
groove	Creates the effect of an outline carved into the page
ridge	Creates the effect of an outline raised from the page
inset	Creates the effect of an outline embedded in the page
outset	Creates the effect of an outline coming out of the page
double	Outline is a double line

All of the outline styles can be combined into the shorthand property

```
outline: width color style;
```

just as you did with the margin, padding, and border styles. Note that there are no separate outline styles for left, right, top, or bottom. The outline always surrounds an entire element.

Outlines often are used to highlight interesting or important page content. Another use is to diagram your layout as an aid in page design. Because outlines take up no space, you can use them to mark the size and location of every page element by using the following style rule:

```
* {
    outline: 1px solid red;
}
```

REFERENCE

Adding an Outline

- To add an outline around an element, use the style property

```
outline: width color style;
```

where *width*, *color*, and *style* are the outline width, outline color, and outline style, respectively.

You'll try this now with the Cycle Pathology page to highlight the placement of each of the page elements you've displayed thus far.

To view the layout structure:

▶ **1.** Return to the **cp_styles.css** file in your text editor.

▶ **2.** At the bottom of the file, insert the following style rule:

```
* {
    outline: 1px solid red;
}
```

▶ **3.** Save your changes to the file and then reload **cycle.htm** in your Web browser. As shown in Figure 4-47, each element in the page is outlined in red, showing its exact width, height, and location under your current design.

| Figure 4-47 | Outlining the page layout |

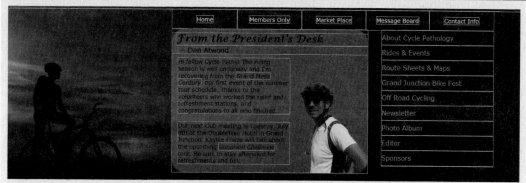

Vaclav Volrab/Shutterstock.com

▶ **4.** Return to the **cp_styles.css** file in your text editor and remove the style rule you created in Step 2. Save your changes to the file.

Putting It All Together

The next part of the Cycle Pathology page is the article written by Kathy Rawlings about cycling on Rim Rock Drive. The article is contained within a `section` element with the id *story* along with a figure box showing a cyclist on Rim Rock Drive. Dan wants the story section aligned with the president's message, with the article and the figure box placed side-by-side. To format these elements, you'll use all of the CSS tools you've learned about so far.

First, you'll edit the reset style sheet to re-display the story section and its contents; then you'll set the location of these elements in the Web page.

To display the story section:

▶ **1.** Return to the **cp_reset.css** file in your text editor and then go to the style rule at the bottom of the file that hides page elements. Remove the selector *#story* and the comma that follows it from the style rule, and then save your changes to the file.

▶ **2.** Return to the **cp_styles.css** file in your style sheet.

3. At the bottom of the file, add the following style rule to align the story section directly below the president's message, separated by a 20-pixel vertical margin:

```
/* Story section styles */

#story {
    background-color: gray;
    background-color: rgba(255, 255, 255, 0.8);
    clear: left;
    float: left;
    margin: 20px 0px 0px 33%;
    width: 66%;
}
```

4. Below the style rule you just added, add the following two style rules to float the article and figure box side-by-side, with each one taking up about half of the width of the story section:

```
/* Article styles */

#story article {
    border-right: 1px solid black;
    float: left;
    width: 50%;
}

/* Figure box styles */

#story figure {
    float: left;
    width: 49%;
}
```

Figure 4-48 highlights and further describes the new style rules you just entered into the style sheet.

Figure 4-48   **Styles for the story section**

displays the story section when the left margin is clear; floats the section on the left with a top margin of 20 pixels and a left margin of 33%; sets the background color to gray or semi-transparent white

```
/* Story section styles */

#story {
    background-color: gray;
    background-color: rgba(255, 255, 255, 0.8);
    clear: left;
    float: left;
    margin: 20px 0px 0px 33%;
    width: 66%;
}
```

floats the article on the left within the story section with a solid right border; sets the width of the article to half of the story section width

```
/* Article styles */

#story article {
    border-right: 1px solid black;
    float: left;
    width: 50%;
}
```

floats the figure box on the left with a width of about half that of the story section

```
/* Figure box styles */

#story figure {
    float: left;
    width: 49%;
}
```

5. Save your changes to the file and then reload **cycle.htm** in your Web browser. Figure 4-49 shows the placement of the story section as well as the Rim Rock Drive article and figure box within it.

Figure 4-49	Placement of the story section

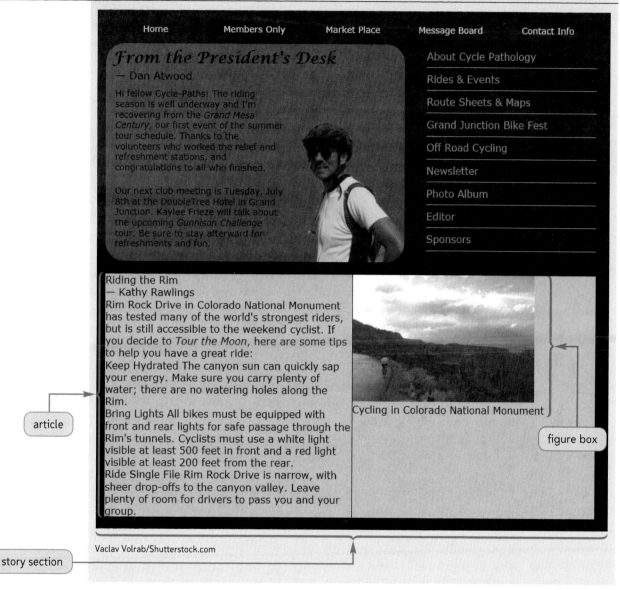

Vaclav Volrab/Shutterstock.com

The first part of the Rim Rock Drive article you'll format is the heading group. Dan wants the h1 and h2 headings displayed in a light brown font on a dark brown background. Furthermore, he wants the heading group resized to 90 pixels high with a background image of Kathy Rawlings displayed in the bottom-right corner of the box. You'll format the article heading now.

To format the article heading:

1. Return to the **cp_styles.css** file in your text editor. Directly below the style rule for the `story article` selector, insert the following rules to format the size, background, and text of the article heading group:

```
#story article hgroup {
    background: rgb(97, 30, 2) url(rawlings.png) bottom right
no-repeat;

    -o-background-size: contain;
    -moz-background-size: contain;
    -webkit-background-size: contain;
    background-size: contain;

    color: rgb(145, 98, 78);
    color: rgba(255, 255, 255, 0.3);

    height: 90px;
    text-indent: 10px;
}
```

2. Set the size of the `h1` heading in the article to 158% of the default font size, and set the kerning to 3 pixels by adding the following rule directly below the rule you created in Step 1:

```
#story article hgroup h1 {
    font-size: 158%;
    letter-spacing: 3px;
}
```

3. Finally, set the size of the `h2` headings to 105% of the default font size by adding the following style rule directly below the rule you created in Step 2:

```
#story article hgroup h2 {
    font-size: 105%;
}
```

Figure 4-50 shows the newly added style rules.

Figure 4-50   **Formatting the article heading**

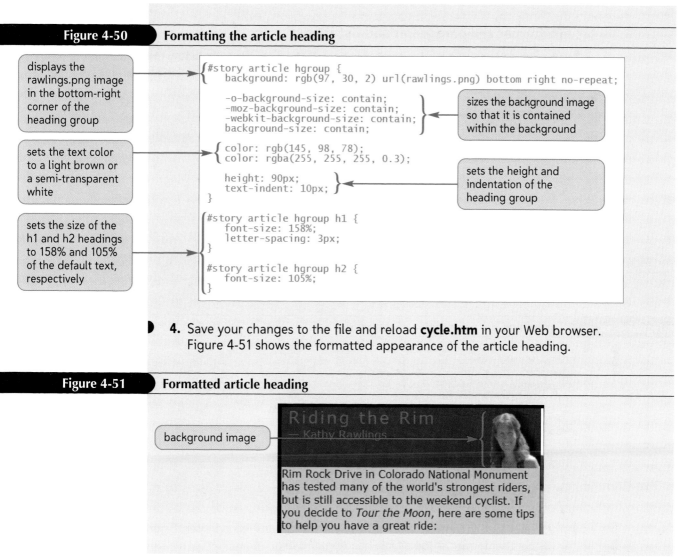

displays the rawlings.png image in the bottom-right corner of the heading group

```
#story article hgroup {
    background: rgb(97, 30, 2) url(rawlings.png) bottom right no-repeat;

    -o-background-size: contain;
    -moz-background-size: contain;
    -webkit-background-size: contain;
    background-size: contain;

    color: rgb(145, 98, 78);
    color: rgba(255, 255, 255, 0.3);

    height: 90px;
    text-indent: 10px;
}

#story article hgroup h1 {
    font-size: 158%;
    letter-spacing: 3px;
}

#story article hgroup h2 {
    font-size: 105%;
}
```

sizes the background image so that it is contained within the background

sets the text color to a light brown or a semi-transparent white

sets the height and indentation of the heading group

sets the size of the h1 and h2 headings to 158% and 105% of the default text, respectively

▶ **4.** Save your changes to the file and reload **cycle.htm** in your Web browser. Figure 4-51 shows the formatted appearance of the article heading.

Figure 4-51   **Formatted article heading**

background image

Riding the Rim
— Kathy Rawlings

Rim Rock Drive in Colorado National Monument has tested many of the world's strongest riders, but is still accessible to the weekend cyclist. If you decide to *Tour the Moon*, here are some tips to help you have a great ride:

Next, you'll format the paragraph and unordered list text. Dan wants the font size of both of these elements to be 80% of the default font size. He also wants you to increase the margin space around the paragraphs and list items.

To format the paragraph and list items:

1. Return to the **cp_styles.css** file in your text editor. Directly below the style rule for the h2 heading you created in the last set of steps, add the following rules (see Figure 4-52):

```
#story article p {
    font-size: 80%;
    margin: 10px;
}

#story article ul li {
    font-size: 80%;
    margin: 15px 25px;
}

#story article ul li strong {
    font-weight: bold;
}
```

Figure 4-52	Formatting the paragraph and unordered list

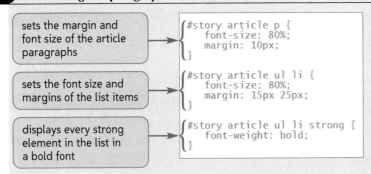

sets the margin and font size of the article paragraphs

```
#story article p {
    font-size: 80%;
    margin: 10px;
}
```

sets the font size and margins of the list items

```
#story article ul li {
    font-size: 80%;
    margin: 15px 25px;
}
```

displays every strong element in the list in a bold font

```
#story article ul li strong {
    font-weight: bold;
}
```

2. Save your changes and reload **cycle.htm** in your Web browser. Figure 4-53 shows the final format of the article heading and text.

Figure 4-53	Formatted article heading and text

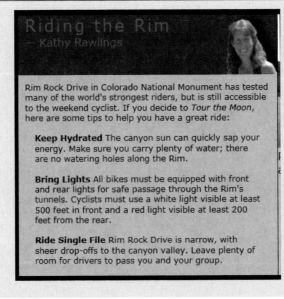

Riding the Rim
— Kathy Rawlings

Rim Rock Drive in Colorado National Monument has tested many of the world's strongest riders, but is still accessible to the weekend cyclist. If you decide to *Tour the Moon*, here are some tips to help you have a great ride:

Keep Hydrated The canyon sun can quickly sap your energy. Make sure you carry plenty of water; there are no watering holes along the Rim.

Bring Lights All bikes must be equipped with front and rear lights for safe passage through the Rim's tunnels. Cyclists must use a white light visible at least 500 feet in front and a red light visible at least 200 feet from the rear.

Ride Single File Rim Rock Drive is narrow, with sheer drop-offs to the canyon valley. Leave plenty of room for drivers to pass you and your group.

Finally, you'll format the contents of the figure box. One of these items is the inline image displaying the cyclist on Rim Rock Drive. You'll change the inline image into a block element and then center it horizontally within the figure box by setting its left and right margins to `auto` (see the Insight Box *Keeping It Centered* from earlier in this session for details on this setting). Dan also wants the size of the image to be based on the size of the figure box. Therefore, you'll set the image width to 80% of the figure box width so that browsers will determine the height automatically. You'll also add a 5-pixel-wide light brown inset border, and you'll center the figure caption, reduce its font size, and display the caption text in italic.

To format the figure box:

▶ **1.** Return to the **cp_styles.css** file in your text editor. At the bottom of the style sheet, insert the following rules (see Figure 4-54):

```
#story figure img {
    border: 5px inset rgb(227, 168, 145);
    display: block;
    margin: 30px auto 10px;
    width: 80%;
}

#story figure figcaption {
    font-size: 75%;
    font-style: italic;
    text-align: center;
}
```

Figure 4-54 Style rules for the image and figure caption

```
/* Figure box styles */

#story figure {
    float: left;
    width: 49%;
}

#story figure img {
    border: 5px inset rgb(227, 168, 145);
    display: block;
    margin: 30px auto 10px;
    width: 80%;
}

#story figure figcaption {
    font-size: 75%;
    font-style: italic;
    text-align: center;
}
```

displays the image as a block, centered in the figure box, 80% of the width of the box, and with a light brown inset border

displays the caption in small italic and centered in the figure box

▶ **2.** Save your changes and then reload **cycle.htm** in your Web browser. Figure 4-55 shows the current state of the story section.

Figure 4-55 | **Formatted figure box**

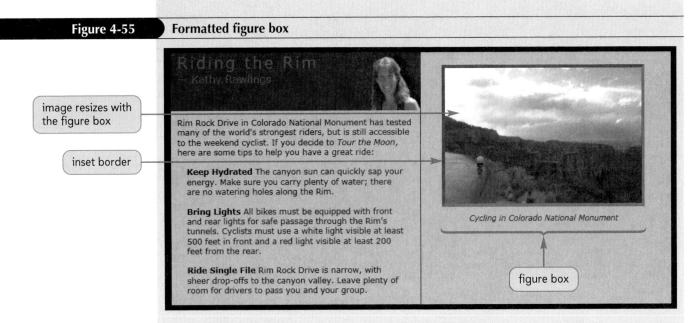

- image resizes with the figure box
- inset border
- *Cycling in Colorado National Monument*
- figure box

Riding the Rim
— Kathy Rawlings

Rim Rock Drive in Colorado National Monument has tested many of the world's strongest riders, but is still accessible to the weekend cyclist. If you decide to *Tour the Moon*, here are some tips to help you have a great ride:

Keep Hydrated The canyon sun can quickly sap your energy. Make sure you carry plenty of water; there are no watering holes along the Rim.

Bring Lights All bikes must be equipped with front and rear lights for safe passage through the Rim's tunnels. Cyclists must use a white light visible at least 500 feet in front and a red light visible at least 200 feet from the rear.

Ride Single File Rim Rock Drive is narrow, with sheer drop-offs to the canyon valley. Leave plenty of room for drivers to pass you and your group.

3. Resize the browser window and verify that the Rim Rock Drive image resizes along with the figure box.

You've completed your work on margins, padding space, and borders, and you've learned how to add special visual effects to your page elements through the use of rounded and elongated corners. The Cycle Pathology Web page is not finished yet, however; you still have to display the page header and the list of upcoming cycling events. You'll complete these tasks and others in the next session.

REVIEW

Session 4.2 Quick Check

1. Provide a style rule to set the margin space around the `header` element to 20 pixels above and below, and 30 pixels to the left and right.
2. Provide a style property that sets the padding space around every `article` element to 10 pixels on every side.
3. Provide a style rule to display every `footer` element with a 5-pixel solid red top border.
4. You want the `h1` heading with the id *mainHeading* to be displayed with a double green border 8 pixels wide. Provide the style rule.
5. Provide a style rule to display all hypertext links within a navigation list as block elements with a gray background, and with rounded corners 10 pixels in radius. Your rule should be accessible under CSS3 and all browser extensions.
6. Provide a style rule to display all `div` elements with elongated corners that have a 15-pixel horizontal radius and a 5-pixel vertical radius. Your code should work with all browser extensions and browsers that support CSS3.
7. What is the difference between a border and an outline?
8. Describe how the following style rule would differ in application between Internet Explorer running in Quirks mode and Internet Explorer running in Standards mode:

```
#mainHead {
   border: 10px solid blue;
   padding: 5px;
   width: 550px;
}
```

SESSION 4.3 VISUAL OVERVIEW

```
position: absolute;
top:        70px;
left:       50px;
```

The **position** property defines how objects should be placed. In this case, the object is placed with **absolute positioning**, **70 pixels** from the top edge of the browser window, and **50 pixels** from the left edge.

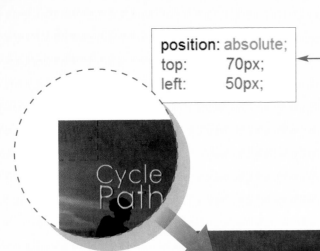

The **overflow** property defines how browsers should handle content that overflows the allotted width and height. In this case, the browser **automatically** adds scroll bars as needed to view any hidden content.

```
overflow: auto;
```

The **width** and **height** properties define the size of the element. These values set the width to **30%** of the browser window and the height to **450 pixels**.

```
width:  30%;
height: 450px;
```

Home   Members Only   Market Place

Cycle Pathology

From the President's Desk
— Dan Atwood

Hi fellow Cycle-Paths! The riding season is well underway and I'm recovering from the *Grand Mesa Century*, our first event of the summer tour schedule. Thanks to the volunteers who worked the relief and refreshment stations, and congratulations to all who finished.

Our next club meeting is Tuesday, July 8th at the DoubleTree Hotel in Grand Junction. Kaylee Frieze will talk about the upcoming *Gunnison Challenge* tour. Be sure to stay afterward for refreshments and fun.

Upcoming Events

... Fruita Canyon View Park and choose the Century or Metric Century ride. The $35 entry fee includes breakfast, support vehicles, rest station refreshments, and a post-ride meal.

July 12 *Tour the Palisades*

The Wine Tour season starts with our annual tour of the Fruit & Wine Trail. Stay afterward to enjoy samples of local wine from the valley.

July 26 *Gunnison Challenge*

Join us for this non-competitive tour through the Black Canyon of the Gunnison. Proceeds from the event benefit the Montrose Medical Mission.

August 9 *Steamboat Springs Rally*

Come to the Steamboat Ski Mountain for this epic 60-mile ride across the Continental Divide. A second ride has been added for those interested in enjoying the cross-country trails within the Steamboat ski area.

Riding the Rim
— Kathy Rawlings

Rim Rock Drive in Colorado National Monument has tested many of the world's strongest riders, but is still accessible to the weekend cyclist. If you decide to *Tour the Moon*, here are some tips to help you have a great ride:

Keep Hydrated The canyon sun can quickly sap your energy. Make sure you carry plenty of water; there are no watering holes along the Rim.

Bring Lights All bikes must be equipped with front and rear lights for safe passage through the Rim's tunnels. Cyclists must use a white light visible at least 500 feet in front and a red light visible at least 200 feet from the rear.

Ride Single File Rim Rock Drive is narrow, with sheer drop-offs to the canyon valley. Leave plenty of room for drivers to pass you and your group.

Cycle Pathology ◇ 100 Redstone Drive ◇ Grand Junction

POSITIONING ELEMENTS

The **clip** property defines a clipping rectangle that crops the object's **top**, **right**, **bottom**, and **left** edges.

clip: rect(100px, 420px, 350px, 50px);

Market Place   Message Board   Contact Info

About Cycle Pathology

Rides & Events

Route Sheets & Maps

Grand Junction Bike Fest

Off Road Cycling

Newsletter

Photo Album

Editor

Sponsors

Cycling In Colorado National Monument

Drive   Grand Junction, CO 81501   (970) 555 - 8944

z-index: 2;

The **z-index** property stacks overlapping objects with the highest z-index value placed on top of the others.

ional Monument

Positioning Objects

One page section you haven't added to the Cycle Pathology home page is the `header` element, which contains the group logo. Dan would like the header moved to the top-left corner of the page.

The ability to position an object was one of the first enhancements to the original CSS1 specifications. Collectively, the various positioning styles were known as **CSS-Positioning**, or more commonly, **CSS-P**. CSS-P became part of the specification for CSS2, and positioning styles were some of the first CSS2 styles to be adopted by browsers.

To place an element at a specific position, you use the style properties

```
position: type;
top: value;
right: value;
bottom: value;
left: value;
```

where `type` indicates the type of positioning applied to the element, and the `top`, `right`, `bottom`, and `left` properties indicate the coordinates of the top, right, bottom, and left edges of the element, respectively. In practice, usually only the left and top coordinates are specified because the right and bottom coordinates can be inferred given the element's height and width. Coordinates can be expressed in any of the CSS measuring units.

The `position` property has five possible values: `static` (the default), `absolute`, `relative`, `fixed`, and `inherit`. In static positioning, browsers place an element based on where it would naturally flow within the document. This is essentially the same as not using any CSS positioning at all. Browsers ignore any values specified for the `left` or `top` properties under static positioning.

REFERENCE

Positioning an Object with CSS

- To position an object at a specific coordinate, use the style properties

```
position: type;
top: value;
right: value;
bottom: value;
left: value;
```

where `type` indicates the type of positioning applied to the object (`absolute`, `relative`, `static`, `fixed`, or `inherit`), and the `top`, `right`, `bottom`, and `left` properties indicate the coordinates of the object.

Absolute Positioning

Absolute positioning places an element at specific coordinates either in the page or within a container element. For example, the style rule

```
header {
    position: absolute;
    left: 100px;
    top: 50px;
}
```

places the `header` element at the coordinates (100, 50), meaning 100 pixels to the right and 50 pixels down from upper-left corner of the page or the element that contains the header. Once an element has been moved using absolute positioning, it affects the placement of other objects in the Web page. To explore how absolute positioning affects page layout, you'll use a demo that explores the effect of different positioning options on page design.

To explore absolute positioning:

1. Use your Web browser to open the **demo_positioning.htm** file from the tutorial.04\demo folder.

   The demo page contains two colored boxes that you can move by changing the values in two sets of list boxes. The boxes are initially set to their default position, which is within the flow of the other elements in the page. To make it easier to place the boxes at specific positions, a grid marked in pixels has been added to the page background.

2. Select **absolute** from the list box for the outer box, and then press the **Tab** key.

3. Enter **275** in the left box, and then press the **Tab** key. Enter **350** in the top box, and then press the **Tab** key again. As shown in Figure 4-56, the red outer box is placed at the page coordinates (275, 350).

| Figure 4-56 | Viewing absolute positioning |

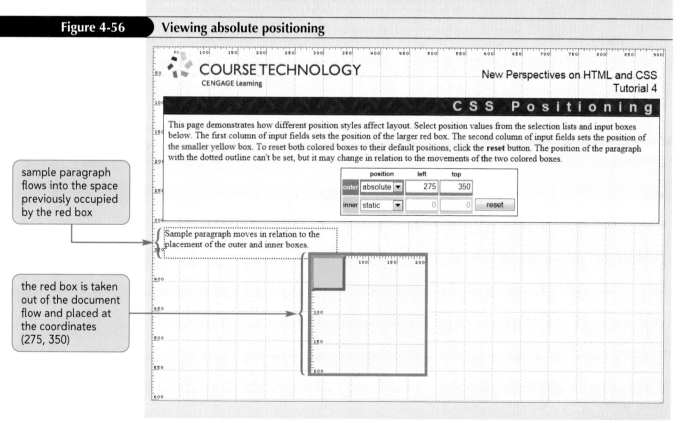

sample paragraph flows into the space previously occupied by the red box

the red box is taken out of the document flow and placed at the coordinates (275, 350)

Absolute positioning takes an element out of the normal document flow, so that any subsequent content flows into the space previously occupied by the element. Note that on the demo page, the sample paragraph moves up into the space that was previously occupied by the red outer box.

The location of the object depends on the context in which absolute positioning has been applied. If the object is contained within another object that has been placed using the `position` property, then those two objects are placed as a single unit and the nested object's coordinates are based on the position of the containing object. On the other hand, if the object is nested within containers that don't have a `position` property, then that object is placed relative to the browser window itself.

To see this effect in action, return to the demo page.

To view absolute positioning with a nested object:

▶ **1.** Within the demo page, select **absolute** from the list box for the inner element.

▶ **2.** Enter **90** in the left box for the inner object and **75** for the top box. As shown in Figure 4-57, the inner yellow box is placed at the coordinates (90, 75) within the outer box. It is *not* placed at the coordinates (90, 75) in the browser window.

Figure 4-57	Positioning a nested object

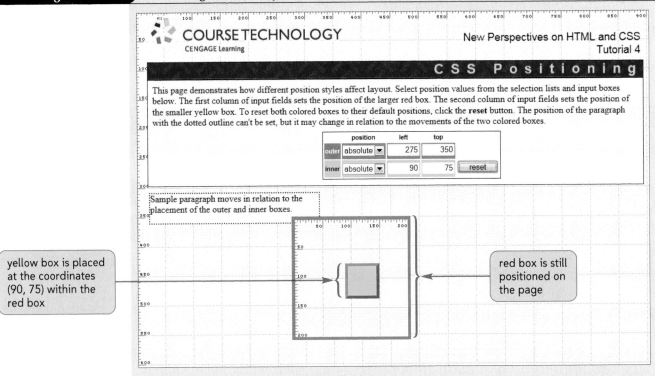

yellow box is placed at the coordinates (90, 75) within the red box

red box is still positioned on the page

Next, you'll examine what occurs when the outer box is no longer placed in the Web page using a positioning style.

▶ **3.** Select **static** from the list box for the outer element.

As shown in Figure 4-58, the red outer box is returned to its default position in the normal document flow, and the yellow inner box is placed at the coordinates (90, 75) in the browser window.

TIP

You can enter negative values for the top and left styles to move page elements up and to the left from their default locations.

Figure 4-58   **Absolute positioning for a nested object within a static container**

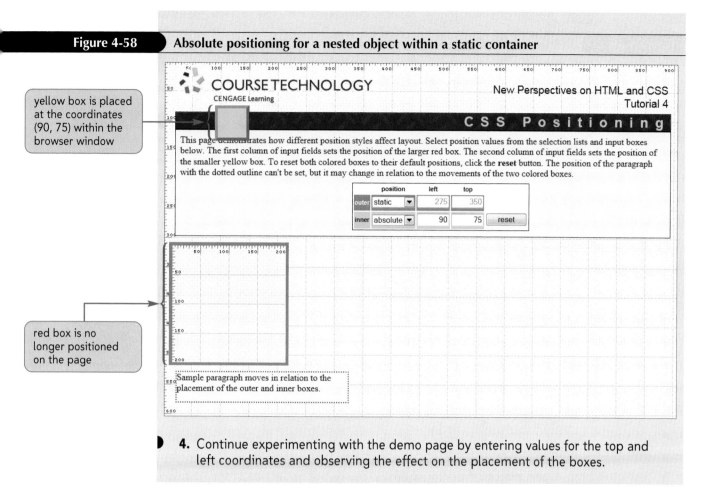

yellow box is placed at the coordinates (90, 75) within the browser window

red box is no longer positioned on the page

▶ **4.** Continue experimenting with the demo page by entering values for the top and left coordinates and observing the effect on the placement of the boxes.

Next, you'll examine how to place objects using relative positioning.

Relative Positioning

Relative positioning is used to move an element relative to where the browser would have placed it if no positioning had been applied. For example, the style

```
position: relative;
left: 100px;
top: 50px
```

places an element 100 pixels to the right and 50 pixels down from its normal placement in a browser window. A relatively positioned object is still part of the normal document flow; its placement is simply adjusted from its default location. You'll return to the demo page to explore the impact and uses of relative positioning.

To explore relative positioning:

▶ **1.** Click the **reset** button within the demo page to return both boxes to their default locations in the Web page.

▶ **2.** Select **relative** from the list box for the outer element, and then enter **275** for the left value and **50** for the top value. As shown in Figure 4-59, the outer box moves 275 pixels to the right and 50 pixels down from its default location.

Figure 4-59 **Relative positioning**

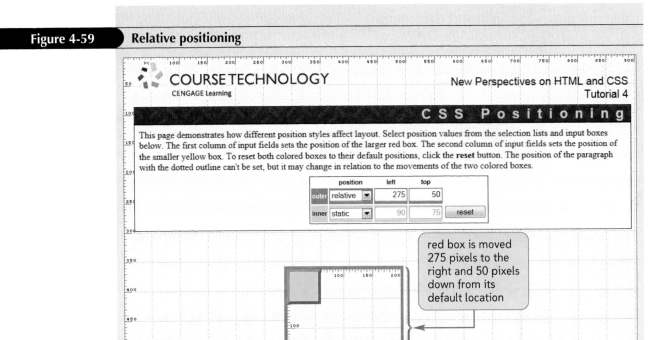

paragraph retains its position in the document flow

red box is moved 275 pixels to the right and 50 pixels down from its default location

Also note that the sample paragraph does not flow into the space previously occupied by the colored boxes. The layout of the rest of the page is unaffected because the red box and its contents are still part of the normal document flow.

3. Explore other combinations of absolute and relative positioning to see their effects on the layout of the demo page.

In many Web page layouts, you might want to absolutely position an object nested within a container element, but you don't want to move the container itself. In those cases, you simply can apply the style

```
position: relative;
```

to the container element without specifying the top and left coordinates. The browser assumes a default value of 0 for these missing coordinates and leaves the container in its default position in the normal document flow; however, any absolute positioning you apply to a nested element still will be applied relative to the top-left corner of the container element.

You can use this fact to center one object within another. If you know the total widths and heights of the nested object and its container, the center location of the nested object corresponds to the following coordinates:

$$\text{horizontal center} = \frac{\textit{container object width}}{2} - \frac{\textit{nested object width}}{2}$$

$$\text{vertical center} = \frac{\textit{container object height}}{2} - \frac{\textit{nested object height}}{2}$$

Note that the widths and heights are determined by calculating the sum of the widths and heights of the content, padding, and border space of each object. Try this by using positioning to center the yellow box within the red box.

To center an object within another object:

▶ **1.** With the red box still relatively positioned, enter **0** for the left and top position to place the object at its default positioning in the normal document flow.

▶ **2.** Select **absolute** for the yellow box.

Because the yellow box is 60 pixels wide by 60 pixels high and the red box is 200 pixels wide by 200 pixels high, you can center it within the red box by placing it at the coordinates (70, 70).

▶ **3.** Enter **70** for both the left and top coordinates (see Figure 4-60).

Figure 4-60 ▶ Centering one object within another

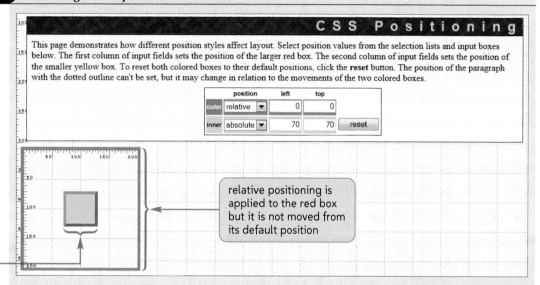

absolute positioning is used to center the yellow box within the red box

relative positioning is applied to the red box but it is not moved from its default position

---

Creating Drop Caps with CSS

A popular design element is the **drop cap**, which consists of an enlarged initial letter in a body of text that drops down into the text body, like the first letter of this sentence. To create a drop cap, you increase the font size of an element's first letter and float it on the left margin. Drop caps also generally look better if you decrease the line height of the first letter, enabling the surrounding content to better wrap around the letter. Finding the best combination of font size and line height is a matter of trial and error; and unfortunately, what looks best in one browser might not look as good in another. The following style rule works well in applying a drop cap to the paragraph element:

```
p:first-letter {
    font-size: 400%;
    float: left;
    line-height: 0.8;
}
```

With older browsers that do not support the first-letter pseudo-element, you have to mark the first letter using a span element. For additional design effects, you can change the font face of the drop cap to a cursive or decorative font.

Fixed and Inherited Positioning

An element placed with absolute or relative positioning scrolls with the document content. Alternatively, you can fix an element at a specific spot in the browser window while the document scrolls by setting the value of the position property to fixed. Note that older browsers might not support fixed positioning, so you should use it with some caution if it is a crucial part of your Web page layout.

You also can assign the position property to inherit so that an element inherits the position value of its parent element. You'll explore both positioning styles on the demo page.

To explore fixed and inherited positioning:

▶ **1.** Click the **reset** button within the demo page to return both boxes to their default locations in the Web page.

▶ **2.** Select **fixed** from the list box for the outer element, and then enter **300** for the left and top values.

The red box is moved out of the document flow and placed at the window coordinates (300, 300). The sample paragraph moves up into the space previously occupied by the red box.

Trouble? If you are running an older browser, you might not see any change in the position of the red box.

▶ **3.** Select **inherit** from the list box for the inner element, and then enter **600** for the left value and **300** for the top value.

The yellow box inherits the position style of its parent. In this case, it uses fixed positioning and is placed to the right of the outer red box.

Trouble? If your browser does not support the inherit position style, fix the position of the inner box by choosing fixed from the list box for the inner object.

▶ **4.** Resize the browser window so it's small enough to force the browser to display vertical and horizontal scroll bars. Scroll through the document and verify that the two color boxes remain fixed at the same location within the window (see Figure 4-61).

| Figure 4-61 | Fixed and inherited position |

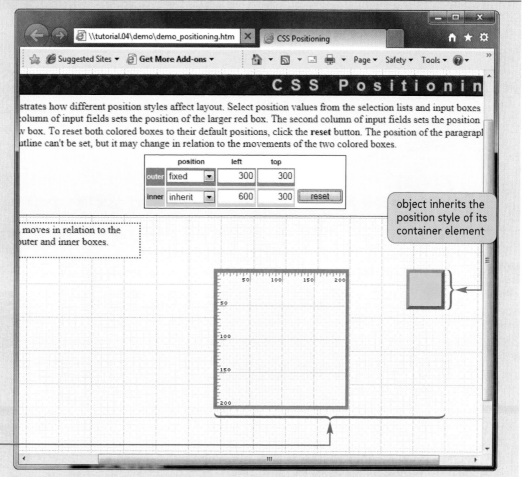

object inherits the position style of its container element

objects remain fixed in the browser window even as the document scrolls behind them

5. Continue to experiment with different positioning combinations. Close the demo page when you're finished.

Now that you've seen how to work with the positioning styles, you'll place the `header` element for the Cycle Pathology page at the coordinates (20, 20) using absolute positioning.

To place the page header:

1. Return to the **cp_reset.css** file in your text editor and remove the selector *header* and the comma that follows it from the style rule at the bottom of the file that hides the page elements. Save your changes to the file.

2. Go to the **cp_styles.css** file in your text editor. Directly below the style rule for the `body` selector near the top of the page, insert the following style rule (see Figure 4-62):

```
/* Styles for the Page Header */

header {
   position: absolute;
   top: 20px;
   left: 20px;
}
```

Figure 4-62   **Setting the position of the page header**

```
body {
    background: black url(bike_bg.png) top left no-repeat;
    width: 95%;
    min-width: 1000px;
    max-width: 1400px;
}


/* Styles for the Page Header */

header {
    position: absolute;
    top: 20px;
    left: 20px;
}
```

header placed with
absolute positioning

3. Save your changes to the file and then reload **cycle.htm** in your Web browser. As shown in Figure 4-63, the graphic image for the Cycle Pathology logo appears in the top-left corner of the browser window.

Figure 4-63   **Page header positioned at the top-left corner of the page**

logo placed at the
coordinates (20, 20)

Vaclav Volrab/Shutterstock.com

Next, you'll place the sidebar listing the upcoming cycling events at the left edge of the browser window directly below the graphic image of the cyclist standing before the sunset.

To place the sidebar:

1. Go to the **cp_reset.css** file in your text editor and remove the selector *aside* and the comma that follows it from the style rule at the bottom of the file, leaving only the *footer* selector. Save your changes to the file.

2. Return to the **cp_styles.css** file in your text editor. At the bottom of the file, insert the following style rule to place the `aside` element halfway down the left edge of the page (see Figure 4-64):

```
/* Sidebar styles */

aside {
   color: rgb(145, 98, 78);

   position: absolute;
   top: 400px;
   left: 10px;

   width: 30%;
}
```

Figure 4-64   Formatting the sidebar listing upcoming events

displays the text in a light brown font

places the sidebar 400 pixels from the top of the page and 10 pixels from the left edge

sets the sidebar width to 30%

```
/* Sidebar styles */

aside {
   color: rgb(145, 98, 78);

   position: absolute;
   top: 400px;
   left: 10px;

   width: 30%;
}
```

3. Save your changes to the file and then reload **cycle.htm** in your Web browser. As shown in Figure 4-65, the sidebar describing the upcoming rides starts halfway down the left edge of the page.

Figure 4-65   Sidebar of upcoming events

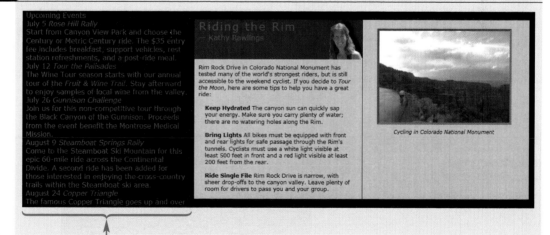

Upcoming Events
July 5 *Rose Hill Rally*
Start from Canyon View Park and choose the Century or Metric Century ride. The $35 entry fee includes breakfast, support vehicles, rest station refreshments, and a post-ride meal.
July 12 *Tour the Palisades*
The Wine Tour season starts with our annual tour of the *Fruit & Wine Trail*. Stay afterward to enjoy samples of local wine from the valley.
July 26 *Gunnison Challenge*
Join us for this non-competitive tour through the Black Canyon of the Gunnison. Proceeds from the event benefit the Montrose Medical Mission.
August 9 *Steamboat Springs Rally*
Come to the Steamboat Ski Mountain for this epic 60-mile ride across the Continental Divide. A second ride has been added for those interested in enjoying the cross-country trails within the Steamboat ski area.
August 24 *Copper Triangle*
The famous Copper Triangle goes up and over

Riding the Rim
Kathy Rawlings

Rim Rock Drive in Colorado National Monument has tested many of the world's strongest riders, but is still accessible to the weekend cyclist. If you decide to *Tour the Moon*, here are some tips to help you have a great ride:

Keep Hydrated The canyon sun can quickly sap your energy. Make sure you carry plenty of water; there are no watering holes along the Rim.

Bring Lights All bikes must be equipped with front and rear lights for safe passage through the Rim's tunnels. Cyclists must use a white light visible at least 500 feet in front and a red light visible at least 200 feet from the rear.

Ride Single File Rim Rock Drive is narrow, with sheer drop-offs to the canyon valley. Leave plenty of room for drivers to pass you and your group.

Cycling in Colorado National Monument

sidebar

The sidebar consists of h1 and h2 headings and paragraphs that describe each ride. You'll style these elements now.

To format the sidebar content:

1. Return to the **cp_styles.css** file in your text editor. At the bottom of the file, insert the following style rules for the h1, h2, and p elements in the aside element:

```
aside h1 {
    font-size: 105%;
    font-weight: bold;
    margin-bottom: 25px;
    text-align: center;
}

aside h2 {
    font-size: 85%;
    font-weight: bold;
}

aside p {
    font-size: 75%;
    margin: 15px;
}
```

Figure 4-66 highlights and describes the new style rules.

Figure 4-66 Formatting the sidebar elements

displays the h1 heading in bold and 105% of the size of the default text; centers the heading and increases the bottom margin to 25 pixels

```
aside h1 {
    font-size: 105%;
    font-weight: bold;
    margin-bottom: 25px;
    text-align: center;
}

aside h2 {
    font-size: 85%;
    font-weight: bold;
}

aside p {
    font-size: 75%;
    margin: 15px;
}
```

displays the h2 headings in bold and 85% of the size of the default text

displays paragraphs at 75% of the size of the default text with a 15-pixel margin

2. Save your changes to the file and then reload **cycle.htm** in your Web browser. Figure 4-67 shows part of the formatted aside element.

Figure 4-67 Formatted sidebar

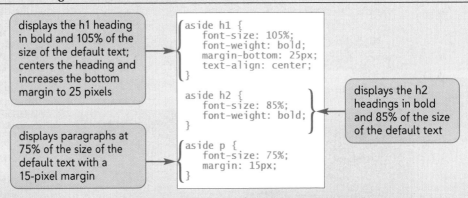

Absolute Positioning and Element Widths

In Figure 4-64, you set the width of the aside element to 30%—but 30% of what? Percentages usually are based on the size of the container element. The 33% left margin you assigned to the president's message in Figure 4-27 represented a length that was 33% of the width of the Web page because the president's message was nested within the body element. The 50% width assigned to the article element in Figure 4-48 represented 50% of the width of the section element because the article was nested within the section.

However, the aside element, while nested within the body element in the HTML file, has been placed in the Web page using absolute positioning, and that takes it out of the normal document flow. The 30% width represents 30% of the width of the container element, but only if that container also has been placed using either absolute or relative positioning. If not, the percentage is based on the width of the browser window itself. This is the same effect you saw earlier in the demo when the position of the inner object depended on whether the outer object itself also had been placed using absolute or relative positioning.

In a fluid layout, you want the sizes of all the page sections to be based on the same thing so that they all are resized the same way. To fix this in the Cycle Pathology Web page, you'll place the entire page body using relative positioning. Recall that you simply can apply the style position: relative to any page element to place it at its default location; the key difference will be that the width of the aside element will be based on the width of the page body rather than the browser window.

To position the entire page body:

1. Return to the **cp_styles.css** file and locate the style rule for the body selector near the top of the page.

2. Add the following property to the style rule as shown in Figure 4-68:

   ```
   position: relative;
   ```

Figure 4-68   Applying relative positioning to the page body

```
body {
    background: black url(bike_bg.png) top left no-repeat;
    position: relative;
    width: 95%;
    min-width: 1000px;
    max-width: 1400px;
}
```

3. Save your changes to the file and then reload the **cycle.htm** file in your Web browser. Change the size of your browser window and verify that the width of the aside element changes proportionally along with the widths of the other page elements.

Dan likes the appearance of the Upcoming Events sidebar, but he feels it's too long and would like you to reduce the height of the object so that it appears within the boundaries of the browser window.

Problem Solving: Principles of Design

Good Web page design is based on the same common principles found in other areas of art, which include balance, unity, contrast, rhythm, and emphasis. A pleasing layout involves the application of most, if not all, of these principles, which are detailed below:

- **Balance** is the distribution of elements. It's common to think of balance in terms of **symmetrical balance**, in which similar objects offset each other like items on a balance scale; but you often can achieve more interesting layouts through **asymmetrical balance**, in which one large page object is balanced against two or more smaller objects.
- **Unity** is the ability to combine different design elements into a cohesive whole. This is accomplished by having different elements share common colors, font styles, and sizes. One way to achieve unity in a layout is to place different objects close to each other, forcing your viewers' eyes to see these items as belonging to a single unified object.
- **Contrast** consists of the differences among all of the page elements. To create an effective design, you need to vary the placement, size, color, and general appearance of the objects in the page so that your viewers' eyes aren't bored by the constant repetition of a single theme.
- **Rhythm** is the repetition or alternation of a design element in order to provide a sense of movement, flow, and progress. You can create rhythm by tiling the same image horizontally or vertically across the page, by repeating a series of elements that progressively increase or decrease in size or spacing, or by using elements with background colors of the same hue but that gradually vary in saturation or lightness.
- **Emphasis** involves working with the focal point of a design. Readers need a few key areas to focus on. It's a common design mistake to assign equal emphasis to all page elements. Without a focal point, there is nothing for your viewers' eyes to latch onto. You can give a page element emphasis by increasing its size, by giving it a contrasting color, or by assigning it a prominent position in the page.

We usually have an intuitive sense of what works and what doesn't in page design, though often we can't say why. These design principles are important because they provide a context in which to discuss and compare designs. If your page design doesn't feel like it's working, evaluate it in light of these principles to identify where it might be lacking.

Working with Overflow and Clipping

The `aside` element is as long as it is because it must display several upcoming events. You can set a smaller height using the `height` property, but what would that do to the content that wouldn't fit under the reduced size?

When you force an element into a specified height and width, you can define how browsers should handle content that overflows allotted space using the style

```
overflow: type;
```

where *type* is `visible` (the default), `hidden`, `scroll`, or `auto`. A value of `visible` instructs browsers to increase the height of an element to fit the overflow content, which is what browsers normally do. The `hidden` value keeps the element at the specified height and width, but cuts off excess content. The `scroll` value keeps the element at the specified dimensions, but adds horizontal and vertical scroll bars to allow users to scroll through the overflow. Finally, the `auto` value keeps the element at the specified size, adding scroll bars only as they are needed. Figure 4-69 shows examples of the effects of each overflow value on content that is too large for its space.

Figure 4-69	Values of the overflow property

Working with Content Overflow and Clipping

- To specify how browsers should handle content that overflows an element's boundary, use the style

    ```
    overflow: type;
    ```

    where *type* is visible (to expand the element height to match the content), hidden (to hide the excess content), scroll (to always display horizontal and vertical scroll bars), or auto (to display scroll bars if needed).

- To specify how browsers should handle content that overflows in the horizontal direction, use the following style:

    ```
    overflow-x: type;
    ```

- To specify how browsers should handle content that overflows in the vertical direction, use the following style:

    ```
    overflow-y: type;
    ```

- To clip an element's content, use the style

    ```
    clip: rect(top, right, bottom, left);
    ```

    where *top*, *right*, *bottom*, and *left* define the boundaries of the clipping rectangle.

You decide to limit the height of the aside element to 450 pixels and to set the overflow property to auto so that browsers display scroll bars as needed.

To define the overflow style for the `aside` **element:**

▶ **1.** Return to **cp_styles.css** in your text editor and scroll down the style rule for the `aside` selector near the bottom of the file.

▶ **2.** Add the following styles, as shown in Figure 4-70:

```
height: 450px;
overflow: auto;
```

Figure 4-70	Setting the height and overflow properties

```
aside {
    color: rgb(145, 98, 78);

    position: absolute;
    top: 400px;
    left: 10px;

    width: 30%;
    height: 450px;
    overflow: auto;
}
```

scroll bars are displayed automatically if the content overflows the space

height of the aside element is set to 450 pixels

▶ **3.** Save your changes to the file and then reload **cycle.htm** in your Web browser. As shown in Figure 4-71, a scroll bar is added to the `aside` element.

Figure 4-71	aside element with scroll bar

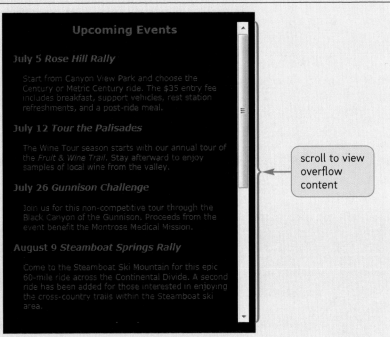

scroll to view overflow content

▶ **4.** Verify that you can view the entire list of upcoming events by scrolling through the contents of the Upcoming Events sidebar.

Trouble? To scroll through the `aside` element using a mobile device like an iPad, you must use the two-finger scroll gesture on the contents of the sidebar.

Horizontal Overflow and White Space

Scroll bars for overflow content are usually placed vertically so that you scroll down to view the extra content. In some page layouts, however, you may want to view content in a horizontal rather than a vertical direction. You can accomplish this by adding the following style properties to the element:

```
overflow: auto;
white-space: nowrap;
```

The `white-space` property defines how browsers should handle white space in the rendered document. The default is to collapse consecutive occurrences of white space into a single blank space, and to automatically wrap text to a new line if it extends beyond the width of the container. However, you can set the `white-space` property of the element to `nowrap` to keep inline content on a single line, preventing line wrapping. With the contents thus confined to a single line, browsers will display only horizontal scroll bars for the overflow content. Other values of the `white-space` property include `normal` (for default handling of white space), `pre` (to preserve all white space from the HTML file), and `pre-wrap` (to preserve white space but to wrap excess content to a new line).

Clipping an Element

Closely related to the `overflow` property is the `clip` property, which allows you to define a rectangular region through which an element's content can be viewed. Anything that lies outside the boundary of the rectangle is hidden. The syntax of the `clip` property is

```
clip: rect(top, right, bottom, left);
```

where `top`, `right`, `bottom`, and `left` define the coordinates of the clipping rectangle. For example, a clip value of `rect(10, 175, 125, 75)` defines a clip region whose top and bottom edges are 10 and 125 pixels from the top of the element, and whose right and left edges are 175 and 75 pixels from the left side of the element. See Figure 4-72.

Figure 4-72   **Clipping an element**

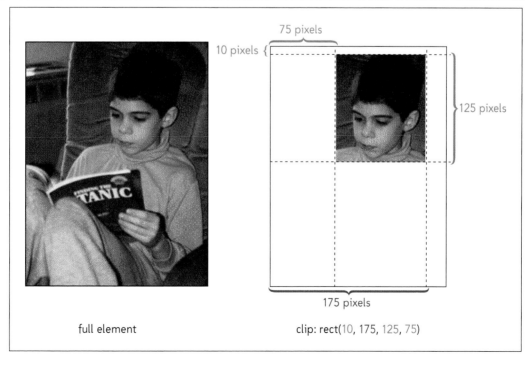

75 pixels

10 pixels {

125 pixels

175 pixels

full element   clip: rect(10, 175, 125, 75)

The *top*, *right*, *bottom*, and *left* values also can be set to *auto*, which matches the specified edge of the clipping region to the edge of the parent element. For example, a clip value of *rect(10, auto, 125, 75)* creates a clipping rectangle whose right edge matches the right edge of the parent element. To remove clipping completely, apply the style *clip: auto*. Clipping can only be applied when the object is placed using absolute positioning.

Semi-Transparent Images

The background image of Dan Atwood in the president's message section contains a transparent background to allow the color and background of the president's message box to show through. Transparent backgrounds are supported in the PNG and GIF image formats, but not in JPEG images. The GIF image format represents an older standard that can support a basic color palette of only 256 colors. The newer png format supports the complete color palette of 16.7 million colors and also supports the alpha channel, enabling designers to use transparent or semi-transparent colors.

Check with the documentation for your graphics software to learn how you can create transparent or semi-transparent colors for use in your Web site designs.

Stacking Elements

Positioning elements can sometimes lead to objects that overlap each other. By default, elements that are loaded later by the browser are displayed on top of elements that are loaded earlier. In addition, elements placed using CSS positioning are stacked on top of elements that are not. To specify a different stacking order, use the style property

```
z-index: value;
```

where *value* is a positive or negative integer, or the keyword *auto*. As shown in Figure 4-73, objects are stacked based on their z-index values, with the highest z-index values placed on top. A value of *auto* allows browsers to determine the stacking order using the default rules.

Figure 4-73　　Using the z-index property to stack elements

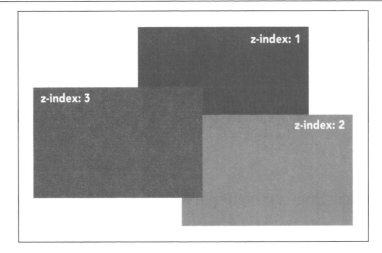

The *z-index* property works only for elements that are placed with absolute positioning. Also, an element's z-index value determines its position relative only to other elements that share a common parent; the style has no impact when applied to elements

with different parents. Figure 4-74 shows a diagram in which the object with a high z-index value of 4 is still covered because it is nested within another object that has a low z-index value of 1.

Figure 4-74   **Nesting stacked elements**

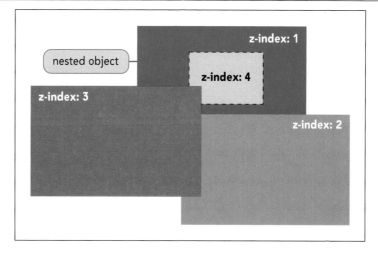

You do not need to include the z-index property in your style sheet as none of the page elements are stacked upon another.

The only remaining page section to include in the Cycle Pathology home page is the page footer and the Cycle Pathology address. You'll display the footer only after the left margin is clear of floating elements, and you'll apply a left margin of 33%. You'll also center the address text in the footer, remove any italic from the font style, and reduce the font size. Add these styles to the Cycle Pathology style sheet now.

To style the page footer and address:

1. Go to the **cp_reset.css** file in your text editor. Scroll to the bottom of the file and delete the entire style rule that hides page elements—which contains only the footer selector now—along with its style comment. No page elements should now be hidden in the page. Close the file, saving your changes.

2. Return to the **cp_styles.css** file in your text editor. At the bottom of the file, insert the following style rules for the page footer:

```
/* Page footer styles */

footer {
   clear: left;
   margin-left: 33%;
   width: 66%;
}
```

3. Directly below the footer style rule, add the following style rule for the address element:

```
footer address {
   color: rgb(182, 182, 92);
   font-size: 80%;
   font-style: normal;
   padding-top: 10px;
   text-align: center;
}
```

Figure 4-75 shows and describes the newly inserted style rules.

Figure 4-75 **Styles for the page footer and address**

floats the footer on the left margin after it clears the story section; sets the left margin to 33% of the page width

```
/* Page footer styles */

footer {
    clear: left;
    margin-left: 33%;
    width: 66%;
}
```

displays the address in a small normal style light yellow font; centers the text with a top padding of 10 pixels

```
footer address {
    color: rgb(182, 182, 92);
    font-size: 80%;
    font-style: normal;
    padding-top: 10px;
    text-align: center;
}
```

▶ **4.** Close the file, saving your changes, and then reload **cycle.htm** in your Web browser. Figure 4-76 shows the final appearance of the Cycle Pathology home page.

Figure 4-76 **Final Cycle Pathology home page**

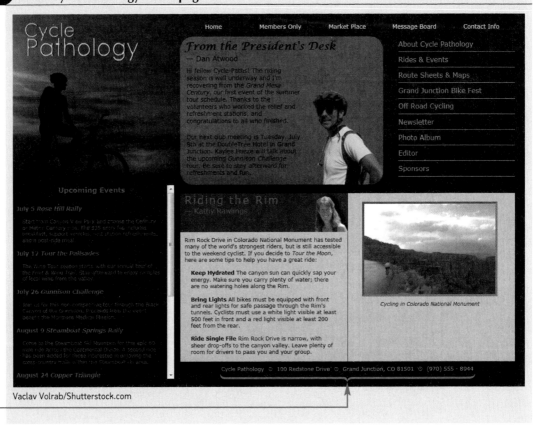

page footer and address

Vaclav Volrab/Shutterstock.com

Dan is pleased with the final design of the home page. He'll continue to work with the page and test it against different browsers and screen resolutions to verify that it's usable under different situations. He'll get back to you with future projects as he continues to overhaul the design of the entire Cycle Pathology Web site.

REVIEW

Session 4.3 Quick Check

1. Provide a style rule to place an element with the id *logo* at the coordinates (150, 75) using absolute positioning.
2. Provide a style rule to move the `header` element 5% down and 10% to the right of its default position.
3. Provide a style rule to fix a page element with the id *watermark* at the screen coordinates (400, 300).
4. Explain the difference between absolute and relative positioning in how they impact the placement of other elements in the Web page.
5. A navigation list has been set with a height of 300 pixels. Provide a style rule to show scroll bars only if there are too many entries in the navigation list to display within the space provided.
6. An inline image with the id *logo_img* is 400 pixels wide by 300 pixels high and needs to be clipped by 10 pixels on each edge. Provide a style rule to accomplish this.
7. One element has a z-index value of 1; a second element has a z-index value of 5. Will the second element always be displayed on top of the first? Explain why or why not.

Practice the skills you learned in the tutorial using the same case scenario.

PRACTICE

Review Assignments

Data Files needed for the Review Assignments: alisha.png, cp_logo2.png, modernizr-1.5.js, racetxt.css, rosetxt.htm, slide01.png-slide08.png

Dan wants your help in designing a layout for a Cycle Pathology Web page that describes one of the group's upcoming tours. He would like you to use a flexible layout with a list of navigation links displayed on the left 20% of the page, with the remaining 80% of the page width devoted to page content. He also wants the page to contain a slide show of images from previous events displayed with a horizontal scroll bar. Figure 4-77 shows a preview of the page you'll create for Dan.

Figure 4-77 Cycle Pathology tour page

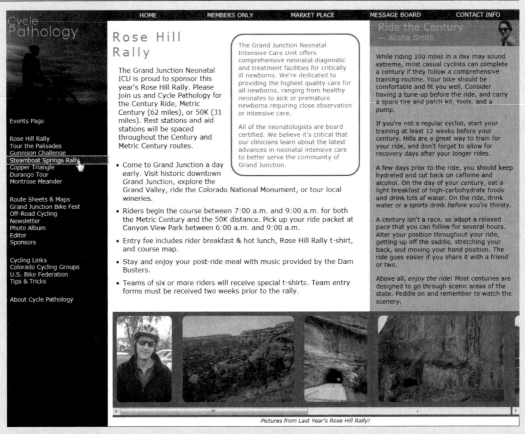

Vaclav Volrab/Shutterstock.com

Complete the following:

1. Use your text editor to open the **rosetxt.htm** and **racetxt.css** files from the tutorial.04\review folder. Enter *your name* and *the date* in the comment section of each file and then save them as **rose.htm** and **race.css**, respectively.

2. Go to the **rose.htm** file in your text editor and take some time to review the content and structure of the file. Link the file to the **race.css** style sheet and then save your changes to the file.

3. Return to the **race.css** file in your text editor. Add a style rule to display the `header`, `article`, `aside`, `figure`, `figcaption`, `hgroup`, `section`, and `nav` elements as blocks.

4. Create a style rule to set the default style for every element so that every element: a) is displayed in a Verdana, Geneva, or sans-serif font; b) has a font size of 100%; and c) has a padding and margin space of 0 pixels.

5. Remove the underlining from every hypertext link within a `nav` element.

6. Create a style rule for the page body that: a) positions the page using relative positioning; and b) sets the page width to 98% of the width of the browser window in a range from 1000 pixels up to 1400 pixels.

7. Create a style rule for the `header` element that: a) places the header at the coordinates (0, 0) using absolute positioning; b) sets the width to 20% of the page body; c) changes the background color to black; and d) adds a 500-pixel padding space to the bottom of the element.

8. For inline images within a `header` element, set the width to 100% of the width of the header.

9. Set the width of the horizontal navigation list to 80% with a left margin of 20%. For list items within the horizontal navigation list, add styles to: a) display each list item as a block floated on the left; b) set the width of each list item to 20%; c) set the background color to the value (49, 38, 31); d) set the upper and lower padding space to 5 pixels; e) horizontally center the list item text; and f) transform the text to uppercase letters, setting the font size to 85%.

10. Set the color of hypertext links in the horizontal navigation list to white. If the user hovers the mouse pointer over the link, change the color to the value (215, 181, 151).

11. For every list item in the vertical navigation list, set the font size to 85% and remove the list style marker. If the list item belongs to the *newgroup* class, add a top padding space of 25 pixels to add a bigger gap between that list item and the previous list item.

12. For every hypertext link within the vertical navigation list, set the font color to white, set the `display` property to block, and indent the text 10 pixels. If the user hovers the mouse pointer over the hypertext link, change the background color to the value (51, 51, 51) and add a 2-pixel solid outline with the color value (215, 181, 151).

13. Add the following styles to the main section of the page: a) float the main section on the left margin once the left margin has been clear of previously floated objects; b) set the size of the left margin to 21%; c) set the size of the top margin to 20 pixels; and d) set the width of the main section to 49% of the page body.

14. For `h1` headings that are direct children of the main section, add styles to: a) set the text color to the value (189, 131, 82); b) set the font size to 180% with normal weight; and c) set the letter spacing to 5 pixels.

15. Set the margins of paragraphs within the main section to 15 pixels. For the unordered list within the main section: a) display a disc marker; b) set the margin around the entire unordered list to 25 pixels; and c) set the bottom margin of each list item to 10 pixels.

16. For the `aside` element, create a style rule to: a) add a 3-pixel solid border with the color value (149, 91, 42) and set the text color to the value (149, 91, 42); b) float the `aside` element on the right with a margin of 10 pixels; c) set the width to 50% of the width of the main section; and d) add a rounded border with a radius of 30 pixels. For paragraphs within the `aside` element, set the font size to 90% and the margin to 20 pixels.

17. For the `article` element, create a style rule to: a) float the element on the left with a width of 29% and a left margin of 1%; and b) set the background color to the value (215, 181, 151).

18. For the header group within the `article` element, create a style rule to: a) display a background color with the value (189, 131, 82) with the background image *alisha.png* displayed in the bottom-right corner with no tiling; b) set the text color to the value (215, 181, 151); c) set the bottom margin to 10 pixels; d) set the height to 60 pixels; and e) indent the text 20 pixels. Set the size of `h1` headings within the header group to 150% with normal weight. Set the size of `h2` headings to 110% with normal weight.

19. For paragraphs within the `article` element, add styles to: a) set the font size to 90%; and b) set the margin to 15 pixels.

20. For the figure box, create a style rule to: a) float the figure box on the left once the left margin is clear; b) add a 21% left margin; c) set the width of the figure box to 79%; and d) set the background color to the value (149, 91, 42).

21. For the `div` element within the figure box, set the browser to display scroll bars automatically if the content overflows the assigned space, and use the `white-space` property to prevent the content from wrapping to a new line.

22. For inline images within the figure box: a) set the margin to 10 pixels; and b) add rounded corners with a radius of 10 pixels.

23. For the figure caption within the figure box, create a style rule to: a) set the background to white; b) set the font size to 80%, displayed in italic and centered; and c) set the top margin to 5 pixels.

24. Add descriptive comments to the style sheet to identify the style rules for the different sections of the Web page.

25. Save your changes to the file and then open **rose.htm** in your Web browser. Verify that the layout and design of the page resemble that shown in Figure 4-77. View your Web page under several different browser window widths to verify that the fluid layout correctly changes in response.

26. Submit your completed files to your instructor, in either printed or electronic form, as requested.

*Apply your
knowledge of
CSS to create
an elastic layout
along with a
drop cap and
an irregular
line wrap.*

APPLY

Case Problem 1

**Data Files needed for this Case Problem: arlogo.png, historytxt.css,
lincoln01.png-lincoln10.png, lincolntxt.htm, modernizr-1.5.js**

American Rhetoric   Professor Annie Chiu teaches rhetoric and history at White Sands
College. She has asked for your help in designing a companion Web site for her course
in American Rhetoric. She's given you the content and graphics for a sample page containing an excerpt from the second inaugural address by Abraham Lincoln. She wants
you to create an elastic layout for the Web page so that it appears the same for different
font sizes. Figure 4-78 shows a preview of the page you'll design for her.

Figure 4-78   Lincoln page

Complete the following:

1. In your text editor, open the **historytxt.css** and **lincolntxt.htm** files from the
   tutorial.04\case1 folder. Enter *your name* and *the date* in the comment section of
   each file. Save the files as **history.css** and **lincoln.htm**, respectively.
2. Return to the **lincoln.htm** file in your text editor and take some time to review the
   content and structure of the file. Link the document to the **history.css** style sheet.
   Close the file, saving your changes.

3. Go to the **history.css** file in your text editor. Create a style rule to display the `header`, `section`, and `nav` elements as blocks.

4. Set the default padding and margin space for every element to 0 pixels.

5. Define a style rule for the `header` element to: a) set the background color to the value (51, 51, 51); b) center the contents of the `header` element; and c) set the width to 55 em. Set the height of the inline image within the header to 4 em.

6. Float the navigation list on the left page margin, setting the width to 15 em and the background color to the value (51, 51, 51).

7. For list items within the navigation list, create a style rule to: a) set the typeface to Century Gothic or sans-serif; b) set the font size to 0.7 em; c) remove the list markers; d) set the line height to 1.4 em; and e) set the left and bottom margins to 1 em and 1.2 em, respectively.

8. For hypertext links within the navigation list, set the text color to the value (212, 212, 212) and remove the underlining. When the user hovers the mouse pointer over these links, change the text color to white.

9. For the speech section of the page, create a style rule to: a) set the background color to the value (212, 212, 212); b) set the width to 40 em and float the section on the left; and c) display the text in a Palatino Linotype, Book Antiqua, Palatino, or serif font.

10. For the `h1` heading within the speech section, create a style rule to: a) set the background color to the value (51, 51, 51); b) set the text color to the value (212, 212, 212) and the font size to 2 em; and c) center the text.

11. For the paragraphs within the speech section, set the font size to 0.9 em and the margin size to 1 em.

⊕ **EXPLORE** 12. Annie wants to create a drop-cap effect for the first letter in the first line of the first paragraph in the speech section. Using the `first-of-type` pseudo-class and the `first-letter` pseudo-element in your style rule selector, create this drop cap by: a) floating the first letter on the left; b) setting the font size and line height to 4 em and 0.8 em, respectively; c) setting the right margin to 0.3 em; d) setting the right and bottom padding to 0.2 em; and e) adding a solid black border 0.02 em in width to the right and bottom edge of the letter.

13. Display the text of the first line of the first paragraph in the speech section in upper-case letters.

⊕ **EXPLORE** 14. Next, you'll create the irregular line wrap shown in Figure 4-78. Stack the 10 slices of the Lincoln image by creating a style rule for the inline image elements within the speech section to: a) float each image on the right once the right margin is clear; and b) set the height of each image to 4 em.

15. Add appropriate style comments to your file to document your work and then save your changes.

16. Open the **lincoln.htm** file in your Web browser. Verify that the layout resembles that shown in Figure 4-78. (Note: Safari for the Macintosh does not at the time of this writing support the `first-line` pseudo-class with uppercase letters. Also, you might notice a slight difference in the layout with browsers running on the Macintosh, iPhone, or iPad.)

⊕ **EXPLORE** 17. Using the Options or Preferences dialog box of your browser, increase and decrease the browser's default font size. Verify that as the font size changes, the layout and size of the inline images in the page change in proportion.

18. Submit your completed files to your instructor, in either printed or electronic form, as requested.

Apply your knowledge of CSS to create a fixed layout design for a pizzeria Web site.

CHALLENGE

Case Problem 2

Data Files needed for this Case Problem: modernizr-1.5.js, notice.png, pizzatxt.css, rblogo.png, redballtxt.htm, redbar.png, slice.png, toppings.png

Red Ball Pizza Alice Nichols is the owner of Red Ball Pizza, a well-established pizzeria in Ormond Beach, Florida. She's asked for your help in creating a design for the company's Web site. After discussing the issue with Alice, you settle on a fixed width layout. Alice has created a sample home page for you to work on. She's already created all of the content and the graphics. She needs your help with the design. Figure 4-79 shows a preview of the page you'll create for her.

Figure 4-79   Red Ball Pizza

Complete the following:

1. In your text editor, open the **pizzatxt.css** and **redballtxt.htm** files from the tutorial.04\case2 folder. Enter *your name* and *the date* in the comment section of each file. Save the files as **pizza.css** and **redball.htm**, respectively.

2. Return to the **redball.htm** file in your text editor. Take some time to review the content and structure of the document, and then link the file to the **pizza.css** style sheet. Close the file, saving your changes.

3. Go to the **pizza.css** file in your text editor. Create a style rule to display the `header`, `section`, `aside`, `footer`, and `nav` elements as blocks.

4. Set the default padding and margin size to 0 pixels.

5. Create a style for the `body` element to: a) set the background color to red; and b) set the font family to Verdana, Geneva, or sans-serif.

⊕ EXPLORE   6. The entire content of the page has been enclosed in a `div` container element with the id *container*. Create a style rule for this container to: a) set the width to 1000 pixels; b) center the container in the browser window by setting the top/bottom margins to 0 pixels and the left/right margins to `auto`; c) display a 1-pixel solid black border on the left and right edges; and d) set the background color to white and display the *redbar.png* image file as the background image, placing the image file in the top-left corner of the container and tiling it in the vertical direction only.

7. Change the background color of the `header` element to white and set its height to 100 pixels.

8. Create a style rule for the horizontal navigation list to: a) set the height to 70 pixels and the width to 100%; and b) set the background color to white.

9. For each list item within the horizontal navigation list, create a style rule to: a) set the background color to white; b) set the font size to 16 pixels, the height and the line height to 50 pixels, and the width to 180 pixels; c) display the item as a block and float it on the left; d) set the left and right margins to 5 pixels; and e) horizontally center the contents.

⊕ EXPLORE   10. For each hypertext link within a list item in the horizontal navigation list, create a style rule to: a) display the link as a block; b) set the background color to red and the text color to white; c) create elongated corners with a horizontal radius of 30 pixels and a vertical radius of 25 pixels (use progressive enhancement to support browser extensions); and d) remove the text underlining. If a user hovers a mouse pointer over these links, change the background color to the value (255, 101, 101) and the text color to black.

11. Create a style rule for the vertical navigation list to: a) float it on the left only when the left margin is clear; and b) set the width to 200 pixels.

12. For list items within the vertical navigation list, create a style rule to: a) remove the list item marker; b) indent the text 20 pixels; and c) set the top and bottom margins to 20 pixels.

13. For hypertext links within the vertical navigation list, set the text color to white and remove the text underlining. When a user hovers the mouse pointer over these links, change the text color to black.

14. The main content of the Web page is contained in a `section` element with the id *main*. Create a style rule for this element to: a) change the background color to the value (255, 211, 211); b) float the element on the left; and c) set the width to 600 pixels.

15. For paragraphs that are direct children of the main section, set the font size to 20 pixels and the margin to 15 pixels.

⊕**EXPLORE** 16. For inline images within the main section, create a style rule to: a) float the image on the right; b) set the margin to 15 pixels; c) set the width to 350 pixels; and d) set the radius of the bottom-left corner to 350 pixels (use progressive enhancement to support the Mozilla and WebKit browser extensions).

17. Alice has included six coupons in the home page that have been nested within `div` elements belonging to the *coupon* class. For each *coupon* `div` element: a) add a 5-pixel dashed black border; b) float the coupons on the left; c) set the width to 170 pixels and the height to 150 pixels; and d) set the top and bottom margins to 20 pixels, and the left and right margins to 10 pixels.

⊕**EXPLORE** 18. To the style rule for the coupons, add style properties to create the following two background images: a) place the *slice.png* image in the center of the coupon without tiling; and b) place the *notice.png* image in the bottom-right corner of the coupon without tiling. Set the background color of the coupon to white.

19. For `h1` headings within the coupons, add a style rule to: a) set the text color to white on a background with the color value (192, 0, 0); b) set the font size to 16 pixels and the kerning to 2 pixels; c) center the text; d) set the height to 25 pixels; and e) display the text in small caps.

20. For paragraphs within the coupons, create a style rule to: a) set the font size to 14 pixels; b) center the text; and c) set the margin to 5 pixels.

21. Alice has placed interesting tidbits about pizza in an `aside` element. Float the `aside` element on the left with a width of 200 pixels.

22. For `h1` headings within the `aside` element, create a style rule to: a) set the text color to the value (192, 0, 0); b) set the font size to 20 pixels and the kerning to 2 pixels; c) set the font weight to normal; and d) center the text of the headings.

23. For list items within the `aside` element, create a style rule to: a) set the background color to the value (255, 135, 135); b) add round corners with a 5-pixel radius; c) set the text color to black; d) remove the list style maker; and e) set the margin to 10 pixels and the padding to 5 pixels.

24. Display the `footer` element when the left margin is clear, and set the size of the left margin to 200 pixels.

25. For the `address` element within the `footer` element, create a style rule to: a) add a 1-pixel solid red border to the top of the element; b) change the text color to red; c) set the font size to 10 pixels, set the font style to normal, and center the address text; and d) set the top margin to 25 pixels and the bottom padding to 20 pixels.

26. Add style comments throughout your style sheet to document your work and then save your changes.

27. Open the **redball.htm** file in your Web browser and verify that the design and layout resemble that shown in Figure 4-79.

28. Submit your completed files to your instructor, in either printed or electronic form, as requested.

Explore how to use CSS to create an interactive map with popup boxes.

CHALLENGE

Case Problem 3

Data Files needed for this Case Problem: bluebar.png, image0.jpg–image9.jpg, longstxt.htm, lpmap.jpg, maptxt.css, modernizr-1.5.js

Longs Peak Interactive Map   Longs Peak is one of the most popular attractions of Rocky Mountain National Park (RMNP). Each year during the months of July, August, and September, thousands of people climb Longs Peak by the Keyhole Route to reach the 14,255-foot summit. Ron Bartlett, the head of the RMNP Web site team, has asked for your help in creating an interactive map of the Keyhole Route. The map will be installed at electronic kiosks in the park's visitor center. Ron envisions a map with 10 numbered waypoints along the Keyhole Route, displaying a popup photo and description when a mouse pointer hovers over one of the numbered points. Figure 4-80 shows a preview of the online map with the first waypoint highlighted by the user.

Figure 4-80   Longs Peak interactive map

Complete the following:

1. Open the **longstxt.htm** and **maptxt.css** files in your text editor. Add *your name* and *the date* to the comment section of each file, and save the files as **longs.htm** and **map.css**, respectively.

2. Return to the **longs.htm** file in your text editor. Take some time to study the content and structure of the document. Link the file to the **map.css** style sheet and then close the file, saving your changes.

3. Go to the **map.css** style sheet.

4. Create a style rule to display the `nav`, `section`, `figure`, and `figcaption` elements as blocks.

⊕ EXPLORE

5. The estimated time that a hiker should arrive at each waypoint has been marked with the `time` element. Create another style rule to display the `time` element inline.

6. Set the margin and padding space of every element to 0 pixels.

7. Set the font family for the page body to Verdana, Geneva, or sans-serif.

8. The entire content of the page is nested within a `div` element with the id *page*. Create a style rule for this element to: a) set the background color to the value (255, 255, 128) and display the background image file, *bluebar.png*, tiled vertically along the left edge; b) add a ridged 15-pixel-wide border with a color value of (70, 76, 222); c) add rounded corners with a radius of 50 pixels; d) set the width and height to 900 pixels and 750 pixels, respectively; and e) horizontally center the `div` element within the browser window, setting its top margin to 10 pixels, setting its bottom margin to 200 pixels, and using `auto` for the left and right margins.

9. Float the vertical navigation list on the left margin with a width of 230 pixels. For each list item within the navigation list, remove the list markers, set the top and bottom margins to 25 pixels, and set the left and right margins to 20 pixels. Set the font color of hypertext links within the navigation list to white, and to yellow in response to the hover event. Remove the underlining from the hypertext links.

10. The description of the map is contained within the `section` element with the id *summary*. Float the summary section on the left with a left margin of 30 pixels and a width of 600 pixels.

11. Create a style rule for the `h1` heading within the summary section to: a) set the text color to the value (70, 76, 222); b) set the font size to 24 pixels, with normal weight and kerning set to 5 pixels; and c) set the margin to 20 pixels.

12. For paragraphs within the summary section, set the margin to 10 pixels.

13. The interactive map has been enclosed in a `section` element with the id *map*. For the map section, create a style rule to: a) place it using relative positioning (do not specify the top or left coordinate); b) set the background color to white, with the *lpmap.jpg* image file as the background image placed in the top-left corner with no tiling; c) add a 1-pixel-wide solid black border; d) float the section on the left with a left margin of 30 pixels; and e) set the width and height to 600 pixels and 294 pixels, respectively.

✦ EXPLORE   14. Each of the popup boxes has been placed within a figure box. Initially, these popup boxes should be clipped so that only the number is shown. Create a style rule for the `figure` element to: a) set the background color to the value (70, 76, 222); b) set the text color to white; c) set the width to 150 pixels; d) add rounded corners with a radius of 15 pixels; e) position the figure box using absolute positioning (but do not specify a top or left coordinate); f) set the z-index value to 1; and g) clip the content using a clipping rectangle that is 20 pixels wide by 20 pixels high and situated in the top-left corner of the figure box.

✦ EXPLORE   15. If a user hovers the mouse pointer over a figure box, then remove the clipping rectangle and increase the z-index value to 2 (so that it appears on top of other objects).

16. For the figure caption within each figure box, set the font size to 12 pixels and the margin to 10 pixels.

17. Set the text color of each `time` element within each figure box to yellow.

18. Each of the 10 figure boxes has an id, ranging from point0 to point9. Set the (left, top) coordinates of the figure boxes as follows:

point0 at (560, 60)
point1 at (277, 90)
point2 at (175, 0)
point3 at (110, 115)
point4 at (55, 165)
point5 at (5, 180)
point6 at (15, 222)
point7 at (50, 245)
point8 at (100, 245)
point9 at (90, 220)

19. Save your changes to the file and then open **longs.htm** in your Web browser. Verify that the placement of the waypoints follows the locations shown in Figure 4-80. Confirm that when you hover your mouse over each of the 10 waypoints, a description of the waypoint appears on the top of the trail map.

20. Submit your completed files to your instructor, in either printed or electronic form, as requested.

CREATE

Case Problem 4

Data Files needed for this Case Problem: address.txt, blake.jpg, cougar.jpg, links1.txt, links2.txt, modernizr-1.5.js, papertxt.css, parch.jpg, parch2.jpg, parktxt.htm, pcglogo.jpg, story1.txt–story4.txt

The Park City Gazette   Park City, Colorado, is a rural mountain community noted for its ski slopes and fishing holes. Kevin Webber is the editor of the weekly *Park City Gazette*. The paper recently redesigned its printed layout, and Kevin wants you to do the same thing for the online version. He's prepared several files containing sample text from recent articles and a few lists of links that usually appear in the front page of the newspaper's Web site. He's also provided you with image files that can be used for the paper's logo and background. Your job will be to use all of these pieces to create a sample Web page for him to evaluate.

Complete the following:

1. Use your text editor to open the **parktxt.htm** and **papertxt.css** files from the tutorial.04\case4 folder. Add *your name* and *the date* in the comment section of each file. Save the files as **park.htm** and **paper.css**, respectively.
2. Using the content of the address, links, and story text files, create the content and structure of the *park.htm* file. You are free to supplement the material in these text files with additional content of your own if appropriate. Use the # symbol for the value of the `href` attribute in your hypertext links because you will be linking to pages that don't actually exist.
3. Link the *park.htm* file to the **paper.css** style sheet file and then save your changes.
4. Go to the **paper.css** style sheet file and create a layout for your *Park City Gazette* sample page. The layout should be based on a fluid design that will render well on page widths from 1000 up to 1400 pixels.
5. The specifics of the page design are up to your imagination and skill, but must include the following features:
   - use of the `display` property
   - application of `width` and `height` style properties
   - floated elements and cleared elements
   - defined margin and padding spaces as well as maximum and minimum widths
   - border styles
   - rounded or elongated corners
   - use of progressive enhancement along with one or more browser style extensions
   - a tiled or non-tiled background image
   - an example of relative or absolute positioning
6. Test your layout and design on a variety of devices, browsers, and screen resolutions to ensure that your sample page is readable under different conditions.
7. Submit your completed files to your instructor, in either printed or electronic form, as requested.

ENDING DATA FILES

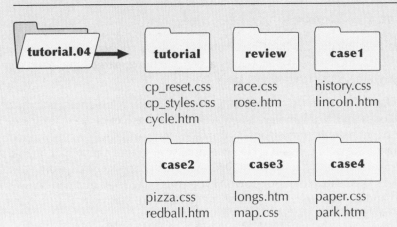

tutorial.04 →

tutorial
cp_reset.css
cp_styles.css
cycle.htm

review
race.css
rose.htm

case1
history.css
lincoln.htm

case2
pizza.css
redball.htm

case3
longs.htm
map.css

case4
paper.css
park.htm

TUTORIAL 5

Working with Tables and Columns

Creating a Radio Program Schedule

Case | *KPAF Radio*

Kyle Mitchell is the program director at KPAF, a public radio station broadcasting out of Bismarck, North Dakota. To remain viable, it's important for the station to continue to have a presence on the Web. With this in mind, Kyle has begun upgrading the KPAF Web site. He envisions a site in which listeners have quick and easy access to information about the station and its programs.

The Web site includes pages listing the KPAF morning, afternoon, and evening schedules. Kyle decides that this information is best conveyed to the listener in a table, with each column of the table displaying one day's program schedule and each row displaying the broadcast times for the various KPAF programs. Kyle has never created a Web table, so he's come to you for help in designing a Web page describing the KPAF evening schedule. Kyle wants the table you create to be easy to read and informative. He also wants you to add table styles that will enhance the appearance of the Web page.

STARTING DATA FILES

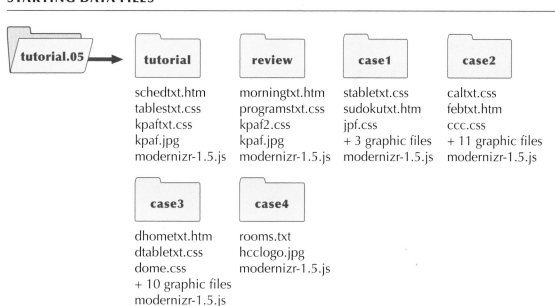

tutorial.05 →

tutorial
schedtxt.htm
tablestxt.css
kpaftxt.css
kpaf.jpg
modernizr-1.5.js

review
morningtxt.htm
programstxt.css
kpaf2.css
kpaf.jpg
modernizr-1.5.js

case1
stabletxt.css
sudokutxt.htm
jpf.css
+ 3 graphic files
modernizr-1.5.js

case2
caltxt.css
febtxt.htm
ccc.css
+ 11 graphic files
modernizr-1.5.js

case3
dhometxt.htm
dtabletxt.css
dome.css
+ 10 graphic files
modernizr-1.5.js

case4
rooms.txt
hcclogo.jpg
modernizr-1.5.js

SESSION 5.1 VISUAL OVERVIEW

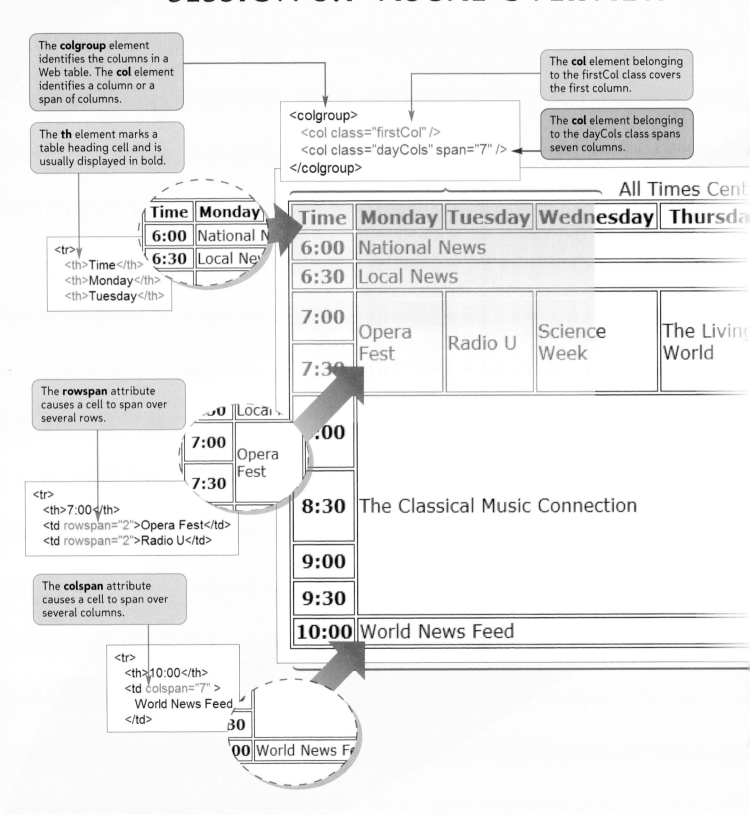

The **colgroup** element identifies the columns in a Web table. The **col** element identifies a column or a span of columns.

The **col** element belonging to the firstCol class covers the first column.

The **col** element belonging to the dayCols class spans seven columns.

The **th** element marks a table heading cell and is usually displayed in bold.

```
<colgroup>
  <col class="firstCol" />
  <col class="dayCols" span="7" />
</colgroup>
```

```
<tr>
  <th>Time</th>
  <th>Monday</th>
  <th>Tuesday</th>
```

The **rowspan** attribute causes a cell to span over several rows.

```
<tr>
  <th>7:00</th>
  <td rowspan="2">Opera Fest</td>
  <td rowspan="2">Radio U</td>
```

The **colspan** attribute causes a cell to span over several columns.

```
<tr>
  <th>10:00</th>
  <td colspan="7" >
    World News Feed
  </td>
```

All Times Cent

Time	Monday	Tuesday	Wednesday	Thursda
6:00	National News			
6:30	Local News			
7:00	Opera Fest	Radio U	Science Week	The Living World
7:30				
8:30	The Classical Music Connection			
9:00				
9:30				
10:00	World News Feed			

STRUCTURE OF A WEB TABLE

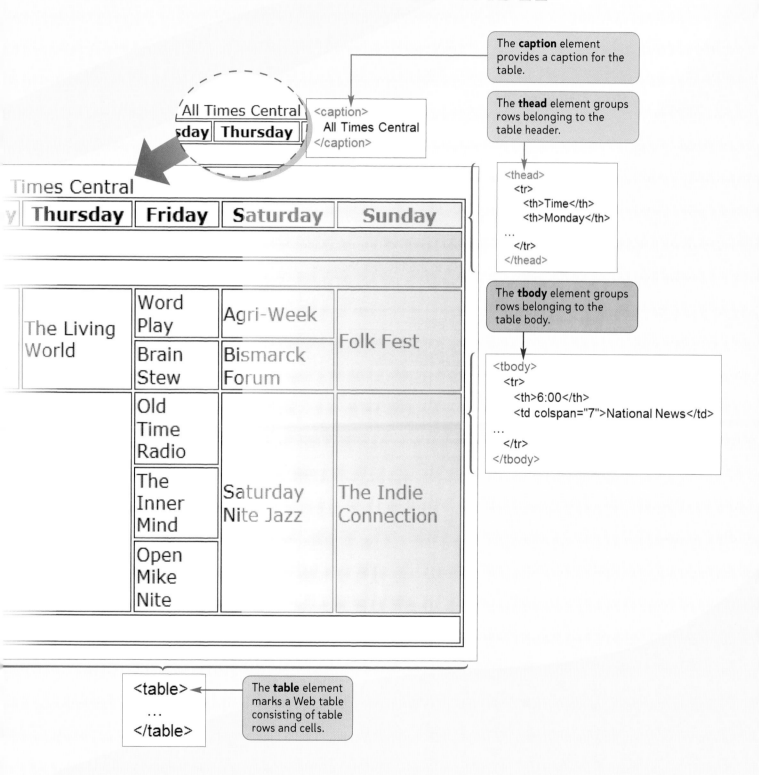

The **caption** element provides a caption for the table.

```
<caption>
   All Times Central
</caption>
```

The **thead** element groups rows belonging to the table header.

```
<thead>
   <tr>
      <th>Time</th>
      <th>Monday</th>
   ...
   </tr>
</thead>
```

The **tbody** element groups rows belonging to the table body.

```
<tbody>
   <tr>
      <th>6:00</th>
      <td colspan="7">National News</td>
   ...
   </tr>
</tbody>
```

```
<table>
   ...
</table>
```

The **table** element marks a Web table consisting of table rows and cells.

Introducing Web Tables

You meet with Kyle in his office at KPAF to discuss the design of the new Web site. Kyle already has created a basic Web page displaying the KPAF logo and a list of links to other pages and to upcoming shows. Open this file now.

To open the KPAF Web page:

▶ 1. In your text editor, open the **schedtxt.htm** and **kpaftxt.css** files, located in the tutorial.05\tutorial folder. Enter *your name* and *the date* in the comment section of each file. Save the files as **schedule.htm** and **kpaf.css**, respectively, in the same folder.

▶ 2. Review the **schedule.htm** file in your text editor to become familiar with its content and structure. Insert the following `link` element directly above the closing `</head>` tag:

```
<link href="kpaf.css" rel="stylesheet" type="text/css" />
```

▶ 3. Save your changes to the file and then open the **schedule.htm** file in your Web browser. Figure 5-1 shows the current appearance of the Web page.

| Figure 5-1 | Initial nightly schedule page |

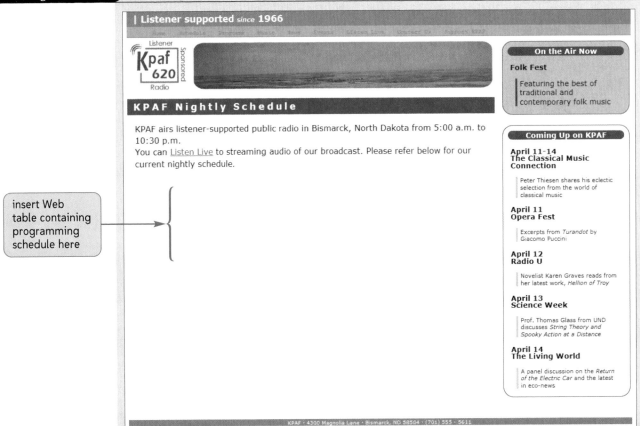

insert Web table containing programming schedule here

▶ 4. Go to the **kpaf.css** style sheet in your text editor. Review the styles and compare them to the elements contained within the *schedule.htm* file to fully understand Kyle's design for the schedule page.

Kyle wants you to add KPAF's nightly schedule, which runs from 6:00 p.m. to 10:30 p.m., to this Web page. The contents of the table are shown in Figure 5-2.

Figure 5-2 **KPAF nightly schedule**

Time	Monday	Tuesday	Wednesday	Thursday	Friday	Saturday	Sunday
6:00	National News	National News	National News	National News	National News	National News	National News
6:30	Local News	Local News	Local News	Local News	Local News	Local News	Local News
7:00	Opera Fest	Radio U	Science Week	The Living World	Word Play	Agri-Week	Folk Fest
7:30					Brain Stew	Bismarck Forum	
8:00	The Classical Music Connection				Old Time Radio	Saturday Nite Jazz	The Indie Connection
8:30					The Inner Mind		
9:00					Open Mike Nite		
9:30							
10:00	World News Feed	World News Feed	World News Feed	World News Feed	World News Feed	World News Feed	World News Feed

To create this program listing, you first have to understand the HTML table structure.

Marking Tables and Table Rows

Each Web table consists of a `table` element containing a collection of table rows. The general structure is

```
<table>
   <tr>
      table cells
   </tr>
   <tr>
      table cells
   </tr>
...
</table>
```

where `<table>` marks the `table` element, `<tr>` marks each row, and *table cells* are the cells within each row. Note that the dimension or size of the table is defined by the number of `tr` elements and the number of cells within those rows. Tables are considered block-level elements; so when rendered by a browser, they appear on a new line in the Web page. Like other block-level elements, you can float tables and resize them using the same styles you've already studied.

REFERENCE

Defining a Table Structure

- To mark a Web table, enter

  ```
  <table>rows</table>
  ```

  where *rows* are the rows of the table.
- To mark a table row, enter

  ```
  <tr>cells</tr>
  ```

  where *cells* are the table cells contained within the row.
- To mark a cell containing a row or column heading, enter

  ```
  <th>content</th>
  ```

  where *content* is the content of the heading.
- To mark a cell containing table data, enter

  ```
  <td>content</td>
  ```

  where *content* is the content of the table data.

Kyle's proposed Web table from Figure 5-2 contains 10 rows; the first row contains the days of the week, and the nine rows that follow list the KPAF shows from 6:00 p.m. to 10:30 p.m. in half-hour intervals. For now, you'll insert **tr** elements for just the first three rows of the table. You'll also include a class attribute, placing the table in the *schedule* class of elements to distinguish it from other tables on the KPAF Web site.

To insert the Web table:

▶ 1. Return to the **schedule.htm** file in your text editor.

▶ 2. Directly above the closing **</section>** tag, insert the following code, as shown in Figure 5-3:

```
<table class="schedule">
    <tr>
    </tr>
    <tr>
    </tr>
    <tr>
    </tr>
</table>
```

Figure 5-3   Marking a table and table rows

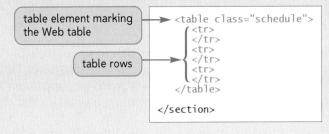

At this point, you have a table with three rows but no content. Your next task is to add table cells to each of those rows.

Marking Table Headings and Table Data

There are two types of table cells: those that contain headings and those that contain data. Table headings, the cells that identify the contents of a row or column, are marked using the th element. You can place a table heading anywhere in a table, but you'll most often place one at the top of a column or at the beginning of a row. Most browsers display table headings in a bold font, centered within the table cell.

Kyle wants you to mark the cells in the first row of the radio schedule as headings because the text identifies the contents of each column. He also wants the first cell in each of the remaining rows to be marked as a heading because these cells display the time. You'll start by adding heading cells to the first three rows of the schedule table.

To insert the table headings:

1. In the first table row of the Web table you just created in the *schedule.htm* file, insert the following th elements:

```
<th>Time</th>
<th>Monday</th>
<th>Tuesday</th>
<th>Wednesday</th>
<th>Thursday</th>
<th>Friday</th>
<th>Saturday</th>
<th>Sunday</th>
```

2. In the second row of the table, insert the following heading:

```
<th>6:00</th>
```

3. In the third table row, insert the following heading:

```
<th>6:30</th>
```

Figure 5-4 shows the revised code in the schedule table.

Figure 5-4   **Inserting table heading cells**

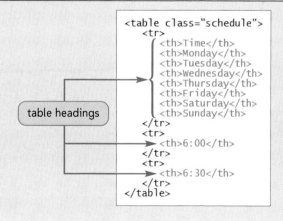

The other type of table cell is a data cell, which is marked using the td element and is used for any content that is not considered a heading. Most browsers display table data as unformatted text, left-aligned within the cell.

TIP

To place an empty table cell anywhere within a row, insert the `<td> </td>` tag into the row.

KPAF airs the national and local news at 6:00 and 6:30, respectively, every night of the week. You'll use table data cells to insert the names of the KPAF programs.

To insert table data for the next two rows of the table:

1. Within the second table row, add the following seven td elements after the initial th element:

   ```
   <td>National News</td>
   <td>National News</td>
   <td>National News</td>
   <td>National News</td>
   <td>National News</td>
   <td>National News</td>
   <td>National News</td>
   ```

2. Within the third table row, insert another seven td elements after the initial th element:

   ```
   <td>Local News</td>
   <td>Local News</td>
   <td>Local News</td>
   <td>Local News</td>
   <td>Local News</td>
   <td>Local News</td>
   <td>Local News</td>
   ```

   Figure 5-5 shows the newly inserted HTML code.

Figure 5-5 Inserting table data

3. Save your changes to the file, and then refresh the **schedule.htm** file in your Web browser. Figure 5-6 shows the current appearance of the program schedule. The headings are in bold and centered, and the table data is in a normal font and left-aligned.

Figure 5-6 **Viewing the Web table**

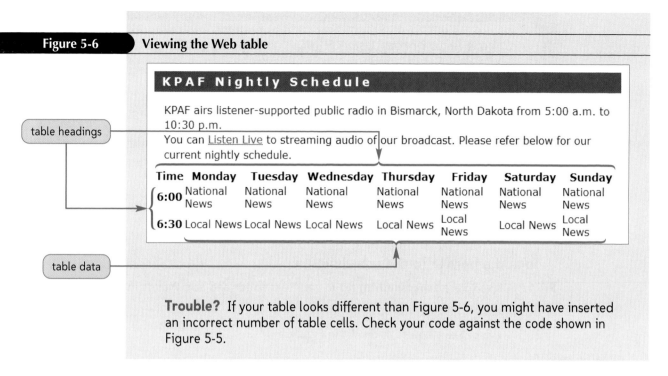

table headings

table data

KPAF Nightly Schedule

KPAF airs listener-supported public radio in Bismarck, North Dakota from 5:00 a.m. to 10:30 p.m.

You can <u>Listen Live</u> to streaming audio of our broadcast. Please refer below for our current nightly schedule.

Time	Monday	Tuesday	Wednesday	Thursday	Friday	Saturday	Sunday
6:00	National News	National News	National News	National News	National News	National News	National News
6:30	Local News	Local News	Local News	Local News	Local News	Local News	Local News

Trouble? If your table looks different than Figure 5-6, you might have inserted an incorrect number of table cells. Check your code against the code shown in Figure 5-5.

The table you created for Kyle has three rows and eight columns. Remember that the number of columns is determined by the maximum number of cells within each row. If one row has four cells and another row has five, the table will have five columns. The row with only four cells will have an empty space at the end, where the fifth cell should be.

Adding a Table Border

By default, no gridlines are displayed in a Web table, making it difficult to see the table structure. You decide the table would be easier to read with gridlines marking each cell in the table. In the next session, you'll learn how to do this using CSS. But for now, you'll use the HTML `border` attribute

```
<table border="value">
   ...
</table>
```

where `value` is the width of the table border in pixels. Figure 5-7 shows how different border values affect the appearance of a sample table.

Figure 5-7 **Tables with different border sizes**

internal gridlines have the same width

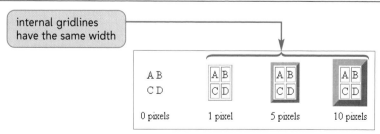

| A B | A B | A B | A B |
| C D | C D | C D | C D |

0 pixels   1 pixel   5 pixels   10 pixels

Note that the `border` attribute does not control the width of the internal gridlines that separate individual table cells. However, to display internal gridlines, you must add a border to the table. You can change the width of internal gridlines by changing the space between table cells, an issue you'll examine in the next session.

REFERENCE

Adding a Table Border Using HTML

• To add a border to a Web table using HTML, use the border attribute

```
<table border="value"> ... </table>
```

where *value* is the size of the border in pixels.

You decide to add a 1-pixel border to the schedule table. As a result of the addition of the border, browsers also will insert gridlines around each of the table cells.

To add a border to the schedule:

1. Return to the **schedule.htm** file in your text editor and add the attribute

   border="1"

   to the table element as shown in Figure 5-8.

Figure 5-8   Adding a table border

```
<table class="schedule" border="1">
    <tr>
        <th>Time</th>
        <th>Monday</th>
        <th>Tuesday</th>
        <th>Wednesday</th>
        <th>Thursday</th>
        <th>Friday</th>
        <th>Saturday</th>
        <th>Sunday</th>
    </tr>
```

table cells will be surrounded by a 1-pixel-wide border

2. Save your changes to the file, and then reload the **schedule.htm** file in your Web browser. Figure 5-9 shows the revised table with the added border and internal gridlines.

Figure 5-9   Web table borders and cell gridlines

Time	Monday	Tuesday	Wednesday	Thursday	Friday	Saturday	Sunday
6:00	National News	National News	National News	National News	National News	National News	National News
6:30	Local News	Local News	Local News	Local News	Local News	Local News	Local News

INSIGHT

Table Border Colors

Most browsers display a table border in gray, in a raised style that gives the border a 3D effect. There is no HTML attribute to change the border style, but many browsers allow you to change the color by adding the `bordercolor` attribute to the `table` element, using the syntax

```
<table border="value" bordercolor="color"> ... </table>
```

where `color` is either a recognized color name or a hexadecimal color value. For example, the following HTML code adds a 10-pixel blue border to a table:

```
<table border="10" bordercolor="blue"> ... </table>
```

The exact appearance of the table border differs among browsers. Internet Explorer, Google Chrome, and Safari display the border in a solid blue color; Firefox displays the border in a raised style using two shades of blue; and Opera does not support the `bordercolor` attribute at all. Thus, you should not rely on getting a consistent border color across all browsers with this attribute.

The `bordercolor` attribute has been deprecated by the World Wide Web Consortium (W3C) and is being gradually phased out. The recommended method is to use one of the CSS border styles discussed in Tutorial 4; however, you may still see this attribute used in many older Web pages.

Spanning Rows and Columns

Reviewing the schedule from Figure 5-2, you notice that several programs are longer than a half hour, and some are repeated across several days. For example, national news and local news air every day at 6:00 and 6:30, respectively. Likewise, from Monday through Thursday, the hour from 7:00 to 8:00 is needed for the shows Opera Fest, Radio U, Science Week, and The Living World, respectively. And finally, The Classical Music Connection airs Monday through Thursday for two hours from 8:00 to 10:00. Rather than repeat the names of programs in all of the half-hour slots, Kyle would prefer that the table cells stretch across those hours and days so that the text must be entered only once.

To do this, you create a spanning cell, which is a single cell that occupies more than one row or one column in the table. Spanning cells are created by adding either or both of the following `rowspan` and `colspan` attributes

```
rowspan="rows" colspan="columns"
```

to a `th` or `td` element, where `rows` is the number of rows that the cell should cover and `columns` is the number of columns. The spanning starts in the cell where you put the `rowspan` and `colspan` attributes, and goes downward and to the right from that cell. For example, to create a data cell that spans two columns and three rows, you'd enter the `td` element as follows:

```
<td colspan="2" rowspan="3"> ... </td>
```

It's important to remember that when a cell spans multiple rows or columns, it pushes other cells down or to the right. If you want to maintain the same number of rows and columns in your table, you must adjust the number of cells in a row or column that includes a spanning cell. To account for a column-spanning cell, you have to reduce the number of cells in the current row. For example, if a table is supposed to cover five columns, but one of the cells in the row spans three columns, you need only three cell elements in that row: two cells that occupy a single column each and one cell that spans the remaining three columns.

Creating a Spanning Cell

• To create a table cell that spans several columns, add the attribute

```
colspan="columns"
```

to the cell, where *columns* is the number of columns covered by the cell.
• To create a table cell that spans several rows, add the attribute

```
rowspan="rows"
```

to the cell, where *rows* is the number of rows covered by the cell.

To see how column-spanning cells work, you'll replace the cells for the National News and Local News programs that currently occupy seven cells each with a single cell spanning seven columns in each row.

To create cells that span several columns:

1. Return to the **schedule.htm** file in your text editor and add the attribute

   ```
   colspan="7"
   ```

   to the second table cell in both the second and third rows of the table.

2. Delete the remaining six table cells in both the second and third table rows. Figure 5-10 shows the revised code for the schedule table.

> You must remove table cells from the table row when you add a cell that spans several columns or else the cell contents won't align properly within the columns.

Figure 5-10   Marking cells to span several columns

```
<table class="schedule" border="1">
    <tr>
        <th>Time</th>
        <th>Monday</th>
        <th>Tuesday</th>
        <th>Wednesday</th>
        <th>Thursday</th>
        <th>Friday</th>
        <th>Saturday</th>
        <th>Sunday</th>
    </tr>
    <tr>
        <th>6:00</th>
        <td colspan="7">National News</td>
    </tr>
    <tr>
        <th>6:30</th>
        <td colspan="7">Local News</td>
    </tr>
</table>
```

remaining six cells in each row deleted

each cell spans seven columns

3. Save your changes to the file, and then refresh the **schedule.htm** file in your Web browser. Figure 5-11 shows the revised appearance of the Web table.

Figure 5-11   **Column-spanning cells**

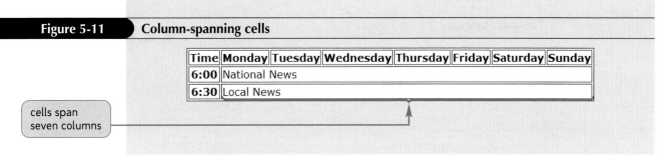

cells span
seven columns

To make the cells for the hour-long shows on Monday through Thursday, you'll need to span two rows, which lengthens the height of each cell. For row-spanning cells, you need to remove extra cells from the rows below the spanning cell. Consider the table shown in Figure 5-12, which contains three rows and four columns. The first cell spans three rows. You need four table cells in the first row, but only three in the second and third rows. This is because the spanning cell from row one occupies a position reserved for a cell that would normally appear in those rows.

Figure 5-12   **Row-spanning cell**

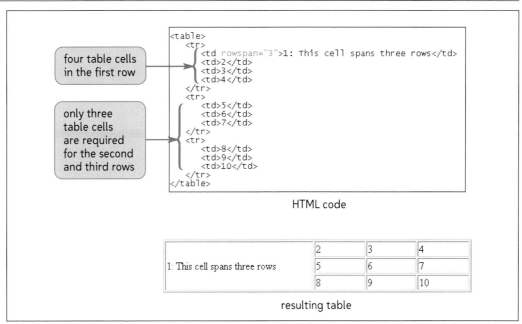

four table cells
in the first row

only three
table cells
are required
for the second
and third rows

HTML code

resulting table

The 7:00 to 8:00 section of the KPAF schedule contains several programs that run for an hour. To insert these programs, you'll create row-spanning cells that span two rows in the schedule table. To keep the columns lined up, you must reduce the number of cells entered in the subsequent row.

To span several table rows:

1. Return to the **schedule.htm** file in your text editor and add the following row to the bottom of the schedule table:

```
<tr>
    <th>7:00</th>
    <td rowspan="2">Opera Fest</td>
    <td rowspan="2">Radio U</td>
    <td rowspan="2">Science Week</td>
    <td rowspan="2">The Living World</td>
    <td>Word Play</td>
    <td>Agri-Week</td>
    <td rowspan="2">Folk Fest</td>
</tr>
```

2. Add the following code for the next row, which adds table cells only for the two programs that start at 7:30:

```
<tr>
    <th>7:30</th>
    <td>Brain Stew</td>
    <td>Bismarck Forum</td>
</tr>
```

Figure 5-13 shows the code for the two new table rows.

Figure 5-13) **Inserting cells that span two rows**

```
                <tr>
                    <th>6:30</th>
                    <td colspan="7">Local News</td>
                </tr>
                <tr>
                    <th>7:00</th>
                    <td rowspan="2">Opera Fest</td>
                    <td rowspan="2">Radio U</td>
                    <td rowspan="2">Science Week</td>
                    <td rowspan="2">The Living World</td>
                    <td>Word Play</td>
                    <td>Agri-Week</td>
                    <td rowspan="2">Folk Fest</td>
                </tr>
                <tr>
                    <th>7:30</th>
                    <td>Brain Stew</td>
                    <td>Bismarck Forum</td>
                </tr>
            </table>
```

cells span two rows

3. Save your changes to the file, and then refresh the **schedule.htm** file in your Web browser. As shown in Figure 5-14, the Sunday through Thursday 7:00 p.m. programs span two table rows, indicating that they last an hour.

Figure 5-14   Schedule table with several one-hour programs spanning two rows

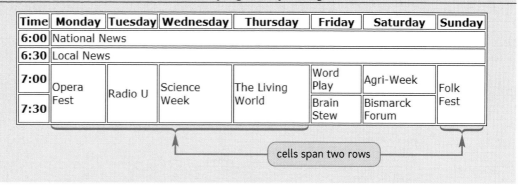

The final part of the evening schedule includes the program The Classical Musical Connection, which spans two hours on Monday through Thursday. Like the news programs, you don't want to repeat the name of the show each day; and like the five hour-long programs you just entered, you don't want to repeat the name of the show in each half-hour cell. Kyle suggests that you use both the `colspan` and `rowspan` attributes to create a table cell that spans four rows and four columns.

Other programs in the 8:00 to 10:00 time slots, such as Saturday Nite Jazz and The Indie Connection, also span four rows, but only one column. The last program aired before KPAF signs off is the World News Feed, which is played every night from 10:00 to 10:30. You'll add these and the other late evening programs to the schedule table now.

To add the remaining KPAF evening programs:

1. Return to the **schedule.htm** file in your text editor and enter the following table row for programs airing starting at 8:00:

```
<tr>
    <th>8:00</th>
    <td rowspan="4" colspan="4">The Classical Music Connection</td>
    <td>Old Time Radio</td>
    <td rowspan="4">Saturday Nite Jazz</td>
    <td rowspan="4">The Indie Connection</td>
</tr>
```

2. The Inner Mind is the only program that starts at 8:30 during the week. Add the 8:30 starting time and the program listing to the table using the following row:

```
<tr>
    <th>8:30</th>
    <td>The Inner Mind</td>
</tr>
```

3. The only program that starts at 9:00 is Open Mike Nite. Add the following row to the table to display this program in the schedule:

```
<tr>
    <th>9:00</th>
    <td rowspan="2">Open Mike Nite</td>
</tr>
```

▶ **4.** There are no programs that start at 9:30, so you'll add the table row but without any programs listed. Add the following row:

```
<tr>
   <th>9:30</th>
</tr>
```

▶ **5.** Complete the schedule table by adding the last table row for the World News Feed occurring every night from 10:00 to 10:30. This single program occupies a single row and spans seven columns. Add the following row:

```
<tr>
   <th>10:00</th>
   <td colspan="7">World News Feed</td>
</tr>
```

Figure 5-15 shows the code completing the structure of the schedule table.

Figure 5-15 ▶ **Adding the remaining KPAF evening programs**

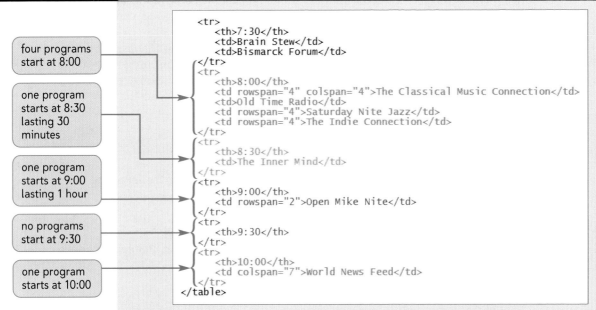

four programs
start at 8:00

one program
starts at 8:30
lasting 30
minutes

one program
starts at 9:00
lasting 1 hour

no programs
start at 9:30

one program
starts at 10:00

```
<tr>
   <th>7:30</th>
   <td>Brain Stew</td>
   <td>Bismarck Forum</td>
</tr>
<tr>
   <th>8:00</th>
   <td rowspan="4" colspan="4">The Classical Music Connection</td>
   <td>Old Time Radio</td>
   <td rowspan="4">Saturday Nite Jazz</td>
   <td rowspan="4">The Indie Connection</td>
</tr>
<tr>
   <th>8:30</th>
   <td>The Inner Mind</td>
</tr>
<tr>
   <th>9:00</th>
   <td rowspan="2">Open Mike Nite</td>
</tr>
<tr>
   <th>9:30</th>
</tr>
<tr>
   <th>10:00</th>
   <td colspan="7">World News Feed</td>
</tr>
</table>
```

▶ **6.** Save your changes to the file, and then reload the **schedule.htm** file in your Web browser. Figure 5-16 shows the complete evening schedule of programs offered by KPAF.

Figure 5-16	The complete KPAF evening schedule

Time	Monday	Tuesday	Wednesday	Thursday	Friday	Saturday	Sunday
6:00	National News						
6:30	Local News						
7:00	Opera Fest	Radio U	Science Week	The Living World	Word Play	Agri-Week	Folk Fest
7:30					Brain Stew	Bismarck Forum	
8:00	The Classical Music Connection				Old Time Radio	Saturday Nite Jazz	The Indie Connection
8:30					The Inner Mind		
9:00					Open Mike Nite		
9:30							
10:00	World News Feed						

The Web table you created matches the printout of KPAF's evening schedule. Kyle likes the clear structure of the table. He notes that many KPAF listeners tune into the station over the Internet, listening to KPAF's streaming audio feed. Because those listeners might be located in different time zones, Kyle suggests that you add a caption to the table indicating that all times in the schedule are based on the Central Time Zone.

Creating a Table Caption

Table captions are another part of the basic table structure and are marked using the `caption` element

```
<table>
   <caption>content</caption>
   ...
</table>
```

where *content* is the content contained within the caption. You can nest text-level elements within a `caption` element. For example, the following code marks the text *Program Schedule* using the `em` element:

```
<table>
   <caption><em>Program Schedule</em></caption>
   ...
</table>
```

Only one caption is allowed per Web table, and the `caption` element must be listed directly after the opening `<table>` tag.

Creating a Table Caption

• To create a table caption, add the caption element directly below the opening
 `<table>` tag using the syntax

 `<caption>content</caption>`

 where *content* is the content of the table caption.

Add Kyle's suggested caption to the program schedule.

To create a caption for the program schedule:

▶ **1.** Return to the **schedule.htm** file in your text editor and insert the following
 caption element directly below the opening tag, as shown in Figure 5-17:

 `<caption>All Times Central</caption>`

Figure 5-17 Inserting a table caption

```
<table class="schedule" border="1">
    <caption>All Times Central</caption>
    <tr>
        <th>Time</th>
        <th>Monday</th>
        <th>Tuesday</th>
        <th>Wednesday</th>
        <th>Thursday</th>
        <th>Friday</th>
        <th>Saturday</th>
        <th>Sunday</th>
    </tr>
```

▶ **2.** Save your changes to the file and refresh the **schedule.htm** file in your Web
 browser. As shown in Figure 5-18, Kyle's suggested caption appears centered
 above the Web table.

Figure 5-18   **Table caption for the KPAF programming schedule**

caption

All Times Central

Time	Monday	Tuesday	Wednesday	Thursday	Friday	Saturday	Sunday
6:00	National News						
6:30	Local News						
7:00	Opera Fest	Radio U	Science Week	The Living World	Word Play	Agri-Week	Folk Fest
7:30					Brain Stew	Bismarck Forum	
8:00	The Classical Music Connection				Old Time Radio	Saturday Nite Jazz	The Indie Connection
8:30					The Inner Mind		
9:00					Open Mike Nite		
9:30							
10:00	World News Feed						

Although table captions might lie outside of the borders of a Web table, they are still part of the Web table's structure. This means that they inherit any styles associated with the table. For example, if you create a style for the `table` element that sets the font color to red, the caption text also will be displayed in a red font. You'll explore how to apply styles to table captions in the next session.

INSIGHT

Aligning a Caption with HTML

A table caption is treated as a block element and by default placed directly above the table, but you can change the placement of the caption in HTML using the following `align` attribute:

```
<caption align="position">content</caption>
```

In this code, *position* can be either `top`, `bottom`, `left`, or `right`, to place the caption above, below, or to the left or right sides of the table, respectively.

The interpretation of the `left` and `right` values is not consistent among the major browsers. Firefox places the captions to the left or right of the Web table. Internet Explorer and Opera still place the caption above the table, but horizontally align the caption text to the left or right. Safari and Chrome ignore the `align` attribute altogether.

The `align` attribute is another example of a presentational attribute that has been deprecated in favor of style sheets, though you'll still often find it used on Web sites, both old and new. However, the best practice is to align the caption not in the HTML file, but in a style sheet using the `caption-side` property.

Marking Row Groups

You can combine sections of rows into row groups in which each row group represents a different collection of table data or information. HTML supports three row groups: one to mark the header rows, another for the body rows, and a third for the footer rows. The syntax to create these three row groups is

```
<table>
   <thead>
      table rows
   </thead>
   <tfoot>
      table rows
   </tfoot>
   <tbody>
      table rows
   </tbody>
</table>
```

where *table rows* are rows from the Web table. For example, the following code marks two rows as belonging to the table header row group:

```
<thead>
   <tr>
      <th colspan="2">KPAF Programs</th>
   </tr>
   <tr>
      <th>Time</th>
      <th>Program</th>
   </tr>
</thead>
```

TIP

The table header, table body, and table footer all must contain the same number of columns.

Order is important. The `thead` element must appear first, and then the `tfoot` element, and finally the `tbody` element. A table can contain only one `thead` element and one `tfoot` element, but it can include any number of `tbody` elements. The reason the table body group appears last, rather than the footer group, is to allow the browser to render the footer before receiving what might be numerous groups of table body rows.

One purpose of row groups is to allow you to create different styles for groups of rows in your table. Any style that you apply to the `thead`, `tbody`, or `tfoot` element is inherited by the rows those elements contain. Row groups also are used for tables in which table body contents are made up of imported data from external data sources such as databases or XML documents. In those situations, a single table can span several Web pages, with different imported content displayed in the table body in each page but the same table header and table footer bracketing each page of content.

REFERENCE

Creating Row Groups

- Row groups must be entered in the following order: table header rows, table footer rows, and then table body rows.
- To create a row group consisting of header rows, add the element

```
<thead>
    rows
</thead>
```

within the table, where *rows* are the row elements within the table header.
- To create a row group consisting of footer rows, add the following element:

```
<tfoot>
    rows
</tfoot>
```

- To create a row group consisting of rows used in the body of the table, add the following element:

```
<tbody>
    rows
</tbody>
```

A table can contain multiple table body row groups.

To indicate the structure of the schedule table, you decide to use the `thead` element to mark the header row in the program schedule, and the `tbody` element to mark the rows that include the broadcast times of each program. You do not need to specify a footer for this table.

To mark the row groups:

1. Return to the **schedule.htm** file in your text editor and enclose the first row of the table within an opening and closing set of `<thead>` tags.

2. Enclose the remaining rows of the table within an opening and closing set of `<tbody>` tags. Figure 5-19 shows the markup tags for the two new row groups.

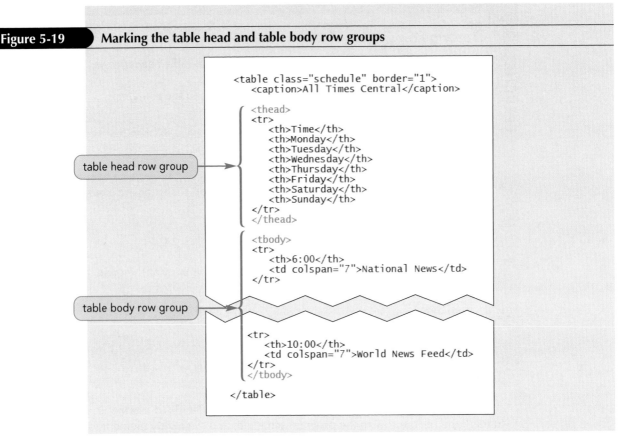

Figure 5-19   Marking the table head and table body row groups

Marking Column Groups

As you've seen, there is no HTML tag to mark table columns—the columns are created implicitly from the number of cells within each row. However, once browsers determine the columns, you can reference the columns through the use of column groups. Column groups give you the ability to assign a common format to all of the cells within a given column. Column groups are defined using the `colgroup` element

```
<colgroup>
    columns
</colgroup>
```

where *columns* are the individual columns with the group. The columns themselves are referenced using the following `col` element:

```
<col />
```

Once you create a column group, you can add `id` or `class` attributes to identify or classify individual columns. For example, the following code creates a column group consisting of three columns, each with a different class name:

```
<colgroup>
    <col class="column1" />
    <col class="column2" />
    <col class="column3" />
</colgroup>
```

The browser applies any style specified for the col element to cells within the corresponding column in the Web table. Thus, to style these three columns with different background colors, you could apply the following style rules:

```
col.column1 {background-color: red;}
col.column2 {background-color: blue;}
col.column3 {background-color: yellow;}
```

In this example, browsers would display the first table column with a background color of red, the second with blue, and the third with yellow. Note that not all CSS styles can be applied to table columns. You'll explore column styles in more detail in the next session.

The col element also supports the span attribute, allowing a column reference to cover several table columns. The syntax of the span attribute is

```
<col span="value" />
```

where value is the number of columns spanned by the col element. Thus, the column structure

```
<colgroup>
    <col class="column1" />
    <col class="nextColumns" span="2" />
</colgroup>
```

references a group of three columns; the first column belongs to the *column1* class and the next two columns belong to the *nextColumns* class. Note that you also can apply the span attribute to a column group itself. The following code uses two column groups to also reference three columns, the first belonging to the *column1* class and the last two belonging to the *nextColumns* class:

```
<colgroup class="column1"></colgroup>
<colgroup class="nextColumns" span="2"></colgroup>
```

Notice that in this case there are no col elements within the column group. Browsers will assume the number of columns indicated by the span attribute; if no span attribute is present, a column group is assumed to have only one column.

REFERENCE

Creating Column Groups

- To create a column group, add the element

```
<colgroup>
    columns
</colgroup>
```

to the Web table, where *columns* are col elements representing individual columns within the group.

- To define a column or columns within a column group, use the col element

```
<col span="value" />
```

where *value* is the number of defined columns. The span attribute is not required if only one column is defined.

Now that you've seen how columns can be referenced through the use of column groups, you'll create a column group for the programming table. You'll mark the first column containing the broadcast times for the different KPAF programs using a `col` element with the class name *firstCol*, and mark the remaining seven columns containing the daily program listings with a `col` element spanning seven columns and identified with the class name *dayCols*. These groupings will allow you to format the two sets of columns in different ways later on in the next session.

To mark the column groups:

▸ **1.** Return to the **schedule.htm** file in your text editor.

▸ **2.** Directly below the `caption` element, insert the following `colgroup` element, as shown in Figure 5-20:

```
<colgroup>
    <col class="firstCol" />
    <col class="dayCols" span="7" />
</colgroup>
```

Figure 5-20 | Inserting a column group

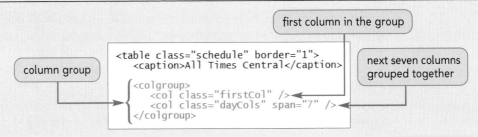

▸ **3.** Save your changes to the file.

▸ **4.** Creating row groups and column groups defines the table's structure but should not alter its appearance. To confirm that the row and column groups have not modified the table's appearance, refresh the **schedule.htm** file in your browser. Verify that the table layout is the same as that shown earlier in Figure 5-18.

PROSKILLS

Problem Solving: Using Tables for Page Layout

Table cells can contain any HTML elements including headings, lists, inline images, and even other tables. Because of the flexibility of tables in organizing content, before the widespread adoption of CSS for page layout, tables also were used to design the layout of entire pages. Using tables for page layout is strongly discouraged for several reasons:

- *Tabular layouts violate the purpose of HTML.* A basic philosophy of Web page design is that HTML code should indicate the structure of a document, but not how the document should be rendered by browsers. Tables take control of layout from style sheets, putting page design back into the HTML file.
- *Table layouts are difficult to revise.* Imagine a complex table layout consisting of two columns with several levels of additional tables nested within each column. Now imagine having to revise that table structure, changing it into a three-column layout. This would not be an easy task because the page content would be intertwined with the page layout. Further, imagine the difficulty of having to repeat that design change for dozens of pages across a large Web site. By contrast, a layout created with a properly designed style sheet is much easier to maintain and revise because it is separate from the page content.
- *Tables take longer to render.* Unless the size of every element in a table is specified, browsers need to first load the table content and then run algorithms to determine how to size each element of the table. This can be time-consuming for large, complex tables that involve many cells and nested elements.
- *Table layouts are code-heavy.* Creating a visually striking table layout often requires several levels of nested table cells, rows, and columns. The ratio of HTML code to actual page content thus becomes more heavily weighted toward the HTML code, resulting in a document that takes longer to load and that can be difficult to interpret by people who need to edit the underlying code.
- *Tables can be inaccessible to users with disabilities.* Aural or Braille browsers recite the Web page content line-by-line down through the file, but tables convey information both horizontally and vertically. The result is that information that is easily understood visually is unintelligible aurally. On the other hand, with style sheets an aural style could be designed that would better convey such information aurally.

Because CSS is so widely supported, there is little reason to use tables for page layout. However, Web table layouts will not disappear immediately. So as a Web page designer, you must be conversant with both approaches—especially if you are called upon to support older browser versions or have the task of maintaining the code of an older Web site that involves table layouts.

Adding a Table Summary

Nonvisual browsers, such as aural browsers that often are used by visually impaired people, can't display tables, and it's cumbersome for users to listen to each cell being read. For these situations, it is useful to include a summary of a table's contents. While a caption and the surrounding page text usually provide clues about a table and its contents, the summary attribute allows you to include a more detailed description. The syntax of the summary attribute is

```
<table summary="description"> ... </table>
```

where *description* is a text string that describes the table's content and structure. The summary attribute fulfills the same role that the alt attribute accomplishes for inline images: providing a textual (aural) alternative to essentially visual material. A user running a screen reader or other type of aural browser first will hear the summary of the table's contents, which can aid in interpreting the subsequent reading of the table's content.

Kyle definitely wants the KPAF Web page to be accessible to users with all types of disabilities, and he asks that you include a summary description of the program schedule.

To add a summary to the table:

1. Return to the **schedule.htm** file in your text editor.

2. Within the opening `<table>` tag, insert the following attribute, as shown in Figure 5-21:

   ```
   summary="This table contains the nightly KPAF program schedule
   aired from Bismarck, North Dakota. Program times are laid
   out in thirty-minute increments from 6:00 p.m. to
   10:00 p.m., Monday through Sunday night."
   ```

TIP

In some browsers, you can view the summary description by right-clicking the table and selecting Properties from the shortcut menu.

Figure 5-21 Inserting a table summary

table summary →

```
<table class="schedule" border="1"
       summary="This table contains the nightly KPAF program schedule
                aired from Bismarck, North Dakota. Program times are laid
                out in thirty-minute increments from 6:00 p.m. to
                10:00 p.m., Monday through Sunday night.">
   <caption>All Times Central</caption>
```

3. Save your changes to the file and then reload the **schedule.htm** file in your Web browser. Verify that the summary description does not appear in the browser window.

Creating Tables with Preformatted Text

As you learned in Tutorial 1, browsers strip out white space from the HTML code when they render Web pages. You can force browsers to keep certain white space by marking your document text as preformatted text, in which browsers display the spacing and line breaks exactly as you enter them. Preformatted text is created using the pre element

```
<pre>content</pre>
```

where *content* is the text that will appear preformatted in browsers. One use of preformatted text is to quickly create tables that are neatly laid out in rows and columns. For example, the code

```
<pre>
Time    Friday       Saturday
====    ==========   ==============
7:30    Brain Stew   Bismarck Forum
</pre>
```

is displayed by browsers exactly as typed, with the spaces as shown:

```
Time    Friday       Saturday
====    ==========   ==============
7:30    Brain Stew   Bismarck Forum
```

Preformatted text is displayed by browsers in a monospace font in which each letter takes up the same amount of space. One of the advantages of monospace fonts that make them useful for entering tabular data is that the relative space between characters is unchanged as the font size increases or decreases. This means that if the font size of the above table were increased or decreased, the columns still would line up.

Although you probably should use the table element to display most of your data, you might consider using preformatted text for simple and quick text tables.

You've completed your work laying out the basic structure of the KPAF program schedule. The next thing Kyle wants you to focus on is formatting the table to look attractive and professional. In the next session, you'll explore how to apply design styles to make a Web table interesting and attractive.

Session 5.1 Quick Check

1. How is the number of columns in a Web table determined?
2. How does a browser usually render text marked with the `<th>` tag?
3. Specify the HTML attribute to add a 10-pixel-wide border to a Web table.
4. A table data cell contains the text *Monday* and should stretch across two rows and three columns. Provide the HTML code for the cell.
5. What adjustment do you have to make when a cell spans multiple columns?
6. Captions usually appear above or below their Web tables. Explain why a caption is still part of a table's structure.
7. What are the three table row groups, and in what order must they be specified in the code?
8. Specify the code to create a column group in which the first two columns belong to the *introCol* class and the next three columns belong to the *col1*, *col2*, and *col3* classes, respectively.
9. What is the purpose of the `table summary` attribute?

SESSION 5.2 VISUAL OVERVIEW

The **column-count** property sets the number of columns.

The **column-gap** property sets the space between columns.

The **column-rule** property adds a dividing line between columns.

```
p {
    column-count: 2;
    column-gap: 20px;
    column-rule: 2px solid purple;
}
```

```
table {
    border-collapse: collapse;
}
```

The **border-collapse** property merges adjacent borders into one border.

The thead selector applies to the table header row group.

```
table  thead {
    background-color: rgb(203, 50, 203);
    color: white;
    color: rgba(255, 255, 255, 0.5);
}
```

The style rule displays the header row in semi-transparent white on a purple background.

The col.firstCol selector applies to the first column group.

```
table col.firstCol {
    background-color: yellow;
    width: 7%;
}
```

The style rule displays the first column with a background color of yellow and a width 7% of the width of the table.

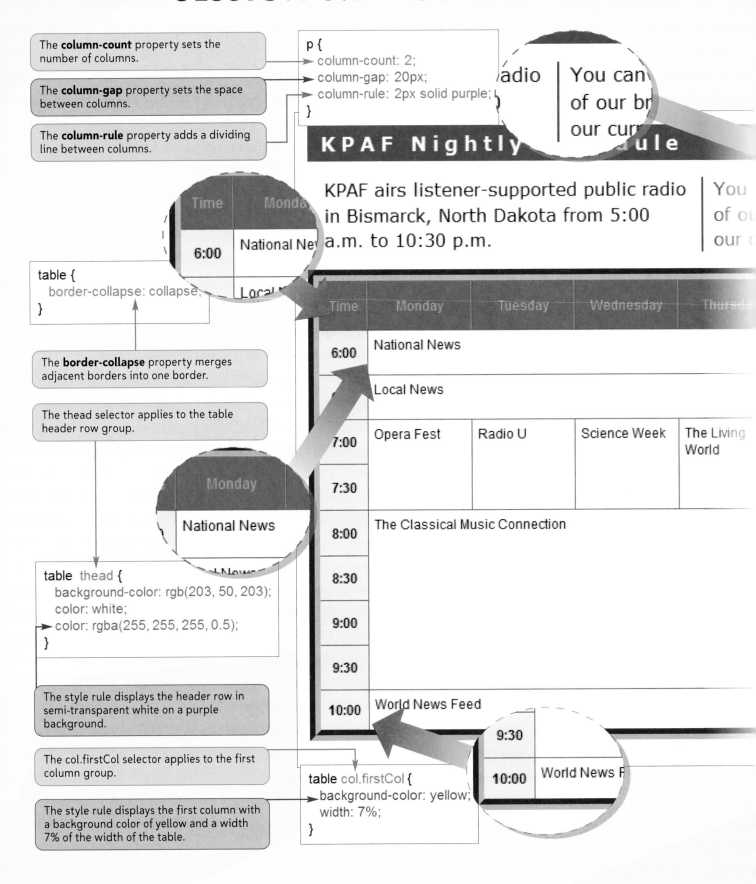

KPAF airs listener-supported public radio in Bismarck, North Dakota from 5:00 a.m. to 10:30 p.m.

Time	Monday	Tuesday	Wednesday	Thursday
6:00	National News			
	Local News			
7:00	Opera Fest	Radio U	Science Week	The Living World
7:30				
8:00	The Classical Music Connection			
8:30				
9:00				
9:30				
10:00	World News Feed			

WEB TABLE STYLES

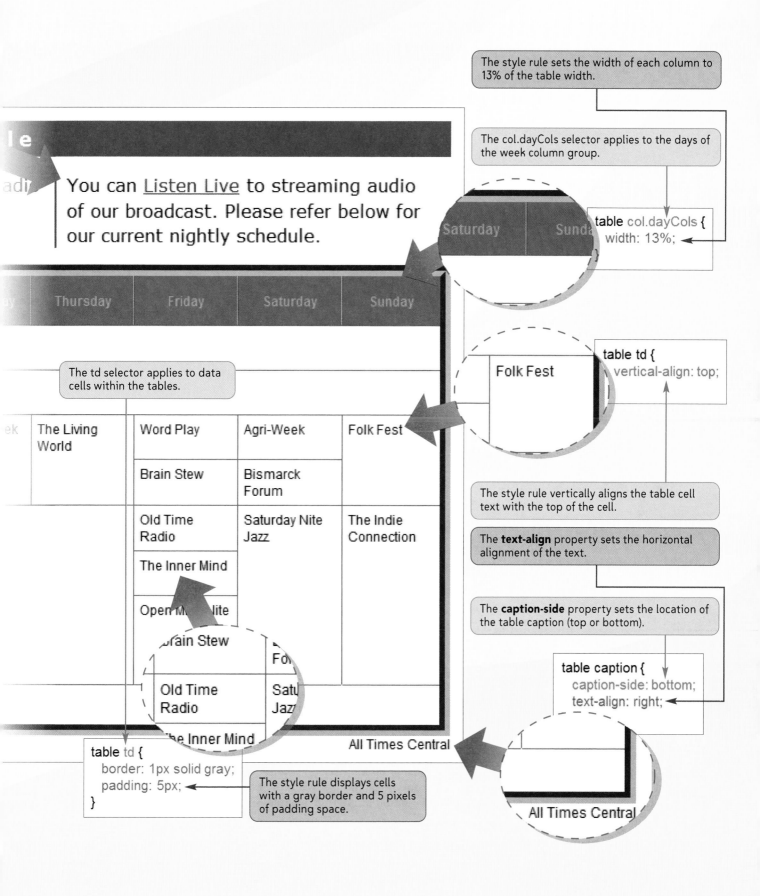

The style rule sets the width of each column to 13% of the table width.

The col.dayCols selector applies to the days of the week column group.

```
table col.dayCols {
    width: 13%;
```

You can <u>Listen Live</u> to streaming audio of our broadcast. Please refer below for our current nightly schedule.

| | Thursday | Friday | Saturday | Sunday |

```
table td {
    vertical-align: top;
```

The td selector applies to data cells within the tables.

	The Living World	Word Play	Agri-Week	Folk Fest
		Brain Stew	Bismarck Forum	
		Old Time Radio	Saturday Nite Jazz	The Indie Connection
		The Inner Mind		
		Open Mind Nite		

Folk Fest

The style rule vertically aligns the table cell text with the top of the cell.

The **text-align** property sets the horizontal alignment of the text.

The **caption-side** property sets the location of the table caption (top or bottom).

```
table caption {
    caption-side: bottom;
    text-align: right;
```

All Times Central

```
table td {
    border: 1px solid gray;
    padding: 5px;
}
```

The style rule displays cells with a gray border and 5 pixels of padding space.

All Times Central

Formatting Tables with HTML Attributes

After specifying the content and structure of the program schedule, you and Kyle are ready to format the table's appearance. There are two approaches to formatting Web tables: using HTML attributes, and using CSS styles. Because you'll see both approaches used on the Internet, you'll examine both techniques, starting with the HTML attribute approach.

Setting Cell Spacing with HTML

Web tables are one of the older HTML page elements, predating the introduction of Cascading Style Sheets. Because of this, HTML has long supported several attributes for controlling the layout and appearance of a table. In the last session, you used one of those attributes, the `border` attribute, to create a table border and display internal table gridlines. The next attribute you'll consider controls the amount of space between table cells. By default, most browsers separate cells by a 2-pixel space. To set a different spacing value, you add the `cellspacing` attribute

```
<table cellspacing="value"> ... </table>
```

to the `table` element, where `value` is the size of the cell spacing in pixels. If you have applied a border to your table, changing the cell spacing value also impacts the size of the internal gridlines. Figure 5-22 shows how different cell spacing values affect the appearance of the table border and internal gridlines. Note that if the cell spacing is set to 0 pixels, many browsers still display an internal gridline that results from the drop shadow that those browsers apply to cell and table borders.

| Figure 5-22 | Cell spacing values |

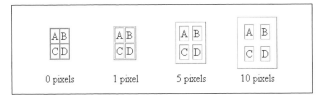

Cell spacing essentially sets the outside margins of table cells. Unlike the CSS `margin` style, you can specify cell spacing values only in pixels and not in other measuring units. You also can't set different cell spacing values for the different sides of a cell. In addition, the effect of setting the cell spacing value is limited by the width allotted to the entire table; browsers ignore cell spacing values that would push a table beyond its defined width.

Setting Cell Padding with HTML

Related to cell spacing is the padding between cell contents and the cell border. In HTML, you set the padding space using the `cellpadding` attribute

```
<table cellpadding="value"> ... </table>
```

where `value` is the size of the cell padding. Like the `cellspacing` attribute, the `cellpadding` attribute applies to every cell in a table. Figure 5-23 shows the impact of various cell padding values on a table's appearance. Cell padding is similar to the CSS `padding` style, though there is no option to define padding values for different sides of the cell. Also, as for the `cellspacing` attribute, values of the `cellpadding` attribute can be expressed only in pixels and not in other units of measure.

Figure 5-23   Cell padding values

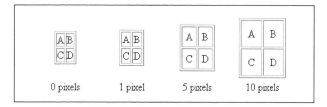

0 pixels   1 pixel   5 pixels   10 pixels

REFERENCE

Setting Cell Spacing and Cell Padding with HTML

- To define the space between table cells, add the `cellspacing` attribute

  `<table cellspacing="value"> ... </table>`

  to the `table` element, where *value* is the space between table cells in pixels.
- To define the padding within table cells, add the `cellpadding` attribute

  `<table cellpadding="value"> ... </table>`

  to the `table` element, where *value* is the size of the padding space in pixels.

Kyle would like you to experiment with how the `cellpadding` and `cellspacing` attributes might affect the appearance of the program schedule, so you'll add these two attributes to the `table` element, setting the cell spacing to 3 pixels and the cell padding to 5 pixels.

To set the cell spacing and cell padding:

1. Return to the **schedule.htm** file in your text editor.

2. Within the opening `<table>` tag, insert the following attributes, as shown in Figure 5-24:

   `cellspacing="3" cellpadding="5"`

Figure 5-24   Setting the cell spacing and padding values

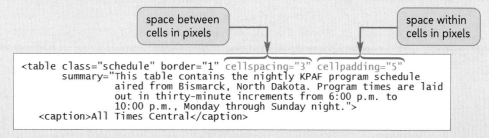

space between cells in pixels

space within cells in pixels

```
<table class="schedule" border="1" cellspacing="3" cellpadding="5"
       summary="This table contains the nightly KPAF program schedule
       aired from Bismarck, North Dakota. Program times are laid
       out in thirty-minute increments from 6:00 p.m. to
       10:00 p.m., Monday through Sunday night.">
   <caption>All Times Central</caption>
```

3. Save your changes to the file and then reopen **schedule.htm** in your Web browser. As shown in Figure 5-25, the spaces between and within the table cells have increased from their default values.

Figure 5-25   Increased padding and spacing within the Web table

All Times Central

Time	Monday	Tuesday	Wednesday	Thursday	Friday	Saturday	Sunday
6:00	National News						
6:30	Local News						
7:00	Opera Fest	Radio U	Science Week	The Living World	Word Play	Agri-Week	Folk Fest
7:30					Brain Stew	Bismarck Forum	
8:00	The Classical Music Connection				Old Time Radio	Saturday Nite Jazz	The Indie Connection
8:30					The Inner Mind		
9:00					Open Mike Nite		
9:30							
10:00	World News Feed						

Setting Table Widths and Heights in HTML

You can use HTML to set the overall width and height of a table and of the individual cells within the table. By default, the width of a table ranges from the minimum necessary to display all the cell contents without line wrapping, up to the width of the container element. To set the width of a table to a specific value, you add the width attribute

```
<table width="value"> ... </table>
```

to the table element, where value is the width either in pixels or as a percentage of the width of the containing element. If the containing element is the page itself, you can set the table to fill the entire page width by specifying a width value of 100%. You still can never reduce a table to a width smaller than is required to display the content or larger than the width of its container. For example, if table content requires a width of 450 pixels, then browsers will ignore any width attribute that attempts to set a smaller table size.

Many browsers also support the height attribute, which has the syntax

```
<table height="value"> ... </table>
```

where value is the height of the table either in pixels or as a percentage of the height of the containing element. Even though the height attribute is widely supported for the table element, it is not part of the specifications for any version of HTML or XHTML. Like the width attribute, the height attribute indicates only the minimum height of the table. If table content cannot fit into the specified height, the table height increases to accommodate the content.

You also can set the widths of individual columns by applying the width attribute to either an individual column or a column group. For example, the HTML code

```
<colgroup width="100" span="7">
</colgroup>
```

sets the width of each of the seven columns in the column group to 100 pixels. To specify different column widths, you apply the `width` attribute to individual `col` elements as in the following code:

```
<colgroup>
   <col width="50" />
   <col width="100" span="5" />
   <col width="50" />
</colgroup>
```

This code sets the widths of the five middle columns to 100 pixels, but sets the widths of the first and seventh columns to 50 pixels each. Column widths also can be expressed as a percentage of the total width of a table. A column width of 50% causes a column to occupy half of the table width. Column widths always are limited by the total width of the table and by the content of each cell. For example, if you try to set the width of each column in a five-column table to 200 pixels, but only 800 pixels of space are available, browsers will reduce the column widths to fit the content.

In the code for many Web tables, you might see the `width` attribute applied to individual table cells. This is another way to set the width of an entire column because the remaining cells in a column where one cell has a `width` attribute also will adopt that width to keep the column cells aligned. Even so, the width value for a single cell might be overridden by browsers if other cells in the column require a larger width to display their content. With the introduction of column groups, there is little need to apply the `width` attribute to individual table cells. Also, the W3C has deprecated the use of the `width` attribute with the `td` and `th` elements. As you might expect, however, you still will see it supported by many of the current browsers.

TIP

Width and height values always should be thought of as minimum widths and heights because they will be overridden whenever the content of the table requires it.

Setting Row Heights with HTML

You can use HTML to set row heights by applying the `height` attribute

```
<tr height="value"> ... </tr>
```

to the `tr` element, where *value* is the height of the row in pixels. Internet Explorer also allows you to specify height values as a percentage of the height of the table. The `height` attribute is not part of the W3C specifications, but most browsers support it. Like setting the column width by setting the width of an individual cell, you also can set row height by applying the `height` attribute to an individual cell within a row. This approach also is supported by most browsers even though it has been deprecated by the W3C.

Formatting Table Borders with HTML

In the last session, you used the `border` attribute to add a border around the table and each of the table cells. You can modify the placement of the table borders using table frames and table rules. A **table frame** specifies which sides of the table (or which sides of the table cells) will have borders. To apply a frame to a table, you apply the `frame` attribute

```
<table border="value" frame="type"> ... </table>
```

to the `table` element, where *value* is the width of the table border and *type* is `box` (the default), `above`, `border`, `below`, `hsides`, `vsides`, `lhs`, `rhs`, or `void`. Figure 5-26 displays the impact of each of these frame options.

Figure 5-26 **Values of the frame attribute**

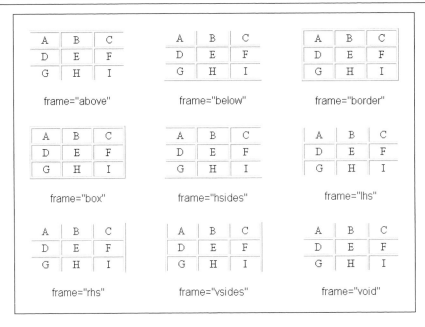

A **table rule** specifies how the internal gridlines are drawn within a table. To apply a table rule, you add the `rules` attribute to the `table` element using the syntax

```
<table border="value" rules="type"> ... </table>
```

where *type* is `all` (the default), `cols`, `groups`, `none`, or `rows`. Figure 5-27 displays the impact of each of these `rules` attribute values on the placement of the internal table gridlines.

Figure 5-27 **Values of the rules attribute**

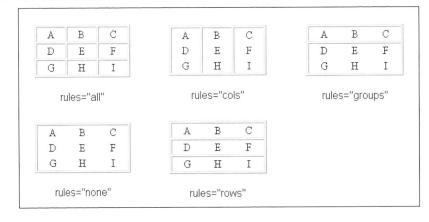

By combining `frame` and `rules` values, you can duplicate many of the same effects you could achieve using the CSS `border-style` property, which you'll explore shortly. Some Web page authors prefer to work with these HTML attributes because they enable them to set the appearance of the table borders from within the `<table>` tag rather than through an external style sheet.

Aligning Cell Contents with HTML

The final set of HTML table attributes you'll examine before looking at the CSS table styles are those attributes that control how content is aligned within each table cell. By default, browsers center the contents of table header cells horizontally and left-align the contents of table data cells. You can specify a different horizontal alignment using the `align` attribute, which has the syntax

```
align="position"
```

where *position* is `left`, `center`, `right`, `justify`, or `char`. The `align` attribute can be applied to table rows, row groups, columns, column groups, or individual table cells. For example, when applied to the column group

```
<colgroup>
   <col align="left" />
   <col span="6" align="right" />
</colgroup>
```

the `align` attribute left-aligns the first column of the Web table and right-aligns the remaining six columns.

When you apply the `align` attribute to the `table` element itself, it aligns the entire table with the surrounding page content but does not affect the alignment of the cells within the table. The `align` attribute has been deprecated for use with the `table` element, but not for the row, column, and cell elements within a table.

Vertical Alignment in HTML

You also can use HTML to vertically align the contents of each table cell. The default is to place the text in the middle of the cell. To choose a different placement, you apply the `valign` attribute using the syntax

```
valign="position"
```

where *position* is `top`, `middle`, `bottom`, or `baseline`. The `top`, `middle`, and `bottom` options align the content with the top, middle, and bottom borders of the cell, respectively. The `baseline` option places the text near the bottom of the cell, but aligns the bases of each letter. The `valign` attribute can be applied to table rows, row groups, columns, and column groups to set the vertical alignment of several cells at once.

Kyle feels that having the program names placed in the middle of each cell makes the program schedule more difficult to read. He prefers to have all of the program names lined up with the top of the cells. To change the cell alignment for all of the cells in the table body, you'll apply the `valign` attribute to the `tbody` row group.

To vertically align the text in the table:

1. Return to the **schedule.htm** file in your text editor.

2. Within the opening `<tbody>` tag, insert the following attribute, as shown in Figure 5-28:

```
valign="top"
```

Figure 5-28   **Applying the valign attribute**

aligns the text of cells in the table body with the top of each cell

```
<tbody valign="top">
<tr>
    <th>6:00</th>
    <td colspan="7">National News</td>
</tr>
```

> **3.** Save your changes to the file and then reload or refresh the **schedule.htm** file in your Web browser. As shown in Figure 5-29, the text is aligned at the top of the cells.

Figure 5-29   **Cell content aligned with the top of each cell**

Time	Monday	Tuesday	Wednesday	Thursday	Friday	Saturday	Sunday
6:00	National News						
6:30	Local News						
7:00	Opera Fest	Radio U	Science Week	The Living World	Word Play	Agri-Week	Folk Fest
7:30					Brain Stew	Bismarck Forum	
8:00	The Classical Music Connection				Old Time Radio	Saturday Nite Jazz	The Indie Connection
8:30					The Inner Mind		
9:00					Open Mike Nite		
9:30							
10:00	World News Feed						

Kyle likes the appearance of the program table. He notes, however, that this is only the evening schedule; he plans to create Web pages for the morning and afternoon schedules as well. To ensure that the tables match each other, you'll have to insert the various HTML attributes into each table's markup tags. Kyle would rather use CSS so he can easily apply the formatting he likes to all of the schedules at once using an external style sheet. He suggests that you explore the CSS table styles before continuing your design of the evening schedule.

Formatting Tables with CSS

Starting with CSS2, Cascading Style Sheets included support for Web tables. As browser support for these styles has grown, CSS gradually has replaced the HTML attributes you've just reviewed; although you will still frequently see those HTML attributes used on the Web. Kyle suggests that you replace the HTML table attributes with an external style sheet that he can apply to all of the program schedule tables on the KPAF Web site.

To create the style sheet:

1. Open the **tablestxt.css** file from the tutorial.05\tutorial folder. Enter **your name** and **the date** in the comment section of the file. Save the file as **tables.css** in the same folder.

2. Return to the **schedule.htm** file in your text editor and insert the following `link` element directly above the closing `</head>` tag:

   ```
   <link href="tables.css" rel="stylesheet" type="text/css" />
   ```

3. Because you'll be replacing the HTML attributes with CSS styles, delete the `border`, `cellpadding`, and `cellspacing` attributes from the opening `<table>` tag.

4. Delete the `valign` attribute from the opening `<tbody>` tag.

5. Save your changes to the file.

TIP

Don't combine HTML table attributes and CSS table styles in the same Web table design. Choose one or the other to avoid conflicts in the two approaches.

Now that you've linked the *schedule.htm* file to the *tables.css* style sheet and you've removed the old HTML table attributes, you're ready to begin creating the style sheet. You'll start with styles for the table border.

Table Border Styles

The first styles you'll apply to the program schedule are the border styles. Web tables use the same border styles you already used with other page elements in Tutorial 4. Unlike the HTML `border` attribute, you can apply one set of borders to a Web table itself and another set of borders to the individual cells within the table. You decide to add a 10-pixel purple border in the outset style around the entire schedule table. You'll also add a 1-pixel solid gray border around each cell within the table.

To add the table border styles:

1. Return to the **tables.css** file in your text editor. Add the following style to apply a border to the entire Web table:

   ```
   /* Styles for the schedule table */

   table.schedule {
      border: 10px outset rgb(153, 0, 153);
   }
   ```

2. Add the following style to apply borders to each table cell (see Figure 5-30):

   ```
   table.schedule th, table.schedule td {
      border: 1px solid gray;
   }
   ```

Figure 5-30   **Setting the table border styles**

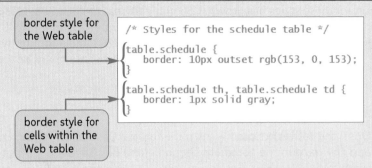

border style for the Web table

```
/* Styles for the schedule table */

table.schedule {
    border: 10px outset rgb(153, 0, 153);
}

table.schedule th, table.schedule td {
    border: 1px solid gray;
}
```

border style for cells within the Web table

Notice that the style sheet uses contextual selectors to apply these styles only to the schedule table and not to other tables that might exist on the KPAF Web site.

3. Save your changes to the style sheet and then reload the **schedule.htm** file in your Web browser. As shown in Figure 5-31, borders have been added to the entire table and to each table cell.

Figure 5-31   **Table and cell borders**

All Times Central

Time	Monday	Tuesday	Wednesday	Thursday	Friday	Saturday	Sunday
6:00	National News						
6:30	Local News						
7:00	Opera Fest	Radio U	Science Week	The Living World	Word Play	Agri-Week	Folk Fest
7:30					Brain Stew	Bismarck Forum	
8:00	The Classical Music Connection				Old Time Radio	Saturday Nite Jazz	The Indie Connection
8:30					The Inner Mind		
9:00					Open Mike Nite		
9:30							
10:00	World News Feed						

CSS provides two ways of drawing table borders. The default is to draw separate borders around the table cells and the entire table. The other approach is to collapse the borders in upon each other. Figure 5-32 shows the impact of both style choices.

Figure 5-32   **Separate and collapsed borders**

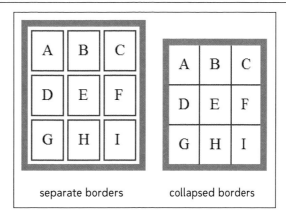

To determine whether to use the separate or collapsed borders model, you apply the style

```
border-collapse: type;
```

to the `table` element, where *type* is either `separate` (the default) or `collapse`. One of the key differences between the separate and collapsed borders models is that under the separate borders model, you can apply borders only to the table itself or to table cells. Under the collapsed borders model, any table object can have a border, including table rows, row groups, columns, and column groups. If the separate borders model is used, you can specify the distance between the borders by applying the style

```
border-spacing: value;
```

to the `table` element, where *value* is the space between the borders in one of the CSS units of measure. For example, the following style specifies that all borders within the table should be separated by a distance of 10 pixels:

```
table {
   border-collapse: separate;
   border-spacing: 10px;
}
```

The separate borders model, therefore, has the same effect as the HTML `cellspacing` attribute in providing additional space between table cells.

In the collapsed borders model, there is no space between borders; in fact, the adjacent borders are merged together to form a single line. It's important to understand that the borders are not simply moved together, but rather they are combined into a single border. For example, if two adjacent 1-pixel-wide borders are collapsed together, the resulting border is not 2 pixels wide, but only 1 pixel wide.

The situation is more complicated when adjacent borders have different widths, styles, or colors. How would you merge a double red border and a solid blue border into a single border of only one color and style? Those kinds of differences must be reconciled before the two borders can be merged. CSS employs the following five rules, listed in decreasing order of importance, to determine the style of a collapsed border:

1. If either border has a border style of `hidden`, the collapsed border is hidden.
2. A border style of `none` is overridden by any other border style.
3. If neither border is hidden, the style of the wider border takes priority over the narrower.

4. If the two borders have the same width but different styles, the border style with the highest priority is used. Double borders have the highest priority, followed by solid, dashed, dotted, ridge, outset, groove, and finally inset borders.

5. If the borders differ only in color, the color from the table object with the highest priority is used. The highest priority color belongs to the border surrounding individual table cells; followed by the borders for table rows, row groups, columns, and column groups; and finally the border around the entire table.

Any situation not covered by these rules is left to browsers to determine which border dominates when collapsing the two borders. Figure 5-33 provides an example of the first rule in action. In this example, the border around the entire table is hidden but a 1-pixel blue border is assigned to the cells within the table. When collapsed, any cell borders that are adjacent to the table border adopt the hidden border property.

Figure 5-33 **Reconciling hidden borders**

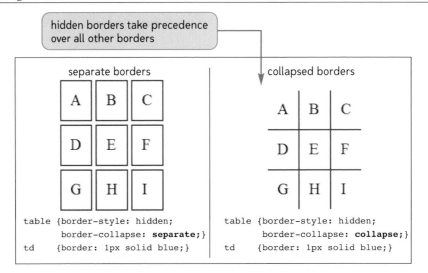

Figure 5-34 shows what happens when two borders of the same width but different styles meet. In this case, because of Rule 4, the table cell borders with the double blue lines take precedence over the solid red lines of the table border when the two borders are collapsed into one.

| Figure 5-34 | Reconciling different border styles |

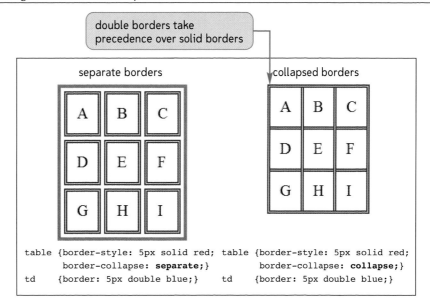

Although the collapsed borders model appears more complicated at first, the rules are reasonable and allow for a wide variety of border designs.

REFERENCE

Setting Table Borders with CSS

- To define the border model used by a table, apply the table style

  `border-collapse: type;`

  where `type` is separate (the default) to keep all borders around cells and the table itself apart, or `collapse` to merge all adjacent borders.
- To set the space between separated borders, apply the table style

  `border-spacing: value;`

  where `value` is the space between the borders in any of the CSS units of measure.

For the KPAF program schedule, Kyle thinks the table would look better if there were no space between the table cells. He asks you to collapse the borders.

To collapse the cell borders:

1. Return to the **tables.css** file in your text editor. Add the following style to the `table` element, as shown in Figure 5-35:

   `border-collapse: collapse;`

Figure 5-35   Adding the border-collapse style

collapses adjacent borders in
the table into a single border

```
table.schedule {
    border: 10px outset rgb(153, 0, 153);
    border-collapse: collapse;
}
```

> **2.** Save your changes to the style sheet and then reload **schedule.htm** in your Web browser. Figure 5-36 shows the revised table design with the collapsed borders layout.

Figure 5-36   Schedule table with collapsed borders

Time	Monday	Tuesday	Wednesday	Thursday	Friday	Saturday	Sunday
			All Times Central				

Time	Monday	Tuesday	Wednesday	Thursday	Friday	Saturday	Sunday
6:00	National News						
6:30	Local News						
7:00	Opera Fest	Radio U	Science Week	The Living World	Word Play	Agri-Week	Folk Fest
7:30					Brain Stew	Bismarck Forum	
8:00	The Classical Music Connection				Old Time Radio	Saturday Nite Jazz	The Indie Connection
8:30					The Inner Mind		
9:00					Open Mike Nite		
9:30							
10:00	World News Feed						

Notice that the browser still uses the purple outset style for the border around the entire table. This is due to Rule 3 above. Because the border around the entire table is 10 pixels wide, it takes priority over the 1-pixel-wide borders around the individual table cells under the collapsed borders model.

Applying Styles to Rows and Columns

Kyle doesn't like the appearance of the table text. He suggests changing it to a sans-serif font that is 0.75 em units in size. He also suggests that the text in the header row be displayed in a semi-transparent white font on a purple background, and that the first column of the schedule, which contains the program times, appear on a light yellow background.

You can apply these styles to the row groups and column groups you created in the last session. Recall that the header row is part of the thead row group (see Figure 5-19), and that the first column of the table belongs to the *firstCol* class of columns (see Figure 5-20).

Thus, to apply Kyle's suggested styles, you could add the following declarations to the *tables.css* style sheet:

```
table.schedule {
    font-family: Arial, Helvetica, sans- serif;
    font-size: 0.75em;
}

table.schedule thead {
    background-color: rgb(203, 50, 203);
    color: white;
    color: rgba(255, 255, 255, 0.5);
}

table.schedule col.firstCol {
    background-color: rgb(255, 255, 192);
}
```

However, you notice a contradiction between these styles. The first cell in the schedule table belongs to both the header row and the first column. Will this cell have a purple background or a yellow background? Which style has precedence? Table objects, like other parts of CSS, have levels of precedence in which the more specific object takes priority over the more general. Figure 5-37 shows a diagram of the different levels of precedence in the Web table structure.

Figure 5-37   Levels of precedence in Web table styles

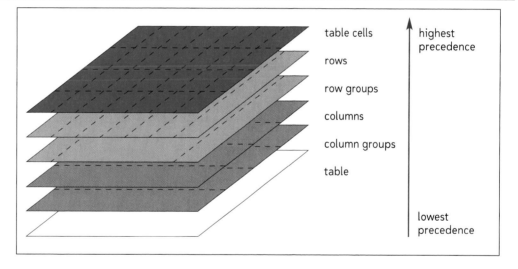

The most general styles are those applied to the entire table. Those styles are overruled by styles that are applied to column groups and then to columns. The next level up in precedence contains those styles applied to row groups and then to rows. The highest level of precedence is given to those styles applied to table cells. Be aware that not all style properties are supported by different layers of the table structure. In particular, columns and column groups accept only four CSS style properties: `border`, `background`, `width`, and `visibility`. If you want to apply a different CSS style property, you have to apply it to the cells within those columns.

Applying Styles to Cells within Rows

You can overcome the limits placed on the CSS styles available to columns and column groups by using pseudo-classes to identify specific cells within a row. For example, the selector

```
tbody tr td:first-of-type
```

matches all of the data cells listed first in any table body row. To match the cells listed last, you use the following selector:

```
tbody tr td:last-of-type
```

With pseudo-classes, you can apply the full range of CSS styles not available to columns and column groups. For example, the `text-align` property is not available for use with columns, but you can use the `last-of-type` pseudo-class to right-align the contents of the last cell in a row as follows:

```
tbody tr td:last-of-type {
    text-align: right;
}
```

For other cells, you can use the `nth-of-type` pseudo-class. Thus, the selector

```
tbody tr td:nth-of-type(7)
```

matches the seventh cell in the table rows. As long as you don't use spanning cells in these rows, this will also match the seventh column in the table.

Under Kyle's proposed style rules, the first cell should have a purple background because row groups take priority over columns or column groups. To verify that this is the case, add Kyle's proposed styles to the *tables.css* style sheet.

To set the text and background styles in the schedule table:

1. Return to the **tables.css** file in your text editor. Add the following styles to the style rule for the `table.schedule` selector:

   ```
   font-family: Arial, Helvetica, sans-serif;
   font-size: 0.75em;
   ```

2. At the bottom of the file, add the following style rule for the header of the schedule table:

   ```
   /* Table header styles */

   table.schedule thead {
       background-color: rgb(203, 50, 203);
       color: white;
       color: rgba(255, 255, 255, 0.5);
   }
   ```

3. Finally, add the following style for the first column of the schedule table:

   ```
   /* Styles for the first column */

   table.schedule col.firstCol {
       background-color: rgb(255, 255, 192);
   }
   ```

   Figure 5-38 highlights the new style rules in the style sheet.

Figure 5-38	Adding font and color styles to the schedule table

font styles for the table text

styles for the table header row group

styles for the first column of the table

```
table.schedule {
    border: 10px outset rgb(153, 0, 153);
    border-collapse: collapse;
    font-family: Arial, Helvetica, sans-serif;
    font-size: 0.75em;
}

table.schedule th, table.schedule td {
    border: 1px solid gray;
}


/* Table header styles */

table.schedule thead {
    background-color: rgb(203, 50, 203);
    color: white;
    color: rgba(255, 255, 255, 0.5);
}


/* Styles for the first column */

table.schedule col.firstCol {
    background-color: rgb(255, 255, 192);
}
```

4. Save your changes to the style sheet and then reload **schedule.htm** in your Web browser. The revised table design is shown in Figure 5-39.

Figure 5-39	Reformatted schedule table

table caption inherits the text styles from the table

As expected, the cell in the first column of the header row does indeed have a purple, rather than a light yellow, background. Also note that all of the cells in the table and the table caption have adopted the smaller sans-serif font. This is because the font style you entered for the schedule table is inherited by all table objects unless a different font style is specified.

Creating Banded Rows and Columns

A popular table design is to create table rows of alternating background colors to make it easier for users to read and locate information in a table. Before CSS3, this could be accomplished in CSS only by first assigning one class name to even-numbered rows and another class name to odd-numbered rows, and then applying different background styles to those classes.

However, with CSS3 you can create banded rows using the nth-of-type pseudo-class. For example, to create a table in which the background colors alternate between yellow on the odd-numbered rows and light green on the even-numbered rows, you could apply the following style rules to your table:

```
tr:nth-of-type(odd) {
    background-color: yellow;
}
tr:nth-of-type(even) {
    background-color: rgb(145, 255, 145);
}
```

The same technique can be used to create banded columns of different background colors. The style rules

```
colgroup col:nth-of-type(odd) {
    background-color: yellow;
}
colgroup col:nth-of-type(even) {
    background-color: rgb(145, 255, 145);
}
```

format a Web table so that the odd-numbered columns have a yellow background and the even-numbered columns are displayed against a light green background. Note that this technique assumes that none of the col elements span more than one column.

Like most CSS3 styles, these techniques might not be supported by older browsers, so you should design workarounds for those browsers.

Using the Width and Height Styles

Reducing the font size and changing the font family have resulted in a more compact table, but Kyle thinks it could be difficult to read and wonders if you could enlarge the table. Recall that browsers set table width to use the page space efficiently, never making tables wider than necessary to display the content. You can use the CSS width property to specify a different table size. Widths are expressed in one of the CSS units of measure or as a percentage of the containing element. Kyle suggests that you set the width of the table to 100% so that it covers the entire width of the section element that contains it.

To set the width of the table:

1. Return to the **tables.css** file in your text editor. Add the following style to the `table` element, as shown in Figure 5-40:

```
width: 100%;
```

Figure 5-40 Setting the width of the schedule table

```
table.schedule {
   border: 10px outset rgb(153, 0, 153);
   border-collapse: collapse;
   font-family: Arial, Helvetica, sans-serif;
   font-size: 0.75em;
   width: 100%;
}
```

2. Save your changes to the file and then reload **schedule.htm** in your Web browser. Figure 5-41 shows the layout of the enlarged table.

Figure 5-41 Table width set to 100%

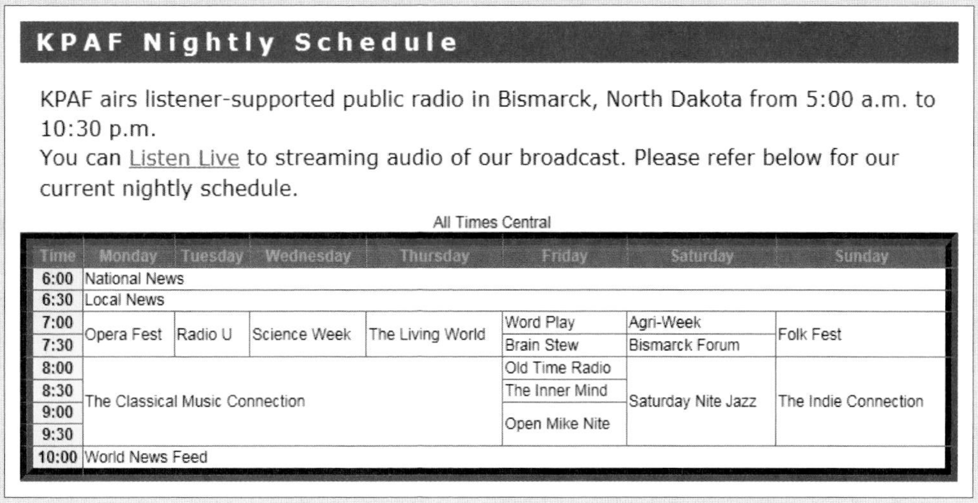

KPAF Nightly Schedule

KPAF airs listener-supported public radio in Bismarck, North Dakota from 5:00 a.m. to 10:30 p.m.
You can Listen Live to streaming audio of our broadcast. Please refer below for our current nightly schedule.

All Times Central

Time	Monday	Tuesday	Wednesday	Thursday	Friday	Saturday	Sunday
6:00	National News						
6:30	Local News						
7:00	Opera Fest	Radio U	Science Week	The Living World	Word Play	Agri-Week	Folk Fest
7:30					Brain Stew	Bismarck Forum	
8:00	The Classical Music Connection				Old Time Radio	Saturday Nite Jazz	The Indie Connection
8:30					The Inner Mind		
9:00					Open Mike Nite		
9:30							
10:00	World News Feed						

You notice that the column widths are inconsistent, with very little width given to the Time column and varying widths given to different days of the week. This results from browsers allotting space to each column as a function of the column's content. A Web browser will attempt to fit the most content possible within each column without having the text wrap to a new line. This means that columns with more text are wider than those with less text. When the width of the entire table is increased, the added space is divided evenly among the table columns.

TIP

Always set the total width of table columns to be less than 100% of the table width to allow space for table borders and padding.

You can set column widths using the same CSS `width` property you applied to the table itself. The column width is expressed either in a CSS unit of measure or as a percentage of the entire width of the table. You decide to set the width of the first column to 7% of the entire table width, while setting each of the seven remaining columns to 13% of the table width. Added together, 98% of the table width will be allotted to the eight table columns. The remaining table width is reserved for table and cell borders.

You'll set the column widths by applying the `width` property to the two column groups. The specified widths are then applied to the individual columns within those groups. The style rules are:

```
table.schedule col.firstCol {
    width: 7%;
}

table.schedule col.dayCols {
    width: 13%;
}
```

Add these styles to the *tables.css* style sheet.

To set the width of the table columns:

▶ **1.** Return to the **tables.css** file in your text editor. Add the following style to the style rule for the *firstCol* selector:

```
width: 7%;
```

▶ **2.** Directly below the style rule for the *firstCol* selector, add the following style rule to set the widths of the columns in the *dayCols* class to 13%, as shown in Figure 5-42:

```
/* Styles for the remaining columns */

table.schedule col.dayCols {
    width: 13%;
}
```

Figure 5-42	Setting the widths of the schedule table columns

the first column is 7% of the table width

each of the remaining seven columns is 13% of the table width

```
/* Styles for the first column */

table.schedule col.firstCol {
    background-color: rgb(255, 255, 192);
    width: 7%;
}

/* Styles for the remaining columns */

table.schedule col.dayCols {
    width: 13%;
}
```

▶ **3.** Save your changes to the file and then reload **schedule.htm** in your Web browser. Figure 5-43 shows the revised layout of the table.

Figure 5-43   **Revised table column widths**

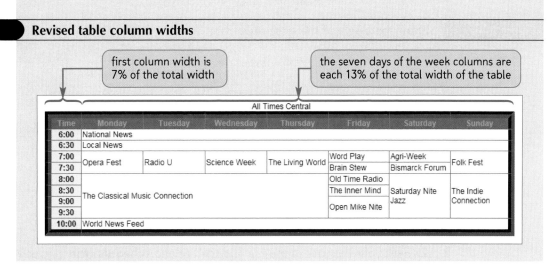

Kyle also wants you to increase the heights of the table rows to provide more visual space for the table contents. Heights are set using the CSS `height` property. You can apply heights to entire table rows or to individual table cells. You also can use the height style to set the height of an entire table. As with the `width` property, the `height` property should be interpreted as the minimum height for these table objects because the browser will enlarge the table, table row, or table cell if the content requires it.

You decide to set the height of the rows in the table header to 50 pixels and the height of the rows in the table body to 40 pixels. The styles to do this are as follows:

```
table.schedule thead tr {
    height: 50px;
}

table.schedule tbody tr {
    height: 40px;
}
```

Note that you don't apply the `height` property to the row groups themselves because that would set the width of the entire group and not the individual rows within the group.

To set the height of the table rows:

1. Return to the **tables.css** file in your text editor and add the following styles directly below the style rule for the `table.schedule thead` selector, as shown in Figure 5-44:

```
table.schedule thead tr {
    height: 50px;
}

/* Table body styles */

table.schedule tbody tr {
    height: 40px;
}
```

Figure 5-44 **Setting the height of the table rows**

```
table.schedule thead {
    background-color: rgb(203, 50, 203);
    color: white;
    color: rgba(255, 255, 255, 0.5);
}
```

height of the row within the table header →

```
table.schedule thead tr {
    height: 50px;
}
```

```
/* Table body styles */
```

heights of the rows within the table body →

```
table.schedule tbody tr {
    height: 40px;
}
```

▶ **2.** Save your changes to the file and then reload **schedule.htm** in your Web browser. Verify that the heights in the table header and table body have changed.

With the increased row height, Kyle would like all of the program names in the schedule to be vertically aligned with the tops of the cell borders as you did earlier with the `valign` HTML attribute. The equivalent CSS style is the `vertical-align` property introduced in Tutorial 3. Kyle also wants to increase the padding within each cell to add more space between the program names and the cell border. You'll add styles to do this.

To place the program names at the top of each table cell:

▶ **1.** Return to the **tables.css** file in your text editor and add the following style rule, as shown in Figure 5-45:

```
table.schedule tbody td {
    padding: 5px;
    vertical-align: top;
}
```

Figure 5-45 **Vertically aligning the table data cells in the table body**

```
/* Table body styles */

table.schedule tbody tr {
    height: 40px;
}

table.schedule tbody td {
    padding: 5px;
    vertical-align: top;
}
```

▶ **2.** Save your changes to the file, and then reload **schedule.htm** in your Web browser. As shown in Figure 5-46, the program names now are placed at the top of each cell, and the padding space between the program names and the cell borders has been increased.

Figure 5-46	Revised table layout

table header row is 50 pixels high

table body rows are each 40 pixels high

cell text is aligned with the top of each cell

Notice that only the data cells within the table body rows are placed at the top of the cell. The header cells still are centered vertically because they were not included in the contextual selector you specified in the style sheet.

Caption Styles

TIP

Firefox supports caption-side values of left and right to place the caption directly to the left or right of a Web table.

Kyle likes the new table design. His only remaining suggestion is that you align the table caption with the bottom-right corner of the table. Browsers usually place captions above the table, but you can specify the caption location using the caption-side property, which has the syntax

```
caption-side: position;
```

where *position* is either top (the default) or bottom to place the caption below the Web table. To align the caption text horizontally, you use the CSS text-align property. Thus, to place the schedule caption in the bottom-right corner of the table, you would enter the following CSS styles:

```
caption-side: bottom;
text-align: right;
```

Formatting a Table Caption with CSS

• To position a table caption, apply the property

  caption-side: *position*;

  where *position* is top or bottom.

Add this style to the *tables.css* style sheet.

To apply a style to the table caption:

1. Return to the **tables.css** file in your text editor and add the following style rule to the bottom of the file (see Figure 5-47):

```
/* Styles for the table caption */

table.schedule caption {
    caption-side: bottom;
    text-align: right;
}
```

Figure 5-47	Setting the caption position

```
/* Styles for the table caption */
table.schedule caption {
    caption-side: bottom;
    text-align: right;
}
```

displays the caption in the bottom-right corner of the table

2. Save your changes and then reload the **schedule.htm** file in your Web browser. As shown in Figure 5-48, the caption should now appear in the bottom-right corner of the table.

Figure 5-48	Table caption in the bottom-right corner

| 9:30 | | | | |
| 10:00 | World News Feed | | | |

All Times Central

Applying Table Styles to Other Page Elements

As you can see, tables are useful for displaying information in an organized structure of rows and columns. Tables are so useful, in fact, that there's no reason to limit the table structure to Web tables. Using the CSS `display` property, you can apply a table layout to other HTML elements, such as paragraphs, block quotes, or lists. Figure 5-49 describes the various CSS table display styles and their HTML equivalents.

Figure 5-49   Table display styles

Display Style	Equivalent HTML Element
display: table;	table (treated as a block-level element)
display: table-inline;	table (treated as an inline element)
display: table-row;	tr
display: table-row-group;	tbody
display: table-header-group;	thead
display: table-footer-group;	tfoot
display: table-column;	col
display: table-column-group;	colgroup
display: table-cell;	td or th
display: table-caption;	caption

For example, the following definition list contains definitions of two networking terms:

```
<dl>
   <dt>bandwidth</dt>
   <dd>A measure of data transfer speed over a network</dd>
   <dt>HTTP</dt>
   <dd>The protocol used to communicate with Web servers</dd>
</dl>
```

Rather than accepting the default browser layout for this list, it might be useful to display the text in a table. However, you don't want to lose the meaning of the markup tags. After all, HTML is designed to mark content, but not indicate how browsers should render that content. To display this definition list as a table, you could enclose each set of terms and definitions within a `div` element as follows:

```
<dl>
   <div>
      <dt>bandwidth</dt>
      <dd>A measure of data transfer speed over a network</dd>
   </div>
   <div>
      <dt>HTTP</dt>
      <dd>The protocol used to communicate with Web servers</dd>
   </div>
</dl>
```

You then could apply the following style sheet to the list, treating the entire definition list as a table—the `div` elements as table rows, and the definition terms and descriptions as table cells within those rows:

```
dl     {display: table; border-collapse: collapse; width: 300px;}
dl div {display: table-row;}
dt, dd {display: table-cell; border: 1px solid black;
        vertical-align: top; padding: 5px;}
```

As Figure 5-50 shows, when viewed in a Web browser, the definition list looks exactly as if it were created using HTML table elements.

Figure 5-50 Applying table styles to a definition list

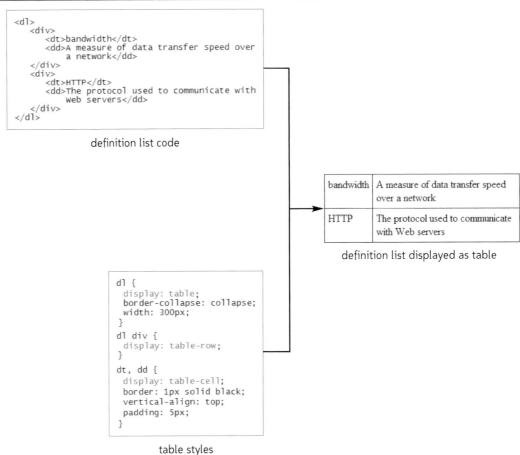

```
<dl>
    <div>
        <dt>bandwidth</dt>
        <dd>A measure of data transfer speed over
            a network</dd>
    </div>
    <div>
        <dt>HTTP</dt>
        <dd>The protocol used to communicate with
            Web servers</dd>
    </div>
</dl>
```

definition list code

bandwidth	A measure of data transfer speed over a network
HTTP	The protocol used to communicate with Web servers

definition list displayed as table

```
dl {
  display: table;
  border-collapse: collapse;
  width: 300px;
}
dl div {
  display: table-row;
}
dt, dd {
  display: table-cell;
  border: 1px solid black;
  vertical-align: top;
  padding: 5px;
}
```

table styles

In the same way, you can display other page elements in tabular form as long as the markup tags are nested in a way that mimics a table structure.

Written Communication: Designing Effective Web Tables

The primary purpose of a Web table is to convey data to the reader in a compact, easily understood way. You can apply several design principles to your Web tables to make them more effective at presenting data to interested readers:

- *Contrast the data cells from the header cells.* Make it easy for readers to understand your data by highlighting the header column or row in a different color or font size.
- *Avoid spanning rows and columns unless necessary.* Usability studies have shown that information can be gleaned quickly when presented in a simple grid layout. Unless data calls for it, don't break the grid by unnecessarily spanning a cell across the grid.
- *Break the monotony with icons.* If you are repeating the same phrase or word within a single row or column, consider replacing the text with an icon that conveys the same message. For example, in a table that describes the features of a product, use a check mark to indicate whether a particular feature is supported, rather than the words *yes* or *no*.
- *Alternate the row colors.* A large table with dozens of rows can be difficult for readers to scan and interpret. Consider using alternative background colors for the table rows to break the monotony and reduce eye strain.
- *Don't overwhelm the eye with borders.* Cell borders should be used only when they aid users by separating one cell from another. If they're not needed for this purpose, they actually can distract from the data. Rather than using borders, apply ample spacing to your cells to differentiate one data cell from another.
- *Keep it brief.* A table should not extend beyond what will fit compactly within the user's browser window. If your table is too extensive, consider breaking it into several tables that focus on different areas of information.

A Web table is judged not on its appearance but on its readability. This can best be accomplished by using a simple design whose features convey relevant information to readers. A good table gives users the data they want as quickly as possible and makes it easy to compare one value with another.

Creating Columnar Layouts

Kyle likes the design of the program schedule table. The only remaining change he wants you to make to the Web page is to break up the introductory paragraph into columns. Kyle feels that the lines of text in the paragraph are too long, making them difficult to quickly scan and read.

There are several ways to break page content into columns. You can separate the content into different block elements and float them as you did with the content in Tutorial 4. You also can nest the content in a two-column table with a single table row. Both of these options suffer from forcing the column layout to be static, as the content of each column is specified in the HTML markup tags. Ideally, in a column layout, the content should flow automatically from one column to the next as new text is inserted or old text is deleted. A third option that provides for a dynamic column layout is to use the column styles from CSS3. This is the approach you'll take.

TIP

Usability studies have shown that between 8 and 12 words is the ideal line length to enhance reading comprehension.

CSS3 Column Styles

Multi-column layouts are created with CSS3 by setting either the number of columns or the width of each column. To set the number of columns, you use the `column-count` property

```
column-count: number;
```

where `number` is the number of columns in the layout. Thus, the style rule

```
p {
    column-count: 3;
}
```

lays out the content from all paragraphs in three columns of equal width. Browsers calculate the width of each column so that the three columns extend across the paragraph. For example, a paragraph that is 600 pixels wide would be broken up into three columns of about 200 pixels each.

Alternately, you can set the width of each column by using the `column-width` property

```
column-width: width;
```

where `width` is the width of the column expressed in one of the CSS units of measure or as a percentage of the width of the element. The style rule

```
p {
    column-width: 200px;
}
```

creates a column layout in which each column is 200 pixels wide. The total number of columns will be based on how many 200-pixel-wide columns can fit into the space reserved for the paragraph. A paragraph that is 800 pixels wide could fit four columns. Because the columns must be whole columns, an 850-pixel-wide paragraph would still only fit four columns, with an extra 50 pixels of space left over.

By default, the gap between columns is 1 em in size, but you can specify a different gap using the `column-gap` property

```
column-gap: width;
```

where `width` is the width of the gap. You also can separate columns using a graphic border with the property

```
column-rule: border;
```

where `border` is the format of the border following the same syntax used with the CSS `border` property introduced in Tutorial 4. For example, the style

```
column-rule: 1px double red;
```

creates a 1-pixel-wide double red border. Column rules don't take up any space in the page layout; if they are wider than the specified gap, they will overlap the content of the columns. Like the `border` property, you can break up the `column-rule` property into the `column-rule-color`, `column-rule-width`, and `column-rule-style` properties to specify the color, width, and style of the dividing line, respectively.

Finally, you can extend content across columns using the `column-span` property

```
column-span: span;
```

where *span* is either `1` (to prevent spanning) or `all` (to enable spanning across all of the columns). In the following style rule, the contents of the `section` element are displayed in three columns but the `h1` heading within that section spans across the three columns:

```
section {
    column-count: 3;
}
section h1 {
    column-span: all;
}
```

Currently, the `column-span` property is not supported by any browser.
The `width` and `count` column styles can be combined into the shorthand property

```
columns: width count;
```

where *width* is the width of each column and *count* is the number of columns in the layout. For example, the style rule

```
section {
    columns: 250px 3;
}
```

creates a three-column layout for the `section` element with each column 250 pixels wide.

Browser Extensions to Columns

The column styles were first introduced in 2001 as part of the working draft of the proposed CSS3 specifications. However, they were not immediately adopted by the browser market. At the time of this writing, the only browsers that support column styles are Firefox, Google Chrome, and Safari, and all three do so through the use of browser extensions. Thus, to create a three-column layout for the paragraphs on your Web site that would be accepted by these browsers, you would use progressive enhancement with the following style rule:

```
p {
    -moz-column-count: 3;
    -webkit-column-count: 3;
    column-count: 3;
}
```

The browser extensions for the `column-width` and `column-rule` properties are expressed in the same way using the `-moz-` or `-webkit-` prefixes. Other column style properties have not been adopted by the market yet, and currently Internet Explorer and Opera do not support column styles at all. If you have to support those browsers, you should not design a layout that relies on multiple columns in order to be readable.

REFERENCE

Designing Columnar Layouts with CSS3

- To specify the number of columns in the layout, use

  ```
  column-count: number;
  ```

  where *number* is the number of columns in the layout.
- To specify the width of the columns, use

  ```
  column-width: width;
  ```

  where *width* is the width of the columns expressed in one of the CSS units of measure or as a percentage of the width of the element.
- To set the size of the gap between columns, use

  ```
  column-gap: width;
  ```

  where *width* is the width of the gap.
- To add a border between the columns, use

  ```
  column-rule: border;
  ```

  where *border* is the format of the border.
- To specify the width and number of columns in a single style property, use

  ```
  columns: width count;
  ```

  where *width* is the width of each column and *count* is the total number of columns in the layout.
- For specific browsers, add the –moz– vendor prefix for Firefox and the –webkit– prefix for Safari and Chrome to these style properties.

Kyle suggests that you use browser extensions and the CSS3 column style properties to display the introductory paragraph in a two-column layout with a gap width of 20 pixels and a purple divider. Add this style rule to the *tables.css* style sheet.

To display the introductory paragraph in two columns:

▶ **1.** Return to the **tables.css** file in your text editor and add the following style rule to the bottom of the file (see Figure 5-51):

```
/* Two column layout for the introductory paragraph */

section#main p {
   -moz-column-count: 2;
   -webkit-column-count: 2;
    column-count: 2;

   -moz-column-gap: 20px;
   -webkit-column-gap: 20px;
    column-gap: 20px;

   -moz-column-rule: 2px solid rgb(153, 0, 153);
   -webkit-column-rule: 2px solid rgb(153, 0, 153);
    column-rule: 2px solid rgb(153, 0, 153);
}
```

Figure 5-51 Applying a two-column style

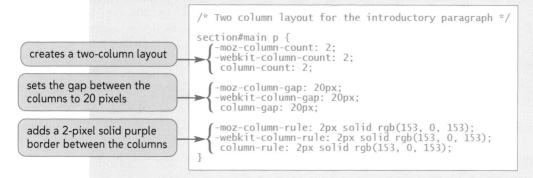

creates a two-column layout

sets the gap between the columns to 20 pixels

adds a 2-pixel solid purple border between the columns

```
/* Two column layout for the introductory paragraph */

section#main p {
    -moz-column-count: 2;
    -webkit-column-count: 2;
    column-count: 2;

    -moz-column-gap: 20px;
    -webkit-column-gap: 20px;
    column-gap: 20px;

    -moz-column-rule: 2px solid rgb(153, 0, 153);
    -webkit-column-rule: 2px solid rgb(153, 0, 153);
    column-rule: 2px solid rgb(153, 0, 153);
}
```

▶ **2.** Close the file, saving your changes, and then reload the **schedule.htm** file in your Web browser. Figure 5-52 shows the completed design of the nightly schedule page as it appears in Google Chrome.

Figure 5-52 Final KPAF nightly schedule page

two-column layout for the introductory paragraph

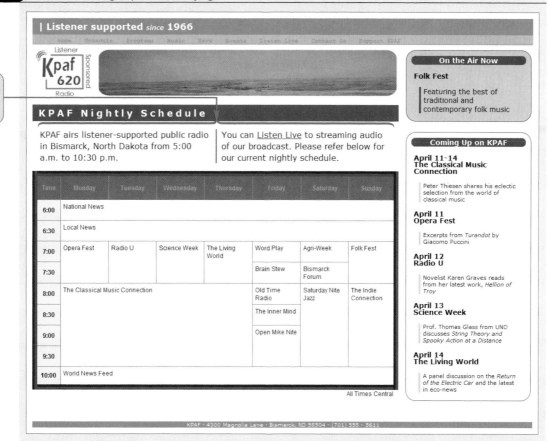

Trouble? At the time of this writing, no columns will appear if you are running Internet Explorer or Opera.

▶ **3.** Close any open files and then submit your completed HTML and CSS documents to your instructor, in either printed or electronic form, as requested.

Setting Manual Column Breaks

By default, browsers automatically break the content within a columnar layout in a way that keeps the columns roughly the same height. To create manual column breaks, CSS3 introduced the following style properties:

```
break-before: column;
break-after: column;
```

A column break created with one of these properties is placed directly before or after the element specified in the style rule selector, respectively. For example, the following style rule inserts a column break directly after any br element that appears within a paragraph:

```
p br {
    break-after: column;
}
```

CSS3 also provides styles to suppress column breaks with the following properties:

```
break-before: avoid-column;
break-after: avoid-column;
break-inside: avoid-column;
```

Thus, the following style rule prevents a column break from occurring within a blockquote element:

```
blockquote {
    break-inside: avoid-column;
}
```

No browser currently supports these manual column breaks. WebKit (used in Safari and Chrome) provides the column break properties

```
-webkit-column-break-before: type;
-webkit-column-break-after: type;
```

where *type* is always (to force a column break), avoid (to suppress a column break), inherit (to inherit the style of the container element), or auto (the default, which inserts a column break automatically when needed). Unfortunately, although they are part of the WebKit specifications, these styles to introduce manual column breaks are not currently implemented in any browser.

Kyle is pleased with the work you've done on the programming schedule page. He'll discuss your final design with other people at the station and get back to you with future projects.

Session 5.2 Quick Check

REVIEW

1. What HTML attribute do you add to the `table` element to set the space between cells to 10 pixels?

2. Specify the CSS style to collapse all adjacent borders within a Web table into single borders.

3. Two table cells have adjacent borders. One cell has a 5-pixel-wide double border and the other cell has a 6-pixel-wide solid border. If the table borders are collapsed, what type of border will the two cells share?

4. In the case of conflicting styles, which has highest precedence: the style of the row group or the style of the column group?

5. What style would you use to align the content of all table header cells with the bottoms of the cells?

6. What style would you use to display the table caption in the bottom-left corner of the table?

7. Provide a style rule to display the paragraphs within all `article` elements in three columns separated by a 1-pixel solid black border.

8. Provide a style rule to display the contents of all `div` elements belonging to the *columns* class in a columnar layout with the column widths set to 250 pixels and the space between the columns set to 10 pixels.

Practice the skills you learned in the tutorial using the same case scenario.

PRACTICE

Review Assignments

Data Files needed for the Review Assignments: kpaf.jpg, kpaf2.css, modernizr-1.5.js, morningtxt.htm, programstxt.css

Kyle has had a chance to work with the KPAF nightly schedule page. He wants you to make a few changes to the layout and apply the new design to a page that displays the KPAF morning schedule. Kyle already has entered much of the Web page content and style. He wants you to complete his work by creating and designing the Web table for the morning schedule. Figure 5-53 shows a preview of the morning schedule page.

Figure 5-53   **KPAF morning schedule**

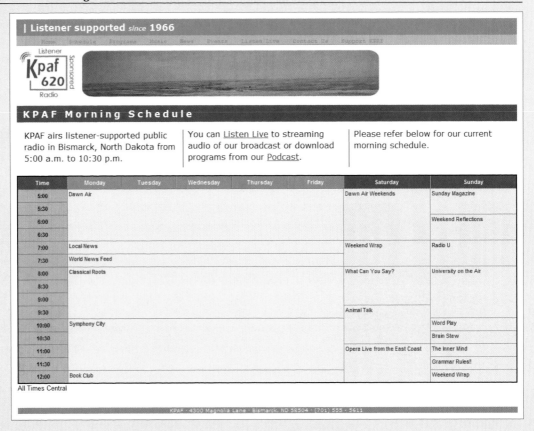

Complete the following:

1. Use your text editor to open the **morningtxt.htm** and **programstxt.css** files from the tutorial.05\review folder. Enter *your name* and *the date* in the comment section of each file. Save the files as **morning.htm** and **programs.css**, respectively, in the same folder.

2. Go to the **morning.htm** file in your text editor. Insert links to the **kpaf2.css** and **programs.css** style sheets.

3. Scroll down the file and directly below the paragraph element, insert a Web table with the class name **programs**.

4. Add a table caption containing the text **All Times Central**.

5. Below the caption, create a column group containing three columns. The first `col` element should have the class name **timeColumn**. The second `col` element should have the class name **wDayColumns** and span five columns in the table. The last `col` element should have the class name **wEndColumns** and span two columns.

6. Insert the following summary for the table: **Lists the morning programs aired by KPAF from 5:00 a.m. to 12:00 p.m. (central time)**.

7. Add the table header row group containing the headings shown in Figure 5-53.

8. Enter the table body row group containing the times and names of the different KPAF programs from 5:00 a.m. to 12:00 p.m., Monday through Sunday, in half-hour intervals. Create row- and column-spanning cells to match the layout of the days and times shown in Figure 5-53.

9. Close the morning.htm file, saving your changes.

10. Go to the **programs.css** file in your text editor. Create a style rule for the programs table to: a) set the width of the table to 100%; b) add a 2-pixel solid black border that is collapsed around the table; and c) set the font family to the following list of fonts: Arial, Verdana, and sans-serif.

11. Create a style rule to align the table caption with the bottom-left corner of the table. Set the caption font size to 0.8 em.

12. Create a style rule for all table data cells in the table body of the programs table to: a) set all table cells to a font size of 0.7 em; b) vertically align the text of all table data cells with the top of the cell; c) add a 1-pixel solid gray border around every cell, and d) setting the padding space to 2 pixels.

13. Set the height of all table rows to 25 pixels.

14. Display the header row group in white font with a background color of (105, 177, 60).

15. For table header cells within the header row group, set the font size to 0.7 em and add a 1-pixel solid gray border. For the first table header cell in the header row group, set the background color to the value (153, 86, 7). Use the `nth-of-type` pseudo-class to set the background color of the seventh and then the eighth table header cells in the header row group to the value (153, 0, 153).

16. Add the following style rules for the three column groups in the table: a) set the width of the timeColumn column group to 10% with a background color of (215, 205, 151); b) set the width of the wDayColumns column group to 11% with a background color of (236, 255, 211); and c) set the width of the wEndColumns column group to 17% with a background color of (255, 231, 255).

17. Create a three-column layout for the introductory paragraph within the intro section with three columns in the layout separated by a gap of 20 pixels with a 1-pixel solid black divider.

18. Add style comments throughout the style sheet to document your work, and then save your changes.

19. Open the **morning.htm** file in your Web browser and verify that the table layout and design resemble that shown in Figure 5-53. (Note: If you are using Internet Explorer or Opera, you will not see the three-column layout for the introductory paragraph.)

20. Submit your completed files to your instructor, in either printed or electronic form, as requested.

APPLY

Apply your knowledge of Web tables and table styles to create a puzzle page with nested tables.

Case Problem 1

Data Files needed for this Case Problem: gold.jpg, green.jpg, jpf.css, jpf.jpg, modernizr-1.5.js, stabletxt.css, sudokutxt.htm

The Japanese Puzzle Factory   Rebecca Peretz has a passion for riddles and puzzles. Her favorites are the Japanese logic puzzles that have become very popular in recent years. Rebecca and a few of her friends have begun work on a new Web site called *The Japanese Puzzle Factory (JPF)*, where they plan to create and distribute Japanese-style puzzles. Eventually, the JPF Web site will include interactive programs to enable users to solve the puzzles online, but for now Rebecca is interested only in the design and layout of the pages. You've been asked to help by creating a draft version of the Web page describing the Sudoku puzzle. Figure 5-54 shows a preview of the design and layout you'll create for Rebecca.

Figure 5-54   The Japanese Puzzle Factory Sudoku page

Rebecca has created some of the content and designs for this page. Your task is to complete the page by entering the code and styles for the Sudoku table, as well as adding some background images to other sections of the page layout.

Complete the following:

1. Use your text editor to open the files **stabletxt.css** and **sudokutxt.htm** from the tutorial.05\case1 folder. Enter *your name* and *the date* in the comment section of each file. Save the files as **stable.css** and **sudoku.htm**, respectively, in the same folder.

2. Return to the **sudoku.htm** file in your text editor. Add links to the **jpf.css** and **stable. css** style sheets.

3. Scroll down to the section element. Directly below the opening `<section>` tag, insert a `table` element that will be used to display the Sudoku puzzle. Give the `table` element the class name **spuzzle**.

4. Add a caption to the spuzzle table containing the text **Sudoku**.

5. Create a table head row group containing a single row. The row should display 10 heading cells. The first heading cell should be blank and the remaining nine cells should display the digits from 1 to 9.

6. Create the table body row group containing nine table rows with the first cell in each row containing a table heading cell displaying the letters A through I.

7. After the initial table heading cell in the first, fourth, and seventh rows, insert three table data cells spanning three rows and three columns each. Altogether, these nine data cells will store the nine 3×3 boxes that are part of the Sudoku puzzle.

8. In the first row of the table body, put the three table data cells in the greenBox, goldBox, and greenBox classes, respectively. In the fourth row, the three data cells belong to the goldBox, greenBox, and goldBox classes. In the seventh row, the three data cells belong to the greenBox, goldBox, and greenBox classes.

⊕ EXPLORE 9. Go to each of the nine table data cells you created in the last two steps. Within each data cell, insert a nested table belonging to the subTable class. Within each nested table, insert three rows and three columns of data cells. Enter the digits from Figure 5-54 in the appropriate table cells. Where there is no digit, leave the table cell empty.

10. Save your changes to the file, and then go to the **stable.css** style sheet in your text editor.

11. Create a style rule to collapse the borders of the spuzzle and subTable tables.

12. Add a 5-pixel outset gray border to the table data cells within the spuzzle table.

13. Set the font size of table header cells within the spuzzle table to 8 pixels and the font color to gray.

14. Set the height of table header cells within the table body row group of the spuzzle table to 40 pixels.

15. For table data cells within the subTable table, add the following styles: a) set the font size to 20 pixels and the font color to blue; b) set the width and height to 40 pixels and center the cell text both horizontally and vertically; and c) add a 1-pixel solid black border around the cell.

⊕ EXPLORE 16. For table data cells nested within the goldBox class of table data cells, display the background image file *gold.jpg* centered within the cell and not tiled. (Hint: Use background position values of 50% for both the horizontal and vertical directions.)

17. For table data cells nested within the greenBox class of data cells, set the background image to the *green.jpg* file, once again centered within the cell without tiling.

18. Add descriptive comments throughout your style sheet to document your work.

19. Save your changes to the file and then reload **sudoku.htm** in your Web browser. Verify that the layout and design of the Sudoku table resemble that shown in Figure 5-54.

20. Submit your completed files to your instructor, in either printed or electronic form, as requested.

APPLY

Apply your knowledge of CSS and Web tables to create a calendar table for a community civic center.

Case Problem 2

Data Files needed for this Case Problem: bottom.jpg, bottomleft.jpg, bottomright.jpg, caltxt.css, ccc.css, ccc.jpg, febtxt.htm, left.jpg, modernizr-1.5.js, right.jpg, tab.jpg, tabred.jpg, top.jpg, topleft.jpg, topright.jpg

The Chamberlain Civic Center   Lewis Kern is an events manager at the Chamberlain Civic Center in Chamberlain, South Dakota. The center is in the process of updating its Web site, and Lewis has asked you to work on the pages detailing events in the upcoming year. He's asked you to create a calendar page for the month of February. Lewis wants the page design to catch the reader's eye, so he suggests that you create a Web table with a background showing a spiral binding. The spiral binding graphic must be flexible enough to accommodate calendars of different sizes, so you'll build the borders by using eight different background images that are placed on the four corners and four sides of the table. The February calendar must list the following events:

- Every Sunday, the Carson Quartet plays at 1:00 p.m. ($8)
- February 1, 8:00 p.m.: Taiwan Acrobats ($16/$24/$36)
- February 5, 8:00 p.m.: Joey Gallway ($16/$24/$36)
- February 7-8, 7:00 p.m.: West Side Story ($24/$36/$64)
- February 10, 8:00 p.m.: Jazz Masters ($18/$24/$32)
- February 13, 8:00 p.m.: Harlem Choir ($18/$24/$32)
- February 14, 8:00 p.m.: Chamberlain Symphony ($18/$24/$32)
- February 15, 8:00 p.m.: Edwin Drood ($24/$36/$44)
- February 19, 7:00 p.m.: The Yearling ($8/$14/$18)
- February 21, 8:00 p.m.: An Ellington Tribute ($24/$32/$48)
- February 22, 8:00 p.m.: Othello ($18/$28/$42)
- February 25, 8:00 p.m.: Madtown Jugglers ($12/$16/$20)
- February 28, 8:00 p.m.: Ralph Williams ($32/$48/$64)
- March 1, 8:00 p.m.: Othello ($18/$28/$42)

Lewis wants the weekend events (Friday and Saturday night) to be displayed with a light red background. A preview of the page you'll create is shown in Figure 5-55.

Figure 5-55   The Chamberlain Civic Center February calendar

the Chamberlain Civic Center

| Home | Events | Box Office | Facilities | Directions | Contact Us |

Coming in February

February will be another banner month at the Chamberlain Civic Center with a two day performance of the Tony Award winning musical, West Side Story by the Broadway Touring Company. Tickets are going fast, so order yours today.

Celebrate Valentine's Day with the Chamberlain Symphony and their special selection of classical music for lovers. The next day, exercise your mind by attending the Charles Dickens classic, The Mystery of Edwin Drood.

Jazz lovers have a lot to celebrate in February with a visit from the Jazz Masters on February 10th, and

then on February 21st, enjoy the music of The Duke with an Ellington Tribute performed by the Jazz Company of Kansas City.

Pins, bottles, plates, and chairs are flying at the Chamberlain Civic Center in February. The Taiwan Acrobats return with another amazing performance. Then, on February 25th, the Madtown Jugglers get into the act with their unique blend of comedy, juggling, and madness.

Enjoy a classical brunch every Sunday in February with music provided by the Carson Quartet. Seating is limited, so please order your table in advance.

Events in February at the CCC

Sun	Mon	Tue	Wed	Thu	Fri	Sat
26	27	28	29	30	31	1 Taiwan Acrobats 8 pm $16/$24/$36
2 Carson Quartet 1 pm $8	3	4	5 Joey Gallway 8 pm $16/$24/$36	6	7 West Side Story 7 pm $24/$36/$64	8 West Side Story 7 pm $24/$36/$64
9 Carson Quartet 1 pm $8	10 Jazz Masters 8 pm $18/$24/$32	11	12	13 Harlem Choir 8 pm $18/$24/$32	14 Chamberlain Symphony 8 pm $18/$24/$32	15 Edwin Drood 8 pm $24/$36/$44
16 Carson Quartet 1 pm $8	17	18	19 The Yearling 7 pm $8/$14/$18	20	21 An Ellington Tribute 8 pm $24/$32/$48	22 Othello 8 pm $18/$28/$42
23 Carson Quartet 1 pm $8	24	25 Madtown Jugglers 8 pm $12/$16/$20	26	27	28 Ralph Williams 8 pm $32/$48/$64	1 Othello 8 pm $18/$28/$42

The Chamberlain Civic Center   2011 Canyon Drive   Chamberlain, SD 53725   (605)555-8741

Complete the following:

1. In your text editor, open the **caltxt.css** and **febtxt.htm** files from the tutorial.05\case2 folder. Enter *your name* and *the date* in the comment section of each file. Save the files as **calendar.css** and **feb.htm**, respectively.

2. Go to the **feb.htm** file in your text editor. Create links to the **calendar.css** and **ccc.css** style sheets.

3. Scroll down to the events `section` element. Within the element, insert a table with the class name **calendar**. Add the table caption **Events in February at the CCC** to the calendar.

4. Create a column group for the calendar consisting of two `col` elements. The first `col` element should belong to the weekdays class and span five columns. The second `col` element should belong to the weekends class and span two columns.

5. Create a table header row group consisting of one row of table headings displaying the three-letter abbreviations for the days of the week, starting with *Sun* and ending with *Sat*.

6. Create a table body row group containing the days in the month of February. The row group should contain five rows and seven columns of table data cells. There are no spanning cells in any of the rows or columns.

7. Each table data cell should have the following content:
   - The day of the month should be marked as an `h3` heading (refer to Figure 5-55 for the starting and ending days in the calendar).
   - On the days when there is a CCC event, enter the event information as a definition list with the name of the event marked as a `dt` element, and the time and price of the event each marked with a `dd` element.

8. Save your changes to the file and then go to the **calendar.css** file in your text editor. Create a style rule for the calendar table to: a) create separate borders for the different parts of the table with a 5-pixel space between the borders; b) set the font size to 8 pixels; c) set the top margin to 20 pixels, the bottom margin to 5 pixels, and the left and right margins to `auto`; d) set the padding space to 40 pixels; and e) set the width to 650 pixels.

⟐ EXPLORE
9. In the style rule you created in the previous step, add a style that specifies multiple background images for the calendar table in the following order:
   - the *topleft.jpg* image in the top-left corner of the table with no tiling
   - the *topright.jpg* image in the top-right corner with no tiling
   - the *bottomleft.jpg* image in the bottom-left corner with no tiling
   - the *bottomright.jpg* image in the bottom-right corner with no tiling
   - the *top.jpg* image in the top-left corner, tiled only in the horizontal direction
   - the *left.jpg* image in the top-left corner, tiled only in the vertical direction
   - the *right.jpg* image in the top-right corner, tiled only in the vertical direction
   - the *bottom.jpg* image in the bottom-left corner, tiled only in the horizontal direction

10. Create a style rule to center the table caption along the top of the calendar table and do the following: a) set the bottom padding to 10 pixels; b) set the font size to 16 pixels; c) set the kerning to 3 pixels; and d) set the width to 650 pixels.

11. Set the width of the table columns to 14% of the width of the table. For columns belonging to the weekends class, change the background color to the value (255, 232, 232).

12. For table heading cells in the table header row group, set the background color to red, the font color to white, and the letter spacing to 5 pixels.

13. Set the height of the table row within the table header row group of the calendar table to 5%. Set the height of the table rows within the table body row group to 19% each.

14. Add a 1-pixel solid gray border to every table data cell within the calendar table. Set the vertical alignment of the cell content to the top of the cell.

15. Set the font size of h3 headings within the data table cells of the calendar table to 8 pixels.

16. The paragraphs in the summary section are enclosed within a div element. Create a style rule for this div element to: a) display the contents in a columnar layout with the column width set to 300 pixels; b) set the column gap to 20 pixels; and c) add a 1-pixel solid black divider rule between columns.

17. Save your changes to the file and then open **feb.htm** in your Web browser. Verify that the layout and design of the page resemble that shown in Figure 5-55. (Note: If you are running Internet Explorer or Opera, you might not see multiple columns in the description of the upcoming February events.)

18. Submit your completed files to your instructor, in either printed or electronic form, as requested.

CHALLENGE

Explore additional CSS table styles and pseudo-class techniques by designing a products table for a manufacturer of geodesic domes.

Case Problem 3

Data Files needed for this Case Problem: bottom.jpg, bottomleft.jpg, bottomright.jpg, dhomelogo.png, dhometxt.htm, dome.css, dtabletxt.css, left.jpg, modernizr-1.5.js, right.jpg, tableback.png, top.jpg, topleft.jpg, topright.jpg

dHome, Inc.   Olivia Moore is the director of advertising for dHome, one of the nation's newest manufacturers of geodesic dome houses. She's hired you to work on the company's Web site. Olivia has provided you with all of the text you need for the Web page, and your job is to design the page's layout. You'll start by designing a draft of the company's home page. Olivia wants the page to include information about dHome's pricing structure for various dome models. The page also contains links to other pages on the Web site.

Olivia also wants you to add some visual effects to the table's appearance. She would like a semi-transparent table background showing the pattern of a geodesic dome, and she would like banded rows colored with alternating bands of semi-transparent white and green. Finally, she'd like you to add rounded corners to the table using some graphic image files she's created.

A preview of the design you'll create for Olivia is shown in Figure 5-56.

Figure 5-56   **dHome Web page**

dHome is the leading manufacturer of dome structures in the world. Our domes are built to exacting standards using the highest quality materials. We've been building domes for over 35 years and have a proven track record of providing quality homes at reasonable prices.

A dome house provides you with a totally new living experience in a spacious and open environment. Imagine a curved ceiling more than 20 feet high with skylights bringing the beauty of the outdoors into your home.

Domes are stronger and safer than conventional homes, and their design provides more stability against hurricanes, tornados, and earthquakes. Dome houses are also more energy efficient. A dome home has approximately 30 to 50% less roof and wall area exposed to the elements than conventional homes, resulting in reduced energy costs. The spherical space also provides for a natural air flow, minimizing cold spots and increasing interior comfort.

Building Models

Model	Total Sq. Ft.	Sphere Size	Price
Class IA	4700 square ft.	50 ft. 5/8 sphere	$150,000
Class IB	4100 square ft.	35 ft. 5/8 sphere	$125,000
Class IIA	3700 square ft.	50 ft. 5/8 sphere	$112,000
Class IIB	3100 square ft.	35 ft. 5/8 sphere	$97,000
Class IIIA	2600 square ft.	45 ft. 5/8 sphere	$84,000
Class IIIB	2200 square ft.	35 ft. 5/8 sphere	$73,000

Call us about custom pricing!

DHOME INC. • 8312 INDUSTRIAL WAY • OWENSBORO, KY 42302 • 270 - 555 - 7811

Judy Crawford/Shutterstock.com
Brad Sauter/Shutterstock.com

Complete the following:

1. Use your text editor to open the **dhometxt.htm** and **dtabletxt.css** files from the tutorial.05\case3 folder. Enter *your name* and *the date* in the comment section of each file. Save the files as **dhome.htm** and **dtable.css**, respectively.

2. Go to the **dhome.htm** file in your text editor. Create links to the **dome.css** and **dtable.css** style sheets.

3. Scroll down to the `section` element. Above the paragraphs within that element, insert a table with the class name *domeSpecs*. Add a table summary with the text **A table describing six dome models sold by dHome, Inc.** and add the table caption **Building Models**.

4. Create a column group containing three `col` elements with class names of *firstColumn*, *middleColumns*, and *lastColumn*. The *middleColumns* `col` element should span two columns in the table.

5. Create a table header row group containing a single table row with four table heading cells. The cells should contain the headings **Model**, **Total Sq. Ft.**, **Sphere Size**, and **Price**.

6. Insert a table footer row group containing a single row and three data cells. The first and third cells should be left blank. The middle cell should contain the text **Call us about custom pricing!** and should span two columns.

7. Create a table body row group consisting of six table rows with four cells each. Insert the model, square feet, sphere size, and price values from Figure 5-56.

8. Save your changes to the **dhome.htm** file and then go to the **dtable.css** file in your text editor.

9. Create a style for the `domeSpecs` table that: a) sets the font size to 16 pixels; b) sets the bottom and left margins to 20 pixels; c) floats the table on the right; and d) collapses the border.

⊕ EXPLORE 10. Add code to the style rule from the previous step to display the file *tableback.png* as the table background aligned with the bottom-right corner without tiling. Set the size of the background image to cover the table.

11. For every data cell in the `domeSpecs` table, set the top and bottom padding to 0 pixels and the left and right padding to 5 pixels.

12. Create a style rule for the table caption to: a) set the font size to 18 pixels and the kerning to 5 pixels; b) center the caption text above the table; and c) set the bottom margin to 10 pixels.

13. For the table header row group, create a style rule to: a) display a 2-pixel solid gray bottom border; and b) display the image file *top.jpg* tiled horizontally across the top of the row group.

14. Set the height of the table row in the header row group to 40 pixels.

15. For heading cells within the header row group: a) set the top/bottom padding to 0 pixels and the left/right padding to 5 pixels; and b) set the kerning to 2 pixels.

⊕ EXPLORE 16. Olivia wants a graphic image used for the top-left and top-right corners of the table header row group. Use the `first-of-type` pseudo-class to set the background image of the first heading cell in the header row group, placing the image file *topleft.jpg* in the top-left corner of the cell with no tiling. In the same way, use the `last-of-type` pseudo-class to place the image file *topright.jpg* as the background image for the last heading cell in the table header row group, positioning the image in the top-right corner of the cell with no tiling.

17. Create a style rule for the table footer row group that: a) adds a 2-pixel solid gray top border; b) centers the text of the row group; and c) adds the background image file *bottom.jpg* repeated horizontally along the bottom of the row group.

18. Set the height of the table rows within the table footer row group to 40 pixels.

19. As with the table header row group, add background graphic images to the corners of the footer. Use the `first-of-type` pseudo-class to add the image file *bottomleft.jpg* as the background image for the first data cell in the table footer row group, set along the bottom-left corner without tiling. Use the `last-of-type` pseudo-class to add the image file *bottomright.jpg* as the background image of the last data cell in the table footer row group, positioning it along the bottom-right corner of that cell without tiling.

20. Create a style rule for the table rows within the table body row group that: a) sets the height of each row to 50 pixels; and b) adds a 1-pixel dotted gray bottom border.

21. As with the table header and table footer row groups, create a graphic border for the first and last cells in each row of the table body row group. Use the `first-of-type` pseudo-class to display the image file *left.jpg* as the background image for the first data cell in each row, positioned at the top-left corner and tiled vertically. Use the `last-of-type` pseudo-class to display the image file *right.jpg* as the background image for the last data cell, positioned along the top-right corner of the cell and tiled vertically. In addition, for the last data cell in every row of the table body row group, right-align the cell contents.

⊕ EXPLORE 22. Olivia would like the table to display semi-transparent banded rows. Use the `nth-of-type` pseudo-class to display every even row in the body section with the background color (152, 228, 215) at 60% opacity. In the same way, display every odd row in the body section with the background color (255, 255, 255) at 60% opacity.

23. Set the width of the `firstColumn` column group to 22% of the table width. Set the width of the columns in the `middleColumns` column group to 28% of the table width. Finally, set the width of the `lastColumn` column group to 22% of the width of the table.

24. Add style comments to document your work.

25. Save your changes to the file and then open **dhome.htm** in your Web browser. Verify that the appearance of the product information table matches that shown in Figure 5-56. (Note: If you are using earlier versions of the major browsers, you will not see the semi-transparent effect in the rows and in the table background, nor will you see rounded graphic corners and edges.)

26. Submit your completed files to your instructor, in either printed or electronic form, as requested.

Test your knowledge of CSS to create a Web table listing room reservations at a popular conference center.

CREATE

Case Problem 4

Data Files needed for this Case Problem: hcclogo.jpg, modernizr-1.5.js, rooms.txt

Hamilton Conference Center   Yancy Inwe is the facilities manager at the Hamilton Conference Center in Hamilton, Ohio. The conference center, a general-use facility for the community, hosts several organizations and clubs as well as special events and shows by local vendors. The center recently upgraded its intranet capabilities, and Yancy would like to create a Web site where employees and guests can easily track which conference rooms are available and which are being used. She would like this information displayed in a Web table that lays out the room use for seven rooms and halls from 8:00 a.m. to 5:00 p.m. in half-hour increments. Eventually, this process will be automated by the conference's Web server; but for now, she has come to you for help in setting up a sample Web page layout and design.

Complete the following:

1. Use your text editor to create an HTML file named **conference.htm** and two style sheets named **hcc.css** and **schedule.css**. Enter *your name* and *the date* in a comment section of each file. Include any other comments you think aptly document the purpose and content of the files. Save the files in the tutorial.05\case4 folder.

2. Use the text files provided to create a Web page containing the reservation information. The design of the Web page is up to you, and you may supplement your Web page with any material you feel is appropriate. Place the styles for the page layout in the **hcc.css** style sheet.

3. Create a table containing the room reservation information. The table structure should contain the following elements:
   - a table caption and summary
   - table row and column groups
   - examples of row- and/or column-spanning cells
   - examples of both table heading and table data cells

4. Create a style for your table in the **schedule.css** style sheet. The layout and appearance of the table are up to you, but the table should include the following:
   - a border style applied to one or more table objects
   - a style that defines whether the table borders are separate or collapsed
   - styles applied to table rows and column groups
   - use of horizontal and vertical alignment of the table cell contents
   - different widths applied to different table columns
   - styles applied to the table caption

5. Document your style choices with appropriate comments.

6. Add a columnar layout to one section of your document. The number of columns and its appearance are up to you.

7. Submit your completed files to your instructor, in either printed or electronic form, as requested.

ENDING DATA FILES

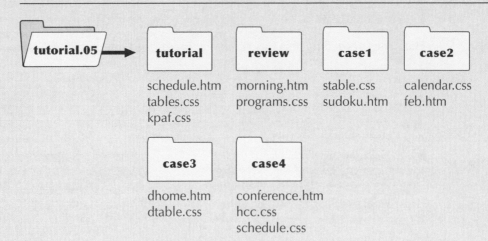

tutorial.05 →

tutorial
schedule.htm
tables.css
kpaf.css

review
morning.htm
programs.css

case1
stable.css
sudoku.htm

case2
calendar.css
feb.htm

case3
dhome.htm
dtable.css

case4
conference.htm
hcc.css
schedule.css

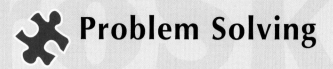

Problem Solving

Assessing Alternatives

At most any job, you'll regularly find yourself confronting questions or problems and needing to identify and choose among alternative solutions. Once you have a clear idea of the problem, a systematic approach can help you identify the path forward that best fits your needs.

Step #1: Determine Feasible Alternatives

In this step, document criteria by which you'll evaluate each course of action. Then, brainstorm on possible solutions by collecting as many ideas as possible about how to correct the problem. Write them all down. Don't discount any ideas as too radical, expensive, or impossible to achieve. In fact, don't even attempt to evaluate the ideas at all! Instead, encourage creative thinking. Ask "what if?"—What if we had unlimited resources? What if we had new skills? Be sure to include as many people or groups as necessary, since whatever solution is selected will need the buy-in of these same individuals and groups later on. Without their ownership, even the best alternative could end up failing.

Step #2: Collect Information Needed to Evaluate Alternatives

This step is where the pros and cons of each idea are evaluated. For each alternative developed in step #1, additional information will be needed to fill out the solution. Don't assume you know it all! Obtaining additional information will involve going back to people you spoke with at the outset to seek their input on the choices. It also may require securing financial information from other divisions in the organization, learning about operation schedules, documenting human resources constraints or training needs, or sourcing some market research intelligence to be able to verify observations or anecdotal evidence provided during initial data collection about the problem. You'll likely start to see relationships between the collected information that can provide insights into the feasibility of the possible solutions.

Step #3: Evaluate Each Alternative

Document both the benefits and costs of all alternatives, whether quantitative (cost savings) or qualitative (employee morale). Spreadsheet software often helps problem solvers track and quantify merits and drawbacks. Consider the resources required—financial, human, or other capital such as equipment. Are they affordable? Is there enough time to implement the different solutions? There may be risks involved with some alternatives; what are they? What would be the consequences if the chosen solution didn't work? The best choice is to go with the solution that offers the greatest reward for the least amount of risk. In some cases, the solution may require developing a "Plan B" to fall back on in case the chosen solution fails to solve the problem.

Step #4: Select an Alternative

Don't get stuck trying to select a solution that addresses every aspect of a problem, especially if it is complex. Rarely are solutions perfect. Instead, consider the effect each alternative course of action may have as the change ripples through the organization. Will the resulting change generate positive results and meet the criteria established at the

ProSkills

outset of the problem-solving process? Will the chosen alternative resolve the problem in the long term? What is realistic, given the merits and drawbacks identified in step #3? Make a choice and then develop the detailed plans to implement it. Also think about how to manage the transition or change from the old approach or process to the new one. Will employees require special training? Does a special newsletter with updates need to be distributed so people are well informed? Are there rumors that need to be dispelled, or undercurrents of unrest that may affect the alternative?

PROSKILLS

Research, Evaluate, and Implement Design Techniques

The Web is a valuable source of information, and it is particularly valuable for those who want to learn how to create and design Web sites. Each Web site presents an opportunity to study how other Web page designers solved problems involving layout and design. In addition, most Web designers are eager to share the methods, the techniques, and sometimes the tricks they've used to get the most out of HTML, CSS, and an occasional uncooperative browser. In this exercise, you'll use the skills and tasks you learned in Tutorials 3 through 5 to create a Web site on a hobby or personal interest of yours. First, you'll research and evaluate the techniques of published Web page designers.

Note: Please be sure *not* to include any personal information of a sensitive nature in the files you create to be submitted to your instructor for this exercise. Later on, you can update the files with such information for your personal use.

1. The W3C specifications for HTML5 and CSS3 represent a "gold standard" by which all browsers are rated. Conduct a Web search to determine the browsers that provide the best support for the W3C specifications. Which browsers provide the poorest level of support?

2. Deprecated elements and attributes are features of HTML that have been replaced, usually by CSS styles. Examine five different deprecated elements or attributes and explain what they were intended to accomplish and what has replaced them under the current specifications for HTML and CSS.

3. Web designers have come up with a variety of approaches to creating two-, three-, and four-column layouts. Search the Web for the pages of Web designers and report on the different techniques designers have used to create these classic layouts.

4. Many of the CSS3 styles are replacing coding techniques used in older browsers. Search the Web and explain how you would create rounded corners without using the `border-radius` property from CSS3.

5. Locate a Web page whose content and layout you enjoy. Take some time to download the underlying HTML and CSS code, and reconstruct exactly how the Web designer created the page. A few caveats: Be respectful about your use of copyrighted material, and avoid large and over-complicated Web sites. A site for a large company or organization would be difficult to interpret.

6. When you're finished studying the page's code, recreate the layout and design techniques in a page describing one of your hobbies or interests. As much as possible, try to duplicate the look and feel of the site that you studied.

7. Save your completed Web site and the answers from your research, and submit them to your instructor, in either printed or electronic form, as requested.

TUTORIAL 6

OBJECTIVES

Session 6.1
- Explore how Web forms interact with Web servers
- Create form elements
- Create field sets and legends
- Create input boxes and form labels

Session 6.2
- Create selection lists
- Create option buttons
- Create text area boxes
- Create check boxes
- Apply styles to Web forms

Session 6.3
- Explore HTML5 data types
- Create spinners and range sliders
- Create form buttons
- Validate form data

Creating a Web Form

Designing a Survey Form

Case | *Red Ball Pizza*

Alice Nichols is the owner of Red Ball Pizza, a popular pizzeria in Ormond Beach, Florida. She wants to conduct an online survey of Red Ball customers and has asked for your help in designing a prototype for the survey form. The form should record customer information as well as each customer's perception of his or her last experience at the restaurant. Alice wants the form to include different tools to ensure that each user enters valid data. Once a customer completes the form, the information will be sent to the Red Ball server for processing.

Note: Several tasks in this tutorial will not work on all browsers. In order to see all of the features covered in this chapter, check your work on a wide variety of browsers as you proceed through the steps.

STARTING DATA FILES

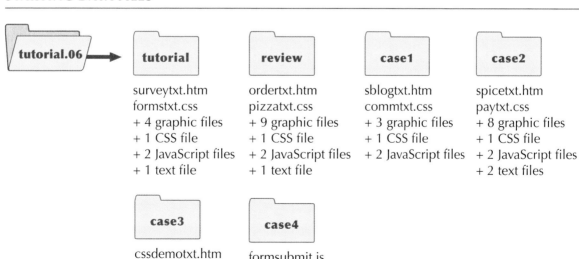

tutorial.06 →

tutorial
surveytxt.htm
formstxt.css
+ 4 graphic files
+ 1 CSS file
+ 2 JavaScript files
+ 1 text file

review
ordertxt.htm
pizzatxt.css
+ 9 graphic files
+ 1 CSS file
+ 2 JavaScript files
+ 1 text file

case1
sblogtxt.htm
commtxt.css
+ 3 graphic files
+ 1 CSS file
+ 2 JavaScript files

case2
spicetxt.htm
paytxt.css
+ 8 graphic files
+ 1 CSS file
+ 2 JavaScript files
+ 2 text files

case3
cssdemotxt.htm
+ 2 graphic files
+ 2 CSS files
+ 2 JavaScript files

case4
formsubmit.js
modernizr-1.5.js
+ 3 graphic files

SESSION 6.1 VISUAL OVERVIEW

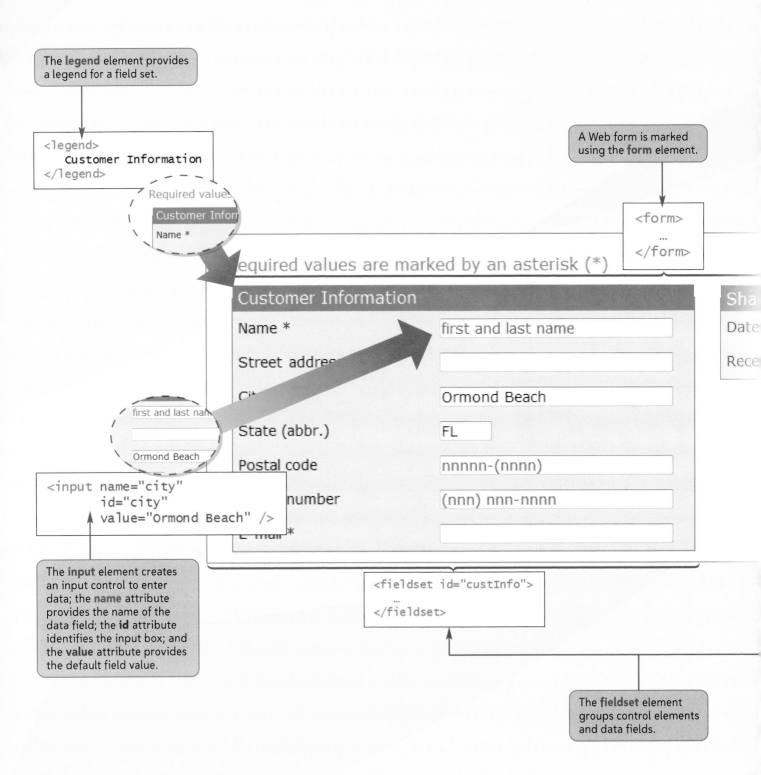

The **legend** element provides a legend for a field set.

```
<legend>
    Customer Information
</legend>
```

A Web form is marked using the **form** element.

```
<form>
   ...
</form>
```

Required values are marked by an asterisk (*)

Customer Information

Name *	first and last name
Street address	
City	Ormond Beach
State (abbr.)	FL
Postal code	nnnnn-(nnnn)
number	(nnn) nnn-nnnn
E-mail *	

The **input** element creates an input control to enter data; the **name** attribute provides the name of the data field; the **id** attribute identifies the input box; and the **value** attribute provides the default field value.

```
<input name="city"
       id="city"
       value="Ormond Beach" />
```

```
<fieldset id="custInfo">
   ...
</fieldset>
```

The **fieldset** element groups control elements and data fields.

PARTS OF A WEB FORM

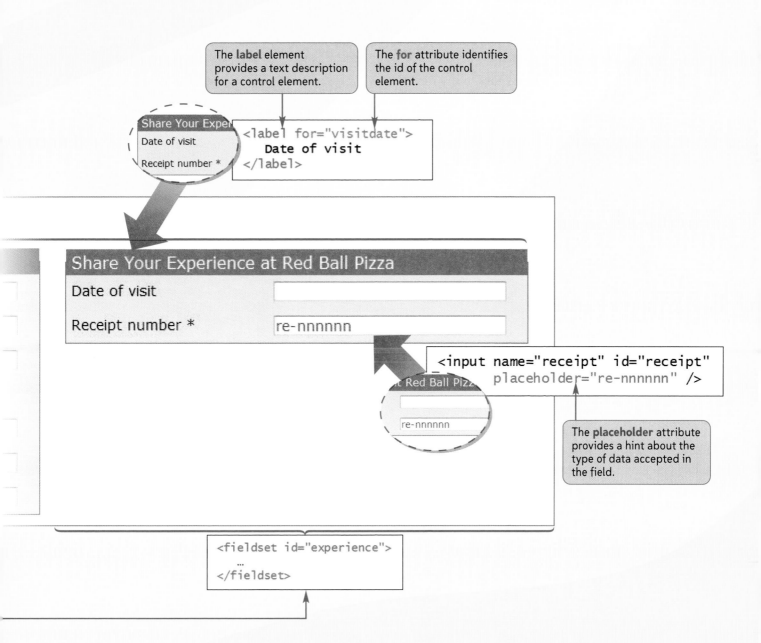

The **label** element provides a text description for a control element.

The **for** attribute identifies the id of the control element.

```
<label for="visitdate">
    Date of visit
</label>
```

Share Your Experience at Red Ball Pizza

Date of visit

Receipt number *   re-nnnnnn

```
<input name="receipt" id="receipt"
    placeholder="re-nnnnnn" />
```

The **placeholder** attribute provides a hint about the type of data accepted in the field.

```
<fieldset id="experience">
    ...
</fieldset>
```

Introducing Web Forms

You meet with Alice to discuss the proposed survey page for the Red Ball Pizza Web site. She already has created the Web page containing the company logo, header text, and footer. You'll open her file now.

To open the survey form page:

▶ 1. In your text editor, open **surveytxt.htm** from the tutorial.06\tutorial folder. Enter *your name* and *the date* in the comment section. Save the file as **survey.htm**.

▶ 2. Review the **survey.htm** file in your text editor to become familiar with its content and structure.

▶ 3. Open **survey.htm** in your Web browser. The initial page is shown in Figure 6-1.

Figure 6-1  Initial survey page

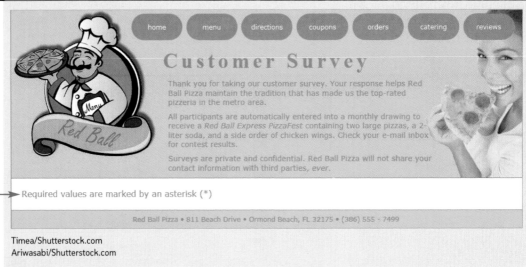

survey form will go here

Timea/Shutterstock.com
Ariwasabi/Shutterstock.com

Alice has sketched the survey form that she would like to display on the restaurant's Web site. Figure 6-2 shows her sketch.

Figure 6-2   Proposed survey form

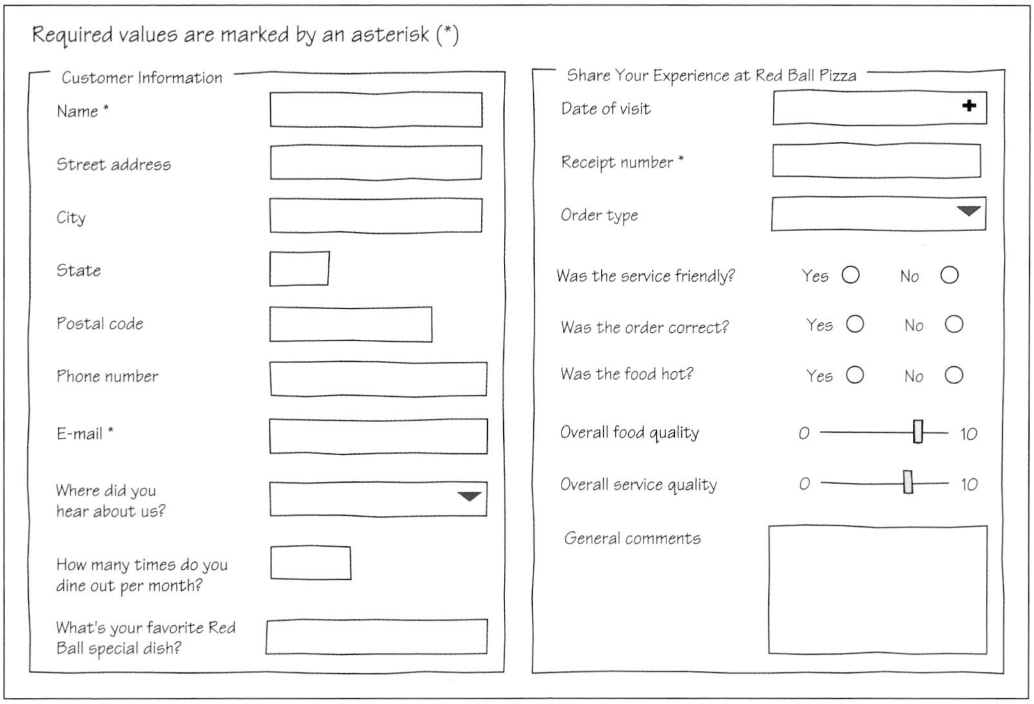

The form is divided into two topical areas. The area on the left includes elements requesting contact information from the customer, including the customer's name, phone number, and e-mail address. The right side of the form contains questions regarding the customer's treatment at Red Ball Pizza and his or her opinion of the food and service.

Parts of a Web Form

Each piece of information entered into a form is stored in a **field**, and the data is known as the **field value**. In some fields, users are free to enter anything they choose, while other fields are limited to a set of allowed values. Users enter or select a field value using **control elements**, which are buttons, boxes, lists, and so on, that provide a way of associating a field value with a particular field. HTML supports the following control elements:

- **input boxes** for text and numerical entries
- **option buttons**, also called **radio buttons**, for selecting a single option from a predefined list
- **selection lists** for long lists of options, usually appearing in a drop-down list box
- **check boxes** for questions limited to true/false or yes/no responses
- **text areas** for extended entries that can include several lines of text

HTML5 introduced the following control elements:

- **color pickers** to choose colors from an array of color values
- **calendar pickers** to select dates and times from a calendar or clock
- **spin boxes** for specifying numeric values from sets of numbers
- **sliders** for selecting numeric values from ranges of possible values

At the time of this writing, these HTML5 control elements are not supported by all current browsers; you'll explore browser support in more detail later in this tutorial. Alice's proposed survey form includes several examples of these different control elements, each one associated with a particular field. Note that some fields in the survey form are **required fields**, meaning that before the form data can be submitted, users must enter values for those fields. Alice's survey form includes required fields for recording the customer name, his or her e-mail address, and the receipt number of the order so that the restaurant can match up each survey response with a specific customer order.

Forms and Server-Based Programs

Before you start work on the survey form, you should understand how such data is processed on the Web. As shown in Figure 6-3, a Web form is used to collect information, but the data itself is usually stored and analyzed by a program running on a Web server.

Figure 6-3	Interaction between a Web form and a Web server

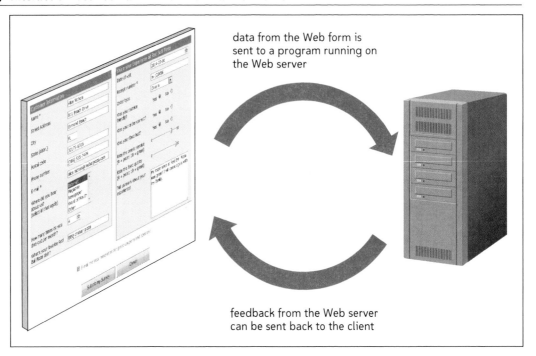

data from the Web form is sent to a program running on the Web server

feedback from the Web server can be sent back to the client

A form designer might not have permission to create or edit programs that run on Web servers. Instead, the designer usually receives instructions about how to interact with the server programs; these instructions usually include a list of fields that are required by a program and a description of the types of values expected in those fields.

There are several reasons to restrict direct access to these programs. The primary reason is that when you run a server-based program, you are interacting directly with the server environment. Mindful of the security risks that computer hackers present and the drain on system resources caused by large numbers of programs running simultaneously, system administrators are understandably careful to maintain strict control over their servers and systems. Otherwise, people could use malicious code to inject programming into the server and possibly change the prices of items or degrade the performance of the server.

Server-based programs are written in a variety of languages. The earliest and most common of these programs are Common Gateway Interface (CGI) scripts, written in a language called Perl. Other popular languages widely used today for writing server-based programs include the following:

- ASP/ASP.NET
- ColdFusion
- C/C++
- Java
- PHP
- Python
- Ruby

Which language your Web form will interact with depends on your Web server. You can check with your ISP or system administrator to find out what programs are available, and what rights and privileges you have in accessing them.

Alice is already working with a programmer on designing the program that will interpret the survey results. You will not have access to that program, so Alice just wants you to work with the Web form portion of this process. Other users will test your Web form to verify that the information is being collected and processed correctly.

Creating a Web Form

Now that you're familiar with the way form data is stored and analyzed, you can begin to work on the survey form. A Web form is inserted into a page using the `form` element

```
<form attributes>
   content
</form>
```

where `attributes` is the attributes that name the form and control how it is processed, and `content` is the content of the form. Forms typically contain many of the control elements that were listed earlier, but also can contain page elements such as tables, paragraphs, inline images, and headings. A `form` element can be placed anywhere within the body of a Web page, and a single page can contain multiple `form` elements.

Form attributes tell browsers the location of the server-based program to be with on the form's data, how that data is to be transferred to the script, and other processing information. However, these attributes are not needed when designing the form, and it's actually useful to omit them at first. This prevents you from accidentally running the program on an unfinished form, causing the Web server to process incomplete information. After you've finalized the form's appearance, you can add the attributes required by the server program. You'll have a chance to do this in the last session of this tutorial.

Two attributes identify the form: the `id` attribute and the `name` attribute. Naming a form is useful for pages that contain multiple forms so you can differentiate one form from another, and it is required for some server-based programs that need to reference a particular form by name. The `id` attribute is used to uniquely identify the `form` element among the different page elements. The syntax of both of these attributes is

```
<form name="name" id="id"> … </form>
```

where `name` is the name of the form and `id` is the id of the form. In many cases, you'll use the same value for both the `id` and `name` attributes.

REFERENCE

Inserting a Web Form

• To insert a Web form, add

```
<form attributes>
   content
</form>
```

to the body of the Web page, where `attributes` is the attributes that identify the form and control how it is processed, and `content` is the content of the form.

• To identify the form, add the attributes

```
id="id" name="name"
```

to the opening `<form>` tag, where `id` is the form id and `name` is the form name.

You'll add a `form` element to the survey page within the main section of the page.

To add the `form` element:

▶ **1.** Return to the **survey.htm** file in your text editor. Directly above the closing `</section>` tag, insert the following `form` element as shown in Figure 6-4:

```
<form id="survey" name="survey">
</form>
```

Figure 6-4 **Inserting a form element**

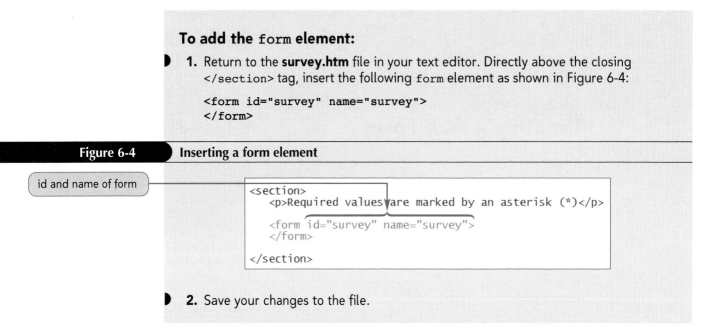

id and name of form

```
<section>
    <p>Required values are marked by an asterisk (*)</p>

    <form id="survey" name="survey">
    </form>

</section>
```

▶ **2.** Save your changes to the file.

Interacting with a Web Server

Another set of form attributes specifies where to send the form data and how to send it. You indicate this information by adding the `action`, `method`, and `enctype` attributes to the `form` element, as follows

```
<form action="url" method="type" enctype="type"> ... </form>
```

where `url` specifies the filename and location of the program that processes the form, the `method` attribute specifies how Web browsers should send data to the server, and the `enctype` attribute specifies the format of the data stored in the fields.

The `method` attribute has two possible values: `get` and `post`. The **get method**, the default, appends the form data to the end of the URL specified in the `action` attribute. The **post method**, on the other hand, sends form data in a separate data stream. Each method has its uses. Web searches often use the get method because the search parameters become part of the URL and thus can be bookmarked for future searching using the same parameters. However, this also can result in a long and cumbersome URL if several fields and field values are attached to the URL, and it may even result in data being truncated if the URL text string becomes too long. There is also a security risk in having name/value pairs attached to a URL that easily can be read by others. Your Web site administrator can supply the necessary information about which of the two methods you should use when accessing the scripts running on its server.

The `enctype` attribute determines how the form data should be encoded as it is sent to the server. Figure 6-5 describes the three most common encoding types.

| Figure 6-5 | Values of the enctype attribute |

Value	Description
application/x-www-form-urlencoded	The default format. In this format, form data is transferred as a long text string in which spaces are replaced with the + character and nontext characters (such as tabs and line breaks) are replaced with their hexadecimal code values. Field names are separated from their field values with an = symbol.
multipart/form-data	Used when sending files to a server. In this format, spaces and nontext characters are preserved, and data elements are separated using delimiter lines. The action type of the form element must be set to post for this format.
text/plain	Form data is transferred as plain text with no encoding of spaces or nontext characters. This format is most often used when the action type of the form element is set to mailto.

Alice tells you that your survey form will be processed by the CGI script located at the URL *http://www.redballpizza.com/cgi-bin/survey* (a fictional address) using the post method. You do not have to specify a value for the enctype attribute because the default value of application/x-www-form-urlencoded is appropriate. Add this information to the form element now.

To add attributes to the form element:

1. Return to the **survey.htm** file and add the following attributes to the form element, as shown in Figure 6-6:

   ```
   action="http://www.redballpizza.com/cgi-bin/survey"
   method="post"
   ```

| Figure 6-6 | Setting the form attributes |

```
<form id="survey" name="survey"
      action="http://www.redballpizza.com/cgi-bin/survey"
      method="post">
```

2. Save your changes to the file.

Because *www.redballpizza.com/cgi-bin/survey* does not correspond to a real CGI script running on the Web and thus cannot process the survey form you'll create in this tutorial, you'll add a JavaScript program named *formsubmit.js* to handle the form. The purpose of this program is to intercept the contents of the form before the browser attempts to contact the CGI script. The script also will report whether or not the data contained in the survey form has been correctly filled out. You'll add a link to this script now.

To link to the *formsubmit.js* JavaScript program:

▶ **1.** Return to the **survey.htm** file in your text editor.

▶ **2.** Go to the head section of the document. Directly below the `script` element that accesses the *modernizr.js* file, insert the following code, as shown in Figure 6-7:

```
<script src="formsubmit.js"></script>
```

Figure 6-7	Linking to the formsubmit.js file

```
<meta charset="UTF-8" />
<title>Customer Survey</title>
<script src="modernizr-1.5.js"></script>
<script src="formsubmit.js"></script>

<link href="rb.css" rel="stylesheet" />
```

▶ **3.** Save your changes to the file.

Now that you've added the `form` element to the survey page, you can start populating the survey form with control elements and other form features. You'll start by adding field sets.

Creating a Field Set

A Web form like the survey form can have dozens of different fields. One way of organizing a form is to group similar fields into **field sets**. When rendered by a browser, a field set is usually displayed with a box enclosing the fields in the set. Field sets are created using the `fieldset` element

```
<fieldset id="id">
    controls
</fieldset>
```

where *id* identifies the field set and *controls* is the control elements associated with fields within the field set. The *id* value is not required, but it is useful in distinguishing one field set from another. Alice wants you to organize the form into two field sets named `custInfo` and `experience`.

Creating a Field Set

• To create a field set, add the element

```
<fieldset id="id">
    controls
</fieldset>
```

to the form, where *id* identifies the field set and *controls* is the control elements associated with fields within the field set.

• To add a legend to a field set, nest the element

```
<legend>text</legend>
```

within the `fieldset` element, where *text* is the text of the legend.

To insert a field set:

1. Within the `form` element in the **survey.htm** file, insert the following two field sets, as shown in Figure 6-8:

```
<fieldset id="custInfo">
</fieldset>

<fieldset id="experience">
</fieldset>
```

Figure 6-8 **Inserting field sets**

```
<form id="survey" name="survey"
      action="http://www.redballpizza.com/cgi-bin/survey"
      method="post">

    <fieldset id="custInfo">
    </fieldset>

    <fieldset id="experience">
    </fieldset>

</form>
```

2. Save your changes to the file.

Every field set can contain a legend describing its contents. The syntax of the `legend` element is

```
<legend>text</legend>
```

where *text* is the text of the legend. The `legend` element can contain only text and no other page elements. Based on Alice's sketch from Figure 6-2, you'll add the legend text *Customer Information* and *Share Your Experience at Red Ball Pizza* to the two field sets you just created.

To insert legends for the field sets:

1. Within the first field set in the *survey.htm* file, insert the following `legend` element:

```
<legend>Customer Information</legend>
```

2. In the second field set, insert the following `legend` element:

```
<legend>Share Your Experience at Red Ball Pizza</legend>
```

Figure 6-9 highlights the revised text in the HTML file.

Figure 6-9   ▶   **Inserting field set legends**

```
<form id="survey" name="survey"
      action="http://www.redballpizza.com/cgi-bin/survey"
      method="post">

    <fieldset id="custInfo">
       <legend>Customer Information</legend>
    </fieldset>

    <fieldset id="experience">
       <legend>Share Your Experience at Red Ball Pizza</legend>
    </fieldset>

</form>
```

▶ **3.** Save your changes to the file and then refresh the **survey.htm** file in your Web browser. Figure 6-10 shows the current appearance of the form.

Figure 6-10   ▶   **Viewing field sets and legends**

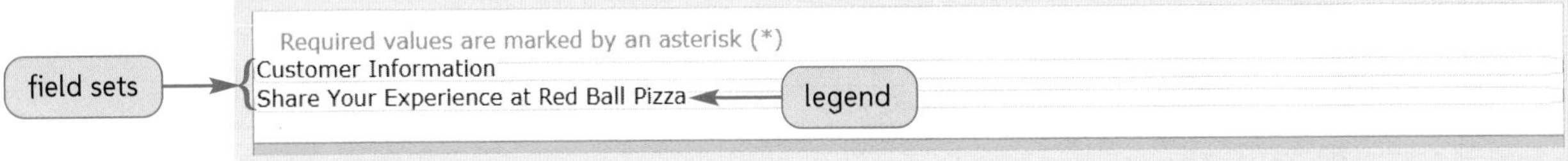

Required values are marked by an asterisk (*)
field sets → Customer Information
Share Your Experience at Red Ball Pizza ◀— legend

Field sets are block elements that expand to accommodate their content. The field sets you added are currently empty, so they appear small and narrow on the survey page. By default, browsers display the legend text in the upper-left corner of the field set box. However, you can use CSS positioning styles to move the legend and format its appearance. Next, you'll add control elements and other content to the two field sets.

Creating Input Boxes

Most of the control elements in which users either type or select a data value are marked as input elements using the `<input>` tag

```
<input type="type" name="name" id="id" />
```

where *type* specifies the type of input control, the `name` attribute provides the name of the field associated with the control element, and the `id` attribute identifies the control element itself. When the form data is submitted to the server, the server program pairs the field name with the field value; thus you almost always need a `name` attribute if you are submitting the form to a server. The `id` attribute is required only when you need to reference the control element itself, as you might if you intend to apply a CSS style rule to modify the appearance of the control element. In this tutorial, you'll supply both a `name` and an `id` attribute for every control, and you'll set them to the same value.

HTML 4 supports 10 different input types, which are described in Figure 6-11; HTML5 adds 13 new input types that you'll explore later in this tutorial.

TIP

If no `type` attribute is included, browsers assume that an input control is a text input box.

Figure 6-11	**Input box data types**

Type	Displays	General Appearance
button	A button that can be clicked to perform an action from a script	Run Program
checkbox	A check box that can be clicked by the user	☐ ☑
file	A Browse button to locate and select a file	C:\survey.htm Browse...
hidden	A hidden field, not viewable on the form	
image	An inline image that can be clicked to perform an action from a script	👤
password	An input box that hides text entered by the user	••••••
radio	An option button that can be clicked by the user	◉ ◉
reset	A button that resets the form when clicked	Cancel Form
submit	A button that submits the form when clicked	Submit Form
text	An input box that displays text entered by the user	Alice Nichols

REFERENCE

Creating an Input Control

- To create an input box for text entry, add the element

  ```
  <input type="type" name="name" id="id" />
  ```

  to the Web form, where `type` specifies the type of input control, the `name` attribute provides the name of the field associated with the control element, and the `id` attribute identifies the control element itself.

The first controls you'll add to the survey form will be seven text input boxes in which each customer can enter a name, street address, city, state, postal code, phone number, and e-mail address. You'll associate these input boxes with data fields named *custname*, *street*, *city*, *state*, *zip*, *phone*, and *email*, respectively. Before each input box you'll insert a text string that describes its contents.

To add the input boxes for the customer information:

1. Return to the **survey.htm** file. Within the `custInfo` field set, insert the following code as shown in Figure 6-12:

```
Name *
<input name="custname" id="custname" />

Street address
<input name="street" id="street" />

City
<input name="city" id="city" />

State (abbr.)
<input name="state" id="state" />

Postal code
<input name="zip" id="zip" />

Phone number
<input name="phone" id="phone" />

E-mail *
<input name="email" id="email" />
```

Figure 6-12 Inserting input boxes to record customer information

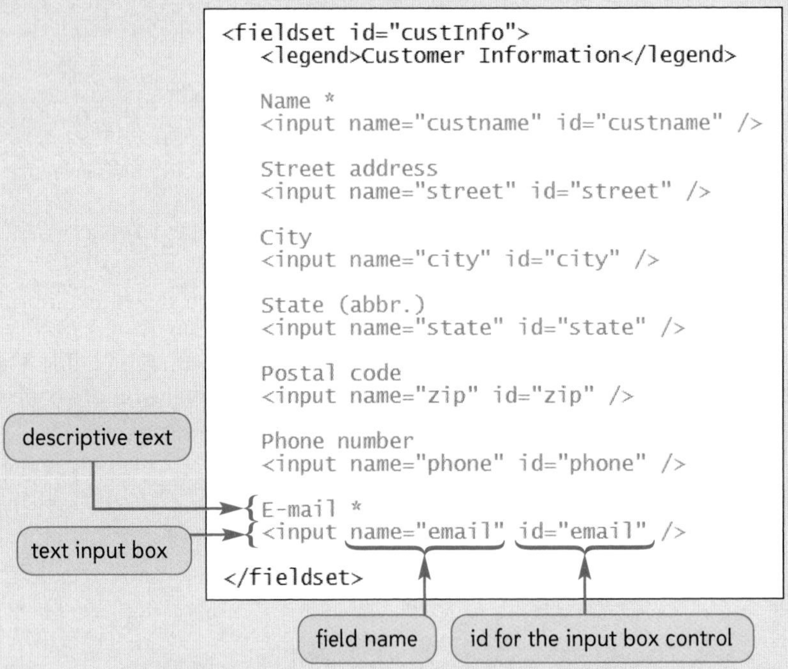

Note that the asterisks next to the Name and E-mail text entries tell users that these fields are required. Later on in this tutorial, you'll learn how to make it mandatory that users enter data into required fields.

2. Save your changes to the file.

Next, you'll add text input boxes for the date of the customer's visit to Red Ball Pizza and the receipt number of the order. The names for these data fields are *visitdate* and *receipt*, respectively.

To add the input boxes for the customer information:

1. Within the Share Your Experience at Red Ball Pizza field set, insert the following input boxes (see Figure 6-13):

```
Date of visit
<input name="visitdate" id="visitdate" />

Receipt number *
<input name="receipt" id="receipt" />
```

Figure 6-13   Inserting input boxes to record the customer's experience

```
<fieldset id="experience">
    <legend>Share Your Experience at Red Ball Pizza</legend>

    Date of visit
    <input name="visitdate" id="visitdate" />

    Receipt number *
    <input name="receipt" id="receipt" />

</fieldset>
```

2. Save your changes to the file and then refresh **survey.htm** in your Web browser.

3. Test the controls by typing your ***first and last name*** in the Name input box. Figure 6-14 shows the newly inserted control elements in the form with sample text in the custname field.

Figure 6-14   Input boxes with sample customer name

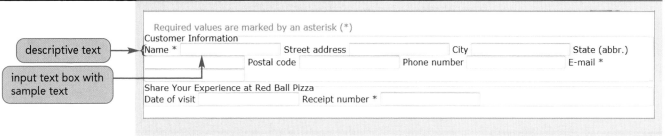

Note that browsers treat all form control elements as text-level elements, so the input boxes that you created for the survey form appear within the same line rather than in separate blocks.

Navigating Forms with Access Keys

You activate control elements like input boxes either by clicking them with your mouse button or by tabbing from one control element to another. As your forms get longer, you might want to give users the ability to jump to a particular input box. This can be done with an access key. An **access key** is a single key on the keyboard that you type in conjunction with the Alt key commonly used for Windows users, or the control key for Mac users, to jump to a spot in the Web page. You create an access key by adding the `accesskey` attribute to an element. For example, to create an access key for the `custName` input box, you would enter the following code:

```
<input name="custName" id="custName" accesskey="l" />
```

If a user types Alt+l (or control+l for Mac users), the cursor automatically moves to the `custName` input box. Note that you must use letters that are not reserved by your browser. For example, Alt+f is used by many browsers including Internet Explorer to access the File menu and thus should not be used for an access key.

Access keys also can be used with hypertext links and are particularly helpful to users with impaired motor skills who find it difficult to use a mouse.

Adding Field Labels

In the last set of steps, you entered descriptive text alongside the input boxes to indicate the purpose of each input box to users. However, nothing in the HTML code explicitly associates that text with the input box. To associate text with a control element, you enclose the descriptive text within a `label` element as follows

```
<label for="id">label text</label>
```

where *id* is the value of the `id` attribute of the control element associated with the label, and *label text* is the text of the label. For example, the following code associates the label text *Street address* with the `street` control element:

```
<label for="street">Street address</label>
<input id="street" />
```

One effect of associating a label with a control element is that clicking the label automatically moves the cursor into the control element.

Using the `for` attribute explicitly associates the label with the relevant control element. You also can make this association implicitly by nesting the control element within the label as in the following code:

```
<label>
   Street address
   <input id="street" />
</label>
```

Notice that you do not need to include a `for` attribute when you nest the control element within the label element.

Which approach you take depends on how you want to lay out a form's contents. When you use the `for` attribute, you can place the label text anywhere within the Web page and it still will be associated with the control element. However, by nesting the control element within the label, you can treat both the control element and its label as a single object, which can make form layout easier because you can move both the label text and the control element as a single unit around the page. Depending on the layout of your Web form, you might use both approaches.

TIP

You can "turn off" a control element, preventing the user from entering data, by adding the attribute `disabled="disabled"` to the element.

REFERENCE

Creating a Field Label

- To explicitly associate a text label with a control element, use the `label` element and the `for` attribute

    ```
    <label for="id">label text</label>
    ```

    where *id* is the id of the control element.
- To implicitly associate a text label with a control element, nest the control element within the `label` element as follows

    ```
    <label>
        label text
        control
    </label>
    ```

    where *control* is the control element. You do not have to include a `for` attribute.

You'll use the `label` element and the `for` attribute to associate the descriptive text you've entered in the survey form with the relevant input boxes.

To apply the field labels:

▶ **1.** Return to the **survey.htm** file in your text editor.

▶ **2.** Go to the customer information field set and enclose the text string *Name* * within a `label` element, associating it with the `custname` input box as follows:

```
<label for="custname">Name *</label>
```

▶ **3.** Repeat this process for the remaining descriptive text strings in the two field sets, using the `for` attribute to associate each label with the corresponding input box. Figure 6-15 shows the revised code in the file, highlighting the different values of the `for` attribute.

Figure 6-15 Adding form labels

```
<fieldset id="custInfo">
    <legend>Customer Information</legend>

    <label for="custname">Name *</label>
    <input name="custname" id="custname" />

    <label for="street">Street address</label>
    <input name="street" id="street" />

    <label for="city">City</label>
    <input name="city" id="city" />

    <label for="state">State (abbr.)</label>
    <input name="state" id="state" />

    <label for="zip">Postal code</label>
    <input name="zip" id="zip" />

    <label for="phone">Phone number</label>
    <input name="phone" id="phone" />

    <label for="email">E-mail *</label>
    <input name="email" id="email" />

</fieldset>

<fieldset id="experience">
    <legend>Share Your Experience at Red Ball Pizza</legend>

    <label for="visitdate">Date of visit</label>
    <input name="visitdate" id="visitdate" />

    <label for="receipt">Receipt number *</label>
    <input name="receipt" id="receipt" />

</fieldset>
```

label associated with the visitdate input box

label element

4. Save your changes to the file and then refresh the **survey.htm** file in your Web browser.

5. Test the labels by clicking each label and verifying that the cursor appears within the corresponding control element.

Setting the autocomplete *Attribute*

Many browsers include an autocomplete feature that automatically fills in input form values if they are based on previously filled out forms. For example, a user who routinely fills in his or her street address in a multitude of Web forms can enable the browser to remember the information and to insert it automatically when the browser encounters another street address field in another form.

The autocomplete feature is a useful time-saver in most cases, but it also can be a security risk for a personal computer located in a public place. After all, you may not want to have a private credit card number or password automatically filled in by a browser on a computer that other people will be using.

One way to prevent this problem is by implementing the HTML5 autocomplete attribute. The autocomplete attribute can be added to a form or input element to turn off (or turn on) the form complete feature. For example, the input element

```
<input name="creditcardnumber" autocomplete="false" />
```

prevents browsers from automatically filling in the creditcardnumber field, even if they have credit card data handy. Currently, the autocomplete attribute is supported by Opera and Firefox, but not by Safari, Chrome, or Internet Explorer. However, you may want to consider using it if you want to add another level of security to confidential information.

Applying a Style Sheet to a Web Form

Alice stops by to see your progress on the survey form. In its current state, the form is difficult to read and she wants you to replace the default styles for the form with your own customized style sheet. First, she wants the two field sets to be floated side-by-side within the main section of the page and resized to be about half the width of the Web page. You'll add a style rule to an external style sheet file to modify the appearance of these field sets.

To create the form style sheet:

1. Use your text editor to open the **formstxt.css** file from the tutorial.06\tutorial folder. Enter **your name** and **the date** in the comment section of the file, and then save it as **forms.css** in the same folder.

2. Below the comment section, add the following style rule as shown in Figure 6-16:

```
/* Field set styles */

fieldset {
   background-color: rgb(255, 246, 205);
   border: 1px solid rgb(233, 69, 0);
   float: left;
   margin: 10px 0px 10px 2.5%;
   width: 46%;
}
```

Figure 6-16 **Styles for the form field sets**

sets the background color of
each field set to a medium yellow

adds a 1-pixel-wide solid
red border to each field set

floats each field set on the left

sets the width of
each field set to
46% of the total
page width

```
/* Field set styles */

fieldset {
    background-color: rgb(255, 246, 205);
    border: 1px solid rgb(233, 69, 0);
    float: left;
    margin: 10px 0px 10px 2.5%;
    width: 46%;
}
```

sets the margins around the field sets

Next, you'll change the style of the field set legends, defining each legend to appear as white text on a medium-red background.

To add a style rule for the field set legends:

1. Directly below the style for the field set selector, add the following style rule as shown in Figure 6-17:

```
legend {
    background-color: rgb(233, 69, 0);
    color: white;
    padding: 3px 0px;
    text-indent: 5px;
    width: 100%;
}
```

Figure 6-17 **Styles for the field set legends**

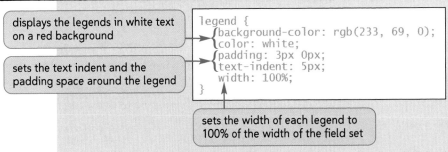

displays the legends in white text
on a red background

sets the text indent and the
padding space around the legend

```
legend {
    background-color: rgb(233, 69, 0);
    color: white;
    padding: 3px 0px;
    text-indent: 5px;
    width: 100%;
}
```

sets the width of each legend to
100% of the width of the field set

2. Save your changes to the file.

Finally, since the default style for labels and input controls is to display them inline, they appear to run together on the form. Alice suggests that you instead display them as blocks and float them side-by-side within the two field sets to make them easier to read.

To define a style for the labels and input controls:

1. At the bottom of the style sheet, add the following style rule for the form labels (see Figure 6-18):

```
/* Label styles */

label {
    clear: left;
    display: block;
    float: left;
    font-size: 0.9em;
    margin: 7px 4% 7px 5px;
    width: 40%;
}
```

Figure 6-18   **Styles for the field labels**

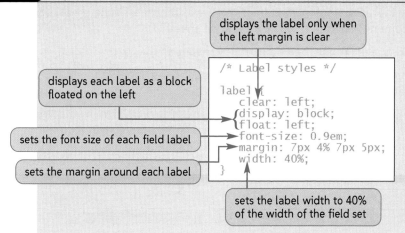

displays the label only when the left margin is clear

displays each label as a block floated on the left

sets the font size of each field label

sets the margin around each label

```
/* Label styles */

label {
    clear: left;
    display: block;
    float: left;
    font-size: 0.9em;
    margin: 7px 4% 7px 5px;
    width: 40%;
}
```

sets the label width to 40% of the width of the field set

2. Below the style rule you just created, add the following style rule for input controls (see Figure 6-19):

```
/* Input control styles */

input {
    display: block;
    float: left;
    font-size: 0.9em;
    margin: 7px 0px;
    width: 50%;
}
```

| Figure 6-19 | Styles for input controls |

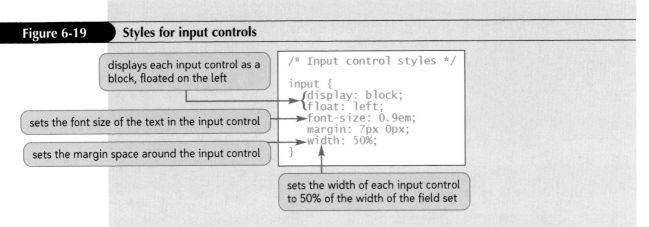

displays each input control as a block, floated on the left

sets the font size of the text in the input control

sets the margin space around the input control

```
/* Input control styles */

input {
    display: block;
    float: left;
    font-size: 0.9em;
    margin: 7px 0px;
    width: 50%;
}
```

sets the width of each input control to 50% of the width of the field set

▶ **3.** Save your changes to the **forms.css** file and then return to the **survey.htm** file in your text editor.

▶ **4.** Below the `link` element that links the file to the *rb.css* style sheet, add the following element to link to the *forms.css* style sheet:

```
<link href="forms.css" rel="stylesheet" />
```

Now you'll view the effect of your fieldset, legend, label, and input styles on the appearance of the survey form.

▶ **5.** Save your changes to the file and then refresh **survey.htm** in your Web browser. Figure 6-20 shows the revised appearance of the Web form.

| Figure 6-20 | Revised format of the survey form |

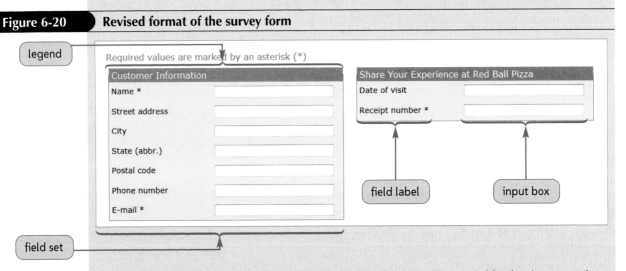

legend

Required values are marked by an asterisk (*)

Customer Information
- Name *
- Street address
- City
- State (abbr.)
- Postal code
- Phone number
- E-mail *

Share Your Experience at Red Ball Pizza
- Date of visit
- Receipt number *

field label   input box

field set

Trouble? If your form does not match that shown in Figure 6-20, check your style sheet code against that shown in Figures 6-16 through 6-19. Make sure you have not mistyped a style property or forgotten to separate one style from another with a semicolon.

Not all of the input boxes need to have a width of 50%. The input box for the `state` field only needs to be large enough to display the two-letter abbreviation of the state name. You'll reduce the width of this input box now.

To reduce the width of the `state` field input box:

▶ **1.** Return to the **forms.css** file in your text editor and add the following style rule at the bottom of the file (see Figure 6-21):

```
input#state {
    width: 50px;
}
```

| Figure 6-21 | Setting the width of the state input box |

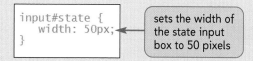

▶ **2.** Save your changes to the file and then refresh **survey.htm** in your Web browser. Verify that the width of the input box for the `state` field has been reduced.

Another way to set the width of an input box is by adding the following `size` attribute to the `input` element

```
size="chars"
```

where *chars* is the width of the input box in characters. For example, the HTML code

```
<input name="state" size="2" />
```

sets the size of the input box for the state field to two characters in width. Note that this is not an exact measure because the width of individual characters varies depending on the typeface and font style.

Defining Default Values and Placeholders

More than 90% of Red Ball Pizza customers come from Ormond Beach in Florida. Rather than forcing these customers to enter the same city and state information in the survey form, Alice wants you to specify Ormond Beach, FL as the default city and state values. To define a default value, you add the attribute

```
value="value"
```

to any form control, where `value` is the default field value that initially will appear in the control when the form is opened by the browser. For example, the following input control sets the default value of the `city` field to *Ormond Beach*:

```
<input name="city" value="Ormond Beach" />
```

REFERENCE

Defining a Default Field Value

• To define the default value of a field, add the attribute

```
value="value"
```

to the control element, where `value` is the default value assumed by a browser unless a user enters a different value.

You'll add the `value` attribute to the `city` and `state` input boxes, setting the default values of the fields to *Ormond Beach* and *FL*, respectively.

To set the default `city` and `state` field values:

▶ **1.** Return to the **survey.htm** file in your text editor and scroll down to the `input` element for the `city` field. Add the attribute `value="Ormond Beach"` to the `<input>` tag.

▶ **2.** Add the attribute `value="FL"` to the `<input>` tag for the `state` field. Figure 6-22 highlights the revised HTML code for the two input boxes.

| Figure 6-22 | Defining default values for the city and state fields |

default value for the city field

```
<label for="city">City</label>
<input name="city" id="city" value="Ormond Beach" />

<label for="state">State (abbr.)</label>
<input name="state" id="state" value="FL" />
```

default value for the state field

▶ **3.** Save your changes to the file and then refresh **survey.htm** in your Web browser. Verify that the input boxes for the `city` and `state` fields show the text values *Ormond Beach* and *FL*, respectively.

Starting with HTML5, you can also populate your input boxes with placeholders. A **placeholder** is a text string that appears within the control element and provides users with information about the kind of information accepted by the field. To create a placeholder, add the attribute

```
placeholder="text"
```

to the control element, where *text* is the text of the placeholder. For example, the following `input` element for the `phone` field provides guidance to users about the format in which phone numbers can be entered:

```
<input name="phone" placeholder="(nnn) nnn-nnnn" />
```

When a browser displays the form, the text *(nnn) nnn-nnnn* will appear grayed out in the phone input box. This text will indicate to a customer reading the form that he or she should enter a phone number, including both the area code and the seven-digit number.

Unlike a default field value, a placeholder is not stored in the data field and is not sent to the server as a field value. The placeholder automatically disappears as soon as a user selects the input box. At the time of this writing, all current browsers except Internet Explorer support placeholders.

Alice wants you to add placeholders to the `custname, postal code, phone number,` and `receipt` input boxes; the placeholders should provide information to customers about the types of data they should enter and the expected formats. You'll add the placeholders now.

To create placeholders for the survey form:

▶ **1.** Return to the **survey.htm** file in your text editor and scroll to the `input` element for the `custname` field. Add the following attribute to the `<input>` tag:

```
placeholder="first and last name"
```

▶ **2.** Add the attribute `placeholder="nnnnn (-nnnn)"` to the `input` element for the `zip` field.

▶ **3.** Add the attribute `placeholder="(nnn) nnn-nnnn"` to the `input` element for the `phone` field.

▶ **4.** Finally, add the attribute `placeholder="re-nnnnnn"` to the `input` element for the `receipt` field. Figure 6-23 highlights the newly added code in the survey form.

Figure 6-23 Adding placeholders to the survey form

```
<fieldset id="custInfo">
    <legend>Customer Information</legend>

    <label for="custname">Name *</label>
    <input name="custname" id="custname"
           placeholder="first and last name" />

    <label for="street">Street address</label>
    <input name="street" id="street" />

    <label for="city">City</label>
    <input name="city" id="city" value="Ormond Beach" />

    <label for="state">State (abbr.)</label>
    <input name="state" id="state" value="FL" />

    <label for="zip">Postal code</label>
    <input name="zip" id="zip"
           placeholder="nnnnn (-nnnn)" />

    <label for="phone">Phone number</label>
    <input name="phone" id="phone"
           placeholder="(nnn) nnn-nnnn" />

    <label for="email">E-mail *</label>
    <input name="email" id="email" />

</fieldset>

<fieldset id="experience">
    <legend>Share Your Experience at Red Ball Pizza</legend>

    <label for="visitdate">Date of visit</label>
    <input name="visitdate" id="visitdate" />

    <label for="receipt">Receipt number *</label>
    <input name="receipt" id="receipt"
           placeholder="re-nnnnnn"/>

</fieldset>
```

placeholder text for the phone field

▶ **5.** Save your changes to the file and then refresh **survey.htm** in your Web browser. As shown in Figure 6-24, placeholder text has been added to the `custname`, `zip`, `phone`, and `receipt` input boxes. Notice that placeholder text is distinguished from default text by appearing in a grayed-out font.

Figure 6-24 **Viewing default values and placeholder text**

Customer Information

Name *	first and last name
Street address	
City	Ormond Beach
State (abbr.)	FL
Postal code	nnnnn (-nnnn)
Phone number	(nnn) nnn-nnnn
E-mail *	

Share Your Experience at Red Ball Pizza

Date of visit	
Receipt number *	re-nnnnnn

default value for the state field

placeholder text for the receipt input box

Trouble? If you are using Internet Explorer or Firefox, you might not see any placeholders in the survey form.

▶ **6.** Click in the input boxes that contain placeholders. Notice that the placeholders disappear as soon as you click each input box.

PROSKILLS

Decision Making: Using HTML5 Form Attributes

HTML5 offers several useful features such as the `placeholder` attribute, but the specification is still new and not universally supported in the browser market. This poses a problem for Web designers who must decide whether or not to use such attributes.

One school of thought holds that differences in appearance and functionality between one browser and the next confuse users and make it more difficult to manage the operations of a Web form. Thus, a feature like the HTML5 `placeholder` attribute should not be used. If a Web designer needs placeholders in a Web form, they should be created using a JavaScript program that can be applied uniformly across browsers and browser versions.

The opposing view holds that the best design is one that uses each browser to its utmost capabilities, and proposes that a Web designer cheats users when the designer decides to forgo an HTML feature that enhances the user experience, like the `placeholder` attribute. Moreover, the Web will only gain in the long run as more HTML5 features are employed because increasing their use will encourage more rapid support of HTML5 across the browser market.

To decide between these two approaches, you must evaluate whether the HTML5 feature you're adding is critical to understanding and using your Web form. Do placeholders add useful, but not essential, information for users? If so, there is little to be lost by adding them. However, even if you want all users to have placeholders in their forms, applying the `placeholder` attribute still can be useful as a quick and easy way of developing a prototype of your form for testing. Later, as you reach the final phase of development, you can replace it with a JavaScript program that extends placeholders to all users.

You've finished the initial stage of developing the survey form. Alice is pleased with the form's appearance and content. In the next session, you'll extend the form by adding new fields and control elements, including selection lists, option buttons, and check boxes.

Session 6.1 Quick Check

1. Provide the code to create a form with the name *registration* that accesses the CGI script at *www.redballpizza.com/cgi-bin/registration* using the post method.

2. What different roles do the `name` and `id` attributes assume when applied to the following `input` element?

   ```
   <input id="lastName" name="lastName" />
   ```

3. Provide the code to create a field set containing the legend text *Contact Information*.

4. Provide the code to create an input box for the data field `custPassword` that will prevent the text of the user's password from being displayed on the screen as it is typed.

5. What are two ways of associating a field label with a control element?

6. Provide the code to create a field label with the text *User Name* that is associated with the input box with the id `userinput`.

7. Provide the code to create an input box for the `country` field with the default text *United States*.

8. Provide the code to create an input box for the `socialSecurity` field. Use HTML attributes to set the width of the box to 11 characters and to display the placeholder text *nnn-nn-nnnn*.

SESSION 6.2 VISUAL OVERVIEW

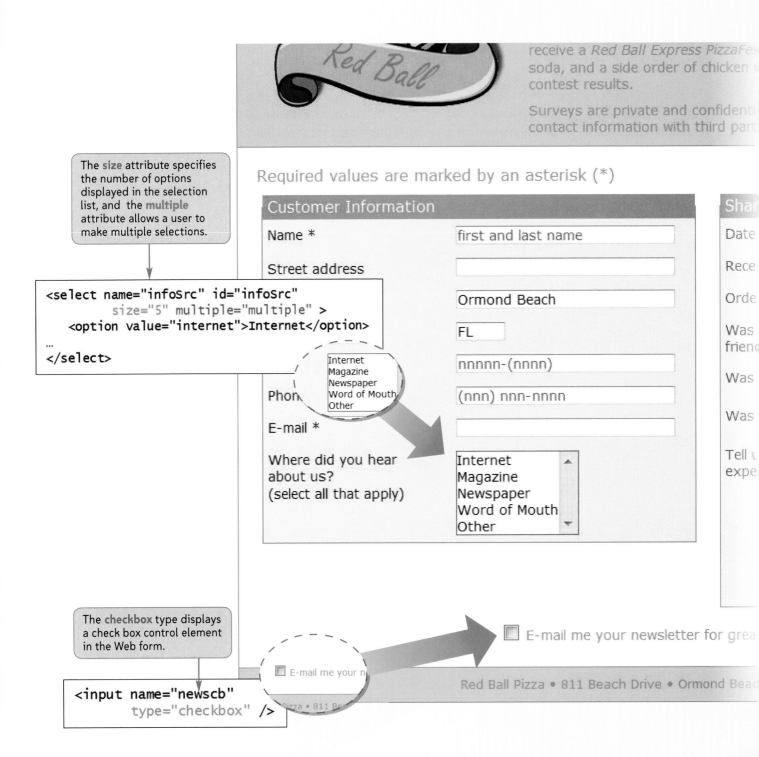

The **size** attribute specifies the number of options displayed in the selection list, and the **multiple** attribute allows a user to make multiple selections.

```
<select name="infoSrc" id="infoSrc"
        size="5" multiple="multiple" >
  <option value="internet">Internet</option>
...
</select>
```

Required values are marked by an asterisk (*)

Customer Information

Name *   first and last name

Street address

Ormond Beach

FL

nnnnn-(nnnn)

Phon   (nnn) nnn-nnnn

E-mail *

Where did you hear   Internet
about us?   Magazine
(select all that apply)   Newspaper
                          Word of Mouth
                          Other

Internet
Magazine
Newspaper
Word of Mouth
Other

The **checkbox** type displays a check box control element in the Web form.

```
<input name="newscb"
       type="checkbox" />
```

☐ E-mail me your newsletter for grea

☐ E-mail me your n

Red Ball Pizza • 811 Beach Drive • Ormond Bea

Timea/Shutterstock.com

SELECTION LISTS AND OPTION BUTTONS

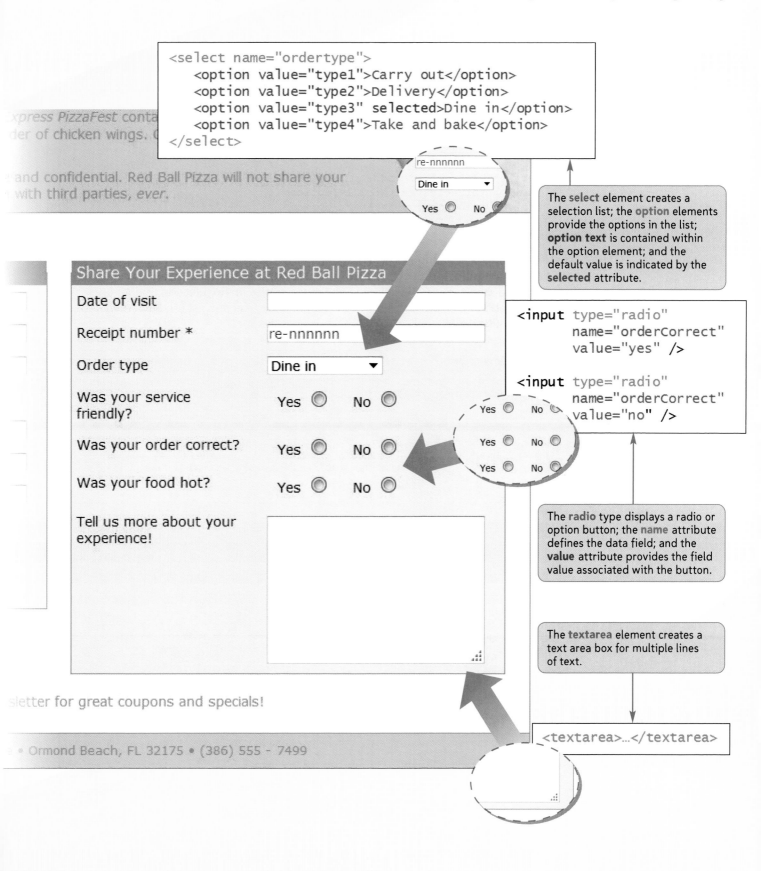

```
<select name="ordertype">
    <option value="type1">Carry out</option>
    <option value="type2">Delivery</option>
    <option value="type3" selected>Dine in</option>
    <option value="type4">Take and bake</option>
</select>
```

The **select** element creates a selection list; the **option** elements provide the options in the list; **option text** is contained within the option element; and the default value is indicated by the **selected** attribute.

```
<input type="radio"
       name="orderCorrect"
       value="yes" />

<input type="radio"
       name="orderCorrect"
       value="no" />
```

The **radio** type displays a radio or option button; the **name** attribute defines the data field; and the **value** attribute provides the field value associated with the button.

The **textarea** element creates a text area box for multiple lines of text.

```
<textarea>...</textarea>
```

Share Your Experience at Red Ball Pizza

Date of visit

Receipt number *   re-nnnnnn

Order type   Dine in

Was your service friendly?   Yes   No

Was your order correct?   Yes   No

Was your food hot?   Yes   No

Tell us more about your experience!

Creating a Selection List

The next part of the survey form records how customers place their orders from Red Ball Pizza. A customer order can be placed in one of four ways: pickup; delivery; dine in; or in the case of pizzas, uncooked pizzas that customers can take home and bake. Alice doesn't want customers to enter their order types into an input box because different customers will enter this information in different ways, and the large variety of spellings and text will make it difficult to group and analyze the survey results. Instead, she wants each user to select the order type from a predetermined group of options. This can be accomplished using a selection list.

A selection list is a list box that presents users with a group of possible field values for the data field. It's created using the HTML code

```
<select name="name" id="id">
   <option value="value1">text1</option>
   <option value="value2">text2</option>
   . . .
</select>
```

where the `name` and `id` attributes provide the name of the data field and identify the selection list control, respectively; `value1`, `value2`, etc. are the possible values of the data field; and `text1`, `text2`, etc. are the text of the entries in the selection list that users see on the Web form. Figure 6-25 shows an example of a selection list used to record each user's political affiliation.

Figure 6-25	Creating a selection list

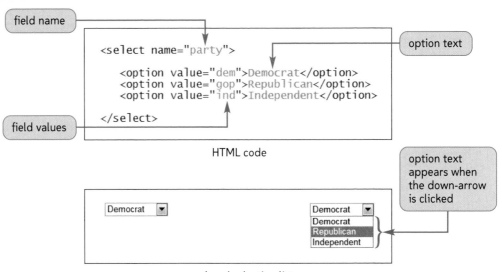

HTML code

rendered selection list

Notice that the field value does not have to match the option text. In most cases, the option text will be more expansive and descriptive to make it easier for users, while the corresponding value will be brief and succinct for use with the server program analyzing the form data.

REFERENCE

Creating a Selection List

- To create a selection list, add the elements

```
<select name="name">
    <option value="value1">text1</option>
    <option value="value2">text2</option>
    ...
</select>
```

to the Web form, where *name* is the name of the field associated with the selection list; *value1*, *value2*, etc. are the possible field values; and *text1*, *text2*, etc. are the entries displayed in the selection list.
- To specify the default value, add the following attribute to one of the *option* elements:

```
selected="selected"
```

- To set the number of options displayed at one time in the selection list, add the attribute

```
size="value"
```

to the `select` element, where *value* is the number of options displayed in the selection list at any one time.
- To allow users to make multiple selections, add the attribute

```
multiple="multiple"
```

to the `select` element.

You'll add a selection list to the Red Ball Pizza survey form to record the type of order placed by the customer, storing the value in the `ordertype` field. The program that will analyze these results will use the field values `type1`, `type2`, `type3`, or `type4`, but the option text in the selection list will read *Carry out, Delivery, Dine in,* and *Take and bake,* respectively.

To create the selection list:

1. Return to the **survey.htm** file in your text editor and scroll down to the bottom of the second field set.

2. Directly before the closing `</fieldset>` tag, add the following code (see Figure 6-26):

```
<label for="ordertype">Order type</label>
<select name="ordertype" id="ordertype">
    <option value="type1">Carry out</option>
    <option value="type2">Delivery</option>
    <option value="type3">Dine in</option>
    <option value="type4">Take and bake</option>
</select>
```

Figure 6-26   **Creating the ordertype selection list**

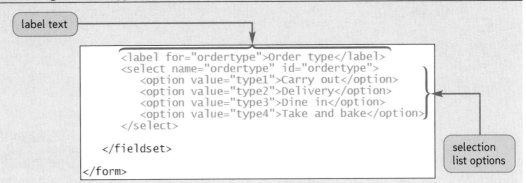

label text

```
<label for="ordertype">Order type</label>
<select name="ordertype" id="ordertype">
    <option value="type1">Carry out</option>
    <option value="type2">Delivery</option>
    <option value="type3">Dine in</option>
    <option value="type4">Take and bake</option>
</select>

</fieldset>

</form>
```

selection list options

3. Save your changes to the file.

You'll also want to set the style of the `select` element so that, like the input boxes you created in the last session, it's floated alongside its label, and its font size and margin space are set to match the layout of the survey form.

4. Go to the **forms.css** file in your text editor. At the bottom of the file, add the following code as shown in Figure 6-27:

```
/* Selection list styles */

select {
    display: block;
    float: left;
    font-size: 0.9em;
    margin: 7px 0px;
}
```

Figure 6-27   **Style rule for the select element**

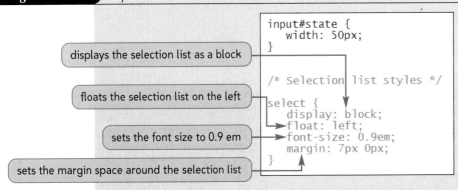

displays the selection list as a block

floats the selection list on the left

sets the font size to 0.9 em

sets the margin space around the selection list

```
input#state {
    width: 50px;
}

/* Selection list styles */

select {
    display: block;
    float: left;
    font-size: 0.9em;
    margin: 7px 0px;
}
```

TIP

The default width of the selection list is equal to the width of the longest selection option; you can set a different width using the CSS `width` property.

5. Save your changes to the style sheet file and then open the **survey.htm** file in your Web browser. The survey form now displays a selection list for the type of order (see Figure 6-28). Click the selection list arrow and verify that all of the order type options are shown.

Figure 6-28   **Order type selection list**

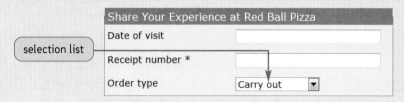

Trouble? Depending on your browser, the selection list may appear slightly different from the one shown in Figure 6-28.

The first option in a selection list is the field's default value. To specify a different default value and to display a different option from the selection list, add the `selected` attribute to the `option` element as follows:

```
<option selected="selected" value="value">text</option>
```

Browsers also will accept the `selected` attribute without an attribute value, appearing as follows:

```
<option selected value="value">text</option>
```

However, this syntax is not supported in XHTML documents. To be consistent across the different markup languages, this book always includes an attribute value, even when that attribute value does nothing more than repeat the attribute name.

Alice knows that most of the survey respondents dine in at the restaurant. Although the options in the Order type selection list are displayed in alphabetical order, she would like the *Dine in* option selected by default.

To specify the default value for the selection list:

▶ **1.** Return to the **survey.htm** file in your text editor and add the `selected="selected"` attribute to the *Dine in* option (see Figure 6-29).

Figure 6-29   **Specifying the selected option**

the *Dine in* option will appear selected by default

```
<label for="ordertype">Order type</label>
<select name="ordertype" id="ordertype">
    <option value="type1">Carry out</option>
    <option value="type2">Delivery</option>
    <option value="type3" selected="selected">Dine in</option>
    <option value="type4">Take and bake</option>
</select>
```

▶ **2.** Save your changes to the file and then reopen **survey.htm** in your Web browser. Verify that the *Dine in* option is preselected in the order type list.

Setting the Size of the Selection List

By default, selection lists display only the currently selected option value. You can change the number of options displayed by applying the `size` attribute

```
<select size="value"> ... </select>
```

to the `select` element, where *value* is the number of options that the selection list displays at one time. By specifying a `size` value greater than 1, you change the selection list from a drop-down list box to a list box with a scroll bar that allows users to scroll through the selection options. If you set the `size` attribute equal to the number of options in the selection list, the scroll bar either is not displayed or is dimmed, as shown in Figure 6-30.

Figure 6-30 | **Setting the size of the selection list**

Alice has another selection list to add to the survey form, recording where the customer heard of Red Ball Pizza. The survey presents the user with five options: the Internet, a magazine, a newspaper, word of mouth, or other. Alice wants you to display all of the options by setting the value of the `size` attribute to 5.

To set the selection list size:

1. Return to the **survey.htm** file in your text editor and add the following label and selection list directly below the `email` field (see Figure 6-31):

```
<label>Where did you hear about us?</label>
<select name="infoSrc" id="infoSrc" size="5">
   <option value="internet">Internet</option>
   <option value="mag">Magazine</option>
   <option value="news">Newspaper</option>
   <option value="word">Word of Mouth</option>
   <option value="other">Other</option>
</select>
```

Figure 6-31 | **Creating the infoSrc selection list**

> setting the size of the selection list to five options

```
<label for="email">E-mail *</label>
<input name="email" id="email" />

<label>Where did you hear about us?</label>
<select name="infoSrc" id="infoSrc" size="5">
   <option value="internet">Internet</option>
   <option value="mag">Magazine</option>
   <option value="news">Newspaper</option>
   <option value="word">Word of Mouth</option>
   <option value="other">Other</option>
</select>
```

2. Save your changes to the file and then reopen **survey.htm** in your Web browser. As shown in Figure 6-32, the selection list appears with all five options displayed.

Figure 6-32   **List box for listing the information source**

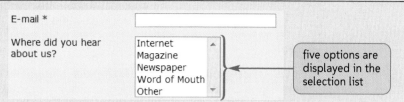

E-mail *

Where did you hear about us?

Internet
Magazine
Newspaper
Word of Mouth
Other

five options are displayed in the selection list

Trouble? Depending on your browser, you might not see a scroll bar next to the list of options.

Allowing for Multiple Selections

In the code you just entered, customers were limited to a single option. However, Alice is aware that a customer could have heard about Red Ball Pizza from more than one source. She would like customers to be able to select more than one option if applicable. Multiple selections can be applied to a selection list by adding the `multiple` attribute to the `select` element as follows:

```
<select multiple="multiple"> … </select>
```

As with the `selected` attribute discussed earlier, you also can apply the `multiple` attribute without an attribute value and most browsers will interpret it correctly.

There are two ways for users to select multiple items from a selection list. For noncontiguous selections, users can press and hold the Ctrl key (or the command key on a Mac) while making the selections. For a contiguous selection, users can select the first item, press and hold the Shift key, and then select the last item in the range. This selects the two items as well as all the items between them.

If you decide to use a multiple selection list in a form, be aware that the form sends a name/value pair to the server for each option the user selects from the list. Verify that your server-based program can handle a single field with multiple values before using a multiple selection list.

You'll add the ability to select multiple options to the `infoSrc` field you just created.

To allow for multiple selections:

1. Return to the **survey.htm** file in your text editor and then add the following text to the `label` element for the `infoSrc` selection list:

   ```
   <br />(select all that apply)
   ```

2. Add the attribute `multiple="multiple"` to the `select` element. Figure 6-33 highlights the newly added code.

Figure 6-33   **Allowing for multiple selections**

revised label text

```
<label>Where did you hear about us? <br />(select all that apply)</label>
<select name="infoSrc" id="infoSrc" size="5" multiple="multiple">
   <option value="internet">Internet</option>
   <option value="mag">Magazine</option>
   <option value="news">Newspaper</option>
   <option value="word">Word of Mouth</option>
   <option value="other">Other</option>
</select>
```

users can select multiple options

3. Save your changes to the file and then reopen **survey.htm** in your Web browser. Verify that you can now select multiple items from the information source list using the ctrl+click, command+click, or shift+click keyboard and mouse combinations.

Grouping Selection Options

In long selection lists, it can be difficult for users to locate a particular option value. You can organize selection list options by placing them in option groups using the `optgroup` element

```
<select>
   <optgroup label="label1">
      <option>text1</option>
      <option>text2</option>
...
   </optgroup>
   <optgroup label="label2">
      <option>text1</option>
      <option>text2</option>
...
   </optgroup>
</select>
```

where *`label1`*, *`label2`*, and so forth are the labels for the different groups of options. The text of the label appears in the selection list above each group of items but is not a selectable item from the list. Figure 6-34 shows an example of a selection list in which the options are divided into two groups.

Figure 6-34 Organizing a selection list with option groups

HTML code

```
<label for="party">Candidate</label>
<select name="party">

   <optgroup label="Democrat">
      <option value="d1">Tim Harris</option>
      <option value="d2">Gary Nielsen</option>
      <option value="d3">Kate Paulenty</option>
   </optgroup>

   <optgroup label="Republican">
      <option value="r1">Barbara Alt</option>
      <option value="r2">Peter Trudea</option>
      <option value="r3">Maria Sandoval</option>
   </optgroup>

</select>
```

rendered selection list

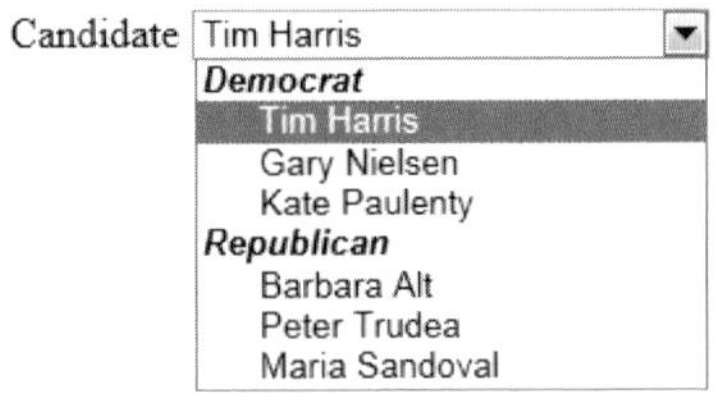

The appearance of the option group label is determined by the browser. You can apply a style to an entire option group including its label, but there is no CSS style to change the appearance of the option group label alone.

Alice does not need you to use an option group for her survey form because the number of options is so small.

INSIGHT

Creating Passwords and Hidden Fields

Fields and field values are not always visible to users. For sensitive data such as passwords or credit card numbers, you can display an input box using the `password` data type

```
<input name="name" type="password" />
```

where *name* is the field name. Any information that a user enters will be displayed as a series of dots or asterisks, protecting the information from prying eyes.

Another way of hiding information is with a hidden field, which is created using an `input` element with the hidden data type, as follows

```
<input name="name" type="hidden" value="value" />
```

where *value* is the value stored in the field. With a hidden field, both the field value and the input control are hidden from the user. Hidden fields are used for fields that have a predefined value that will be used by the script processing the Web form. Even though hidden fields are not displayed by browsers, the field values still can be read by examining the source code; for this reason, you should not put any sensitive information in a hidden field.

Creating Option Buttons

In the next part of the form, Alice wants to ask customers general questions about their experiences at the restaurant. She wants to know whether the service was friendly, whether orders were recorded correctly, and if the food was delivered hot. She suggests that you present these questions using option buttons.

Option buttons, also called radio buttons, are like selection lists in that they limit users to a set of possible values; but unlike selection lists, the options appear as separate control elements on the form. Option buttons are created using the `input` element with the `type` attribute set to a value of `radio` as follows

```
<input type="radio" name="name" value="value1" />
<input type="radio" name="name" value="value2" />
<input type="radio" name="name" value="value3" />
...
```

where *name* is the name of the data field associated with the option buttons, and *value1*, *value2*, *value3*, etc. are the field values associated with each option. When multiple option buttons are applied to the same data field, browsers treat them as a group, and selecting one option button automatically deselects all of the others. Figure 6-35 shows an example of a Web form that uses an option button group to indicate political party affiliations.

Figure 6-35 **Creating a group of option buttons**

```
HTML code   <fieldset>
                <legend>Party Affiliation<legend>

                <label for="demOption">Democrat</label>
                <input type="radio" name="party" id="demOption" value="dem" />

                <label for="repOption">Republican</label>
                <input type="radio" name="party" id="repOption" value="rep" />

                <label for="indOption">Independent</label>
                <input type="radio" name="party" id="indOption" value="ind" />

            </fieldset>
```

rendered option buttons

Party Affiliation
Democrat ◉ Republican ◉ Independent ◉

In this sample code, all of the option buttons are associated with the `party` field with values of `dem`, `rep`, and `ind`, respectively. The option buttons are organized within a field set, and each label within the field set is linked to a specific option button control using the `for` and `id` attributes. When you link a label to an option button, users can select the option by clicking either the label or the option button. For example, clicking on the label text *Democrat* would cause a browser to select the `demoOption` option button.

REFERENCE

Creating a Group of Option Buttons

- To create a group of option buttons associated with a single field, add the `input` elements

```
<input type="radio" name="name" value="value1" />
<input type="radio" name="name" value="value2" />
<input type="radio" name="name" value="value3" />
...
```

  where *name* is the name of the data field, and *value1*, *value2*, *value3*, etc. are the field values associated with each option.
- To specify the default option, add the `checked` attribute to the `input` element as follows:

```
checked="checked"
```

You'll create option buttons now for the `serviceFriendly` field to record whether a customer was treated well by the Red Ball Pizza staff. To keep the control elements for the option buttons organized as a group, you'll nest them and their labels within a `fieldset` element with the class name `optionGroup`.

To create option buttons:

1. Return to the **survey.htm** file in your text editor and then scroll down to the second field set. Directly after the `ordertype` selection list, add the following code (see Figure 6-36):

```
<label>Was your service friendly?</label>
<fieldset class="optionGroup">
   <label for="sYes">Yes</label>
   <input type="radio" name="serviceFriendly" id="sYes"
          value="yes" />

   <label for="sNo">No</label>
   <input type="radio" name="serviceFriendly" id="sNo"
          value="no" />
</fieldset>
```

Make sure you use the same field name for the different radio buttons within the group so that browsers treat them all as part of the same field.

Figure 6-36 **Option button group for the serviceFriendly field**

field set containing the label and option buttons

label associated with the option button control

option button for the serviceFriendly field

```
        <option value="type4">Take and bake</option>
</select>

<label>Was your service friendly?</label>
<fieldset class="optionGroup">
   <label for="sYes ">Yes</label>
   <input type="radio" name="serviceFriendly" id="sYes"
          value="yes" />

   <label for="sNo">No</label>
   <input type="radio" name="serviceFriendly" id="sNo"
          value="no" />
</fieldset>
```

2. Save your changes to the file and then reopen **survey.htm** in your Web browser. Figure 6-37 shows the current appearance of the option buttons.

Figure 6-37 **Rendered option buttons**

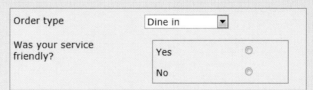

3. Click each option button and confirm that clicking one option button deselects the other. Also verify that when you click the labels next to the option buttons, the option buttons become selected.

The appearance of the option buttons and the field set box is partly based on the CSS styles you created for the `fieldset` and `input` elements in the last session. The option buttons take up more space than necessary and you think they would look better if they were all on a single line. To accomplish this, you'll create style rules to display the labels and option buttons as inline elements, reduce their widths, resize their margins, and prevent them from floating. You'll also remove the border from the `fieldset` element that contains the option button labels and controls.

To revise the styles for the option button group:

▶ **1.** Go to the **forms.css** file in your text editor.

▶ **2.** At the bottom of the file, insert the following style rules as shown in Figure 6-38:

```
/* Option button styles */

fieldset.optionGroup {
   border-width: 0px;
}

fieldset.optionGroup label {
   display: inline;
   float: none;
   margin: 0px 3px 0px 0px;
   width: 30px;
}

fieldset.optionGroup input {
   display: inline;
   float: none;
   margin: 0px 20px 0px 0px;
   width: 20px;
}
```

Figure 6-38 Style rules for the option button group

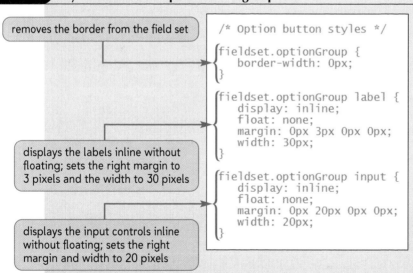

removes the border from the field set

displays the labels inline without floating; sets the right margin to 3 pixels and the width to 30 pixels

displays the input controls inline without floating; sets the right margin and width to 20 pixels

▶ **3.** Save your changes to the file and then reopen the **survey.htm** file in your Web browser. Figure 6-39 shows the revised appearance of the option button group.

Figure 6-39 Revised appearance of the option button group

Trouble? In some browsers, the label text will not wrap to a new line.

There are two other option button groups that Alice wants in the survey form: one to find out whether the customer's order was delivered correctly, and the other to find out if the food was presented hot. You'll add these option button groups now.

To add the remaining option button groups:

1. Return to the **survey.htm** file in your text editor.
2. Directly below the `fieldset` element for the `serviceFriendly` field, add the following HTML code (see Figure 6-40):

```
<label>Was your order correct?</label>
<fieldset class="optionGroup">
   <label for="oYes">Yes</label>
   <input type="radio" name="orderCorrect" id="oYes"
          value="yes" />

   <label for="oNo">No</label>
   <input type="radio" name="orderCorrect" id="oNo"
          value="no" />
</fieldset>

<label>Was your food hot?</label>
<fieldset class="optionGroup">
   <label for="hotYes">Yes</label>
   <input type="radio" name="foodHot" id="hotYes"
          value="yes" />

   <label for="hotNo">No</label>
   <input type="radio" name="foodHot" id="hotNo"
          value="no" />
</fieldset>
```

Figure 6-40 **Option button groups for the orderCorrect and foodHot fields**

```
   <input type="radio" name="serviceFriendly" id="sNo"
          value="no" />
</fieldset>

<label>Was your order correct?</label>
<fieldset class="optionGroup">
   <label for="oYes">Yes</label>
   <input type="radio" name="orderCorrect" id="oYes"
          value="yes" />

   <label for="oNo">No</label>
   <input type="radio" name="orderCorrect" id="oNo"
          value="no" />
</fieldset>
<label>Was your food hot?</label>
<fieldset class="optionGroup">
   <label for="hotYes">Yes</label>
   <input type="radio" name="foodHot" id="hotYes"
          value="yes" />

   <label for="hotNo">No</label>
   <input type="radio" name="foodHot" id="hotNo"
          value="no" />
</fieldset>
```

field set for the orderCorrect field

field set for the foodHot field

3. Save your changes to the file and then reopen the **survey.htm** file in your Web browser. Figure 6-41 shows all of the option button groups in the survey form.

Figure 6-41   **Completed option button groups**

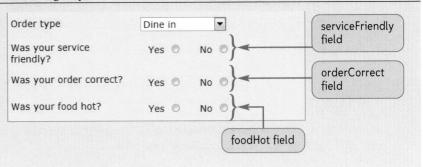

By default, an option button is unselected; however, you can set an option button to be selected when a form opens by adding the `checked` attribute to the `input` element as follows:

```
<input type="radio" name="name" checked="checked" />
```

You also can enter the `checked` attribute without an attribute value, and most browsers will be able to interpret your code.

Creating a Text Area Box

Alice wants the survey form to include a place where customers can enter extended comments about Red Ball Pizza. She wants customers to be able to enter several lines of text. Because an input box is limited to a single line of text, it would not be appropriate to enter those comments in an input box. Instead, you can create a control element that allows for extended text entries using the `textarea` element

```
<textarea name="name">
    text
</textarea>
```

where *text* is default text that is placed in the text area box. You do not have to specify default text and can leave the text box empty. Many browsers also support the `placeholder` attribute introduced in the last session to provide additional hints to users about what to enter into the text box.

Browsers determine the default size of a text area box. Most browsers create a box that is about 20 characters long and two or three lines high. You can set the dimensions of a text area box using the CSS `width` and `height` style properties. HTML also supports the `row` and `cols` attributes to set the size of the box, as follows

TIP

The rows and cols attributes are required under strict applications of XHTML.

```
<textarea rows="value" cols="value"> ... </textarea>
```

where the `rows` attribute specifies the number of lines in the text area box and the `cols` attribute specifies the number of characters per line.

As you type text into a text area box, the text automatically wraps to a new line as it extends beyond the box's width. If more text is entered into a box than can be displayed, the browser automatically adds horizontal and vertical scroll bars to the box. You can determine whether the locations of line wrapping are included in the field value by using the `wrap` attribute

```
<textarea wrap="type"> ... </textarea>
```

where *type* is either `hard` or `soft`. In a hard wrap, information about where the text begins a new line is included with the data field value, while in a soft wrap this information is not included. When a hard wrap is used, the `cols` attribute also needs to be specified. Many browsers also support the `off` wrap type to prevent browsers from wrapping text within a text area box, though it is not part of any HTML specification. The default value of the `wrap` attribute is `soft`.

REFERENCE

Creating a Text Area Box

- To create a text area box for multiple lines of text, use the element

```
<textarea name="name">
    text
</textarea>
```

where *name* is the name of the field associated with the text area box and *text* is the default text that appears in the box.

- To specify the dimensions of the box, add the attributes

```
rows="value" cols="value"
```

to the `textarea` element, where the `rows` attribute specifies the number of lines in the text area box and the `cols` attribute specifies the number of characters per line.

- To specify how the field value should handle wrapped text, use the attribute

```
wrap="type"
```

where *type* is either `hard` (to include the locations of the line wraps) or `soft` (to ignore line wrap locations).

You'll add a `textarea` element to the survey form to store the customer comments. You'll also set the width and the height of the element using a CSS style rule.

To create the comments text area box:

1. Return to the **survey.htm** file in your text editor.

2. Directly below the `fieldset` element for the `foodHot` option group you just created, enter the following code (see Figure 6-42):

```
<label for="comments">Tell us more about your experience!</label>
<textarea name="comments" id="comments"></textarea>
```

Figure 6-42   Creating a text area control

```
            <label for for="hotNo">No</label>
            <input type="radio" name="foodHot" id="hotNo"
                    value="no" />
        </fieldset>

        <label for= "comments ">Tell us more about your experience!</label>
        <textarea name="comments" id="comments"></textarea>
    </fieldset>
```

comments field

▶ **3.** Save your changes to the file and then return to the **forms.css** file in your text editor.

▶ **4.** At the bottom of the style sheet file, insert the following style rule as shown in Figure 6-43:

```
/* Text area styles */

textarea {
    display: block;
    font-size: 0.9em;
    float: left;
    height: 150px;
    margin: 10px 0px;
    width: 50%;
}
```

Figure 6-43 Style rule for the text area box

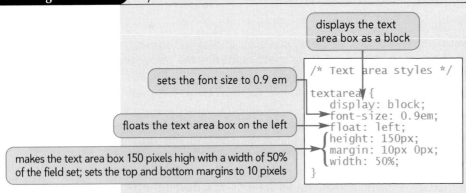

displays the text area box as a block

sets the font size to 0.9 em

floats the text area box on the left

makes the text area box 150 pixels high with a width of 50% of the field set; sets the top and bottom margins to 10 pixels

```
/* Text area styles */

textarea {
    display: block;
    font-size: 0.9em;
    float: left;
    height: 150px;
    margin: 10px 0px;
    width: 50%;
}
```

▶ **5.** Save your changes to the file and then reopen the **survey.htm** file in your Web browser. Figure 6-44 shows the newly added text area box.

Figure 6-44 Text area box

▶ **6.** Type some sample text into the text area box and verify that the text wraps to a new line as you exceed the width of the box.

Trouble? Line wraps do not occur in the middle of words. If you find your sample text is not wrapping to a new line, make sure you are entering individual words rather than a long character string.

Tab Indexing and Autofocus

Typically, users navigate through a Web form using the Tab key, which moves the cursor from one field to another in the order that the field tags are entered into the HTML file.

You can specify an alternate order by adding the `tabindex` attribute to any control element in your form. When each element is assigned a tab index number, the cursor moves through the fields from the lowest index number to the highest. For example, to assign the tab index number 1 to the `name` field from the survey form, you would enter the following `tabindex` attribute to the control element:

```
<input name="name" tabindex="1" />
```

This code would ensure that the cursor is in the `name` field when the form is first opened. (Fields with 0 or negative tab indexes are omitted from the tab order entirely.)

Another way to ensure that a particular field is selected when a Web form is initially opened is to use the `autofocus` attribute. The HTML code

```
<input name="name" autofocus="autofocus" />
```

automatically places the cursor in the input box for the `name` field when the form is loaded by a browser. The `autofocus` attribute was introduced in HTML5 and thus might not be supported by older browsers.

Older browsers that do not support tab indexing or the `autofocus` attribute simply ignore them and open a file without giving the focus to any control element. When a user tabs through the form, the tab order will reflect the order of the items in the HTML file.

Creating Check Boxes

A survey form like the one you're creating for Red Ball Pizza serves two purposes. One, of course, is to receive customer feedback; the other is to remain in contact with the consumer base. Red Ball Pizza has an e-mail newsletter that it sends out to subscribers, detailing the latest news about the restaurant and informing patrons about upcoming events and special deals. Alice wants to give customers filling out the survey form a way of subscribing to the newsletter. This can be done using a check box.

You use a check box control in situations where you are verifying the presence or absence of something; in this case, whether or not a customer is interested in receiving e-mail from the restaurant. Check boxes are created using the `input` element with the `type` attribute set to `checkbox`, as follows:

```
<input type="checkbox" name="name" value="value" />
```

The `value` attribute contains the value of the field when the check box is checked. If no value is provided, the value `on` is used by default. For example, the following code creates a check box for determining whether a user is a member of the Democratic party:

```
<label for="dem">Democrat?</label>
<input type="checkbox" name="dem" id="dem" value="yes" />
```

If the check box is selected, the browser will submit a name-value pair of `dem-yes` to the script running on the Web server. A name-value pair is sent to the server only when the check box is checked by the user. If it is not checked, then nothing is sent to the server.

By default, check boxes are not selected. To preselect a check box, add the `checked` attribute to the `input` element as follows:

```
checked="checked"
```

As with the `multiple` and `selected` attributes, you also can use the `checked` attribute without an attribute value.

REFERENCE

Creating a Check Box

- To create a check box, add the element

  ```
  <input type="checkbox" name="name" value="value" />
  ```

  to the Web form, where *name* is the name of the data field and *value* is the data field value if the check box is selected.
- To specify that a check box is selected by default, add the following attribute to the input element:

  ```
  checked="checked"
  ```

You'll add a check box below the two field sets asking customers whether they would like to receive the Red Ball Pizza e-mail newsletter.

To create a check box inviting customers to subscribe:

1. Return to the **survey.htm** file in your text editor.

2. Directly above the closing `</form>` tag, insert the following code (see Figure 6-45):

```
<label id="newsletter">
   <input type="checkbox" name="newscb" />
   E-mail me your newsletter for great coupons and specials!
</label>
```

Figure 6-45 Creating a check box for the newscb field

```
        <label for="comments">Tell us more about your experience!</label>
        <textarea name="comments" id="comments"></textarea>

    </fieldset>

    <label id="newsletter">
        <input type="checkbox" name="newscb" />
        E-mail me your newsletter for great coupons and specials!
    </label>

</form>
```

3. Save your changes to the file.

Next, you'll design a style rule for the label text and check box control.

To create a style rule for the label text and check box control:

1. Go to the **forms.css** file in your text editor.

2. At the bottom of the file, insert the following style rules (see Figure 6-46):

```css
/* Check box styles */

#newsletter {
    color: rgb(233, 69, 0);
    float: none;
    margin: 10px auto;
    text-align: center;
    width: 90%;
}

#newsletter input {
    display: inline;
    float: none;
    width: 20px;
}
```

Figure 6-46   Style rules for the label and check box

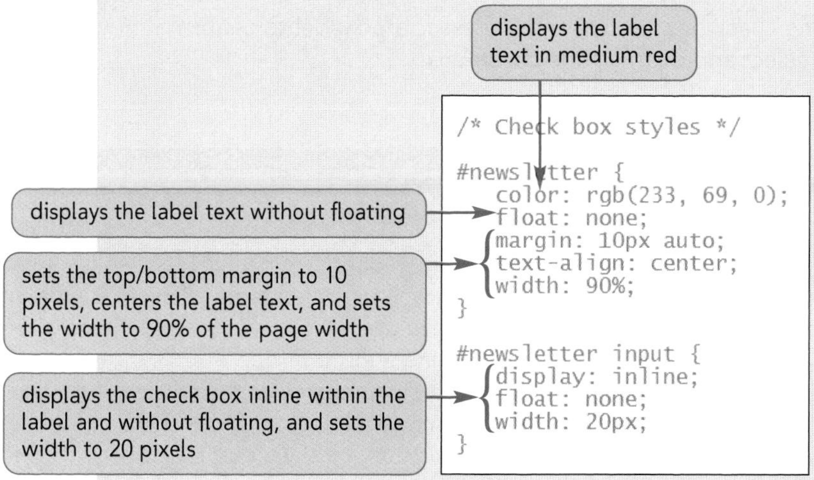

displays the label text in medium red

displays the label text without floating

sets the top/bottom margin to 10 pixels, centers the label text, and sets the width to 90% of the page width

displays the check box inline within the label and without floating, and sets the width to 20 pixels

```css
/* Check box styles */

#newsletter {
    color: rgb(233, 69, 0);
    float: none;
    margin: 10px auto;
    text-align: center;
    width: 90%;
}

#newsletter input {
    display: inline;
    float: none;
    width: 20px;
}
```

3. Save your changes to the style sheet and then refresh **survey.htm** in your Web browser. Figure 6-47 shows the current state of the Web form.

Figure 6-47　**Current appearance of the survey form**

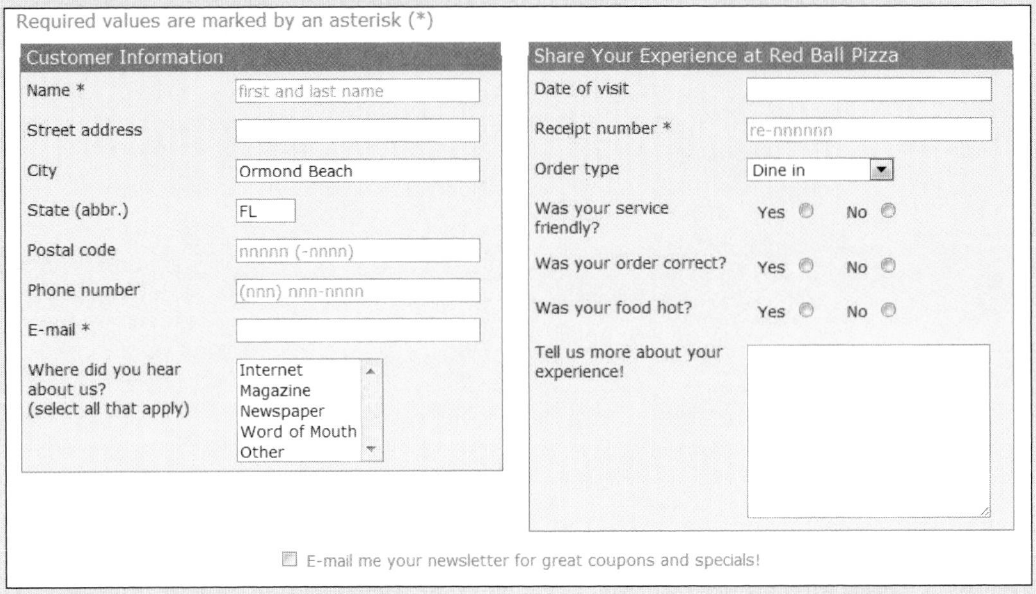

> **4.** Click the check box control and the associated label to confirm that you can alternately select and deselect the check box.

Written Communication: Creating Effective Forms

Web forms are one of the main ways of getting feedback from your users, so it's important for the forms to be friendly and easy to use. A well-designed form often can be the difference between a new customer and a disgruntled user who leaves your site to go elsewhere. Here are some tips to remember when designing a form:

- Mark fields that are required, but also limit their number. Don't overwhelm your users with requests for information that is not really essential. Keep your forms short and to the point.
- Use the autofocus attribute to place users automatically into the first field of your form, rather than forcing them to click that field.
- Many users will navigate through your form using the Tab key. Make sure that your tab order is logical and easy for users to follow.
- Provide detailed instructions about what users are expected to do. Don't assume that your form is self-explanatory.
- If you ask for personal data and financial information, provide clear assurances that the data will be secure. If possible, provide a link to a Web page describing your security practices.
- If you need to collect a lot of information, break the form into manageable sections spread out over several pages. Allow users to easily move backward and forward through the form without losing data. Provide information to users indicating where they are as they progress through your pages.
- Clearly indicate what users will receive once a form is submitted, and provide feedback on the Web site and through e-mail that tells them when their data has been successfully submitted.

Finally, every Web form should undergo usability testing before it is made available to the general public. Weed out any mistakes and difficulties before your users see the form.

PROSKILLS

You've greatly extended the scope of the survey form through the use of selection lists, option buttons, text area boxes, and check boxes. In the next session, you'll continue to work on the survey form by exploring many of the new HTML5 data types, and you'll learn how to validate the form data to ensure that users enter their data correctly.

REVIEW

Session 6.2 Quick Check

1. Provide the code to create a selection list for the `State` field limited to the option text *California, Nevada, Oregon,* and *Washington.*

2. What attribute would you add to the code in the previous question to make *Oregon* the default value for the `State` field?

3. For the code in Question 1, what attribute would you add to the code to display all of the possible field values in the selection list?

4. How would you modify the code in Question 1 to allow for multiple selections?

5. Specify the code to create two option buttons for the `Computer` field with the values `PC` and `Mac`.

6. In the previous question, what attribute would you add to the code to make `PC` the default value for the `Computer` field?

7. Specify the code to create a text area box for the `Memo` field that displays 10 lines of text, each of which displays up to 40 characters.

8. Specify the code to create a check box and a label for the `Computer` field. The text of the label should be *I use a PC* and the value of the check box should be `Yes`.

SESSION 6.3 VISUAL OVERVIEW

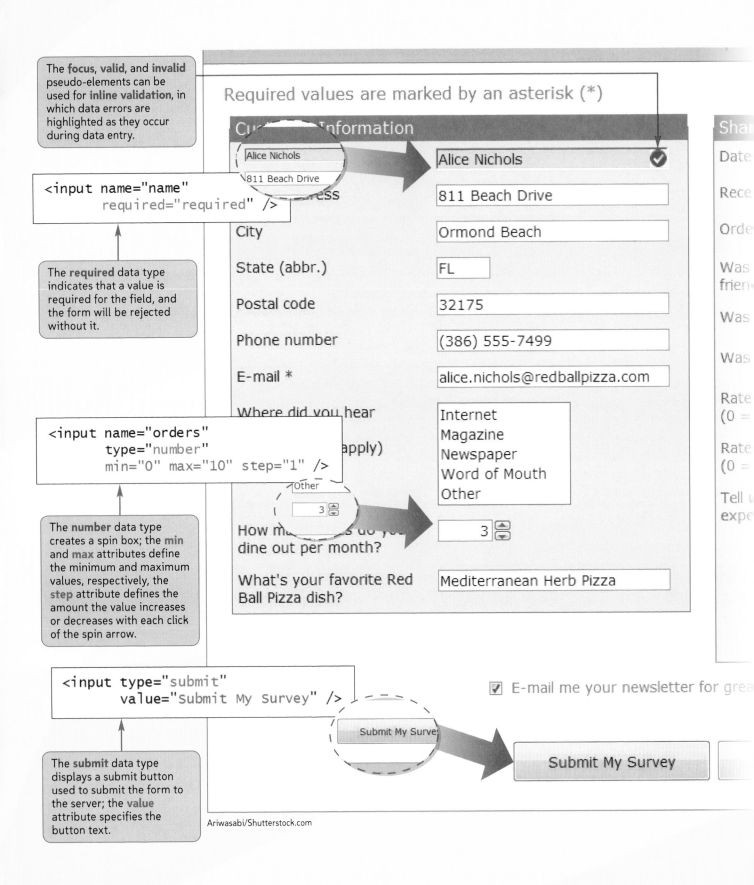

The **focus**, **valid**, and **invalid** pseudo-elements can be used for **inline validation**, in which data errors are highlighted as they occur during data entry.

```
<input name="name"
        required="required" />
```

The **required** data type indicates that a value is required for the field, and the form will be rejected without it.

```
<input name="orders"
        type="number"
        min="0" max="10" step="1" />
```

The **number** data type creates a spin box; the **min** and **max** attributes define the minimum and maximum values, respectively, the **step** attribute defines the amount the value increases or decreases with each click of the spin arrow.

```
<input type="submit"
        value="Submit My Survey" />
```

The **submit** data type displays a submit button used to submit the form to the server; the **value** attribute specifies the button text.

Required values are marked by an asterisk (*)

Customer Information

Alice Nichols	Alice Nichols ✓
811 Beach Drive	811 Beach Drive
City	Ormond Beach
State (abbr.)	FL
Postal code	32175
Phone number	(386) 555-7499
E-mail *	alice.nichols@redballpizza.com

Where did you hear (apply)

Internet
Magazine
Newspaper
Word of Mouth
Other

Other
3

How m... ...do you dine out per month? 3

What's your favorite Red Ball Pizza dish? Mediterranean Herb Pizza

Sha...

Date
Rece
Orde
Was
frien
Was
Was
Rate
(0 ...
Rate
(0 ...
Tell ...
expe...

☑ E-mail me your newsletter for grea...

Submit My Surve

Submit My Survey

Ariwasabi/Shutterstock.com

HTML5 DATA TYPES

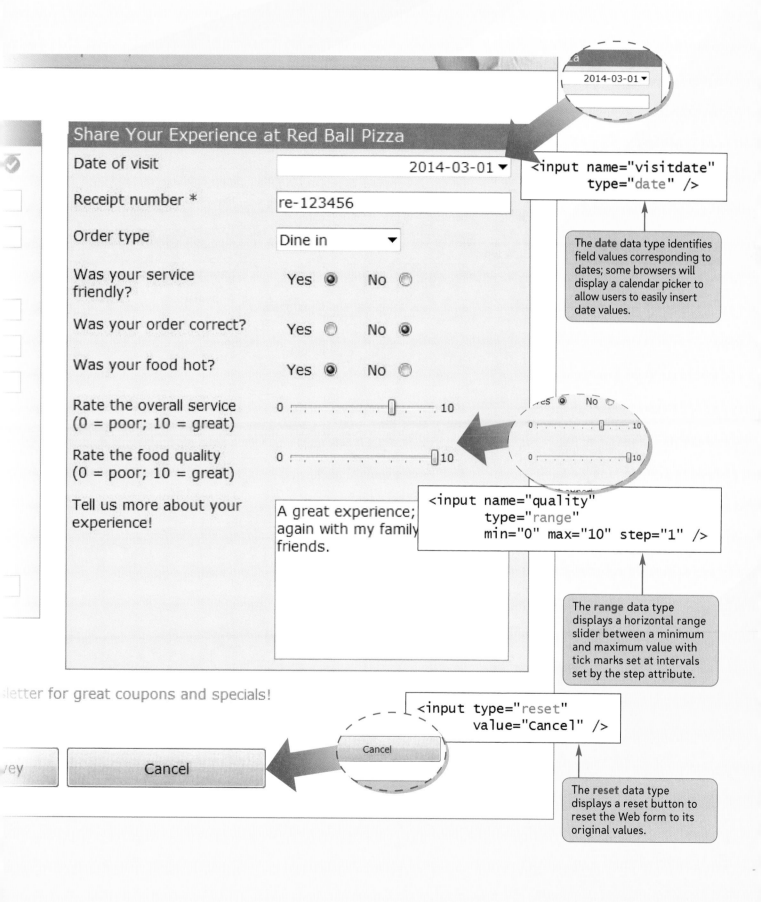

```
<input name="visitdate"
       type="date" />
```

The **date** data type identifies field values corresponding to dates; some browsers will display a calendar picker to allow users to easily insert date values.

```
<input name="quality"
       type="range"
       min="0" max="10" step="1" />
```

The **range** data type displays a horizontal range slider between a minimum and maximum value with tick marks set at intervals set by the step attribute.

```
<input type="reset"
       value="Cancel" />
```

The **reset** data type displays a reset button to reset the Web form to its original values.

Exploring HTML5 Data Types

Alice has had a chance to review your work on the survey form. She has several new fields to add to the survey form, including a data field for the number of times a customer dines out per month, and data fields in which the customer can provide a numeric rating of Red Ball Pizza's food and service quality.

Alice wants numbers stored in these fields, but so far your survey form has only recorded text values. However, HTML5 introduced 13 new data types, including data types for numeric values. These new data types are not uniformly supported across the browser market at the time of this writing, but you can still use many of them today.

Figure 6-48 summarizes the new data types provided by HTML5. The images of the input controls are taken from the Opera Web browser, which currently has the best support for the new data types. Other browsers have mixed levels of support. At the time of this writing, Internet Explorer does not support the new HTML5 data types at all. However, as HTML5 increases in popularity, this will rapidly change and Web designers will be able to use them with greater confidence.

Figure 6-48   HTML5 data types

Type	Description	General Appearance
color	An RGB color value that can be selected from a color picker dialog box	
date	A date (year, month, day) with no specified time zone	
datetime	A date and time (year, month, day, hour, minute, second, fraction of a second) with the time zone set to Coordinated Universal Time (UTC)	
datetime-local	A date and time (year, month, day, hour, minute, second, fraction of a second) with no specified time zone	
email	An e-mail address or list of e-mail addresses	nichols@redballpizza.com
month	A date consisting of a year and a month	
number	A numeric value	5
range	A numeric value selected from a defined range of values	
search	A text string usually used for performing searches	local pizza ✕
tel	A telephone number	(365) 555 - 7499
time	A time value (hour, minute, seconds, fractional seconds)	01:45
url	A URL of a Web site or Internet resource	http://www.redballpizza.com
week	A date consisting of a year number and a week number	

All of these data types are used with the `input` element. For example, to create an input box for e-mail addresses, you would use the `input` element

```
<input type="email" name="name" />
```

where *name* is the name of the data field in which you want to store an e-mail address. You'll explore these different data types in more detail now.

The `email`, `tel`, and `url` Data Types

The `email`, `tel`, and `url` data types are used for storing e-mail addresses, telephone numbers, and Web addresses, respectively. The input controls for these data types appear as simple text boxes. However, touch screen devices that use virtual keyboards can alter the keyboard layout in response to different data types. Figure 6-49 shows the iPad virtual keyboard layout for the `text`, `email`, `tel`, and `url` data types. Note that the layout for the `email` data type includes the addition of the @ character, which is a part of all e-mail addresses. The layout for the `tel` data type displays a row of numbers for easy typing of a telephone number. Finally, the keyboard layout for the `url` data type displays characters such as the / and : characters that are often used in URLs, as well as a key that automatically inserts the *.com* text string.

Figure 6-49   **Virtual keyboards for different data types**

type="text"

type="email"

type="tel"

type="url"

If an input box is opened by an older browser that doesn't support one of the new HTML5 data types, the browser simply treats the data field as basic text. Thus, there is little reason not to use one of the new data types. Older browsers can't display anything but a simple text box anyway; but with newer browsers, you can enhance the user experience by employing a more descriptive data type.

You'll return to the Red Ball Pizza survey form now to change the data type of the `email` and `phone` fields to use the `email` and `tel` data types.

To apply the `email` and `tel` data types:

1. Return to the **survey.htm** file in your text editor.

2. Scroll down to the `input` element for the `phone` field and insert the attribute `type="tel"`.

3. Insert the attribute `type="email"` into the `input` element for the `email` field. Figure 6-50 highlights the newly added code.

| Figure 6-50 | Applying the tel and email data types |

input box contains a telephone number

```
<label for="phone">Phone number</label>
<input name="phone" id="phone" type="tel"
       placeholder="(nnn) nnn-nnnn" />

<label for="email">E-mail *</label>
<input name="email" id="email" type="email" />
```

input box contains an e-mail address

4. Save your changes to the file.

5. If you have access to a mobile device that uses a virtual keyboard, access the **survey.htm** file and verify that the keyboard layout changes when the focus is placed on the input boxes for the phone and email fields.

   Trouble? At the time of this writing, not all mobile devices alter their virtual keyboard layouts for different HTML5 data types.

Specifying Dates and Times

Next, Alice wants you to set the data type of the visitdate field to date. For browsers that support the date type, this will bring up a calendar widget from which users can select a date. The date data type is only one of five date types used for entering date and time values; date is used for recording a calendar date as a text string in the format yyyy-mm-dd where yyyy is the four-digit year value, mm is the two-digit month value, and dd is the two-day day-of-the-month value.

The various date and time data types do not have a lot of support in the browser market at the time of this writing. Only Opera displays a calendar widget, while Google Chrome for Windows currently provides a box with spin arrows that can be used to enter a date value. Some handheld devices such as the BlackBerry provide a calendar scroll for selecting a date and/or time.

You'll change the data type of the visitdate field to date now.

To change the data type of the visitdate field:

1. Return to the **survey.htm** file in your text editor.

2. Locate the input element for the visitdate field and insert the attribute **type="date"** as shown in Figure 6-51.

Figure 6-51 ▶ **Applying the date data type**

```
<fieldset id="experience">
    <legend>Share Your Experience at Red Ball Pizza</legend>

    <label for="visitdate">Date of visit</label>
    <input name="visitdate" id="visitdate" type="date" />
```

(input box contains a date)

  ▶ **3.** Save your changes to the file.

  ▶ **4.** If you have access to the Opera, Chrome for Windows, or BlackBerry browser, or another browser that supports calendar data types, open the **survey.htm** file in the browser and click the input box for the date of the customer's visit to Red Ball Pizza. As shown in Figure 6-52, Opera displays a calendar object from which a user can select the date of the visit.

Figure 6-52 ▶ **Calendar widget in the Opera browser**

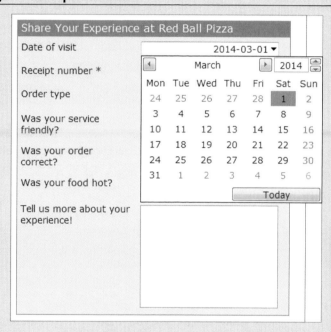

Trouble? If you are using other browsers, the input box might be treated as a text box with no calendar object displayed.

Browsers that don't support the various date and time data types display text boxes just as they did before the introduction of HTML5. Once again, nothing is lost by switching to one of the new date and time data types, and something is gained for customers using one of the browsers that support those types.

Using the number Data Type

Next, you'll record the number of times a typical Red Ball Pizza customer dines out per month. Because this is a numeric value, Alice wants you to use the number data type. Input boxes with the number data type are displayed using a **spinner control** in which users click an up or down arrow to increase or decrease the field value, respectively.

The default effect of clicking the spin arrow is to change the field value by one unit. You can specify a different amount for the value to change and identify the minimum and maximum values of the field using the step, min, and max attributes, as follows

```
<input name="name" type="number" value="value"
       step="value" min="value" max="value" />
```

where the value attribute provides the default field value, the step attribute indicates the amount by which the field value changes when a user clicks the spin arrow, the min attribute defines the minimum possible value, and the max attribute defines the maximum possible value of the field.

Creating Spinner Controls and Range Sliders

- To create a spinner control for numeric data, enter the input element

```
<input name="name" type="number" value="value"
       step="value" min="value" max="value" />
```

where the value attribute provides the default field value, the step attribute indicates the amount by which the field value changes when a user clicks the spin arrow, the min attribute defines the minimum possible value, and the max attribute defines the maximum possible value of the field.

- To create a range slider control for numeric data, use the following input element:

```
<input name="name" type="range" value="value"
       step="value" min="value" max="value" />
```

You'll add a new field to the survey form named ordersPerMonth that queries customers about how often they dine out; you'll set its default value to 1 and set the field value to range from 0 up to 10 in steps of 1 unit.

To create a number data type:

▶ 1. Return to the **survey.htm** file in your text editor.

▶ 2. Directly below the selection list for the infoSrc field, insert the following HTML code (see Figure 6-53):

```
<label for="ordersPerMonth">
   How many times do you dine out per month?
</label>
<input name="ordersPerMonth" id="ordersPerMonth"
       type="number" value="1"
       min="0" max="10" step="1" />
```

Figure 6-53 Applying a number data type

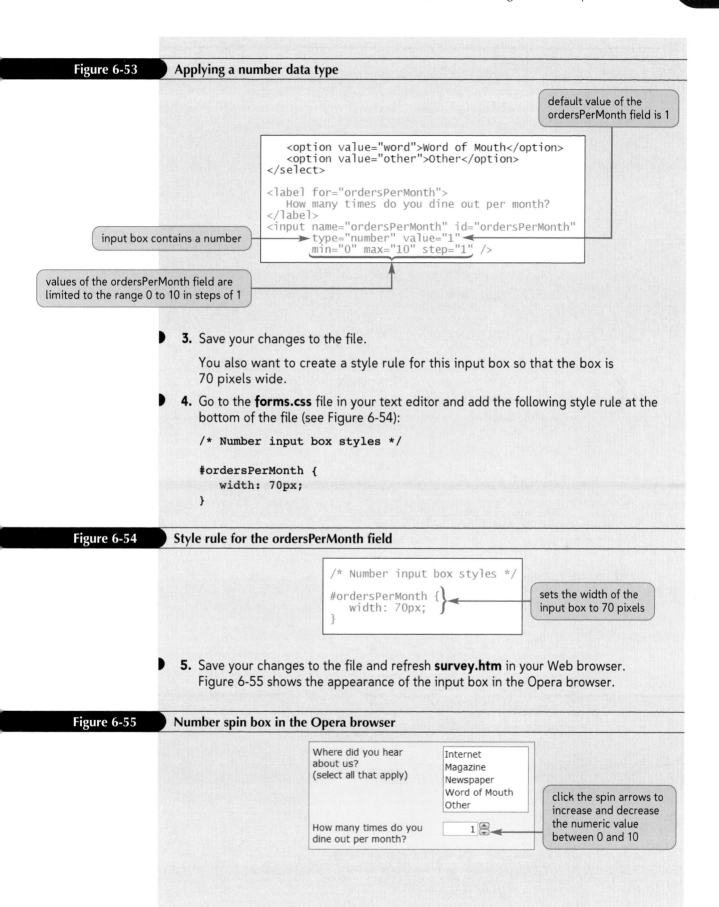

default value of the ordersPerMonth field is 1

```
        <option value="word">Word of Mouth</option>
        <option value="other">Other</option>
</select>

<label for="ordersPerMonth">
    How many times do you dine out per month?
</label>
<input name="ordersPerMonth" id="ordersPerMonth"
       type="number" value="1"
       min="0" max="10" step="1" />
```

input box contains a number

values of the ordersPerMonth field are limited to the range 0 to 10 in steps of 1

▶ **3.** Save your changes to the file.

You also want to create a style rule for this input box so that the box is 70 pixels wide.

▶ **4.** Go to the **forms.css** file in your text editor and add the following style rule at the bottom of the file (see Figure 6-54):

```
/* Number input box styles */

#ordersPerMonth {
    width: 70px;
}
```

Figure 6-54 Style rule for the ordersPerMonth field

```
/* Number input box styles */

#ordersPerMonth {
    width: 70px;
}
```

sets the width of the input box to 70 pixels

▶ **5.** Save your changes to the file and refresh **survey.htm** in your Web browser. Figure 6-55 shows the appearance of the input box in the Opera browser.

Figure 6-55 Number spin box in the Opera browser

Where did you hear about us? (select all that apply)

Internet
Magazine
Newspaper
Word of Mouth
Other

How many times do you dine out per month? 1

click the spin arrows to increase and decrease the numeric value between 0 and 10

Trouble? Depending on your browser, you might not see spin arrows next to the input box.

▶ **6.** If they're displayed in your browser, click the **up** and **down spin arrows** to verify that you can increase and decrease the value in the input box by 1 unit, and that the field value is limited to the range 0 to 10.

Browsers that do not support the number data type also ignore the step, min, and max attributes, so they have no effect in those browsers and the input box is treated as just another text box.

Specifying a Numeric Range with the range Data Type

Recall that Alice also wants to give customers the ability to rate Red Ball Pizza service and food quality on a numeric scale from 0 to 10. To describe this set of numbers, you can use the range data type

```
<input name="name" type="range" value="value"
       min="value" max="value" step="value" />
```

where *name* is the name of the data field, the value attribute provides the default field value, the min attribute provides the minimum possible value, the max attribute provides the maximum value, and the step value provides the size of the steps between the minimum and maximum. For example, the following HTML5 code creates a range box for the saturation field that covers a range of values from 0 to 100 in steps of 5 with a default value of 50:

```
<input name="saturation" type="range" value="50"
       min="0" max="100" step="5" />
```

The range data type is rendered differently from the number data type. Rather than a spin box, the control object is a slider in which the data value is selected by sliding a marker horizontally across a bar. Currently, the Opera, Safari, and Chrome browsers support the range data type while the Firefox and Internet Explorer browsers do not, treating range boxes as text boxes designed for simple text input.

You'll create a range slider now for the serviceRating and qualityRating fields, which are designed to record the customer's rating of Red Ball Pizza's service and food quality.

To create the two range boxes:

▶ **1.** Return to the **survey.htm** file in your text editor.

▶ **2.** Directly above the label for the textarea element, insert the following code as shown in Figure 6-56:

```
<label>Rate the overall service<br />
       (0 = poor; 10 = great)</label>
<input name="service" id="service" type="range" value="5"
       min="0" max="10" step="1" />

<label>Rate the food quality<br />
       (0 = poor; 10 = great)</label>
<input name="quality" id="quality" type="range" value="5"
       min="0" max="10" step="1" />
```

Figure 6-56   **Adding input elements with the range data type**

```
<label>Rate the overall service<br />
       (0 = poor; 10 = great)</label>                    range data type
<input name="service" id="service" type="range" value="5"
       min="0" max="10" step="1" />

<label>Rate the food quality<br />
       (0 = poor; 10 = great)</label>
<input name="quality" id="quality" type="range" value="5"
       min="0" max="10" step="1" />

<label for="comments">Tell us more about your experience!</label>
<textarea name="comments" id="comments"></textarea>
```

quality values range from 0 to 10 in steps of 1

3. Save your changes to the file and then refresh the **survey.htm** file in your Web browser. Figure 6-57 shows the appearance of the two sliders in the Opera Web browser. Notice that the default value of 5 is represented by placing the slider marker in the exact center of the 0 to 10 range.

Figure 6-57   **Range slider in the Opera browser**

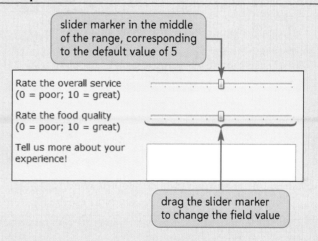

slider marker in the middle of the range, corresponding to the default value of 5

Rate the overall service
(0 = poor; 10 = great)

Rate the food quality
(0 = poor; 10 = great)

Tell us more about your experience!

drag the slider marker to change the field value

4. Drag the marker on the slider back and forth to confirm that the widget works as expected.

Trouble? If you are running Firefox or Internet Explorer, you might only see a text box with a default value of 5.

A problem with the range slider is that the minimum and maximum values represented on the slider bar are not displayed on the widget, so there is no indication of what value is actually being selected and stored in the data field. To add that information, you'll insert a label directly before and directly after the range slider to tell users that the minimum value on the slider represents a 0 and the maximum value represents a 10.

To add descriptive labels to the range slider:

1. Return to the **survey.htm** file in your text editor.

2. Directly before the `input` element for the service range slider, insert the following `label` element:

   ```
   <label class="sliderLabel">0</label>
   ```

3. Directly after the `input` element for the service range slider, insert the following `label` element:

   ```
   <label class="sliderLabel">10</label>
   ```

4. Repeat Steps 2 and 3 for the `input` element for the food quality range slider. Figure 6-58 highlights the revised code.

Figure 6-58 Adding descriptive labels to the range slider

```
<label>Rate the overall service<br />
       (0 = poor; 10 = great)</label>
<label class="sliderLabel">0</label>
<input name="service" id="service" type="range" value="5"
       min="0" max="10" step="1" />
<label class="sliderLabel">10</label>

<label>Rate the food quality<br />
       (0 = poor; 10 = great)</label>
<label class="sliderLabel">0</label>
<input name="quality" id="quality" type="range" value="5"
       min="0" max="10" step="1" />
<label class="sliderLabel">10</label>
```

Next, you have to create a style rule for these new labels so that they appear alongside the range sliders. You also have to resize the labels and the sliders to make them fit within the width of the field set.

5. Go to the **forms.css** file in your text editor. At the bottom of the file, insert the following style rules as shown in Figure 6-59. Note that you have to specifically *not* clear the label text so that it floats alongside the other objects within that line on the form.

```
/* Range slider styles */

label.sliderLabel {
   clear: none;
   font-size: 0.7em;
   margin: 10px 0px;
   text-align: center;
   width: 10px
}

input[type="range"] {
   width: 150px;
}
```

Figure 6-59   **Style rules for the range slider**

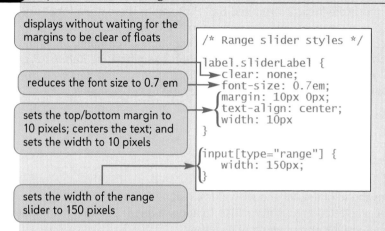

displays without waiting for the margins to be clear of floats

reduces the font size to 0.7 em

sets the top/bottom margin to 10 pixels; centers the text; and sets the width to 10 pixels

sets the width of the range slider to 150 pixels

```
/* Range slider styles */

label.sliderLabel {
    clear: none;
    font-size: 0.7em;
    margin: 10px 0px;
    text-align: center;
    width: 10px;
}

input[type="range"] {
    width: 150px;
}
```

6. Save your changes to the file and then refresh **survey.htm** in your Web browser. Figure 6-60 shows the appearance of the range slider in the Opera browser.

Figure 6-60   **Range slider in the Opera browser**

Rate the overall service   0 ⌐·······◻······· 10
(0 = poor; 10 = great)

Rate the food quality   0 ⌐·······◻······· 10
(0 = poor; 10 = great)

Exploring Form Controls with JavaScript Libraries

INSIGHT

With the current lack of cross-browser support for many of the HTML5 form elements, you should only use them if they are not essential to reading and successfully completing your Web form. On the other hand, if your form requires the use of a spin box or a range slider, you should confine yourself to HTML 4 or XHTML elements and create your own control elements from a JavaScript library.

JavaScript libraries or JavaScript frameworks enhance HTML by adding elements and controls created using the JavaScript language. Among the most popular frameworks are jQuery, MooTools, Dojo Toolkit, and Yahoo! UI Library. Each provides the tools to create enhanced form control objects such as sliders and spin boxes.

To use these tools, you have to download the JavaScript source file for the library and usually another JavaScript program that creates the control object. Most of the libraries work with the input elements already present in your Web form and will include documentation about how you should modify the markup tags to take advantage of a specific JavaScript library. If you do use a JavaScript library, be aware that your users must have JavaScript enabled to be able to use those enhanced control objects.

Suggesting Options with Data Lists

The last data field that Alice wants added to the survey form is a text box in which customers can indicate their favorite Red Ball Pizza dish. There are a lot of possible answers and Alice doesn't want to limit the options to a selection list, but she does want to provide suggestions to customers as they type their entries. For example, as the user types a *B*, Alice would like the text box to display entries such as *Big Kahuna Pizza* or *BBQ Chicken Pizza* (both of which are Red Ball Pizza specials that start with *B*).

You can create this effect using the HTML5 `datalist` element

```
<datalist id="id">
   <option value="value" />
   <option value="value" />
...
</datalist>
```

where *id* is the id of the list and the values assigned to the different `option` elements provide the suggested entries in the list. To apply a `datalist` to a text input box, add the `list` attribute to the `input` element as follows

```
<input name="name" list="id" />
```

where *id* references the id of the data list. For example, to create an input box for the `favDish` field that offers a few suggested items, you could enter the following HTML5 code:

```
<input name="favDish" list="dishes" />
<datalist id="dishes">
   <option value="Antipasto Pizza" />
   <option value="Big Kahuna Pizza" />
   <option value="BBQ Chicken Pizza" />
</datalist>
```

The options in the `dishes` data list are just suggestions. The customer is not obligated to accept any options and can type a dish of his or her own choosing. Currently, the `list` attribute and the `datalist` element are supported only by the Firefox and Opera browsers. Other browsers that encounter this code ignore both the attribute and the element, and treat the input box as just another text box.

REFERENCE

Creating and Applying a Data List

- To create a data list of possible values, enter the HTML code

```
<datalist id="id">
   <option value="value" />
   <option value="value" />
...
</datalist>
```

where the `value` attribute provides the text of the possible values in the data list.
- To reference the data list from an input control, add the `list` attribute

```
<input name="name" list="id" />
```

where *id* references the id of the data list structure.

Add an input box for the `favDish` field to the survey form now and augment it with a data list of suggested Red Ball Pizza dishes.

To create a data list:

▶ **1.** Return to the **survey.htm** file in your text editor. Directly below the input box for the `ordersPerMonth` field, insert the following code (see Figure 6-61):

```
<label for="favDish">What's your favorite Red Ball dish?</label>
<input name="favDish" id="favDish" list="dishType" />
<datalist id="dishType">
   <option value="Antipasto Pizza" />
   <option value="Big Kahuna Pizza" />
   <option value="BBQ Chicken Pizza" />
   <option value="Mediterranean Herb Pizza" />
   <option value="Pasta Rolls" />
   <option value="Pesto Artichoke Pizza" />
   <option value="Sal's Stuffed Pizza" />
   <option value="Wing'd Pizza" />
</datalist>
```

Figure 6-61	Adding a data list

accesses the dishType data list

data list of text options

```
<input name="ordersPerMonth" id="ordersPerMonth"
       type="number" value="1"
       min="0" max="10" step="1" />

<label for="favDish">What's your favorite Red Ball dish?</label>
<input name="favDish" id="favDish" list="dishType" />
<datalist id="dishType">
   <option value="Antipasto Pizza" />
   <option value="Big Kahuna Pizza" />
   <option value="BBQ Chicken Pizza" />
   <option value="Mediterranean Herb Pizza" />
   <option value="Pasta Rolls" />
   <option value="Pesto Artichoke Pizza" />
   <option value="Sal's Stuffed Pizza" />
   <option value="Wing'd Pizza" />
</datalist>
```

▶ **2.** Save your changes to the file and then reopen **survey.htm** in the Firefox or Opera Web browser.

▶ **3.** Click the input box for the `favDish` field and type the letter **p**. In Opera, the browser displays a list of two menu items that begin with the letter P (see Figure 6-62). In Firefox, the browser displays any option that contains the letter P, not just options that begin with the letter P.

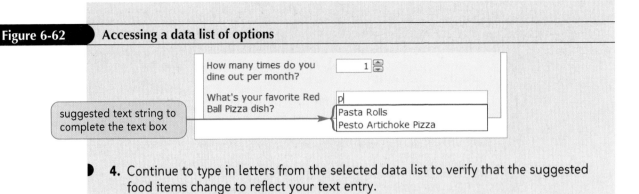

Figure 6-62 — Accessing a data list of options

suggested text string to complete the text box

How many times do you dine out per month? [1]

What's your favorite Red Ball Pizza dish? [p]
Pasta Rolls
Pesto Artichoke Pizza

▶ **4.** Continue to type in letters from the selected data list to verify that the suggested food items change to reflect your text entry.

Now that you've completed all of the fields for the survey form, you'll next examine how to submit the form for processing. To do that, you'll create a form button.

Creating Form Buttons

So far, all of your control elements have involved entering field values. Another type of control element is one that performs an action. In forms, this is usually done with **form buttons**, each of which performs one of three actions:

• Run a command from a program linked to the Web page.
• Submit the form to the program running on the server.
• Reset the form to its starting values.

The first type of button you'll examine is the command button.

Creating a Command Button

A **command button** runs a command that affects the contents of the Web page or the Web browser itself. Command buttons are created by applying the `button` attribute to the `input` element

```
<input type="button" value="text" />
```

where *text* is the text that appears on the button. To associate an action with a command button, you link the button to a program that runs when the command button is clicked using the `onclick` attribute, as follows

```
<input type="button" value="text" onclick="program" />
```

where *program* is the name of the program. In most cases, the program is stored in a JavaScript file that is linked to the Web page. For example, the `input` element

```
<input type="button" value="Run Program" onclick="setup()" />
```

creates a command button that runs the JavaScript program `setup()` when the button is clicked. You won't be applying command buttons to the survey page.

Creating Submit and Reset Buttons

The two other kinds of form buttons are submit and reset buttons. A **submit button** submits a form to the server for processing when clicked. Clicking a **reset button** resets the form, changing all field values to their original default values and deleting any values that a user might have entered into the form. The syntax for creating these two buttons is

```
<input type="submit" value="text" />
<input type="reset" value="text" />
```

where once again the value attribute defines the text that appears on the button.

REFERENCE

Creating Form Buttons

- To create a form button to run a command, use the element

  ```
  <input type="button" value="text" onclick="program" />
  ```

  where *text* is the text that appears on the button and *program* is the program that is run in response to the user clicking the button.
- To create a form button to submit the form and its fields and values to a script, use the following element:

  ```
  <input type="submit" value="text" />
  ```

- To create a form button to reset the form to its default values and appearance, use the following element:

  ```
  <input type="reset" value="text" />
  ```

Alice wants the survey form to include both a submit button and a reset button. The submit button, which she wants labeled *Submit My Survey*, will send the form data to the server for processing when clicked. The reset button, which she wants labeled *Cancel*, will erase the user's input and reset the fields to their default values.

To add the submit and reset buttons to the survey form:

1. Return to the **survey.htm** file in your text editor.

2. Scroll to the bottom of the file. Directly above the closing </form> tag, insert the following code (see Figure 6-63):

```
<p>
    <input type="submit" value="Submit My Survey" />
    <input type="reset" value="Cancel" />
</p>
```

Figure 6-63   **Creating submit and reset buttons**

submit button type

reset button type

```
<p>
    <input type="submit" value="Submit My Survey" />
    <input type="reset" value="Cancel" />
</p>
</form>
```

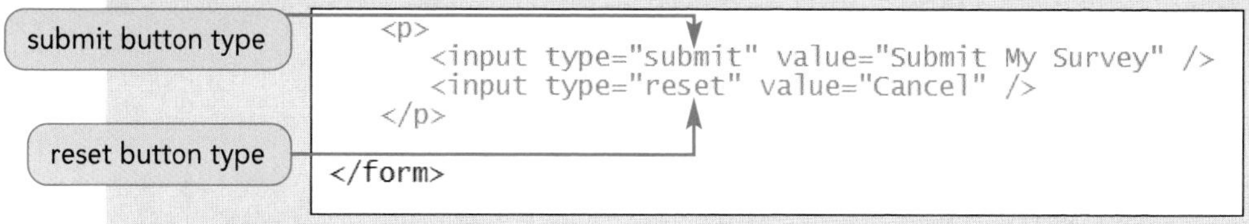

3. Save your changes to the file.

   Next, you'll create style rules so that the submit and reset buttons appear centered below the rest of the form content.

4. Go to the **forms.css** file in your text editor. At the bottom of the file, insert the following code, as shown in Figure 6-64:

```
/* Button styles */

form p {
    text-align: center;
}

input[type="submit"], input[type="reset"] {
    display: inline;
    float: none;
    height: 40px;
    width: 200px;
}
```

Figure 6-64 **Style rules for the submit and reset buttons**

centers the paragraph containing the two form buttons

displays the buttons inline rather than as blocks

displays the buttons without floating

sets the button height to 40 pixels

sets the button width to 200 pixels

```
/* Button styles */

form p {
    text-align: center;
}

input[type="submit"], input[type="reset"] {
    display: inline;
    float: none;
    height: 40px;
    width: 200px;
}
```

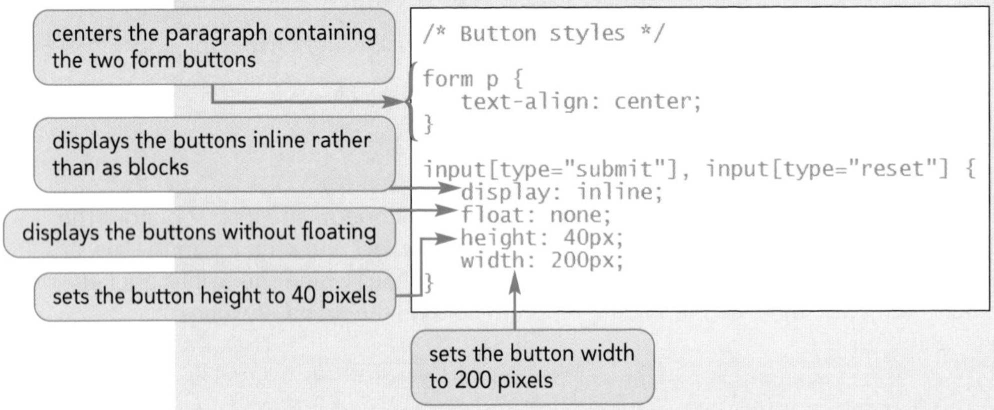

5. Save your changes to the file and then refresh the **survey.htm** file in your Web browser. Figure 6-65 shows the completed Web page with all of the form elements and controls.

Figure 6-65	Final layout of the survey page as displayed by Opera

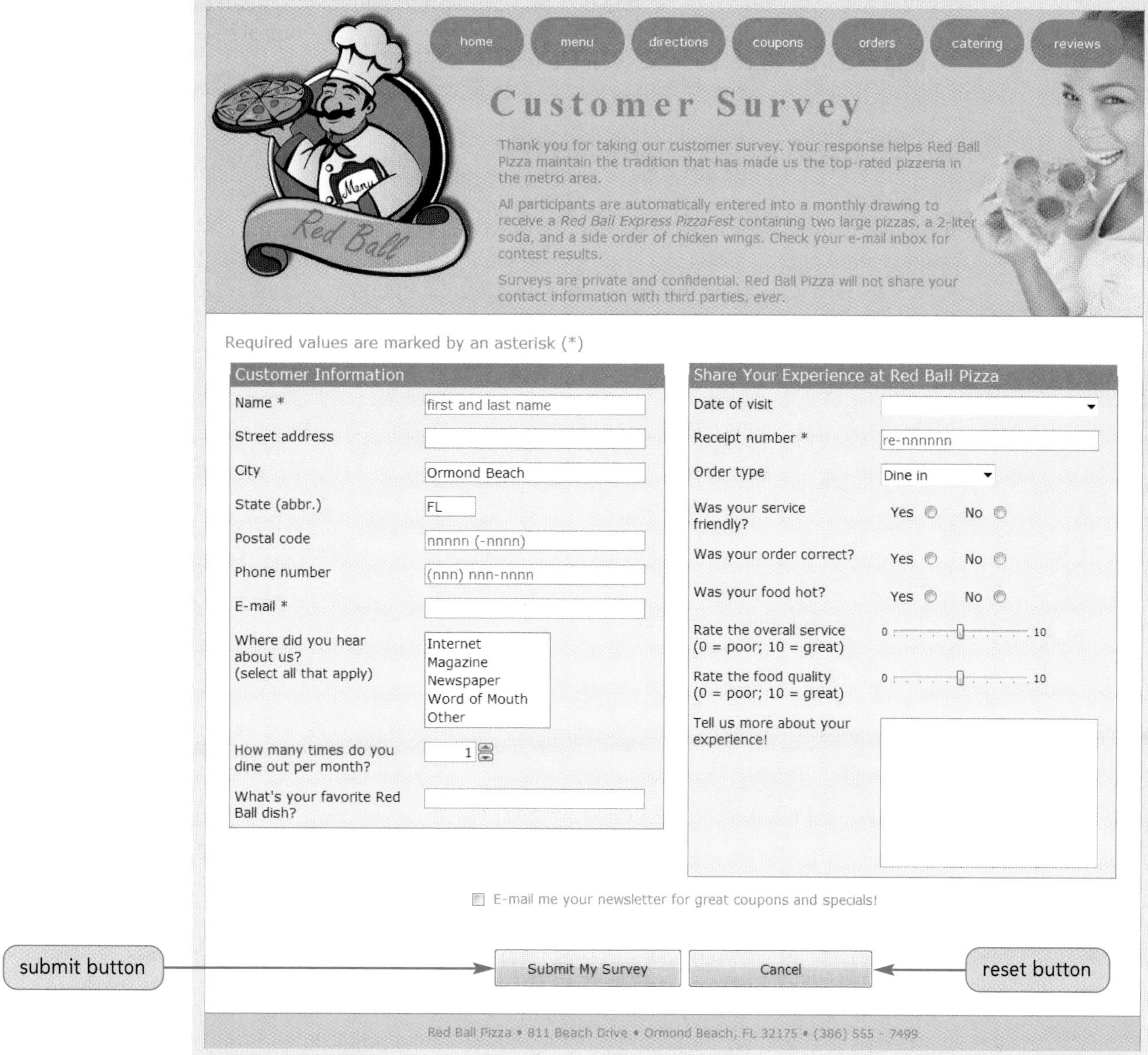

Timea/Shutterstock.com
Ariwasabi/Shutterstock.com

▶ **6.** Enter some sample data into the form and then click the **Cancel** button to test the actions of your reset button. Verify that the form is reset to its initial state and default values. You'll test the actions of the submit button shortly.

Designing a Custom Button

The text of a command, submit, or reset button is determined by the `value` attribute. You are only allowed to specify the text displayed on the button; you can't add other elements such as an inline image to the button value. For more control over a button's appearance, you can use the `button` element as follows

```
<button type="text">
   content
</button>
```

where the `type` attribute specifies the button type (`submit`, `reset`, or `button`—for creating a command button) and *content* is page elements displayed within the button. The page content can include formatted text, inline images, and other design elements supported by HTML. Figure 6-66 shows an example of a button that contains both formatted text and an inline image.

Figure 6-66   **Creating a custom button**

HTML code

```
<button type="button">

   <img src="home.png" />
   Return to the <br /> Home Page

</button>
```

custom button

You will not need a custom button in the survey form.

Validating a Web Form

The final part of your work on the survey form is to test your ability to submit values from the form. Data values often need to be tested or **validated** before they can be used. Validation can occur after the data is sent to the server with **server-side validation**, and it also can be tested on a user's own computer via **client-side validation** before sending it to the server. Whenever possible, you should supplement your server-side validation with client-side validation to reduce the workload on the server. For example, in a payment form, you'll want to verify that a user has entered a valid credit card number and completed all of the fields required for payment before submitting the data to the server. Sending an invalid payment to the server slows down the process and puts an extra burden on a server that may be dealing with hundreds or thousands of transactions every hour.

HTML5 includes several attributes that can be used to perform client-side validation. At the time of this writing, Opera, Firefox, and Google Chrome support client-side validation under HTML5; Internet Explorer and Safari do not. Once again, if client-side validation is an essential part of your Web site design, use a JavaScript library like jQuery or a program of your own creation to perform the validation on the user's computer. However, you also can supplement these programs with HTML5's built-in validation attributes.

The first HTML5 attribute you'll examine can be used to ensure that the user completes all required fields.

Indicating Required Values

In the survey form, Alice has indicated that the `custname`, `email`, and `receipt` fields all must be completed for the survey to be valid. If any of those fields are left blank, she wants the browser to notify the user of the missing data and cancel the submission. You can indicate that a field is required by adding the following `required` attribute to the control element:

```
required="required"
```

If a required field is left blank and the submit button is clicked, the browser will cancel the submission and display an error message.

REFERENCE

Validating Field Values

- To indicate that a field is required, add the `required="required"` attribute to the control element.
- To validate an e-mail address, set the data type to `email`. To validate a Web address, set the data type to `url`.
- To validate that a text input box follows a character pattern, add the attribute

  ```
  pattern="regex"
  ```

  where *regex* is a regular expression that defines the character pattern.

To see how validation works with HTML5, add the `required` attribute to the `custname`, `email`, and `receipt` fields.

To apply and test the `required` attribute:

1. Return to the **survey.htm** file in your text editor.

2. Add the attribute `required="required"` to the `input` element for the `custname` field at the top of the form.

3. Scroll down to the `input` element for the `email` field and then add the attribute `required="required"`.

4. Go to the `receipt` field and then add the attribute `required="required"` to the `input` element. Figure 6-67 highlights the newly added code.

Figure 6-67 Marking required fields

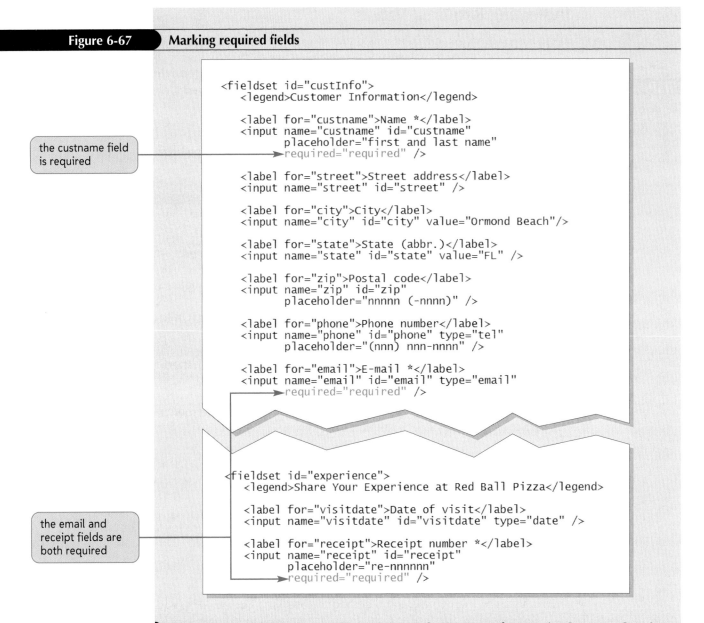

the custname field is required

the email and receipt fields are both required

```
<fieldset id="custInfo">
   <legend>Customer Information</legend>

   <label for="custname">Name *</label>
   <input name="custname" id="custname"
          placeholder="first and last name"
          required="required" />

   <label for="street">Street address</label>
   <input name="street" id="street" />

   <label for="city">City</label>
   <input name="city" id="city" value="Ormond Beach"/>

   <label for="state">State (abbr.)</label>
   <input name="state" id="state" value="FL" />

   <label for="zip">Postal code</label>
   <input name="zip" id="zip"
          placeholder="nnnnn (-nnnn)" />

   <label for="phone">Phone number</label>
   <input name="phone" id="phone" type="tel"
          placeholder="(nnn) nnn-nnnn" />

   <label for="email">E-mail *</label>
   <input name="email" id="email" type="email"
          required="required" />
```

```
<fieldset id="experience">
   <legend>Share Your Experience at Red Ball Pizza</legend>

   <label for="visitdate">Date of visit</label>
   <input name="visitdate" id="visitdate" type="date" />

   <label for="receipt">Receipt number *</label>
   <input name="receipt" id="receipt"
          placeholder="re-nnnnnn"
          required="required" />
```

▶ **5.** Save your changes to the file and then refresh **survey.htm** in the Opera or Google Chrome browser.

▶ **6.** Leaving the form blank, click the **Submit My Survey** button. As shown in Figure 6-68, in the Google Chrome browser for Windows, the browser does not submit the form but displays an error message for the first invalid field it encounters.

Figure 6-68	Data validation error message in Google Chrome

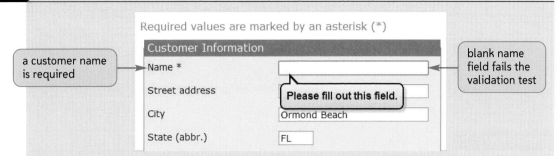

Trouble? If you are running Internet Explorer or Safari, you might not see an error message.

▶ **7.** Enter **Alice Nichols** in the Name box and then click the **Submit My Survey** button again. Verify that the browser displays an error message next to the blank input box for the `email` field.

▶ **8.** Enter **alice.nichols@redballpizza.com** in the E-mail box and submit the form again. Verify that an error message now appears next to the input box for the `receipt` field.

▶ **9.** Enter **re-123456** in the Receipt number box and submit the form one last time. Verify that no error messages are displayed by the browser, and that the browser displays a dialog box with the message *No invalid data detected. Will retain data for further testing.*

The dialog box you encountered in Step 9 is not part of HTML5 or your Web browser; it comes from the *formsubmit.js* JavaScript file you linked to back in the first session. The message appears only once you've passed all of the HTML5 validation checks.

▶ **10.** Click the **OK** button to close the dialog box and return to the Web page.

Note that all of your data values have been preserved in the survey form. This is also a feature of the *formsubmit.js* JavaScript file to avoid re-typing field values as you continue to test the Web page.

Validating Based on Data Type

The new data types supported by HTML5 also can be used for data validation. For example, a data field with the `number` data type will be rejected if non-numeric data is entered. Similarly, fields marked using the `email` and `url` fields will be rejected if a user provides an invalid e-mail address or Web site URL.

E-mail addresses must be entered in the form *username@domain*. Verify that your browser rejects an invalid e-mail address by attempting to enter erroneous data in the `email` field.

To test the `email` field:

▶ **1.** Click the input box for the `email` field and change the text of the e-mail address to **Alice Nichols**.

▶ **2.** Click the **Submit My Survey** button.

▶ **3.** The browser rejects your text entry because it does not match the pattern of an e-mail message. Figure 6-69 shows the appearance of the error message in the Firefox browser.

Figure 6-69	Entering an invalid e-mail address

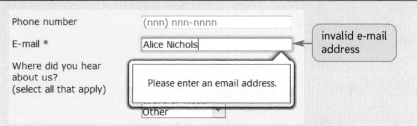

▶ **4.** Change the text of the input box back to **alice.nichols@redballpizza.com** and re-submit the form. Verify that no validation errors are reported.

A browser that supports the `date` data type also rejects invalid dates if they are not in the form *yyyy-mm-dd*. However, a browser that supports the `date` data type also provides a calendar widget to allow for the easy submission of valid dates. Currently, only the Google Chrome and Opera browsers provide validation checks on date values.

Testing for a Valid Pattern

Several fields in the survey form are required to follow a specified pattern of characters. For example, the receipt numbers from Red Ball Pizza all follow the pattern `re-nnnnnn` where *n* is a single digit. Thus, a receipt labeled re-123456 would be considered valid, but receipt numbers such as 123456 or re-1234 would not. Other field values are limited to a set of possible character patterns. A U.S. phone number might be entered as (386) 555 - 7499, or 555-7499, or 3865557499. United States postal codes can be entered as 32175, or in the nine-digit format as 32175-6316. However, a phone number would not be valid without at least seven numbers, and a postal code would not be valid if it were written with other than five or nine numbers.

To test whether a field value follows a valid pattern of characters, you can test the character string against a regular expression. A **regular expression** or **regex** is a concise description of a character pattern. It is beyond the scope of this tutorial to discuss the syntax of regular expressions; but to validate a text value against a regular expression, add the attribute

```
pattern="regex"
```

to the control element, where `regex` is the regular expression pattern. For example, the following code tests the value of the `receipt` field against the regular expression `^re\-\d{6}$`:

```
<input name="receipt" pattern="^re\-\d{6}$" />
```

This regular expression will cause browsers to reject any value for the `receipt` field that is not exactly in the form `re-nnnnnn`, where *n* is a single digit.

Alice has obtained some regular expressions for phone numbers, postal codes, and
Red Ball Pizza receipt numbers. You'll add these regular expression patterns to the
phone, zip, and receipt fields, and then test them in your browser. Note that some of
the regular expressions are long and complicated, and you must type them exactly as
written. If you make a mistake, you can copy the text of the regular expressions from the
regex.txt file in the tutorial.06/tutorial folder.

To apply and test regular expression patterns:

1. Return to the **survey.htm** file in your text editor.

2. Within the input element for the zip field, insert the following regular expression
   pattern that tests for the presence of a five- or nine-digit postal code:

   `pattern="^\d{5}(\-\d{4})?$"`

3. Go to the input element for the phone field. Change the data type from
   type="tel" to **type="text"** and add the following attribute that tests for a valid
   phone number pattern:

   `pattern="^\d{10}$|^(\(\d{3}\)\s*)?\d{3}[\s-]?\d{4}$"`

4. Scroll down to the input element for the receipt field and insert the following
   attribute that tests for a valid receipt number:

   `pattern="^re\-\d{6}$"`

   Figure 6-70 highlights the revised text in the file.

Figure 6-70   Specifying character patterns with regular expressions

regular expression
for a five- or
nine-digit postal code

regular expression
for a phone number

regular expression
for a Red Ball Pizza
receipt number

5. Save your changes to the file and then refresh **survey.htm** in your Web browser.
   Enter some text in the Name input box.

6. Type **321** in the input box for the postal code and then submit the form. As shown
   in Figure 6-71, the browser rejects the field value because it does not match the
   pattern of either a five-digit or a nine-digit postal code.

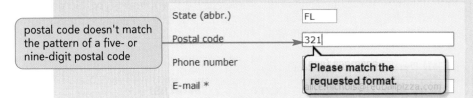

Figure 6-71 **Entering an invalid postal code**

Trouble? If your browser does not reject the invalid postal code, it might not support character pattern validation. Currently, only some versions of the Firefox, Opera, and Google Chrome browsers support validation of character patterns.

7. Change the value of the `zip` field to **32175** and then resubmit the form. Verify that the form is submitted without error.

8. Try entering values for the `phone` and `receipt` fields that do not match the character patterns for phone numbers or receipt numbers, verifying that the form is rejected when invalid values are entered.

9. Enter **(386) 555-7499** for the phone field and **re-123456** for the receipt field and submit the form.

You also can use HTML to define the maximum number of characters in a field using the `maxlength` attribute

```
<input name="name" maxlength="value" />
```

where `length` is the maximum number of characters. This is not an HTML5 attribute and thus *is* supported by all browsers. For example, to limit the value of the `zip` field to five characters only, you'd enter the following HTML code:

```
<input name="zip" maxlength="5" />
```

Note that the `maxlength` attribute does not define what type of characters can be entered into the `zip` field. A user could enter the text string *abcde* as easily as *32175*.

Applying Inline Validation

One disadvantage with the current validation checks is that they all occur *after* a user has completed and submitted the form. It is extremely annoying for a user to go back to an already completed form to fix an error. Studies have shown that users are less likely to make errors and can complete a form faster if they are informed of data entry errors as they occur. The technique of immediate data validation and reporting of errors is known as **inline validation**.

Using the `focus` Pseudo-Class

One way of integrating inline validation into a Web form is to create style rules that change the appearance of each control element based on the validity of the data it contains. This can be done using some of the CSS3 pseudo-classes described in Figure 6-72.

Figure 6-72	Pseudo-classes for Web form controls

Pseudo-Class	Matches
checked	Check boxes or options that are checked
default	The default user control element
disabled	Control elements that are disabled
enabled	Control elements that are enabled
focus	Control elements that have the focus (are actively selected) in the form
indeterminate	Check boxes or option buttons whose toggle states (checked or unchecked) cannot be determined
in-range	Control elements whose values are within each field's range of values (between the min and max attribute values)
invalid	Control elements whose values fail validation tests
optional	Control elements that are optional (not required) in the Web form
out-of-range	Control elements whose values are outside each field's range of values (outside of the min and max attribute values)
required	Control elements that are required in the Web form
valid	Control elements whose values pass validation tests

For example, to create styles for all of the option buttons in a form that are checked, you could apply the checked pseudo-class, as in the style rule

```
input[type="radio"]:checked {
    styles
}
```

where *styles* is the CSS styles applied to checked option buttons.

The first pseudo-class you'll apply to the survey form will be used to change the background color of any element that has the focus. **Focus** refers to the state in which an element has been clicked by the user, making it the active control element on the form. You may have noticed that some browsers highlight or add a glowing border around control elements that have the focus. Alice would like the control elements that have the focus to be displayed with a light green background color.

To apply the focus pseudo-class:

▶ **1.** Return to the **forms.css** file in your text editor.

▶ **2.** At the bottom of the file, insert the following style rule, as displayed in Figure 6-73:

```
/* Validation styles */

input:focus, select:focus, textarea:focus {
    background-color: rgb(220, 255, 220);
}
```

Figure 6-73 | **Style rule for elements that have the focus**

selector for input, select, and textarea elements that have the focus

```
/* Validation styles */
input:focus, select:focus, textarea:focus {
    background-color: rgb(220, 255, 220);
}
```

changes the background color to light green

▶ **3.** Save your changes to the file and then refresh **survey.htm** in your Web browser.

▶ **4.** Click the input box for the street field and verify that the background color changes to a light green as the input box receives the focus (see Figure 6-74).

Figure 6-74 | **Changed background color for element that has the focus**

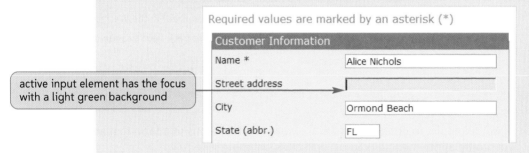

active input element has the focus with a light green background

Note that the focus pseudo-class is supported by all current browsers, so you can feel confident in adding it to your Web forms.

Pseudo-Classes for Valid and Invalid Data

The valid and invalid pseudo-classes can be used to create styles for control elements based on whether the field value associated with a control is valid or invalid. For example, the style rule

```
input:invalid {
    background-color: rgb(255, 220, 220);
}
```

displays all input elements for invalid data with a light red background, while the style rule

```
input:valid {
    background-color: rgb(220, 255, 220);
}
```

displays all input elements for valid data with a light green background. Both of these style rules set the background color whether the input element has the focus or not. Displaying a multitude of input boxes with different background colors can be confusing and distracting to the user, however. To set the background color only when a field is valid or invalid and the input box has the focus, you combine the two pseudo-classes as follows:

```
input:focus:invalid {
    background-color: rgb(255, 220, 220);
}
```

Alice wants you to display all invalid data with a light red background when the input element has the focus. In addition, she wants you to add an image of a red x to the input box background. For valid data, she wants the input box to be displayed with a light green background along with a green check mark image.

To set styles for the valid and invalid data:

1. Return to the **forms.css** file in your text editor. At the bottom of the file, add the following style rule for input boxes containing valid data:

```
input:focus:valid {
    background: rgb(220, 255, 220) url(go.png) bottom right
no-repeat;

    -o-background-size: contain;
    -moz-background-size: contain;
    -webkit-background-size: contain;
    background-size: contain;
}
```

2. Add the following style rule for invalid data:

```
input:focus:invalid {
    background: rgb(255, 232, 233) url(stop.png) bottom right
no-repeat;

    -o-background-size: contain;
    -moz-background-size: contain;
    -webkit-background-size: contain;
    background-size: contain;
}
```

Figure 6-75 displays the content of the new style rules.

Figure 6-75   Style rules for valid and invalid field values

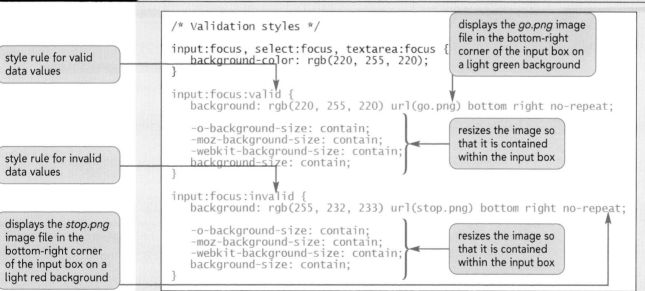

style rule for valid data values

displays the go.png image file in the bottom-right corner of the input box on a light green background

resizes the image so that it is contained within the input box

style rule for invalid data values

displays the stop.png image file in the bottom-right corner of the input box on a light red background

resizes the image so that it is contained within the input box

3. Save your changes to the file and then refresh **survey.htm** in your Web browser.

4. Test the inline validation by typing the postal code value **32175-6136** into the `zip` field. Note that the background of the input box provides immediate visual feedback on whether the data value you enter is currently valid or invalid (see Figure 6-76).

Figure 6-76 Inline validation on the postal code

initial text does not match a valid postal code	Postal code	321 ⊗
five-digit postal code is valid	Postal code	32175 ✓
as the user continues to type, the postal code becomes invalid again	Postal code	32175-61 ⊗
final nine-digit postal code is valid	Postal code	32175-6136 ✓

▶ **5.** Continue to enter different values into the different input boxes and verify the effectiveness of the inline validation tools in providing immediate feedback on the validity of your data.

Trouble? If you're using Internet Explorer or Safari, you might not see a change in the background of the different input boxes as you enter the field values. If you are using Opera, the background image will change but the background color will not.

You've finished the initial work on the survey form. Alice has placed a copy of your files in a folder on the company's Web server, and from there the Web form can continue to be tested to verify that the CGI script and the form work properly together. Alice is pleased with your work on this project and will come back to you for future Web page development for Red Ball Pizza.

Session 6.3 Quick Check

REVIEW

1. Provide the code to create an input box for a field named `homepage` that is used for storing Web site addresses.
2. Provide the code to create a spinner control for the `withdrawal` field that ranges from 20 to 200 in increments of 20 units.
3. Provide the code to create a range slider for the `red` field that ranges from 0 to 255 in increments of 5 units.
4. Provide the code to create an input box named `state` that has the suggested options *Alabama*, *Alaska*, *Arizona*, *Arkansas*, *California*, and *Colorado* from a data list with the id `statelist`.
5. Create a submit button with the text *Send Donation*.
6. Provide the code to create a text input box for the `socSecNum` field and make the field required.
7. The `userAccount` field must follow the regular expression pattern `^\user\-d{4}$`. Provide the code for a text input box that can be validated for this field.
8. Provide a style rule to display all `textarea` elements with the background color `rgb(220, 220, 255)` when they have the focus.

Practice the skills you learned in the tutorial using the same case scenario.

Review Assignments

Data Files needed for the Review Assignments: delivery.png, formsubmit.js, full.png, left.png, modernizr-1.5.js, none.png, okay.png, ordertxt.htm, pizzatxt.css, redball.css, redball.png, regex.txt, right.png, sizes.png, warning.png

Alice wants you to start working on an order form for customers who want to place their orders online using the Red Ball Pizza Web site. She suggests that you create a prototype page in which customers can enter their contact information for delivery and provide the ingredients for the pizza they want Red Ball Pizza to make for them. Alice wants you to validate the Web form as much as possible before it is sent to the Web server. She has created the file *regex.txt*, which contains regular expression patterns for validating the customer's phone number and preferred time of delivery.

A preview of the form you'll create is shown in Figure 6-77 as it appears in the Opera browser.

Figure 6-77	Build Your Own Pizza form

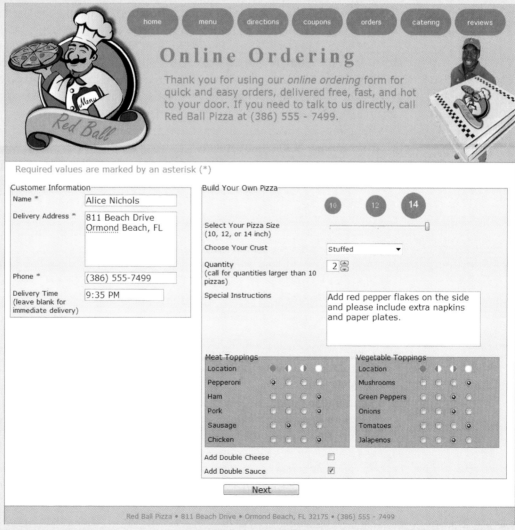

Timea/Shutterstock.com
Stephen Coburn/Shutterstock.com

Complete the following:

1. Use your text editor to open the **ordertxt.htm** and **pizzatxt.css** files from the tutorial.06\review folder included with your Data Files. Enter *your name* and *the date* within the comment section of each file, and then save them as **order.htm** and **pizza.css**, respectively.

2. Go to the **order.htm** file in your text editor. Link the file to the **pizza.css** style sheet file.

3. Directly below the paragraph in the `section` element, insert a `form` element with the name and id `pizza` that has the action *http://www.redballpizza.com/cgi-bin/ buildpizza* and uses the `post` method.

4. Create two field sets with the ids `custInfo` and `buildPizza`, and with the legend text **Customer Information** and **Build Your Own Pizza**, respectively.

5. Within the `custInfo` field set, create a label with the text **Name *** along with a text input box for the `custname` field. Add the placeholder text **First and Last Name** and make the field required.

6. Create a text area box for the `address` field along with the label **Delivery Address ***. Make the `address` field required.

7. Create a label containing the text **Phone *** and text input box for the `phone` field. Add the placeholder text **(nnn) nnn-nnnn** and make the field required. The text of the input box should follow the regular expression pattern `^\d{10}$|^(\(\d{3}\)\s*)?\d{3}[\s-]?\d{4}$`.

8. Create a text input box for the `delTime` field with the label text **Delivery Time (leave blank for immediate delivery)**, with the parenthetical text placed on a new line. Add the placeholder text **hh:mm AM/PM** and specify the regular expression pattern `^([0-9]|1[012]):[0-5][0-9]\s?((a|p)m|(A|P)M)$`.

9. Within the `buildPizza` field set, add the *sizes.png* file as an inline image. Add the id `sizeimage` to the inline image.

10. Create a range slider for the `size` field along with the label text **Select Your Pizza Size (10, 12, or 14 inch)**, placing the parenthetical text on a new line. Set the default value to 12, the minimum value to 10, the maximum to 14, and the step value to 2.

11. Create a selection list for the `crust` field along with the label text **Choose Your Crust**. The selection list should display the option text **Thin**, **Thick**, **Stuffed**, and **Pan** with option values equal to the option text.

12. Create a number spinner for the `quantity` field with the label text **Quantity (call for quantities larger than 10 pizzas)**, with the parenthetical text on a new line. The field has a default value of 1 and ranges from 1 to 10 increments of 1 unit.

13. Create a text area for the `instructions` field with the label text **Special Instructions**.

14. Within the `buildPizza` field set, create two field sets with the ids `meat` and `vegetables`, and with the legend text **Meat Toppings** and **Vegetable Toppings**, respectively.

15. Within the `meat` field set, add a label with the text **Location** followed by four inline images for the *full.png*, *left.png*, *right.png*, and *none.png* files with the alternate text **full**, **left**, **right**, and **none**, respectively.

16. Create a group of four option buttons for the `pepperoni` field with the field values **full**, **left**, **right**, and **none**, respectively. Make the *none* option checked by default. Nest the four option buttons within a `fieldset` element belonging to the *optionGroup* class.

17. Repeat the previous step for the remaining meat toppings, Ham, Pork, Sausage, and Chicken, naming the fields `ham`, `pork`, `sausage`, and `chicken`, respectively.

18. Repeat Steps 15 through 17 for the vegetable toppings within the `vegetables` field set, creating option groups for Mushrooms, Green Peppers, Onions, Tomatoes, and Jalapenos, and naming the fields `mushrooms`, `green peppers`, `onions`, `tomatoes`, and `jalapenos`, respectively.

19. Directly after the `vegetables` field set, create a check box for the `doubleCheese` field with the label text **Add Double Cheese**. Create another check box for the `doubleSauce` field with the label text **Add Double Sauce**.

20. Directly after the `buildPizza` field set, create a submit button with the button text **Next**.

21. Save your changes to the file, and then go to the **pizza.css** file in your text editor and create the styles described in the following steps.

22. Display all field sets with a background color value of (255, 246, 205) and with a solid 1-pixel border with the color value (233, 69, 0). Float the field sets on the left with a 1% margin. Set the width of the `custInfo` field set to 35%, the width of the `buildPizza` field set to 60%, and the widths of the `meat` and `vegetables` field sets to 47% each. Set the background color of the `meat` and `vegetables` field sets to the (237, 178, 74) color value.

23. Set the font size of the field set legends to 0.9 em.

24. Display all labels as blocks with a font size of 0.8 em. Float the labels on the left only when the left margin is clear. Set the label width to 40% of the containing element. Set the top and bottom margins to 5 pixels and set the size of the left padding space to 5 pixels.

25. Display all `input` elements and `textarea` elements as blocks floated on the left. Set the width to 50% with top and bottom margins of 5 pixels. Set the height of the `textarea` elements to 100 pixels.

26. Display all inline images nested within a form as blocks floated on the left with top and bottom margins of 5 pixels.

27. Set the width of the `delTime` input box to 150 pixels.

28. Set the left margin of the `sizeimage` inline image to 40%. Set the width of the `size` field range slider to 200 pixels. Make the background of the `size` field range slider transparent.

29. Float the selection list for the `crust` field on the left with a font size of 0.8 em. Set the top and bottom margins to 5 pixels and the width to 150 pixels.

30. Set the width of the spinner control for the `quantity` field to 40 pixels.

31. Set the width of `fieldset` elements that belong to the *optionGroup* class to 50%. Remove the border from the field set and make the background transparent.

32. Set the width of radio buttons to 30 pixels and the width of check boxes to 20 pixels.

33. Set the width of the submit button to 150 pixels, set the `float` property to `none`, and set the top and bottom margins to 0 pixels and the left and right margins to `auto`.

34. If an `input` element, `select` element, or `textarea` element receives the focus, set the background color to the value (220, 255, 220).

35. If an `input` element receives the focus and is valid, set the background color to the value (220, 255, 220) displaying the background image *okay.png* at the bottom-right corner with no tiling. Size the background image so that it's contained within the input box.

36. Repeat Step 35 for `input` elements that receive the focus and are invalid, setting the background color to the value (255, 232, 233) and the background image to the file *warning.png*.

37. Save your changes to the file and then load the **order.htm** file in your Web browser, preferably a browser that has good support for HTML5 forms such as Opera or Google Chrome. Test the form by confirming that it shows warnings for all invalid data values and for required fields that have no values.

38. Submit your completed files to your instructor, in either printed or electronic form, as requested.

Apply your
knowledge of
Web forms and
CSS to create
a comments
form for a sports
blogging page.

APPLY

Case Problem 1

Data Files needed for this Case Problem: blog.css, commtxt.css, formsubmit.js, go.png, modernizr-1.5.js, sblogo.jpg, sblogtxt.htm, stop.png

Sblogger   Sports enthusiast Steve Lavent is working on a Web site called *Sblogger* that will contain articles and commentary on the world of sports. He's asked for your help in designing the page on which users can submit their own comments on the articles that Steve posts to his blog. Your job will be to create a prototype for the commentary form, and to include HTML code and CSS styles to help validate user input. A preview of the Web form you'll create is shown in Figure 6-78.

Figure 6-78	Sblogger comments form

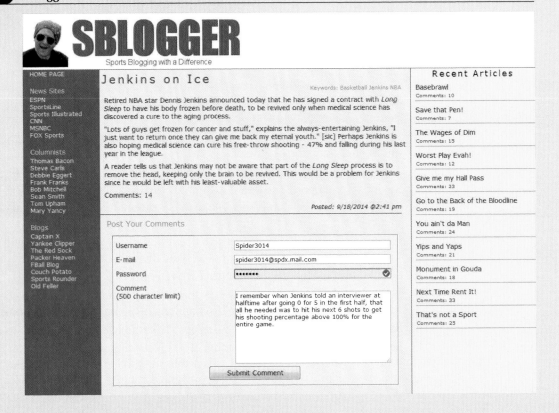

Complete the following:

1. In your text editor, open the **sblogtxt.htm** and **commtxt.css** files from the tutorial.06\case1 folder included with your Data Files. Enter *your name* and *the date* in the comment section of the file. Save the files as **sblogger.htm** and **comments.css**, respectively.

2. Go to the **sblogger.htm** file in your text editor and review the contents and structure of the document. Link the file to the **comments.css** style sheet.

3. Scroll down to the h2 heading title *Post Your Comments*, and directly below this heading insert a `form` element with the action *www.sblogger/cgi-bin/subcomments* using the `post` method.

4. Within the `form` element, create a field set with the name and id `commentFS`.

5. Create a `label` element with the text **Username**. Within the `label` element, insert an input box for the `username` field. Make the field required and add the title **Supply your username**.

6. Create a `label` element with the text **E-mail**. Within the `label` element, insert an input box for the `email` field. Set the data type to `email` and make the field required. Add the title **Supply a valid e-mail address**.

7. Create a `label` element with the text **Password** containing an input box for the `password` field. Set the data type to `password` and make the field required. Add the title **You must provide your password**.

⊕ **EXPLORE**

8. Create a `label` element with the text **Comment (500 character limit)**, placing the parenthetical text on a new line, and within the `label` element insert a text area box for the `commentBox` field. Limit the number of characters that can be typed into the text area box to 500 characters.

9. Add a submit button with the text **Submit Comment**.

10. Save your changes to the file and then go to the **comments.css** file in your text editor. Create style rules for the styles described in the following steps.

11. Display the field set with a background color of (245, 245, 255). Set the top and bottom margins to 15 pixels and the left and right margins to `auto`. Add 5 pixels of padding and set the width of the field set to 90%.

12. Display labels as blocks floated on the left once the left margin is clear of elements. Set the font size to 0.9 em and the width to 100%. Set the top and bottom margins to 5 pixels.

13. Display input boxes and text area boxes as blocks floated on the right margin. Set the font size to 0.9 em and the width to 55%. Set the left and right margins to 10 pixels. In addition, set the height of text area boxes to 150 pixels.

14. Display the submit button as a block once both margins are clear. Do not float the submit button. Set the dimensions of the button to 200 pixels wide by 30 pixels high. Set the top and bottom margins to 5 pixels, and the left and right margins to `auto`.

15. When input boxes and text area boxes receive the focus, change the background color to the value (225, 225, 240).

16. When input boxes receive the focus and are valid, change the background color to (225, 240, 225) and display the background image *go.png* in the bottom-right corner of the box with no tiling. Resize the background image so that it is contained within the input box.

17. When input boxes receive the focus and are invalid, change the background color to (240, 225, 225) and display the background image *stop.png* in the bottom-right corner of the box with no tiling. Resize the background image so that it's contained within the input box.

18. Close the style sheet file, saving your changes.

19. Open **sblogger.htm** in your Web browser and test the form. Verify that you cannot leave the `username`, `email`, and `password` fields blank and still submit the form. Also verify that the form is rejected if an invalid e-mail address is submitted in the `email` field.

⊕ **EXPLORE**

20. If you have access to the Google Chrome browser, test the Web page in that browser and verify that the title text you entered for the input boxes in Steps 5 through 7 is included in the error box supplied by the browser when those input boxes fail the validation test.

21. Submit your completed files to your instructor, in either printed or electronic form, as requested.

Apply your knowledge of Web forms and CSS to create a payment form for a salt and spice online grocery store.

APPLY

Case Problem 2

Data Files needed for this Case Problem: diners.png, discover.png, formsubmit.js, go.png, master.png, modernizr-1.5.js, paytxt.css, regex.txt, sb.css, sbback.png, sblogo.png, spicetxt.htm, state.txt, stop.png, visa.png

The Spice Bowl Rita Sato is the manager of the Web development team for The Spice Bowl, a new online grocery store specializing in gourmet spices. She's asked you to work on the Web forms for the site. The first form you'll create is a payment form in which customers enter their billing address and credit card data. She wants you to include validation tests for customers' postal codes, phone numbers, e-mail addresses, and credit card numbers. A preview of the form you'll create is shown in Figure 6-79.

Figure 6-79	The Spice Bowl payment form

Complete the following:

1. In your text editor, open the **spicetxt.htm** and **paytxt.css** files from the tutorial.06\case2 folder included with your Data Files. Enter ***your name*** and ***the date*** in the comment section of each file. Save the files as **spice.htm** and **payment.css**, respectively.

2. Go to the **spice.htm** file in your text editor and review the contents and structure of the document. Link the file to the **payment.css** style sheet.

3. Scroll down to the `h1` heading *Payment Form*, and below it insert a `form` element with the action *http://www.thespicebowlcorp.com/cgi-bin/payment* using the `post` method.

4. Within the form, create three field sets with the ids `billing`, `creditcard`, and `info`, and with the legend text **Billing Information (required)**, **Credit Card (required)**, and **Additional Information**, respectively.

5. Within the `billing` field set, create input boxes for the customer's first name, last name, street address, second line of the street address, and city with the field names `fName`, `lName`, `street`, `street2`, and `city`, respectively. Add field labels for these input boxes as shown in Figure 6-79.

6. Create a selection list for the `state` field containing two-letter abbreviations of the state names. You can find a list of state abbreviations in the *state.txt* file. Add the label text **State**.

7. Create an input box for the `zip` field along with the label text **ZIP/Postal Code**. The pattern of the field value should match the regular expression for postal codes. You can use the regular expression patterns listed in the *regex.txt* data file.

8. Create an input box for the `country` field along with the label text **Country**. Make the default value of the field equal to the text string **United States**.

9. Create an input box for the `phone` field along with the label text **Phone**. The pattern of the field value should match the regular expression for phone numbers.

10. All of the fields within the `billing` field set should be marked as required fields with the exception of the `street2` field.

11. Within the `creditcard` field set, create a field set belonging to the class *optionGroup*. Within this field set, create four label elements. Within each label, create an option button belonging to the `ccard` field followed by an inline image belonging to one of four credit card companies. The field values associated with the four option buttons are *diners*, *discover*, *master*, and *visa*, and the inline images are *diners.png*, *discover.png*, *master.png*, and *visa.png*, respectively.

12. Directly below the `optionGroup` field set, create an input box for the `ccardnumber` field along with the label text **Credit Card Number**. The text of the field value should match the regular expression for credit card numbers found in the *regex.txt* file.

13. Add a label containing the text **Expiration Date** followed by a selection list for the `ccardmonth` field that contains the first entry **--Month--** followed by the text for each individual month in chronological order from **January (01)** through **December (12)**. Also add a selection list for the `ccardyear` field with the first entry **--Year--** followed by year values for **2014** through **2018**.

14. Add a label containing the text **CSC** followed by an input box for the `csc` field. The `csc` field should be limited to three characters, follow the regular expression pattern `^\d{3}$` and display the placeholder text **nnn**.

15. Make all of the fields within the `creditCard` field set required fields.

16. Within the `info` field set, create a label containing the text **Contact Email** followed by an input box for the `email` field that uses the `email` data type.

17. Add a label containing the text **Special Notes** followed by a text area box for the `notes` field.

18. At the bottom of the form, directly above the closing `</form>` tag, insert a submit button with the button text **Submit Order**.

19. Save your changes to the file, and then go to the **payment.css** file and add styles rules for the different form elements as described in the following steps.

20. Display all field sets without borders and with a 5-pixel margin. Display all field set legends with a background color of (239, 198, 145) and a text color of black. Set the top and bottom margins to 10 pixels and indent the legend text 20 pixels. Set the width of the legend to 100% of the width of the field set. Finally, add rounded borders to the legend, 10 pixels in radius.

21. Display all labels as blocks, floated on the left margin once the left margin is clear. Set the font size to 0.8 em and align the label text to the right. Set the top and bottom margins to 2 pixels, and set the left and right margins to 5 pixels. Set the width of the labels to 25%.

22. Display all `input` elements as blocks, floated on the left with a font size of 0.9 em and a width of 60%. Set the top and bottom margins to 2 pixels, and set the left and right margins to 0 pixels.

23. Display all `select` elements as blocks floated on the left with a font size of 0.9 em and a margin of 2 pixels.

24. Display all `textarea` elements as blocks floated on the left with a font size of 0.9 em, a height of 75 pixels, and a width of 60%.

25. Set the left margin of the field set belonging to the *optionGroup* class to 25%. For `label` elements nested within the `optionGroup` field set: a) display the labels inline; b) do not float the labels; and c) set the label width to 100 pixels.

26. Display option buttons inline with no floating. Set the margin of the option buttons to 0 pixels and the width to 20 pixels.

27. Set the width of the input box for the `csc` field to 50 pixels.

28. For the submit button, add the following styles: a) set the background color to the value (239, 198, 145); b) do not float the input box; c) set the dimensions of the button to 150 pixels wide by 30 pixels high; d) set the top and bottom margins to 10 pixels, and set the left and right margins to `auto`; and e) add a rounded border with a 15-pixel radius.

29. When `input`, `select`, and `textarea` elements receive the focus, change the background color to the value (255, 218, 165).

30. When an `input` element receives the focus and is invalid, change the background color to the value (255, 245, 215) and display the *stop.png* background image file in the bottom-right corner of the input box with no tiling.

31. When an `input` element receives the focus and is valid, change the background color to the value (215, 255, 215) and display the *go.png* image in the bottom-right corner of the input box with no tiling.

32. Save your changes to the style sheet.

33. Open the **spice.htm** file in your Web browser. Verify that you cannot submit the form without all required fields filled out, and without phone number, e-mail address, and CSC values entered in the proper format.

✛ EXPLORE 34. Verify the validation checks for the credit card number by confirming that the form rejects the following credit card numbers (which are not valid card numbers):
- 31012345678901
- 6012123456789019
- 5912345678901235
- 8123456789012349

✛ EXPLORE 35. Further verify the validation checks for the credit card number by confirming that the form accepts the following credit card numbers (which are valid card numbers):
- 30312345678901
- 6011123456789019
- 5112345678901235
- 4123456789012349

36. Submit your completed files to your instructor, in either printed or electronic form, as requested.

Apply your knowledge of Web forms to design a form for a demo page displaying the impact of different CSS text styles.

CHALLENGE

Case Problem 3

Data Files needed for this Case Problem: back.png, cssdemotxt.htm, cssforms.css, modernizr-1.5.js, rundemo.js, wm.css, wmlogo.png

WidgetMage   Anna Lopez is the founder of WidgetMage, a Web site that specializes in designing small demos and applications for Web sites. Anna has asked you to work on creating a CSS demo page in which users can interactively select style values and see their effects on the page. Anna already has the JavaScript code written to make the demo page work and a style sheet for the Web form. She wants you to finish her project by writing the HTML code for the Web form. A preview of the page you'll create is shown in Figure 6-80. In this page, you'll enter sample text into a text area box and then select style values from the form controls in the page. The page shown in Figure 6-80 is based on the Opera browser.

Figure 6-80   WidgetMage CSS demo page in Opera

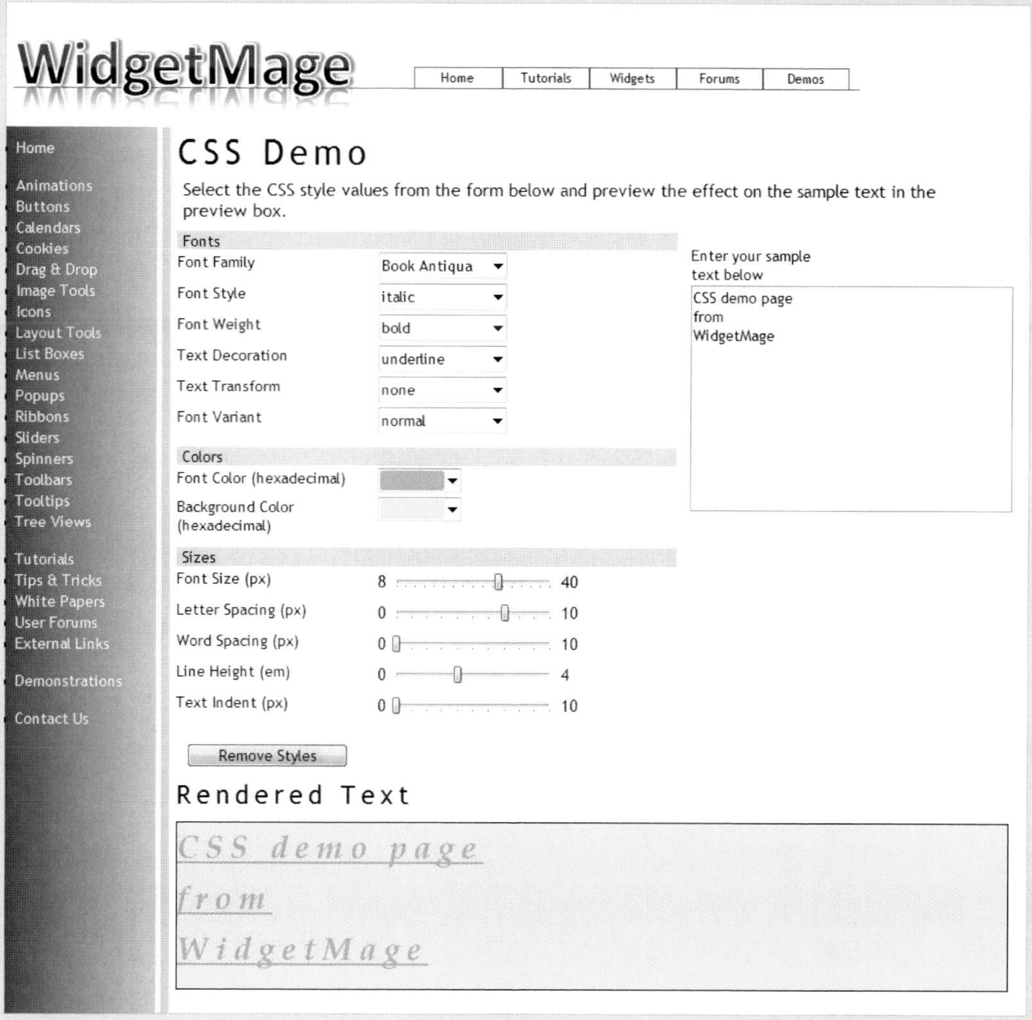

Complete the following:

1. In your text editor, open the **cssdemotxt.htm** file from the tutorial.06\case3 folder included with your Data Files. Enter *your name* and *the date* in the comment section of the file. Save the file as **cssdemo.htm**.

2. Review the contents and structure of the document. Link the file to the **cssforms.css** style sheet.

3. Directly below the paragraph within the `section` element, insert a `form` element. You do not have to specify an action or a method.

4. Create field sets with ids equal to `textstring`, `fonts`, `colors`, and `sizes`. Do not add a legend to the `textstring` field set. For the three remaining field sets, add the legend text **Fonts**, **Colors**, and **Sizes**, respectively.

   Note: In the steps that follow, make sure you add both an `id` attribute and a `name` attribute to each input box, selection list, or text area box, giving the same value to both attributes. Also, make sure that you enter the name-id values in lowercase letters. Finally, make sure that every selection list has both option text and option values set to the same text string.

EXPLORE 5. Within the `textstring` field set, insert a label containing the text **Enter your sample text below**, followed by a text area box. The text area box should have the name and id value `sampletext`. Set the text area so that it automatically receives the focus when the page is loaded, and set its tab index value to 1. Set the line wrap within the text area box to `hard` to preserve any line breaks within the text area box.

6. Within the `fonts` field set, insert a label containing the text **Font Family** followed by a selection list for the `fontfamily` field. Add the following options to the selection list: **default**, **serif**, **sans-serif**, **monospace**, **cursive**, **fantasy**, **Arial**, **'Book Antiqua'**, **'Courier New'**, **Geneva**, **Helvetica**, **Impact**, **Palatino**, and **'Times New Roman'**. Set the option values equal to the option text, including the single quotes where required for the font name.

EXPLORE 7. For the options created for the `fontfamily` selection list, enclose the generic font names in an option group with the label **generic** and the specific fonts within an option group with the label **specific**.

8. After the `fontfamily` selection list, insert a label with the text **Font Style**. Add a selection list for the `fontstyle` field with the option text and option values equal to **normal**, **italic**, and **oblique**.

9. Add a label with the text **Font Weight** along with a selection list for the `fontweight` field containing the option values and option text **normal** and **bold**.

10. Add a label with the text **Text Decoration** along with a selection list for the `textdecoration` field containing the option values and option text **none**, **line-through**, **overline**, and **underline**.

11. Add a label with the text **Text Transform** along with a selection list for the `texttransform` field containing the option values and option text **none**, **capitalize**, **lowercase**, and **uppercase**.

12. Add a label with the text **Font Variant** along with a selection for the `fontvariant` field containing the option text and values **normal** and **small-caps**.

EXPLORE 13. Within the `colors` field set, add a label with the text **Font Color (hexadecimal)**. Add an input box for the `color` field. Set the data type of the input box to `color`. Set the default value to the text string **#000000**. Add the placeholder text **#rrggbb**.

14. Add a label containing the text **Background Color (hexadecimal)** followed by an input box for the `backgroundcolor` field. Set the data type of the input box to `color`. Set the default value to the text string **#FFFFFF**. Add the placeholder text **#rrggbb**.

15. Within the `sizes` field set, add a label containing the text **Font Size (px)** followed by a range slider for the `fontsize` field. Set the default value of the `fontsize` field to 14, the minimum to 8, and the maximum to 40. The range slider should move from the minimum to the maximum in steps of 1 unit.

16. Create range sliders for the next four items in the `sizes` field set. Figure 6-81 lists the label text, field names, and ranges of the range sliders in the CSS demo page. Add appropriate range labels before and after the range sliders as indicated in Figure 6-80.

Figure 6-81   Range sliders in the CSS demo page

Field	Label Text	Default	Range
fontsize	Font Size (px)	14	8 - 40 by 1
letterspacing	Letter Spacing (px)	0	0 - 10 by 1
wordspacing	Word Spacing (px)	0	0 - 10 by 1
lineheight	Line Height (em)	1	0 - 4 by 0.2
textindent	Text Indent (px)	0	0 - 10 by 1

EXPLORE

17. Directly after the `sizes` field set, add a command button containing the text **Remove Styles** and the id `removestyles`.

18. Scroll to the top of the file. Within the `head` element, add a `script` element to connect to the *rundemo.js* file.

19. Save your changes to the file.

20. Open the **cssdemo.htm** file in a Web browser that supports range sliders. Test the form by entering sample text into the text area box near the top of the form. Verify that when you tab out of the text area box, the text appears in the rendering box at the bottom of the page.

21. Change the style of the rendered text by selecting options and values from the style controls on the form.

EXPLORE

22. If you have access to Opera or another Web browser that supports the `color` data type, verify that you can change the font and background color using a color picker. If your browser does not support the `color` data type, change the colors by entering hexadecimal values for the font color and background color fields.

23. Submit your completed files to your instructor, in either printed or electronic form, as requested.

Test your knowledge of Web forms by creating an order form for an online computer store.

RESEARCH

Case Problem 4

Data Files needed for this Case Problem: formsubmit.js, go.png, mclogo.jpg, modernizr-1.5.js, stop.png

Millennium Computers You are employed at Millennium Computers, a discount mail-order company specializing in computers and computer components. Your supervisor, Sandy Walton, has asked you to create an order form Web page so that customers can purchase products online. Your order form is for computer purchases only. There are several options for customers to consider when purchasing computers from Millennium. Customers can choose from the following:

- Processor Speed: 3.2 GHz, 4 GHz, 5.2 GHz
- Memory: 1 GB, 2 GB, 4 GB, 8 GB
- Monitor Size: 15", 17", 19", 21"
- Hard Drive: 240 GB, 500 GB, 750 GB, 1 TB
- DVD Burner: yes/no
- Tuner Card: yes/no
- Media Card Reader: yes/no

Complete the following:

1. Use your text editor to create an HTML file named **pc.htm** and two style sheets named **mill.css** and **oform.css**. Enter *your name* and *the date* in a comment section in each file. Include any other comments you think will aptly document the purpose and content of the files. Save the files in the tutorial.06\case4 folder included with your Data Files.

2. Design a Web page for Millennium Computers. Insert any styles you create in the *mill.css* style sheet. You are free to use the *mclogo.jpg* file and whatever text or images you wish to complete the look and content of the Web page.

3. Within the **pc.htm** file, insert a Web form containing the following elements:
   - Input boxes for the customer's first name, last name, street address, city, state, zip code, and phone number. The field names should be `fName`, `lName`, `street`, `city`, `state`, `zip`, and `phone`, respectively.
   - Selection lists for the processor speed, memory, monitor size, and hard drive size. The field names should be `pSpeed`, `mem`, `monitor`, and `hd`, respectively. The option values should match the option text.
   - Option buttons for the DVD burner, tuner card, and media card reader options. The field names should be `dvd`, `tuner`, and `mCard`, respectively.
   - A check box for the `warranty` field that asks whether customers want the 24-month extended warranty.
   - A text area box requesting additional information or comments on the order.
   - Three form buttons: a submit button with the text **Send Order**, a reset button with the text **Cancel Order**, and a command button with the text **Contact Me**.
   - Add validation checks marking all of the customer contact fields as required.
   - Use regular expression patterns to ensure that each user enters his or her zip code and phone number in the correct format.

4. Name the form `cOrder` and add attributes so the form is submitted using the `post` method to the CGI script located at *http://www.mill_computers.com/orders/process.cgi*.

5. Create a style for your form in the **oform.css** style sheet. The layout and appearance of the form are up to you. It should include style rules to highlight input boxes that receive the focus, and it should employ inline validation for missing or incorrectly entered data.

6. Test your Web site on a variety of browsers to ensure your design works under different conditions.

7. Submit your completed files to your instructor, in either printed or electronic form, as requested.

ENDING DATA FILES

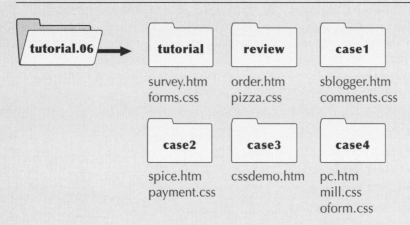

tutorial.06 → tutorial
survey.htm
forms.css

review
order.htm
pizza.css

case1
sblogger.htm
comments.css

case2
spice.htm
payment.css

case3
cssdemo.htm

case4
pc.htm
mill.css
oform.css

OBJECTIVES

Session 7.1
- Learn about sound file formats and properties
- Embed a sound clip using the `audio` element
- Embed a sound clip using the `embed` element

Session 7.2
- Learn about video file formats and properties
- Embed a video clip using the `video` element
- Embed a video clip using the `object` element
- Explore how to use Shockwave Flash players
- Explore how to embed YouTube videos

Session 7.3
- Explore the history of Java
- Embed a Java applet and other Objects

Designing a Multimedia Web Site

Enhancing a Document with Sound, Video, and Applets

Case | *Jumbo Popcorn*

Maxine Michaels is a movie buff and has a special fondness for classic movies. To pursue her interests, she's started *Jumbo Popcorn*, a Web site of articles, reviews, and news about the cinema.

Maxine wants to enhance her Web site with sound and video clips of famous movie moments. She's asked you to help complete a sample page describing the 1951 classic movie *Royal Wedding*, starring Fred Astaire and Jane Powell.

Note: Some tasks require you to have Adobe Flash and Apple QuickTime.

STARTING DATA FILES

tutorial	review	case1	case2
jumbotxt.htm	astairetxt.htm	rftxt.htm	roadtxt.htm
clipstxt.css	embedtxt.css	+ 2 graphic files	+ 1 graphic file
+ 7 graphic files	+ 8 graphic files	+ 6 media files	+ 3 media files
+ 5 media files	+ 6 media files	+ 1 CSS file	+ 1 CSS file
+ 1 CSS file	+ 1 CSS file	+ 1 JavaScript file	+ 1 JavaScript file
+ 1 class file	+ 1 class file		
+ 1 text file	+ 1 text file		
+ 1 JavaScript file	+ 1 JavaScript file		

case3	case4
fractaltxt.htm	bysoinfo.txt
+ 3 graphic files	schedule.txt
+ 3 media files	+ 2 graphic files
+ 4 class files	+ 3 media files
+ 1 CSS file	+ 1 class file
+ 1 JavaScript file	+ 1 JavaScript file

SESSION 7.1 VISUAL OVERVIEW

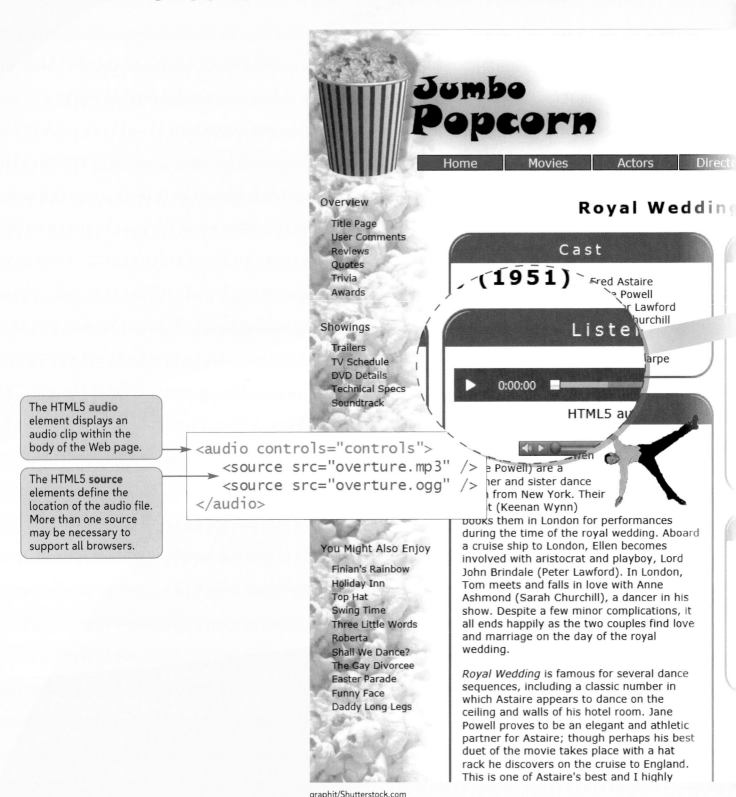

The HTML5 **audio** element displays an audio clip within the body of the Web page.

The HTML5 **source** elements define the location of the audio file. More than one source may be necessary to support all browsers.

```
<audio controls="controls">
    <source src="overture.mp3" />
    <source src="overture.ogg" />
</audio>
```

Overview

Title Page
User Comments
Reviews
Quotes
Trivia
Awards

Showings

Trailers
TV Schedule
DVD Details
Technical Specs
Soundtrack

You Might Also Enjoy

Finian's Rainbow
Holiday Inn
Top Hat
Swing Time
Three Little Words
Roberta
Shall We Dance?
The Gay Divorcee
Easter Parade
Funny Face
Daddy Long Legs

Royal Wedding

Cast
(1951)
Fred Astaire
Jane Powell
Peter Lawford
Sarah Churchill

Listen

0:00:00

HTML5 audio

(Jane Powell) are a brother and sister dance team from New York. Their agent (Keenan Wynn) books them in London for performances during the time of the royal wedding. Aboard a cruise ship to London, Ellen becomes involved with aristocrat and playboy, Lord John Brindale (Peter Lawford). In London, Tom meets and falls in love with Anne Ashmond (Sarah Churchill), a dancer in his show. Despite a few minor complications, it all ends happily as the two couples find love and marriage on the day of the royal wedding.

Royal Wedding is famous for several dance sequences, including a classic number in which Astaire appears to dance on the ceiling and walls of his hotel room. Jane Powell proves to be an elegant and athletic partner for Astaire; though perhaps his best duet of the movie takes place with a hat rack he discovers on the cruise to England. This is one of Astaire's best and I highly

graphit/Shutterstock.com

Gl0ck/Shutterstock.com

PLAYING WEB AUDIO

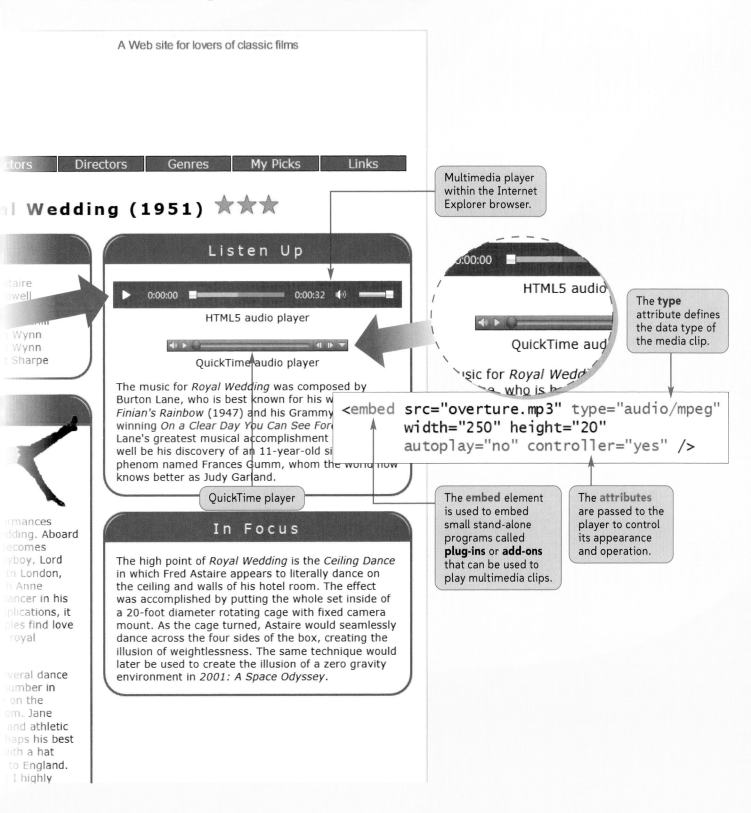

A Web site for lovers of classic films

ctors | Directors | Genres | My Picks | Links

l Wedding (1951) ★★★

Listen Up

▶ 0:00:00 ━━━ 0:00:32 ◀◁)) ━━━

HTML5 audio player

◀◁)) ▶ ━━━ ◀◁ ▷▶ ▼

QuickTime audio player

The music for *Royal Wedding* was composed by Burton Lane, who is best known for his w Finian's Rainbow (1947) and his Grammy winning *On a Clear Day You Can See For* Lane's greatest musical accomplishment well be his discovery of an 11-year-old si phenom named Frances Gumm, whom the world now knows better as Judy Garland.

QuickTime player

In Focus

The high point of *Royal Wedding* is the *Ceiling Dance* in which Fred Astaire appears to literally dance on the ceiling and walls of his hotel room. The effect was accomplished by putting the whole set inside of a 20-foot diameter rotating cage with fixed camera mount. As the cage turned, Astaire would seamlessly dance across the four sides of the box, creating the illusion of weightlessness. The same technique would later be used to create the illusion of a zero gravity environment in *2001: A Space Odyssey*.

Multimedia player within the Internet Explorer browser.

:00:00 ━━━

HTML5 audio

◀◁)) ▶ ━━━

QuickTime aud

usic for *Royal Wedd* e, who is h

The **type** attribute defines the data type of the media clip.

```
<embed src="overture.mp3" type="audio/mpeg"
width="250" height="20"
autoplay="no" controller="yes" />
```

The **embed** element is used to embed small stand-alone programs called **plug-ins** or **add-ons** that can be used to play multimedia clips.

The **attributes** are passed to the player to control its appearance and operation.

staire owell
Wynn
Wynn
Sharpe

rmances dding. Aboard ecomes yboy, Lord In London, h Anne ancer in his plications, it les find love royal

veral dance umber in on the om. Jane and athletic aps his best th a hat to England. I highly

Introducing Multimedia on the Web

You and Maxine sit down to discuss her new cinema Web site. She's completed much of the work on the *Royal Wedding* Web page and wants to show you her progress. You'll open her file now.

To view Maxine's page:

▶ 1. In your text editor, open the **jumbotxt.htm** file from the tutorial.07\tutorial folder. Enter *your name* and *the date* in the comment section of the file. Save the file as **jumbo.htm**.

▶ 2. Review the contents of the **jumbo.htm** file in your text editor to become familiar with its content and structure.

▶ 3. Open **jumbo.htm** in your Web browser. The initial page is shown in Figure 7-1.

Figure 7-1   The initial Royal Wedding page

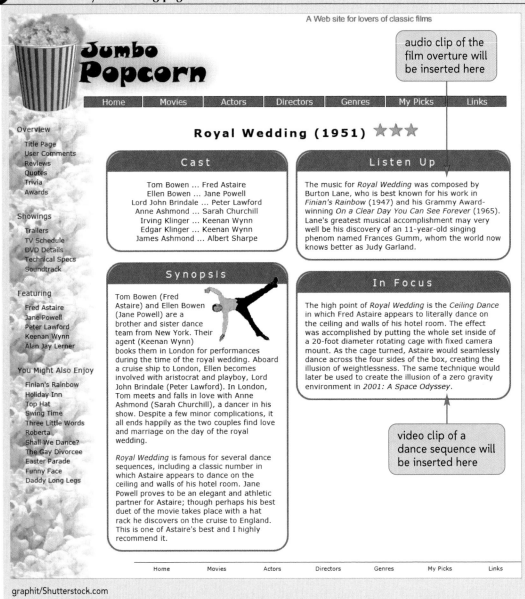

graphit/Shutterstock.com

Gl0ck/Shutterstock.com

Royal Wedding is one of a handful of Metro-Goldwyn-Mayer productions from the early 1950s whose original copyrights were never renewed. This means that versions of the movie are now in the public domain and that Maxine can add production stills, sound clips, and video clips from the film to her Web page without worrying about the copyright. One of her audio clips contains the first few seconds from the film's overture. She would like to add that clip to the Listen Up box in the upper-right corner of the Web page. She also has a brief excerpt from a Fred Astaire dance number that she wants to add to the In Focus box in the lower-right corner of the page.

Multimedia Sites and Bandwidth

One of the most important factors in the application of multimedia on the Web is bandwidth. **Bandwidth** is a measure of the amount of data that can be sent through a communication pipeline each second. In the early days of the Web, efforts to include multimedia elements on Web sites were hampered by low-bandwidth connections, as most users connected to the Internet over slow landlines. Under those conditions, a Web site containing more than one or two short multimedia clips would be inaccessible to most users.

This situation changed because of two developments. One was high-speed Internet access being made more available to the general public through the use of cable modems and DSL. The second development was the reduction of the file size of multimedia clips, without sacrificing sound or video quality, through the use of file compression technology. Paired together, the two developments made multimedia much more accessible to most Internet users, eventually resulting in the creation of one of the most popular sites on the Web, YouTube, which is solely dedicated to the creation and dissemination of user-created video.

Understanding Plug-Ins

Multimedia is displayed within a Web page in a fashion similar to an inline image. The controls to play a media clip are also displayed as part of the Web page. To play a multimedia file, a browser often will have access to a plug-in or add-on—an extra component accessed by the browser to provide a feature or capability not included with the browser. The most commonly used plug-ins for multimedia files include Windows Media Player, the QuickTime plug-in for video and audio clips, and Adobe Flash Player for video, audio, and animation.

However, starting with the widespread adoption of HTML5, many browsers now include built-in support for audio and video files, removing the need for plug-ins. You'll work with the HTML5 multimedia elements as well as some plug-ins to add the multimedia content to the *Royal Wedding* page, starting with adding an audio clip. Before you add that audio clip, you'll first learn about the various audio formats available for the Web and explore the differences in their sound quality and file size.

Exploring Digital Audio

If you want to add sound to your Web site, it's helpful to understand some of the issues involved in converting sound into a format that can be played on your users' computers and over their Internet connections. Sound is composed of combinations of sound waves; and every sound wave can be described on the basis of two components—amplitude and frequency. Figure 7-2 shows a basic sound wave. The **amplitude** is the height of the sound wave and it relates to the sound's volume—the higher the amplitude, the louder the sound. The **frequency** is the speed at which the sound wave moves and it relates to the sound's pitch—the higher the frequency, the higher the pitch.

Figure 7-2   A simple sound wave

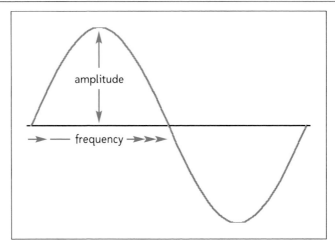

When you hear sound, your ears hear a continuously varying signal created by the vibrations on your eardrum; to store that sound in a computer file, it must be converted into discrete pieces or **bits** of information. A digital recording of that sound takes measurements of the sound wave at different moments in time; each measurement is called a **sample**. The number of samples taken per second is called the **sampling rate**, a value that is measured in kilohertz (kHz). As shown in Figure 7-3, a higher sampling rate means that more samples are taken per second, resulting in a digital recording that more closely matches the original sound. There is a trade-off, however, as increasing the sampling rate also increases the size of a sound file. This might not be a problem with a CD recording, but it can be an issue when transferring sound over an Internet connection, where it's important to keep file sizes compact.

Figure 7-3   **Different sampling rates**

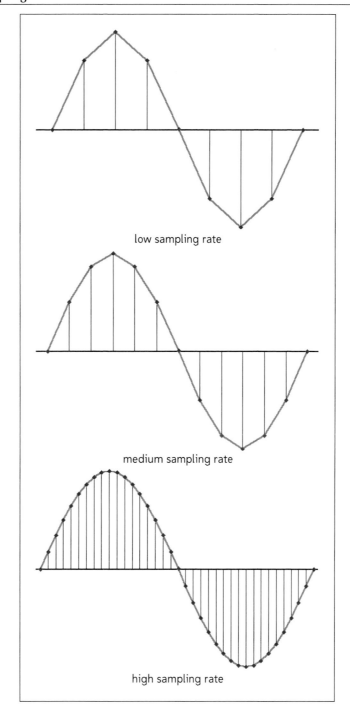

low sampling rate

medium sampling rate

high sampling rate

A second factor in converting sound to digital form is the sample resolution. **Sample resolution** or **bit depth** indicates the precision in measuring the sound within each sample. Three commonly used sample resolution values are 8 bit, 16 bit, and 32 bit. As shown in Figure 7-4, increasing the sample resolution creates a digital sound file that represents the analog signal more accurately, but this results in a larger file. For most applications, saving sound files at the 16-bit resolution provides a good balance between sound quality and file size.

Figure 7-4 Different sampling resolutions

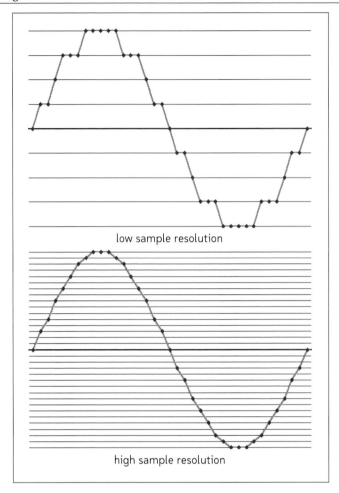

low sample resolution

high sample resolution

Another factor affecting audio quality is the number of sound channels. Typically, the choice is between stereo (two channels) or monaural (a single channel). Stereo provides a richer sound than mono, but with the trade-off of approximately doubling the size of the sound file.

The size of an audio clip is therefore related to the sampling rate, the sample resolution, and the number of channels. The total size can be expressed in terms of the **bit rate**, which is the number of bits of data required for each second of sound. For music stored on compact discs, the bit rate is determined by multiplying the sampling rate by the sample resolution by the number of channels. A typical CD track has a bit rate value of 1411 Kbps, which is too high for practical use on the Web. Therefore, sound files used on the Web must employ **file compression**, a process that reduces the size of the audio file but sometimes at the expense of sound quality. The most common file compression format is the MP3 format used throughout the Web as well as on portable music players and cell phones. MP3s can achieve near-CD-quality sound at bit rates of 192 to 320 Kbps. The standard bit rate for MP3s is 192 Kbps, which results in some minor sound degradation but also requires only 13% of the size required for CD-quality sound. If a sound clip involves spoken words and not music, even greater sound compression can be used without affecting the overall quality of the recording.

Audio Formats under HTML5

The MP3 format is one of three file formats currently supported by the browsers that support HTML5. The other two formats are the WAV format and Ogg Vorbis. Figure 7-5 describes each of these formats.

Figure 7-5   Audio formats in HTML5

Format	Description
MP3	The most popular format for downloading and storing music, MP3 compresses sound files to roughly one-tenth the size of uncompressed files while maintaining good audio quality. However, the MP3 format is proprietary and not royalty-free, which can be a hindrance to audio distributors.
Ogg Vorbis	A file compression format designed for Web audio, Ogg Vorbis is an open source and royalty-free format. In general, Ogg Vorbis provides better sound quality than MP3, especially at lower bitrates. However, few portable players support Ogg Vorbis, while the MP3 format has almost universal support.
WAV	The original audio format for Windows PCs, WAV is commonly used for storing uncompressed CD-quality sound. In this format, a WAV file requires about 10 megabytes per minute of sound, making it impractical as a format for Web audio for all but the shortest audio clips.

A great deal of controversy has surrounded the selection of a common audio format for HTML5. The original HTML5 specifications in January 2007 explicitly called on browsers to support the Ogg Vorbis format because it is royalty-free and thus would allow for the quick development and publishing of audio products for the Web. However, not all browser vendors went along with this proposal; Apple in particular refused to implement Ogg Vorbis in its Safari browser, citing the lack of support for that format on portable media players and its doubts about its sound quality. Microsoft also declined to support Ogg Vorbis. These events led to a revision of the HTML5 audio specification, changing the proposal to a general guideline for a common audio format without supporting one format over another. All of this leaves Web developers stuck amid the three audio formats, none of which are supported by every browser. Figure 7-6 describes the support among the major browsers for MP3, Ogg Vorbis, and WAV at the time of this writing.

Figure 7-6   Audio formats supported by HTML5 audio

Browser	WAV	Ogg Vorbis	MP3
Internet Explorer			✓
Firefox	✓	✓	
Safari	✓		✓
Chrome	✓	✓	✓
Opera	✓	✓	

Thus, to provide a cross-browser solution for her users, Maxine needs to supply two versions of every audio clip: one in MP3 format and the other in Ogg Vorbis format. Maxine does not want to create a WAV version of her audio clips because that format, being uncompressed, would not be suitable for streaming audio over the Web.

Exploring Other Audio Formats

Audio formats other than MP3, Ogg Vorbis, and WAV are available to you through the use of plug-ins. One of the oldest audio formats is the **AU** format, also called the *mu-law* format, which is used primarily on UNIX workstations. AU sound files have 8-bit sample resolutions, use a sampling rate of 8 kHz, and are recorded in mono. The **RealAudio** format was one of the first formats that allowed for streaming audio over low- to high-bandwidth connections. RealAudio files tend to be much smaller than AU and WAV files, but the sound quality is usually not as good. Windows Media Player supports the **WMA (Windows Media Audio)** format. WMA is a proprietary audio format developed by Microsoft to compete with MP3s, offering comparable or better levels of compression and audio quality.

Finally, a popular music format is the **MIDI (Musical Instrument Digital Interface)** format, which synthesizes musical sounds through the use of mathematical functions describing the pitch, length, and volume of each note. MIDI files are much smaller than music stored in other audio formats: A MIDI composition lasting several minutes is less than 20 kilobytes in size, while a similar file in WAV format would be several megabytes in size, and a comparable MP3 would be only several hundred kilobytes in size. However, the MIDI format is limited to instrumental music and cannot be used for general sounds, such as speech.

Using the HTML5 audio Element

Maxine has created a 30-second sound clip from the overture of *Royal Wedding* and stored it in two sound files named *overture.mp3* and *overture.ogg*. The file is a monaural recording with a sample rate of 44 kHz and a bit rate of 96 Kbps, which she feels is adequate for use on her Web site. To embed her audio clip under HTML5, you apply the audio element

```
<audio src="url" />
```

where `url` specifies the location of the audio file. For example, the code

```
<audio src="overture.mp3" />
```

loads an audio clip from the *overture.mp3* file.

Understanding the source Element

Because you have to provide audio clips in both the MP3 and Ogg Vorbis formats, you must include two sources for the audio element. You can do this by inserting multiple source elements as follows

```
<audio>
    <source src="url1" />
    <source src="url2" />
...
</audio>
```

where *url1*, *url2*, etc. are the possible sources of the audio clip. A browser will attempt to load the audio files, stopping at the first file format that it supports. Versions of the Apple operating system before iOS4.0 did not support multiple source elements, viewing only the first source element. Because Apple devices support only the MP3 format, you always should start your list with the MP3 version of your audio clip.

Adding HTML5 Audio

• To add an audio clip under HTML5, use the audio element

```
<audio>
   <source src="url1" />
   <source src="url2" />
   …
</audio>
```

where *url1*, *url2*, etc. are the possible sources of the audio clip.

Use the audio and source elements to add an audio clip of the overture from *Royal Wedding* to Maxine's Web page.

To add an audio clip:

1. Return to the **jumbo.htm** file in your text editor.

2. Scroll down to the h2 heading, *Listen Up*, and below it insert the following audio and source elements (see Figure 7-7):

```
<audio>
   <source src="overture.mp3" />
   <source src="overture.ogg" />
</audio>
```

Figure 7-7   **Inserting the audio element**

```
<article>
   <h2>Listen Up</h2>

   <audio>
      <source src="overture.mp3" />
      <source src="overture.ogg" />
   </audio>
```

source for the MP3 file version

source for the Ogg Vorbis version

3. Save your changes to the file.

By adding the audio element, you've embedded the audio clip in the Web page, but you haven't provided any means for users to interact with the audio file. You can do that by setting the attributes of the audio element.

Attributes of the audio Element

Figure 7-8 lists the attributes associated with the HTML5 audio element. For example, to display controls for an audio clip, you add the following controls attribute to the audio element:

```
<audio controls="controls"> … </audio>
```

Note that you can leave off the value and simply include the name of the control attribute; however, that is not valid syntax for XHTML documents. This book will continue to follow the convention of always including attribute values even when they're not strictly required by most browsers.

Figure 7-8   Attributes of the audio element

Attribute	Description
autoplay="autoplay"	Starts playing the audio clip as soon as it is downloaded
controls="controls"	Displays the audio controls in the Web page
loop="loop"	Automatically restarts the audio clip when it is finished playing
preload="type"	Specifies whether the audio clip should be preloaded by the browser, where type is auto (to load the entire clip), metadata (to preload only descriptive data about the clip), or none (not to preload the audio clip)
src="url"	Specifies the source of the audio clip, where url is the location and name of the audio file

You can create a background sound for your Web page by adding the following audio element to your HTML file:

```
<audio controls="controls" autoplay="autoplay" loop="loop">...</audio>
```

The audio file starts playing automatically when the page is loaded and then loops back to the beginning when the end of the clip is reached to start playing again.

By default, audio controls are displayed in-line with text-level elements. To display the controls as a block, you must apply a style rule to the audio element. You'll add controls to the overture clip now and then create a style rule for the audio element.

TIP

Provide background sound only when you have the audio controls prominently displayed on your page so that users have a way of turning off the music.

To add controls to the audio clip:

▶ **1.** Add the attribute controls="controls" to the audio element, as shown in Figure 7-9.

Figure 7-9   Adding audio controls

```
<audio controls="controls">          ◀───  display controls
   <source src="overture.mp3" />           for the embedded
   <source src="overture.ogg" />           audio clip
</audio>
```

▶ **2.** Scroll to the top of the file and add the following link element directly below the link to the *jp.css* style sheet:

```
<link href="clips.css" rel="stylesheet" />
```

▶ **3.** Save your changes to the file, and then open the **clipstxt.css** file in your text editor. Enter **your name** and **the date** in the comment section of the file, and then save it as **clips.css**.

TIP

At the time of this writing, the Opera browser has a software bug that requires audio controls displayed as blocks to include a background color.

4. Add the following style rule to the file (see Figure 7-10):

```
/* Multimedia control styles */

audio {
    background-color: white;
    display: block;
    margin: 5px auto;
    width: 95%;
}
```

Figure 7-10   **Styles for the audio clip**

```
/* Multimedia control styles */

audio {
    background-color: white;
    display: block;
    margin: 5px auto;
    width: 95%;
}
```

sets the width to 95% of the containing element, centered horizontally

displays the controls as blocks on a white background

5. Save your changes to the file, and then reload **jumbo.htm** in your Web browser. Figure 7-11 shows the appearance of the audio controls under six browsers.

Figure 7-11   **The audio player as rendered by different browsers**

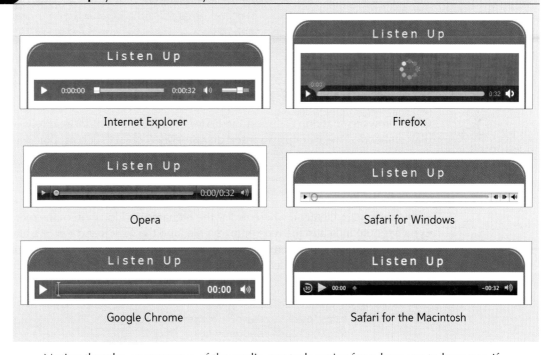

Internet Explorer

Firefox

Opera

Safari for Windows

Google Chrome

Safari for the Macintosh

Notice that the appearance of the audio controls varies from browser to browser. If you want your audio and video controls to share a uniform look, you must create your own using form elements along with a JavaScript program to manage the actions of the control buttons.

Verbal Communication: Tips for Effective Web Audio

Enhancing your Web site with audio clips can be an effective way to provide information and entertainment for your users and customers. However, it must be used judiciously to avoid annoying users. Here are some tips to keep in mind when using Web audio:

- *Avoid background music.* Remember that many customers multitask when using the Web and are often listening to their own music and audio files. Don't annoy them by inserting your audio clip over theirs.
- *Give users control.* Turn off the autoplay feature of your audio player. Let each user choose whether or not to play your audio clip.
- *Provide a mute button.* Your users might be accessing your site at work or in a public place where audio is inappropriate. Always give users the ability to pause, stop, and—above all—mute the audio.
- *Download on demand.* A page that is slow to load often will be skipped. Don't slow the loading of your Web page by automatically downloading sound and video files. Download them when a user clicks on the player and not before.
- *Keep it short.* If you use sound to supplement different visual effects in your Web page, keep the clips short in duration. Don't force your users to listen to long clips.
- *Use the right frequency.* The human ear hears sounds in the range from 1 kilohertz to 5 kilohertz. Keep your audio clips in this frequency range for the most effective playback.
- *Accommodate hearing-impaired customers.* The Web is an important source of information for the hard of hearing. Always provide alternatives for those who can't hear your site's audio content.

Finally, every feature on your Web site, including sound, should have a reason for being there. An audio clip should provide users with important information that cannot be conveyed in any other way. Don't add sound simply to impress your users. In the end, they will be more interested in the site's content.

Working with Embedded Objects

Older browsers that don't support the HTML5 `audio` element instead rely on plug-ins to play embedded media clips. To insert an embedded object such as a media player, you can nest the `embed` element

```
<embed src="url" type="mime"
       width="value" height="value" />
```

within the `audio` element, where `url` is the filename and location of the media clip, the `type` attribute indicates the type of media file, and the `width` and `height` attributes specify the width and height of the embedded object in pixels, respectively. For example, the following code creates an embedded object for the *overture.mp3* file that is 250 pixels wide by 10 pixels high:

```
<audio src="overture.mp3">
   <embed src="overture.mp3" type="audio/mpeg"
          width="250" height="10" />
</audio>
```

Notice that the `embed` element is nested within the HTML5 `audio` element. Any browser encountering this code will first attempt to load the audio clip via the HTML5 `audio` element; but if the browser doesn't recognize the `<audio>` tag, it then will attempt to load the clip using the `embed` element.

MIME Types

Embedded objects are not limited to audio and video files. They also can be used for other objects such as images, interactive programs, and even other Web pages. A **Multipurpose Internet Mail Extensions (MIME) type** identifies the type of data contained in a file and provides information about how that data should be interpreted. One common MIME type you've used since Tutorial 1 is `text/css`, which identifies a text file as containing CSS style declarations. As you saw in the previous example, the MIME type for MP3 files is `audio/mpeg`. Figure 7-12 lists the MIME types for other sound file formats and players.

Figure 7-12   **Audio MIME types**

Format	File Extension	MIME Type
AU	.au	audio/basic
MIDI	.mid	audio/mid
MP3	.mp3	audio/mpeg
Ogg Vorbis	.ogg	audio/ogg
RealAudio	.ra	audio/x-pn-realaudio
SND	.snd	audio/basic
Shockwave Flash	.swf	application/x-shockwave-flash
WAV	.wav	audio/wav

REFERENCE

Using the embed *Element*

- To embed an object using the embed element, add the code

```
<embed src="url" type="mime"
       width="value" height="value" />
```

to the HTML file, where `url` is the filename and location of the media clip, the `type` attribute indicates the type of media file, and the `width` and `height` attributes specify the width and height of the embedded object in pixels, respectively.

You'll add an embed element to the *Royal Wedding* page, nesting it within the audio clip you created in the last set of steps.

To add the embedded object:

▶ **1.** Return to the **jumbo.htm** file in your text editor and add the following code, as shown in Figure 7-13:

```
<embed src="overture.mp3" type="audio/mpeg"
       height="20" width="250" />
```

Figure 7-13   **Adding the embed element**

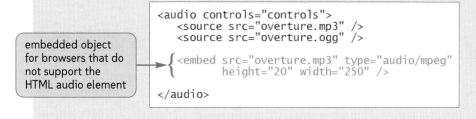

embedded object for browsers that do not support the HTML audio element

```
<audio controls="controls">
    <source src="overture.mp3" />
    <source src="overture.ogg" />
    <embed src="overture.mp3" type="audio/mpeg"
           height="20" width="250" />
</audio>
```

▶ **2.** Save your changes to the file.

Next, you'll revise the style rule for the `audio` element so that the content of the `audio` element, including any embedded content, is horizontally centered.

▶ **3.** Return to the **clips.css** file in your text editor, and then add the style `text-align: center;` to the audio style rule (see Figure 7-14).

Figure 7-14	Revising the audio style rule

```
audio {
    background-color: white;
    display: block;
    margin: 5px auto;
    text-align: center;
    width: 95%;
}
```

▶ **4.** Save your changes to the file.

Before viewing the embedded object in the Jumbo Popcorn Web page, you first must set additional attributes.

INSIGHT

MIME Types

The MIME type designation was first introduced as a way of attaching nontextual content to e-mail messages. With the growth of the World Wide Web, the use of MIME types expanded to include the flow of information across the Web. Each MIME type uses a header that indicates the type of data content. The header has the general form

  type/*subtype*

where *type* is the general data type and *subtype* is a special classification of data within that type. The possible values for *type* are `application`, `audio`, `image`, `message`, `model`, `multipart`, `text`, and `video`. Within these types there can be dozens or hundreds of subtypes. The subtype value for an object sometimes can be determined by examining the file extension of the object. For example, a JPEG image is identified as `image/jpeg`. However, note that different file extensions can be associated with the same MIME type. JPEG image files can end in .jpe, .jfif, .jpg, or .jpeg, but all are designated as `image/jpeg`.

MIME types also include information that tells users' computers how to handle and interpret object data. Most operating systems give an administrator the ability to associate MIME types with specific programs. You can view and change these associations in the Windows Control Panel or Mac Finder. For example, you can direct your computer to associate `image/jpeg` content with a particular graphics program, which tells the operating system always to use that graphics program to open files containing `image/jpeg` content. Note that any changes you make in the Control Panel or Finder might impact how your browser handles and displays multimedia content.

Plug-In Attributes

The `src`, `type`, `height`, and `width` attributes constitute the basic HTML attributes for the `embed` element, but they do not specify how users interact with the embedded object. To provide that information, you must use attributes that are specific to the plug-in that will be used to display the object. For many users, an embedded MP3 audio clip such as the

Royal Wedding overture will be played by Apple's QuickTime Player. To control the actions and appearance of the QuickTime plug-in, you can use the attributes listed in Figure 7-15.

Figure 7-15   **Attributes of the QuickTime plug-in**

Attribute	Description
`autoplay="value"`	Specifies whether the clip should start playing automatically when the page loads, where `value` equals `true` or `false`
`bgcolor="color"`	Sets the background color for the space allotted to the object
`controller="value"`	Specifies whether or not to show the object controls, where `value` equals `true` or `false`
`endtime="hh:mm:ss"`	Specifies the time in the clip at which playback ends
`href="url"`	Specifies the page to load when a user clicks on the object
`loop="value"`	Specifies whether to play the clip in a continuous loop, where `value` equals `true`, `false`, or `palindrome` (to play backward and then forward)
`src="url"`	Specifies the source of the clip
`starttime="hh:mm:ss"`	Specifies the time in the clip at which playback begins
`volume="value"`	Sets the initial audio volume, where `value` ranges from 0 to 255

For example, the embed element

```
<embed src="overture.mp3" autoplay="no" controller="yes" />
```

keeps browsers from automatically playing the overture clip when the page is loaded, and adds the QuickTime controls so that users can pause, rewind, modify the volume, or scroll through the audio contents. Modify the embed element now to add attributes to control the playback of the audio clip.

To add attributes for the QuickTime Player:

▶ **1.** Return to the **jumbo.htm** file in your text editor, and then add the following attributes to the `<embed>` tag (see Figure 7-16):

```
autoplay="no" controller="yes"
```

Figure 7-16   **Adding attributes for the QuickTime plug-in**

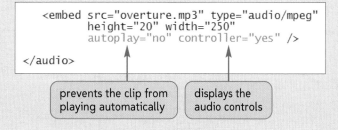

```
<embed src="overture.mp3" type="audio/mpeg"
       height="20" width="250"
       autoplay="no" controller="yes" />
</audio>
```

prevents the clip from playing automatically   displays the audio controls

▶ **2.** Save your changes to the file.

▶ **3.** Load the **jumbo.htm** file in a Web browser that does not support HTML5.

You can use a version of the Internet Explorer browser before IE9 for this step. If you have IE9 or a later version, you can display the page using the standards of older browser versions by pressing the **F12** key to open the browser developer tools and pressing **Alt+8** or **Alt+7** to switch to the Internet Explorer 8 or Internet Explorer 7 mode. Switch back to the IE9 version by pressing **Alt+9**. Figure 7-17 shows the appearance of the embedded clip using the QuickTime Player.

Figure 7-17 **QuickTime plug-in viewed in Internet Explorer 8**

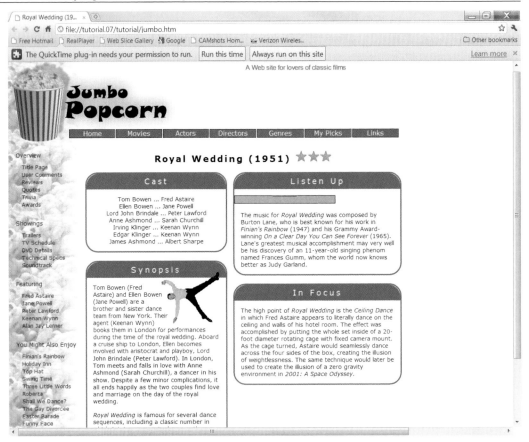

4. Click the **play** button of the embedded QuickTime Player to play the excerpt from the *Royal Wedding* overture.

5. If you switched Internet Explorer 9 to IE8 or IE7 mode, switch it back to IE9 mode.

If you open the page with a browser that supports neither the HTML5 `audio` element nor the QuickTime plug-in, you will not see any audio clip in your browser, or you may be prompted to install or activate the QuickTime plug-in (see Figure 7-18).

Figure 7-18 **QuickTime plug-in error message**

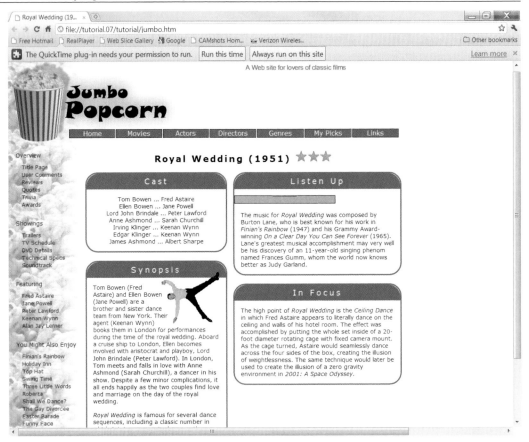

graphit/Shutterstock.com

Gl0ck/Shutterstock.com

Thus, the great problem with embedded objects is that they rely on each user to have a certain piece of software installed in addition to a Web browser. One goal of introducing multimedia support in HTML5 was to avoid this problem by making the insertion of audio and video content as easy and seamless as inserting inline images.

The Long Journey of the <embed> Tag

The <embed> tag originally was introduced by the Netscape browser in the 1990s as a way of embedding multimedia content and external programs. At the same time, Internet Explorer was attempting to do the same thing with its own object element. Ultimately, the object element (which you'll learn more about in the next session) was adopted as the HTML 4 standard and the embed element never became part of any HTML specification.

That should have ended the embed element; however, the way that Internet Explorer employed the object element was inconsistent with other browsers. That meant that cumbersome workarounds were required to create multimedia code that would work across all browsers. The most popular workaround involved nesting an embed element within an object element because even though it wasn't part of *any* official HTML specification, every browser still supported the embed element. However, if a developer wanted to write XHTML code, such workarounds were not allowed because the embed element could not be used at all, and so even more complicated solutions were sought.

Into this mess entered HTML5 with the guiding principle that the specifications for the new language should reflect how HTML is used in the browser community. Based on that consideration, HTML5 *included* the embed element as a legitimate HTML element. Of course, as HTML5 gains broader acceptance on the Web and elements such as the audio element gain acceptance, the need for the embed element will fade, just at the point when it gained legitimacy.

Maxine is pleased with your work on the *overture.mp3* sound clip. In the next session, you'll use the same techniques to embed a video clip in her Web page.

Session 7.1 Quick Check

1. Define the terms *bandwidth*, *sampling rate*, *sample resolution*, and *bit rate*.
2. What are the three audio formats supported by current browsers that support HTML5?
3. Provide the HTML code to create an audio clip for the *royal.mp3* and *royal.ogg* audio files. Give users control over playing the audio clip.
4. Provide the HTML code to play the audio clip *soundtrack.mp3* as a background sound that plays continuously when the page is opened by a browser.
5. What is the MIME type for a WAV file?
6. Provide the HTML code to insert the *royal.mp3* file using the embed element. Display controls for the embedded object and have it start automatically when the page loads, beginning 5 seconds into the clip.

SESSION 7.2 VISUAL OVERVIEW

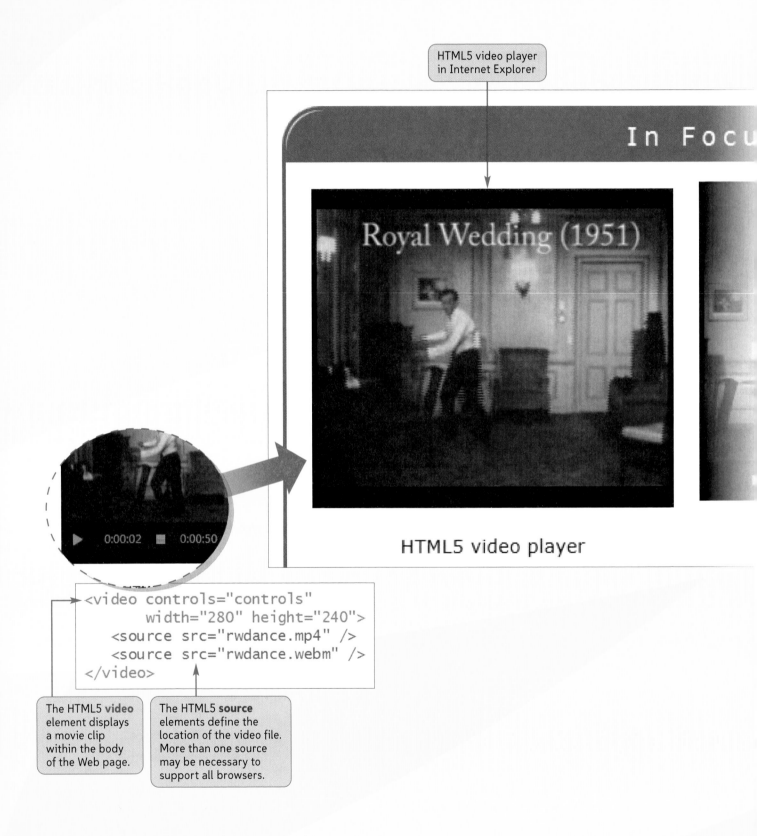

HTML5 video player in Internet Explorer

Royal Wedding (1951)

In Focu

▶ 0:00:02 ■ 0:00:50

HTML5 video player

```
<video controls="controls"
       width="280" height="240">
  <source src="rwdance.mp4" />
  <source src="rwdance.webm" />
</video>
```

The HTML5 **video** element displays a movie clip within the body of the Web page.

The HTML5 **source** elements define the location of the video file. More than one source may be necessary to support all browsers.

PLAYING WEB VIDEO

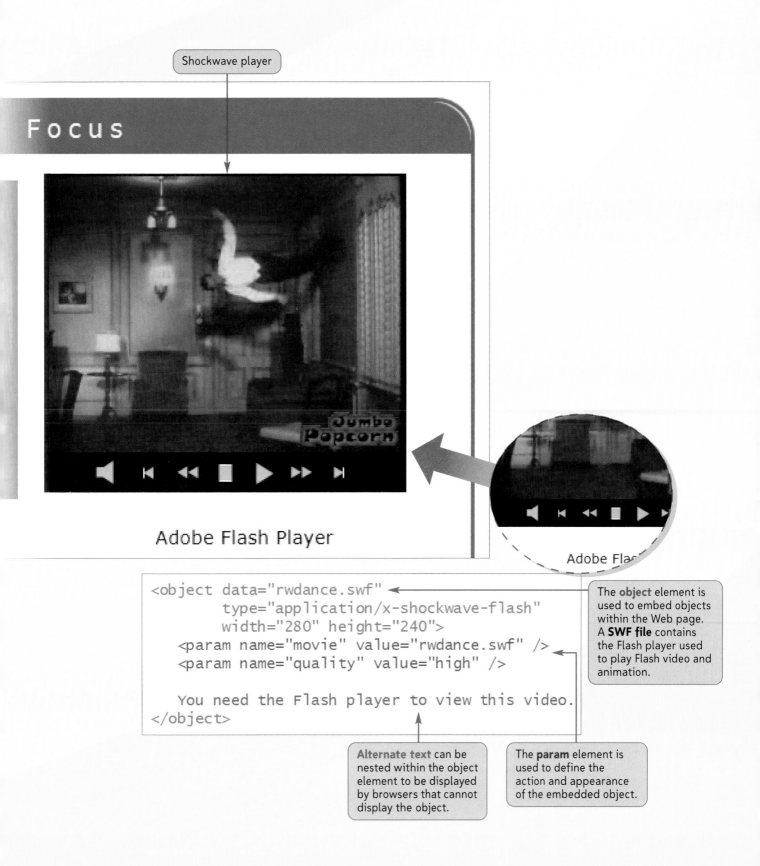

Shockwave player

Focus

Adobe Flash Player

```
<object data="rwdance.swf"
        type="application/x-shockwave-flash"
        width="280" height="240">
  <param name="movie" value="rwdance.swf" />
  <param name="quality" value="high" />

  You need the Flash player to view this video.
</object>
```

The **object** element is used to embed objects within the Web page. A **SWF file** contains the Flash player used to play Flash video and animation.

Alternate text can be nested within the object element to be displayed by browsers that cannot display the object.

The **param** element is used to define the action and appearance of the embedded object.

Exploring Digital Video

Maxine's next task for you is to embed a video clip on her Web page of Fred Astaire dancing in *Royal Wedding*. Video has become one of the most popular methods of sharing information on the Web. Before embedding Maxine's video clip, you'll first examine some of the issues involved in working with digital video on the Web.

Bit Rates and Video Quality

A video is composed of a series of single images or **frames** that are played in rapid succession to create the illusion of motion. Many frames are sized to have width-to-height ratios or **aspect ratios** of 4:3, though theatrical releases typically have aspect ratios of 1.85:1 or 2.39:1. The two most common frame sizes for the Web are 160 × 120 pixels and 320 × 240 pixels; frame sizes as large as 640 × 480 pixels or more are becoming more common as connection speeds increase. Online movie sites such as Netflix, Hulu, and Amazon Instant Video offer high-definition movies at resolutions of 1280 × 720.

The speed at which one frame in a video is replaced by the next is called the **frame rate**, commonly expressed in frames per second (fps). Higher frame rates usually, but not always, result in a smoother animation. DVDs typically render video at 24 fps; frame rates of 10 to 15 fps, commonly used on the Web, still can result in videos of good quality.

However, the frame rate is not the only factor that determines the quality of a video playback. A more important factor is the **video bit rate**, which is the amount of data that has to be processed by the video player each second. Video bit rates are defined in megabits per second (mbps) or kilobits per second (kbps). DVD-quality video has bit rates of about 4 to 8 mbps, while Blu-ray video requires roughly 25 mbps. Most Web video has a bit rate of about 800 kbps, which is slightly less than 1 mbps. Movie Web sites typically require bit rates of 2 to 3 mbps.

It is a mistake to assume that a higher bit rate always results in better video quality. You also must take into account the bandwidth of the connection to your Web site. The bandwidth must be large enough to accommodate the amount of information processed each second to smoothly play the video. If a user attempts to play a video with too high of a bit rate, the playback will be choppy and uneven as the connection tries in vain to keep up with the pace of the clip.

File Formats and Codecs

Video size can be greatly reduced through the use of file compression. When a compressed video is replayed, each frame is decompressed as it is rendered by the video player. The software that compresses and decompresses a media clip is called a **codec** (short for *compression/decompression*). Some codecs create smaller video files but at the expense of choppier playback. Video editing software allows you to choose the codec for a video clip, but you might need to experiment to determine which codec provides the best file compression without sacrificing video quality. During the last 15 years, advances in video technology and increases in computer processor speed have allowed for codecs that greatly reduce video size, resulting in high-quality video at data rates that are reasonable even under lower bandwidths.

Each codec is stored within a file called a **container file**. Figure 7-19 lists four popular container files along with some of the codecs they support. Note that a single file format might support several different possible codecs. You should not confuse the video file format with the codec of the clip it contains; for example, a Flash video file might contain a video clip that has been compressed using either the H.264 or the VP6 codec.

Figure 7-19   Video formats

File Format	File Extension	MIME Type	Video Codec(s)	Description
Flash Video	.flv	video/x-flv	VP6 Sorenson Spark H.264	A proprietary file format developed by Adobe to deliver video over the Internet using the popular Adobe Flash Player
MP4	.mp4	video/mpeg	MPEG-4 H.264	A widely-used proprietary format developed by Apple with versions of the H.264 codec used in all of Apple's mobile devices
Ogg Theora	.ogv	video/ogg	Theora	An open source format developed by the Xiph.org Foundation that uses the Theora codec as an alternative to the MPEG-4 codec
WebM	.webm	video/webm	VP8	An open source format introduced by Google to provide royalty-free video and audio to be used with the HTML5 video element

Video Formats under HTML5

As with audio support, the introduction of video in HTML5 involved determining what video formats would be supported in the new standard. The original HTML5 specifications called on browsers to support the Ogg Theora format in the same way that Ogg Vorbis was to be the designated audio format. As with the audio recommendation, this was rescinded in later specifications. Currently, three video formats are supported across current browsers: Ogg Theora, MP4, and WebM. Both Ogg Theora and WebM are royalty-free formats, allowing for free and open use by video developers. The H.264 codec is the most widely used codec and is used by Apple in its mobile devices and iTunes software. Complicating matters is the fact that Google decided in 2011 to discontinue support for H.264 in its Chrome browser, instead opting to develop the WebM format. Figure 7-20 lists the support for the different video formats at the time of this writing.

Figure 7-20   Video formats supported by HTML5 video

Browser	MP4	Ogg Theora	WebM
Internet Explorer	✓		
Firefox		✓	✓
Safari	✓		
Chrome		✓	✓
Opera		✓	✓

What this means for you as a Web page author is that currently under HTML5, you need two versions of your video files: one in MP4 format and the other in either WebM or Ogg Theora. This situation is reminiscent of the battle between Betamax and VHS in the 1980s for dominance of the home video market. Unfortunately, these differences in format support make it more difficult for the Web to quickly move to the HTML5 standard for embedded video.

Using the HTML5 `video` Element

Maxine has decided to go ahead with using HTML5 to embed the video clip from *Royal Wedding* in her Web page. She has created versions of the clip in MP4 format and in WebM format. To add a video to a Web page in HTML5, the code is similar to what you used with the `audio` element

```
<video>
   <source src="url1" />
   <source src="url2" />
 ...
</video>
```

where *url1*, *url2*, etc. are the possible sources of the video clip. As with sources for the `audio` element, a browser uses the first source it finds in a format it supports.

REFERENCE

Adding Video in HTML5

- To add a video clip with HTML5 use

```
<video>
   <source src="url1" />
   <source src="url2" />
 ...
</video>
```

where *url1*, *url2*, etc. are the possible sources of the video clip.

You'll add the *Royal Wedding* video to Maxine's page now.

To add the *Royal Wedding* video:

1. Return to the **jumbo.htm** file in your Web browser.

2. Directly below the h2 heading, *In Focus*, insert the following code (see Figure 7-21):

```
<video>
    <source src="rwdance.mp4" />
    <source src="rwdance.webm" />
</video>
```

You must include the video source in both the MP4 and WebM formats to ensure support across all of the major browsers.

Figure 7-21	Using the HTML5 video element

```
<article>
    <h2>In Focus</h2>

    <video>
        <source src="rwdance.mp4" />
        <source src="rwdance.webm" />
    </video>
</article>
```

file version in MP4 format →

file version in WebM format ←

3. Save your changes to the file.

The video element supports many of the same attributes as the audio element. For example, to display video controls, you add the attribute controls="controls" to the <video> tag. Figure 7-22 describes the other video attributes supported in HTML5.

Figure 7-22	Attributes of the video element

Attribute	Description
audio="muted"	Mutes the audio track of the video clip
autoplay="autoplay"	Starts playing the video clip as soon as it is downloaded
controls="controls"	Displays the video controls
height="value"	Sets the height of the video clip in pixels
loop="loop"	Automatically restarts the video clip when it is finished playing
poster="url"	Specifies the url of an image that represents the video
preload="type"	Specifies whether the video clip should be preloaded by the browser, where type is auto (to load the entire clip), metadata (to preload only descriptive data about the clip), or none (not to preload the video clip)
src="url"	Specifies the source of the video clip, where url is the location and name of the video file
width="value"	Specifies the width of the video clip in pixels

As you did with the audio clip, add controls to the video clip, format the style of the video clip, and then display it in your browser.

To display the *Royal Wedding* video:

▶ **1.** Within the opening `<video>` tag, insert the attribute `controls="controls"` as shown in Figure 7-23.

Figure 7-23 | **Adding controls to the video element**

```
<video controls="controls">
        <source src="rwdance.mp4" />
        <source src="rwdance.webm" />
</video>
```
← displays player controls with the video

▶ **2.** Save your changes to the file, and then go to the **clips.css** file in your text editor.

▶ **3.** Add the selector, `video` to the style rule (see Figure 7-24).

Figure 7-24 | **Style rule for the video element**

```
audio, video {
        background-color: white;
        display: block;
        margin: 5px auto;
        text-align: center;
        width: 95%;
}
```

▶ **4.** Save your changes to the file, and then reload **jumbo.htm** in your Web browser. The browser displays the video clip along with the video controls. As shown in Figure 7-25, different browsers have slightly different video players.

Figure 7-25 | **The video player as rendered by different browsers**

Internet Explorer

Firefox

Opera

Safari for Windows

Google Chrome

Safari for the Macintosh

▶ **5.** Click the **play** button on your browser's video player and confirm that you can play the video clip within the Web page.

Adding Video Captions with Web Tracks

One goal of HTML5 is to make the Web more accessible to all users. To this end, in 2010 HTML5 introduced the ability to time-synchronize audio and video clips with text using the `track` element

```
<video attributes>
   <track kind="type" src="url" label="text" />
</video>
```

where the `kind` attribute defines the kind of text track associated with the audio or video clip, the `src` attribute provides the location and filename of the track text, and the `label` attribute provides a title for the text track. The `kind` attribute has the following five possible values—`subtitles` (for foreign language subtitles), `captions` (for closed-captioning), `descriptions` (to augment the audio or video with textual information), `chapters` (used to divide the audio or video track into topical sections), and `metadata` (for meta information that can be used with a program script).

Currently, the proposed format for time-synchronized text is **WebVTT** (**Web Video Text Tracks**). A WebVTT file consists of several time entries, each marked with a time stamp. As the audio or video clip is played, the entries are displayed and synchronized alongside the `audio` or `video` element. WebVTT also allows a developer to place captions at specific locations within a video clip and to format the caption text using CSS.

The following code shows how HTML5 could augment the *Royal Wedding* dance clip with a commentary track from the *commentary.vtt* file:

```
<video controls="controls">
   <source="rwdance.mp4" />
   <track kind="description" src="commentary.vtt" label="Commentary"
/>
</video>
```

Currently, the `track` element and WebVTT are not supported by the browser market. However, this will change in the upcoming years as HTML5 gains wider acceptance and the W3C finalizes the specifications for Web tracks.

Introducing the `object` Element

For browsers that don't support the HTML5 `video` element, you once again must nest an embedded object. To do this, you'll use the `object` element.

The `object` element was introduced in the specifications for HTML 4 for the purpose of marking any kind of nontextual content. The `object` element replaced the `embed` element, which was widely supported though never part of the previous HTML specifications released by the W3C. The syntax of the object element is

```
<object attributes>
   parameters
</object>
```

where *attributes* define the object and *parameters* is values passed to the object controlling the object's appearance and actions. The `object` element can be used with almost any type of content, from sound and video clips to graphic images, PDF files, and even the content of other Web pages. Figure 7-26 describes some of the attributes associated with the `object` element.

Figure 7-26	Attributes of the object element

Attribute	Description
data="*url*"	Specifies the source of the file used in the object
form="*name*"	Specifies the name of the form that the object belongs to (HTML5)
height="*value*"	Sets the height of the object in pixels
name="*name*"	Provides a unique name for the object
type="*mime*"	Identifies the MIME type of the data within the object
usemap="*url*"	Associates the object with a client-side image map
width="*value*"	Sets the width of the object in pixels

For example, the following `object` element could be used in place of the `embed` element you used earlier to insert the *overture.mp3* audio clip:

```
<object data="overture.mp3" type="audio/mpeg"
        height="20" width="250">
</object>
```

Most objects also use parameters that define how users interact with the object; you declare these parameters with the element

```
<param name="name" value="value" />
```

where the `name` attribute is the name of the parameter and the `value` attribute provides the parameter's value. To embed a QuickTime Player using the `object` element, you could define the source of the audio clip by adding the following `param` element:

```
<object data="overture.mp3" type="audio/mpeg"
        height="20" width="250">
   <param name="src" value="overture.mp3" />
</object>
```

Note that the filename is provided twice—once as an attribute of the `object` element, and a second time with the `param` element. This is because browsers differ on whether they use the `data` attribute or the `param` element. Also note that there is no standard list of HTML parameter names and values. They differ based on the object being embedded and the browsers you need to support in your Web page. However, the `name` parameter should be supported by most browsers.

Working with Flash

Maxine will use the `object` element to place a Flash video in her Web page. There are two main file formats involved in creating a Flash video. The first is the **FLV** or **Flash Video** file that contains a video clip that will be displayed by **Adobe Flash Player**. The Flash Video file is often embedded within a Shockwave Flash file. A **Shockwave Flash** or **SWF** file contains the video, audio, animations, interactive scripts, program controls, and other features that provide real-time interactive animation for the viewer. One advantage of a SWF file is that programmers can create their own players, containing video controls tailored to the specific needs of their Web site. It's not uncommon to observe Web sites containing players reflecting the Web site's content or design. For example, video played with YouTube's player displays the YouTube logo in the lower-right corner of each frame.

Flash and Apple

Within the last several years, Adobe Flash became the dominant format for embedding video on the Web because Adobe Flash Player was free and available on a variety of different platforms and operating systems. However in April 2010, Steve Jobs, CEO of Apple, explained that Apple would not support Flash on its mobile devices, including the iPhone, iPod, and iPad. Among the reasons cited, Jobs included his concerns that a) Flash was proprietary, a fact that inhibits the future development of multimedia on the Web; b) Flash was not secure or reliable and adversely affects the performance of mobile devices; c) Flash was a significant drain on battery life; and d) Flash was designed for PCs using a mouse interface and could not be adapted to the touch interface found on mobile devices. Rather than relying on Flash, Jobs advocated the continuing development of open standards for Web video including the rapid adoption of HTML5.

However, thousands of Web sites had made considerable investments in Flash and were not happy with the prospect of significantly retooling their sites. In response, in March 2011, Adobe released a tool to convert Flash files to HTML5-compatible formats so they run on Apple's mobile devices. Also, Flash is supported on several mobile operating systems, such as the Android platform for mobile devices.

Users running older browsers will not be able to use HTML5 video; so for complete cross-browser support, you'll make a Flash version of the *Royal Wedding* clip available to users. Maxine has created an Adobe Flash Player file named *rwdance.swf* containing both the video clip and the controls to run it.

Embedding a Flash Player

To embed a Flash Player, you use the `object` element

```
<object data="url"
        type="application/x-shockwave-flash"
        width="value" height="value">
   <param name="movie" value="url" />
   parameters

</object>
```

where *url* is the location and filename of the SWF file, and *parameters* is other parameter elements that manage the appearance and actions of the player. Notice that you always must include at least the `movie` parameter to identify the video file to be played in the Flash player.

REFERENCE

Adding a Flash Player File

- To add a Flash player (.swf) file, use the `object` element

```
<object data="url"
        type="application/x-shockwave-flash"
        width="value" height="value">
   <param name="movie" value="url" />
   parameters

</object>
```

   where *url* is the location and filename of the SWF file, and *parameters* is other parameter elements that manage the appearance and actions of the player.

You'll nest an `object` element within the `video` element you just created to display a Flash Player for the *rwdance.swf* file, setting the dimensions of the player to 280 pixels wide by 239 pixels high.

To embed a Flash player file:

1. Return to the **jumbo.htm** file in your text editor.
2. Within the `video` element, insert the following `object` element as shown in Figure 7-27:

```
<object data="rwdance.swf"
        type="application/x-shockwave-flash"
        width="280" height="239">
   <param name="movie" value="rwdance.swf" />
</object>
```

Figure 7-27 Nesting a Flash player using the object element

```
<video controls="controls">
     <source src="rwdance.mp4" />
     <source src="rwdance.webm" />

     <object data="rwdance.swf"
             type="application/x-shockwave-flash"
             width="280" height="239">
        <param name="movie" value="rwdance.swf" />
     </object>

</video>
```

Shockwave Flash player file

Shockwave Flash MIME type

3. Save your changes to the file.

Before running your Flash video, you'll first add a few more parameters to the Flash player.

Working with Flash Parameters

The `movie` parameter is only one of the Flash player parameters. Figure 7-28 describes some of the other parameters associated with Adobe Flash Player, along with their values.

Figure 7-28	Parameters of the Flash player

Name	Value(s)	Description
bgcolor	#rrggbb	color name	Sets the background color of the Flash player
flash-var	text	Contains text values that are passed to the Flash player as variables to control the behavior and content of the movie
id	text	Identifies the embedded Flash movie so that it can be referenced
loop	true	false	Plays the movie in a continuous loop
menu	true	false	Displays the full Flash popup when a user right-clicks the movie
name	text	Names the embedded Flash movie so that it can be referenced
play	true	false	Starts playing the movie automatically when the page loads
quality	low	autolow	autohigh	medium	high	best	Sets the playback quality of the movie; low values favor playback speed over display quality; high values favor display quality over playback speed
scale	showall	noborder	exactfit	Defines how the movie clip is scaled within the defined space; a value of showall makes the entire clip visible in the specified area without distortion; a value of noborder scales the movie to fill the specified area, without distortion but possibly with some cropping; a value of exactfit makes the entire movie visible in the specified area without trying to preserve the original aspect ratio
wmode	window	opaque	transparent	Sets the appearance of the Flash player against the page background; a value of window causes the movie to play within its own window in the page; a value of opaque hides everything in the page behind the clip; a value of transparent allows the page background to show through transparent colors in the movie

For example, if you wanted to set the playback quality of a Flash movie to high, you would add the following parameter to the object element:

```
<param name="quality" value="high" />
```

Note that Flash movies with high display quality may suffer from ragged playback, so you must test your video clips to ensure that the speed of each clip is still sufficient for viewers.

Maxine suggests that you set the playback quality of the *rwdance.swf* clip to high. She also asks you to change the menu settings so that viewers see only the brief version of the popup menu rather than the full version. Using a brief Flash popup menu is a standard approach on the Web so that viewers cannot change the playback settings chosen by the clip's author.

To add parameters to the Flash Player:

▶ **1.** Add the following parameters to the `object` element for the *rwdance.swf* file, as shown in Figure 7-29:

```
<param name="quality" value="high" />
<param name="menu" value="false" />
```

Figure 7-29   Adding parameters to the Flash player

```
<object data="rwdance.swf"
        type="application/x-shockwave-flash"
        width="280" height="239">
    <param name="movie" value="rwdance.swf" />
    <param name="quality" value="high" />
    <param name="menu" value="false" />
</object>
```

parameters of the Flash player

▶ **2.** Save your changes to the file and then reload **jumbo.htm** in a Web browser that does not support HTML5 but does support Adobe Flash player. If you are running Internet Explorer, you can press the **F12** key and change the browser and document mode to Internet Explorer 7 or Internet Explorer 8.

▶ **3.** Click the **play** button on the player to verify that the Flash player works properly within your browser. Figure 7-30 shows the appearance of the Flash player and the *Royal Wedding* clip.

Figure 7-30   Flash player displaying the Royal Wedding clip

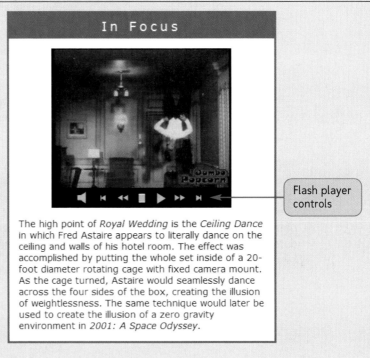

Flash player controls

The high point of *Royal Wedding* is the *Ceiling Dance* in which Fred Astaire appears to literally dance on the ceiling and walls of his hotel room. The effect was accomplished by putting the whole set inside of a 20-foot diameter rotating cage with fixed camera mount. As the cage turned, Astaire would seamlessly dance across the four sides of the box, creating the illusion of weightlessness. The same technique would later be used to create the illusion of a zero gravity environment in *2001: A Space Odyssey*.

▶ **4.** Right-click the embedded video and verify that the popup menu has only two entries—Settings and About Adobe Flash Player.

Trouble? On a Macintosh you might not see the two entries in the popup menu.

▶ **5.** If you changed the settings of your Internet Explorer browser, press the **F12** key and change them back to use more current browser settings.

The Flash Player that Maxine created for her Web site has a few interesting features. She customized the video control buttons, and she placed the Jumbo Popcorn logo in the lower-right corner of the player. This demonstrates a few of the features of Flash that have made it so popular for designers who want to customize the multimedia on their Web sites.

Nesting a Hypertext Link

Finally, Maxine is concerned about browsers that don't support HTML5 video or Shockwave Flash. For those users, you can create a hypertext link directing them to a location where they can download and install the Flash player. The link should be nested within the `object` element, which itself is nested within the `video` element; thus, only users who run browsers supporting neither HTML5 video nor the Flash player will see the link.

To add the hypertext link:

1. Return to the **jumbo.htm** file in your text editor.

2. Directly after the last `parameter` element, insert the following hypertext link as shown in Figure 7-31:

```
You must have the
<a href="http://www.adobe.com/products/shockwaveplayer/">
   Shockwave Player
</a>
to play the video clip.
```

Figure 7-31 | Code nested within the object element

```
<object data="rwdance.swf"
        type="application/x-shockwave-flash"
        width="280" height="239">
   <param name="movie" value="rwdance.swf" />
   <param name="quality" value="high" />
   <param name="menu" value="false" />
   You must have the
   <a href="http://www.adobe.com/products/shockwaveplayer/">
      Shockwave Player
   </a>
   to play the video clip.
</object>
```

code used by browsers that support neither HTML5 nor Flash

3. Save your changes to the file, and then return to a Web browser that does not support HTML5 video.

4. If necessary, disable the Shockwave Player add-on from the browser, and then reload the **jumbo.htm** file. As shown in Figure 7-32, the browser should now display a hypertext link to the site where users can download the Shockwave Player.

| Figure 7-32 | Content displayed when Flash is not available |

hypertext link
displayed by browsers
that support neither
HTML5 nor Flash

In Focus

You must have the Shockwave Player to play
the video clip.

The high point of *Royal Wedding* is the *Ceiling Dance*
in which Fred Astaire appears to literally dance on the
ceiling and walls of his hotel room. The effect was
accomplished by putting the whole set inside of a 20-
foot diameter rotating cage with fixed camera mount.
As the cage turned, Astaire would seamlessly dance
across the four sides of the box, creating the illusion
of weightlessness. The same technique would later be
used to create the illusion of a zero gravity
environment in *2001: A Space Odyssey*.

▶ **5.** Re-enable the Shockwave Player add-on in your browser if necessary.

Embedding Videos from YouTube

With hundreds of millions of videos stored online, the most popular site to view and share
videos is YouTube. In May 2010 alone, more than 14.6 billion videos were viewed by visitors
to the site (*www.comscore.com/Press_Events/Press_Releases/2010/6/comScore_Releases_
May_2010_U.S._Online_Video_Rankings*), accounting for 43.1% of videos viewed online.

YouTube videos are embedded using either the YouTube Shockwave Flash player file
(.swf) or, depending on each user's device and playing preferences, an HTML5 video
player. The general syntax of the HTML code is

```
<object width="value" height="value">
    <param name="movie" value="url" />
    parameters
    <embed src="url"
           type="application/x-shockwave-flash"
           width="value" height="value"
           parameters />
</object>
```

where *url* is the URL of the video stored on the YouTube Web site, and *parameters*
is parameters that control the actions and appearance of the YouTube video player. The
URL for a YouTube video has the general form *http://www.youtube.com/id?parameters*,
where *id* is the id of the video itself and *parameters* is a list of parameters that control
the actions and appearance of the player. The parameters are entered into the URL as
parameter=value, with multiple parameter/value pairs separated from one another with
an ampersand (&) symbol. Figure 7-33 lists some of the YouTube parameters that can be
entered into a URL.

Figure 7-33	Parameters of the YouTube player

Parameter	Default Value	Description
autoplay=0|1	0	Indicates whether to play the video automatically (1) or to wait for the user to press the play button (0)
controls=0|1	1	Removes the player controls (0) or displays them (1)
fs=0|1	0	Enables the user to play the video full screen (1) or not (0)
hd=0|1	0	Causes the high-definition version of the video to play (1) or not (0)
loop=0|1	0	Sets the video to repeat (1) or to play only once (0)
playlist=list		Plays a list of videos, where list is a comma-separated list of videos
rel=0|1	1	Indicates whether to display a list of related YouTube videos (1) or to disable that feature (0)
start=value		Starts the video playback value seconds into the video

For example, the following URL identifies a unique YouTube video, allows users to play the video in full-screen mode, and displays a list of related videos when the clip is finished:

```
http://www.youtube.com/v/iaN8M0pDOeM?fs=1&rel=1
```

The complete HTML code is as follows:

```
<object width="640" height="349">
   <param name="movie"
    value="http://www.youtube.com/v/iaN8M0pDOeM?fs=1&rel=1" />
   <param name="allowFullScreen" value="true" />
   <embed src="http://www.youtube.com/v/iaN8M0pDOeM?fs=1&rel=1"
          type="application/x-shockwave-flash"
          width="640" height="349"
          allowFullScreen="true" />
</object>
```

Notice that you also can include the allowFullScreen parameter either as a param element or as an attribute of the embed element to turn on full-screen viewing of the video.

Starting in 2010, YouTube also began providing alternate embedding code to support browsers using HTML5 that do not support Flash. The general syntax is

```
<iframe type="text/html" width="value" height="value"
        src="url"
        frameborder="0" parameters>
</iframe>
```

TIP

You can learn more about the iframe element in the appendices.

where once again url identifies the YouTube video and parameters controls the appearance and actions of the YouTube player. The iframe element is used to store inline frames, which are windows into the content of another Web page or Internet resource.

YouTube makes it very easy to generate the code required to embed its videos. You simply can click the Share button below a video on the YouTube Web site and copy the HTML code displayed by YouTube into the appropriate location in your HTML file. Please note that any videos submitted to YouTube are still subject to copyright restrictions and are removed if those restrictions are violated.

The `object` Element and ActiveX

Internet Explorer supports a technology called ActiveX to play embedded media. **ActiveX** employs reusable software components that can be run from within a variety of Windows programs. For example, a programmer could create an ActiveX component to display a drop-down list box to be run within Internet Explorer, and that same component could be run from within Microsoft Word or Microsoft Excel. Another ActiveX component could be created to play video clips or sound files.

There are literally thousands of ActiveX components available to programmers and end users. The problem is that ActiveX is a technology designed only for Windows, and thus you cannot rely solely upon it if you're developing a program or Web site that will be used under a variety of operating systems. ActiveX components can be accessed using the `object` element once you have installed the ActiveX control on your computer.

The `classid` Attribute

Each ActiveX component is identified by a unique string of characters called the **class id**. The class id value is determined by the developer of the ActiveX control. Figure 7-34 lists the class id values for several ActiveX controls that can be used with multimedia players.

Figure 7-34   ActiveX class ids

ActiveX Control	Class id
Flash Shockwave Player	D27CDB6E-AE6D-11cf-96B8-444553540000
QuickTime Player	02BF25D5-8C17-4B23-BC80-D3488ABDDC6B
RealAudio Player	CFCDAA03-8BE4-11cf-B84B-0020AFBBCCFA
Windows Media Player	6BF52A52-394A-11d3-B153-00C04F79FAA6
Java applet	8AD9C840-044E-11D1-B3E9-00805F499D93

To insert a specific ActiveX control into your Web page, you must add the `classid` attribute

```
classid="clsid:id"
```

to the `object` element, where `id` is the class id of the ActiveX control. For example, to insert the ActiveX control for the QuickTime Player, you would add the following `classid` attribute to the `<object>` tag:

```
classid="clsid:02BF25D5-8C17-4B23-BC80-D3488ABDDC6B"
```

Class id values are not case sensitive, so you can use upper- or lowercase letters in your HTML code; however, you do have to enter the entire class id string with no omissions or errors. Given the length of a class id text string, this makes writing code for ActiveX objects a bit cumbersome. You can find the class id values for each ActiveX control by viewing the developer's documentation.

The codebase Attribute

When a browser encounters a plug-in or an ActiveX control that it doesn't recognize, it usually leaves a blank space where the embedded object normally would appear. One way of dealing with this problem is to provide browsers with information about where a working version of the plug-in or control can be downloaded. This is done by adding the codebase attribute

```
codebase="url"
```

to the object element, where url is the filename and location of the program. In some cases, these programs are stored in installation files called **cab** or **cabinet files**, which automatically install the necessary software on users' computers. You usually can find the location of installation programs in the developer's documentation. For instance, for the ActiveX QuickTime Player, the URL for the cabinet file is *www.apple.com/qtactivex/qtplugin.cab*. Thus, to embed an object using the ActiveX version of the QuickTime Player, you would enter the code

```
<object classid="clsid:02BF25D5-8C17-4B23-BC80-D3488ABDDC6B"
        codebase="http://www.apple.com/qtactivex/qtplugin.cab">

    parameters

</object>
```

in your Web page, where *parameters* is the object parameters associated with the QuickTime video player. When Internet Explorer encounters this object, it first attempts to insert the ActiveX QuickTime control into the Web page. If it can't find an ActiveX control on the computer with that class id value, it then accesses the cab file at the URL specified in the codebase attribute and prompts the user to install the ActiveX control from that location. This frees the user from having to search for the program file.

Both the classid and codebase attributes were part of the specifications for the object element in HTML4; however, they are not part of the specifications for the object element in HTML5 and thus might not be supported by future browser versions.

PROSKILLS

Problem Solving: Tips for Effective Web Video

Web video is one of the most important mediums for conveying information and advertising products and services. With inexpensive hardware and sophisticated video editing software, almost anyone can be a movie producer with free, instant distribution available through the Web. However, this also means you have a lot of competition to get noticed and it's essential that your videos be polished and professional. Here are some things to keep in mind when creating a Web video:

- *Keep it short.* Studies have shown that Web users have an attention span of about 4 seconds. If they don't receive valuable information within that time, they'll go to a different site. This means your Web video must get to the point quickly and keep users' attention. Also recognize that most users will not watch your entire video, so make your key points *early.*
- *Keep the image simple.* Your video probably will be rendered in a tiny frame, so make your content easier to view by shooting close-ups. Avoid wide-angle shots that will make your subject even smaller to the user's eye. Avoid complex backgrounds and distracting color schemes.
- *Keep the human element.* Eye-tracking studies have shown that people naturally gravitate to human faces for information and emotional content. Use tight shots in which the narrator speaks directly into the camera.
- *Use effective lighting.* Light should be projected onto the subject. Avoid relying solely on overhead lights, which can create distracting facial shadows. Video compression can result in loss of detail; thus, make sure you use bright lighting on key areas to highlight and focus users' attention on the important images in your video.
- *Follow the rule of thirds.* Avoid static layouts by imagining the frame divided into a 3 × 3 grid. Balance items of interest along the lines of the intersection in the grid rather than centered within the frame. If interviewing a subject, leave ample headroom at the top of the frame.
- *Avoid pans and zooms.* Excessive panning and zooming can make your Web video appear choppy and distorted, and unnecessary movement slows down the video stream.

Finally, consider investing in professional Web video services that can storyboard an idea for you, and that have the experience and expertise to create a finished product that will capture and keep the attention of users and customers.

Maxine is pleased with the work you've done embedding the video in several different formats in the *Royal Wedding* page. In the next session, you'll explore how to work with program applets by adding a scrolling marquee to Maxine's page.

Session 7.2 Quick Check

REVIEW

1. Define the terms *frame, frame rate, video bit rate,* and *codec*.
2. Why does saving Web video at a high frame rate and video bit rate not always result in high-quality video playback?
3. What is a container file? Which three container file formats are currently supported under HTML5 video?
4. Provide the code to insert the file *trailer.mp4* or *trailer.webm* as an HTML5 video.
5. Describe some of the benefits and limitations of using Shockwave Flash to embed Web video.
6. Provide the code to embed the file *trailer.swf* as a Web page object. Set the dimensions of the Flash player to 350 pixels wide by 150 pixels high.
7. What parameter would you enter to cause the Flash player to start playing the movie automatically when the page loads?

SESSION 7.3 VISUAL OVERVIEW

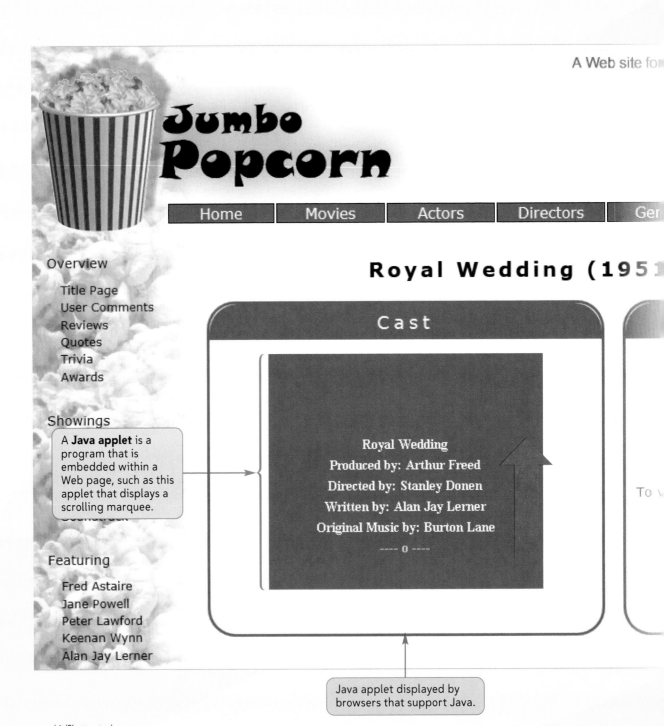

A **Java applet** is a program that is embedded within a Web page, such as this applet that displays a scrolling marquee.

Java applet displayed by browsers that support Java.

graphit/Shutterstock.com

Gl0ck/Shutterstock.com

EMBEDDING AN APPLET

```
<object type="application/x-java-applet"
                   width="250" height="250">
  <param name="code" value="CreditRoll.class" />

  <param name="fontsize" value="14" />
  <param name="bgcolor" value="A27029" />
  <param name="textcolor" value="FFFFFF" />
  <param name="text1" value="Royal Wedding" />
  <param name="text2" value="Produced by: Arthur Freed" />
  ...

     Tom Bowen ... Fred Astaire<br />
     Ellen Bowen ... Jane Powell<br />
     Lord John Brindale ... Peter Lawford<br />
     Anne Ashmond ... Sarah Churchill<br />
     Irving Klinger ... Keenan Wynn<br />
     Edgar Klinger ... Keenan Wynn<br />
     James Ashmond ... Albert Sharpe

     <br /><br />
     To view a scrolling marquee, get the latest
     <a href="http://java.sun.com/products/plugin/downloads">
        Java Plug-in.
     </a>
</object>
```

The **object element** contains the CreditRoll.class applet embedded within the Web page.

Parameters for the applet are defined using the param element.

Nested within the object element is **alternate content** that is displayed by browsers that do not support Java.

A Web site f...

...rs   Ge...

g (195...

Cast

Tom Bowen ... Fred Astaire
Ellen Bowen ... Jane Powell
Lord John Brindale ... Peter Lawford
Anne Ashmond ... Sarah Churchill
Irving Klinger ... Keenan Wynn
Edgar Klinger ... Keenan Wynn
James Ashmond ... Albert Sharpe

To view a scrolling marquee, get the latest Java Plug-in.

Content displayed by browsers that don't support Java.

Introducing Java

Maxine has included a cast list for *Royal Wedding* on her Web site. Currently, the list displays only a few of the actors and actresses from the movie. Maxine would like to expand the list to include more of the cast as well as the director, producers, and writers; however, doing so would result in a list so long that it would ruin her page layout. Instead of a long list, Maxine envisions a scrolling cast list mimicking the credits that appear at the end of a movie. Maxine has seen scrolling text on other Web sites and wonders if you could add a similar feature to her Web page. You can do so with a programming language called Java.

As with many computing innovations, Java came from some unexpected sources. In the early 1990s, programmers at Sun Microsystems envisioned a day when common appliances and devices, such as refrigerators, toasters, and garage door openers, would be networked and controllable using a single operating system. Such an operating system would need to be portable because it obviously would need to be able to work with a wide variety of devices. The programmers began development on such an operating system and based it on a language called Oak. The project did not succeed at that point (perhaps the world was not ready for toasters and refrigerators to communicate), but the initial work on Oak was so promising that Sun Microsystems saw its potential for use on the Internet. Oak was modified in 1995 and renamed **Java**.

Java programs are stored in executable files called **class files**, which have the file extension *.class*. Some Java applications might require several class files to run properly. Each class file is run within a **Java Virtual Machine**, a software program that runs the class file and returns the results to the user's computer. Java Virtual Machines can be created for different operating systems, so a Java program can be run from any operating system, including UNIX, Windows, DOS, and Mac OS. Just as Web pages were designed at the beginning to be platform-independent, so was Java, and it became a natural fit for use on the Web. Web browsers soon began supporting Java Virtual Machines and Web developers began using Java to add interactive features to their Web sites.

A Java program is not a stand-alone application, but instead runs in conjunction with a hosting program such as a Web browser. The program is therefore a mini application or **applet**. When a user connects to a Web page containing a Java applet, the applet is downloaded along with the Web page from the Web server; but the applet itself runs within the Java Virtual Machine on the user's computer. This frees up the Web server for other tasks, as shown in Figure 7-35.

Figure 7-35   Applets and Java Virtual Machines

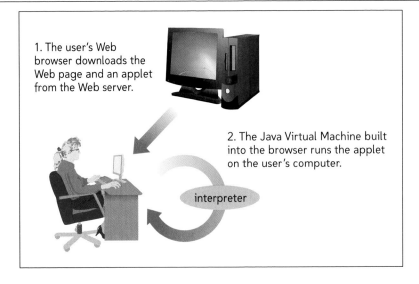

1. The user's Web browser downloads the Web page and an applet from the Web server.

2. The Java Virtual Machine built into the browser runs the applet on the user's computer.

interpreter

Applets are embedded within Web pages just like the sound and video clips you embedded in the first two sessions of this tutorial. The applet runs within an applet window, which can be resized and positioned anywhere within the page.

Libraries of Java applets are available on the Web. Some applets are free to download and use for non-commercial purposes. In other cases, programmers charge a fee for the use of their applets. You can find Java applets for a variety of tasks, including stock market tickers, games, animations, and utilities for your browser or Web page. The popularity of Java has declined in recent years as more and more of its features can be duplicated with Flash or JavaScript. The programming enhancements provided with HTML5 also will result in an even more reduced need for Java. However, for the moment, Maxine still wants to use a Java applet with her sample page.

Working with Java Applets

Java applets are embedded with the same `object` element you used in the last session to embed a Flash player. The general syntax of an embedded Java applet is

```
<object type="application/x-java-applet"
        width="value" height="value">

   <param name="code" value="url" />
   parameters
</object>
```

where the `width` and `height` attributes define the dimensions of the applet window, `url` specifies the location and filename of the Java file (usually the class file), and `parameters` represents the parameters associated with running the applet.

Embedding a Java Applet

Maxine has located a Java applet to display text in a scrolling marquee. The name of the class file is *CreditRoll.class*. You'll embed this applet in her Web page both as an ActiveX object for Internet Explorer and as a plug-in for non-IE browsers.

REFERENCE

Embedding a Java Applet

- To embed a Java applet, use the `object` element

```
<object type="application/x-java-applet"
        width="value" height="value">

   <param name="code" value="url" />
   parameters
</object>
```

where the `width` and `height` attributes define the dimensions of the applet window, `url` specifies the location and filename of the Java file (usually the class file), and `parameters` represents the parameters associated with running the applet.

To embed the Java applet:

▶ **1.** Return to the **jumbo.htm** file in your text editor, and then scroll up to the paragraph listing the cast members.

▶ **2.** Directly above the cast list within the paragraph, insert the following code for the `object` element:

```
<object type="application/x-java-applet"
        width="250" height="250">

<param name="code" value="CreditRoll.class" />
```

▶ **3.** After the cast list, insert the closing `</object>` tag. Figure 7-36 highlights the newly inserted code.

Figure 7-36 **Object element for Java applet**

```
<section class="middle">

    <article>
        <h2>Cast</h2>
        <p>
                                                    Java MIME type

            <object type="application/x-java-applet"
                    width="250" height="250">

                <param name="code" value="CreditRoll.class" />

                Tom Bowen ... Fred Astaire<br />
                Ellen Bowen ... Jane Powell<br />
                Lord John Brindale ... Peter Lawford<br />
                Anne Ashmond ... Sarah Churchill<br />
                Irving Klinger ... Keenan Wynn<br />
                Edgar Klinger ... Keenan Wynn<br />
                James Ashmond ... Albert Sharpe

            </object>
        </p>
    </article>
```

class file containing Java applet

▶ **4.** Save your changes to the file.

Notice that you kept the cast list that Maxine previously entered in this document nested within the `object` element. If this page is opened by a browser that does not support Java, the browser will ignore the `object` and `param` elements but will still display the abbreviated cast list.

Inserting Java Parameters

The CreditRoll applet contains several parameters that define the text being scrolled, the speed of the scrolling, and the font and background styles. Figure 7-37 describes the parameters used by the CreditRoll applet.

Figure 7-37	Parameters of the CreditRoll.class

Parameter	Description
bgcolor	The background color of the applet window, expressed as a hexadecimal color value
fadezone	The text in the applet window fades in and out as it scrolls; this parameter sets the size of the area in which the text fades (in pixels)
textcolor	The color value of the text in the applet window
font	The font used for the scrolling text in the applet window
textx	Each line of text in the applet window requires a separate textx parameter, where x is the line number; for example, the parameter text1 sets the text for the first line in the applet window, text2 sets the text for the second line in the applet window, and so forth
url	Specifies the Web page that is opened if the applet window is clicked
repeat	Specifies whether the text in the applet window is repeated; setting this parameter's value to yes causes the text to scroll continuously
speed	The speed at which the text scrolls, expressed in milliseconds between each movement
vspace	The space between each line of text, in pixels
fontsize	The point size of the text in the applet window

Maxine would like the credit roll to appear in a 12-point white font on a brown background. She suggests setting the speed of the scrolling to 100, which is 100 milliseconds or 1/10 of a second between each movement of the text. She wants 3 pixels of space between each line of text and a fadezone value of 20 pixels. The scrolling should run continuously. Add these parameters and values to the object code for the CreditRoll applet.

To insert the parameters for the CreditRoll applet:

1. Add the following parameters directly above the text for the cast list to set the font style of the scrolling text:

```
<param name="fontsize" value="12" />
<param name="bgcolor" value="A27029" />
<param name="textcolor" value="FFFFFF" />
```

2. Add the following parameters to set the scrolling speed, the space between the lines of text, and the size of the fadezone:

```
<param name="speed" value="100" />
<param name="vspace" value="3" />
<param name="fadezone" value="20" />
```

3. Finally, set the CreditRoll applet to repeatedly scroll the text without stopping by adding the following parameter, as shown in Figure 7-38:

```
<param name="repeat" value="yes" />
```

Figure 7-38	Adding parameters for font style and scrolling

```
<object type="application/x-java-applet"
        width="250" height="250">


    <param name="code" value="CreditRoll.class" />

    <param name="fontsize" value="12" />
    <param name="bgcolor" value="A27029" />
    <param name="textcolor" value="FFFFFF" />

    <param name="speed" value="100" />
    <param name="vspace" value="3" />
    <param name="fadezone" value="20" />

    <param name="repeat" value="yes" />

    Tom Bowen ... Fred Astaire<br />
    Ellen Bowen ... Jane Powell<br />
    Lord John Brindale ... Peter Lawford<br />
    Anne Ashmond ... Sarah Churchill<br />
    Irving Klinger ... Keenan Wynn<br />
    Edgar Klinger ... Keenan Wynn<br />
    James Ashmond ... Albert Sharpe

</object>
```

parameters of the CreditRoll applet

▶ **4.** Save your changes to the file.

Next, you must specify the text of the rolling marquee. The credit roll text is entered into parameters named **text***x*, where *x* is the number of the line in the credit roll. Because of the length of the cast list, parameters named *text1* through *text19* already have been created for you and stored in a separate file in the tutorial.07\tutorial folder.

The CreditRoll applet also supports a parameter named **url** that adds a link to the credit roll, opening a Web page when a user clicks the applet window. Maxine suggests that you link the credit roll to a Web page from the Internet Movie Database describing *Royal Wedding*. The URL of the Web page is *www.imdb.com/title/tt0043983/*.

You'll add parameters for the credit roll text and the URL to the embedded applet now.

To add the scrolling text and URL:

▶ **1.** Use your text editor to open the **creditlist.txt** file from the tutorial.07\tutorial folder included with your Data Files and copy the parameter text. Close the file.

▶ **2.** Return to the **jumbo.htm** file in your text editor and paste the copied parameter text directly below the `<param>` tag for the `repeat` parameter.

▶ **3.** Add the following parameter to set the URL associated with the CreditRoll applet:

```
<param name="url" value="http://www.imdb.com/title/tt0043983" />
```

Figure 7-39 shows the revised code of the file.

Figure 7-39	Specifying the marquee text

```
<param name="repeat" value="yes" />

<param name="text1" value="Royal Wedding" />
<param name="text2" value="Produced by: Arthur Freed" />
<param name="text3" value="Directed by: Stanley Donen" />
<param name="text4" value="Written by: Alan Jay Lerner" />
<param name="text5" value="Original Music by: Burton Lane" />
<param name="text6" value="---- o ----" />
<param name="text7" value="" />
<param name="text8" value="Fred Astaire ... Tom Bowen" />
<param name="text9" value="Jane Powell ... Ellen Bowen" />
<param name="text10" value="Peter Lawford ... Lord John Brindale" />
<param name="text11" value="Sarah Churchill ... Anne Ashmond" />
<param name="text12" value="Keenan Wynn ... Irving Klinger" />
<param name="text13" value="Keenan Wynn ... Edgar Klinger" />
<param name="text14" value="Albert Sharpe ... James Ashmond" />
<param name="text15" value="Eddie ... Wilson Benge" />
<param name="text16" value="Charles Gordon ... Francis Bethencourt" />
<param name="text17" value="Dick ... William Cabanne" />
<param name="text18" value="Harry ... Jimmy Fairfax" />
<param name="text19" value="Billy ... John Hedloe" />

<param name="url" value="http://www.imdb.com/title/tt0043983" />

Tom Bowen ... Fred Astaire<br />
Ellen Bowen ... Jane Powell<br />
Lord John Brindale ... Peter Lawford<br />
Anne Ashmond ... Sarah Churchill<br />
Irving Klinger ... Keenan Wynn<br />
Edgar Klinger ... Keenan Wynn<br />
James Ashmond ... Albert Sharpe
```

4. Save your changes to the file, and then reload **jumbo.htm** in your Web browser. Verify that the Cast box contains a scrolling marquee of the cast from *Royal Wedding*. Figure 7-40 shows the completed Web page with all of the embedded objects.

Figure 7-40   Completed Royal Wedding page

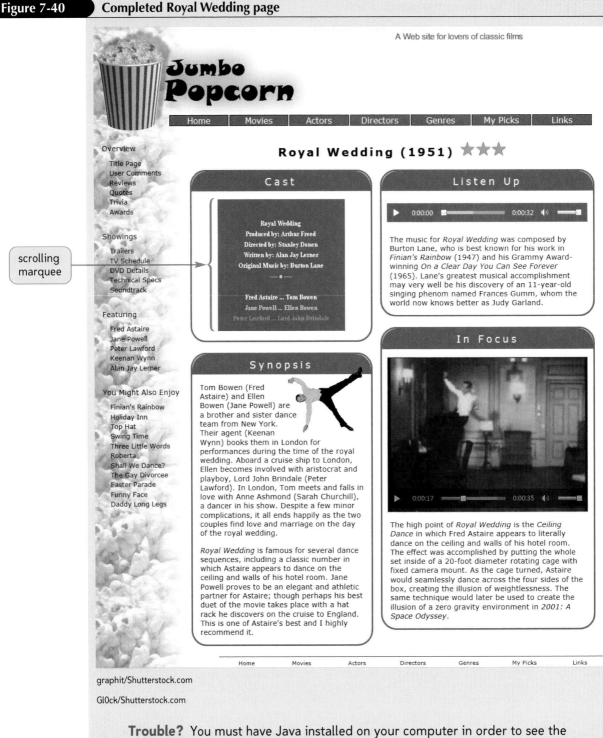

graphit/Shutterstock.com

GlOck/Shutterstock.com

Trouble? You must have Java installed on your computer in order to see the scrolling marquee. You can download Java from *www.java.com*. After downloading and installing the plug-in, you may be required to restart your browser.

5. Click the scrolling marquee box and verify that your Web browser opens a Web page from the Internet Movie Database describing the film.

You show Maxine the scrolling marquee, which she likes very much. She asks how the page will appear for users who don't have Java. You tell her that the page will show the abbreviated cast list used earlier. That text is still present in the Web page, though it won't be displayed if the CreditRoll applet can be run.

Maxine also wants you to include a hyperlink for users that informs them of the missing Java applet and tells them where they can download a version of Java to run on their machines.

To provide installation support for Java:

▶ **1.** Return to the **jumbo.htm** file in your text editor.

▶ **2.** Scroll down the file and add the following code after the last cast entry, as shown in Figure 7-41:

```
<br /><br />
To view a scrolling marquee, get the latest
<a href="http://www.java.com">
    Java Plug-in.
</a>
```

Figure 7-41	Specifying alternate text to the Java applet

```
            Tom Bowen ... Fred Astaire<br />
            Ellen Bowen ... Jane Powell<br />
            Lord John Brindale ... Peter Lawford<br />
            Anne Ashmond ... Sarah Churchill<br />
            Irving Klinger ... Keenan Wynn<br />
            Edgar Klinger ... Keenan Wynn<br />
            James Ashmond ... Albert Sharpe

            <br /><br />
            To view a scrolling marquee, get the latest
            <a href="http://www.java.com">
                Java Plug-in.
            </a>

        </object>
```

display a link to the Java Web site for browsers that don't have Java installed

▶ **3.** Close the file, saving your changes.

▶ **4.** Reload the **jumbo.htm** file in your Web browser and use the settings on your browser to temporarily disable the Java applet. As shown in Figure 7-42, your browser should now display the abbreviated cast list and a link to the Web site where users can download and install Java.

Figure 7-42 **Alternate text as rendered in the Web page**

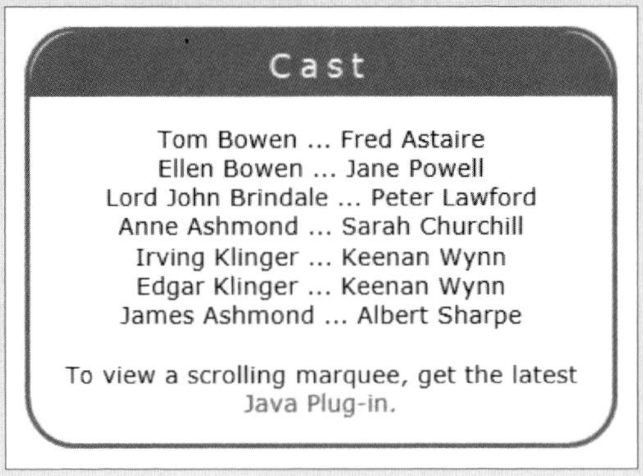

```
                        C a s t

            Tom Bowen ... Fred Astaire
            Ellen Bowen ... Jane Powell
     Lord John Brindale ... Peter Lawford
       Anne Ashmond ... Sarah Churchill
         Irving Klinger ... Keenan Wynn
        Edgar Klinger ... Keenan Wynn
       James Ashmond ... Albert Sharpe

     To view a scrolling marquee, get the latest
                  Java Plug-in.
```

▶ **5.** Re-enable the Java applet in your browser.

Embedding Java with the `applet` Element

If you are working with legacy pages containing old HTML code, you might encounter Java programs embedded in the page with the `applet` element

```
<applet code="url" width="value" height="value" alt="text">
   parameters
</applet>
```

where `url` is the location and name of the Java class file, the `width` and `height` attributes set the dimensions of the applet window, the `alt` attribute defines alternate text to be displayed by the browser if it doesn't support Java, and `parameters` represents the parameters associated with the applet. For example, to embed the *CreditRoll.class* applet using the `applet` element, you could enter the code

```
<applet code="CreditRoll.class" width="250" height="250">
   parameters
</applet>
```

with `parameters` employing the same `<param>` tags you used with the `object` element. The `<applet>` tag was never part of the W3C specifications for HTML and XHTML, and is gradually being phased out by current browsers.

Conditional Comments with Internet Explorer

One challenge in creating cross-browser Web sites is the fact that Internet Explorer often interprets code differently from other Web browsers. This was particularly true with embedded audio and video clips for which Internet Explorer used ActiveX technology to embed its multimedia player. Sometimes the easiest way to reconcile the two approaches was to run one set of code for Internet Explorer and another set of code for the other browsers. This could be done using **conditional comments** that employ the syntax

```
<!--[if condition IE version]>
   HTML code
<![endif]-->
```

where `condition` is a condition that is either true or false, `version` is the version number of an IE browser, and `HTML code` is code that will be run if the condition is true. If you want to run code only for Internet Explorer (regardless of the version), you would enter the following code:

```
<!--[if IE]>
   HTML code
<![endif]-->
```

If a non-IE browser encounters this code structure, it interprets the whole structure as one long HTML comment and does not attempt to parse any of the HTML code within the comment tags. You also can mark code to be run only if a browser is *not* Internet Explorer using the following structure:

```
<![if !IE]>
   HTML code
<![endif]>
```

One use of conditional comments was to create one opening `<object>` tag for Internet Explorer involving the use of ActiveX, and a different opening `<object>` tag for every other browser. For example, the following code uses conditional comments to create two possible sets of `<object>` tags for IE and non-IE browsers in order to embed a Java applet:

```
<!--[if IE]>
   <object type="application/x-java-applet"
    width="260" height="130"
    classid="clsid:8AD9C840-044E-11D1-B3E9-00805F499D93">
<![endif]-->

<![if !IE]>
   <object type="application/x-java-applet"
           width="260" height="130">
<![endif]>
```

The main difference between the two `<object>` tags is that the Internet Explorer version uses the `classid` attribute in order to access the ActiveX object for running Java. Other browsers, not requiring ActiveX, do not require that attribute.

With more recent versions of Internet Explorer supporting more of the W3C standards for CSS and HTML, and with the widespread adoption of HTML5, there is less of a need for conditional comments than before. You may still encounter them when working with the code for older Web pages, however.

Embedding Other Objects

So far in this tutorial, you've embedded sound clips, video clips, and Java applets. In fact, any type of content can be embedded using the `object` element; the original vision of the `object` element was to act as a general container for any content not directly entered into the HTML code of the Web page. Maxine suggests that you explore a few examples.

Inserting Inline Images

You can use the `<object>` tag to insert all of your inline images. One advantage of entering images as embedded objects is that you can apply markup tags for the alternate text. For example, the inline image

```
<img src="jplogo.jpg" alt="Jumbo Popcorn"
     width="300" height="200" />
```

can be replaced with the following embedded object:

```
<object data="jplogo.jpg" type="image/jpeg"
        width="300" height="200">
   <h1>Jumbo Popcorn</h1>
</object>
```

Another advantage of treating images as embedded objects is that you can provide users with different formats of the same graphic image. For example, the code

```
<object data="jplogo.png" type="image/png">
   <object data="jplogo.jpg" type="image/jpg">
      <h1>Jumbo Popcorn</h1>
   </object>
</object>
```

allows browsers to first display the Jumbo Popcorn logo in PNG format. If a browser does not support that format, the browser displays the logo as a JPEG. Finally, if the browser does not support either format or is a non-graphical browser, it displays the text *Jumbo Popcorn* marked as an `h1` heading.

You also can nest videos and inline images. For example, you can embed a video clip and nest an image object within the video clip, allowing browsers to choose which type of object to display.

Embedding an HTML File

Web pages themselves can be embedded as objects. To embed a Web page, you use the `<object>` tags

```
<object data="url" type="text/html"
        width="value" height="value">
</object>
```

where *url* is the URL of the HTML file to be embedded. When you embed a Web page, that file is displayed within the dimensions specified by the `width` and `height` attributes. Browsers automatically add horizontal and vertical scroll bars to allow users to scroll around the document. Figure 7-43 shows an example that Maxine might want to use on the Jumbo Popcorn Web site, showing a preview of the contents of the IMDB Web site (*www.imdb.com/title/tt0043983/*) describing *Royal Wedding*.

| Figure 7-43 | Embedded object containing external page |

graphit/Shutterstock.com

Gl0ck/Shutterstock.com

You also can embed Web pages using inline frames with the `iframe` element

```
<iframe src="url" width="value" height="value">
   alternate content
</iframe>
```

where `alternate content` is the content that is displayed for browsers that don't support inline frames. Thus, the following `iframe` element displays the content of the *Royal Wedding* page at the IMDB Web site in a frame that is 400 pixels wide and 200 pixels high:

```
<iframe src="http://www.imdb.com/title/tt0043983/"
   width="400" height="200">
</iframe>
```

Browsers support either the `object` element or the `iframe` element for embedded Web pages. The `iframe` element is more commonly used on the Web; but if you are writing your code in compliance with the strict application of XHTML, you should use the `object` element.

PROSKILLS

Problem Solving: Making Multimedia Content Accessible

Users with impaired vision, hearing, or motor skills may find it difficult to work with sites that offer embedded content. One survey has shown that 71% of users who employ screen readers found it difficult to work with Flash players and Java applets (*http://webaim.org/projects/screenreadersurvey2/*). In fact, that survey ranked Flash as the technology that presented the greatest obstacles when used with screen readers. There are several things you can do to make your Web site more accessible to all users without sacrificing content.

Adobe Flash Professional software includes development tools to make the Flash player more accessible. For example, this Flash software allows you to augment your multimedia with captions that can be added to either FLV or H.264 video. The captioning tools also support the Unicode character map for international closed captioning. The latest Flash player at the time of this writing, Adobe Flash Player 10, offers support for keyboard navigation so that users are not required to interact with the player using a mouse. If you are designing content using Flash, you should avail yourself of these tools.

There are also tools available to allow Java to interact more effectively with screen readers. One of these tools, the Java Access Bridge, integrates Java with the assistive technologies in the Microsoft Windows operating system, which then can be used by different screen readers to allow visually impaired users to interact with Java.

In the end, the best practice is to provide your users with alternatives. Always nest multiple levels of multimedia content so that users with different needs can retrieve your content at some level. If necessary, create multiple versions of the same page for users with different needs and abilities.

You've completed your work on Maxine's sample page describing the *Royal Wedding* movie. She likes the media clips and Java applet you've inserted in the Web page, and looks forward to adding more features.

Session 7.3 Quick Check

REVIEW

1. What is a Java Virtual Machine?
2. What are class files?
3. Specify the code you would enter to display the *stockmarket.class* applet as an embedded object that is 500 pixels wide by 400 pixels high.
4. What are conditional comments and when are they necessary?
5. Specify the code to embed the image file *logo.jpg* as an object with a width of 200 pixels and a height of 100 pixels. If a browser does not support embedded objects, have it display the text *Millennium Computers* as an h2 heading.
6. Specify the code to display the HTML file *glossary.htm* as an embedded object that is 400 pixels wide by 200 pixels high.
7. Provide the code to display the same embedded object described in the previous question using an inline frame.

Practice the skills
you learned in
the tutorial using
the same case
scenario.

PRACTICE

Review Assignments

Data Files needed for the Review Assignments: astairetxt.htm, CreditRoll.class, embedtxt.css, fa1.gif-fa5.gif, fabio.css, fasong.mp3, fasong.ogg, fasong.swf, filmlist.txt, hatrack.mp4, hatrack.swf, hatrack.webm, jplogo.png, modernizr-1.5.js, popcorn.jpg, threestars.jpg

Maxine has been working on the Jumbo Popcorn Web site for several weeks now. She has come back to you for help with completing another page. This page will feature the life of Fred Astaire. She has created a sound clip and a video clip that she wants you to embed in the Web page. She's also interested in creating another scrolling marquee, this one listing some of the many movies that Fred Astaire starred in during his life. A preview of the page you'll create is shown in Figure 7-44.

Figure 7-44 Fred Astaire biography page

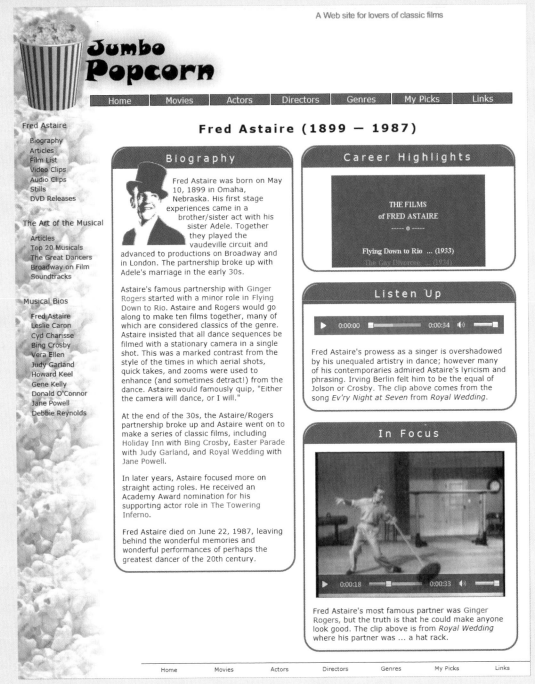

graphit/Shutterstock.com

Gl0ck/Shutterstock.com

Complete the following:

1. Use your text editor to open the **astairetxt.htm** and **embedtxt.css** files from the tutorial.07\review folder included with your Data Files. Enter *your name* and *the date* in the comment section of each file. Save the files as **astaire.htm** and **embed.css**, respectively, in the same folder.

2. Go to the **astaire.htm** file in your text editor. Add a link to the **embed.css** file in the document head.

3. Scroll down the file and locate the `article` element below the Career Highlights heading. Within this article, Maxine would like to insert a rolling marquee displaying a list of classic Fred Astaire movies. Insert an embedded object to display the CreditRoll applet. Set the dimensions of the applet window to 300 pixels wide by 175 pixels high.

4. Add the following parameters to the CreditRoll applet:
   a. Set the value of the `code` parameter to the *CreditRoll.class* file.
   b. Display the marquee text in a 14-point font with a background hexadecimal color value of #996600 and a text color of #FFFFFF.
   c. Set the scrolling speed to 150, the `vspace` value to 3 pixels, and the `fadezone` value to 10 pixels. Have the marquee repeat the scrolling without stopping.
   d. When users click the marquee, have the browser display the IMDB Fred Astaire biography located at *www.imdb.com/name/nm0000001*.

5. Copy and paste the parameters from the *filmlist.txt* file (located in the tutorial.07\ review folder included with your Data Files) to insert the marquee text.

6. For browsers that do not support Java, display the brief list of Astaire movies found in the original data file, followed by a hypertext link to the page *www.java.com*.

7. Scroll down the file and locate the article with the Listen Up heading. Directly below this heading, insert an `audio` element using the *fasong.mp3* and *fasong.ogg* files. Have the `audio` element show player controls.

8. Within the `audio` element, insert an `object` element containing the *fasong.swf* Flash player file. Set the width of the Flash player to 350 pixels wide by 50 pixels high. Within the `object` element, insert a hypertext link to the *fasong.mp3* file with the hypertext caption *Ev'ry Night at Seven (mp3)*.

9. Scroll down to the article containing the In Focus heading and directly below the heading insert a `video` element containing the *hatrack.mp4* and *hatrack.webm* files. Display the player controls along with the video clip.

10. Within the `video` element, insert an `object` element for the *hatrack.swf* Flash player file. Set the width of the player to 280 pixels and the height to 239 pixels.

11. Within the `object` element, insert text informing users that they need the Shockwave player if they don't have it installed in order to play the Shockwave file. Link your statement to the Web page URL *http://www.adobe.com/products/shockwaveplayer*.

12. Save your changes to the file.

13. Go to the **embed.css** file in your text editor. Create a style rule to display `audio` and `video` elements as blocks that are 90% in width. Set the top/bottom margin to 5 pixels and the left/right margins to `auto`.

14. Display `object` elements as blocks with the top/bottom margins set to 5 pixels and the left/right margins set to `auto`.

15. Close the file, saving your changes.

16. Open the **astaire.htm** file in your Web browser. Verify that you can play the embedded sound file and movie file, and that the CreditRoll applet starts automatically within the page.

17. View the page in a browser that does not support HTML5 but does support Flash player. Verify that you can play the audio and video clips from the Flash players. Disable Flash support in your browser and verify that the page displays a message describing the two clips with the recommendation that the user have Flash installed.

18. Submit your completed files to your instructor, in either printed or electronic form, as requested.

Apply your knowledge of multimedia to create a poetry page with audio samples from an American poet.

APPLY

Case Problem 1

Data Files needed for this Case Problem: devotion.mp3, devotion.ogg, devotion.swf, fireice. mp3, fireice.ogg, fireice.swf, modernizr-1.5.js, poetry.css, rfback.png, rflogo.gif, rftxt.htm

American Poetry 121   Professor Debra Li of the English Department at Carston University in Columbia, Mississippi, has asked you to help her create a Web page devoted to the works of the poet Robert Frost for her American Poetry 121 class. With your help, she has created a Web page that contains a short biography of the poet and the complete text of two of his works. Professor Li would like to add sound clips of the two poems to the page so that her students can listen to Frost's poetry as well as read it. She also wants to add an embedded YouTube video clip. Figure 7-45 shows a preview of the page you'll create for her.

Figure 7-45	The Robert Frost Web page

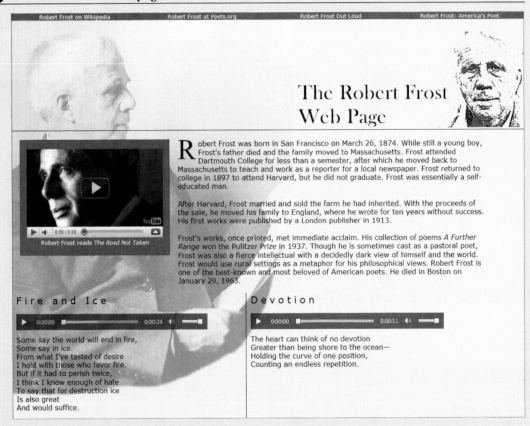

Complete the following:

1. Use your text editor to open the **rftxt.htm** file from the tutorial.07\case1 folder included with your Data Files. Enter *your name* and *the date* in the comment section of the file. Save the file as **rf.htm** in the same folder.

⊕ **EXPLORE**

2. Scroll down to the `figure` element directly after the page header. Within the `figure` element, create an `object` element linking to the YouTube video *www.youtube.com/v/ie2Mspukx14* and add parameters to the URL to disable the ability of users to display the video in full-screen mode. Set the width and height of the object to 320 pixels by 200 pixels. Within the `object` element, nest an `embed` element linking to the same YouTube video with the same parameters.

3. Scroll down to the first poem section. Directly below the Fire and Ice h2 heading, insert an audio element with *fireice.mp3* and *fireice.ogg* as the source files. Display the audio controls.

4. Within the audio element, nest an object element for the *fireice.swf* Flash player. Set the width and height to 345 pixels by 21 pixels.

5. Within the object element, nest an embed element for the *fireice.swf* file, setting the dimensions again to 345 pixels wide by 21 pixels high.

6. Go to the next poem section. Directly below the Devotion h2 heading, insert nested audio, object, and embed elements (as you did for Steps 3 through 5) for the *devotion.mp3*, *devotion.ogg*, and *devotion.swf* files.

7. Save your changes to the file.

8. Open the **rf.htm** file in your Web browser. Verify that you can play the YouTube video only within the YouTube player, and that the ability to play the clip in full-screen mode has been disabled.

9. Verify that you can play the two poetry audio clips in an HTML5-enabled browser.

10. Reopen the page in a browser that doesn't support HTML5 but does support Shockwave Flash. Verify that you can play the two audio clips within a Flash player.

11. Submit your completed files to your instructor, in either printed or electronic form, as requested.

Apply your knowledge of embedded video to create a travel guide page with a video tour.

Case Problem 2

Data Files needed for this Case Problem: modernizr-1.5.js, roadtxt.htm, rw.css, rwlogo.jpg, trailridge.mp4, trailridge.swf, trailridge.webm

Roadways   Karen Upton loves to travel and spends more than half of the year behind the wheel exploring byways and roadways for her online travel guide, Roadways. Karen's Web site is a place where others who share her passion for travel can gather to share stories, advice, and their love for travel. Karen would like to upgrade her site by adding video tours of some of her favorite roadways. She's come to you for help in adding this feature to her site. Karen presents you with a sample page; she already has created the video and descriptive text for Trail Ridge Road, the highest paved continuous highway in the United States. A preview of the page you'll create for Karen is shown in Figure 7-46.

Figure 7-46	Roadways Web page

Home

Classic Rides

   North America
   South America
   Europe
   Asia
   Africa
   Australia

Tips and Traps

   Maintenance
   Weather
   Law
   Enforcement
   Local Customs

The Mailbag

   Hot Topics
   Chat
   Archives
   FAQs

Contact Me

Travelling the Scenic Byways of the World

Trail Ridge Road

Trail Ridge Road covers the stretch of U.S. Highway 34 from Rocky Mountain National Park near Estes Park, Colorado in the east to Grand Lake, Colorado in the west. The road reaches a maximum elevation of 12,183 feet near Fall River Pass. Trail Ridge Road is the highest paved continuous highway in the United States, spending 10 miles above the tundra line. The road is closed from late fall until early summer due to the snowpack at the higher elevations.

A simulated drive from Estes Park to the Alpine Visitor Center

Travellers on Trail Ridge Road climb 4,000 feet in a matter of minutes. The changes that occur en route are dramatic. The drive begins in a forest of aspen and ponderosa pine, but the terrain will soon change to forests of fir and spruce. At 11,000 feet, drivers will encounter treeline and the last stunted trees which soon yield to heavy winds and the alpine tundra.

As you drive, be sure to stop and take in the views at Rainbow Curve, Many Parks Curve, and at Forest Canyon Overlook. On clear days, you can gaze north to Wyoming and east down to the cities along the Front Range. Looking south and west you can gaze further into the heart of the Rocky Mountains. Reserve at least half a day for the drive between Estes Park and Grand Lake.

Complete the following:

1. Use your text editor to open the **roadtxt.htm** file from the tutorial.07\case2 folder included with your Data Files. Enter ***your name*** and ***the date*** in the comment section of the file. Save the file as **roadways.htm** in the same folder.

2. Scroll down to the `figure` element and within the element insert a `video` element for the two source files *trailridge.mp4* and *trailridge.webm*. Display the controls with the video clip. Set the width and height of the video clip to 320 pixels by 260 pixels.

3. Nest within the `video` element an `object` element to display the Flash player file *trailridge.swf*. Set the dimensions of the Flash player to 320 pixels wide by 260 pixels high.

4. If the user's browser doesn't support HTML5 video or Shockwave Flash, display the message, *To play this clip you need the Shockwave Player.* Include a link to the Web site where users can download the player.

5. Save your changes to the file, and then load the **roadways.htm** file in a browser that supports HTML5 video. Verify that you can play the video clip of the drive up Trail Ridge Road.

6. Display the file in a browser that doesn't support HTML5 but does support Flash. Verify that you can view and play the Flash video of the ride up Trail Ridge Road.

7. Disable Flash in your browser and verify that the browser displays the message that you need to get Adobe Flash Player.

8. Re-enable Flash in your browser. Submit your completed files to your instructor, in either printed or electronic form, as requested.

Explore how to use a Java applet to create a Web page describing the mathematics of fractals.

CHALLENGE

Case Problem 3

Data Files needed for this Case Problem: Cmplx.class, Controls.class, fback.jpg, flogo.jpg, FracPanel.class, fractaltxt.htm, fstyles.css, Mandel.class, mandel.mp4, mandel.swf, mandel.webm, modernizr-1.5.js, zoom.png

Franklin High School   Fractals are geometric objects that closely model the seemingly chaotic world of nature. Doug Hefstadt, a mathematics teacher at Franklin High School in Lake Forest, Illinois, has just begun a unit on fractals for his senior math class. He's used the topic of fractals to construct a Web page to be placed on the school network, and he needs your help to complete the Web page. He has a video clip of a fractal that he wants placed in the Web page, along with a Java applet that allows students to interactively explore the Mandelbrot Set, a type of fractal object. He wants your assistance with putting these two objects in his Web page. A preview of the page you'll create is shown in Figure 7-47.

Figure 7-47   Fractals Web page

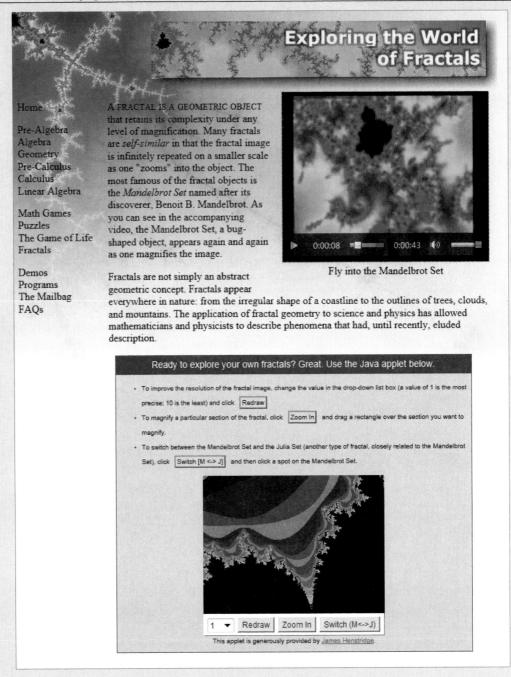

Complete the following:

1. Use your text editor to open the **fractaltxt.htm** file from the tutorial.07\case3 folder included with your Data Files. Enter **your name** and **the date** in the comment section of the file. Save the file as **fractal.htm** in the same folder.

⊕ EXPLORE

2. Scroll down to the `figure` element. Directly above the figure caption, insert a `video` element. Set the width and height of the video to 320 pixels by 260 pixels. Add attributes to display the *zoom.png* file as a poster image for the video, and have the video automatically loop back to the beginning when played. Display the *mandel.mp4* and *mandel.webm* video files in the player. Display the video controls in the player.

3. Within the `video` element, nest an `object` element displaying the *mandel.swf* Flash player. Add an attribute and a parameter to loop the player back to the beginning when played.

4. If the browser does not support the Flash player, display a message telling the user that he or she must have the Shockwave player. Include a link to the Web site where the user can download the player.

✦EXPLORE 5. Scroll down to the `article` element. Within the paragraph in this element, insert an `object` element containing the Java applet for the *Mandel.class* file; set the width of the Java window to 280 pixels and the height to 240 pixels.

6. If the browser does not support Java, have it display the text *Your browser does not support Java applets* in place of the *Mandel.class* applet.

7. Save your changes to the file.

8. Open the Web page in an HTML5-enabled browser and verify that the video plays correctly.

9. Open the Web page in a browser that does not support HTML5 but does support Flash, and verify that you can play the Flash video. If the browser does not support HTML5 and Flash, verify that the browser displays a message indicating that the user should install Flash. Re-enable Flash if you disabled it.

✦EXPLORE 10. Test the fractal applet to verify that you can use it to zoom into the Mandelbrot Set at different levels of magnification.

11. Disable Java support and verify that the browser displays a message indicating that you should install Java. Re-enable Java support in the browser.

12. Submit your completed files to your instructor, in either printed or electronic form, as requested.

Test your knowledge of embedded media by creating a multimedia Web page for a youth orchestra.

RESEARCH

Case Problem 4

Data Files needed for this Case Problem: beethoven.mp3, beethoven.ogg, beethoven. swf, byso.jpg, bysoinfo.txt, bysologo.jpg, CreditRoll.class, modernizr-1.5.js, schedule.txt

Boise Youth Symphony Orchestra The Boise Youth Symphony Orchestra (BYSO) is one of the premier young people's orchestras in the United States. Denise Young, the BYSO artistic director, has asked you to help create a Web site that contains information about the orchestra. Denise has a short excerpt from the first movement of Beethoven's Symphony No. 8 in F Major, Op. 93 that the orchestra played in its most recent spring concert. She would like you to embed the clip in the Web page. She also has a schedule of upcoming events and concerts that she would like displayed in a scrolling marquee.

Complete the following:

1. Use your text editor to create an HTML file named **byso.htm** and a style sheet named **bstyles.css**. Enter *your name* and *the date* in a comment section of each file. Include any other comments you think will aptly document the purpose and content of the files. Save the files in the tutorial.07\case4 folder included with your Data Files.

2. Go to the **byso.htm** file in your text editor and design the Web page using the files you've been given and any other supplements you have. Place all of your styles in the **bstyles.css** style sheet.

3. The page should contain the audio clip from Beethoven's Symphony No. 8. Provide the clip to the user in MP3 and OGG format using the HTML5 `audio` element. For browsers that don't support HTML5, provide the audio clip in a Flash player using the SWF format. For browsers that support none of these formats, display a hypertext link to the *beethoven.mp3* file.

4. Use the schedule information from the *schedule.txt* file to create a scrolling marquee of upcoming BYSO events. The exact parameter values are left up to you. Set the URL of the CreditRoll applet to *www.cityofboise.org*.

5. If a user's browser does not support Java at all, have the Web page display a message indicating this fact and suggesting that Java be installed to view the marquee. Include a hypertext link to a Web site where Java can be downloaded and installed.

6. Save your changes to the file and view the page in your Web browser. Verify that you can play both media clips and view the scrolling marquee under a variety of browser configurations.

7. If you are working on your own computer or have permission to turn off support within your browser for embedded media and Java, turn off that support temporarily and verify that the page degrades well, showing the hypertext links and the message about installing Java.

8. Submit your completed files to your instructor, in either printed or electronic form, as requested.

ENDING DATA FILES

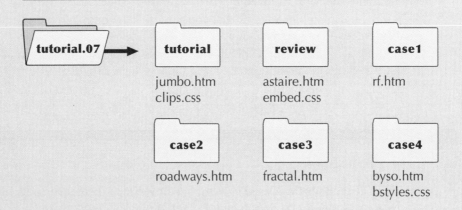

tutorial.07 → tutorial
jumbo.htm
clips.css

review
astaire.htm
embed.css

case1
rf.htm

case2
roadways.htm

case3
fractal.htm

case4
byso.htm
bstyles.css

TUTORIAL 8

Enhancing a Web Site with Advanced CSS

Designing for Special Effects, Print Media, and the Mobile Web

OBJECTIVES

Session 8.1
- Create text and box shadows
- Work with IE filters
- Rotate an object using CSS3
- Create linear gradients

Session 8.2
- Apply a border image
- Set the opacity of a page object
- Apply a style to a media device
- Create and apply print styles

Session 8.3
- Define the visual viewport
- Create a media query
- Create styles for mobile devices in portrait and landscape mode

Case | *Tree and Book*

Kevin Whitmore is the founder of Tree and Book, a social networking Web site for people interested in documenting their family histories, creating online photo albums, and posting stories and information about members of their extended families. He has come to you for help in upgrading the site's design. Kevin wants to take advantage of some of the CSS styles that can be used to add interesting visual effects to his Web pages and to create styles for printed and mobile output.

STARTING DATA FILES

tutorial.08 →

tutorial
effectstxt.css
mobiletxt.css
printtxt.css
treebooktxt.htm
+ 2 CSS files
+ 10 graphic files
+ 2 text files
+ 1 JavaScript file

review
dfeffectstxt.css
dfmobiletxt.css
dfprinttxt.css
dubcektxt.htm
+ 2 CSS files
+ 12 graphic files
+ 1 JavaScript file

case1
dweffectstxt.css
dwprinttxt.css
recipetxt.htm
+ 2 CSS files
+ 4 graphic files
+ 1 JavaScript file

case2
wceffectstxt.css
wcmobiletxt.css
willettxt.htm
+ 3 CSS files
+ 23 graphic files
+ 18 HTML files
+ 1 JavaScript file

case3
sweffectstxt.css
swprinttxt.css
messtxt.htm
+ 2 CSS files
+ 8 graphic files
+ 1 JavaScript file

case4
listing.txt
+ 10 graphic files
+ 1 JavaScript file

demo
demo_box_shadows.htm
demo_ie_filters.htm
demo_linear_gradients.htm
demo_radial_gradients.htm
demo_repeat_linear_gradients.htm
demo_repeat_radial_gradients.htm
demo_text_shadows.htm
demo_transformations.htm
demo_transformations3d.htm
+ 4 graphic files

SESSION 8.1 VISUAL OVERVIEW

The text-shadow property adds a drop shadow to a text string; the first parameter sets the shadow color; the next two parameters specify the horizontal and vertical offsets; and the last parameter sets the size of the shadow blur.

```
text-shadow:
green 3px 4px 5px;
```

The box-shadow property adds a drop shadow to any element; the parameters match those for the text-shadow property.

```
box-shadow:
gray 3px 4px 5px;
```

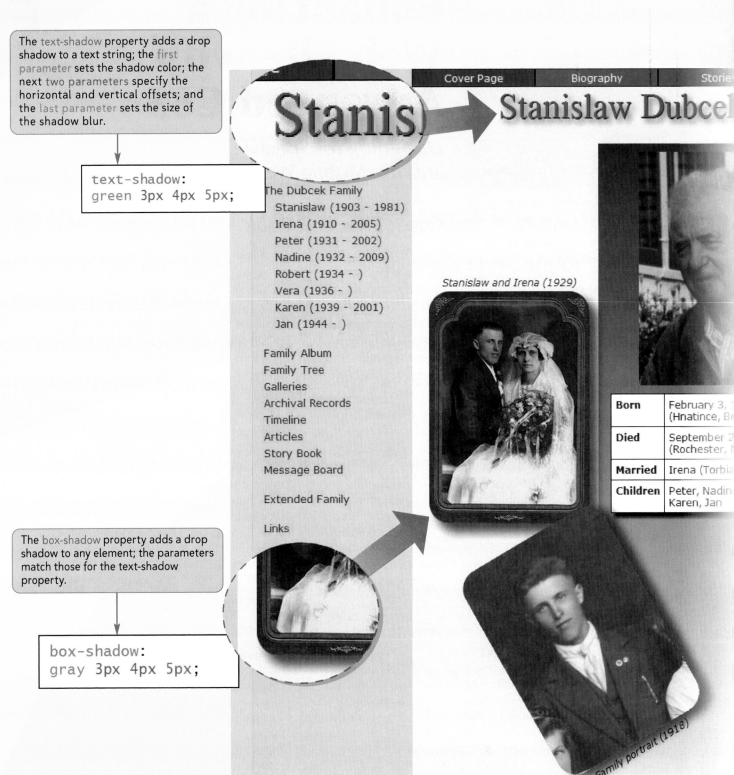

Cover Page   Biography   Stories

Stanis)

Stanislaw Dubcel

The Dubcek Family
  Stanislaw (1903 – 1981)
  Irena (1910 – 2005)
  Peter (1931 – 2002)
  Nadine (1932 – 2009)
  Robert (1934 –)
  Vera (1936 –)
  Karen (1939 – 2001)
  Jan (1944 –)

Family Album
Family Tree
Galleries
Archival Records
Timeline
Articles
Story Book
Message Board

Extended Family

Links

Stanislaw and Irena (1929)

Born	February 3, (Hnatince, B
Died	September 2 (Rochester, N
Married	Irena (Torbia
Children	Peter, Nadin Karen, Jan

Family portrait (1918)

VISUAL EFFECTS WITH CSS3

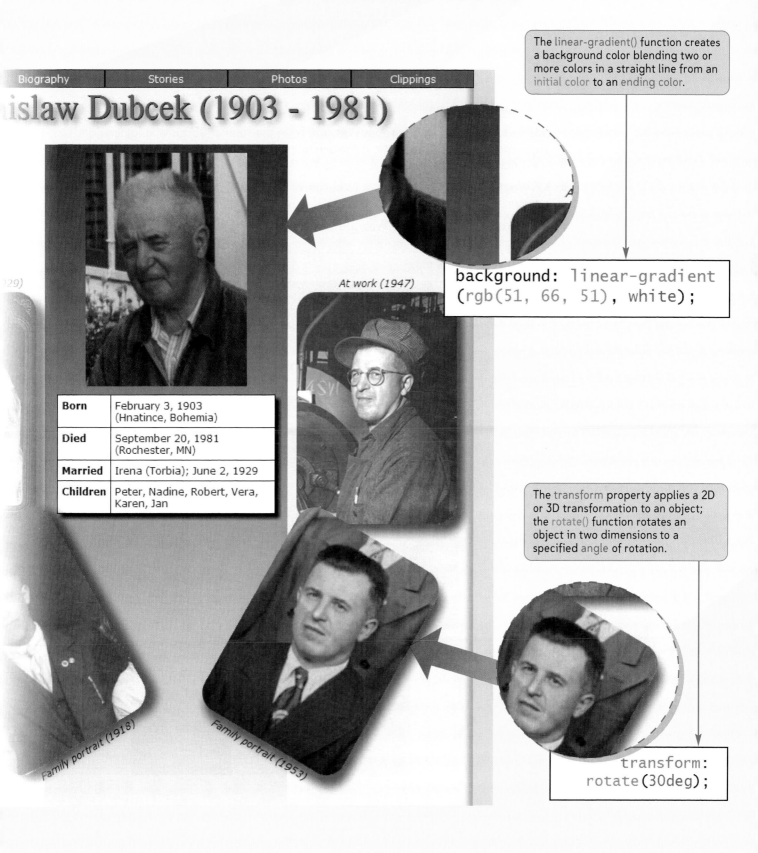

The linear-gradient() function creates a background color blending two or more colors in a straight line from an initial color to an ending color.

```
background: linear-gradient
(rgb(51, 66, 51), white);
```

The transform property applies a 2D or 3D transformation to an object; the rotate() function rotates an object in two dimensions to a specified angle of rotation.

```
transform:
rotate(30deg);
```

...islaw Dubcek (1903 - 1981)

Biography   Stories   Photos   Clippings

At work (1947)

Born	February 3, 1903 (Hnatince, Bohemia)
Died	September 20, 1981 (Rochester, MN)
Married	Irena (Torbia); June 2, 1929
Children	Peter, Nadine, Robert, Vera, Karen, Jan

Family portrait (1918)

Family portrait (1953)

Creating Drop Shadows with CSS3

You meet with Kevin to discuss his ideas for a new design for Tree and Book. He wants you to create a Web page design that can be applied to all pages on his Web site. Your design will be based on a sample page that Kevin created. You'll open Kevin's sample page now.

To view Kevin's page:

1. In your text editor, open **treebooktxt.htm** from the tutorial.08\tutorial folder. Enter **your name** and **the date** in the comment section of the file. Save the file as **treebook.htm**.

2. Review the file in your text editor to become familiar with its content and structure.

3. Open **treebook.htm** in your Web browser. The initial page is shown in Figure 8-1.

Figure 8-1	The initial Tree and Book page

sabri deniz kizil/Shutterstock.com
okicoki/Shutterstock.com

The sample page that Kevin has chosen contains biographical information about and photos of Kevin's great-grandfather, Stanislaw Dubcek, an immigrant to the United States who settled and raised a family in the Midwest. Kevin feels that the current appearance of the page is dull and uninteresting, and he sketches out some ideas to give the page more visual appeal (see Figure 8-2).

Figure 8-2   **Kevin's proposed design changes**

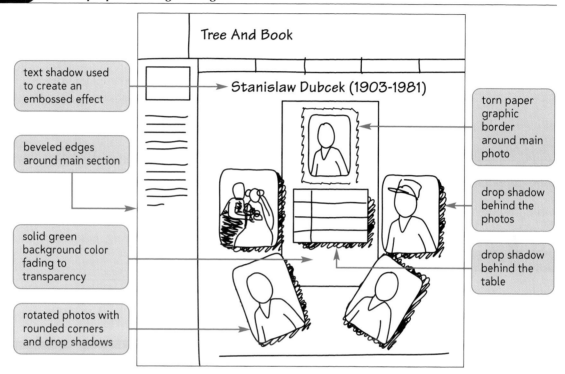

Kevin wants you to add the following visual effects to the cover page:

- drop shadows around the page heading, Web table, and page photos
- a green background around the main article that gradually fades out in the vertical direction
- the two family portrait photos rotated 30° clockwise and counter-clockwise from their default orientations
- a semi-transparent filter added to the photos of Stanislaw Dubcek
- a torn page border around the main photo

To create these visual effects, you'll use some CSS3 and browser-specific styles. You'll start by using CSS3 to create drop shadows around the page heading, Web table, and page photos.

Creating a Text Shadow

Kevin wants to augment the appearance of the h1 heading *Stanislaw Dubcek (1903 - 1981)* by adding a drop shadow around each of the letters. Drop shadows can be added using the text-shadow style

```
text-shadow: color offsetX offsetY blur;
```

where *color* is the color of the shadow, and *offsetX* and *offsetY* are the distance of the shadow from the text in the horizontal and vertical directions, respectively. Positive values for *offsetX* and *offsetY* move the shadow to the right and down from the text, while negative values move the shadow to the left and up.

The `blur` parameter defines the amount of space the shadow text is stretched, creating a blurred effect. The larger the `blur` value, the less distinct are the borders of the shadow image. The default `blur` value is 0 pixels for a text shadow that has very hard and distinct edges. The `text-shadow` style

```
text-shadow: red 10px 5px 15px;
```

creates a red text shadow that is 10 pixels to the right and 5 pixels down from the text with a blur size of 15 pixels.

You can apply multiple shadows to the same text by specifying different shadow styles separated by commas as follows

```
text-shadow: shadow, shadow, shadow, … ;
```

where `shadow` is a text shadow style. Multiple shadows are applied from first to last with the first shadow listed displayed on top of the succeeding shadows. Thus the style

```
text-shadow: red 10px 5px 15px,
             blue -5px -10px 5px;
```

applies two shadows: a red shadow with the parameter values described above, and a blue shadow that is placed 5 pixels to the left and 10 pixels above the text with a 5-pixel blur. The blue shadow is put down first, with the red shadow on top of it.

Figure 8-3 shows examples of applying the `text-shadow` style to achieve a variety of different effects using single and multiple shadows.

Figure 8-3   **Examples of text shadows**

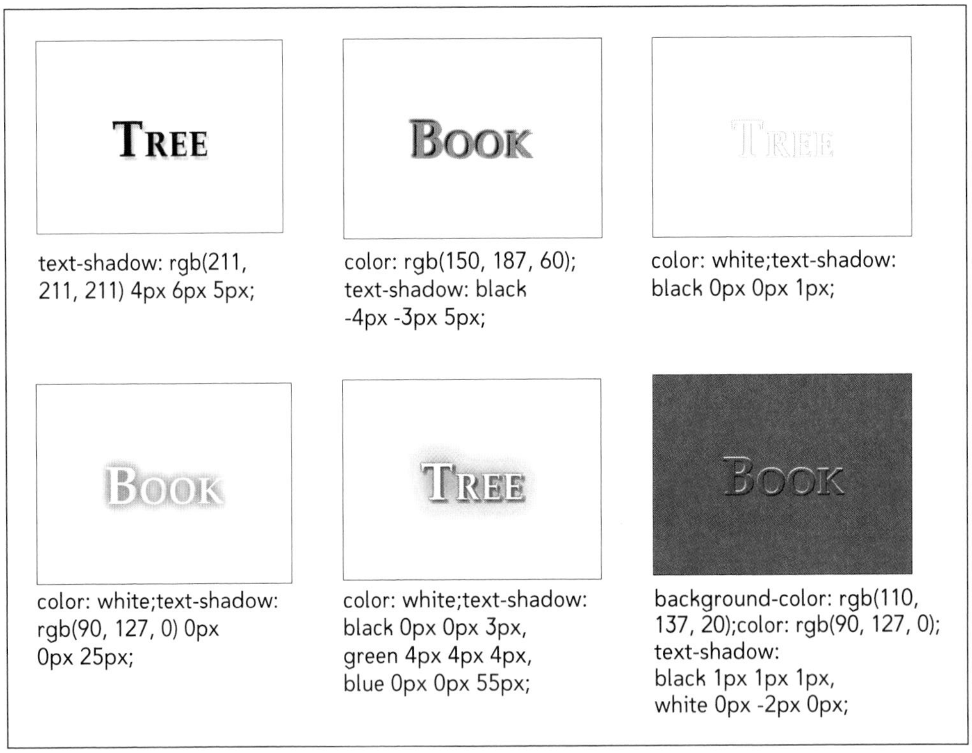

text-shadow: rgb(211, 211, 211) 4px 6px 5px;

color: rgb(150, 187, 60); text-shadow: black -4px -3px 5px;

color: white;text-shadow: black 0px 0px 1px;

color: white;text-shadow: rgb(90, 127, 0) 0px 0px 25px;

color: white;text-shadow: black 0px 0px 3px, green 4px 4px 4px, blue 0px 0px 55px;

background-color: rgb(110, 137, 20);color: rgb(90, 127, 0); text-shadow: black 1px 1px 1px, white 0px -2px 0px;

TIP

To remove a `text-shadow`, set the value of the text-shadow style to none.

You can also explore the `text-shadow` style using the *demo_text_shadows.htm* file in the tutorial.08/demo folder.

Creating Text and Box Shadows

- To create a text shadow, apply the style

  ```
  text-shadow: color offsetX offsetY blur;
  ```

  where *color* is the color of the shadow, *offsetX* and *offsetY* are the displacements of the shadow from the text in the horizontal and vertical directions, and *blur* is the size of the blurring effect.
- To apply a drop shadow to a page element, use the style

  ```
  box-shadow: [inset] color offsetX offsetY blur [spread];
  ```

  where the optional `inset` keyword places the shadow within the object, and the optional *spread* value increases or decreases the size of the shadow relative to the size of the object.

At the time of this writing, no version of Internet Explorer supports the `text-shadow` style. Shortly you'll learn how to create such text shadows using an Internet Explorer browser extension. But for Kevin's Web site, you'll use the CSS3 `text-shadow` style to apply an embossed effect to the `h1` heading in the document—making it appear as if the letters in the heading are raised out from the page.

To apply the `text-shadow` style:

1. In your text editor, open the **effectstxt.css** file from the tutorial.08/tutorial folder. Enter **your name** and **the date** in the comment section of the file. Save the file as **effects.css**.

2. Below the comment section, enter the following style rule as shown in Figure 8-4:

   ```
   /* Heading text style */

   section#main h1 {
     color: rgb(90, 127, 0);
     text-shadow: black 1px 1px 0px,
                  rgba(90, 127, 0, 0.7) 5px 5px 10px;

   }
   ```

Figure 8-4   **Adding text shadows to the h1 heading**

displays a black shadow 1 pixel down and to the right from the text

changes the font color to medium green

displays a semi-transparent green shadow 5 pixels down and to the right with a 10-pixel blur radius

```
/* Heading text style */

section#main h1 {
  color: rgb(90, 127, 0);
  text-shadow: black 1px 1px 0px,
               rgba(90, 127, 0, 0.7) 5px 5px 10px;
}
```

3. Save your changes to the file.

4. Return to the **treebook.htm** file in your text editor. Directly below the `link` element for the *layout.css* style sheet, insert another `link` element that links the document to the **effects.css** style sheet file.

> **5.** Save your changes, and then reopen the **treebook.htm** file in a non-Internet Explorer browser that supports CSS3. Figure 8-5 shows the current appearance of the page heading in the Google Chrome browser.

Figure 8-5	Heading text with an embossed effect

Next, you'll add shadows to other page elements.

Creating a Box Shadow

The CSS3 style to add a drop shadow to any page object is

```
box-shadow: [inset] color offsetX offsetY blur [spread];
```

where `color`, `offsetX`, `offsetY`, and `blur` have the same meanings as they do for text shadows.

The `inset` keyword is an optional keyword to display shadows within the object. The meanings of the `offsetX` and `offsetY` values are switched when used with inset shadows. Positive `offsetX` and `offsetY` values move the inset shadow to the left and up, while negative values move the shadow to the right and down. For example, the `box-shadow` style

```
box-shadow: inset rgb(231, 231, 231) 5px 5px 10px;
```

creates a light gray border in the *upper-left* interior corner of the object and *not* the lower-right corner.

Finally, the default size of the box shadow is equal to the size of the object; however, the optional `spread` value allows you to increase or decrease the size of the shadow relative to the size of the element. The `box-shadow` style

```
box-shadow: rgb(211, 211, 252) 0px 10px 5px 20px;
```

creates a light blue shadow 10 pixels below the object but 20 pixels larger in width and height. To decrease the size of the shadow, you use a negative value for the `spread` parameter.

As with the `text-shadow` style, you can apply multiple box shadows by creating a comma-separated list of shadow values as follows

```
box-shadow: shadow, shadow, … ;
```

where `shadow` is a shadow style. Once again, shadows are applied in the order listed, with the initial shadows displayed on top of subsequent shadows. Figure 8-6 shows some applications of the `box-shadow` style. You can also view an interactive demo of the `box-shadow` style using the *demo_box_shadows.htm* file in the tutorial.08/demo folder.

Figure 8-6	Examples of box shadows

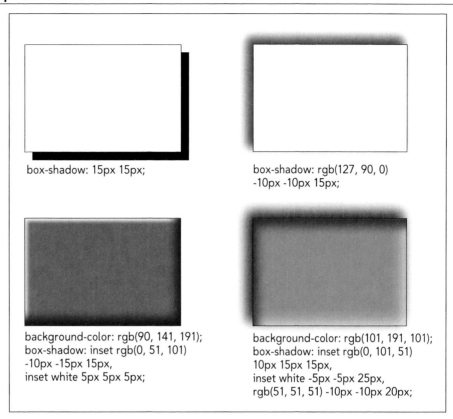

box-shadow: 15px 15px;

box-shadow: rgb(127, 90, 0)
-10px -10px 15px;

background-color: rgb(90, 141, 191);
box-shadow: inset rgb(0, 51, 101)
-10px -15px 15px,
inset white 5px 5px 5px;

background-color: rgb(101, 191, 101);
box-shadow: inset rgb(0, 101, 51)
10px 15px 15px,
inset white -5px -5px 25px,
rgb(51, 51, 51) -10px -10px 20px;

The `box-shadow` style was originally introduced as a browser extension under Mozilla and WebKit. To provide the greatest cross-browser support for your box shadows, you should always use all browser extensions. For example, the following code applies the Mozilla, WebKit, and CSS3 styles to add a light gray box shadow to the `heading` element:

```
heading {
    -moz-box-shadow: rgba(51, 51, 51, 0.3) 5px 5px 15px;
    -webkit-box-shadow: rgba(51, 51, 51, 0.3) 5px 5px 15px;
     box-shadow: rgba(51, 51, 51, 0.3) 5px 5px 15px;
}
```

TIP

The color value can be placed either before or after the shadow offsets and dimensions. If no color is specified, the browser creates a black shadow.

Note that versions of Internet Explorer before version 9 do not support the `box-shadow` style.

Kevin wants several box shadows added to his Web page. He would like each of the four photos to have rounded corners with a box shadow in the lower-right corner. He also wants a shadow added to the table of biographical data about Stanislaw Dubcek. Finally, he wants to add an inset shadow to the entire main section of the page, to give it a beveled appearance.

To add box shadows to the page elements:

1. Return to the **effects.css** file in your text editor.

2. At the bottom of the file, insert the following style rule to create rounded corners and drop shadows for every inline image within a figure box:

```
/* Box shadow styles */

figure img {

    -moz-border-radius: 25px;
    -webkit-border-radius: 25px;
    border-radius: 25px;

    -moz-box-shadow: rgba(0, 0, 0, 0.6) 10px 10px 15px;
    -webkit-box-shadow: rgba(0, 0, 0, 0.6) 10px 10px 15px;
    box-shadow: rgba(0, 0, 0, 0.6) 10px 10px 15px;

}
```

3. Add the following style rule to create an interior beveled border for the entire main section element:

```
section#main {
    -moz-box-shadow: inset rgba(0, 0, 0, 0.3) -5px -5px 10px;
    -webkit-box-shadow: inset rgba(0, 0, 0, 0.3) -5px -5px 10px;
    box-shadow: inset rgba(0, 0, 0, 0.3) -5px -5px 10px;
}
```

4. Finally, add the following style rule to apply a drop shadow to the Web table nested within the main section. Figure 8-7 highlights the revised code in the style sheet.

```
section#main table {
    -moz-box-shadow: black 5px 5px 5px;
    -webkit-box-shadow: black 5px 5px 5px;
    box-shadow: black 5px 5px 5px;
}
```

Figure 8-7   **Adding box shadows to page elements**

adds rounded borders to images within figure boxes

adds a semi-transparent black shadow to the lower-right corner of the figure with a blur radius of 15 pixels

adds an interior drop shadow to the lower-right corner of the main section with a blur radius of 10 pixels

adds a black shadow to the lower-right corner of the table within the main section

```
/* Box shadow styles */

figure img {

    -moz-border-radius: 25px;
    -webkit-border-radius: 25px;
    border-radius: 25px;

    -moz-box-shadow: rgba(0, 0, 0, 0.6) 10px 10px 15px;
    -webkit-box-shadow: rgba(0, 0, 0, 0.6) 10px 10px 15px;
    box-shadow: rgba(0, 0, 0, 0.6) 10px 10px 15px;
}

section#main {
    -moz-box-shadow: inset rgba(0, 0, 0, 0.3) -5px -5px 10px;
    -webkit-box-shadow: inset rgba(0, 0, 0, 0.3) -5px -5px 10px;
    box-shadow: inset rgba(0, 0, 0, 0.3) -5px -5px 10px;
}

section#main table {
    -moz-box-shadow: black 5px 5px 5px;
    -webkit-box-shadow: black 5px 5px 5px;
    box-shadow: black 5px 5px 5px;
}
```

5. Save your changes to the file, and then reload the **treebook.htm** file in your Web browser. Figure 8-8 displays the current appearance of the main section of the page.

Figure 8-8   Box shadows in the *Tree and Book* page

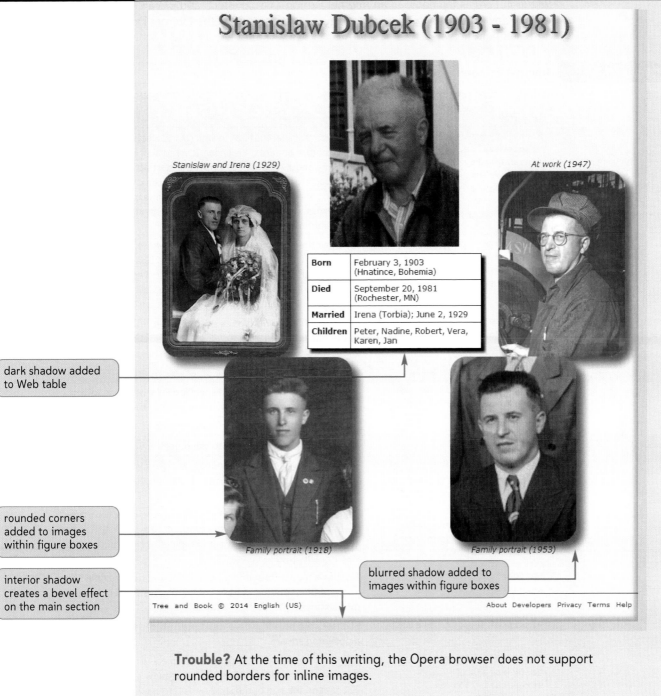

dark shadow added to Web table

rounded corners added to images within figure boxes

interior shadow creates a bevel effect on the main section

blurred shadow added to images within figure boxes

Trouble? At the time of this writing, the Opera browser does not support rounded borders for inline images.

Next, you'll explore how to create text shadows and box shadows using the Internet Explorer browser.

Introducing Internet Explorer Filters

Not until version 9 did Internet Explorer start to support the CSS3 collection of visual styles; and even then, its support was incomplete. However, since Internet Explorer 5.5, the browser has supported the use of visual effects through the application of the `filter` style

```
filter: progid:DXImageTransform.Microsoft.filter(param);
```

where `filter` is the name of an Internet Explorer visual effect, and `param` is the parameters (if any) that apply to that effect. Figure 8-9 lists some of the Internet Explorer filters and their parameters.

Figure 8-9 Internet Explorer filters

IE Filter	Description
`Alpha(style=type, opacity=value, finishOpacity=value, startX=value, finishX=value, startY=value, finishY=value)`	Applies a transparent filter in which `style` sets the direction of the filter (0 = uniform, 1 = linear, 2 = radial, 3 = rectangular); `opacity` and `finishOpacity` set the starting and ending opacity values, respectively; and `startX`, `finishX`, `startY`, and `finishY` set the starting and finishing points in the horizontal and vertical directions, respectively, as percentages of the width and height of the object
`BasicImage(rotation=0|1|2|3, opacity=0-1, mirror=0|1, invert=0|1, xRay=0|1, grayscale=0|1)`	Modifies the appearance of the object, where `rotation` rotates the object (0=0°, 1=90° 2=180°, 3=270°), `opacity` sets the opacity of the object, and the remaining parameters, if their values are set to 1, create a mirror image, invert the object, apply an X-ray effect, or display the object in grayscale
`Blur(pixelRadius=value, makeShadow=true|false, shadowOpacity=0-1)`	Blurs the object, where `pixelRadius` determines the amount of the blurring, and `makeShadow` and `shadowOpacity` apply shadowing to the blur effect
`Chroma(color=#rrggbb)`	Makes a specified color in the object transparent
`DropShadow(color=#rrggbb, offX=value, offY=value)`	Creates a drop shadow of the specified color with a length of `offX` in the horizontal direction and `offY` in the vertical direction
`Emboss()`	Applies an embossing effect to the object
`Engrave()`	Applies an engraving effect to the object
`Glow(color=#rrggbb, strength=1-255)`	Applies a glowing border around the object with the size of the glow determined by `strength` and the glow's color determined by `color`
`Gradient(gradientType=0|1, startColorStr=#rrggbb, endColorStr=#rrggbb)`	Applies a color gradient to the object, where `gradientType` determines the direction of the gradient (0 = vertical, 1 = horizontal), and `startColorStr` and `endColorStr` indicate the starting and ending colors
`MotionBlur(direction=angle, strength=1-255)`	Applies a motion blur effect, where `direction` provides the angle of the motion and `strength` indicates the length of the motion lines
`Pixelate(maxSquare=value)`	Pixelates the object, where `maxSquare` is the width in pixels of a pixelated square
`Shadow(direction=angle, color=#rrggbb, strength=1-255)`	Applies a simple drop shadow to the object with the angle of the shadow specified by `direction`, the shadow's color indicated by `color`, and the size of the shadow determined by `strength`
`Wave(freq=value, lightStrength=value, phase=value, strength=value)`	Applies a sine-wave distortion to the object; the appearance of the wave is determined by the four parameters

In order to bring the `filter` style into compliance with the syntax for CSS browser extensions, Microsoft introduced the following `-ms-filter` browser extension starting with Internet Explorer version 8:

```
-ms-filter: "progid:DXImageTransform.Microsoft.filter(param)";
```

Note that the text of the `-ms-filter` browser extension is the same as the text of the Internet Explorer `filter` style. For complete support across all versions of Internet Explorer, you should include both formats, starting with the `-ms-filter` browser extension form for the current browsers, followed by the `filter` style for versions of Internet Explorer before version 8.

Figure 8-10 shows examples of some of the Internet Explorer filters applied to a sample image.

Figure 8-10   **Examples of IE filters**

Alpha(style=2)   BasicImage(invert=1)   Emboss()

Engrave()   Pixelate(maxSquare=10)   Wave(freq=3, strength=10)

TIP

The `filter` style should be entered on a single line with no hard returns within the code; otherwise, Internet Explorer will not be able to correctly parse the style statement.

You can also view an interactive demo of the Internet Explorer filter styles using the *demo_ie_filters.htm* file in the tutorial.08/demo folder.

Internet Explorer filters can be applied only to objects that have a defined layout on the page. This can be achieved by floating an object, specifying the object's width or height, or placing the object using absolute or fixed positioning. In addition, page elements that are responsible for arranging their own content will always have a defined layout; this includes objects such as tables, table cells, table rows, inline images, embedded objects, and the entire page body itself.

The `Shadow` and `DropShadow` Filters

Internet Explorer supports two styles for applying shadows to objects: the `Shadow` filter and the `DropShadow` filter. The `Shadow` filter has the syntax

```
Shadow(direction=angle, strength=value, color=color)
```

where the `direction` parameter measures the angle of shadow in degrees clockwise from 0° (directly above the object), the `strength` parameter indicates the extent of the shadow blurring, and the `color` parameter specifies the hexadecimal color value of the shadow. For example, the style

```
filter: progid:DXImageTransform.Microsoft.Shadow(direction=135,
strength=10, color=#7F7F7F);
```

creates a gray shadow with a strength of 10 units located at a direction of 135°.
The `DropShadow` filter creates a solid shadow with no blurring and has the syntax

```
DropShadow(color=color, offX=value, offY=value)
```

TIP

Use a direction value of 45 for shadows located in the upper-right corner, 135 for lower-right shadows, 225 for lower-left shadows, and 315 for upper-left shadows.

where *color* once again is a hexadecimal color value, and `offX` and `offY` specify the offset of the shadow from the object in the horizontal and vertical directions, respectively. For example, the filter style

```
filter: progid:DXImageTransform.Microsoft.DropShadow(color=#FF0000,
offX=5, offY=10);
```

places a red drop shadow 5 pixels to the right and 10 pixels down from the element. Figure 8-11 shows examples of the `Shadow` and `DropShadow` filters applied to a sample image.

Figure 8-11 **Applying the Shadow and DropShadow IE filters**

filter:
progid:DXImageTransform.
Microsoft.Shadow
(direction=135,
strength=20,
color=#0000FF);

filter:
progid:DXImageTransform.
Microsoft.DropShadow
(color=#0000FF, offX=-10,
offY=-10);

REFERENCE

Applying an Internet Explorer Filter

• To apply an Internet Explorer filter, add the style

```
filter: progid:DXImageTransform.Microsoft.filter(param);
```

where `filter` is the name of an Internet Explorer visual effect, and `param` is the parameters that apply to that effect.

• To apply an Internet Explorer filter in compliance with correct CSS syntax, add the following style:

```
-ms-filter: "progid:DXImageTransform.Microsoft.filter(param)";
```

Combining Several Filters

Several Internet Explorer filters can be combined to apply multiple visual effects to the same object. The syntax is

```
filter: filter1 filter2 … ;
```

where *filter1*, *filter2*, etc. are the Internet Explorer filters. Filters are added in the order in which they appear in the filter style. For example, the following style combines the Wave filter and the Shadow filter to create the effect shown in Figure 8-12:

```
filter: progid:DXImageTransform.Microsoft.Wave(freq=2,strength=10),
        progid:DXImageTransform.Microsoft.Shadow(direction=135,
        strength=20, color=#5A7F00);
```

Figure 8-12   **Combining two IE filters**

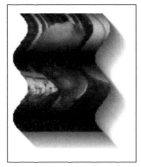

```
filter: progid:DXImageTransform.Microsoft.Wave(freq=2,strength=10),
progid:DXImageTransform.Microsoft.Shadow(direction=135, strength=20,
color=#5A7F00);
```

Note that you cannot combine filters by adding multiple filter statements as you do with multiple CSS style lines. When Internet Explorer encounters more than one `filter` statement, the last one listed supersedes all of the previous filters.

You discuss with Kevin the issue of using the Internet Explorer filters on the Tree and Book Web site. You decide that adding support for this browser-specific feature would complicate the development and maintenance of the Web site, and you opt to develop the Web site based only on CSS3 standards.

Rotating an Object

Kevin feels that the four photos are too tightly bunched on the page. He would like you to add some space and visual flow to the page by rotating the lower-left photo 30° counter-clockwise and the lower-right photo 30° clockwise. To rotate a page object, you can use the CSS3 `transform` *styles*.

The `transform` Styles

Styles that modify the placement or orientation of a page object are organized under the `transform` style

```
transform: effect(params);
```

where *effect* is the transformation function that will be applied to the object, and *params* are any parameters required by the transformation. Figure 8-13 describes some of the CSS3 transformation functions.

Figure 8-13 CSS3 2D transformation functions

Transformation Function	Description
translate(offX, offY)	Moves the object offX pixels to the right and offY pixels down
translateX(offX)	Moves the object offX pixels to the right
translateY(offY)	Moves the object offY pixels down
scale(x, y)	Resizes the object by a factor of x horizontally and a factor of y vertically
scaleX(x)	Resizes the object by a factor of x horizontally
scaleY(y)	Resizes the object by a factor of y horizontally
skew(angleX, angleY)	Skews the object by the specified angle, angleX, horizontally and angleY degrees vertically
skewX(angleX)	Skews the object by the specified angle, angleX, horizontally
skewY(angleY)	Skews the object by the specified angle, angleY, vertically
rotate(angle)	Rotates the object by the specified angle clockwise
matrix(n, n, n, n, n, n)	Applies a 2D transformation based on a matrix of six values

For example, to rotate an object 30° clockwise, you apply the following `rotate()` function:

```
transform: rotate(30deg);
```

To rotate an object counter-clockwise, you use a negative value for the angle of rotation. Thus, the style

```
transform: rotate(-60deg);
```

rotates the object 60° counter-clockwise.

Figure 8-14 displays the effects of other transformation functions.

Figure 8-14 Examples of CSS3 transformation functions

transform: translate(10px, -15px);

transform: scale(0.8, 0.5);

transform: skew(25deg, -10deg);

transform: rotate(45deg);

You can view an interactive demo of all of the CSS3 transformation effects in the *demo_transformations.htm* file in the tutorial.08/demo folder.

REFERENCE

Rotating an Element

- To rotate a page element, apply the style

```
transform: rotate(angle);
```

where *angle* is the angle of rotation.

Each of the transformations was originally implemented as a browser extension. So to create a cross-browser transformation, you should use the extensions for the Opera, Mozilla, WebKit, and Microsoft browser engines before the application of the CSS3 style. You'll use the `rotate()` function now to rotate the bottom two figures in Kevin's Web page.

To rotate a page object:

1. Return to the **effects.css** file in your text editor.

2. At the bottom of the file, insert the following style rule to rotate the figure box for the lower-left photo 30° counter-clockwise:

```
/* Rotate styles */


figure#photo4 {
    -o-transform: rotate(-30deg);
    -moz-transform: rotate(-30deg);
    -webkit-transform: rotate(-30deg);
    -ms-transform: rotate(-30deg);
    transform: rotate(-30deg);
}
```

3. Add the following style rule to rotate the figure box for the lower-right photo 30° clockwise:

```
figure#photo5 {
    -o-transform: rotate(30deg);
    -moz-transform: rotate(30deg);
    -webkit-transform: rotate(30deg);
    -ms-transform: rotate(30deg);
    transform: rotate(30deg);
}
```

Figure 8-15 highlights the new style code.

Figure 8-15 **Applying the rotate transformation**

rotates the photo 30° counter-clockwise; uses browser extensions to support all browsers

```
/* Rotate styles */

figure#photo4 {
    -o-transform: rotate(-30deg);
    -moz-transform: rotate(-30deg);
    -webkit-transform: rotate(-30deg);
    -ms-transform: rotate(-30deg);
    transform: rotate(-30deg);
}
```

rotates the photo 30° clockwise

```
figure#photo5 {
    -o-transform: rotate(30deg);
    -moz-transform: rotate(30deg);
    -webkit-transform: rotate(30deg);
    -ms-transform: rotate(30deg);
    transform: rotate(30deg);
}
```

4. Save your changes to the file, and then reload **treebook.htm** in your Web browser. As shown in Figure 8-16, the bottom two figure boxes should be rotated on the rendered page.

Figure 8-16 **Rotated photos**

Born	February 3, 1903 (Hnatince, Bohemia)
Died	September 20, 1981 (Rochester, MN)
Married	Irena (Torbia); June 2, 1929
Children	Peter, Nadine, Robert, Vera, Karen, Jan

The -ms-transform browser extension is supported only by Internet Explorer version 9 and above. For older versions of Internet Explorer, you have to use the Internet Explorer Matrix filter to rotate a page object.

General Transformations with Matrices

The translation, scale, skew, and rotate effects can all be combined in a single transformation style using the `matrix()` function, which has the syntax

```
transform: matrix(n, n, n, n, n, n)
```

where each n refers to a specific value in a 3×3 transformation matrix. To fully understand how to use a transformation matrix, you have to study matrix theory, which is beyond the scope of this book. However, you can use some basic patterns to achieve different visual effects. For example, to translate a page object, use the function

```
matrix(0, 0, 0, 0, offX, offY)
```

where $offX$ and $offY$ are the translations in the horizontal and vertical directions, respectively. To scale an object, use

```
matrix(x, 0, 0, y, 0, 0)
```

where x and y are the scale factors in the horizontal and vertical directions, respectively. To rotate an object, use

```
matrix(cos(angle), sin(angle), -sin(angle), cos(angle), 0, 0)
```

where $angle$ is the angle of rotation. Finally, to skew an object, use

```
matrix(1, tan(angleY), tan(angleX), 1, 0, 0)
```

where $angleY$ is the skew angle in the vertical direction, and $angleX$ is the skew angle in the horizontal direction. Note that CSS doesn't support the `cos()`, `sin()`, or `tan()` functions, so you have to calculate these values yourself. You can combine all of these effects within the same `matrix()` function. For example, the function

```
matrix(2, 0, 0, 2, 10, 20)
```

doubles the size of the object and moves it 10 pixels to the right and 20 pixels down. Once you have mastered the `matrix()` function, you can use it for all of your object transformations.

Transformations in Three Dimensions

CSS3 also supports a collection of three-dimensional (3D) transformation functions. With the addition of a third spatial axis, you can create effects in which an object appears to zoom toward and away from users, or rotate in three-dimensional space. Three-dimensional transformations assume the existence of three spatial axes: an x-axis that runs horizontally across the page, a y-axis that runs vertically, and a z-axis that comes straight off the page toward and away from users, as illustrated in Figure 8-17. Positive z-values come out of the page toward users, while negative z-values recede away from users.

Figure 8-17   A 3D view of a page object

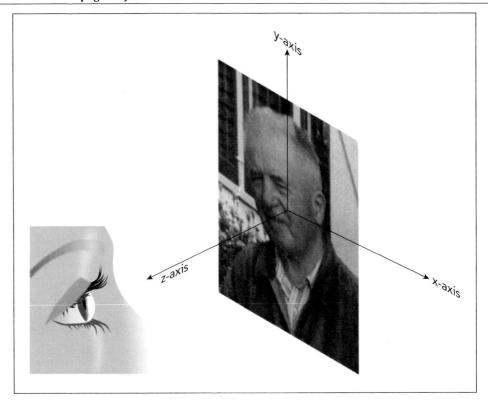

In addition to the three spatial axes, you specify the size of the **perspective** effect, which is how rapidly objects appear to recede from or advance toward users for different values of z. The lower the perspective value, the more extreme the distortion.

Figure 8-18 describes some of the 3D transformation functions supported under CSS3.

Figure 8-18   CSS3 3D transformation functions

Transform Function	Description
translate3d(offX, offY, offZ)	Moves the object offX pixels horizontally, offY pixels vertically, and offZ pixels along the z-axis
translateZ(offZ)	Moves the object offZ pixels along the z-axis
rotate3d(x, y, z, angle)	Rotates the object around the three-dimensional vector (x, y, z) at an angle of angle
rotateZ(angle)	Rotates the object around the z-axis at an angle of angle
scale3d(x, y, z)	Resizes the object by a factor of x horizontally, a factor of y vertically, and a factor of z along the z-axis
scaleZ(z)	Resizes the object by a factor of z along the z-axis
perspective(p)	Sets the size of the perspective effect to p
matrix3d(n, n, ..., n)	Applies a 3D transformation based on a matrix of 16 values

For example, the following 3D transformation sets the perspective effect to 150 and rotates the object 30° around the x-axis:

```
transform: perspective(150) rotateX(30deg)
```

Figure 8-19 shows how you can use the `perspective()` and `rotate3d()` functions to create other effects in which an object appears to rotate toward or away from users.

| Figure 8-19 | Rotating an object in three dimensions |

transform: perspective(150)
rotateX(60deg);

transform:
perspective(100)
rotateY(30deg);

transform: perspective(100)
rotate3d(1, -1.5, -1, 35deg);

You can explore how to achieve 3D transformations using the *demo_transformations3d.htm* file in the tutorial.08/demo folder. Note, however, that at the time of this writing, these 3D visual effects are supported only by Safari and Google Chrome, and only through the use of the WebKit browser extension. Thus, you will not be applying them to Kevin's document.

Applying a Color Gradient

Next, Kevin wants you to add background colors to the `article` element in his Web page. So far, you've worked with foregrounds and backgrounds consisting of a single color; but Kevin wants a background with a **color gradient**, in which one color gradually blends into another or, if transparent colors are used, fades away altogether. For example, Kevin wants a background that starts out in solid green and gradually fades away. One challenge of creating color gradients is that different browsers employ different styles to achieve the gradient effect, and there are several options that control the number of colors involved, the direction of the gradient, and how many times a particular color gradient is repeated within the object. Before modifying Kevin's document, you'll first examine the CSS3 gradient functions and their browser extensions.

Creating Linear Gradients with CSS3

One type of gradient is a **linear gradient** in which the color blending proceeds horizontally or vertically across an object's background. The CSS3 function to create a vertical linear gradient has the basic syntax

```
linear-gradient(color1, color2, …)
```

in which *color1*, *color2*, etc. are the colors that blend into each other moving from the top of the object to the bottom. Figure 8-20 shows a simple color gradient in which the background color blends from red to yellow and finally to blue.

Figure 8-20   A vertical color gradient of three colors

background: linear-gradient(red, yellow, blue)

TIP

For browsers that support multiple background images, you can create interesting visual effects by using semi-transparent colors to overlay several gradients or to overlay gradients with back-ground images.

Gradients are treated like images and thus are used with any CSS style that accepts images, such as the `background`, `background-image`, and `list-style-image` properties. The gradient applied to the object in Figure 8-20 is created using the `background` style.

To change the direction of a gradient, you can add a `position` or `angle` parameter to the `linear-gradient()` function as follows

```
linear-gradient(position || angle, color1, color2, …)
```

where *position* defines the starting point of the first color, and *angle* is the direction in which the gradient is pointed. The starting point is expressed using the keywords `top`, `bottom`, `left`, and `right`. If no position is given, the gradient is assumed to start from the top of the object and proceed vertically downward. Thus, the following function creates a gradient that starts from the top-left corner of the object and transitions from blue into white as it proceeds down to the bottom-right corner:

```
linear-gradient(top left, blue, white)
```

The other option is to define the angle of the gradient. Angles are laid out in a counter-clockwise direction with an angle of 0° equating to a gradient that moves horizontally across the object from the left to the right, a 90° angle representing a gradient that moves vertically up from the bottom to the top, 180° moving horizontally from the right to the left, and finally 270° for a gradient that moves vertically down from the top to the bottom (see Figure 8-21).

Figure 8-21   Gradient directions expressed as angles

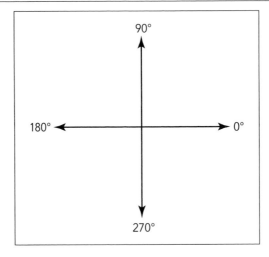

For example, the following function creates a gradient that moves diagonally across the object at a 45° angle starting from the bottom-left corner and moving toward the top-right corner:

```
linear-gradient(45deg, blue, white)
```

Angles also can be expressed using negative values, in which case the angles are laid out in a clockwise direction. If no angle is specified, the browser determines the gradient direction based on the location of the starting position. Figure 8-22 shows examples of different gradients you can create using the `linear-gradient()` function.

Figure 8-22   **Color gradients from different starting positions and angles**

background:
linear-gradient(left, red, yellow, blue)

background:
linear-gradient(bottom right, red, yellow, blue)

background:
linear-gradient(65deg, red, yellow, blue)

By default, the colors from the color list are evenly distributed across the gradient. You can specify the location of each color by adding **color stops** to the `linear-gradient()` function using the syntax

```
linear-gradient(position || angle, color-stop, color-stop, …)
```

where *color-stop* specifies the color and distance of the color from the starting position. For example, the function

```
linear-gradient(orange, yellow 50px, green 100px)
```

starts the gradient with orange, places yellow 50 pixels down from the top of the object, and finally places green 100 pixels down from the top. Anything more than 100 pixels away from the starting orange color will be displayed in the same shade of green.

Color stops also can be specified as percentages of the width of the color gradient space, as illustrated in the function

```
linear-gradient(left, orange 30%, yellow 40%, green 50%)
```

which starts the color orange at 30% of the object's width, yellow at 40%, and green at 50%. Before the 30% point, the background is a solid orange; and beyond the 50% point, the background is solid green. Figure 8-23 shows an example of a color gradient using multiple color stops to create a banded effect.

Figure 8-23 **A linear gradient with color stops**

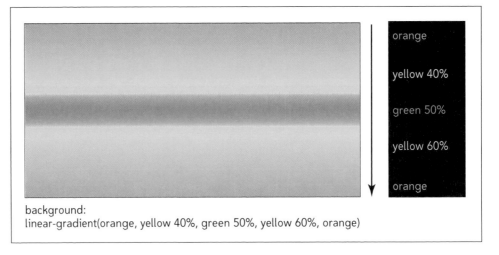

```
background:
linear-gradient(orange, yellow 40%, green 50%, yellow 60%, orange)
```

Note that if no color stop is assigned to the first color in the list, it is placed at the 0% position; and if no color stop is assigned to the last color in the list, it is placed at the 100% position.

You can try creating your own linear gradients using the *demo_linear_gradients.htm* file in the tutorial.08/demo folder.

Creating Radial Gradients with CSS3

The other type of gradient supported by CSS3 is a **radial gradient** in which color blending starts from a single point within the object and proceeds outward in a circular or elliptical shape, as shown in Figure 8-24.

Figure 8-24 **A radial color gradient of three colors**

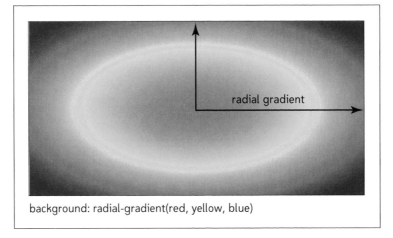

```
background: radial-gradient(red, yellow, blue)
```

To create a radial gradient in CSS3, use the `radial-gradient()` function

```
radial-gradient(center, shape size, color-stop, color-stop, … )
```

where *center* is the position of the radial gradient's center, *shape* is the gradient's shape, *size* is the size of the gradient, and each occurrence of *color-stop* is a color and its position within the radial gradient. If you don't define the position of the color stops, they are evenly distributed across the gradient.

The default starting position is the horizontal and vertical center of the object, but you also can specify the starting position using the keywords `top`, `bottom`, `left`, `right`, and center; or you can set the starting position explicitly using a percentage or one of the CSS units of measure.

The default shape of a radial gradient is `ellipse` with the specific dimensions based on the size of the containing object and the size of the gradient. For example, if the object is taller than it is wide, the radial gradient will be as well, appearing in the form of an elongated circle. You also can specify the gradient shape as `circle`, so that the gradient takes the shape of a perfect circle regardless of the object's dimensions.

By default, a radial gradient covers the entire object with the last color placed at the corner farthest from the center of the gradient. You can set a different stopping point using the following keywords:

- `closest-side:`   Stop at the side closest to the gradient's center.
- `closest-corner:`   Stop at the corner closest to the gradient's center.
- `farthest-side:`   Stop at the side farthest from the gradient's center.
- `farthest-corner:` Stop at the corner farthest from the gradient's center.
- `contain:`   Contain the gradient entirely within the object (synonymous with `closest-side`).
- `cover:`   Cover the entire object with the gradient (synonymous with `farthest-corner`).

You also can explicitly set the size of the radial gradient using pixels or percentages. Figure 8-25 shows examples of different radial gradients created using the `radial-gradient()` function.

Figure 8-25   **Radial gradients from different starting positions and shapes**

background:
radial-gradient
(left top, center, red,
blue, green)

background:
radial-gradient
(center, closest-side, red,
blue, green)

background:
radial-gradient(right, red
30%, yellow 35%, blue 40%)

You can explore how to define your own radial gradients using the *demo_radial_gradients.htm* page in the tutorial.08/demo folder.

Defining Gradients with Browser Extensions

The syntax of linear and radial gradients is not yet finalized at the time of this writing, and support for gradients is uneven in the current browser market. To support the widest range of browsers, you should use browser extensions in your style sheets. The `linear-gradient()` and `radial-gradient()` functions were based on Mozilla's `-moz-linear-gradient()` and `-moz-radial-gradient()` functions. Beginning in 2010, WebKit also began supporting the `linear-gradient()` and `radial-gradient()` functions as a browser extension, preceded by the `-webkit-` prefix.

However, before 2010, installations of WebKit used the function

```
-webkit-gradient(linear, start, stop, from(color), color-
stop(percent, color), to(color) )
```

to create linear gradients, where *start* provides the starting location of the gradient, *stop* defines the gradient's stopping location, *color* is a color value or color name, and the `color-stop()` function identifies the location and color of an intermediate color in the gradient. For example, the linear gradient

```
linear-gradient(left, yellow, blue)
```

would be written in WebKit's `gradient()` function as follows:

```
-webkit-gradient(linear, left center, right center, from(yellow),
to(blue) )
```

Note that for the *start* and *stop* values, you must specify both the horizontal and vertical positions. A vertical linear gradient with multiple color stops such as

```
linear-gradient(orange, yellow 50%, green 60%)
```

would be entered as

```
-webkit-gradient(linear, center top, center 60%, from(orange),
color-stop(50%, yellow), to(green))
```

The WebKit `gradient()` function can have multiple color stops, but the location can be entered only as a percentage of the object's width.

WebKit also supports radial gradients using the function

```
-webkit-gradient(radial, inner-center, inner-radius, outer-center,
outer-radius, from(color), color-stop(percent, color), to(color))
```

where *inner-center* and *outer-center* set the centers of the first and last color in the color list, respectively; *inner-radius* sets the endpoint of the first color; and *outer-radius* sets the starting point of the last color. The values for *inner-center* and *outer-center* can be expressed in pixels, as a percentage of the width and height of the object, or by using a keyword; while the values for the *inner-radius* and *outer-radius* can be expressed only in pixels. Figure 8-26 shows an example of a linear gradient and a radial gradient created using the WebKit `gradient()` function.

Figure 8-26 Gradients using the WebKit gradient() function

```
background:
-webkit-gradient(linear, 0% 100%, 100% 80%,
from(blue), to(yellow));
```

```
background:
-webkit-gradient(radial, center center, 10, center
center, 60,
from(orange), color-stop(30%, yellow), to(green));
```

TIP

Unlike the CSS `radial-gradient()` function, you can create only circular radial gradients with WebKit's `gradient()` function.

Opera did not support gradients until version 11, which was released in March 2011. With the release of Opera 11.1, you can use both the `linear-gradient()` and `radial-gradient()` functions if you include the `-o-` browser prefix.

At the time of this writing, Internet Explorer 10 (currently in Beta) supports the `-ms-linear-gradient()` and `-ms-radial-gradient()` functions employing the same syntax as the CSS3 functions. For earlier versions of Internet Explorer, you can create a gradient only using the filter

```
Gradient(gradientType=type, startColorStr=#rrggbb,
   endColorStr=#rrggbb)
```

where *type* is either 0 for a vertical gradient or 1 for a horizontal gradient, `startColorStr` indicates the starting color, and `endColorStr` indicates the ending color. Color values must be entered as hexadecimals. The Internet Explorer filter allows for transparent colors using the nonstandard hexadecimal string *#aarrggbb*, where **aa** is the opacity value of the color in hexadecimal. An alpha value of 00 is used for completely transparent colors, while a value of FF is used for completely opaque colors. Thus, the `Gradient` filter

```
Gradient(gradientType=0, startColorStr=#33D333,
   endColorStr=#005A7F00)
```

creates a vertical gradient that starts with a fully opaque dark green and blends into a fully transparent medium green. Note that the `Gradient` filter does not support radial gradients, nor does it allow for color stops within a gradient or for linear gradients in directions other than horizontal or vertical.

REFERENCE

Creating a Gradient

- To create a linear gradient, apply the function

```
linear-gradient(position || angle, color-stop, color-stop, …)
```

where *position* is the starting point of the gradient using the keywords `left`, `right`, `top`, and `bottom`; *angle* is the angle of the gradient; and *color-stop* is the position and color of each color (entered as *color position*).

- To create a radial gradient, apply the function

```
radial-gradient(center, shape size, color-stop, color-stop, …)
```

where *center* is the position of the radial gradient's center, *shape* is the gradient's shape, *size* is the size of the gradient, *color* is the initial color at the center, and *color-stop* is a color and its position within the radial gradient.

- To create a linear gradient in WebKit, apply the function

```
-webkit-gradient(linear, start, stop, from(color), color-
stop(percent, color), to(color))
```

where *start* provides the starting location of the gradient, *stop* defines the gradient's stopping location, *color* is a color value or color name, and the `color-stop()` function identifies the location and color of an intermediate color in the gradient.

- To create a radial gradient in WebKit, apply the function

```
-webkit-gradient(radial, inner-center, inner-radius, outer-center,
outer-radius, from(color), color-stop(percent, color), to(color))
```

where *inner-center* and *outer-center* set the centers of the first and last color in the color list, respectively; *inner-radius* sets the endpoint of the first color; and *outer-radius* sets the starting point of the last color.

- To create a linear gradient in Internet Explorer, apply the filter

```
Gradient(gradientType=type, startColorStr=#rrggbb,
endColorStr=#rrggbb)
```

where *type* is either 0 for a vertical gradient or 1 for a horizontal gradient, `startColorStr` indicates the starting color, and `endColorStr` indicates the ending color.

Obviously, to provide cross-browser support for gradients, you need to cover all of the possible browser extensions as well as the CSS gradient functions. Given the complexity of creating cross-browser gradient styles, you and Kevin agree to limit your style sheet to the CSS3 gradient functions. You'll use the `linear-gradient()` function to add a vertical gradient to the `article` element.

To create a linear gradient:

▶ 1. Return to the **effects.css** file in your text editor. At the bottom of the file, insert the following style rule as shown in Figure 8-27:

```
/* Style rule to add a dark green vertical gradient to the
   background of the article element */

article {
   background: -o-linear-gradient(black, rgb(51,101,51) 20%, white
80%);
   background: -ms-linear-gradient(black, rgb(51,101,51) 20%, white
80%);
   background: -moz-linear-gradient(black, rgb(51,101,51) 20%, white
80%);
   background: -webkit-linear-gradient(black, rgb(51,101,51) 20%,
white 80%);
   background: linear-gradient(black, rgb(51,101,51) 20%, white 80%);
}
```

Figure 8-27	Defining a linear gradient

vertical linear gradient starting with the color black, placing dark green 20% down the gradient, and ending with white 80% down the gradient

```
/* Style rule to add a dark green vertical gradient to the
   background of the article element */

article {
   background: -o-linear-gradient(black, rgb(51,101,51) 20%, white 80%);
   background: -ms-linear-gradient(black, rgb(51,101,51) 20%, white 80%);
   background: -moz-linear-gradient(black, rgb(51,101,51) 20%, white 80%);
   background: -webkit-linear-gradient(black, rgb(51,101,51) 20%, white 80%);
   background: linear-gradient(black, rgb(51,101,51) 20%, white 80%);
}
```

▶ 2. Save your changes to the file, and then reopen the **treebook.htm** file in your browser. Figure 8-28 shows the vertical gradient as it appears in the Google Chrome browser.

| Figure 8-28 | Linear gradient applied to the article element |

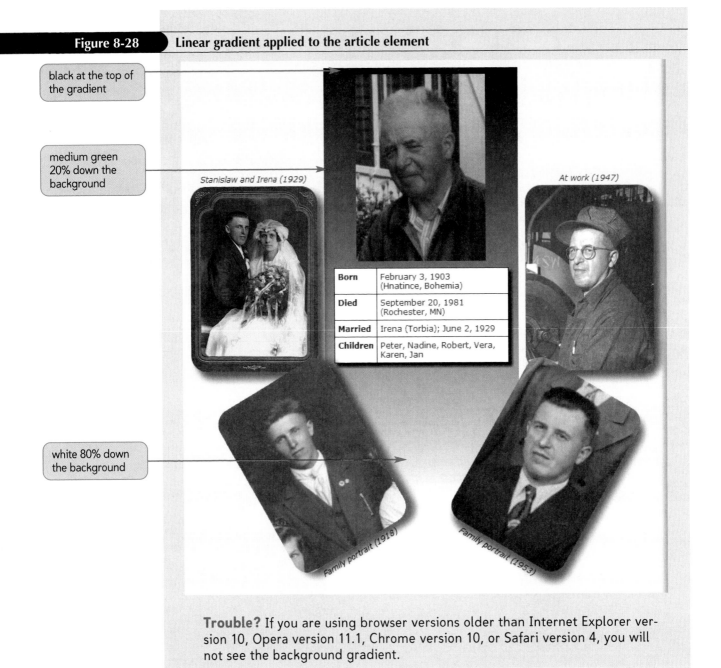

black at the top of the gradient

medium green 20% down the background

white 80% down the background

Stanislaw and Irena (1929)

At work (1947)

Born	February 3, 1903 (Hnatince, Bohemia)
Died	September 20, 1981 (Rochester, MN)
Married	Irena (Torbia); June 2, 1929
Children	Peter, Nadine, Robert, Vera, Karen, Jan

Family portrait (1918)

Family portrait (1953)

Trouble? If you are using browser versions older than Internet Explorer version 10, Opera version 11.1, Chrome version 10, or Safari version 4, you will not see the background gradient.

Repeating a Gradient

As you add more color stops, a gradient definition becomes unwieldy and complicated to write and use. One alternative is to repeat the gradient design. In CSS3, you can repeat linear and radial gradients using the functions

```
repeating-linear-gradient(definition)
repeating-radial-gradient(definition)
```

where *definition* describes the gradient's appearance using the same parameters in the `linear-gradient()` and `radial-gradient()` functions. The only requirement is that a stopping position is required for the last color in the list that is less than the size of the object background. When the last color is reached, the gradient starts over again. For example, the linear gradient

```
repeating-linear-gradient(white, black 10%)
```

creates a vertical gradient that starts with white fading to black and then repeats that pattern every 10% of the height of the object. Figure 8-29 shows some other examples of repeating gradients.

Figure 8-29   **Repeating a gradient**

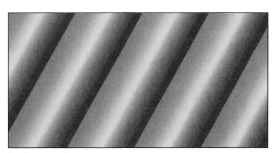

background:
repeating-linear-gradient(-30deg, red,
yellow 10%, blue 20%);

background:
repeating-radial-gradient(bottom, circle, red,
yellow 10%, blue 20%);

TIP

You cannot repeat gradients with the WebKit `gradient()` function or the Internet Explorer Gradient filter.

You can experiment with the `repeating-linear-gradient()` and `repeating-radial-gradient()` functions using the *demo_repeat_linear_gradients.htm* and *demo_repeat_radial_gradients.htm* Web pages in the tutorial.08/demo folder.

Written Communication: How to Use Visual Effects

The CSS3 styles can add striking visual effects to your Web site; but as you've seen, many of them are not completely supported by all browsers. Even if a current browser version supports those styles, there is no guarantee that your users will be running up-to-date browsers. This leaves you with the dilemma of when and how to use these styles. Here are some tips to keep in mind when applying visual effects to your Web site:

- Because not every user will be able to see a particular visual effect, design your page so that it is still readable to users with or without the visual effect.
- Be aware that some visual effects that flicker or produce strobe-like effects can cause discomfort and even photo-epileptic seizures in susceptible individuals. Avoid clashing color combinations and optical illusions that can cause these conditions.
- If you need to create a cross-browser solution, use the Internet Explorer filters and WebKit style functions to support older versions of Internet Explorer, Chrome, and Safari.
- Consider using graphic images to create your visual effects. For example, rather than using the CSS3 gradient functions, create a background image file containing the gradient effect of your choice.

No matter how you employ visual effects on your Web site, remember that the most important part of your site is its content. Do not let visual effects distract from your content and message.

Kevin appreciates the drop shadow, rotated photos, and background gradients you've added to his Web page. He thinks they give the document visual appeal. He has a few more visual effects he wants you to add, and he wants you to create a style sheet for the printed version of his page. You'll accomplish these tasks in the next session.

Session 8.1 Quick Check

REVIEW

1. Provide a CSS3 style rule to add a red shadow to the text of all `h1` headings in your Web page. The shadow should be offset 5 pixels to the left and 10 pixels down, and should have a blur value of 7 pixels.

2. Provide a CSS3 style rule to add a black box shadow to all `aside` elements in your Web page. The box shadow should be placed 2 pixels to the left and 5 pixels above the element with a blur value of 10 pixels.

3. Provide a CSS3 style rule to add an interior black box shadow to the page footer. The interior shadow should be displayed in the lower-right corner of the object offset by 10 pixels in the horizontal direction and 15 pixels in the vertical direction. Set the blur value to 5 pixels.

4. Provide the Internet Explorer filter to display a shadow with the hexadecimal color value #FF00FF, with the strength of 15 and at an angle of 60°.

5. Provide a CSS3 style rule to rotate all inline images 45° counter-clockwise.

6. Provide a CSS3 style rule to add a horizontal linear gradient to the background of the `header` element in the Web page document. The gradient should start at the object's left edge with the color red and move to the right with a color stop of yellow 30% of the way across the element, ending at the right edge with the color green.

7. Provide a CSS3 style rule to add a linear gradient to the background of the `nav` element, starting at the top-right corner with the color blue and ending in the bottom-left corner with the color white.

8. Provide a CSS3 style rule to add a circular radial gradient to the background of the `article` element. The gradient should be placed at the left-center side of the element starting with the color blue and blending into yellow. The gradient should halt at the closest corner.

9. Provide a CSS3 style rule to repeat a radial gradient of black and white bands in the background of the `section` element. The gradient should be an ellipse centered at the bottom-right corner of the element, with the white color stop placed 20 pixels from the start of the gradient.

SESSION 8.2 VISUAL OVERVIEW

The media attribute specifies the device(s) associated with a style sheet.

```
<link href="print.css"
  rel="stylesheet" media="print" />
```

Stani

Stanislaw Dubcek (1903 - 1981)

```
@page {
    size: 8.5in 11in portrait;
}
```

The size property defines the size and orientation of the page.

An @page rule defines the properties of the page box containing the content to be printed.

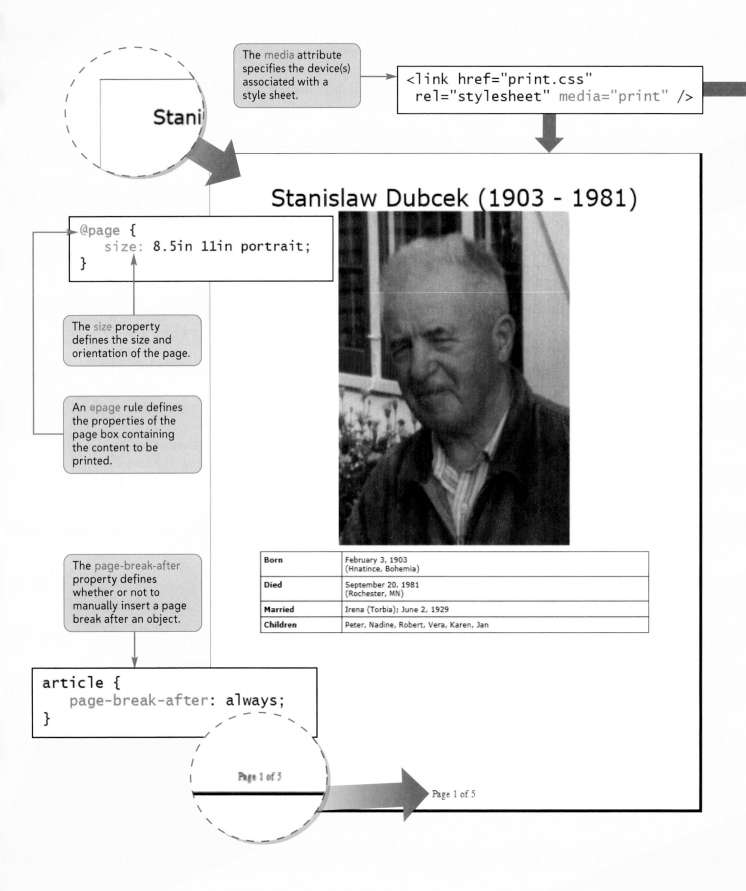

Born	February 3, 1903 (Hnatince, Bohemia)
Died	September 20, 1981 (Rochester, MN)
Married	Irena (Torbia); June 2, 1929
Children	Peter, Nadine, Robert, Vera, Karen, Jan

The page-break-after property defines whether or not to manually insert a page break after an object.

```
article {
    page-break-after: always;
}
```

Page 1 of 5

DESIGNING FOR PRINTED MEDIA

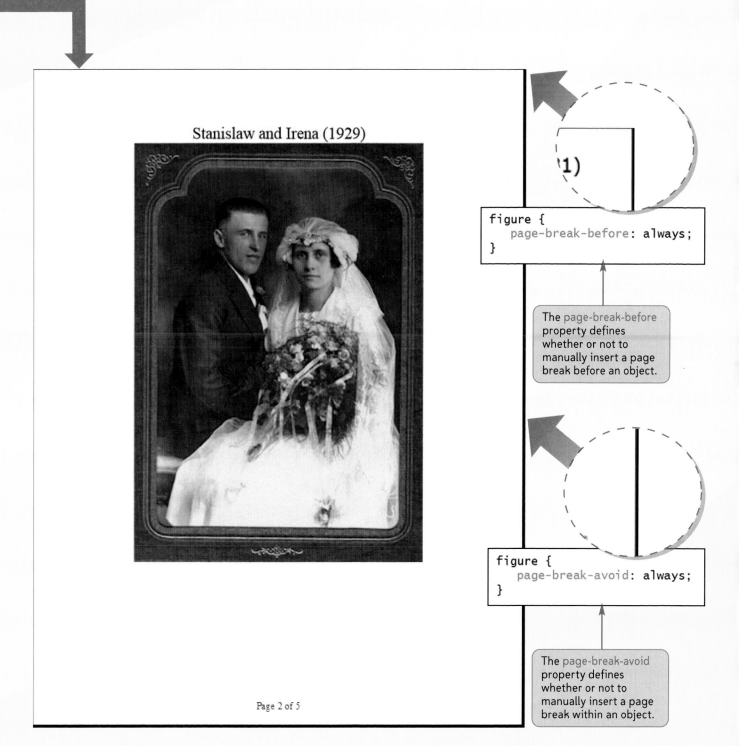

Stanislaw and Irena (1929)

```
figure {
    page-break-before: always;
}
```

The page-break-before property defines whether or not to manually insert a page break before an object.

```
figure {
    page-break-avoid: always;
}
```

The page-break-avoid property defines whether or not to manually insert a page break within an object.

Page 2 of 5

Applying a Border Image

Kevin wants you to change the appearance of the main photo of his great-grandfather by adding a graphic border that will make the photo look like it came from a torn piece of paper. Starting with CSS3, graphic borders can be created from any image file. To create a graphic border, imagine an image file sliced into nine pieces as displayed in Figure 8-30.

Figure 8-30   **Slicing an image to create a border image**

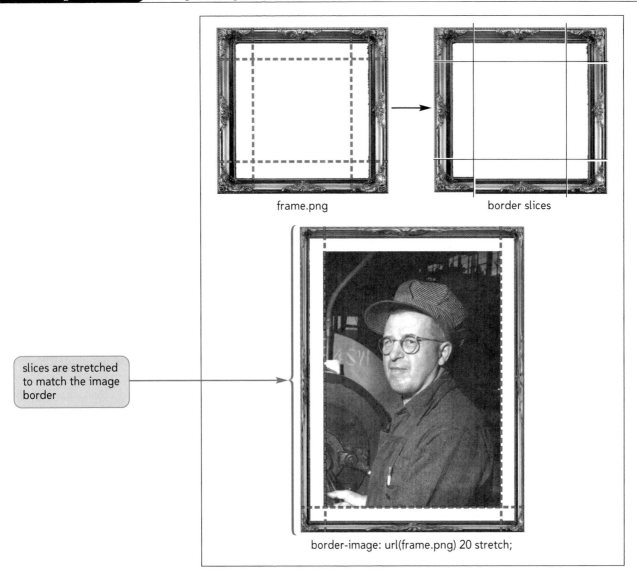

frame.png   border slices

slices are stretched to match the image border

border-image: url(frame.png) 20 stretch;

The nine pieces consist of four corners, four sides, and the interior piece. The interior piece is ignored (it's where the content of the object will appear), the four corners become the corners of the border, and the four sides are stretched or tiled to fill in the four sides of the border. Graphic borders are applied to an object using the CSS3 style

```
border-image: url(url) slice repeat;
```

where *url* is the source of the border image file, *slice* is the size of the border image cut off to create the borders, and *repeat* indicates whether the side borders should be stretched to cover the object's four sides or tiled. For example, the style

```
border-image: url(frame.png) 10 stretch;
```

cuts a 10-pixel-wide border slice from the *frame.png* image file. The four sides are stretched to cover the length of the four sides of the object. Note that you do not include the px measurement unit when indicating the size of the slice. Slices can be expressed only in pixels or as a percent of the width and height of the border image. You can set different size slices for each of the four sides. For instance, the style

```
border-image: url(frame.png) 5 10 15 25 stretch;
```

slices the border image 5 pixels on the top side, 10 pixels on the right, 15 pixels on the bottom, and 25 pixels on the left side. The slice sizes follow the same syntax used with all border widths. Thus, the style

```
border-image: url(frame.png) 5% 10% stretch;
```

slices the border image 5% of the image's height on the top and bottom sides, and 10% of the image's width on the left and right sides.

The `repeat` parameter value controls how browsers use the border image to fill in the sides of the object and has the following values:

- `stretch:`   The border slices are stretched to fill the border.
- `repeat:`   The border slices are tiled to fill the border.
- `round:`   The border slices are tiled to fill the border; if they don't fill the border with an integer number of tiles, the image is rescaled until they do.
- `space:`   The border slices are tiled to fill the border; if they don't fill the area with an integer number of tiles, extra space is distributed around the tiles.

You can apply different repeat values to different sides of the border. For example, the style

```
border-image: url(frame.png) 10 stretch repeat;
```

stretches the border slices on the top and bottom, but tiles the border slices on the left and right.

REFERENCE

Adding a Border Image

- To use a graphic image as an element border, apply the style

  ```
  border-image: url(url) slice repeat;
  ```

  where *url* is the source of the border image file, *slice* is the size of the slice cut from the border image file, and *repeat* indicates whether the border slices should be stretched to cover the object's four sides or tiled.

The torn paper image that Kevin wants to use as a border image has been saved in the *borderimg.png* file. You'll use the `border-image` style now to add this border around the main photo in Kevin's Web page. Kevin suggests that you tile the border image sides using the `repeat` keyword. Opera, Firefox, Chrome, and Safari all support border images as browser extensions; however, at the time of this writing, no version of Internet Explorer does.

To add the border image:

1. Return to the **effects.css** file in your text editor.

2. At the bottom of the file, insert the following style rule as shown in Figure 8-31:

```
/* Border image style */

article img {
   border-width: 10px;

   -o-border-image: url("borderimg.png") 50 repeat;
   -moz-border-image: url("borderimg.png") 50 repeat;
   -webkit-border-image: url("borderimg.png") 50 repeat;
   border-image: url("borderimg.png") 50 repeat;
}
```

Figure 8-31	Adding a border image

```
/* Border image style */

article img {
    border-width: 10px;            sets the width of the
                                   border to 10 pixels

    -o-border-image: url("borderimg.png") 50 repeat;
    -moz-border-image: url("borderimg.png") 50 repeat;
    -webkit-border-image: url("borderimg.png") 50 repeat;
    border-image: url("borderimg.png") 50 repeat;
}
```

cuts 50-pixel-wide border slices from the *borderimg.png* file; tiles the top, right, bottom, and left side images

3. Save your changes to the file.

4. Reload **treebook.htm** in your Web browser. As shown in Figure 8-32, a torn paper border image appears around the main photo in the page.

Figure 8-32   **Torn paper border image around the main photo**

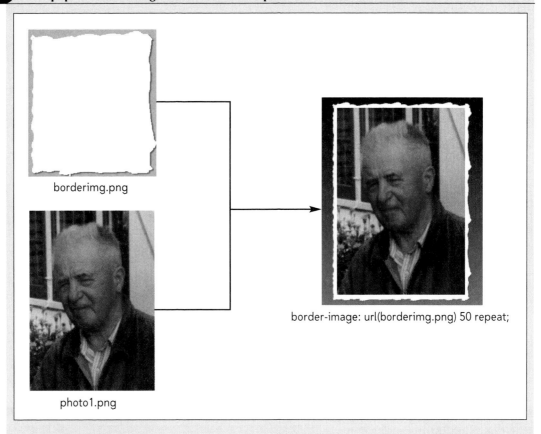

borderimg.png

photo1.png

border-image: url(borderimg.png) 50 repeat;

Trouble? If you are running Internet Explorer, you will not see a torn paper border around the photo.

Creating Semi-Transparent Objects

The last visual effect that Kevin wants you to add to the Tree and Book Web page is to make the two photos at the bottom of the page, which have the ids *photo4* and *photo5*, appear semi-transparent so that part of the background gradient appears through the photos. You've already worked with semi-transparent colors for several different projects. CSS3 also supports the style

```
opacity: value;
```

to make any page object semi-transparent, where *value* ranges from 0 (completely transparent) up to 1 (completely opaque).

Creating a Semi-Transparent Object

• To create a semi-transparent object, apply the style

    opacity: *value*;

where *value* ranges from 0 (completely transparent) up to 1 (completely opaque).
• To create a semi-transparent object under Internet Explorer version 8 or earlier, apply the filter

    Alpha(opacity=*value*)

where *value* ranges from 0 (completely transparent) up to 100 (completely opaque).

You'll use this style now to set the opacity of the two photos to 0.7.

To set the opacity of the photos:

1. Return to the **effects.css** file in your text editor.
2. At the bottom of the file, insert the following style rule, as shown in Figure 8-33:

```
/* Styles for semi-transparent images */

figure#photo4, figure#photo5 {

    opacity: 0.7;
}
```

Figure 8-33 Setting the opacity

sets the opacity of the two bottom photos to 70%

```
/* Styles for semi-transparent images */
figure#photo4, figure#photo5 {
    opacity: 0.7;
}
```

3. Save your changes to the file, and then reload **treebook.htm** in your Web browser. Figure 8-34 shows the final appearance of the Web page.

| Figure 8-34 | The final Tree and Book page as viewed in Google Chrome |

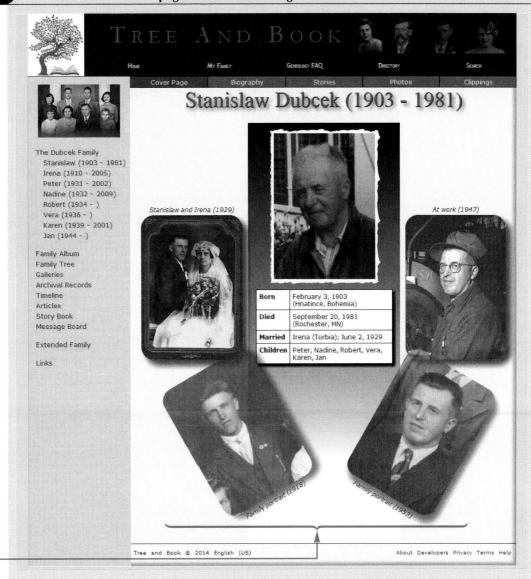

semi-transparent photos

sabri deniz kizil/Shutterstock.com
okicoki/Shutterstock.com

Trouble? If you are running Internet Explorer version 8 or earlier, you will not see a semi-transparent effect applied to the two bottom photos.

Versions of Internet Explorer before version 9 do not support the `opacity` property. To support earlier versions of Internet Explorer, you can set the opacity of the entire object using the `Alpha` filter

```
Alpha(opacity=value)
```

where *value* ranges from 0 (transparent) to 100 (opaque).

Using the `Alpha` *Filter to Create Transparent Gradients*

Internet Explorer's `Alpha` filter also can be used to create gradient effects in which a page object appears to fade away in a linear, radial, or rectangular direction. The general syntax of the `Alpha` filter is

```
Alpha(style=type, opacity=value, finishOpacity=value, startX=value,
finishX=value, startY=value, finishY=value)
```

where `type` is equal to 0 (for a uniform opacity), 1 (for a linear gradient), 2 (for a radial gradient), or 3 (for a rectangular gradient); `opacity` and `finishOpacity` provide the opacity values on a scale of 0 to 100; and `startX`, `finishX`, `startY`, and `finishY` indicate the starting and ending points of the gradient as percentages of the object's width and height on a scale of 0 to 100.

For example, to create a linear gradient that fades out from the top-left corner down to the bottom-right corner, you would apply the following filter:

```
Alpha(style=1, opacity=100, finishOpacity=0, startX=0, finishX=100,
startY=0, finishY=100)
```

To create a radial gradient in which the object appears to fade out from the center, you would apply the following filter:

```
Alpha(style=2)
```

Internet Explorer would apply a default opacity value of 100 to the object's center and 0 to the object's edges. If you don't specify a style value, Internet Explorer assumes a uniform opacity.

Working with Different Media Devices

Many visitors to the Tree and Book Web site like to print out portrait pages like the one Kevin has created for his great-grandfather. However, these users often find that the pages don't print well. Most users would prefer to print the photos and accompanying text without the page header, navigation list, and page footer.

Kevin could create two versions of his page—one for computer screens and the other for printouts—but he would like to avoid having multiple versions of the same document on his Web site. He would much prefer to use separate style sheets: one that is designed for users viewing the page on their computer screens, and another for printed output. Kevin wants you to investigate how this could be done.

Media Devices

When a user prints a Web page, the Web browser and its built-in styles prepare the document for the printer. The user also has some control over that process: for example, he or she can determine the size of the page margins or the content of the printout's header or footer. However, beyond these and similar parameters, the user cannot control what parts of the page are printed or how they are to be best laid out on the printed page.

CSS2 and subsequent versions of CSS have given more control to Web page authors to create output styles designed for particular devices. To do this, you can apply the `media` attribute

```
media="devices"
```

to either a `style` element or a `link` element in your HTML file, where `devices` is a list of media devices to which the style sheet should be applied. Figure 8-35 describes the different devices supported by the `media` attribute.

Figure 8-35	Media devices

Device	Used For
all	All output devices (the default)
braille	Braille tactile feedback devices
embossed	Paged Braille printers
handheld	Mobile devices with small screens and limited bandwidth
print	Printers
projection	Projectors
screen	Computer screens
speech	Speech and sound synthesizers
tty	Fixed-width devices such as teletype machines and terminals
tv	Television-type devices with low resolution, color, and limited scrollability

For example, to specify that aural browsers should render your Web page using the *sounds.css* style sheet, you could enter the following `link` element in the HTML file:

```
<link href="sounds.css" type="text/css" media="speech" />
```

In the same way, you would use the following `media` attribute in an embedded style sheet to indicate that its styles are intended for aural devices:

```
<style type="text/css" media="speech">
   ...
</style>
```

The `media` attribute also can contain a comma-separated list of media types. The following `link` element points to a style sheet designed for both print and projection media:

```
<link href="output.css" type="text/css" media="print, projection" />
```

Style sheets cascade through the media types in the same way they cascade through a document tree. A style sheet in which the output device is not specified is applied to all devices, unless it is superseded by a style designed for a particular device. When no value is given to the `media` attribute, any style defined in the embedded or external style sheet is used for all media, where applicable.

The `@media` and `@import` Rules

It's not always convenient to maintain several different style sheets for the same document. In place of several style sheets, you can use a single style sheet broken down into different sections for each media type. This is done using the rule

```
@media devices {
   styles
}
```

where *devices* is the supported media types and *styles* is the style rules associated with those devices. For example, the following style sheet is broken into four sections with different styles for screen, print, handheld, and television media:

```
@media screen   { body {font-size: 1em;}  h1 {font-size: 2em;}  }
@media print    { body {font-size: 12pt;} h1 {font-size: 16pt;} }
@media handheld { body {font-size: 8px;}  h1 {font-size: 12px;} }
@media tv    { body {font-size: 20px;} h1 {font-size: 18px;} }
```

In this style sheet, the font size is smallest for a handheld device (which presumably has a limited screen area) and largest for a television (which is usually viewed from a greater distance). Similar to the `media` attribute, the `@media` rule also allows you to place media types in a comma-separated list, as in the following declaration:

```
@media screen, print, handheld, tv {
    h1 {font-family: sans-serif;}
}
```

Both the `media` attribute and the `@media` rule come with their own benefits and disadvantages. The `@media` rule enables you to consolidate all of your styles within a single style sheet; however, this consolidation can result in larger and complicated files. The alternative—placing media styles in different sheets—can make those sheets easier to maintain; however, if you change the design of your site, you might have to duplicate your changes across several style sheets.

Finally, you can specify media devices when importing one style sheet into another. The `css` rule

```
@import url(screen.css) screen;
```

imports the *screen.css* style sheet file in the current style sheet only when the browser device is a screen.

Media Groups

The distinction among the different media devices is not always immediately clear. For example, how is projection media different from screen media? The difference lies in what kind of output can be sent to the media. All output devices can be described based on some common properties. CSS uses **media groups** to describe how different media devices render content. There are four media groups based on the following characteristics:

- continuous or paged
- visual, audio, or tactile
- grid (for character grid devices) or bitmap
- interactive (for devices that allow user interaction) or static (for devices that allow no interaction)

Figure 8-36 shows how all output media are categorized based on the four media groups. For example, a printout is paged (because the output comes in discrete units or pages), visual, bitmap, and static (you can't interact with it). A computer screen, on the other hand, is continuous, visual, and bitmap, and can be either static or interactive.

Figure 8-36	Media groups

Device	continuous/paged	visual/audio/tactile	grid/bitmap	interactive/static
braille	continuous	tactile	grid	both
embossed	paged	tactile	grid	both
handheld	both	visual	both	both
print	paged	visual	bitmap	static
projection	paged	visual	bitmap	static
screen	continuous	visual	bitmap	both
speech	continuous	audio	N/A	both
tty	continuous	visual	grid	both
tv	both	visual, audio	bitmap	both

Media groups help identify which CSS styles are appropriate for different devices. For example, the `font-size` property belongs to the visual media group because it describes the visual appearance of the document content; and as indicated in Figure 8-36, this means you can use the `font-size` property with handheld, print, projection, screen, TTY, and TV devices. However, it would have no meaning to—and would in fact be ignored by—devices whose output consists of Braille or audio output. On the other hand, the `pitch` property, which is used to define the pitch or frequency of a speaking voice, belongs to the audio media group and is supported by speech and TV devices. By studying the media groups, you can identify the properties that apply to different media devices.

Creating Styles for Different Devices

- To create a style sheet for a specific media device, add the attribute

  ```
  media = "devices"
  ```

  to either the `link` element or the `style` element, where *devices* is one or more of `braille`, `embossed`, `handheld`, `print`, `projection`, `screen`, `speech`, `tty`, `tv`, or `all`. If you don't specify a media device, the style sheet applies to all devices. Multiple media types should be entered in a comma-separated list.
- To create a style for specific media from within a style sheet, add the rule

  ```
  @media devices {styles}
  ```

  where *styles* is the style rules that are applied to the different page elements displayed by those media devices.

Now that you've seen how to define the style sheet for a particular media device, you decide to create one for printed output.

To create a style sheet for print media:

1. Use your text editor to open the **printtxt.css** style sheet from the tutorial.08\ tutorial folder included with your Data Files. Enter **your name** and **the date** in the comment section of the file.

2. Save the file as **print.css** in the same folder.

Kevin wants you to use the print style sheet for print devices. He wants the other style sheets to be applied to screen devices with the exception of the base style sheet, which should be applied to all devices. You'll use the `media` attribute now to associate each style sheet with the appropriate device.

To apply the `media` attribute:

▶ **1.** Return to the **treebook.htm** file in your text editor.

▶ **2.** Add the attribute `media="screen"` to the `link` elements for the *layout.css* and *effects.css* style sheets.

▶ **3.** Directly below the `link` element for the *effects.css* style sheet, add the following `link` element:

```
<link href="print.css" rel="stylesheet" media="print" />
```

Figure 8-37 highlights the newly added code.

Figure 8-37   **Specifying the media device for each style sheet**

```
<title>Tree and Book</title>
<script src="modernizr-1.5.js"></script>

<link href="base.css" rel="stylesheet" />
<link href="layout.css" rel="stylesheet" media="screen" />
<link href="effects.css" rel="stylesheet" media="screen" />
<link href="print.css" rel="stylesheet" media="print" />
```

base style sheet is used by all devices

load the style sheets only for screen devices

load the style sheet only for print devices

▶ **4.** Save your changes to the file, and then reload the **treebook.htm** file in your Web browser. Confirm that the appearance of the page has not changed. It should not change because your Web browser is treated as screen media, and you haven't changed the style sheet for that media type.

Now that you've identified a style sheet to be used with printed or paged output, you are ready to create your print styles. The first style rule you'll make is to hide the page header, navigation lists, and page footer by setting their display properties to `none`.

To hide the page header, navigation lists, and page footer:

▶ **1.** Return to the **print.css** file in your text editor.

▶ **2.** Add the following style rule as shown in Figure 8-38:

```
/* Hide page elements that will not be printed */

header, nav, footer {
   display: none;
}
```

Figure 8-38	Hiding page elements in the printed output

```
/* Hide page elements that will not be printed */

header, nav, footer {
   display: none;
}
```

does not display the
contents of the header,
nav, and footer elements

▶ **3.** Save your changes to the file, and then reload **treebook.htm** in your Web browser. Verify that the appearance of the page as displayed on your screen has not changed.

▶ **4.** Either print the Web page from within your browser, or use your browser's Print Preview command to preview the printed version of the page. Figure 8-39 shows how the initial page appears when printed.

Figure 8-39 **Printout of the first page**

Stanislaw Dubcek (1903 - 1981)

Born	February 3, 1903 (Hnatince, Bohemia)
Died	September 20, 1981 (Rochester, MN)
Married	Irena (Torbia); June 2, 1929
Children	Peter, Nadine, Robert, Vera, Karen, Jan

Stanislaw and Irena (1929)

Trouble? The initial page of your printout might not resemble that shown in Figure 8-39. Each browser has its own set of styles for rendering printed output. Some browsers will include headers and footers to display the page title, URL, and page number, and others will not.

Kevin likes the printout you created; however, he wants the main photo to appear on the first page along with the table of biographic information, and he wants the four figure boxes to be resized and placed on their own pages alongside their captions. To do this, you'll have to place a page break in the middle of the document directly after the `article` element containing the main photo and Web table. Although page breaks are not supported by media types such as computer screens, they are supported in printed output and for projection devices.

Using Print Styles

CSS defines printed pages by extending the CSS box model described in Tutorial 4 to incorporate the entire page in a page box. As shown in Figure 8-40, the **page box** is composed of two areas: the page area, which contains the content of the document, and the margin area, which contains the space between the printed content and the edges of the page.

Figure 8-40   **The page box**

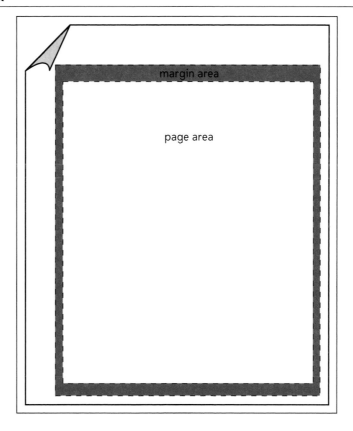

As with the box model, you can specify the size of a page box, the page margins, the internal padding, and other features. The style rules for a page box are contained within the `@page` rule

```
@page {styles}
```

where `styles` is the styles applied to the page. For example, the following `@page` rule sets the page margin for the printed output to 0.5 inches:

```
@page {
   margin: 0.5in;
}
```

A page box does not support all of the measurement units you've used with the other elements. For example, pages do not support the em or ex measurement units. In general, you should use measurement units that are appropriate to the dimensions of your page, such as inches or centimeters.

Page Pseudo-Classes

If a Web page covers several printed pages, you might want to define different styles for different pages. You can do this with pseudo-classes that reference specific pages. The syntax to reference a page pseudo-class uses the rule

```
@page:pseudo-class {styles}
```

where *pseudo-class* is `first` for the first page of the printout, `left` for the pages that appear on the left in double-sided printouts, or `right` for pages that appear on the right in double-sided printouts.

For example, if you are printing on both sides of the paper, you might want to create mirror images of the margins for the left and right pages of the printout. The following styles result in pages in which the inner margin is set to 5 centimeters and the outer margin is set to 2 centimeters:

```
@page:left {margin: 3cm 5cm 3cm 2cm;}
@page:right {margin: 3cm 2cm 3cm 5cm;}
```

Page Names and the Page Property

To define styles for pages other than the first, left, or right, you first must create a **page name** for those styles as follows

```
@page name {styles}
```

where *name* is the label assigned to the page style. The following code defines a page style named *large_margins* used for pages in which the page margin is set at 10 centimeters on each side:

```
@page large_margins {margin: 10cm}
```

Once you define a page name, you can apply it to any grouping element in your document. The content of the element will appear on its own page, with the browser automatically inserting page breaks before and after the element if required. To assign a page name to an element, you use the `page` property

```
selector {
    page: name;
}
```

where *selector* identifies the element that will be displayed on the page, and *name* is the name of a defined page. For example, the style

```
blockquote {
    page: large_margins;
}
```

causes all block quotes to be displayed on their own separate pages using the styles defined for the large_margins page.

Setting the Page Size

Because printed media can vary in size and orientation, one style property supported by the page box is the `size` property that allows Web authors to define the default dimensions of a printed page as well as whether pages should be printed in portrait or landscape orientation. The syntax of the `size` property is

```
size: width height orientation
```

where *width* and *height* are the width and height of the page, and *orientation* is the orientation of the page (`portrait` or `landscape`). If you don't specify the orientation, browsers assume a portrait orientation. Thus, to format a page as a standard-size page in landscape orientation with a 1-inch margin, you would apply the following style rule:

```
@page {
    size: 8.5in 11in landscape;
    margin: 1in;
}
```

If you don't set the orientation value, browsers print the output in portrait by default. Note that users can override the page sizes and orientations chosen by a Web page author because users may choose different settings when actually printing the page.

You also can replace the width, height, and orientation values with the keyword `auto` (to let browsers determine the page dimensions) or `inherit` (to inherit the page size from the parent element). If a page does not fit into the dimensions specified by the `@page` styles, browsers either rotate the page box 90° or scale the page box to fit the sheet size.

REFERENCE

Setting the Page Size

- To define a page box for a printout that indicates the page size, margins, and orientation, use the style rule

  ```
  @page {styles}
  ```

  where *styles* is the styles that define the page.
- To set the page size and orientation, use the style property

  ```
  size: width height orientation;
  ```

  where *width* and *height* are the width and height of the page, and *orientation* is the orientation of the page (`portrait` or `landscape`).

You'll use the `@page` rule to define the print layout of the Tree and Book page. Kevin suggests that you set the page size to 8.5 × 11 inches, in portrait orientation, with 0.5-inch margins.

To set the style of the printed page:

1. Return to the **print.css** file in your text editor.

2. As shown in Figure 8-41, add the following rule at the top of the style sheet, directly after the initial comments:

```
@page {
    size: 8.5in 11in portrait;
    margin: 0.5in;
}
```

Figure 8-41   Setting the page size with the @page rule

```
@page {
    size: 8.5in 11in portrait;
    margin: 0.5in;
}

/* Hide page elements that will not be printed */
```

▶ **3.** Save your changes to the file.

INSIGHT

Printing Hypertext Links

The great appeal of the Web is the ability to quickly navigate from document to document using hypertext links. This advantage is lost when a user views a printed version of a page. Because hypertext links within the main content of the page are often underlined, you may want to remove that underlining to make your printed version easier to read.

However, readers of the printed version might also want to know the URLs of those links so that they can view those sites at a later date. You can use CSS to automatically add the URL of each link to the printed version using the following style rule:

```
a:after {
    content: " (" attr(href) ") ";
}
```

This style rule uses the `after` pseudo-element along with the `content` property and the `attr()` function to append the text of the `href` attribute to each hyperlink. Using this style rule, the hypertext link

```
Visit the <a href="www.treebook.com">Tree and Book</a> Web site.
```

would appear in the printed version of the document as follows:

```
Visit the Tree and Book (www.treebook.com) Web site.
```

You should be careful when using this technique with all of your hypertext links. Appending the text of a long and complicated URL will make your text difficult to read and will probably not help your users very much. Several JavaScript tools are available on the Web to give you more options for how your URLs should be printed, including scripts that automatically append all URLs as footnotes at the end of the printed document.

Working with Page Breaks

When a document is sent to a printer, the browser determines the location of the page breaks unless that information is included as part of the print style. To specify a page break that occurs either before or after a page element, you apply the style properties

```
page-break-before: type;
page-break-after: type;
```

where *type* has the following possible values:

- `always`:   to always place a page break before or after the element
- `avoid`:   to never place a page break

- `left:`   to place a page break where the next page will be a left page
- `right:`   to place a page break where the next page will be a right page
- `auto:`   to allow the printer to determine whether or not to insert a page break
- `inherit:`   to insert the page break style from the parent element

For example, if you wanted every `h1` heading to start a new page, you would apply the following style rule:

```
h1 {
    page-break-before: always;
}
```

Likewise, if you wanted block quotes to always appear on their own pages, you could place a page break before and after the `blockquote` element using the following style rule:

```
blockquote {
    page-break-before: always;
    page-break-after: always;
}
```

Preventing a Page Break

Sometimes you want to keep printers from inserting a page break inside of an element. This usually occurs when you have a long string of text that you don't want broken into two pages. You can prevent printers from inserting a page break by using the style property

```
page-break-inside: type;
```

where *type* is `auto`, `inherit`, or `avoid`. Thus, to prevent a block quote from appearing on two separate pages, you could apply the following style:

```
blockquote {
    page-break-inside: avoid;
}
```

Note that the `avoid` type does not guarantee that there will not be a page break within the element. If the content of an element exceeds the dimensions of the sheet of paper on which it's being printed, the browser will be forced to insert a page break.

Working with Widows and Orphans

Even with the three page break properties, there will be situations where a printer has to divide the contents of an element across two pages. This can result in the presence of widows and orphans. A **widow** occurs when only a few ending lines of an element appear at the top of a page while the bulk of the content appears on the preceding page. An **orphan** is just the opposite: It occurs when only a few beginning lines of an element appear at the bottom of a page, while the bulk of the content is placed on the following page. Leaving one or two lines stranded on a page either as a widow or an orphan makes the material more difficult to read and is considered poor page design. To control the appearance of widows and orphans, CSS provides the two properties

```
widow: value;
orphan: value;
```

where *value* is the number of lines that must appear within the element before a page break can be inserted by the printer. The default value is 2, which means that the printer can strand a widow or an orphan only if the widow or orphan includes at least two lines of text.

TIP

You can repeat the same element across several pages, displaying it as a page header or footer, by setting its `position` property to `fixed`.

If you wanted to increase the size of widows and orphans to three lines for the paragraphs in a document, you could apply the style rule

```
p {
   widow: 3;
   orphan: 3;
}
```

and printers would not insert a page break if fewer than three lines of a paragraph would be stranded at either the top or the bottom of the page.

How Browsers Set Automatic Page Breaks

Browsers establish page breaks automatically unless you manually specify the page breaks with CSS. By default, browsers insert page breaks using the following guidelines:
- Insert all of the manual page breaks as indicated by the `page-break-before`, `page-break-after`, and `page-break-inside` properties.
- Break the pages as few times as possible.
- Make all pages that don't have a forced page break appear to have the same height.
- Avoid page breaking inside a grouping element that has a border.
- Avoid breaking inside a table.
- Avoid breaking inside of a floating element.

Only after attempting to satisfy these constraints are the Web page designer's recommendations for the widow and orphan styles applied.

You can combine all of the page styles described above to provide the greatest control over the appearance of your printed document. The following styles display all `blockquote` elements on an 8.5-×-11 inch sheet on a single page in landscape orientation:

```
@page quote_page {
   8.5in 11in landscape;
}
blockquote {
   page: quote_page;
   page-break-before: always;
   page-break-inside: avoid;
   page-break-after: always;
}
```

Setting Page Breaks

REFERENCE

- To insert a page break before an element, use the style property

  ```
  page-break-before: type;
  ```

  where *type* is `always` to always place a page break, `avoid` to never place a page break, `left` to force a page break where the succeeding page will be a left page, `right` to force a page break where the succeeding page will be a right page, `auto` to allow browsers to determine whether or not to insert a page break, or `inherit` to inherit the page break style of the parent element.

- To insert a page break after an element, use the property

  ```
  page-break-after: type;
  ```

  where *type* has the same values as the `page-break-before` style.

- To apply a page break inside an element, use the property

  ```
  page-break-inside: type;
  ```

  where *type* is `auto`, `inherit`, or `avoid`.

Now that you've seen how to insert page breaks into printed output, you can insert a manual page break into Kevin's document. Kevin wants the contents of the `article` element to appear on the first page, and he wants a page break added directly after the article. He also wants to prohibit browsers from inserting page breaks within the `article` element. Now, you'll add style rules to the *print.css* style sheet to control these page breaks.

To control the placement of page breaks in the document:

1. At the bottom of the *print.css* style sheet, insert the following style rule as shown in Figure 8-42:

   ```
   /* Setting the page breaks in the document */

   article {
       display: block;
       page-break-after: always;
       page-break-inside: avoid;
   }
   ```

Figure 8-42   Defining page breaks within the printed output

```
/* Setting the page breaks in the document */

article {
    display: block;
    page-break-after: always;
    page-break-inside: avoid;
}
```

avoids adding page breaks within the article element

always adds a page break after the article element

2. Save your changes to the style sheet.

To complete the style sheet for printed output, you'll add style rules for the heading and figure boxes. Kevin suggests that you increase the font size of the `h1` heading to 28 points and set the width of the photo to 4 inches, centering both on the page. You'll add these styles to the style sheet now.

To format the contents of the first page:

▶ **1.** At the bottom of the style sheet, insert the following style rule for the h1 heading:

```
/* Styles for the h1 heading */

h1 {
    font-size: 28pt;
    text-align: center;
    width: 100%;
}
```

▶ **2.** Next, insert the following style rule for the main photo:

```
/* Styles for the main photo */

#photo1 {
    display: block;
    margin: 0in auto;
    width: 4in;
}
```

Figure 8-43 highlights the new style rules in the file.

Figure 8-43 **Styles for the h1 heading and main photo**

```
/* Styles for the h1 heading */

h1 {
    font-size: 28pt;                          expresses font sizes
    text-align: center;                       in points, not pixels
    width: 100%;
}

/* Styles for the main photo */

#photo1 {
    display: block;
    margin: 0in auto;                         uses inches to define
    width: 4in;                               the margin and
}                                             width of the photo
```

▶ **3.** Save your changes to the file.

Finally, Kevin wants each figure box to appear on its own page. As with the `article` element, you'll add a page break after each `figure` element and instruct browsers to avoid placing page breaks within each figure box. You'll also create style rules to set the width of each figure box image and the font size of each caption.

To create styles for the figure boxes:

▶ **1.** At the bottom of the style sheet, add the following style rule to place each figure box on its own page:

```
/* Styles for the figure boxes */

figure {
    display: block;
    text-align: center;
    page-break-after: always;
    page-break-inside: avoid;
}
```

2. Add the following style rules to set the width of figure box images to 5 inches and the font size of captions to 20 points:

```
figure img {
    width: 5in;
}

figure figcaption {
    font-size: 20pt;
}
```

3. Finally, add the following style rule to avoid adding a page break after the last figure box:

```
figure:last-of-type {
    page-break-after: avoid;
}
```

Figure 8-44 highlights the newly added styles.

Figure 8-44   **Figure box styles**

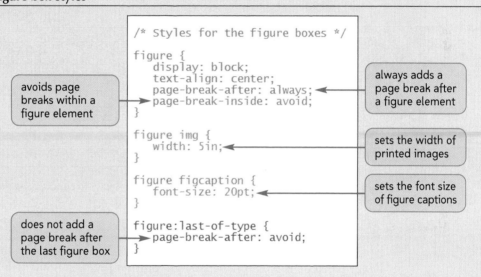

4. Save your changes to the style sheet file.

5. Reload the **treebook.htm** file in your Web browser, and then either print the file or view the file in a Print Preview window. Figure 8-45 shows a preview of the five pages that should be in the printout.

Figure 8-45   **Printed output**

Written Communication: Tips for Effective Printing

One challenge of printing a Web page is that what works very well on the screen often fails when transferred to the printed page. For example, some browsers suppress printing background images, so that white text on a dark background, which appears fine on the computer monitor, is unreadable when printed. Following are some tips and guidelines you should keep in mind when designing the printed version of your Web page:

- *Remove the clutter.* A printout should contain only information that is of immediate use to the reader. Page elements such as navigation lists, banners, and advertising should be removed, leaving only the main articles and images from your page.
- *Measure for printing.* Use only those measuring units in your style sheet that are appropriate for printing, such as points, inches, centimeters, and millimeters. Avoid expressing widths and heights in pixels because those can vary with printer resolution.
- *Use serif fonts.* Serif fonts such as Times New Roman and Georgia were originally designed for printed material because the serifs make text easier to read at smaller font sizes. Use serif fonts for your body text, reserving sans-serif fonts such as Helvetica and Arial only for headers.
- *Design for white.* Because many browsers suppress the printing of background images and some users do not have access to color printers, create a style sheet that assumes black text on a white background.
- *Avoid absolute positioning.* Absolute positioning is designed for screen output. When printed, an object placed at an absolute position will be displayed on the first page of your printout, potentially making your text unreadable.
- *Give the user a choice.* Some readers will still want to print your Web page exactly as it appears on the screen. To accommodate them, you can use one of the many JavaScript tools available on the Web that allows readers to switch between your screen and print style sheets.

Finally, a print style sheet is one aspect of Web design that works better in theory than in practice. Many browsers provide only partial support for the CSS print styles, so you should always test your designs on a variety of browsers and browser versions. In general, you will have the best results with a basic style sheet rather than one that tries to implement a complicated and involved print layout.

You've seen how to use the `media` attribute for printing. Another goal of the `media` attribute is to provide an easy way of creating style sheets designed for handheld devices such as mobile phones and PDAs. In a perfect world, all mobile browsers would respond only to style sheets written with the `handheld` device type, but that is not what has occurred. Support for the `handheld` device type is mixed and inconsistently implemented.

Some mobile browsers read only style sheets written for handheld devices; others load a handheld style sheet if one exists, but apply a screen style if it is the only one available. A third group of mobile browsers loads *both* the screen style sheet and the handheld style sheet, and then attempts to reconcile any differences between them.

Finally, most of the newer mobile browsers simply ignore the `handheld` device type altogether, treating a handheld device as simply another screen device, albeit with a much smaller screen. Thus, even though `handheld` is a CSS media device type, it is not practical to rely on it.

How, then, do you design your Web site for mobile browsers? In the next session, you'll solve this problem through the use of media queries.

Session 8.2 Quick Check

1. Provide a CSS3 style rule to add a border image around every `blockquote` element. The image should be taken from a 15-pixel-wide slice of the *borders.png* file. Have the side images stretch to fit the border space, and set the border width to 10 pixels.

2. Provide a CSS3 style rule to display the `aside` element at 80% opacity.

3. What HTML attribute should you use to apply a style sheet to an aural device such as a screen reader?

4. Which media devices belong to the continuous and visual groups?

5. Which media types would be most appropriate for Web browsers designed for the visually impaired?

6. Provide a style to set the page size of a printed document to 11 inches wide by 14 inches high in landscape orientation with 1.5-inch margins.

7. Provide a style rule to insert a page break before every `h1` heading in a document.

8. In page design, what is a widow? What is an orphan?

SESSION 8.3 VISUAL OVERVIEW

A media query specifies the media device and the properties of that device.

```
<link href="mobile.css" rel="stylesheet"
  media="screen and (max-width: 500px)" />
```

The viewport meta tag sets the size of the viewport in the mobile device.

```
<meta name="viewport"
  content="width-device-width,
  initial-scale=1.0,
  maximum-scale=1.0" />
```

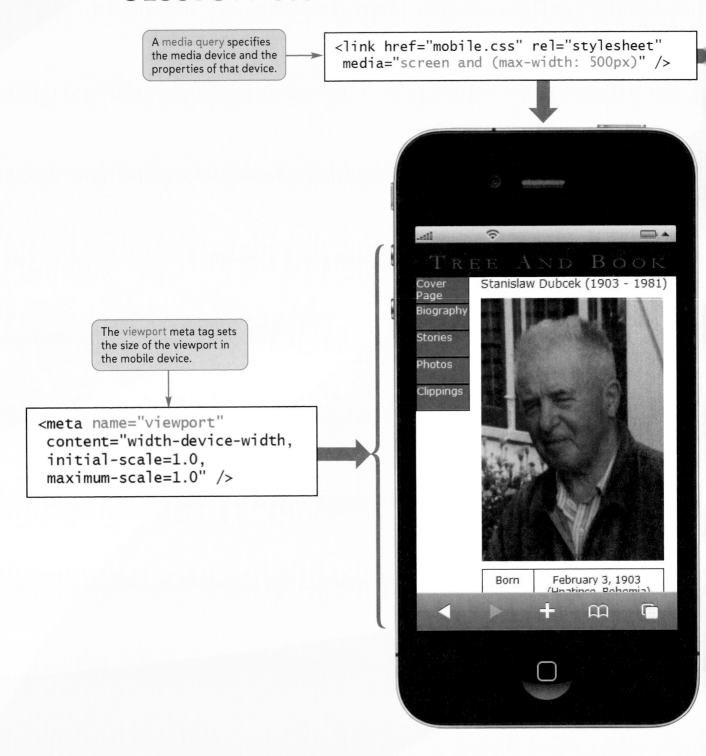

```
@media screen and
(orientation: portrait)
```

DESIGNING FOR THE MOBILE WEB

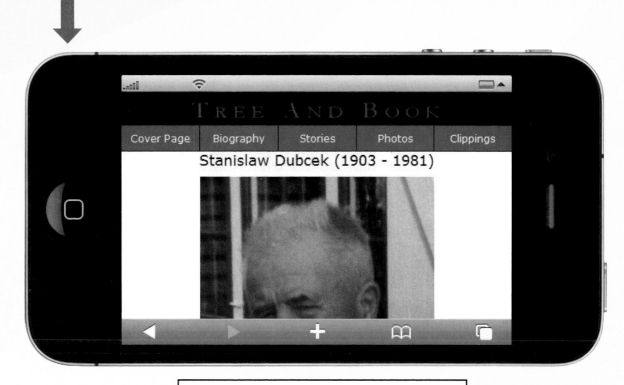

```
@media screen and
(orientation: landscape)
```

To create a style for portrait or landscape mode, use the orientation feature.

Designing for the Mobile Web

Kevin has had a chance to upload his sample page to a server and view it on his mobile device. The page rendered correctly on his device, but in full-screen view it was small and difficult to read; and if he zoomed into the page, only a small portion was visible (see Figure 8-46).

Figure 8-46 The Tree and Book page as it appears on a mobile device

sabri deniz kizil/Shutterstock.com
okicoki/Shutterstock.com

Kevin is not happy with either viewing option and would like you to design a style sheet appropriate for the smaller screens found on most mobile devices and cell phones. As with the print style sheet you created in the last session, Kevin wants to limit the amount of content displayed in the mobile version of his sample page and design the page to reduce the amount of scrolling required by readers. In general, the goal of mobile Web design is not to recreate the desktop experience on a smaller scale on mobile devices, but rather to re-envision the page design and content in a form that is suitable for devices with smaller screens and limited bandwidth.

Kevin suggests that you create a mobile design that focuses only on the photos and biographical information about his great-grandfather. Figure 8-47 shows a preview of how he would like his sample page to appear on a typical mobile device. Notice that Kevin wants one design for when the page is displayed in portrait mode and another for landscape mode.

Figure 8-47   Preview of Kevin's proposed mobile design

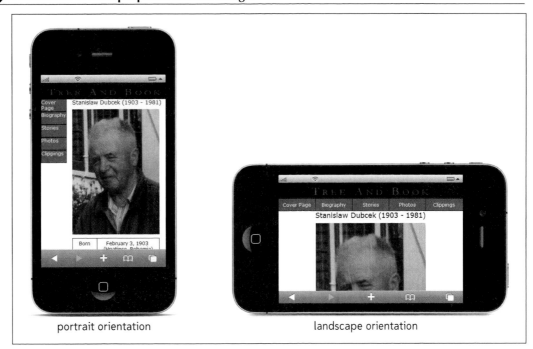

portrait orientation   landscape orientation

Testing a Mobile Design

The easiest way to create and test a mobile design is to go out and purchase all of the popular mobile devices on the market and load your page on each one. Though this is the easiest, it's also the most expensive! While a Web designer may have one smartphone, it's uncommon to have 10. The next best thing to having the actual device is to acquire an **SDK** or **software development kit**, which is a set of development tools that you can use to create applications for software programs, devices, or hardware platforms. SDKs are available for download for all major mobile devices. With the SDKs, you can develop and test your Web site designs and create your own custom mobile Web apps without actually owning the hardware device.

To assist you in developing your mobile application, most SDKs also include an **emulator**, which is a software program that runs on a desktop computer and emulates the actions of another hardware device. With an emulator, you can run many smartphone apps right on your PC or Mac. A simpler version of an emulator is a **simulator**, which simulates some of the behavior of a device but does not emulate the operations of the hardware. Figure 8-48 lists some of the SDKs, emulators, and simulators available on the Web at the time of this writing.

Figure 8-48   **Mobile SDKs, emulators, and simulators**

Emulator and Simulator	Description	URL
Adobe Device Central	A suite of emulators for a variety of mobile devices	www.adobe.com/products/devicecentral.html
Android SDK	SDK for Android development (Mac OS X, Windows, Linux)	developer.android.com/sdk
Firefox Mobile Emulator	Emulator for mobile version of Firefox, also known as Fennec, developed for Nokia and Android	developer.mozilla.org/En/Mobile
iPhone SDK	SDK and emulator for the iPhone (Mac OS X only)	developer.apple.com/
iPhoney	iPhone simulator that allows developers to test their Web sites on a 320 × 480 pixel screen	www.marketcircle.com/iphoney/
iPad Emulator	Online emulator for iPad developers	www.ipad-emulator.com
MobiOne Studio	iPhone emulator for Windows (free trial period with option to purchase)	www.genuitec.com/mobile/
Opera Mini Simulator	Java applet that simulates the Opera mobile browser	www.opera.com/mini/demo
Opera Mobile Emulator	Emulator for mobile version of Opera	www.opera.com/developer/tools
HP webOS SDK	Emulator for webOS devices	developer.palm.com
Windows Phone Emulator	Developer tools for the Windows Phone	create.msdn.com/en-US/

Another way to test your mobile design is to submit it to a testing lab. A site such as MobiReady (*ready.mobi*) tests your mobile Web site design and provides screen shots and optimization tips. To test your site, you may have to submit personal information including your e-mail address, phone number, and street address. Be aware that many testing labs are not free. To view Kevin's mobile design in this session, you will not need to have a mobile device or an emulator, but you may find one useful.

Configuring the Viewport

Mobile devices can display pages written for the larger screens found on desktop computers; but as Kevin discovered, too often the resulting pages are difficult to read and navigate. Therefore, to optimize Kevin's sample page for the mobile Web, you first must learn how Web pages designed for a computer desktop get adapted for use on a mobile device.

The contents of a Web page are displayed within a window known as the **viewport**. On a desktop computer, the viewport is equivalent to the browser window; with printed material, the viewport is the page box. Browsers on mobile devices support two kinds of viewports: a **visual viewport** containing the Web page content that appears on the screen, and a **layout viewport** containing the complete content of the page, some of which is hidden from the user (see Figure 8-49).

Figure 8-49   The visual and layout viewports

visual viewport

layout viewport

sabri deniz kizil/Shutterstock.com
okicoki/Shutterstock.com

Most of the time, users interact with Web pages on mobile devices without being aware of the two viewports. When a user pans through a page, he or she is scrolling through the contents of the visual viewport. Zooming out of the page to view more of the page content has the effect of displaying more of the layout viewport within the visual viewport, at the expense of decreasing the font size and making the text difficult to read. If a user zooms completely out, displaying the entire page within the screen, the layout viewport coincides with the visual viewport.

The size of the layout viewport is set by the browser running on the mobile device. For example, the mobile version of Safari running on the iPhone has a layout viewport width of 980 pixels, the Opera Mini browser uses an 850-pixel-wide layout viewport, and Android's default Web browser employs a layout viewport that is 974 pixels wide. These are the default values; layout viewports increase in width based on the layout of the Web page being viewed. The apparent width of the visual viewport, on the other hand, does not change, as it is based on the physical size of the device screen.

The distinction between the visual viewport and the layout viewport is important because mobile browsers render Web pages based on the size of the layout viewport, not the visual viewport. This is done so that Web sites designed for larger desktop displays will translate quickly and easily to smaller mobile screens. For example, although the iPhone screen is only 320 pixels wide, the mobile browser running on the iPhone acts as if the device was 980 pixels or more in width. This is why Kevin's document is so difficult to view on a mobile display. Thus, to optimize your Web site for mobile display, you first should set the width of the layout viewport to match the width of the device's screen. Once that is done, you can create a style sheet that matches the screen width of the mobile device. You set the layout viewport using a `meta` element.

The Viewport meta Element

The viewport meta element was introduced by Apple for use with the iPhone as a way of setting the properties of the layout viewport. Although not part of the HTML specifications, most current mobile browsers support this meta element, which has the syntax

```
<meta name="viewport" content="properties" />
```

where *properties* is the media features of the layout viewport. Web designers may choose different widths and heights based on the content of the pages on their Web sites. Kevin wants a layout viewport that matches the width of the device screen. To accomplish this, you'll apply the following meta element to his document:

```
<meta name="viewport" content="width=device-width, initial-scale=1.0, maximum-scale=1.0" />
```

In this meta element, the device-width keyword is used to return the width of the device's screen, whatever that may be. For a mobile device like the iPhone, this sets the width of the layout viewport to 320 pixels; other devices have different widths. The initial-scale and maximum-scale parameters are set to 1 so that the page layout is always scaled to match the resolution of the device screen. You'll add this meta element to Kevin's document now.

To add the viewport meta element:

1. Return to the **treebook.htm** file in your text editor.

2. Directly below the meta element that defines the character set, add the following element as shown in Figure 8-50:

```
<meta name="viewport" content="width=device-width,
             initial-scale=1.0, maximum-scale=1.0" />
```

Figure 8-50 Adding the viewport meta element

```
<meta charset="UTF-8" />
<meta name="viewport" content="width=device-width,
                        initial-scale=1.0, maximum-scale=1.0" />

<title>Tree and Book</title>
<script src="modernizr-1.5.js"></script>
```

3. Save your changes to the file.

Now that you've set the width of the layout viewport to match the device width, you'll begin creating a style sheet for your mobile devices. You'll add this style sheet now.

To create the mobile style sheet:

1. Use your text editor to open the **mobiletxt.css** file from the tutorial.08/tutorial folder. Enter *your name* and *the date* in the comment section of the file.

2. Save the file as **mobile.css**.

Before you can link Kevin's document to this style sheet, you have to set the conditions under which browsers will apply it to Kevin's sample page. You do this through media queries.

Introducing Media Queries

In the last session, you learned how to use the media attribute to associate style sheets with particular devices such as screens and printers. However, in a world in which screens can vary from small handheld devices only a few inches wide to large flat screen monitors 30 inches or more across, it's often more important to know about the properties of a device itself rather than what kind of device it is. For this reason, CSS3 introduced **media queries** to allow Web designers to associate style sheets not just with devices, but with devices that have specific screen sizes, color resolutions, page orientations, and other display features.

The media Attribute in CSS3

A media query uses the same media attribute, @media, and @import rules that were discussed in the last session. The syntax, though, is different, having the form

```
media = "devices and|or (features)"


@media devices and|or (features) {
   styles
}

@import url(url) devices and|or (features)
```

where *devices* is a list of media devices and *features* is a list of display features and their values found on those devices. The and and or keywords are used to create media queries that involve different devices or different features, or combinations of both. Figure 8-51 details some of the specific features supported in CSS3.

Figure 8-51   **Media features**

Feature	Description
aspect-ratio	The ratio of the width of the display area to the height of the display
color	The number of bits per color component of the output device; if the device does not support color, the value is 0
color-index	The number of colors supported by the output device
device-aspect-ratio	The ratio of the device-width value to the device-height value
device-height	The height of the rendering surface of the output device: for continuous media, this is the height of the screen; for paged media, this is the height of the page
device-width	The width of the rendering surface of the output device: for continuous media, this is the width of the screen; for paged media, this is the width of the page
grid	Whether the output device employs a grid or a bitmap: if the output device uses a grid (as in a TTY terminal or a phone display with only one fixed font), the value is 1; otherwise, the value is 0
height	The height of the display area of the output device: for continuous media, this is the height of the browser window including the scroll bars; for paged media, this is the height of the page box
monochrome	The number of bits per pixel in the device's monochrome frame buffer
orientation	The general description of the aspect ratio: equal to portrait when the height of the display area is greater than the width; equal to landscape otherwise
resolution	The resolution of the output device in pixels, expressed in either dpi (dots per inch) or dpcm (dots per centimeter)
scan	The scanning process used by the device; equal to either progressive or interlace
width	The width of the display area of the output device: for continuous media, this is the width of the browser window including the scroll bars; for paged media, this is the width of the page box

Each feature is entered into a media query using the format

```
(feature: value)
```

where *feature* is the name of a media feature, and *value* is the value that must be matched before the browser can load the style sheet or apply a group of styles to the page. For example, the following link element loads the *screen1.css* style sheet file only when the output device is a screen and the screen width is equal to 320 pixels:

```
<link href="screen1.css" rel="stylesheet"
        media="screen and (device-width: 320px)" />
```

All of the media features in Figure 8-51 with the exception of the grid, orientation, and scan features also accept the min- and max- prefixes, where min- expresses a range that is greater than or equal to the specified value, and max- indicates a range that is less than or equal to the value provided. Thus, the following @media rule applies the enclosed styles only when the output device is a screen and the width of the viewport is at most 700 pixels:

```
@media screen and (max-width: 700px) {
    styles
}
```

TIP

For mobile devices, the width and height features refer to the width and height of the layout viewport, not the visual viewport.

In the same way, the following @media rule applies style rules only on a screen device with a width of 400 pixels or more:

```
@media screen and (min-width: 400px) {
    styles
}
```

REFERENCE

Creating a Media Query

- To create a media query for loading a style sheet, add the media attribute

  media = "*devices* and|or (*features*)"

  to the link element, where *devices* is a list of media devices, and *features* is a list of display features and their values as found on those devices.
- To apply a media query to a collection of style rules, apply the @media rule

  @media *devices* and|or (*features*) {
      styles
  }

  in your style sheet, where *styles* is those styles applied to the specified devices and features.
- To import a style sheet based on a media query, apply the following @import rule:

  @import url(*url*) *devices* and|or (*features*)

Writing a Feature Expression

You can combine multiple media queries using logical operators such as and, not, and or. For example, the @import rule

```
@import(mobile.css) all and (min-width: 320px and max-width: 480px);
```

imports the *mobile.css* style sheet file only when the width of the output device is between 320 and 480 pixels (inclusive), while the statement

```
@import(tall.css) print and (orientation: portrait and min-height:
9in);
```

imports the *tall.css* file only for print devices whose orientation is portrait with a minimum height in the page box of 9 inches.

Some media features are directed toward devices that do not have a particular property or characteristic. This is done by applying the not operator, as in the following example:

```
<link href = "example.css" rel = "stylesheet"
      media = "not screen and (max-width: 480px)" />
```

The not operator acts to negate whatever follows in the expression. In this case, the initial expression (without the not operator) matches screen devices with maximum widths of 480 pixels; negating the expression matches any device that's not a screen or does not have a maximum width of 480 pixels.

Several media queries can be combined in a comma-separated list. If at least one of the media queries is true, the entire expression is treated as true; otherwise, it's treated as false. Thus, the expression

```
@media screen and (device-aspect-ratio: 16/9), projection and
(device-aspect-ratio: 16/9) {
    styles
}
```

TIP

If you attempt to apply a feature to a device that doesn't support it, the media query always returns the value false.

loads the style rules only if the device is a screen or a projector with a device aspect ratio of 16 to 9.

If no value is specified for a media feature, browsers assume a value of 0. This is useful as a shorthand method of testing whether a particular feature is present or not. For instance, the media query

```
media = screen and (color)
```

matches screen devices that can display color. If you don't specify a media device, browsers assume that the query applies to all devices; thus, the query

```
media = (color)
```

matches any device that supports color.

Finally, for older browsers that do not support media queries, CSS3 provides the `only` keyword to hide style sheets from those browsers. For example, when an older browser processes the `link` element

```
<link href = "color.css" rel = "stylesheet" media = "only screen and
(color)" />
```

it initially encounters the `only` keyword and interprets it as an unsupported device name, and thus does not load the *color.css* style sheet file. Newer browsers that support media queries recognize the `only` keyword and continue to load the style sheet for screen devices that support color.

Choosing a Media Query for the Mobile Web

Now that you've seen how to write a media query, you'll create one for the mobile style sheet so that the style sheet is loaded only for devices with small screen widths. As mobile devices increase in size and capability, one challenge for Web designers is deciding at what point mobile devices end and tablet and desktop devices begin. For example, the original iPhone had a screen width of 320 pixels in portrait mode and 480 pixels in landscape mode; but other mobile devices support slightly larger widths, up to the iPhone 4 with a screen dimension of 640 × 960 pixels. For Kevin's document, you decide to apply the mobile style sheet for screen widths of up to 500 pixels; beyond that, you'll apply the desktop style sheets that you've been using throughout the course of this tutorial.

REFERENCE

Writing a Feature Expression

- To associate a style sheet with screen devices that are less than or equal to a specific width, use the query

  ```
  media = "screen and (max-width: value)"
  ```

  where *value* is the maximum allowable width of the screen's viewport.
- To associate a style sheet with screen devices that are greater than or equal to a specific width, use the query

  ```
  media = "screen and (min-width: value)"
  ```

  where *value* is the minimum allowable width of the screen's viewport.
- To associate a style sheet with screen devices that fall within a range of screen widths, use the following query:

  ```
  media = "screen and (min-width: value and max-width: value)"
  ```

- To associate a style sheet with screen devices in portrait or landscape mode, use the query

  ```
  media = "screen and (orientation: type)"
  ```

  where *type* is either portrait or landscape.

Link Kevin's document to the mobile style sheet now, and add media queries to associate each style sheet file with the correct device and viewport width.

To create a media query for the mobile style sheet:

1. Return to the **treebook.htm** file in your text editor.

2. Within the `link` elements for the *layout.css* and *effects.css* files, add the media query `and (min-width: 501px)` to the value of the `media` attribute.

3. Directly above the closing `</head>` tag, insert the following `link` element:

```
<link href="mobile.css" rel="stylesheet" media="only screen and
(max-width: 500px)" />
```

Notice that you use the `only` keyword to hide this style sheet from older browsers that do not support media queries. Figure 8-52 highlights the newly added code in the file.

Figure 8-52 **Applying media queries**

applies the style sheet when the screen
viewport width is greater than 500 pixels

```
<link href="base.css" rel="stylesheet" />
<link href="layout.css" rel="stylesheet" media="screen and (min-width: 501px)" />
<link href="effects.css" rel="stylesheet" media="screen and (min-width: 501px)" />
<link href="print.css" rel="stylesheet" media="print" />
<link href="mobile.css" rel="stylesheet" media="only screen and (max-width: 500px)" />
```

applies the mobile style sheet only when the
screen viewport width is 500 pixels or less

Versions of Internet Explorer before version 9 do not support media queries and fail to load a style sheet if a `media` attribute includes a media query. To accommodate older versions of Internet Explorer, you'll place `link` elements for the *layout.css* and *effects.css* style sheets within a set of conditional comments. See the Tutorial 7 Insight box *Conditional Comments with Internet Explorer* for a review of IE's conditional comments feature.

To place the `link` elements for Internet Explorer:

1. Directly below the `link` element for the *effects.css* style sheet, insert the following code as shown in Figure 8-53:

```
<!-- Style sheet links for Internet Explorer prior to version 9 -->
<!--[if lt IE 9]>
    <link href="layout.css" rel="stylesheet" media="screen" />
    <link href="effects.css" rel="stylesheet" media="screen" />
<![endif]-->
```

Figure 8-53 Media style sheets for Internet Explorer prior to version 9

```
<link href="base.css" rel="stylesheet" />
<link href="layout.css" rel="stylesheet" media="screen and (min-width: 501px)" />
<link href="effects.css" rel="stylesheet" media="screen and (min-width: 501px)" />

<!-- Style sheet links for Internet Explorer prior to Version 9 -->
<!--[if lt IE 9]>
  <link href="layout.css" rel="stylesheet" media="screen" />
    <link href="effects.css" rel="stylesheet" media="screen" />
<![endif]-->

<link href="print.css" rel="stylesheet" media="print" />
<link href="mobile.css" rel="stylesheet" media="only screen and (max-width: 500px)" />
```

Internet Explorer prior to version 9 loads the style sheets for all device screens

2. Save your changes to the file and then reload **treebook.htm** in your Web browser. Verify that the appearance of the page has not changed.

3. You can test the effect of the media query without having access to a mobile device by changing the width of the browser window. Reduce the browser window now and verify that when the width is less than or equal to 500 pixels, the Web page is displayed using only the current mobile style sheet. See Figure 8-54.

Figure 8-54 Page layout at browser window width less than or equal to 500 pixels

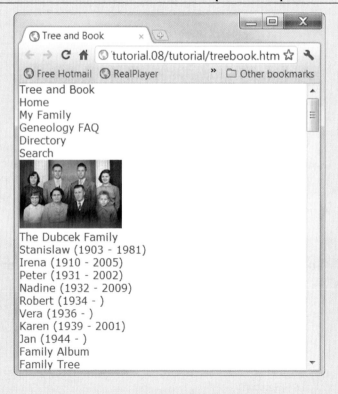

4. If you have access to a mobile device or emulator and can install your Web site on a Web server, upload the contents of the Tree and Book Web site to your server and verify that the appearance of the page resembles that shown in Figure 8-54.

With the media queries in place, you are ready to create the mobile style sheet.

INSIGHT

Not All Pixels Are Equal

Pixels are a basic unit of measurement in Web design, but there are two types of pixels to be aware of. One is a **device pixel**, which refers to the actual physical pixel on a screen. The other is a **CSS pixel**, which is the fundamental unit in CSS measurements. The difference between device pixels and CSS pixels is easiest to understand when you zoom into and out of a Web page. For example, the following style creates an `aside` element that is 300 CSS pixels wide:

```
aside: {width: 300px;}
```

However, the element is not necessarily 300 device pixels. If a user zooms into the Web page, the apparent size of the article increases as measured by device pixels but remains 300 CSS pixels wide, resulting in 1 CSS pixel being represented by several device pixels. The number of device pixels matched to a single CSS pixel is known as the **device-pixel ratio**. For example, when a page is zoomed at a factor of 2x, the device-pixel ratio is 2, with a single CSS pixel represented by a 2 × 2 square of device pixels.

One area where the difference between device pixels and CSS pixels becomes important is in the development of Web sites optimized for displays with high device-pixel ratios. One such device is the iPhone 4 with the Retina display, which is capable of displaying images at a device-pixel density of 326 pixels per inch. Designers can optimize their Web sites for devices like the iPhone 4 by creating one set of style sheets for low-resolution displays and another for high-resolution displays. The high-resolution style sheet would load extremely detailed, high-resolution images, while the low-resolution style sheet would load lower resolution images better suited to devices that are limited to smaller device-pixel ratios. For example, the media query

```
<link href="retina.css" rel="stylesheet"
    media="only screen and (-webkit-min-device-pixel-ratio: 2)" />
```

loads the *retina.css* style sheet file for high-resolution screen devices that have device-pixel ratios of at least 2. Note that currently the `device-pixel-ratio` media feature is only supported by WebKit, but this will change as more high-resolution devices become available in the mobile market.

Creating a Mobile Style Sheet

For the mobile version of his sample page, Kevin wants you to hide the `h1` heading and navigation list in the header, the vertical navigation list, and the page footer, leaving only the header logo, photos, and navigation links to other pages about Stanislaw Dubcek's life. He also wants you to replace the current banner logo with a new one sized to fit on a smaller screen, and to set the font size and alignment of the figure box captions. You'll make these changes now.

To begin designing the mobile style sheet:

▶ 1. Return to the **mobile.css** file in your text editor. At the bottom of the file, insert the following style rule:

```
/* Hide page elements that will not be displayed */

header h1, header nav, section nav.vertical, footer {
   display: none;
}
```

▶ **2.** Add the following style rule to format the appearance of the header banner:

```
/* Header styles */
header {
   background: rgb(18, 15, 12) url(tblogo_sm.png) center center
no-repeat;

   -o-background-size: contain;
   -moz-background-size: contain;
   -webkit-background-size: contain;
   background-size: contain;

   height: 50px;
   width: 100%;
}
```

▶ **3.** Add the following style rule for the figure box captions (see Figure 8-55):

```
/* Figure box caption styles */

figure figcaption {
   font-size: 12px;
   text-align: center;
}
```

Figure 8-55   **Initial mobile styles**

```
/* Hide page elements that will not be displayed */

header h1, header nav, section nav.vertical, footer {
   display: none;
}

/* Header styles */

header {
   background: rgb(18, 15, 12) url(tblogo_sm.png) center center no-repeat;

   -o-background-size: contain;
   -moz-background-size: contain;
   -webkit-background-size: contain;
   background-size: contain;

   height: 50px;
   width: 100%;
}

/* Figure box caption styles */

figure figcaption {
   font-size: 12px;
   text-align: center;
}
```

▶ **4.** Save your changes to the file, and then reload the **treebook.htm** file in either your resized Web browser window or a mobile device. Figure 8-56 shows part of the page as it appears in a reduced browser window.

Figure 8-56 | **Revised layout with new header banner**

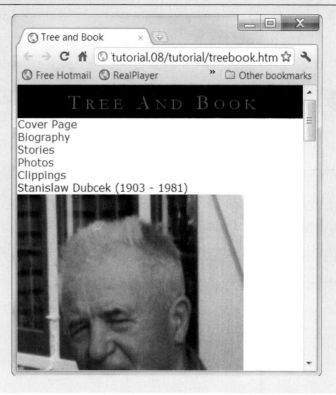

The styles of the remaining page elements depend on whether the page is being viewed in portrait or landscape orientation. You'll use media queries to create a different set of style rules for each situation.

Designing for Portrait Orientation

To create styles for a screen in portrait orientation, you can use the media query

```
@media screen and (orientation: portrait) {
   styles
}
```

where *styles* is the portrait style rules. You'll use this @media rule now to create styles for mobile devices in portrait orientation.

To create an @media rule for portrait orientation:

▶ **1.** Return to the **mobile.css** file in your text editor.

▶ **2.** Enter the following code at the bottom of the file:

```
/* Mobile styles under portrait orientation */

@media screen and (orientation: portrait) {


}
```

3. Save your changes to the file.

4. To avoid needing to type all of the style rules that apply under portrait orientation, they have been saved for you in a text file. Open the **portrait.txt** file now in your text editor, and then copy and paste the code from that file within the curly braces of the @media rule you just created in the mobile style sheet. See Figure 8-57.

Figure 8-57   **Inserting an @media rule for screens in portrait orientation**

media query for portrait orientation

styles implemented when the screen is in portrait orientation

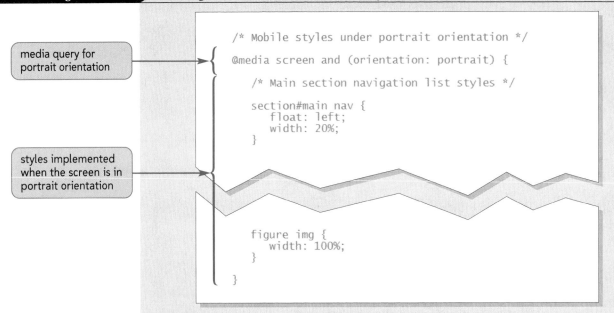

```
/* Mobile styles under portrait orientation */

@media screen and (orientation: portrait) {

    /* Main section navigation list styles */

    section#main nav {
        float: left;
        width: 20%;
    }



    figure img {
        width: 100%;
    }

}
```

5. Save your changes to the **mobile.css** style sheet file, and then reopen the **treebook.htm** file in your browser window or mobile device. To place your browser window in portrait mode, resize the window so that it is longer than it is wide with a maximum width of 500 pixels. Figure 8-58 shows the appearance of the page in a resized browser window.

Figure 8-58   Web page under portrait orientation

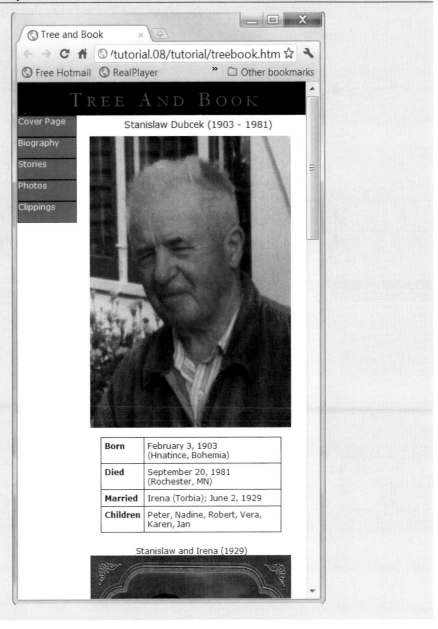

Designing for Landscape Orientation

To define styles under landscape orientation, you use the same @media rule, setting the orientation to landscape. You'll add this @media rule now.

To create the landscape style rules:

▶ **1.** Return to the **mobile.css** file in your text editor. At the end of the file, insert the following code:

```
/* Mobile styles under landscape orientation */

@media screen and (orientation: landscape) {


}
```

▶ **2.** Save your changes to the file.

▶ **3.** Copy the code from the **landscape.txt** file and paste it within the @media rule for landscape orientation. See Figure 8-59.

Figure 8-59 ▶ **Inserting an @media rule for screens in landscape orientation**

media query for landscape orientation

styles implemented when the screen is in landscape orientation

```
/* Mobile styles under landscape orientation */

@media screen and (orientation: landscape) {

    /* Main section navigation list styles */

    section#main nav {
        width: 100%;
    }



    figure img {
        width: 100%;
    }

}
```

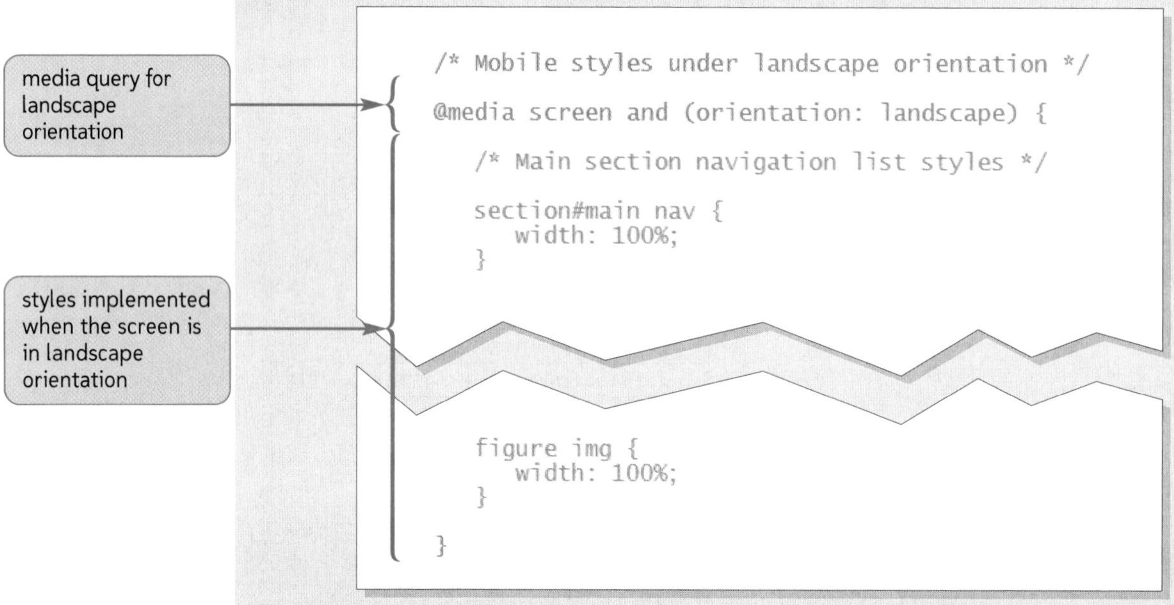

▶ **4.** Save your changes to the file, and then reload **treebook.htm** in your browser window or mobile device. Resize the browser window so that its width is 500 pixels or less, and the width of the browser window is greater than the height. If you are using a mobile device or emulator, flip the device into landscape orientation. Figure 8-60 shows the layout of the page under landscape orientation.

Figure 8-60   Web page under landscape orientation

5. Scroll through the page and verify that the four photos beneath the Web table appear in a 2 × 2 grid.

Trouble? If your mobile browser displays the full desktop layout when you view the page in landscape orientation, it might be due to the width of the viewport. Some larger mobile phones display pages at screen widths of 600 pixels or more in landscape mode.

Most current mobile browsers support the `orientation` feature; however, this is not always the case with older browsers. Instead, for those browsers, you determine when a user has switched between portrait and landscape orientation based on the width of the screen. One common standard is to assume that any mobile device with a screen width of 320 pixels or less is being held in portrait orientation. Thus, for older mobile browsers, you can use the media query

```
@media screen and (max-width: 320px) {
    styles
}
```

where *styles* is those style rules applied when the screen width is 320 pixels or less. For landscape orientation, you use the following media query for screen widths in excess of 320 pixels:

```
@media screen and (min-width: 321px) {
    styles
}
```

Note that the landscape media query should only be used once you have ascertained that a mobile device is in use with a screen width of about 500 pixels or less; otherwise, you'll apply these styles for any device whose screen width exceeds 320 pixels.

PROSKILLS

Problem Solving: Optimizing Your Site for the Mobile Web

The mobile browser market is a rapidly evolving and growing field with more new devices and apps being introduced and purchased each month. Market analysis from Juniper Research (*juniperresearch.com*) estimates that the number of mobile Web users will grow from 577 million in 2008 to more than 1.7 billion by the end of 2013. Adapting your Web sites for the mobile Web is not a luxury, but a necessity.

A good mobile design matches the needs of consumers. Mobile users need quick access to main sources of information without a lot of the extra material often found in the desk-top versions of their favorite sites. Here are some things to keep in mind as you create your mobile designs:

• *Keep it simple.*   To accommodate the smaller screen sizes and slower connection speeds, scale down each page to a few key items and articles. Users are looking for quick and obvious information from their mobile sites.
• *Resize your images.*   Downloading several images can bring a mobile device to a crawl. Reduce the number of images in your mobile design, and use a graphics package to resize the images so they are optimized in quality and size for a smaller screen.
• *Scroll vertically.*   Readers can more easily read your page when they only have to scroll vertically. Limit yourself to one column of information in portrait orientation and two columns in landscape.
• *Make your links accessible.*   Clicking a small hypertext link is extremely difficult to do on a mobile device with a touch screen interface. Create hypertext links that are easy to locate and activate.

Above all, test your site on a variety of devices and under different conditions. Mobile devices vary greatly in size, shape, and capability. What works on one device might fail utterly on another. Testing your code on a desktop computer is only the first step; you may also need access to the devices themselves. Even emulators cannot always capture the nuances involved in the performance of an actual mobile device.

You show Kevin the completed Web site, which he loads on his mobile device. He's pleased with the work you've done in developing several different designs for the same document, ranging from special visual effects, to print styles, to mobile styles. Kevin will continue to work on the design of the Tree and Book Web site and will need your help in future projects.

Session 8.3 Quick Check

1. What is an SDK? An emulator? A simulator?
2. On mobile devices, what is the difference between the visual viewport and the layout viewport?
3. Provide a media query to match screen devices that are at least 320 pixels wide.
4. Provide a media query to match screen devices between 320 and 480 pixels in width.
5. What is the purpose of the `only` keyword?
6. Provide a media query to match screen or print devices that support color.
7. Provide a media query to match a screen device in landscape orientation or with a screen width of at least 400 pixels.

Practice the skills you learned in the tutorial using the same case scenario.

PRACTICE

Review Assignments

Data Files needed for the Review Assignments: dfbase.css, dfeffectstxt.css, dflayout. css, dfmobiletxt.css, dfprinttxt.css, dubcektxt.htm, family.png, link01.png - link08.png, modernizr-1.5.js, paper.png, tblogo.png, tblogo_sm.png

Kevin has created another sample document summarizing the history of the Dubcek family. He would like to use CSS3 to add some visual effects to his page, including drop shadows, gradients, and opacity filters. He also wants you to design a style sheet for the printed document and another style sheet for mobile devices. Kevin has already written several of the style rules he wants to apply to his document, but he needs you to complete the process.

A preview of the page as it appears on a desktop computer is shown in Figure 8-61.

Figure 8-61   Dubcek family page

sabri deniz kizil/Shutterstock.com

okicoki/Shutterstock.com

Complete the following:

1. Use your text editor to open the **dubcektxt.htm** and **dfeffectstxt.css** files from the tutorial.08\review folder included with your Data Files. Enter *your name* and *the date* within the comment section of each file, and then save them as **dubcek.htm** and **dfeffects.css**, respectively.

2. Go to the **dubcek.htm** file in your text editor. Take some time to study the contents and structure of the document, and then link the file to **dfeffects.css** using a media query for only screen devices that are at least 501 pixels wide. Also add a media query to the link element for the **dflayout.css** style sheet file, matching that style sheet to only screen devices that are at least 501 pixels wide.

3. Create a conditional comment for Internet Explorer version 8 and earlier. Within the conditional comment, create links to the **dflayout.css** and **dfeffects.css** style sheets. For each style sheet, specify screen as the media device. Save your changes to the file.

4. Go to the **dfeffects.css** file in your text editor. The navigation list of links to each family member has the id *familyLinks*. Format the appearance of this navigation list by adding an inset box shadow that is black in color with an opacity of 0.6. Place the inset shadow within the right edge of the element with a horizontal offset of 10 pixels, a vertical offset of 0 pixels, and a blurring effect of 15 pixels.

5. Add box shadows to the images within the familyLinks list; make the shadows black in color with 0.6 opacity. The shadows should be offset 10 pixels horizontally and vertically with a blur of 15 pixels.

6. Every time the user hovers over an image in the familyLinks list, rotate the image 5° counter-clockwise and set the opacity to 1.0.

7. Apply a horizontal gradient to the article element that moves from the left to the right, starting with the color value (151, 151, 151) and ending with the color value (231, 231, 231). Include browser extensions for all major browsers.

8. Add two text shadows to the h1 heading. The first shadow should be black with a horizontal and vertical offset of 1 pixel and a 0-pixel blur. The second shadow should have the color value (30, 57, 0) with an opacity of 0.8. The offset should be 5 pixels in the horizontal and vertical directions with a 10-pixel blur.

9. Add a border image to the family image within the article element. Use the file paper.png with a slice value of 70 pixels, tiled along the sides. Set the width of the border to 10 pixels.

10. Save your changes to the style sheet, and then go to the **dubcek.htm** file in your Web browser and verify that the design effects resemble those shown in Figure 8-61. Hover your mouse pointer over the list of linked images and verify that they rotate 5° counter-clockwise in response.

11. Figure 8-62 shows a preview of the print style sheets that you'll create for Kevin's document. To create this file, open the **dfprinttxt.css** file from the tutorial.08/review folder in your text editor. Add *your name* and *the date* in the comment section of the file, and then save it as **dfprint.css**.

Figure 8-62 Dubcek family printouts

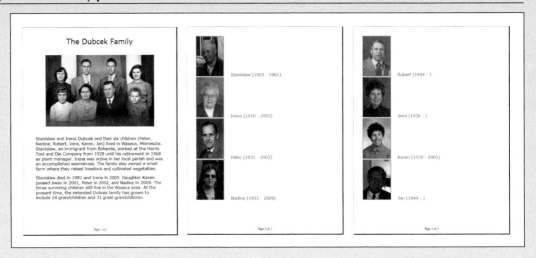

12. Directly after the initial style comments, insert an @page rule to set the size of the printed page to 8.5 inches by 11 inches in portrait orientation with a margin of 0.5 inches.

13. At the bottom of the file, insert a style rule for the article element to avoid page breaks within the element and always add a page break after the element.

14. Add a style rule for the list items in the familyLinks navigation list to avoid page breaks within and after each item.

15. For the last list item in the familyLinks navigation list, insert a style rule to avoid adding a page break.

16. Close the file, saving your changes. Return to the **dubcek.htm** file in your text editor. Add a link to the **dfprint.css** style sheet file, using print as the media device. Save your changes to the file.

17. Print the **dubcek.htm** file or view it in your Print Preview window and verify that the page layout resembles that shown in Figure 8-62.

18. Figure 8-63 shows how Kevin wants his document to appear on a mobile device in portrait and landscape modes. Open the **dfmobiletxt.css** file from the tutorial.08/ review folder. Enter *your name* and *the date* in the comment section of the file, and then save it as **dfmobile.css**.

Figure 8-63   Dubcek mobile view

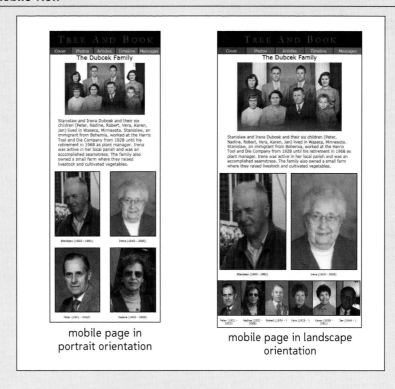

mobile page in portrait orientation

mobile page in landscape orientation

19. Kevin has already written the general style rules for the document. He wants you to create specific style rules for when the document is displayed in portrait and landscape orientation. At the bottom of the file, insert an `@media` rule with a media query to match a screen device in portrait orientation. Within this `@media` rule, create a style rule for list items within the familyLinks navigation list to: a) display the list items as blocks; b) set the width to 40%; c) set the top and bottom margins to 5 pixels, and set the left and right margins to 5%; and d) float the list items on the left.

20. Create an `@media` rule for screen devices in landscape orientation. Within the `@media` rule, create a style rule for list items belonging to the parentList class to: a) display the items as blocks; b) set the width to 45%; c) set the top and bottom margins to 5 pixels, and set the left and right margins to 2%; and d) float the items on the left.

21. Also within the `@media` rule for landscape orientation, add a style rule for list items belonging to the childList class to: a) display the items as blocks; b) set the width to 16%; c) set the top and bottom margins to 5 pixels, and set the left and right margins to 0.2%; and d) float the items on the left.

22. Save your changes to the file.

23. Return to the **dubcek.htm** file in your text editor. In the head section of the file, insert a `meta` element to set the viewport of the file to match the device width.

24. Add a link to the **dfmobile.css** style sheet file, loading the style sheet only for screen elements that are less than or equal to 500 pixels in width. Save your changes to the file.

25. Open the **dubcek.htm** file in a mobile device or your Web browser. Verify that as you resize the browser window or view the mobile device, the layout resembles that shown in Figure 8-63 for both portrait and landscape orientation.

26. Submit your completed files to your instructor.

Apply your knowledge of CSS3 and print styles to design a recipe page.

APPLY

Case Problem 1

Data Files needed for this Case Problem: dw.png, dwbase.css, dweffectstxt.css, dwlayout.css, dwprinttxt.css, halfstar.png, modernizr-1.5.js, recipetxt.htm, star.png, torte.jpg

dessertWeb   Amy Wu has asked for your help in redesigning her Web site, *dessertWeb*, taking advantage of some of the new CSS3 styles. The *dessertWeb* Web site is a cooking site for people who want to share dessert recipes and learn about cooking in general. In addition to redesigning the site's appearance, she wants you to create a print style sheet so that users can easily print out recipes and ingredient lists without having to print the headers, footers, and navigation lists that appear on each Web page. Figure 8-64 shows a preview of the screen version of the page.

Figure 8-64	dessertWeb page

Complete the following:

1. In your text editor, open the **recipetxt.htm** and **dweffectstxt.css** files from the tutorial.08\case1 folder included with your Data Files. Enter *your name* and *the date* in the comment section of each file. Save the files as **recipe.htm** and **dweffects.css**, respectively.

2. Go to the **dweffects.css** file in your text editor. Create a style rule for the body element to add two box shadows. One shadow should be placed on the right edge of the page body with the color value (211, 211, 211) and an opacity of 0.5. Set the horizontal offset to 10 pixels, the vertical offset to 0 pixels, and the blur to 15 pixels. Create the same drop shadow on the left edge of the page body as well.

3. Apply the following style rules to each list item in the horizontal navigation list of the page header: a) set the background color to the value (224, 238, 238); b) add rounded corners 10 pixels in radius; and c) create two inset box shadows: one white shadow located in the upper-left corner offset 3 pixels in the horizontal and vertical direction with a blur of 2 pixels, and the other, a shadow in the lower-right corner with a color value of (147, 207, 207) offset 5 pixels in the horizontal and vertical direction with a blur of 5 pixels.

4. Add box shadows to the article element with the following properties: a) create an inset box shadow in the lower-right corner with a color value of (171, 171, 171), offset 15 pixels in the horizontal and vertical direction, and with a blur of 75 pixels; and b) create an external shadow located in the lower-right corner with a color value of (101, 101, 101), offset 5 pixels in the vertical and horizontal direction with a blur of 5 pixels.

EXPLORE

5. Add a horizontal background gradient to the blockquote element with the following properties: a) set the gradient to go from the left to the right starting with the color value (166, 230, 230), having a color stop at the 5% point with a value (231, 231, 231), and ending with the color value (255, 255, 255) 15% of the way across the block quote; b) create the same color gradient using the WebKit gradient() function with a color stop for the middle color occurring at the 33% point; and c) using the Internet Explorer Gradient filter, create a horizontal gradient that starts with the hexadecimal color value DEF4F4 and ends with the value FFFFFF.

6. Save your changes to the file, and then return to the **recipe.htm** file in your text editor. Add a link to the **dweffects.css** style sheet file. Specify that the *dwlayout.css* and *dweffects.css* style sheets should be used with screen devices.

7. Save your changes to the document, and then view the page in your Web browser. Verify that the appearance of the page resembles that shown in Figure 8-64. (Note: If you are using Internet Explorer version 8 or earlier, your page will show only the gradient effect around the block quotes, and the gradient will go from light teal to white.)

8. Figure 8-65 shows a preview of the printed version of the recipe page, displaying the recipe description and ingredients on the first page and the directions on the second page. In your text editor, open the **dwprinttxt.css** file from the tutorial.08/case1 folder. Enter *your name* and *the date* in the comment section of the file, and then save it as **dwprint.css**.

Figure 8-65   Printout of recipe

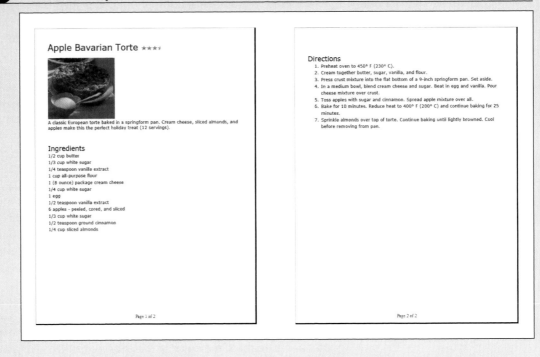

9. Set the page size of the printout to 8.5 × 11 inches in portrait orientation with a margin of 0.5 inch.

10. Hide the following page elements on the printout: page header, left section, right section, all navigation lists, the `aside` element, the page footer, the `h2` element nested within a heading group, and the last paragraph in the `article` element.

11. Set the font size of all `h1` headings to 200% with a bottom margin of 0.2 inches. Set the font size of all `h2` elements to 150% with a top margin of 0.5 inches.

12. Set the line height of all list items to 1.5 em.

13. Set the left margin of all ordered lists to 0.5 inches, displaying a decimal value.

14. Set a page break to always occur before the last `h2` element in the page.

15. Save your changes to the file, and then return to the **recipe.htm** file in your text editor. Add a link to the **dwprint.css** style sheet file, setting the style sheet to be used with a print device.

16. Save your changes to the document, and then view the printed version of the file or preview the printed version in your Web browser. Verify that the contents and layout resemble that shown in Figure 8-65.

17. Submit your completed files to your instructor.

Apply your knowledge of CSS3 and mobile styles to design a page for a golf course.

APPLY

Case Problem 2

Data Files needed for this Case Problem: arrow.png, gray.png, h01.htm – h18.htm, hole01.jpg – hole18.jpg, holes.css, modernizr-1.5.js, wcback.png, wcbase.css, wceffectstxt.css, wclayout.css, wcmobiletxt.css, willet.jpg, willet.png, willettxt.htm

Willet Creek Golf Course   Willet Creek is a popular golf course resort in central Idaho. You've been asked to work on the design of the resort's Web site by Michael Carpenter, the head of promotion for the resort. He would like you to add some CSS3 visual effects for drop shadows and gradients. Figure 8-66 shows a preview of the screen version of the Web page.

Figure 8-66	**Willet Creek page**

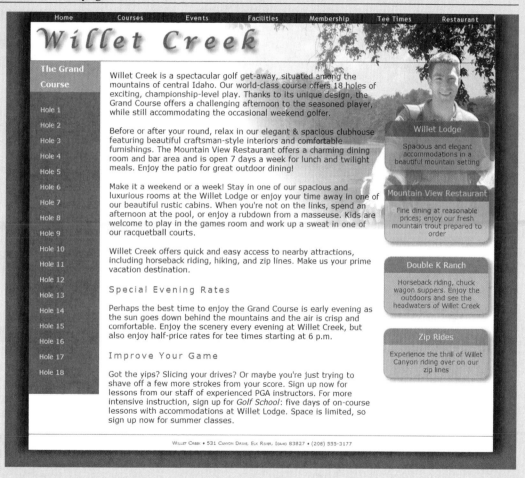

Complete the following:

1. In your text editor, open the **willettxt.htm** and **wceffectstxt.css** files from the tutorial.08\case2 folder included with your Data Files. Enter *your name* and *the date* in the comment section of each file. Save the files as **willet.htm** and **wceffects. css**, respectively.

2. Go to the **wceffects.css** file and create a shadow effect for the body element. The effect should contain two box shadows, both with a color value of (31, 61, 31) and an opacity of 0.9. Place the first shadow with a horizontal offset of 20 pixels, a vertical offset of 0 pixels, and a blur of 25 pixels. Do the same for the second shadow, except place the shadow with a horizontal offset of −20 pixels.

◆ EXPLORE

3. Set the opacity of the `div` elements nested within the `aside` elements to 75%. Use both the CSS3 `opacity` style and the IE `Alpha` filter. Add a box shadow that has a color value of (101, 101, 101) with an opacity of 0.7. Set the horizontal and vertical offsets to 5 pixels and the blur to 10 pixels. You do not have to add an IE filter for the box shadow.

4. Save your changes to the file, and then return to the **willet.htm** file in your text editor. Add a link to the **wceffects.css** style sheet file, using the style sheet for screen devices that have a minimum width of 501 pixels. Add the same media query for the **wclayout.css** style sheet file.

5. Use an Internet Explorer conditional comment for versions of IE before version 9 to link to the **wclayout.css** and **wceffects.css** style sheet files for screen devices.

6. Save your changes to the document, and then open the **willet.htm** file in your Web browser. Verify that the appearance and layout of your page resemble those shown in Figure 8-66.

7. Many golfers playing the courses at Willet Creek like to receive information and advice about each hole. Michael would like you to create a mobile version of the Web page so that golfers with mobile devices can view information about the course during their rounds. Figure 8-67 shows a preview of the Web app you'll create.

Figure 8-67 **Willet Creek mobile view**

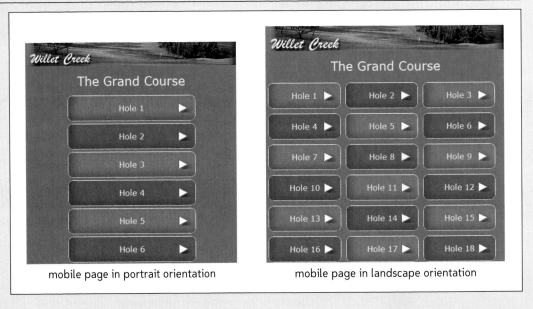

mobile page in portrait orientation   mobile page in landscape orientation

8. Open the **wcmobiletxt.css** file from the tutorial.08/case2 folder in your text editor. Enter *your name* and *the date* in the comment section of the file, and then save it as **wcmobile.css**.

9. Within the style sheet file, add a style rule to hide the navigation list in the header, the inline image in the header, the main section, the `aside` element, and the page footer.

10. Set the background color to the value (107, 140, 80).

11. For the `header` element, create a style rule to: a) change the background color to the value (151, 201, 151) with the image file *willet.jpg* placed in the left-center of the background with no tiling; b) set the size of the background image to `contain`; c) set the width to 100%; and d) set the height to 50 pixels.

12. The navigation list containing links to each of the 18 holes in the Grand Course has the id *holes*. Create a style rule to set the width of this navigation list to 100%.

13. For `h1` elements within the holes navigation list, create a style rule to: a) set the font size to 25 pixels; b) set the font color to white; c) set the margin to 15 pixels; and d) center the text of the heading.

14. For list items in the holes navigation list, create a style rule to: a) display the items as blocks; b) add the background image file *arrow.png* to the right-center of the background with no tiling; c) set the width to 60% and the height to 50 pixels; d) add top and bottom margins of 5 pixels, and add left and right margins of `auto`; e) add a 1-pixel-wide solid white border to each list item and create rounded borders with a radius of 10 pixels; and f) add inset box shadows to the list items with a color value of (51, 51, 51) and an opacity of 50% (the inset shadows should appear in the lower-left corner of each list item with a horizontal offset of 10 pixels, a vertical offset of 5 pixels, and a blur of 20 pixels).

15. For hypertext links within each list item, add a style rule to: a) display the link as blocks; b) set the width to 100% and the line height to 50 pixels; c) set the font color to white; and d) horizontally center the text of the link.

EXPLORE

16. For odd-numbered list items, set the background color to the value (187, 105, 123). (Hint: Use the pseudo-class `nth-of-type(odd)`.) For even-numbered list items, set the background color to the value (150, 80, 100).

17. The preceding styles will be applied by default to the page in portrait orientation. Create an `@media` rule for the page in landscape orientation.

18. Add the following style rule for list items displayed in landscape orientation: a) set the width to 30%; b) float the list items on the left; and c) set the margins to 5 pixels.

19. Save your changes to the style sheet, and then return to the **willet.htm** file in your text editor.

20. Within the **willet.htm** file, insert a viewport `meta` element.

21. Create a link to the **wcmobile.css** file to be accessed by only screen devices with maximum widths of 500 pixels.

22. Save your changes to the file, and then open the **willet.htm** file in your mobile device or with your browser window resized to a width of less than 500 pixels. Verify that for smaller screen widths, the mobile version of the page is displayed. Further verify that the layout of the links to individual holes changes depending on whether the page is in portrait or landscape orientation.

23. Submit your completed files to your instructor.

Apply your knowledge of CSS3 and print styles to design an astronomy Web site.

CHALLENGE

Case Problem 3

Data Files needed for this Case Problem: m01.jpg, m13.jpg, m16.jpg, m20.jpg, m27.jpg, m31.jpg, messier.png, messtxt.htm, modernizr-1.5.js, skyweb.png, swbase.css, sweffectstxt.css, swlayout.css, swprinttxt.css

SkyWeb   Dr. Andrew Weiss of Central Ohio University maintains an astronomy site called *SkyWeb* for the students in his class. On his Web site, he discusses many aspects of astronomy and stargazing. He wants your help with one page that involves the Messier catalog, which lists the deep sky objects of particular interest to professional and amateur astronomers.

Dr. Weiss wants you to modify the appearance of his page by adding several radial gradients to the page background, giving the illusion of deep sky objects on a medium gray background. Figure 8-68 shows a preview of the design you'll create for Dr. Weiss.

Figure 8-68   SkyWeb page with radial gradients

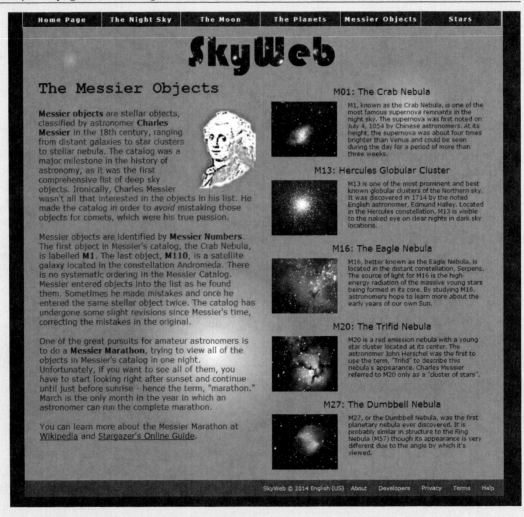

Complete the following:

1. In your text editor, open the **messtxt.htm** and **sweffectstxt.css** files from the tutorial.08\case3 folder included with your Data Files. Enter *your name* and *the date* in the comment section of each file. Save the files as **messier.htm** and **sweffects.css**, respectively.

EXPLORE

2. Go to the **sweffects.css** file. Create a style rule for the body element to add a radial gradient background using the CSS3 `radial-gradient()` function. For the function, set the horizontal and vertical centers of the gradient to 40% and 70%, respectively. Display a circular gradient with the size that extends to the nearest corner. Have the gradient go from a solid white center to a color value of (171, 171, 171) with an opacity of 0.5. Set the color stop of the outer color to 50%.

EXPLORE

3. Add two more CSS3 radial gradients to the body background in a comma-separated list. Use the same colors that you used in the first radial gradient. The next gradient should be centered at (80%, 20%) with a circular shape that extends to the nearest corner. Add a color stop of 20% to the second radial gradient. For the third radial gradient, set the center at (10%, 10%) and set the shape to an ellipse extended to the nearest side. Set the color stop of the outer color to 25%.

4. Duplicate the background style you created for different browsers by adding the appropriate browser extensions.

EXPLORE

5. For WebKit browsers, create the radial gradients using the `gradient()` function. Use the same inner and outer colors as you did for the CSS3 `radial-gradient()` function. Set up the three radial gradients as follows:

   a. Place the inner and outer centers of the first gradient at the point (40%, 70%). Set the inner and outer radii to 0 and 180, respectively.

   b. Place the inner and outer centers of the second gradient at the point (80%, 20%). Set the inner and outer radii to 0 and 90, respectively.

   c. Place the inner and outer centers of the third gradient at the point (10%, 10%). Set the inner and outer radii to 0 and 20, respectively.

6. Save your changes to the style sheet, and then return to the **messier.htm** file in your text editor. Create a link to the **sweffects.css** style sheet file.

7. Save your changes to the document, and then view it in your Web browser. Verify that three radial gradients appear in the background of the Web page. (Note: If you are using a version of Internet Explorer before version 10, you will not see any radial gradients.)

8. Dr. Weiss also wants you to create a print style sheet to display the summary of Messier objects on the first page with a description of each Messier object on its own page. Figure 8-69 shows a preview of the design of the printed page.

Figure 8-69   Printout of SkyWeb page

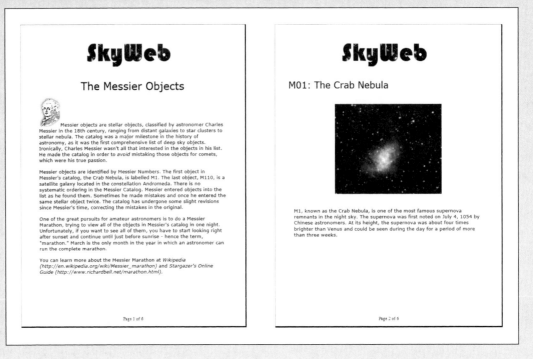

Use your text editor to open the **swprinttxt.css** file. Enter *your name* and *the date* in the comment section of the file, and then save it as **swprint.css**.

9. Set the page size of the printout to 8.5 × 11 inches in portrait orientation with a margin of 0.5 inches.

10. Hide the navigation list and the footer in the printout.

⊕ EXPLORE 11. Dr. Weiss wants the SkyWeb logo to appear at the top of every page. Create a style rule for the inline image within the page header, placing the image using fixed positioning and setting the location of the image to 0 inches from the top edge and 2 inches from the left edge. (Note: WebKit browsers including Google Chrome and Safari do not support the display of headers on each page using fixed positioning.)

12. Display every `article` element with a top padding space of 1.5 inches. Add page breaks after every article and avoid placing page breaks within the article.

13. Display paragraphs within each article with a font size of 13 points and a margin of 0.2 inches.

14. Display the `h1` heading within the left section in a 28-point font and horizontally centered on the page.

15. For `h1` headings within the right section, set the font size to 24 points.

16. Add the following style rule for inline images within the right section: a) display the image as a block; b) set the width of the image to 4 inches; and c) set the top and bottom margins to 0.5 inches, and set the left and right margins to `auto`.

17. Display every hypertext link in black and in italic.

⊕ EXPLORE 18. Dr. Weiss wants the printout to show the URL of every hypertext link. For every hypertext link, use the `after` pseudo-class and the `content` style property to add the text of the link's URL in the format *(url)*, where *url* is the text of the link's *href* attribute.

19. Save your changes to the style sheet, and then return to the **messier.htm** file in your text editor. Add a link to the **swprint.css** style sheet file.

20. Set the media of the **swlayout.css** and **sweffects.css** style sheet files to the screen device. Set the media of the **swprint.css** style sheet file to the print device.

21. Save your changes to the file, and then open it in your Web browser. Print the page or preview the printed version in your browser. Verify that: a) the article describing Messier objects appears on the first page; b) each subsequent page contains the image and description of a single Messier object; c) the SkyWeb logo appears at the top of each page as a page header; and d) the `url` of each of the two hypertext links appears in parentheses after the link text.

22. Submit your completed files to your instructor.

Test your knowledge of CSS3, print, and mobile styles by designing the home listings for an online realty Web site.

RESEARCH

Case Problem 4

Data Files needed for this Case Problem: brlogo.png, img01.jpg - img09.jpg, listing.txt, modernizr-1.5.js

Browyer Realty   Linda Browyer is the owner of Browyer Realty, a real estate company operating in Owatonna, Minnesota. She's asked you to help create a style design for the pages on her site that describe residential listings. Linda has already written up sample content for a listing and collected images of the property. She needs you to create the HTML file and write up the style sheets.

Complete the following:

1. Use your text editor to create an HTML file named **browyer.htm** that will contain the document describing the property. Also, create a style sheet file named **brbase.css** that will contain basic styles that will be used by all devices, **breffects.css** that will contain special visual effects, **brlayout.css** that will contain the page layout design for desktop screen devices, **brprint.css** for print styles, and **brmobile.css** for mobile devices. Add the appropriate comments and documentation to each file.

2. Create the content of the **browyer.htm** file using the contents of the **listing.txt** text file as a guide.

3. Design the page layout of your document in the **brlayout.css** file.

4. Add CSS3 visual effects to your document using the **breffects.css** style sheet. The effects are left to you to choose, but they should include examples of the following:
   - a linear or radial gradient, written using the CSS3 `linear-gradient()` or `radial-gradient()` function
   - a text shadow using the CSS3 `text-shadow` property
   - drop shadows using the CSS3 `box-shadow` property and either the IE `DropShadow` or `Shadow` filter
   - a rotated object using the CSS3 `rotate` property
   - semi-transparent objects using the opacity style and the IE `Alpha` filter

5. Linda wants users to be able to view a nice printout of her sample listing. Place the print styles in the **brprint.css** file. Include an example of the `@page` rule and several examples of styles that either place or suppress page breaks.

6. Linda also wants potential clients to be able to view the sample listings in a format appropriate for mobile devices. Create the styles for mobile devices in the **brmobile.css** file. Your style sheet should include different rules depending on whether a device is in portrait or landscape orientation.

7. Link your Web document to your style sheets. Include the appropriate media queries to match each style sheet with the correct device and device width. Include a `meta` element to set the width of the viewport.

8. Place any style sheets to be used by Internet Explorer version 8 or earlier within a conditional comment.

9. Test your completed project on a variety of browsers, devices, and screen conditions.

10. Submit your completed files to your instructor, in either printed or electronic form, as requested.

ENDING DATA FILES

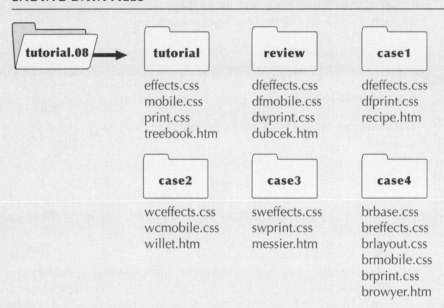

tutorial.08 →

tutorial
effects.css
mobile.css
print.css
treebook.htm

review
dfeffects.css
dfmobile.css
dwprint.css
dubcek.htm

case1
dfeffects.css
dfprint.css
recipe.htm

case2
wceffects.css
wcmobile.css
willet.htm

case3
sweffects.css
swprint.css
messier.htm

case4
brbase.css
breffects.css
brlayout.css
brmobile.css
brprint.css
browyer.htm

Working with XHTML

Creating a Well-Formed, Valid Document

OBJECTIVES

Session 9.1
- Describe the history and theory of XHTML
- Understand the rules for creating valid XHTML documents
- Apply a DTD to an XHTML document
- Apply the XHTML namespace
- Explore the relationship between HTML5 and XHTML

Session 9.2
- Test an XHTML document under the transitional DTD
- Test an XHTML document under the strict DTD
- Explore the use of character and parsed character data

Case | *Wizard Works Fireworks*

Wizard Works is one of the largest sellers of brand-name and customized fireworks in the central states. Its Web site generates the bulk of the company's sales. Tom Blaska, the head of advertising for Wizard Works, helps develop the content and design of the company's Web site. Because the Web site has been around for many years, some of the code dates back to the earliest versions of HTML. Tom is examining how to integrate the Web site code with XML documents that the company uses for storing and processing customer information and orders. He would like you to modify the HTML code so that it is written in XHTML, an XML version of HTML. He also would like you to find ways to verify that the code used by Wizard Works meets XHTML standards.

STARTING DATA FILES

tutorial.09 → **tutorial**
workstxt.htm
wwtxt.css
+ 4 graphic files
+ 1 text file

review
founttxt.htm
wstylestxt.css
+ 2 graphic files
+ 1 text file

case1
breaktxt.htm
dinnrtxt.htm
lunchtxt.htm
kdstylestxt.css
+ 4 graphic files
+ 1 text file

case2
gargtxt.htm
maah5txt.htm
maah5txt.css
maatxt.css
+ 5 graphic files
+ 1 text file
+ 1 JavaScript file

case3
quadtxt.xhtml
+ 1 CSS file
+ 3 graphic files
+ 1 text file

case4
7 text files
+ 1 graphic file

SESSION 9.1 VISUAL OVERVIEW

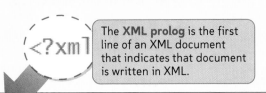

The **XML prolog** is the first line of an XML document that indicates that document is written in XML.

The DOCTYPE or DTD indicates the XML vocabulary used in the document and defines the syntax rules of the language.

The **default namespace** indicates the default XML vocabulary for elements and attributes in the document.

In an XHTML document, every non-empty element must have a closing tag.

```
<?xml version="1.0" encoding="UTF-8" ?>

<!DOCTYPE html PUBLIC "-//W3C//DTD XHTML
    "http://www.w3.org/TR/xhtml1/DTD/xhtm

<html xmlns="http://www.w3.org/1999/xht
    <head>
        <meta http-equiv="Content-type" conte

            <!--
                New Perspectives on HTML and C
                Tutorial 9
                Tutorial Case

                Wizard Works Fireworks
                Author: Tom Blaska
                Date:    3/1/2014

                Filename:        works.htm
                Supporting files: back.jpg, fi

            -->

            <title>Wizard Works</title>

        <link href="ww.css" rel="styleshe
    </head>
```

STRUCTURE OF AN XHTML DOCUMENT

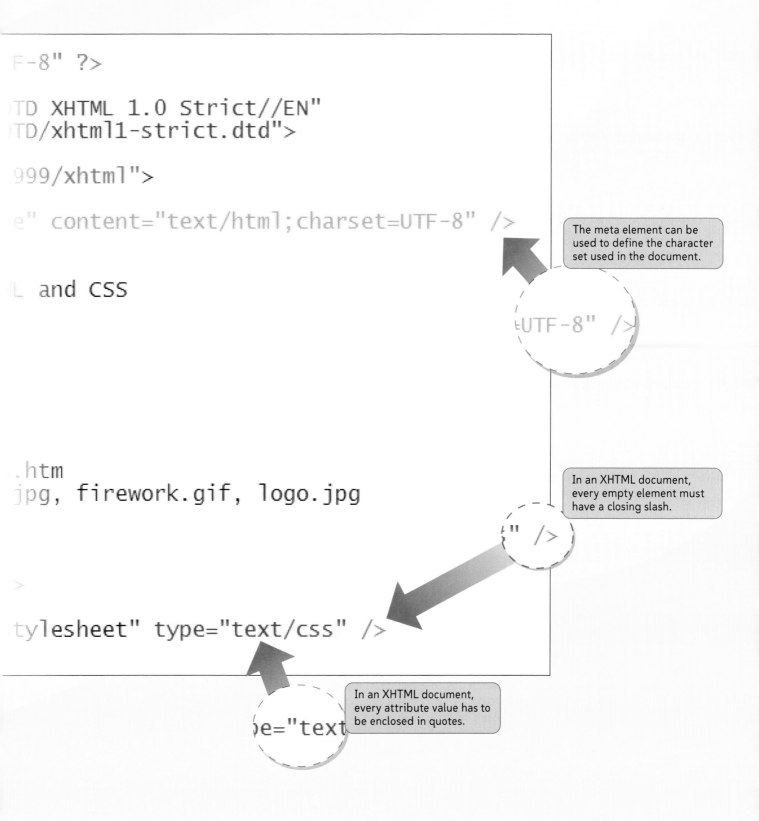

```
F-8" ?>

TD XHTML 1.0 Strict//EN"
TD/xhtml1-strict.dtd">

999/xhtml">

e" content="text/html;charset=UTF-8" />
```

The meta element can be used to define the character set used in the document.

`UTF-8" />`

```
L and CSS




.htm
jpg, firework.gif, logo.jpg
```

In an XHTML document, every empty element must have a closing slash.

`" />`

```
>

tylesheet" type="text/css" />
```

In an XHTML document, every attribute value has to be enclosed in quotes.

`e="text`

Introducing XHTML

Thus far, you've worked with documents written to correspond with the specifications of HTML5. However, other versions of HTML have applications both on the Web and in the business world. One of these versions is XHTML. Before you can create your first XHTML document, it's important to understand some of the history of the language. XHTML has its beginnings in SGML.

SGML

Standard Generalized Markup Language (SGML) is a markup language introduced in 1980 that describes the structure and content of documents or of any type of information that is readable by machines. SGML is device-independent and system-independent, meaning that documents written in SGML can be used, in theory, on almost any type of device under almost any type of operating system. SGML has been and remains the chosen vehicle for creating structured documents in businesses and government organizations of all sizes. Think of the daunting task involved in documenting all of the parts used in a jet airplane while at the same time organizing those documents so that engineers, mechanics, and developers can use them to quickly retrieve and edit information they need. SGML provides tools to manage documentation projects of this magnitude.

However, because of its power, scope, and flexibility, SGML is a difficult language to learn and apply. The official specification for SGML is more than 150 pages long and covers some scenarios and cases that are rarely encountered by even the most experienced programmer. This means that the use of SGML is limited to organizations that can afford the cost and overhead of maintaining complex SGML environments. For example, SGML is not intended for the World Wide Web, where Web page authors need a language that is easy to use.

HTML as an SGML Application

SGML is more often used in creating **SGML applications**, which are markup languages that are based on the SGML architecture and that can be applied to specific, not general, types of information. One such SGML application is HTML. Because HTML is an SGML application, it shares several properties of SGML, such as device-independence, which is why the same Web page can be rendered by PCs, cell phones, printers, and screen readers.

One problem that developers confronted early on in the history of HTML was that Web browsers supported their own unique flavors of HTML to provide customers with new and useful features not available with other browsers. For example, the `iframe` element was originally introduced in the Internet Explorer browser as a way of embedding the contents of one page within another. Although this extension was later adopted into the official HTML specifications by the World Wide Web Consortium (W3C), many other extensions were not adopted—such as Internet Explorer's `marquee` element, which was used to create blocks of scrolling text. The opposite is also true: Some specifications proposed by the W3C are adopted by only a few browsers. The result was a confusing mixture of competing HTML standards—one kind of HTML for each browser and, even worse, for each browser version. Although browser-specific elements and attributes increased the scope and power of HTML, they did so at the expense of clarity. Web designers could no longer create Web sites without taking a lot of time and effort to ensure their sites worked across various browsers and browser versions.

Another issue that complicated the development of HTML was that browsers allowed page authors to be lax in their use of syntax. For example, the following code does not follow HTML specifications because the `h1` element has not been closed with an ending `</h1>` tag:

```
<body>
   <h1>Web Page Title
</body>
```

Although this code does not follow the correct syntax, most browsers still render it correctly. Likewise, the following code would likely be interpreted correctly even though the `colspan` attribute value is not enclosed in quotation marks:

```
<td colspan=2>Heading</td>
```

Although a browser that is very forgiving of mistakes in syntax might seem beneficial to Web page designers, this behavior also affects the browser design. By making allowances for inconsistently applied HTML code, the source code for the browser itself must be larger and more complex to deal with all contingencies. This can become an issue for browsers that run on handheld devices, which are more limited in the space they allot for software. Because of these concerns, several developers began to push for a version of HTML in which syntax rules would be more strictly enforced. This was done by making HTML into an XML vocabulary.

XML and XHTML

Extensible Markup Language (XML) can be thought of as "SGML light"—a language like SGML used to create markup languages but without SGML's complexity and size. XML has been used to create specialized markup languages called XML vocabularies such as MathML for mathematical content, CML for documenting chemical structures, and MusicML for describing musical scores. Individual users can also create their own markup languages tailored for specific needs. For instance, the following code is an excerpt from a MusicML document describing Mozart's *Piano Sonata in A Major*:

```
<work>
   <work-number>K. 331</work-number>
   <work-title>Piano Sonata in A Major</work-title>
</work>
<identification>
   <creator type="composer">Wolfgang Amadeus Mozart</creator>
   <rights>Copyright 2003 Recordare LLC</rights>
</identification>
```

Aside from the different tag names, the appearance and structure of this document are very similar to what you've seen with HTML; this should not be a surprise because both are markup languages. XHTML is another example of an XML vocabulary. As with HTML and XML, the W3C maintains the specifications and standards for XHTML. Figure 9-1 summarizes the different versions of XHTML.

Figure 9-1   Versions of XHTML

Version	Date Released	Description
XHTML 1.0	2001	This version is a reformulation of HTML 4.01 as an XML vocabulary, bringing the rigor of XML to Web document code.
XHTML 1.1	2002	A minor update to XHTML 1.0 that allows for modularity and simplifies writing extensions to the language.
XHTML 2.0	Discontinued in 2009	A follow-up version to XHTML 1.1; XHTML 2.0 was not backward compatible with earlier XHTML versions and was discontinued due to lack of support.
XHTML5	In development	A version of HTML5 written as an XML vocabulary; unlike XHTML 2.0, XHTML5 will be backward compatible with earlier XHTML versions.

The initial version of XHTML was XHTML 1.0, an XML vocabulary based on the specifications for HTML 4.0. A follow-up version, XHTML 1.1, provided a restructuring of XHTML 1.0 in which different elements are placed within programming modules. This allowed browser developers to support only those parts of XHTML 1.1 that were relevant to their products. For example, a browser developed for people who are visually impaired would not need to support purely visual aspects of XHTML.

After XHTML 1.1, the W3C supported the development of XHTML 2.0, which was designed to be a complete departure from the earlier XHTML versions. In fact, XHTML 2.0 documents would not be backward compatible and thus would not be able to be rendered on older browsers. Because of this aspect, XHTML 2.0 received little support in the browser market and work on it was discontinued in 2009, leaving HTML5 as the de facto Web document standard for the future. Because the final specifications for HTML5 are still being developed, XHTML5 is in the experimental stage at the time of this writing.

Creating an XHTML Document

Because XHTML documents are also considered XML documents, the first line of an XHTML file contains a statement called a **prolog** that indicates the document adheres to the syntax rules of XML. The form of the XML prolog is

```
<?xml version="value" encoding="type" ?>
```

where the version attribute indicates the XML version of the document and the encoding attribute specifies its character encoding. For XHTML documents, you set the value of the version attribute to 1.0. The encoding type depends on the character set being used. For example, if a document is saved using the UTF-8 character set, you would apply the following XML prolog:

```
<?xml version="1.0" encoding="UTF-8" ?>
```

With XHTML documents, you also can include the character encoding using the meta element

```
<meta http-equiv="Content-type" content="text/html;charset="type" />
```

where type is once again the character encoding. Thus, the meta element

```
<meta http-equiv="Content-type" content="text/html;charset="UTF-8" />
```

defines the content type as using the UTF-8 character set.

REFERENCE

Adding an XML Prolog

• To declare that a document is written in XML, enter

```
<?xml version="value" encoding="type" ?>
```

as the first line of the file, where the version attribute indicates the XML version of the document and the encoding attribute specifies the character encoding.
• For XHTML documents, use the following prolog:

```
<?xml version="1.0" encoding="type" ?>
```

You also should add the meta element

```
<meta http-equiv="Content-type" content="text/html;charset="type" />
```

where once again type specifies the character encoding.

You meet with Tom to discuss changing the Wizard Works home page to an XHTML document form. He has brought a sample file from the company's Web site for you to examine. The document is more than 10 years old and relies on several HTML elements that are no longer part of the current specifications. It also includes code that does not follow correct HTML syntax. You'll change the document to XHTML format, starting by adding an XML prolog.

To add a prolog to the sample document:

▶ **1.** Use your text editor to open the **workstxt.htm** and **wwtxt.css** files from the tutorial.09\tutorial folder included with your Data Files. Enter *your name* and *the date* in the comment section of each file, and then save them as **works.htm** and **ww.css**, respectively, in the same folder.

▶ **2.** At the top of the **works.htm** file, insert the following XML prolog:

```
<?xml version="1.0" encoding="UTF-8" ?>
```

▶ **3.** Directly after the opening <head> tag, insert the following meta element as shown in Figure 9-2, followed by a blank line:

```
<meta http-equiv="Content-type" content="text/html;charset=UTF-8" />
```

Figure 9-2	Inserting the XML prolog and meta element

```
<?xml version="1.0" encoding="UTF-8" ?>
<html>
   <head>
      <meta http-equiv="Content-type" content="text/html;charset=UTF-8" />
```

▶ **4.** Save your changes to the file, and then open the file in your Web browser. Figure 9-3 shows the layout and content of the page.

Figure 9-3	Wizard Works legacy page

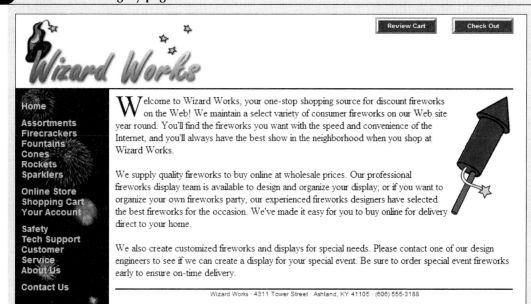

Creating Well-Formed Documents

To ensure that XML documents follow specific rules for content and structure, they can be evaluated with an **XML parser**, which is a program that checks each document for errors in syntax and content, and reports any errors it finds. Parsers can be stand-alone programs or they can be built into a Web browser. Many Web browsers include built-in XML parsers.

An XML document that employs the correct syntax is known as a **well-formed document**. Figure 9-4 illustrates the parsing process.

Figure 9-4	Testing for well-formedness

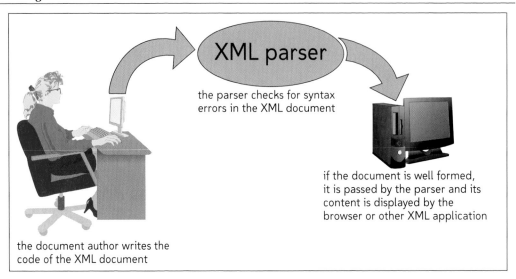

XML parser

the parser checks for syntax errors in the XML document

if the document is well formed, it is passed by the parser and its content is displayed by the browser or other XML application

the document author writes the code of the XML document

Browsers usually accept HTML documents that violate HTML syntax as long as the violation is not too severe. However, an XML parser rejects any XML document that is not well formed. For example, the sample code described earlier

```
<body>
    <h1>Web Page Title
</body>
```

is an example of code that is not well formed because it violates the basic rule that every two-sided tag must have both an opening and closing tag. When you write XHTML code, it's important to be familiar with all of the rules of proper syntax. Figure 9-5 lists seven syntax requirements that all XML documents (and therefore all XHTML documents) must follow.

Figure 9-5   **Rules for well-formed XML**

Rule	Incorrect	Correct
Element names must be lowercase.	`<P>This is a paragraph.</P>`	`<p>This is a paragraph.</p>`
Elements must be properly nested.	`<p>This text is <b>bold.</p></b>`	`<p>This text is <b>bold.</b></p>`
All elements must be closed.	`<p>This is the first paragraph.` `<p>This is the second paragraph.`	`<p>This is the first paragraph.</p>` `<p>This is the second paragraph.</p>`
Empty elements must be terminated.	`This is a line break. `	`This is a line break. `
Attribute names must be lowercase.	`<td ALIGN="right">`	`<td align="right">`
Attribute values must be quoted.	`<table width=620>`	`<table width="620">`
Attributes must have values.	`<option selected>`	`<option selected="selected">`

In addition to the rules specified in Figure 9-5, all XML documents must also include a single root element that contains all other elements. For XHTML, that root element is the `html` element. You should already be familiar with most of these rules because you've been working with well-formed HTML since Tutorial 1. However, if you examine older Web pages, you may find document code that violates this basic syntax, but which most browsers nonetheless support.

In some older HTML documents, you might find cases of **attribute minimization**, a situation in which some attributes lack attribute values. XHTML does not allow attribute minimization. Figure 9-6 lists the minimized attributes found in some HTML documents, along with the XHTML-compliant versions of these attributes.

Figure 9-6   **Attribute minimization in HTML and XHTML**

HTML	XHTML
`compact`	`compact="compact"`
`checked`	`checked="checked"`
`declare`	`declare="declare"`
`readonly`	`readonly="readonly"`
`disabled`	`disabled="disabled"`
`selected`	`selected="selected"`
`defer`	`defer="defer"`
`ismap`	`ismap="ismap"`
`nohref`	`nohref="nohref"`
`noshade`	`noshade="noshade"`
`nowrap`	`nowrap="nowrap"`
`multiple`	`multiple="multiple"`
`noresize`	`noresize="noresize"`

For example, in HTML, the following code can be used to indicate that a radio button should be selected by default:

```
<input type="radio" checked>
```

In XHTML, this code would be rewritten as follows:

```
<input type="radio" checked="checked" />
```

Failure to make this change would cause the XHTML document to be rejected as not well formed. Note that in HTML5, either form is accepted: You can write such an attribute either with the attribute value or without.

Creating Valid XHTML Documents

In addition to being tested for well-formedness, XML documents also can be checked to see if they are valid. A **valid document** is a well-formed document that also contains only those elements, attributes, and other features that have been defined for the XML vocabulary that it uses. For example, if the code

```
<body>
   <mainhead>Web Page Title</mainhead>
</body>
```

were entered into an XHTML file, the code would be considered well formed because it complies with the syntax rules of XML—but it would not constitute valid XHTML code because XHTML does not have a `mainhead` element. To specify the correct content and structure for a document, the developers of an XML-based language can create a collection of rules called the **document type definition** or **DTD**. As shown in Figure 9-7, an XML parser tests the content of a document against the rules in the DTD. If the document does not conform to those rules, the parser rejects the document as not valid.

Figure 9-7	Testing for validity

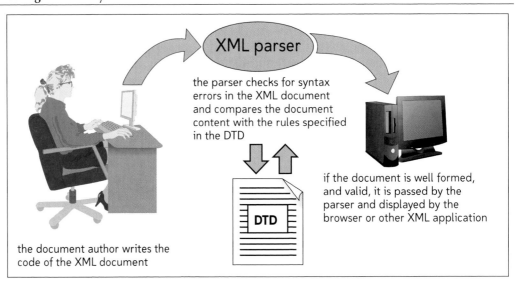

XML parser

the parser checks for syntax errors in the XML document and compares the document content with the rules specified in the DTD

DTD

if the document is well formed, and valid, it is passed by the parser and displayed by the browser or other XML application

the document author writes the code of the XML document

For example, an XML document for a business might contain elements that store the name of each product in inventory. The DTD for that document could require that each product name element be accompanied by an `id` attribute value, and that no products share the same name or id. An XML parser would reject any XML document that didn't satisfy those rules, even if the document was well formed. In this way, XML differs from HTML, which does not include a mechanism to force Web page authors to adhere to rules for syntax and content.

Transitional, Frameset, and Strict DTDs

There are several different DTDs associated with HTML and XHTML documents. Some DTDs represent older versions of HTML. For example, if you want to create a document that is validated only against the standards of HTML 2.0, a DTD is available for this purpose. However, for Tom's document, you'll focus on the following DTDs used with XHTML 1.0:

- *transitional*: The transitional DTD supports many presentational features of HTML, including the deprecated elements and attributes. It is best used for older documents that contain deprecated features.
- *frameset*: The frameset DTD is used for documents containing frames, and also supports deprecated elements and attributes (for a discussion of frames, see Appendix E).
- *strict*: The strict DTD does not allow any presentational features or deprecated HTML elements and attributes, and does not support frames or inline frames. It is best used for documents that must conform strictly to the latest standards.

If you need to validate the HTML or XHTML code found in older Web sites, you should use the transitional DTD, which recognizes deprecated elements and attributes such as the `font` element and the `bgcolor` attribute. If you need to support older browsers in a framed Web site, you should use the frameset DTD. If you want to weed out any use of deprecated features and you have no need to support frames, then you should use the strict DTD.

All three DTDs require that the following elements be present in every valid XHTML document:

- `html`
- `head`
- `title`
- `body`

Although the `html`, `head`, and `body` elements are generally expected under HTML, XHTML requires that every valid document include the `title` element as well. XML parsers reject any XHTML document that omits the `title` element.

However, there are also elements that are allowed in one DTD but not in another. For example, the following elements are not allowed under the strict DTD for XHTML 1.0:

- `applet`
- `basefont`
- `center`
- `dir`
- `font`
- `isindex`
- `menu`
- `noframes`
- `s`
- `strike`
- `u`

But these elements are allowed in the transitional DTD, and you often will encounter them in the code with older Web pages. The frameset DTD supports these elements as well as the `frame`, `frameset`, and `noframes` elements. Therefore, the code

```
<font color="red">Wizard Works</font>
```

which uses the deprecated `font` element to format text, would be considered valid code under the transitional and frameset DTDs but not under the strict DTD.

In addition to prohibiting the use of certain elements, the strict DTD also requires a particular document structure. For example, you cannot nest a block-level element within an inline element. Figure 9-8 lists the prohibited child elements under the strict DTD.

| Figure 9-8 | Child elements prohibited under the strict DTD |

Element	Prohibited Children
inline elements	any block-level element
body	a, abbr, acronym, b, bdo, big, br, button, cite, code, dfn, em, i, img, input, kbd, label, map, object, q, samp, select, small, span, strong, sub, sup, textarea, tt, var
button	button, form, fieldset, iframe, input, isindex, label, select, textarea
blockquote	a, abbr, acronym, b, bdo, big, br, button, cite, code, dfn, em, i, img, input, kbd, label, map, object, q, samp, select, small, span, strong, sub, sup, textarea, tt, var
form	a, abbr, acronym, b, bdo, big, br, cite, code, dfn, em, form, i, img, kbd, map, object, q, samp, small, span, strong, sub, sup, tt, var
label	label
pre	big, img, object, small, sub, sup

Thus, the following code would be disallowed under the strict DTD because it places an inline image as a child of the body element:

```
<body>
    <img src="logo.jpg" alt="Wizard Works" />
</body>
```

However, you could make this code compliant with the strict DTD by placing the inline image within a paragraph, as follows:

```
<body>
    <p>
        <img src="logo.jpg" alt="Wizard Works" />
    </p>
</body>
```

The goal of this rule is to enforce the inline nature of the img element. Because an inline image is displayed inline within a block element such as a paragraph, it should not be found outside of that context. For the same reason, form elements such as the input or select elements should be found only within a form, not outside of one under the strict DTD.

The Valid Use of Attributes

DTDs also include different rules for attributes and their use. Under the strict DTD, deprecated attributes are not allowed. A list of these prohibited attributes with their corresponding elements is displayed in Figure 9-9.

| Figure 9-9 | Prohibited attributes under the XHTML strict DTD |

Element	Prohibited Attributes
a	target
area	target
base	target
body	alink, bgcolor, link, text, vlink
br	clear
caption	align
div	align
dl	compact
form	name, target
hn	align
hr	align, noshade, size, width
img	align, border, hspace, name, vspace
input	align
li	type, value
link	target
map	name
object	align, border, hspace, vspace
ol	compact, start
p	align
pre	width
script	language
table	align, bgcolor
td	bgcolor, height, nowrap, width
th	bgcolor, height, nowrap, width
tr	bgcolor
ul	type, compact

Many of the attributes listed in Figure 9-9 are called **presentational attributes** because they define how browsers should render the associated elements in Web pages. Note that all of the attributes listed in Figure 9-9 are supported in the transitional and frameset DTDs. Therefore, the code

```
<img src="logo.jpg" alt="Wizard Works" align="left" />
```

which uses the align attribute to float an inline image on the left margin of the page, would not be valid under the strict DTD because the align attribute is prohibited; however, it would be allowed under the frameset and transitional DTDs. To make this code valid under all three DTDs, you could replace the align attribute with the CSS float property.

The strict DTD also requires the use of the id attribute in place of the name attribute for several elements. For example the following tags that you might see in older HTML code

```
<a name="top">
<form name="order" action="http://www.wizworks.com/order">
<img name="logo" alt="logo image" />
<map name="parkmap" />
```

would be written in XHTML under the strict DTD as follows:

```
<a id="top">
<form id="order" action="http://www.wizworks.com/order">
<img id="logo" alt="logo image" />
<map id="parkmap" />
```

TIP

The transitional and frameset DTDs also require the use of the id attribute, but do not reject documents that contain both the name and id attributes. For those DTDs, it's best to include both attributes if you want to make your code backward compatible.

Whereas some attributes are prohibited, others are required. A list of the required attributes and the elements they're associated with is shown in Figure 9-10.

Figure 9-10	Required XHTML attributes

Element	Required Attributes
applet	height, width
area	alt
base	href
basefont	size
bdo	dir
form	action
img	alt, src
map	id
meta	content
optgroup	label
param	name
script	type
style	type
textarea	cols, rows

For example, an inline image is valid only if it contains both the `src` and `alt` attributes, and a `form` element is valid only if it contains an `action` attribute.

Although the list of rules for well-formed and valid documents may seem long and onerous, these rules simply reflect good coding practice. You would not, for example, want to create a Web page without a page title, or an inline image without alternate text. In addition to being required for valid well-formed code, there are many advantages to using DTDs. Perhaps their most significant advantage is the help they provide in trouble-shooting documents. If you create or edit your XHTML code by hand, you can easily make mistakes in syntax, content, or structure. Using a DTD is required if you want to test your document against the set of rules that govern XML.

Inserting the DOCTYPE Declaration

To specify which DTD is used by an XML document, you add a DOCTYPE declaration directly after the XML prolog. The syntax is

```
<!DOCTYPE root type "id" "url">
```

where *root* is the name of the root element of the document, *type* identifies the type of DTD (either PUBLIC or SYSTEM), *id* is an id associated with the DTD, and *url* is the location of an external file containing the DTD rules. For XHTML documents, you set the *root* value to html and the *type* value to PUBLIC.

Figure 9-11 lists the complete DOCTYPE declarations for different versions of HTML and XHTML. Note that you can validate a document not only against different versions of XHTML 1.0, but even against different W3C specifications for HTML as far back as HTML 2.0; this can be beneficial if you need to develop code for older browsers that do not support current standards. You can access the most recent versions of these DTDs on the W3C Web site.

Figure 9-11	DTDs for different versions of HTML and XHTML

DTD	DOCTYPE
HTML 2.0	`<!DOCTYPE html PUBLIC "-//IETF//DTD HTML 2.0//EN">`
HTML 3.2	`<!DOCTYPE html PUBLIC "-//W3C//DTD HTML 3.2 Final//EN">`
HTML 4.01 strict	`<!DOCTYPE html PUBLIC "-//W3C//DTD HTML 4.01//EN` `"http://www.w3.org/TR/html4/strict.dtd">`

HTML 4.01 transitional	`<!DOCTYPE html PUBLIC`
	`"-//W3C//DTD HTML 4.01 Transitional//EN"`
	`"http://www.w3.org/TR/html4/loose.dtd">`

HTML 4.01 frameset	`<!DOCTYPE html PUBLIC "-//W3C//DTD HTML 4.01 Frameset//EN"` `"http://www.w3.org/TR/html4/frameset.dtd">`
HTML5	`<!DOCTYPE html>`
XHTML 1.0 strict	`<!DOCTYPE html PUBLIC "-//W3C//DTD XHTML 1.0 Strict//EN"` `"http://www.w3.org/TR/xhtml1/DTD/xhtml1-strict.dtd">`

XHTML 1.0 transitional	`<!DOCTYPE html PUBLIC`
	`"-//W3C//DTD XHTML 1.0 Transitional//EN"`
	`"http://www.w3.org/TR/xhtml1/DTD/xhtml1-transitional.dtd">`

XHTML 1.0 frameset	`<!DOCTYPE html PUBLIC "-//W3C//DTD XHTML 1.0 Frameset//EN"` `"http://www.w3.org/TR/xhtml1/DTD/xhtml1-frameset.dtd">`
XHTML 1.1	`<!DOCTYPE html PUBLIC "-//W3C//DTD XHTML 1.1//EN"` `"http://www.w3.org/TR/xhtml11/DTD/xhtml11.dtd">`
XHTML5	`<!DOCTYPE html>`

REFERENCE

Setting the Document DTD

- To apply the XHTML 1.0 strict DTD, add the following line after the XML declaration:

```
<!DOCTYPE html PUBLIC "-//W3C//DTD XHTML 1.0 Strict//EN"
    "http://www.w3.org/TR/xhtml1/DTD/xhtml1-strict.dtd">
```

- To apply the XHTML 1.0 transitional DTD, use the following:

```
<!DOCTYPE html PUBLIC "-//W3C//DTD XHTML 1.0 Transitional//EN"
    "http://www.w3.org/TR/xhtml1/DTD/xhtml1-transitional.dtd">
```

- To apply the XHTML 1.0 frameset DTD, use the following:

```
<!DOCTYPE html PUBLIC "-//W3C//DTD XHTML 1.0 Frameset//EN"
    "http://www.w3.org/TR/xhtml1/DTD/xhtml1-frameset.dtd">
```

- For HTML5 or XHTML5 documents, use the following:

```
<!DOCTYPE html>
```

Tom suggests that you associate the Wizard Works Web site with the transitional DTD for XHTML 1.0. To do that, you'll add the DOCTYPE declaration for XHTML 1.0 transitional. Because the code for a DOCTYPE declaration can be long and complicated, a text file with the declarations from Figure 9-11 has been created for you to copy from.

To insert a DOCTYPE declaration:

▶ **1.** In your text editor, open the **dtd_list.txt** file from the tutorial.09\tutorial folder included with your Data Files.

Make sure you copy the text of the DTD exactly.

▶ **2.** Copy the DOCTYPE declaration for the XHTML 1.0 transitional DTD—the fourth DTD from the bottom of the file.

▶ **3.** Close the file, and then return to the **works.htm** file in your text editor.

▶ **4.** Directly after the XML prolog, paste the copied DOCTYPE declaration. Figure 9-12 highlights the revised code in the file.

Figure 9-12 **Insert the DOCTYPE declaration**

```
<?xml version="1.0" encoding="UTF-8" ?>

    <!DOCTYPE html PUBLIC "-//W3C//DTD XHTML 1.0 Transitional//EN"
        "http://www.w3.org/TR/xhtml1/DTD/xhtml1-transitional.dtd">
<ht.....
    <head>
        <meta http-equiv="Content-type" content="text/html;charset=UTF-8" />
```

▶ **5.** Save your changes to the file.

Setting the XHTML Namespace

As noted earlier, XHTML is only one of hundreds of XML vocabularies. In some situations, a document author may want to combine elements and attributes from different vocabularies in the same document. For example, a mathematician might want to combine features of the MathML vocabulary with features from XHTML in a single compound document. Each element or attribute that belongs to a particular language is part of that language's **namespace**. There are two types of namespaces: default and local. For now, you'll focus only on the default namespace. A **default namespace** is the namespace that is assumed to be applied, by default, to any element or attribute in the document. To declare a default namespace, you add the `xmlns` (XML namespace) attribute

```
<root xmlns="namespace">
```

to the markup tag for the document's root element, where *root* is the name of the root element and *namespace* is the namespace id. Every XML vocabulary has a unique namespace id. For example, if you wish to declare that the elements in your document belong to the XHTML namespace by default, you add the following attribute to the opening `<html>` tag:

```
<html xmlns="http://www.w3.org/1999/xhtml">
```

TIP

There is no syntax for declaring namespaces in HTML5.

The namespace id for XHTML looks like a URL, but it's not treated as one by XML parsers. The id can actually be any string of characters as long as it uniquely identifies the document namespace. For XHTML, it was decided to use `http://www.w3.org/1999/xhtml` as the unique identifier.

REFERENCE

Defining a Default Namespace

- To define a default namespace for an XML document, add the attribute

  ```
  <root xmlns="namespace">
  ```

  to the document's root element, where *root* is the name of the root element and *namespace* is the namespace id for the default namespace.
- To set the default namespace for an XHTML document, add the following `xmlns` attribute to the `html` element:

  ```
  <html xmlns="http://www.w3.org/1999/xhtml">
  ```

If you don't intend to combine different XML-based languages within the same document, it's still a good idea to add a namespace to an XHTML file to explicitly identify the XML vocabulary in use. In practical terms, though, an XHTML document is still interpretable by most browsers without a namespace. Tom would like you to add the XHTML default namespace to his *works.htm* file.

To add the XHTML namespace:

1. Locate the opening `<html>` tag in the **works.htm** file.

2. Within the tag, insert the following attribute, as shown in Figure 9-13:

   ```
   xmlns="http://www.w3.org/1999/xhtml"
   ```

Figure 9-13 Declaring the XHTML namespace

```
<?xml version="1.0" encoding="UTF-8" ?>

<!DOCTYPE html PUBLIC "-//W3C//DTD XHTML 1.0 Transitional//EN"
  "http://www.w3.org/TR/xhtml1/DTD/xhtml1-transitional.dtd">

<html xmlns="http://www.w3.org/1999/xhtml">
   <head>
      <meta http-equiv="Content-type" content="text/html;charset=UTF-8" />
```

3. Save your changes to the file.

INSIGHT

Local Namespaces in Compound Documents

One feature of XML is the ability to combine several languages into a single document. For the elements of the different languages to coexist, you assign one language as the default namespace for the document so that all elements are assumed to belong to that language. Elements that do not belong to the default namespace belong instead to a **local namespace**.

To define a local namespace, you add the attribute

```
xmlns:prefix="namespace"
```

to the root element of the XML document, where *prefix* is the prefix you'll use to mark elements in this local namespace, and *namespace* is the namespace id. Every XML-based language has a unique namespace id. For example, to declare a local namespace for MathML within an XHTML document, you would add the following code to the `html` element:

```
<html xmlns:ml="http://www.w3.org/1998/math/MathML">
```

This code sets the prefix for the namespace to the character string `ml`. Once you define a namespace prefix, you place individual elements in that namespace by adding the prefix to the element name in each markup tag as follows

```
<prefix:element> ... </prefix:element>
```

where *prefix* is the prefix for the local namespace and *element* is the name of the element within that local namespace. For example, the following code contains the paragraph element from XHTML and the `mi`, `mo`, and `mn` elements from MathML, all coexisting within a single document:

```
<p>
    <ml:mi>x</ml:mi>
    <ml:mo>+</ml:mo>
    <ml:mn>1</ml:mn>
</p>
```

Different browsers provide varying levels of support for different markup languages. For instance, at the time of this writing, only Firefox and Opera provide built-in support for MathML. The only requirement is that filenames including MathML elements use either the *.xml* or *.xhtml* extension. Internet Explorer supports MathML through the use of a browser add-in. WebKit browsers such as Safari and Google Chrome are promising to provide built-in support for MathML in the near future.

MathML is also part of the design specifications for HTML5, and currently Firefox and Opera both support MathML without the use of namespaces or namespace prefixes.

HTML5 and XHTML

HTML5 was developed to be backward compatible with earlier versions of HTML, and also to support the common application of HTML syntax. The result is that many syntax rules enforced in XHTML documents are not enforced in HTML5. Figure 9-14 summarizes some of the differences between HTML5 and XHTML.

Figure 9-14	HTML5 vs. XHTML

Syntax Issue	HTML5	XHTML
Attribute minimization	Attributes need not have attribute values.	All attributes must have attribute values.
Attribute names	Attribute names are not case sensitive.	Attribute names must be lowercase.
Attribute values	Unquoted attribute values are allowed.	All attribute values must be enclosed in quotes.
DOCTYPE	A DOCTYPE is required in the form <!DOCTYPE html >	The DOCTYPE is optional.
Element names	Element names are not case sensitive.	Element names must be lowercase.
Empty element tags	A closing slash may or may not be used with an empty element tag.	Empty element tags must include a closing slash.
Error validation	In HTML5 there are no well-formedness constraints; no errors are fatal.	Well-formedness errors are fatal.
Namespace prefixes	Namespace prefixes are not supported in HTML5.	Namespace prefixes are supported in XHTML.
Namespaces	Elements and attributes for known vocabularies (HTML, SVG, and MathML) are implicitly assigned.	Namespaces must be explicitly declared using the xmlns attribute.
Processing instructions	HTML5 does not support processing instructions and instead treats the enclosed text as a comment.	Allows the use of processing instructions closed with ?>

The rules for HTML5 are much more open than for XHTML. For example, an HTML5 document is considered valid regardless of whether attributes have attribute values, whether attribute names and element names are in lowercase letters, or whether empty element tags have closing slashes. Even though HTML5 does not have the same syntax requirements as XHTML, you should follow the general XHTML syntax rules in case you need to work with XHTML or XML documents in the future.

Note that with XHTML, you cannot use the HTML5 structural elements including the header, footer, nav, section, article, aside, hgroup, figure, and figcaption elements. One alternative to using those elements is to use div elements, and identify the purpose of each div element using an id attribute. Thus, under XHTML, you can use the following div element to make a page header:

```
<div id="header"> … </div>
```

However, there is no specification in XHTML to use one id value over another. A different author might use an id value of *head* or *title*. Syntactical elements such as the header element are one of the chief advantages of HTML5 in that they provide a common structure for Web pages.

Written Communication: Updating a Legacy Page

Revamping a Web site can be an expensive and time-consuming process. It's not surprising, therefore, that many businesses use Web sites that are based on HTML code that is more than 10 years old, involving elements and attributes that have long been deprecated. However, trying to piggyback new content on old code often can result in code that is cumbersome and difficult to interpret, making it even more difficult and expensive to update the site in the future.

When your business decides to update its legacy pages, here are some things you should consider doing:

- *Always add a DTD.* Whether or not you plan to validate your Web site, always add a DTD to ensure that the browser renders the page in Standards mode rather than Quirks mode. If you update your site to HTML5, use the basic `<!DOCTYPE html>` DTD.
- *Use standard syntax.* Even though HTML5 supports variations in syntax, your code will be easier to maintain if you adopt standard syntax rules such as always using lowercase element and attribute names, providing attribute values for every attribute, and closing empty elements with a closing slash.
- *Replace all presentation elements.* Older Web sites will be filled with presentational elements such as the `font`, `center`, and `u` elements. Replace these with CSS styles.
- *Replace all presentational attributes.* Attributes such as `width`, `align`, and `color` should be replaced with CSS styles.
- *Use CSS for layout.* A common practice with older Web sites is to use tables for page layout. Replace all tabular layouts with CSS layout styles.

Despite the work and expense involved, upgrading your company's Web site will pay for itself in the long run. The updated site will be easier to use and maintain, and will be more easily adaptable to design changes in the future.

With the addition of the XHTML namespace, you have converted Tom's original HTML document into XHTML format. In the next session, you'll test this document to determine whether it passes the W3C tests for well-formedness and validity.

Session 9.1 Quick Check

REVIEW

1. What is a well-formed document? What is a valid document?
2. Why is the following code not well formed?

```
<img src="logo.jpg" alt="Wizard Works">
```

How would you correct it?

3. Why is the following code not well formed?

```
<input type="radio" disabled />
```

How would you correct it?

4. Why is the following code not valid under strict XHTML?

```
<blockquote>
    For more information go to the <a href="faq.
htm">FAQ page</a>
</blockquote>
```

Suggest a correction for the problem.

5. Why is the following code not valid under strict XHTML?

```
<img src="logo.jpg" alt="Wizard Works" align="right" />
```

How would you fix it?

6. Why is the following code not valid under transitional XHTML?

```
<map name="parkmap"> ... </map>
```

Suggest a change to the code that would correct the problem and make the code backward compatible with older browsers.

7. What declaration would you add to an XHTML document to associate it with the XHTML strict DTD?
8. What statement do you add to the start of a file to declare it as an XML document?

SESSION 9.2 VISUAL OVERVIEW

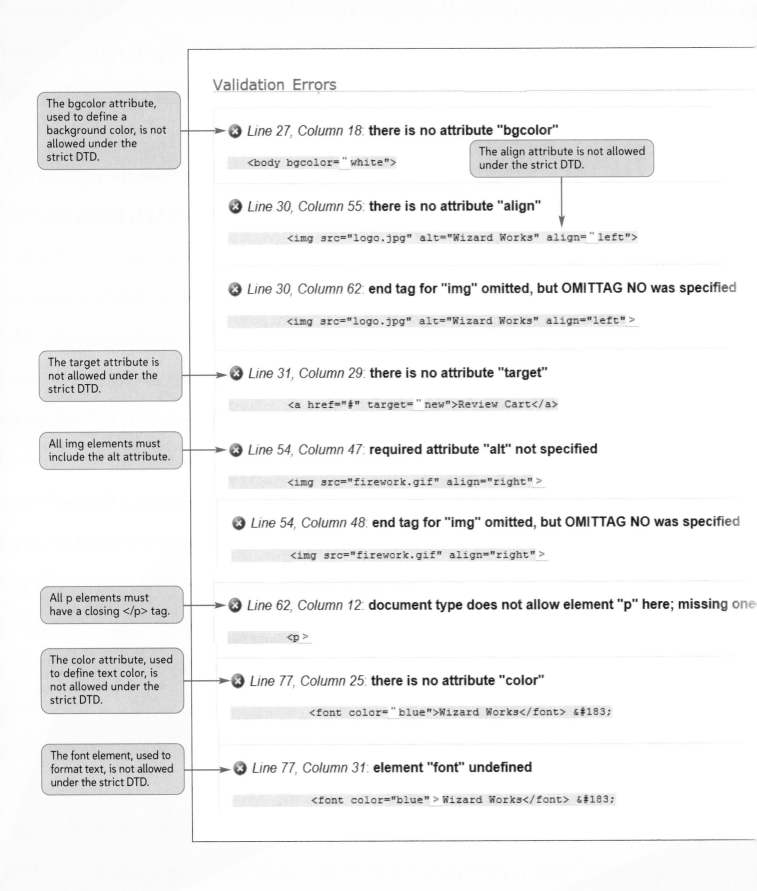

Validation Errors

The bgcolor attribute, used to define a background color, is not allowed under the strict DTD.

❌ *Line 27, Column 18*: **there is no attribute "bgcolor"**

```
<body bgcolor="white">
```

The align attribute is not allowed under the strict DTD.

❌ *Line 30, Column 55*: **there is no attribute "align"**

```
<img src="logo.jpg" alt="Wizard Works" align="left">
```

❌ *Line 30, Column 62*: **end tag for "img" omitted, but OMITTAG NO was specified**

```
<img src="logo.jpg" alt="Wizard Works" align="left">
```

The target attribute is not allowed under the strict DTD.

❌ *Line 31, Column 29*: **there is no attribute "target"**

```
<a href="#" target="new">Review Cart</a>
```

All img elements must include the alt attribute.

❌ *Line 54, Column 47*: **required attribute "alt" not specified**

```
<img src="firework.gif" align="right">
```

❌ *Line 54, Column 48*: **end tag for "img" omitted, but OMITTAG NO was specified**

```
<img src="firework.gif" align="right">
```

All p elements must have a closing </p> tag.

❌ *Line 62, Column 12*: **document type does not allow element "p" here; missing one**

```
<p>
```

The color attribute, used to define text color, is not allowed under the strict DTD.

❌ *Line 77, Column 25*: **there is no attribute "color"**

```
<font color="blue">Wizard Works</font> &#183;
```

The font element, used to format text, is not allowed under the strict DTD.

❌ *Line 77, Column 31*: **element "font" undefined**

```
<font color="blue">Wizard Works</font> &#183;
```

VALIDATING AN XHTML DOCUMENT

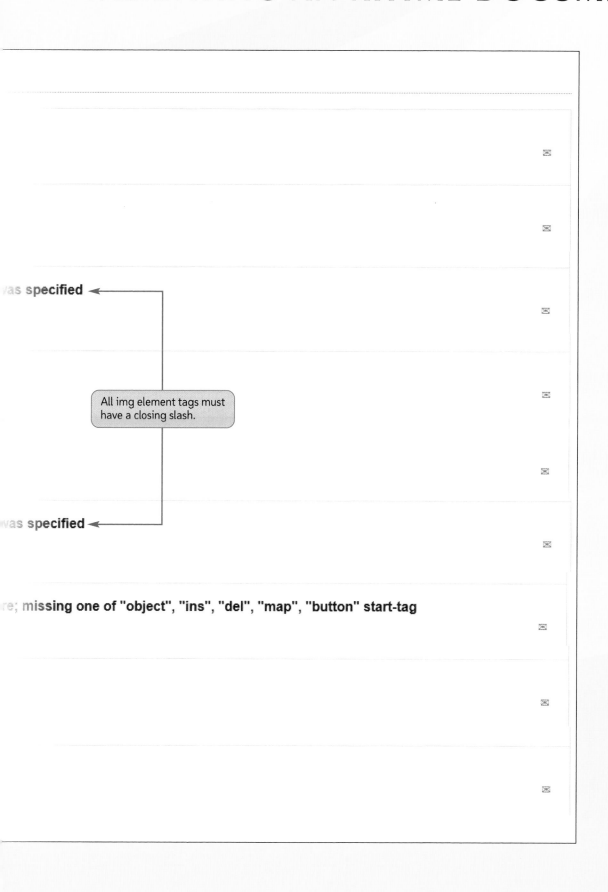

was specified

All img element tags must have a closing slash.

was specified

re; missing one of "object", "ins", "del", "map", "button" start-tag

Validating Under XHTML Transitional

In the last session, you converted Tom's Web page document from HTML format into XHTML format. By adding the DOCTYPE declaration and XML namespace, you can test whether the document is well formed and valid. To test the document, you must submit the file to an XML parser that will generate a report listing any errors in the document. Several parsers are available on the Web. You'll use the one hosted on the W3C Web site.

To access the W3C validator page:

▶ **1.** Use your browser to open the Web page at *http://validator.w3.org*.

▶ **2.** Click the **Validate by File Upload** tab in the Web page.

> **Trouble?** Depending on the current format of the validator page, it might not exactly match the figures and screen shots in this session. Use whatever buttons or forms exist in the Web page.

▶ **3.** Click the **Browse** or **Choose File** button, and then locate the **works.htm** file from the tutorial.09\tutorial folder included with your Data Files.

▶ **4.** Select the file, and then click the **Open** or **Choose** button. The filename and path will be displayed in the File input box, as shown in Figure 9-15.

| Figure 9-15 | Selecting a file for validation |

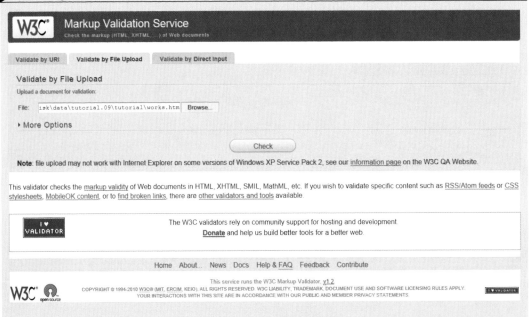

TIP

You can test a different DTD in the validator page without editing the file by clicking the More Options link, and then selecting the DTD from the Document Type list box.

▶ **5.** Click the **Check** button. The validator reports several errors in the file, as shown in Figure 9-16.

Figure 9-16 | **Results of the validation test under XHTML 1.0 transitional**

> **6.** Scroll down the Web page to read the validator's summary of the errors.

The validator reports a total of nine errors. This doesn't mean that there are nine separate mistakes in the file. In some cases, the same mistake results in several errors being noted in the report; and fixing one mistake can result in several of the errors reported by the validator being resolved. In a large error list, it's unlikely that you can fix everything at once. It's best to fix the most obvious mistakes first to reduce the size of the list, leaving the more subtle errors to be fixed last. Tom wants you to examine the error list in more detail. The first error reported was the following:

Line 31, column 62: **end tag for "img" omitted, but OMITTAG NO was specified**

```
<img src="logo.jpg" alt="Wizard Works" align="left">
```

TIP

The exact line number and column number might differ depending on how you entered text into the document.

When the validator reports that the end tag for an element is missing, it means that either a two-sided tag is missing an end tag, or a one-sided tag was improperly entered. This is a syntax error and indicates that the document is not well formed. If you examine the code for the *logo.jpg* inline image, you'll notice that the img element was not written as a one-sided tag. This is a common problem with older HTML code, in which tags for empty elements use the same form as the opening tags of two-sided tags. Note that even though the tag was improperly entered, the page was still rendered correctly by the browser earlier in the tutorial. This is because browsers usually can render a Web page even when it violates XHTML syntax.

Another error reported by the validator indicates a problem with the document's validity:

Line 55, column 47: **required attribute "alt" not specified**

```
<img src="firework.gif" align="right">
```

This is an inline image without the alt attribute. Because the alt attribute is required for all inline images within an XHTML document, omitting it results in an error. This inline image was also not inserted using a one-sided tag, resulting in a second syntax error. You'll fix these errors and resubmit the file for testing.

To fix and resubmit the file:

> **1.** Return to the **works.htm** file in your text editor.

> **2.** Locate the img element for the *logo.jpg* file, and then change it to a one-sided tag using the proper syntax.

3. Locate the img element for the *firework.gif* image, add the attribute

   alt=""

   and then change the tag to a one-sided tag. Figure 9-17 shows the revised code in the file.

Figure 9-17 Modifying the img elements in the document

```
<div id="head">
   <img src="logo.jpg" alt="Wizard Works" align="left" />
   <a href="#" target="new">Review Cart</a>
   <a href="#" target="new">Check Out</a>
</div>

<div id="linklist">
   <a href="#">Home</a>
   <a href="#" class="newgroup">Assortments</a>
   <a href="#">Firecrackers</a>
   <a href="#">Fountains</a>
   <a href="#">Cones</a>
   <a href="#">Rockets</a>
   <a href="#">Sparklers</a>
   <a href="#" class="newgroup">Online Store</a>
   <a href="#">Shopping Cart</a>
   <a href="#">Your Account</a>
   <a href="#" class="newgroup">Safety</a>
   <a href="#">Tech Support</a>
   <a href="#">Customer Service</a>
   <a href="#">About Us</a>
   <a href="#" class="newgroup">Contact Us</a>
</div>

<div id="main">
   <img src="firework.gif" align="right" alt="" />
   <p class="firstp">
      Welcome to Wizard Works, your one-stop shopping source for discount
      fireworks on the Web! We maintain a select variety of consumer fireworks
      on our Web site year round. You'll find the fireworks you want with the
      speed and convenience of the Internet, and you'll always have the best
      show in the neighborhood when you shop at Wizard Works.
```

syntax error for one-sided <img /> tag corrected

required alt attribute for img element added and syntax error fixed

4. Save your changes to the file.

5. Return to your Web browser, and then refresh or reload the Web page to resubmit the validation check on the *works.htm* file. You might be queried as to whether or not you wish to resend the previous information. If so, click the **Retry** or **OK** button.

   Trouble? If clicking the Refresh or Reload button does not resubmit the page for testing, you can click the Browse button on the form to reselect the *works.htm* file from the tutorial.09\tutorial folder and then click the Revalidate button.

   Figure 9-18 shows the new validation report.

Figure 9-18 Results of the second validation test

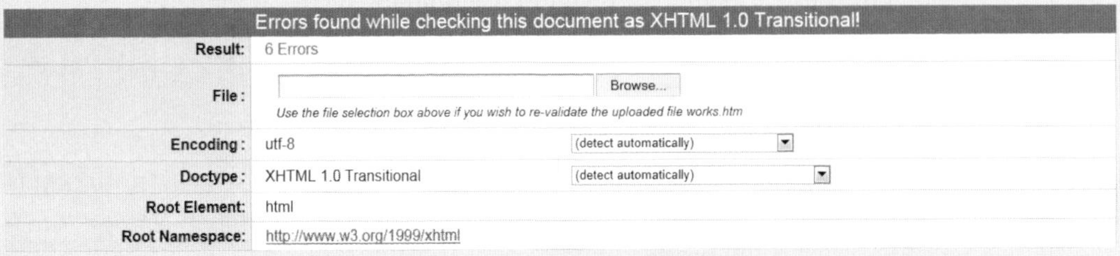

	Errors found while checking this document as XHTML 1.0 Transitional!
Result:	6 Errors
File :	[ ] Browse... *Use the file selection box above if you wish to re-validate the uploaded file works.htm*
Encoding :	utf-8 (detect automatically)
Doctype :	XHTML 1.0 Transitional (detect automatically)
Root Element:	html
Root Namespace:	http://www.w3.org/1999/xhtml

By fixing these two elements, you reduced the size of the error list from nine to six items. You can trim that down even more. The first error in the latest list states

Line 63, column 12: **document type does not allow element "p" here; missing one of "object", "applet", "map", "iframe", "button", "ins", "del" start-tag**

        `<p≥`

which can indicate that an element has been improperly nested within a paragraph element—but read on. Another error states

Line 84, column 12: **tag for "p" omitted, but OMITTAG NO was specified**

        `</div≥`

which indicates that the paragraph element was not properly closed due to the absence of the closing `</p>` tag. In this case, the same mistake has caused both errors. Because the paragraph element is not closed, it appears that other elements have been improperly placed inside of it. By adding the closing tag, both errors should be corrected.

To fix the errors in the Web page paragraphs:

▶ **1.** Return to the **works.htm** file in your text editor.

▶ **2.** Locate the three paragraph elements in the main section, and then add a closing `</p>` tag to each paragraph, as shown in Figure 9-19.

Figure 9-19   Closing the paragraph elements

```
<div id="main">
   <img src="firework.gif" align="right" alt="" />
   <p class="firstp">
      Welcome to Wizard Works, your one-stop shopping source for discount
      fireworks on the Web! We maintain a select variety of consumer fireworks
      on our Web site year round. You'll find the fireworks you want with the
      speed and convenience of the Internet, and you'll always have the best
      show in the neighborhood when you shop at Wizard Works.</p>

   <p>
      We supply quality fireworks to buy online at wholesale prices. Our
      professional fireworks display team is available to design and organize
      your display; or if you want to organize your own fireworks party, our
      experienced fireworks designers have selected the best fireworks for the
      occasion. We've made it easy for you to buy online for delivery direct
      to your home.</p>

   <p>
      We also create customized fireworks and displays for special needs. Please
      contact one of our design engineers to see if we can create a display for
      your special event. Be sure to order special event fireworks early to ensure
      on-time delivery.</p>
```

closing `</p>` tags added to the three paragraphs

▶ **3.** Save your changes, and then return to the W3C validator page. Click the **Refresh** or **Reload** button in your browser to redo the validation check. As shown in Figure 9-20, the page should now pass the validation check under the XHTML 1.0 transitional DTD.

Figure 9-20 **Successful validation under XHTML 1.0 transitional**

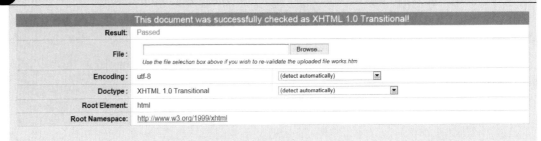

Testing Under XHTML Strict

Now that the Web page has passed the validation check for XHTML 1.0 transitional, Tom wants the page tested under XHTML 1.0 strict. To perform this test, you'll change the DOCTYPE declaration to use the strict XHTML 1.0 DTD.

To change the DOCTYPE declaration:

1. In your text editor, reopen the **dtd_list.txt** file from the tutorial.09\tutorial folder. Copy the DOCTYPE declaration for XHTML 1.0 strict, and then close the file.
2. Return to the **works.htm** file in your text editor.
3. Paste the copied DOCTYPE declaration into the file, replacing the previous declaration for XHTML 1.0 transitional. Figure 9-21 highlights the revised code in the file.

Figure 9-21 **Pasting the XHTML 1.0 strict DTD**

```
<?xml version="1.0" encoding="UTF-8" ?>

<!DOCTYPE html PUBLIC "-//W3C//DTD XHTML 1.0 Strict//EN"
  "http://www.w3.org/TR/xhtml1/DTD/xhtml1-strict.dtd">

<html xmlns="http://www.w3.org/1999/xhtml">
   <head>
      <meta http-equiv="Content-type" content="text/html;charset=UTF-8" />
```

With the new DOCTYPE declaration pasted into the *works.htm* file, you can retest the document using the same validator page on the W3C Web site.

To test the file under the strict DTD:

1. Save your changes to the **works.htm** file.
2. Return to the W3C validator page. Click the **Refresh** or **Reload** button in your browser to redo the validation check. As shown in Figure 9-22, the page fails the test under XHTML 1.0 strict.

TIP

You can view extended comments on your page errors by checking the Verbose Output check box in the validator page, and then clicking the Revalidate button.

Figure 9-22   **Results of the XHTML 1.0 strict validation test**

	Errors found while checking this document as XHTML 1.0 Strict!
Result:	5 Errors
File:	[ ] Browse...
	Use the file selection box above if you wish to re-validate the uploaded file works.htm
Encoding:	utf-8 (detect automatically) ▾
Doctype:	XHTML 1.0 Strict (detect automatically) ▾
Root Element:	html
Root Namespace:	http://www.w3.org/1999/xhtml

Five errors are reported by the W3C validator page. The first two are:
Line 28, column 14: **there is no attribute "bgcolor"**

```
<body bgcolor="white">
```

Line 31, column 55: **there is no attribute "align"**

```
<img src="logo.jpg" alt="Wizard Works" align="left" />
```

Both errors reference presentational attributes that are not supported under the XHTML 1.0 strict DTD. The first attribute, `bgcolor`, is used to set the background color of the Web page. The `align` attribute referenced in the second error message is used to float the inline image on the left page margin. You can fix both errors by removing the attributes and replacing them with style properties.

To replace the attributes with styles:

1. Return to the **works.htm** file in your Web browser, and then delete the attribute

   `bgcolor="white"`

   from the opening `<body>` tag.

2. Go down two lines in the file, and then delete the attribute

   `align="left"`

   from the `<img />` tag for the *logo.jpg* file.

3. Scroll down the file, and then delete the attribute

   `align="right"`

   from the `<img />` tag for the *firework.gif* graphic.

4. Save your changes to the file, and then open the **ww.css** file in your text editor.

5. Add the following style rule to the `body` element to replace the actions of the `bgcolor` attribute you deleted in Step 1:

   `background-color: white;`

6. Within the style rule for the `#head img` selector, add the following property to float the image on the left margin:

   `float: left;`

7. Next, add the following style rule to float inline images within the `#main` selector on the right margin:

   ```
   #main img {
      float: right;
   }
   ```

Figure 9-23 highlights the revised code in the style sheet file.

Figure 9-23   Modifying the style sheet

```
body {
    background-image: url(back.jpg);
    background-repeat: repeat-y;
    font-size: 16px;
    margin: 0px;
    position: absolute;
    background-color: white;
}

#head {
    background-color: white;
    border-bottom: 2px solid black;
    font-size: 16px;
    font-family: sans-serif;
    margin: 0px;
    padding-top: 5px;
    position: absolute;
    text-align: right;
    top: 0px;
    left: 0px;
    width: 800px;
}

#head img {
    margin: 0px;
    float: left;
}

#main img {
    float: right;
}
```

▸ **8.** Save your changes to the file, and then return to the W3C validator page in your Web browser. Refresh or reload the **works.htm** page, and then verify that the number of errors in the page has dropped to three.

The next error reported by the validator is:
Line 32, column 29: **there is no attribute "target"**

```
<a href="#" target="_new">Review Cart</a>
```

The `target` attribute is not supported in XHTML strict, so it will have to be removed from the Web page. This means that if Tom wants to work with XHTML strict, he will not be able to direct his hypertext links to new browser windows or tabs.

To remove the `target` attribute:

▸ **1.** Return to the **works.htm** file in your Web browser.

▸ **2.** Delete the attribute

`target="_new"`

from the hypertext links for Review Cart and Check Out located at the top of the Web page body.

▸ **3.** Save your changes to the file, and then reload or refresh the W3C validator page in your Web browser. The number of errors in the Web page has dropped to two.

The `target` Attribute and Strict XHTML

The decision not to support the `target` attribute under strict XHTML was a controversial one. Many Web page designers prefer to have some links open in new browser windows or tabs, rather than in the window or tab that displays their site, to allow users to stay at their site while also browsing on other sites.

One problem is that the ability to open a new window or tab is strictly browser-dependent. For example, cell phones and PDAs don't support opening new windows, and those devices are becoming increasingly important tools for viewing the Web. Another argument is that the action of opening a link in a new window should be left to each user's preference; it should not be forced on users by Web site designers. Most browsers provide users the ability to choose where to open links, and that is where the decision should reside. Finally, there is the opinion that opening new browser windows for users is actually confusing to new users, who can get lost as the number of open windows increases with each site they visit.

However, despite these reasons, many Web designers still want to direct links to new browser windows. One way to allow a link to be opened in a new window but still retain valid code under XHTML strict is to use JavaScript to open the link. The following code shows a JavaScript command that can be added to any hypertext link to force the link to open in a new window:

```
<a href="url" onclick="window.open(this.href); return false;"
   onkeypress="window.open(this.href); return false;">
   linked text
</a>
```

Note that for this approach to work, the user's browser must have JavaScript enabled. This is the default state for most browsers. However, if JavaScript is not enabled, the JavaScript code will be ignored and the link will open in the current browser window or tab.

The last two errors in the *works.htm* file involve using the `color` attribute and the `<font>` tag. The reported errors are as follows:

Line 78, column 25: **there is no attribute "color"**

```
<font color="blue">Wizard Works</font> &#183;
```

Line 78, column 31: **element "font" undefined**

```
<font color="blue">Wizard Works</font> &#183;
```

To fix this problem, you'll remove the unsupported `color` attribute and `font` element, replacing them with the following span element and inline style:

```
<span style="color: blue">Wizard Works</span> &#183;
```

You'll make this change now to the *works.htm* file.

To replace the `font` element and `color` attribute:

▶ 1. Return to the **works.htm** file in your text editor.

▶ 2. Scroll to the bottom of the file, and then replace

```
<font color="blue">Wizard Works</font>
```

with the following, as shown in Figure 9-24:

```
<span style="color: blue">Wizard Works</span> &#183;
```

Figure 9-24 | **Replacing the font element and color attribute**

```
<address>
    <span style="color: blue">Wizard Works</span> &#183;
    4311 Tower Street &#183;
    Ashland, KY  41105 &#183;
    (606) 555-3188
</address>
```

 3. Save your changes to the file, and then reload or refresh the W3C validator page in your Web browser. As shown in Figure 9-25, the validator should now report that the code for the *works.htm* file passes validation under XHTML strict.

Figure 9-25 | **Successful validation under XHTML strict**

	This document was successfully checked as XHTML 1.0 Strict!		
Result:	Passed		
File :		Browse...	
	Use the file selection box above if you wish to re-validate the uploaded file works.htm		
Encoding :	iso-8859-1	(detect automatically)	▼
Doctype :	utf-8	(detect automatically)	▼
Root Element:	html		
Root Namespace:	http://www.w3.org/1999/xhtml		

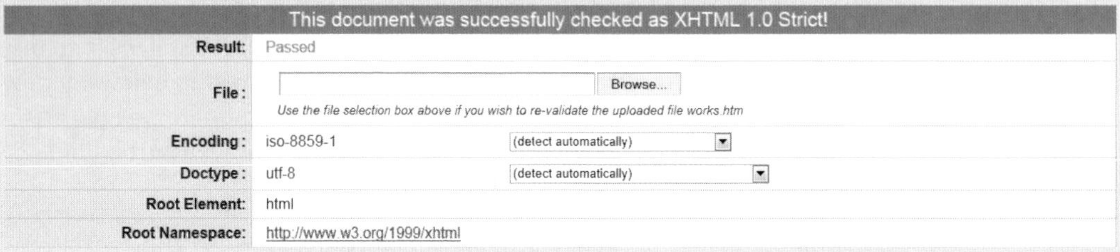

Once your document passes the validation test, you might want to make a note of this fact in your Web page. The W3C provides code that you can paste into your document to let others know that your document matches all of the validation tests. Tom suggests that you add this code to the Wizard Works Web page.

To insert the W3C validation notice:

 1. Scroll to the bottom of the W3C validator page, and then select the code sample directly to the right of the validation icon image.

 2. Click **Edit** from your browser menu, and then click **Copy**.

 3. Return to the **works.htm** file in your text editor, and then paste the following code directly below the closing `</address>` tag, as shown in Figure 9-26:

```
<p>
    <a href="http://validator.w3.org/check?uri=referer">
        <img src="http://www.w3.org/Icons/valid-xhtml10"
            alt="Valid XHTML 1.0 Strict" height="31" width="88" />
    </a>
</p>
```

Indent the code to make it easier to read.

Figure 9-26 | **Inserting code for the W3C validation icon**

```
    <p>
        <a href="http://validator.w3.org/check?uri=referer">
        <img src="http://www.w3.org/Icons/valid-xhtml10" alt="Valid XHTML 1.0 Strict"
            height="31" width="88" /></a>
    </p>

    </div>
</body>
```

▶ **4.** Save your changes to the **works.htm** file, and then close it.

▶ **5.** Reopen **works.htm** in your Web browser. As shown in Figure 9-27, the validation icon appears in the lower-right corner of the page.

Figure 9-27   Final Wizard Works page

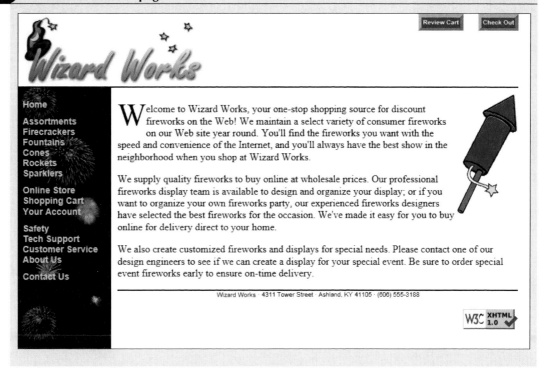

You show the completed Web page to Tom. He's pleased with your work on updating the file to meet the specifications for XHTML. He is sure that these changes will help the Web site in the future as the company tries to stay current with the latest developments in XHTML.

Using Embedded Style Sheets in XHTML

Although XHTML and HTML files are simple text documents, not all text is the same. XML distinguishes between two types of text: parsed character data and unparsed character data. **Parsed character data**, or **PCDATA**, is text that is processed (parsed) by a browser or parser. The following code is an example of PCDATA:

```
<title>Wizard Works</title>
```

When a browser encounters this string of characters, it processes it and uses that information to set the text displayed in the browser's title bar. With PCDATA in an XML document, you cannot enter character symbols such as <, >, and & directly into a document as text because they are used to process information. The < and > symbols are used to mark the beginning and end of an element tag; the & symbol is used to mark special characters. If you want to display a < symbol in your document, for example, you must use the special character symbol <.

Unparsed character data, or **CDATA**, is text that is not processed by a browser or parser. In CDATA, you can use any character you like without worrying about it being misinterpreted—browsers and parsers essentially ignore it. The DTDs for XML and XHTML specify whether a given element contains CDATA or PCDATA. Most elements contain PCDATA, which prevents document authors from putting symbols such as < into the element content.

The distinction between these two types of data also has an impact on embedded style sheets. The content of an embedded style sheet is treated as PCDATA, meaning that a parser attempts to process the information contained in the style sheet's characters. This can cause problems if the style sheet contains a character that could be processed by the parser. For example, the following embedded style sheet contains the > character, which a parser would interpret as the end of an element tag:

```
<style type="text/css">
   p > img {
      float: left;
   }
</style>
```

An XML parser encountering this code would invalidate the document (assuming that the code didn't crash the page entirely). This problem also occurs with JavaScript (a topic you'll cover in the next tutorial), in which the <, >, and & symbols are frequently used.

One way of dealing with this problem is to create a section called a **CDATA section**, which marks a block of text as CDATA so that parsers ignore any text within it. The syntax of a CDATA section is

```
<![CDATA[
   text
]]>
```

where *text* is the content that you want treated as CDATA. To apply a CDATA section to your style sheet, you could place the CDATA section within the style element as follows:

```
<style type="text/css">
   <![CDATA[
      p > img {
         float: left;
      }
   ]]>
</style>
```

The problem with this solution is that many browsers do not understand or recognize CDATA sections, and this could cause problems in displaying your page. In the end, the best solution is often to replace all embedded style sheets in XHTML documents with external style sheets. This has the added advantage of completely removing style from content because all the styles are placed in separate files. Note that this is not an issue if an embedded style sheet doesn't contain any characters that can't be processed by an XML parser.

PROSKILLS

Decision Making: Are Standards Necessary?

Browsers are very forgiving of lapses in syntax. In fact, this is one of the reasons that non-programmers were able to quickly create their own Web pages in the early days of the World Wide Web. Part of the conflict between XHTML 2.0 and HTML5 was over whether it was crucial to future Web development to enforce syntax rules in the next generation of Web sites. It was a debate that HTML5, with its support for flexibility in enforcing syntax rules, decisively won.

In light of this, you may wonder if it's really important to validate a document and follow syntax rules when browsers are so accommodating. In fact, there are several good reasons to enforce syntax rules and follow good coding practices:

- Although many browsers accommodate variations in syntax, not all browsers do so and not always in the same way. However, when you follow the syntax rules of the W3C, all browsers enforce those rules and in the same way.
- Web pages tend to be rendered more quickly when they use good syntax because browsers don't have to interpret poorly written code.
- If a browser renders one of your pages incorrectly, it's easier to debug the page if it's written in compliance with standard syntax. Many Web developers do a validation check as part of the debugging process to locate errors in the code.
- In a working group where several people are tasked with maintaining the same Web site code, you need to have a common set of rules to avoid confusion and mistakes. Why not use the rules set down by the W3C?
- Even if you are writing a page in HTML5, your business might also need to create XML-based documents. Given the similarity between the two markup languages, it's easier for everyone to use the same set of syntax rules.

Even if you're writing your code in HTML5, it's best to follow the syntax rules of XHTML. This does not mean you have to run a validation check every time or add a namespace or an XML prolog; but you should use XHTML standards such as lowercasing element and attribute names, and always provide attribute values enclosed within quotes.

REVIEW

Session 9.2 Quick Check

1. An XHTML transitional validation test reports the following error:
   Line 51, column 3: **tag for "br" omitted, but OMITTAG NO was specified**
   ```
   <br>
   ```
   Suggest a possible cause of the error and how you would correct it.
2. A validation test under XHTML 1.0 strict reports the following error:
   Line 59, column 12: **there is no attribute "align"**
   ```
   <p align="left">
   ```
   Suggest a possible cause of the error and how you would correct it.
3. A validation test under XHTML 1.0 strict reports the following error:
   Line 22, column 14: **there is no attribute "name"**
   ```
   <form name="orders">
   ```
   Suggest a possible cause of the error and how you would correct it.
4. Suggest how to write code for a hypertext link to open in a new browser window and still be valid under the XHTML strict DTD.
5. What is the difference between PCDATA and CDATA?
6. Why would you want to place an embedded style sheet within a CDATA section?

Practice the skills you learned in the tutorial using the same case scenario.

PRACTICE

Review Assignments

Data Files needed for the Review Assignments: back.jpg, dtd_list.txt, founttxt.htm, logo. jpg, wstylestxt.css

Tom has another legacy page containing an order form that he wants you to modify so that it complies with the syntax rules for XHTML strict. The file contains some older HTML elements and syntax, so he wants you to confirm that the file is well formed and valid after you've updated it for XHTML. Figure 9-28 shows a preview of the completed Web page.

| Figure 9-28 | Wizard Works order page |

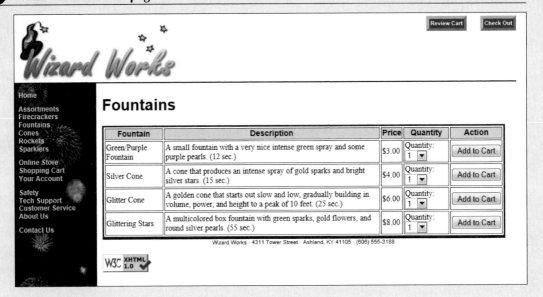

Complete the following:

1. Use your text editor to open the **founttxt.htm** and **wstylestxt.css** files from the tutorial.09\review folder included with your Data Files. Enter *your name* and *the date* in the comment sections of the files, and then save them as **fountain.htm** and **wstyles.css**, respectively.

2. Insert an XML prolog at the top of the *fountain.htm* file, setting the version number to 1.0 and the character encoding to UTF-8.

3. Below the XML prolog, insert a DOCTYPE declaration indicating that this document conforms to the XHTML 1.0 strict DTD (you can copy the code for this declaration from the *dtd_list.txt* file in the tutorial.09\review folder).

4. Set the default namespace for the document to the XHTML namespace.

5. Use a validator to test whether the document is well formed and valid under the XHTML 1.0 strict DTD.

6. Fix any errors reported by the validator. Note that when this form should have an `action` attribute equal to *http://wizardworksstore.com/cgi/cart*.

7. If any deprecated presentational attributes are found, replace them with an equivalent style added to the bottom of the *wstyles.css* style sheet. Document your new styles.

8. After the document passes XHTML 1.0 strict, add the W3C XHTML 1.0 icon to the bottom of the page directly below the `address` element. Save your changes, and then view the page in your Web browser to ensure that it still looks like Figure 9-28.

9. Submit your completed files to your instructor, in either printed or electronic form, as requested.

Use the skills you learned in this tutorial to convert an online menu to XHTML format.

APPLY

Case Problem 1

Data Files needed for this Case Problem: breakfst.jpg, breaktxt.htm, dinner.jpg, dinnrtxt.htm, dtd_list.txt, kdstylestxt.css, lunch.jpg, lunchtxt.htm, tan.jpg

Kelsey's Diner   You've been asked to update legacy Web pages for Kelsey's Diner, a popular restaurant in Worcester, Massachusetts. Cindy Towser, the manager of the diner, would like the pages that display her breakfast, lunch, and dinner menus updated so that they comply with XHTML standards under the strict DTD. A preview of one menu page is shown in Figure 9-29.

| Figure 9-29 | Kelsey's Diner breakfast menu |

Complete the following:

1. Use your text editor to open the **breaktxt.htm**, **lunchtxt.htm**, **dinnrtxt.htm**, and **kdstylestxt.css** files from the tutorial.09\case1 folder. Enter *your name* and *the date* in the comment section of each file, and then save the files as **breakfast.htm**, **lunch.htm**, **dinner.htm**, and **kdstyles.css**, respectively, in the same folder.

2. Go to the **breakfast.htm** file in your text editor, and then insert an XML prolog at the top of the file. Set the XML version to 1.0 and the encoding type to UTF-8.

3. After the XML prolog, insert a DOCTYPE declaration for the XHTML 1.0 strict DTD.

4. Set the default namespace of the document to the XHTML namespace.

5. Add a link to the **kdstyles.css** style sheet.

6. Test the file on a validator and make a note of the errors reported. Here are some possible ways to fix the errors:

   - Convert any deprecated presentational attributes to a CSS style, adding the style to the *kdstyles.css* style sheet file.
   - Correct syntax errors for one-sided tags.
   - Replace any prohibited attributes (such as the `name` attribute) with an equivalent valid attribute.
   - The `map` element requires both an `id` and a `name` attribute to be valid under the strict DTD and to work under all major browsers.

7. Save your changes to the **breakfast.htm** file, and then continue to test the file until it passes the XHTML 1.0 strict validation test.

8. Add the icon that indicates the page passes the DTD for XHTML 1.0 strict in a paragraph directly below the definition list.

9. Repeat Steps 2 through 8 for the **lunch.htm** and **dinner.htm** files.

10. Test the completed Web site on your browser, and then verify that you can move among the pages by clicking the image map links in the logo at the top of the page.

11. Submit your completed files to your instructor, in either printed or electronic form, as requested.

Use the skills you've learned in this tutorial to update an old product page.

APPLY

Case Problem 2

Data Files needed for this Case Problem: cassini.jpg, dtd_list.txt, gargtxt.htm, gbar.jpg, glogo.jpg, maa.jpg, maah5txt.css, maah5txt.htm, maatxt.css, modernizr-1.5.js, oneil.jpg

Middle Age Arts   Nicole Swanson is the head of the Web site team at Middle Age Arts, a company that creates and sells replicas of historical European works of art for home and garden use. She has recently started a project to update the old HTML code in the site's many pages. She's asked you to update the page describing the company's collection of decorative gargoyles. She wants the page to comply with XHTML 1.0 strict standards. Figure 9-30 shows a preview of the completed Web page.

Figure 9-30   **Gargoyle Collection page**

Complete the following:

1. Use your text editor to open the **gargtxt.htm** and **maatxt.css** files from the tutorial.09\case2 folder included with your Data Files. Enter *your name* and *the date* in the comment sections, and then save the files as **gargoyle.htm** and **maa.css**, respectively.

2. Go to the **gargoyle.htm** file in your text editor, and then insert an XML prolog at the top of the file. Use the standard attribute defaults for an XHTML file.

3. After the XML prolog, insert a DOCTYPE declaration for the XHTML 1.0 strict DTD.

4. Set the default namespace of the document to the XHTML namespace.

5. Link the file to the **maa.css** style sheet.

6. Test the file in the validator. Fix the errors as follows:

   - Convert the attributes for the `body` element into style rules in the *maa.css* style sheet. (Hint: The `link`, `alink`, and `vlink` attributes can be replaced with pseudo-classes to set the colors of all hyperlinks, active links, and visited links in the Web page, respectively, to white.)
   - Create a style rule in the *maa.css* style sheet to set the background color and width of the different tables and table cells in the page layout. (Hint: Use the id values to identify the different table cells and embedded tables.)
   - Use proper syntax for any empty elements.
   - Create style rules to set the color and text alignment of the `h4` elements in the document.
   - Ensure that all two-sided tags are properly closed.
   - Replace the use of the `align` attribute with the `float` style for the two inline images aligned on the right margin of their container.
   - Remove all deprecated elements and attributes.

7. Continue to validate your document until it passes the validation test for XHTML 1.0 strict. Once it passes, add an icon indicating that it has passed in a paragraph at the bottom of the file.

8. Legacy pages often used tables to define the page layout. Nicole suggests that you also create another version of this page in HTML5 that employs only CSS layout styles. Open the **maah5txt.htm** and **maah5txt.css** files in your text editor. Enter *your name* and *the date* in the comment section of each file, and then save them as **maah5.htm** and **maah5.css**, respectively.

9. As best you can, recreate the appearance of the Gargoyle Collection Web page in HTML5 format and using CSS styles.

⊕ EXPLORE   10. Write a summary comparing the structure and complexity of the document design using Web tables to the document design using HTML5 and CSS. Which one is easier to maintain and document for others?

11. Submit your completed files to your instructor, in either printed or electronic form, as requested.

Explore how to combine elements from XHTML and MathML in a single document.

CHALLENGE

Case Problem 3

Data Files needed for this Case Problem: back.jpg, math.css, mathml.txt, mhlogo.jpg, quadtxt.xhtml, side.jpg

Math High   Professor Laureen Cole of Coastal University, owner of the Web site Math High, has been studying the XML vocabulary MathML and how it can be used to display mathematical equations and information. She's asked you to create an XHTML document that contains elements from both XHTML and MathML. A preview of the page that you'll create is shown in Figure 9-31.

Figure 9-31   Math High page

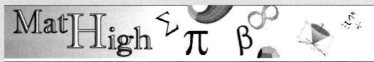

Basic Math

Pre-Algebra

Algebra

Geometry

Trigonometry

Statistics

Calculus

Advanced Math

Math Games

Puzzles

Math History

Solving the Quadratic Equation

A **quadratic equation** is a polynomial equation of the second degree, having the general form:

$$ax^2 + bx + c = 0$$

The letters a, b and c are called coefficients: a is the coefficient of x^2, b is the coefficient of x, and c is the constant coefficient. A quadratic equation has two complex roots (i.e., solutions for the unknown term x). In some cases, these roots can have the same value. The roots can also belong to the realm of **complex numbers**. The values of the roots can be computed using the **quadratic formula** as shown below:

$$x = \frac{-b \pm \sqrt{b^2 - 4ac}}{2a}$$

For example, the roots of the quadratic equation

$$2x^2 - 14x + 20 = 0$$

can be determined by first substituting 2 for a, -14 for b, and 20 for c

$$x = \frac{14 \pm \sqrt{(-14)^2 - 4(2)(20)}}{2(2)}$$

and then solving the expression, which gives the roots of the equation as either $x = 5$ or $x = 2$.

Created using MathML and XHTML

Complete the following:

1. Use your text editor to open the **quadtxt.xhtml** file from the tutorial.09\case3 folder included with your Data Files. Enter *your name* and *the date* in the comment section of the file. Save the file as **quad.xhtml** in the same folder.

2. Add an XML prolog at the top of the document.

⊕ EXPLORE 3. Within the `html` element, insert two namespace declarations: one for the XHTML namespace and the other for the MathML namespace (*http://www.w3.org/1998/ math/MathML*). Make XHTML the default namespace for the document and make MathML a local namespace with the prefix *m*.

⊕ EXPLORE 4. Scroll down the document to the paragraph element with the id *eq1*. Within this paragraph, copy and paste the MathML elements from the *mathml.txt* file for the first equation.

5. Repeat Step 4 for the paragraphs with ids from *eq2* through *eq4*.

⊕ EXPLORE 6. For each MathML element, add the MathML namespace prefix *m* to indicate that these elements are part of the MathML vocabulary.

7. Close the file, saving your changes.

⊕ EXPLORE 8. Open the **quad.xhtml** file in a browser that provides built-in support for MathML. At the time of this writing, that includes the Firefox and Opera browsers. Verify that your page resembles that shown in Figure 9-31.

9. Submit your completed files to your instructor, in either printed or electronic form, as requested.

RESEARCH

Test your knowledge of XHTML by creating a well-formed, valid document for an educational site.

Case Problem 4

Data Files needed for this Case Problem: address.txt, astro.txt, chem.txt, dtd_list.txt, elect.txt, eng.txt, mwslogo.gif, physics.txt

Maxwell Scientific   Maxwell Scientific is a Web site that sells science kits and educational products. Chris Todd, the head of the Web site development team, is leading an effort to update the company's Web site. He has given you some text files and graphic images. You may supplement this material with any additional files and resources at your disposal. Your job will be to develop this material into a Web site that is compliant with XHTML 1.0 strict standards. To ensure that the completed Web page is both well formed and valid, he wants you to test it on a validator before submitting it to him.

Complete the following:

1. Use your text editor to create the following files in the tutorial.09\case4 folder: **astro.htm**, **chem.htm**, **elect.htm**, **eng.htm**, **physics.htm**, and **mw.css**. Include *your name* and *the date* in a comment section for each file, along with a description of the purpose of the file.

2. Use the content from the *address.txt*, *astro.txt*, *chem.txt*, *elect.txt*, *eng.txt*, and *physics.txt* files to create the content of each Web page. The design of the Web site and each individual page is up to you. Store any styles you create in the *mw.css* style sheet file you created in Step 1.

3. Each page should be designed as an XHTML 1.0 strict document. Include all necessary declarations and namespaces.

4. Test all of your pages against a validator to ensure that each page fulfills the requirements of the XHTML 1.0 strict DTD.

5. Submit your completed files to your instructor, in either printed or electronic form, as requested.

ENDING DATA FILES

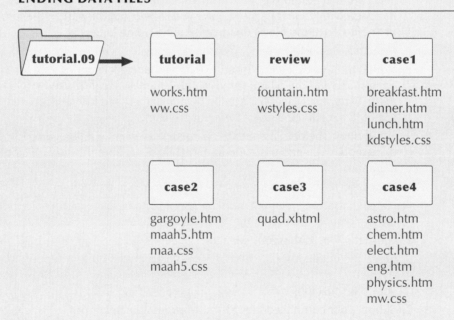

tutorial.09 →

tutorial
works.htm
ww.css

review
fountain.htm
wstyles.css

case1
breakfast.htm
dinner.htm
lunch.htm
kdstyles.css

case2
gargoyle.htm
maah5.htm
maa.css
maah5.css

case3
quad.xhtml

case4
astro.htm
chem.htm
elect.htm
eng.htm
physics.htm
mw.css

Programming with JavaScript

Hiding E-Mail Addresses on a Library Web Site

Case | *Monroe Public Library*

Kate Howard is the head of technical services at Monroe Public Library in Monroe, Ohio. One of her jobs is to maintain the library's Web site. In previous years, the library has made its staff directory, including e-mail links to library employees, available online. Kate thinks that this is an important part of making the library more accessible to everyone. However, Kate has become concerned about the security issues involved with making the staff's e-mail addresses so accessible. Kate is aware that e-mail addresses can be scanned from an HTML file and used to send junk mail to the recipients.

She would like to have some way of scrambling the e-mail addresses within the HTML code while still making them viewable when the page is rendered by a Web browser. Kate has approached you for help in writing a program to accomplish this.

STARTING DATA FILES

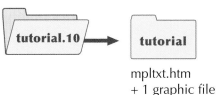

tutorial.10 ➝

tutorial
mpltxt.htm
+ 1 graphic file
+ 1 style sheet
+ 2 JavaScript files

review
mpl2txt.htm
+ 11 graphic files
+ 1 style sheet
+ 2 JavaScript files

case1
skymaptxt.htm
+ 26 graphic files
+ 1 style sheet
+ 2 JavaScript files

case2
fronttxt.htm
+ 7 graphic files
+ 1 style sheet
+ 3 JavaScript files

case3
todaytxt.htm
+ 1 graphic file
+ 2 style sheets
+ 7 HTML files
+ 2 JavaScript files

case4
1 graphic file
2 JavaScript files

SESSION 10.1 VISUAL OVERVIEW

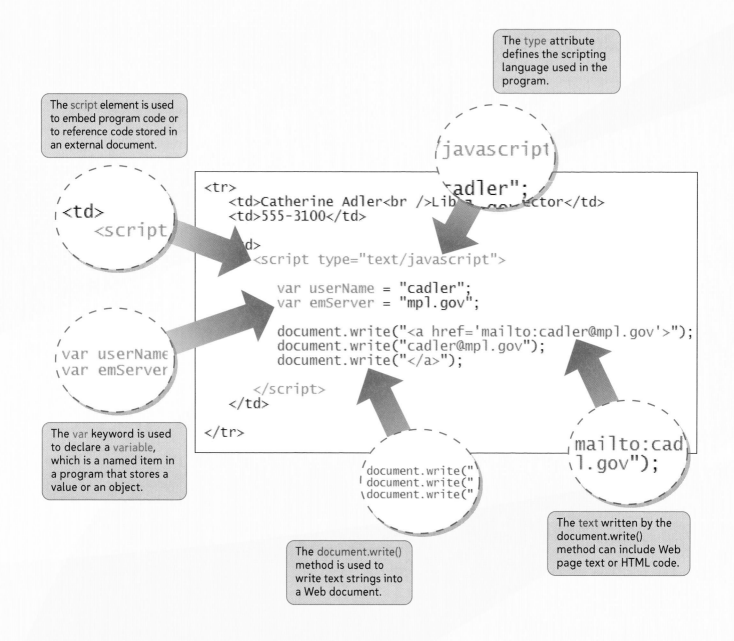

The script element is used to embed program code or to reference code stored in an external document.

The type attribute defines the scripting language used in the program.

The var keyword is used to declare a variable, which is a named item in a program that stores a value or an object.

The document.write() method is used to write text strings into a Web document.

The text written by the document.write() method can include Web page text or HTML code.

```
<tr>
    <td>Catherine Adler<br />Library Director</td>
    <td>555-3100</td>
    <td>
    <script type="text/javascript">

    var userName = "cadler";
    var emServer = "mpl.gov";

    document.write("<a href='mailto:cadler@mpl.gov'>");
    document.write("cadler@mpl.gov");
    document.write("</a>");

    </script>
    </td>
</tr>
```

USING JAVASCRIPT VARIABLES

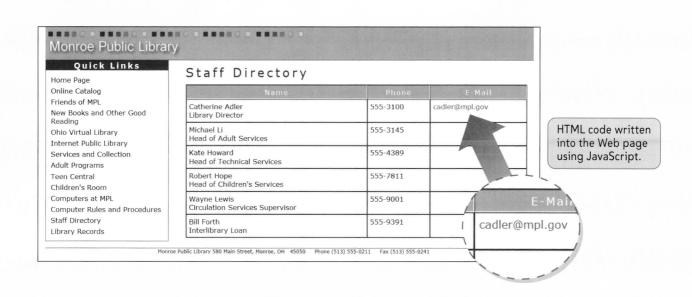

Monroe Public Library

Quick Links

Home Page
Online Catalog
Friends of MPL
New Books and Other Good Reading
Ohio Virtual Library
Internet Public Library
Services and Collection
Adult Programs
Teen Central
Children's Room
Computers at MPL
Computer Rules and Procedures
Staff Directory
Library Records

Staff Directory

Name	Phone	E-Mail
Catherine Adler Library Director	555-3100	cadler@mpl.gov
Michael Li Head of Adult Services	555-3145	
Kate Howard Head of Technical Services	555-4389	
Robert Hope Head of Children's Services	555-7811	
Wayne Lewis Circulation Services Supervisor	555-9001	
Bill Forth Interlibrary Loan	555-9391	

Monroe Public Library 580 Main Street, Monroe, OH 45050   Phone (513) 555-0211   Fax (513) 555-0241

HTML code written into the Web page using JavaScript.

E-Mail

cadler@mpl.gov

Introducing JavaScript

You meet with Kate to discuss her goals regarding the e-mail addresses on the library's staff directory page. She shows you the content and page layout she has created.

To view Kevin's page:

▶ **1.** Use your text editor to open **mpltxt.htm** from the tutorial.10\tutorial folder included with your Data Files. Enter *your name* and *the date* in the comment section at the top of the file and save the file as **mpl.htm** in the same folder.

▶ **2.** Take some time to scroll through the document to become familiar with its contents and structure.

▶ **3.** Open **mpl.htm** in your Web browser. Figure 10-1 shows the initial appearance of the Web page.

| Figure 10-1 | Monroe Public Library staff page |

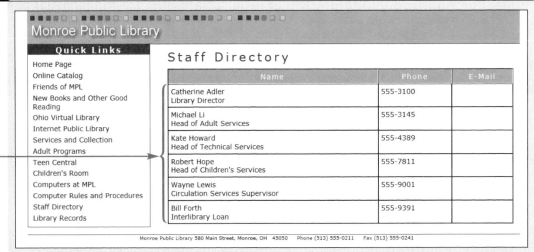

Note that the staff directory table contains a column in which Kate wants to insert a link to each employee's e-mail address; right now the column is empty.

Although the staff directory page has proven invaluable in making library employees more responsive to the needs of the public, Kate is concerned about the security risks of putting e-mail addresses in the directory. Kate is most concerned about spam. **Spam** is essentially junk e-mail—messages that advertise products and services not requested by the recipient. A **spammer** is a person who sends these unsolicited e-mails, sometimes in bulk e-mailings involving tens of thousands of recipients. Aside from the annoyance of receiving unsolicited e-mail, spam costs companies thousands—and sometimes millions—of dollars each year by consuming valuable resources on mail servers and other devices forced to process the messages. Spam also reduces productivity by forcing employees to wade through numerous spam messages every day to find messages that are truly relevant. Even if your spam filter hides unwanted e-mails from you, their mere existence costs millions of dollars each year in the time spent by mail servers processing them.

One way that spammers collect e-mail addresses is through the use of e-mail harvesters. An **e-mail harvester** is a program that scans documents, usually Web pages, looking for e-mail addresses. Any e-mail address a harvester finds within the code of a document is added to a database, which can then be used for sending spam. Thus, by putting the staff's e-mail addresses in the HTML code for the staff directory, as in Figure 10-2, Kate would also be making them available to e-mail harvesters.

Figure 10-2   **Viewing e-mail addresses in the HTML file**

e-mail addresses in the staff directory

```
<tr>
   <td>Catherine Adler<br />Library Director</td>
   <td>555-3100</td>
   <td><a href="mailto:cadler@mpl.gov">cadler@mpl.gov</a>
   </td>
</tr>
<tr>
   <td>Michael Li<br />Head of Adult Services</td>
   <td>555-3145</td>
   <td><a href="mailto:mikeli@mpl.gov">mikeli@mpl.gov</a>
   </td>
</tr>
<tr>
   <td>Kate Howard<br />Head of Technical Services</td>
   <td>555-4389</td>
   <td><a href="mailto:khoward@mpl.gov">khoward@mpl.gov</a>
   </td>
</tr>
```

Kate would like you to scramble the e-mail addresses so that they don't appear within the Web page code; however, as shown in Figure 10-3, she'd like the e-mail addresses to be unscrambled when a browser loads and renders the page for a user. This mechanism will thwart most e-mail harvesters examining the document's HTML code while making the addresses available to users viewing the page on the Web. Note that some e-mail harvesters can still view both the underlying code and the page as they are rendered by a browser, so the proposed scrambling method will not be 100% effective. However, because this technique will thwart many e-mail harvesters, Kate accepts it as a compromise solution.

Figure 10-3   **Scrambling e-mail addresses**

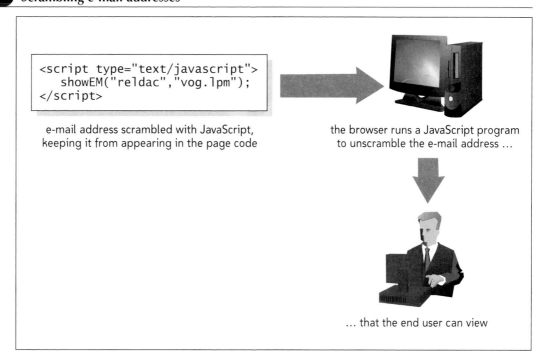

```
<script type="text/javascript">
   showEM("reldac","vog.lpm");
</script>
```

e-mail address scrambled with JavaScript, keeping it from appearing in the page code

the browser runs a JavaScript program to unscramble the e-mail address ...

... that the end user can view

Neither HTML nor XHTML has features that allow you to scramble and unscramble the e-mail addresses from Kate's staff directory. This is not a standard function of Web browsers either. Therefore, you'll have to write a program to do this. Kate doesn't want library patrons to have to download any special applications; she wants the scrambling and unscrambling to happen behind the scenes of the library Web page. After some discussion, you decide that JavaScript is well suited to this task. You'll start on this project by first finding out just what JavaScript is and how to use it.

Server-Side and Client-Side Programming

Programming on the Web comes in two types: server-side programming and client-side programming. In **server-side programming**, a program is placed on the server that hosts a Web site. The program is then used to modify the contents and structure of Web pages. In some cases, users can interact with the program, requesting that specific information be displayed on a page, but the interaction is done remotely from the user to the server. See Figure 10-4.

Figure 10-4	Server-side programming

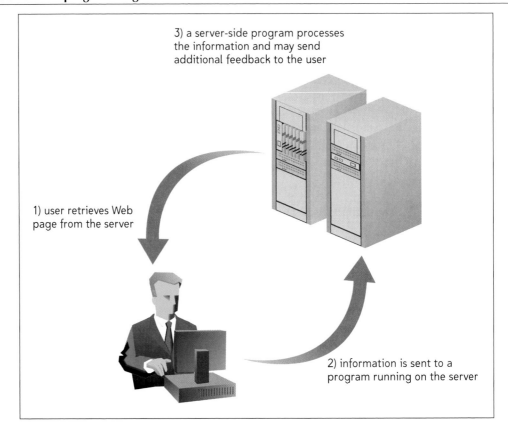

3) a server-side program processes the information and may send additional feedback to the user

1) user retrieves Web page from the server

2) information is sent to a program running on the server

There are advantages and disadvantages to this approach. A program running on a server can be connected to a database containing information not usually accessible to end users, enabling them to perform tasks not available on their own computers. This enables Web pages to support such features as online banking, credit card transactions, and discussion groups. However, server-side programs use Web server resources, and in some cases a server's system administrator might place limitations on access to server-side programs to prevent users from continually accessing the server and potentially overloading the system. If the system is overloaded, an end user might have to sit through long delays as the server-side program handles multiple requests for information and action.

Client-side programming solves many of these problems by running programs on the user's own computer rather than remotely off the server. See Figure 10-5.

Figure 10-5   Client-side programming

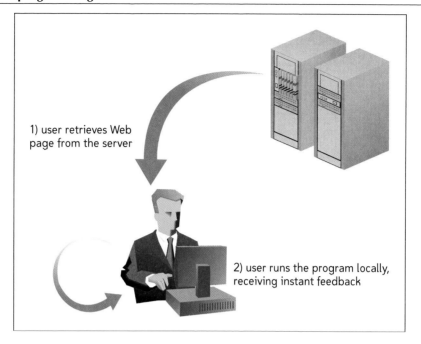

1) user retrieves Web page from the server

2) user runs the program locally, receiving instant feedback

Computing is thereby distributed so that the server is not overloaded with program-related requests. Client-side programs also tend to be more responsive because users do not have to wait for data to be sent over the Internet to a Web server. However, client-side programs can never completely replace server-side programming. For example, tasks such as running a search or processing a purchase order must be run from a central server because only the server contains the database needed to complete these types of operations.

In many cases, a combination of server-side and client-side programming is used. For example, Web forms typically use client-side programs to validate a user's entries—such as ensuring that all address information has been completely entered—and use server-side programs to submit the validated form for further processing—such as sending a purchase order to a central database. See Figure 10-6.

Figure 10-6 Combining client-side and server-side programming

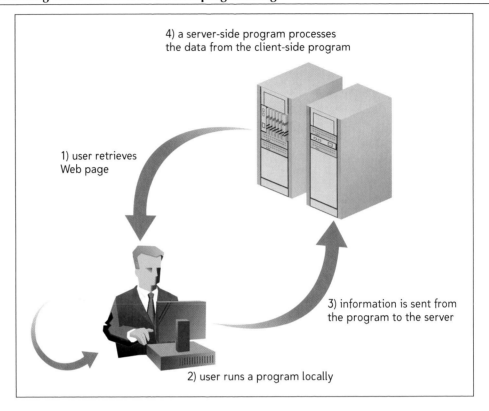

In this tutorial you'll work only with client-side programming. However, it's important to be aware that in many cases, a complete Web programming environment includes both client-side and server-side elements.

The Development of JavaScript

Several programming languages can be run on the client side. One popular client-side programming language is Java in which code is stored within stand-alone programs known as **Java applets**. However, creating a Java applet required access to the Java Development Kit (JDK), so nonprogrammers found it difficult to write their own applets.

Another client-side programming language is **JavaScript**, which despite in similarity in name, differs markedly from Java in several important ways. Java is a **compiled language**, meaning that the program code must be submitted to a compiler that manipulates it, translating the code into a more basic language that machines can understand. For Java, this compiled code is the Java applet. Therefore, to write and run a program written in a compiled language, you need both the compiler and an application or operating system that can run the compiled code.

JavaScript, on the other hand, is an **interpreted language**, meaning that the program code is executed directly without compiling. You need only two things to use JavaScript: 1) a text editor to write the JavaScript commands, and 2) a Web browser to run the commands and display the results. This means that JavaScript code can be inserted directly into an HTML file, or placed in a separate text file that is linked to a Web page. Figure 10-7 summarizes some of the key differences between Java and JavaScript.

| Figure 10-7 | Comparing Java and JavaScript |

Java	JavaScript
A compiled language	An interpreted language
Requires the JDK (Java Development Kit) to create an applet	Requires a text editor
Requires a Java virtual machine or interpreter to run an applet	Requires a browser that can interpret JavaScript code
Applet files are distinct from HTML files	Programs can be embedded within HTML files
Source code is hidden from users	Source code is accessible to users
Powerful, requiring programming knowledge and experience	Simpler, requiring less programming knowledge and experience
Secure; programs cannot write content to a hard disk	Secure; programs cannot write content to a hard disk; however, there are more security holes than in Java
Compiled code runs on the client side computer within an applet window	Code run on the client side computer directly within the Web browser

Through the years, JavaScript has undergone several revisions. Included with the introduction of HTML5 are several new JavaScript components and features that are not supported in older browsers. Because of this, you need to test your JavaScript code on a variety of browsers and platforms in the same way you test your HTML and CSS code.

Working with the `script` Element

A JavaScript program can be placed directly in an HTML file or it can be saved in an external text file. Placing JavaScript code in a Web page file means that users need to retrieve only one file from the server. In addition, because the code and the page it affects are both within the same file, it can be easier to locate and fix programming errors. However, if you place the code in a separate file, the programs you write can be shared by the different pages on your Web site in the same way that an external style sheet can be shared among several Web pages. In this tutorial, you'll work with JavaScript code entered into an HTML file as well as code stored in an external file. You'll first examine how to insert JavaScript code directly into an HTML file.

Creating a `script` Element

Scripts can be embedded anywhere within an HTML file using the `script` element

```
<script type="mime-type">
   script commands
</script>
```

where *mime-type* defines the language in which the script is written and *script commands* represents commands written in the scripting language. The **type** attribute is required for XHTML documents and should be used for HTML5 documents as well. The MIME type for JavaScript programs is `text/javascript`, meaning that to embed a JavaScript program, you would use the following form:

```
<script type="text/javascript">
   JavaScript commands
</script>
```

In earlier versions of HTML, the `language` attribute was used in place of the `type` attribute to indicate the script language. Thus if you are working with legacy pages you might see the following `script` element used to embed a JavaScript program:

```
<script language="JavaScript">
   JavaScript commands
</script>
```

The `language` attribute has been deprecated and is not supported in either HTML5 or XHTML, so you should use the `type` attribute in its place if you want to conform to the current standards.

Note that the `script` element can be used with programming languages other than JavaScript. Other client-side scripting languages are identified by using a different value for the type attribute. For example, if you use VBScript from Microsoft, the MIME type is text/vbscript. You won't use VBScript in this tutorial.

REFERENCE

Embedding a Script

- To place a `script` element in a Web page, insert the two-sided tag

  ```
  <script type="mime-type">
     script commands
  </script>
  ```

  where *mime-type* defines the language in which the script is written and *script commands* represents commands written in the scripting language.
- For JavaScript programs, set `mime-type` to `text/javascript`.

Placing the `script` Element

When a browser encounters a `script` element within a file, it treats any lines within the element as commands to be run, processing the commands in the order in which they appear within the file. There is no limit to the number of `script` elements that you can use within a Web page. Scripts can be placed in either the head section or the body section of a document. When placed in the body section, a browser interprets and runs them as it loads the different elements of the Web page. Although a single page can contain many `script` elements, the browser still works with them as a single unit. As a result, JavaScript content that is placed in one `script` element can be referenced within other `script` elements in the HTML file.

Writing a JavaScript Statement

Now that you've reviewed some of the basic concepts surrounding JavaScript, you'll examine how to enter JavaScript code. Every JavaScript program consists of a series of statements. Each **statement**—also known as a **command**—is a single line that indicates an action for the browser to take. A statement should end in a semicolon, employing the following syntax

```
JavaScript statement;
```

where *JavaScript statement* is the code that the browser runs. The semicolon is the official way of notifying the browser that it has reached the end of the statement. Most browsers are very forgiving and still interpret most statements correctly even if you neglect to include the ending semicolon. However, it is good programming practice to include the semicolons, and some browsers require them.

JavaScript and XML Parsers

Embedding JavaScript code within an XHTML file can lead to problems because XHTML parsers attempt to process the symbols in JavaScript code. Character symbols such as angle brackets (< >) and the ampersand (&) are often used in JavaScript programs and can lead to a page being rejected by an XHTML parser. To avoid this problem, you can place your JavaScript code within a CDATA section as follows:

```
<script type="text/javascript">
<![CDATA[
   JavaScript code
]]>
</script>
```

where *JavaScript code* is the code that makes up the JavaScript program. The CDATA section marks the text of the JavaScript code as data that should not be processed by XHTML parsers. Unfortunately, CDATA sections are not well supported by current browsers.

Another alternative is not to embed your scripts within XHTML files at all, but instead to place them in external files. This practice has the added advantage of separating program code from page content. If you need to create valid XHTML documents, this is probably the best solution.

Writing Output to a Web Document

The first JavaScript program you'll add to Kate's document is a program that writes the text of an e-mail address into the Web page. Although you could enter the e-mail address directly, you'll use this opportunity to experiment with JavaScript. You'll also build on this simple statement as you progress through the rest of the tutorial. You'll insert the e-mail address for Catherine Adler as the first entry in the staff directory. Her e-mail address is *cadler@mpl.gov*. To write this text to the Web document, you'll insert the following statement:

```
<script type="text/javascript">
   document.write("cadler@mpl.gov");
</script>
```

The document.write() statement tells browsers to send the text string *cadler@mpl.gov* to the Web page document. To see how your browser applies this command, you'll enter the script element and command into Kate's mpl.htm file now.

To write text to the Web page using JavaScript:

1. Return to the **mpl.htm** file in your text editor.

2. Locate the table cell after the entry for Catherine Adler and insert the following code, as shown in Figure 10-8:

```
<script type="text/javascript">
   document.write("cadler@mpl.gov");
</script>
```

Figure 10-8   **Embedding a script element**

```
<tr>
    <td>Catherine Adler<br />Library Director</td>
    <td>555-3100</td>
    <td>
        <script type="text/javascript">
            document.write("cadler@mpl.gov");
        </script>
    </td>
</tr>
```

script to write content to the Web document

3. Save your changes to the file and then reload **mpl.htm** in your Web browser. As shown in Figure 10-9, the text of Catherine's e-mail address should appear in the staff directory.

Figure 10-9   **Text generated by JavaScript**

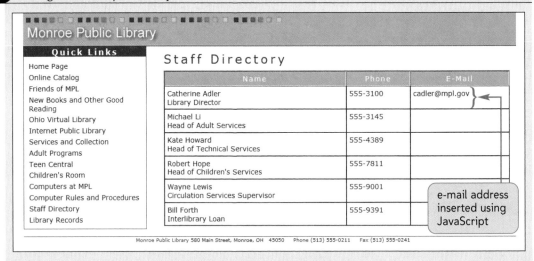

e-mail address inserted using JavaScript

Trouble? Internet Explorer might display a yellow alert bar at the top of the browser window with a warning that it has restricted access to active content for security reasons. This is done to enable users to prevent their browsers from running unwanted scripts. To run the script, click the information bar and choose Allow Blocked Content from the pop-up menu, and then click **Yes** in the dialog box that follows.

Note that the placement of the `script` element tells the browser where to place the new text. Because the `script` element is placed between the opening and closing `<td>` tags, the text generated by the script is placed there as well. In more advanced JavaScript programs you can direct your output to specific locations in the Web page document, but that's beyond the scope of this tutorial.

The `document.write()` Method

In JavaScript, many commands involve working with objects in the Web page and browser. An **object** is any item—from the browser window itself to a document displayed in the browser to an element displayed within the document. Even the mouse pointer, the window scrollbars, or a browser application itself can be treated as an object. A **method** is a process by which JavaScript manipulates or acts upon the properties of an object. The `document.write()` method, which you just used to display the e-mail text, is one of the basic ways in JavaScript to send output to a Web document. In this case, you've used the `write()` method to write new text into the `document` object. The `document.write()` method has the general syntax

```
document.write("text");
```

where *text* is a string of characters that you want written to a Web document. The text string can include HTML tags. For example, the following statement writes the text *Monroe Public Library* marked as an `h1` heading into a document:

```
document.write("<h1>Monroe Public Library</h1>");
```

When a browser encounters this statement, it places the text and the markup tags in the document and renders that text as if it had been entered directly into the HTML file.

Kate wants the e-mail addresses in the staff directory to appear as hypertext links. This requires placing the e-mail addresses within `<a>` tags and adding the `href` attribute value indicating the destination of each link. For example, the code to create a link for Catherine Adler's e-mail address is

```
<a href="mailto:cadler@mpl.gov">cadler@mpl.gov</a>
```

Writing this text string requires you to include quotation marks around the `href` attribute value. Because text strings created with the `document.write()` method must be enclosed in quotes as well, you have to place one set of quotes within another. This is done by using both single and double quotation marks. If you want to write a double quotation mark as part of the code sent to the document, you enclose the quotation marks within single quotation marks. To write single quotation marks, you enclose them within a set of double quotation marks. The type of quotation mark to be written to the Web page must always be different from the type of quotation marks that enclose it. If you try to enclose double quotes within another set of double quotes, browsers won't know where the quoted text string begins and ends. The following JavaScript code encloses the `href` attribute value in single quotes and uses double quotes to mark the entire text to be written to the Web page document:

```
document.write("<a href='mailto:cadler@mpl.gov'>");
document.write("cadler@mpl.gov");
document.write("</a>");
```

Note that this example places the entire code into three separate `document.write()` commands. Although you could use one long text string, it might be more difficult to read and to type without making a mistake. A browser treats these consecutive commands as one long string of text to be written into the document.

REFERENCE

Writing to a Web Page

- To write text to a Web page with JavaScript, use the method

  ```
  document.write("text")
  ```

  where *text* is the HTML code to be written to the Web page.

You're ready to add the code for the link to Catherine Adler's e-mail address.

To write the e-mail link for Catherine Adler:

▶ **1.** Return to the **mpl.htm** file in your text editor.

▶ **2.** Directly after the opening `<script>` element you added earlier, insert the following command:

```
document.write("<a href='mailto:cadler@mpl.gov'>");
```

▶ **3.** Directly before the closing `</script>` tag, insert the following command:

```
document.write("</a>");
```

Figure 10-10 shows the revised code in the file.

Figure 10-10　**Inserting several document.write() commands**

```
<tr>
    <td>Catherine Adler<br />Library Director</td>
    <td>555-3100</td>
    <td>
        <script type="text/javascript">
            document.write("<a href='mailto:cadler@mpl.gov'>");
            document.write("cadler@mpl.gov");
            document.write("</a>");
        </script>
    </td>
</tr>
```

▶ **4.** Save your changes and then reopen **mpl.htm** in your Web browser.

▶ **5.** Hover your mouse pointer over the e-mail address to verify that it is a link. As shown in Figure 10-11, the link to the e-mail address should appear in the browser's status bar.

Figure 10-11　**Viewing an e-mail link**

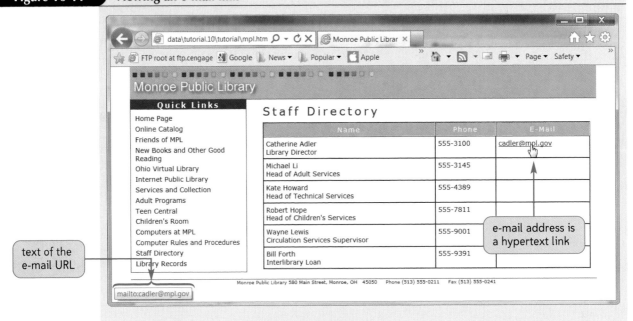

Trouble? If the link does not appear, verify that you included the opening and closing quotation marks in the JavaScript commands you just entered.

Understanding JavaScript Syntax

Besides always including semicolons at the end of each statement, there are some other syntax rules you should keep in mind when writing JavaScript statements. JavaScript is case sensitive, so you must pay attention to whether or not letters are capitalized. For example, the following statements are not equivalent as far as JavaScript is concerned:

```
document.write("</a>");
Document.write("</a>");
```

The first command writes the HTML tag `</a>` to a Web page document. The second command is not recognized by browsers as a legitimate command and results in an error message. Figure 10-12 shows the error message generated by the Internet Explorer browser. The browser does not recognize the word `Document` (as opposed to `document`) and so cannot process the command. You'll examine how to handle this type of error later in this tutorial.

Figure 10-12	Error message resulting from improper case

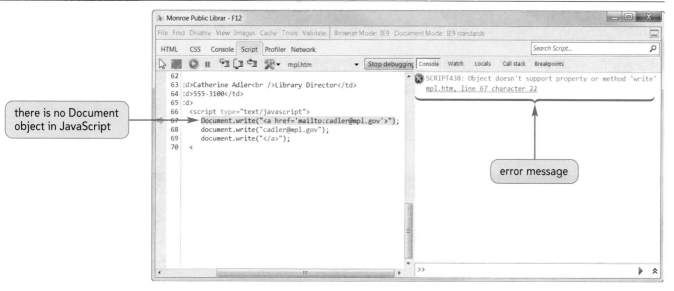

there is no Document object in JavaScript

error message

Like HTML, JavaScript ignores most occurrences of extra white space, so you can indent your code to make it easier to read. You can see examples of this in Figure 10-10, where the newly entered statements are indented several spaces to make the commands stand out from the opening and closing `<script>` tags.

However, unlike HTML, you must be careful about line breaks occurring within a statement. A line break cannot be placed within the name of a JavaScript command or within a quoted text string without causing an error in the code. For example, the following line break is not allowed:

```
document.write("<a href='mailto:cadler@mpl.gov'>
cadler@mpl.gov
</a>");
```

It is good practice not to break a statement into several lines if you can avoid it. If you must break a long statement into several lines, you can indicate that the statement continues on the next line using a backslash, as follows:

```
document.write("<a href='mailto:cadler@mpl.gov'> \
cadler@mpl.gov \
</a>");
```

If the line break occurs within a quoted text string, you can also break the string into several distinct text strings placed over several lines by adding a plus symbol (+) at the end of each line, as follows:

```
document.write("<a href='mailto:cadler@mpl.gov'>" +
"cadler@mpl.gov" +
"</a>");
```

The + symbol used in this command combines several text strings into a single text string. However, breaking a single statement into several lines is usually not recommended because of the possibility of introducing errors into the code. It should be done only with very long and complicated statements.

INSIGHT

Supporting Non-JavaScript Browsers

For browsers that don't support scripts or that have their support for client-side scripts disabled, you can specify alternative content using the noscript element

```
<noscript>
    alternative content
</noscript>
```

where *alternative content* is the content a browser should display in place of accessing and running the script. For example, the following code displays a text message indicating that the page requires the use of JavaScript:

```
<script type="text/javascript">
    JavaScript statements
</script>
<noscript>
    <p>This page requires JavaScript. Please turn on JavaScript
        if your browser supports it and reload the page.
    </p>
</noscript>
```

Browsers that support client-side scripts and have that support enabled ignore the content of the noscript element. Note that the noscript element is not supported under XHTML strict.

Working with Variables

Because you used a specific text string with the document.write(), the code did little more than what you could have accomplished by entering the e-mail link directly into an HTML tag. JavaScript is much more powerful and versatile when used in conjunction with variables. A **variable** is a named item in a program that stores a data value—such as a number or text string—or an object—such as a part of the Web document or browser. Variables are useful because they can store information created in one part of a program and use that information elsewhere. Variable values can also change as a program runs, enabling the program to display different values under varying conditions.

Declaring a Variable

You introduce variables in your code by declaring them. **Declaring** a variable tells the JavaScript interpreter to reserve memory space for the variable. To declare a variable you use the var keyword

```
var variable;
```

where *variable* is the name assigned to the variable. For example, the following statement creates a variable named *emLink*:

```
var emLink;
```

You can declare multiple variables by entering the variable names in a comma-separated list. The following statement declares three variables named emLink, userName, and emServer:

```
var emLink, userName, emServer;
```

JavaScript imposes the following limits on variable names:

- The first character must be either a letter or an underscore character (_).
- The remaining characters can be letters, numbers, or underscore characters.
- Variable names cannot contain spaces.
- You cannot use words that JavaScript has reserved for other purposes; for example, you cannot name a variable document.

TIP

To avoid programming errors, use a consistent pattern for case in variable names.

Like other aspects of the JavaScript language, variable names are case sensitive. The variable names emLink and emlink represent two different variables. One common programming mistake is to forget this important fact and to use uppercase and lowercase letters interchangeably in variable names.

Assigning a Value to a Variable

Once a variable has been created or declared, you can assign it a value. The statement to assign a value to a variable is

```
variable = value;
```

where *variable* is the variable name and *value* is the value assigned to the variable. For example, the following statement stores the text string *cadler* in the *userName* variable:

```
userName = "cadler";
```

You can combine the variable declaration and the assignment of a value in a single statement. The following statements declare the userName and emServer variables, and set their initial values:

```
var userName = "cadler", emServer = "mpl.gov";
```

TIP

To make your code easier to interpret, place all of your variable declarations at the beginning of your program.

Note that declaring a variable with the **var** statement is not required in JavaScript. The first time you use a variable, JavaScript creates the variable in computer memory. The following statement both creates the director variable (if it has not already been declared in a previous statement) and assigns it an initial value:

```
director = "Catherine Adler";
```

Although it's not required, it's considered good programming style to use a **var** statement to declare all of your variables. Doing so helps you keep track of the variables a program uses and also makes it easier for others to read and interpret your code.

Declaring a JavaScript Variable

REFERENCE

- To declare a JavaScript variable, use the statement

  `var variable;`

  where `variable` is the name assigned to the variable.
- To declare a JavaScript variable and set its initial value, use

  `var variable = value;`

  where `value` is the initial value of the variable.

Using what you've learned about variables, you're ready to add two variables to the script you started earlier. The first variable, userName, will store the text string *cadler*, which is Catherine Adler's username on the library's mail server. The second variable, emServer, will store the text string *mpl.gov*, which is the domain name of the mail server. Later you'll revise this code to place different values in these variables, but you'll start with these two fixed values. By breaking up Catherine Adler's e-mail address into two parts, you'll make it easier to hide the e-mail address from e-mail harvesters later on.

To create two JavaScript variables:

▶ **1.** Return to the **mpl.htm** file in your text editor.

▶ **2.** Locate the `script` element you created earlier. Directly below the opening `<script>` tag, insert the following code, as shown in Figure 10-13:

```
var userName = "cadler";
var emServer = "mpl.gov";
```

Figure 10-13   Declaring JavaScript variables

```html
<tr>
    <td>Catherine Adler<br />Library Director</td>
    <td>555-3100</td>
    <td>
        <script type="text/javascript">
            var userName = "cadler";
            var emServer = "mpl.gov";

            document.write("<a href='mailto:cadler@mpl.gov'>");
            document.write("cadler@mpl.gov");
            document.write("</a>");
        </script>
    </td>
</tr>
```

▶ **3.** Save your changes to the file.

Working with Data Types

So far, the examples you've explored have used variables that store text strings. However, JavaScript variables can store different types of information. The type of information stored in a variable is referred to as its **data type**. JavaScript supports the following data types:

- numeric value
- text string
- Boolean value
- null value

A **numeric value** is any number, such as 13, 22.5, or -3.14159. Numbers can also be expressed in scientific notation, such as 5.1E2 for the value 5.1×10^2 (or 510). Numeric values are specified without any quotation marks. Thus, if you wished to store the value 2007 in the year variable, you would use the statement

```
year = 2007;
```

rather than

```
year = "2007";
```

A **text string** is any group of characters, such as *Hello* or *Happy Holidays!* or *421 Sunrise Lane*. Text strings must be enclosed within either double or single quotation marks, but not a mix of both. The string value *'Hello'* is acceptable, but the string value *"Hello'* is not.

A **Boolean value** indicates the truth or falsity of a statement. There are only two Boolean values: *true* and *false*. For example, the following statement sets the value of the useSafari variable to *true* and the value of the useIE variable to *false*:

```
useSafari = true;
useIE = false;
```

Boolean values are most often used in programs that must act differently based on different conditions. The useSafari variable cited above might be used in a program that tests whether a user is running the Safari browser. If the value is set to *true*, the program might be written to run differently for the user than if the value were set to *false*.

Finally, a **null value** indicates that no value has yet been assigned to a variable. This can be done explicitly using the keyword *null* in assigning a value to a variable, as in the statement

```
emLink = null;
```

or implicitly by simply declaring the variable without assigning it a value, as follows:

```
var emLink;
```

In either case, the emLink variable would have a null value until it was assigned a value using one of the other data types.

In JavaScript, a variable's data type is always determined by the context in which it is used. This means that a variable can switch from one data type to another within a single program. In the following two statements, the Month variable starts out as a numeric variable with an initial value of 5, but then becomes a text string variable containing the text March:

```
Month = 5;
Month = "March";
```

A programming language like JavaScript, in which variables are not strictly tied to specific data types, is referred to as a **weakly typed language**. Some other programming languages, known as **strongly typed languages**, force the programmer to explicitly identify a variable's data type. In those languages, the above code would result in an error because a given variable would not be able to switch from one data type to another.

TIP

In a weakly type language, variables which are not strictly tied to specific data types are called variant data types.

A weakly typed language relieves programmers from the task of assigning data types to variables. However, this can lead to unpredictable results if you aren't careful. For example, in JavaScript the + symbol can be used with either numeric values or text strings. When used with numeric values, it returns the sum of the values; thus, the statement

```
var total = 5 + 4;
```

stores the value *9* in the total variable. When used with text strings, however, the + symbol combines the strings, meaning that the statement

```
var emLink = "cadler" + "@" + "mpl.gov";
```

stores the text string *cadler@mpl.gov* in the emLink variable. Note that when used with both a text string and a numeric value, the + symbol treats the numeric value as a text string; thus, the following statements

```
x = 5;
y = "4";
z = x+y;
```

result in the text string *54* being stored in the z variable, because the y variable stores *4* as a text string, not a number. This result is not readily apparent from the code without a prior understanding of how JavaScript handles text and numeric values. This is one of the limitations of a weakly typed language, in which data types are sometimes inferred by the rules of the language and not explicitly set by the programmer.

To see how the + symbol works with text string variables, you'll add a third variable to your script: the emLink variable, which will be used to store the complete e-mail address for Catherine Adler by combining the userName variable with the emServer variable.

To create the *emLink* variable:

1. Return to the **mpl.htm** file in your text editor.

2. Directly below the command to create the emServer variable, insert the following command, as shown in Figure 10-14:

```
var emLink = userName + "@" + emServer;
```

Figure 10-14   Creating the emLink variable

the emLink variable combines the text values of the userName and emServer variables

```
<script type="text/javascript">
    var userName = "cadler";
    var emServer = "mpl.gov";
    var emLink = userName + "@" + emServer;

    document.write("<a href='mailto:cadler@mpl.gov'>");
    document.write("cadler@mpl.gov");
    document.write("</a>");
</script>
```

3. Save your changes to the file.

After you've created a variable, you can use it in JavaScript statements in place of the value it contains. For example, the following code uses the value of the libName variable to write the text string *Monroe Public Library* to a Web page:

```
var libName = "Monroe Public Library";
document.write(libName);
```

You can also use the + symbol to combine a variable with a text string and then write the combined text string to the document. The following statements use the libName variable and the `document.write()` method to write the text string *<p>Welcome to the Monroe Library</p>* to the Web document:

```
var libName = "Monroe Library";
document.write("<p>Welcome to the " + libName + "</p>");
```

You can use the `document.write()` method with the variables you've already created to write the hypertext link for Catherine Adler's e-mail address. The code is as follows:

```
document.write("<a href='mailto:" + emLink + "'>");
document.write(emLink);
document.write("</a>");
```

If the text string *cadler@mpl.gov* is stored in the emLink variable, these commands will write the following HTML to the Web page:

```
<a href='mailto:cadler@mpl.gov'>
caldler@mpl.gov
</a>
```

Notice that the `document.write()` method nests single quotes within double quotes so that the HTML code written to the Web page places the value of the `href` attribute within a set of single quotation marks. You'll add this JavaScript code to the Web page now, replacing the previous commands.

To replace the `document.write()` commands in the script:

1. Return to the **mpl.htm** file in your text editor.

2. Replace the three `document.write()` statements in the script with the following code, as shown in Figure 10-15:

```
document.write("<a href='mailto:" + emLink + "'>");
document.write(emLink);
document.write("</a>");
```

> Make sure that you enclose single quotes within a set of double quotes so that the single quotes appear in the rendered HTML code.

Figure 10-15   **Writing the value of the emLink variable to the Web page**

```
<script type="text/javascript">
    var userName = "cadler";
    var emServer = "mpl.gov";
    var emLink = userName + "@" + emServer;

    document.write("<a href='mailto:" + emLink + "'>");
    document.write(emLink);
    document.write("</a>");
</script>
```

3. Save your changes to the file and then reload **mpl.htm** in your Web browser. The hypertext link for Catherine Adler's e-mail address should remain unchanged from what was shown earlier in Figure 10-11.

PROSKILLS

Written Communication: Writing Better JavaScript Code

In working environments, the maintenance of a program or script is often shared among several individuals. The program you write today might be the responsibility of one of your colleagues next month. Thus, an important goal in writing program code is to make it intelligible to other users so that they can easily maintain and update it. Here are some tips to help you write better JavaScript code:

- **Use consistent variable names**: One common source of error is misnamed variables. You can avoid this problem by being consistent in the use of upper- and lowercase letters in your variable names.
- **Make the code easier to read with whitespace**: Crowded commands and statements are difficult to read and edit. Use whitespace and indented text generously to make your code more legible to others.
- **Keep your lines compact**: Long text strings can wrap to new lines in your text editor, making the text difficult to read. Strive to keep your lines to 80 characters or less. When a statement doesn't fit on a single line, break it to a new line at a point that maximizes readability.
- **Comment your work**: Like HTML and CSS, JavaScript supports the use of comments. Always comment your work, documenting the purpose of each variable.
- **Declare all of your variables**: Though JavaScript is a weakly-typed language that will automatically create your variables as soon as they are used in a statement, you should still explicitly declare all of your variables at the top of your program.

As your scripts become longer and more complicated you can also simplify your code through the use of functions and external JavaScript files. You'll explore these concepts in more detail in the next session.

You've entered the initial code for the JavaScript program and learned how to work with objects, methods, and variables. In the next session you'll complete your program by working with JavaScript functions and files. You'll also learn how to use browser tools to locate and fix errors that may appear in your code.

Session 10.1 Quick Check

1. What is a client-side program? What is a server-side program?
2. What tag do you enter in your HTML code to create a `script` element for the JavaScript programming language?
3. What JavaScript command would you enter to write the following tag to a Web document?

   ```
   <h2 id="sub">Public Library</h2>
   ```

4. Why would the following command produce an error message?

   ```
   document.Write("Monroe Public Library");
   ```

5. What code should you enter in an HTML file to write the following HTML code for browsers that don't support JavaScript?

   ```
   <p><i>JavaScript required</i></p>
   ```

6. Specify the JavaScript command to declare a variable named weekday with an initial value equal to the text string *Friday*.
7. Describe two uses of the + symbol.
8. What are the four data types supported by JavaScript?
9. Specify the JavaScript command to write the code

   ```
   <img src='file' alt='' />
   ```

   to a Web page, where *file* is the value stored in the fileName variable.

SESSION 10.2 VISUAL OVERVIEW

A function is a collection of commands that performs an action or returns a value.

A function can contain parameters, which are variables associated with the function.

Single-line comments are prefaced by the // characters and are used to add comments in-line with JavaScript code.

```
function showEM(
    /*
        The showEM
        e-mail ad
```

```
(userName,emServer)

M() function displ
```

```
// rever
// rever
```

```
    The showE
    e-mail ad
    The text
    reverse
```

```
function showEM(userName,emServer) {
    /*
        The showEM() function displays a link to the user's
        e-mail address.
        The text of the user and e-mail server names are entered in
        reverse order to thwart e-mail harvesters.
    /

    userName = stringReverse(userName); // reverse the text of the userName parameter
    emServer = stringReverse(emServer); // reverse the text of the emServer parameter

    var emLink = userName + emServer; // combine the text of userName and emServer

    document.write("<a href=    to:" + emLink + "'>");
    document.write(emLink);
    document.write("</a>");
}
```

Multi-line comments are enclosed within the /* and */ symbols, and are used to add comments as blocks of text.

```
erse(userName)
erse(emServer)
```

A function can be called using the statement function(*values*), where function is the function name and *values* represents one or more values passed to the function parameters.

WRITING JAVASCRIPT FUNCTIONS

> HTML code written by calling the showEM() function.

```
<script type="text/javascript">
    showEM("reldac","vog.lpm");
</script>
```

Staff Directory

Name	Phone	E-Mail
Catherine Adler Library Director	555-3100	cadler@mpl.gov
Michael Li Head of Adult Services	555-3145	mikeli@mpl.gov
Kate Howard Head of Technical Services	555-4389	khoward@mpl.gov
Robert Hope Head of Children's Services	555-7811	rhope@mpl.gov
Wayne Lewis Circulation Services Supervisor	555-9001	wlewis@mpl.gov
Bill Forth Interlibrary Loan	555-9391	bforth@mpl.gov

Writing a JavaScript Function

So far, in writing code for the staff directory page, you've focused on the e-mail address of only one person. However, five other individuals are listed in the staff directory. If you wanted to use JavaScript to write the e-mail links for the rest of the directory, you could duplicate the code you used for Catherine Adler's entry five more times. However, JavaScript provides a simpler way of repeating multiple instances of code that share a common pattern and structure.

When you want to reuse the same JavaScript commands throughout your Web page, you store the commands in a function. A function is a collection of commands that performs an action or returns a value. Every function includes a function name that identifies it, and a set of commands that are run when the function is called. Some functions also require parameters, which are variables associated with the function. The general syntax of a JavaScript function is

```
function function_name(parameters){
    JavaScript commands
}
```

where *function_name* is the name of the function, *parameters* is a comma-separated list of variables and values used in the function, and *JavaScript commands* is the set of statements run by the function. Function names, like variable names, are case sensitive. For example, weekDay and WEEKDAY are treated as different function names. As with variable names, a function name must begin with a letter or underscore (_) and cannot contain any spaces. The following code is an example of a function named showMsg() that writes a paragraph to a Web document:

```
function showMsg() {
    document.write("<p>Welcome to the Monroe Library</p>");
}
```

Note that there are no parameters to this function, so it always writes the same text string to the Web page. However, you could store the name of the library as a parameter of the function. For example the following code stores the name of the library in the libName parameter and then references that parameter value in writing the text string to the Web page:

```
function showMsg(libName) {
    document.write("<p>Welcome to the " + libName +"</p>");
}
```

Thus, if the libName parameter contained the text string *Monroe Public Library*, then the following HTML code would be written to the Web document.

```
<p>Welcome to the Monroe Public Library</p>
```

If you alter the value of the libName parameter, the HTML code would be altered to match.

Rather than rewriting the code for generating the e-mail link for each person in the staff directory, you'll put the commands in the following showEM() function:

```
function showEM(userName, emServer) {
    var emLink = userName + "@" + emServer;
    document.write("<a href='mailto:" + emLink + "'>");
    document.write(emLink);
    document.write("</a>");
}
```

Compare the code for this function to the script you created in Figure 10-15. Note that userName and emServer variables from that earlier code appear here as parameters of the showEM() function. You'll add the showEM() function to the document head of the mpl.htm file now.

TIP

Organize your functions by placing them all within the document head rather than scattered throughout the Web page.

To insert the showEM() function:

▶ **1.** Return to the **mpl.htm** file in your text editor.

▶ **2.** Directly above the closing `</head>` tag, insert the following `script` element and function, as shown in Figure 10-16:

```
<script type="text/javascript">
    function showEM(userName,emServer) {
        var emLink = userName + "@" + emServer;
        document.write("<a href='mailto:" + emLink + "'>");
        document.write(emLink);
        document.write("</a>");
    }
</script>
```

Figure 10-16   Inserting the showEM() function

```
<link href="mplstyles.css" rel="stylesheet" />

<script type="text/javascript">
    function showEM(userName, emServer) {
        var emLink = userName + "@" + emServer;
        document.write("<a href='mailto:" + emLink + "'>");
        document.write(emLink);
        document.write("</a>");
    }
</script>
```

Calling a Function

When a browser encounters a function, it bypasses it without executing any of the code contained within the function. The code is executed only when called by another JavaScript command. If the function has any parameters, the initial values of the parameters are set when the function is called. The expression to call a function and run the commands it contains has the form

```
function_name(parameter values)
```

where *function_name* is the name of the function and *parameter values* is a comma-separated list of values that match the parameters of the function. For example, to call the showMsg() function described earlier using the text string *Monroe Public Library* as the value of the libName parameter, you would run the command

```
showMsg("Monroe Public Library");
```

resulting in the following HTML code being written to the document (see Figure 10-17):

```
<p>Welcome to the Monroe Public Library</p>
```

Figure 10-17 **Calling a JavaScript function**

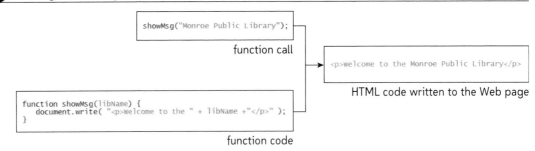

Parameter values can also themselves be variables. The following commands store the library name in a text string variable named libText and call the showMsg() function using that variable as the parameter value:

```
var libText="Cutler Public Library";
showMsg(libText);
```

As a result, the following HTML code would be written to the Web document:

```
<p>Welcome to the Cutler Public Library</p>
```

Functions can be called repeatedly with different parameter values to achieve different results. For example, the following code calls the showMsg() function twice with different parameter values to display two welcome paragraphs—one for the Monroe Public Library and one for the Cutler Public Library:

```
var libText = "Monroe Public Library";
showMsg(libText);
var libText2 = "Cutler Public Library";
showMsg(libText2);
```

You can call the showEM() function that you just entered to display the hypertext link for Catherine Adler's e-mail address. The command is

```
showEM("cadler","mpl.gov");
```

As a result of this command, the userName parameter would contain a text string of *cadler* and the emServer parameter would contain the text string *mpl.gov*. You're ready to replace the commands you entered earlier to write the hypertext link for Catherine Adler's e-mail address by calling the showEM() function.

To call the showEM() function:

▶ **1.** Return to the **mpl.htm** file in your text editor and then scroll down the file to the `script` element containing the JavaScript code for Catherine Adler's e-mail address.

▶ **2.** Replace all of the commands within the `script` element with the following command, as shown in Figure 10-18:

```
showEM("cadler","mpl.gov");
```

Figure 10-18   **Calling the showEM() function**

```
<tr>
    <td>Catherine Adler<br />Library Director</td>
    <td>555-3100</td>
    <td>

        <script type="text/javascript">
            showEM("cadler","mpl.gov");
        </script>

    </td>
</tr>
```

> **3.** Save your changes to the file and then reload **mpl.htm** in your Web browser. The link to Catherine Adler's e-mail address should once again appear in the staff table, unchanged from what you saw earlier in Figure 10-11.

Using the function call gives the same result as the code you used earlier. However, the great advantage is that you can reuse the showEM() function for other e-mail addresses in the staff directory simply by changing the parameter values. You don't have to reenter all four of the program lines. For longer programs this greatly simplifies the code.

REFERENCE

Creating and Calling a JavaScript Function

- To create a JavaScript function that performs an action, insert the structure

```
function function_name(parameters){
    JavaScript commands
}
```

where *function_name* is the name of the function, *parameters* is a comma-separated list of variable names used in the function, and *JavaScript commands* is the set of statements run by the function.

- To create a JavaScript function that returns a value, use

```
function function_name(parameters){
    JavaScript commands
    return value;
}
```

where *value* is the value returned by the function.

- To call a JavaScript function, run the command

```
function_name(values)
```

where *function_name* is the name of the JavaScript function and *values* is a comma-separated list of values for the parameters of the function.

Kate asks you to call the showEM() function for the other e-mail addresses in the staff table.

To add the remaining e-mail addresses:

▶ **1.** Return to the **mpl.htm** file in your text editor.

▶ **2.** Locate the entry for Michael Li. His e-mail address is *mikeli@mpl.gov*. Add the following `script` element to the empty table cell that directly follows the Michael Li entry:

```
<script type="text/javascript">
    showEM("mikeli","mpl.gov");
</script>
```

▶ **3.** Kate Howard's e-mail address is *khoward@mpl.gov*. Insert the following `script` element in the empty table cell for her entry in the staff directory:

```
<script type="text/javascript">
    showEM("khoward","mpl.gov");
</script>
```

Trouble? You can use the copy and paste feature of your text editor because the additions you'll make to the file in these steps are so similar. If you're not sure where to place these script elements, refer to Figure 10-19.

▶ **4.** Robert Hope's e-mail address is *rhope@mpl.gov*. Enter the following `script` element for his entry:

```
<script type="text/javascript">
    showEM("rhope","mpl.gov");
</script>
```

▶ **5.** Wayne Lewis's e-mail address is *wlewis@mpl.gov*. Enter the following `script` element in the empty table cell for his entry:

```
<script type="text/javascript">
    showEM("wlewis","mpl.gov");
</script>
```

▶ **6.** Bill Forth's e-mail address is *bforth@mpl.gov*. Enter the following code in the empty table cell for his entry:

```
<script type="text/javascript">
    showEM("bforth","mpl.gov");
</script>
```

Figure 10-19 shows the revised code in the mpl.htm file.

Figure 10-19   Inserting the remaining e-mail addresses

```
<tr>
   <td>Michael Li<br />Head of Adult Services</td>
   <td>555-3145</td>
   <td>
      <script type="text/javascript">
         showEM("mikeli","mpl.gov");
      </script>
   </td>
</tr>
<tr>
   <td>Kate Howard<br />Head of Technical Services</td>
   <td>555-4389</td>
   <td>
      <script type="text/javascript">
         showEM("khoward","mpl.gov");
      </script>
   </td>
</tr>
<tr>
   <td>Robert Hope<br />Head of Children's Services</td>
   <td>555-7811</td>
   <td>
      <script type="text/javascript">
         showEM("rhope","mpl.gov");
      </script>
   </td>
</tr>
<tr>
   <td>Wayne Lewis<br />Circulation Services Supervisor</td>
   <td>555-9001</td>
   <td>
      <script type="text/javascript">
         showEM("wlewis","mpl.gov");
      </script>
   </td>
</tr>
<tr>
   <td>Bill Forth<br />Interlibrary Loan</td>
   <td>555-9391</td>
   <td>
      <script type="text/javascript">
         showEM("bforth","mpl.gov");
      </script>
   </td>
</tr>
```

▶ **7.** Save your changes to the file and then reload **mpl.htm** in your Web browser.
Figure 10-20 shows the complete list of e-mail addresses in the staff directory.
Verify that each e-mail address is a hypertext link by hovering your mouse pointer
over the address text and then observing the destination of the link in the browser's status bar.

Figure 10-20 | Complete list of e-mail address links

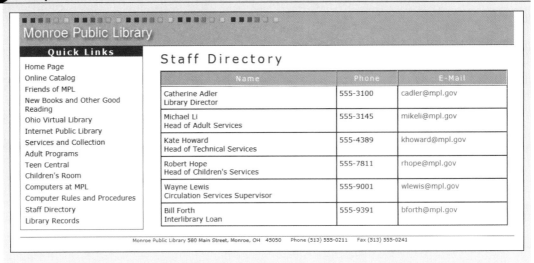

Creating a Function to Return a Value

You created the showEM() function to perform the action of writing a text string to your Web document. The other use of a function is to return a calculated value. For a function to return a value, it must include a `return` statement as follows:

```
function function_name(parameters){
   JavaScript commands
   return value;
}
```

where *value* is the calculated value that is returned by the function. For example, the following CalcArea() function calculates the area of a rectangular region by multiplying the region's length and width:

```
function CalcArea(length, width) {
   var area = length*width;
   return area;
}
```

In this function, the value of the area variable is returned by the function. You can call the function to retrieve this value. The following code uses the function to calculate the area of a rectangle whose dimensions are 8 × 6 units:

```
var x = 8;
var y = 6;
var z = CalcArea(x,y);
```

The first two commands assign the values *8* and *6* to the x and y variables, respectively. The values of both of these variables are then sent to the CalcArea() function as the values of the length and width parameters. The CalcArea() function uses these values to calculate the area, which it then returns, assigning that value to the z variable. As a result of these commands, a value of 48 is assigned to the z variable.

Functions that return a value can be placed within larger expressions. For example, the following code calls the CalcArea() function within an expression that multiplies the area value by 2:

```
var z = CalcArea(x,y)*2;
```

When this command is run, the value of the CalcArea() function is returned, multiplied by 2, and then stored in the z variable. Using the above parameter values, the value of the z variable is 96.

Functions and Variable Scope

As you've seen, the commands within a function are run only when the function is called. This has an impact on how variables within the function are treated. Every variable you create has a property known as **scope**, which indicates where you can reference the variable within the Web page. A variable's scope can be either local or global. A variable created within a JavaScript function has **local scope** and can be referenced only within that function. Variables with local scope are sometimes referred to as **local variables**. In the function you created in this session, the emLink variable has local scope and can be referenced only within the showEM() function. Parameters such as the userName and emServer parameters from the showEM() function also have local scope and are not recognized outside of the function in which they're used. When the showEM() function stops running, those variables and their values are not held in the computer memory and their values can no longer be accessed.

Variables not declared within functions have **global scope** and can be referenced from within all script elements on a Web page. Variables with global scope are often referred to as **global variables**.

Accessing an External JavaScript File

You show your work on the staff directory to Kate. She's happy that you were able to use JavaScript to generate the e-mail addresses, but she's still concerned that the text of each employee's username and mail server are present in the document as parameter values of the showEM() function. She would like to have those values hidden from any e-mail harvesters that might be scanning the document code. You discuss the issue with a programmer friend who sends you a file containing the following function:

```
function stringReverse(textString) {
   if (!textString) return '';
   var revString='';

   for (i = textString.length-1; i>=0; i--)
      revString += textString.charAt(i);

   return revString;
}
```

Interpreting the code contained within this function is beyond the scope of this tutorial, but for now it is sufficient to know in general what the function does. The function has a single parameter named textString, which stores a string of characters. The function then creates a variable named revString that stores the characters from textString in reverse order, and that reversed text string is returned by the function. For example, if you called the function in the statements

```
userName = stringReverse("reldac");
emServer = stringReverse("vog.lpm");
```

the userName variable would store the text string *cadler*, and the emServer variable would store the text string *mpl.gov* (the text strings *reldac* and *vog.lpm* in reverse order). You show this function to Kate and she agrees that this will be sufficient to hide the actual username and server name from most e-mail address harvesters.

The stringReverse() function has already been entered for you and stored in a file named *spam.js*. To access JavaScript code and functions placed in external files, you employ the same `script` element you use to insert JavaScript commands directly into a document. The code to access an external script file is

```
<script src="url" type="mime-type"></script>
```

where `url` is the URL of the external document and `mime-type` is the language of the code in the external script file. For example, to access the code in the spam.js file, you would add the following script element to your Web document:

```
<script src="spam.js" type="text/javascript"></script>
```

It's a common practice for JavaScript programmers to create libraries of functions located in external files that are easily accessible to pages on the entire Web site. Any new functions added to the external file are then instantly accessible to each Web page without having to edit the contents of those pages. External files containing JavaScript commands and functions always have the file extension .js to distinguish them from files containing script commands from other languages.

When a browser encounters a `script` element that points to an external file, it loads the contents of the external file into the Web document just as if the programmer had entered the code from the external file directly into the Web file. See Figure 10-21.

TIP

Place all script elements that reference external files in the document head so that those programs are immediately loaded by the Web browser and can be referenced by any code within the Web page.

Figure 10-21   **Using an external script file**

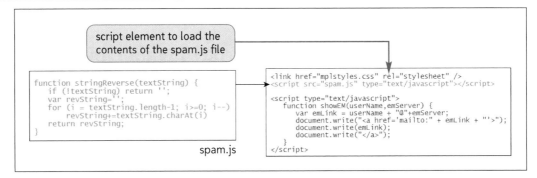

Accessing an External JavaScript File

REFERENCE

• To access the code stored in an external file, add the script element

```
<script src="url" type="mime-type"></script>
```

to the Web page, where `url` is the URL of the external document and `mime-type` is the language of the code in the external script file.
• For JavaScript files, set the `mime-type` to *text/javascript*.

You'll insert a `script` element into the staff directory page to access the code from the spam.js file.

To access the code in the spam.js file:

1. Return to the **mpl.htm** file in your text editor.

2. Directly below the `link` element in the head section of the document, insert the following `script` element, as shown in Figure 10-22:

```
<script src="spam.js" type="text/javascript"></script>
```

Figure 10-22 | Inserting a link to the spam.js script file

```
<link href="mplstyles.css" rel="stylesheet" />
<script src="spam.js" type="text/javascript"></script>
```

Next you want to confirm that the stringReverse() function from the spam.js file is working correctly. To test the function, you'll call it to reverse the text string values of the userName and emServer parameters in the showEM() function.

To test the stringReverse() function:

1. Scroll down to the showEM() function.

2. Insert the following two lines of code at the top of the function, as shown in Figure 10-23:

   ```
   userName = stringReverse(userName);
   emServer = stringReverse(emServer);
   ```

Figure 10-23 | Calling the stringReverse() function

reverses the order of characters in the userName and emServer parameter values

```
<script type="text/javascript">
   function showEM(userName,emServer) {

      userName = stringReverse(userName);
      emServer = stringReverse(emServer);

      var emLink = userName + "@"+emServer;
      document.write("<a href='mailto:" + emLink + "'>");
      document.write(emLink);
      document.write("</a>");
   }
</script>
```

3. Save your changes to the file, and then reload **mpl.htm** in your Web browser. As shown in Figure 10-24, the text of the username and mail server portions of each employee's e-mail address appears reversed on the Web page.

Figure 10-24 | Staff directory with the e-mail addresses reversed

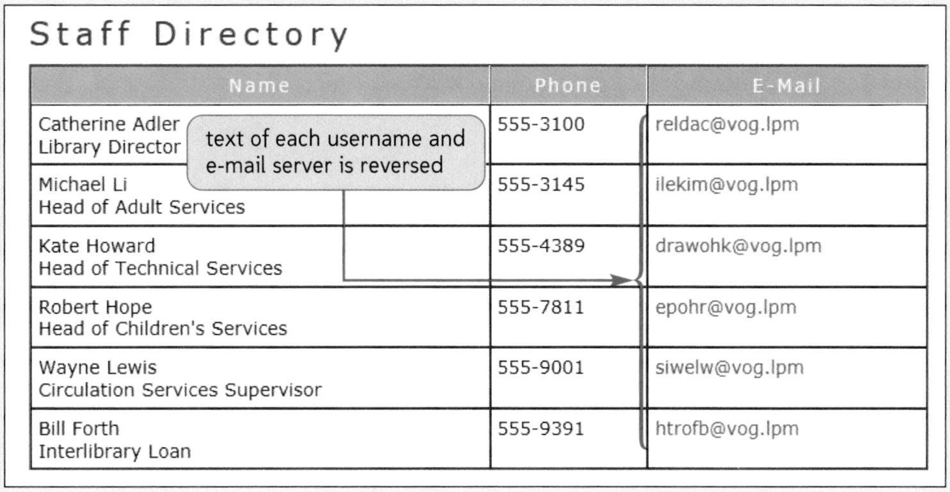

Staff Directory

Name	Phone	E-Mail
Catherine Adler Library Director	555-3100	reldac@vog.lpm
Michael Li Head of Adult Services	555-3145	ilekim@vog.lpm
Kate Howard Head of Technical Services	555-4389	drawohk@vog.lpm
Robert Hope Head of Children's Services	555-7811	epohr@vog.lpm
Wayne Lewis Circulation Services Supervisor	555-9001	siwelw@vog.lpm
Bill Forth Interlibrary Loan	555-9391	htrofb@vog.lpm

text of each username and e-mail server is reversed

The stringReverse() function appears to be working correctly. Of course, you don't want the e-mail addresses to be reversed in the rendered document; you want those addresses to appear correctly. Instead, you want the code within the document reversed to thwart e-mail harvesters. This means that you need to enter the usernames and e-mail server names in reverse order.

To change the userName and emServer parameter values:

▶ **1.** Return to the **mpl.htm** file in your text editor.

▶ **2.** Scroll down the file to the `script` element for Catherine Adler's e-mail address and change the value of the userName parameter from *cadler* to **reldac**. Change the value of the emServer parameter from *mpl.gov* to **vog.lpm**.

▶ **3.** Change the parameter values for Michael Li's e-mail address to **ilekim** and **vog.lpm**.

▶ **4.** Change the parameter values for Katherine Howard's e-mail address to **drawohk** and **vog.lpm**.

▶ **5.** Change the parameter values for Robert Hope's e-mail address to **epohr** and **vog.lpm**.

▶ **6.** Change the parameter values for Wayne Lewis's e-mail address to **siwelw** and **vog.lpm**.

▶ **7.** Finally, change the parameter values for Bill Forth's e-mail address to **htrofb** and **vog.lpm**. Figure 10-25 highlights the revised code in the file.

Figure 10-25 | **Entering the reversed userName and emServer parameter values**

```
<tr>
    <td>Catherine Adler<br />Library Director</td>
    <td>555-3100</td>
    <td>
        <script type="text/javascript">
            showEM("reldac","vog.lpm");
        </script>
    </td>
</tr>

<tr>
    <td>Michael Li<br />Head of Adult Services</td>
    <td>555-3145</td>
    <td>
        <script type="text/javascript">
            showEM("ilekim","vog.lpm");
        </script>
    </td>
</tr>
<tr>
    <td>Kate Howard<br />Head of Technical Services</td>
    <td>555-4389</td>
    <td>
        <script type="text/javascript">
            showEM("drawohk","vog.lpm");
        </script>
    </td>
</tr>
<tr>
    <td>Robert Hope<br />Head of Children's Services</td>
    <td>555-7811</td>
    <td>
        <script type="text/javascript">
            showEM("epohr","vog.lpm");
        </script>
    </td>
</tr>
<tr>
    <td>Wayne Lewis<br />Circulation Services Supervisor</td>
    <td>555-9001</td>
    <td>
        <script type="text/javascript">
            showEM("siwelw","vog.lpm");
        </script>
    </td>
</tr>
<tr>
    <td>Bill Forth<br />Interlibrary Loan</td>
    <td>555-9391</td>
    <td>
        <script type="text/javascript">
            showEM("htrofb","vog.lpm");
        </script>
    </td>
</tr>
```

▶ 8. Save your changes to the file and reload **mpl.htm** in your Web browser. As shown in Figure 10-26, the text characters of the e-mail addresses for staff members now appear in the correct order.

Figure 10-26 Final staff directory page

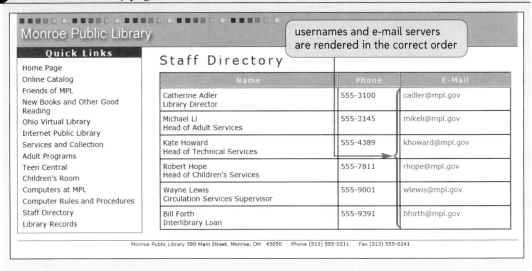

You review your progress with Kate. As she scans through the code in the HTML file, she's pleased to note that none of the e-mail addresses for the six staff members appears in any readable form. By breaking the e-mail addresses into two parts (the userName and emServer parts) and entering the text in reverse order, you have effectively hidden the actual addresses from e-mail harvesting programs.

Commenting JavaScript Code

Kate is pleased to see how JavaScript can unscramble the e-mail addresses and present them to users in a readable form. However, she is concerned that in the future, she might forget how this program is designed to work. She would like you to add some comments to the code you created.

Inserting Single-Line and Multiline Comments

Commenting your code is an important programming practice. It helps other people who examine your code to understand what your programs are designed to do and how they work. It can even help you in the future when you return to edit the programs you've written and need to recall the programming choices you made. Comments can be added to scripts as either single or multiple lines. The syntax of a single-line comment is

```
// comment text
```

where *comment text* is the JavaScript comment. Single-line comments can be placed within the same line as a JavaScript command, making it easier to interpret each command in your code. The following is an example of a JavaScript statement that includes a single-line comment:

```
document.write(emLink); // write e-mail address to the Web page
```

For more extended comments, you place the comment text on several lines using the following structure:

```
/*
    comment text spanning
    several lines
*/
```

The following is an example of a multiline comment applied to a JavaScript program:

```
/*
   The showEM() function displays a link to the user's e-mail
   address.
   The text of the user and e-mail server names are entered in
   reverse order to thwart e-mail harvesters.
*/
```

REFERENCE

Inserting JavaScript Comments

• To insert a single-line comment into a JavaScript program, use

```
// comment text
```

where *comment text* is the JavaScript comment. Single-line comments can be placed on the same line as a JavaScript command.

• To insert several lines of comments, use the following structure:

```
/*
   comment text spanning
   several lines
*/
```

Kate would like you to add comments to the showEM() function you created.

To add comments to your JavaScript code:

▶ **1.** Return to the **mpl.htm** file in your text editor.

▶ **2.** Add the following multiline comment directly below the opening function statement for the showEM() function:

```
/*
   The showEM() function displays a link to the user's
   e-mail address.
   The text of the user and e-mail server names are entered in
   reverse order to thwart e-mail harvesters.
*/
```

▶ **3.** Add the following single-line comment to the end of the line that reverses the value of the userName parameter:

```
// reverse the text of the userName parameter
```

▶ **4.** Add the following comment to the end of the line that reverses the value of the emServer parameter:

```
// reverse the text of the emServer parameter
```

▶ **5.** Finally, add the following comment to the end of the line creating the emLink variable:

```
// combine the text of userName and emServer
```

Figure 10-27 displays these comments in the mpl.htm file.

Figure 10-27 Adding comments to the showEM() function

```
<script type="text/javascript">
    function showEM(userName,emServer) {
        /*
            The showEM() function displays a link to the user's
            e-mail address.
            The text of the user and e-mail server names are entered in
            reverse order to thwart e-mail harvesters.
        */

        userName = stringReverse(userName); // reverse the text of the userName parameter
        emServer = stringReverse(emServer); // reverse the text of the emServer parameter

        var emLink = userName + "@"+emServer; // combine the text of userName and emServer
        document.write("<a href='mailto:" + emLink + "'>");
        document.write(emLink);
        document.write("</a>");
    }
</script>
```

▶ **6.** Close the **mpl.htm** file, saving your changes.

▶ **7.** Reopen **mpl.htm** in your Web browser and verify that you have not introduced any errors by adding comments to the showEM() function.

You show the commented version of the showEM() function to Kate. She agrees that it will help her better remember the purpose of the function and how the function works.

Debugging Your JavaScript Programs

As you work with JavaScript, you will inevitably encounter scripts that fail to work because of an error in the code. To fix a problem with a program, you need to debug it. **Debugging** is the process of searching code to locate a source of trouble. To debug a program, you must first determine the type of error present in your code.

There are three types of errors: load-time errors, run-time errors, and logical errors. A **load-time error** occurs when a script is first loaded by a browser. As the page loads, the browser reads through the code looking for mistakes in syntax. For example, suppose you had neglected to include the closing parenthesis, as in the following command from the showEM() function:

```
document.write("</a>";
```

In this case, you would be making a mistake in the syntax of the `document.write()` method. When a load-time error is uncovered, the JavaScript interpreter halts loading the script. Depending on the browser, an error message might also appear. Figure 10-28 shows the message generated by the above error in the Firefox Error Console. An error message can include the line number and character number of the error. This does not mean that the error occurred at this location in the document—the source of the trouble could be much earlier in the script. The message simply indicates the location at which the JavaScript interpreter was forced to cancel loading the script.

Figure 10-28   Reporting a load-time error in the Firefox Error Console

A **run-time error** occurs after a script has been successfully loaded and is being executed by a browser. In a run-time error, the mistake occurs when the browser cannot complete a line of code. One common source of a run-time error is mislabeling a variable name. For example, the line of code

```
document.write(emlink);
```

in the showEM() function would result in the run-time error shown from the Internet Explorer browser in Figure 10-29.

Figure 10-29   Reporting a run-time error in Internet Explorer

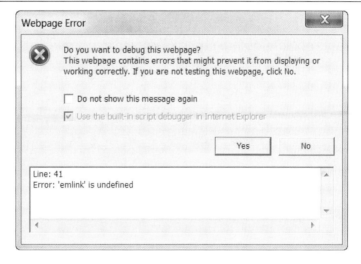

The mistake in this line of code is that there is no variable named emlink in the showEM() function—the variable name should be emLink (recall that variable names are case sensitive). When a browser attempts to write the contents of the emlink variable to the Web document, it discovers that no such variable exists and reports the run-time error. When a JavaScript interpreter catches a run-time error, it halts execution of the script and displays an error message indicating the location where it was forced to quit.

Logical errors are free from syntax and structural mistakes, but result in incorrect results. A logical error is often the hardest to fix and sometimes requires you to meticulously trace every step of your code to detect the mistake. Suppose you had incorrectly entered the line of code to create the emLink variable, placing the server name before the username, as follows:

```
var emLink = emServer + "@" + userName;
```

In this case, a browser would display the list of e-mail addresses as shown in Figure 10-30.

Figure 10-30 Results of a logical error

Staff Directory

Name	Phone	E-Mail
Catherine Adler Library Director	555-3100	mpl.gov@cadler
Michael Li Head of Adult Services	555-3145	mpl.gov@mikeli
Kate Howard Head of Technical Services	555-4389	mpl.gov@khoward
Robert Hope Head of Children's Services	555-7811	mpl.gov@rhope
Wayne Lewis Circulation Services Supervisor	555-9001	mpl.gov@wlewis
Bill Forth Interlibrary Loan	555-9391	mpl.gov@bforth

> usernames and e-mail server names are displayed in the wrong order

Although the browser did not report any mistakes, this is obviously not the way Kate wants e-mail addresses displayed!

PROSKILLS

Problem Solving: Fixing Common Programming Mistakes

When you begin writing JavaScript programs, you will invariably encounter mistakes in your code. Some common sources of programming error include:

- **Misspelling a variable name**: For example, if you named a variable `ListPrice`, then misspellings or incorrect capitalization—such as `listprice`, `ListPrices`, or `list_price`—will result in the program failing to run correctly.
- **Mismatched parentheses or braces**: The following code results in an error because the function lacks the closing brace:

```
function Area(width, height) {
    var size = width*height;
```

- **Mismatched quotes**: If you neglect the closing quotes around a text string, JavaScript treats the text string as an object or variable, resulting in an error. The following code results in an error because the closing double quote is missing from the `firstName` variable:

```
var firstName = "Sean';
var lastName = "Lee";
document.write(firstName+" " + lastName);
```

- **Missing quotes**: When you combine several text strings using the + symbol, you might neglect to quote all text strings. For example, the following code generates an error because of the missing quotes around the `<br />` tag:

```
document.write("MidWest Student Union" + <br />);
```

As you become more experienced in writing JavaScript code, you'll be able to quickly spot these types of errors, making it easier for you to debug your programs.

Debugging Tools and Techniques

There are several techniques you can employ to avoid making programming mistakes and to quickly locate the mistakes you do make. One is to write **modular code**, which is code that breaks up a program's different tasks into smaller, more manageable chunks. A common strategy when creating modular code is to use functions that perform a few simple tasks. The different functions can then be combined and used in a variety of ways.

If you encounter a logical error in which the incorrect results are displayed by the browser, you can monitor the changing values of your variables using an alert dialog box. An **alert dialog box** is a dialog box generated by JavaScript that displays a text message with an OK button. Clicking the OK button closes the dialog box, allowing the browser to resume running the JavaScript code. The command to create an alert dialog box is

```
alert(text);
```

where `text` is the text string that you want displayed in the dialog box. You can also use a variable name in place of a text string. For example, the command

```
alert(emLink);
```

displays the current value of the `emLink` variable. Figure 10-31 shows the appearance of this dialog box for the first entry in the library staff directory. Alert dialog boxes are useful in determining what is happening to your variable values while a program is running.

Figure 10-31   Alert dialog box

Browsers also offer various tools for debugging JavaScript programs. In Internet Explorer you can open the Developer Tools window by pressing the F12 key. From this window you can run a script debugger to locate and describe any load-time or run-time errors in your code, as shown in Figure 10-32.

Figure 10-32   Internet Explorer Developer Tools window

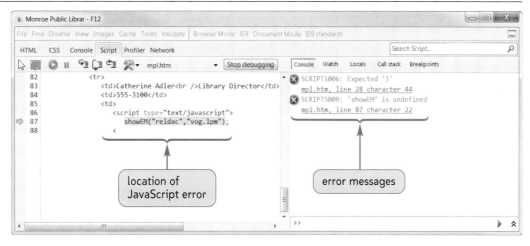

Firefox provides the Firefox Error Console shown in Figure 10-33, which displays all of the errors generated within the current document. To view the console, click Web Developer and Error Console from the Tools menu. Within the Error Console is an Evaluate box in which you can insert JavaScript commands to evaluate your code and variable values at the point at which the error occurred.

Figure 10-33 **Firefox Error Console and document source window**

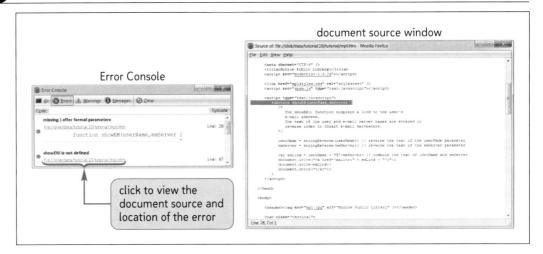

To view the developer tools under Google Chrome, you click the Customize and control button located in the upper-right corner of the browser window, click Tools, and then click Developer Tools. As Figure 10-34 shows, Chrome opens a pane at the bottom of the browser window that contains tools to work with the document, the style sheets, and any JavaScript programs.

| Figure 10-34 | Google Chrome developer tools pane |

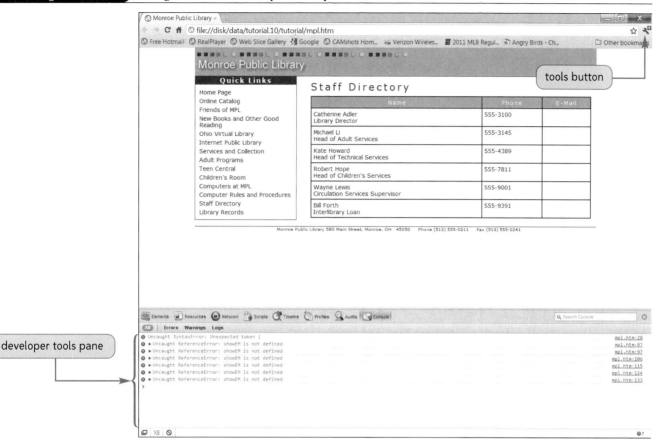

Safari for Windows also contains developer tools in its Web Inspector window. To view the Web Inspector window, click the Menu icon in the upper-right corner of the browser window and then click Develop and Show Error Console. With Safari for the Macintosh, you first have to enable the Safari Develop menu by clicking Safari, clicking Preferences, and then within the Advanced tab checking Show Develop menu in the menu bar. Once the menu is enabled, you click the Show Error Console button to view any JavaScript errors in your code. Figure 10-35 shows the errors listed in the Console tab of the Web Inspector window.

| Figure 10-35 | Safari Web Inspector window |

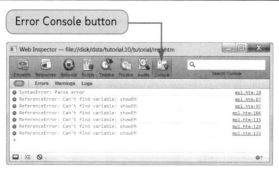

To learn how to use all of the various developer tools, read the online help information for your browser.

You've now completed your work on the staff directory for the Monroe Public Library. Kate will call you again as other issues with the library's Web site arise.

Session 10.2 Quick Check

REVIEW

1. Write a JavaScript function named CalcVol() to calculate the volume of a rectangular solid. The function should have three parameters named x, y, and z, and should return the value of a variable named Vol that is equal to x*y*z.
2. Write the JavaScript statement to call the CalcVol() function with values of x = 3, y = 10, and z = 4, storing the result of the function in a variable named TotalVol.
3. What is variable scope?
4. Specify the HTML code to access the JavaScript file *library.js*.
5. Specify the code to enter the single-line JavaScript comment *Library of JavaScript functions*.
6. Specify the code to enter following multiline JavaScript comment:

```
The library.js file contains a collection of
JavaScript functions for use with the file index.htm
```

7. What code would you enter to display the value of the userName variable in an alert dialog box?
8. What are the three types of errors generated by mistakes in a JavaScript program?

Practice the skills you learned in the tutorial using the same case scenario.

Review Assignments

Data Files needed for the Review Assignments: 0.png - 9.png, modernizr-1.5.js, mpl.jpg, mpl2txt.htm, mplstyles.css, random.js

Kate has a new assignment for you. One of the pages on the Monroe Public Library Web site is the library records page, which contains sensitive information about library patrons and the books they have checked out. Kate has created a Web form in which a staff member enters a username and password before getting access to the library records. However, Kate has heard that some hackers create programs that search for Web forms that open confidential pages. One technique of these hackers is to have automated programs that submit thousands of username/password combinations, hoping to break into the system. Kate knows that some sites use human input validation to thwart these programs.

Human input validation is a technique that requires the entry of a piece of information that humans can easily enter, but automated programs cannot. One approach is to display a completely automated public Turing test to tell computers and humans apart (CAPTCHA) requesting that each user enter the numbers or letters being displayed on the screen. Because most automated programs can't "see" images, they cannot answer this question; most humans, on the other hand, can enter the requested information without trouble. Kate suggests you write a program that shows five images, each displaying a random number between 0 and 9. In addition to entering a username and password, users will be required to enter the numbers they see on the screen. Figure 10-36 shows a preview of the completed Web page.

Figure 10-36   Library records page

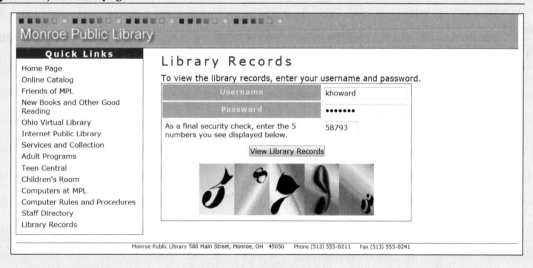

Your job is to write a script to display the random images. The images have been stored in files named *0.png* through *9.png*. To help you, Kate has located a file that contains a JavaScript function to return a random integer from 0 to a specified number, which is represented by the size parameter. The name of the function is randomInteger, so to call the function, you use the command

```
randomInteger(size)
```

For example, to return a random integer from 0 to 5, you would run the command

```
randomInteger(5)
```

The randomInteger() function has been saved for you in the *random.js* file.

Complete the following:

1. Use your text editor to open **mpl2txt.htm** from the tutorial.10\review folder included with your Data Files. Enter *your name* and *the date* in the comment section of the file and save the file as **mpl2.htm** in the same folder.

2. In the head section, just above the closing `</head>` tag, insert a `script` element that accesses the code in the *random.js* file.

3. Add an embedded `script` element for the code that you'll add to the mpl2.htm file.

4. Within the embedded `script` element, create a function named showImg(). The purpose of this function is to write an inline image tag into the current document. The function has no parameters. Add the following statements to the function:

   a. Add the following multiline comment to the start of the function, just below the opening `showImg()` function statement:

      The showImg() function displays a random image from the 0.png through 9.png files. The random image is designed to thwart hackers attempting to enter the library records database by requiring visual confirmation.

   b. Declare a variable named **imgNumber** equal to the value returned by the randomInteger() function. Use **9** as the value of the size parameter in the randomInteger() function.

   c. After the statement that creates the imgNumber variable append the following single-line comment:

      Return a random number from 0 to 9.

   d. Insert a command that writes the text

      ```
      <img src='imgNumber.png' alt='' />
      ```

      to the document, where *imgNumber* is the value of the imgNumber variable.

5. Scroll down to the bottom of the file and locate the last table cell in the document. Within this empty table cell, insert a `script` element.

6. Within the `script` element, call the `showImg()` function five times. You do not need to specify a parameter value.

7. Save your changes to the file.

8. Open **mpl2.htm** in your Web browser. Verify that each time you refresh the Web page, a different sequence of five image numbers appears at the bottom of the Web form. Debug your code as necessary using any of the tools or techniques described in this tutorial.

9. Submit your completed files to your instructor.

Use the skills you learned in this tutorial to create an online star map.

APPLY

Case Problem 1

Data Files needed for the Case Problem: datetime.js, mask.gif, modernizr-1.5.js, sky0.jpg - sky23.jpg, skymaptxt.htm, skyweb.css, skyweb.jpg

SkyWeb Astronomy   Dr. Andrew Weiss of Central Ohio University maintains an astronomy page called SkyWeb for his students. On his Web site he discusses many aspects of astronomy and stargazing. One of the tools of the amateur stargazer is a planisphere, which is a handheld device composed of two flat disks: one disk shows a map of the constellations, and the other disk contains a window corresponding to the part of the sky that is visible at a given time and date. When a user rotates the second disk to the current date and time, the constellations that appear in the window correspond to the constellations currently visible in the nighttime sky.

Dr. Weiss has asked for your help in constructing an online planisphere for his Web site. He has created 24 different sky chart image files, named *sky0.jpg* through *sky23.jpg*, that represent 24 different rotations of the nighttime sky. He has also created an image containing a transparent window through which a user can view a selected sky chart. A preview of the completed Web page is shown in Figure 10-37.

Figure 10-37   **SkyWeb planisphere page**

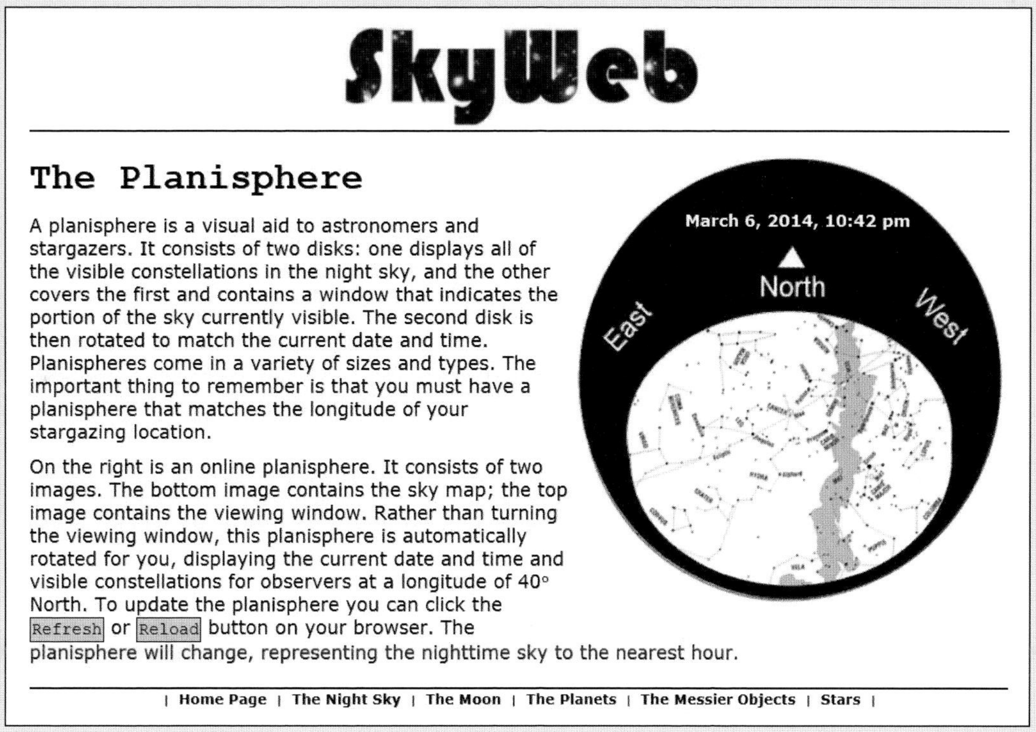

Dr. Weiss has designed the page layout. He needs your help in creating JavaScript code to display the current date and time and to display the correct sky chart for that date and time. To do this, you've been provided with two functions:

- The showDateTime() function returns the current date and time in the text string

    Month Day, Year, hour:minute am/pm

    where *Month* is the name of the current month, *Day* is the current day, *Year* is the current year, *hour* is the current hour, *minute* is the current minute, and am/pm changes based on the current time.

- The getMap() function returns a number from 0 to 23. The number matches the number of the sky map image to show based on the current date and time.

Both functions have been placed in an external JavaScript file named *datetime.js*.

Complete the following:

1. Use your text editor to open the **skymaptxt.htm** file from the tutorial.10\case1 folder included with your Data Files. Enter *your name* and *the date* in the comment section of the file. Save the file as **skymap.htm** in the same folder.

2. Directly below the link element in the head section, insert a script element accessing the *datetime.js* file.

3. Below the `script` element, insert another `script` element that contains statements to do the following:

   a. Insert a multiline comment containing the following text:

   ```
   timeStr is a text string containing the current date and time
   mapNum is the number of the map to display in the planisphere
   ```

   b. Declare a variable named **timeStr** equal to the value returned from the showDateTime() function.

   c. Declare a variable named **mapNum** equal to the value returned from the get-Map() function.

4. Scroll down the file to the `div` element with id value *maps* and replace the line

   ```
   <img id="sky" src="sky0.jpg" alt="" />
   ```

   with a `script` element that writes the following HTML code:

   ```
   <img id='sky' src='skymapNum.jpg' alt='' />
   ```

   where *mapNum* is the value of the mapNum variable.

5. Scroll down a few lines and replace the date/time value *January 1, 2014, 12:00 a.m.* with a script element that writes the value of the timeStr variable to the Web page.

6. Save your changes to the file and then open **skymap.htm** in your Web browser. Verify that the planisphere displays the current date and time.

⊕ EXPLORE

7. If you're able to modify the date/time settings on your computer, change the date and time and then reload or refresh the page to verify that the date/time value changes and that the map also changes. Debug your code as necessary.

8. Submit your completed files to your instructor.

Use JavaScript to display random banner ads.

APPLY

Case Problem 2

Data Files needed for the Case Problem: ad1.jpg - ad5.jpg, ads.js, fp.jpg, fronttxt.htm, logo.jpg, modernizr-1.5.js, random.js, styles.css

Ridgewood Herald Tribune Maria Ramirez manages advertising accounts for the Ridgewood *Herald Tribune* in Ridgewood, New Jersey. To offset the cost of the paper's Web site, Maria is selling ad space on the company's home page. She is looking at creating banner ads to be displayed on the paper's masthead, with each ad linked to the advertiser's Web site. Because ad space on the paper's home page is the most valuable, Maria has decided to sell space to five companies, with the selection of the banner ad determined randomly each time a user opens the page.

Maria has asked for your help in writing the JavaScript code to display banner ads randomly. She has provided a collection of functions that will be useful to you.

- The randInt() function returns random integers from 1 to n. To call the randInt() function, use the following expression:

  ```
  randInt(n)
  ```

- The adDescription() function returns the description of the nth ad from a list of ad descriptions. To call the function, use the following expression:

  ```
  adDescription(n)
  ```

- The adLink() function returns the URL of the nth ad of the collection. To call the function, use the following expression:

  ```
  adLink(n)
  ```

The *random.js* file contains the randInt() function. The *ads.js* file contains the adDescription() and adLink() functions. Figure 10-38 shows a preview of the completed Web page with one of the random banner ads displayed at the top of the page.

Figure 10-38   **Ridgewood Herald Tribune rotating ads**

Complete the following:

1. Use your text editor to open the **fronttxt.htm** file from the tutorial.10\case2 folder included with your Data Files. Enter *your name* and *the date* in the comment section of the file. Save the file as **front.htm** in the same folder.

2. After the `link` element in the head section, insert a `script` element accessing the functions in the *random.js* file.

3. Insert another `script` element accessing the functions in the *ads.js* file.

4. Scroll down the file to the `div` element with the id *ads*. Replace the content of the div element with a `script` element containing the following statements:

   a. Declare a variable named `rNumber` equal to the value returned from the `randInt()` function using **5** as the parameter value. Append the following comment to the statement:

   ```
   generate a random integer from 1 to 5
   ```

   b. Declare a variable named `rAd` equal to the text string returned from the `adDescription()` function using `rNumber` as the parameter value. Append the following comment to the statement:

   ```
   description of the random ad
   ```

   c. Declare a variable named `rLink` equal to the URL returned from the `adLink()` function using `rNumber` as the parameter value. Append the following comment:

   ```
   URL of the random ad
   ```

      d. Insert a command to write the HTML code

```
<a href="url">
   <img src="adn.jpg" alt="description"/>
</a>
```

      to the Web document, where *url* is the value of the `rLink` variable, *n* is the value of the `rNumber` variable, and *description* is the value of the `rAd` variable.

5. Save your changes to the file.

6. Open **front.htm** in your Web browser. Refresh the Web page multiple times, verifying that different banner ads appear each time the page is refreshed. Debug your code as necessary.

7. Submit your completed files to your instructor.

Explore how to write a script to display the daily calendar of events at a student union.

CHALLENGE

Case Problem 3

Data Files needed for the Case Problem: back.jpg, friday.htm, functions.js, modernizr-1.5.js, monday.htm, mw.css, saturday.htm, schedule.css, sunday.htm, thursday.htm, todaytxt.htm, tuesday.htm, wednesday.htm

MidWest Student Union   Sean Lee manages the Web site for the student union at MidWest University in Salina, Kansas. The student union provides daily activities for the students on campus. As Web site manager, part of Sean's job is to keep the Web site up to date on the latest activities sponsored by the union. At the beginning of each week, she revises a set of seven Web pages detailing the events for each day in the upcoming week.

Sean would like the Web site to display the current day's schedule in an inline frame within the Web page titled Today at the Union. To do this, her Web page must be able to determine the day of the week and then load the appropriate file into the frame. She would also like the Today at the Union page to display the current day and date. Figure 10-39 shows a preview of the page she wants you to create.

Figure 10-39   MidWest Student Union daily events

Sean has created the layout of the page, and she needs you to write the scripts to insert the current date and the calendar of events for the current day. To assist you, she has located two functions:

- The showDate() function returns a text string containing the current date in the format *Weekday, Month Day, Year*. The function has no parameter values.
- The weekDay() function returns a text string containing the name of the current weekday, from Sunday through Saturday. This function also has no parameter values.

The two functions are stored in an external JavaScript file named *functions.js*. The daily schedules have been stored in files named *sunday.htm* through *saturday.htm*.

Complete the following:

1. Use your text editor to open the **todaytxt.htm** file from the tutorial.10\case3 folder included with your Data Files. Enter *your name* and *the date* in the comment section of the file and save it as **today.htm**.

2. In the head section just above the closing </head> tag, insert a script element accessing the *functions.js* file.

3. Scroll down the file and locate the div element with the id *dateBox*. Within this element insert a script element. The script should run the following two commands:

   a. Write the following HTML code to the Web page:

      ```
      Today is <br />
      ```

   ⊕ EXPLORE

   b. Write the text string returned by the showDate() function to the Web document.

4. Scroll down the file and locate the h1 heading with the text *Today at the Union*. Within the empty paragraph that follows this heading, insert another script element. Within the script element, do the following:

   a. Insert the following multiline comment:

      ```
      Display the daily schedule in an inline frame.

      Daily schedules are stored in the files sunday.
      htm through saturday.htm.
      ```

   ⊕ EXPLORE

   b. Insert a command to write the HTML code

      ```
      <iframe src='weekday.htm'></iframe>
      ```

      to the Web page, where *weekday* is the text string returned by the weekDay() function.

5. Save your changes to the document.

6. Open **today.htm** in your Web browser. Verify that it shows the current date and that the daily schedule matches the current weekday.

⊕ EXPLORE

7. If you have the ability to change your computer's date and time, change the date to different days of the week and reload (not simply refresh) the Web page. Verify that the date and the daily schedule change to match the new date you selected. Debug your code as necessary.

8. Submit your completed files to your instructor.

RESEARCH

Test your knowledge of JavaScript by creating a splash screen displaying famous birthdays.

Case Problem 4

Data Files needed for this Case Problem: functions.js, logo.jpg, modernizr-1.5.js

HappyBirthdayNews.com   Linda Chi is the owner of a Web site called *HappyBirthdayNews.com* that specializes in birthday gifts and memorabilia. To make her site more interesting for users, Linda wants to create an opening screen that displays the current date and a famous birthday occurring on that date. She has asked for your help in writing the JavaScript code to generate the welcome message. She has designed the page's style and content, and has also located the following JavaScript functions:

- The showDate() function returns the current date as the text string *Weekday, Month Day, Year*, where *Weekday* is the day of the week, *Month* is the name of the month, *Day* is the day of the month, and *Year* is the four-digit year value. The showDate() function has no parameters.
- The dayNumber() function returns the day number of the current date, ranging from 1 (the first day of the year) to 366 (the last day of the year). The dayNumber() function has no parameters.
- The showBirthDay() function returns a text string describing a famous birthday on the given date. The function has a single parameter—day, which is equal to the day number of the famous birthday you want to view.

The three functions have already been saved for you in a file named *functions.js*. Figure 10-40 shows one possible solution to this problem.

Figure 10-40   **Happy Birthday page**

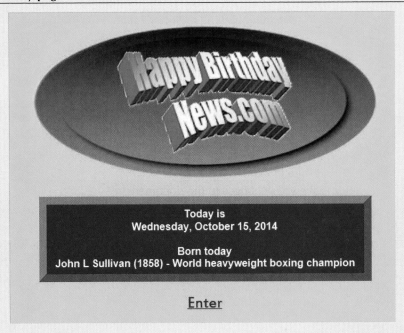

Complete the following:

1. Use your text editor to create the file **birthday.htm** and save it in the tutorial.10\case4 folder included with your Data Files. Create a comment section containing **your name** and **the date** as well as a brief description of the Web page.
2. Design the birthday.htm page as the opening page of the *HappyBirthdayNews.com* Web site. The content and design of the site are up to you. You can use the *logo.jpg* graphic file as the logo for the Web site and supplement it with any other content or graphics you find.

3. Place all of the styles used for your Web page in an external file named **styles.css**. Create a comment section containing *your name* and *the date* as well as a brief description of the style sheet.

4. Link your style sheet file to the HTML document.

5. Use your knowledge of JavaScript to add the following features to the Web page:

   a. A page element that displays the current date

   b. A page element that displays the name of a famous person born on that date

   c. Comments that document each of the variables you use in writing your JavaScript code and any functions you create

6. Save your changes to the file and then open it in your Web browser. Verify that the page displays the current date and a famous person's birthday for that date.

7. If you're able to change the date on your computer's clock, change the date and then reload the Web page. Verify that the page displays the new date and a new famous birthday. Debug your code as necessary.

8. Submit your completed files to your instructor.

ENDING DATA FILES

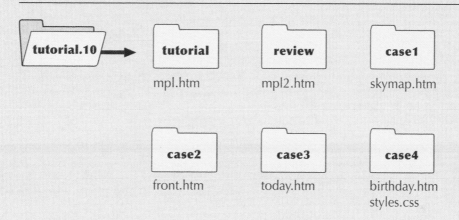

tutorial.10 → tutorial
mpl.htm

review
mpl2.htm

case1
skymap.htm

case2
front.htm

case3
today.htm

case4
birthday.htm
styles.css

Teamwork

Working With a Team

Especially in large organizations, working as Web developer requires the ability to work skillfully as part of a team. To be a better team member, it helps to understand some of the roles common in teamwork, as well as how to identify problems that may crop up on teams.

Roles You Might Play

If a team is to be successful for any length of time, members must see the value in both their contribution and what the team gets out of it. This means two important requirements must be met: task performance and social satisfaction. The job of task performance is usually handled by one or more members who are task specialists. Task specialists spend a lot of time and effort ensuring that the team achieves its goals. Often, they are the ones to initiate ideas, give opinions, gather information, sort and cull details, and provide the spark that keeps the team on track.

The socioemotional role is handled by individuals who strengthen the team's social bonds. This is often done through encouragement, empathy, conflict resolution, compromise, and tension reduction. Have you ever been in a group that had conflict and someone stepped in to tell a joke or soften the blow of criticism? That person held the socioemotional role.

Both of these roles are important for healthy teamwork. It's like the saying, "All work and no play makes Jack a dull boy." Jack as the task specialist needs the complementary skills of the more social Jill to handle the socioemotional side of things for a healthy balance.

The task specialist and socioemotional roles are important to teams. However, most teams will have other roles as well, including team leaders, work coordinators, idea people, and critics. These roles are not mutually exclusive. For example, the team leader might also be a task specialist, while the idea person also fills the socioemotional role. As your teamwork commences, these positions will be filled—maybe even by you. On a team, no single role is more or less important than the others. The progress and results the team achieves depend on how well the roles mesh in getting the work done.

Performance Problems

Not every team works smoothly. Sometimes, individuals have their own agendas that run counter to the goals of the team. Others disengage and don't participate at all. This particular problem is called *social loafing*, and is usually the most common human issue teams struggle to overcome. People who are assigned to teams against their will, or when they don't have the skill or ability to contribute, may end up "free-riding" on the work of the rest of the team. They get the credit but they didn't do anything to deserve it. Does this sound familiar?

Teams may also suffer from other performance problems, such as:

- Personality conflicts or power struggles
- Different or incompatible work styles
- Lack of clear goals or direction
- Communication breakdowns

PROSKILLS

What can you do if a performance problem emerges? If the issue is trivial, you can try to ignore it. When it's important to come to a consensus quickly, try working out a compromise, with each party giving a bit. For situations where the outcome is too important and compromise won't work, a collaboration approach could be the solution where the two parties bargain and negotiate their way to a consensus that lets both win. Accommodation - giving in for the greater good of the group - might work if the problematic parties are both in the wrong and want to resolve the point so the team can move on. Only when a situation is urgent and you need to get your way should you compete against team members to move forward.

Research How the Web Has Changed

The Web is constantly changing, offering users new and innovative ways of presenting information and exchanging data. Some of the greatest innovations do not always come from large and well-financed companies, but from entrepreneurs who see ways of bringing something new to the Internet community. In this exercise you will work in a team to explore the dynamic world of the Web.

Note: Please be sure *not* to include any personal information of a sensitive nature in the files you create to be submitted to your instructor for this exercise. Later on, you can update the files with such information for your personal use.

1. Assemble a group to research the history and development of some of the most important sites on the Web, with each member choosing a different site. Have each member prepare a report exploring what new features those sites brought to the Web. For example, how did sites such as Google, MySpace, and YouTube change our perceptions of the Internet? What features did these sites offer that had not previously been part of the Web?

2. Have your team members explore the impact that new technology has had on Web page development and the development of HTML5. Focus on the impact of MP3 players, cell phones, and high-speed wireless connections.

3. The World Wide Web Consortium (W3C) develops standards for the browser market to follow. One of the challenges for a Web site designer is to accommodate differences in browser support for the W3C standards. Write a report summarizing the level of browser support for the W3C's specifications for HTML5 and CSS3. The report should include any methods to resolve differences between the W3C specifications and the browser's level of support. Assign each team member a different Web browser to investigate.

4. When a Web site changes its content, it's useful to be able to notify users of that fact. One way of informing users of new and interesting material is by creating a feed of the site using RSS. Have your team explore the concepts behind RSS, including the use of RSS in creating audio and video feeds for podcasts.

5. All information on the Web is stored on Web servers. Users interact with the Web using Web browsers run on their PCs and Macintoshes. One approach to make communication between the server and the browser more seamless is called AJAX. Have a member of your team do a Web search on AJAX technology and report how AJAX has affected the way users interact with Web servers.

ProSkills

6. How is the Web changing? Have your team examine some of the latest trends in the development of the Web. Research the goals of the languages currently in development by the W3C. How will these new languages change the way people design Web sites in the future?

7. Assume that you're a designer who wishes to create a Web site that reports on issues involved with Web page design and changes to the Web. Have your team create a Web site that summarizes what you've learned about the changing nature of the Web. The design and content of the Web site is up to your team, but the site should include the following features:

   - At least three pages, one each describing a different aspect of the changing nature of the Web
   - A convenient list of links to enable users to quickly access topics of interest on your Web site
   - Links to all external sites containing the information you've gathered
   - At least one external style sheet used by all of the pages on your Web site
   - At least one Web table listing some of the information you've gathered for your report
   - A Web form in which users can sign up for a newsletter about the changing nature of the Web and HTML
   - An audio or video clip introducing your site's contents to the viewer (if you have the ability to create or locate a clip)

   Have one group of your team work on the page content and another group work on the page design.

8. Submit your completed files from your team to your instructor in electronic or printed form as requested. Clearly identify which members of your team were responsible for which parts of the final product.

HTML

OBJECTIVES

- Insert an image with an irregular line wrap
- Insert and format a Web table
- Insert and format an `aside` element
- Embed MP3, Ogg, and SWF sound clips
- Insert and format a Web form

Creating a Music School Web Site

Case | *Young Notes*

Brenda Li is the owner of Young Notes, a private music school that recently opened in Brownwood, Texas. She has asked for your help in setting up the school's Web site. Eventually the Web site will be extensive, covering all of the services offered by the school; but for now, Brenda wants you to create a site with five Web pages. The first page will contain the site's home page, describing the Young Notes school. The second page will contain a description of the lessons offered by the school and will include a Web table with a fee schedule. The third page will list a few members of the Young Notes staff. Brenda wants the staff biographies to appear within an inline frame in the Web page. The fourth page will contain a list of upcoming Young Notes concerts and recitals. Brenda wants you to include a sound clip from last year's Honors Award Concert in this page. The last page will display a Web form that potential students and their parents can use to request more information about Young Notes.

Brenda has created much of the site's content and many of the site's styles. She needs you to add a graphical image of a Young Notes student, a table with information on lessons, an inline frame for the staff biographies, a sound clip from last year's concert, and a form for prospective students and their families to fill out to get more information about the school. She also needs you to insert styles into her style sheets for these new elements and to link the Web pages together. Once you're finished, she will use your work as a starting point for planning the final version of the site.

STARTING DATA FILES

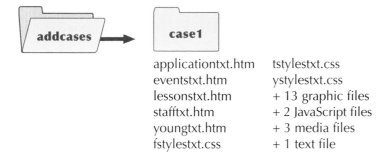

addcases → case1

applicationtxt.htm
eventstxt.htm
lessonstxt.htm
stafftxt.htm
youngtxt.htm
fstylestxt.css

tstylestxt.css
ystylestxt.css
+ 13 graphic files
+ 2 JavaScript files
+ 3 media files
+ 1 text file

Complete the following:

1. Use your text editor to open the **applicationtxt.htm**, **eventstxt.htm**, **fstylestxt.css**, **lessonstxt.htm**, **stafftxt.htm**, **tstylestxt.css**, **youngtxt.htm**, and **ystylestxt.css** files from the addcases\case1 folder included with your Data Files. Enter *your name* and *the date* in the comment section of each file. Save the files as **application.htm**, **events. htm**, **fstyles.css**, **lessons.htm**, **staff.htm**, **tstyles.css**, **young.htm**, and **ystyles.css**, respectively, in the same folder.

2. Go to the **young.htm** file in your text editor. This file contains the Young Notes home page. Brenda wants you to add a graphic of a student to the page with an irregular line wrap around the image. Figure AC1-1 shows a preview of the completed page.

Figure AC1-1   Young Notes home page

3. To insert the graphic, add five inline image elements before the first paragraph directly after the initial `h1` element. Set the source of the inline images to the **student1.jpg** through **student5.jpg** files. Specify an empty text string for the `alt` attribute. Set the value of the `class` attribute for the five images to **irregularWrap**.

4. Close the file, saving your changes.

5. Go to the **ystyles.css** style sheet in your text editor. At the bottom of the file, insert a style to float all `img` elements belonging to the *irregularWrap* class on the right margin, but only when the right margin is clear of other floating elements. Set the margin around those image elements to **0 pixels**

6. Save your changes to the style sheet, and then open the **young.htm** file in your Web browser. Verify that the page resembles that shown in Figure AC1-1, and that the text of the home page wraps around the graphic files that constitute the student image.

7. Go to the **lessons.htm** file in your text editor. This file contains a short summary of the music lessons offered by Young Notes. Figure AC1-2 shows a preview of the completed Web page you'll create for Brenda.

Figure AC1-2   Young Notes lessons page

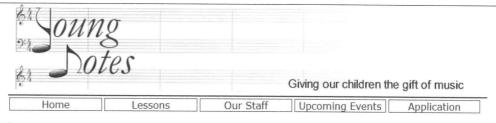

8. Near the bottom of the file, directly above the last paragraph, insert a Web table containing the following elements:

   a. A table heading row group consisting of one row with three heading cells containing the text **Lesson**, **Per Term**, and **Per Year**.

   b. A table body row group containing three rows of table data cells with the values shown in Figure AC1-2.

   c. A column group containing one column element belonging to the *firstCol* class and another column element belonging to the *feeColumns* class. The *feeColumns* column group should span two columns in the Web table.

9. Link the **lessons.htm** file to the **tstyles.css** style sheet and then close the file, saving your changes.

10. Go to the **tstyles.css** file in your text editor. Add the following styles to the style sheet:

   a. Set the font size of the `table` element to **14 pixels**. Add a **10-pixel outset** border with the color value **(68, 76, 169)** around the table. Set the table borders to **collapse** in case of conflicts with other borders. Center the table horizontally in the page by setting the top and bottom margins to **10 pixels**, and the left and right margins to `auto`. Set the width of the table to **400 pixels**.

 b. Set the background color of the table heading row group to **ivory**.

 c. Vertically align the text of all table header and table data cells with the top of the cell. Add **5 pixels** of padding to those cells. Surround those cells with a **1-pixel-wide** solid black border.

 d. Right-align the contents of the second and third data cells within each row. (Hint: Use the `nth-of-type` pseudo-class in your selector.)

 e. Change the background color of table columns belonging to the *feeColumns* class to the value **(232, 232, 255)**.

11. Close the file, saving your changes, and then in your browser, view the lessons page. Verify that the layout and format of the Web table resemble that shown in Figure AC1-2.

 The *staff.htm* file contains the code for the Young Notes staff page. The biographies of four staff members will appear within an `aside` element. The code for the four bio sketches has already been created for you. Figure AC1-3 shows a preview of the completed staff page.

Figure AC1-3   **Young Notes staff page**

12. To create the style for the biographical sketches, return to the **ystyles.css** file in your text editor. At the bottom of the file, add a style rule for the `aside` element that sets the height of the element to **250 pixels**. Have browsers automatically display scroll bars if the element's content exceeds the 250-pixel height.

13. Save your changes to the style sheet, and then view the **staff.htm** file in your browser. Verify that your page resembles that shown in Figure AC1-3.

14. Go to the **events.htm** file in your text editor. This file lists the upcoming events sponsored by Young Notes. Brenda wants you to add an embedded sound clip from a concert performed last year. Figure AC1-4 shows a preview of the page with the embedded sound clip.

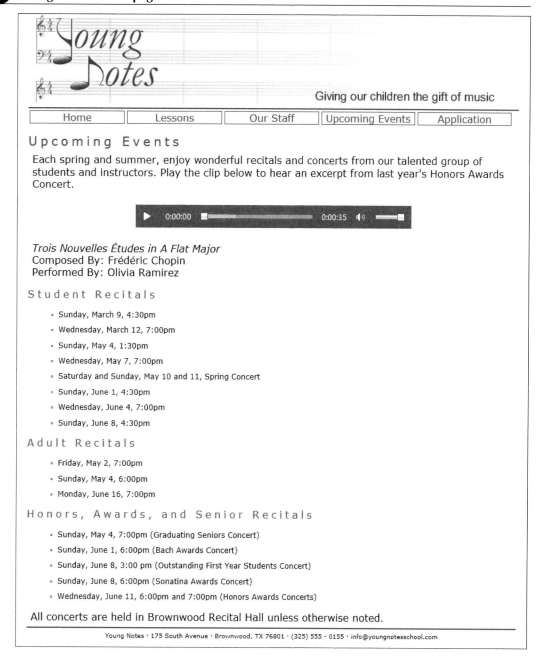

15. Within the second paragraph directly above the `cite` element, insert an `audio` element using the *chopin.mp3* and *chopin.ogg* files as sources. Display the audio controls along with the audio.

16. For browsers that do not support the HTML5 `audio` element, insert within that element an `object` element **350 pixels** wide by **21 pixels** high to play the *chopin.swf* file.

17. For browsers that do not support the `object` element, nest within that element an `embed` element to play the *chopin.swf* file. Specify the MIME type of the `embed` element as a Shockwave Flash player.

18. Save your changes to the file, and then return to the **ystyles.css** file in your text editor. Add a style rule to the bottom of the file to display the `audio`, `object`, and `embed` elements as blocks. Center those three elements by setting the top and bottom margins to **15 pixels**, and the left and right margins to `auto`.

19. Close the **ystyles.css** file, saving your changes. Go to the events page in your Web browser and verify that the embedded sound clip appears above the citation as displayed in Figure AC1-4.

20. View the Web page in an older browser that does not support HTML5 audio. Verify that you can still play the audio within a Shockwave Flash player.

21. Go to the **application.htm** file in your text editor. In this file, you'll insert a Web form that prospective students and their families can fill out and submit to obtain more information about Young Notes. Figure AC1-5 shows a preview of the Web form you'll create.

Figure AC1-5   **Young Notes application form**

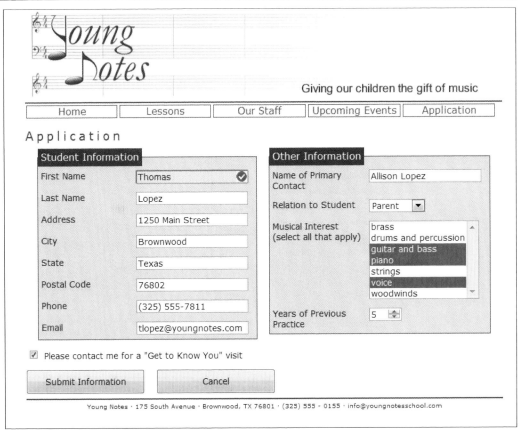

22. Within the document head, add a `script` element for the *formsubmit.js* file in order to process the form if you submit it to the server by mistake.

23. Directly below the Application `h1` heading, insert a `form` element. Set the name and id of the form to **interestForm**. Have the form access the CGI script located at *www.youngnotesschool.com/cgi-bin/interest* using the post method.

24. Create a field set with the id **contactFields** and the legend text **Student Information**. Within the field set, do the following:

    a. Insert a label with the text **First Name**, associated with the **fName** field. Add an input box for the **fName** field directly after the label.

    b. Insert a label with the text **Last Name**, associated with the **lName** field. Add an input box for the **lName** field directly after the label.

    c. Insert a label with the text **Address**, associated with the **address** field. Add an input box for the **address** field directly after the label.

    d. Insert a label with the text **City**, associated with the **city** field. Add an input box for the **city** field directly after the label.

e. Insert a label with the text **State**, associated with the **state** field. Add an input box for the **state** field directly after the label with a default value of **Texas**.

f. Insert a label with the text **Postal Code**, associated with the **zip** field. Add an input box for the **zip** field directly after the label. Using the regular expression pattern in the *regex.txt* file, define the character pattern for the field. Add the placeholder text **nnnnn (-nnnn)**.

g. Insert a label with the text **Phone**, associated with the **phone** field. Add an input box for the **phone** field directly after the label. Define the data type of the phone field as **tel**. Using the regular expression pattern in the *regex.txt* file, define the character pattern for the phone field. Add the placeholder text **(nnn) nnn-nnnn**.

h. Insert a label containing the text **Email**, associated with the **email** field. Add an input box for the **email** field directly after the label. Define the data type of the field as **email**.

i. Make the fName, lName, address, city, state, and phone fields required fields.

j. Below the contactFields field set, insert another field set with the id **otherFields**. Add the legend text **Other Information**.

25. Add the following to the otherFields field set:

a. Insert a label containing the text **Name of Primary Contact**, associated with the **pcontact** field. After the label, insert an input box for the **pcontact** field. Add the placeholder text **Parent or guardian**.

b. Insert a label containing the text **Relation to Student**, associated with the **ctype** field. After the label, insert a selection list for the **ctype** field containing the options **Parent** and **Guardian**. The values for the two options also should be **Parent** and **Guardian**, respectively.

c. Insert a label containing the text **Musical Interest (select all that apply)**, associated with the **interest** field. After the label, insert a selection list containing the text shown in Figure AC1-5. The option values associated with text are: **brass**, **drums**, **guitar**, **piano**, **strings**, **voice**, and **woodwinds**. Set the size of the selection list to seven entries and allow users to select multiple options from the list.

d. Insert a label containing the text **Years of Previous Practice**, associated with the **years** field. Add an input box for the **years** field with a default value of **0**. Set the data type of the input box to **number**, and set the minimum possible value to **0** and the maximum possible value to **12**.

e. After the otherFields field set, insert a check box field named **call**. Next to the check box, insert a label containing the text **Please contact me for a "Get to Know You" visit**. Assign the `label` element to the call field.

26. Below the check box label, insert a submit button containing the text **Submit Information**, and then insert a cancel button containing the text **Cancel**.

27. Link the application page to the *fstyles.css* style sheet. Close the file, saving your changes.

28. Go to the **fstyles.css** file in your text editor. Add the following to the style sheet:

a. For every field set, create a style rule to: i) set the background color to the value **(231, 231, 255)**; ii) add a 1-pixel solid border with a color value of **(67, 76, 169)**; iii) float the field set on the left margin; iv) set the top margin to **10 pixels**, the right margin to **0 pixels**, the bottom margin to **10 pixels**, and the left margin to **2.5%**; and v) set the width to **46%**.

b. For every legend, create a style rule to: i) set the background color to the value **(67, 76, 169)**; ii) set the font color to **white**; and iii) set the padding to **5 pixels**.

c. For every label, add a style rule to: i) float the label on the left margin when the left margin is clear; ii) display the label as a block; iii) set the font size to **0.9 em**; iv) set the top and bottom margins to **7 pixels**, the right margin to **4%**, and the left margin to **5 pixels**; and v) set the width of the label to **40%**.

d. For every `input` element, create a style rule to: i) display the element as a block floated on the left margin; ii) set the font size to **0.9 em**; iii) set the top and bottom margins to **7 pixels**, and the left and right margins to **0 pixels**; and iv) set the width to **50%**.

e. For every selection list, add a style rule to: i) display the selection list as a block floated on the left margin; ii) set the font size to **0.9 em**; and iii) set the top and bottom margins to **7 pixels**, and the left and right margins to **0 pixels**.

f. Set the width of the input box for the `years` field to **50 pixels**.

g. Set the width of the check box for the `call` field to **25 pixels**, displayed only when the left margin is clear.

h. Set the width of the label directly after the call check box to **auto**, and set the value of the `clear` style property to **none**.

i. Display the input box for the submit button only when the left margin is clear of floating objects.

j. For both the submit and reset buttons, create a style rule to: i) set the height to **40 pixels** and the width to **200 pixels**; and ii) set the right margin to **20 pixels**.

k. Set the background color of all input boxes and selection lists to **ivory** when they receive the focus.

l. If an input box receives the focus and contains a valid value, then display the background color value **(220, 255, 220)** with the background image *go.png* displayed in the bottom-right corner with no tiling. Have the background image contained within the input box.

m. If an input box receives the focus and is not valid, then display the background color value **(255, 232, 233)** with the background image *stop.png* displayed in the bottom-right corner with no tiling. Have the background image contained within the input box.

29. Save your changes to the style sheet file, and then go to the application page on the Young Notes Web site. Verify that the layout and content of the application form resemble that shown in Figure AC1-5. Verify that you cannot enter invalid data values or leave required fields with no value. (Note: On some browsers, you will not be able to test the validation requirements of the form, and the input box for the `years` field will not appear as a spin box.)

30. Submit your completed files to your instructor, in either printed or electronic form, as requested.

ENDING DATA FILES

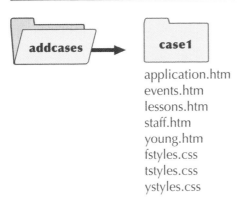

addcases → case1

application.htm
events.htm
lessons.htm
staff.htm
young.htm
fstyles.css
tstyles.css
ystyles.css

ADDITIONAL CASE 2

OBJECTIVES

- Apply shadow and gradient effects to a Web page
- Create a drop-cap for a starting paragraph
- Generate content with JavaScript
- Create a style sheet for printed output
- Create a style sheet for mobile devices

Creating a Culinary Web Site

Case | *Cornucopia Online*

Gary Kendrick is the owner and manager of a shop selling gourmet products. Gary's company began under the name Cornucopia and is based in his hometown of Bristol, Connecticut. The store originally was a small shop in which Gary raised and sold turkeys—still a main feature of the company. As the company grew in popularity, Gary branched out into other fields and products, eventually moving its operations to the Web under the name Cornucopia Online.

The company has been in operation for several years, and Gary is looking at revising the Web site's design and layout. He has hired you as part of his Web site development team. Some work on the new design has already been completed; he would like you to complete the design of the site's home page and work on the Recipe of the Week page.

Because of the store's origins in selling turkeys and other poultry, Gary is aware that Thanksgiving and the holidays are a busy time for Cornucopia Online. So, besides the HTML code you'll write, Gary also wants you to add a JavaScript program to the site's home page that will display a countdown message informing customers of the number of days remaining until Thanksgiving.

STARTING DATA FILES

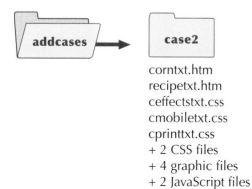

addcases → case2

corntxt.htm
recipetxt.htm
ceffectstxt.css
cmobiletxt.css
cprinttxt.css
+ 2 CSS files
+ 4 graphic files
+ 2 JavaScript files

Figure AC2-1 shows a preview of the site's home page.

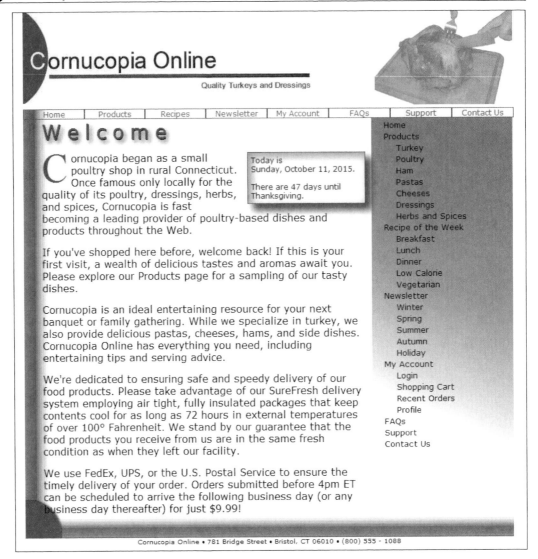

Complete the following:

1. Use your text editor to open the **corntxt.htm** and **ceffectstxt.css** files from the addcases\case2 folder. Enter *your name* and *the date* in the comment section of each file, and then save the files as **corn.htm** and **ceffects.css**, respectively.

2. Take some time to view the **corn.htm** file in your text editor to become familiar with its contents and structure. Link the file to the *ceffects.css* style sheet file and save your changes to the file.

3. Go to the **ceffects.css** file in your text editor. Create a style for the background of the header element to: a) set the background color to white; b) display the *back.png* file in the upper-right corner of the element with no tiling; and c) set the size of the background image to contain. Use browser extensions when required.

4. Add two text shadows to the h1 heading within the article element. The first shadow should be black with a 1-pixel offset in the horizontal and vertical directions, and a blur size of 0 pixels. The second shadow should use the semi-transparent color (127, 90, 0) with an opacity of 0.7, horizontal and vertical offsets of 5 pixels, and a blur size of 10 pixels.

5. Add a linear gradient to the background of the ul element within the vertical navigation list. The gradient should start in the upper-right corner of the element with the semi-transparent color (170, 90, 27) and an opacity of 0.7. The second color in the gradient should be the semi-transparent value (16, 77, 61) with an opacity of 0.4 placed at a color stop of 50%. The last color value should be the semi-transparent value (255, 255, 255) with an opacity of 0.4 placed at a color stop of 85%. Use browser extensions to cover all browsers.

6. Add three backgrounds to the section element:
   a. The first background should display the *corner.png* image in the lower-left corner with no tiling.
   b. The second background should be a linear gradient starting at the left edge with the semi-transparent value (170, 90, 27) and an opacity of 0.7, followed by the semi-transparent color (16, 77, 61) with an opacity of 0.7 placed at the 2% color stop. The last color value should be (255, 255, 255) with an opacity of 0.1 placed at the 5% color stop.
   c. The third background should use the same colors and color stops as in Step 6b except that the gradient should start from the bottom of the element.
   Make sure you use browser extensions to cover all browsers.

7. Gary also wants to create a drop-cap effect for the first paragraph of text in the home page. Create a style rule for the first letter of the first paragraph within the section element to do the following: a) set the font color to the value (170, 90, 27) with a font size of 400%; b) set the font family to Times New Roman or serif; c) float the letter on the left margin; and d) set the top margin to 15 pixels, the right and bottom margins to 5 pixels, and the left margin to 0 pixels.

8. Save your changes to the style sheet file, and then return to the **corn.htm** file in your text editor.

9. Gary wants to display the number of days until Thanksgiving, and he has located some JavaScript functions to display the current date and to calculate the number of days until Thanksgiving from the current date. The function to display the current date is named showDate(). The function to calculate the days until Thanksgiving is called daysToThanksgiving(). He's stored both of these functions in the *tday.js* file. Insert a script element pointing to the *tday.js* external JavaScript file.

10. Scroll down to the h1 heading within the article element, and then insert an aside element directly after the h1 heading.

11. Within the aside element, insert a script element that contains several document.write() commands to write the HTML code

```
Today is<br />
date.
<br /><br /> There are
days
days until Thanksgiving.
```

   to the Web page, where *date* is the text returned by the showDate() function, and *days* is the text returned by the daysToThanksgiving() function. Neither function requires a parameter value.

12. Close the **corn.htm** file, saving your changes.

13. Return to the **ceffects.css** file in your text editor. At the bottom of the file, insert a style rule for the aside element you just created. The style rule should do the following:
   a. Add a 1-pixel solid border with a color value of (127, 90, 0).
   b. Add two box shadows to the element. The color value of the first value should be (0, 0, 0) with an opacity of 0.6, a vertical and horizontal offset of 10 pixels, and a blur of 15 pixels. The second shadow should be inset with a color value of

(127, 90, 0) and an opacity of 0.5, a horizontal and vertical offset of 5 pixels, and a blur of 20 pixels. Use browser extensions so that your styles are cross-browser compatible.

   c. Set the width of the element to 180 pixels with a margin of 10 pixels and a padding space of 5 pixels.

   d. Float the element on the right margin.

   e. Set the font size to 12 pixels.

14. Save your changes to the style sheet file, and then open **corn.htm** in your Web browser. Verify that the layout resembles that shown earlier in Figure AC2-1. (Note: If you are running Internet Explorer Version 9 or earlier, you will not see the gradient backgrounds in the `section` element and vertical navigation list.) Verify that the `aside` element displays the current date and the number of days until Thanksgiving.

15. Next, Gary wants you to create print styles for his sample recipe page and apply other style sheets for screen media. Use your text editor to open the **recipetxt.htm** and **cprinttxt.css** files from the addcases\case2 folder. Enter *your name* and *the date* in the comment section of each file, and then save them as **recipe.htm** and **cprint.css**, respectively.

16. Go to the **recipe.htm** file in your text editor. Add a media query to the `link` elements for the *clayout.css* and *ceffects.css* style sheet files so that the browser applies these style sheets only for screen media, and only when the minimum width of the screen is 501 pixels.

17. Create an IE conditional comment to apply the *clayout.css* and *ceffects.css* style sheets for screen media when the version of Internet Explorer is earlier than version 9.

18. Below the IE conditional comment, insert a link to the *cprint.css* style sheet file to be used for print media.

19. Save your changes to the file, and then open the **recipe.htm** file in your Web browser. Figure AC2-2 shows the appearance of the Web page in the Google Chrome browser. (Note: Other browsers should appear similar except for Internet Explorer version 9 and earlier, which does not support linear gradient backgrounds.)

Figure AC2-2   Cornucopia Online recipe page

20. Go to the **cprint.css** file in your text editor. Add a rule to set the page size to 8.5 inches by 11 inches in portrait mode. Set the page margin to 0.3 inches.

21. Create a style rule to hide the `header`, `nav`, and `footer` elements.

22. For `h1` headings within the `article` element, create a style rule to: a) set the font size to 18 points; b) set the font weight to bold; and c) set the bottom margin to 0.2 inches and all other margins to 0 inches.

23. For `h2` headings within the `article` element, create a style rule to: a) set the font size to 16 points; b) set the font weight to bold; and c) set the top and bottom margins to 0.2 inches, and the left and right margins to 0 inches.

24. For paragraphs within the `article` element, create a style rule to set the font size to 14 points and the margin to 0.1 inches.

25. For unordered lists within the `article` element, create a style rule to: a) set the font size to 12 points; b) set the list style type to `disc`; c) set the left margin to 0.3 inches; and d) avoid page breaks within the list.

26. Repeat the style rule in the previous step for ordered lists within the `article` element, except set the list style type to `decimal`.

27. Save your changes to the file, and then view a print preview or a printout of the recipe page in your browser. Verify that the layout and content of the page resemble that shown in Figure AC2-3.

Figure AC2-3   **Print version of the recipe page**

Grilled Turkey

Take your turkey outside this year and let your grill do the cooking. Grilled turkey is deliciously crisp with a tangy smoked flavor. Properly treated, turkey on the grill doesn't take any longer than turkey cooked in an oven.

Ingredients

- 1 turkey, 12 to 14 lbs.
- 8-10 garlic cloves
- 2 cups lightly packed Italian parsley leaves
- 1 Tbsp. kosher salt
- 2 tsp. freshly ground black pepper
- 2 tsp. chili powder
- 2 oranges
- 1 stick unsalted butter
- 2-4 cups reduced-sodium chicken stock
- 1 large onion
- 1 large carrot

Instructions

1. Remove neck and giblets from turkey cavity. Rinse turkey under cold water and pat dry with paper towels.
2. Finely chop garlic and parsley and place in a small bowl. Add salt, pepper, and chili powder. Add grated orange zest.
3. Mix in softened butter until all ingredients in the bowl are evenly distributed.
4. Starting from neck-end of turkey, carefully separate skin from the breast meat. Push about half of butter mixture onto breast meat under skin and spread it out evenly.
5. Cover top and sides of turkey with remaining butter mixture. Season turkey with salt and pepper.
6. Quarter oranges and place sections in the turkey cavity. Use a trussing clamp to turn wings back, holding neck skin in place. Tie together with a cotton string.
7. Put 2 cups of chicken stock, onion, and carrot inside a heavy-duty roasting pan. Place turkey, breast side up, on a roasting rack, and set rack inside pan. Cook the turkey over indirect medium heat to an internal temperature of 350°.
8. Grill turkey for two to three hours, checking every half hour to verify that the roasting pan has not dried out. If pan looks dry, moisten it with the remaining chicken stock.
9. Turkey is done when the internal temperature in the thighs is 180° and the internal temperature of the breast is 170°.
10. Transfer to a cutting board and let sit for 20 to 30 minutes before carving.
11. Use drippings as a base for a turkey gravy.

Serves 10 to 12.

28. Gary also wants a mobile version of the sample recipe page so customers can view the ingredients and instructions on a mobile device while cooking in the kitchen. Use your text editor to open the **cmobiletxt.css** file, and then enter *your name* and *the date* in the comment section. Save the file as **cmobile.css**.

29. Return to the **recipe.htm** file in your text editor. Below the link to the *cprint.css* style sheet, insert a link to the *cmobile.css* style sheet file, to be used only for screen media and only for screens that have a maximum width of 500 pixels.

30. Below the `meta` element, insert another `meta` element that sets the width of the viewport to match the device width with an initial scale value of 1.0 and a maximum scale value of 1.0 as well.

31. Save your changes to the file, and then return to the **cmobile.css** file in your text editor.

32. Create a style rule to hide the `img` element within the `header` element, and to hide the `nav` element, the `footer` element, and any paragraphs in the document.

33. Create a style rule for the `header` element to: a) set the width to 100%; b) set the height to 80 pixels; c) use the *cornlogo.jpg* file as the background image with no tiling; and d) set the size of the background image to `contain`.

34. Set the font of `h1` headings within the `article` element to a 16-pixel bold font with a bottom margin of 10 pixels.

35. Set the font of `h2` headings within the `article` element to a 14-pixel bold font with top and bottom margins of 10 pixels, and left and right margins of 0 pixels.

36. For all unordered and ordered lists within the `article` element, set the font size to 10 pixels and the left margin to 20 pixels. Set the list style type of the unordered lists to `disc` and the list style type of the ordered lists to `decimal`.

37. Save your changes to the file, and then reopen the **recipe.htm** file in your Web browser. Reduce the width of the browser window at or below 500 pixels, and verify that the layout and content of the page change.

38. Submit your completed files to your instructor, in either printed or electronic form, as requested.

ENDING DATA FILES

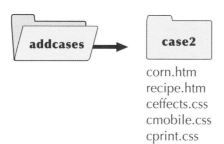

corn.htm
recipe.htm
ceffects.css
cmobile.css
cprint.css

OBJECTIVES

- Create a complete Web site from scratch
- Manage a collection of Web site style sheets
- Manage different HTML5 and CSS3 features on an integrated Web site

Creating a Web Site for a Climbing School

Case | *Cliff Hangers*

One of the most popular climbing schools and touring agencies in Colorado is Cliff Hangers. Located in Boulder, Cliff Hangers specializes in teaching beginning through advanced climbing techniques. The school also sponsors several climbing tours, leading individuals on some of the most exciting climbs in North America.

Debbie Chen is the owner of the school, and she is always looking for ways to market her programs and improve the visibility of the school. She has asked you to help her upgrade the school's Web site. You'll start by working on a smaller version of the Web site that you'll present to Debbie as a sample of what you hope to accomplish for the entire site. Your sample Web site will contain six pages: a home page, a page describing the lessons offered by the school, a page describing tours offered by the school, a page describing the Cliff Hangers staff, a page containing a survey form for interested customers, and a page describing the school's operating philosophy.

STARTING DATA FILES

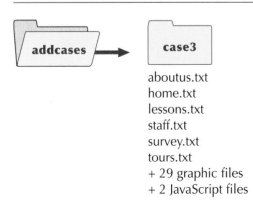

addcases → case3

aboutus.txt
home.txt
lessons.txt
staff.txt
survey.txt
tours.txt
+ 29 graphic files
+ 2 JavaScript files

Complete the following:

1. Use your text editor to create the following HTML5 files: **aboutus.htm**, **form.htm**, **home.htm**, **lessons.htm**, **staff.htm**, and **tours.htm**. Create a comment section within each file that lists *your name* and *the date*, and provides a description of the page and the files that it uses.

2. Use your text editor to create the following CSS style sheet files: **aboutus.css**, **form.css**, **home.css**, **lessons.css**, **staff.css**, and **tours.css**. Create a comment section within each file that lists *your name* and *the date*. Create another style sheet file named **chbase.css** that will contain the basic style rules for all of your pages.

3. Within the **home.htm** file, create a Web page that will serve as the home page for the Cliff Hangers Web site. Use the contents of the *home.txt* file as the contents of your page. You are free to supplement this and all of your pages with additional content and graphics that seem appropriate to you. Use *chbase.css* and *home.css* to design the appearance of your page. The designs and layout you employ on your Web site are up to you. Your Web site should be written based on HTML5 and CSS3 specifications.

4. In the **aboutus.htm** file, construct a Web page that describes the philosophy of the Cliff Hangers climbing school using the contents of the *aboutus.txt* file for inspiration. Put design styles for this page in the **aboutus.css** file.

5. In the **lessons.htm** file, create the code for a Web page that describes the different lessons offered by the school using the *lessons.txt* file as a guide. Put design styles for this page in the **lessons.css** file.

6. In the **staff.htm** file, create the Web page that describes the Cliff Hangers staff using the information from the *staff.txt* file. Put design styles for this page in the **staff.css** file.

7. In the **tours.htm** file, create the Web page that describes tours offered by the school using the information from the *tours.txt* file. Put design styles for this page in the **tours.css** file.

8. In the **form.htm** file, create a survey form for prospective customers of the Cliff Hangers school, basing the form on the contents of the *survey.txt* file. The following field names should be used in the form:
   a. **custname** to record the customer's name
   b. **email** to record the customer's e-mail address
   c. **infoSrc** to record where the customer heard about Cliff Hangers
   d. **experience** to record the number of years of climbing experience, ranging from 0 to 10
   e. **interest** to record the area of climbing interest
   f. **custType** to record whether the customer is interested in lessons, tours, or both
   g. **comments** to record general comments from the customer
   h. **elist** to record whether the customer wants to subscribe to the e-mail list

9. The form should be sent to the CGI script at *www.cliffhangerschool.com/survey* using the post method.

10. Place your form styles in the **form.css** file.

11. Incorporate examples of the following design features on your Web site:
    a. HTML5 structural elements including a header, navigation list, and figure box
    b. hypertext links between Web pages and within a Web page
    c. a Web table formatted using CSS styles
    d. one or more floated elements or images
    e. HTML5 data types and attributes within your survey form
    f. an HTML5 spinner or slider input box
    g. placeholder text within your survey form

    h. CSS3 styles to create rounded or elongated corners, linear or radial gradients, box or text shadows, and multiple background images

    i. CSS3 validation styles to check for invalid data entry or required fields that are left blank

12. Show that you know how to access an external JavaScript file by employing the *modernizr-1.5.js* and *formsubmit.js* files on the Web site.

13. Comment your work in both your HTML and CSS files so that others can understand your code and your choices for design and content.

14. Submit your completed files to your instructor, in either printed or electronic form, as requested.

ENDING DATA FILES

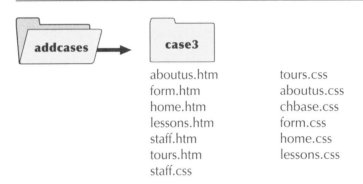

aboutus.htm	tours.css
form.htm	aboutus.css
home.htm	chbase.css
lessons.htm	form.css
staff.htm	home.css
tours.htm	lessons.css
staff.css	

OBJECTIVES

Session 11.1
- Describe the history of XML and the uses of XML documents
- Understand XML vocabularies
- Define well-formed and valid XML documents, and describe the basic structure of an XML document
- Create an XML declaration
- Work with XML comments
- Work with XML parsers and understand how Web browsers work with XML documents

Session 11.2
- Create XML elements and attributes
- Work with character and entity references
- Describe how XML handles parsed character data, character data, and white space
- Create an XML processing instruction to apply a style sheet to an XML document
- Declare a default namespace for an XML vocabulary and apply the namespace to an element

Creating an XML Document

Developing a Document for SJB Pet Boutique

Case | *SJB Pet Boutique*

SJB Pet Boutique in Delafield, Wisconsin, creates beautiful jewelry and clothing accessories "for pets and their humans." The boutique's top two best-selling items are holiday pet costumes, and matching pet collar and human necklace pendants.

During the past year, the boutique has received more requests for custom work. The owners would like to further develop this aspect of their business by making it available on the SJB Pet Boutique Web site. Patricia Dean manages the boutique's Web site. She has been investigating using Extensible Markup Language to organize information about the boutique's product line and the custom work offered. **Extensible Markup Language (XML)** is a markup language that can be extended and modified to match the needs of the document author and the data being recorded. XML has some advantages in presenting structured content such as descriptions of available customizations. Data stored in an XML document can be integrated with the boutique's Web site. Through the use of style sheets, Patricia can present XML data in a way that would be attractive to potential customers.

The boutique's Web site already takes advantage of many of the latest Web standards, including HTML5 and CSS. Patricia would like to gradually incorporate XML into the Web site and increase the use of style sheets. As a first step, she has asked for your help in creating a document that will display a small part of the boutique's inventory using XML.

STARTING DATA FILES

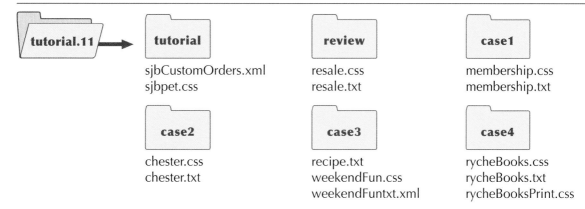

tutorial.11 → tutorial

sjbCustomOrders.xml
sjbpet.css

review

resale.css
resale.txt

case1

membership.css
membership.txt

case2

chester.css
chester.txt

case3

recipe.txt
weekendFun.css
weekendFuntxt.xml

case4

rycheBooks.css
rycheBooks.txt
rycheBooksPrint.css

SESSION 11.1 VISUAL OVERVIEW

The **prolog** contains the XML declaration, optional comment lines, optional processing instructions, and an optional document type declaration.

The XML **declaration** indicates that the document is written in XML and specifies the version of XML used.

The encoding attribute identifies the character set used in the document.

The standalone attribute indicates whether the document contains any references to external files.

Comments in the prolog provide additional information about what a document will be used for and how it was created.

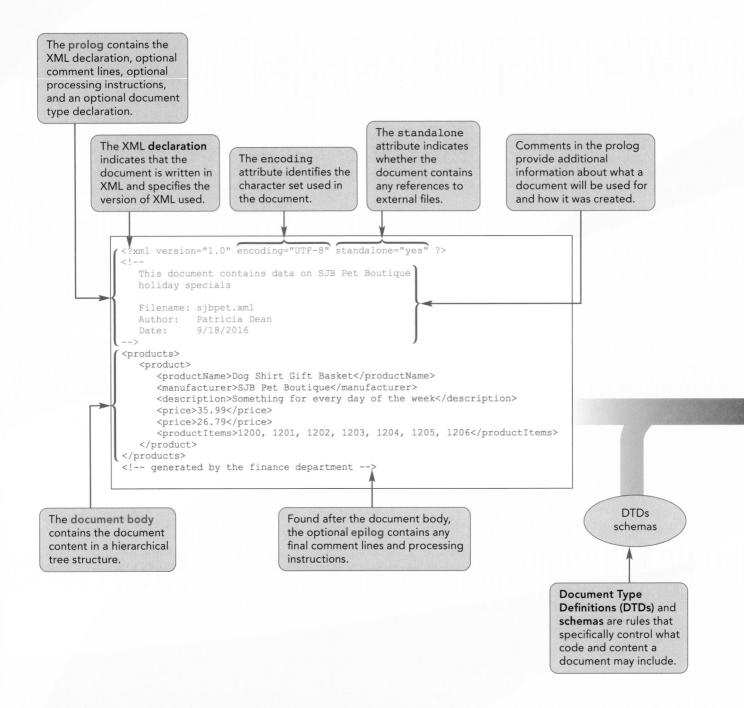

```
<?xml version="1.0" encoding="UTF-8" standalone="yes" ?>
<!--
    This document contains data on SJB Pet Boutique
    holiday specials

    Filename: sjbpet.xml
    Author:   Patricia Dean
    Date:     9/18/2016
-->
<products>
    <product>
        <productName>Dog Shirt Gift Basket</productName>
        <manufacturer>SJB Pet Boutique</manufacturer>
        <description>Something for every day of the week</description>
        <price>35.99</price>
        <price>26.79</price>
        <productItems>1200, 1201, 1202, 1203, 1204, 1205, 1206</productItems>
    </product>
</products>
<!-- generated by the finance department -->
```

The **document body** contains the document content in a hierarchical tree structure.

Found after the document body, the optional **epilog** contains any final comment lines and processing instructions.

DTDs schemas

Document Type Definitions (DTDs) and **schemas** are rules that specifically control what code and content a document may include.

XML OVERVIEW

A **valid document** is an XML document that is well formed and satisfies the rules of a DTD or schema.

An **XML parser** or **XML processor** interprets a document's code and verifies that it satisfies the W3C specifications.

A **well-formed document** has no syntax errors and satisfies the general specifications for XML code defined by the World Wide Web Consortium (W3C).

XML parser

Most major browsers display XML content in a hierarchical format by default.

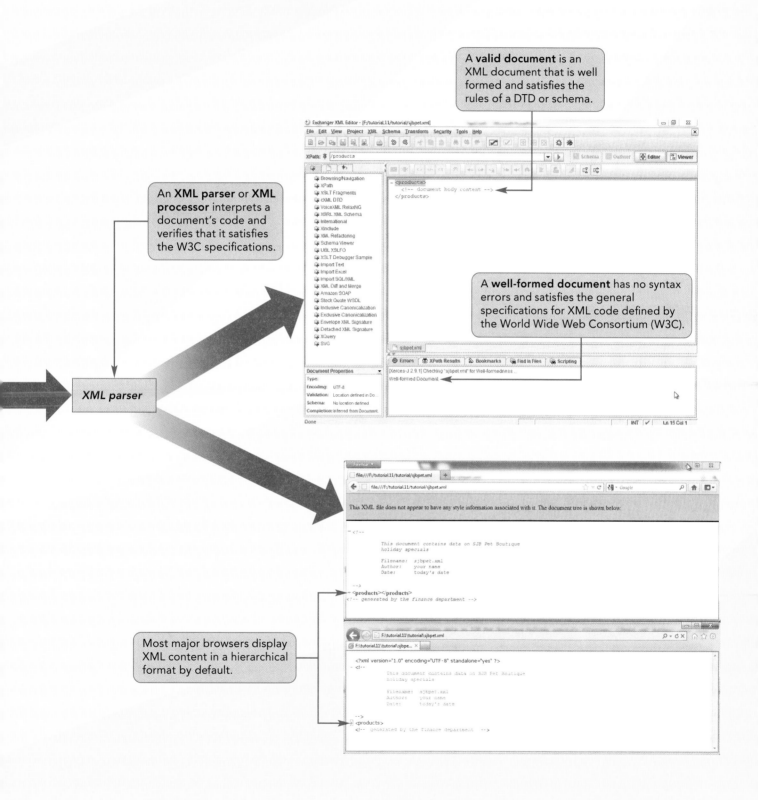

Introducing XML

The following short history lesson may help you better understand how XML fits in with today's technologies.

The Roots of XML

XML has its roots in **Standard Generalized Markup Language (SGML)**, a language introduced in the 1980s that describes the structure and content of any machine-readable information. SGML is device-independent and system-independent. In theory, this means that documents written in SGML can be used on almost any type of device under almost any type of operating system. SGML has been the chosen vehicle for creating structured documents in businesses and government organizations of all sizes.

Even though SGML provides tools to manage enormous projects, it is a difficult language to learn and to apply because of its power, scope, and flexibility. XML can be thought of as a lightweight version of SGML. Like SGML, XML is a language used to create vocabularies for other markup languages, but it does not have SGML's complexity and expansiveness. XML is a markup language that is extensible, so it can be modified to match the needs of the document author and the data being recorded. The standards for XML are developed and maintained by the World Wide Web Consortium (W3C). When the W3C started planning XML, it established a number of design goals for the language. The syntax rules of XML are easy to learn and easy to use as shown in Figure 11-1.

| Figure 11-1 | Highlights of XML syntax rules |

Syntax Rule	Application
Every XML element must have a closing tag.	Every element must have a closing tag. A self-closing tag is permitted.
XML tags are case sensitive.	Opening and closing tags (or start and end tags) must be written with the same case.
XML elements must be properly nested.	All elements can have child (sub) elements. Child elements must be in pairs and be correctly nested within their respective parent element.
Every XML document must have a root element.	Every XML document must contain a single tag pair that defines the root element. All other elements must be nested within the root element.
XML elements can have attributes in name-value pairs.	Each attribute name within the same element can occur only once. Each attribute value must be quoted.
Some characters have a special meaning in XML.	The use of certain characters is restricted. If these characters are needed, entity references or character references may be used. References always begin with the character "&" (which is specially reserved) and end with the character ";".
XML allows for comments.	Comments cannot occur prior to the XML Declaration. Comments cannot be nested.

XML Today

XML was originally created to structure, store, and transport information. Today, XML is still used for that purpose and has become the most common tool for data transmission among various applications. XML is used across a variety of industries, including accounting, banking, human resources, medical records, information technology, and insurance. Generally, it is used in all major Web sites, including major Web services.

XML with Software Applications and Languages

Currently, many software applications such as Microsoft Excel and Microsoft Word, and server languages such as Java, .NET, Perl, and PHP, can read and create XML files. As of the 2007 releases of Microsoft Office and OpenOffice, users can exchange data among Office applications and enterprise systems using XML and file compression technologies. Not only are the documents universally accessible, but the use of XML also reduces the risk of damaged files. Figure 11-2 shows Excel's built-in mechanism for importing an XML file into an Excel spreadsheet.

Figure 11-2	Importing XML data into Excel 2010

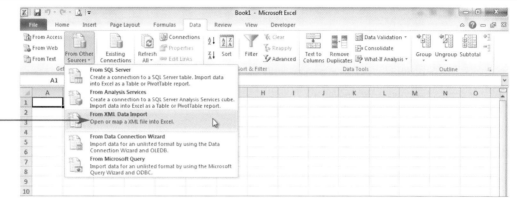

feature in Excel 2010 to import XML data from an external source

XML and Databases

Databases store data, and XML is widely used for data interchange. All major databases, including Microsoft Access, Oracle, and MySQL, can read and create XML files. The fact that XML isn't platform-dependent gives the language flexibility as technologies change.

XML and relational databases are tightly woven together in most Web applications. However, the two use distinctly different models to structure data. The relational model used by relational databases is based on two-dimensional tables, which have no hierarchy and no significant order. By contrast, XML is based on hierarchical trees in which order is significant. In the relational model, neither hierarchy nor sequence may be used to model information. In XML, hierarchy and sequence are the main methods used to represent information. This is one of the more fundamental differences between the two models, but there are more.

On Web pages, XML is very useful because the structure of XML closely matches the structure used to display the same information in HTML. Both HTML and XML use tags in similar ways, often creating distinctly hierarchical structures to present data to users. Most of the data for Web pages comes from relational databases and it must be converted to appropriate XML hierarchies for use in Web pages. For these reasons, it makes more sense to see XML as a tool that works in conjunction with databases, rather than as a competitor to them. Major databases support easy-to-use integration with XML. For instance, Figure 11-3 shows how Access has incorporated easy XML importing and exporting of data.

Figure 11-3 Importing XML-formatted data into Access

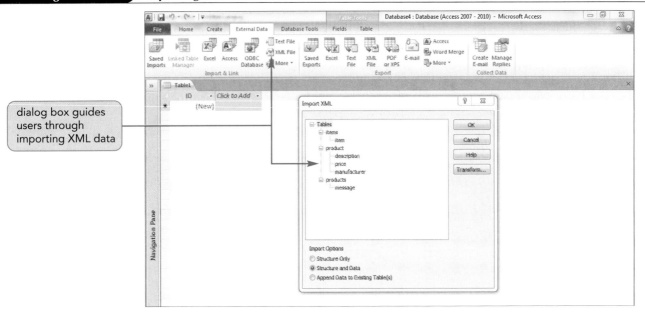

dialog box guides users through importing XML data

XML and Mobile Development

It is highly doubtful that when members of the W3C got together to discuss XML, they even considered mobile device development and the importance that XML would play in this area. In fact, mobile device platforms such as Google's Android and Apple's iOS use XML in a variety of ways.

In iOS, Apple has built in the ability to import and export data classes in XML format. This makes it very easy to transfer information via XML. A popular use of XML in the iPhone is in a preference list or property list—commonly abbreviated as p-list—to organize data into named properties and lists of values, as shown in Figure 11-4.

Figure 11-4 iOS p-list file written in XML

```
<?xml version="1.0" encoding="UTF-8"?>
<!DOCTYPE plist PUBLIC "-//Apple Computer//DTD PLIST 1.0//EN"
        "http://www.apple.com/DTDs/PropertyList-1.0.dtd">
<plist version="1.0">
   <dict>
      <key>Accessories</key>
      <string>Collar Tag</string>
      <key>Shirt</key>
      <string>Week Day</string>
      <key>Bowls</key>
      <string>Ceramic 2 Holder</string>
   </dict>
</plist>
```

Android uses XML for screen layout and for working with data. Android provides a straightforward XML vocabulary for laying out content on the screen, allowing creation of XML layouts for different screen orientations, different device screen sizes, and different languages. Declaring an Android layout in XML makes it easier to visualize the structure of a user interface. Figure 11-5 shows an example of how Android uses XML to lay out the screen.

Figure 11-5   **Android layout definitions written in XML**

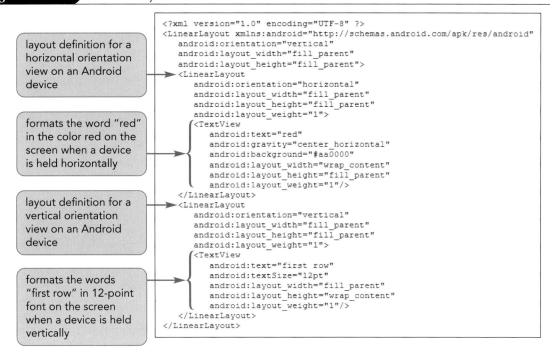

layout definition for a horizontal orientation view on an Android device

formats the word "red" in the color red on the screen when a device is held horizontally

layout definition for a vertical orientation view on an Android device

formats the words "first row" in 12-point font on the screen when a device is held vertically

```
<?xml version="1.0" encoding="UTF-8" ?>
<LinearLayout xmlns:android="http://schemas.android.com/apk/res/android"
    android:orientation="vertical"
    android:layout_width="fill_parent"
    android:layout_height="fill_parent">
<LinearLayout
    android:orientation="horizontal"
    android:layout_width="fill_parent"
    android:layout_height="fill_parent"
    android:layout_weight="1">
<TextView
    android:text="red"
    android:gravity="center_horizontal"
    android:background="#aa0000"
    android:layout_width="wrap_content"
    android:layout_height="fill_parent"
    android:layout_weight="1"/>
</LinearLayout>
<LinearLayout
    android:orientation="vertical"
    android:layout_width="fill_parent"
    android:layout_height="fill_parent"
    android:layout_weight="1">
<TextView
    android:text="first row"
    android:textSize="12pt"
    android:layout_width="fill_parent"
    android:layout_height="wrap_content"
    android:layout_weight="1"/>
</LinearLayout>
</LinearLayout>
```

Creating an XML Vocabulary

HTML is an SGML application and is the foundation of Web development. Like SGML, XML can be used to create **XML applications** or **vocabularies**, which are markup languages tailored to contain specific pieces of information. If Patricia wanted to create a vocabulary for the items in the SJB Pet Boutique product catalog, she might use XML to store the product information in the following format:

```
<productName>Dog Shirt Gift Basket</productName>
<manufacturer>SJB Pet Boutique</manufacturer>
<description>Something for every day of the week
</description>
<price currency="USD">$35.99</price>
<price currency="EUR"> 26.79</price>
<productItems>1200, 1201, 1202, 1203, 1204, 1204, 1205, 1206
</productItems>
```

You'll explore the structure and syntax of this document further in the next session, but you can already infer a lot about the type of information this document contains even without knowing much about XML. You can quickly see that this file contains data on a product named "Dog Shirt Gift Basket," including its manufacturer, its description, its two selling prices, and the product numbers of the items it includes.

The productName, manufacturer, description, price, and productItems elements in this example do not come from any particular XML specification; rather, they are custom elements that Patricia might create specifically for one of the SJB Pet Boutique documents.

Patricia could create additional elements describing things such as the product number, the seller name, and the quantity on hand. In this way, Patricia could create her own XML vocabulary that deals specifically with product, manufacturer, and inventory data.

You'll start your work for Patricia by examining an XML document and comparing the similarities between HTML and XML documents.

Like HTML documents, XML documents can be created and viewed with a basic text editor such as Notepad or TextEdit. More sophisticated XML editors are available, and using them can make it easier to design and test documents. One such editor, Exchanger XML Editor, is used in some figures and steps later in this tutorial. You can download Exchanger XML Editor for free at *www.exchangerxml.com/editor/downloads.html*. However, you can complete the project in this tutorial with a basic text editor.

To open an XML document in a text or XML editor:

▶ **1.** In a text editor or XML editor, open **sjbCustomOrders.xml** from the tutorial.11\ tutorial folder where your data files are located. Figure 11-6 shows the contents of the sjbCustomOrders.xml document for the first order.

Figure 11-6   **Opening an XML document**

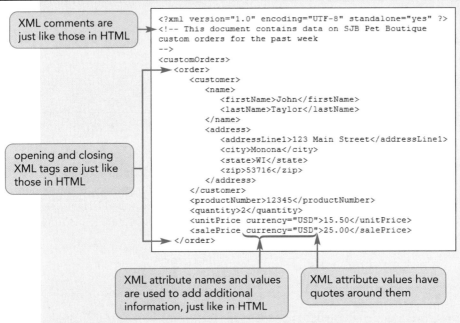

XML comments are just like those in HTML

opening and closing XML tags are just like those in HTML

XML attribute names and values are used to add additional information, just like in HTML

XML attribute values have quotes around them

```
<?xml version="1.0" encoding="UTF-8" standalone="yes" ?>
<!-- This document contains data on SJB Pet Boutique
custom orders for the past week
-->
<customOrders>
   <order>
      <customer>
         <name>
            <firstName>John</firstName>
            <lastName>Taylor</lastName>
         </name>
         <address>
            <addressLine1>123 Main Street</addressLine1>
            <city>Monona</city>
            <state>WI</state>
            <zip>53716</zip>
         </address>
      </customer>
      <productNumber>12345</productNumber>
      <quantity>2</quantity>
      <unitPrice currency="USD">15.50</unitPrice>
      <salePrice currency="USD">25.00</salePrice>
   </order>
```

▶ **2.** Examine the code, noting the similarities between an XML document and an HTML document, such as comments and opening and closing tags. You'll explore each aspect of an XML document's structure in the next session.

▶ **3.** Close the file.

Standard XML Vocabularies

If Patricia wanted to share the vocabulary that she uses for SJB Pet Boutique with other companies, she might use a standard vocabulary that is accepted throughout the industry. You can think of a **standard vocabulary** as a set of XML tags for a particular industry or business function. As XML has grown in popularity, standard vocabularies continue to be developed across a wide range of disciplines.

For example, chemists need to describe chemical structures containing hundreds of atoms bonded to other atoms and molecules. To meet this need, an XML vocabulary called **Chemical Markup Language (CML)** was developed, which codes molecular information. Figure 11-7 shows an example of a CML document used to store information on the ammonia molecule.

Figure 11-7 Ammonia molecule described using CML

```
<molecule id="Ammonia">
    <formula>N H3</formula>
    <atomArray>
        <atom id="a1">
            <string builtin="elementType">N</string>
        </atom>
        <atom id="a2">
            <string builtin="elementType">H</string>
        </atom>
        <atom id="a3">
            <string builtin="elementType">H</string>
        </atom>
        <atom id="a4">
            <string builtin="elementType">H</string>
        </atom>
    </atomArray>
    <bondArray>
        <bond id="b1">
            <string builtin="atomRef">a1</string>
            <string builtin="atomRef">a2</string>
        </bond>
        <bond id="b2">
            <string builtin="atomRef">a1</string>
            <string builtin="atomRef">a3</string>
        </bond>
        <bond id="b3">
            <string builtin="atomRef">a1</string>
            <string builtin="atomRef">a4</string>
        </bond>
    </bondArray>
</molecule>
```

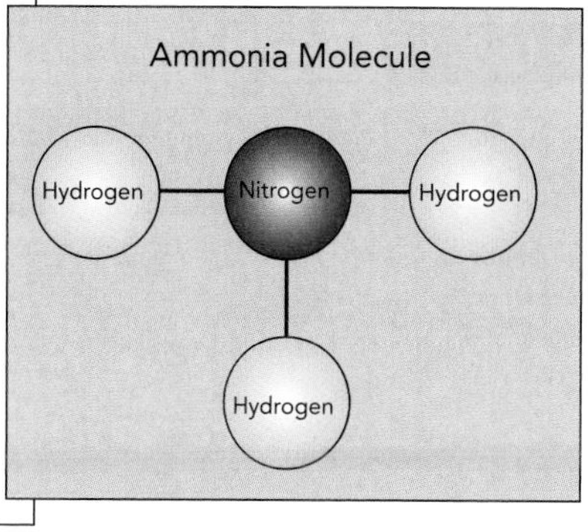

One of the more important XML vocabularies on the Internet is **Really Simple Syndication (RSS)**, which is the language used for distributing news articles or any content that changes on a regular basis. Subscribers to an RSS feed can receive periodic updates using a software program called a **feed reader** or an **aggregator**. Most current browsers contain some type of built-in feed reader to allow users to retrieve and view feeds from within the browser window. Most RSS feeds contain just links, headlines, or brief synopses of new information. Because an RSS file is written in XML, the RSS code follows the conventions of all XML documents. Figure 11-8 shows a segment of an RSS document.

| Figure 11-8 | RSS document |

the item element contains news story information

the title element defines the title of the story

the description element contains a brief description of the news story

the link element defines the hyperlink to the story

```
<channel>
    <title>SJB Pet Boutique</title>
    <link>http://www.sjbpetboutique.com</link>
    <description>Everything for a pet and their owner</description>
    <item>
        <title>Holiday Fun</title>
        <link>http://www.sjbpetboutique.com/holiday</link>
        <description>New holiday products in stock</description>
    </item>
    <item>
        <title>Specials</title>
        <link>http://www.sjbpetboutique.com/specials</link>
        <description>New specials from SJB</description>
    </item>
    <item>
        <title>Clearance</title>
        <link>http://www.sjbpetboutique.com/clearance</link>
        <description>Clearance specials from SJB</description>
    </item>
</channel>
```

Figure 11-9 lists a few of the many vocabularies that have been developed using XML.

| Figure 11-9 | XML vocabularies |

XML Vocabulary	Description
Bioinformatic Sequence Markup Language (BSML)	Coding of bioinformatic data
Extensible Hypertext Markup Language (XHTML)	HTML written as an XML application
Mathematical Markup Language (MathML)	Presentation and evaluation of mathematical equations and operations
Music Markup Language (MML)	Display and organization of music notation and lyrics
Weather Observation Definition Format (OMF)	Distribution of weather observation reports, forecasts, and advisories
Really Simple Syndication (RSS)	Distribution of news headlines and syndicated columns
Synchronized Multimedia Integration Language (SMIL)	Editing of interactive audiovisual presentations involving streaming audio, video, text, and any other media type
Voice Extensible Markup Language (VoiceXML)	Creation of audio dialogues that feature synthesized speech, digitized audio, and speech recognition
Wireless Markup Language (WML)	Coding of information for smaller-screened devices, such as PDAs and cell phones

TIP

You can learn more about several standard XML vocabularies at the W3C site, *www.w3.org/XML/*.

One of the more important XML vocabularies is XHTML (Extensible Hypertext Markup Language), which is a reformulation of HTML as an XML application. You'll examine some properties of XHTML as you learn more about XML in the upcoming tutorials. Don't worry if you find all of these acronyms and languages a bit overwhelming.

DTDs and Schemas

For different users to share a vocabulary effectively, rules must be developed that specifically control what code and content a document from that vocabulary might contain. This is done by attaching either a Document Type Definition (DTD) or a schema to the XML document containing the data. Both DTDs and schemas contain rules for how data in a document vocabulary should be structured. A DTD defines the structure of the data and, very broadly, the types of data allowable. A schema more precisely defines the structure of the data and specific data restrictions.

For example, Patricia can create a DTD or schema to require her documents to list the name, the manufacturer, a description, a list of prices, and a list of product items for each product in the SJB Pet Boutique inventory. DTDs and schemas are not required, but they can be quite helpful in ensuring that your XML documents follow a specific vocabulary. The standard vocabularies listed in Figure 11-9 all have DTDs to ensure that people in a given industry or area all work from the same guidelines.

To create a DTD or a schema, you simply need access to a basic text editor. You'll explore how to create DTDs and schemas in later tutorials.

Well-Formed and Valid XML Documents

To ensure a document's compliance with XML rules, it can be tested against two standards—whether it's well formed, and whether it's valid. A well-formed document contains no syntax errors and satisfies the general specifications for XML code as laid out by the W3C. At a minimum, an XML document must be well formed or it will not be readable by programs that process XML code.

If an XML document is part of a vocabulary with a defined DTD or schema, it also must be tested to ensure that it satisfies the rules of that vocabulary. A well-formed XML document that satisfies the rules of a DTD or schema is said to be a valid document. In this tutorial, you'll look only at the basic syntax rules of XML to create well-formed documents. You'll learn how to test documents for validity in later tutorials.

PROSKILLS

Problem Solving: Designing for Efficiency and Effectiveness

Although XML can do many different things, it is used most effectively to communicate data. In this respect, XML and databases go hand-in-hand—XML communicates data, and databases store data. XML delivers structured information in a generic format that's independent of how that information is used. As a result, the data does not rely on any particular programming language or software. XML developers have the freedom to work with a wide range of applications, devices, and complementary languages. A much larger benefit to the structural and logical markup is the ability to reuse portions of the information easily in any context where the information is structurally valid. Because XML focuses on communicating the data, the overall structure is simple and easy to design and maintain. This approach allows for a high level of efficiency and effectiveness, which in the long term reduces the amount of time and money spent on development and maintenance.

Creating an XML Document

Now that you're familiar with the history and theory of XML, you're ready to create your first XML document.

The Structure of an XML Document

An XML document consists of three parts—the prolog, the document body, and the epilog. As shown in Figure 11-10, the prolog includes the following parts:

- **XML declaration**: indicates that the document is written in the XML language
- **Processing instructions** (optional): provide additional instructions to be run by programs that read the XML document
- **Comment lines** (optional): provide additional information about the document contents
- **Document type declaration (DTD)** (optional): provides information about the rules used in the XML document's vocabulary

Figure 11-10   **Structure of a prolog**

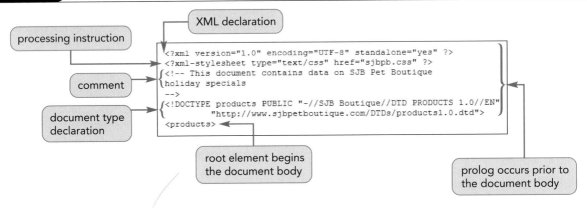

The document body, found immediately after the prolog, contains the document's content in a hierarchical tree structure. Following the document body is an optional epilog, which contains any final comments or processing instructions.

The XML Declaration

The XML declaration is the first part of the prolog as well as the first line in an XML document. It signals to the program reading the file that the document is written in XML, and it provides information about how that code is to be interpreted by the program. The syntax of the XML declaration is

```
<?xml version="version number" encoding="encoding type"
      standalone="yes|no" ?>
```

where *version number* is the version of the XML specification being used in the document and *encoding type* identifies the character set used in the document. The default version value is 1.0. Although you can also specify a version value of 1.1, only a few programs support XML 1.1. With the growth of the Web, XML 1.1 was implemented to allow almost any Unicode character to be used in object names. **Unicode** is a computing industry standard for the consistent encoding, representation, and handling of text expressed in most of the world's written languages. Unicode can be implemented using different character encodings; the most commonly used encodings are UTF-8 and UTF-16. Aside from forward compatibility with the Unicode standard in XML 1.1, there is not much difference between the 1.0 and 1.1 specifications, and most programmers still use the default version, 1.0. If you include the `standalone` or `encoding` attribute, you must include the `version` attribute.

Because different languages use different character sets, the `encoding` attribute allows XML to be used across a range of written languages. The default encoding scheme is UTF-8, which includes the characters used in almost all widely used written languages. However, a number of encoding schemes predate UTF-8, and some are still in use. If your XML document is intended for use with a system that uses a different encoding scheme, you might need to specify the scheme. For example, setting the `encoding` value to `ISO-8859-1` tells a program reading the document that characters from the ISO-8859-1 (Latin-1) character set are being used in the document. The ISO-8859-1 character set has largely been replaced by UTF-8, but some systems and applications still use ISO-8859-1 encoding.

Finally, the `standalone` attribute indicates whether the document contains any references to external files. A standalone value of `yes` indicates that the document is self-contained, and a value of `no` indicates that the document requires additional information from external documents. The default value is `no`.

REFERENCE

Creating an XML Declaration

- To create an XML declaration, enter the code

  ```
  <?xml ?>
  ```

  in the first line of an XML document.
- To specify a version of XML to use, enter the code

  ```
  version="version number"
  ```

  after the opening `<?xml` tag, where *version number* is either 1.0 or 1.1.
- To specify a character encoding, enter the code

  ```
  encoding="encoding type"
  ```

  after the `version` attribute-value pair, where *encoding type* identifies the character set used in the document.
- To indicate whether the document is a standalone document, enter the code

  ```
  standalone="yes|no"
  ```

  after the `encoding` attribute-value pair, where the value `yes` or `no` indicates whether access to external files will be needed when processing the document.

Therefore, a sample XML declaration might appear as follows:

```
<?xml version="1.0" encoding="ISO-8859-1" standalone="yes" ?>
```

This declaration indicates that the XML version is 1.0, the ISO-8859-1 encoding scheme is being used, and the document is self-contained. If you instead entered the XML declaration

```
<?xml version="1.0" ?>
```

a processor would apply the default UTF-8 encoding scheme and the default `standalone` value of `no`.

Because XML is case sensitive, you cannot change the code to uppercase letters. The following code would generate an error because it is entered in uppercase.

Not well-formed code:

```
<?XML VERSION="1.0" ENCODING="ISO-8859-1" STANDALONE="YES" ?>
```

You also must ensure the quotation marks are included around the values in a declaration. The following XML declaration would result in an error because it is missing the quotation marks around the `version`, `encoding`, and `standalone` attribute values.

Not well-formed code:

```
<?xml version=1.0 encoding=ISO-8859-1 standalone=yes ?>
```

The optional attributes for the XML declaration cannot be switched around. The following code would result in an error because the `standalone` attribute must come after the `encoding` attribute.

Not well-formed code:

```
<?xml version="1.0" standalone="yes" encoding="ISO-8859-1" ?>
```

The following statements are samples of well-formed options for coding an XML declaration:

Well-formed code:

```
<?xml version="1.0" standalone="yes" ?>
<?xml version="1.1" standalone="no" ?>
<?xml version="1.0" encoding="UTF-8" ?>
<?xml version="1.1" encoding="UTF-8" ?>
```

Now that you've learned how to structure an XML declaration, you'll begin creating your first XML document by writing the prolog for an XML document to be used by SJB Pet Boutique.

To create the basic structure of an XML document:

▶ **1.** Use your text editor to open a blank document.

Trouble? Some XML editors ask what type of XML document you want to create. If you are using Exchanger XML Editor for this step, choose "Default XML Document."

Be sure to include both question marks; otherwise, browsers will not recognize the declaration statement.

▶ **2.** Type the following line of code into your document:

```
<?xml version="1.0" encoding="UTF-8" standalone="yes" ?>
```

▶ **3.** Press the **Enter** key, and then compare your code to Figure 11-11.

Figure 11-11 Adding the XML declaration

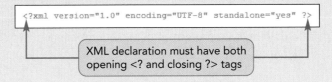

```
<?xml version="1.0" encoding="UTF-8" standalone="yes" ?>
```

XML declaration must have both opening <? and closing ?> tags

▶ **4.** Save your document as **sjbpet.xml** in the tutorial.11\tutorial folder.

Trouble? Some editors, such as Notepad, automatically assign the .txt extension to text files. To specify the .xml extension in Notepad, type sjbpet.xml in the File name box, click All Files from the Save as type list box, and then click the Save button. If you're using a different text editor, consult that program's documentation.

Inserting Comments

Patricia wants you to include information in the document about its purpose and contents. Comments are one way of doing this. They can appear anywhere in the prolog after the XML declaration. Comments in the prolog provide additional information about what the document will be used for and how it was created. Generally speaking, comments are ignored by programs reading the document and do not affect the document's contents or structure.

To insert a comment in an XML document, enter

```
<!-- comment -->
```

where *comment* is the text of the comment. Comments cannot be placed before the XML declaration and cannot be embedded within tags or other comments. You should avoid using the two dashes (--) anywhere in a comment except at the beginning and the end. If you have a comment that will occupy more than one line, you can continue the comment on as many lines as you need. All text after `<!--` is considered a comment until the close of the comment tag, which is signaled by the two dashes. Anything within comments is effectively invisible, so only code outside of the comments needs to be valid and well formed.

You'll add comments to the sjbpet.xml file describing its contents and purpose.

To insert an XML comment:

1. In the sjbpet.xml file, enter the following comment lines directly below the XML declaration as shown in Figure 11-12, pressing the **Enter** key after each line, replacing the text *your name* and *today's date* with your name and the current date, respectively, and indenting as shown:

```
<!--
    This document contains data on SJB Pet Boutique
    holiday specials

    Filename:  sjbpet.xml
    Author:    your name
    Date:      today's date
-->
```

Figure 11-12   **Adding a comment to the XML document**

comment must begin after the XML declaration

multi-line comment describing the document

```
<?xml version="1.0" encoding="UTF-8" standalone="yes" ?>
<!--
    This document contains data on SJB Pet Boutique
    holiday specials

    Filename:  sjbpet.xml
    Author:    Patricia Dean
    Date:      9/18/2016
-->
```

> **2.** Directly below the comment closing tag, add the following code:

```
<products>
   <!-- document body content -->
</products>
```

This code serves as a placeholder for the document body.

Trouble? Exchanger XML Editor automatically adds the closing HTML tag after you type the starting tag. Be sure to type the element content before the closing tag.

> **3.** Add a comment to the document's epilog by placing the following text directly below the closing `</products>` tag, as shown in Figure 11-13:

```
<!-- generated by the finance department -->
```

Figure 11-13 Adding a comment to the epilog

```
<?xml version="1.0" encoding="UTF-8" standalone="yes" ?>
<!--
   This document contains data on SJB Pet Boutique
   holiday specials

   Filename: sjbpet.xml
   Author:   Patricia Dean
   Date:     9/18/2016
-->
<products>
   <!-- document body content -->
</products>
<!-- generated by the finance department -->
```

a placeholder for the document body

the epilog is found after the closing tag of the document body and is a single-line comment in this example

> **4.** Save your changes to the sjbpet.xml document.

Patricia is pleased that you've created a basic XML document so quickly. Next, you'll add the content.

Commenting an XML Document

INSIGHT

Although a developer should easily be able to read and understand the code of an XML document, it's good practice to include comments in a document's prolog. Typically, these comments summarize the contents of the XML data. If there's anything special about the original creation of the XML document, that information should be included as well.

Some businesses have very specific standards for how comments should be coded within a document. These rules might even dictate where opening and closing tags for a comment are coded. For example, you might encounter coding standards that require single-line and multi-line comments to have the opening tag, comments, and closing tag on separate lines, as in the following code:

```
<!--
    single-line comment or multi-line comment
-->
```

Likewise, you might see coding standards that allow a single-line comment to have the opening and closing tags on the same line, as follows:

```
<!-- single-line comment -->
```

Processing an XML Document

Now that you've created the very basic content for Patricia's pet store document, you can work with browsers to display that content.

XML Parsers

A program that reads and interprets an XML document is called an XML processor or XML parser, or simply a **processor** or **parser**. A parser has several functions. First, a parser interprets a document's code and verifies that it satisfies all the XML specifications for document structure and syntax. XML parsers are strict. If even one tag is omitted or one lowercase character should be uppercase, a parser reports an error and rejects the document. This might seem excessive, but that rigidity was built into XML to eliminate viewers' ability to interpret how the code is displayed—much like HTML gives Web browsers wide discretion in interpreting markup code. A second function of a parser is to interpret PCDATA in a document and resolve any character or entity references found within the document. Finally, an XML document might contain processing instructions that tell a parser exactly how the document should be read and interpreted. A third job of a parser is to interpret these instructions and carry them out. Figure 11-14 illustrates the parsing process from document creation to final presentation.

Figure 11-14   **XML parsing process**

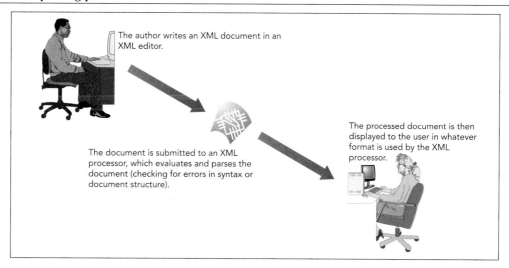

The author writes an XML document in an XML editor.

The document is submitted to an XML processor, which evaluates and parses the document (checking for errors in syntax or document structure).

The processed document is then displayed to the user in whatever format is used by the XML processor.

TIP

Because XML, by definition, includes no predefined elements, browsers can't apply default styles to elements as they do to HTML content; instead, they default to showing the document's tree structure.

The current versions of all major Web browsers include an XML parser of some type. When an XML document is submitted to a browser, the XML parser built into the browser first checks for syntax errors. If it finds none, the browser then displays the contents of the document. Older browsers might display only the data content; newer browsers display both the data and the document's tree structure. Current versions of Internet Explorer, Chrome, and Firefox display XML documents in an expandable/collapsible outline format that allows users to hide nested elements. This is supported by a built-in extensible style sheet, which you'll learn more about in later tutorials. The various parts of a document might be color coded within the browser, making the document easier to read and interpret. Opera displays raw XML that is not expandable/collapsible, but is color coded. Safari parses the XML; in order to view the raw XML in Safari, you must select the View Source command.

You're ready to test whether the sjbpet.xml document is well formed. To test for well-formedness, you'll use an XML parser to compare the XML document against the rules established by the W3C. The Web has many excellent sources for parsers that check for well-formedness, including Web sites to which you can upload an XML document. Several editors check XML code for well-formedness as well, including Exchanger XML Editor.

NOTE: The following steps use Exchanger XML Editor to check Patricia's sjbpet. xml document for well-formedness and view it. If you're using a different XML editor, consult that program's documentation and follow those steps to check your document for well-formedness. If you don't have access to an XML editor, you can upload your document to validator.w3.org *just as you would an HTML document.*

To check the sjbpet.xml file for well-formedness using Exchanger XML Editor:

▶ **1.** If necessary, open **sjbpet.xml** in Exchanger XML Editor.

As shown in Figure 11-15, the editor reports on the Errors tab at the bottom of the window that the sjbpet.xml file is well formed.

Figure 11-15 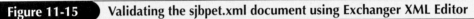 **Validating the sjbpet.xml document using Exchanger XML Editor**

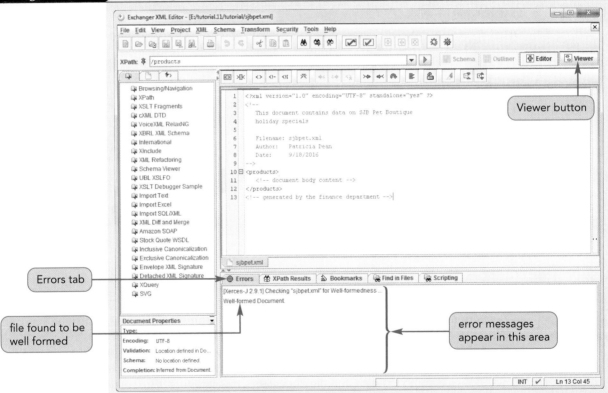

Trouble? If you do not see a message in the Errors tab at the bottom of the window, press the F5 key (or, if that doesn't work, Fn+F5).

Trouble? If an error is reported on the Errors tab, there is an error in the XML code. Check your XML code against the sjbpet.xml code shown in Figure 11-15. Your code must match exactly, including the use of uppercase and lowercase letters. Fix any discrepancies, be sure to save your changes, and then reexamine the Errors tab for information.

▶ **2.** In the top right corner of the Exchanger window, click the **Viewer** button. As shown in Figure 11-16, the editor switches to Viewer view and displays the contents of the document in outline form.

Figure 11-16   **Viewing the sjbpet.xml document using Exchanger XML Editor**

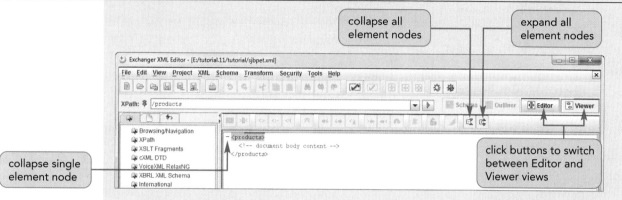

Trouble? If you are unable to switch to the Viewer view, it might be because the document is not well formed. Verify that your code matches the code in Figure 11-15 and then switch to the Viewer view.

▶ **3.** Click the **minus (–)** in front of the `<products>` tag. The Viewer collapses the comment nested within the `<products>` tag.

▶ **4.** Click the **plus (+)** in front of the `<products>` tag. The Viewer expands to show the comment nested within the `<products>` tag.

▶ **5.** In the top right corner of the Exchanger window, click the **Editor** button to switch back to Editor view.

▶ **6.** Press **Ctrl+S** to save your work.

Most Web browsers also function as XML parsers. To see how Patricia's basic document is displayed, you'll open it now in your browser.

To view the sjbpet.xml file in your browser:

▶ **1.** Open the **sjbpet.xml** document in your Web browser. Different browsers display XML content differently. Figure 11-17 shows the contents of the file as it appears in current versions of Firefox, Internet Explorer, and Chrome at the time this book was published. In Safari, the window is blank because the browser displays only the content of an XML document, and your document is currently empty.

Figure 11-17 | **Displaying the sjbpet.xml document in Firefox, Internet Explorer, and Chrome**

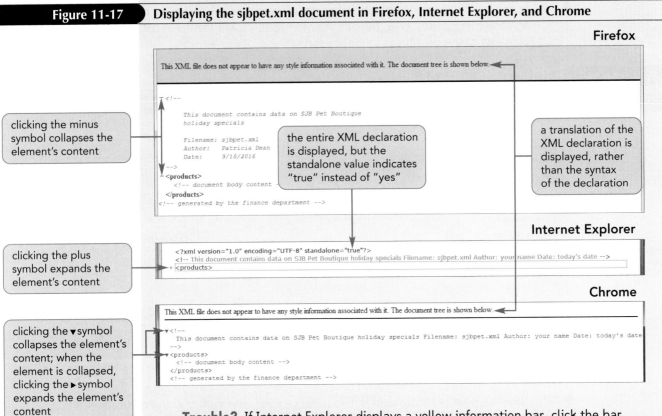

clicking the minus symbol collapses the element's content

the entire XML declaration is displayed, but the standalone value indicates "true" instead of "yes"

a translation of the XML declaration is displayed, rather than the syntax of the declaration

clicking the plus symbol expands the element's content

clicking the ▼symbol collapses the element's content; when the element is collapsed, clicking the ▶symbol expands the element's content

Trouble? If Internet Explorer displays a yellow information bar, click the bar, select Allow Blocked Content, and then click Yes in the Security Warning dialog box to fully display the file.

Trouble? If the sjbpet.xml file opened in another application instead of your browser, XML documents are probably associated with that application on your system. To instead open an XML document in your browser, locate the file in your file manager, right-click the filename, point to Open with, and then click the name of your browser in the list of available programs.

Trouble? In Windows 8, Internet Explorer may not be configured to open XML files stored locally. If you're using Windows 8, you may need to use a different browser, such as Firefox or Chrome, to complete the steps in this tutorial.

2. If you are running a browser that displays the contents of the document in outline form, click the **minus (–)** or the **down-pointing triangle (▼)** in front of the `<products>` tag. The browser collapses the comment nested within the `products` element.

3. Click the **plus (+)** or the **right-pointing triangle (▶)** in front of the `<products>` tag. The browser expands the comment nested within the `products` element.

Because the XML file is well formed, the browser has no trouble rendering the document content. Patricia now wants to see how browsers respond to an XML document that is not well formed. She asks you to intentionally introduce an error into the sjbpet.xml file to verify that the error is flagged by the browser.

To see the result of an error in the sjbpet.xml file:

▶ **1.** Return to the **sjbpet.xml** document in your XML editor.

▶ **2.** Change the second to the last line of the file from `</products>` to `</PRODUCTS>`.

Once you make this change, your document is no longer well formed because element names are case sensitive and a closing tag must match its opening tag.

▶ **3.** Save the changes to your document. As shown in Figure 11-18, Exchanger XML Editor identifies the error and details on the Errors tab.

Figure 11-18   **Error from a document that is not well formed**

line error indicator

error message indicating the line, column, and validation error

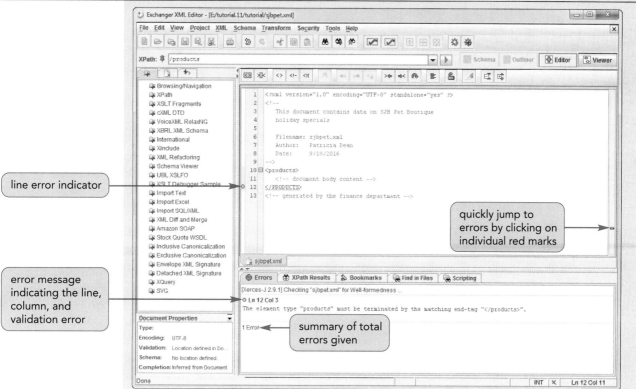

quickly jump to errors by clicking on individual red marks

summary of total errors given

▶ **4.** Refresh or reload the **sjbpet.xml** document in your Web browser. Figure 11-19 shows the contents of the file as it appears in Firefox, Chrome, and Safari.

| Figure 11-19 | Firefox, Chrome, and Safari renderings of a document that is not well formed |

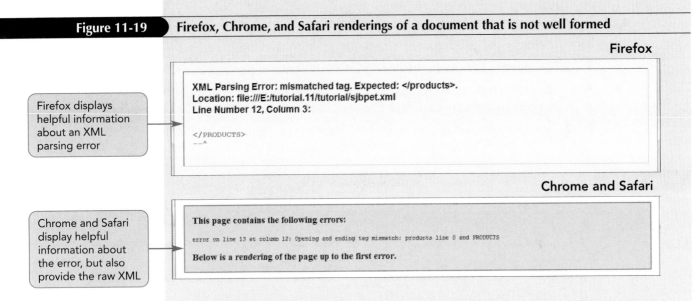

Firefox

Firefox displays helpful information about an XML parsing error

XML Parsing Error: mismatched tag. Expected: </products>.
Location: file:///E:/tutorial.11/tutorial/sjbpet.xml
Line Number 12, Column 3:

</PRODUCTS>
--^

Chrome and Safari

Chrome and Safari display helpful information about the error, but also provide the raw XML

This page contains the following errors:

error on line 13 at column 12: Opening and ending tag mismatch: products line 0 and PRODUCTS

Below is a rendering of the page up to the first error.

Trouble? Recent versions of Internet Explorer handle case-sensitivity of XML and CSS differently from all other browsers and show a blank window. To display the error message in Internet Explorer, press the F12 key to open the developer tools if they are not open at the bottom of the window, click Browser Mode on the Developer Tools menu bar, and then click Internet Explorer 8. The error message should now appear.

5. Return to your XML editor and then replace </PRODUCTS> with </products>. This returns the code to its original, well-formed state.

6. Save your changes to the document, and then verify that the error message is replaced with an indication that the document is well formed.

7. Refresh or reload the **sjbpet.xml** document in your Web browser, and then verify that the browser displays the document contents without any errors.

You have created a well-formed XML document containing a prolog, the shell for the document body, and an epilog. In the next session, you'll focus your attention on adding the contents of the document body.

Session 11.1 Quick Check

REVIEW

1. Define the term "extensible." How does the concept of extensibility relate to XML?
2. What is SGML and why was it not used for authoring pages on the Web?
3. What is an SGML application? Provide one example of an SGML application.
4. Name three limitations of HTML that led to the development of XML.
5. What is an XML vocabulary? Provide an example of an XML vocabulary.
6. What are the three parts of an XML document?
7. Provide an XML declaration that specifies that the document supports XML version 1.0, uses the ISO-8859-1 encoding scheme, and does not require information from other documents.
8. Write the XML code that creates a comment with the text "Data extracted from the sjbpetboutique.com database".
9. What is an XML parser?
10. What happens if you attempt to open an XML document in an XML parser when that document contains syntax errors?

SESSION 11.2 VISUAL OVERVIEW

You link a CSS document to an XML document using a **processing instruction**, which is a command that provides an instruction to XML parsers.

Every XML document must contain one and only one **root element**, which contains all the other elements in the document.

A **CDATA section** is a large block of text that XML treats as character data only. Character data (CDATA) is not processed, but instead is treated as pure data content.

A child element is nested completely within another element, known as its parent element.

An **attribute** stores additional information about an element and has a value surrounded by a matching pair of single or double quotes.

Sibling elements are children to the same parent element.

Parsed character data (PCDATA) consists of all those characters that XML treats as parts of the code of an XML document.

```xml
<?xml version="1.0" encoding="UTF-8" standalone="yes" ?>
<?xml-stylesheet type="text/css" href="sjbpet.css" ?>
<!--
    This document contains data on SJB Pet Boutique
    holiday specials

    Filename: sjbpet.xml
    Author:   Patricia Dean
    Date:     9/18/2016
-->
<products xmlns="http://example.com/sjbpetboutique/produc
    <message>
      <![CDATA[
        At SJB Pet Boutique we are constantly striving t
        our customers (and their humans) the highest qual
        products at very competitive prices. Welcome in
        the holidays' festivities by coming to SJB Pet
        Boutique for your holiday accessories. "Somethin
        you & something for your human."

        Don't forget to get your SJBTracks stamps for
        even more di$count$!!
      ]]>
    </message>
    <product>
      <productName>Dog Shirt Gift Basket</productName>
      <manufacturer>SJB Pet Boutique</manufacturer>
      <description>Something for every day of the week</des
      <price currency="USD">$35.99</price>
      <price currency="EUR">&#8364;26.79</price>
      <productItems>1200, 1201, 1202, 1203, 1204, 1205, 12
    </product>
    <product>
      <productName>Cat Curiosity Basket</productName>
      <manufacturer>SJB Pet Boutique</manufacturer>
      <description>Playtime morning, noon, and night</descr
      <price currency="USD">$15.99</price>
      <price currency="EUR">&#8364;11.90</price>
      <productItems>4430, 6500, 4434</productItems>
    </product>
    ...
</products>
```

STRUCTURING AN XML DOCUMENT

A **Uniform Resource Identifier (URI)** is a text string that uniquely identifies a resource; one version of a URI is the Uniform Resource Locator (URL), which is used to identify the location of a resource on the Web, and the other is a **Uniform Resource Name (URN)**, which provides a persistent name for a resource, independent of that resource's location.

```
" encoding="UTF-8" standalone="yes" ?>
pe="text/css" href="sjbpet.css" ?>

ntains data on SJB Pet Boutique


.xml
ia Dean
2016

tp://example.com/sjbpetboutique/products">


 Boutique we are constantly striving to give
rs (and their humans) the highest quality
 very competitive prices. Welcome in
ys' festivities by coming to SJB Pet
r your holiday accessories. "Something for
hing for your human."

t to get your SJBTracks stamps for
di$count$!!



Dog Shirt Gift Basket</productName>
>SJB Pet Boutique</manufacturer>
Something for every day of the week</description>
cy="USD">$35.99</price>
cy="EUR">&#8364;26.79</price>
>1200, 1201, 1202, 1203, 1204, 1205, 1206</productItems>

Cat Curiosity Basket</productName>
>SJB Pet Boutique</manufacturer>
Playtime morning, noon, and night</description>
cy="USD">$15.99</price>
cy="EUR">&#8364;11.90</price>
>4430, 6500, 4434</productItems>
```

A namespace is a defined collection of element and attribute names.

Character references in XML work the same as character references in HTML.

Working with Elements

The document body in an XML document is made up of elements that contain data to be stored in the document. Elements are the basic building blocks of XML files. An element can have text content and child element content. The content is stored between an opening tag and a closing tag, just as in HTML. The syntax of an XML element with text content is

```
<element>content</element>
```

where `element` is the name given to the element and `content` represents the text content of the element. The opening tag is `<element>`, and `</element>` is the closing tag. Element names usually are selected by XML authors to describe element contents. Element names might be established already if an author is using a particular XML vocabulary, such as VoiceXML. As you saw in the last session, Patricia can store the name of a manufacturer using the following line of code:

```
<manufacturer>SJB Pet Boutique</manufacturer>
```

There are a few important points to remember about XML elements:

- Element names are case sensitive, which means that, for example, `itemnumber`, `itemNumber`, and `ItemNumber` are unique elements.
- Element names must begin with a letter or the underscore character (_) and may not contain blank spaces. Thus, you cannot name an element `Item Number`, but you can name it `Item_Number`.
- Element names cannot begin with the string *xml* because that group of characters is reserved for special XML commands.
- The name in an element's closing tag must exactly match the name in the opening tag.
- Element names can be used more than once, so the element names can mean different things at different points in the hierarchy of an XML document.

The following element text would result in an error because the opening tag is capitalized and the closing tag is not, meaning that they are not recognized as the opening and closing tags for the same element.

Not well-formed code:

```
<MANUFACTURER>SJB Pet Boutique</manufacturer>
```

REFERENCE

Creating XML Elements

- To create an XML element, use the syntax

  ```
  <element>content</element>
  ```

  where `element` is the name given to the element, `content` represents the text content of the element, `<element>` is the opening tag, and `</element>` is the closing tag.
- To create an empty XML element with a single tag, use the following syntax:

  ```
  <element />
  ```

- To create an empty XML element with a pair of tags, use the syntax

  ```
  <element></element>
  ```

Empty Elements

Not all elements contain content. An open element or empty element is an element with no content. White space, such as multiple spaces or a tab, is not considered content. An empty element tag usually is entered using a one-sided tag that obeys the syntax

```
<element />
```

where *element* is the name of the empty element. Alternatively, you can enter an empty element as a two-sided tag with no content, as follows:

```
<element></element>
```

Most programmers prefer the one-sided tag syntax to avoid confusion with two-sided tags, which normally have content.

All of the following are examples of empty elements:

```
<sample1 />
<sample2></sample2>
<sample3>  </sample3>
<sample4>

</sample4>
```

Empty XML elements are similar to HTML's collection of empty elements, such as the `<br />` tag for line breaks or the `<img />` tag for inline graphics.

If empty elements have no content, why use them in an XML document? One reason is to mark certain sections of the document for programs reading it. For example, Patricia might use an empty element to distinguish one group of products from another. Empty elements can also contain attributes that can be used to store information. Finally, empty elements can be used to reference external documents containing non-textual data in much the same way that the HTML `<img />` tag is used to reference image files.

Nesting Elements

In addition to text content, elements also can contain other elements. An element contained within another element is said to be a nested element. For instance, in the following example, multiple elements are nested within the `product` element:

```
<product>
   <productName>Dog Shirt Gift Basket</productName>
   <manufacturer>SJB Pet Boutique</manufacturer>
   <description>Something for every day of the week</description>
   <price>35.99</price>
   <price>26.79</price>
   <productItems>1200, 1201, 1202, 1203, 1204, 1205, 1206
   </productItems>
</product>
```

Like HTML, XML uses familial names to refer to the hierarchical relationships between elements. A nested element is a child element of the element in which it is nested—its parent element. Elements that are side-by-side in a document's hierarchy are sibling elements. In the example in Figure 11-20, the `productName`, `manufacturer`, `description`, `price`, and `productItems` elements are siblings to each other, and each of these elements is also a child of the `product` element.

Figure 11-20 **Parent, child, and sibling elements**

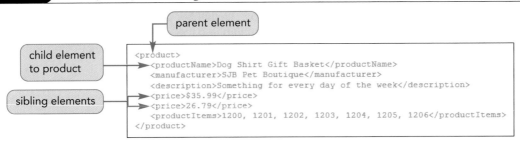

A common syntax error in creating an XML document is improperly nesting one element within another. Just as in XHTML, XML does not allow the opening and closing tags of parent and child elements to overlap. For this reason, the following XML code is not considered well formed because the `productName` element does not completely enclose the `manufacturer` element.

Not well-formed code:

```
<productName>Dog Shirt Gift Basket<manufacturer>SJB Pet Boutique
</productName></manufacturer>
```

To make the code well formed, the closing `</productName>` tag should be moved after the `</manufacturer>` tag to prevent any overlap of the element tags, as follows:

Well-formed code:

```
<productName>Dog Shirt Gift Basket<manufacturer>SJB Pet Boutique
</manufacturer></productName>
```

This syntax is correct because both `manufacturer` tags are within the opening and closing tags of the parent `productName` element.

The Element Hierarchy

The familial relationship of parent, child, and sibling extends throughout the entire document body. All elements in the body are children of a single element called the root element or **document element**. Figure 11-21 shows a sample XML document with its hierarchy represented in a tree diagram. The root element in this document is the `products` element. Note that the XML declaration and comments are not included in the tree structure of the document body.

Figure 11-21   **Code for an XML document along with its corresponding tree diagram**

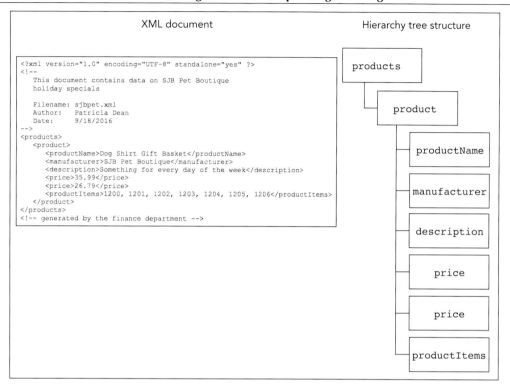

An XML document must include a root element to be considered well formed. The following document code is not well formed because it lacks a single root element containing all other elements in the document body.

Not well-formed code:

```
<?xml version="1.0" encoding="UTF-8" standalone="yes" ?>
<!--
   This document contains data on SJB Pet Boutique
   holiday specials
-->
<productName>Dog Shirt Gift Basket</productName>
<manufacturer>SJB Pet Boutique</manufacturer>
<description>Something for every day of the week</description>
<price>35.99</price>
<price>26.79</price>
<productItems>1200, 1201, 1202, 1203, 1204, 1205, 1206
</productItems>
```

PROSKILLS

Written Communication: Writing Code Visually

Including comments in a file is one way of communicating information about the file contents to other developers. The way you visually arrange your code is another way to communicate with other developers. Technically, child and sibling elements do not have to be coded on separate lines; parsers do not care. Thus, the following code, while challenging to understand at a glance, is considered well formed:

```
<product><productName>Dog Shirt Gift Basket</productName>
<manufacturer>SJB Pet Boutique</manufacturer><description>
Something for every day of the week</description><price>35.99
</price><price>26.79</price><productItems>1200, 1201, 1202,
1203, 1204, 1205, 1206</productItems></product>
```

However, by indenting the code and placing siblings on their own lines, you can visually reveal the hierarchy relationships and add a dimension of visual communication to your code. The following code is the same as the previous example, but now line breaks and indents have been added:

```
<product>
    <productName>Dog Shirt Gift Basket</productName>
    <manufacturer>SJB Pet Boutique</manufacturer>
    <description>Something for every day of the week
    </description>
    <price>35.99</price>
    <price>26.79</price>
    <productItems>1200, 1201, 1202, 1203, 1204, 1205, 1206
    </productItems>
</product>
```

Although the elements are coded exactly the same in both instances, a programmer would spend a lot more time identifying the parent, child, and sibling relationships in the first coding sample. By including simple line breaks and tabs in your documents, you can communicate the structure of your document in a way that complements written comments.

Charting the Element Hierarchy

A quick way to view the overall structure of a document body is to chart the elements in a tree structure like the one shown in Figure 11-21. This can become confusing, however, when a single element has several children of the same type. For example, the `product` element in Figure 11-21 contains two `price` elements within it. Other product descriptions might have differing numbers of `price` elements using this layout. It would be useful to have a general tree diagram that indicates whether a particular child element can occur zero times, once, or several times within a parent. Figure 11-22 displays the shorthand code you will see in the tree diagrams in this and subsequent tutorials to indicate the general structure of the document body.

Figure 11-22   **Charting the number of child elements**

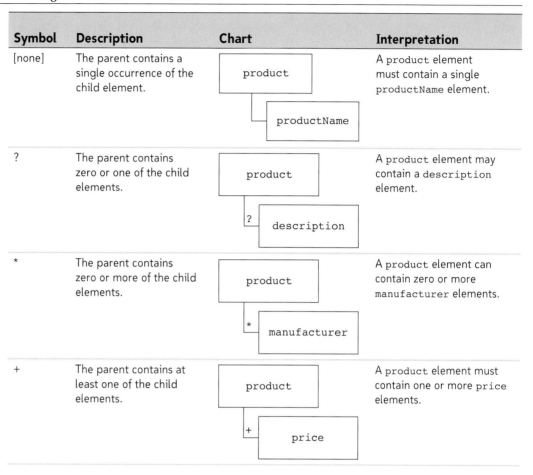

Symbol	Description	Chart	Interpretation
[none]	The parent contains a single occurrence of the child element.	product → productName	A product element must contain a single productName element.
?	The parent contains zero or one of the child elements.	product → ? description	A product element may contain a description element.
*	The parent contains zero or more of the child elements.	product → * manufacturer	A product element can contain zero or more manufacturer elements.
+	The parent contains at least one of the child elements.	product → + price	A product element must contain one or more price elements.

Figure 11-23 shows how these symbols apply to the structure of the XML document you will create for SJB Pet Boutique.

Figure 11-23 **Charting the sjbpet.xml document**

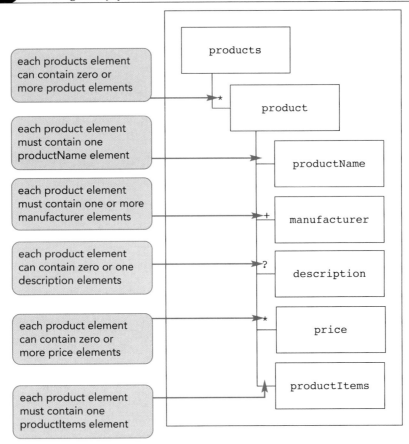

The symbols ?, *, and + are part of the code used in creating DTDs to validate XML documents. Using these symbols in a tree diagram prepares you to learn more about DTDs later on.

Writing the Document Body

Now that you've reviewed some of the aspects of XML elements, you're ready to use them in an XML document. You've already started creating the sjbpet.xml document, which will describe the SJB Pet Boutique's holiday specials. Patricia would like you to add information on the products shown in Figure 11-24 to this document. Patricia has indicated that no current XML vocabulary exists that meets her data requirements. Because you'll create your own XML vocabulary for this document, you'll use descriptive element names for all of the element items.

Figure 11-24	**Product descriptions for the SJB Pet Boutique holiday specials**

Product Name	Manufacturer	Description	Price	Product Items
Dog Shirt Gift Basket	SJB Pet Boutique	Something for every day of the week	35.99 26.79	1200, 1201, 1202, 1203, 1204, 1205, 1206
Cat Curiosity Basket	SJB Pet Boutique	Playtime morning, noon, and night	15.99 11.90	4430, 6500, 4434
Piggy Snuggle Basket	ACME		17.50 13.03	3230, 3232
Dog Snuggle Basket	ACME		14.25 10.61	3230, 3232, 3250

The `products` element will be the root element of the document. The `productName`, `manufacturer`, `description`, `price`, and `productItems` elements all will be children of a parent `product` element for each item.

To add the products to the XML document:

1. If you took a break after the previous session, make sure the **sjbpet.xml** document is open in your editor.

2. Delete the code `<!-- document body content -->` from the document. You'll replace it with the actual document body content.

3. Between the opening and closing `<products>` tags, insert the following code, as shown in Figure 11-25, pressing the **Enter** key at the end of each line and indenting as shown:

```
<product>
   <productName>Dog Shirt Gift Basket</productName>
   <manufacturer>SJB Pet Boutique</manufacturer>
   <description>Something for every day of the week
   </description>
   <price>35.99</price>
   <price>26.79</price>
   <productItems>1200, 1201, 1202, 1203, 1204, 1205, 1206
   </productItems>
</product>
<product>
   <productName>Cat Curiosity Basket</productName>
   <manufacturer>SJB Pet Boutique</manufacturer>
   <description>Playtime morning, noon, and night
   </description>
   <price>15.99</price>
   <price>11.90</price>
   <productItems>4430, 6500, 4434</productItems>
</product>
<product>
   <productName>Piggy Snuggle Basket</productName>
   <manufacturer>ACME</manufacturer>
   <price>17.50</price>
   <price>13.03</price>
   <productItems>3230, 3232</productItems>
</product>
```

```
<product>
    <productName>Dog Snuggle Basket</productName>
    <manufacturer>ACME</manufacturer>
    <price>14.25</price>
    <price>10.61</price>
    <productItems>3230, 3232, 3250</productItems>
</product>
```

Figure 11-25   **Adding elements to the XML document body**

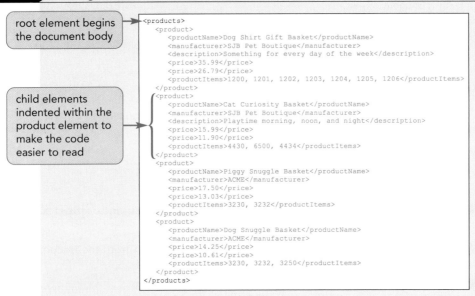

root element begins the document body

child elements indented within the product element to make the code easier to read

```
<products>
    <product>
        <productName>Dog Shirt Gift Basket</productName>
        <manufacturer>SJB Pet Boutique</manufacturer>
        <description>Something for every day of the week</description>
        <price>35.99</price>
        <price>26.79</price>
        <productItems>1200, 1201, 1202, 1203, 1204, 1205, 1206</productItems>
    </product>
    <product>
        <productName>Cat Curiosity Basket</productName>
        <manufacturer>SJB Pet Boutique</manufacturer>
        <description>Playtime morning, noon, and night</description>
        <price>15.99</price>
        <price>11.90</price>
        <productItems>4430, 6500, 4434</productItems>
    </product>
    <product>
        <productName>Piggy Snuggle Basket</productName>
        <manufacturer>ACME</manufacturer>
        <price>17.50</price>
        <price>13.03</price>
        <productItems>3230, 3232</productItems>
    </product>
    <product>
        <productName>Dog Snuggle Basket</productName>
        <manufacturer>ACME</manufacturer>
        <price>14.25</price>
        <price>10.61</price>
        <productItems>3230, 3232, 3250</productItems>
    </product>
</products>
```

4. Save your changes to the **sjbpet.xml** document.

Trouble? If your editor indicates that your document is no longer well formed, check each line of code associated with an error message against the code in Step 3 and fix any errors. Save your work and, if necessary, repeat until the editor indicates that the document is well formed.

You've finished adding the product elements and their child elements. Next, you'll add attributes to the sjbpet.xml document.

Working with Attributes

Every element in an XML document can contain one or more attributes. An attribute describes a feature or characteristic of an element. The syntax for adding an attribute to an element is

```
<element attribute="value"> ... </element>
```

where `attribute` is the attribute's name and `value` is the attribute's value. In the case of a one-sided element tag, the syntax is as follows:

```
<element attribute="value" />
```

Attribute values are text strings. Therefore, an attribute value always must be enclosed within either single or double quotes. For example, if Patricia wants to include the currency as an attribute of the `price` element, she could enter the following code:

```
<price currency="USD">35.99</price>
```

Alternatively, she could instead use single quotes, as follows:

```
<price currency='USD'>35.99</price>
```

Because they're considered text strings, attribute values may contain spaces and almost any character other than the less than (<) and greater than (>) symbols. You can choose any name for an attribute as long as it meets the following rules:

• An attribute name must begin with a letter or an underscore (_).
• Spaces are not allowed in attribute names.
• Like an element name, an attribute name should not begin with the text string *xml*.

An attribute name can appear only once within an element. Like all other aspects of XML, attribute names are case sensitive, and incorrect case is a common syntax error found in attributes. An attribute named `Currency` is considered distinct from an attribute named `currency`, so it's important to be consistent in your case when naming attributes.

REFERENCE

Adding an Attribute to an Element

• To add an attribute to an element, use the syntax

```
<element attribute="value"> … </element>
```

where *element* is the name given to the element, *attribute* is the attribute's name, and *value* is the attribute's value.

• To add an attribute to a single-sided tag, use the syntax

```
<element attribute="value" />
```

• To specify multiple attributes for a single element, use the syntax

```
<element attribute1="value1" attribute2="value2" …> … </element>
```

where *attribute1* is the first attribute's name, *value1* is the first attribute's value, *attribute2* is the second attribute's name, *value2* is the second attribute's value, and so on. Each attribute is separated by a space.

Most of SJB Pet Boutique's business is in the U.S., but the company also has a sizable customer base in Ireland. For this reason, the XML document includes the prices for each item both in the U.S. dollar and in Ireland's currency, the euro. Patricia would like to specify the currency as an attribute of each `price` element instead of as a separate element. She wants to use the abbreviation USD for prices in U.S. dollars and EUR for prices in euros. Figure 11-26 shows the currency for each `price` element in the sjbpet.xml document.

Figure 11-26   Currency values for price elements

Product Name	Price	Currency
Dog Shirt Gift Basket	35.99	USD
	26.79	EUR
Cat Curiosity Basket	15.99	USD
	11.90	EUR
Piggy Snuggle Basket	17.50	USD
	13.03	EUR
Dog Snuggle Basket	14.25	USD
	10.61	EUR

You'll modify the sjbpet.xml document to include a `currency` attribute with the proper value for each `price` element.

To add the `currency` attribute to each `price` element:

1. Return to the **sjbpet.xml** document in your editor.

2. Locate the first `price` element for the first product, which has a value of 35.99.

TIP

Make sure you enclose the value of the attribute within double quotes.

3. Directly before the > in the `price` element's opening tag, insert a space and then type **currency="USD"**.

4. Repeat Steps 2 and 3 to add `currency` attributes to the remaining `price` elements, using the values found in Figure 11-26. Figure 11-27 shows the updated code.

Figure 11-27 **Number attributes added to document body**

```
<products>
  <product>
    <productName>Dog Shirt Gift Basket</productName>
    <manufacturer>SJB Pet Boutique</manufacturer>
    <description>Something for every day of the week</description>
    <price currency="USD">35.99</price>
    <price currency="EUR">26.79</price>
    <productItems>1200, 1201, 1202, 1203, 1204, 1205, 1206</productItems>
  </product>
  <product>
    <productName>Cat Curiosity Basket</productName>
    <manufacturer>SJB Pet Boutique</manufacturer>
    <description>Playtime morning, noon, and night</description>
    <price currency="USD">15.99</price>
    <price currency="EUR">11.90</price>
    <productItems>4430, 6500, 4434</productItems>
  </product>
  <product>
    <productName>Piggy Snuggle Basket</productName>
    <manufacturer>ACME</manufacturer>
    <price currency="USD">17.50</price>
    <price currency="EUR">13.03</price>
    <productItems>3230, 3232</productItems>
  </product>
  <product>
    <productName>Dog Snuggle Basket</productName>
    <manufacturer>ACME</manufacturer>
    <price currency="USD">14.25</price>
    <price currency="EUR">10.61</price>
    <productItems>3230, 3232, 3250</productItems>
  </product>
</products>
```

attribute name and value are defined in the opening tag of each element

5. Save the changes to your document.

Elements vs. Attributes

It's not always clear when to use an attribute value rather than inserting a new element. For example, the following code provides currency information about each `price` element using an attribute:

```
<price currency="USD">35.99</price>
<price currency="EUR">26.79</price>
```

However, you could instead insert the currency information for each `price` element as a sibling element using the following format:

```
<price>35.99</price>
<currency>USD</currency>
<price>26.79</price>
<currency>EUR</currency>
```

Either style is acceptable. Some developers argue that attributes never should be used because they increase a document's complexity. Their rationale is that when information is placed as an element rather than as an attribute within an element, it's more easily accessible by programs reading a document.

A general rule of thumb is that if all of the XML tags and their attributes were removed from a document, the remaining text should comprise the document's content or information. In this scenario, if an attribute value is something you want displayed, it really should be placed in an element, as in the second example above. However, if an attribute is not necessary in order to understand the document content, you can safely keep it as an attribute placed within an element, as in the first example above.

Another rule of thumb is that attributes should be used to describe data, but should not contain data themselves. However, this can be a difficult distinction to make in most cases.

So which should you use? Different developers have different preferences, and there's no right answer. However, when you're in doubt, it's probably safest to use an element.

Using Character and Entity References

Next, Patricia would like you to make sure that the symbols for the item prices display in browsers. Figure 11-28 displays the prices of the four products with the corresponding currency symbols.

Figure 11-28   **Product prices**

Product	U.S. Price	Ireland Price
Dog Shirt Gift Basket	$35.99	€26.79
Cat Curiosity Basket	$15.99	€11.90
Piggy Snuggle Basket	$17.50	€13.03
Dog Snuggle Basket	$14.25	€10.61

To insert characters such as the € symbol, which is not available on a standard U.S. keyboard, you use a numeric character reference, also known simply as a **character reference**. The syntax for a character reference is

```
&#nnn;
```

where *nnn* is a character number from the ISO/IEC character set. The **ISO/IEC character set** is an international numbering system for referencing characters from virtually any language. Character references in XML work the same as character references in HTML.

Because it can be difficult to remember the character numbers for different symbols, some symbols also can be identified using a character entity reference—also known simply as an **entity reference**—using the syntax

`&entity;`

where *entity* is the name assigned to the symbol.

Make sure to start every character or entity reference with an ampersand (&) and end with a semicolon (;). Figure 11-29 lists a few of the commonly used character and entity references.

Figure 11-29   **Character and entity references**

Symbol	Character Reference	Entity Reference	Description
>	>	>	Greater than
<	<	<	Less than
'	&#27;	'	Apostrophe (single quote)
"	&#22;	"	Double quote
&	&	&	Ampersand
©	©	©	Copyright
®	®	®	Registered trademark
™	™		Trademark
°	°		Degree
£	£		Pound
€	€	€	Euro
¥	¥	¥	Yen

Notice that not all symbols have both character and entity references.

REFERENCE

Inserting Character and Entity References

- To insert a character reference into an XML document, use

  `&#nnn;`

  where *nnn* is a character reference number from the ISO/IEC character set.
- To insert an entity reference, use

  `&entity;`

  where *entity* is a recognized entity name.

A common mistake made in XML documents is to forget that XML processors interpret the ampersand symbol (&) as the start of a character reference and not as a character. Often, XML validators catch such mistakes. For example, the following code results in an error message because the ampersand symbol is not followed by a recognized character reference number or entity name.

Not well-formed code:

```
<manufacturer>Hills & Barton</manufacturer>
```

To avoid this error, you need to use the `&#38;` character reference or the `&amp;` entity reference in place of the ampersand symbol, as follows:

Well-formed code:

```
<manufacturer>Hills &amp; Barton</manufacturer>
```

Character references are sometimes used to store the text of HTML code within an XML element. For example, to store the HTML tag `<img src="sjblogo.jpg" />` in an element named `htmlCode`, you need to use character references `&#60;` and `&#62;` to reference the < and > symbols contained in the HTML tag. The following code accomplishes this:

```
<htmlCode>&#60;img src="sjblogo.jpg" /&#62;</htmlCode>
```

The following code would not give the same result.

Not well-formed code:

```
<htmlCode><img src="sjblogo.jpg" /></htmlCode>
```

When encountering this code, an XML processor would attempt to interpret `<img src="sjblogo.jpg" />` as an empty element within the document and not as the content of the `htmlCode` element.

The character reference for the € symbol is `&#8364;`. You'll use this character reference now to add Ireland's currency symbol to the second `price` element for each product. You'll also use the keyboard to add the $ symbol to the first price element for each product.

To insert the dollar symbol and the euro character reference into the `price` elements:

1. Return to the **sjbpet.xml** document in your text editor.

2. Within the first `product` element, click after the opening tag for the first `price` element, and then type the $ character.

3. Within the first `product` element, click after the opening tag for the second `price` element, and then type `&#8364;`

4. Repeat Steps 2 and 3 for each of the remaining three `product` elements, as shown in Figure 11-30. You should insert both the $ character and the character reference a total of four times within the document.

Figure 11-30 $ and euro symbol character reference inserted

```
<products>
    <product>
        <productName>Dog Shirt Gift Basket</productName>
        <manufacturer>SJB Pet Boutique</manufacturer>
        <description>Something for every day of the week</description>
        <price currency="USD">$35.99</price>
        <price currency="EUR">&#8364;26.79</price>
        <productItems>1200, 1201, 1202, 1203, 1204, 1205, 1206</productItems>
    </product>
    <product>
        <productName>Cat Curiosity Basket</productName>
        <manufacturer>SJB Pet Boutique</manufacturer>
        <description>Playtime morning, noon, and night</description>
        <price currency="USD">$15.99</price>
        <price currency="EUR">&#8364;11.90</price>
        <productItems>4430, 6500, 4434</productItems>
    </product>
    <product>
        <productName>Piggy Snuggle Basket</productName>
        <manufacturer>ACME</manufacturer>
        <price currency="USD">$17.50</price>
        <price currency="EUR">&#8364;13.03</price>
        <productItems>3230, 3232</productItems>
    </product>
    <product>
        <productName>Dog Snuggle Basket</productName>
        <manufacturer>ACME</manufacturer>
        <price currency="USD">$14.25</price>
        <price currency="EUR">&#8364;10.61</price>
        <productItems>3230, 3232, 3250</productItems>
    </product>
</products>
```

character reference starts with & and ends with;

▶ **5.** Save your changes to the document.

▶ **6.** If necessary, start your Web browser and then open the **sjbpet.xml** document. As Figure 11-31 shows, each occurrence of the € character reference is converted into a € symbol.

Figure 11-31 € symbol rendered in browser

```
- <products>
    - <product>
        <productName>Dog Shirt Gift Basket</productName>
        <manufacturer>SJB Pet Boutique</manufacturer>
        <description>Something for every day of the week</description>
        <price currency="USD">$35.99</price>
        <price currency="EUR">€26.79</price>
        <productItems>1200, 1201, 1202, 1203, 1204, 1205, 1206</productItems>
    </product>
    - <product>
        <productName>Cat Curiosity Basket</productName>
        <manufacturer>SJB Pet Boutique</manufacturer>
        <description>Playtime morning, noon, and night</description>
        <price currency="USD">$15.99</price>
        <price currency="EUR">€11.90</price>
        <productItems>4430, 6500, 4434</productItems>
    </product>
    - <product>
        <productName>Piggy Snuggle Basket</productName>
        <manufacturer>ACME</manufacturer>
        <price currency="USD">$17.50</price>
        <price currency="EUR">€13.03</price>
        <productItems>3230, 3232</productItems>
    </product>
    - <product>
        <productName>Dog Snuggle Basket</productName>
        <manufacturer>ACME</manufacturer>
        <price currency="USD">$14.25</price>
        <price currency="EUR">€10.61</price>
        <productItems>3230, 3232, 3250</productItems>
    </product>
</products>
```

browser replaces each occurrence of € with € symbol

Understanding Text Characters and White Space

As you've seen from working on the sjbpet.xml document, XML documents consist only of text characters. However, text characters fall into three categories—parsed character data, character data, and white space. In order to appreciate how programs like browsers interpret XML documents, it's important to understand the distinctions among these categories.

Parsed Character Data

Parsed character data (PCDATA) consists of all those characters that XML treats as parts of the code of an XML document. This includes characters found in the following:

- the XML declaration
- the opening and closing tags of an element
- empty element tags
- character or entity references
- comments

Parsed character data also can be found in other XML features that you'll learn about in later tutorials, such as processing instructions and document type declarations.

The presence of PCDATA can cause unexpected errors to occur within a document. XML treats any element content as potential PCDATA because elements may contain other elements. This means that symbols such as &, <, or >, which are all used in creating markup tags or entity references, are extracted and the appropriate content is used in your program. For example, the following line would result in an error because the greater than symbol (>) in the temperature value would be viewed as the end of a markup tag.

Not well-formed code:

```
<temperature> > 98.6 degrees</temperature>
```

Because the greater than symbol does not have any accompanying markup tag characters, the document would be rejected for being not well formed. To correct this error, you would have to replace the greater than symbol with either the character reference `&#62;` or the entity reference `&gt;`. The correct temperature value would then be entered as follows:

Well-formed code:

```
<temperature>&gt;98.6 degrees</temperature>
```

If you instead wanted to display the above line without it being parsed, you would code it as follows:

```
&lt;temperature&gt; &gt;98.6 degrees&lt;/temperature&gt;
```

Character Data

After you account for parsed character data, the remaining symbols constitute a document's actual contents, known as character data. Character data is not processed, but instead is treated as pure data content. One purpose of character and entity references is to convert PCDATA into character data. For example, when the program reading an XML document encounters the entity reference `&gt;`, it converts it to the corresponding character data symbol **>**.

White Space

The third type of character that an XML document can contain is white space. White space refers to nonprintable characters such as spaces (created by pressing the spacebar), new line characters (created by pressing the Enter key), or tab characters (created by pressing the Tab key). Processors reading an XML document must determine whether white space represents actual content or is used to make the code more readable. For example, the code you've entered in the SJB Pet Boutique document is indented to make it more readable to users. However, this does not have any impact on how the XML document's contents or structure are interpreted.

HTML applies **white space stripping**, in which consecutive occurrences of white space are treated as a single space. White space stripping allows HTML authors to format a document's code to be readable without affecting the document's appearance in browsers. As a result of white space stripping, the HTML code

```
<p>This is a
    paragraph.</p>
```

is treated the same as

```
<p>This is a paragraph.</p>
```

White space is treated slightly differently in XML. Technically, no white space stripping occurs for element content, which means that the content of the XML element

```
<paragraph>This is    a
      Paragraph.</paragraph>
```

is interpreted as

```
This is    a
      Paragraph.
```

This preserves both the new line character and all of the blank spaces.

However, the majority of browsers today transform XML code into HTML, and in the process apply white space stripping to element content. Thus, in browsers such as Internet Explorer, Firefox, or Chrome, the contents of the above XML element would be displayed as

```
This is a paragraph.
```

When white space appears in places other than element content, XML treats it in the following manner:

- White space is ignored when it is the only character data between element tags; this allows XML authors to format their documents to be readable without affecting the content or structure.
- White space is ignored within a document's prolog and epilog, and within any element tags.
- White space within an attribute value is treated as part of the attribute value.

In summary, white space in an XML document is generally ignored unless it is part of the document's data.

TIP

Not all browsers parse white space in the same way, so be sure to preview your documents in a variety of browsers.

Creating a CDATA Section

Sometimes an XML document needs to store significant blocks of text containing the < and > symbols. For example, what if you wanted to place all of the text from this tutorial into an XML document? If there were only a few < and > symbols, it might not be too much work to replace them all with < and > character references, or with < and > entity references. However, given the volume of text in this tutorial, it would be cumbersome to replace all of the < and > symbols with the associated character or entity references, and the code itself would be difficult to read.

As an alternative to using character references, you can place text into a CDATA section. A CDATA section is a block of text that XML treats as character data only. The syntax for creating a CDATA section is

```
<![CDATA [
    character data
]]>
```

A CDATA section may contain most markup characters, such as <, >, and &. In a CDATA section, these characters are interpreted by XML parsers or XML editors as text rather than as markup commands. A CDATA section

- may be placed anywhere within a document.
- cannot be nested within other CDATA sections.
- cannot be empty.

The only sequence of symbols that may not occur within a CDATA section is]] because this is the marker ending a CDATA section.

The following example shows an element named `htmlCode` containing a CDATA section used to store several HTML tags:

```
<htmlCode>
    <![CDATA[
        <h1>SJB Pet Boutique</h1>
        <h2>Fashion for Pets and Their Humans</h2>
    ]]>
</htmlCode>
```

The text in this example is treated by XML as character data, not PCDATA. Therefore, a processor would not read the <h1> and <h2> character strings as element tags. You might find it useful to place any large block of text within a CDATA section to protect yourself from inadvertently inserting a character such as the ampersand symbol that would be misinterpreted by an XML processor.

Patricia would like you to insert a message element into the sjbpet.xml document that describes the purpose and contents of the document. You'll use a CDATA section for this task.

To create a CDATA section:

1. Return to the **sjbpet.xml** document in your XML editor.

2. Insert a blank line below the opening `<products>` tag, and then enter the following code, pressing **Enter** at the end of each line, as shown in Figure 11-32:

```
<message>
  <![CDATA[
    At SJB Pet Boutique we are constantly striving to give
    our customers (and their humans) the highest quality
    products at very competitive prices. Welcome in
    the holidays' festivities by coming to SJB Pet
    Boutique for your holiday accessories. "Something for
    you & something for your human."

    Don't forget to get your SJBTracks stamps for
    even more di$count$!!
  ]]>
</message>
```

Figure 11-32 Adding a CDATA section

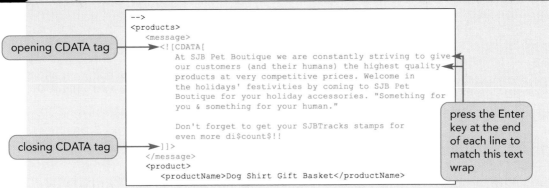

opening CDATA tag

closing CDATA tag

press the Enter key at the end of each line to match this text wrap

```
-->
<products>
    <message>
        <![CDATA[
            At SJB Pet Boutique we are constantly striving to give
            our customers (and their humans) the highest quality
            products at very competitive prices. Welcome in
            the holidays' festivities by coming to SJB Pet
            Boutique for your holiday accessories. "Something for
            you & something for your human."

            Don't forget to get your SJBTracks stamps for
            even more di$count$!!
        ]]>
    </message>
    <product>
        <productName>Dog Shirt Gift Basket</productName>
```

▶ **3.** Save the changes to your document.

▶ **4.** Verify that your document is well formed, and correct any errors if necessary.

Trouble? In Exchanger XML Editor, if an error is shown on the Errors tab, there is an error in the XML code. Check your XML code against the sjbpet.xml code shown in Figure 11-32. Your newly added code should match exactly, including the use of uppercase and lowercase letters. Fix any discrepancies, be sure to save your changes, and then reexamine the Errors tab for validation information.

▶ **5.** In Exchanger XML Editor, click the **Viewer** button in the upper-right corner of the application. As shown in Figure 11-33, the white space is preserved within the CDATA section of the sjbpet.xml contents.

Figure 11-33 Viewing the sjbpet.xml document using Exchanger XML Editor

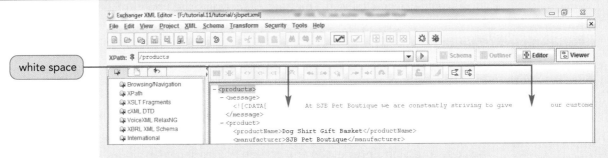

white space

Trouble? If you are unable to switch to the Viewer view, it may be because the document is not well formed. Verify that your code matches the code in Figure 11-32 and then switch to the Viewer view.

Trouble? If you're using a text editor without a preview mode, you'll explore the display of the CDATA content in a browser in the next set of steps.

▶ **6.** In Exchanger XML Editor, click the **Editor** button in the upper-right corner of the application to return to Editor view.

You've completed your work to create Patricia's XML document. Next, you'll display the document in a Web browser.

CDATA Cans and Cannots

INSIGHT

New authors of XML documents often mistakenly use CDATA to protect data from being treated as ordinary character data during processing. Character data is character data, regardless of whether it is expressed via a CDATA section or ordinary markup. CDATA blocks can be very useful as long as you keep a few CDATA rules in mind.

You *can* use CDATA blocks when you want to include large blocks of special characters as character data. This saves the time it would take to replace characters with their corresponding entity references. However, keep in mind the size of the CDATA sections. If you serve XML files through a Web service, you must ensure that client applications can handle potentially large data transfers without timing out or blocking their user interfaces. You also should make sure your server can accept large upstream transfers from clients sending XML data. Sending large blocks of data from the browser in this manner can be error-prone and tends to lock up valuable resources on the server and the client. You also should keep in mind that many users may be using mobile platforms, and there may be implications with attempting such large data transfers.

You *cannot* expect to keep markup untouched just because it looks as though it would be securely concealed inside a CDATA section. New programmers often assume that they can hide JavaScript or HTML markup by putting it inside a CDATA section. The content is still there, but it's treated as text.

You *cannot* use XML comments in a CDATA section. The literal text of the comment tags and comment text, such as <!-- December special events -->, is passed directly to the application or screen.

You *cannot* nest a CDATA section inside another CDATA section. While processing the XML document, the nested section end marker]]> is encountered before the real section end, which can cause a parser to assume that the nested section marker is the end of your CDATA section. This might cause a parser error when it subsequently hits the real section end.

CDATA has its own special rules. If you master them, CDATA can be a very powerful tool for your XML documents.

To see how Patricia's document is displayed with all of the added content, you'll open it in your Web browser.

To view thse *sjbpet.xml* file in your browser:

1. In your Web browser, refresh or reload the **sjbpet.xml** document.

2. Locate the `message` element. Because different browsers display XML content differently, in the CDATA section, the CDATA tags and white space might or might not be shown in a given browser. Figure 11-34 shows the contents of the file as it appears in Firefox, Chrome, and Internet Explorer. Safari and Opera display CDATA sections in a way similar to Chrome.

Figure 11-34 Displaying the sjbpet.xml document in Firefox and Chrome

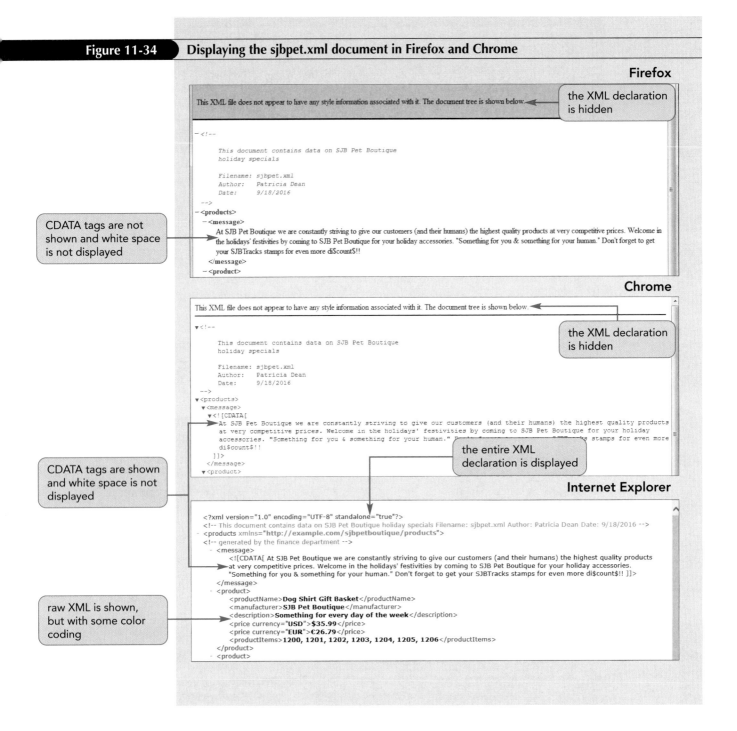

Formatting XML Data with CSS

Patricia appreciates your work on the XML document. She would like to share this type of information with other users and place it on the Web. However, she does not want to display the contents in the default hierarchical format shown in Figure 11-34. She would instead like to have the data formatted in a visually attractive way.

In contrast to HTML documents, XML documents do not include any information about *how* they should be rendered. Rendering is determined solely by the parser processing the document. As seen previously, different browsers render XML differently when an XML document does not indicate how its data is to be formatted or displayed. If you want to have control over the document's appearance, you have to physically link the document to a style sheet. The XML document and the style sheet are then combined by an XML parser to render a single formatted document as shown in Figure 11-35.

Figure 11-35	**Combining an XML document and a style sheet**

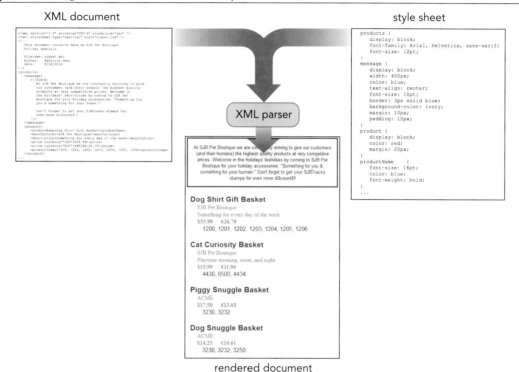

rendered document

Applying a Style to an Element

Cascading Style Sheets (CSS), the style sheet language developed for use with HTML on the Web, also can be used with the elements in any XML document. CSS styles are applied to an XML element using the style declaration

```
selector {
    attribute1: value1;
    attribute2: value2;
    ...
}
```

where *selector* identifies an element (or a set of elements with each element separated by a comma) from the XML document; *attribute1*, *attribute2*, and so on are CSS style attributes; and *value1*, value2, and so forth are values of the CSS styles. For example, the following style declaration displays the text of the `author` element in a red boldface type:

```
author {
    color: red;
    font-weight: bold;
}
```

Creating and Attaching a Style to an Element in an XML Document

- To create a style rule for an element, use the syntax

```
selector {
    attribute1: value1;
    attribute2: value2;
    …
}
```

where *selector* identifies an element (or a set of elements, with each element separated by a comma) from the XML document; *attribute1*, *attribute2*, and so on are CSS style attributes; and *value1*, *value2*, and so forth are values of the CSS styles.

- To attach a CSS style sheet to an XML document, insert the processing instruction

```
<?xml-stylesheet type="text/css" href="url" media="type" ?>
```

within the XML document's prolog, where *url* is the name and location of the CSS file, and the value of the optional *media* attribute describes the type of output device to which the style sheet should be applied. If no *media* value is specified, a default value of *all* is used.

Patricia already has generated a style sheet for the elements of the sjbpet.xml file and stored the styles in an external style sheet named sjbpet.css. To see how the styles in this style sheet will affect the appearance of the sjbpet.xml document, you must link the XML document to the style sheet.

Inserting a Processing Instruction

You create a link from an XML document to a style sheet by using a processing instruction. A processing instruction is a command that tells an XML parser how to process the document. Processing instructions have the general form

```
<?target instruction ?>
```

where *target* identifies the program (or object) to which the processing instruction is directed and *instruction* is information that the document passes on to the parser for processing. Usually the instruction takes the form of attributes and attribute values. For example, the basic processing instruction to link the contents of an XML document to a style sheet is

```
<?xml-stylesheet type="style" href="url" media="type" ?>
```

where *style* is the type of style sheet the XML processor will be accessing, *url* is the name and location of the style sheet, and *type* is the type of output device to which the style sheet is to be applied. In this example, `xml-stylesheet` is the processing instruction's target, and the other items within the tag are processing instructions that identify the type, location, and output media for the style sheet. For a style sheet, the value of the `type` attribute should be `text/css`. The most commonly used `media` types are `screen` and `print`. If no `media` value is specified, a default value of `all` is used. The following example applies a style sheet called main.css to all output devices:

```
<?xml-stylesheet type="text/css" href="main.css" media="all" ?>
```

The same processing instruction for all output devices could be coded as follows:

```
<?xml-stylesheet type="text/css" href="main.css" ?>
```

Multiple processing instructions can exist within the same XML document for different media types. The following example shows two processing instructions being included within the same document:

```
<?xml-stylesheet type="text/css" href="main.css" media="screen" ?>
<?xml-stylesheet type="text/css" href="myPrint.css"
                 media="print" ?>
```

If you prefer to avoid using the media attribute, the @media and @import rules for CSS can be used instead. The following example uses the screen media type and the print media type within the same CSS file:

```
@media screen {
    product {
        font-size:   12pt;
    }
}
@media print {
    product {
        font-size:   10pt;
    }
}
```

The above CSS applies a 12-point font size to the product element if the information is displayed on a screen, but applies a 10-point font size to the product element if the information is sent to a printer.

You'll add a processing instruction to the sjbpet.xml file to access the styles in the sjbpet.css file.

To link the sjbpet.xml file to the sjbpet.css style sheet:

1. Return to the **sjbpet.xml** document in your text editor.

2. Below the XML declaration in the prolog, insert the following processing instruction (see Figure 11-36), making sure not to include a space after the first question mark, and also making sure to include a space before the final question mark:

```
<?xml-stylesheet type="text/css" href="sjbpet.css" ?>
```

Figure 11-36   **Inserting the processing instruction**

processing instruction for connecting to the sjbpet.css style sheet →

```
<?xml version="1.0" encoding="UTF-8" standalone="yes" ?>
<?xml-stylesheet type="text/css" href="sjbpet.css" ?>
<!--
    This document contains data on SJB Pet Boutique
    holiday specials

    Filename:  sjbpet.xml
    Author:    Patricia Dean
    Date:      9/18/2016
-->
```

3. Save the changes to your document.

4. Refresh or reload the **sjbpet.xml** document in your Web browser. Figure 11-37 shows the sjbpet.xml file in a browser with the sjbpet.css style sheet applied to the file's contents. The browser uses the specified style sheet in place of its default styles.

Figure 11-37	The sjbpet.xml document with style sheet applied

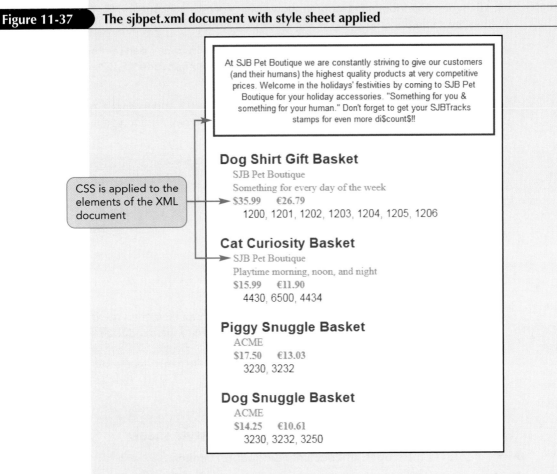

At SJB Pet Boutique we are constantly striving to give our customers (and their humans) the highest quality products at very competitive prices. Welcome in the holidays' festivities by coming to SJB Pet Boutique for your holiday accessories. "Something for you & something for your human." Don't forget to get your SJBTracks stamps for even more di$count$!!

Dog Shirt Gift Basket
SJB Pet Boutique
Something for every day of the week
$35.99   €26.79
1200, 1201, 1202, 1203, 1204, 1205, 1206

Cat Curiosity Basket
SJB Pet Boutique
Playtime morning, noon, and night
$15.99   €11.90
4430, 6500, 4434

Piggy Snuggle Basket
ACME
$17.50   €13.03
3230, 3232

Dog Snuggle Basket
ACME
$14.25   €10.61
3230, 3232, 3250

CSS is applied to the elements of the XML document

Trouble? If some content is formatted differently, it is most likely due to minor rendering differences among browsers and will not cause a problem.

INSIGHT

Creating Style Sheets for XML with XSL

CSS is only one way of applying a style to the contents of an XML document. Another way is to use **Extensible Stylesheet Language (XSL)**, which is a style sheet language developed specifically for XML. XSL is actually an XML vocabulary, so any XSL style sheet must follow the rules of well-formed XML. XSL works by transforming the contents of an XML document into another document format. For example, an XSL style sheet can be used to transform the contents of an XML document into an HTML file that can be displayed in any Web browser. In addition, the HTML code generated by an XSL style sheet could itself be linked to a CSS file.

XSL is not limited to generating HTML code; an XML document instead could be transformed into another XML document.

Web browsers often use internal XSL style sheets to display XML documents. The outline form of Patricia's document shown in Figure 11-34 is actually the XML document as transformed by the XSL style sheet built into each browser's XML parser. This style sheet is used by the browser unless a different style sheet is specified by a processing instruction in the XML document.

You've finished creating the XML vocabulary for the holiday specials products at SJB Pet Boutique. Patricia anticipates creating future documents that combine elements from this vocabulary with elements from other XML vocabularies. She'd like you to ensure that you'll be able to distinguish elements in one vocabulary from elements in another vocabulary. XML enables you to do this using namespaces.

Working with Namespaces

A namespace is a defined collection of element and attribute names. For example, the collection of element and attribute names from Patricia's products vocabulary could define a single namespace. Applying a namespace to an XML document involves two steps:

1. Declare the namespace.
2. Identify the elements and attributes within the document that belong to that namespace.

Declaring a Namespace

To declare a namespace for an element within an XML document, you add an attribute within the opening tag for the element using the syntax

```
<element xmlns:prefix="uri"> ... </element>
```

where *element* is the element in which the namespace is declared, *prefix* is a string of characters that you'll add to element and attribute names to associate them with the declared namespace, and *uri* is a Uniform Resource Identifier (URI)—a text string that uniquely identifies a resource. In this case, the URI is the declared namespace. For example, the following code declares a namespace with the URI *http://example.com/sjbpetboutique/products* and associates that URI with the prefix prd within the products element:

```
<products xmlns:prd="http://example.com/sjbpetboutique/products">
...
</products>
```

The number of namespace attributes that can be declared within an element is unlimited. In addition, a namespace that has been declared within an element can be applied to any descendant of the element. Some XML authors add all namespace declarations to a document's root element so that each namespace is available to all elements within the document.

Applying a Default Namespace

You can declare a default namespace by omitting the prefix in the namespace declaration. Any descendant element or attribute is then considered part of this namespace unless a different namespace is declared within one of the child elements. The syntax to create a default namespace is

```
<element xmlns="uri"> ... </element>
```

For instance, to define the http://example.com/sjbpetboutique/products namespace as the default namespace for all elements in the document, you could use the following root element:

```
<products xmlns="http://example.com/sjbpetboutique/products">
```

In this case, all elements in the document, including the products element, are considered part of the http://example.com/sjbpetboutique/products namespace.

REFERENCE

Declaring a Namespace

- To declare a namespace for an element within an XML document, add the `xmlns:prefix` attribute to the opening tag of the element using the syntax

  `<element xmlns:prefix="uri"> ... </element>`

  where `element` is the element in which the namespace is declared, `prefix` is the namespace prefix, and `uri` is the URI of the namespace.
- To declare a default namespace, add the `xmlns` attribute without specifying a prefix, as follows:

  `<element xmlns="uri"> ... </element>`

The advantage of default namespaces is that they make the code easier to read and write because you do not have to add the namespace prefix to each element. The disadvantage, however, is that an element's namespace is not readily apparent from the code. Still, many compound documents use a default namespace that covers most of the elements in the document, and assign namespace prefixes to elements from other XML vocabularies. A **compound document** is an XML document composed of elements from other vocabularies or schemas. For example, you may combine elements from HTML and XML vocabularies. You'll learn how to work with compound documents in future tutorials.

INSIGHT

Understanding URIs

The URI used in namespaces looks like a Web address used to create a link to a Web site; however, that is not its purpose. The purpose of a URI is simply to provide a unique string of characters that identify a resource.

One version of a URI is the Uniform Resource Locator (URL), which is used to identify the location of a resource (such as a Web page) on the Web. There is a good reason to also use URLs as a basis for identifying namespaces. If an XML vocabulary is made widely available, the namespace associated with that vocabulary must be unique. URLs serve as a built-in mechanism on the Web for generating unique addresses. For example, assume that the home page of Patricia's company, SJB Pet Boutique, has the Web address

`http://example.com/sjbpetboutique`

This address provides customers with a unique location to access all of SJB Pet Boutique's online products. To ensure the uniqueness of any namespaces associated with the vocabularies developed for SJB Pet Boutique documents, it makes sense to use the SJB Pet Boutique Web address as a foundation. Note that although a URI doesn't actually need to point to a real site on the Web, it's often helpful to place documentation at the site identified by a URI so users can go there to learn more about the XML vocabulary being referenced.

The use of URLs is widely accepted in declaring namespaces, but you can use almost any unique string identifier, such as SJBPetBoutiqueProductNS or P2205X300x. The main requirement is that a URI is unique so that it is not confused with the URIs of other namespaces.

Patricia wants you to declare a default namespace for the products vocabulary. You'll declare the namespace in the root element of the sjbpet.xml file. The URI for the namespace is *http://example.com/sjbpetboutique/products*. This URI does not point to an actual site on the Web, but it does provide a unique URI for the namespace.

To declare a default namespace:

▶ **1.** Return to the **sjbpet.xml** file in your text editor.

▶ **2.** Within the opening `<products>` tag, insert the following default namespace declaration, as shown in Figure 11-38:

```
xmlns="http://example.com/sjbpetboutique/products"
```

Figure 11-38	The sjbpet.xml document with default namespace applied

```
<?xml version="1.0" encoding="UTF-8" standalone="yes" ?>
<?xml-stylesheet type="text/css" href="sjbpet.css" ?>
<!--
    This document contains data on SJB Pet Boutique
    holiday specials

    Filename: sjbpet.xml
    Author:   Patricia Dean
    Date:     9/18/2016
-->
<products xmlns="http://example.com/sjbpetboutique/products">
    <message>
```

default namespace added to the root element

▶ **3.** Press **Ctrl+S** to save your work.

▶ **4.** Reload or refresh **sjbpet.xml** in your Web browser. If you're using any major browser, the Web page should look unchanged from Figure 11-37.

Trouble? If your browser reports a syntax error, return to the sjbpet.xml file in your text editor, ensure that the namespace is within the opening tag of the root element, save any changes, and then repeat Step 4.

Patricia is very happy with the work you've done. She'll show your work to the other members of her Web team, and if they need more XML documents created in the future, they'll get back to you.

REVIEW

Session 11.2 Quick Check

1. What is the error in the following code?

   `<Title>Grilled Steak</title>`

2. What is the root element?
3. What are sibling elements?
4. What is parsed character data?
5. Name three ways to insert the ampersand (&) symbol into the contents of an XML document without it being treated as parsed character data.
6. What is a CDATA section?
7. What is a processing instruction?
8. What code links an XML document to a style sheet file named standard.css?
9. What is a namespace?
10. What attribute would you add to a document's root element to declare a default namespace with the URI *http://ns.doc.book*?

Review Assignments

Data Files needed for the Review Assignments: resale.css, resale.txt

Patricia would like you to create another document for the SJB Pet Boutique resale business. She has provided you with a text file that she'd like you to convert to XML. Figure 11-39 outlines the structure of the final document that she wants you to create.

Figure 11-39	The SJB Pet Boutique resale tree hierarchy

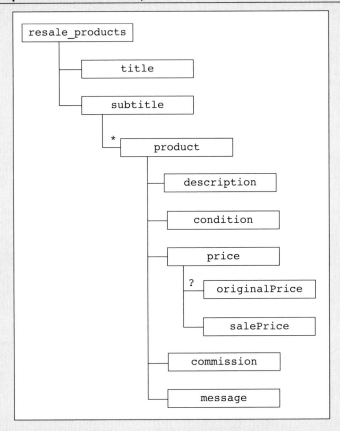

Patricia also would like the final document displayed using the provided *resale.css* style sheet, as shown in Figure 11-40.

| **Figure 11-40** | The resale.xml document in the browser |

> # Resale Products
> *Latest Offerings*
>
> ## 8" Hamster Travel Cage
> Good
> - $35
> - $15
> - 15%
>
> ## Dog and Cat Doorstop
> Excellent
> - $70
> - $20
> - 10%
>
> ## Puppy Dog Rhinestone Collar
> Excellent
> - $25
> - $10
> - 15%
>
> ## 30" Kitty Travel Cage
> New
> - $40
> - $35
> - 20%
>
> Interested in resale? The SJB Pet Boutique will publish for resale select items purchased at our store that you or your owner have outgrown. All sales are "as-is" condition. A commission is charged for listing the item for resale. If your resale item is sold and you purchase a new item at our store using the money from the sale of the item, you can save 50% off our commission price! ☺

Complete the following:

1. Using your text editor, open the **resale.txt** file located in the tutorial.11\review folder included with your Data Files.
2. Save the document as **resale.xml**.
3. Create a prolog at the top of the document indicating that this is an XML document using the UTF-8 encoding scheme, and that it is a standalone document.
4. Create processing instructions to link the *resale.xml* document to the **resale.css** style sheet.
5. On a new line below the XML declaration, insert a comment containing the text **SJB Pet Boutique resale products, latest offerings**

   Filename: resale.xml
   Author: *your name*
   Date: *today's date*
   where *your name* is your first and last names, and *today's date* is the current date.
6. Enclose the document body content in a root element named `resale_products`.
7. Mark the text *Resale Products* with an element named `title`.
8. Mark the text *Latest Offerings* with an element named `subtitle`.
9. There are four new resale products. Create an element named `product`, which will contain all of the information about each product within a single product element.
10. Each `product` element should now contain five detail lines about each product, as shown in Figure 11-40.
11. Mark the first line of each product with an element named `description`, which contains a description of the product.

12. Mark the second line of each product with an element named `condition`, which contains data regarding the condition of the product.

13. Mark the third line of each product with an element named `originalPrice,` which will contain data regarding the original price of the product.

14. Mark the fourth line of each product with an element named `salePrice`, which will contain data regarding the resale price of the product.

15. Mark the fifth line of each product with an element named `commission`, which will contain data regarding the commission percentage to be earned on the sale.

16. Create a parent element named `price` for the child elements `originalPrice` and `salePrice`.

17. At the bottom of the document is a message to clients who are interested in resale. Enclose this message in a CDATA section and place the CDATA section within an element named `message`.

18. Patricia wants a smiley face (☺) to be displayed at the end of the contents of the `message` element. Delete the colon and closing parenthesis (`:)`) at the end of the message text. Outside the CDATA section but within the `message` element, add the character reference `&#9786;`. (Note: The reference must be outside the CDATA section in order for parsers to translate it.)

19. Within the opening `<resale_products>` tag, insert a default namespace declaration to place all elements in the **http://example.com/sjbpetboutique/resale** namespace.

20. Save your changes to the **resale.xml** document.

21. Open the **resale.xml** document in your Web browser. Compare the results to Figure 11-40. If your output does not match the expected output, correct any errors and refresh your browser to verify changes.

22. Submit your completed files to your instructor, in either printed or electronic form, as requested.

Apply your knowledge of XML to mark up blog entries.

APPLY

Case Problem 1

Data Files needed for this Case Problem: membership.css, membership.txt

MSN Baseball Fan Club   The MSN Baseball Fan Club is an online fan club based in Madison, Wisconsin. Anyone can be a member of the club; the only prerequisite is that the person is a fan of Madison baseball. Members have voted to add to the current Web site a page to display each club member's blog entries. The club wants the output displayed with a style sheet, which one of the members has provided. Figure 11-41 outlines the structure of the document you will create, and Figure 11-42 shows the document displayed with a style sheet.

Figure 11-41   **Baseball membership tree hierarchy of combined documents**

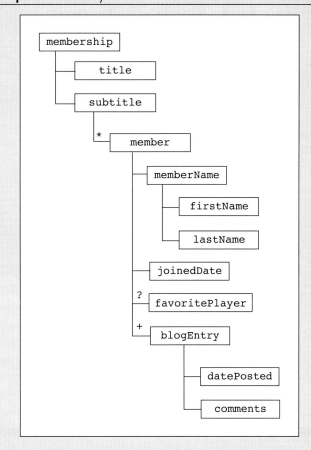

Figure 11-42   **The membership.xml document displayed using the membership.css style sheet**

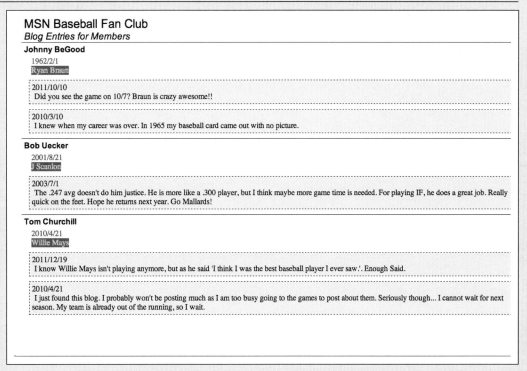

Complete the following:

1. Using your text editor, open the **membership.txt** file located in the tutorial.11\case1 folder included with your Data Files.

2. Save the document as **membership.xml**.

3. Create a prolog at the top of the *membership.xml* document indicating that this is an XML document using the UTF-8 encoding scheme, and that it is a standalone document.

4. Create a processing instruction to link the *membership.xml* document to the **membership.css** style sheet.

5. Directly below the XML declaration, insert a comment containing the text **MSN Baseball Fan Club Blog Entries**

   Filename: membership.xml
   Author: *your name*
   Date: *today's date*

   where *your name* is your first and last names, and *today's date* is the current date.

6. Enclose the document body content in a root element named `membership`.

7. Enclose the text *MSN Baseball Fan Club* in an element named `title`.

8. Enclose the text *Blog Entries for Members* in an element named `subtitle`.

9. Three members have had data collected for the document. Enclose the information about each member within an element named `member`.

   Each `member` element should contain four detail lines about the member, as shown in Figure 11-42, prior to adding the blog content. Be sure the `member` element encloses all information about a member, including his blog entry(ies).

10. Mark the first line of each `member` element, which contains the member's first name, with an element named `firstName`.

11. Mark the second line of each `member` element, which contains the member's last name, with an element named `lastName`.

12. For each member, create a parent element named `memberName` that contains `firstName` and `lastName` as child elements.

13. Mark the third line of each member's information, which contains the date the member joined the fan club, with an element named `joinedDate`.

14. Mark the fourth line of each member's information, which contains the name of the member's favorite player, with an element named `favoritePlayer`.

15. Each member has at least one blog entry, which contains a date and a comment as shown in Figure 11-42. Enclose each date and comment within a `blogEntry` element. You may need to add more than one `blogEntry` element for a member who has multiple blog entries.

16. Enclose the date associated with each blog entry in a `datePosted` element.

17. Enclose the contents of each `comments` element in a CDATA section, with the `<comments>` tags outside of the CDATA section.

18. Insert a namespace declaration to add all the elements in the document body to the **http://example.com/msnmembball/membership** namespace.

19. Save your changes to the membership.xml document.

20. Open the membership.xml document in your Web browser and compare the output to Figure 11-42. If necessary, correct any errors and re-verify the output in the browser.

21. Submit your completed files to your instructor, in either printed or electronic form, as requested.

*Apply your
knowledge of
XML to structure
menu data.*

APPLY

Case Problem 2

Data Files needed for this Case Problem: chester.css, chester.txt

Chester's Restaurant   Chester's Restaurant is located in the quaint town of Hartland,
Minnesota. Jasmine Pup, the owner and operator, wants to display the recently revamped
breakfast menu on the Web. She wants you to apply an existing style sheet to the document so the menu is nicely formatted on the Web. She has saved the menu information
to a text file and needs you to convert the document to XML. Figure 11-43 outlines the
structure of the document you will create, and Figure 11-44 shows the document displayed with a style sheet.

Figure 11-43	Chester's breakfast menu tree hierarchy

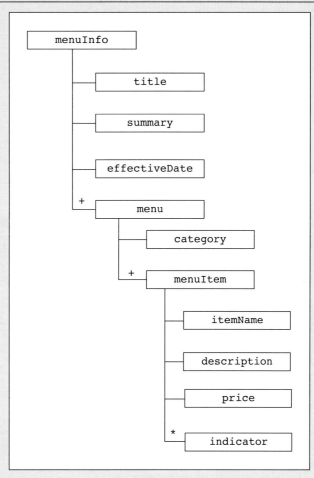

Figure 11-44	The chester.xml document displayed using the chester.css style sheet

Chester's Breakfast Menu

If you've been craving an authentic homestyle country breakfast, look no further than Chester's! We've got your breakfast favorites served up just the way you like them!!

03/12/2016

Traditional Favorites

- **Rise n' Shine**
  Two Eggs* cooked to order with Grits, Gravy and Homemade Buttermilk Biscuits along with real Butter and the best fresh jam available. Served with your choice of Fresh Fruit or Hashbrown Casserole and Smoked Sausage Patties, Turkey Sausage Patties or Thick-Sliced Bacon.
  7.95

- **Fresh Mornin' Sampler**
  Low-Fat Vanilla Yogurt and Seasonal Fruit topped with our Honey Granola mix of Almonds and Dried Fruit. Served with a Wild Maine Blueberry Muffin or an Apple Bran Muffin.
  6.95 ♥ ♦ ♠

Lite and Quick

- **Oatmeal Breakfast**
  Our Oatmeal is served warm with your choice of Fried Apples, Pecans, Raisins, Fresh Sliced Bananas or 100% Pure Natural Syrup. Also, served with your choice of Apple Bran Muffin or Wild Maine Blueberry Muffin. Available all day.
  6.95 ♥ ♦ ♠

- **Chester's Meat Platter**
  Country Ham, Pork Chops or Steak* grilled to order, Three Eggs* cooked to order served with Cottage Cheese, Smoked Sausage Patties, Turkey Sausage Patties or Thick-Sliced Bacon.
  12.95 ♨

Complete the following:

1. Using your text editor, open the **chester.txt** file located in the tutorial.11\case2 folder included with your Data Files.

2. Save the document as **chester.xml**.

3. Create a prolog at the top of the document indicating that this is an XML document using the UTF-8 encoding scheme, and that it is a standalone document.

4. Create a processing instruction to link the *chester.xml* document to the **chester.css** style sheet.

5. Directly below the XML declaration, insert a comment containing the text

   Chester's Restaurant Breakfast Menu

Filename:	**chester.xml**
Author:	*your name*
Date:	*today's date*

   where *your name* is your first and last names, and *today's date* is the current date.

6. Enclose the document body content in a root element named **menuInfo**.

7. Enclose the text *Chester's Breakfast Menu* in an element named **title**.

8. Enclose the three lines of text beginning with *If you've been craving* in an element named **summary**. Enclose the content for each **summary** element in a CDATA section.

9. Enclose the date found after the text *Effective thru* in an element named **effectiveDate**.

10. Add an attribute called **text** to the **effectiveDate** element with a value of **Effective thru**.

11. The menu information is divided into two categories. Add the first opening tag for the parent element called **menu** to the document on the line before the text *Traditional Favorites*. Add the closing tag for the first menu element and the opening tag for the second menu element on the line before the text *Lite and Quick*. Add the closing tag for the second menu element on the last line of the document.

12. Each menu category contains a description to be marked with a **category** element. Mark the text *Traditional Favorites* in the first menu element with a **category** element, and then mark the text *Lite and Quick* in the second menu element with another **category** element.

13. Each menu category also contains one or more child menu items and their associated information. On the next line below each **category** element, add a parent element named **menuItem**. Create element tags for each of the following child elements and place them within each **menuItem** parent element:

    a. Mark the first line of each menu category with an element named **itemName**, which will contain the name of the item on the menu. Be sure to place this element within the **menuItem** parent element.

    b. Mark the second piece of information for each menu category with an element named **description**, which will give a detailed description of what the menu item consists of. There may be several lines for the description. The content of the **description** element should be enclosed within a CDATA section. Be sure to place this element within the **menuItem** parent element.

    c. Mark the third piece of information for each menu category with an element named **price**, which will indicate the purchase price of the item. Be sure to place this element within the **menuItem** parent element.

    d. Mark the fourth piece of information for each menu category with an element named **indicator**, which contains optional text indicators that flag the menu item under one or more of the following subcategories:

       - ♥ *Heart Healthy*: character reference ♥
       - ♦ *Low Sodium*: character reference ♦
       - ♠ *Vegan*: character reference ♠
       - ♨ *Low Carb*: character reference ♨

       Because each menu item could fall under none or several categories, the number of indicator elements will vary. If a menu item includes an **indicator** element, use the appropriate character reference to display the symbol for the indicator instead of displaying the text description. Be sure to place this element within the **menuItem** parent element.

    e. Because others might not be familiar with the character references, include a single-line comment containing the text description for each character reference after the closing tag for each **indicator** element.

    f. If there are more **menuItem** elements, repeat Steps 13a–13e.

14. Add the namespace **http://example.com/chestershartland/menu** to the opening tag of the root element.

15. Save your changes to the **chester.xml** document.

16. Open the **chester.xml** document in your Web browser and compare the output to Figure 11-44. If necessary, correct any errors and then re-verify the output in the browser.

17. Submit your completed files to your instructor, in either printed or electronic form, as requested.

Explore how to debug an XML document.

CHALLENGE

Case Problem 3

Data Files needed for this Case Problem: recipe.txt, weekendFun.css, weekendFuntxt.xml

Weekend Fun Snacks Cleo Coal is creating a Web site called *Weekend Fun Snacks*. The site will list her picks of the best and easiest recipes for kids to cook on the weekend (or anytime). Cleo has been entering recipe information into an XML document. However, she has run into some problems and has come to you for help. Cleo would like your help with cleaning up her XML document so it displays in a browser with her style sheet. Once you've corrected the XML document, she also would like you to add a new recipe to the document. Figure 11-45 displays a preview of the document's contents when all corrections are made and the new recipe is added.

Figure 11-45   **The corrected weekendFun.xml document**

Complete the following:

1. Using Exchanger XML Editor or your text editor, open the **weekendFuntxt.xml** file located in the tutorial.11\case3 folder included with your Data Files.

2. Save the document as **weekendFun.xml**, and then note the initial error reported. If you don't have access to an XML editor, use an online XML code checker, such as http://validator.w3.org, to identify the first error in the code.

⊕ EXPLORE

3. Using the information provided by the editor, locate and correct the first error.

4. Save the modifications to **weekendFun.xml**.

5. If the browser reports another error, repeat Steps 3 and 4 until all errors are corrected. The following are some errors to look for:
   - misspelled element names
   - missing quotes
   - misplaced closing tags
   - missing closing tags
   - invalid namespace

6. Save the modifications to **weekendFun.xml**.

7. Open the document in your browser.

8. Verify that the style sheet has been applied. If not, edit and reload the document in the Web browser.

⊕ EXPLORE

9. Modify the prolog at the top of the document to indicate that the document uses the UTF-8 encoding scheme, and that it is a standalone document.

⊕ EXPLORE

10. Copy and paste the content from the **recipe.txt** document into the **weekendFun.xml** document as a new recipe. Using the existing recipe vocabulary as your guide, modify the newly added recipe data to use the vocabulary for the data.

11. Save the modifications to **weekendFun.xml**.

12. Reload the document in the browser.

13. Verify that all of the information for the new recipe is included as shown in Figure 11-45.

⊕ EXPLORE

14. Draw the tree structure for the contents of the *weekendFun.xml* document. Each document can have many recipes, an optional description, at least one ingredient, an optional measurement, and at least one direction. Each other element occurs one time.

15. Submit your completed files to your instructor, in either printed or electronic form, as requested.

Test your knowledge of XML by creating an XML document for an online bookstore.

CREATE

Case Problem 4

Data Files needed for this Case Problem: rycheBooks.css, rycheBooks.txt, rycheBooksPrint.css

Ryche Books   David Ryche is the owner and operator of Ryche Books, which is an online bookstore that specializes in hard-to-find books. He often receives phone calls regarding his current stock of books and he would like this information available to his customers at his Web site. He has created a text file that contains data about his current inventory of books. He would like your help with converting his text file to an XML document and then displaying that information in a Web browser. Figure 11-46 gives a preview of the document's contents in a browser, and Figure 11-47 shows a print preview of the document's contents.

Figure 11-46   The browser output for the rycheBooks.xml document

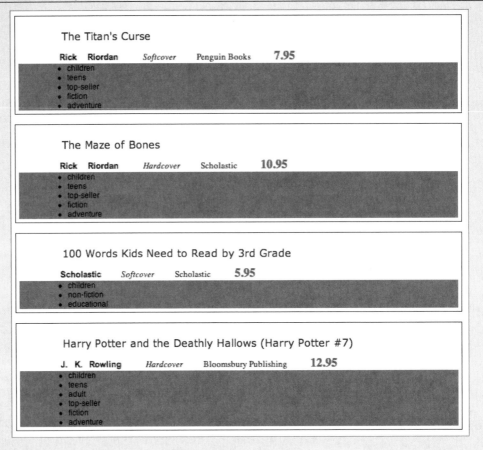

Figure 11-47   The print preview output for the rycheBooks.xml document

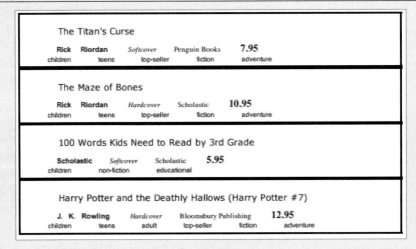

Complete the following:

1. Using your text editor, open the **rycheBooks.txt** file, which is located in the tutorial.11\case4 folder included with your Data Files.

2. Save the document as **rycheBooks.xml**.

3. At the top of the document, add code indicating that this is an XML document using the UTF-8 encoding scheme, and that it is a standalone document.

4. Create processing instructions to link the XML document to the **rycheBooks.css** style sheet for screen media, and to the **rycheBooksPrint.css** style sheet for print media.

5. Within the document's prolog, include the filename, your name, today's date, and the purpose of the document in a comment.

6. Mark up the contents of the document using the following specifications:
   - The root element of the document should be named **books**.
   - The **books** element should contain multiple occurrences of a child element named **book**.
   - Each **book** element should have a single attribute named **ISBN** containing the International Standard Book Number (ISBN) of the book. (Note: The ISBN begins with the letter I, which is followed by several numeric digits.)
   - Each **book** element should have six child elements: **title**, **author**, **type**, **publisher**, **sellPrice**, and **categories**.
     - The **title** element should contain the book's title.
     - The **author** element should contain three child elements: **firstName**, **middleName**, and **lastName**. Each author name should be divided accordingly and stored in these elements. (Note: If the author is a business name such as *Scholastic*, it will not have all three child elements.)
     - The **type** element should contain the book's cover type: **hardcover** or **softcover**.
     - The **publisher** element should contain the name of the book's publisher.
     - The **sellPrice** element should contain the book's selling price.
     - The **categories** element should contain at least one child element called **category**. A book may have multiple **category** elements.

⊕ EXPLORE

7. Add a default namespace for the books vocabulary using an appropriate URI.

8. Save your changes to the **rycheBooks.xml** document.

9. Open the **rycheBooks.xml** document in your Web browser and compare the output to Figure 11-46.

10. If your Web browser reports any syntax errors, locate and correct each error using the information from the Web browser. Save any modifications to **rycheBooks.xml** and reload the document in your browser.

11. Verify that the style sheet is also properly applied to print media. To verify the print media style sheet, use the print preview feature of your browser and compare the output to Figure 11-47. If necessary, correct any errors and re-verify the output in the browser.

12. Submit your completed files to your instructor, in either printed or electronic form, as requested.

ENDING DATA FILES

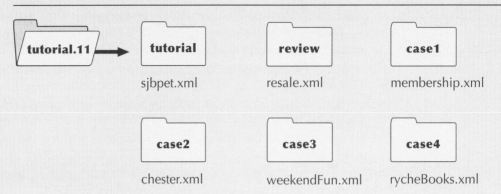

tutorial.11 → tutorial
sjbpet.xml

review
resale.xml

case1
membership.xml

case2
chester.xml

case3
weekendFun.xml

case4
rycheBooks.xml

Validating Documents with DTDs

Creating a Document Type Definition for Map Finds For You

Case | Map Finds For You

Benjamin Mapps works at Map Finds For You, an online store that sells mass-produced and custom map products. Map Finds For You sells more than 1000 map products ranging from maps of the present-day world to detailed historical maps. Some are available in both paper and electronic formats. Part of Benjamin's job at Map Finds For You is to record information about the store's customers, including the individual orders they place.

Benjamin is starting to use XML to record this information, and he has created a sample XML document containing information on customers and their orders. Benjamin knows that his document needs to be well formed, following the XML syntax rules exactly, but he also wants the document to follow certain rules regarding content. For example, data on each customer must include the customer's name, phone number, and address. Each customer order must contain a complete list of the items purchased and include the date the order was placed. You will create an XML document for Benjamin that adheres to both the rules of XML and the rules Benjamin has set up for the document's content and structure.

Note: To complete this tutorial, you need access to a recent version of a major browser, such as Internet Explorer, Firefox, or Chrome, as well as an XML parser capable of validating an XML document based on a DTD.

STARTING DATA FILES

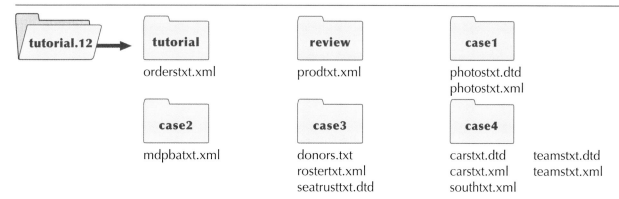

tutorial.12 → **tutorial**

orderstxt.xml

review

prodtxt.xml

case1

photostxt.dtd
photostxt.xml

case2

mdpbatxt.xml

case3

donors.txt
rostertxt.xml
seatrusttxt.dtd

case4

carstxt.dtd
carstxt.xml
southtxt.xml

teamstxt.dtd
teamstxt.xml

SESSION 12.1 VISUAL OVERVIEW

> The name of the root element follows the word DOCTYPE and must match the root element of the document.

> The DOCTYPE, or document type declaration, must be added to the document prolog after the XML declaration and before the document's root element.

> The declaration statements for an internal DTD are included within opening and closing brackets.

> The closing > for the DOCTYPE must be placed after the closing].

```
Date:     12/11/2016

Filename:              orders.xml
Supporting Files:
-->
<!DOCTYPE customers
[
    <!ELEMENT customers (customer+)>

    <!ELEMENT customer (name, address, ph

    <!ELEMENT name (#PCDATA)>

    <!ELEMENT address (#PCDATA)>
    <!ELEMENT phone (#PCDATA)>
    <!ELEMENT email (#PCDATA)>
    <!ELEMENT orders (order+)>

    <!ELEMENT order (orderDate, items)>

    <!ELEMENT orderDate (#PCDATA)>
    <!ELEMENT items (item+)>

    <!ELEMENT item (itemPrice, itemQty)>

    <!ELEMENT itemPrice (#PCDATA)>
    <!ELEMENT itemQty (#PCDATA)>

]>
<customers>
    <customer custID="cust201">
        <name title="Mr.">John Michael</na
        <address>
            <![CDATA[
```

> An **element type declaration**, or simply **element declaration**, specifies an element's name and the element's content model.

THE STRUCTURE OF A DTD

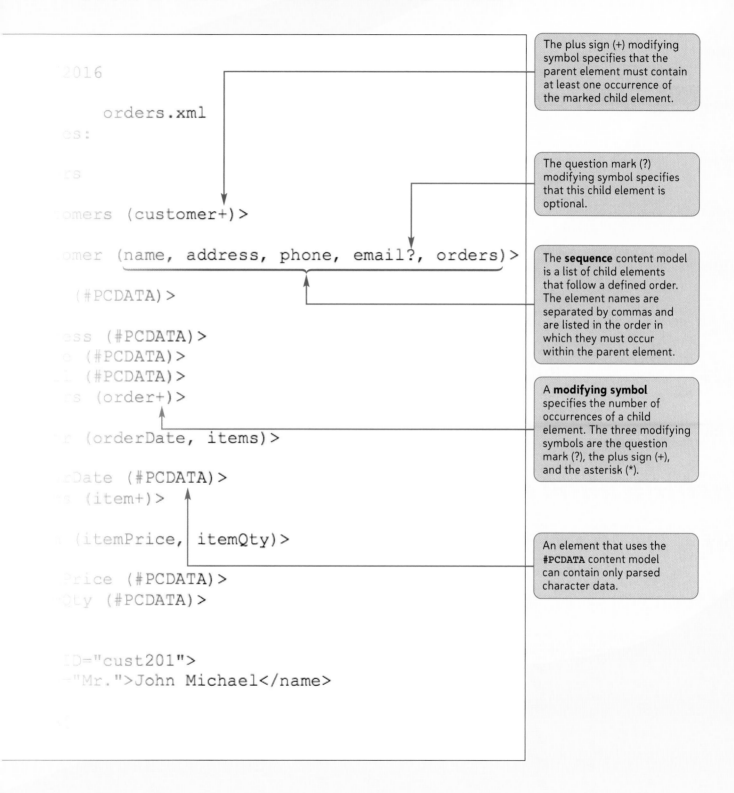

2016

    orders.xml

es:

s

omers (customer+)>

omer (name, address, phone, email?, orders)>

(#PCDATA)>

ss (#PCDATA)>
(#PCDATA)>
(#PCDATA)>
s (order+)>

r (orderDate, items)>

Date (#PCDATA)>
s (item+)>

(itemPrice, itemQty)>

rice (#PCDATA)>
ty (#PCDATA)>

D="cust201">
"Mr.">John Michael</name>

The plus sign (+) modifying symbol specifies that the parent element must contain at least one occurrence of the marked child element.

The question mark (?) modifying symbol specifies that this child element is optional.

The **sequence** content model is a list of child elements that follow a defined order. The element names are separated by commas and are listed in the order in which they must occur within the parent element.

A **modifying symbol** specifies the number of occurrences of a child element. The three modifying symbols are the question mark (?), the plus sign (+), and the asterisk (*).

An element that uses the **#PCDATA** content model can contain only parsed character data.

Creating a Valid Document

Benjamin has created a sample document that contains information about Map Finds For You's customers. To keep the information to a manageable size, Benjamin limited the document to three customers and their orders. Figure 12-1 shows a table of the information he entered for those customers.

Figure 12-1 | **Customer orders table**

Customer		Orders		Item	Qty	Price	Sale Item
name:	Mr. John Michael	orderID:	or1089	WM100PL	1	39.95	N
custID:	cust201	orderBy:	cust201	WM101P	2	19.90	Y
address:	41 West Plankton Avenue Orlando, FL 32820	orderDate:	8/11/2016				
phone:	(407) 555-3476						
email:	jk@example.net						
name:	Mr. Dean Abernath	orderID:	or1021	WM100PL	1	29.95	N
custID:	cust202	orderBy:	cust202	WM105L	1	19.95	N
address:	200 Bear Avenue	orderDate:	8/1/2016				
	Front Royal, VA 22630	orderID:	or1122	H115E	2	24.90	Y
phone:	(540) 555-1788	orderBy:	cust202	H115F	1	14.95	N
email:	dabernath@example.com	orderDate:	10/1/2016				
name:	Riverfront High School	orderID:	or1120	WM140P	2	78.90	N
custID:	cust203	orderBy:	cust203				
address:	1950 West Magnolia Drive	orderDate:	9/15/2016				
	River Falls, WI 54022						
phone:	(715) 555-4022						
email:							

For each customer, Benjamin has recorded the customer's name, ID, address, phone number, and email address. Each customer has placed one or more separate orders. For convenience, Benjamin has grouped each customer order within an orders element. For each order, Benjamin recorded the order's ID number, customer ID number, and date. Finally, for each item ordered, he entered the item number, the quantity, the price of the item, and whether the item was on sale. Benjamin placed this information in an XML document, which you will open now.

To open the orders document:

1. Use your text editor or XML editor to open **orderstxt.xml** from the tutorial.12\tutorial folder where your data files are located.

2. Enter **your name** and **today's date** in the comment section of the file, and then save the file as **orders.xml**. Figure 12-2 shows the contents of the *orders.xml* document for the first customer.

Figure 12-2   **First customer in the orders.xml document**

```
<customer custID="cust201">
    <name title="Mr.">John Michael</name>
    <address>
        <![CDATA[
        41 West Plankton Avenue
        Orlando, FL  32820
        ]]>
    </address>
    <phone>(407) 555-3476</phone>
    <email>jk@example.net</email>
    <orders>
        <order orderID="or1089" orderBy="cust201">
            <orderDate>8/11/2016</orderDate>
            <items>
                <item itemNumber="WM100PL">
                    <itemPrice saleItem="N">39.95</itemPrice>
                    <itemQty>1</itemQty>
                </item>
                <item itemNumber="WM101P">
                    <itemPrice saleItem="Y">19.90</itemPrice>
                    <itemQty>2</itemQty>
                </item>
            </items>
        </order>
    </orders>
</customer>
```

Trouble? The figures in this tutorial show the code in Exchanger XML Editor, but you can complete the steps in any code editor or basic text editor. An XML editor such as Exchanger XML Editor can verify that your code is both well formed and valid. Many free general-purpose code editors, such as Notepad++ and Komodo Edit, can check that your code is well formed, and you can upload the code to an online service like *http://validator.w3.org* to confirm that the code is valid.

▶ **3.** Compare the elements and attributes entered in the document with the table shown in Figure 12-1, noticing whether each piece of data is coded as an element or an attribute.

▶ **4.** If you're using Exchanger XML Editor, click **XML** on the menu bar, and then click **Check Well-formedness**. This setting ensures that you don't see validation errors until your document is ready for validation.

Some elements in Benjamin's document, such as the name and phone elements, should appear only once for each customer, while other elements, such as the order and item elements, can appear multiple times. The email element is optional: Two customers have email addresses and one customer does not. The itemPrice and itemQty elements each appear once per item element.

Benjamin created the diagram shown in Figure 12-3 to better illustrate the structure of the elements and attributes in his document. Recall that the + symbol in front of an element indicates that at least one child element must be present in the document, and the ? symbol indicates the presence of zero children or one child. Benjamin's diagram shows that the customers, orders, and items elements must have at least one customer, order, or item child, respectively, and that the email element is optional. Benjamin also indicated the presence of element attributes in blue below the relevant element names. An attribute name in square brackets ([ ]) is optional; all other attributes are required.

Figure 12-3   **Structure of the orders.xml document**

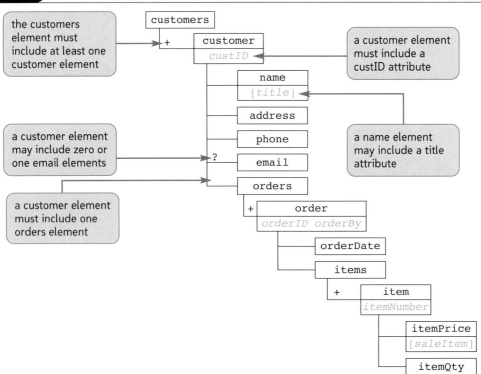

To keep accurate and manageable records, Benjamin must maintain this structure in his document. He wants to ensure that the customer information includes the address and phone number for each customer, the items each customer ordered, and the date each order was placed. In XML terms, this means that the document must be not only well formed, but also valid.

Declaring a DTD

One way to create a valid document is to design a document type definition, or DTD, for the document. Recall that a DTD is a collection of rules that define the content and structure of an XML document. Used in conjunction with an XML parser that supports data validation, a DTD can:

- Ensure that all required elements are present in the document.
- Prevent undefined elements from being used in the document.
- Enforce a specific data structure on document content.
- Specify the use of element attributes and define their permissible values.
- Define default values for attributes.
- Describe how parsers should access non-XML or nontextual content.

A DTD is attached to an XML document by using a statement called a document type declaration, which is more simply referred to as a DOCTYPE. The DOCTYPE must be added to the document prolog after the XML declaration and before the document's root element. The purpose of the DOCTYPE is to either specify the rules of the DTD or provide information to the parser about where those rules are located. Each XML document can have only one DOCTYPE.

Because DTDs can be placed either within an XML document or in an external file, you can divide a DOCTYPE into two parts—an internal subset and an external subset. A DOCTYPE can include either or both of these parts. The **internal subset** contains the rules and declarations of the DTD placed directly into the document, using the form

```
<!DOCTYPE root
[
    statements
]>
```

where `root` is the name of the document's root element and `statements` represents the declarations and rules of the DTD.

For example, the root element of the *orders.xml* document is `customers`, so a DOCTYPE in the *orders.xml* document has to specify `customers` as the value for the `root` parameter, as follows:

```
<!DOCTYPE customers
[
    statements
]>
```

TIP

The root value in a DOCTYPE must exactly match the name of the XML document's root element; otherwise, parsers will reject the document as invalid.

When the DTD is located in an external file, the DOCTYPE includes an **external subset** that indicates the location of the file. Locations can be defined using either a system identifier or a public identifier. With a **system identifier**, you specify the location of the DTD file. A DOCTYPE using a system identifier has the form

```
<!DOCTYPE root SYSTEM "uri">
```

where `root` is again the document's root element and `uri` is the URI of the external file. For example, if Benjamin placed the DTD for the *orders.xml* document in an external file named *rules.dtd*, he could access it using the following DOCTYPE:

```
<!DOCTYPE customers SYSTEM "rules.dtd">
```

Understanding URIs

The URI used in DOCTYPEs looks like a Web address used to create a link to a Web site; however, that is not its purpose. The purpose of a URI is simply to provide a unique string of characters that identify a resource.

One version of a URI is the Uniform Resource Locator (URL), which is used to identify the location of a resource (such as a Web page) on the Web—for instance, *http://www.example.com*. One reason to use URLs as a basis for identifying DTDs is that URLs serve as a built-in mechanism on the Web for generating unique addresses. If an XML vocabulary is made widely available, the DTD associated with that vocabulary needs to be unique. So, to ensure the uniqueness of any DTDs associated with the vocabularies developed for documents used by a specific company, it makes sense to use the company's Web address as a foundation. Note that, although a URI doesn't actually need to point to a real site on the Web, it is often helpful to place documentation at the site identified by the URI so users can go there to learn more about the XML vocabulary being referenced.

The use of URLs in declaring DTDs is widely accepted, but you can use almost any unique string identifier, such as MapFindsForYouModelNS or WM140PL. The main requirement is that a URI is unique so that it is not confused with the URIs of other DTDs.

When an XML vocabulary becomes widely used, developers seek to make the DTD easily accessible. This is done by creating a name for the DTD; this name is called a **public identifier** or a **formal public identifier**. The public identifier, which is optional, provides XML parsers with information about the DTD, including the owner or author of the DTD and the language in which the DTD is written. The syntax of a DOCTYPE that has only an external subset and involves a public identifier is

```
<!DOCTYPE root PUBLIC "id" "uri">
```

where *root* is the document's root element, *id* is the public identifier, and *uri* is the system location of the DTD. The system location is included in case the XML parser cannot process the document solely based on the information provided by the public identifier. In one sense, the public identifier acts like the namespace URI because it doesn't specify a physical location for the DTD; instead, it provides the DTD with a unique name that can be recognized by an XML parser. For example, XHTML documents that conform strictly to version 1.0 standards employ the following DOCTYPE:

```
<!DOCTYPE html PUBLIC "-//W3C//DTD XHTML 1.0 Strict//EN"
          "http://www.w3.org/TR/xhtml1/DTD/xhtml1-strict.dtd">
```

The public identifier is -//W3C//DTD XHTML 1.0 Strict//EN, a string of characters that XML parsers recognize as the identifier for the XHTML strict DTD. An XML parser that recognizes this public identifier can use it to try to retrieve the DTD associated with the XML vocabulary used in the document. If the parser cannot retrieve the DTD based on the public identifier, it can access it from the system location provided by the *uri* value, which is http://www.w3.org/TR/xhtml1/DTD/xhtml1-strict.dtd. As you can see, the system location acts as a backup to the public identifier. Most standard XML vocabularies such as XHTML and RSS have public identifiers. However, a customized XML vocabulary such as the one Benjamin created for Map Finds For You may not have a public identifier.

Written Communication: Interpreting Public Identifiers

A public identifier is simply a public name given to a DTD that an XML parser can use to process and validate the document. The parser can use the public identifier to find the latest version of the DTD on the Internet. Each public identifier name has the structure

```
standard//owner//description//language
```

where *standard* indicates whether the DTD is a recognized standard, *owner* is the owner or developer of the DTD, *description* is a description of the XML vocabulary for which the DTD is developed, and *language* is a two-letter abbreviation of the language employed by the DTD. For example, the identifier for the XHTML 1.0 Strict vocabulary

```
-//W3C//DTD XHTML 1.0 Strict//EN
```

can be interpreted in the following manner:

- The initial – character tells the parser that the DTD is not a recognized standard. DTDs that are approved ISO (Internal Organization for Standardization) standards begin with the string ISO, whereas DTDs that are approved non-ISO standards begin with the + symbol.
- The next part of the id, W3C, indicates that this DTD is owned and developed by the W3C (World Wide Web Consortium).
- The description content, DTD XHTML 1.0 Strict, specifies that this standard is used for the XHTML 1.0 Strict vocabulary.
- Finally, the closing EN characters indicate that the DTD is written in English.

  If an XML parser has an internal catalog for working with public identifiers, it can use the information contained in the public identifier to work with the DTD. However, parsers are not required to work with public identifiers, so you should always include system locations for your public DTDs to support parsers that do not work with public identifiers.

When writing code, you might create DOCTYPEs with both internal and external subsets. A DTD that is shared among many different XML documents would be placed within an external file, whereas rules or declarations specific to an individual XML document would be placed within the internal subset. A DOCTYPE that combines both internal and external subsets and references a system identifier has the following form:

```
<!DOCTYPE root SYSTEM "uri"
[
   declarations
]>
```

If the DTD has a public identifier, then the DOCTYPE has the following form:

```
<!DOCTYPE root PUBLIC "id" "uri"
[
   declarations
]>
```

When a DOCTYPE contains both an internal and an external subset, the internal subset takes precedence over the external subset when conflict arises between the two. This is useful when an external subset is shared among several documents. The external subset would define some basic rules for all of the documents, and the internal subset would define rules that are specific to each document, as illustrated in Figure 12-4.

Figure 12-4 **Internal and external DTDs**

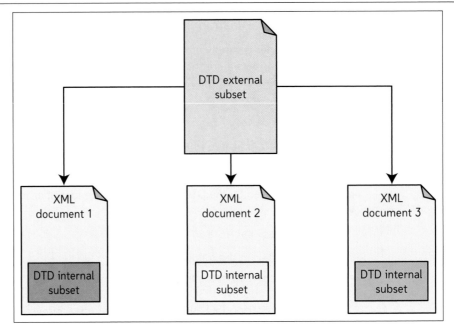

In this way, internal and external DTDs work in the same manner as embedded and external style sheets. An XML environment composed of several documents and vocabularies might use both internal and external DTDs.

REFERENCE

Declaring a DTD

- To declare an internal DTD subset, use the DOCTYPE

```
<!DOCTYPE root
[
    declarations
]>
```

where *root* is the name of the document's root element and *declarations* represents the statements that constitute the DTD.

- To declare an external DTD subset with a system location, use the DOCTYPE

```
<!DOCTYPE root SYSTEM "uri">
```

where *uri* is the URI of the external DTD file.

- To declare an external DTD subset with a public location, use the DOCTYPE

```
<!DOCTYPE root PUBLIC "id" "uri">
```

where *id* is the public identifier of the DTD.

Writing the Document Type Declaration

Benjamin wants you to place the DTD directly in his XML document so he can easily compare the DTD to the document content. You'll start by inserting a blank DOCTYPE into the *orders.xml* file.

To insert a DOCTYPE into the *orders.xml* document:

The DOCTYPE must be located within the prolog, which is before the document body.

1. Directly above the opening `<customers>` tag, insert the following DOCTYPE, as shown in Figure 12-5:

```
<!DOCTYPE customers
[

]>
```

Figure 12-5   Blank DOCTYPE inserted

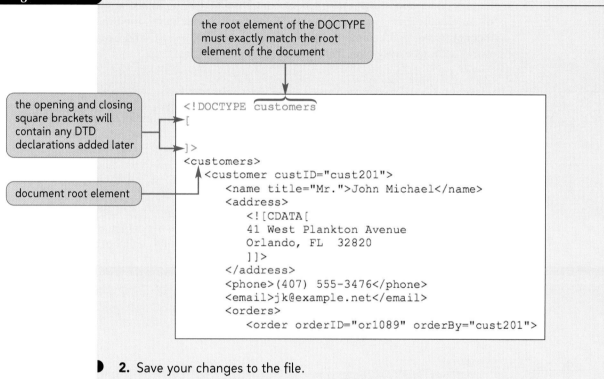

the root element of the DOCTYPE must exactly match the root element of the document

the opening and closing square brackets will contain any DTD declarations added later

document root element

```
<!DOCTYPE customers
[
]>
<customers>
   <customer custID="cust201">
      <name title="Mr.">John Michael</name>
      <address>
         <![CDATA[
         41 West Plankton Avenue
         Orlando, FL  32820
         ]]>
      </address>
      <phone>(407) 555-3476</phone>
      <email>jk@example.net</email>
      <orders>
         <order orderID="or1089" orderBy="cust201">
```

2. Save your changes to the file.

Now that you've added a DOCTYPE to Benjamin's document, you can begin adding statements to the DTD to define the structure and content of his XML vocabulary.

Declaring Document Elements

In a valid document, every element must be declared in the DTD. An element type declaration, or element declaration, specifies an element's name and indicates what content the element can contain. It can even specify the order in which elements appear in the document. The syntax of an element declaration is

```
<!ELEMENT element content-model>
```

TIP

Element declarations must begin with <!ELEMENT in all uppercase letters, and not <!Element or <!element.

where *element* is the name of the element and *content-model* specifies what type of content the element contains. The element name is case sensitive, so if the element name is VENDORS, it must be entered as VENDORS (not Vendors or vendors) in the element declaration. Remember that element names cannot contain any spaces or reserved symbols such as < or >. The `content-model` value can be one of three specific keywords (`ANY`, `EMPTY`, `#PCDATA`), or one of two content descriptions (sequence, `#PCDATA` with sequence), as follows:

- `ANY`: The element can store any type of content or no content at all.
- `EMPTY`: The element cannot store any content.
- `#PCDATA`: The element can contain only parsed character data.
- Sequence: The element can contain only child elements.
- `#PCDATA` with sequence: The element can store both parsed character data and child elements.

Generally, elements contain parsed character data or child elements. For example, in Benjamin's document, the `phone` element contains a text string that stores a customer's phone number, which is parsed character data. On the other hand, the `customer` element contains five child elements (`name`, `address`, `phone`, `email`, and `orders`). The following sections explore the five content types in more detail.

Elements Containing Any Type of Content

The most general type of content model is ANY, which allows an element to store any type of content. The syntax to allow any element content is

```
<!ELEMENT element ANY>
```

For example, the declaration

```
<!ELEMENT vendor ANY>
```

in the DTD would allow the `vendor` element to contain any type of content, or none at all. Any of the following content in the XML document would satisfy this element declaration:

```
<vendor>V12300 Mapping Down the Road</vendor>
```

or

```
<vendor />
```

or

```
<vendor>
   <number>PLBK70</number>
   <name>Mapping Down the Road</name>
</vendor>
```

Allowing an element to contain any type of content has little value in document validation. After all, the idea behind validation is to enforce a particular set of rules on elements and their content; allowing any content defeats the purpose of these rules.

Empty Elements

The EMPTY content model is reserved for elements that store no content. The syntax for an empty element declaration is

```
<!ELEMENT element EMPTY>
```

The element declaration

```
<!ELEMENT shelf EMPTY>
```

would require the `shelf` element to be entered as an empty element, as follows:

```
<shelf />
```

Including content in an element that uses the EMPTY content model would cause XML parsers to reject the document as invalid.

Elements Containing Parsed Character Data

Recall that parsed character data, or PCDATA, is text that is parsed by a parser. The #PCDATA content model value is reserved for elements that can store parsed character data, which are declared as follows:

```
<!ELEMENT element (#PCDATA)>
```

For example, the declaration

```
<!ELEMENT name (#PCDATA)>
```

permits the following element in an XML document:

```
<name>John Michael</name>
```

An element declaration employing the #PCDATA content model value does not allow for child elements. As a result, the name element

Not valid code:

```
<name>
    <first>John</first>
    <last>Michael</last>
</name>
```

is not considered valid because child elements are not considered parsed character data.

REFERENCE

Specifying Types of Element Content

- To declare an element that may contain any type of content, insert the declaration

  ```
  <!ELEMENT element ANY>
  ```

  where *element* is the element name.
- To declare an empty element containing no content whatsoever, use the following declaration:

  ```
  <!ELEMENT element EMPTY>
  ```

- To declare an element that may contain only parsed character data, use the following declaration:

  ```
  <!ELEMENT element (#PCDATA)>
  ```

The name, address, phone, email, orderDate, itemPrice, and itemQty elements in the *orders.xml* document contain only parsed character data. You'll add declarations for these elements to the DTD.

To declare elements containing parsed character data in the *orders.xml* document:

1. Within the DOCTYPE, insert the following element declarations, as shown in Figure 12-6:

   ```
   <!ELEMENT name (#PCDATA)>
   <!ELEMENT address (#PCDATA)>
   <!ELEMENT phone (#PCDATA)>
   <!ELEMENT email (#PCDATA)>
   <!ELEMENT orderDate (#PCDATA)>
   <!ELEMENT itemPrice (#PCDATA)>
   <!ELEMENT itemQty (#PCDATA)>
   ```

Figure 12-6 **Element declarations**

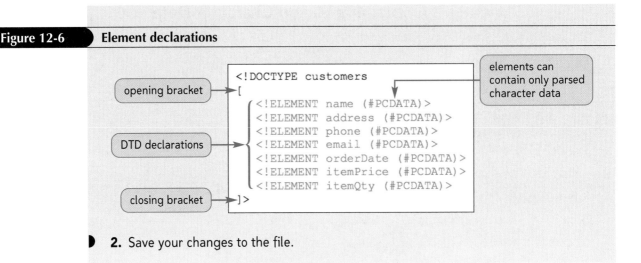

▶ **2.** Save your changes to the file.

Working with Child Elements

Next, you'll consider how to declare an element that contains only child elements. The syntax for such a declaration is

```
<!ELEMENT element (children)>
```

where *element* is the parent element and *children* is a listing of its child elements. The simplest form for the listing consists of a single child element associated with a parent. For example, the declaration

```
<!ELEMENT customer (phone)>
```

indicates that the `customer` element can contain only a single child element named `phone`. The following code would be invalid under this element declaration because the customer element contains two child elements—`name` and `phone`:

```
<customer>
   <name>John Michael</name>
   <phone>(407) 555-3476</phone>
</customer>
```

For content that involves multiple child elements, you can specify the elements in a sequence or you can specify a choice of elements.

Specifying an Element Sequence

A sequence is a list of elements that follow a defined order. The syntax to specify child elements in a sequence is

```
<!ELEMENT element (child1, child2, ...)>
```

where *child1*, *child2*, etc., represents the sequence of child elements within the parent. The order of the child elements in an XML document must match the order defined in the element declaration. For example, the following element declaration defines a sequence of three child elements for each `customer` element:

```
<!ELEMENT customer (name, phone, email)>
```

Under this declaration, the following code is valid:

```
<customer>
    <name>John Michael</name>
    <phone>(407) 555-3476</phone>
    <email>jk@example.net</email>
</customer>
```

However, even though the elements and their contents are identical in the following code, the code is not valid because the sequence doesn't match the defined order:

```
<customer>
    <name>John Michael</name>
    <email>jk@example.net</email>
    <phone>(407) 555-3476</phone>
</customer>
```

Specifying an Element Choice

Rather than defining a sequence of child elements, the element declaration can define a choice of possible elements. The syntax used to specify an element choice is

```
<!ELEMENT element (child1 | child2 | ...)>
```

where *child1*, *child2*, etc., are the possible child elements of the parent. For example, the following declaration allows the `customer` element to contain either the `name` or the `company` element:

```
<!ELEMENT customer (name | company)>
```

Based on this declaration, either of the following code samples is valid:

```
<customer>
    <name>John Michael</name>
</customer>
```

or

```
<customer>
    <company>Mapping Down the Road</company>
</customer>
```

However, under this declaration, a `customer` element cannot include both the `name` and `company` elements because the choice model allows only one of the child elements listed.

An element declaration can combine both a sequence and a choice of child elements. For example, the following declaration limits the `customer` element to three child elements, the first of which is either the `name` or the `company` element, followed by the `phone` and then the `email` element:

```
<!ELEMENT customer ((name | company), phone, email)>
```

Under this declaration, both of the following code samples are valid:

```
<customer>
    <name>Lea Ziegler</name>
    <phone>(813)555-8931</phone>
    <email>LZiegler@example.net</email>
</customer>
```

or

```
<customer>
    <company>VTech Productions</company>
    <phone>(813)555-8931</phone>
    <email>LZiegler@example.net</email>
</customer>
```

However, a `customer` element that does not start with either a `name` element or a `company` element followed by the `phone` and `email` elements would be invalid.

Specifying Child Elements

- To specify the sequence of child elements, use the declaration

  `<!ELEMENT element (child1, child2, ...)>`

  where `child1, child2, ...` is the order in which the child elements must appear within the parent element.
- To allow for a choice of child elements, use the declaration

  `<!ELEMENT element (child1 | child2 | ...)>`

  where `child1, child2, ...` are the possible children of the parent element.
- To combine a choice and a sequence of child elements in the same declaration, specify the choice elements within an additional set of parentheses, in the appropriate place within the sequence, as in the following code:

  `<!ELEMENT element ((child1 | child2 | ...), child3, child4, ...)>`

Modifying Symbols

So far, all the content models you have seen assume that each child element occurs once within its parent. If you need to specify duplicates of the same element, you could repeat the element name in the list. For example, the following element declaration indicates that the `customer` element must contain two `phone` elements:

```
<!ELEMENT customer (phone, phone)>
```

However, it's rare that you specify the exact number of duplicate elements. Instead, DTDs use more general numbering with a modifying symbol that specifies the number of occurrences of each element. The three modifying symbols are the question mark (?), the plus sign (+), and the asterisk (*). These are the same symbols you saw when creating a tree diagram for an XML document. As before, the ? symbol indicates that an element occurs zero times or one time, the + symbol indicates that an element occurs at least once, and the * symbol indicates that an element occurs zero times or more. There are no other modifying symbols. If you want to specify an exact number of child elements, such as the two `phone` elements discussed above, you must repeat the element name the appropriate number of times.

In the *orders.xml* document, the `customers` element must contain at least one element named `customer`. The element declaration for this is

```
<!ELEMENT customers (customer+)>
```

As this code demonstrates, a modifying symbol is placed directly after the element it modifies. You can also include modifying symbols in element sequences. For example, in Benjamin's document, each `customer` element contains the `name`, `address`, `phone`, and `email` elements, but the `email` element is optional, occurring either zero times or one time. The element declaration for this is

```
<!ELEMENT customer (name, address, phone, email?)>
```

The three modifying symbols can also modify entire element sequences or choices. You do this by placing the character immediately following the closing parenthesis of the sequence or choice. For example, the declaration

```
<!ELEMENT order (orderDate, items)+>
```

indicates that the child element sequence (`orderDate, items`) can be repeated one or more times within each `order` element. Of course, each time the sequence is repeated, the `orderDate` element must appear first, followed by the `items` element.

When applied to a choice model, the modifying symbols allow for multiple combinations of each child element. The declaration

```
<!ELEMENT customer (name | company)+>
```

allows any of the following lists of child elements:

```
name
company
name, company
name, name, company
name, company, company, name
```

The only requirement is that the combined total of `name` and `company` elements be greater than zero.

Applying Modifying Symbols

- To specify that an element can appear zero times or one time, use

  item?

  in the element declaration in the DTD, where *item* is an element name or a sequence or choice of elements.
- To specify one or more occurrences of an item, use

  item+
- To specify zero or more occurrences of an item, use

  *item**

Now that you've seen how to specify the occurrences of child elements, you'll add these declarations to the DTD for Benjamin's document. The declarations can be entered in any order, but you'll insert the declarations in the order in which the elements appear in the document. You'll also insert blank lines between groups of declarations to make the code easier to read.

To declare the child elements:

1. In the DTD of the *orders.xml* file, on the line below the opening bracket, insert the following element declaration, followed by a blank line:

   ```
   <!ELEMENT customers (customer+)>
   ```

   This declaration specifies that the root `customers` element must contain at least one `customer` element.

2. Above the `name` declaration, insert the following declaration followed by a blank line:

   ```
   <!ELEMENT customer (name, address, phone, email?, orders)>
   ```

   This declaration specifies that a `customer` element must contain, in order, a `name` element, an `address` element, and a `phone` element; it may then contain an `email` element; and then it must contain an `orders` element.

3. Below the declaration for the `email` element, insert the following declaration:

   ```
   <!ELEMENT orders (order+)>
   ```

This declaration specifies that an `orders` element must contain at least one `order` element.

▶ **4.** Below the `orders` declaration, insert a blank line followed by the following declaration:

```
<!ELEMENT order (orderDate, items)>
```

This declaration specifies that each `order` element must contain an `orderDate` element and an `items` element.

▶ **5.** Below the `orderDate` declaration, insert the following declaration:

```
<!ELEMENT items (item+)>
```

This declaration specifies that each `items` element must contain at least one `item` element.

▶ **6.** Below the `items` declaration, insert a blank line followed by the following declaration:

```
<!ELEMENT item (itemPrice, itemQty)>
```

This declaration specifies that the `item` element must contain the `itemPrice` and `itemQty` elements.

▶ **7.** Add a blank line after the `name` declaration, the `order` declaration, and the `item` declaration. Figure 12-7 shows the completed element declarations in the DTD.

Figure 12-7   **Declarations for the child elements**

customers element must contain one or more customer elements

```
<!DOCTYPE customers
[
    <!ELEMENT customers (customer+)>

    <!ELEMENT customer (name, address, phone, email?, orders)>

    <!ELEMENT name (#PCDATA)>

    <!ELEMENT address (#PCDATA)>
    <!ELEMENT phone (#PCDATA)>
    <!ELEMENT email (#PCDATA)>
    <!ELEMENT orders (order+)>

    <!ELEMENT order (orderDate, items)>

    <!ELEMENT orderDate (#PCDATA)>
    <!ELEMENT items (item+)>

    <!ELEMENT item (itemPrice, itemQty)>

    <!ELEMENT itemPrice (#PCDATA)>
    <!ELEMENT itemQty (#PCDATA)>
]>
```

customer element must contain the name, address, and phone elements in that order; may then contain the email element; and then must contain the orders element

orders element must contain one or more order elements

order element must contain the orderDate element and then the items element

items element must contain one or more item elements

item element must contain the itemPrice element and then the itemQty element

▶ **8.** Save your changes to the file.

To see how these element declarations represent the structure of the document, compare Figure 12-7 with the tree diagram shown earlier in Figure 12-3.

DTDs and Mixed Content

An XML element is not limited to either parsed character data or child elements. If an element contains both, its content is known as **mixed content**. For example, the `title` element in the following code contains both the text of the title and a collection of `subtitle` elements:

```
<title>The Adventures of Sherlock Holmes
   <subtitle>The Sign of Four</subtitle>
   <subtitle>by Sir Arthur Conan Doyle</subtitle>
</title>
```

To declare mixed content in a DTD, you use the following declaration:

```
<!ELEMENT element (#PCDATA | child1 | child2 | ...)*>
```

This declaration applies the * modifying symbol to a choice of parsed character data or child elements. Because the * symbol is used with a choice list, the element can contain any number of occurrences of child elements or text strings of parsed character data, or it can contain no content at all. For example, the declaration

```
<!ELEMENT title (#PCDATA | subtitle)*>
<!ELEMENT subtitle (#PCDATA)>
```

allows the `title` element to contain any number of text strings of parsed character data interspersed by `subtitle` elements. The `subtitle` elements themselves can contain only parsed character data.

Because they are very flexible, elements with mixed content do not add much defined structure to a document. You can specify only the names of the child elements, and you cannot constrain the order in which those child elements appear or control the number of occurrences for each element. An element might contain only text or it might contain any number of child elements in any order. For this reason, it is best to avoid working with mixed content if you want a tightly structured document.

At this point you've defined a structure for the elements in the *orders.xml* file. You will declare the attributes associated with those elements in the next session.

Session 12.1 Quick Check

1. What code would you enter to connect an XML document with the root element `Inventory` to a DTD stored in the file *books.dtd*?
2. What declaration would you enter to allow the `book` element to contain any content?
3. What declaration would you enter to specify that the `video` element is empty?
4. What declaration would you enter to indicate that the `book` element can contain only parsed character data?
5. What declaration would you enter to indicate that the `book` element can contain only a single child element named `author`?
6. What declaration would you enter to indicate that the `book` element can contain one or more child elements named `author`?
7. What declaration would you enter to allow the `part` element to contain a sequence that begins with a choice of the `partNum` or `partName` child elements, followed by child elements named `description` and then `price`?

SESSION 12.2 VISUAL OVERVIEW

The third term in an attribute-list declaration specifies the name of the attribute.

The fourth term in an attribute-list declaration specifies the data type of the attribute.

An **attribute-list declaration**, or simply **attribute declaration**, lists the names of all the attributes associated with a specific element. It also specifies the data type of each attribute, indicates whether each attribute is required or optional, and provides a default value for each attribute, if necessary.

The second term in an attribute-list declaration specifies the name of the element to which the attribute applies.

```
<!DOCTYPE customers
[
   <!ELEMENT customers (customer+)>

   <!ELEMENT customer (name, address, phone, ema
   <!ATTLIST customer custID ID #REQUIRED>

   <!ELEMENT name (#PCDATA)>
   <!ATTLIST name title (Mr. | Mrs. | Ms.) #IMP

   <!ELEMENT address (#PCDATA)>
   <!ELEMENT phone (#PCDATA)>
   <!ELEMENT email (#PCDATA)>
   <!ELEMENT orders (order+)>

   <!ELEMENT order (orderDate, items)>
   <!ATTLIST order orderID ID #REQUIRED>
   <!ATTLIST order orderBy IDREF #REQUIRED>

   <!ELEMENT orderDate (#PCDATA)>
   <!ELEMENT items (item+)>

   <!ELEMENT item (itemPrice, itemQty)>
   <!ATTLIST item itemNumber CDATA #REQUIRED>

   <!ELEMENT itemPrice (#PCDATA)>
   <!ATTLIST itemPrice saleItem (Y | N) "N">
   <!ELEMENT itemQty (#PCDATA)>
]>
```

DEFINING ATTRIBUTES WITHIN A DTD

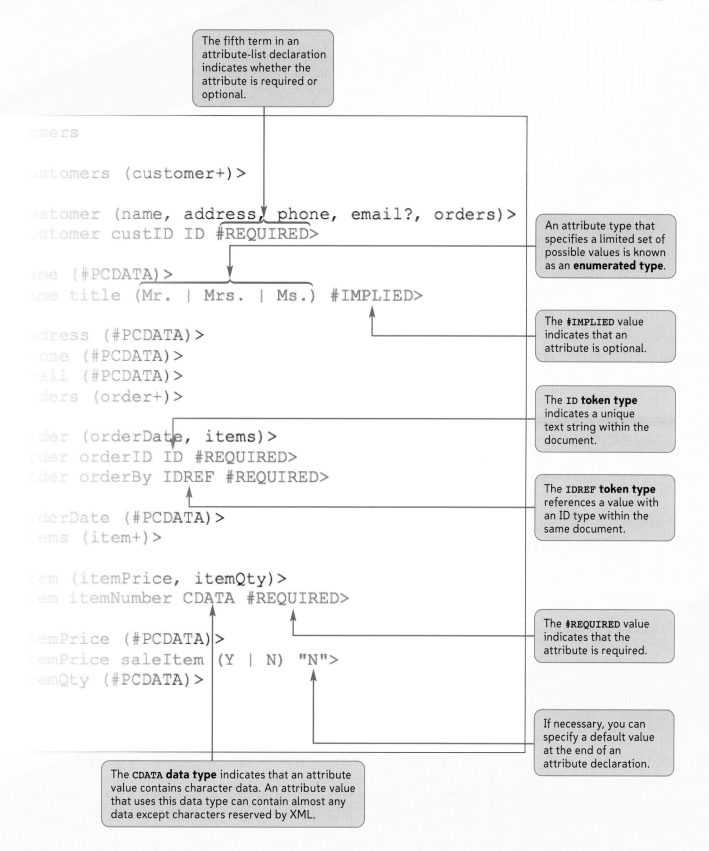

The fifth term in an attribute-list declaration indicates whether the attribute is required or optional.

An attribute type that specifies a limited set of possible values is known as an **enumerated type**.

The **#IMPLIED** value indicates that an attribute is optional.

The **ID** token type indicates a unique text string within the document.

The **IDREF** token type references a value with an ID type within the same document.

The **#REQUIRED** value indicates that the attribute is required.

If necessary, you can specify a default value at the end of an attribute declaration.

The **CDATA data type** indicates that an attribute value contains character data. An attribute value that uses this data type can contain almost any data except characters reserved by XML.

```
omers

ustomers (customer+)>

ustomer (name, address, phone, email?, orders)>
ustomer custID ID #REQUIRED>

ame (#PCDATA)>
ame title (Mr. | Mrs. | Ms.) #IMPLIED>

ddress (#PCDATA)>
one (#PCDATA)>
ail (#PCDATA)>
ders (order+)>

der (orderDate, items)>
der orderID ID #REQUIRED>
der orderBy IDREF #REQUIRED>

derDate (#PCDATA)>
ems (item+)>

em (itemPrice, itemQty)>
em itemNumber CDATA #REQUIRED>

emPrice (#PCDATA)>
emPrice saleItem (Y | N) "N">
emQty (#PCDATA)>
```

Declaring Attributes

In the previous session, you defined the structure of Benjamin's document by declaring all the elements in the *orders.xml* document and indicating what type of content each element could contain. However, the tree structure shown in Figure 12-3 also includes attributes for some elements. For the document to be valid, you must also declare all the attributes associated with the elements. You must indicate whether each attribute is required or optional, and you must indicate what kinds of values are allowed for each attribute. Finally, you can indicate whether each attribute has a default value associated with it. Figure 12-8 describes all the attributes that Benjamin intends to use in the *orders.xml* document along with the properties of each attribute.

Figure 12-8   **Properties of attributes used in orders.xml**

Element	Attribute	Description	Required?	Allowable Values
customer	custID	customer ID number	Yes	character data
name	title	title associated with the customer's name	No	"Mr.", "Mrs.", or "Ms."
order	orderID	order ID number	Yes	character data
	orderBy	ID of the customer placing the order	Yes	character data
item	itemNumber	item number	Yes	character data
itemPrice	saleItem	whether item price is a sale price	No	"Y" or "N" (default)

For example, every `customer` element must have a `custID` attribute to record the customer ID value. If a `custID` attribute is omitted from a `customer` element, the document is invalid.

To enforce attribute properties, you must add an attribute-list declaration to the document's DTD for each element that includes attributes. An attribute-list declaration:

• lists the names of all the attributes associated with a specific element
• specifies the data type of each attribute
• indicates whether each attribute is required or optional
• provides a default value for each attribute, if necessary

The syntax for declaring a list of attributes is

```
<!ATTLIST element attribute1 type1 default1
               attribute2 type2 default2
               ... >
```

where *element* is the name of the element associated with the attributes; *attribute1*, *attribute2*, etc., are the names of attributes; *type1*, *type2*, etc., are the attributes' data types; and *default1*, *default2*, etc., indicate whether each attribute is required and whether it has a default value. In practice, declarations for elements with multiple attributes are often easier to interpret if the attributes are declared separately rather than in one long declaration. The following is an equivalent form in the DTD:

```
<!ATTLIST element attribute1 type1 default1>
<!ATTLIST element attribute2 type2 default2>
...
```

XML parsers combine the different statements into a single attribute-list declaration. If a processor encounters more than one declaration for the same attribute, it ignores the second statement. Attribute-list declarations can be located anywhere within the document type declaration; however, it is often easiest to work with attribute declarations that are located adjacent to the declaration for the element with which they are associated.

Declaring Attributes in a DTD

- To declare a list of attributes associated with an element, enter the declaration

  ```
  <!ATTLIST element attribute1 type1 default1
                    attribute2 type2 default2
                    ...>
  ```

  or

  ```
  <!ATTLIST element attribute1 type1 default1>
  <!ATTLIST element attribute2 type2 default2>
  ...
  ```

  where `element` is the element associated with the attributes; `attribute1`, `attribute2`, etc., are the names of attributes; `type1`, `type2`, etc., are the attributes' data types; and `default1`, `default2`, etc., indicate whether each attribute is required and whether it has a default value.

- To indicate that an attribute contains character data, use

  `attribute CDATA`

  where `attribute` is the name of the attribute.

- To constrain an attribute value to a list of possible values, use

  `attribute (value1 | value2 | value3 | ...)`

  where `value1`, `value2`, etc., are allowed values for the attribute.

- To indicate that an attribute contains ID values, use

  `attribute ID`

- To indicate that an attribute contains a white space–separated list of ID values, use

  `attribute IDS`

- To indicate that an attribute contains a reference to an ID value, use

  `attribute IDREF`

- To indicate that an attribute contains a white space–separated list of references to ID values, use

  `attribute IDREFS`

- To constrain an attribute to an XML name containing only letters, numbers, and the punctuation symbols underscore (_), hyphen (-), period (.), and colon (:), but no white space, use

  `attribute NMTOKEN`

- To constrain an attribute to a white space–separated list of XML names, use

  `attribute NMTOKENS`

As a first step in adding attributes to the DTD for the *orders.xml* document, you will declare the names of the attributes and the elements they are associated with in the document.

Note: Because you are not yet going to include the data type and default values for the attributes, these attribute declarations are incomplete and would be rejected by any XML parser. You'll fix this later in this session.

To declare the attributes in the *orders.xml* document:

▶ **1.** If you took a break after the previous session, make sure the *orders.xml* file is open in your editor.

▶ **2.** Insert a new line below the `customer` element declaration, enter the following declaration, and then insert a new line:

    `<!ATTLIST customer custID>`

    This declaration indicates that the `customer` element can contain an attribute named `custID`.

▶ **3.** Insert a new line below the declaration for the `name` element, enter the following declaration, and then insert a new line:

    `<!ATTLIST name title>`

    This declaration indicates that the `name` element can contain a `title` attribute.

▶ **4.** On the blank line below the declaration for the `order` element, insert the following two declarations on new lines, and then insert a new line:

    `<!ATTLIST order orderID>`
    `<!ATTLIST order orderBy>`

    These declarations indicate that the `order` element can contain attributes named `orderID` and `orderBy`.

▶ **5.** On the blank line below the declaration for the `item` element, enter the following attribute declaration, and then insert a blank line:

    `<!ATTLIST item itemNumber>`

    This declaration indicates that the `item` element can contain an attribute named `itemNumber`.

▶ **6.** Insert a blank line below the declaration for the `itemPrice` element, and then enter the following declaration:

    `<!ATTLIST itemPrice saleItem>`

    This declaration indicates that the `itemPrice` element can contain an attribute named `saleItem`. Figure 12-9 shows the revised code including the attribute-list declarations.

Figure 12-9 | **Declarations for the attribute names**

> you can place an attribute-list declaration anywhere within the DOCTYPE, but placing it after the relevant element declaration helps organize your code

```
<!DOCTYPE customers
[
   <!ELEMENT customers (customer+)>

   <!ELEMENT customer (name, address, phone, email?, orders)>
   <!ATTLIST customer custID>

   <!ELEMENT name (#PCDATA)>
   <!ATTLIST name title>

   <!ELEMENT address (#PCDATA)>
   <!ELEMENT phone (#PCDATA)>
   <!ELEMENT email (#PCDATA)>
   <!ELEMENT orders (order+)>

   <!ELEMENT order (orderDate, items)>
   <!ATTLIST order orderID>
   <!ATTLIST order orderBy>

   <!ELEMENT orderDate (#PCDATA)>
   <!ELEMENT items (item+)>

   <!ELEMENT item (itemPrice, itemQty)>
   <!ATTLIST item itemNumber>

   <!ELEMENT itemPrice (#PCDATA)>
   <!ATTLIST itemPrice saleItem>
   <!ELEMENT itemQty (#PCDATA)>
]>
```

7. Save your changes to the file.

Trouble? When you save changes, your XML editor may indicate that the document contains an error and is no longer well formed. This is because the attribute-list declarations you entered are not yet complete. You'll fix this error by completing the declarations in the steps that follow.

Working with Attribute Types

The next step in defining these attributes is to specify the type of data each attribute can contain. Attribute values can consist only of character data, but you can control the format of those characters. Figure 12-10 lists the different data types that DTDs support for attribute values. Each data type gives you a varying degree of control over an attribute's content. You will investigate each of these types in greater detail, starting with character data.

Figure 12-10	**Attribute types**

Attribute Value	Description
CDATA	Any character data except characters reserved by XML
enumerated list	A list of possible attribute values
ID	A unique text string
IDREF	A reference to an ID value
IDREFS	A list of ID values separated by white space
ENTITY	A reference to an external unparsed entity
ENTITIES	A list of entities separated by white space
NMTOKEN	An accepted XML name
NMTOKENS	A list of XML names separated by white space
NOTATION	The name of a notation defined in the DTD

Character Data

Attribute values specified as character data (CDATA) can contain almost any data except characters reserved by XML for other purposes, such as <, >, and &. To declare an attribute value as character data, you add the CDATA data type to the attribute declaration with the syntax

> `<!ATTLIST element attribute CDATA default>`

TIP

You'll learn more about default attribute values later in this tutorial.

where the optional term `default` specifies a default value. For example, the item number of each item in Benjamin's document is expressed in character data. To indicate this in the DTD, you would add the CDATA attribute type to the declaration for the itemNumber attribute as follows:

> `<!ATTLIST item itemNumber CDATA>`

Any of the following attribute values are allowed under this declaration because they all contain character data:

```
<item itemNumber="340-978"> ... </item>
<item itemNumber="WMPro"> ... </item>
<item itemNumber="WM101PL"> ... </item>
```

In Benjamin's document, the attribute itemNumber contains character data. You'll add this information to its attribute declaration.

To specify that the itemNumber attribute contains character data:

1. In the *orders.xml* file, within the attribute-list declaration for itemNumber, just before the closing >, type a **space**, and then type **CDATA** as shown in Figure 12-11.

| **Figure 12-11** | **Character data type added to the attribute-list declaration** |

```
<!ELEMENT orderDate (#PCDATA)>
<!ELEMENT items (item+)>

<!ELEMENT item (itemPrice, itemQty)>
<!ATTLIST item itemNumber CDATA>          ← specifies that
                                            attribute values
<!ELEMENT itemPrice (#PCDATA)>              are composed of
<!ATTLIST itemPrice saleItem>               character data
<!ELEMENT itemQty (#PCDATA)>
]>
```

▶ **2.** Save your changes to the file.

Even though you may work with attribute values that will use only numbers as data, it's not possible to declare that an attribute's values must contain only a certain type of characters, such as integers or numbers. To indicate that an attribute value must be an integer or a number, you use schemas—a topic you will study in a later tutorial.

Enumerated Types

The CDATA data type allows for almost any string of characters, but in some cases you want to restrict an attribute to a set of possible values. For example, Benjamin uses the `title` attribute to indicate the title by which a customer chooses to be addressed. He needs to restrict the `title` attribute to values of "Mr.", "Mrs.", or "Ms." An attribute type that specifies a limited set of possible values is known as an enumerated type. The general form of an attribute declaration that uses an enumerated type is

```
<!ATTLIST element attribute (value1 | value2 | value3 | ...)
          default >
```

where *value1*, *value2*, etc., are allowed values for the specified attribute. To limit the value of the `title` attribute to "Mr." or "Mrs." or "Ms.", Benjamin can include an enumerated type, as in the following declaration:

```
<!ATTLIST name title (Mr. | Mrs. | Ms.)>
```

Under this declaration, any `title` attribute whose value is not "Mr.", "Mrs.", or "Ms." causes parsers to reject the document as invalid. You'll add this enumerated type to the DTD along with an enumerated type to specify the enumerated values for the `title` attribute of the `name` element.

To declare enumerated data types for the two `title` attributes:

▶ **1.** Within the `title` attribute declaration for the `name` element, just before the closing >, type a **space** and then type **(Mr. | Mrs. | Ms.)**.

▶ **2.** Within the `saleItem` attribute declaration for the `itemPrice` element, just before the closing >, type a **space** and then type **(Y | N)**. Figure 12-12 shows the revised DTD.

Figure 12-12 Attributes with enumerated data types

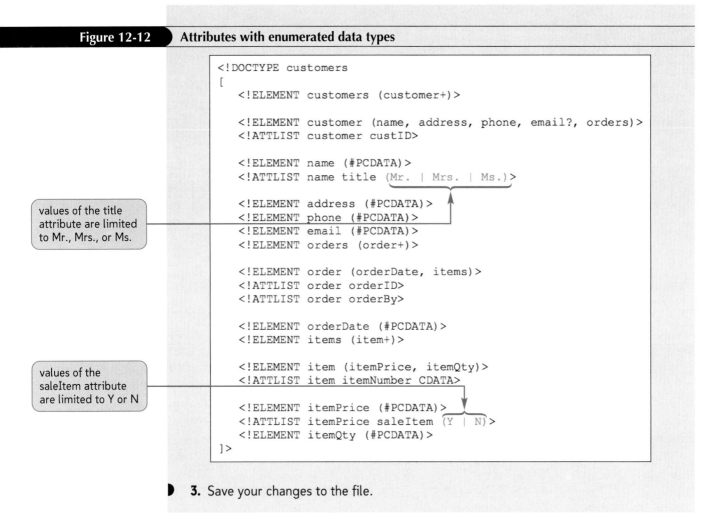

values of the title attribute are limited to Mr., Mrs., or Ms.

values of the saleItem attribute are limited to Y or N

▶ **3.** Save your changes to the file.

Another type of enumerated type is a notation. A **notation** associates the value of an attribute with a `<!NOTATION>` declaration that is inserted elsewhere in the DTD. Notations are used when an attribute value refers to a file containing nontextual data, such as a graphic image or a video clip. You will learn more about notations and how to work with nontextual data in the next session.

Tokenized Types

Tokenized types are character strings that follow certain specified rules for format and content; these rules are known as **tokens**. DTDs support four kinds of tokens—ID, ID reference, name token, and entity.

An **ID token** is used when an attribute value must be unique within a document. In Benjamin's document, the `customer` element contains the `custID` attribute, which stores a unique ID for each customer. To prevent users from entering the same `custID` value for different customers, Benjamin can define the attribute type for the `custID` attribute as follows:

```
<!ATTLIST customer custID ID>
```

Under this declaration, the following elements are valid:

```
<customer custID="cust201"> ... </customer>
<customer custID="cust202"> ... </customer>
```

However, the following elements occurring in the same document would not be valid because the same custID value is used more than once:

```
<customer custID="cust201"> ... </customer>
<customer custID="cust201"> ... </customer>
```

When an ID value is declared in a document, other attribute values can reference it using the IDREF token. An attribute declared using the **IDREF token** must have a value equal to the value of an ID attribute located somewhere in the same document. This enables an XML document to contain cross-references between one element and another.

For example, the order element in Benjamin's document has an attribute named orderBy, which contains the ID of the customer who placed the order. Assuming the custID value of the customer element is defined using the ID token, Benjamin can ensure that the orderBy value refers to an actual customer by using the following declaration:

```
<!ATTLIST order orderBy IDREF>
```

When an XML parser encounters this attribute, it searches the XML document for an ID value that matches the value of the orderBy attribute. If one of the attribute values doesn't have a matching ID value in the document, the parser rejects the document as invalid. However, you cannot specify that an XML parser limit its search to only particular elements or attributes. Any attribute that has been declared by the data type ID is a candidate for an ID reference.

An attribute can contain multiple IDs and ID references in a list, with entries separated by white space. For example, Benjamin might list all the orders made by a certain customer as an attribute of the customer element as in the following sample code:

```
<customer orders="or1089 or1021 or1122">
   ...
   <order orderID="or1089"> ... </order>
   <order orderID="or1021"> ... </order>
   <order orderID="or1122"> ... </order>
   ...
</customer>
```

Each ID listed in the orders attribute must match an ID value located elsewhere in the document. If one does not, Benjamin would want the document to be declared invalid.

To declare that an attribute contains a list of IDs, you apply the IDS attribute type to the attribute declaration as follows:

```
<!ATTLIST element attribute IDS default>
```

To declare that an attribute contains a list of ID references, you use the IDREFS attribute type as follows:

```
<!ATTLIST element attribute IDREFS default>
```

For the code sample above, to indicate that the orders attribute contains a list of ID references and to indicate that the orderID attribute contains IDs, you would enter the following attribute declarations in the DTD:

```
<!ATTLIST customer orders IDREFS>
<!ATTLIST order orderID ID>
```

As with the IDREF token, all of the IDs listed in an IDREFS token must be found in an ID attribute located somewhere in the file; otherwise, parsers will reject the document as invalid. However, nothing in the attribute declaration defines in which attributes the referenced ID will be located. So, although the orders attribute defined above must reference an ID value, it is not required to find that ID value only in the order attribute.

In Benjamin's document, the custID and orderID attributes contain ID values, while the orderBy attribute contains a reference to the customer ID. You'll declare the custID and orderID attributes as ID data types, and the orderBy attribute as an IDREF data type.

To declare attributes as IDs and ID references:

1. Within the custID attribute declaration, before the closing >, type a **space** and then type ID. This ensures that each custID value in the document is unique.

2. Repeat Step 1 for the orderID attribute declaration.

3. Within the orderBy attribute declaration, before the closing >, type a **space** and then type IDREF. This ensures that each orderBy value references an ID value somewhere in the document. See Figure 12-13.

Figure 12-13 Attribute IDs and IDREF added

each custID value must be unique in the document

each orderID value must be unique in the document

each value of the orderBy attribute must match an ID value somewhere in the document

```
<!DOCTYPE customers
[
    <!ELEMENT customers (customer+)>

    <!ELEMENT customer (name, address, phone, email?, orders)>
    <!ATTLIST customer custID ID>

    <!ELEMENT name (#PCDATA)>
    <!ATTLIST name title (Mr. | Mrs. | Ms.)>

    <!ELEMENT address (#PCDATA)>
    <!ELEMENT phone (#PCDATA)>
    <!ELEMENT email (#PCDATA)>
    <!ELEMENT orders (order+)>

    <!ELEMENT order (orderDate, items)>
    <!ATTLIST order orderID ID>
    <!ATTLIST order orderBy IDREF>

    <!ELEMENT orderDate (#PCDATA)>
    <!ELEMENT items (item+)>

    <!ELEMENT item (itemPrice, itemQty)>
    <!ATTLIST item itemNumber CDATA>

    <!ELEMENT itemPrice (#PCDATA)>
    <!ATTLIST itemPrice saleItem (Y | N)>
    <!ELEMENT itemQty (#PCDATA)>
]>
```

4. Save your changes to the file.

The **NMTOKEN**, or name token, data type is used with character data whose values must meet almost all the qualifications for valid XML names. NMTOKEN data types can contain letters and numbers, as well as the underscore (_), hyphen (-), period (.), and colon (:) symbols, but not white space characters such as blank spaces or line returns. However, while an XML name can start only with a letter or an underscore, an NMTOKEN data type can begin with any valid XML character.

The limits on the NMTOKEN data type make name tokens less flexible than character data, which can contain white space characters. If Benjamin wants to make sure that an attribute value is always a valid XML name, he can use the NMTOKEN type instead of the CDATA type. For instance, he could use an NMTOKEN data type for an attribute whose value would always be a date stored in ISO date format (such as 2016-05-20). Specifying this data type would exclude obviously erroneous data, including anything with a string or a date separated by slashes (which are disallowed characters in an XML name).

When an attribute contains more than one name token, you define the attribute using the **NMTOKENS** data type and separate the name tokens in the list with blank spaces.

Working with Attribute Defaults

The final part of an attribute declaration is the attribute default, which defines whether an attribute value is required, optional, assigned a default, or fixed. Figure 12-14 shows the entry in the attribute-list declaration for each of these four possibilities.

Figure 12-14	Attribute defaults

Attribute Default	Description
#REQUIRED	The attribute must appear with every occurrence of the element.
#IMPLIED	The attribute is optional.
"default"	The attribute is optional. If an attribute value is not specified, a validating XML parser will supply the default value.
#FIXED "default"	The attribute is optional. If an attribute value is specified, it must match the default value.

Figure 12-8 showed how Benjamin outlined the properties for the attributes in the *orders.xml* document. Based on this outline, a customer ID value is required for every customer. To indicate this in the DTD, you'd add the #REQUIRED value to the attribute declaration, as follows:

```
<!ATTLIST customer custID ID #REQUIRED>
```

On the other hand, Benjamin does not always record whether a customer wants to be addressed as Mr., Mrs., or Ms., so you'd add the #IMPLIED value to the title attribute to indicate that this attribute is optional. The following shows the complete attribute declaration for the title attribute:

```
<!ATTLIST name title (Mr. | Mrs. | Ms.) #IMPLIED>
```

Based on this declaration, if an XML parser encounters a name element without a title attribute, it doesn't invalidate the document but it assumes a blank value for the attribute instead.

Another attribute from Benjamin's document is the saleItem attribute, which indicates whether the itemPrice value is a sale price. The saleItem attribute is optional; however, unlike the title attribute, which gets a blank value if omitted, Benjamin wants XML parsers to assume a value of N if no value is specified for the saleItem attribute. The complete attribute declaration for the saleItem attribute is

```
<!ATTLIST itemPrice saleItem (Y | N) "N">
```

The last type of attribute default is #FIXED *default*, which fixes the attribute to the value specified by *default*. If you omit a #FIXED attribute from the corresponding element, an XML parser supplies the default value. If you include the attribute, the attribute value must equal *default* or the document is invalid.

TIP

If you specify a default value for an attribute, omit #REQUIRED and #IMPLIED from the attribute declaration so parsers don't reject the DTD.

Specifying an Attribute Default

- For an attribute that must appear with every occurrence of the element, insert the attribute default

  `#REQUIRED`

  within the attribute declaration.
- For an optional attribute, insert

  `#IMPLIED`
- For an optional attribute that has a value of *default* when omitted, insert

  `"default"`
- For an optional attribute that must be fixed to the value *default*, insert

  `#FIXED "default"`

Now that you've seen how to work with attribute defaults, you'll complete the attribute declarations by adding the default specifications.

To specify attribute defaults in the *orders.xml* document:

1. Within the `custID` attribute-list declaration, before the closing >, type a **space** and then type **#REQUIRED**. This indicates that this is a required attribute.

2. Repeat Step 1 for the `orderID`, `orderBy`, and `itemNumber` attribute-list declarations.

3. Within the `title` attribute-list declaration, before the closing >, type a **space** and then type **#IMPLIED**. This indicates that `title` is an optional attribute.

4. Within the `saleItem` attribute-list declaration, before the closing >, type a **space** and then type **"N"**. This indicates that this is the default value of the attribute if no attribute value is entered in the document. Figure 12-15 shows the final form of all of the attribute declarations in the DTD.

Figure 12-15   **Attribute defaults**

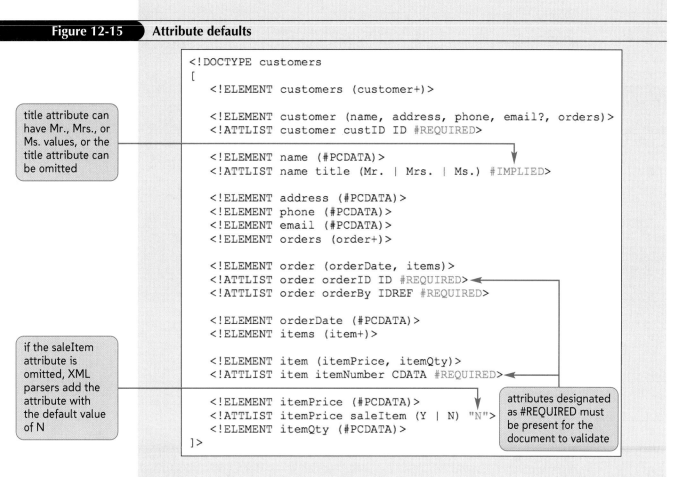

title attribute can have Mr., Mrs., or Ms. values, or the title attribute can be omitted

if the saleItem attribute is omitted, XML parsers add the attribute with the default value of N

attributes designated as #REQUIRED must be present for the document to validate

```
<!DOCTYPE customers
[
    <!ELEMENT customers (customer+)>

    <!ELEMENT customer (name, address, phone, email?, orders)>
    <!ATTLIST customer custID ID #REQUIRED>

    <!ELEMENT name (#PCDATA)>
    <!ATTLIST name title (Mr. | Mrs. | Ms.) #IMPLIED>

    <!ELEMENT address (#PCDATA)>
    <!ELEMENT phone (#PCDATA)>
    <!ELEMENT email (#PCDATA)>
    <!ELEMENT orders (order+)>

    <!ELEMENT order (orderDate, items)>
    <!ATTLIST order orderID ID #REQUIRED>
    <!ATTLIST order orderBy IDREF #REQUIRED>

    <!ELEMENT orderDate (#PCDATA)>
    <!ELEMENT items (item+)>

    <!ELEMENT item (itemPrice, itemQty)>
    <!ATTLIST item itemNumber CDATA #REQUIRED>

    <!ELEMENT itemPrice (#PCDATA)>
    <!ATTLIST itemPrice saleItem (Y | N) "N">
    <!ELEMENT itemQty (#PCDATA)>
]>
```

▶ **5.** Save your changes to the file. If you're using an XML editor, the document should once again be recognized as well formed.

Validating an XML Document

You are ready to test whether the *orders.xml* document is valid under the rules Benjamin has specified. To test for validity, an XML parser must be able to compare the XML document with the rules established in the DTD. The Web has many excellent sources for validating parsers, including Web sites in which you can upload an XML document for free to have it validated against an internal or external DTD. Several editors provide XML validation as well.

    The following steps describe how to use Exchanger XML Editor to validate Benjamin's *orders.xml* document.

To validate the *orders.xml* file:

▶ **1.** If necessary, use Exchanger XML Editor to open the **orders.xml** file.

    Trouble? If you don't have access to Exchanger XML Editor, you can upload your document to *http://validator.w3.org*, just as you would an HTML document, to validate its content against the DTD. As long as the document is found to be valid, you can ignore any warnings generated.

2. On the menu bar, click **XML** and then on the submenu click **Validate**. As shown in Figure 12-16, the Errors tab reports that the *orders.xml* file is a valid document.

Figure 12-16 **Validation results in Exchanger XML Editor**

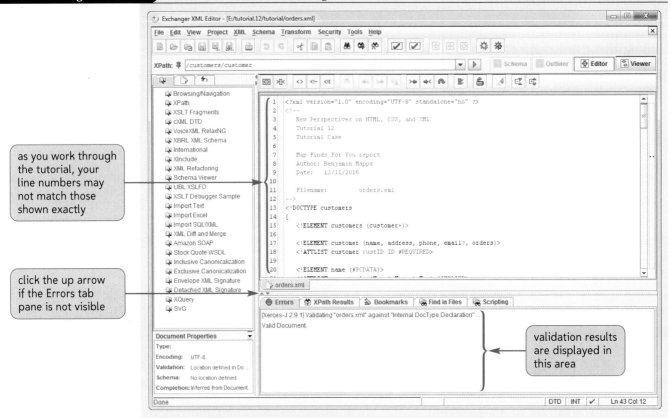

as you work through the tutorial, your line numbers may not match those shown exactly

click the up arrow if the Errors tab pane is not visible

validation results are displayed in this area

Trouble? If the Errors tab isn't visible, click the small up arrow in the lower-left corner of the pane displaying the document code.

Trouble? If a validation error is reported in the Errors tab, there is an error in the DTD code. Check your DTD code against the *orders.xml* code shown in Figure 12-15. Your code should match exactly, including the use of uppercase and lowercase letters. Fix any discrepancies, be sure to save your changes, revalidate, and then reexamine the Errors tab for validation information.

3. If necessary, save your changes to the file.

TIP

You can also press F7 (Windows) or fn+F7 (Mac) to validate a document in Exchanger XML Editor.

Although the file is valid, it is a good learning experience to place a few intentional errors in your XML code to see how validation errors are discovered and reported. You'll add the following errors to your document:

- Include an element not listed in the DTD.
- Include an attribute not listed in the DTD.
- Provide a value for an attribute declared as an ID reference that does not reference any ID value in the document.

Each of these errors should cause the document to be rejected by your XML parser as invalid.

To add intentional errors to the *orders.xml* file:

▶ **1.** Return to the **orders.xml** file in your editor.

▶ **2.** Scroll down to the first customer, John Michael, and then, directly below the `phone` element, insert a blank line and type the following new `cell` element:

```
<cell>(603) 555-1221</cell>
```

XML parsers will flag this as an error because the element is not declared in the DTD.

▶ **3.** Scroll down to the first `order` element, with the `orderID` value or1089, click just before the closing >, insert a **space**, and then type the following new attribute:

```
orderType="online"
```

XML parsers will flag this as an error because the attribute is not declared in the DTD.

▶ **4.** Within the same `order` element, change the value of the `orderBy` attribute from cust201 to **cust210**. Because no ID attribute entered into this document has the value cust210, the XML parser will flag this as an error. Figure 12-17 highlights the new and revised code in the document.

Figure 12-17   Intentional errors added to the orders.xml file

```
<customers>
   <customer custID="cust201">
      <name title="Mr.">John Michael</name>
      <address>
         <![CDATA[
         41 West Plankton Avenue
         Orlando, FL   32820
         ]]>
      </address>
      <phone>(407) 555-3476</phone>
      <cell>(603) 555-1221</cell>
      <email>jk@example.net</email>
      <orders>
         <order orderID="or1089" orderBy="cust210" orderType="online">
            <orderDate>8/11/2016</orderDate>
            <items>
```

cell element has not been declared in the DTD as an element or as a child of customer

cust210 attribute value does not match any ID listed in the document

orderType attribute has not been declared in the DTD

▶ **5.** Save your changes to the file.

Next, you'll again validate the *orders.xml* file to test whether an XML parser catches the errors and reports them. You added three intentional errors, but it is not unusual for one error to generate more than one error message. Therefore, it is a good idea to revalidate a document after correcting each error.

To validate the revised *orders.xml* file:

▶ **1.** On the menu bar, click **XML**, and then on the submenu, click **Validate**. The parser reports two errors due to the addition of the cell element. First, the parser is expecting an element named cell to be defined. Additionally, because cell was not listed as a child element for the customer element in the DTD, another error message regarding the customer content type not matching is generated. Because of these errors and the additional errors generated from the other changes, the *orders.xml* file is rejected. See Figure 12-18.

Figure 12-18	Validation errors due to an invalid document

a red circle containing an x is displayed next to the number of each line that contains a validation error

each error message indicates the line and column where the error occurs

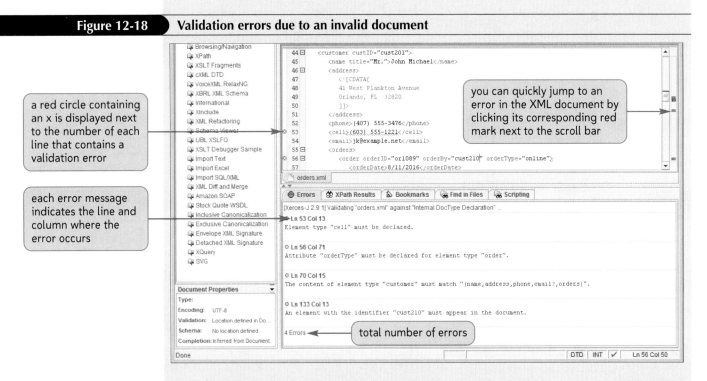

you can quickly jump to an error in the XML document by clicking its corresponding red mark next to the scroll bar

total number of errors

Trouble? If the validation errors are not appearing, check your code against Figure 12-18 and be sure they match exactly, save the file again to ensure that the errors you added are saved, and then re-validate the document.

Note that in Exchanger XML Editor, a red circle containing an x is displayed next to the number of each line that contains a validation error. In addition, you can quickly jump to an error in the XML document by clicking its corresponding red mark next to the scroll bar.

▶ **2.** In the *orders.xml* code, remove the cell element that you entered in the previous set of steps, and then save your changes to the file.

▶ **3.** Press **F7** (Windows) or **fn+F7** (Mac) to validate the file again, and then, if necessary, scroll down the error listing. Two errors have been eliminated. Now the first error being identified involves the undeclared attribute orderType. See Figure 12-19.

Figure 12-19   **Reduced list of errors**

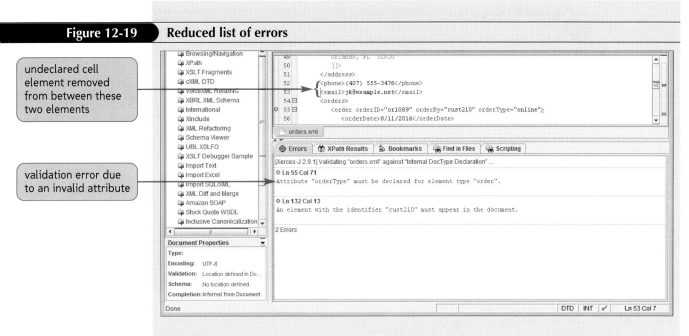

undeclared cell element removed from between these two elements

validation error due to an invalid attribute

▶ **4.** Remove the `orderType` attribute and its attribute value from the first `order` element, and then save your changes to the file.

▶ **5.** Press **F7** (Windows) or **fn**+**F7** (Mac) to validate the file again, and then, if necessary, scroll down the error listing. Another error has been eliminated. As Figure 12-20 shows, the validator finds only one remaining error in the document: The cust210 value does not reference any ID value found in the document.

Figure 12-20   **Final validation error**

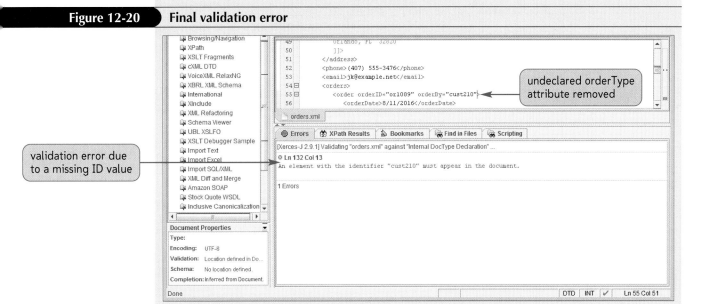

undeclared orderType attribute removed

validation error due to a missing ID value

▶ **6.** Change the `orderBy` attribute value for the first `order` element from cust210 back to **cust201**, and then save your changes to the file.

▶ **7.** Press **F7** (Windows) or **fn**+**F7** (Mac) to validate the file again, and then verify that the validator reports no errors in the *orders.xml* file.

PROSKILLS

Problem Solving: Reconciling DTDs and Namespaces

One drawback with DTDs is that they are not namespace-aware, so you cannot create a set of validation rules for elements and attributes belonging to a particular namespace. To get around this limitation, you can work with namespace prefixes, applying a validation rule to an element's qualified name. For example, if the phone element is placed in the customers namespace using the cu namespace prefix

```
<cu:phone>(407) 555-3476</cu:phone>
```

then the element declaration in the DTD would need to include the same element name qualification:

```
<!ELEMENT cu:phone (#PCDATA)>
```

In essence, the DTD treats a qualified name as the complete element name including the namespace prefix, colon, and local name. It doesn't recognize the namespace prefix as significant. Any namespace declarations in a document must also be included in the DTD for a document to be valid. This is usually done using a FIXED data type for the namespace's URI. For example, if the root element in a document declares the customers namespace using the attribute value

```
<cu:customers xmlns:cu="http://example.com/mapfindsforyou/
customers">
```

then the DTD should include the following attribute declaration:

```
<!ATTLIST cu:customers xmlns:cu CDATA #FIXED "http://example.com/
mapfindsforyou/customers">
```

The drawback to mixing namespaces and DTDs is that you must know the namespace prefix used in an XML document, and the DTD must be written to conform to that namespace. This makes it difficult to perform validation on a wide variety of documents that might employ any number of possible namespace prefixes. In addition, there is no way of knowing what namespace a prefix in the DTD points to because DTDs do not include a mechanism for matching a prefix to a namespace URI. It is also difficult to validate a compound document using standard vocabularies such as XHTML because you cannot easily modify the standard DTDs to accommodate the namespaces in your document.

If you need to validate compound documents that employ several namespaces, a better solution is to use schemas, which are validation tools that do support namespaces.

In this session, you defined the content and structure of Benjamin's document in a DTD. In the next session, you will work with entities and nontextual content in the DTD and learn about the DTDs associated with some of the standard XML vocabularies.

Session 12.2 Quick Check

REVIEW

1. What attribute declaration creates an optional `title` attribute within the `book` element and specifies text string content for the `title` attribute?

2. A `play` element has a required attribute named `type`, which can have one of four possible values—`Romance`, `Tragedy`, `History`, and `Comedy`. Provide the appropriate attribute declaration for the `type` attribute.

3. What is the main difference between an attribute with the CDATA type and one with the NMTOKEN type?

4. A `book` element has a required ID attribute named `ISBN`. Provide the appropriate attribute declaration for the `ISBN` attribute.

5. An `author` element has an optional attribute named `booksBy`, which contains a white space–separated list of ISBNs for the books the author has written. If `ISBN` is an ID attribute for another element in the document, what declaration would you use for the `booksBy` attribute?

6. A `book` element has an optional attribute named `inStock` that can have the value `yes` or `no`. The default value is `yes`. What is the declaration for the `inStock` attribute?

SESSION 12.3 VISUAL OVERVIEW

> A comment within a DTD uses the same syntax as in XML and XHTML code.

> When naming an entity, follow the same guidelines as for naming an XML element.

> The value of an entity is contained within quotation marks.

DTD code

```
<!DOCTYPE customers
[
    <!-- Item code descriptions inserted as general entities -->
    <!ENTITY WM100PL "World map outlining countries and capitals; poster-size, laminated paper">
    <!ENTITY WM101P "World map outlining countries and capitals; poster-size, paper">
    <!ENTITY WM105L "World map outlining countries and populations; laminated paper">
    <!ENTITY WM140P "World map focusing on land and water features; paper roll">
    <!ENTITY H115E "United States hiking map including elevations; electronic">
    <!ENTITY H115F "United States hiking map including elevations; folded paper">

    <!ELEMENT customers (customer+)>

    <!ELEMENT customer (name, address, phone, email?, orders)>
    <!ATTLIST customer custID ID #REQUIRED>
```

> Entities that are used within an XML document are known as **general entities**. An entity whose content is found within the DTD is known as an **internal entity**, and a **parsed entity** references text that can be readily interpreted by an application reading the XML document.

XML code

```
<customers>
    <customer custID="cust201">
        <name title="Mr.">John Michael</name>
        <address>
            <![CDATA[
            41 West Plankton Avenue
            Orlando, FL  32820
            ]]>
        </address>
        <phone>(407) 555-3476</phone>
        <cell>(603) 555-1221</cell>
        <email>jk@example.net</email>
        <orders>
            <order orderID="or1089" orderBy="cust210" orderType="online">
                <orderDate>8/11/2016</orderDate>
                <items>
                    <item itemNumber="WM100PL">
                        <desc>&WM100PL;</desc>
                        <itemPrice saleItem="N">39.95</itemPrice>
                        <itemQty>1</itemQty>
                    </item>
                    <item itemNumber="WM101P">
                        <desc>&WM101P;</desc>
                        <itemPrice saleItem="Y">19.90</itemPrice>
                        <itemQty>2</itemQty>
                    </item>
                </items>
            </order>
        </orders>
    </customer>
```

> An entity reference starts with an ampersand (&) and ends with a semicolon (;).

ENTITIES AND COMMENTS IN A DTD

> An entity reference is replaced by its value when an XML document is parsed.

Parsed XML document

```xml
<?xml version="1.0" encoding="UTF-8"?>
<!-- New Perspectives on HTML, CSS, and XML Tutorial 12 Tutorial Case Map Finds For You report Author: Benjamin
Mapps Date: 12/11/2016 Filename: orders.xml -->
<!DOCTYPE customers>
<customers>
    <customer custID="cust201">
        <name title="Mr.">John Michael</name>
        <address>
            <![CDATA[ 41 West Plankton Avenue Orlando, FL 32820 ]]>
        </address>
        <phone>(407) 555-3476</phone>
        <email>jk@example.net</email>
        <orders>
            <order orderBy="cust201" orderID="or1089">
                <orderDate>8/11/2016</orderDate>
                <items>
                    <item itemNumber="WM100PL">
                        <desc>World map outlining countries and capitals; poster-size, laminated paper</desc>
                        <itemPrice saleItem="N">39.95</itemPrice>
                        <itemQty>1</itemQty>
                    </item>
                    <item itemNumber="WM101P">
                        <desc>World map outlining countries and capitals; poster-size, paper</desc>
                        <itemPrice saleItem="Y">19.90</itemPrice>
                        <itemQty>2</itemQty>
                    </item>
                </items>
            </order>
        </orders>
    </customer>
```

Introducing Entities

In the *orders.xml* document, Benjamin inserted item numbers for the different items ordered by customers. For example, the first customer in the file, Mr. John Michael, ordered two items with the item codes WM100PL and WM101P. Each of these item numbers is associated with a longer text description of the product. Figure 12-21 shows the item code and item description for each of the items in the *orders.xml* file.

Figure 12-21	Item codes and descriptions

Item Codes	Description
WM100PL	World map outlining countries and capitals; poster-size, laminated paper
WM101P	World map outlining countries and capitals; poster-size, paper
WM105L	World map outlining countries and populations; laminated paper
WM140P	World map focusing on land and water features; paper roll
H115E	United States hiking map including elevations; electronic
H115F	United States hiking map including elevations; folded paper

Benjamin wants some way to include the longer text descriptions of these items in his document without having to enter them into each order, which might result in some typographical errors. You can do this with entities. You have already worked with entities to insert special character strings into an XML document. XML supports the following five built-in entities:

- `&amp;` for the & character
- `&lt;` for the < character
- `&gt;` for the > character
- `&apos;` for the ' character
- `&quot;` for the " character

When an XML parser encounters one of these entities, it can display the corresponding character symbol. With a DTD, you can create a customized set of entities corresponding to text strings such as Benjamin's product descriptions, files, or nontextual content that you want referenced by the XML document. When an XML parser encounters one of your customized entities, it will also be able to display the corresponding character text.

Working with General Entities

TIP

For a long text string that will be repeated throughout an XML document, avoid data entry errors by placing the text string in its own entity.

To create a customized entity, you add it to the document's DTD. An entity is classified based on three factors—where it will be applied, where its content is located, and what type of content it references. Entities that are used within an XML document are known as general entities. Another type of entity, a **parameter entity**, is used within a DTD. You will work with parameter entities later in this session.

Entities can reference content found either in an external file or within the DTD itself. An entity that references content found in an external file is called an **external entity**, whereas an entity whose content is found within the DTD is known as an internal entity.

Finally, the content referenced by an entity can be either parsed or unparsed. A parsed entity references text that can be readily interpreted, or parsed, by an application reading the XML document. Parsed entities are used when text is repeated often, and can reference characters, words, phrases, paragraphs, or entire documents. The only requirement is that the text be well formed. An entity that references content that either is nontextual or cannot be interpreted by an XML parser is an **unparsed entity**. One example of an unparsed entity is an entity that references a graphic image file.

Different types of entities are declared slightly differently based on the above three factors. For Benjamin's product codes, you'll declare general parsed internal entities.

Creating Parsed Entities

To create a parsed internal entity, you add the entity declaration

```
<!ENTITY entity "value">
```

to the DTD, where *entity* is the name assigned to the entity and *value* is the text string associated with the entity. The entity name follows the same rules that apply to all XML names: It can have no blank spaces and must begin with either a letter or an underscore. The entity value itself must be well-formed XML text. This can be a simple text string or it can be well-formed XML code. For example, to store the product description for the product with the item code WM100PL, you would add the following entity to the document's DTD:

```
<!ENTITY WM100PL "World map outlining countries and capitals;
poster-size, laminated paper">
```

You can add markup tags to any entity declaration by including them in the entity value, as follows:

```
<!ENTITY WM100PL "<desc>World map outlining countries and capitals;
poster-size, laminated paper</desc>">
```

Any text is allowed to be used for an entity's value as long as it corresponds to well-formed XML. Thus, a document containing the following entity declaration would not be well formed because the declaration lacks the closing `</desc>` tag in the entity's value:

Not well-formed code:

```
<!ENTITY WM100PL "<desc>World map outlining countries and capitals;
poster-size, laminated paper">
```

Entity values must be well formed without reference to other entities or document content. You couldn't, for example, place the closing `</desc>` tag in another entity declaration or within the XML document itself. Although tags within entity references are allowed, this is not a recommended practice.

For longer text strings that would not easily fit within the value of an entity declaration, you can place the content in an external file. To create a parsed entity that references content from an external file using a system identifier, such as a filename or URI, you use the declaration

```
<!ENTITY entity SYSTEM "uri">
```

where *entity* is again the entity's name, SYSTEM indicates the content is located in an external file, and *uri* is the URI of the external file containing the entity's content. For instance, the following entity declaration references the content of the *description.xml* file:

```
<!ENTITY WM100PL SYSTEM "description.xml">
```

The *description.xml* file must contain well-formed XML content. However, it should not contain an XML declaration. Because an XML document can contain only one XML declaration, placing a second one in a document via an external entity results in an error.

An external entity can also reference content from an external file using a public identifier with the declaration

```
<!ENTITY entity PUBLIC "id" "uri">
```

where PUBLIC indicates the content is located in a public location, *id* is the public identifier, and *uri* is the system location of the external file (included in case an XML parser doesn't recognize the public identifier). An entity declaration referencing a public location might look like the following:

```
<!ENTITY WM100PL PUBLIC "-//MFY// WM100PL INFO" "description.xml">
```

In this case, the public identifier -//MFY// WM100PL INFO is used by an XML parser to load the external content corresponding to the WM100PL entity. If that identifier is not recognized, the parser falls back to the system location of the *description.xml* file. In this way, external entities behave like DOCTYPEs that reference external DTDs from either public or system locations.

Declaring and Referencing Parsed Entities

- To declare a parsed internal entity, use the declaration

  ```
  <!ENTITY entity "value">
  ```

  where *entity* is the entity's name and *value* is the entity's value.
- To declare a parsed external entity from a system location, use the declaration

  ```
  <!ENTITY entity SYSTEM "uri">
  ```

  where *uri* is the URI of the external file containing the entity value.
- To declare a parsed external entity from a public location, use the declaration

  ```
  <!ENTITY entity PUBLIC "id" "uri">
  ```

  where *id* is the public identifier for the external file.
- To reference a general entity within an XML document, enter

  ```
  &entity;
  ```

  where *entity* is the entity name declared in the DTD associated with the XML document.

Referencing a General Entity

After a general entity is declared in a DTD, it can be referenced anywhere within the body of the XML document. The syntax for referencing a general entity is the same as for referencing one of the five built-in XML entities, namely

```
&entity;
```

where *entity* is the entity's name as declared in the DTD. For example, if the WM100PL entity is declared in the DTD as

```
<!ENTITY WM100PL "World map outlining countries and capitals;
poster-size, laminated paper">
```

you could reference the entity's value in the XML document within a desc element as follows:

```
<desc>&WM100PL;</desc>
```

Any XML parser encountering this entity reference would be able to expand the entity into its referenced value, resulting in the following parsed code:

```
<desc>World map outlining countries and capitals; poster-size,
laminated paper</desc>
```

The fact that the entity's value is expanded into the code of the XML document is one reason why entity values must correspond to well-formed XML code. Because of the way entities are parsed, you cannot include the & symbol as part of an entity's value. XML parsers interpret the & symbol as a reference to another entity and attempt to resolve the reference. If you need to include the & symbol, you should use the built-in entity reference `&amp;`. You also cannot use the % symbol in an entity's value because, as you'll learn later in this session, this is the symbol used for inserting parameter entities.

At the time of this writing, none of the major browsers support the use of external entities in combination with DTDs. These browsers use a built-in XML parser that does not support resolution of external entities. The reason is that if an entity declaration is placed in a file on a remote Web server, the XML parser must establish a TCP/IP connection with the remote file, which might not always be possible. The major browsers consider such a connection to be a potential security risk. Thus, to ensure that an XML document can be properly read and rendered, browsers require entities to be part of the internal DTD.

Next, you'll declare parsed entities for all the product codes in the *orders.xml* document. You'll place the declarations within the internal DTD. You'll also add a declaration to the DTD for the `desc` element, which will contain the entities within the document code.

To create the entity declarations in an internal DTD:

▶ **1.** If you took a break after the previous session, make sure the **orders.xml** file is open in your text editor.

▶ **2.** Add the following entity declarations below the opening square bracket in the DOCTYPE declaration statement, as shown in Figure 12-22:

```
<!ENTITY WM100PL "World map outlining countries and capitals;
                  poster-size, laminated paper">
<!ENTITY WM101P "World map outlining countries and capitals;
                  poster-size, paper">
<!ENTITY WM105L "World map outlining countries and populations;
                  laminated paper">
<!ENTITY WM140P "World map focusing on land and water features;
                  paper roll">
<!ENTITY H115E "United States hiking map including elevations;
                  electronic">
<!ENTITY H115F "United States hiking map including elevations;
                  folded paper">
```

Figure 12-22 | **Creating general entities**

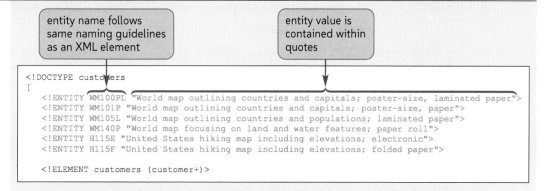

▶ **3.** Scroll down to the element definition for the `item` element, place the insertion point after the opening parenthesis for the list of child elements and before the `itemPrice` element name, and then type **desc** followed by a comma and a space.

▶ **4.** Insert a blank line before the `itemPrice` element definition, and then type the following new element definition on the blank line you just created:

```
<!ELEMENT desc (#PCDATA)>
```

Figure 12-23 shows the updated code in the DTD.

Figure 12-23 **Adding a new element to the DTD**

new desc element
specified as a child
of the item element

new desc element
added

```
<!ELEMENT items (item+)>

  <!ELEMENT item (desc, itemPrice, itemQty)>
  <!ATTLIST item itemNumber CDATA #REQUIRED>

  <!ELEMENT desc (#PCDATA)>
  <!ELEMENT itemPrice (#PCDATA)>
  <!ATTLIST itemPrice saleItem (Y | N) "N">
  <!ELEMENT itemQty (#PCDATA)>
]>
```

▶ **5.** Save the **orders.xml** file.

Now that you've defined the entities, you'll insert entity references to Benjamin's item description codes in the body of the XML document.

To add entity references:

▶ **1.** Scroll down to the `customer` element for the first customer, John Michael, and then directly below the opening tag for the first `item` element, enter the following new desc element:

```
<desc>&WM100PL;</desc>
```

Notice that the entity reference is the value of the `itemNumber` attribute for the preceding `item` element, with & at the start and ; at the end.

▶ **2.** Directly below the opening tag for the second `item` element for John Michael, add the following new desc element:

```
<desc>&WM101P;</desc>
```

Figure 12-24 shows the revised code for John Michael's orders.

Figure 12-24	Revised order information for John Michael

```
<customer custID="cust201">
    <name title="Mr.">John Michael</name>
    <address>
        <![CDATA[
        41 West Plankton Avenue
        Orlando, FL  32820
        ]]>
    </address>
    <phone>(407) 555-3476</phone>
    <cell>(603) 555-1221</cell>
    <email>jk@example.net</email>
    <orders>
        <order orderID="or1089" orderBy="cust210" orderType="online">
            <orderDate>8/11/2016</orderDate>
            <items>
                <item itemNumber="WM100PL">
                    <desc>&WM100PL;</desc>
                    <itemPrice saleItem="N">39.95</itemPrice>
                    <itemQty>1</itemQty>
                </item>
                <item itemNumber="WM101P">
                    <desc>&WM101P;</desc>
                    <itemPrice saleItem="Y">19.90</itemPrice>
                    <itemQty>2</itemQty>
                </item>
            </items>
        </order>
    </orders>
</customer>
```

desc element containing the general entity reference for the item description

general entity reference begins with an ampersand and ends with a semicolon

Be sure to include an ampersand (&) at the start of each entity reference and a semicolon (;) at the end of each one; otherwise, parsers will not correctly interpret them as entity references.

3. Insert a desc child element within each of the four item elements for Dean Abernath, each containing an ampersand (&) followed by the value of the itemNumber attribute for the preceding item element and then a semicolon (;), as shown in Figure 12-25.

Figure 12-25	Revised order information for Dean Abernath

```
<email>dabernath@example.net</email>
<orders>
   <order orderID="or1021" orderBy="cust202">
      <orderDate>8/1/2016</orderDate>
      <items>
         <item itemNumber="WM100PL">
            <desc>&WM100PL;</desc>
            <itemPrice>29.95</itemPrice>
            <itemQty>1</itemQty>
         </item>
         <item itemNumber="WM105L">
            <desc>&WM105L;</desc>
            <itemPrice>19.95</itemPrice>
            <itemQty>1</itemQty>
         </item>
      </items>
   </order>
   <order orderID="or1122" orderBy="cust202">
      <orderDate>10/1/2016</orderDate>
      <items>
         <item itemNumber="H115E">
            <desc>&H115E;</desc>
            <itemPrice saleItem="Y">24.90</itemPrice>
            <itemQty>2</itemQty>
         </item>
         <item itemNumber="H115F">
            <desc>&H115F;</desc>
            <itemPrice saleItem="N">14.95</itemPrice>
            <itemQty>1</itemQty>
         </item>
      </items>
   </order>
</orders>
```

▶ **4.** Repeat Step 3 for the one remaining item element for the last customer, Riverfront High School. Figure 12-26 shows the revised code for the Riverfront High School order.

Figure 12-26	Revised order information for Riverfront High School

```
<phone>(715) 555-4022</phone>
<orders>
   <order orderID="or1120" orderBy="cust203">
      <orderDate>9/15/2016</orderDate>
      <items>
         <item itemNumber="WM140P">
            <desc>&WM140P;</desc>
            <itemPrice>78.90</itemPrice>
            <itemQty>2</itemQty>
         </item>
      </items>
   </order>
</orders>
```

▶ **5.** Save the **orders.xml** file.

Now that you've added the entity references to Benjamin's document, you can verify that their values are resolved in your Web browser.

▶ **6.** Open **orders.xml** in a Web browser. When viewed in a browser that uses an outline format for XML files, the values of all seven product codes are displayed. Figure 12-27 shows the document in Internet Explorer.

Figure 12-27	The orders.xml file displayed in a browser

```
<?xml version="1.0" encoding="UTF-8"?>
<!-- New Perspectives on HTML, CSS, and XML Tutorial 12 Tutorial Case Map Finds For You report Author: Benjamin Mapps Date: 12/11/2016
Filename: orders.xml -->
<!DOCTYPE customers>
- <customers>
  - <customer custID="cust201">
      <name title="Mr.">John Michael</name>
    - <address>
        <![CDATA[ 41 West Plankton Avenue Orlando, FL 32820 ]]>
      </address>
      <phone>(407) 555-3476</phone>
      <email>jk@example.net</email>
    - <orders>
      - <order orderBy="cust201" orderID="or1089">
          <orderDate>8/11/2016</orderDate>
        - <items>
          - <item itemNumber="WM100PL">
              <desc>World map outlining countries and capitals; poster-size, laminated paper</desc>
              <itemPrice saleItem="N">39.95</itemPrice>
              <itemQty>1</itemQty>
            </item>
          - <item itemNumber="WM101P">
              <desc>World map outlining countries and capitals; poster-size, paper</desc>
              <itemPrice saleItem="Y">19.90</itemPrice>
              <itemQty>2</itemQty>
            </item>
          </items>
        </order>
      </orders>
    </customer>
```

parser translation of the &WM100PL; entity reference you entered in the desc element

Trouble? If your browser displays a warning message about the content of your file, click the necessary button(s) to allow the content to be parsed and displayed. Some browsers treat XML files with suspicion for computer security reasons; but because you created this file, you don't need to be concerned about opening it.

So far, you've placed all your entity declarations internally within the *orders.xml* document. However, you can also externally link declarations rather than defining them internally. There are two methods for linking to external declarations—revising the DOCTYPE to link to an external DTD file and using a parameter entity.

Working with Parameter Entities

Just as you use a general entity when you want to insert content into an XML document, you use a **parameter entity** when you want to insert content into the DTD itself. You can use parameter entities to break a DTD into smaller chunks, or **modules**, that are placed in different files. Imagine a team of programmers working on a DTD for a large XML vocabulary such as XHTML, containing hundreds of elements and attributes. Rather than placing all the declarations within a single file, individual programmers could work on sections suited to their expertise. Then a project coordinator could use parameter entities to reference the different sections in the main DTD. Parameter entities also enable XML programmers to reuse large blocks of DTD code, which saves them from retyping the same code multiple times.

The declaration to create a parameter entity is similar to the declaration for a general entity, with the syntax

```
<!ENTITY % entity "value">
```

where *entity* is the name of the parameter entity and *value* is the text referenced by the parameter entity. Like general entities, parameter entities can also reference external content in either system or public locations. The declarations for external parameter entities are

```
<!ENTITY % entity SYSTEM "uri">
```

and

```
<!ENTITY % entity PUBLIC "id" "uri">
```

where *id* is a public identifier for the parameter entity and *uri* is the location of the external file containing DTD content.

For example, the following code shows an internal parameter entity for a collection of elements and attributes:

```
<!ENTITY % books
   "<!ELEMENT Book (Title, Author)>
    <!ATTLIST Book Pages CDATA #REQUIRED>
    <!ELEMENT Title (#PCDATA)>
    <!ELEMENT Author (#PCDATA)>"
>
```

If you instead placed the elements and attributes referenced in the previous code in an external DTD file named *books.dtd*, you could use an external parameter entity to access the content of that document as follows:

```
<!ENTITY % books SYSTEM "books.dtd">
```

After a parameter has been declared, you can reference it within the DTD using the statement

```
%entity;
```

where *entity* is the name assigned to the parameter entity. Parameter entity references can be placed only where a declaration would regularly occur, such as within an internal or external DTD. You *cannot* insert a parameter entity reference within the element content of an XML document. For example, to reference the books parameter entity described above, you would enter the following line into the DTD:

```
%books;
```

Figure 12-28 shows how parameter entities can be used to combine DTDs from multiple files into a single (virtual) DTD.

TIP

Note that when declaring a parameter entity, you include a space after the %; but when referencing a parameter entity, there is no space between the % and the entity name.

Figure 12-28 Creating a combined DTD using parameter entities

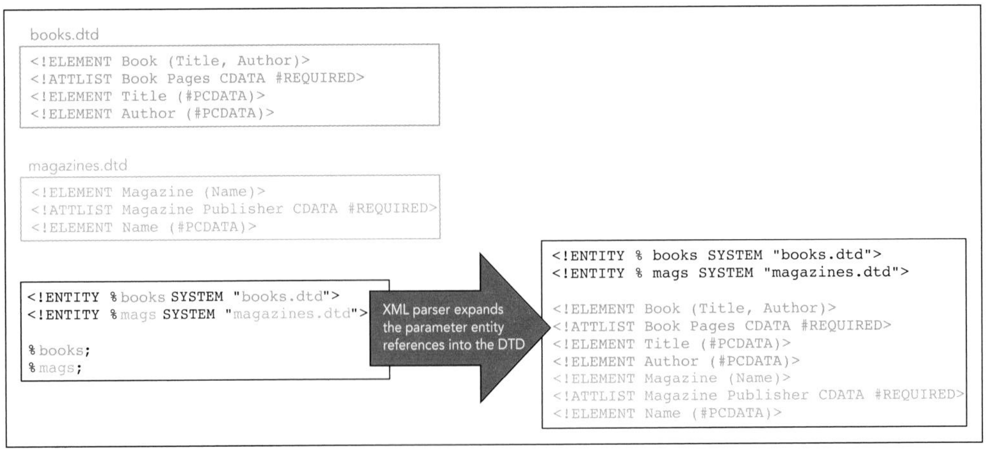

In the figure, two parameter entities—`%books;` and `%mags;`—are used to combine the contents of *books.dtd* and *magazines.dtd* into a master document.

Declaring and Referencing Parameter Entities

- To declare an internal parameter entity, add the line
  ```
  <!ENTITY % entity "value">
  ```
  to the DTD, where `entity` is the entity name and `value` is the entity value.
- To declare an external parameter entity for a system location, use
  ```
  <!ENTITY % entity SYSTEM "uri">
  ```
  where `uri` is the location of the external file containing DTD content.
- To declare an external parameter entity for a public location, use
  ```
  <!ENTITY % entity PUBLIC "id" "uri">
  ```
  where `id` is the public identifier.
- To reference a parameter entity, add the statement
  ```
  %entity;
  ```
  to the DTD, where `entity` is the name of the parameter entity.

Inserting Comments into a DTD

Benjamin is pleased with your work on creating the DTD for the sample XML document. However, he is concerned that the code in the DTD might be confusing to other programmers. He suggests that you add a comment. Comments in a DTD follow the same syntax as comments in XML. The specific form of a DTD comment is

```
<!-- comment -->
```

where `comment` is the text of the DTD comment. White space is ignored within a comment, so you can spread comment text over several lines without affecting DTD code.

Teamwork: Documenting Shared Code with Comments

When you're working on a large project with other developers to create a DTD, including comments in your code is important to help other team members quickly understand the code you've written. You can use comments to indicate changes you've made to existing code, to flag code that may need future changes, and simply to document what you've done and when. Although a DTD doesn't require comments, using them to document your work can make you a more valuable team member and increase your group's efficiency.

You'll add a comment now to the *orders.xml* DTD to summarize its content.

To add a comment to the DTD:

▸ **1.** Return to the **orders.xml** file in your text editor.

▶ **2.** Within the DTD, after the opening bracket and above the first general entity (for the WM100PL item code), insert a blank line, and then enter the following comment:

```
<!-- Item code descriptions inserted as general entities -->
```

Figure 12-29 shows the final form of the DTD for the *orders.xml* file.

Figure 12-29 **DTD comment added**

```
<!DOCTYPE customers
[
    <!-- Item code descriptions inserted as general entities -->
    <!ENTITY WM100PL "World map outlining countries and capitals; poster-size, laminated paper">
    <!ENTITY WM101P "World map outlining countries and capitals; poster-size, paper">
    <!ENTITY WM105L "World map outlining countries and populations; laminated paper">
    <!ENTITY WM140P "World map focusing on land and water features; paper roll">
    <!ENTITY H115E "United States hiking map including elevations; electronic">
    <!ENTITY H115F "United States hiking map including elevations; folded paper">

    <!ELEMENT customers (customer+)>
```

▶ **3.** Save your changes to the **orders.xml** file, and then close the file.

Creating Conditional Sections

When you're creating a new DTD, it can be useful to try out different combinations of declarations. You can do this by using a **conditional section**, which is a section of the DTD that is processed only in certain situations. The syntax for creating a conditional section is

```
<![keyword[
    declarations
]]>
```

where *keyword* is either INCLUDE (for a section of declarations that you want parsers to interpret) or IGNORE (for the declarations that you want parsers to pass over). For example, the following code creates two sections of declarations—one for the Magazine element and its child elements, and another for the Book element and its child elements—and instructs parsers to ignore the Magazine-related elements and interpret the Book-related elements:

```
<![IGNORE[
    <!ELEMENT Magazine (Name)>
    <!ATTLIST Magazine Publisher CDATA #REQUIRED>
    <!ELEMENT Name (#PCDATA)>
]]>

<![INCLUDE[
    <!ELEMENT Book (Title, Author)>
    <!ATTLIST Book Pages CDATA #REQUIRED>
    <!ELEMENT Title (#PCDATA)>
    <!ELEMENT Author (#PCDATA)>
]]>
```

An XML parser processing this DTD would run the declarations related to the Book element, but would ignore the declarations related to the Magazine element. As you experiment with a DTD's structure, you can enable a section by changing its keyword from IGNORE to INCLUDE.

One effective way of creating IGNORE sections is to create a parameter entity that defines whether those sections should be included, and to use the value of the entity as the keyword for the conditional sections. For example, the following UseFullDTD entity has a value of IGNORE, which causes the conditional section that follows it to be ignored by XML parsers:

```
<!ENTITY % UseFullDTD "IGNORE">

<![ %UseFullDTD; [
   <!ELEMENT Magazine (Name)>
   <!ATTLIST Magazine Publisher CDATA #REQUIRED>
   <!ELEMENT Name (#PCDATA)>
]]>
```

By changing the value of UseFullDTD from IGNORE to INCLUDE, you can add any conditional section that uses this entity reference to the document's DTD. This enables you to switch multiple sections in the DTD on and off by editing a single line in the file, which is most useful when several conditional sections are scattered throughout a long DTD. Rather than locating and changing each conditional section, you can switch the sections on and off by changing the parameter entity's value.

Conditional sections can be applied only to external DTDs. Both sets of code samples above that illustrate conditional sections would need to be located in external files, rather than in the internal subset of a DTD. Although they may be useful in other contexts, you cannot apply them to the DTD in Benjamin's document because it uses only an internal DTD.

Working with Unparsed Data

So far in this session, you've created entities for character data. For a DTD to validate either binary data, such as images or video clips, or character data that is not well formed, you need to work with unparsed entities. Because an XML parser cannot work with these types of data directly, a DTD must include instructions for how to treat an unparsed entity.

The first step is to declare a **notation**, which identifies the data type of the unparsed data. A notation must supply a name for the data type and provide clues about how applications should handle the data. Notations must reference external content (because that content must contain nontextual data that is, by definition, not well formed) and you must specify an external location. One option is to use a system location, which you specify with the code

```
<!NOTATION notation SYSTEM "uri">
```

where *notation* is the notation's name and *uri* is a system location that gives the XML parser clues about how the data should be handled. The other option is to specify a public location, using the declaration

```
<!NOTATION notation PUBLIC "id" "uri">
```

where *id* is a public identifier recognized by XML parsers. The URI for the resource can either refer to a program that can work with the unparsed data or specify the actual data type. For example, if Benjamin wanted to include references in the *orders.xml* document to graphic image files stored in the PNG format, he could enter the following notation in the document's DTD:

```
<!NOTATION png SYSTEM "paint.exe">
```

Because an XML parser doesn't know how to handle graphic data, this notation associates the *paint.exe* program with the png data type. If you don't want to specify a particular program, you could instead indicate the data type using its MIME type value with the following notation:

```
<!NOTATION png SYSTEM "image/png">
```

In this case, an XML parser associates the `png` notation with the `image/png` data type as long as the operating system already knows how to handle PNG files. After a notation is declared, you can create an unparsed entity that references specific items that use that notation. The syntax to declare an unparsed entity is

```
<!ENTITY entity SYSTEM "uri" NDATA notation>
```

where `entity` is the name of the entity referencing the notation, `uri` is the URI of the unparsed data, and `notation` is the name of the notation that defines the data type for the XML parser. Again, you can also provide a public location for the unparsed data if an XML parser supports it, using the following form:

```
<!ENTITY entity PUBLIC "id" "uri" NDATA notation>
```

For example, the following declaration creates an unparsed entity named WM100PLIMG that references the graphic image file *WM100PL.png*:

```
<!ENTITY WM100PLIMG SYSTEM "WM100PL.png" NDATA png>
```

This declaration references the `png` notation created above to provide the data type.

After you create an entity to reference unparsed data, that entity can be associated with attribute values by using the ENTITY data type in each attribute declaration. If Benjamin wanted to add an `image` attribute to every `item` element in the *orders.xml* document, he could insert the following attribute declaration in the DTD:

```
<!ATTLIST item image ENTITY #REQUIRED>
```

With this declaration added, Benjamin could then add the image attribute to the XML document, using the WM100PLIMG entity as the attribute's value, as follows:

```
<item image="&WM100PLIMG;">
```

It's important to understand precisely what this code does and does not accomplish. It tells XML parsers what kind of data is represented by the WM100PLIMG entity, and it provides clues about how to interpret the data stored in the WM100PL.png file—but it does not tell parsers anything else. Whether an application reading the XML document opens another application to display the image file depends solely on the program itself. Remember that the purpose of XML is to create structured documents, but not necessarily to tell programs how to render the data in a document. If a validating XML parser reads the `<item>` tag described above, it probably wouldn't try to read the graphic image file, but it might check to see whether the file is in the expected location. By doing so, the parser would confirm that the document is complete in its content and in all its references to unparsed data.

Current Web browsers do not support mechanisms for validating and rendering unparsed data declared in the DTDs of XML documents, so you will not add this feature to the *orders.xml* file.

Declaring an Unparsed Entity

- To declare an unparsed entity, first declare a notation for the data type used in the entity, using the syntax

  ```
  <!NOTATION notation SYSTEM "uri">
  ```

  where *notation* is the name of the notation and *uri* is a system location that defines the data type or a program that can work with the data type.
- To specify a public location for the notation, use the declaration

  ```
  <!NOTATION notation PUBLIC "id" "uri">
  ```

  where *id* is a public identifier for the data type associated with the notation.
- To associate a notation with an unparsed entity, use the declaration

  ```
  <!ENTITY entity SYSTEM "uri" NDATA notation>
  ```

  where *entity* is the name of the entity, *uri* is the system location of a file containing the unparsed data, and *notation* is the name of the notation that defines the data type.
- For a public location of the unparsed entity, use the following declaration:

  ```
  <!ENTITY entity PUBLIC "id" "uri" NDATA notation>
  ```

Validating Standard Vocabularies

All of your work in this tutorial involved the custom XML vocabulary developed by Benjamin for orders submitted to Map Finds For You. Most of the standard XML vocabularies in popular use are associated with existing DTDs. To validate a document used with a standard vocabulary, you usually must access an external DTD located on a Web server or rely upon a DTD built into your XML parser. Figure 12-30 lists the DOCTYPEs for some popular XML vocabularies.

Figure 12-30	DOCTYPEs for standard vocabularies

Vocabulary	DOCTYPE
XHTML 1.0 Strict	`<!DOCTYPE html PUBLIC "-//W3C//DTD XHTML 1.0 Strict//EN" "http://www.w3.org/TR/xhtml1/DTD/xhtml1-strict.dtd">`
XHTML 1.0 Transitional	`<!DOCTYPE html PUBLIC "-//W3C//DTD XHTML 1.0 Transitional//EN" "http://www.w3.org/TR/xhtml1/DTD/xhtml1-transitional.dtd">`
XHTML 1.1	`<!DOCTYPE html PUBLIC "-//W3C//DTD XHTML 1.1//EN" "http://www.w3.org/TR/xhtml11/DTD/xhtml11.dtd">`
MathML 1.01	`<!DOCTYPE math SYSTEM "http://www.w3.org/Math/DTD/mathml1mathml.dtd">`
MathML 2.0	`<!DOCTYPE math PUBLIC "-//W3C//DTD MathML 2.0//EN" "http://www.w3.org/Math/DTD/mathml2/mathml2.dtd">`
SVG 1.1 Basic	`<!DOCTYPE svg PUBLIC "-//W3C//DTD SVG 1.1 Basic//EN" "http://www.w3.org/Graphics/SVG/1.1/DTD/svg11-basic.dtd">`
SVG 1.1 Full	`<!DOCTYPE svg PUBLIC "-//W3C//DTD SVG 1.1//EN" "http://www.w3.org/Graphics/SVG/1.1/DTD/svg11.dtd">`
SMIL 1.0	`<!DOCTYPE smil PUBLIC "-//W3C//DTD SMIL 1.0//EN" "http://www.w3.org/TR/REC-smil/SMIL10.dtd">`
SMIL 2.0	`<!DOCTYPE SMIL PUBLIC "-//W3C//DTD SMIL 2.0//EN" "http://www.w3.org/TR/REC-smil/2000/SMIL20.dtd">`
VoiceXML 2.1	`<!DOCTYPE vxml PUBLIC "-//W3C//DTD VOICEXML 2.1//EN" "http://www.w3.org/TR/voicesml21/vxml.dtd">`

For example, to validate an XHTML document against the XHTML 1.0 Strict standard, you would add the following code to the document header:

```
<?xml version="1.0" encoding="UTF-8" standalone="no" ?>
<!DOCTYPE html PUBLIC "-//W3C//DTD XHTML 1.0 Strict//EN"
    "http://www.w3.org/TR/xhtml1/DTD/xhtml1-strict.dtd">
```

The W3C provides an online validator at *http://validator.w3.org* that you can use to validate HTML, XHTML, MathML, SVG, and other XML vocabularies. The validator works with files placed on the Web or uploaded via a Web form.

The DTDs of most standard vocabularies are available online for inspection. Studying the DTDs of other XML vocabularies is a great way to learn how to design your own. Figure 12-31 shows the part of the DTD for XHTML 1.0 that sets the syntax rules for the br (line break) element.

Figure 12-31   **XHTML 1.0 Strict DTD for the br element**

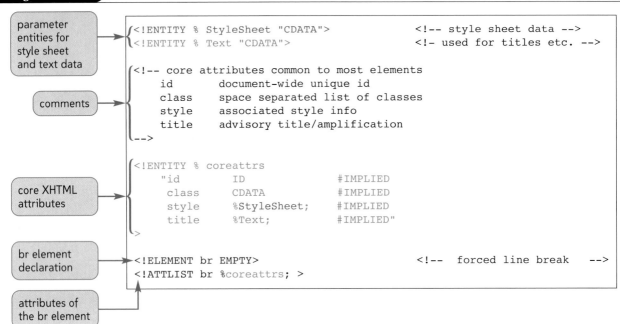

This DTD includes substantial use of parameter entities to allow the same set of attributes to be shared among the many elements of XHTML. For example, the coreattrs parameter entity contains a list of core attributes used by most XHTML elements. The StyleSheet and Text parameter entities contain code that sets the data types for style sheets and title attributes, respectively. From the DTD, you can quickly see that the four core attributes of XHTML are the id, class, style, and title attributes. You can also see that although they are available to almost all elements in the XHTML language, they are not required attributes. The specifications for the br element are fairly simple. Other elements of the XHTML language have more complicated rules, but all are based on the principles discussed in this tutorial.

INSIGHT

Advantages and Disadvantages of DTDs

DTDs are the common standard for validating XML documents, but they do have some serious limitations. Because a DTD is not written in the XML language, XML parsers must support the syntax and language requirements needed to interpret DTD code. DTDs are also limited in the data types they support. For example, you cannot specify that the value of an element or an attribute be limited only to integers or to text strings entered in a specific format; nor can you specify the structure of a document beyond a general description of the number or choice of child elements. Finally, DTDs do not support namespaces and thus are of limited value in compound documents.

However, DTDs are a recognized and long-supported standard. Therefore, you should have little problem finding parsers and applications to validate your XML documents based on DTDs. DTDs also support entities, providing a mechanism for referencing nontextual content from your XML files.

If the limitations of DTDs are a severe hindrance to validating your XML documents, another standard—schemas—provides support for an extended list of data types and can be easily adapted to compound documents involving several namespaces.

You've completed your work on Benjamin's document. He will use the DTD you developed to ensure that any new data added to the *orders.xml* document conforms to the standards you established.

REVIEW

Session 12.3 Quick Check

1. What is the difference between a general entity and a parameter entity?
2. What is the difference between a parsed entity and an unparsed entity?
3. What declaration stores the text string `<Title>Hamlet</Title>` as a general entity named `Play`? What command references this entity in a document?
4. What declaration stores the contents of the *plays.xml* file as a general entity named `Plays`?
5. What code stores the contents of the *plays.dtd* file as a parameter entity named `Works`?
6. What is a notation?
7. How do you reference the image file *shakespeare.gif* in an unparsed entity named `Portrait`? Assume that this entity is using a notation named `GIF`.

Review Assignments

Data File needed for the Review Assignments: prodtxt.xml

Benjamin needs your help with a document that lists some of Map Finds For You's map products. Figure 12-32 shows the tree structure of Benjamin's XML document.

Figure 12-32   **Structure of the products document**

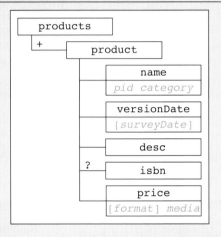

The document contains a root element named **products** with one or more occurrences of the **product** element containing information on map products. The **product** element contains five child elements—**name**, **versionDate**, **desc**, an optional **isbn**, and **price**. The **name** element stores the name of the product and supports two attributes—**pid**, the ID number of the product; and **category**, the type of product (**historical**, **state**, or **parks**). The **versionDate** element also supports an optional **surveyDate** attribute that indicates the date of the map survey, if known. The **desc** element stores a description of the product. The optional **isbn** element stores the ISBN for the product. The **price** element stores the name of the product and supports two attributes—**format**, the format of the product (**flat** or **raised**) with a default of **flat**; and **media**, the media type of the product (**paper** or **electronic**).

For this document, Benjamin wants to enforce a document structure to ensure that information recorded in the document is valid. Therefore, your task will be to create the DTD for the document.

Complete the following:

1. Using your text editor, open the **prodtxt.xml** file from the tutorial.12\review folder provided with your Data Files, enter *your name* and *today's date* in the comment section of the file, and then save the file as **products.xml**.

2. In the **products.xml** file, insert an internal DTD for the root element **products** directly after the comment section and before the opening <products> tag.

3. Within the internal DTD, declare the following items:

   a. The **products** element, containing at least one occurrence of the child element **product**

   b. The **product** element, containing five child elements in the sequence **name**, **versionDate**, **desc**, an optional **isbn**, and **price**

   c. The **name**, **versionDate**, **desc**, **isbn**, and **price** elements, each containing parsed character data

4. Add the following attribute declarations to the product file:

   a. For the name element, a required **pid** attribute as an ID

   b. For the name element, a required **category** attribute equal to **historical**, **state**, or **parks**

   c. For the versionDate element, an optional **surveyDate** attribute containing the date of the survey

   d. For the price element, an optional **format** attribute equal to either **flat** or **raised**, with a default of **flat**

   e. For the price element, a required **media** attribute equal to either **paper** or **electronic**

5. On the same line as the format attribute definition, insert a comment containing the text **format default is flat**.

6. Save your changes to the **products.xml** file, and then use Exchanger XML Editor or another XML tool to verify that the document is well formed.

7. Validate the document. If necessary, correct errors one at a time and revalidate until the document is valid.

8. Submit your completed and validated project to your instructor, in either printed or electronic form, as requested.

Apply the skills you learned in this tutorial to validate a historical society's photo catalog.

APPLY

Case Problem 1

Data Files needed for this Case Problem: photostxt.dtd, photostxt.xml

The Our Lady of Bergen Historical Society   Sharon Strattan is an archivist at the Our Lady of Bergen Historical Society in Bergenfield, New Jersey. The historical society is exploring how to transfer its listings to XML format, and Sharon has begun by creating a sample document of the society's extensive collection of photos. A schematic of the vocabulary she's developing is shown in Figure 12-33.

Figure 12-33   **Structure of the photos document**

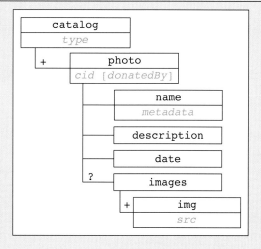

The vocabulary Sharon designed has a root element named **catalog** containing one or more **photo** elements. Each **photo** element contains the name of the photo, a description, the estimated date the photo was taken, and, in some cases, a list of image files containing scans of the original photo. Sharon also added attributes to indicate the type of collection the photos come from, the collection ID for each photo, who donated the photo, a list of keywords (metadata) associated with the photo, and the source of any image file. You'll assist Sharon by creating a DTD based on her XML vocabulary, and then you'll use the DTD to validate her sample document.

Complete the following:

1. Using your text editor, open **photostxt.dtd** and **photostxt.xml** from the tutorial.12\case1 folder provided with your Data Files, enter *your name* and *today's date* in the comment section of each file, and then save the files as **photos.dtd** and **photos.xml**, respectively.

2. In the **photos.dtd** file, declare the following elements:

   a. The `catalog` element, containing one or more `photo` elements

   b. The `photo` element, containing the following sequence of child elements—`name`, `description`, `date`, and (optionally) `images`

   c. The `name`, `description`, and `date` elements, containing only parsed character data

   d. The `images` element, containing one or more `img` elements

   e. The `img` element, containing empty content

3. Declare the following attributes in the DTD:

   a. The `type` attribute, a required attribute of the `catalog` element, containing a valid XML name (*Hint*: Use the NMTOKEN data type.)

   b. The `cid` attribute, a required ID attribute of the `photo` element

   c. The `donatedBy` attribute, an optional attribute of the `photo` element, containing character data

   d. The `metadata` attribute, a required attribute of the `name` element, containing a list of valid XML names (*Hint*: Use the NMTOKENS data type.)

   e. The `src` attribute, a required attribute of the `img` element, containing character data

4. Save your changes to the **photos.dtd** file.

5. In the **photos.xml** file, directly after the comment section, insert a DOCTYPE that references the system location *photos.dtd*.

6. Save your changes to the **photos.xml** file.

7. Verify that the *photos.xml* file is well formed, and then validate it. Revalidate after correcting each error in the code, if necessary, until the document passes validation. (*Hint*: Because this document uses an external DTD, you must correct any validation errors related to the DTD in the *photos.dtd* file.) Note that you cannot use *http://validator.w3.org* to validate an XML file against a nonpublic external DTD file, so you must use a program such as Exchanger to validate this file.

8. Submit your completed and validated project to your instructor, in either printed or electronic form, as requested.

Apply the skills you learned in this tutorial to validate a document containing pipe band data.

APPLY

Case Problem 2

Data File needed for this Case Problem: mdpbatxt.xml

Midwest Developmental Pipe Band Association   Jacob St. John works as a coordinator for the Midwest Developmental Pipe Band Association (MDPBA), and is responsible for coordinating competitions for the MDPBA's many developmental pipe bands in the midwestern United States. A pipe band is a musical group consisting of pipe players and drummers. Pipe bands are traditional in Great Britain, as well as in other parts of the world that have received British cultural influence. Part of Jacob's job is to maintain a document that lists competition entries for each pipe band. Jacob has asked for your help in creating XML documents that maintain a consistent document structure. He has created a sample document describing five pipe bands. The document lists the competition program for each pipe band. Each program includes exactly two events in which each band plays one or more tunes. One event type is a March, Strathspey, & Reel (MSR). The other event type is a Medley event. Figure 12-34 shows a tree diagram for the vocabulary.

Figure 12-34 Structure of the mdpba document

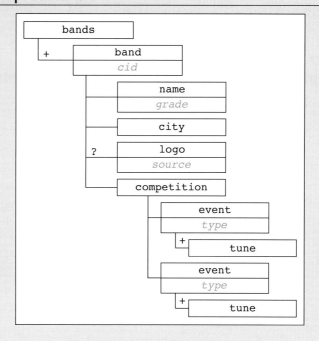

The document also contains an optional `logo` element that stores information about graphic files of the pipe band logos. Any DTD you create for this document also must work with the unparsed data contained in these graphic files.

Complete the following:

1. Using your text editor, open **mdpbatxt.xml** from the tutorial.12\case2 folder provided with your Data Files, enter *your name* and *today's date* in the comment section of the file, and then save the file as **mdpba.xml**.

2. Review the contents of the *mdpba.xml* file. Directly after the comment section, insert a DOCTYPE that includes DTD statements for the following elements:
   a. The **bands** element, containing at least one occurrence of the child element `band`
   b. The **band** element, containing child elements in the sequence `name`, `city`, `logo` (optional), and `competition`
   c. The **name** and **city** elements, containing parsed character data
   d. The **logo** element as an empty element
   e. The **competition** element, containing exactly two child elements named `event`
   f. The **event** element, containing at least one occurrence of the child element `tune`
   g. The **tune** element, containing parsed character data

3. Declare the following required attributes in the DTD:
   a. The **band** element should contain a single required attribute named `cid` containing an ID value.
   b. The **name** element should contain a required attribute named `grade` with values limited to `1`, `2`, `3`, `4`, `5`, `juvenile`, and `novice`.
   c. The **logo** element should contain a required entity attribute named `source`.
   d. The **event** element should contain a required attribute named `type` with values limited to `MSR` or `Medley`.

EXPLORE 4. Declare a notation named `JPG` with a system location equal to `image/jpg`.

EXPLORE 5. Create two unparsed entities within the internal subset to the DTD. Each entity should reference the `JPG` notation. The first entity should be named **celtic** and reference the *celtic.jpg* file. The second entity should be named **badger** and reference the *badger.jpg* file.

6. Save your changes to the **mdpba.xml** file.

7. Verify that the document is well formed and then validate it.

8. Submit your completed and validated project to your instructor, in either printed or electronic form, as requested.

Case Problem 3

Data Files needed for this Case Problem: donors.txt, rostertxt.xml, seatrusttxt.dtd

The Save Exotic Animals Trust Sienna Woo is the donor coordinator for the Save Exotic Animals Trust (SEA Trust), a charitable organization located in central Florida. One of her responsibilities is to maintain a membership list of people in the community who have donated to SEA Trust. Donors can belong to one of four categories—Friendship, Patron, Sponsor, or Founder. The categories assist Sienna in marketing SEA Trust's fundraising goals and in developing strategies to reach those goals.

Currently, most of the data that Sienna has compiled resides in text files. To make the fundraising campaign strategies more effective, she wants to convert this data into an XML document and ensure that the resulting document follows some specific guidelines. You will create the XML document for her.

Complete the following:

1. Using your text editor, open the **rostertxt.xml** and **seatrusttxt.dtd** files from the tutorial.12\case3 folder provided with your Data Files, insert ***your name*** and ***today's date*** in the comment section of each file, and then save the files as **roster.xml** and **seatrust.dtd**, respectively.

2. Add the data stored in the **donors.txt** file in the tutorial.12\case3 folder to the *roster.xml* file as the document content, and then add XML elements to structure the data in the *roster.xml* file as follows: (*Note*: You should ignore any validation or well-formedness errors flagged by your editor until the document is finished.)

    a. A root element named **roster** should contain several **donor** elements.

    b. Each **donor** element should contain the following child elements, which should appear no more than once within the **donor** element, except as noted—**name**, **address**, **phone** (one or more), **email** (optional), **donation**, **method**, and **effectiveDate**.

    c. The **phone** element should contain an attribute named **type** that identifies the phone type—**home**, **work**, or **cell**. This should be a required attribute for each **phone** element.

    d. The **donor** element should contain an attribute named **level** that identifies the donor level—**friendship**, **patron**, **sponsor**, or **founder**. This should be a required attribute for each **donor** element.

3. In the **seatrust.dtd** file, create a DTD based on the structure you created in the *roster.xml* file. Save and close the **seatrust.dtd** file.

4. Apply your DTD to the contents of the *roster.xml* file. Save your changes to the **roster.xml** file.

5. Verify that the *roster.xml* file is well formed and valid.

6. Submit your completed and validated project to your instructor, in either printed or electronic form, as requested.

Explore how to use both DTDs and namespaces in a compound document.

CHALLENGE

Case Problem 4

Data Files needed for this Case Problem: carstxt.dtd, carstxt.xml, southtxt.xml, teamstxt.dtd, teamstxt.xml

South Racing   Danika Francis tracks team cars for South Racing's racing teams. As part of her job, she has created several XML vocabularies dealing with team series and the cars available to race in them. She wants to create a compound document combining information from the teams and cars vocabularies. She also wants to validate any data entered into her documents, and she asks you to develop DTDs. Because she is creating compound documents that combine elements from the teams and cars namespaces, she needs the DTDs to work with namespaces. Figure 12-35 shows the tree structure of the compound document.

| **Figure 12-35** | **Structure of the compound document** |

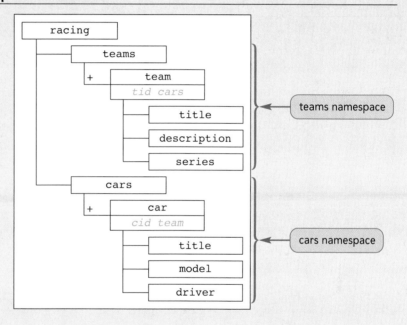

Danika wants you to create separate DTDs for the teams and cars namespaces, and then use entities to read the information from different XML documents into a master compound document. Figure 12-36 shows a schematic of the file relationships in Danika's proposed project.

Figure 12-36 **File relationships for the compound document**

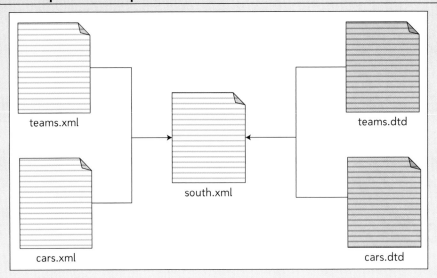

Complete the following:

1. Using your text editor, open the **carstxt.dtd**, **carstxt.xml**, **southtxt.xml**, **teamstxt.dtd**, and **teamstxt.xml** files from the tutorial.12\case4 folder, enter *your name* and *today's date* in the comment section of each file, and then save the files as **cars.dtd**, **cars.xml**, **south.xml**, **teams.dtd**, and **teams.xml**, respectively.

2. In the **teams.xml** file, place all the elements in the namespace **http://example.com/southracing/teams** with the namespace prefix **t**. Save your changes to the file.

3. In the **cars.xml** file, place all the elements in the namespace **http://example.com/southracing/cars** with the namespace prefix **c**. Save your changes to the file.

⊕ EXPLORE 4. In the **teams.dtd** file, add the following element declarations (making sure to include the namespace prefix **t** with all of the element names):

   a. The `teams` element, containing at least one child element named `team`

   b. The `team` element, containing the following sequence of child elements: `title`, `description`, and `series`

   c. The `title`, `description`, and `series` elements, containing parsed character data

⊕ EXPLORE 5. Add an attribute declaration to the `teams` element to declare the **http://example.com/southracing/teams** namespace as a fixed value.

6. Add the following attribute declarations to the `team` element:

   a. An ID attribute named `tid`

   b. An attribute named `cars`, containing a list of ID references

7. Save your changes to the **teams.dtd** file.

⊕ EXPLORE 8. In the **cars.dtd** file, add the following element declarations (making sure all element references in the document include the **c** namespace prefix):

   a. The `cars` element, containing at least one child element named `car`

   b. The `car` element, containing the following sequence of child elements: `title`, `model`, and `driver`

   c. The `title`, `model`, and `driver` elements, containing parsed character data

⊕ EXPLORE 9. Add an attribute declaration to the `cars` element to declare the **http://example.com/southracing/cars** namespace as a fixed value.

10. Add the following attribute declarations to the `car` element:
    a. An ID attribute named **cid**
    b. A **team** attribute containing a list of ID references

11. Save your changes to the **cars.dtd** file.

12. In the **south.xml** file, add the root element **racing** to the document belonging to the default namespace **http://example.com/southracing**.

⊕ **EXPLORE** 13. Between the comment section and the opening `<racing>` tag, insert an internal DTD subset with the following declarations:
    a. The **racing** element, containing the two child elements **t:teams** and **c:cars**
    b. A fixed attribute of the **racing** element declaring the **http://example.com/southracing** namespace
    c. A parameter entity named **teamsDTD** pointing to the *teams.dtd* file
    d. A parameter entity named **carsDTD** pointing to the *cars.dtd* file
    e. An external entity named **teamsList** pointing to the *teams.xml* file
    f. An external entity named **carsList** pointing to the *cars.xml* file

⊕ **EXPLORE** 14. At the end of the internal DTD subset, insert references to the **teamsDTD** and **carsDTD** parameters.

15. Within the **racing** element, insert references to the **teamsList** and **carsList** entities.

16. Save your changes to the **south.xml** file, and then close it.

17. Verify that all the documents are well formed and valid.

18. Submit your completed and validated project to your instructor, in either printed or electronic form, as requested.

ENDING DATA FILES

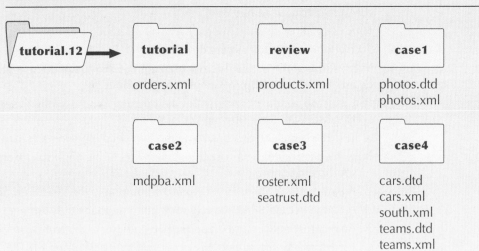

tutorial.12 → tutorial
orders.xml

review
products.xml

case1
photos.dtd
photos.xml

case2
mdpba.xml

case3
roster.xml
seatrust.dtd

case4
cars.dtd
cars.xml
south.xml
teams.dtd
teams.xml

TUTORIAL **13**

OBJECTIVES

Session 13.1
- Compare schemas and DTDs
- Explore different schema vocabularies
- Declare simple type elements and attributes
- Declare complex type elements
- Apply a schema to an instance document

Session 13.2
- Work with XML Schema data types
- Derive new data types for text strings, numeric values, and dates
- Create data types for patterned data using regular expressions

Validating Documents with Schemas

Creating a Schema for the ATC School of Information Technology

Case | *ATC School of Information Technology*

Sabrina Lincoln is an academic advisor for the School of Information Technology at Austin Technical College (ATC) in Austin, Utah, where she advises students in the information technology programs. Sabrina wants to use XML to create structured documents containing information on the different programs and the students enrolled in those programs. Eventually, the XML documents can be used as a data resource for the center's intranet, enabling faculty advisors to view program and student data online.

Accuracy is important to ATC, and Sabrina needs to know that the data she enters is error free. In particular, she must be able to confirm that the student data in her XML documents matches the criteria for the programs. Sabrina also needs to create documents from the various XML vocabularies she's created. For example, she may need to create a document that combines student information with information on the programs themselves.

DTDs cannot fulfill Sabrina's needs because DTDs have a limited range of data types and provide no way to deal with numeric data. Also, DTDs and namespaces do not mix well. However, schemas can work with a wide range of data types and do a better job of supporting namespaces than DTDs. In this tutorial, you'll develop schemas for the XML document that Sabrina has created.

STARTING DATA FILES

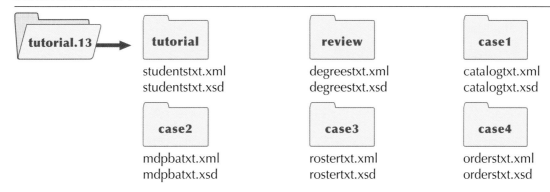

tutorial.13 → **tutorial**
studentstxt.xml
studentstxt.xsd

review
degreestxt.xml
degreestxt.xsd

case1
catalogtxt.xml
catalogtxt.xsd

case2
mdpbatxt.xml
mdpbatxt.xsd

case3
rostertxt.xml
rostertxt.xsd

case4
orderstxt.xml
orderstxt.xsd

SESSION 13.1 VISUAL OVERVIEW

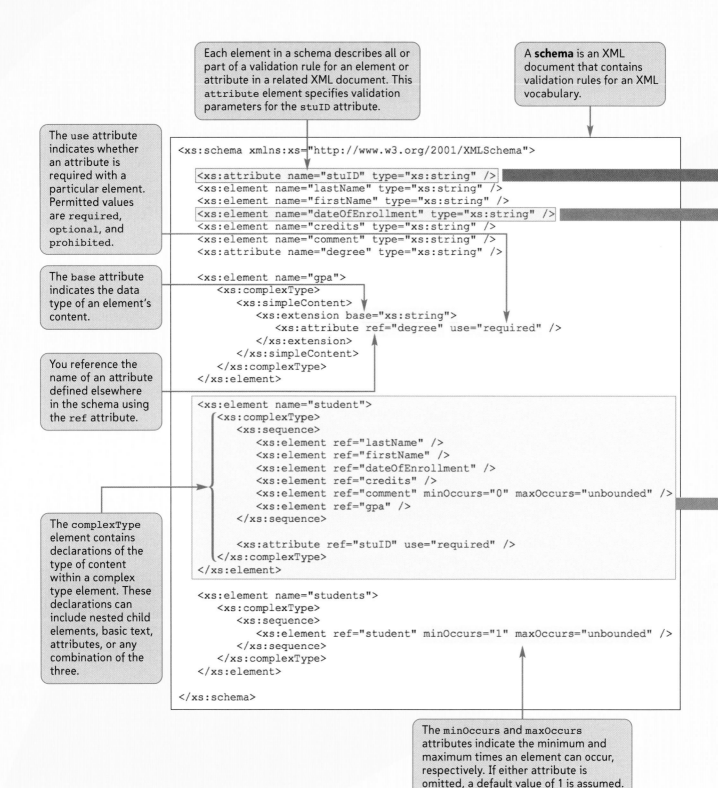

Each element in a schema describes all or part of a validation rule for an element or attribute in a related XML document. This `attribute` element specifies validation parameters for the stuID attribute.

A **schema** is an XML document that contains validation rules for an XML vocabulary.

The use attribute indicates whether an attribute is required with a particular element. Permitted values are required, optional, and prohibited.

The base attribute indicates the data type of an element's content.

You reference the name of an attribute defined elsewhere in the schema using the ref attribute.

The complexType element contains declarations of the type of content within a complex type element. These declarations can include nested child elements, basic text, attributes, or any combination of the three.

```
<xs:schema xmlns:xs="http://www.w3.org/2001/XMLSchema">

  <xs:attribute name="stuID" type="xs:string" />
  <xs:element name="lastName" type="xs:string" />
  <xs:element name="firstName" type="xs:string" />
  <xs:element name="dateOfEnrollment" type="xs:string" />
  <xs:element name="credits" type="xs:string" />
  <xs:element name="comment" type="xs:string" />
  <xs:attribute name="degree" type="xs:string" />

  <xs:element name="gpa">
    <xs:complexType>
      <xs:simpleContent>
        <xs:extension base="xs:string">
          <xs:attribute ref="degree" use="required" />
        </xs:extension>
      </xs:simpleContent>
    </xs:complexType>
  </xs:element>

  <xs:element name="student">
    <xs:complexType>
      <xs:sequence>
        <xs:element ref="lastName" />
        <xs:element ref="firstName" />
        <xs:element ref="dateOfEnrollment" />
        <xs:element ref="credits" />
        <xs:element ref="comment" minOccurs="0" maxOccurs="unbounded" />
        <xs:element ref="gpa" />
      </xs:sequence>

      <xs:attribute ref="stuID" use="required" />
    </xs:complexType>
  </xs:element>

  <xs:element name="students">
    <xs:complexType>
      <xs:sequence>
        <xs:element ref="student" minOccurs="1" maxOccurs="unbounded" />
      </xs:sequence>
    </xs:complexType>
  </xs:element>

</xs:schema>
```

The minOccurs and maxOccurs attributes indicate the minimum and maximum times an element can occur, respectively. If either attribute is omitted, a default value of 1 is assumed.

STRUCTURE OF A BASIC SCHEMA

An XML document to which a schema is applied is known as an **instance document** because it represents a specific instance of the rules defined in the schema.

```
<students xmlns:xsi="http://www.w3.org/2001/XMLSchema-instance"
          xsi:noNamespaceSchemaLocation="students.xsd">
  <student stuID="SI890-041-02">
      <lastName>Berstein</lastName>
      <firstName>Cynthia</firstName>
      <dateOfEnrollment>2016-05-22</dateOfEnrollment>
      <credits>12</credits>
      <gpa degree="MP">3.81</gpa>
  </student>

  <student stuID="SI771-121-10">
      <lastName>Boothe</lastName>
      <firstName>Jennifer</firstName>
      <dateOfEnrollment>2016-11-24</dateOfEnrollment>
      <credits>38</credits>
      <comment>Applied for summer studies internship</comment>
      <gpa degree="WPA">3.14</gpa>
  </student>

  <student stuID="SI815-741-03">
      <lastName>Bowen</lastName>
      <firstName>Kristi</firstName>
      <dateOfEnrollment>2016-04-25</dateOfEnrollment>
      <credits>19</credits>
      <gpa degree="MP">3.88</gpa>
  </student>

  <student stuID="SI701-891-05">
      <lastName>Sanchez</lastName>
      <firstName>Rosario</firstName>
      <dateOfEnrollment>2016-08-14</dateOfEnrollment>
      <credits>14</credits>
      <comment>Applied for student tutor</comment>
      <comment>Applied for Women in IT Scholarship</comment>
      <gpa degree="WPA">3.89</gpa>
  </student>

  <student stuID="SI805-891-08">
      <lastName>Russeon</lastName>
      <firstName>Alison</firstName>
      <dateOfEnrollment>2016-09-14</dateOfEnrollment>
      <credits>15</credits>
      <gpa degree="WPA">2.76</gpa>
  </student>
</students>
```

A **simple type** contains a single value such as the value of an attribute or the textual content of an element. The dateOfEnrollment element is a simple type because it includes only textual content.

A **complex type** contains two or more values or elements placed within a defined structure. The student element is a complex type because it contains an attribute as well as multiple child elements.

Introducing XML Schema

You and Sabrina meet at the School of Information Technology to discuss her work for Austin Technical College. She has brought along a file named *students.xml*, which contains a list of students accepted into programs within the school. You'll open this file now.

To open the *students.xml* document:

▶ **1.** Use your text editor to open **studentstxt.xml** from the tutorial.13\tutorial folder provided with your Data Files, enter **your name** and **today's date** in the comment section, and then save the file as **students.xml**.

▶ **2.** Examine the contents of the document, paying close attention to the order of the elements and the values of the elements and attributes.

Figure 13-1 shows the tree structure of the XML vocabulary used in the document. For each student element in the document, Sabrina inserted the attribute stuID. The attribute contains the student's assigned student number. In addition, Sabrina has collected each student's last and first names, date of enrollment, credits, and GPA. Each student element can also contain multiple comment elements for any additional information that an advisor wants to add.

Figure 13-1   **Structure of the students vocabulary**

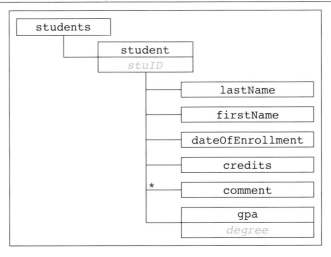

The *students.xml* file contains information on a few students in the information technology programs, but eventually it will contain more entries. As more students are added, Sabrina wants the document to require that the data for each student meet eligibility guidelines for the specified program of study. For example, students' GPAs must be at least 2.0 on a 4.0 scale, and every student must have a valid student ID number. For the initial faculty advising rollout, students must be enrolled in either the Mobile Programmer or Web Programmer/Analyst programs. Your task is to set up a validation system for this document.

The Limits of DTDs

DTDs are commonly used for validation largely because of XML's origins as an offshoot of SGML. SGML originally was designed for text-based documents, such as reports and technical manuals. As long as data content is limited to simple text, DTDs work well for validation. However, as XML began to be used for a wider range of document content, developers needed an alternative to DTDs.

One complaint about DTDs is their lack of data types. For example, Sabrina can declare a gpa element in the DTD, but she cannot specify that the gpa element may contain only numbers or that those numbers must fall within a specified range of values. Likewise, she can declare a dateOfEnrollment element, but a DTD cannot require that element to contain only dates. DTDs simply do not provide the control over data that Sabrina requires. DTDs also do not recognize namespaces, so they are not well suited to compound documents in which content from several vocabularies needs to be validated. This is a concern for Sabrina because her job at the ATC will involve developing several XML vocabularies that often will be combined into a single document.

Finally, DTDs employ a syntax called **Extended Backus–Naur Form (EBNF)**, which is different from the syntax used for XML. This means that a document's author must be able to work not only with the syntax of XML, but with EBNF as well. For developers who want to work with only one language, this could be a concern.

Because of XML's extensibility, you can instead use XML itself to document the structure and content of other XML documents. This is the idea behind schemas.

Schemas and DTDs

A schema is an XML document that contains validation rules for an XML vocabulary. When applied to a specific XML file, the document to be validated is called the instance document because it represents a specific instance of the rules defined in the schema. Schemas have several advantages over DTDs. XML parsers need to understand only XML, so all the tools used to create an instance document can also be applied to designing the schema. Schemas also support more data types, including data types for numbers and dates as well as custom data types for special needs. Additionally, schemas are more flexible than DTDs in dealing with elements that contain both child elements and text content, and they provide support for namespaces, making it easier to validate compound documents. Figure 13-2 summarizes some of the most significant differences between schemas and DTDs.

Figure 13-2   **Comparison of schemas and DTDs**

Feature	Schemas	DTDs
Document language	XML	Extended Backus Naur Form (EBNF)
Standards	multiple standards	one standard
Supported data types	44 (19 primitive + 25 derived)	10
Customized data types	yes	no
Mixed content	easy to develop	difficult to develop
Namespaces	completely supported	only namespace prefixes are supported
Entities	no	yes

If schemas are so useful, why do you need DTDs? First, DTDs represent an older standard for XML documents and are more widely supported. DTDs are simpler to create and maintain than schemas because the language itself is easier to work with. This is partly due to the fact that DTDs are more limited than schemas. Thus, DTDs are easier to set up for basic documents that don't require much validation. Figure 13-3 compares a simple DTD to its equivalent basic schema.

Figure 13-3 Comparison of simple DTD and simple schema

Schema Vocabularies

Unlike DTDs, a single standard doesn't exist for schemas. Instead, several schema vocabularies have been created to serve the needs of different XML developers. Because schemas are written in XML, a **schema vocabulary** is simply an XML vocabulary created for the purpose of describing schema content. Figure 13-4 describes some schema vocabularies.

| **Figure 13-4** | **Schema vocabularies** |

Schema	Description
XML Schema	The most widely used schema standard, XML Schema is developed and maintained by the W3C, and is designed to handle a broad range of document structures. It is also referred to as XSD.
Document Definition Markup Language (DDML)	One of the original schema languages, DDML (originally known as XSchema) was created to replicate all DTD functionality in a schema. DDML does not support any data types beyond what could be found in DTDs.
XML Data	One of the original schema languages, XML Data was developed by Microsoft to replace DTDs.
XML Data Reduced (XDR)	XDR is a subset of the XML Data schema, and was primarily used prior to the release of XML Schema.
Regular Language description for XML (RELAX)	A simple alternative to the W3C's XML Schema standard, RELAX provides much of the same functionality as DTDs, with additional support for namespaces and data types. RELAX does not support entities or notations.
Tree Regular Expressions for XML (TREX)	A TREX schema specifies a pattern for an XML document's structure and content, and thus identifies a class of XML documents that match the pattern. TREX has been merged with RELAX into RELAX NG.
RELAX NG (Regular Language for XML Next Generation)	RELAX NG is the current version of RELAX, combining the features of RELAX and TREX.
Schematron	The Schematron schema represents documents using a tree pattern, allowing support for document structures that might be difficult to represent in traditional schema languages.

Support for a particular schema depends solely on the XML parser being used for validation. Before applying any of the schemas listed in Figure 13-4, you must verify the level of support offered by your application for that particular schema. XML Schema, developed by the W3C in March 2001, is the most widely adopted schema standard. Although this tutorial focuses primarily on XML Schema, many of the concepts involved with XML Schema can be applied to the other schema vocabularies.

Starting a Schema File

A DTD can be placed within an instance document or within an external file. A schema, however, is always placed in an external file. XML Schema filenames end with the *.xsd* file extension. Sabrina has created a blank XML Schema file for you to work on. You'll open her file now.

To start work on the XML Schema file:

1. Use your text editor to open **studentstxt.xsd** from the tutorial.13\tutorial folder, and then enter *your name* and *today's date* in the comment section.

   Trouble? If you open the file in an XML editor, such as Exchanger, you may see an error message indicating that the document is not well formed and contains a premature end of file. In later steps, after you add your first validation rule to this file, the error should be resolved. For now, there's no need to worry about it.

2. Save the file as **students.xsd**.

The root element in any XML Schema document is the `schema` element. For a parser to recognize that a document is written in the XML Schema vocabulary, the `schema` element must include a declaration for the XML Schema namespace using the URI *http://www.w3.org/2001/XMLSchema*. The general structure of an XML Schema file is

```
<?xml version="1.0" ?>
<schema xmlns="http://www.w3.org/2001/XMLSchema">
   content
</schema>
```

where *content* is the list of elements and attributes that define the rules of the instance document. By convention, the namespace prefix xsd or xs is assigned to the XML Schema namespace to identify elements and attributes that belong to the XML Schema vocabulary. Keeping well-defined namespaces in an XML Schema document becomes very important when you start creating schemas for compound documents involving several namespaces. Therefore, the usual form of an XML Schema document is

```
<?xml version="1.0" ?>
<xs:schema xmlns:xs="http://www.w3.org/2001/XMLSchema">
   content
</xs:schema>
```

This tutorial assumes a namespace prefix of xs when discussing the elements and attributes of the XML Schema language. However, you can choose to use a different prefix in your own XML Schema documents. You can also set XML Schema as the document's default namespace, which eliminates the need for a prefix. The only requirement is that you be consistent in the use of a namespace prefix.

REFERENCE

Creating a Schema

- To create an XML Schema document, insert the structure

```
<?xml version="1.0" ?>
<schema xmlns="http://www.w3.org/2001/XMLSchema">
   content
</schema>
```

in the file, where *content* consists of the XML Schema elements and attributes used in defining the rules for the instance document.
- To apply a namespace prefix (customarily xs or xsd) to the elements and attributes of the XML Schema vocabulary, use the following structure:

```
<xs:schema xmlns:xs="http://www.w3.org/2001/XMLSchema">
   content
</xs:schema>
```

You'll add the root `schema` element to the *students.xsd* file now, using the xs namespace prefix to place it in the XML Schema namespace.

To insert the schema element in the *students.xsd* file:

▶ **1.** Directly below the comment section, insert the following code, as shown in Figure 13-5:

```
<xs:schema xmlns:xs="http://www.w3.org/2001/XMLSchema">
</xs:schema>
```

Figure 13-5	XML Schema root element

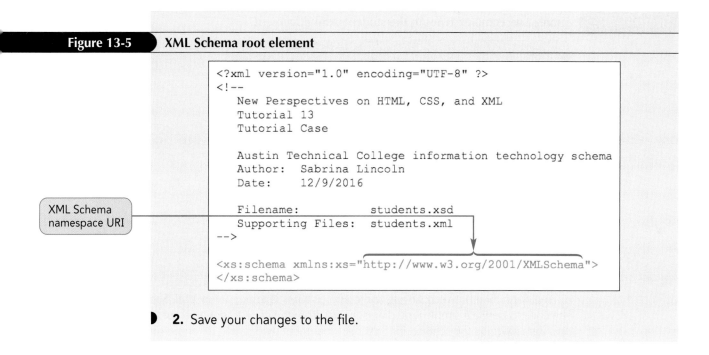

XML Schema namespace URI

```
<?xml version="1.0" encoding="UTF-8" ?>
<!--
    New Perspectives on HTML, CSS, and XML
    Tutorial 13
    Tutorial Case

    Austin Technical College information technology schema
    Author:  Sabrina Lincoln
    Date:    12/9/2016

    Filename:           students.xsd
    Supporting Files:   students.xml
-->

<xs:schema xmlns:xs="http://www.w3.org/2001/XMLSchema">
</xs:schema>
```

▶ **2.** Save your changes to the file.

Understanding Simple and Complex Types

XML Schema supports two types of content—simple and complex. A simple type contains only text and no nested elements. Examples of simple types include all attributes, as well as elements with only textual content. A complex type contains two or more values or elements placed within a defined structure. Examples of complex types include an empty element that contains an attribute, and an element that contains child elements. Figure 13-6 shows examples of both simple and complex types.

Figure 13-6	Simple and complex types

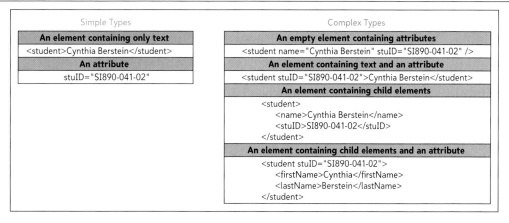

Simple Types	Complex Types
An element containing only text	**An empty element containing attributes**
<student>Cynthia Berstein</student>	<student name="Cynthia Berstein" stuID="SI890-041-02" />
An attribute	**An element containing text and an attribute**
stuID="SI890-041-02"	<student stuID="SI890-041-02">Cynthia Berstein</student>
	An element containing child elements
	<student> <name>Cynthia Berstein</name> <stuID>SI890-041-02</stuID> </student>
	An element containing child elements and an attribute
	<student stuID="SI890-041-02"> <firstName>Cynthia</firstName> <lastName>Berstein</lastName> </student>

The *students.xml* file contains several examples of simple and complex types, which are listed in Figure 13-7. Note that all attributes in the document are, by default, simple types. The `students`, `student`, and `gpa` elements are complex types because they contain either nested child elements or attributes. The `lastName`, `firstName`, `dateOfEnrollment`, `credits`, and `comment` elements are all simple types because each contains only element text.

Figure 13-7   **Simple and complex types in the students.xml document**

Item	Contains	Content Type
students	nested child elements	complex
student	nested child elements	complex
stuID	an attribute value	simple
lastName	element text	simple
firstName	element text	simple
dateOfEnrollment	element text	simple
credits	element text	simple
comment	element text	simple
gpa	an attribute	complex
degree	an attribute value	simple

The distinction between simple and complex types is important in XML Schema because the code to define a simple type differs greatly from the code to define a complex type. You'll start writing the schema for Sabrina's document by defining all of the simple types found in the *students.xml* file.

Defining a Simple Type Element

An element in the instance document containing only text and no attributes or child elements is defined in XML Schema using the `<xs:element>` tag

```
<xs:element name="name" type="type" />
```

where *name* is the name of the element in the instance document and *type* is the type of data stored in the element. The data type can be one of XML Schema's built-in data types, or it can be a data type defined by the schema author. If you use a built-in data type, you must indicate that it belongs to the XML Schema namespace because it is a feature of the XML Schema language. Therefore, the code to use a built-in data type is

```
<xs:element name="name" type="xs:type" />
```

where *type* is a data type supported by XML Schema. Note that if you use a different namespace prefix or declare XML Schema as the default namespace for the document, the prefix will be different.

Perhaps the most commonly used data type in XML Schema is `string`, which allows an element to contain any text string. For example, in the *students.xml* file, the `lastName` element contains the text of the student's last name. To indicate that this element contains string data, you would add the following element to the XML Schema file:

```
<xs:element name="lastName" type="xs:string" />
```

Another popular data type in XML Schema is `decimal`, which allows an element to contain a decimal number.

REFERENCE

Defining a Simple Type Element

- To define a simple type element, enter

```
<xs:element name="name" type="type" />
```

where *name* is the element name in the instance document and *type* is the data type.
- To use a data type built into the XML Schema language, place *type* in the XML Schema namespace as follows:

```
<xs:element name="name" type="xs:type" />
```

For now, you'll define the data type of each simple type element as a simple text string. You'll revise these declarations in the next session, when you examine the wide variety of data types supported by XML Schema as well as learn how to define your own data types.

To declare the simple type elements:

1. Within the schema root element, insert the following simple type elements, as shown in Figure 13-8, making sure to match the case:

```
<xs:element name="lastName" type="xs:string" />
<xs:element name="firstName" type="xs:string" />
<xs:element name="dateOfEnrollment" type="xs:string" />
<xs:element name="credits" type="xs:string" />
<xs:element name="comment" type="xs:string" />
```

Figure 13-8	Elements defined as simple types

simple type elements

element contains only a simple text string

2. Save your changes to the file.

Defining an Attribute

The other simple type content found in Sabrina's document consists of attribute values. To define an attribute in XML Schema, you use the `<xs:attribute>` tag

```
<xs:attribute name="name" type="type" default="default"
              fixed="fixed" />
```

where *name* is the name of the attribute, *type* is the data type, *default* is the attribute's default value, and *fixed* is a fixed value for the attribute. The *default* and *fixed* attributes are optional. You use the *default* attribute to specify a default attribute value, which is applied when no attribute value is entered in the instance document; you use the *fixed* attribute to fix an attribute to a specific value.

Attributes use the same collection of data types that simple type elements do. For example, the following code defines the `degree` attribute and indicates that it contains a text string with a default value of WPA:

```
<xs:attribute name="degree" type="xs:string" default="WPA" />
```

REFERENCE

Defining an Attribute

- To define an attribute, use the syntax

```
<xs:attribute name="name" type="type" default="default"
          fixed="fixed" />
```

where *name* is the attribute name in the instance document, *type* is the data type of the attribute, *default* specifies a default value for the attribute when no attribute value is entered in the instance document, and *fixed* fixes the attribute to a specific value. The *default* and *fixed* values are optional.

- For data types that are part of the XML Schema vocabulary, place *type* in the XML Schema namespace, as follows:

```
<xs:attribute name="name" type="xs:type" default="default"
          fixed="fixed" />
```

The *students.xml* file uses two attributes—`stuID` and `degree`. Neither of these attributes has a default value or a fixed value. You'll add the attribute declarations to the schema file below the element declarations you just created.

To define the attributes used in the *students.xml* file:

▶ **1.** Add the following attribute definition on a new line above the first element definition:

```
<xs:attribute name="stuID" type="xs:string" />
```

As in a DTD, the declarations in a schema can be placed in any order. However, you can make your code easier to understand by keeping your declarations organized. Because the second attribute you'll declare occurs near the end of the XML code for each record, you'll place it below the other declarations.

▶ **2.** Add the following attribute definition on a new line below the last element definition, and then compare your code to Figure 13-9:

```
<xs:attribute name="degree" type="xs:string" />
```

Figure 13-9	Attributes defined as simple types

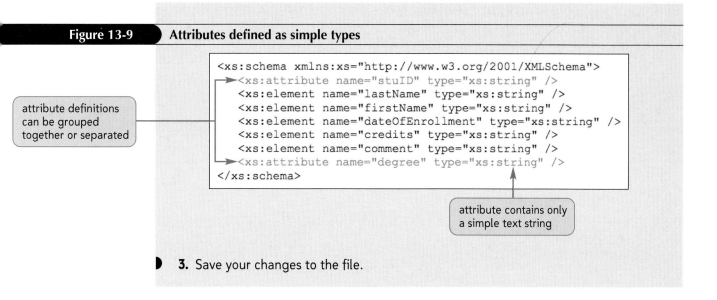

attribute definitions can be grouped together or separated

attribute contains only a simple text string

3. Save your changes to the file.

Defining a Complex Type Element

The two attributes you defined are not yet associated with any elements in Sabrina's document. To create those associations, you must first define the element containing each attribute. Because those elements contain attributes, they are considered complex type elements. The basic structure for defining a complex type element with XML Schema is

```
<xs:element name="name">
    <xs:complexType>
        declarations
    </xs:complexType>
</xs:element>
```

where *name* is the name of the element and *declarations* represents declarations of the type of content within the element. This content could include nested child elements, basic text, attributes, or any combination of the three. As shown in Figure 13-6, the following four complex type elements usually appear in an instance document:

• An empty element containing only attributes
• An element containing text content and attributes but no child elements
• An element containing child elements but no attributes
• An element containing both child elements and attributes

XML Schema uses a different code structure for each of these four possibilities. You'll start by looking at the definition for an empty element that contains one or more attributes.

Defining an Element Containing Only Attributes

The code to define the attributes of an empty element is

```
<xs:element name="name">
   <xs:complexType>
       attributes
   </xs:complexType>
</xs:element>
```

where *name* is the name of the empty element in the instance document and *attributes* is the set of simple type elements that define the attributes associated with the empty element. For example, the empty `student` element

```
<student name="Cynthia Berstein" gpa="3.81"/>
```

has two attributes—`name` and `gpa`. The code for this complex type element has the following structure:

```
<xs:element name="student">
   <xs:complexType>
       <xs:attribute name="name" type="xs:string" />
       <xs:attribute name="gpa" type="xs:decimal" />
   </xs:complexType>
</xs:element>
```

The order of the attribute declarations is unimportant. XML Schema allows attributes to be entered in any order within a complex type element.

Defining an Element Containing Attributes and Basic Text

If an element in the instance document contains attributes and text content but no child elements, the structure that declares the element and the attributes takes a different form. In these cases, the definition needs to indicate that the element contains simple content and a collection of one or more attributes. The structure of the element definition is

```
<xs:element name="name">
   <xs:complexType>
       <xs:simpleContent>
           <xs:extension base="type">
               attributes
           </xs:extension>
       </xs:simpleContent>
   </xs:complexType>
</xs:element>
```

where *type* is the data type of the element's content (or `xs:type` if the data type is part of the XML Schema vocabulary) and *attributes* represents a list of the attributes associated with the element. The purpose of the `simpleContent` element in this code is to indicate that the element contains only text and no nested child elements. The `<xs:extension>` tag is used to extend this definition to include the list of attributes. The `simpleContent` and `extension` elements are important tools used by XML Schema to derive new data types and to define complex content. For the *students.xml* document, you'll use them to define the `gpa` element, which is a complex type element that contains a text value and is associated with an attribute. The following is a sample of the type of content stored in this element:

```
<gpa degree="WPA">3.81</gpa>
```

The following code defines this element and associates it with the `degree` attribute:

```
<xs:element name="gpa">
   <xs:complexType>
      <xs:simpleContent>
         <xs:extension base="xs:string">
            <xs:attribute name="degree" type="xs:string" />
         </xs:extension>
      </xs:simpleContent>
   </xs:complexType>
</xs:element>
```

In this code, the `base` attribute in the `<xs:extension>` element sets the data type for the `gpa` element. At this point, you're assuming that the `gpa` element contains a text string. This code also sets the data type of the `degree` attribute to `xs:string`, indicating that it contains a text string.

Referencing an Element or Attribute Definition

You've already defined the `degree` attribute in the *students.xsd* file. You could revise the code to nest that attribute definition within the definition of the `gpa` element. However, XML Schema allows for a great deal of flexibility in writing complex types.

Rather than repeating that earlier attribute declaration within the `gpa` element, you can create a reference to it. The code to create a reference to an element definition is

```
<xs:element ref="elemName" />
```

where *elemName* is the name used in the element definition. Likewise, the code to create a reference to an attribute definition is

```
<xs:attribute ref="attName" />
```

where *attName* is the name used in the attribute definition. The following code defines the `degree` attribute and then references the definition from within the `gpa` element:

```
<xs:attribute name="degree" type="xs:string" />

<xs:element name="gpa">
   <xs:complexType>
      <xs:simpleContent>
         <xs:extension base="xs:string">
            <xs:attribute ref="degree" />
         </xs:extension>
      </xs:simpleContent>
   </xs:complexType>
</xs:element>
```

REFERENCE

Defining a Complex Type Element

- To define an empty element containing one or more attributes, use

```
<xs:element name="name">
   <xs:complexType>
      attributes
   </xs:complexType>
</xs:element>
```

where *name* is the element name and *attributes* represents a list of attributes associated with the element.

- To define an element containing text content and one or more attributes, use

```
<xs:element name="name">
   <xs:complexType>
      <xs:simpleContent>
         <xs:extension base="type">
            attributes
         </xs:extension>
      </xs:simpleContent>
   </xs:complexType>
</xs:element>
```

where *type* is the data type of the text content of the element.

- To define an element containing only nested child elements, use

```
<xs:element name="name">
   <xs:complexType>
      <xs:compositor>
         elements
      </xs:compositor>
   </xs:complexType>
</xs:element>
```

where *elements* is a list of the child elements, and *compositor* is sequence, choice, or all.

- To define an element containing both attributes and nested child elements, use

```
<xs:element name="name">
   <xs:complexType>
      <xs:compositor>
         elements
      </xs:compositor>
         attributes
   </xs:complexType>
</xs:element>
```

You'll add the definition of the gpa element to the *students.xsd* file now.

To define the gpa element:

▶ **1.** In the *students.xsd* file, below the declaration for the degree attribute, add the following complex type declaration, as shown in Figure 13-10:

```
<xs:element name="gpa">
   <xs:complexType>
      <xs:simpleContent>
         <xs:extension base="xs:string">
            <xs:attribute ref="degree" />
         </xs:extension>
      </xs:simpleContent>
   </xs:complexType>
</xs:element>
```

| Figure 13-10 | Complex type element containing text and an attribute |

```
<xs:schema xmlns:xs="http://www.w3.org/2001/XMLSchema">

   <xs:attribute name="stuID" type="xs:string" />
   <xs:element name="lastName" type="xs:string" />
   <xs:element name="firstName" type="xs:string" />
   <xs:element name="dateOfEnrollment" type="xs:string" />
   <xs:element name="credits" type="xs:string" />
   <xs:element name="comment" type="xs:string" />
   <xs:attribute name="degree" type="xs:string" />

   <xs:element name="gpa">
      <xs:complexType>
         <xs:simpleContent>
            <xs:extension base="xs:string">
               <xs:attribute ref="degree" />
            </xs:extension>
         </xs:simpleContent>
      </xs:complexType>
   </xs:element>

</xs:schema>
```

ref attribute value uses name defined for the degree attribute

the text content of the gpa element is a simple text string

▶ **2.** Save your changes to the file.

Defining an Element with Nested Children

Next, you'll examine complex elements that contain nested child elements but no attributes or text. To define this type of complex element, you use the structure

```
<xs:element name="name">
   <xs:complexType>
      <xs:compositor>
         elements
      </xs:compositor>
   </xs:complexType>
</xs:element>
```

where *name* is the name of the element, *compositor* is a value that defines how the child elements appear in the document, and *elements* is a list of the nested child elements. You can choose any of the following compositors to define how the child elements display in the document:

- `sequence`—requires the child elements to appear in the order listed in the schema
- `choice`—allows any *one* of the child elements listed to appear in the instance document
- `all`—allows any of the child elements to appear in any order in the instance document; however, each may appear only once, or not at all

For example, the following code assigns four child elements—`street`, `city`, `state`, and `country`—to the `address` element:

```
<xs:element name="address">
   <xs:complexType>
      <xs:sequence>
         <xs:element name="street" type="xs:string" />
         <xs:element name="city" type="xs:string" />
         <xs:element name="state" type="xs:string" />
         <xs:element name="country" type="xs:string" />
      </xs:sequence>
   </xs:complexType>
</xs:element>
```

Because the definition uses the `sequence` compositor, the document is invalid if the `address` element doesn't contain all the listed child elements in the order specified.

The following definition allows the `sponsor` element to contain an element named `parent` or an element named `guardian`:

```
<xs:element name="sponsor">
   <xs:complexType>
      <xs:choice>
         <xs:element name="parent" type="xs:string" />
         <xs:element name="guardian" type="xs:string" />
      </xs:choice>
   </xs:complexType>
</xs:element>
```

Because the definition uses the `choice` compositor, the `sponsor` element can contain either element, but not both.

Finally, the following definition uses the `all` compositor to allow the `Family` element to contain elements named `Father` and/or `Mother`:

```
<xs:element name="Family">
   <xs:complexType>
      <xs:all>
         <xs:element name="Father" type="xs:string" />
         <xs:element name="Mother" type="xs:string" />
      </xs:all>
   </xs:complexType>
</xs:element>
```

It is also acceptable for the `Family` element to contain neither a `Father` nor a `Mother` element.

TIP

A complex element can contain only one all compositor; you cannot combine the all compositor with the choice or sequence compositor.

The choice and sequence compositors can be nested and combined. For example, the following definition uses two choice compositors nested within a sequence compositor to require the Account element to contain either the Person or the Company element followed by either the Cash or the Credit element:

```
<xs:element name="Account">
    <xs:complexType>
        <xs:sequence>
            <xs:choice>
                <xs:element name="Person" type="xs:string" />
                <xs:element name="Company" type="xs:string" />
            </xs:choice>
            <xs:choice>
                <xs:element name="Cash" type="xs:string" />
                <xs:element name="Credit" type="xs:string" />
            </xs:choice>
        </xs:sequence>
    </xs:complexType>
</xs:element>
```

Defining an Element Containing Nested Elements and Attributes

The next complex element you'll consider is an element containing both child elements and attributes. To define an element with this kind of content, you use the structure

```
<xs:element name="name">
    <xs:complexType>
        <xs:compositor>
            elements
        </xs:compositor>
        attributes
    </xs:complexType>
</xs:element>
```

where *name* is the name of the element; *compositor* is either sequence, choice, or all; *elements* represents a list of child elements nested within the element; and *attributes* represents a list of attribute definitions associated with the element. This is the same structure used for elements containing nested children except that a list of attributes is included. For example, the student element from Sabrina's *students.xml* file contains two attributes (stuID and degree) and six child elements (lastName, firstName, dateOfEnrollment, comment, credits, and gpa). Because you've already defined the content for the stuID attribute and the six child elements, you can insert references to those earlier definitions in the code, as follows:

```
<xs:element name="student">
    <xs:complexType>
        <xs:sequence>
            <xs:element ref="lastName" />
            <xs:element ref="firstName" />
            <xs:element ref="dateOfEnrollment" />
            <xs:element ref="credits" />
            <xs:element ref="comment" />
            <xs:element ref="gpa" />
        </xs:sequence>
```

```
        <xs:attribute ref="stuID" />
    </xs:complexType>
</xs:element>
```

You'll add this definition of the student element to the *students.xsd* file now.

To define the student element in the *students.xsd* file:

▸ **1.** Below the definition of the gpa element, insert the following code, as shown in Figure 13-11:

```
<xs:element name="student">
    <xs:complexType>
        <xs:sequence>
            <xs:element ref="lastName" />
            <xs:element ref="firstName" />
            <xs:element ref="dateOfEnrollment" />
            <xs:element ref="credits" />
            <xs:element ref="comment" />
            <xs:element ref="gpa" />
        </xs:sequence>

        <xs:attribute ref="stuID" />
    </xs:complexType>
</xs:element>
```

Figure 13-11   **Element containing both child elements and attributes**

```
<xs:element name="gpa">
    <xs:complexType>
        <xs:simpleContent>
            <xs:extension base="xs:string">
                <xs:attribute ref="degree" />
            </xs:extension>
        </xs:simpleContent>                sequence indicates
    </xs:complexType>                      that the contained
</xs:element>                              elements must be in
                                           the specified order
<xs:element name="student">
    <xs:complexType>
        <xs:sequence>◀
            <xs:element ref="lastName" />
            <xs:element ref="firstName" />
child elements of     <xs:element ref="dateOfEnrollment" />
the student element   <xs:element ref="credits" />
            <xs:element ref="comment" />
            <xs:element ref="gpa" />
        </xs:sequence>

        <xs:attribute ref="stuID" />
    </xs:complexType>
</xs:element>
```

▸ **2.** Save your changes to the file.

The only element from the *students.xml* file you haven't yet declared is the root students element. This element has no attributes but does contain the student element as a child. The definition of this element references the definition of the student element that you created earlier:

```
<xs:element name="students">
   <xs:complexType>
      <xs:sequence>
         <xs:element ref="student" />
      </xs:sequence>
   </xs:complexType>
</xs:element>
```

You'll add this definition to the file now.

To define the students element in the *students.xsd* file:

1. Below the definition of the student element, insert the following code, as shown in Figure 13-12:

```
<xs:element name="students">
   <xs:complexType>
      <xs:sequence>
         <xs:element ref="student" />
      </xs:sequence>
   </xs:complexType>
</xs:element>
```

Figure 13-12   Element containing only a child element

```
<xs:element name="student">
    <xs:complexType>
        <xs:sequence>
            <xs:element ref="lastName" />
            <xs:element ref="firstName" />
            <xs:element ref="dateOfEnrollment" />
            <xs:element ref="credits" />
            <xs:element ref="comment" />
            <xs:element ref="gpa" />
        </xs:sequence>

        <xs:attribute ref="stuID" />
    </xs:complexType>
</xs:element>

<xs:element name="students">
    <xs:complexType>
        <xs:sequence>
            <xs:element ref="student" />
        </xs:sequence>
    </xs:complexType>
</xs:element>
```

the only child element of the root students element is the student element

2. Save your changes to the file.

Specifying Mixed Content

One limitation of using DTDs is their inability to define mixed content. An element is said to have **mixed content** when it contains both a text string and child elements. You can specify the child elements with a DTD, but you cannot constrain their order or number. XML Schema gives you more control over mixed content. To specify that an element contains both text and child elements, you add the `mixed` attribute to the `<complexType>` tag. When the `mixed` attribute is set to the value `true`, XML Schema assumes that the element contains both text and child elements. The structure of the child elements can then be defined with the conventional method. For example, assume you were working on a document containing the following XML content:

```
<summary>
    Student <firstName>Cynthia</firstName>
    <lastName>Berstein</lastName> is enrolled in an IT
    degree program and has completed <credits>12</credits>
    credits since 01/01/2012.
</summary>
```

You could declare the summary element for this document in a schema file using the following complex type:

```
<element name="summary">
    <complexType mixed="true">
        <sequence>
            <element name="firstName" type="string" />
            <element name="lastName" type="string" />
            <element name="credits" type="string" />
        </sequence>
    </complexType>
</element>
```

In an element with mixed content, XML Schema allows text content to appear before, between, and after any child element.

At this point, you have defined all of the simple and complex types in Sabrina's document. Next, you'll refine your schema by adding code that defines exactly how these simple and complex types are used and what kind of data they can contain.

Indicating Required Attributes

An attribute may or may not be required with a particular element. To indicate whether an attribute is required, the `use` attribute can be added to the statement that assigns the attribute to an element. The general syntax of the `use` attribute is

```
<xs:element name="name">
    <xs:complexType>
        element content
        <xs:attribute properties use="use" />
    </xs:complexType>
</xs:element>
```

where *use* is one of the following three values:

- `required`—The attribute must always appear with the element.
- `optional`—The use of the attribute is optional with the element.
- `prohibited`—The attribute cannot be used with the element.

For example, in Sabrina's document, the degree attribute is required with every gpa element. To force the instance document to follow this rule, you add the use attribute to the definition of the degree attribute, as follows:

```
<xs:attribute name="degree" type="xs:string" use="required" />
```

If you neglect to add the use attribute to an element declaration, XML parsers assume that the attribute is optional. The use attribute is applied only when assigning an attribute to a specific element from the instance document. After all, an attribute might be required for one element and optional for another.

The two attributes in Sabrina's document—stuID and degree—are both required for the document to be valid. You will indicate this in the schema by specifying the use of each attribute.

To indicate required attributes in the *students.xsd* file:

▶ **1.** Within the code that defines the gpa element, locate the xs:attribute tag for the degree attribute, and then add the code use="required" to the tag. This code indicates that the degree attribute is required for the gpa element.

▶ **2.** Within the code that defines the student element, locate the xs:attribute tag for the stuID attribute, and then add the code use="required" to the tag. This code indicates that the stuID attribute is required for the student element. Figure 13-13 highlights the revised code in the schema.

Figure 13-13   **Attributes designated as required**

```
<xs:element name="gpa">
    <xs:complexType>
        <xs:simpleContent>
            <xs:extension base="xs:string">
                <xs:attribute ref="degree" use="required" />
            </xs:extension>
        </xs:simpleContent>
    </xs:complexType>
</xs:element>
```

the gpa element requires the use of the degree attribute

```
<xs:element name="student">
    <xs:complexType>
        <xs:sequence>
            <xs:element ref="lastName" />
            <xs:element ref="firstName" />
            <xs:element ref="dateOfEnrollment" />
            <xs:element ref="credits" />
            <xs:element ref="comment" />
            <xs:element ref="gpa" />
        </xs:sequence>

        <xs:attribute ref="stuID" use="required" />
    </xs:complexType>
</xs:element>
```

the student element requires the use of the stuID attribute

▶ **3.** Save your changes to the file.

Specifying the Number of Child Elements

The previous code samples assumed that each element in the list appeared once and only once. This is not always the case. For example, Sabrina's document contains information on one or more students, so you need to allow for one or more `student` elements. To specify the number of times an element appears in the instance document, you can apply the `minOccurs` and `maxOccurs` attributes to the element definition, using the syntax

```
<xs:element name="name" type="type" minOccurs="value"
            maxOccurs="value" />
```

where the value of the `minOccurs` attribute defines the minimum number of times the element can occur, and the value of the `maxOccurs` attribute defines the maximum number of times the element can occur. For example, the following element declaration specifies that the `student` element must appear at least once and may appear no more than three times in the instance document:

```
<xs:element name="student" type="xs:string" minOccurs="1"
            maxOccurs="3" />
```

TIP

A minOccurs value of 0 with a maxOccurs value of unbounded is equivalent to the * character in a DTD. Likewise, values of 1 and unbounded are equivalent to the + character, and values of 0 and 1 are equivalent to the ? character.

Any time the `minOccurs` attribute is set to 0, an element is optional. The `maxOccurs` attribute can be any positive value, or it can have a value of `unbounded` for unlimited occurrences of the element. If a value is specified for the `minOccurs` attribute but the `maxOccurs` attribute is missing, the value of the `maxOccurs` attribute is assumed to be equal to the value of the `minOccurs` attribute. Finally, if both the `minOccurs` attribute and the `maxOccurs` attribute are missing, the element is assumed to occur only once.

The `student` element occurs one or more times in Sabrina's document, and the `comment` element occurs zero or more times. All the other elements occur only once. You'll add the appropriate `minOccurs` and `maxOccurs` values to the schema now for the `student` and `comment` elements.

To set the occurrences of the `student` and `comment` elements in the *students.xsd* file:

Be sure to add the minOccurs and maxOccurs attributes to the comment element reference within the definition for the student element, and *not* within the definition of the comment element at the start of the schema.

▶ 1. In the *students.xsd* file, within the code that defines the `student` element, locate the `xs:element` tag that references the `comment` element, and then add the code `minOccurs="0" maxOccurs="unbounded"` to the tag. This code allows for zero or more occurrences of the `comment` element.

▶ 2. Within the code that defines the `students` element, locate the `xs:element` tag that references the `student` element and then add the code `minOccurs="1" maxOccurs="unbounded"` to the tag. This code allows for one or more occurrences of the `student` element. Figure 13-14 highlights the new code in the schema.

Figure 13-14   **The minOccurs and maxOccurs values**

```
<xs:schema xmlns:xs="http://www.w3.org/2001/XMLSchema">

   <xs:attribute name="stuID" type="xs:string" />
   <xs:element name="lastName" type="xs:string" />
   <xs:element name="firstName" type="xs:string" />
   <xs:element name="dateOfEnrollment" type="xs:string" />
   <xs:element name="credits" type="xs:string" />
   <xs:element name="comment" type="xs:string" />
   <xs:attribute name="degree" type="xs:string" />

   <xs:element name="gpa">
      <xs:complexType>
         <xs:simpleContent>
            <xs:extension base="xs:string">
               <xs:attribute ref="degree" use="required" />
            </xs:extension>
         </xs:simpleContent>
      </xs:complexType>
   </xs:element>

   <xs:element name="student">
      <xs:complexType>
         <xs:sequence>
            <xs:element ref="lastName" />
            <xs:element ref="firstName" />
            <xs:element ref="dateOfEnrollment" />
            <xs:element ref="credits" />
            <xs:element ref="comment" minOccurs="0" maxOccurs="unbounded" />
            <xs:element ref="gpa" />
         </xs:sequence>

         <xs:attribute ref="stuID" use="required" />
      </xs:complexType>
   </xs:element>

   <xs:element name="students">
      <xs:complexType>
         <xs:sequence>
            <xs:element ref="student" minOccurs="1" maxOccurs="unbounded" />
         </xs:sequence>
      </xs:complexType>
   </xs:element>

</xs:schema>
```

the comment element can occur any number of times, or not at all, within the student element

the student element must occur one or more times within the students element

   3. Save your changes to the file.

Validating a Schema Document

You're ready to test whether the *students.xsd* document validates. The Web has many excellent sources for validating parsers including Web sites such as the W3C's, where you can upload or paste schema code to have it validated. Several editors provide schema validation as well.

    The following steps use Exchanger XML Editor to validate Sabrina's *students.xsd* document.

To validate the *students.xsd* file:

▶ **1.** If necessary, open **students.xsd** in Exchanger XML Editor.

▶ **2.** Click **Schema** on the Menu bar, and then click **Validate XML Schema**. As shown in Figure 13-15, the error console reports that the *students.xsd* file is valid.

Figure 13-15	XML Schema validation

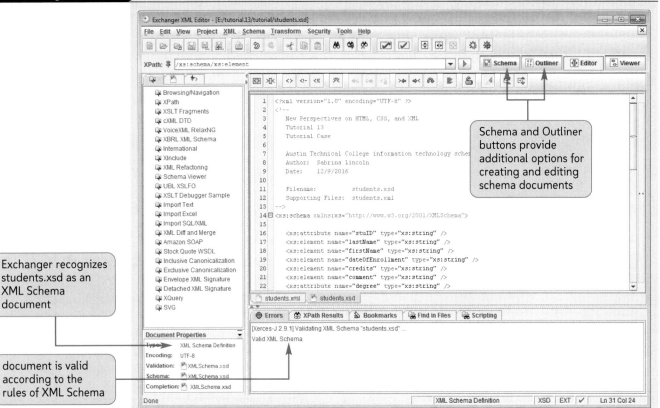

Trouble? If a validation error is reported in the Errors tab, there is an error in the schema. Check your schema code against the *students.xsd* code shown in Figure 13-14. Your code should match exactly, including the use of uppercase and lowercase letters. Fix any discrepancies, be sure to save your changes, validate the schema again, and then reexamine the Errors tab for validation information.

Trouble? If your Exchanger XML Editor window doesn't match the one shown in Figure 13-15, close *students.xsd* and reopen it.

Now that you've confirmed that your schema is valid, you can apply it to your XML document.

Applying a Schema to an Instance Document

To attach a schema to an instance document, you declare the XML Schema instance namespace in the instance document, and then you specify the location of the schema file. To declare the XML Schema instance namespace, you add the following attribute to the root element of the instance document:

```
xmlns:xsi="http://www.w3.org/2001/XMLSchema-instance"
```

Although the prefix `xsi` is commonly used for the XML Schema Instance namespace, you can specify a different prefix in your documents.

You add a second attribute to the root element to specify the location of the schema file. The attribute you use depends on whether the instance document is associated with a namespace. If the document is not associated with a namespace, you add the attribute

```
xsi:noNamespaceSchemaLocation="schema"
```

to the root element, where *schema* is the location and name of the schema file. Note that the attribute requires the `xsi` namespace prefix because the attribute itself is from the XML Schema Instance namespace.

PROSKILLS

Teamwork: Working with Multiple Schema Documents

Especially on a large project involving multiple programmers, it can be useful to create multiple schema documents rather than a single large schema document. You can use the `xs:include` element within an XML Schema document to include the contents of another schema document. For instance, a project might break up into two teams—one creating *customer.xsd*, a schema for customer content, and another creating *products.xsd*, a schema for order information. To validate against the contents of both of these schemas, you'd create a master schema file for your project and add the following two lines of code to it:

```
<xs:include schemaLocation="customer.xsd" />
<xs:include schemaLocation="products.xsd" />
```

Using the `xs:include` element enables you to validate instance documents against the validation rules defined in multiple XML Schema documents.

Sabrina has not yet placed the contents of her *students.xml* document in a namespace, so you'll add the following attribute to the root `students` element:

```
xsi:noNamespaceSchemaLocation="students.xsd"
```

To apply the *students.xsd* schema to the *students.xml* document:

▶ 1. Return to the **students.xml** file in your editor.

▶ 2. Within the opening tag for the `students` element, add the following attributes, as shown in Figure 13-16:

```
xmlns:xsi="http://www.w3.org/2001/XMLSchema-instance"
xsi:noNamespaceSchemaLocation="students.xsd"
```

Figure 13-16 Schema applied to a document without a namespace

XML Schema instance namespace

```
<students xmlns:xsi="http://www.w3.org/2001/XMLSchema-instance"
          xsi:noNamespaceSchemaLocation="students.xsd">
   <student stuID="SI890-041-02">
      <lastName>Berstein</lastName>
      <firstName>Cynthia</firstName>
      <dateOfEnrollment>2016-05-22</dateOfEnrollment>
      <credits>12</credits>
      <gpa degree="MP">3.81</gpa>
   </student>
</students>
```

name of the schema document

▶ **3.** Save your changes to the file.

Now that you've applied your schema to Sabrina's instance document, you can validate the document against the rules defined in the *students.xsd* file. To validate the document, you use an XML parser. Although the following steps use the validator within Exchanger XML Editor, you can also validate using one of the free or commercial XML validating parsers available on the Web.

To validate the *students.xml* document:

▶ **1.** If necessary, open **students.xml** in Exchanger XML Editor.

▶ **2.** Click the **Viewer** button in the upper-right corner of the window.

▶ **3.** Click **XML** on the menu bar, and then click **Validate**. As shown in Figure 13-17, the error console reports that the *students.xml* file is a valid document.

Figure 13-17 Validation results for the students.xml file

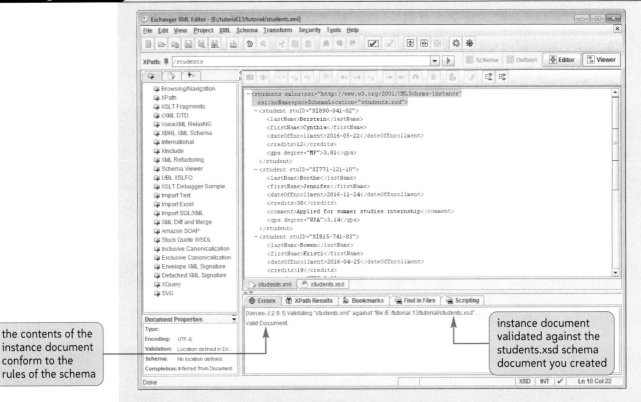

the contents of the instance document conform to the rules of the schema

instance document validated against the students.xsd schema document you created

Trouble? If a validation error is reported in the Errors tab and your schema validated successfully in the earlier steps, then there is an error in the namespace attributes you entered in the instance document. Check your *students.xml* code against the namespace attributes shown in Figure 13-16. Your code should match exactly, including the use of uppercase and lowercase letters. Fix any discrepancies, save your changes, and then revalidate.

Sabrina suggests that you add an intentional error to the *students.xml* file to confirm that the document is rejected as invalid. To do this, you'll add a second `credits` element to the first student's data. Because the schema you wrote permits only one `credits` element per student, this should result in an invalid document.

To add an error to the *students.xml* file:

▶ **1.** Return to the **students.xml** file in Exchanger XML Editor, and then click the **Editor** button in the upper-right corner.

▶ **2.** Within the `student` element containing information on Cynthia Berstein, add the following code, as shown in Figure 13-18:

```
<credits>14</credits>
```

| Figure 13-18 | Second credits element added to the students.xml file |

```
<students xmlns:xsi="http://www.w3.org/2001/XMLSchema-instance"
          xsi:noNamespaceSchemaLocation="students.xsd">
    <student stuID="SI890-041-02">
        <lastName>Berstein</lastName>
        <firstName>Cynthia</firstName>
        <dateOfEnrollment>2016-05-22</dateOfEnrollment>
        <credits>12</credits>
        <credits>14</credits>
        <gpa degree="MP">3.81</gpa>
    </student>
```

a second credits element is not valid according to the schema

▶ **3.** Save your changes to the file.

▶ **4.** Click **XML** on the Menu bar, and then click **Validate**. The document is rejected as invalid due to the extra `credits` element. See Figure 13-19.

Figure 13-19 **Validation error**

suspected line with error is marked

line number and column number identifying the suspected location of the error

error count replaces "Valid Document" message

description of the error

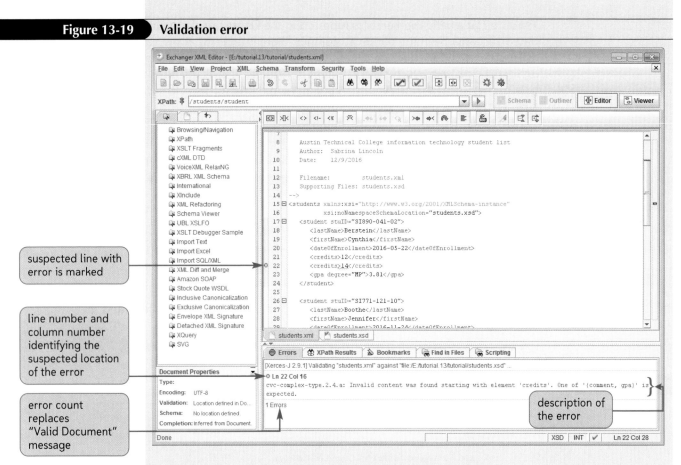

▶ **5.** If necessary, click on the error message on the Errors tab to scroll the code in the editor to display the line containing the error. A red circle containing a white x marks the line containing the error.

▶ **6.** Delete the line `<credits>14</credits>` and then save your changes to the file.

▶ **7.** Click **XML** on the Menu bar, and then click **Validate**. The error console once again reports that the *students.xml* file is a valid document.

Sabrina is pleased with the initial work you've done on designing a schema for the *students.xml* document. In the next session, you'll implement additional validation rules that Sabrina would like applied to her document as you learn about data types.

Session 13.1 Quick Check

REVIEW

1. What is a schema? What is an instance document?
2. How do schemas differ from DTDs?
3. What is a simple type? What is a complex type?
4. How do you declare a simple type element named `Address` that contains string data?
5. How do you declare a complex type element named `Address` that contains, in order, the child elements `Apartment` (optional), `City`, `State`, and `Zip`? (Assume that the `Apartment`, `City`, `State`, and `Zip` elements are simple type elements containing text strings.)
6. The `Book` element contains simple text and a `Title` attribute. What code would you enter into a schema file to define this complex type element?
7. What code would you enter into a schema to create a reference to an attribute named `studentID`?
8. What attributes would you add to the root element of an instance document to attach it to a schema file named *schema1.xsd*? Assume that no namespace has been assigned to the schema file, and that you're using the XML Schema vocabulary.

SESSION 13.2 VISUAL OVERVIEW

The string data type is a **built-in data type**, which is part of the XML Schema language. The string data type is an example of a **primitive data type** (also called a **base type**), which is a subgroup of built-in data types that are not defined in terms of other types.

The siType data type is a **user-derived data type**, which is a data type defined by a schema's author.

```
<?xml version="1.0" encoding="UTF-8" ?>
<xs:schema xmlns:xs="http://www.w3.org/2001/XMLSchema">

    <xs:attribute name="stuID" type="siType" />
    <xs:element name="lastName" type="xs:string" />
    <xs:element name="firstName" type="xs:string" />
    <xs:element name="dateOfEnrollment" type="xs:date" />
    <xs:element name="credits" type="creditsType" />
    <xs:element name="comment" type="xs:string" />
    <xs:attribute name="degree" type="degreeType" />

    <xs:simpleType name="siType">
        <xs:restriction base="xs:ID">
            <xs:pattern value="SI\d{3}-\d{3}-\d{2}" />
        </xs:restriction>
    </xs:simpleType>

    <xs:element name="gpa">
        <xs:complexType>
            <xs:simpleContent>
                <xs:extension base="gpaType">
                    <xs:attribute ref="degree" use="required" />
                </xs:extension>
            </xs:simpleContent>
        </xs:complexType>
    </xs:element>
```

A regular expression is a text string that defines a character pattern.

A **pattern** is a constraining facet that limits data to a general pattern.

A **character type** is a representation of a specific type of character. For instance, \d is the character type for a single digit.

VALIDATING WITH DATA TYPES

The `integer` data type is an example of a **derived data type**, which is one of 25 built-in data types that are developed from one of the base types.

minInclusive is a constraining facet that constrains the data to be greater than a minimum value. A **constraining facet** is a restriction placed on the facets of a preexisting data type.

```
<xs:simpleType name="creditsType">
    <xs:restriction base="xs:integer">
        <xs:minInclusive value="1" />
    </xs:restriction>
</xs:simpleType>

<xs:simpleType name="gpaType">
    <xs:restriction base="xs:decimal">
        <xs:minExclusive value="0" />
        <xs:maxInclusive value="4" />
    </xs:restriction>
</xs:simpleType>

<xs:simpleType name="degreeType">
    <xs:restriction base="xs:string">
        <xs:enumeration value="MP" />
        <xs:enumeration value="WPA" />
    </xs:restriction>
</xs:simpleType>
```

maxInclusive is a constraining facet that constrains the data to be greater than or equal to a minimum value.

A **restricted data type** is a type of derived data type in which a restriction is placed on the facets of a preexisting data type. This code defines the degreeType data type by restricting the string data type to a list of values.

enumeration is a constraining facet that constrains data to a specified list of values.

Validating with Built-In Data Types

The schema you designed for the *students.xml* document uses the `string` data type for all element and attribute content, which allows users to enter any text string into those items. Sabrina wants to ensure that dates are entered in the proper form, that only positive integers are entered for the student credits, and that the student IDs follow a prescribed pattern. You can do all of these using additional data types supported by XML Schema.

XML Schema supports two general categories of data types—built-in and user-derived. A built-in data type is part of the XML Schema language. A user-derived data type is a data type defined by a schema's author. You'll begin your work with data types by exploring the built-in data types in XML Schema.

XML Schema divides its built-in data types into two classes—primitive and derived. A primitive data type, also called a base type, is one of 19 fundamental data types that are not defined in terms of other types. A **derived data type** is one of 25 data types that are developed from one of the base types. Figure 13-20 provides a schematic diagram of all 44 built-in data types.

TIP

All built-in data types are part of the XML Schema vocabulary and must be placed in the XML Schema namespace.

Figure 13-20   XML Schema built-in data types

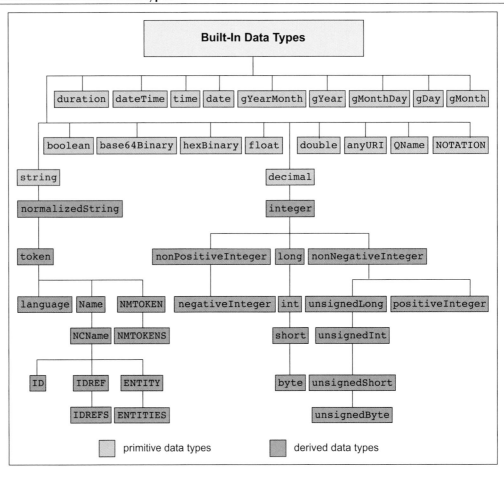

Derived data types share many of the same characteristics as the primitive data types they are derived from, but incorporate one or two additional restrictions or modifications. To see how this is done, you'll examine the string data types.

String Data Types

In the previous session, you used only the primitive `string` data type, allowing almost any text string in the elements and attributes of Sabrina's document. The `string` data type is the most general of XML Schema's built-in data types. For that reason, it is not very useful if you need to exert more control over element and attribute values in an instance document. XML Schema provides several derived data types that enable you to restrict text strings. Figure 13-21 describes some of these data types.

Figure 13-21	Some data types derived from string

Data Type	Description
xs:string	A text string containing all legal characters from the ISO/IEC character set, including all white space characters
xs:normalizedString	A text string in which all white space characters are replaced with blank spaces
xs:token	A text string in which adjoining blank spaces are replaced with a single blank space, and opening and closing spaces are removed
xs:NMTOKEN	A text string containing valid XML names with no white space
xs:NMTOKENS	A list of NMTOKEN data values separated by white space
xs: Name	A text string similar to the NMTOKEN data type except that names must begin with a letter or the colon (:) or hyphen (-) character
xs:NCName	A "noncolonized name," derived from the Name data type but restricting the use of colons anywhere in the name
xs:ID	A unique ID name found nowhere else in the instance document
xs:IDREF	A reference to an ID value found in the instance document
xs:IDREFS	A list of ID references separated by white space
xs:ENTITY	A value matching an unparsed entity defined in a DTD
xs:ENTITIES	A list of entity values matching unparsed entities defined in a DTD

Some of the data types in the list should be familiar from your work with DTDs. For example, the `ID` data type allows text strings containing unique ID values, and the `IDREF` and `IDREFS` data types allow only text strings that contain references to ID values located in the instance document.

REFERENCE

Applying Built-In XML Schema Data Types

- For any string content, use the data type `xs:string`.
- For an ID value, use `xs:ID`.
- For a reference to an ID value, use `xs:IDREF`.
- For a decimal value, use `xs:decimal`.
- For an integer value, use `xs:integer`.
- For a positive integer, use `xs:positiveInteger`.
- For a date in the format *yyyy-mm-dd*, use `xs:date`.
- For a time in the format *hh:mm:ss*, use `xs:time`.

Each student in Sabrina's document has a `stuID` attribute that uniquely identifies the student. You'll apply the `ID` data type to this attribute now.

To apply the ID data type:

▶ **1.** If you took a break after the previous session, make sure the **students.xml** and **students.xsd** files are open in your editor.

▶ **2.** Within the *students.xsd* file, locate the definition for the stuID attribute.

▶ **3.** Change the type value from xs:string to **xs:ID** as shown in Figure 13-22. Just like the string data type, the ID data type is built into XML Schema, so you identify it using the xs namespace prefix.

Figure 13-22   ID data type applied

stuID values must be unique IDs

```
<xs:schema xmlns:xs="http://www.w3.org/2001/XMLSchema">

    <xs:attribute name="stuID" type="xs:ID" />
    <xs:element name="lastName" type="xs:string" />
```

▶ **4.** Save your changes to the **students.xsd** file.

Numeric Data Types

Unlike DTDs, schemas that use XML Schema support numeric data types. Most numeric data types are derived from four primitive data types—decimal, float, double, and boolean. Figure 13-23 describes these and some other XML Schema numeric data types.

Figure 13-23   Numeric data types

Data Type	Description
xs:decimal	A decimal number in which the decimal separator is always a dot (.) with a leading + or - character allowed; no nonnumeric characters are allowed, nor is exponential notation
xs:integer	An integer
xs:nonPositiveInteger	An integer less than or equal to zero
xs:negativeInteger	An integer less than zero
xs:nonNegativeInteger	An integer greater than or equal to zero
xs:positiveInteger	An integer greater than zero
xs:float	A floating point number allowing decimal values and values in scientific notation; infinite values can be represented by -INF and INF; nonnumeric values can be represented by NaN
xs:double	A double precision floating point number
xs:boolean	A Boolean value that has the value true, false, 0, or 1

Sabrina's XML document includes the total credits for each of the students in the information technology programs. She wants you to validate that all the values she entered for the `credits` element are positive integers. Sabrina also entered a numeric score for each student's GPA. The GPA values range from 0 to 4. She wants you to change the data type for the `gpa` element to `decimal`. Because `gpa` is a complex type element containing text and attributes, you'll add the data type to the `base` attribute in the `simpleContent` element. You'll make these changes to your schema document now.

To apply the `positiveInteger` and `decimal` data types:

1. Within the **students.xsd** file, locate the `xs:element` tag for the `credits` element and then change the value of the `type` attribute from `xs:string` to `xs:positiveInteger`.

2. Within the code to define the `gpa` element, locate the opening `xs:extension` tag and then change the value of the `base` attribute from `xs:string` to `xs:decimal`. Figure 13-24 shows the revised code.

Figure 13-24	positiveInteger and decimal data types applied

```
<xs:schema xmlns:xs="http://www.w3.org/2001/XMLSchema">

    <xs:attribute name="stuID" type="xs:ID" />
    <xs:element name="lastName" type="xs:string" />
    <xs:element name="firstName" type="xs:string" />
    <xs:element name="dateOfEnrollment" type="xs:string" />
    <xs:element name="credits" type="xs:positiveInteger" />
    <xs:element name="comment" type="xs:string" />
    <xs:attribute name="degree" type="xs:string" />

    <xs:element name="gpa">
        <xs:complexType>
            <xs:simpleContent>
                <xs:extension base="xs:decimal">
                    <xs:attribute ref="degree" use="required" />
                </xs:extension>
            </xs:simpleContent>
        </xs:complexType>
    </xs:element>
```

values for the gpa element are limited to decimal values

values for the credits element are limited to positive integers

3. Save your changes to the **students.xsd** file.

Data Types for Dates and Times

TIP

To support date strings such as 1/8/2012 or Jan. 8, 2012, you must create your own date type or use a date type library created by another XML developer.

XML Schema provides several data types for dates, times, and durations. However, XML Schema does not allow for any flexibility in the date and time formats it uses. For instance, date values containing a month, day, and year must be entered in the format

`yyyy-mm-dd`

where *yyyy* is the four-digit year value, *mm* is the two-digit month value, and *dd* is the two-digit day value. Month values range from 01 to 12, and day values range from 01 to 31 (depending on the month). The date value

2012-01-08

would be valid under XML Schema, but the date value

2012-1-8

would not be valid because its month and day values are not two-digit integers.
Times in XML Schema must be entered using 24-hour (or military) time. The format is

hh:mm:ss

where *hh* is the hour value ranging from 00 to 23, and *mm* and *ss* are the minutes and
seconds values, respectively, ranging from 00 to 59. No data type exists in XML Schema
for expressing time in the 12-hour AM/PM format. In the `time` data type, each time value
(hours, minutes, and seconds) must be specified. Thus, the time value

15:45

would be invalid because it does not specify a value for seconds. Figure 13-25
summarizes the different data types supported by XML Schema for dates and times.

Figure 13-25   Date and time data types

Data Type	Description
xs:datetime	A date and time entered in the format *yyyy-mm-ddThh:mm:ss* where *yyyy* is the four-digit year, *mm* is the two-digit month, *dd* is the two-digit day, *T* is the time zone, *hh* is the two-digit hour, *mm* is the two-digit minute, and *ss* is the two-digit second
xs:date	A date entered in the format *yyyy-mm-dd*
xs:time	A time entered in the format *hh:mm:ss*
xs:gYearMonthDay	A date based on the Gregorian calendar entered in the format *yyyy-mm-dd* (equivalent to xs:date)
xs:gYearMonth	A date entered in the format *yyyy-mm* (no day is specified)
xs:gYear	A year entered in the format *yyyy*
xs:gMonthDay	A month and day entered in the format *--mm-dd*
xs:gMonth	A month entered in the format *--mm*
xs:gDay	A day entered in the format *---dd*
xs:duration	A time duration entered in the format P*y*Y*m*M*d*D*h*H*m*M*s*S where *y, m, d, h, m,* and *s* are the duration values in years, months, days, hours, minutes, and seconds, respectively; an optional negative sign is also permitted to indicate a negative time duration

Sabrina recorded each student's date of enrollment in her XML document using the
`dateOfEnrollment` element. You'll apply the `date` data type to values of this element to
confirm that she entered all the date values correctly.

To apply the `date` data type:

▶ 1. Within the **students.xsd** file, locate the `xs:element` tag for the
`dateOfEnrollment` element, and then change the data type from `xs:string` to
`xs:date`, as shown in Figure 13-26.

Figure 13-26   date data type applied

```
<xs:schema xmlns:xs="http://www.w3.org/2001/XMLSchema">

    <xs:attribute name="stuID" type="xs:ID" />
    <xs:element name="lastName" type="xs:string" />
    <xs:element name="firstName" type="xs:string" />
    <xs:element name="dateOfEnrollment" type="xs:date" />
    <xs:element name="credits" type="xs:positiveInteger" />
    <xs:element name="comment" type="xs:string" />
    <xs:attribute name="degree" type="xs:string" />
```

dateOfEnrollment values must be entered in the format yyyy-mm-dd

▶ **2.** Save your changes to the **students.xsd** file.

Now that you've added more specific data types to the *students.xsd* file, you'll validate the contents of the *students.xml* file to verify that Sabrina's data matches the rules of the schema.

To validate the *students.xml* file:

▶ **1.** In your XML editor, switch to the **students.xml** file and then click the **Viewer** button in the upper-right corner of the window.

▶ **2.** On the Menu bar, click **XML** and then click **Validate**. The document validates successfully against the schema.

Sabrina suggests that you add a few errors to the *students.xml* file to confirm that the modifications you just made to the schema work as expected. The schema you wrote allows only integer values for `credits` element, and allows only decimal values for the `gpa` element. In addition, date values for the `dateOfEnrollment` must follow a strict pattern. You'll modify the `credits`, `gpa`, and `dateOfEnrollment` values for the first student's data so they don't satisfy these criteria; if the schema works as intended, these changes should result in an invalid document.

To add errors to the *students.xml* file:

▶ **1.** Return to the **students.xml** file in your XML editor, and then click the **Editor** button in the upper-right corner of the window.

▶ **2.** Within the `student` element for Cynthia Berstein, in the `credits` element value, add a **space** after the number 12 and then type the word **credits**. With the additional characters, the value is no longer an integer.

▶ **3.** Within the `gpa` element for the same student, delete the element value 3.81. The empty value does not match the element's `decimal` data type.

▶ **4.** Within the `dateOfEnrollment` element for the same student, delete the leading 0 from the month value so the date reads **2016-5-22**. The date no longer matches the *yyyy-mm-dd* pattern for the `date` data type. Figure 13-27 shows the revised data for the first student in the document.

| Figure 13-27 | Three errors introduced into instance document |

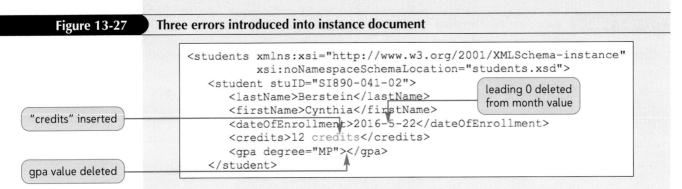

5. Save your changes to the **students.xml** file.

6. On the Menu bar, click **XML**, click **Validate**, and then scroll through the list of errors on the Errors tab. The document is rejected with errors found due to the credits, gpa, and dateOfEnrollment element values you edited no longer matching the schema definitions.

7. In the credits element for the first record, delete the space and the word "credits" that you entered so the value is once again 12; in the gpa element for the first record, enter the value **3.81**; in the dateOfEnrollment element, change the value to read **2016-05-22**; and then save your changes to the file.

8. Revalidate the document and confirm that it passes the validation test.

9. Save your changes to the **students.xml** file.

Deriving Customized Data Types

In addition to the built-in data types you're using, you also need to create some new data types to fully validate Sabrina's document. Sabrina has provided the following additional rules for the elements and attributes in her document:

- The value of the credits element must be at least 1.
- The gpa value must fall between 0 and 4.
- The value of the degree attribute must be either MP or WPA. (The value MP stands for Mobile Programmer, and the value WPA stands for Web Programmer/Analyst.)

Although XML Schema has no built-in data types for these rules, you can use it to derive—or build—your own data types. The code to derive a new data type is

```
<xs:simpleType name="name">
   rules
</xs:simpleType>
```

where *name* is the name of the user-defined data type and *rules* is the list of statements that define the properties of that data type. This structure is also known as a named simple type because it defines simple type content under a name provided by the schema author. You can also create a simple type without a name, which is known as an **anonymous simple type**. The code for an anonymous simple type is easier to create. However, one advantage of creating a named simple type is that you can reference that simple type elsewhere in your schema using the simple type name.

TIP

Just as you can create customized simple types, you can also create customized complex types, which allow you to reuse complex structures in a schema document.

Each new data type must be derived from a preexisting data type found in either XML Schema or a user-defined vocabulary. The following three components are involved in deriving any new data type:

- **value space**—The set of values that correspond to the data type. For example, the value space for a `positiveInteger` data type includes the numbers 1, 2, 3, etc., but not 0, negative integers, fractions, or text strings.
- **lexical space**—The set of textual representations of the value space. For example, a value supported by the `floating` data type, such as 42, can be represented in several ways, including 42, 42.0, or 4.2E01.
- **facets**—The properties that distinguish one data type from another. Facets can include such properties as text string length or a range of allowable values. For example, a facet that distinguishes the `integer` data type from the `positiveInteger` data type is the fact that positive integers are constrained to the realm of positive numbers.

New data types are created by manipulating the properties of these three components. You can do this by:

1. Creating a list based on preexisting data types
2. Creating a union of one or more of the preexisting data types
3. Restricting the values of a preexisting data type

PROSKILLS

Problem Solving: Reusing Code with Named Model Groups and Named Attribute Groups

Named types are not the only structures you can create to be reused in your schemas. Another structure is a named model group. As the name suggests, a **named model group** is a collection, or group, of elements. The syntax for creating a model group is

```
<xs:group name="name">
    elements
</xs:group>
```

where `name` is the name of the model group and `elements` is a collection of element declarations. Model groups are useful when a document contains element declarations or code that you want to repeat throughout the schema.

Like elements, attributes can be grouped into collections called **named attribute groups**. This is particularly useful for attributes that you want to use with several different elements in a schema. The syntax for a named attribute group is

```
<xs:attributeGroup name="name">
    attributes
</xs:attributeGroup>
```

where `name` is the name of the attribute group and `attributes` is a collection of attributes assigned to the group.

You'll start by examining how to create a list data type.

Deriving a List Data Type

A **list data type** is a list of values separated by white space, in which each item in the list is derived from an established data type. You already have seen a couple of examples of list data types found in XML Schema, including the `xs:ENTITIES` and `xs:IDREFS` lists. In these cases, the list data types are derived from XML Schema's `xs:ENTITY` and `xs:IDREF` data types. The syntax for deriving a customized list data type is

```
<xs:simpleType name="name">
   <xs:list itemType="type" />
</xs:simpleType>
```

TIP

A list data type must always use white space as the delimiter. You cannot use commas or other non–white space characters.

where *name* is the name assigned to the list data type and *type* is the data type from which each item in the list is derived. For example, Austin Technical College might decide to include a student's GPA for each semester along with the student's overall GPA. An element containing the GPA information by semester might appear as follows:

```
<semGPA>3.81 3.92 3.3 3.2</semGPA>
```

To create a data type for this information, you could define the following named simple type:

```
<xs:simpleType name="semList">
   <xs:list itemType="xs:decimal" />
</xs:simpleType>
```

In this case, you have a data type named `semList` that contains a list of decimal values. To apply this new data type to the `semGPA` element, you would reference the data type in the definition as follows:

```
<xs:element name="semGPA" type="semList" />
```

Notice that the type value does not have the `xs` namespace prefix because `semList` is not part of the XML Schema vocabulary; it is a named simple type created by the schema author.

Deriving a Union Data Type

A **union data type** is based on the value and/or lexical spaces from two or more preexisting data types. Each base data type is known as a **member data type**. The syntax for deriving a union data type is

```
<xs:simpleType name="name">
   <xs:union memberTypes="type1 type2 type3 ..." />
</xs:simpleType>
```

where *type1*, *type2*, *type3*, etc., are the member types that constitute the union. XML Schema also allows unions to be created from nested simple types. The syntax is

```
<xs:simpleType name="name">
   <xs:union>
      <xs:simpleType>
         rules1
      </xs:simpleType>
      <xs:simpleType>
         rules2
      </xs:simpleType>
      ...
   </xs:union>
</xs:simpleType>
```

where *rules1*, *rules2*, etc., are rules for creating different user-derived data types. For example, when collecting data on semester GPA values, Sabrina might want to specify the type of semester GPA, such as `program`, `genEd`, or `all`. As a result of this variety, the `semGPA` element might look as follows:

```
<semGPA>3.81 program 3.92 all 3.3 genEd 3.2 all</semGPA>
```

To validate this element, which contains a mixture of numeric and descriptive measures, she could create the following derived data type:

```
<xs:simpleType name="semType">
   <xs:union memberTypes="xs:decimal xs:Name" />
</xs:simpleType>
```

Based on this simple type definition, a parser will accept any value as long as it is either a decimal value or a text string of the `Name` data type. Next, Sabrina would use this data type to derive a list type based on the following union data type:

```
<xs:simpleType name="semList">
   <xs:list itemType="semType" />
</xs:simpleType>
```

This list data type would allow the `semGPA` element to contain a list consisting of either decimal values or XML names.

Deriving a Restricted Data Type

The final kind of derived data type is a restricted data type, in which a restriction is placed on the facets of a preexisting data type, such as an `integer` data type that is constrained to fall within a range of values. XML Schema provides 12 constraining facets that can be used to derive new data types; these facets are described in Figure 13-28.

Figure 13-28	Constraining facets

Facet	Description
enumeration	Constrains the data to a specified list of values
length	Specifies the length of the data in characters (for text strings) or items (for lists)
maxLength	Specifies the maximum length of the data in characters (for text strings) or items (for lists)
minLength	Specifies the minimum length of the data in characters (for text strings) or items (for lists)
pattern	Constrains the lexical space of the data to follow a specific character pattern
whiteSpace	Controls the use of blanks in the lexical space of the data; the `whiteSpace` facet has three values—`preserve` (preserve all white space), `replace` (replace all tabs, carriage returns, and line feed characters with blank spaces), and `collapse` (collapse all consecutive occurrences of white space to a single blank space, and remove any leading or trailing white space)
maxExclusive	Constrains the data to be less than a maximum value
maxInclusive	Constrains the data to be less than or equal to a maximum value
minExclusive	Constrains the data to be greater than a minimum value
minInclusive	Constrains the data to be greater than or equal to a minimum value
fractionDigits	Specifies the maximum number of decimal places to the right of the decimal point in the data value
totalDigits	Specifies the maximum number of digits in the data value

Constraining facets are applied to a base type using the structure

```
<xs:simpleType name="name">
   <xs:restriction base="type">
      <xs:facet1 value="value1" />
      <xs:facet2 value="value2" />
      ...
   </xs:restriction>
</xs:simpleType>
```

where *type* is the data type on which the restricted data type is based; *facet1*, *facet2*, etc., are constraining facets; and *value1*, value2, etc., are values for the constraining facets. In Sabrina's document, each student's total credits must be at least 1. You could create a restricted data type using the `minInclusive` facet to restrict the `credits` value to at least 1, as in the following code:

```
<xs:simpleType name="creditsType">
   <xs:restriction base="xs:integer">
      <xs:minInclusive value="1" />
   </xs:restriction>
</xs:simpleType>
```

When applied to the `credits` element, this data type would require each `credits` value to be an integer with a minimum value of 1.

INSIGHT

Constraining Facets vs Form Validation

Like form validation in HTML, constraining facets in an XML schema let you place limits on the allowable values for data in your document. However, while you can use HTML validation to prompt users to correct information they've entered, an XML parser uses a schema to decide whether or not an entire document is valid, and rejects the whole document if it does not adhere to all the rules of the schema, including the constraining facets for specific elements. In short, HTML form validation is a tool to ensure valid collection of data from users, while constraining facets in an XML schema generally serve only as a check on data that has already been collected.

You'll add the `creditsType` data type to the schema and apply it to the `credits` element next.

REFERENCE

Deriving Customized and Patterned Data Types

- To derive a list data type, use

```
<xs:simpleType name="name">
   <xs:list itemType="type" />
</xs:simpleType>
```

where *name* is the name of the custom data type and *type* is the data type on which it is based.

- To derive a union data type, use

```
<xs:simpleType name="name">
   <xs:union memberTypes="type1 type2 type3 ..." />
</xs:simpleType>
```

where *type1*, *type2*, *type3*, etc., are the member types that constitute the union and upon which the custom data type is based. Alternatively, you can use the nested form

```
<xs:simpleType name="name">
   <xs:union>
      <xs:simpleType>
         rules1
      </xs:simpleType>
      <xs:simpleType>
         rules2
      </xs:simpleType>
      ...
   </xs:union>
</xs:simpleType>
```

where *rules1*, *rules2*, etc., are the rules that define the different data types in the union.

- To derive a data type by restricting the values of a preexisting data type, use

```
<xs:simpleType name="name">
   <xs:restriction base="type">
      <xs:facet1 value="value1" />
      <xs:facet2 value="value2" />
      ...
   </xs:restriction>
</xs:simpleType>
```

where *facet1*, *facet2*, etc., are constraining facets; and *value1*, *value2*, etc., are values for the constraining facets.

- To derive a data type based on a regular expression pattern, use

```
<xs:simpleType name="name">
   <xs:restriction base="type">
      <xs:pattern value="regex" />
   </xs:restriction>
</xs:simpleType>
```

where *name* is the name of the derived data type, *type* is a preexisting data type on which the derived type is based, and *regex* is a regular expression defining the pattern of characters in the data.

To create the `creditsType` data type:

▶ **1.** Return to the **students.xsd** file in your editor.

▶ **2.** Below the declaration for the gpa element, insert the following code to constrain the credits element to at least 1:

```
<xs:simpleType name="creditsType">
    <xs:restriction base="xs:integer">
        <xs:minInclusive value="1" />
    </xs:restriction>
</xs:simpleType>
```

Be sure to enter the data type as creditsType without a prefix, and *not* as xs:creditsType because the data type is user-defined.

▶ **3.** In the xs:element tag for the credits element, change the value of the type attribute from xs:positiveInteger to **creditsType**. You do *not* include the xs namespace prefix when referencing the data type because creditsType is not part of the XML Schema vocabulary. Figure 13-29 shows the revised code in the schema.

Figure 13-29 The creditsType data type

credits values must follow the rules of the creditsType simple type

restricted data type with a constraining facet that limits values to integers greater than or equal to 1

```
<xs:schema xmlns:xs="http://www.w3.org/2001/XMLSchema">

    <xs:attribute name="stuID" type="xs:ID" />
    <xs:element name="lastName" type="xs:string" />
    <xs:element name="firstName" type="xs:string" />
    <xs:element name="dateOfEnrollment" type="xs:date" />
    <xs:element name="credits" type="creditsType" />
    <xs:element name="comment" type="xs:string" />
    <xs:attribute name="degree" type="xs:string" />

    <xs:element name="gpa">
        <xs:complexType>
            <xs:simpleContent>
                <xs:extension base="xs:decimal">
                    <xs:attribute ref="degree" use="required" />
                </xs:extension>
            </xs:simpleContent>
        </xs:complexType>
    </xs:element>

    <xs:simpleType name="creditsType">
        <xs:restriction base="xs:integer">
            <xs:minInclusive value="1" />
        </xs:restriction>
    </xs:simpleType>
```

▶ **4.** Save your changes to the **students.xsd** file.

Facets can also be used to define lower and upper ranges for data. In Sabrina's data, GPA values range from 0 to 4, with 0 excluded and 4 included as possible values. You'll create a data type for this interval now using the minExclusive and maxInclusive facets. You'll set the value of the minExclusive facet to 0, and set the value of the maxInclusive facet to 4. You'll name the data type gpaType and apply it to the gpa element.

To derive the `gpaType` data type in the *students.xsd* file:

▶ **1.** Below the code for the `creditsType` simple type, insert the following code:

```
<xs:simpleType name="gpaType">
   <xs:restriction base="xs:decimal">
      <xs:minExclusive value="0" />
      <xs:maxInclusive value="4" />
   </xs:restriction>
</xs:simpleType>
```

This code specifies decimal values greater than 0 and less than or equal to 4.

▶ **2.** Within the code that defines the `gpa` element, locate the opening `xs:extension` tag and then change the value of the `base` attribute from `xs:decimal` to `gpaType`. Do *not* include the `xs` namespace prefix when referencing the data type. See Figure 13-30.

Figure 13-30   **The gpaType data type**

gpa values must follow the rules of the gpaType simple type

```
<xs:element name="gpa">
   <xs:complexType>
      <xs:simpleContent>
         <xs:extension base="gpaType">
            <xs:attribute ref="degree" use="required" />
         </xs:extension>
      </xs:simpleContent>
   </xs:complexType>
</xs:element>

<xs:simpleType name="creditsType">
   <xs:restriction base="xs:integer">
      <xs:minInclusive value="1" />
   </xs:restriction>
</xs:simpleType>

<xs:simpleType name="gpaType">
   <xs:restriction base="xs:decimal">
      <xs:minExclusive value="0" />
      <xs:maxInclusive value="4" />
   </xs:restriction>
</xs:simpleType>
```

restricted data type with a constraining facet that limits values to integers greater than 0, and up to and including 4

▶ **3.** Save your changes to the file.

Sabrina wants values of the `degree` attribute to be limited to either MP or WPA. When permitted content belongs to a set of specific values rather than a range, you can create a list of possible values using the `enumeration` element. The following simple type creates the restriction that Sabrina needs:

```
<xs:simpleType name="degreeType">
   <xs:restriction base="xs:string">
      <xs:enumeration value="MP" />
      <xs:enumeration value="WPA" />
   </xs:restriction>
</xs:simpleType>
```

You'll create this enumerated data type now and apply it to the schema.

To create the `degreeType` data type in the *students.xsd* file:

▶ **1.** Below the code that defines the `gpaType` simple type, insert the following code:

```
<xs:simpleType name="degreeType">
    <xs:restriction base="xs:string">
        <xs:enumeration value="MP" />
        <xs:enumeration value="WPA" />
    </xs:restriction>
</xs:simpleType>
```

▶ **2.** Within the `xs:attribute` element for the `degree` attribute, change the value of the `type` attribute from `xs:string` to `degreeType`. Do *not* include the `xs` namespace prefix when referencing the data type. Figure 13-31 highlights the revised code.

Figure 13-31   The degreeType data type

```
<xs:schema xmlns:xs="http://www.w3.org/2001/XMLSchema">

    <xs:attribute name="stuID" type="xs:ID" />
    <xs:element name="lastName" type="xs:string" />
    <xs:element name="firstName" type="xs:string" />
    <xs:element name="dateOfEnrollment" type="xs:date" />
    <xs:element name="credits" type="creditsType" />
    <xs:element name="comment" type="xs:string" />
    <xs:attribute name="degree" type="degreeType" />
    ...

    <xs:simpleType name="gpaType">
        <xs:restriction base="xs:decimal">
            <xs:minExclusive value="0" />
            <xs:maxInclusive value="4" />
        </xs:restriction>
    </xs:simpleType>

    <xs:simpleType name="degreeType">
        <xs:restriction base="xs:string">
            <xs:enumeration value="MP" />
            <xs:enumeration value="WPA" />
        </xs:restriction>
    </xs:simpleType>
```

degree values must follow the rules of the degreeType simple type

the degreeType data type limits values to "MP" and "WPA"

▶ **3.** Save your changes to the **students.xsd** file.

Before editing your schema further, you'll validate revisions to the schema and then revalidate it after introducing errors in the *students.xml* file and verifying that a parser flags the errors in validation.

To validate revisions to the schema, introduce errors into the *students.xml* file, and then test the validation rules for the schema file:

▶ **1.** Return to the **students.xml** file in Exchanger XML editor, and then, if necessary, click the **Viewer** button.

▶ **2.** Validate your document and confirm that it validates successfully.

Trouble? If any validation errors are listed on the Errors tab, return to the *students.xsd* document and be sure your code matches the code shown in Figures 13-29 through 13-31 exactly. Make changes as needed, save your document, and then return to *students.xml* and revalidate the document until it passes.

▶ **3.** Click the **Editor** button in the upper-right corner.

▶ **4.** Locate the student element for Cynthia Berstein, and then in the gpa element, change the value of the degree attribute to **MPA**. The data for the first student element in the document should match Figure 13-32.

Figure 13-32	Invalid degree value

```
<students xmlns:xsi="http://www.w3.org/2001/XMLSchema-instance"
          xsi:noNamespaceSchemaLocation="students.xsd">
   <student stuID="SI890-041-02">
      <lastName>Berstein</lastName>
      <firstName>Cynthia</firstName>
      <dateOfEnrollment>2016-05-22</dateOfEnrollment>
      <credits>12</credits>
      <gpa degree="MPA">3.81</gpa>
   </student>
```

content changed to invalid value to introduce an error

▶ **5.** Save your changes to the file.

▶ **6.** On the Menu bar, click **XML**, click **Validate**, and then review the error descriptions displayed on the Errors tab. The document is rejected and the parser reports errors because the value of the attribute degree for the element gpa does not match the schema definitions.

▶ **7.** In the gpa element for the first record, change the value of the degree attribute back to **MP**, and then save your changes to the file.

▶ **8.** Revalidate the document and confirm that it passes.

Deriving Data Types Using Regular Expressions

Sabrina has one final restriction to place on data values stored in her student records: Each student's student ID must be entered in the form SI###-###-##, where # is a digit from 0 to 9.

This rule involves the representation of the values, so you need to create a restriction based on the lexical space. One way of doing this is through a regular expression.

Introducing Regular Expressions

A regular expression is a text string that defines a character pattern. Regular expressions can be created to define patterns for many types of data, including phone numbers, postal address codes, and e-mail addresses—and, in the case of Sabrina's document, student IDs. To apply a regular expression in a data type, you create the simple type

```
<xs:simpleType name="name">
   <xs:restriction base="type">
      <xs:pattern value="regex" />
   </xs:restriction>
</xs:simpleType>
```

where *regex* is a regular expression pattern.

The most basic pattern specifies the characters that must appear in valid data. For instance, the following regular expression requires that the value of the data type be the text string *ABC*:

```
<xs:pattern value="ABC" />
```

Any other combination of letters, including the use of lowercase letters, would be invalid.

Instead of a pattern involving specific characters, though, you usually want a more general pattern involving character types, which are representations of different kinds of characters. The general form of a character type is

```
\char
```

where *char* represents a specific character type. Character types can include digits, word characters (any uppercase or lowercase letter, any digit, or the underscore character (_)), boundaries around words, and white space characters. Figure 13-33 describes the code for representing each of these character types.

| Figure 13-33 | Regular expression character types |

Character Type	Description
\d	A digit from 0 to 9
\D	A non-digit character
\w	A word character (an upper- or lowercase letter, a digit, or an underscore (_))
\W	A non-word character
\b	A boundary around a word (a text string of word characters)
\B	The absence of a boundary around a word
\s	A white space character (a blank space, tab, new line, carriage return, or form feed)
\S	A non-white space character
.	Any character

TIP

In a regular expression, the opposite of a character type is indicated by a capital letter. So while \d represents a single digit, \D represents any character that is not a digit.

For example, the character type for a single digit is \d. To create a regular expression representing three digits, you would apply the following pattern:

```
<xs:pattern value="\d\d\d" />
```

Any text string that contains three digits would match this pattern. Thus, the text strings 012 and 921 would both match this pattern, but 1,020 and 54 would not.

For more general patterns, characters can also be grouped into lists called **character sets** that specify exactly what characters or ranges of characters are allowed in the pattern.

The syntax of a character set is

`[chars]`

where *chars* is the set of characters in the character set. For example, the pattern

`<xs:pattern value="[dog]" />`

matches any of the characters d, o, or g. Because characters can be sorted alphabetically or numerically, a character set can also be created for a range of characters using the general syntax

`[char1-charN]`

where *char1* is the first character in the range and *charN* is the last character in the range. To create a range of lowercase letters, you would use the following pattern:

`<xs:pattern value="[a-z]" />`

Any lowercase letter would be matched by this pattern. You can also match numeric ranges. The following pattern matches any digit from 1 to 5:

`<xs:pattern value="[1-5]" />`

Figure 13-34 lists many of the common character sets used in regular expressions.

Figure 13-34   **Common regular expression character sets**

Character Set	Description
`[chars]`	Match any character in the `chars` list
`[^chars]`	Do not match any character in `chars`
`[char1-charN]`	Match any character in the range `char1` through `charN`
`[^char1-charN]`	Do not match any character in the range `char1` through `charN`
`[a-z]`	Match any lowercase letter
`[A-Z]`	Match any uppercase letter
`[a-zA-Z]`	Match any letter
`[0-9]`	Match any digit from 0 to 9
`[0-9a-zA-Z]`	Match any digit or letter

The regular expressions you've looked at so far have involved individual characters. To specify the number of occurrences for a particular character or group of characters, a **quantifier** can be appended to a character type or set. Figure 13-35 lists the different quantifiers used in regular expressions. Some of these quantifiers should be familiar from your work with DTDs.

Figure 13-35   **Regular expression quantifiers**

Quantifier	Description
`*`	Repeat 0 or more times
`?`	Repeat 0 times or 1 time
`+`	Repeat 1 or more times
`{n}`	Repeat exactly *n* times
`{n,}`	Repeat at least *n* times
`{n,m}`	Repeat at least *n* times but no more than *m* times

As you saw earlier, to specify a pattern of three consecutive digits, you can use the following regular expression:

```
\d\d\d
```

Alternatively, you can employ the quantifier {3} using the pattern

```
<xs:pattern value="\d{3}" />
```

which also defines a pattern of three digits. Likewise, to validate a string of uppercase characters of any length, you can use the * quantifier, as follows:

```
<xs:pattern value="[A-Z]*" />
```

Similarly, the following pattern uses the quantifier {0,10} to allow for a text string of uppercase letters from 0 to 10 characters long:

```
<xs:pattern value="[A-Z]{0,10}" />
```

Applying a Regular Expression

You have only scratched the surface of what regular expressions can do. The topic of regular expressions could fill an entire tutorial by itself. However, you have covered enough to be able to implement Sabrina's request that all student ID strings be in the format SI###-###-##, where # is a digit from 0 to 9. The pattern for this expression is

```
<xs:pattern value="SI\d{3}-\d{3}-\d{2}" />
```

where the character type \d represents a single digit, and the quantifiers {3} and {2} indicate that the digits must be in groups of three and two, respectively. Note that the characters SI at the start of the pattern must be matched literally, including capitalization; thus, a student ID value of Si448-996-22 would not match the pattern because the i isn't capitalized. You'll create a data type named siType now based on this pattern.

To derive the siType data type based on a regular expression:

▶ **1.** Return to the **students.xsd** file in your editor, and then directly below the declaration for the degree attribute, insert the following code:

```
<xs:simpleType name="siType">
   <xs:restriction base="xs:ID">
      <xs:pattern value="SI\d{3}-\d{3}-\d{2}" />
   </xs:restriction>
</xs:simpleType>
```

The base data type is xs:ID, indicating that this custom data type will be derived from unique ID values in the document.

▶ **2.** Within the declaration of the stuID attribute, change the value of the type attribute from xs:ID to **siType**. Do *not* include the xs namespace prefix when referencing the data type.

Figure 13-36 shows the revised code for the schema file.

Figure 13-36 | **Declaring and applying the siType data type**

stuID values must follow the rules of the siType simple type

```
<xs:schema xmlns:xs="http://www.w3.org/2001/XMLSchema">

    <xs:attribute name="stuID" type="siType" />
    <xs:element name="lastName" type="xs:string" />
    <xs:element name="firstName" type="xs:string" />
    <xs:element name="dateOfEnrollment" type="xs:date" />
    <xs:element name="credits" type="creditsType" />
    <xs:element name="comment" type="xs:string" />
    <xs:attribute name="degree" type="degreeType" />

    <xs:simpleType name="siType">
      <xs:restriction base="xs:ID">
        <xs:pattern value="SI\d{3}-\d{3}-\d{2}" />
      </xs:restriction>
    </xs:simpleType>
</xs:simpleType>
```

values must be unique IDs of the form SI###-###-##, where # is a digit

▶ **3.** Save your changes to the **students.xsd** file.

Next, you'll validate Sabrina's document to ensure that all the student IDs match the pattern you defined.

To validate the student IDs:

▶ **1.** Return to the **students.xml** file in your XML editor, and then verify that you are in Editor view.

▶ **2.** Within the record for Cynthia Berstein, change the capital letters SI in the `stuID` value to the lowercase letters **si** so it reads si890-041-02. This value doesn't meet the validation criteria for the `siType` data type because the first two letters are lowercase. See Figure 13-37.

Figure 13-37 | **Invalid stuID value**

```
<students xmlns:xsi="http://www.w3.org/2001/XMLSchema-instance"
          xsi:noNamespaceSchemaLocation="students.xsd">
   <student stuID="si890-041-02">
      <lastName>Berstein</lastName>
      <firstName>Cynthia</firstName>
      <dateOfEnrollment>2016-05-22</dateOfEnrollment>
      <credits>12</credits>
      <gpa degree="MP">3.81</gpa>
   </student>
```

first two letters of value changed to lowercase

▶ **3.** Save your changes to the file.

▶ **4.** On the Menu bar, click **XML**, click **Validate**, and then examine the contents of the Errors tab. The document is rejected with errors found because the value of the attribute `stuID` for the element `student` no longer matches the schema definitions.

▶ **5.** Change the `stuID` value for Cynthia Berstein back to **SI890-041-02**, and then save your changes to the file.

▶ **6.** Revalidate the document and confirm that it passes the validation test.

INSIGHT

Deriving Data Types and Inheritance

You can use XML Schema to create a library of new data types, and you can use each new data type you create as the base for creating yet another type. For example, you could start with a data type for integer values, use that to define a new data type for positive integers, use that to define a data type for positive integers between 1 and 100, and so forth. Note that unless you are creating a list or a union, every new type represents a restriction of one or more facets in a preexisting type.

In some cases, you might want to fix a facet so that any new data types based upon it cannot modify it. For example, if Sabrina defined the `credits` data type to have a maximum value of 130, she might want to prevent any data types based on `credits` from being able to change that maximum value. She could do so by applying the `fixed` attribute to the `maxInclusive` facet as follows:

```
<xs:maxInclusive value="130" fixed="true" />
```

As a result of this attribute, any data type based on the `credits` type would have its maximum value set at 130. Because fixing a facet makes a data type library less flexible, it should be used only in situations where changing the facet value would dramatically alter the original meaning of the data type.

You can also use XML Schema to prevent any new data types from being created from an existing data type. This is done using the `final` attribute

```
<xs:simpleType name="name" final="derivation">
    . . .
</xs:simpleType>
```

where *name* is the name of the new data type and *derivation* indicates which methods of creating new data types are prohibited (`list`, `union`, `restriction`, or `all`). For example, the following code defines the `credits` data type and prohibits it from being used in deriving a new data type through a union or a list:

```
<xs:simpleType name="credits" final="union list">
    . . .
</xs:simpleType>
```

When the `final` attribute is omitted or set to an empty text string, XML Schema allows for any kind of derivations of the original type.

Sabrina is pleased with the work you have done on creating a schema for the document describing the students enrolled in the information technology programs at Austin Technical College.

Session 13.2 Quick Check

1. Enter a definition for an element named `Height` containing only decimal data.
2. Enter the attribute definition for the `productIDs` attribute containing a list of ID references.
3. Define a data type named `applicationDates` that contains a list of dates.
4. Define a data type named `Status` that contains either a decimal or a text string.
5. Define a data type named `Party` that is limited to one of the following—Democrat, Republican, or Independent.
6. Define a data type named `Percentage` that is limited to decimal values falling between 0 and 1 (inclusive).
7. Define a data type named `SocSecurity` that contains a text string matching the pattern `###-##-####`, where # is a digit from 0 to 9.

Note: *In the Review Assignments and Case Problems, some XML documents include intentional errors. Part of your job is to find and correct those errors using validation reports from the schemas you create.*

Practice the skills you learned in the tutorial using the same case scenario.

PRACTICE

Review Assignments

Data Files needed for the Review Assignments: degreestxt.xml, degreestxt.xsd

Each department at Austin Technical College must maintain information on the associate's degrees it offers; each associate's degree must be approved by a college authority. Sabrina has created an XML vocabulary containing information about the different degrees offered by the Information Technology department. She wants you to create a schema to validate the degree information. Figure 13-38 shows the structures of the degrees vocabulary that you'll create.

Figure 13-38   The degrees vocabulary structure

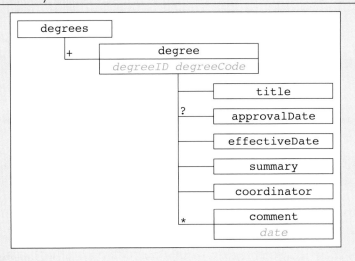

A description of the elements and attributes used in the degrees vocabulary is shown in Figure 13-39.

Figure 13-39   The degrees vocabulary

Element or Attribute	Description
degrees	The root element
degree	The collection of information about a degree
degreeID	The ID number of the degree with the format IT##-###-###, where # is a digit
degreeCode	The in-house code for the degree (MP, SP, or WPA)
title	The title of the degree
approvalDate	The date the degree was approved by the college authority
effectiveDate	The date the degree curriculum becomes effective
summary	The descriptive summary of the degree
coordinator	The currently assigned degree coordinator
comment	A comment regarding the degree
date	The date of the comment

Sabrina already created a document containing a list of degrees currently offered by the Information Technology department. She wants the document validated based on a schema you create.

Complete the following:

1. Using your XML editor, open the **degreestxt.xml** and **degreestxt.xsd** files from the tutorial.13\review folder, enter *your name* and *today's date* in the comment section of each file, and then save the files as **degrees.xml** and **degrees.xsd**, respectively.

2. In the **degrees.xsd** file, add the root schema element to the document and declare the XML Schema namespace using the **xs** prefix, and then save your work.

3. In the **degrees.xml** file, attach the schema file **degrees.xsd** to this instance document, indicating that the schema and instance document do not belong to any namespace, and then save your work.

4. In the **degrees.xsd** file, create the following named simple types:
   a. **idType**, based on the **ID** data type and restricted to the regular expression pattern `IT\d{2}-\d{3}-\d{3}`
   b. **codeType**, based on the **string** data type and restricted to the following values—MP, SP, WPA

5. Declare the **degrees** element containing the child element **degree**.

6. Declare the **degree** element containing the following sequence of nested child elements—**title**, **approvalDate**, **effectiveDate**, **summary**, **coordinator**, and **comment**. Set the following properties for the nested elements:
   a. All of the child elements should contain string data except the **approvalDate** and **effectiveDate** elements, which contain dates. The **degree** element should also support two required attributes—**degreeID** and **degreeCode**. The **degreeID** attribute contains **idType** data, while the **degreeCode** attribute contains **codeType** data.
   b. The **degree** element must occur at least once, but its upper limit is unbounded. The **approvalDate** element is optional. The **comment** element is optional, and it may occur multiple times. All other elements are assumed to occur only once.
   c. Each **comment** element requires a **date** attribute of the **date** data type.

7. Save your changes to the **degrees.xsd** file, and then validate the schema document. Correct any errors you find.

8. Validate the **degrees.xml** file against the schema document you created. Correct any validation errors you discover in the instance document.

9. Submit your completed and validated project to your instructor, in either printed or electronic form, as requested.

Apply the skills you learned in this tutorial to validate a document containing photo data.

APPLY

Case Problem 1

Data Files needed for this Case Problem: catalogtxt.xml, catalogtxt.xsd

The Our Lady of Bergen Historical Society   Sharon Strattan is an archivist at the Our Lady of Bergen Historical Society in Bergenfield, New Jersey. The historical society is exploring how to transfer its listings to XML format, and Sharon has begun by creating a sample document of the society's extensive collection of photos. As part of this process, she's asked for your help in developing the schema that will be used to validate the XML documents. She has created a sample document to work on. Eventually, your work will be used in a much larger system. The structure of the sample document is shown in Figure 13-40.

Figure 13-40   **The catalog vocabulary structure**

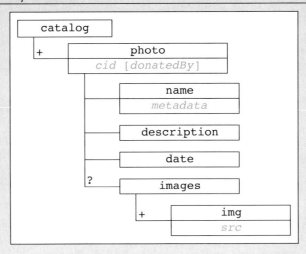

Figure 13-41 describes the elements and attributes in this sample document as well as the rules that govern the data that can be entered into a valid document.

Figure 13-41   **The catalog vocabulary**

Element or Attribute	Description
catalog	The root element
photo	The collection of information about a photo
cid	The ID number of the catalog with the format c####, where # is a digit
donatedBy	The name of the donor
name	The name of the photo
metadata	The metadata for the photo
description	The description of the photo
date	The approximate date of the photo
images	The collection of img elements
img	The element that references the image file
src	The source file containing the image; must end with .jpg

Your job will be to express this document structure and set of rules in terms of the XML Schema language, and then to validate Sharon's document based on the schema you create.

Complete the following:

1. Using your XML editor, open the **catalogtxt.xml** and **catalogtxt.xsd** files from the tutorial.13\case1 folder, enter *your name* and *today's date* in the comment section of each file, and then save the files as **catalog.xml** and **catalog.xsd**, respectively.

2. Go to the **catalog.xsd** file in your text editor. Add the root schema element to the document and declare the XML Schema namespace using the xs prefix.

3. Attach the schema file **catalog.xsd** to the instance document, indicating that the schema and instance document do not belong to any namespace.

4. Create the following named simple types:

   a. **cidType**, based on the ID data type and restricted to the regular expression pattern c\d{4}

   b. **srcType**, based on the string data type and restricted to the regular expression pattern [a-zA-Z0-9]+.jpg

5. Declare the **catalog** element containing the child element photo. The photo element must occur at least once, but its upper limit is unbounded.

6. Declare the **photo** element containing the following sequence of nested child elements—name, description, date, and images. Set the following properties for the nested elements:

   a. All of the child elements should contain string data. The name element should also support the metadata attribute.

   b. The cid attribute is required. The donatedBy attribute is optional.

7. Declare the **img** element. It has no content and contains a required attribute, src.

8. Declare the following attributes and elements:

   a. The attribute metadata must have the string data type.

   b. The attribute cid must have the cidType data type.

   c. The attribute src must have the srcType data type.

   d. The attribute donatedBy must have the string data type.

   e. The element description must have the string data type.

   f. The element date must have the string data type.

9. Save your changes to the **catalog.xsd** file, and then validate the schema. Continue to correct any validation errors you discover until the schema validates.

10. Validate the **catalog.xml** file against the schema. Continue to correct any validation errors you discover until the instance document validates.

11. Submit your completed and validated project to your instructor, in either printed or electronic form, as requested.

Apply the skills you learned in this tutorial to validate a document of pipe band data.

APPLY

Case Problem 2

Data Files needed for this Case Problem: mdpbatxt.xml, mdpbatxt.xsd

Midwest Developmental Pipe Band Association   Jacob St. John works as a coordinator for the Midwest Developmental Pipe Band Association (MDPBA) and is responsible for coordinating competitions for the MDPBA's many developmental pipe bands in the Midwest. Part of Jacob's job is to maintain a document that lists competition entries for each pipe band. As part of this process, he's asked for your help with developing the schema that will be used to validate the XML documents. He has created a sample document to work on. The structure of the sample document is shown in Figure 13-42.

Figure 13-42   **The bands vocabulary structure**

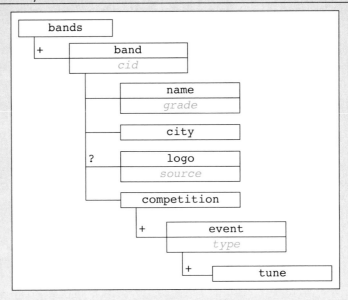

Figure 13-43 describes the elements and attributes in this sample document as well as the rules that govern the data that can be entered into a valid document.

Figure 13-43   **The bands vocabulary**

Element or Attribute	Description
bands	The root element
band	The collection of information about a band
cid	The ID number of the band with the format c####, where # is a digit
name	The name of the band
grade	The grade level at which the band is competing (juvenile, novice, 1, 2, 3, or 4)
city	The home city of the band
logo	The logo image
source	The source file containing the logo image
competition	The collection of information about a competition
event	The collection of information about an event
type	The type of event entered (MSR or Medley)
tune	The name of a tune

Your job will be to express this document structure and set of rules in terms of the XML Schema language, and then to validate Jacob's document based on the schema you create.

Complete the following:

1. Using your XML editor, open the **mdpbatxt.xml** and **mdpbatxt.xsd** files from the tutorial.13\case2 folder, enter *your name* and *today's date* in the comment section of each file, and then save the files as **mdpba.xml** and **mdpba.xsd**, respectively.

2. Go to the **mdpba.xsd** file in your text editor. Add the root schema element to the document and declare the XML Schema namespace using the **xs** prefix.

3. Attach the schema file **mdpba.xsd** to the instance document, indicating that the schema and instance document do not belong to any namespace.

4. Create the following named simple types:

   a. **gradeType**, based on the `string` data type and limited to the enumerated values `novice`, `juvenile`, `1`, `2`, `3`, and `4`

   b. **eType**, based on the `string` data type and limited to the enumerated values `MSR` and `Medley`

   c. **cidType**, based on the `ID` data type and restricted to the regular expression pattern `c\d{4}`

   d. **srcType**, based on the `string` data type and restricted to the regular expression pattern `[a-zA-Z0-9]+.png`

5. Declare the **bands** element containing the child element `band`. The `band` element must occur at least once, but its upper limit is unbounded.

6. Declare the **band** element containing the following sequence of nested child elements—`name`, `city`, `logo`, and `competition`. Set the following properties for the nested elements:

   a. All of the child elements should contain string data. The `name` element should also support the required `grade` attribute.

   b. The `logo` element is optional.

   c. The `band` element must contain the `cid` attribute.

7. Declare the **logo** element, which has no content and contains the required attribute `source`.

8. Declare the **competition** element containing the child element `event`. The `event` element must occur at least once, but its upper limit is unbounded.

9. Declare the **event** element containing the child element `tune`. The `tune` element must occur at least once, but its upper limit is unbounded. The `event` element is required.

10. Declare the following attributes and elements:

    a. The attribute `grade`, which uses the `gradeType` data type

    b. The attribute `type`, which uses the `eType` data type

    c. The attribute `cid`, which uses the `cidType` data type

    d. The attribute `source`, which uses the `srcType` data type

    e. The element `city`, which uses the `string` data type

    f. The element `tune`, which uses the `string` data type

11. Save your changes to the **mdpba.xsd** file, and then validate the schema. Continue to correct any validation errors you discover until the schema validates.

12. Validate the **mdpba.xml** file against the schema. Continue to correct any validation errors you discover until the instance document validates.

13. Submit your completed and validated project to your instructor, in either printed or electronic form, as requested.

Test your knowledge by validating a donation roster.

CREATE

Case Problem 3

Data Files needed for this Case Problem: rostertxt.xml, rostertxt.xsd

The Save Exotic Animals Trust Sienna Woo is the donor coordinator for the Save Exotic Animals Trust (SEA Trust), a charitable organization located in central Florida. One of her responsibilities is to maintain a membership list of people in the community who have donated to SEA Trust. A donor can belong to one of four categories—friendship, patron, sponsor, or founder. A donor's phone number can be classified in one of three categories—home, cell, or work. Each donor's preferred method of contact can be one of three methods—Phone, Personal, or Mail. Sienna has asked for your help with developing a schema to validate the sample XML document that she created. The structure of the sample document is shown in Figure 13-44.

Figure 13-44 The roster vocabulary structure

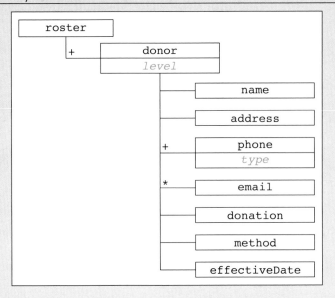

Your job will be to express this document structure in terms of the XML Schema language, and then to validate Sienna's document against the schema you create.

Complete the following:

1. Using your text editor, open the **rostertxt.xml** and **rostertxt.xsd** files from the tutorial.13\case3 folder, enter *your name* and *today's date* in the comment section of each file, and then save the files as **roster.xml** and **roster.xsd**, respectively.

2. Go to the **roster.xsd** file in your text editor. Add the root schema element to the document and declare the XML Schema namespace using the **xs** prefix.

3. Attach the schema file **roster.xsd** to the instance document, indicating that the schema and instance document do not belong to any namespace.

4. Create the following named simple types:
   a. **pType**, based on the **string** data type and limited to the enumerated values home, cell, and work
   b. **methodType**, based on the **string** data type and limited to the enumerated values Phone, Personal, and Mail
   c. **levelType**, based on the **string** data type and limited to the enumerated values founder, sponsor, patron, and friendship

   d. **phoneType**, based on the **string** data type consisting of 14 characters—the first character should be a left opening parenthesis, followed by three digits from 0 to 9, followed by a right closing parenthesis, followed by a space, followed by three digits from 0 to 9, followed by a hyphen, and then four digits from 0 to 9 (*Hint*: Opening and closing parentheses are special characters in creating regular expressions. To include one of these characters in your expression, enter a backslash before it.)

5. Declare the **roster** element containing the child element listed in the vocabulary structure. The child element must occur at least once but its upper limit is unbounded.
   a. Declare the **donor** element containing the sequence of nested child elements shown in the vocabulary structure. Set properties for the minimum and/or maximum occurrences of the donor, phone, and email elements as illustrated in the vocabulary structure. Specify that the donor element must contain the required **level** attribute.
   b. Declare the **phone** element, containing the required attribute **type**.

6. Declare the following attributes and elements:
   a. The attribute `type`, which uses the `pType` data type
   b. The attribute `level`, which uses the `levelType` data type
   c. The element `name`, which uses the `string` data type
   d. The element `address`, which uses the `string` data type
   e. The element `email`, which uses the `string` data type
   f. The element `donation`, which uses the `decimal` data type
   g. The element `effectiveDate`, which uses the `date` data type
   h. The element `method`, which uses the `methodType` data type

7. Save your changes to the **roster.xsd** file, and then validate the schema. Continue to correct any validation errors you discover until the schema validates.

8. Validate the **roster.xml** file against the schema. In response to any validation errors, correct relevant values in the *roster.xml* document to match the schema rules. Continue to correct any validation errors you discover until the instance document validates.

9. Submit your completed and validated project to your instructor, in either printed or electronic form, as requested.

Use the skills you learned in this tutorial to validate an online store's map collection.

CHALLENGE

Case Problem 4

Data Files needed for this Case Problem: orderstxt.xml, orderstxt.xsd

Map Finds For You   Benjamin Mapps is working on an XML document to hold data regarding customers who have placed orders with his store, Map Finds For You. Figure 13-45 shows the structure of the vocabulary employed by the document.

Figure 13-45   **The customers vocabulary structure**

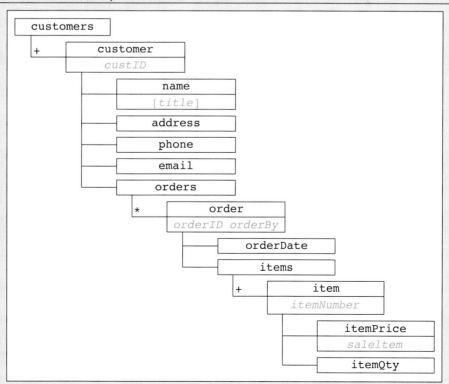

A description of the elements and attributes used for customer data is shown in Figure 13-46.

Figure 13-46   The customers vocabulary

Element or Attribute	Description
customers	The root element
customer	The collection of information about a customer
custID	The ID number of the customer with the format cust###, where # is a digit
name	The name of the customer
title	The title for the customer (Mr., Ms., or Mrs.)
address	The address for the customer
phone	The phone number for the customer
email	The email address for the customer
orders	The collection of information on orders
order	The collection of information on an individual order
orderID	The ID number of the order with the format or###, where # is a digit
orderBy	The ID number of the customer who placed the order
orderDate	The date the order was placed
items	The collection of information on items
item	The collection of information on a specific item
itemNumber	The item number of the item ordered
itemPrice	The price paid for the item
saleItem	Whether the itemPrice was a sale price (Y or N)
itemQty	The quantity of the item ordered

Benjamin needs your help with creating a schema that will validate the data he has already entered and will enter in the future.

Complete the following:

1. Using your text editor, open the **orderstxt.xml** and **orderstxt.xsd** files from the tutorial.13\case4 folder, enter *your name* and *today's date* in the comment section of each file, and then save the files as **orders.xml** and **orders.xsd**, respectively.

2. Go to the **orders.xsd** file in your text editor and insert the root schema element. Declare the XML Schema namespace with **xs** as the namespace prefix.

⊕ EXPLORE 3. Create the following simple data types:

   a. **idType**, based on the ID data type and consisting of the characters cust followed by three digits from 0 to 9

   b. **cidType**, based on the ID data type and consisting of the characters "or" followed by four digits from 0 to 9

   c. **titleType**, based on the string data type and limited to the enumerated values Mr., Ms., and Mrs.

⊕ EXPLORE d. **phoneType**, based on the string data type consisting of a left parenthesis followed by three digits from 0 to 9, followed by a right parenthesis, followed by a space, followed by three digits from 0 to 9, followed by a hyphen, and then four more digits 0 to 9 (*Hint*: Opening and closing parentheses are special characters in creating regular expressions. To include one of these characters in your expression, enter a backslash before it.)

e. **qtyType**, based on the `integer` data type and allowing only numbers with a value of 1 or more

f. **saleType**, based on the `string` data type and limited to the values `Y` and `N`

4. Declare the **customers** complex element type, and then nest the `customer` element within it. The `customer` element must occur at least once, but its upper limit is unbounded.

EXPLORE

5. Set the data types of the elements and attributes of the `customer` element as follows:

   a. The child elements must occur in the sequence `name`, `address`, `phone`, `email`, `orders`. The `name`, `address`, and `email` elements use the `string` data type. The `phone` element uses the `phoneType` data type. The `email` element can occur once or not at all.

   b. The **name** element is a complex type element and uses a data type of `string`. The `name` attribute also contains an optional **title** attribute.

   c. The **orders** element is a complex type element and contains at least one **order** element.

   d. Declare an attribute named **custID**. The `custID` attribute is required and contains `idType` data.

EXPLORE

6. Set the data types of the elements and attributes of the `order` element as follows:

   a. The child elements must occur in the sequence `orderDate`, `items`. The `orderDate` element uses the `date` data type.

   b. The `order` element also contains required `orderID` and `orderBy` attributes containing `cidType` and `IDREF` data types, respectively.

   c. The `items` element is a complex type element and contains at least one `item` element.

EXPLORE

7. Set the data types of the elements and attributes of the `item` element as follows:

   a. The child elements must occur in the sequence `itemPrice`, `itemQty`. The `itemPrice` and `itemQty` elements use the `decimal` and `qtyType` data types, respectively.

   b. The `item` element also contains a required `itemNumber` attribute that uses the `string` data type.

   c. The `itemPrice` element is a complex type element and contains an attribute, `saleItem`, which uses the `saleType` data type and has a default value of `N`.

8. Save your changes to the **orders.xsd** file, and then validate the schema. Continue to correct any validation errors you discover until the schema validates.

9. Validate the **orders.xml** file against the schema. In response to any validation errors, correct relevant values in the **orders.xml** document to match the schema rules. Continue to correct any validation errors you discover until the instance document validates.

10. Submit your completed and validated project to your instructor, in either printed or electronic form, as requested.

ENDING DATA FILES

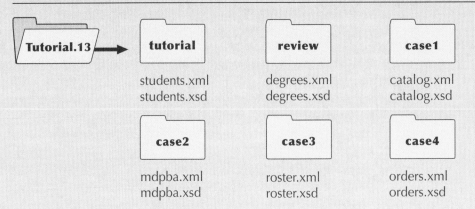

Tutorial.13 → tutorial
students.xml
students.xsd

review
degrees.xml
degrees.xsd

case1
catalog.xml
catalog.xsd

case2
mdpba.xml
mdpba.xsd

case3
roster.xml
roster.xsd

case4
orders.xml
orders.xsd

TUTORIAL 14

OBJECTIVES

Session 14.1
- Explore the Flat Catalog schema design
- Explore the Russian Doll schema design
- Explore the Venetian Blind schema design

Session 14.2
- Attach a schema to a namespace
- Apply a namespace to an instance document
- Import one schema file into another
- Reference objects from other schemas

Session 14.3
- Declare a default namespace in a style sheet
- Specify qualified elements by default in a schema
- Integrate a schema and a style sheet with an instance document

Working with Advanced Schemas

Creating Advanced Schemas for Higher Ed Test Prep

Case | *Higher Ed Test Prep*

Gabby Phelps is an exam study coordinator at Higher Ed Test Prep, an Internet-based company that prepares students for academic exams such as the PSAT, ACT, SAT, and GRE. Gabby wants to use XML to create structured documents containing information about the different exams that she oversees and about the students who are studying for those exams.

Accuracy is important for Higher Ed, so Gabby is using a schema to make sure that the data she enters is error free. Although she has already created a basic schema document, she would like to explore some different schema designs. Gabby also needs to create compound documents from the various XML vocabularies she's created.

STARTING DATA FILES

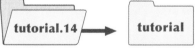

tutorial.14 → **tutorial**
- coursetxt.css
- coursetxt.xsd
- psattxt.xml
- studentsfctxt.xsd
- studentsrdtxt.xsd
- studentstxt.css
- studentstxt.xml
- studentsvbtxt.xsd

review
- coursetxt.css
- coursetxt.xsd
- psattxt.xml
- sessionstxt.css
- sessionstxt.xml
- sessionstxt.xsd

case1
- sitemapPS.xml
- sitemapVS.xml
- sitemapWFS.xml
- sitestxt.xml
- sitestxt.xsd

case2
- menutxt.css
- menutxt.xml
- recipetxt.css
- recipetxt.xml

case3
- atclectxt.xml
- ituneselem.txt

case4
- carstxt.css
- carstxt.xml
- teamstxt.css
- teamstxt.xml

SESSION 14.1 VISUAL OVERVIEW

In a **Flat Catalog design**—sometimes referred to as a **Salami Slice design**—all element and attribute definitions have global scope.

A **Russian Doll design** has only one global element with everything else nested inside of it, much like Russian dolls nest one inside another.

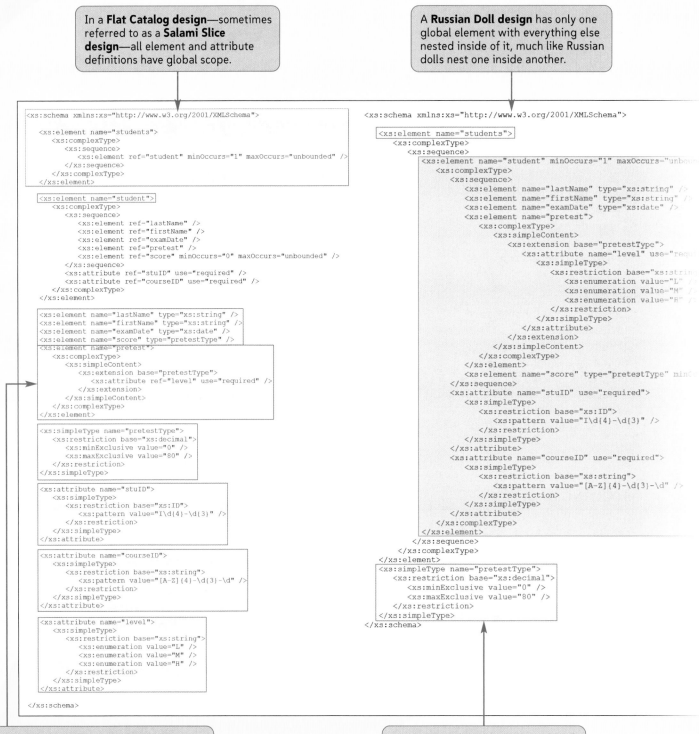

```
<xs:schema xmlns:xs="http://www.w3.org/2001/XMLSchema">

    <xs:element name="students">
        <xs:complexType>
            <xs:sequence>
                <xs:element ref="student" minOccurs="1" maxOccurs="unbounded" />
            </xs:sequence>
        </xs:complexType>
    </xs:element>

    <xs:element name="student">
        <xs:complexType>
            <xs:sequence>
                <xs:element ref="lastName" />
                <xs:element ref="firstName" />
                <xs:element ref="examDate" />
                <xs:element ref="pretest" />
                <xs:element ref="score" minOccurs="0" maxOccurs="unbounded" />
            </xs:sequence>
            <xs:attribute ref="stuID" use="required" />
            <xs:attribute ref="courseID" use="required" />
        </xs:complexType>
    </xs:element>

    <xs:element name="lastName" type="xs:string" />
    <xs:element name="firstName" type="xs:string" />
    <xs:element name="examDate" type="xs:date" />
    <xs:element name="score" type="pretestType" />
    <xs:element name="pretest">
        <xs:complexType>
            <xs:simpleContent>
                <xs:extension base="pretestType">
                    <xs:attribute ref="level" use="required" />
                </xs:extension>
            </xs:simpleContent>
        </xs:complexType>
    </xs:element>

    <xs:simpleType name="pretestType">
        <xs:restriction base="xs:decimal">
            <xs:minExclusive value="0" />
            <xs:maxExclusive value="80" />
        </xs:restriction>
    </xs:simpleType>

    <xs:attribute name="stuID">
        <xs:simpleType>
            <xs:restriction base="xs:ID">
                <xs:pattern value="I\d{4}-\d{3}" />
            </xs:restriction>
        </xs:simpleType>
    </xs:attribute>

    <xs:attribute name="courseID">
        <xs:simpleType>
            <xs:restriction base="xs:string">
                <xs:pattern value="[A-Z]{4}-\d{3}-\d" />
            </xs:restriction>
        </xs:simpleType>
    </xs:attribute>

    <xs:attribute name="level">
        <xs:simpleType>
            <xs:restriction base="xs:string">
                <xs:enumeration value="L" />
                <xs:enumeration value="M" />
                <xs:enumeration value="H" />
            </xs:restriction>
        </xs:simpleType>
    </xs:attribute>

</xs:schema>
```

```
<xs:schema xmlns:xs="http://www.w3.org/2001/XMLSchema">

    <xs:element name="students">
        <xs:complexType>
            <xs:sequence>
                <xs:element name="student" minOccurs="1" maxOccurs="unbou
                    <xs:complexType>
                        <xs:sequence>
                            <xs:element name="lastName" type="xs:string" /
                            <xs:element name="firstName" type="xs:string" /
                            <xs:element name="examDate" type="xs:date" />
                            <xs:element name="pretest">
                                <xs:complexType>
                                    <xs:simpleContent>
                                        <xs:extension base="pretestType">
                                            <xs:attribute name="level" use="requ
                                                <xs:simpleType>
                                                    <xs:restriction base="xs:strin
                                                        <xs:enumeration value="L" /
                                                        <xs:enumeration value="M" /
                                                        <xs:enumeration value="H" /
                                                    </xs:restriction>
                                                </xs:simpleType>
                                            </xs:attribute>
                                        </xs:extension>
                                    </xs:simpleContent>
                                </xs:complexType>
                            </xs:element>
                            <xs:element name="score" type="pretestType" min
                        </xs:sequence>
                        <xs:attribute name="stuID" use="required">
                            <xs:simpleType>
                                <xs:restriction base="xs:ID">
                                    <xs:pattern value="I\d{4}-\d{3}" />
                                </xs:restriction>
                            </xs:simpleType>
                        </xs:attribute>
                        <xs:attribute name="courseID" use="required">
                            <xs:simpleType>
                                <xs:restriction base="xs:string">
                                    <xs:pattern value="[A-Z]{4}-\d{3}-\d" />
                                </xs:restriction>
                            </xs:simpleType>
                        </xs:attribute>
                    </xs:complexType>
                </xs:element>
            </xs:sequence>
        </xs:complexType>
    </xs:element>
    <xs:simpleType name="pretestType">
        <xs:restriction base="xs:decimal">
            <xs:minExclusive value="0" />
            <xs:maxExclusive value="80" />
        </xs:restriction>
    </xs:simpleType>
</xs:schema>
```

An object with **global scope** is a direct child of the root schema element and can be referenced throughout the schema document. Each code block shaded purple in this Visual Overview has global scope.

Russian Doll designs have very few if any global scope declarations. This declaration is the only one other than the root element with global scope in this Russian Doll design schema.

SCHEMA DESIGN COMPARISONS

An object with **local scope** can only be referenced within the object in which it is defined. This code block, shaded green, is the only code with local scope in these schema designs.

A **Venetian Blind design** creates named types and references those types within a single global element.

```
l">


maxOccurs="unbounded">


e="xs:string" />
pe="xs:string" />
="xs:date" />


etestType">
"level" use="required">


n base="xs:string">
tion value="L" />
tion value="M" />
tion value="H" />
on>


pretestType" minOccurs="0" maxOccurs="unbounded" />


ired">


\d{3}" />


required">


ing">
-\d{3}-\d" />
```

```xml
<xsi:schema xmlns:xsi="http://www.w3.org/2001/XMLSchema">

  <xsi:element name="students">
    <xsi:complexType>
      <xsi:sequence>
        <xsi:element name="student" type="sType" minOccurs="1" maxOccurs="unbounded" />
      </xsi:sequence>
    </xsi:complexType>
  </xsi:element>

  <xsi:complexType name="sType">
    <xsi:group ref="childElements" />
    <xsi:attributeGroup ref="studentAtt" />
  </xsi:complexType>

  <xsi:group name="childElements">
    <xsi:sequence>
      <xsi:element name="lastName" type="xsi:string" />
      <xsi:element name="firstName" type="xsi:string" />
      <xsi:element name="examDate" type="xsi:date" />
      <xsi:element name="pretest" type="pretestComplex" />
      <xsi:element name="score" type="pretestType" minOccurs="0" maxOccurs="unbounded" />
    </xsi:sequence>
  </xsi:group>

  <xsi:attributeGroup name="studentAtt">
    <xsi:attribute name="stuID" type="idType" />
    <xsi:attribute name="courseID" type="courseType" />
  </xsi:attributeGroup>

  <xsi:complexType name="pretestComplex">
    <xsi:simpleContent>
      <xsi:extension base="pretestType">
        <xsi:attribute name="level" type="levelType" use="required" />
      </xsi:extension>
    </xsi:simpleContent>
  </xsi:complexType>

  <xsi:simpleType name="pretestType">
    <xsi:restriction base="xsi:decimal">
      <xsi:minExclusive value="0" />
      <xsi:maxExclusive value="80" />
    </xsi:restriction>
  </xsi:simpleType>

  <xsi:simpleType name="idType">
    <xsi:restriction base="xsi:ID">
      <xsi:pattern value="I\d{4}-\d{3}" />
    </xsi:restriction>
  </xsi:simpleType>

  <xsi:simpleType name="courseType">
    <xsi:restriction base="xsi:string">
      <xsi:pattern value="[A-Z]{4}-\d{3}-\d" />
    </xsi:restriction>
  </xsi:simpleType>

  <xsi:simpleType name="levelType">
    <xsi:restriction base="xsi:string">
      <xsi:enumeration value="L" />
      <xsi:enumeration value="M" />
      <xsi:enumeration value="H" />
    </xsi:restriction>
  </xsi:simpleType>

</xsi:schema>
```

A Russian Doll design is often compact, but the multiple levels of nested elements can be confusing and can make it more difficult to debug; it also means the nested element and attribute declarations cannot be reused elsewhere in the schema because they are made locally.

Globally defined complexTypes, simpleTypes, element groups, and attribute groups are used in a Venetian Blind design rather than globally defined elements and attributes. The only exception is the root element global definition.

Designing a Schema

You and Gabby meet to discuss the needs of Higher Ed Test Prep. She has provided you with *students.xml*, which is a file that contains a list of students enrolled in the PSAT Mathematics Course. She has also created three different versions of a schema for the students vocabulary and would like your help with choosing the most appropriate schema design for the needs of Higher Ed Test Prep.

There are many different ways to design a schema. The building blocks of any schema are the XML elements that define the structure; these are known collectively as objects. You can create objects such as named complex types and then reuse them through the schema file, or you can nest one complex type inside of another. The way you design the layout of your schema file can impact how that schema is interpreted and applied to the instance document.

One important issue in schema design is determining the scope of the different objects declared within the schema. XML Schema recognizes two types of scope—global and local. Objects with global scope are direct children of the root schema element and can be referenced throughout the schema document. One advantage of creating objects with global scope is that you can reuse code several times in the same schema file without having to rewrite it. Objects with local scope can be referenced only within the object in which they are defined. It can be an advantage to keep all definitions confined to a local scope rather than referencing them throughout a long document—especially in a large and sprawling schema file—to avoid having to keep track of a large set of global objects. This distinction between global and local scope leads to three basic schema designs—Flat Catalog, Russian Doll, and Venetian Blind.

Flat Catalog Design

In a Flat Catalog design—sometimes referred to as a Salami Slice design—all element and attribute definitions have global scope. Every element and attribute definition is a direct child of the root schema element and thus has been defined globally. The developer can then use references to the set of global objects to build the schema.

You'll open Gabby's *students.xml* file and the Flat Catalog version of the schema for the students vocabulary to explore what a schema that uses this design looks like.

To explore and apply the Flat Catalog version of the schema:

1. In your XML editor, open the **studentstxt.xml** and **studentsfctxt.xsd** files from the tutorial.14\tutorial folder provided with your data files.

2. Within the comment section of each file, enter *your name* and *today's date*, and then save the files as **students.xml** and **studentsfc.xsd**, respectively. The *studentsfc.xsd* file is a Flat Catalog version of the schema for the students vocabulary.

3. Review the contents of the *studentsfc.xsd* document. As shown in Figure 14-1, all elements and attributes have global scope because they are all direct children of the root schema element.

| Figure 14-1 | Schema for students vocabulary using Flat Catalog design |

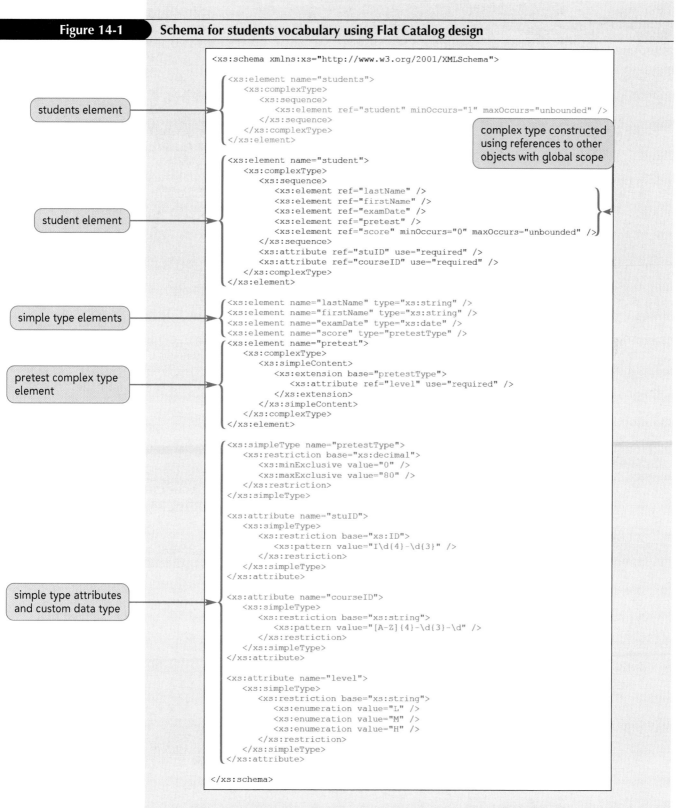

students element

student element

simple type elements

pretest complex type element

simple type attributes and custom data type

```
<xs:schema xmlns:xs="http://www.w3.org/2001/XMLSchema">

  <xs:element name="students">
    <xs:complexType>
      <xs:sequence>
        <xs:element ref="student" minOccurs="1" maxOccurs="unbounded" />
      </xs:sequence>
    </xs:complexType>
  </xs:element>

  <xs:element name="student">
    <xs:complexType>
      <xs:sequence>
        <xs:element ref="lastName" />
        <xs:element ref="firstName" />
        <xs:element ref="examDate" />
        <xs:element ref="pretest" />
        <xs:element ref="score" minOccurs="0" maxOccurs="unbounded" />
      </xs:sequence>
      <xs:attribute ref="stuID" use="required" />
      <xs:attribute ref="courseID" use="required" />
    </xs:complexType>
  </xs:element>

  <xs:element name="lastName" type="xs:string" />
  <xs:element name="firstName" type="xs:string" />
  <xs:element name="examDate" type="xs:date" />
  <xs:element name="score" type="pretestType" />
  <xs:element name="pretest">
    <xs:complexType>
      <xs:simpleContent>
        <xs:extension base="pretestType">
          <xs:attribute ref="level" use="required" />
        </xs:extension>
      </xs:simpleContent>
    </xs:complexType>
  </xs:element>

  <xs:simpleType name="pretestType">
    <xs:restriction base="xs:decimal">
      <xs:minExclusive value="0" />
      <xs:maxExclusive value="80" />
    </xs:restriction>
  </xs:simpleType>

  <xs:attribute name="stuID">
    <xs:simpleType>
      <xs:restriction base="xs:ID">
        <xs:pattern value="I\d{4}-\d{3}" />
      </xs:restriction>
    </xs:simpleType>
  </xs:attribute>

  <xs:attribute name="courseID">
    <xs:simpleType>
      <xs:restriction base="xs:string">
        <xs:pattern value="[A-Z]{4}-\d{3}-\d" />
      </xs:restriction>
    </xs:simpleType>
  </xs:attribute>

  <xs:attribute name="level">
    <xs:simpleType>
      <xs:restriction base="xs:string">
        <xs:enumeration value="L" />
        <xs:enumeration value="M" />
        <xs:enumeration value="H" />
      </xs:restriction>
    </xs:simpleType>
  </xs:attribute>

</xs:schema>
```

complex type constructed using references to other objects with global scope

4. In the **students.xml** document, within the opening <students> tag, add the attribute **xsi:noNamespaceSchemaLocation="studentsfc.xsd"** on its own line, as shown in Figure 14-2. This attribute links the *students.xml* instance document to the *studentsfc.xsd* schema file.

| Figure 14-2 | The students.xml document modified to use studentsfc.xsd schema |

```
<students xmlns:xsi="http://www.w3.org/2001/XMLSchema-instance"
          xsi:noNamespaceSchemaLocation="studentsfc.xsd">
   <student stuID="I8900-041" courseID="PSAT-080-5">
```

name of the Flat Catalog schema document

▶ **5.** Save your changes to the **students.xml** document and then validate it. The document validates successfully against the *studentsfc.xsd* schema.

Russian Doll Design

A Russian Doll design has only one global element with everything else nested inside of it, much like Russian Matryoshka dolls nest one inside another. Russian Doll designs mimic the nesting structure of the elements in an instance document. The root element of the instance document becomes the top element declaration in the schema. All child elements within the root element are similarly nested in the schema. A Russian Doll design is much more compact than a Flat Catalog, but the multiple levels of nested elements can be confusing and can make it more difficult to debug. Also, the element and attribute declarations cannot be reused elsewhere in the schema because aside from the single root element, all object declarations are made locally.

You'll explore the Russian Doll version of the schema for the students vocabulary now and apply it to the *students.xml* instance document.

To explore and apply the Russian Doll version of the schema:

▶ **1.** In your XML editor, open the **studentsrdtxt.xsd** file from the tutorial.14\tutorial folder provided with your data files.

▶ **2.** Within the comment section, enter *your name* and *today's date*, and then save the file as **studentsrd.xsd**. The *studentsrd.xsd* file is a Russian Doll version of the schema for the students vocabulary.

▶ **3.** Review the contents of the *studentsrd.xsd* document, as shown in Figure 14-3.

| Figure 14-3 | Schema for students vocabulary using Russian Doll design |

students element

student element

simple type elements

pretest complex type element

simple type attributes and custom data type

simpleType definition for pretestType is made globally so it can be used with both the pretest and score elements

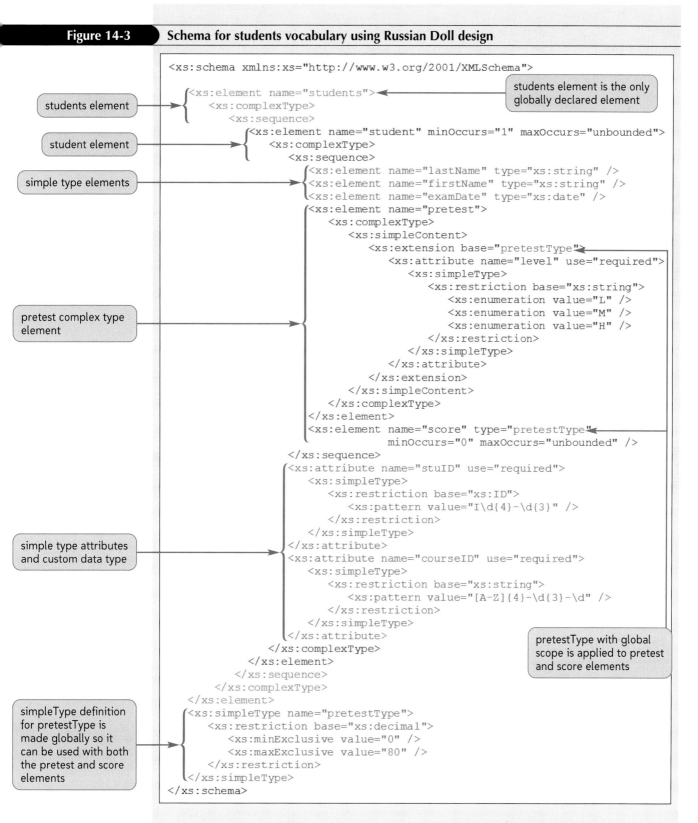

students element is the only globally declared element

pretestType with global scope is applied to pretest and score elements

```
<xs:schema xmlns:xs="http://www.w3.org/2001/XMLSchema">

  <xs:element name="students">
    <xs:complexType>
      <xs:sequence>
        <xs:element name="student" minOccurs="1" maxOccurs="unbounded">
          <xs:complexType>
            <xs:sequence>
              <xs:element name="lastName" type="xs:string" />
              <xs:element name="firstName" type="xs:string" />
              <xs:element name="examDate" type="xs:date" />
              <xs:element name="pretest">
                <xs:complexType>
                  <xs:simpleContent>
                    <xs:extension base="pretestType">
                      <xs:attribute name="level" use="required">
                        <xs:simpleType>
                          <xs:restriction base="xs:string">
                            <xs:enumeration value="L" />
                            <xs:enumeration value="M" />
                            <xs:enumeration value="H" />
                          </xs:restriction>
                        </xs:simpleType>
                      </xs:attribute>
                    </xs:extension>
                  </xs:simpleContent>
                </xs:complexType>
              </xs:element>
              <xs:element name="score" type="pretestType"
                          minOccurs="0" maxOccurs="unbounded" />
            </xs:sequence>
            <xs:attribute name="stuID" use="required">
              <xs:simpleType>
                <xs:restriction base="xs:ID">
                  <xs:pattern value="I\d{4}-\d{3}" />
                </xs:restriction>
              </xs:simpleType>
            </xs:attribute>
            <xs:attribute name="courseID" use="required">
              <xs:simpleType>
                <xs:restriction base="xs:string">
                  <xs:pattern value="[A-Z]{4}-\d{3}-\d" />
                </xs:restriction>
              </xs:simpleType>
            </xs:attribute>
          </xs:complexType>
        </xs:element>
      </xs:sequence>
    </xs:complexType>
  </xs:element>
  <xs:simpleType name="pretestType">
    <xs:restriction base="xs:decimal">
      <xs:minExclusive value="0" />
      <xs:maxExclusive value="80" />
    </xs:restriction>
  </xs:simpleType>
</xs:schema>
```

As Figure 14-3 shows, the only element declaration with global scope is for the students element; all other elements and attributes are declared locally, nested inside of the students element. Also notice that the definition for the pretestType simple type is global because it is defined outside the nested part of the design. This allows the `pretestType` type to be reused in both the `pretest` and `score` elements. Because you can't set both a restriction and an extension to the same element definition, the only way to define the minimum and maximum values for the `pretest` element is by using a globally defined `simpleType` element. This is one area where strictly adhering to the Russian Doll design can be impractical.

▶ 4. Return to the **students.xml** document, and then change the `xsi:noNamespaceSchemaLocation` value from studentsfc.xsd to **studentsrd.xsd** as shown in Figure 14-4.

Figure 14-4   The students.xml document modified to use the studentsrd.xsd schema

```
<students xmlns:xsi="http://www.w3.org/2001/XMLSchema-instance"
          xsi:noNamespaceSchemaLocation="studentsrd.xsd">
    <student stuID="I8900-041" courseID="PSAT-080-5">
```

name of the Russian Doll schema document

▶ 5. Save your changes to the **students.xml** document and then validate it. The document validates successfully against the *studentsrd.xsd* schema.

Venetian Blind Design

A Venetian Blind design is similar to a Flat Catalog except that instead of declaring objects globally, it creates named types, named element groups, and named attribute groups and references those types within a single global element. A Venetian Blind design represents a compromise between Flat Catalogs and Russian Dolls. Although the various element and attribute groups and named types are declared globally (and can be reused throughout the schema), the declarations for the elements and attributes for the instance document are local and nested within element and attribute groups. The XML Schema `group` element is used to assign a name to a list of references to elements or attributes, and then the named group is referenced elsewhere using the `ref` attribute. Only the root element from the instance document—in this case, the `students` element—is defined globally.

You'll explore the Venetian Blind version of the schema for the students vocabulary now and apply it to the *students.xml* instance document.

To explore and apply the Venetian Blind version of the schema:

▶ 1. In your XML editor, open the **studentsvbtxt.xsd** file from the tutorial.14\tutorial folder provided with your data files.

▶ 2. Within the comment section, enter **your name** and **today's date**, and then save the file as **studentsvb.xsd**. The *studentsvb.xsd file* is a Venetian Blind version of the schema for the students vocabulary.

▶ 3. Review the contents of the *studentsvb.xsd* document, noting the use of named types, element groups, and attribute groups, as shown in Figure 14-5.

Figure 14-5 — Schema for students vocabulary using Venetian Blind design

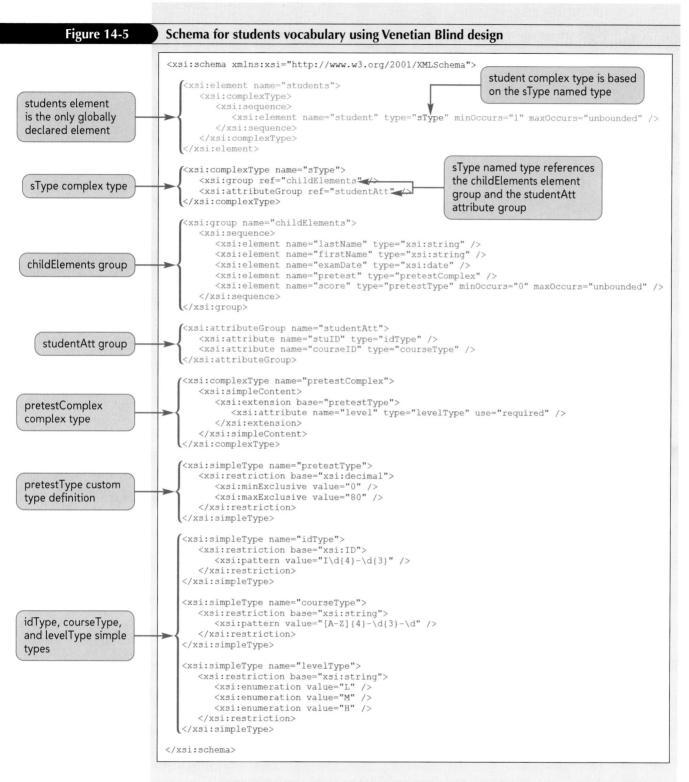

In this layout, the only globally declared element is the students element. All other elements and attributes are placed within element or attribute groups or, in the case of the pretest element's level attribute, within a named complex type.

▶ 4. Return to the **students.xml** document, and then change the xsi:noNamespaceSchemaLocation value from studentsrd.xsd to **studentsvb.xsd** as shown in Figure 14-6.

| Figure 14-6 | The students.xml document modified to use the studentsvb.xsd schema |

```
<students xmlns:xsi="http://www.w3.org/2001/XMLSchema-instance"
          xsi:noNamespaceSchemaLocation="studentsvb.xsd">
    <student stuID="I8900-041" courseID="PSAT-080-5">
```

> name of the Venetian
> Blind schema document

5. Save your changes to the **students.xml** document and then validate it.
The document validates successfully against the *studentsvb.xsd* schema.

PROSKILLS

Decision Making: Deciding Which Schema Design to Use

Which schema layout you use depends on several factors. If a schema contains several lines of code that need to be repeated, you probably should use a Flat Catalog or Venetian Blind design. If you are interested in a compact schema that mirrors the structure of the instance document, you should use a Russian Doll design.

Figure 14-7 summarizes some of the differences among the three schema designs.

| Figure 14-7 | Comparison of schema designs |

Feature	Flat Catalog (Salami Slice)	Russian Doll	Venetian Blind
Global and local declarations	All declarations are global.	The schema contains one single global element; all other declarations are local.	The schema contains one single global element; all other declarations are local.
Nesting of elements	Element declarations are not nested.	Element declarations are nested within a single global element.	Element declarations are nested within a single global element referencing named complex types, element groups, and attribute groups.
Reusability	Element declarations can be reused throughout the schema.	Element declarations can only be used once.	Named complex types, element groups, and attribute groups can be reused throughout the schema.
Interaction with namespaces	If a namespace is attached to the schema, all elements need to be qualified in the instance document.	If a namespace is attached to the schema, only the root element needs to be qualified in the instance document.	If a namespace is attached to the schema, only the root element needs to be qualified in the instance document.

Rather than using the original Flat Catalog design for the schema file, Gabby wants you to continue to work with the Venetian Blind design. She likes the fact that the Venetian Blind layout maintains the flexibility of a Flat Catalog while providing a structure similar to the contents of her instance document. She has also heard that using a Venetian Blind design will make it easier to apply a namespace to the schema and instance document, which you'll explore in the next session.

INSIGHT

The Garden of Eden Schema Design

In addition to the Flat Catalog, Russian Doll, and Venetian Blind layouts, other standardized schema designs exist. One of these, known as the Garden of Eden design, combines the Flat Catalog approach of declaring all elements globally with the Venetian Blind practice of declaring type definitions globally. Although this results in a schema in which all parts are easily reusable, its main trade-off is that it requires more code than either of the designs on which it is based.

REVIEW

Session 14.1 Quick Check

1. List and define the two types of scope for objects in a schema.
2. Name one advantage of each type of scope.
3. What is a Flat Catalog design and how does it differ from a Russian Doll design?
4. What is another name for the Flat Catalog design?
5. What is a Venetian Blind design, and how does it differ from the Flat Catalog and Russian Doll designs?

SESSION 14.2 VISUAL OVERVIEW

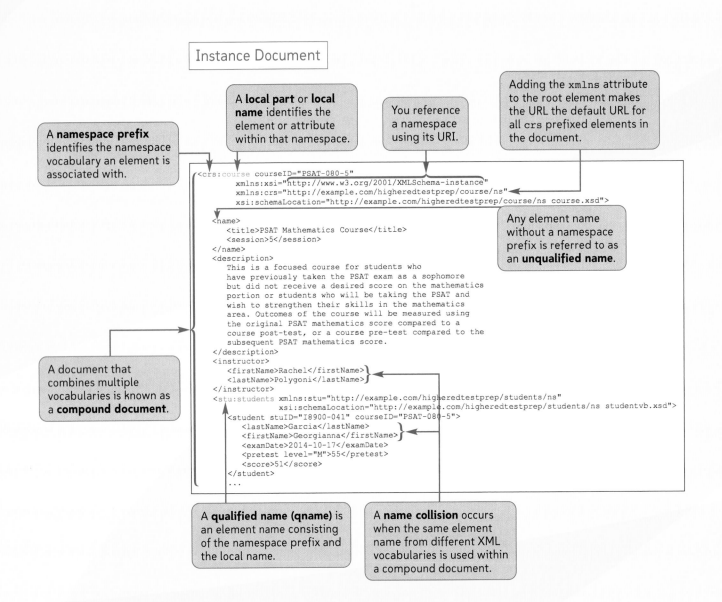

Instance Document

A **namespace prefix** identifies the namespace vocabulary an element is associated with.

A **local part** or **local name** identifies the element or attribute within that namespace.

You reference a namespace using its URI.

Adding the xmlns attribute to the root element makes the URL the default URL for all crs prefixed elements in the document.

```
<crs:course courseID="PSAT-080-5"
        xmlns:xsi="http://www.w3.org/2001/XMLSchema-instance"
        xmlns:crs="http://example.com/higheredtestprep/course/ns"
        xsi:schemaLocation="http://example.com/higheredtestprep/course/ns course.xsd">

    <name>
        <title>PSAT Mathematics Course</title>
        <session>5</session>
    </name>
    <description>
        This is a focused course for students who
        have previously taken the PSAT exam as a sophomore
        but did not receive a desired score on the mathematics
        portion or students who will be taking the PSAT and
        wish to strengthen their skills in the mathematics
        area. Outcomes of the course will be measured using
        the original PSAT mathematics score compared to a
        course post-test, or a course pre-test compared to the
        subsequent PSAT mathematics score.
    </description>
    <instructor>
        <firstName>Rachel</firstName>
        <lastName>Polygoni</lastName>
    </instructor>
    <stu:students xmlns:stu="http://example.com/higheredtestprep/students/ns"
            xsi:schemaLocation="http://example.com/higheredtestprep/students/ns studentvb.xsd">
        <student stuID="I8900-041" courseID="PSAT-080-5">
            <lastName>Garcia</lastName>
            <firstName>Georgianna</firstName>
            <examDate>2014-10-17</examDate>
            <pretest level="M">55</pretest>
            <score>51</score>
        </student>
        ...
```

Any element name without a namespace prefix is referred to as an **unqualified name**.

A document that combines multiple vocabularies is known as a **compound document**.

A **qualified name (qname)** is an element name consisting of the namespace prefix and the local name.

A **name collision** occurs when the same element name from different XML vocabularies is used within a compound document.

A COMPOUND DOCUMENT

> The **import** element combines schemas when the schemas come from different namespaces.

Main Schema Document

```
<xs:schema xmlns:xs="http://www.w3.org/2001/XMLSchema"
           xmlns="http://example.com/higheredtestprep/course/ns"
           targetNamespace="http://example.com/higheredtestprep/course/ns"
           xmlns:stu="http://example.com/higheredtestprep/students/ns">

   <xs:import namespace="http://example.com/higheredtestprep/students/ns"
              schemaLocation="studentsvb.xsd" />
   <xs:element name="course">
      <xs:complexType>
         <xs:sequence>
            <xs:element name="name">
               <xs:complexType>
                  <xs:sequence>
                     <xs:element name="title" type="xs:string" />
                     <xs:element name="session" type="xs:string" />
                  </xs:sequence>
               </xs:complexType>
            </xs:element>
            <xs:element name="description" type="xs:string" />
            <xs:element name="instructor">
               <xs:complexType>
                  <xs:sequence>
                     <xs:element name="firstName" type="xs:string" />
                     <xs:element name="lastName" type="xs:string" />
                  </xs:sequence>
               </xs:complexType>
            </xs:element>
            <xs:element ref="stu:students" />
         </xs:sequence>
         <xs:attribute name="courseID" type="xs:ID" />
      </xs:complexType>
   </xs:element>

</xs:schema>
```

> The `ref` attribute is used to reference an object from an imported schema.

Imported Schema Document

```
<xsi:schema xmlns:xsi="http://www.w3.org/2001/XMLSchema"
            xmlns="http://example.com/higheredtestprep/students/ns"
            targetNamespace="http://example.com/higheredtestprep/students/ns">

   <xsi:element name="students">
      <xsi:complexType>
         <xsi:sequence>
            <xsi:element name="student" type="sType" minOccurs="1" maxOccurs="unbounded" />
         </xsi:sequence>
      </xsi:complexType>
   </xsi:element>

   <xsi:complexType name="sType">
      <xsi:group ref="childElements" />
      <xsi:attributeGroup ref="studentAtt" />
   </xsi:complexType>

   <xsi:group name="childElements">
      <xsi:sequence>
         <xsi:element name="lastName" type="xsi:string" />
         <xsi:element name="firstName" type="xsi:string" />
         <xsi:element name="examDate" type="xsi:date" />
         <xsi:element name="pretest" type="pretestComplex" />
         <xsi:element name="score" type="pretestType" minOccurs="0" maxOccurs="unbounded" />
      </xsi:sequence>
   </xsi:group>

   ...
```

Combining XML Vocabularies

Gabby has been working on a second XML vocabulary—one that documents the features of the different exam courses run by Higher Ed Test Prep. The structure of the course vocabulary is shown in Figure 14-8.

Figure 14-8	Structure of the course vocabulary

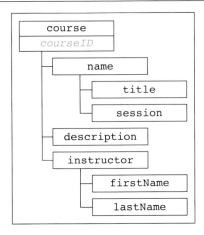

So far, the course vocabulary contains only basic information about each exam course: It records the course ID, name, title, session, and description of the course, and the first and last names of the course's instructor. As Gabby develops additional XML documents using this vocabulary, she will add more elements and attributes to it. Gabby already has created a schema file and an instance document based on this vocabulary. You will open both of those now.

To view the schema file and instance document for the course vocabulary:

▶ 1. Use your XML editor to open the **coursetxt.xsd** file from the tutorial.14\tutorial folder, enter **your name** and **today's date** in the comment section, and then save the file as **course.xsd**.

▶ 2. Review the contents and structure of the course schema shown in Figure 14-9. This schema uses a Russian Doll design, with course being the only element declared globally in the file.

Figure 14-9	Schema for the course vocabulary

```
<xs:schema xmlns:xs="http://www.w3.org/2001/XMLSchema">
   <xs:element name="course">
      <xs:complexType>
         <xs:sequence>
            <xs:element name="name">
               <xs:complexType>
                  <xs:sequence>
                     <xs:element name="title" type="xs:string" />
                     <xs:element name="session" type="xs:string" />
                  </xs:sequence>
               </xs:complexType>
            </xs:element>
            <xs:element name="description" type="xs:string" />
            <xs:element name="instructor">
               <xs:complexType>
                  <xs:sequence>
                     <xs:element name="firstName" type="xs:string" />
                     <xs:element name="lastName" type="xs:string" />
                  </xs:sequence>
               </xs:complexType>
            </xs:element>
         </xs:sequence>
         <xs:attribute name="courseID" type="xs:ID" />
      </xs:complexType>
   </xs:element>
</xs:schema>
```

course is the only element with global scope

Russian Doll design

3. Use your XML editor to open the **psattxt.xml** file from the tutorial.14\tutorial folder, enter *your name* and *today's date* in the comment section, and then save the file as **psat.xml**. The *psat.xml* file contains basic information on a course that helps students improve their PSAT mathematics scores.

Gabby wants to combine the information about the PSAT Mathematics Course and the list of students enrolled in that course in a single compound document. A **compound document** is a document that combines elements from multiple vocabularies. Figure 14-10 shows a schematic diagram of the document Gabby wants to create, involving elements and attributes from both the course and students vocabularies.

Figure 14-10   **Structure of the compound document**

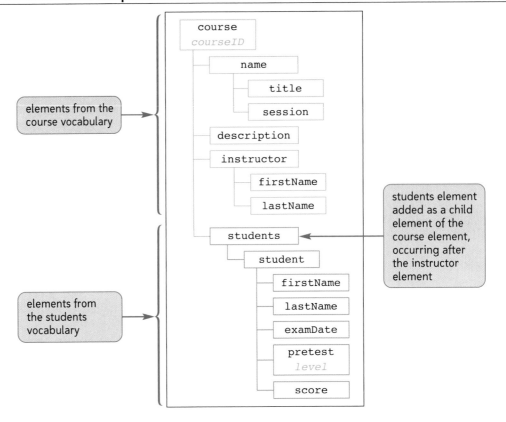

Creating a Compound Document

Gabby wants you to work with her XML files to create a sample compound document that she can use as a model for future projects. You'll start by combining the elements from the students and course vocabularies, storing the result in a new file named *psatstudents.xml*. You'll create this compound document now.

To create the *psatstudents.xml* compound document:

▶ **1.** If necessary, return to the **psat.xml** file in your XML editor, and then save a copy of the file with the name **psatstudents.xml**.

▶ **2.** In the comment section, change the filename to **psatstudents.xml**; in the supporting files list, add the filenames **course.css**, **students.css**, and **studentsvb.xsd**; and then save your changes.

▶ **3.** Return to the **students.xml** file, and then copy the contents of the opening `<students>` tag through the closing `</students>` tag to the Clipboard.

▶ **4.** Return to the **psatstudents.xml** file in your XML editor, and then insert the copied *students.xml* contents below the closing `</instructor>` tag.

Be sure to scroll down and copy all the student information in the *students.xml* file including the closing `</students>` tag, rather than stopping at one of the `</student>` tags.

5. In the opening `<students>` tag, delete both attributes and their values. The `xmlns` attribute declares the XML Schema instance namespace; however, it's unnecessary because the namespace is already declared in the `course` element, which encloses all the contents of this document. In addition, because you'll be using namespaces in this compound document, the `noNamespaceSchemaLocation` is no longer relevant. Figure 14-11 shows the compound document containing elements from both the course and students vocabularies.

Figure 14-11   **Compound document showing information on first and last students**

XML schema instance namespace attribute

```
<course courseID="PSAT-080-5"
        xmlns:xsi="http://www.w3.org/2001/XMLSchema-instance"
        xsi:noNamespaceSchemaLocation="course.xsd">

   <name>
      <title>PSAT Mathematics Course</title>
      <session>5</session>
   </name>
   <description>
      This is a focused course for students who
      have previously taken the PSAT exam as a sophomore
      but did not receive a desired score on the mathematics
      portion or students who will be taking the PSAT and
      wish to strengthen their skills in the mathematics
      area. Outcomes of the course will be measured using
      the original PSAT mathematics score compared to a
      course post-test, or a course pre-test compared to the
      subsequent PSAT mathematics score.
   </description>
   <instructor>
      <firstName>Rachel</firstName>
      <lastName>Polygoni</lastName>
   </instructor>
```

duplicate attributes are deleted from the opening students tag

```
   <students>
      <student stuID="I8900-041" courseID="PSAT-080-5">
         <lastName>Garcia</lastName>
         <firstName>Georgianna</firstName>
         <examDate>2014-10-17</examDate>
         <pretest level="M">55</pretest>
         <score>51</score>
      </student>
```

students element and contents copied from the students.xml document

```
      <student stuID="I8154-741" courseID="PSAT-080-5">
         <lastName>Browne</lastName>
         <firstName>Brenda</firstName>
         <examDate>2014-10-22</examDate>
         <pretest level="L">30</pretest>
      </student>

   </students>
</course>
```

6. Save your changes to the **psatstudents.xml** file.

Notice that after combining the two vocabularies, some elements have the same names: Both the `instructor` and `student` elements contain child elements named `lastName` and `firstName`, as illustrated in Figure 14-12. Gabby would like you to investigate whether this is a problem.

Figure 14-12   **Name collision in a compound document**

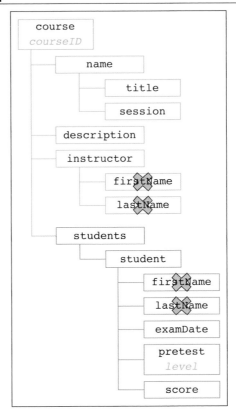

Understanding Name Collision

The duplication of these element names is an example of name collision, which occurs when the same element name from different XML vocabularies is used within a compound document. Higher Ed Test Prep could have been more careful in choosing element names to prevent name collisions among different vocabularies. However, name collisions are often unavoidable. After all, one benefit of XML vocabularies is the ability to use simple element names to describe data. Creating complex element names to avoid name collisions eliminates this benefit. Moreover, there are other XML vocabularies such as XHTML over which Gabby has no control. XHTML element names such as `title` and `address` are certain to be found in thousands of XML vocabularies.

Gabby could also avoid combining elements from different vocabularies in the same document to prevent name collisions; however, this would make XML a poor information tool. Instead, Gabby can use namespaces to distinguish elements in one vocabulary from elements in another vocabulary.

Working with Namespaces in an Instance Document

A namespace is a defined collection of element and attribute names. For example, the collection of element and attribute names from Gabby's courses vocabulary could make up a single namespace. Likewise, the element and attribute names from the students vocabulary could constitute a different namespace. Applying a namespace to an XML document involves two steps:

1. Declare the namespace.
2. Identify the elements and attributes within the document that belong to that namespace.

First, you will review how to declare a namespace.

Declaring and Applying a Namespace to a Document

To declare and apply a namespace to a document, you add the attributes

```
xmlns="uri"
xsi:schemaLocation="uri schema"
```

to an element in the document, where *uri* is the URI of the namespace and *schema* is the location and name of the schema file. For example, the following code declares a namespace with the URI http://example.com/higheredtestprep/course/ns within the course element and applies the schema file *course.xsd* to the document:

```
<course courseID="PSAT-080-5"
        xmlns="http://example.com/higheredtestprep/course/ns"
        xsi:schemaLocation="http://example.com/higheredtestprep/
        course/ns course.xsd">
...
</course>
```

The number of namespace attributes that can be declared within an element is unlimited.

REFERENCE

Declaring and Applying a Namespace in an Instance Document

- To declare a namespace, add the attribute

  ```
  xmlns:prefix="uri"
  ```

  to an element in the document, where *prefix* is the namespace prefix and *uri* is the URI of the namespace.
- To apply a schema file to a namespace you've declared, add the attribute

  ```
  xsi:schemaLocation="uri schema"
  ```

  where *schema* is the location and name of the schema file.
- To apply a namespace to an element, add the namespace prefix

  ```
  <prefix:element> ... </prefix:element>
  ```

  to the element's opening and closing tags, where *prefix* is the namespace prefix and *element* is the local part of the qualified element name. If no prefix is specified, the element is assumed to be part of the default namespace.
- To apply a namespace to an attribute, add the namespace prefix

  ```
  <element prefix:attribute="value"> ... </element>
  ```

  to the attribute name, where *attribute* is the attribute name. By default, an attribute is part of the namespace of its containing element.

Gabby wants you to create namespaces for the course and students vocabularies. You will declare each namespace in the root element of the content it applies to; for the course vocabulary, this is the `course` element, and for the students vocabulary, this is the `students` element. The URIs for the two namespaces will be

http://example.com/higheredtestprep/course/ns
http://example.com/higheredtestprep/students/ns

These URIs do not point to actual sites on the Web, but they do provide unique URIs for the two namespaces.

To declare the course and students namespaces:

1. If necessary, return to the **psatstudents.xml** file in your XML editor.

2. Within the opening `<course>` tag, delete the code `xsi:noNamespaceSchemaLocation="course.xsd"`, and then add the following code to declare the course namespace and specify the location of the schema file:

   ```
   xmlns="http://example.com/higheredtestprep/course/ns"
   xsi:schemaLocation="http://example.com/higheredtestprep/course/ns
   course.xsd"
   ```

3. Within the opening `<students>` tag, add the following code to declare the students namespace and specify the schema location:

   ```
   xmlns="http://example.com/higheredtestprep/students/ns"
   xsi:schemaLocation="http://example.com/higheredtestprep/students/ns
   studentsvb.xsd"
   ```

   Compare your namespace declarations to those in Figure 14-13.

Figure 14-13   Declaring namespaces within a compound document

course namespace declaration

```
<course courseID="PSAT-080-5"
       xmlns:xsi="http://www.w3.org/2001/XMLSchema-instance"
       xmlns="http://example.com/higheredtestprep/course/ns"
       xsi:schemaLocation="http://example.com/higheredtestprep/course/ns course.xsd">

    <name>
        <title>PSAT Mathematics Course</title>
        <session>5</session>
    </name>
    <description>
        This is a focused course for students who
        have previously taken the PSAT exam as a sophomore
        but did not receive a desired score on the mathematics
        portion or students who will be taking the PSAT and
        wish to strengthen their skills in the mathematics
        area. Outcomes of the course will be measured using
        the original PSAT mathematics score compared to a
        course post-test, or a course pre-test compared to the
        subsequent PSAT mathematics score.
    </description>
    <instructor>
        <firstName>Rachel</firstName>
        <lastName>Polygoni</lastName>
    </instructor>
    <students xmlns="http://example.com/higheredtestprep/students/ns"
           xsi:schemaLocation="http://example.com/higheredtestprep/students/ns studentsvb.xsd">
        <student stuID="I8900-041" courseID="PSAT-080-5">
```

location of schema file for the course vocabulary

location of schema file for the students vocabulary

students namespace declaration

4. Save the changes to **psatstudents.xml**.

Applying a Namespace to an Element

In an instance document containing elements from more than one namespace, after you declare the namespaces, you must indicate which elements in the document belong to each namespace. This process involves two steps:

1. Associate the namespace declaration with a prefix.
2. Add the prefix to the tags for each element in the namespace.

To apply an XML namespace to an element, you qualify the element's name. A qualified name, or qname, is an element name consisting of two parts—the namespace prefix that identifies the namespace, and the local part or local name that identifies the element or attribute within that namespace. The general form for applying a qualified name to a two-sided tag is

```
<prefix:element> ... </prefix:element>
```

where *prefix* is the namespace prefix and *element* is the local part. An element name without such a prefix is referred to as an unqualified name. You worked with qualified names previously when specifying elements from the XML Schema vocabulary in a schema file, using the `xs:` or `xsi:` prefix.

Namespaces have a scope associated with them. The scope of a namespace declaration declaring a prefix extends from the beginning of the opening tag to the end of the corresponding closing tag. The namespace declared in a parent element is connected with—or bound to—the defined prefix for that element as well as for all of its child elements. This is true unless the given prefix in the parent is overridden in a child element that has been assigned a different namespace. Some XML authors add all namespace declarations to the document's root element so that the namespace is available to all elements within the document. The association between the namespace and the prefix declared in an element does not apply to the siblings of that element.

A single namespace prefix can be declared as an attribute of an element, as shown in this example:

```
<crs:course courseID="PSAT-080-5"
    xmlns:crs="http://example.com/higheredtestprep/course/ns">
  <name>
     <title>PSAT Mathematics Course</title>
     <session>5</crs:session>
  </name>
  ...
</crs:course>
...
```

The opening `<course>` tag includes both the namespace prefix and the `xmlns` attribute to declare the namespace. This indicates that the course element itself is part of the namespace that it declares.

INSIGHT

Qualified and Unqualified Names

The use of qnames in elements and attributes is controversial because it creates a dependency between the content of the document and its markup. However, in its official position, the W3C doesn't discourage this practice. The syntax for default namespaces was designed for convenience, but they tend to cause more confusion than they're worth. The confusion typically stems from the fact that elements and attributes are treated differently, and it's not immediately apparent that nested elements are being assigned the default namespace identifier. Nevertheless, in the end, choosing between prefixes and default namespaces is mostly a matter of style except when attributes come into play.

In XML Schema, any element or attribute with global scope must be entered as a qualified name (i.e., with a namespace prefix). The reason is that elements and attributes with global scope are attached to the schema's target namespace, while elements and attributes declared locally are not. In the instance document, this is reflected by qualifying those global elements or attributes.

This fact may affect your choice of schema designs. In a Flat Catalog, all elements and attributes are declared globally, so each element and attribute must be qualified in the instance document. Because Venetian Blind and Russian Doll designs have a single global element, only the root element must be qualified in the instance document.

In the *psatstudents.xml* document, you'll use the `crs` prefix for elements from the course namespace and the `stu` prefix for elements from the students namespace. You will apply each namespace to the parent element that belongs to that namespace. There is no need to assign attributes to namespaces, so you will not add prefixes to attributes in the *psatstudents.xml* file.

To apply the courses and students namespaces:

▶ **1.** Verify that the **psatstudents.xml** file is the active file in your XML editor.

▶ **2.** In the opening `<course>` tag, add the prefix **:crs** to the `xmlns` attribute that declares the course namespace so the attribute reads as follows:

`xmlns:crs="http://example.com/higheredtestprep/course/ns"`

This associates the `crs` prefix with the course namespace.

▶ **3.** In the opening `<students>` tag, add the prefix **:stu** to the `xmlns` attribute that declares the students namespace so the attribute reads as follows:

`xmlns:stu="http://example.com/higheredtestprep/students/ns"`

This associates the `stu` prefix with the students namespace.

▶ **4.** In the opening `<course>` tag, insert the **crs:** prefix just before the word `course`, and then repeat for the closing `<course>` tag.

Add the crs: prefix to the closing tag as well as to the opening tag.

Adding the `crs` prefix to the opening and closing `<course>` tags specifies that the `course` element is part of the course namespace.

▶ **5.** In the opening `<students>` tag, insert the **stu:** prefix just before the word `students`, and then repeat for the closing `</students>` tag. Figure 14-14 shows the updated code.

Figure 14-14 | **Declaring namespaces within a compound document**

```
<crs:course courseID="PSAT-080-5"
      xmlns:xsi="http://www.w3.org/2001/XMLSchema-instance"
      xmlns:crs="http://example.com/higheredtestprep/course/ns"
      xsi:schemaLocation="http://example.com/higheredtestprep/course/ns course.xsd">

  <name>
     <title>PSAT Mathematics Course</title>
     <session>5</session>
  </name>
  <description>
     This is a focused course for students who
     have previously taken the PSAT exam as a sophomore
     but did not receive a desired score on the mathematics
     portion or students who will be taking the PSAT and
     wish to strengthen their skills in the mathematics
     area. Outcomes of the course will be measured using
     the original PSAT mathematics score compared to a
     course post-test, or a course pre-test compared to the
     subsequent PSAT mathematics score.
  </description>
  <instructor>
     <firstName>Rachel</firstName>
     <lastName>Polygoni</lastName>
  </instructor>
  <stu:students xmlns:stu="http://example.com/higheredtestprep/students/ns"
            xsi:schemaLocation="http://example.com/higheredtestprep/students/ns studentsvb.xsd">
     <student stuID="I8900-041" courseID="PSAT-080-5">
        <lastName>Garcia</lastName>
        <firstName>Georgianna</firstName>
        <examDate>2014-10-17</examDate>
        <pretest level="M">55</pretest>
        <score>51</score>
     </student>


     <student stuID="I8154-741" courseID="PSAT-080-5">
        <lastName>Browne</lastName>
        <firstName>Brenda</firstName>
        <examDate>2014-10-22</examDate>
        <pretest level="L">30</pretest>
     </student>
  </stu:students>
</crs:course>
```

prefixes associated with namespaces

prefixes applied to opening and closing tags of root elements

You don't have to qualify any of the child elements and attributes of the course element because none of them were declared globally in the *course.xsd* schema file. Only the course element was defined globally, which is why it is the only element that requires a qualified name. The same is true for the students element.

▸ **6.** Save your changes to the **psatstudents.xml** file.

Working with Attributes

Like an element name, an attribute can be qualified by adding a namespace prefix. The syntax to qualify an attribute is

```
<element prefix:attribute="value"> ... </element>
```

where *prefix* is the namespace prefix and *attribute* is the attribute name. For example, the following code uses the crs: prefix to assign both the course element and the courseID attribute to the same course namespace:

```
<crs:course crs:courseID="PSAT-080-5"
    xmlns:xsi="http://www.w3.org/2001/XMLSchema-instance"
    xmlns:crs="http://example.com/higheredtestprep/course/ns">
...
</crs:course>
```

Unlike element names, there is no default namespace for attribute names. Default namespaces apply to elements, but not to attributes. An attribute name without a prefix is assumed to belong to the same namespace as the element that contains it. This means you could write the code listed above without the `crs:` prefix before the `courseID` attribute name and have the same result. In the code that follows, the `courseID` attribute is automatically assumed to belong to the course namespace, even though it lacks the `crs` prefix:

```
<crs:course courseID="PSAT-080-5"
    xmlns:xsi="http://www.w3.org/2001/XMLSchema-instance"
    xmlns:crs="http://example.com/higheredtestprep/course/ns">
...
</crs:course>
```

Because an attribute is automatically associated with the namespace of its element, you rarely need to qualify an attribute name. The only exception occurs when an attribute from one namespace needs to be used in an element from another namespace. For example, XHTML uses the `class` attribute to associate elements belonging to a common group or class. You could attach the `class` attribute from the XHTML namespace to elements from other namespaces. Because the `class` attribute is often used in CSS to apply common formats to groups of elements, using the `class` attribute in other XML elements would apply this feature of CSS to those elements as well.

For Gabby's document, there is no need to assign attributes to namespaces, so you will not specify namespaces for the attributes in the *psatstudents.xml* file.

Now that you've specified namespaces for the root elements of the two vocabularies you're using, you'll use an XML validator to validate your compound document.

To validate the compound document:

1. Use an XML validator to validate the **psatstudents.xml** document. The validator returns a number of errors.

2. Examine the text of the error messages for the reported errors. The first error message says that the target namespace of the schema document is 'null.'

   Trouble? If you're using Exchanger XML Editor and your first error message doesn't say that the target namespace of the schema document is 'null', compare your code to Figures 14-13 and 14-14, fix any errors you find, and then revalidate until the target namespace error is the first error.

Gabby's compound document is invalid because even though the namespaces in the compound document are associated with URIs, the schemas themselves are not. For the instance document to be valid, you must add this information to each schema file associated with it.

Associating a Schema with a Namespace

So far, you've specified the URI http://example.com/higheredtestprep/course/ns as the URI for the course vocabulary and the URI

http://example.com/higheredtestprep/students/ns

as the URI for the students vocabulary in the *psatstudents.xml* compound document. Next, you need to place the schemas themselves in the namespaces.

Targeting a Namespace

To associate the rules of a schema with a namespace, you declare the namespace of the instance document in the schema element and then make that namespace the target of the schema using the `targetNamespace` attribute. The code to set the schema namespace is

```
<xs:schema xmlns:xs="http://www.w3.org/2001/XMLSchema"
           xmlns:prefix="uri"
           targetNamespace="uri">
...
</xs:schema>
```

where *prefix* is the prefix of the namespace and *uri* is the URI of the namespace. The *prefix* value is optional. You can omit it to make the namespace of the instance document the default namespace. For example, to associate Gabby's *studentsvb.xsd* schema file with the namespace of the students vocabulary, you would modify the schema element as follows:

```
<xsi:schema xmlns:xsi="http://www.w3.org/2001/XMLSchema"
            xmlns="http://example.com/higheredtestprep/students/ns"
            targetNamespace="http://example.com/higheredtestprep/students/ns">
...
</xsi:schema>
```

TIP

This code uses the `xsi:` prefix for the XML Schema namespace because that's the prefix Gabby uses in her documents.

Any customized data types, named types, elements, element groups, or attributes created in the schema are considered part of the target namespace. This allows you to make validation rules part of an XML vocabulary. For example, the `pretest` element is part of the students vocabulary, as is the rule that the `pretest` element must have a minimum value of 0 and a maximum value of 80.

REFERENCE

Targeting a Namespace in a Schema and Applying the Namespace to an Instance Document

- To target a schema to a namespace, add the attributes

```
xmlns:prefix="uri"
targetNamespace="uri"
```

to the `schema` element, where *prefix* is the optional prefix of the namespace and *uri* is the URI of the namespace.
- To apply a schema to a document with a namespace, add the attributes

```
xmlns:xsi="http://www.w3.org/2001/XMLSchema-instance"
xmlns:prefix="uri"
xsi:schemaLocation="uri schema"
```

to the instance document's root element, where *prefix* is the namespace prefix, *uri* is the URI of the namespace, and *schema* is the schema file. All global elements and attributes declared in the schema must be qualified in the instance document.

If you use the vocabulary's namespace as the default namespace for the schema, you do not have to qualify any references to those customized objects. On the other hand, if you apply a prefix to the namespace, references to those objects must be qualified by that prefix. Figure 14-15 shows both possibilities—one in which references to objects from the XML Schema vocabulary are qualified, and the other in which XML Schema is the default namespace and references to customized objects are qualified.

Figure 14-15 A schema with and without qualified XML Schema object names

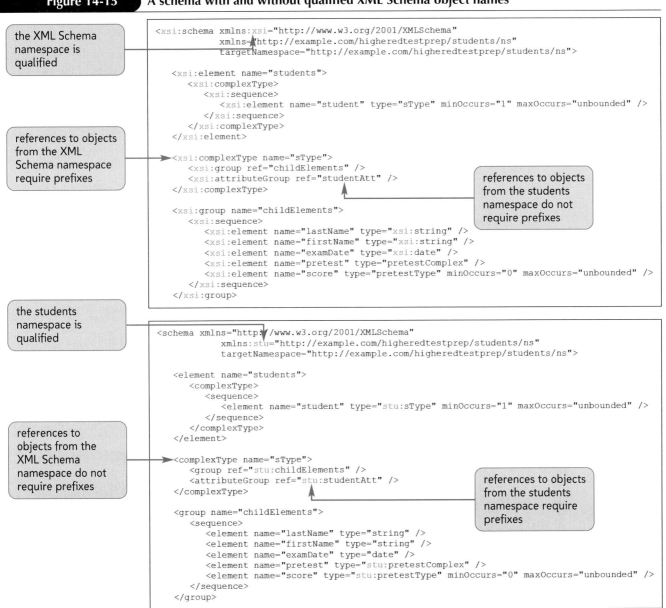

the XML Schema namespace is qualified

references to objects from the XML Schema namespace require prefixes

references to objects from the students namespace do not require prefixes

the students namespace is qualified

references to objects from the XML Schema namespace do not require prefixes

references to objects from the students namespace require prefixes

You will modify Gabby's *studentsvb.xsd* schema file, using http://example.com/higheredtestprep/students/ns as the default and target namespace of the schema. You'll also modify the *course.xsd* schema file using http://example.com/higheredtestprep/course/ns.

To associate each schema with a namespace:

1. Return to the **studentsvb.xsd** document in your XML editor.

2. In the file, add the following attributes to the root schema element, as shown in Figure 14-16:

   ```
   xmlns="http://example.com/higheredtestprep/students/ns"
   targetNamespace="http://example.com/higheredtestprep/students/ns"
   ```

Figure 14-16   Associating the students schema with a namespace

```
<xsi:schema xmlns:xsi="http://www.w3.org/2001/XMLSchema"
            xmlns="http://example.com/higheredtestprep/students/ns"
            targetNamespace="http://example.com/higheredtestprep/students/ns">

  <xsi:element name="students">
```

3. Save your changes to the **studentsvb.xsd** file.

4. In the **course.xsd** file, add the following attributes to the root schema element, as shown in Figure 14-17:

   ```
   xmlns="http://example.com/higheredtestprep/course/ns"
   targetNamespace="http://example.com/higheredtestprep/course/ns"
   ```

Figure 14-17   Associating the course schema with a namespace

```
<xs:schema xmlns:xs="http://www.w3.org/2001/XMLSchema"
           xmlns="http://example.com/higheredtestprep/course/ns"
           targetNamespace="http://example.com/higheredtestprep/course/ns">

  <xs:element name="course">
```

5. Save your changes to the **course.xsd** file, return to **psatstudents.xml** in your XML validator, and then validate the document. The document still fails validation, this time with a message about stu:students not being expected as a child element.

   Trouble? If you receive any validation errors other than the error described in Step 5, compare your code against the preceding figures, fix any errors you find, and then revalidate until you receive only the error described in Step 5.

Gabby is pleased that you've been able to combine both the course and the students namespaces in a single instance document. Your final step will be to combine the schema information for both namespaces in the *course.xsd* schema document. XML Schema includes two methods for achieving this—including and importing schemas.

Including and Importing Schemas

You include a schema file when you want to combine schema files from the same namespace. This might be the case if one schema file contains a collection of customized data types that you want shared among many different files, and another schema file contains a collection of elements and attributes that define the structure of a particular document. To include a schema, you add the element

```
<xsi:include schemaLocation="schema" />
```

as a child of the root `schema` element, where *schema* is the name of the schema file to be included. The effect is to combine the two schema files into a single schema that can then be applied to a specific instance document. In an environment in which large and complex XML vocabularies are developed, different teams might work on different parts of the schema, using the `include` element to combine the different parts into a finished product. Rather than having one large and complex schema file, you can break the schema into smaller, more manageable files that can be shared and combined.

The other way to combine schemas is through importing, which is used when the schemas come from different namespaces. The syntax of the `import` element is

```
<xsi:import namespace="uri" schemaLocation="schema" />
```

where *uri* is the URI of the namespace for the imported schema and *schema* is again the name of the schema file. For example, to import the contents of the students schema into Gabby's course schema, you would add the following `import` element to the *course.xsd* schema file:

```
<xsi:import
    namespace="http://example.com/higheredtestprep/students/ns"
    schemaLocation="studentsvb.xsd" />
```

A schema can contain any number of `include` and `import` elements. Each must be globally declared as a direct child of the root `schema` element.

REFERENCE

Including and Importing Schemas

- To combine schemas from the same namespace, add the element

  ```
  <xsi:include schemaLocation="schema" />
  ```

  as a child of the schema element, where *schema* is the name of the schema file.
- To combine schemas from different namespaces, use

  ```
  <xsi:import namespace="uri" schemaLocation="schema" />
  ```

  where *uri* is the URI of the imported schema's namespace and *schema* is the name of the schema file.

You will use the `import` element to import the *studentsvb.xsd* schema file into the *course.xsd* file.

To import the *studentsvb.xsd* schema file:

1. Return to the **course.xsd** file in your XML editor.

2. Directly below the opening tag of the `schema` element, insert the following `import` element, as shown in Figure 14-18:

```
<xs:import
      namespace="http://example.com/higheredtestprep/students/ns"
      schemaLocation="studentsvb.xsd" />
```

Figure 14-18	Importing a schema file

```
<xs:schema xmlns:xs="http://www.w3.org/2001/XMLSchema"
           xmlns="http://example.com/higheredtestprep/course/ns"
           targetNamespace="http://example.com/higheredtestprep/course/ns">

   <xs:import namespace="http://example.com/higheredtestprep/students/ns"
              schemaLocation="studentsvb.xsd" />
   <xs:element name="course">
```

This element assigns the namespace

   http://example.com/higheredtestprep/students/ns

to the contents of the *studentsvb.xsd* schema document.

3. Save your work, validate the file, and then if necessary troubleshoot any validation errors until the file validates.

Referencing Objects from Other Schemas

After a schema is imported into another schema file, any objects it contains with global scope can be referenced in that file. To reference an object from an imported schema, you must declare the namespace of the imported schema in the `schema` element. You can then reference the object using the `ref` attribute or the `type` attribute for customized simple and complex types.

Gabby wants the `students` element to be placed directly after the `instructor` element in this schema, to match the location where you placed the `students` element and its content in the instance document. You will add the reference to the `students` element to the schema now.

To reference the `students` element in the *course.xsd* file:

TIP

When referencing elements in an imported schema file, the prefix does not have to match the prefix used in the imported schema file.

1. In the **course.xsd** file, add the following namespace declaration to the root `schema` element:

   ```
   xmlns:stu="http://example.com/higheredtestprep/students/ns"
   ```

2. Insert the following element reference directly below the closing `</xs:element>` tag for the `instructor` element declaration, as shown in Figure 14-19:

   ```
   <xs:element ref="stu:students" />
   ```

   This code tells validators that in the sequence of elements within the `course` element, the `students` element from the students namespace should follow the `instructor` element from the course namespace. The element reference is qualified with a namespace prefix to indicate to validators that this reference points to a global object found in the students namespace. Figure 14-19 shows the revised schema code.

Figure 14-19   The course and students schemas combined in a single file

```
<xs:schema xmlns:xs="http://www.w3.org/2001/XMLSchema"
           xmlns="http://example.com/higheredtestprep/course/ns"
           targetNamespace="http://example.com/higheredtestprep/course/ns"
           xmlns:stu="http://example.com/higheredtestprep/students/ns">

   <xs:import namespace="http://example.com/higheredtestprep/students/ns"
           schemaLocation="studentsvb.xsd" />
   <xs:element name="course">
      <xs:complexType>
         <xs:sequence>
            <xs:element name="name">
               <xs:complexType>
                  <xs:sequence>
                     <xs:element name="title" type="xs:string" />
                     <xs:element name="session" type="xs:string" />
                  </xs:sequence>
               </xs:complexType>
            </xs:element>
            <xs:element name="description" type="xs:string" />
            <xs:element name="instructor">
               <xs:complexType>
                  <xs:sequence>
                     <xs:element name="firstName" type="xs:string" />
                     <xs:element name="lastName" type="xs:string" />
                  </xs:sequence>
               </xs:complexType>
            </xs:element>
            <xs:element ref="stu:students" />
         </xs:sequence>
         <xs:attribute name="courseID" type="xs:ID" />
      </xs:complexType>
   </xs:element>

</xs:schema>
```

3. Save the changes to the **course.xsd** document.

4. Return to **psatstudents.xml** in your XML editor.

5. Validate the XML content against the schema. The document passes validation, with the validator drawing rules for content and structure from the two different schema files.

   Trouble? If your *psatstudents.xml* document doesn't validate, compare your *course.xsd* file to Figure 14-19, and then edit your code as necessary until the *psatstudents.xml* document validates.

This example provides a glimpse of the power and flexibility of schemas in working with multiple vocabularies and namespaces. In more advanced applications, large schema structures can be created to validate equally complex XML environments involving dozens of documents and vocabularies. The XML Schema language is also flexible enough to provide control over which elements and attributes are validated, and how they are validated.

Gabby is pleased with the work you have done on creating a schema for the compound document describing the features of the PSAT Mathematics Course and the list of students enrolled in that course. She'll use the document as a model for creating compound documents for other courses.

PROSKILLS

Problem Solving: To Namespace or Not to Namespace?

XML documents can have any format unless specifically tied to a vocabulary. The question of whether or not to namespace often arises. Because namespaces must be added to both the XML document and any associated CSS, adding a namespace prefix requires quite a bit of document customization. Some programmers feel that using namespaces in XML and CSS documents "clutters" the code, and they argue that it would be better to modify any custom vocabularies as much as possible to avoid name collision problems. This would allow the XML and CSS documents to remain more flexible. To avoid namespace collisions, the name of one item (typically the one used less often) would need to be changed to some other name. Although this seems like a simple solution, it could be difficult to implement because there is no master list of all element and attribute names for XML vocabularies. Therefore, you may not always be able to predetermine where every possible name collision will occur. Another approach would be to put unique characters before the names so that the names differ and further name collisions are unlikely to happen. Regardless of which approach you take to avoid namespace collisions, it should be applied consistently throughout the system.

Combining Standard Vocabularies

So far you've worked only with the custom XML vocabularies that Gabby has created for Higher Ed Test Prep. The standard vocabularies that are shared throughout the world, such as XHTML, RSS, and MathML, can also be combined within a single compound document. Many of these standard vocabularies have unique URIs, some of which are listed in Figure 14-20.

Figure 14-20	Namespace URIs for standard vocabularies

Vocabulary	Namespace URI
CML	http://www.xml-cml.org/schema
MathML	http://www.w3.org/1998/Math/MathML
iTunes Podcast	http://www.itunes.com/dtds/podcast-1.0.dtd
SMIL	http://www.w3.org/2001/SMIL20/Language
SVG	http://www.w3.org/2000/svg
VoiceML	http://www.w3.org/2001/vxml
XForms	http://www.w3.org/2002/xforms
XHTML	http://www.w3.org/1999/xhtml

TIP

Internet Explorer versions before IE9 support the combination of MathML with other languages only if an add-in is installed.

As XML has developed as a standard language for sharing markup data, Web browsers have extended and improved their ability to support documents that combine multiple vocabularies. For example, current versions of Internet Explorer, Firefox, Chrome, Safari, and Opera support documents that combine both the XHTML and MathML languages.

INSIGHT

Compound Documents and Podcasting

Podcasting is an area where compound documents are used. Information about the location and content of podcasts is written in the XML vocabulary language RSS. As you learned in an earlier tutorial, RSS is used for syndicating text, video, or audio content. However, if you want to list your podcast on Apple's iTunes Music Store to make it more accessible to the general population, you must add elements that are specific to the needs of iTunes but that are not part of RSS. Therefore, the final podcast document contains elements from both RSS and the iTunes vocabulary.

To declare the iTunes namespace, you add the following attribute to the root `rss` element of the podcast document:

```
<rss version="2.0"
xmlns:itunes="http://www.itunes.com/dtds/podcast-1.0.dtd">
```

After you have declared the iTunes namespace, you can populate the rest of the document with iTunes-specific elements. The following text shows a portion of a compound document describing a podcast channel using elements from both RSS and iTunes:

```
<channel>
    <title>Jazz Pod Sessions</title>
    <link>http://example.com</link>
    <description>Enjoy jazz music from JPS</description>
    <itunes:author>David Hmong</itunes:author>
    <itunes:category text="Music">
       <itunes:category text="Jazz" />
    </itunes:category>
...
</channel>
```

The iTunes-specific elements listed here—author and category—will be displayed in Apple's iTunes Music Store, providing additional information to potential subscribers of the feed. To augment the descriptions of individual episodes, you add iTunes-specific elements to each `<item>` tag in the RSS document. The following shows part of the code for one episode of a podcast:

```
<item>
    <title>Jazz at Carnegie Hall</title>
    <itunes:subtitle>Famous Concerts</itunes:subtitle>
    <itunes:summary>Jazz from Carnegie Hall</itunes:summary>
    <itunes:author>Various</itunes:author>
    <itunes:duration>59:23</itunes:duration>
...
</item>
```

This particular episode highlights famous jazz concerts at Carnegie Hall. The code uses iTunes-specific elements to provide a subtitle for the show, a summary, the show's author, and the duration of the show in minutes and seconds.

The iTunes elements listed here represent only a fraction of the elements you can add to podcast code. You can learn more about podcasting and how to write compound documents involving both RSS and iTunes by visiting Apple's Web site.

REVIEW

Session 14.2 Quick Check

1. What is a name collision?
2. How do namespaces prevent the problem of name collisions?
3. If an attribute name is unqualified, what namespace is it presumed to belong to?
4. How does importing a schema file differ from including a schema file, with respect to the namespace of the schema?
5. How do you reference an object with global scope from an imported schema?

SESSION 14.3 VISUAL OVERVIEW

To link multiple style sheets to a compound document, you add a separate processing instruction for each style sheet.

Elements in an instance document must be qualified to be styled by linked style sheet rules.

The lastName and firstName elements in the course vocabulary are qualified with the crs: prefix and formatted by the style sheet for the course vocabulary.

The lastName and firstName elements in the students vocabulary are qualified with the stu: prefix and formatted by the style sheet for the students vocabulary.

```xml
<?xml-stylesheet type="text/css" href="students.css" ?>
<?xml-stylesheet type="text/css" href="course.css" ?>

<crs:course courseID="PSAT-080-5"
        xmlns:xsi="http://www.w3.org/2001/XMLSchema-instance"
        xmlns:crs="http://example.com/higheredtestprep/course/ns"
        xsi:schemaLocation="http://example.com/higheredtestprep/course/ns course.xsd">

   <crs:name>
       <crs:title>PSAT Mathematics Course</crs:title>
       <crs:session>5</crs:session>
   </crs:name>
   <crs:description>
       This is a focused course for students who
       have previously taken the PSAT exam as a sophomore
       but did not receive a desired score on the mathematics
       portion or students who will be taking the PSAT and
       wish to strengthen their skills in the mathematics
       area. Outcomes of the course will be measured using
       the original PSAT mathematics score compared to a
       course post-test, or a course pre-test compared to the
       subsequent PSAT mathematics score.
   </crs:description>
   <crs:instructor>
       <crs:firstName>Rachel</crs:firstName>
       <crs:lastName>Polygoni</crs:lastName>
   </crs:instructor>

   <stu:students xmlns:stu="http://example.com/higheredtestprep/students/ns"
            xsi:schemaLocation="http://example.com/higheredtestprep/students/ns studentsvb.xsd">
       <stu:student stuID="I8900-041" courseID="PSAT-080-5">
           <stu:lastName>Garcia</stu:lastName>
           <stu:firstName>Georgianna</stu:firstName>
           <stu:examDate>2014-10-17</stu:examDate>
           <stu:pretest level="M">55</stu:pretest>
           <stu:score>51</stu:score>
       </stu:student>

       ...

   </stu:students>
</crs:course>
```

STYLING A COMPOUND DOCUMENT

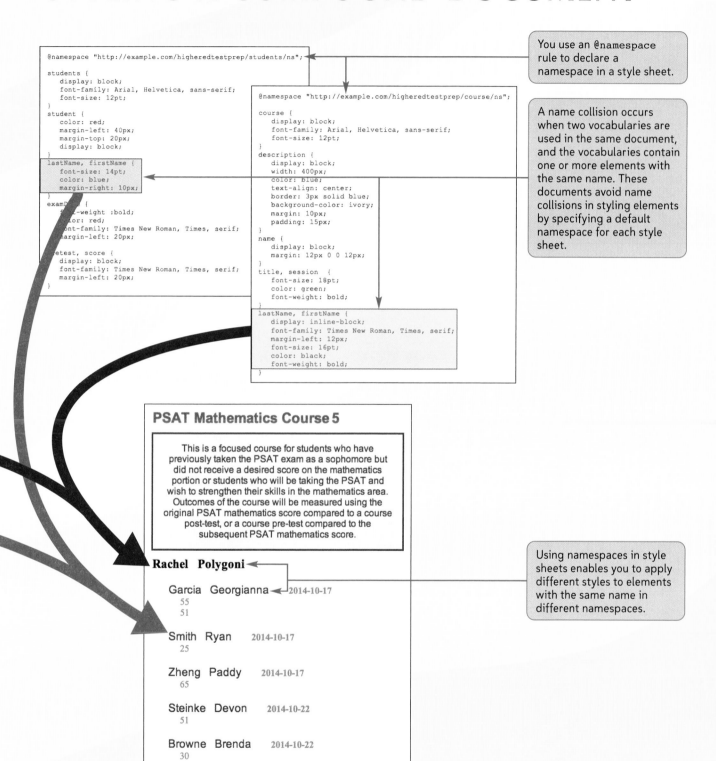

```
@namespace "http://example.com/higheredtestprep/students/ns";

students {
    display: block;
    font-family: Arial, Helvetica, sans-serif;
    font-size: 12pt;
}
student {
    color: red;
    margin-left: 40px;
    margin-top: 20px;
    display: block;
}
lastName, firstName {
    font-size: 14pt;
    color: blue;
    margin-right: 10px;
}
examDate {
    font-weight :bold;
    color: red;
    font-family: Times New Roman, Times, serif;
    margin-left: 20px;
}
pretest, score {
    display: block;
    font-family: Times New Roman, Times, serif;
    margin-left: 20px;
}
```

You use an @namespace rule to declare a namespace in a style sheet.

```
@namespace "http://example.com/higheredtestprep/course/ns";

course {
    display: block;
    font-family: Arial, Helvetica, sans-serif;
    font-size: 12pt;
}
description {
    display: block;
    width: 400px;
    color: blue;
    text-align: center;
    border: 3px solid blue;
    background-color: ivory;
    margin: 10px;
    padding: 15px;
}
name {
    display: block;
    margin: 12px 0 0 12px;
}
title, session  {
    font-size: 18pt;
    color: green;
    font-weight: bold;
}
lastName, firstName {
    display: inline-block;
    font-family: Times New Roman, Times, serif;
    margin-left: 12px;
    font-size: 16pt;
    color: black;
    font-weight: bold;
}
```

A name collision occurs when two vocabularies are used in the same document, and the vocabularies contain one or more elements with the same name. These documents avoid name collisions in styling elements by specifying a default namespace for each style sheet.

PSAT Mathematics Course 5

This is a focused course for students who have previously taken the PSAT exam as a sophomore but did not receive a desired score on the mathematics portion or students who will be taking the PSAT and wish to strengthen their skills in the mathematics area. Outcomes of the course will be measured using the original PSAT mathematics score compared to a course post-test, or a course pre-test compared to the subsequent PSAT mathematics score.

Rachel   Polygoni

Garcia   Georgianna   2014-10-17
55
51

Smith   Ryan   2014-10-17
25

Zheng   Paddy   2014-10-17
65

Steinke   Devon   2014-10-22
51

Browne   Brenda   2014-10-22
30

Using namespaces in style sheets enables you to apply different styles to elements with the same name in different namespaces.

Adding a Namespace to a Style Sheet

In the previous session, you added namespaces to Gabby's new *psatstudents.xml* compound document. To display the contents of this compound document, Gabby wants you to use styles from style sheets that she already uses for the students and course vocabularies. You'll link these files now to the *psatstudents.xml* compound document.

To link the *students.css* and *course.css* style sheets to the *psatstudents.xml* file:

1. Use your XML editor to open **studentstxt.css** and **coursetxt.css** from the tutorial.14/tutorial folder, enter *your name* and *today's date* in the comment section, and then save the files as **students.css** and **course.css**, respectively, in the same folder.

2. Examine the contents of the *students.css* and *course.css* files.

3. If you took a break after the previous session, make sure the **psatstudents.xml** document from the tutorial.14/tutorial folder is open in your XML editor.

4. In the **psatstudents.xml** file, immediately below the comment section, enter the following two processing instructions to link the *students.css* and *course.css* style sheets to the *psatstudents.xml* document, as shown in Figure 14-21:

   ```
   <?xml-stylesheet type="text/css" href="students.css" ?>
   <?xml-stylesheet type="text/css" href="course.css" ?>
   ```

Figure 14-21 Linking the instance document to the style sheets

```
   Filename:          psatstudents.xml
   Supporting Files: course.css, course.xsd, students.css, studentvb.xsd
-->
<?xml-stylesheet type="text/css" href="students.css" ?>
<?xml-stylesheet type="text/css" href="course.css" ?>

<crs:course courseID="PSAT-080-5"
```

5. Save your changes to the **psatstudents.xml** file, and then open the **psatstudents.xml** file in your browser. See Figure 14-22.

Figure 14-22	Compound document with default style sheets applied

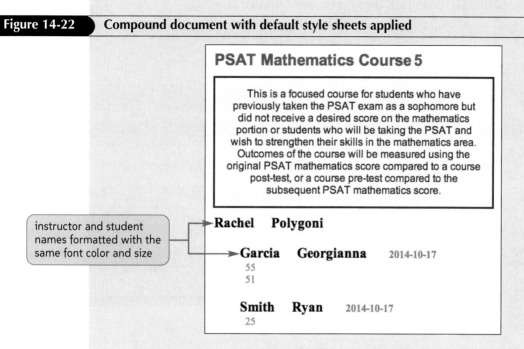

PSAT Mathematics Course 5

This is a focused course for students who have previously taken the PSAT exam as a sophomore but did not receive a desired score on the mathematics portion or students who will be taking the PSAT and wish to strengthen their skills in the mathematics area. Outcomes of the course will be measured using the original PSAT mathematics score compared to a course post-test, or a course pre-test compared to the subsequent PSAT mathematics score.

instructor and student names formatted with the same font color and size

Rachel   Polygoni

Garcia   Georgianna   2014-10-17
55
51

Smith   Ryan   2014-10-17
25

Trouble? If the instructor name and the student names are displayed in blue instead of black in your browser, you entered the link to the *course.css* style sheet before the link to the *students.css* style sheet. To make your code match the figure, edit the code you just added to the instance document so the line referencing *students.css* is first, followed by the line referencing *course.css*, as in Figure 14-21.

The first and last names of the instructor and the students are displayed in the same color, size, and font. Instead, Gabby wants the instructor's name to be visually distinct from the students' names, as shown in the rendered document in Visual Overview 14.3.

The document's appearance is different than expected because the rules in the style sheet documents don't take into account the namespaces of the different elements in the instance document. Your next task is to add namespace support to the style sheets.

Recall that to apply a CSS style to an XML element, you use the style declaration

```
selector {attribute1:value1; attribute2:value2; ...}
```

where `selector` references an element or elements in the XML document. So, to set the width of the `student` element, you could enter the following style declaration:

```
student {width: 150px}
```

If an element has a qualified name such as `stu:student`, you do *not* include the prefix in the selector name, as follows:

Invalid code

```
stu:student {width: 150px}
```

This doesn't work with style sheets because CSS reserves the colon character for pseudo-elements and pseudo-classes. Instead, you must declare a namespace in the style sheet and then reference that namespace in the selector using a different syntax.

Declaring a Namespace in a Style Sheet

To declare a namespace in a style sheet, you add the rule

```
@namespace prefix "uri";
```

to the CSS style sheet, where *prefix* is the namespace prefix and *uri* is the URI of the namespace. Both the prefix and the URI must match the prefix and URI used in the XML document. So, to declare the students namespace in Gabby's *students.css* style sheet, you would add the following rule:

```
@namespace stu "http://example.com/higheredtestprep/students/ns";
```

Note that the prefix (stu) and the URI

```
http://example.com/higheredtestprep/students/ns
```

match the prefix and URI you entered in the previous session.

As with XML documents, the namespace prefix is optional. If the namespace prefix is omitted, the URI in the @namespace rule is considered to be the default namespace for the selectors in the style sheet. Any @namespace rules in the style sheet must come after all @import and @charset rules, and before any style declarations.

INSIGHT

Applying a Namespace to a Selector

After you have declared a namespace in a style sheet, you can associate selectors with that namespace by adding the namespace prefix to each selector name separated with the | symbol, as follows:

```
prefix|selector {attribute1: value1; attribute2: value2; ...}
```

For example, the style declaration

```
stu|lastname {width: 150px}
```

applies a width value of 150px to all lastname elements that belong to the stu namespace. You can also use the wildcard symbol (*) to apply a style to any element within a namespace or to elements across different namespaces. For example, the style declaration

```
stu|* {font-size: 12pt}
```

applies the specified font-size value to any element within the stu namespace. Similarly, the declaration

```
*|student {width: 150px}
```

sets a width of 150 pixels for any element named student from any namespace. If you omit the namespace prefix from a selector, its style is also applied to all namespaces. For example, the declaration

```
student {width: 150px}
```

applies to all elements named student in any namespace.

In the *psatstudents.xml* instance document, the namespace collisions are occurring between the students and course vocabularies. As a result, styles intended for the firstName and lastName elements from one vocabulary are being applied to those elements in the other vocabulary as well. You'll add code to each style sheet now to associate it with a namespace.

REFERENCE

Declaring and Applying a Namespace in a CSS Style Sheet

- To declare a namespace in a CSS style sheet, add the rule

  `@namespace prefix "uri";`

  before any style declarations, where `prefix` is the namespace prefix and `uri` is the namespace URI. If no prefix is specified, the namespace URI is the default namespace for selectors in the style sheet.
- To apply a namespace to a selector, use the form

  `prefix|selector {attribute1: value1; attribute2: value2; ...}`

  where `prefix` is the namespace prefix and `selector` is a selector for an element or group of elements in the document.

You will add `@namespace` rules to the style sheets in the *students.css* and *course.css* files now.

To declare and apply namespaces in the *students.css* and *course.css* style sheets:

1. In the **students.css** style sheet, directly after the comment section, insert the following namespace declaration as shown in Figure 14-23:

   `@namespace "http://example.com/higheredtestprep/students/ns";`

Figure 14-23	Default namespace declared in students.css style sheet

```
*/
@namespace "http://example.com/higheredtestprep/students/ns";

students {
    display: block;
    font-family: Arial, Helvetica, sans-serif;
    font-size: 12pt;
}
```

This code specifies http://example.com/higheredtestprep/students/ns as the default namespace for all selectors in the *students.css* document.

2. Save your changes to the file.

3. In the **course.css** style sheet in your XML editor, directly after the comment section, insert the following namespace declaration as shown in Figure 14-24:

   `@namespace "http://example.com/higheredtestprep/course/ns";`

This code specifies http://example.com/higheredtestprep/course/ns as the default namespace for all selectors in the *course.css* document.

Figure 14-24 Default namespace declared in course.css style sheet

```
*/
@namespace "http://example.com/higheredtestprep/course/ns";

course {
    display: block;
    font-family: Arial, Helvetica, sans-serif;
    font-size: 12pt;
}
```

▶ **4.** Save your changes to the **course.css** style sheet, and then reload **psatstudents.xml** in your browser. As shown in Figure 14-25, none of the text from either namespace is formatted.

Figure 14-25 Unformatted document in browser after declaring style sheet namespaces

PSAT Mathematics Course 5 This is a focused course for students who have previously taken the PSAT exam as a sophomore but did not receive a desired score on the mathematics portion or students who will be taking the PSAT and wish to strengthen their skills in the mathematics area. Outcomes of the course will be measured using the original PSAT mathematics score compared to a course post-test, or a course pre-test compared to the subsequent PSAT mathematics score. Rachel Polygoni
Garcia Georgianna 2014-10-17 55 51 Smith Ryan 2014-10-17 25 Zheng Paddy 2014-10-17 65 Steinke Devon 2014-10-22 51 Browne Brenda 2014-10-22 30

You need to make a couple more changes to your code to enable both schemas and style sheets to work together in your instance document.

As you saw earlier in the tutorial, parsers can associate child elements with namespaces and validate those elements against schemas, based only on a prefix designated for the parent element. However, when browsers apply CSS styles to a default namespace, such as those you declared for the *students.css* and *course.css* style sheets, the browsers expect the name of each element being styled to be qualified. Because all of the elements that you want to style in your instance document are currently inheriting their namespace designations from their parent elements, rather than being qualified themselves, the browser didn't associate any of the styles in the style sheets with elements in the instance document. You'll make two changes in your code to make the elements styleable.

Qualifying Elements and Attributes by Default

You can force all elements and attributes to be qualified, regardless of their scope, by adding the `elementFormDefault` and `attributeFormDefault` attributes

```
<xs:schema
    elementFormDefault="qualify"
    attributeFormDefault="qualify">
...
</xs:schema>
```

to the root `schema` element in the schema file, where *qualify* is either `qualified` or `unqualified`, specifying whether all the elements and attributes of the instance document must be qualified. The default value of both of these attributes is `unqualified` except for globally defined elements and attributes, which must always be qualified. To require all elements to be qualified but not all attributes (other than globally declared attributes), you enter the following code into the schema element:

```
<xs:schema
    elementFormDefault="qualified"
    attributeFormDefault="unqualified">

...
</xs:schema>
```

This is a common setup when you want to explicitly qualify each element name with a namespace prefix.

You can also set the qualification for individual elements or attributes by applying the `form` attribute

```
<xs:element name="name" form="qualify" />
<xs:attribute name="name" form="qualify" />
```

to the definitions in the schema, where *qualify* is again either `qualified` or `unqualified`. For example, the element declaration

```
<xs:element name="student" form="qualified" />
```

requires the `student` element to be qualified in the instance document, whether it has been declared globally or locally in the schema.

Browsers are looking for qualified element names in your instance document, but your schema is configured to expect unqualified names. To make your instance document work with both schemas and style sheets, you'll first add code to the *course.xsd* schema document to specify that all elements should be qualified. Then in your instance document, you'll make all elements qualified by adding prefixes to all elements.

To specify that elements should be qualified and then qualify all elements:

1. In the **course.xsd** schema file, within the opening <schema> tag, insert the following attributes as shown in Figure 14-26, and then save your changes:

```
elementFormDefault="qualified"
attributeFormDefault="unqualified"
```

Figure 14-26	Attributes added to course.xsd schema file

```
<xs:schema xmlns:xs="http://www.w3.org/2001/XMLSchema"
        xmlns="http://example.com/higheredtestprep/course/ns"
        targetNamespace="http://example.com/higheredtestprep/course/ns"
        xmlns:stu="http://example.com/higheredtestprep/students/ns"
        elementFormDefault="qualified" attributeFormDefault="unqualified">

   <xs:import namespace="http://example.com/higheredtestprep/students/ns"
            schemaLocation="studentsvb.xsd" />
```

This code specifies that the schema expects all elements in an instance document to be qualified, and that it does not expect attributes in an instance document to be qualified.

2. In the **studentsvb.xsd** schema file, within the opening <schema> tag, insert the following attributes as shown in Figure 14-27, and then save your changes:

```
elementFormDefault="qualified"
attributeFormDefault="unqualified"
```

Figure 14-27	Attributes added to studentsvb.xsd schema file

```
<xsi:schema xmlns:xsi="http://www.w3.org/2001/XMLSchema"
        xmlns="http://example.com/higheredtestprep/students/ns"
        targetNamespace="http://example.com/higheredtestprep/students/ns"
        elementFormDefault="qualified" attributeFormDefault="unqualified">

   <xsi:element name="students">
```

3. In the **psatstudents.xml** instance document, add the stu: prefix to the opening and closing tags of all elements nested within the students element, add the crs: prefix to the opening and closing tags of all elements within the root course element that are not already qualified with the stu: prefix, and then save your changes. See Figure 14-28.

Figure 14-28 | Namespace prefixes added to elements in compound document

```
<crs:course courseID="PSAT-080-5"
        xmlns:xsi="http://www.w3.org/2001/XMLSchema-instance"
        xmlns:crs="http://example.com/higheredtestprep/course/ns"
        xsi:schemaLocation="http://example.com/higheredtestprep/course/ns course.xsd">

    <crs:name>
        <crs:title>PSAT Mathematics Course</crs:title>
        <crs:session>5</crs:session>
    </crs:name>
    <crs:description>
        This is a focused course for students who
        have previously taken the PSAT exam as a sophomore
        but did not receive a desired score on the mathematics
        portion or students who will be taking the PSAT and
        wish to strengthen their skills in the mathematics
        area. Outcomes of the course will be measured using
        the original PSAT mathematics score compared to a
        course post-test, or a course pre-test compared to the
        subsequent PSAT mathematics score.
    </crs:description>
    <crs:instructor>
        <crs:firstName>Rachel</crs:firstName>
        <crs:lastName>Polygoni</crs:lastName>
    </crs:instructor>

    <stu:students xmlns:stu="http://example.com/higheredtestprep/students/ns"
            xsi:schemaLocation="http://example.com/higheredtestprep/students/ns studentsvb.xsd">
        <stu:student stuID="I8900-041" courseID="PSAT-080-5">
        <stu:lastName>Garcia</stu:lastName>
        <stu:firstName>Georgianna</stu:firstName>
        <stu:examDate>2014-10-17</stu:examDate>
        <stu:pretest level="M">55</stu:pretest>
        <stu:score>51</stu:score>
        </stu:student>

        <stu:student stuID="I7711-121" courseID="PSAT-080-5">
        <stu:lastName>Smith</stu:lastName>
        <stu:firstName>Ryan</stu:firstName>
        <stu:examDate>2014-10-17</stu:examDate>
        <stu:pretest level="L">25</stu:pretest>
        </stu:student>

        <stu:student stuID="I7012-891" courseID="PSAT-080-5">
        <stu:lastName>Zheng</stu:lastName>
        <stu:firstName>Paddy</stu:firstName>
        <stu:examDate>2014-10-17</stu:examDate>
        <stu:pretest level="H">65</stu:pretest>
        </stu:student>

        <stu:student stuID="I8053-891" courseID="PSAT-080-5">
        <stu:lastName>Steinke</stu:lastName>
        <stu:firstName>Devon</stu:firstName>
        <stu:examDate>2014-10-22</stu:examDate>
        <stu:pretest level="M">51</stu:pretest>
        </stu:student>

        <stu:student stuID="I8154-741" courseID="PSAT-080-5">
        <stu:lastName>Browne</stu:lastName>
        <stu:firstName>Brenda</stu:firstName>
        <stu:examDate>2014-10-22</stu:examDate>
        <stu:pretest level="L">30</stu:pretest>
        </stu:student>

    </stu:students>
</crs:course>
```

crs: prefix added to opening and closing tags for all elements in the course namespace

stu: prefix added to opening and closing tags for all elements in the students namespace

4. Reload **psatstudents.xml** in your browser. Now that all the elements are qualified, the lastName and firstName elements for the instructor and the students are formatted using the rules for the course and students namespaces, respectively, as shown in Visual Overview 14.3.

Defining Namespaces with the Escape Character

Not all browsers support the use of the `@namespace` rule. When the specifications for XML 1.0 were first posted, no support existed for namespaces. Several competing proposals were circulated for adding namespace support to XML and CSS. One proposal, which was not adopted but was implemented in the Internet Explorer browser before version 9, was to insert the backslash escape character (\ ) before the colon character in the namespace prefix. So, for older versions of Internet Explorer to apply a style to an element from a particular namespace, you use the declaration

```
prefix\:selector {attribute1:value1; attribute2:value2; ...}
```

where *prefix* is the namespace prefix used in the XML document. For example, the declaration for the `title` element in a products namespace that uses the `prd` prefix is as follows:

```
prd\:title {width: 150px}
```

You can apply the same style to several elements in the namespace by using the * symbol. For example, the following declaration sets the width of all elements in the products namespace to 150 pixels:

```
prd\:* {width: 150px}
```

Other browsers such as Firefox, Opera, and Safari do not support this method with XML documents. If you want to support the widest range of browsers, you must duplicate the styles in the style sheet using both methods.

Gabby is pleased that you were able to apply namespaces to the style sheets and the namespaces. The Web page contains all the data that Gabby wants and is displayed in the way she intended. She'll base future documents for Higher Ed Test Prep on the model document you created.

Session 14.3 Quick Check

1. What code would you add to an XML instance document to link it to the *branding.css* style sheet?
2. What rule would you add to a CSS style sheet to declare a namespace with the URI *http://ns.doc.student* and the namespace prefix `student`?
3. What rule would you add to a CSS style sheet to make the namespace in Question 2 the default namespace for all selectors in the style sheet?
4. In a style sheet that includes the namespace rule in Question 2, how would you modify the selector for the `lastname` element to indicate that it belongs to the namespace with the URI *http://ns.doc.student*?
5. What code would you add to a schema file to force all elements and all attributes to be qualified by default?

Practice the skills you learned in the tutorial using the same case scenario.

PRACTICE

Review Assignments

Data Files needed for the Review Assignments: coursetxt.css, coursetxt.xsd, psattxt.xml, sessionstxt.css, sessionstxt.xml, sessionstxt.xsd

Gabby would like your help with creating another compound document and styling it with CSS. She would like to create a document that combines the description of a single course, using the course vocabulary, with a list of session descriptions for that course, using the sessions vocabulary. She then wants to apply the *course.css* and *sessions.css* styles to the content to produce formatted content in a Web browser. Figure 14-29 shows a preview of the completed document.

Figure 14-29 Final PSAT Writing Skills Course compound document

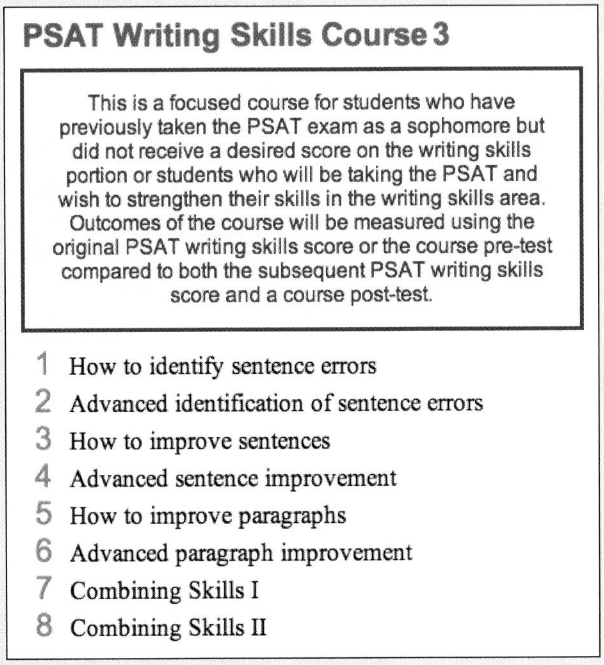

PSAT Writing Skills Course 3

This is a focused course for students who have previously taken the PSAT exam as a sophomore but did not receive a desired score on the writing skills portion or students who will be taking the PSAT and wish to strengthen their skills in the writing skills area. Outcomes of the course will be measured using the original PSAT writing skills score or the course pre-test compared to both the subsequent PSAT writing skills score and a course post-test.

1 How to identify sentence errors
2 Advanced identification of sentence errors
3 How to improve sentences
4 Advanced sentence improvement
5 How to improve paragraphs
6 Advanced paragraph improvement
7 Combining Skills I
8 Combining Skills II

Gabby has already created separate XML documents for the course and sessions content schemas to validate each vocabulary, and style sheets for the different elements in both vocabularies. She needs you to combine the content into a single document, import the sessions schema into the course schema, and edit the style sheets so that they support namespaces.

Complete the following:

1. In your XML editor, open the **psattxt.xml** and **sessionstxt.xml** documents and the **coursetxt.xsd** and **sessionstxt.xsd** schema files located in the tutorial.14\review folder, enter *your name* and *today's date* in the comment section of each file, and then save the files as **psat.xml**, **sessions.xml**, **course.xsd**, and **sessions.xsd**, respectively, in the same folder. Validate the **psat.xml** and **sessions.xml** files to confirm that they're valid.

2. In the **sessions.xml** file, copy the content from the opening `<sessions>` tag through the closing `</sessions>` tag, and then in **psat.xml**, paste the copied content directly before the closing `</course>` tag. Save the file as **psatsessions.xml**. Close the **sessions.xml** file.

3. In **psatsessions.xml**, in the opening `<course>` tag, keep the attribute and value that declare the XML Schema namespace, and then edit the attributes to declare the namespace http://example.com/higheredtestprep/course/ns for the course vocabulary, declare the namespace http://example.com/higheredtestprep/sessions/ns for the sessions vocabulary, and specify the location of the *course.xsd* schema file. Specify the prefix `crs` for the course namespace and the prefix `ses` for the sessions namespace. In the opening `<sessions>` tag, remove all attributes.

4. Qualify the `course` element and the `sessions` element using the prefixes declared in the previous step, and then save your work.

5. In the **course.xsd** file, specify the namespace

   http://example.com/higheredtestprep/course/ns

   for all unqualified names in the schema, and then specify the same namespace as the target namespace. Repeat for the **sessions.xsd** file, using the namespace http://example.com/higheredtestprep/sessions/ns.

6. In the **course.xsd** file, import the **sessions.xsd** file, specifying the http://example.com/higheredtestprep/sessions/ns namespace, declare the prefix `ses` for the sessions namespace, and then add a reference to the `sessions` element from the sessions namespace immediately after the declaration of the `description` element.

7. Save your work in all open files, and then validate **psatsessions.xml**.

8. In your XML editor, open the **coursetxt.css** and **sessionstxt.css** style sheets from the tutorial.14\review folder, enter *your name* and *today's date* in the comment section of each file, and then save the files as **course.css** and **sessions.css**, respectively, in the same folder.

9. In the **course.css** style sheet, declare

   http://example.com/higheredtestprep/course/ns

   as the default namespace. In the **sessions.css** style sheet, declare

   http://example.com/higheredtestprep/sessions/ns

   as the default namespace. Save your changes to both files.

10. In the **course.xsd** and **sessions.xsd** files, specify that elements are qualified by default, and that attributes are unqualified by default. Save your changes to both files.

11. In the **psatsessions.xml** file, add instructions to link to the **course.css** and **sessions.css** style sheets, and then qualify all elements. Save your work and validate the file.

12. Open **psatsessions.xml** in your browser and verify that it matches Figure 14-29.

13. Submit your completed assignment to your instructor, in either printed or electronic form, as requested.

Apply the skills you learned in this tutorial to create a compound document.

APPLY

Case Problem 1

Data Files needed for this Case Problem: sitemapPS.xml, sitemapVS.xml, sitemapWFS.xml, sitestxt.xml, sitestxt.xsd

Weekend Fun Snacks   Cleo Coal created and maintains a Web site called Weekend Fun Snacks, which lists her picks of the best and easiest recipes for kids to cook. The site's popularity convinced her there was room for more specialty recipe sites, so she created two additional Web sites—Primal Snacks, which features snacks appropriate for a paleo or primal diet, and Veg Snacks, which includes quick bites suitable for vegetarians.

Cleo also created a Sitemaps file for each site, which is a document written in XML that provides basic information about each page in a Web site, as well as how all the pages are related. Cleo has submitted her Sitemaps files to Google and other search services to help them better index her sites. However, she also thinks that the Sitemaps content she's created would be useful in a compound document with a custom vocabulary, which would allow her to view information about all the pages on all of her sites in a single page. Cleo asks for your help with creating this compound document.

Figure 14-30 shows a tree diagram highlighting some of the elements from both vocabularies that you'll place in the document.

Figure 14-30   **Tree diagrams of Sitemaps and sites vocabularies**

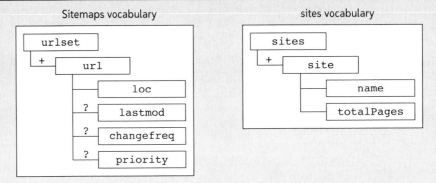

Cleo has provided you with a truncated version of the Sitemaps file for each of her three Web sites as well as another XML file containing the administrative information on her sites. Your job will be to create a compound document combining the features of the two vocabularies.

Complete the following:

1. In your XML editor, open the **sitestxt.xml** and **sitestxt.xsd** files from the tutorial.14\case1 folder, enter *your name* and *today's date* in the comment section of each file, and then save the files as **sites.xml** and **sites.xsd**, respectively, in the same folder.

2. In the **sites.xml** file, add a namespace declaration to the root `sites` element, associating the `xs` prefix with the URI for the XML Schema namespace. Specify the default namespace http://example.com/weekendfunsnacks/sites for the file. Specify **sites.xsd** as the location of the schema for the default namespace.

3. In your XML editor, open the **sitemapPS.xml**, **sitemapVS.xml**, and **sitemapWFS.xml** files from the tutorial.14\case1 folder. These files contain the Sitemaps for Cleo's three Web sites. In the sitemapWFS.xml file, copy the contents from the opening `<urlset>` tag through the closing `</urlset>` tag to the Clipboard, and then paste them into the **sites.xml** file just before the closing `</site>` tag for the Weekend Fun Snacks site. Repeat to copy and paste the content from the sitemapPS.xml file into the `site` element for the Paleo Snacks site, and the content from the **sitemapVS.xml** file into the `site` element for the Veg Snacks site. Save your changes to the **sites.xml** file.

4. In each of the opening `<urlset>` tags you pasted in the previous step, remove the XML Schema namespace declaration and the schema location, leaving the default namespace declaration for each element. Save your work.

5. In the **sites.xsd** file, in the root element, specify the target namespace as http://example.com/weekendfunsnacks/sites, and then associate the prefix `cc` with the target namespace. Associate the prefix `sm` with the namespace http://www.sitemaps.org/schemas/sitemap/0.9. Specify that elements are qualified by default, and that attributes are unqualified by default.

6. Add code to import the schema for the
http://www.sitemaps.org/schemas/sitemap/0.9
namespace from the location
http://www.sitemaps.org/schemas/sitemap/0.9/sitemap.xsd.

7. Immediately following the declaration of the `totalPages` element, add a reference to the `urlset` element from the
   http://www.sitemaps.org/schemas/sitemap/0.9 namespace.
   Save your work.

8. Validate the **sites.xml** file, and then, if necessary, fix any validation errors.

9. Submit your completed compound document to your instructor, in either printed or electronic form, as requested.

Create and style a compound document for a restaurant.

CREATE

Case Problem 2

Data Files needed for this Case Problem: menutxt.css, menutxt.xml, recipetxt.css, recipetxt.xml

Chester's Restaurant   Chester's Restaurant is located in Hartland, Minnesota. Jasmine Pup, the owner and operator, has all the menu information stored in XML files. She also has the recipes for all the menu items stored in XML. She'd like to combine the menu and recipe information for each item into a document formatted with CSS, which would give her an easy-to-read overview of the description and ingredients of each menu item.

Jasmine has asked you to combine the menu and recipe information about one menu item for her approval. Figure 14-31 shows tree diagrams of the subsets of the menu and recipe vocabularies that you'll be using.

Figure 14-31   **Tree diagrams of menu and recipe subsets**

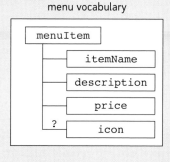
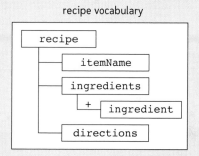

Figure 14-32 shows a preview of the page that you will create.

Figure 14-32   **Preview of menu and recipe document in browser**

Oatmeal Breakfast
　　Our oatmeal is served warm with fresh fruit, pecans, raisins, and 100% maple syrup. Available all
　　day.
　　　6.95 ♠ ♥

　　1/3 c steel cut oats
　　1-1/4 c water
　　1/4 t salt

　　Bring water to a boil. Add salt and oats, stir, and lower heat to lowest setting. Cover and let stand 2
　　hours.

Complete the following:

1. In your XML editor, open **menutxt.xml** and **recipetxt.xml** from the tutorial.14\case2 folder, enter *your name* and *today's date* in the comment section of each file, and then save the documents as **menu.xml** and **recipe.xml**, respectively, in the same folder.

⊕ EXPLORE

2. Review the contents of **menu.xml**, and then create a schema file for the menu vocabulary using the Russian Doll design. Save the schema file to the tutorial.14\case2 folder as **menu.xsd**. Specify the target namespace for the schema and save your changes. In **menu.xml**, specify the location of the schema file and save your changes. Validate **menu.xml** against the schema and then, if necessary, fix any validation errors.

⊕ EXPLORE

3. Review the contents of **recipe.xml**, and then create a schema file for the recipe vocabulary using the Russian Doll design. Save the schema file to the tutorial.14\case2 folder as **recipe.xsd**. Specify the target namespace for the schema and save your changes. In **recipe.xml**, specify the location of the schema file and save your changes. Validate **recipe.xml** against the schema and then, if necessary, fix any validation errors.

4. In the **recipe.xml** file, copy the `recipe` element and its contents to the Clipboard, and then in the **menu.xml** file, paste the recipe contents directly before the closing `</menuItem>` tag. Save a copy of the file as **menurecipe.xml**, and then change the filename listed in the comment section to match.

5. In **menurecipe.xml**, select and assign a prefix to the XML Schema namespace. Select and assign a prefix to the menu namespace specified in the root element of the *menu.xml* file.

6. Select and assign a prefix to the recipe namespace specified in the root element of the **menurecipe.xml** file. Specify the location of the schema file for the menu namespace.

7. Qualify all elements in the **menurecipe.xml** file using the prefixes you defined.

8. In **menu.xsd**, specify that elements are qualified by default and attributes are unqualified by default. Specify the namespace of the menu vocabulary as the target namespace. Assign a prefix to the namespace for the recipe vocabulary. Import the **recipe.xsd** file, and then add a reference to the `recipe` element from the recipe namespace immediately after the definition of the `icon` element. Save your work.

9. In your XML editor, open **menutxt.css** and **recipetxt.css** from the tutorial.14\case2 folder, enter *your name* and *today's date* in the comment section of each file, and then save the documents as **menu.css** and **recipe.css**, respectively, in the same folder.

10. In **menu.css**, specify the namespace for the menu vocabulary as the default namespace, and then save your changes.

11. In **recipe.css**, specify the namespace for the recipe vocabulary as the default namespace, and then save your changes.

12. In **menurecipe.xml**, directly below the comment section, insert a processing instruction that links the document to the **menu.css** style sheet. Insert another processing instruction that links the document to the **recipe.css** style sheet. Save your changes.

13. Validate the **menurecipe.xml** file and then, if necessary, fix any validation errors.

14. Open **menurecipe.xml** in your browser and verify that its appearance matches Figure 14-32.

15. Submit your completed project to your instructor, in either printed or electronic form, as requested.

Use the skills you learned in this tutorial to create a compound document containing elements from the RSS, iTunes, and iTunes U namespaces.

Case Problem 3

Data Files needed for this Case Problem: atclectxt.xml, ituneselem.txt

Austin Technical College   Pia Zhou is a community relations officer for the School of Information Technology at Austin Technical College (ATC) in Austin, Utah. Pia is part of an interdepartmental task force exploring ways to make more ATC courses available online. Her current task is to explore making lectures from a single class available through iTunes U, which is an Apple application that lets instructors distribute course content to students. Pia has asked for your help with creating an initial demonstration document.

iTunes U content is formatted in XML using the RSS vocabulary, supplemented with elements from the custom iTunes and iTunes U vocabularies.

Figure 14-33 shows tree diagrams highlighting some of the elements from the vocabularies that you'll place in the document.

Figure 14-33   **Tree diagrams of RSS and iTunes vocabularies**

RSS 2.0 vocabulary

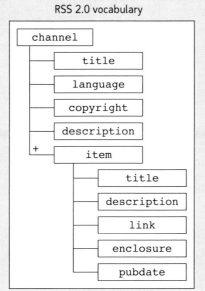

iTunes and iTunes U vocabularies

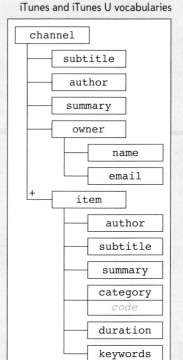

You've already received an RSS file containing the RSS elements and a text file containing iTunes U-related information on the course and lectures. Your job will be to create a compound document combining the features of the two vocabularies. Note that by convention, RSS documents do not declare the RSS namespace.

Complete the following:

1. In your XML editor, open the **atclectxt.xml** file from the tutorial.14\case3 folder, enter ***your name*** and ***today's date*** in the comment section, and then save the file as **atclecture.xml** in the same folder.

2. Add a namespace declaration to the root `rss` element declaring the iTunes namespace http://www.itunes.com/dtds/podcast-1.0.dtd. Use `itunes` as the namespace prefix. Add a second namespace declaration to the root `rss` element declaring the iTunes U namespace http://www.itunesu.com/feed. Use `itunesu` as the namespace prefix.

3. In your XML editor, open the **ituneselem.txt** file from the tutorial.14\case3 folder. This file contains the content for the different iTunes and iTunes U elements. Using this file as a reference, complete the rest of the content in the RSS document.

4. Return to the **atclecture.xml** file in your XML editor. Add the `subtitle`, `author`, and `summary` iTunes elements as child elements of the `channel` element. Place all three elements in the iTunes namespace, and use the text indicated in the **ituneselem.txt** file as the content of the three elements.

5. Below the `description` element, insert the iTunes `owner` element. The `owner` element indicates the owner of the podcast for the iTunes Store. Within the `owner` element, insert two elements named `name` and `email` containing Zakia Choudhry's name and email address, respectively. Make sure these elements belong to the iTunes namespace.

6. Add iTunes elements that describe each lecture in the series. Each lecture is marked with the `item` element. Zakia's document includes four lectures. Add the `author`, `subtitle`, `summary`, `duration`, and `keywords` elements for each of the four lectures.

7. Specify the category of each lecture using the iTunes U `category` element. The name of the category is contained in an attribute of the `category` element named `code`. The `code` attribute for each lecture should have a value of 101102, which corresponds to computer science.

8. Save your changes to the file, and then load **atclecture.xml** in your Web browser. Verify that no errors are reported in the document.

9. Submit your completed compound document to your instructor, in either printed or electronic form, as requested.

Test your knowledge of compound documents by combining data and styles for two vocabularies in a single file.

CREATE

Case Problem 4

Data Files needed for this Case Problem: carstxt.css, carstxt.xml, teamstxt.css, teamstxt.xml

South Racing   Danika Francis tracks team cars for South Racing's racing teams. As part of her job, she has created several XML vocabularies dealing with team series and the cars available to race in them. She has created an XML document containing information on two teams, and another document on cars. She wants to combine this information to create a compound document that includes team information and lists each team's cars. She has already developed a style sheet for each vocabulary. Figure 14-34 shows the tree structures of the teams and cars vocabularies.

Figure 14-34 | **Tree diagrams of combined teams and cars vocabularies**

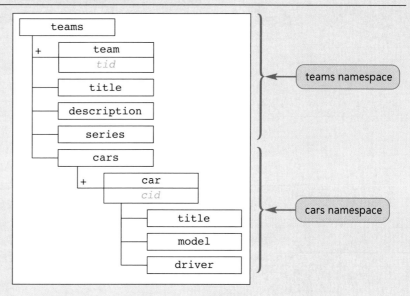

Danika has asked you to create schema documents to validate both vocabularies, and a compound document that incorporates the information and style sheet formatting from both vocabularies. There is some overlap in the element names from the two vocabularies, so you'll have to use namespaces to distinguish the elements from the two vocabularies. Figure 14-35 shows a preview of the page you'll create.

Figure 14-35 | **Completed South Racing document in browser**

Rodas Motorsports
#1 Team in racing Indy
- **Straight Away**
  Nissan
  indy
- **Quick Start**
  General Motors
  indy
- **Stop Blocks Laps**
  Ford
  indy
- **Bendwinder**
  Ford
  412
- **Turn Twister**
  Nissan
  indy

SAM Racing
Top 10 over last 5 years Nascar
- **Straight Away**
  Nissan
  indy
- **Quick Start**
  General Motors
  indy
- **Stop Blocks Laps**
  Ford
  indy
- **Sleeker**
  General Motors
  278
- **84 Racer**
  General Motors
  198

Complete the following:

1. In your XML editor, open the **carstxt.css**, **carstxt.xml**, **teamstxt.css**, and **teamstxt.xml** files from the tutorial.14\case4 folder, enter *your name* and *today's date* in the comment section of each file, and then save the files as **cars.css**, **cars.xml**, **teams.css**, and **teams.xml**, respectively, in the same folder.

2. Create a schema file for each of the two XML files using whichever schema design you choose, and selecting appropriate filenames and namespaces. Validate each XML file against its schema file, and then correct any errors, if necessary, until both instance documents validate.

3. Add a `cars` element after the `series` element for both of the teams. Copy and paste the relevant `cars` elements, along with their children, for each team, as shown in Figure 14-34. Save the compound document as **teamscars.xml**.

4. Associate the schema information with the compound document.

5. Specify the default namespace for each style sheet, and then link the compound document to both style sheets.

6. Validate the compound document and then correct any errors, if necessary, until it validates. Open the document in your browser and verify that it matches Figure 14-35.

7. Submit your completed project to your instructor, in either printed or electronic form, as requested.

ENDING DATA FILES

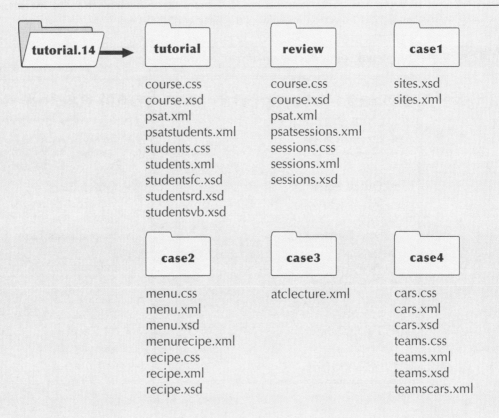

tutorial.14 → **tutorial**
course.css
course.xsd
psat.xml
psatstudents.xml
students.css
students.xml
studentsfc.xsd
studentsrd.xsd
studentsvb.xsd

review
course.css
course.xsd
psat.xml
psatsessions.xml
sessions.css
sessions.xml
sessions.xsd

case1
sites.xsd
sites.xml

case2
menu.css
menu.xml
menu.xsd
menurecipe.xml
recipe.css
recipe.xml
recipe.xsd

case3
atclecture.xml

case4
cars.css
cars.xml
cars.xsd
teams.css
teams.xml
teams.xsd
teamscars.xml

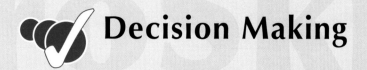

Decision Making

Deciding How to Structure Data with XML

Decision making is a process of choosing between alternative courses of action. The steps involved in evaluating a given alternative include the following:

1. Obtain relevant information.
2. Make predictions about the future.
3. Select the best alternative.
4. Prepare an action plan to implement the alternative.
5. Launch the implementation and monitor the result.
6. Verify the accuracy of the decision and take corrective action, if needed.

For some decisions, you might combine some steps, and you might even skip steps for the simplest decisions.

Obtaining Information, Making Predictions, and Selecting the Best Alternative

In order to effectively evaluate a potential course of action, data and information must be gathered. The relevant information may include quantitative financial factors that can be expressed in monetary or numerical terms, and qualitative factors that cannot be measured in numerical terms. For example, a company thinking about switching to a new system for maintaining electronic data will gather quantitative information related to the costs of the current system, such as staff time, salaried positions, software licensing, and hardware requirements. Additional information may include qualitative information related to factors such as employee morale.

After collecting relevant information, a decision model can be used to help make predictions about how the costs, behaviors, and states of nature beyond the control of the decision maker may influence outcomes. Excel spreadsheets are well suited to the quantitative portion of this task; qualitative variables may be assigned numerical weights so they, too, can be part of the decision model used for predicting potential outcomes.

Using quantitative approaches to making a decision can lead to greater confidence in the choice, but you should not ignore the value of qualitative information. After modeling the decision alternatives and calculating outcomes, selection of the best alternative may require asking additional questions, such as:

- What qualitative factors must be considered in addition to the quantitative analysis, and do they carry enough weight to discount one or more options?
- Does this alternative make sense for the long term?
- Can this alternative be realistically implemented? Think about resources and time frame, for example.
- Will the alternative be acceptable even if the outcome is not perfect, or if some unconsidered factors emerge after implementation?

Proskills

Preparing an Implementation Action Plan

Once the decision has been made, the steps necessary to implement the decision must be determined. The decision maker should have a pretty good idea of what the final outcome should be in order to consider all relevant steps. For example, in the case of moving to a new data storage system, the final outcome is new software and hardware in use company-wide.

One key consideration is the time table for implementation. When will it start? How long will each task take? What tasks must be completed before others start? Can tasks be performed concurrently?

A project manager also must be chosen to help develop and manage the implementation action plan. This person will be held accountable for all tasks, resources, and scheduling to assure the decision is implemented as originally designed.

Key milestones for the implementation must be determined so that successful completion can be tracked. Determining who will be accountable for these milestones can help keep track of completion. The project manager may have overall responsibility for keeping the implementation on budget and on time, but others will play a supporting role in getting work done.

What resources are required for successful implementation? Money? Personnel? Facilities? Are these available in-house, or does external expertise need to be sourced?

Often, the most challenging part of implementing some decisions is dealing with the human and behavioral aspects. Part of the action plan must consider regular communication with all affected parties, including weekly project status updates, scheduled training sessions, and mechanisms for handling inquiries, feedback, or opposition.

Taking Action and Monitoring Results

Once the decision is made, approvals are received, and the action plan is developed, the actual implementation of the plan can begin. As progress is made, completion of the predetermined tasks can be documented and assessed against the schedule. The project manager can then compare actual completion activity against planned activity to be sure the implementation stays on track.

Occasionally, the best-laid plans do veer off-course. In this case, the project manager must be able to determine why, when, and where the tasks fell behind schedule to help set them back on course.

Verifying the Accuracy of the Decision

Once the action plan has been implemented, it is essential to verify that the decision was the correct course of action. The decision maker can assess the effect of the implemented decision by collecting feedback about the changes in operations. For example, in the case of the new electronic data storage system, were the anticipated cost savings achieved? Was the retraining of affected staff managed appropriately?

PROSKILLS

Design and Implement a Custom XML Vocabulary

XML is a powerful tool for developing structured documents whose content can be tested against a collection of rules defined in a DTD or schema. In this exercise, you'll use XML to create a vocabulary, and then you'll create and validate an XML document using your vocabulary by applying the XML skills you've learned in these tutorials.

Note: Please be sure *not* to include any personal information of a sensitive nature in the documents you create to be submitted to your instructor for this exercise. Later on, you can update the data in your database with such information for your own personal use.

1. Design your own XML vocabulary for a field of study that interests you. Your vocabulary should include the following features:
   a. Elements containing textual content
   b. Elements containing child elements
   c. Attributes containing textual content
   d. XML-supported entities
2. Write a summary documenting your vocabulary for other users.
3. Create an instance document based on your XML vocabulary.
4. Write a DTD to validate your instance document based on your vocabulary. Confirm that your instance document passes validation.
5. Write a schema to validate your instance document. Your schema should include the following features:
   a. One or more custom data types
   b. A named complex type
   c. Schema contents laid out in a Venetian Blind design
6. Apply your schema to your instance document and verify that your instance document passes validation.
7. Create a second XML vocabulary in the same field of study as your first. Document your vocabulary for other users.
8. Create a namespace for each of your vocabularies.
9. Create a compound document combining elements and attributes from both of your vocabularies.
10. Create a second schema file to validate the contents of your second XML vocabulary.
11. Apply your combined schemas to your compound document and confirm that the compound document passes validation.
12. Document your code and describe what you've learned from creating your own system of XML documents.
13. Submit your completed project to your instructor as requested.

Color Names with Color Values, and HTML Character Entities

Both HTML and XHTML allow you to define colors using either color names or color values. HTML and XHTML support a list of 16 basic color names. Most browsers also support an extended list of color names, which are listed in Table A-1 in this appendix, along with their RGB and hexadecimal values. The 16 color names supported by HTML and XHTML appear highlighted in the table. Web-safe colors appear in a bold font.

If you want to use only Web-safe colors, limit your RGB values to 0, 51, 153, 204, and 255 (or limit your hexadecimal values to 00, 33, 66, 99, CC, and FF). For example, an RGB color value of (255, 51, 204) would be Web safe, while an RGB color value of (255, 192, 128) would not.

Table A-2 in this appendix lists the extended character set for HTML, also known as the ISO Latin-1 Character Set. You can specify characters by name or by numeric value. For example, you can use either ® or ® to specify the registered trademark symbol, ®. Not all browsers recognize all code names. Some older browsers that support only the HTML 2.0 standard do not recognize × as a code name, for instance. Code names that older browsers might not recognize are marked with an asterisk in Table A-2.

STARTING DATA FILES

There are no starting Data Files needed for this appendix.

Table A-1:
Color names and
corresponding values

Color Name	RGB Value	Hexadecimal Value
aliceblue	(240,248,255)	#F0F8FF
antiquewhite	(250,235,215)	#FAEBD7
aqua	**(0,255,255)**	**#00FFFF**
aquamarine	(127,255,212)	#7FFFD4
azure	(240,255,255)	#F0FFFF
beige	(245,245,220)	#F5F5DC
bisque	(255,228,196)	#FFE4C4
black	**(0,0,0)**	**#000000**
blanchedalmond	(255,235,205)	#FFEBCD
blue	**(0,0,255)**	**#0000FF**
blueviolet	(138,43,226)	#8A2BE2
brown	(165,42,42)	#A52A2A
burlywood	(222,184,135)	#DEB887
cadetblue	(95,158,160)	#5F9EA0
chartreuse	(127,255,0)	#7FFF00
chocolate	(210,105,30)	#D2691E
coral	(255,127,80)	#FF7F50
cornflowerblue	(100,149,237)	#6495ED
cornsilk	(255,248,220)	#FFF8DC
crimson	(220,20,54)	#DC1436
cyan	**(0,255,255)**	**#00FFFF**
darkblue	(0,0,139)	#00008B
darkcyan	(0,139,139)	#008B8B
darkgoldenrod	(184,134,11)	#B8860B
darkgray	(169,169,169)	#A9A9A9
darkgreen	(0,100,0)	#006400
darkkhaki	(189,183,107)	#BDB76B
darkmagenta	(139,0,139)	#8B008B
darkolivegreen	(85,107,47)	#556B2F
darkorange	(255,140,0)	#FF8C00
darkorchid	(153,50,204)	#9932CC
darkred	(139,0,0)	#8B0000
darksalmon	(233,150,122)	#E9967A
darkseagreen	(143,188,143)	#8FBC8F
darkslateblue	(72,61,139)	#483D8B
darkslategray	(47,79,79)	#2F4F4F
darkturquoise	(0,206,209)	#00CED1
darkviolet	(148,0,211)	#9400D3
deeppink	(255,20,147)	#FF1493
deepskyblue	(0,191,255)	#00BFFF
dimgray	(105,105,105)	#696969
dodgerblue	(30,144,255)	#1E90FF
firebrick	(178,34,34)	#B22222
floralwhite	(255,250,240)	#FFFAF0
forestgreen	(34,139,34)	#228B22
fuchsia	**(255,0,255)**	**#FF00FF**

Color Name	RGB Value	Hexadecimal Value
gainsboro	(220,220,220)	#DCDCDC
ghostwhite	(248,248,255)	#F8F8FF
gold	(255,215,0)	#FFD700
goldenrod	(218,165,32)	#DAA520
gray	(128,128,128)	#808080
green	(0,128,0)	#008000
greenyellow	(173,255,47)	#ADFF2F
honeydew	(240,255,240)	#F0FFF0
hotpink	(255,105,180)	#FF69B4
indianred	(205,92,92)	#CD5C5C
indigo	(75,0,130)	#4B0082
ivory	(255,255,240)	#FFFFF0
khaki	(240,230,140)	#F0E68C
lavender	(230,230,250)	#E6E6FA
lavenderblush	(255,240,245)	#FFF0F5
lawngreen	(124,252,0)	#7CFC00
lemonchiffon	(255,250,205)	#FFFACD
lightblue	(173,216,230)	#ADD8E6
lightcoral	(240,128,128)	#F08080
lightcyan	(224,255,255)	#E0FFFF
lightgoldenrodyellow	(250,250,210)	#FAFAD2
lightgreen	(144,238,144)	#90EE90
lightgrey	(211,211,211)	#D3D3D3
lightpink	(255,182,193)	#FFB6C1
lightsalmon	(255,160,122)	#FFA07A
lightseagreen	(32,178,170)	#20B2AA
lightskyblue	(135,206,250)	#87CEFA
lightslategray	(119,136,153)	#778899
lightsteelblue	(176,196,222)	#B0C4DE
lightyellow	(255,255,224)	#FFFFE0
lime	**(0,255,0)**	**#00FF00**
limegreen	(50,205,50)	#32CD32
linen	(250,240,230)	#FAF0E6
magenta	**(255,0,255)**	**#FF00FF**
maroon	(128,0,0)	#800000
mediumaquamarine	(102,205,170)	#66CDAA
mediumblue	(0,0,205)	#0000CD
mediumorchid	(186,85,211)	#BA55D3
mediumpurple	(147,112,219)	#9370DB
mediumseagreen	(60,179,113)	#3CB371
mediumslateblue	(123,104,238)	#7B68EE
mediumspringgreen	(0,250,154)	#00FA9A
mediumturquoise	(72,209,204)	#48D1CC
mediumvioletred	(199,21,133)	#C71585
midnightblue	(25,25,112)	#191970
mintcream	(245,255,250)	#F5FFFA
mistyrose	(255,228,225)	#FFE4E1

Color Name	RGB Value	Hexadecimal Value
moccasin	(255,228,181)	#FFE4B5
navajowhite	(255,222,173)	#FFDEAD
navy	**(0,0,128)**	**#000080**
oldlace	(253,245,230)	#FDF5E6
olive	(128,128,0)	#808000
olivedrab	(107,142,35)	#6B8E23
orange	(255,165,0)	#FFA500
orangered	(255,69,0)	#FF4500
orchid	(218,112,214)	#DA70D6
palegoldenrod	(238,232,170)	#EEE8AA
palegreen	(152,251,152)	#98FB98
paleturquoise	(175,238,238)	#AFEEEE
palevioletred	(219,112,147)	#DB7093
papayawhip	(255,239,213)	#FFEFD5
peachpuff	(255,218,185)	#FFDAB9
peru	(205,133,63)	#CD853F
pink	(255,192,203)	#FFC0CB
plum	(221,160,221)	#DDA0DD
powderblue	(176,224,230)	#B0E0E6
purple	**(128,0,128)**	**#808080**
red	**(255,0,0)**	**#FF0000**
rosybrown	(188,143,143)	#BC8F8F
royalblue	(65,105,0)	#4169E1
saddlebrown	(139,69,19)	#8B4513
salmon	(250,128,114)	#FA8072
sandybrown	(244,164,96)	#F4A460
seagreen	(46,139,87)	#2E8B57
seashell	(255,245,238)	#FFF5EE
sienna	(160,82,45)	#A0522D
silver	(192,192,192)	#C0C0C0
skyblue	(135,206,235)	#87CEEB
slateblue	(106,90,205)	#6A5ACD
slategray	(112,128,144)	#708090
snow	(255,250,250)	#FFFAFA
springgreen	(0,255,127)	#00FF7F
steelblue	(70,130,180)	#4682B4
tan	(210,180,140)	#D2B48C
teal	(0,128,128)	#008080
thistle	(216,191,216)	#D8BFD8
tomato	(255,99,71)	#FF6347
turquoise	(64,224,208)	#40E0D0
violet	(238,130,238)	#EE82EE
wheat	(245,222,179)	#F5DEB3
white	**(255,255,255)**	**#FFFFFF**
whitesmoke	(245,245,245)	#F5F5F5
yellow	**(255,255,0)**	**#FFFF00**
yellowgreen	(154,205,50)	#9ACD32

Table A-2:
HTML character entities

Character	Code	Code Name	Description
	&#09;		Tab
	&#10;		Line feed
	&#32;		Space
!	&#33;		Exclamation mark
"	&#34;	&quot;	Double quotation mark
#	&#35;		Pound sign
$	&#36;		Dollar sign
%	&#37;		Percent sign
&	&#38;	&amp;	Ampersand
'	&#39;		Apostrophe
(	&#40;		Left parenthesis
)	&#41;		Right parenthesis
*	&#42;		Asterisk
+	&#43;		Plus sign
,	&#44;		Comma
-	&#45;		Hyphen
.	&#46;		Period
/	&#47;		Forward slash
0 - 9	0–9		Numbers 0–9
:	&#58;		Colon
;	&#59;		Semicolon
<	&#60;	&lt;	Less than sign
=	&#61;		Equal sign
>	&#62;	&gt;	Greater than sign
?	&#63;		Question mark
@	&#64;		Commercial at sign
A - Z	A–Z		Letters A–Z
[	&#91;		Left square bracket
\	&#92;		Back slash
]	&#93;		Right square bracket
^	&#94;		Caret
_	&#95;		Horizontal bar (underscore)
`	&#96;		Grave accent
a - z	a–z		Letters a–z
{	&#123;		Left curly brace
|	|		Vertical bar
}	&#125;		Right curly brace
~	&#126;		Tilde
‚	&#130;		Comma
ƒ	&#131;		Function sign (florin)
„	&#132;		Double quotation mark
…	&#133;		Ellipsis
†	&#134;		Dagger

Character	Code	Code Name	Description
‡	&#135;		Double dagger
ˆ	&#136;		Circumflex
‰	&#137;		Permil
Š	&#138;		Capital S with hacek
‹	&#139;		Left single angle
Œ	&#140;		Capital OE ligature
	–		Unused
'	&#145;		Single beginning quotation mark
'	&#146;		Single ending quotation mark
"	&#147;		Double beginning quotation mark
"	&#148;		Double ending quotation mark
•	&#149;		Bullet
–	&#150;		En dash
—	&#151;		Em dash
~	&#152;		Tilde
™	&#153;	™*	Trademark symbol
š	&#154;		Small s with hacek
›	&#155;		Right single angle
œ	&#156;		Lowercase oe ligature
Ÿ	&#159;		Capital Y with umlaut
		*	Non-breaking space
¡	&#161;	¡*	Inverted exclamation mark
¢	&#162;	¢*	Cent sign
£	&#163;	£*	Pound sterling
¤	&#164;	¤*	General currency symbol
¥	&#165;	¥*	Yen sign
¦	&#166;	¦*	Broken vertical bar
§	&#167;	§*	Section sign
¨	&#168;	¨*	Umlaut
©	&#169;	©*	Copyright symbol
ª	&#170;	ª*	Feminine ordinal
«	&#171;	«*	Left angle quotation mark
¬	&#172;	¬*	Not sign
	&#173;	­*	Soft hyphen
®	&#174;	®*	Registered trademark
¯	&#175;	¯*	Macron
°	&#176;	°*	Degree sign
±	&#177;	±*	Plus/minus symbol
2	&#178;	²*	Superscript 2
3	&#179;	³*	Superscript 3
´	&#180;	´*	Acute accent
µ	&#181;	µ*	Micro sign
¶	&#182;	¶*	Paragraph sign

Character	Code	Code Name	Description
·	&#183;	·*	Middle dot
ç	&#184;	¸*	Cedilla
1	&#185;	¹*	Superscript 1
º	&#186;	º*	Masculine ordinal
»	&#187;	»*	Right angle quotation mark
¼	&#188;	¼*	Fraction one-quarter
½	&#189;	½*	Fraction one-half
¾	&#190;	¾*	Fraction three-quarters
¿	&#191;	¿*	Inverted question mark
À	&#192;	&Agrave;	Capital A, grave accent
Á	&#193;	&Aacute;	Capital A, acute accent
Â	&#194;	&Acirc;	Capital A, circumflex accent
Ã	&#195;	&Atilde;	Capital A, tilde
Ä	&#196;	&Auml;	Capital A, umlaut
Å	&#197;	&Aring;	Capital A, ring
Æ	&#198;	&Aelig;	Capital AE ligature
Ç	&#199;	&Ccedil;	Capital C, cedilla
È	&#200;	&Egrave;	Capital E, grave accent
É	&#201;	&Eacute;	Capital E, acute accent
Ê	&#202;	&Ecirc;	Capital E, circumflex accent
Ë	&#203;	&Euml;	Capital E, umlaut
Ì	&#204;	&Igrave;	Capital I, grave accent
Í	&#205;	&Iacute;	Capital I, acute accent
Î	&#206;	&Icirc;	Capital I, circumflex accent
Ï	&#207;	&Iuml;	Capital I, umlaut
F	&#208;	Ð*	Capital ETH, Icelandic
Ñ	&#209;	&Ntilde;	Capital N, tilde
Ò	&#210;	&Ograve;	Capital O, grave accent
Ó	&#211;	&Oacute;	Capital O, acute accent
Ô	&#212;	&Ocirc;	Capital O, circumflex accent
Õ	&#213;	&Otilde;	Capital O, tilde
Ö	&#214;	&Ouml;	Capital O, umlaut
×	&#215;	×*	Multiplication sign
Ø	&#216;	&Oslash;	Capital O slash
Ù	&#217;	&Ugrave;	Capital U, grave accent
Ú	&#218;	&Uacute;	Capital U, acute accent
Û	&#219;	&Ucirc;	Capital U, circumflex accent
Ü	&#220;	&Uuml;	Capital U, umlaut
Ý	&#221;	&Yacute;	Capital Y, acute accent
Þ	&#222;	&THORN;	Capital THORN, Icelandic
ß	&#223;	&szlig;	Small sz ligature
à	&#224;	&agrave;	Small a, grave accent
á	&#225;	&aacute;	Small a, acute accent

Character	Code	Code Name	Description
â	&#226;	&acirc;	Small a, circumflex accent
ã	&#227;	&atilde;	Small a, tilde
ä	&#228;	&auml;	Small a, umlaut
å	&#229;	&aring;	Small a, ring
æ	&#230;	&aelig;	Small ae ligature
ç	&#231;	&ccedil;	Small c, cedilla
è	&#232;	&egrave;	Small e, grave accent
é	&#233;	&eacute;	Small e, acute accent
ê	&#234;	&ecirc;	Small e, circumflex accent
ë	&#235;	&euml;	Small e, umlaut
ì	&#236;	&igrave;	Small i, grave accent
í	&#237;	&iacute;	Small i, acute accent
î	&#238;	&icirc;	Small i, circumflex accent
ï	&#239;	&iuml;	Small i, umlaut
ð	&#240;	&eth;	Small eth, Icelandic
ñ	&#241;	&ntilde;	Small n, tilde
ò	&#242;	&ograve;	Small o, grave accent
ó	&#243;	&oacute;	Small o, acute accent
ô	&#244;	&ocirc;	Small o, circumflex accent
õ	&#245;	&otilde;	Small o, tilde
ö	&#246;	&ouml;	Small o, umlaut
÷	&#247;	÷*	Division sign
ø	&#248;	&oslash;	Small o slash
ù	&#249;	&ugrave;	Small u, grave accent
ú	&#250;	&uacute;	Small u, acute accent
û	&#251;	&ucirc;	Small u, circumflex accent
ü	&#252;	&uuml;	Small u, umlaut
ý	&#253;	&yacute;	Small y, acute accent
þ	&#254;	&thorn;	Small thorn, Icelandic
ÿ	&#255;	&yuml;	Small y, umlaut

Making the Web More Accessible

Studies indicate that about 20% of the population has some type of disability. Many of these disabilities do not affect an individual's ability to interact with the Web. However, other disabilities can severely affect an individual's ability to participate in the Web community. For example, on a news Web site, a blind user could not see the latest headlines. A deaf user would not be able to hear a news clip embedded in the site's main page. A user with motor disabilities might not be able to move a mouse pointer to activate important links featured on the site's home page.

Disabilities that inhibit an individual's ability to use the Web fall into four main categories:

- **Visual disability:** A visual disability can include complete blindness, color-blindness, or an untreatable visual impairment.
- **Hearing disability:** A hearing disability can include complete deafness or the inability to distinguish sounds of certain frequencies.
- **Motor disability:** A motor disability can include the inability to use a mouse, to exhibit fine motor control, or to respond in a timely manner to computer prompts and queries.
- **Cognitive disability:** A cognitive disability can include a learning disability, attention deficit disorder, or the inability to focus on large amounts of information.

While the Web includes some significant obstacles to full use by disabled people, it also offers the potential for contact with a great amount of information that is not otherwise cheaply or easily accessible. For example, before the Web, in order to read a newspaper, a blind person was constrained by the expense of Braille printouts and audio tapes, as well as the limited availability of sighted people willing to read the news out loud. As a result, blind people would often only be able to read newspapers after the news was no longer new. The Web, however, makes news available in an electronic format and in real-time. A blind user can use a browser that converts electronic text into speech, known as a **screen reader**, to read a newspaper Web site. Combined with the Web, screen readers provide access to a broader array of information than was possible through Braille publications alone.

> "The power of the Web is in its universality. Access by everyone regardless of disability is an essential aspect."
>
> — Tim Berners-Lee, W3C Director and inventor of the World Wide Web

STARTING DATA FILES

There are no starting Data Files needed for this appendix.

In addition to screen readers, many other programs and devices—known collectively as **assistive technology** or **adaptive technology**—are available to enable people with different disabilities to use the Web. The challenge for the Web designer, then, is to create Web pages that are accessible to everyone, including (and perhaps especially) to people with disabilities. In addition to being a design challenge, for some designers, Web accessibility is the law.

Working with Section 508 Guidelines

In 1973, Congress passed the Rehabilitation Act, which aimed to foster economic independence for people with disabilities. Congress amended the act in 1998 to reflect the latest changes in information technology. Part of the amendment, **Section 508**, requires that any electronic information developed, procured, maintained, or used by the federal government be accessible to people with disabilities. Because the Web is one of the main sources of electronic information, Section 508 has had a profound impact on how Web pages are designed and how Web code is written. Note that the standards apply to federal Web sites, but not to private sector Web sites; however, if a site is provided under contract to a federal agency, the Web site or portion covered by the contract has to comply. Required or not, though, you should follow the Section 508 guidelines not only to make your Web site more accessible, but also to make your HTML code more consistent and reliable. The Section 508 guidelines are of interest not just to Web designers who work for the federal government, but to all Web designers.

The Section 508 guidelines encompass a wide range of topics, covering several types of disabilities. The part of Section 508 that impacts Web design is sub-section 1194.22, titled

§ 1194.22   **Web-based intranet and internet information and applications.**

Within this section are 15 paragraphs, numbered (a) through (p), which describe how each facet of a Web site should be designed so as to maximize accessibility. Let's examine each of these paragraphs in detail.

Graphics and Images

The first paragraph in sub-section 1194.22 deals with graphic images. The standard for the use of graphic images is that

§1194.22 (a)   **A text equivalent for every nontext element shall be provided (e.g., via "alt", "longdesc", or in element content).**

In other words, any graphic image that contains page content needs to include a text alternative to make the page accessible to visually impaired people. One of the simplest ways to do this is to use the `alt` attribute with every inline image that displays page content. For example, in Figure B-1, the `alt` attribute provides the text of a graphical logo for users who can't see the graphic.

Figure B-1   **Using the alt attribute**

```
<img src="jkson.jpg" alt="Jackson Electronics" />
```

Not every graphic image requires a text alternative. For example, a decorative image such as a bullet does not need a text equivalent. In those cases, you should include the `alt` attribute, but set its value to an empty text string. You should never neglect to include the `alt` attribute. If you are writing XHTML-compliant code, the `alt` attribute is required. In other cases, screen readers and other nonvisual browsers will recite the filename of a graphic image file if no value is specified for the `alt` attribute. Since the filename is usually of no interest to the end-user, this results in needless irritation.

The `alt` attribute is best used for short descriptions that involve five words or less. It is less effective for images that require long descriptive text. You can instead link these images to a document containing a more detailed description. One way to do this is with the `longdesc` attribute, which uses the syntax

```
<img src="url" longdesc="url" />
```

where *url* for the `longdesc` attribute points to a document containing a detailed description of the image. Figure B-2 shows an example that uses the `longdesc` attribute to point to a Web page containing a detailed description of a sales chart.

Figure B-2	Using the alt attribute

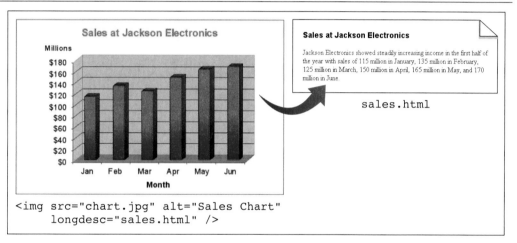

```
<img src="chart.jpg" alt="Sales Chart"
     longdesc="sales.html" />
```

In browsers that support the `longdesc` attribute, the attribute's value is presented as a link to the specified document. However, since many browsers do not yet support this attribute, many Web designers currently use a D-link. A **D-link** is an unobtrusive "D" placed next to the image on the page, which is linked to an external document containing a fuller description of the image. Figure B-3 shows how the sales chart data can be presented using a D-link.

Figure B-3	Using a D-link

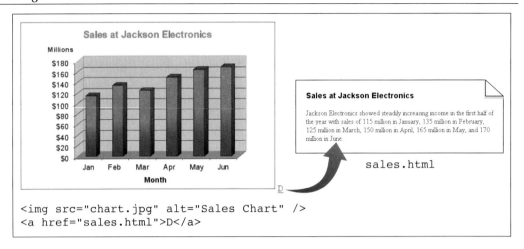

```
<img src="chart.jpg" alt="Sales Chart" />
<a href="sales.html">D</a>
```

To make your pages accessible to visually-impaired users, you will probably use a combination of alternative text and linked documents.

Multimedia

Audio and video have become important ways of conveying information on the Web. However, creators of multimedia presentations should also consider the needs of deaf users and users who are hard of hearing. The standard for multimedia accessibility is

§1194.22 (b)   Equivalent alternatives for any multimedia presentation shall be synchronized with the presentation.

This means that any audio clip needs to be accompanied by a transcript of the audio's content, and any video clip needs to include closed captioning. Refer to your multimedia software's documentation on creating closed captioning and transcripts for your video and audio clips.

Color

Color is useful for emphasis and conveying information, but when color becomes an essential part of the site's content, you run the risk of shutting out people who are color blind. For this reason the third Section 508 standard states that

§1194.22 (c)   Web pages shall be designed so that all information conveyed with color is also available without color, for example from context or markup.

About 8% of men and 0.5% of women are afflicted with some type of color blindness. The most serious forms of color blindness are:

- **deuteranopia**: an absence of green sensitivity; deuteranopia is one example of red-green color blindness, in which the colors red and green cannot be easily distinguished.
- **protanopia**: an absence of red sensitivity; protanopia is another example of red-green color blindness.
- **tritanopia**: an absence of blue sensitivity. People with tritanopia have much less loss of color sensitivity than other types of color blindness.
- **achromatopsia**: absence of any color sensitivity.

The most common form of serious color blindness is red-green color blindness. Figure B-4 shows how each type of serious color blindness would affect a person's view of a basic color wheel.

Figure B-4	**Types of color blindness**

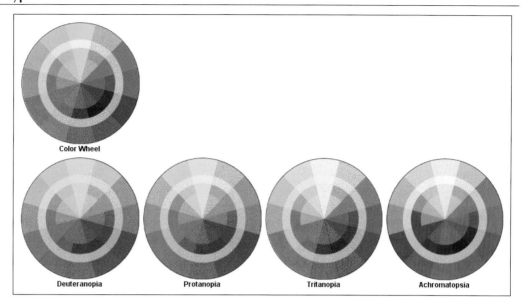

Color combinations that are easily readable for most people may be totally unreadable for users with certain types of color blindness. Figure B-5 demonstrates the accessibility problems that can occur with a graphical logo that contains green text on a red background. For people who have deuteranopia, protanopia, or achromatopsia, the logo is much more difficult to read.

Figure B-5	**The effect of color blindness on graphical content**

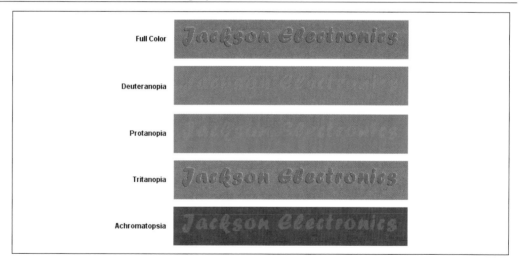

To make your page more accessible to people with color blindness, you can do the following:

- Provide noncolor clues to access your page's content. For example, some Web forms indicate required entry fields by displaying the field names in a red font. You can supplement this for color blind users by marking required fields with a red font *and* with an asterisk or other special symbol.
- Avoid explicit references to color. Don't instruct your users to click a red button in a Web form when some users are unable to distinguish red from other colors.
- Avoid known areas of color difficulty. Since most color blindness involves red-green color blindness, you should avoid red and green text combinations.

- Use bright colors, which are the easiest for color blind users to distinguish.
- Provide a grayscale or black and white alternative for your color blind users, and be sure that your link to that page is easily viewable.

Several sites on the Web include tools you can use to test your Web site for color blind accessibility. You can also load color palettes into your graphics software to see how your images will appear to users with different types of color blindness.

Style Sheets

By controlling how a page is rendered in a browser, style sheets play an important role in making the Web accessible to users with disabilities. Many browsers, such as Internet Explorer, allow a user to apply their own customized style sheet in place of the style sheet specified by a Web page's designer. This is particularly useful for visually impaired users who need to display text in extra large fonts with a high contrast between the text and the background color (yellow text on a black background is a common color scheme for such users). In order to make your pages accessible to those users, Section 508 guidelines state that

§1194.22 (d) **Documents shall be organized so they are readable without requiring an associated style sheet.**

To test whether your site fulfills this guideline, you should view the site without the style sheet. Some browsers allow you to turn off style sheets; alternately, you can redirect a page to an empty style sheet. You should modify any page that is unreadable without its style sheet to conform with this guideline.

Image Maps

Section 508 provides two standards that pertain to image maps:

§1194.22 (e) **Redundant text links shall be provided for each active region of a server-side image map.**

and

§1194.22 (f) **Client-side image maps shall be provided instead of server-side image maps except where the regions cannot be defined with an available geometric shape.**

In other words, the *preferred* image map is a client-side image map, unless the map uses a shape that cannot be defined on the client side. Since client-side image maps allow for polygonal shapes, this should not be an issue; however if you must use a server-side image map, you need to provide a text alternative for each of the map's links. Because server-side image maps provide only map coordinates to the server, this text is necessary in order to provide link information that is accessible to blind or visually impaired users. Figure B-6 shows a server-side image map that satisfies the Section 508 guidelines by repeating the graphical links in the image map with text links placed below the image.

Figure B-6 Making a server-side image map accessible

Client-side image maps do not have the same limitations as server-side maps because they allow you to specify alternate text for each hotspot within the map. For example, if the image map shown in Figure B-6 were a client-side map, you could make it accessible using the following HTML code:

```
<img src="servermap.jpg" alt="Jackson Electronics"
 usemap="#links" />
<map name="links">
   <area shape="rect" href="home.html" alt="home"
    coords="21,69,123,117" />
   <area shape="rect" href="products.html" alt="products"
    coords="156,69,258,117" />
   <area shape="rect" href="stores.html" alt="stores"
    coords="302,69,404,117" />
   <area shape="rect" href="support.html" alt="support"
    coords="445,69,547,117" />
</map>
```

Screen readers or other nonvisual browsers use the value of the `alt` attribute within each `<area />` tag to give users access to each area. However, because some older browsers cannot work with the `alt` attribute in this way, you should also include the text alternative used for server-side image maps.

Tables

Tables can present a challenge for disabled users, particularly for those who employ screen readers or other nonvisual browsers. To render a Web page, these browsers employ a technique called **linearizing**, which processes Web page content using a few general rules:

1. Convert all images to their alternative text.
2. Present the contents of each table one cell at a time, working from left to right across each row before moving down to the next row.
3. If a cell contains a nested table, that table is linearized before proceeding to the next cell.

Figure B-7 shows how a nonvisual browser might linearize a sample table.

| Figure B-7 | Linearizing a table |

table						linearized content
Model	**Processor**	**Memory**	**DVD Burner**	**Modem**	**Network Adapter**	Desktop PCs Model Processor Memory DVD Burner Modem Network Adapter Paragon 2.4 Intel 2.4 GHz 256MB No Yes No Paragon 3.7 Intel 3.7GHz 512MB Yes Yes No Paragon 5.9 Intel 5.9GHz 1024MB Yes Yes Yes
Paragon 2.4	Intel 2.4GHz	256MB	No	Yes	No	
Paragon 3.7	Intel 3.7GHz	512MB	Yes	Yes	No	
Paragon 5.9	Intel 5.9GHz	1024MB	Yes	Yes	Yes	

(Left side row label: **Desktop PCs**)

One way of dealing with the challenge of linearizing is to structure your tables so that they are easily interpreted even when linearized. However, this is not always possible, especially for tables that have several rows and columns or may contain several levels of nested tables. The Section 508 guidelines for table creation state that

§1194.22 (g)   Row and column headers shall be identified for data tables.

and

§1194.22 (h)   Markup shall be used to associate data cells and header cells for data tables that have two or more logical levels of row or column headers.

To fulfill the 1194.22 (g) guideline, you should use the `<th>` tag for any table cell that contains a row or column header. By default, header text appears in a bold centered font; however, you can override this format using a style sheet. Many nonvisual browsers can search for header cells. Also, as a user moves from cell to cell in a table, these browsers can announce the row and column headers associated with each cell. In this way, using the `<th>` tag can significantly reduce some of the problems associated with linearizing.

You can also use the `scope` attribute to explicitly associate a header with a row, column, row group, or column group. The syntax of the `scope` attribute is

```
<th scope="type"> … </th>
```

where `type` is either `row`, `column`, `rowgroup`, or `colgroup`. Figure B-8 shows how to use the `scope` attribute to associate the headers with the rows and columns of a table.

Figure B-8   **Using the scope attribute**

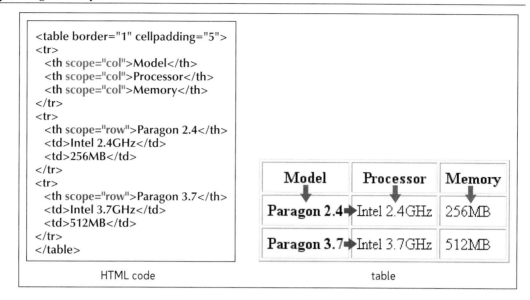

```
<table border="1" cellpadding="5">
<tr>
  <th scope="col">Model</th>
  <th scope="col">Processor</th>
  <th scope="col">Memory</th>
</tr>
<tr>
  <th scope="row">Paragon 2.4</th>
  <td>Intel 2.4GHz</td>
  <td>256MB</td>
</tr>
<tr>
  <th scope="row">Paragon 3.7</th>
  <td>Intel 3.7GHz</td>
  <td>512MB</td>
</tr>
</table>
```

HTML code   table

A nonvisual browser that encounters the table in Figure B-8 can indicate to users which rows and columns are associated with each data cell. For example, the browser could indicate that the cell value "512MB" is associated with the Memory column and the Paragon 3.7 row.

For more explicit references, HTML also supports the headers attribute, which specifies the cell or cells that contain header information for a particular cell. The syntax of the headers attribute is

```
<td headers="ids"> … </td>
```

where ids is a list of id values associated with header cells in the table. Figure B-9 demonstrates how to use the headers attribute.

Figure B-9   **Using the headers attribute**

```
<table>
<tr>
  <th id="c1">Model</th>
  <th id="c2">Processor</th>
  <th id="c3">Memory</th>
</tr>
<tr>
  <th id="r1" headers="c1">Paragon 2.4</th>
  <td headers="r1 c2">Intel 2.4GHz</td>
  <td headers="r1 c3">256MB</td>
</tr>
<tr>
  <th id="r2" headers="c1">Paragon 3.7</th>
  <td headers="r2 c2">Intel 3.7GHz</td>
  <td headers="r2 c3">512MB</td>
</tr>
</table>
```

HTML code   table

Note that some older browsers do not support the scope and headers attributes. For this reason, it can be useful to supplement your tables with caption and summary attributes in order to provide even more information to blind and visually impaired users. See Tutorial 5 for a more detailed discussion of these elements and attributes.

Frame Sites

When a nonvisual browser opens a frame site, it can render the contents of only one frame at a time. Users are given a choice of which frame to open. So, it's important that the name given to a frame indicate the frame's content. For this reason, the Section 508 guideline for frames states that

§1194.22 (i)   Frames shall be titled with text that facilitates frame identification and navigation.

Frames can be identified using either the title attribute or the name attribute, and different nonvisual browsers use different attributes. For example, the Lynx browser uses the `name` attribute, while the IBM Home Page Reader uses the `title` attribute. For this reason, you should use both attributes in your framed sites. If you don't include a `title` or `name` attribute in the frame element, some nonvisual browsers retrieve the document specified as the frame's source and then use that page's title as the name for the frame.

The following code demonstrates how to make a frame site accessible to users with disabilities.

```
<frameset cols="25%, *">
   <frame src="title.htm" title="banner" name="banner" />
   <frameset rows="100, *">
      <frame src="links.htm" title="links" name="links" />
      <frame src="home.htm" title="documents" name="documents" />
   </frameset>
</frameset>
```

Naturally, you should make sure that any document displayed in a frame follows the Section 508 guidelines.

Animation and Scrolling Text

Animated GIFs, scrolling marquees, and other special features can be sources of irritation for any Web user; however, they can cause serious problems for certain users. For example, people with photosensitive epilepsy can experience seizures when exposed to a screen or portion of a screen that flickers or flashes within the range of 2 to 55 flashes per second (2 to 55 Hertz). For this reason, the Section 508 guidelines state that

§1194.22 (j)   Pages shall be designed to avoid causing the screen to flicker with a frequency greater than 2 Hz and lower than 55 Hz.

In addition to problems associated with photosensitive epilepsy, users with cognitive or visual disabilities may find it difficult to read moving text, and most screen readers are unable to read moving text. Therefore, if you decide to use animated elements, you must ensure that each element's flickering and flashing is outside of the prohibited range, and you should not place essential page content within these elements.

Scripts, Applets and Plug-ins

Scripts, applets, and plug-ins are widely used to make Web pages more dynamic and interesting. The Section 508 guidelines for scripts state that

§1194.22 (l)   When pages utilize scripting languages to display content, or to create interface elements, the information provided by the script shall be identified with functional text that can be read by adaptive technology.

Scripts are used for a wide variety of purposes. The following list describes some of the more popular uses of scripts and how to modify them for accessibility:

- **Pull-down menus**: Many Web designers use scripts to save screen space by inserting pull-down menus containing links to other pages in the site. Pull-down menus are usually accessed with a mouse. To assist users who cannot manipulate a mouse, include keyboard shortcuts to all pull-down menus. In addition, the links in a pull-down menu should be repeated elsewhere on the page or on the site in a text format.
- **Image rollovers**: Image rollovers are used to highlight linked elements. However, since image rollovers rely on the ability to use a mouse, pages should be designed so that rollover effects are not essential for navigating a site or for understanding a page's content.
- **Dynamic content**: Scripts can be used to insert new text and page content. Because some browsers designed for users with disabilities have scripting turned off by default, you should either not include any crucial content in dynamic text, or you should provide an alternate method for users with disabilities to access that information.

Applets and plug-ins are programs external to a Web page or browser that add special features to a Web site. The Section 508 guideline for applets and plug-ins is

§1194.22 (m)   **When a Web page requires that an applet, plug-in or other application be present on the client system to interpret page content, the page must provide a link to a plug-in or applet that complies with §1994.21(a) through (i).**

This guideline means that any applet or plug-in used with your Web site must be compliant with sections §1994.21(a) through (i) of the Section 508 accessibility law, which deal with accessibility issues for software applications and operating systems. If the default applet or plug-in does not comply with Section 508, you need to provide a link to a version of that applet or plug-in which does. For example, a Web page containing a Real Audio clip should have a link to a source for the necessary player. This places the responsibility on the Web page designer to know that a compliant application is available before requiring the clip to work with the page.

Web Forms

The Section 508 standard for Web page forms states that

§1194.22 (n)   **When electronic forms are designed to be completed on-line, the form shall allow people using assistive technology to access the information, field elements, and functionality required for completion and submission of the form, including all directions and cues.**

This is a general statement that instructs designers to make forms accessible, but it doesn't supply any specific instructions. The following techniques can help you make Web forms that comply with Section 508:

- **Push buttons** should always include value attributes. The value attribute contains the text displayed on a button, and is rendered by different types of assistive technology.
- **Image buttons** should always include alternate text that can be rendered by nonvisual browsers.
- **Labels** should be associated with any input box, text area box, option button, checkbox, or selection list. The labels should be placed in close proximity to the input field and should be linked to the field using the label element.
- **Input boxes** and **text area boxes** should, when appropriate, include either default text or a prompt that indicates to the user what text to enter into the input box.
- **Interactive form elements** should be triggered by either the mouse or the keyboard.

The other parts of a Web form should comply with other Section 508 standards. For example, if you use a table to lay out the elements of a form, make sure that the form still makes sense when the table is linearized.

Links

It is common for Web designers to place links at the top, bottom, and sides of every page in their Web sites. This is generally a good idea, because those links enable users to move quickly and easily through a site. However, this technique can make it difficult to navigate a page using a screen reader, because screen readers move through a page from the top to bottom, reading each line of text. Users of screen readers may have to wait several minutes before they even get to the main body of a page, and the use of repetitive links forces such users to reread the same links on each page as they move through a site. To address this problem, the Section 508 guidelines state that

§1194.22 (o)   A method shall be provided that permits users to skip repetitive navigation links.

One way of complying with this rule is to place a link at the very top of each page that allows users to jump to the page's main content. In order to make the link unobtrusive, it can be attached to a transparent image that is one pixel wide by one pixel high. For example, the following code lets users of screen readers jump to the main content of the page without needing to go through the content navigation links on the page; however, the image itself is invisible to other users and so does not affect the page's layout or appearance.

```
<a href="#main">
    <img src="spacer.gif" height="1" width="1" alt="Skip to main
content" />
</a>

...

<a name="main"> </a>
page content goes here …
```

One advantage to this approach is that a template can be easily written to add this code to each page of the Web site.

Timed Responses

For security reasons, the login pages of some Web sites automatically log users out after a period of inactivity, or if users are unable to log in quickly. Because disabilities may prevent some users from being able to complete a login procedure within the prescribed time limit, the Section 508 guidelines state that

§1194.22 (p)   When a timed response is required, the user shall be alerted and given sufficient time to indicate that more time is required.

The guideline does not suggest a time interval. To satisfy Section 508, your page should notify users when a process is about to time out and prompt users whether additional time is needed before proceeding.

Providing a Text-Only Equivalent

If you cannot modify a page to match the previous accessibility guidelines, as a last resort you can create a text-only page:

§1194.22 (k)   **A text-only page, with equivalent information or functionality, shall be provided to make a Web site comply with the provisions of this part, when compliance cannot be accomplished in any other way. The content of the text-only pages shall be updated whenever the primary page changes.**

To satisfy this requirement, you should:

- Provide an easily accessible link to the text-only page.
- Make sure that the text-only page satisfies the Section 508 guidelines.
- Duplicate the essential content of the original page.
- Update the alternate page when you update the original page.

By using the Section 508 guidelines, you can work towards making your Web site accessible to everyone, regardless of disabilities.

Understanding the Web Accessibility Initiative

In 1999, the World Wide Web Consortium (W3C) developed its own set of guidelines for Web accessibility called the **Web Accessibility Initiative (WAI)**. The WAI covers many of the same points as the Section 508 rules, and expands on them to cover basic Web site design issues. The overall goal of the WAI is to facilitate the creation of Web sites that are accessible to all, and to encourage designers to implement HTML in a consistent way.

The WAI sets forth 14 guidelines for Web designers. Within each guideline is a collection of checkpoints indicating how to apply the guideline to specific features of a Web site. Each checkpoint is also given a priority score that indicates how important the guideline is for proper Web design:

- **Priority 1:** A Web content developer **must** satisfy this checkpoint. Otherwise, one or more groups will find it impossible to access information in the document. Satisfying this checkpoint is a basic requirement for some groups to be able to use Web documents.
- **Priority 2:** A Web content developer **should** satisfy this checkpoint. Otherwise, one or more groups will find it difficult to access information in the document. Satisfying this checkpoint will remove significant barriers to accessing Web documents.
- **Priority 3:** A Web content developer **may** address this checkpoint. Otherwise, one or more groups will find it somewhat difficult to access information in the document. Satisfying this checkpoint will improve access to Web documents**.**

The following table lists WAI guidelines with each checkpoint and its corresponding priority value. You can learn more about the WAI guidelines and how to implement them by going to the World Wide Web Consortium Web site at *www.w3.org*.

WAI Guidelines	Priority
1. Provide equivalent alternatives to auditory and visual content	
1.1 Provide a text equivalent for every nontext element (e.g., via `alt`, `longdesc`, or in element content). *This includes:* images, graphical representations of text (including symbols), image map regions, animations (e.g., animated GIFs), applets and programmatic objects, ascii art, frames, scripts, images used as list bullets, spacers, graphical buttons, sounds (played with or without user interaction), stand-alone audio files, audio tracks of video, and video.	1
1.2 Provide redundant text links for each active region of a server-side image map.	1
1.3 Until user agents can automatically read aloud the text equivalent of a visual track, provide an auditory description of the important information of the visual track of a multimedia presentation.	1
1.4 For any time-based multimedia presentation (e.g., a movie or animation), synchronize equivalent alternatives (e.g., captions or auditory descriptions of the visual track) with the presentation.	1
1.5 Until user agents render text equivalents for client-side image map links, provide redundant text links for each active region of a client-side image map.	3
2. Don't rely on color alone	
2.1 Ensure that all information conveyed with color is also available without color, for example from context or markup.	1
2.2 Ensure that foreground and background color combinations provide sufficient contrast when viewed by someone having color deficits or when viewed on a black and white screen. [Priority 2 for images, Priority 3 for text].	2
3. Use markup and style sheets and do so properly	
3.1 When an appropriate markup language exists, use markup rather than images to convey information.	2
3.2 Create documents that validate to published formal grammars.	2
3.3 Use style sheets to control layout and presentation.	2
3.4 Use relative rather than absolute units in markup language attribute values and style sheet property values.	2
3.5 Use header elements to convey document structure and use them according to specification.	2
3.6 Mark up lists and list items properly.	2
3.7 Mark up quotations. Do not use quotation markup for formatting effects such as indentation.	2
4. Clarify natural language usage	
4.1 Clearly identify changes in the natural language of a document's text and any text equivalents (e.g., captions).	1
4.2 Specify the expansion of each abbreviation or acronym in a document where it first occurs.	3
4.3 Identify the primary natural language of a document.	3
5. Create tables that transform gracefully	
5.1 For data tables, identify row and column headers.	1
5.2 For data tables that have two or more logical levels of row or column headers, use markup to associate data cells and header cells.	1
5.3 Do not use a table for layout unless the table makes sense when linearized. If a table does not make sense, provide an alternative equivalent (which may be a linearized version).	2
5.4 If a table is used for layout, do not use any structural markup for the purpose of visual formatting.	2

WAI Guidelines	Priority
5.5 Provide summaries for tables.	3
5.6 Provide abbreviations for header labels.	3
6. Ensure that pages featuring new technologies transform gracefully	
6.1 Organize documents so they may be read without style sheets. For example, when an HTML document is rendered without associated style sheets, it must still be possible to read the document.	1
6.2 Ensure that equivalents for dynamic content are updated when the dynamic content changes.	1
6.3 Ensure that pages are usable when scripts, applets, or other programmatic objects are turned off or not supported. If this is not possible, then provide equivalent information on an alternative accessible page.	1
6.4 For scripts and applets, ensure that event handlers are input device-independent.	2
6.5 Ensure that dynamic content is accessible or provide an alternative presentation or page.	2
7. Ensure user control of time-sensitive content changes	
7.1 Until user agents allow users to control flickering, avoid causing the screen to flicker.	1
7.2 Until user agents allow users to control blinking, avoid causing content to blink (i.e., change presentation at a regular rate, such as turning on and off).	2
7.3 Until user agents allow users to freeze moving content, avoid movement in pages.	2
7.4 Until user agents provide the ability to stop the refresh, do not create periodically auto-refreshing pages.	2
7.5 Until user agents provide the ability to stop auto-redirect, do not use markup to redirect pages automatically. Instead, configure the server to perform redirects.	2
8. Ensure direct accessibility of embedded user interfaces	
8.1 Make programmatic elements such as scripts and applets directly accessible or compatible with assistive technologies [Priority 1 if functionality is important and not presented elsewhere, otherwise Priority 2.]	2
9. Design for device-independence	
9.1 Provide client-side image maps instead of server-side image maps except where the regions cannot be defined with an available geometric shape.	1
9.2 Ensure that any element with its own interface can be operated in a device-independent manner.	2
9.3 For scripts, specify logical event handlers rather than device-dependent event handlers.	2
9.4 Create a logical tab order through links, form controls, and objects.	3
9.5 Provide keyboard shortcuts to important links (including those in client-side image maps), form controls, and groups of form controls.	3
10. Use interim solutions	
10.1 Until user agents allow users to turn off spawned windows, do not cause pop-ups or other windows to appear and do not change the current window without informing the user.	2
10.2 Until user agents support explicit associations between labels and form controls, ensure that labels are properly positioned for all form controls with implicitly associated labels.	2
10.3 Until user agents (including assistive technologies) render side-by-side text correctly, provide a linear text alternative (on the current page or some other) for *all* tables that lay out text in parallel, word-wrapped columns.	3
10.4 Until user agents handle empty controls correctly, include default, place-holding characters in edit boxes and text areas.	3
10.5 Until user agents (including assistive technologies) render adjacent links distinctly, include nonlink, printable characters (surrounded by spaces) between adjacent links.	3

WAI Guidelines	Priority
11. Use W3C technologies and guidelines	
11.1 Use W3C technologies when they are available and appropriate for a task and use the latest versions when supported.	2
11.2 Avoid deprecated features of W3C technologies.	2
11.3 Provide information so that users may receive documents according to their preferences (e.g., language, content type, etc.)	3
11.4 If, after best efforts, you cannot create an accessible page, provide a link to an alternative page that uses W3C technologies, is accessible, has equivalent information (or functionality), and is updated as often as the inaccessible (original) page.	1
12. Provide context and orientation information	
12.1 Title each frame to facilitate frame identification and navigation.	1
12.2 Describe the purpose of frames and how frames relate to each other if this is not obvious from frame titles alone.	2
12.3 Divide large blocks of information into more manageable groups where natural and appropriate.	2
12.4 Associate labels explicitly with their controls.	2
13. Provide clear navigation mechanisms	
13.1 Clearly identify the target of each link.	2
13.2 Provide metadata to add semantic information to pages and sites.	2
13.3 Provide information about the general layout of a site (e.g., a site map or table of contents).	2
13.4 Use navigation mechanisms in a consistent manner.	2
13.5 Provide navigation bars to highlight and give access to the navigation mechanism.	3
13.6 Group related links, identify the group (for user agents), and, until user agents do so, provide a way to bypass the group.	3
13.7 If search functions are provided, enable different types of searches for different skill levels and preferences.	3
13.8 Place distinguishing information at the beginning of headings, paragraphs, lists, etc.	3
13.9 Provide information about document collections (i.e., documents comprising multiple pages).	3
13.10 Provide a means to skip over multiline ASCII art.	3
14. Ensure that documents are clear and simple	
14.1 Use the clearest and simplest language appropriate for a site's content.	1
14.2 Supplement text with graphic or auditory presentations where they will facilitate comprehension of the page.	3
14.3 Create a style of presentation that is consistent across pages.	3

Checking Your Web Site for Accessibility

As you develop your Web site, you should periodically check it for accessibility. In addition to reviewing the Section 508 and WAI guidelines, you can do several things to verify that your site is accessible to everyone:

- Set up your browser to suppress the display of images. Does each page still convey all of the necessary information?
- Set your browser to display pages in extra large fonts and with a different color scheme. Are your pages still readable under these conditions?
- Try to navigate your pages using only your keyboard. Can you access all of the links and form elements?
- View your page in a text-only browser. (You can use the Lynx browser for this task, located at *www.lynx.browser.org.*)
- Open your page in a screen reader or other nonvisual browser. (The W3C Web site contains links to several alternative browsers that you can download as freeware or on a short-term trial basis in order to evaluate your site.)
- Use tools that test your site for accessibility. (The WAI pages at the W3C Web site contains links to a wide variety of tools that report on how well your site complies with the WAI and Section 508 guidelines.)

Following the accessibility guidelines laid out by Section 508 and the WAI will result in a Web site that is not only more accessible to a wider audience, but whose design is also cleaner, easier to work with, and easier to maintain.

HTML Elements and Attributes

This appendix provides descriptions of the major elements and attributes of HTML. The elements and attributes represent the specifications of the W3C; therefore, they might not all be supported by the major browsers. Also, in some cases, an element or attribute is not part of the W3C specifications, but instead is an extension offered by a particular browser. Where this is the case, the element or attribute is listed with the supporting browser indicated in parentheses.

Many elements and attributes have been deprecated by the W3C. Deprecated elements and attributes are supported by most browsers, but their use is discouraged. In addition, some elements and attributes have been marked as *obsolete*. The use of both deprecated and obsolete items is not recommended. However, while deprecated items are in danger of no longer being supported by the browser market, obsolete items will probably still be supported by the browser market for the foreseeable future.

Finally, elements and attributes that are new with HTML5 are indicated in the text. Note that some of these elements and attributes are not supported by all browsers and browser versions.

The following data types are used throughout this appendix:

- *char* — A single text character
- *char code* — A character encoding
- *color* — An HTML color name or hexadecimal color value
- *date* — A date and time in the format: *yyyy-mm-dd*T*hh: mm:ssTIMEZONE*
- *id* — An id value
- *lang* — A language type
- *media* — A media type equal to all, aural, braille, handheld, print, projection, screen, tty, or tv
- *integer* — An integer value
- *mime-type* — A MIME data type, such as "text/css"
- *mime-type list* — A comma-separated list of mime-types
- **option1**|*option2*| … — The value is limited to the specified list of *options*, with the default in **bold**
- *script* — A script or a reference to a script
- *styles* — A list of style declarations
- *text* — A text string
- *text list* — A comma-separated list of text strings
- *url* — The URL for a Web page or file
- *value* — A numeric value
- *value list* — A comma-separated list of numeric values

STARTING DATA FILES

There are no starting Data Files needed for this appendix.

General Attributes

Several attributes are common to many page elements. Rather than repeating this information each time it occurs, the following tables summarize these attributes.

Core Attributes

The following attributes apply to all page elements and are supported by most browser versions.

Attribute	Description
class="*text*"	Specifies the class or group to which an element belongs
contenteditable= "*text list*"	Specifies whether the contents of the element are editable (HTML5)
contextmenu="*id*"	Specifies the value of the id attribute on the menu with which to associate the element as a context menu
draggable="true|false"	Specifies whether the element is draggable (HTML5)
dropzone= "copy|move|link"	Specifies what types of content can be dropped on the element and which actions to take with content when it is dropped (HTML5)
hidden="hidden"	Specifies that the element is not yet, or is no longer, relevant and that the element should not be rendered (HTML5)
id="*text*"	Specifies a unique identifier to be associated with the element
spellcheck="true|false"	Specifies whether the element represents an element whose contents are subject to spell checking and grammar checking (HTML5)
style="*styles*"	Defines an inline style for the element
title="*text*"	Provides an advisory title for the element

Language Attributes

The Web is designed to be universal and has to be adaptable to languages other than English. Thus, another set of attributes provides language support. This set of attributes is not as widely supported by browsers as the core attributes are. As with the core attributes, they can be applied to most page elements.

Attribute	Description
dir="**ltr**|rtl"	Indicates the text direction as related to the lang attribute; a value of ltr displays text from left to right; a value of rtl displays text from right to left
lang="*lang*"	Identifies the language used in the page content where *lang* is language code name

Form Attributes

The following attributes can be applied to most form elements or to a Web form itself, but not to other page elements.

Attribute	Description
accesskey="*char*"	Indicates the keyboard character that can be pressed along with the accelerator key to access a form element
disabled="disabled"	Disables a form field for input
tabindex="*integer*"	Specifies a form element's position in a document's tabbing order

Event Attributes

To make Web pages more dynamic, HTML supports event attributes that identify scripts to be run in response to an event occurring within an element. For example, clicking a main heading with a mouse can cause a browser to run a program that hides or expands a table of contents. Each event attribute has the form

```
onevent = "script"
```

where *event* is the name of the event attribute and *script* is the name of the script or command to be run by the browser in response to the occurrence of the event within the element.

Core Events

The general event attributes are part of the specifications for HTML. They apply to almost all page elements.

Attribute	Description
onabort	Loading of the element is aborted by the user (HTML5)
onclick	The mouse button is clicked.
oncontextmenu	The user requested the context menu for the element (HTML5)
ondblclick	The mouse button is double-clicked.
onerror	The element failed to load properly (HTML5)
onkeydown	A key is pressed down.
onkeypress	A key is initially pressed.
onkeyup	A key is released.
onload	The element finishes loading (HTML5)
onmousedown	The mouse button is pressed down.
onmousemove	The mouse pointer is moved within the element's boundaries.
onmouseout	The mouse pointer is moved out of the element's boundaries.
onmouseover	The mouse pointer hovers over the element.
onmouseup	The mouse button is released.
onmousewheel	The user rotates the mouse wheel
onreadystatechange	The element and its resources finish loading (HTML5)
onscroll	The element or document window is being scrolled (HTML5)
onshow	The user requests that the element be shown as a context menu (HTML5)
onsuspend	The browser suspends retrieving data (HTML5)

Document Events

The following list of event attributes applies not to individual elements within the page, but to the entire document as it is displayed within the browser window or frame.

Attribute	Description
onafterprint	The document has finished printing (IE only).
onbeforeprint	The document is about to be printed (IE only).
onload	The page is finished being loaded.
onunload	The page is finished unloading.

Form Events

The following list of event attributes applies to either an entire Web form or fields within a form.

Attribute	Description
onblur	The form field has lost the focus.
onchange	The value of the form field has been changed.
onfocus	The form field has received the focus.
onformchange	The user made a change in the value of a form field in the form (HTML5)
onforminput	The value of a control in the form changes (HTML5)
oninput	The value of an element changes (HTML5)
oninvalid	The form field fails to meet validity constraints (HTML5)
onreset	The form has been reset.
onselect	Text content has been selected in the form field.
onsubmit	The form has been submitted for processing.

Drag and Drop Events

The following list of event attributes applies to all page elements and can be used to respond to the user action of dragging and dropping objects in the Web page.

Attribute	Description
ondrag	The user continues to drag the element (HTML5)
ondragenter	The user ends dragging the element, entering the element into a valid drop target (HTML5)
ondragleave	The user's drag operation leaves the element (HTML5)
ondragover	The user continues a drag operation over the element (HTML5)
ondragstart	The user starts dragging the element (HTML5)
ondrop	The user completes a drop operation over the element (HTML5)

Multimedia Events

The following list of event attributes applies to embedded multimedia elements such as audio and video clips and is used to respond to events initiated during the loading or playback of those elements.

Attribute	Description
oncanplay	The browser can resume playback of the video or audio, but determines the playback will have to stop for further buffering
oncanplaythrough	The browser can resume playback of the video or audio, and determines the playback can play through without further buffering (HTML5)
ondurationchange	The DOM duration of the video or audio element changes (HTML5)
onemptied	The video or audio element returns to the uninitialized state (HTML5)
onended	The end of the video or audio is reached (HTML5)
onloadeddata	The video or audio is at the current playback position for the first time (HTML5)

Attribute	Description
onloadedmetadata	The duration and dimensions of the video or audio element are determined (HTML5)
onloadstart	The browser begins looking for media data in the video or audio element (HTML5)
onpause	The video or audio is paused (HTML5)
onplay	The video or audio playback is initiated (HTML5)
onplaying	The video or audio playback starts (HTML5)
onprogress	The browser fetches data for the video or audio (HTML5)
onratechange	The video or audio data changes (HTML5)
onseeked	A seek operation on the audio or video element ends (HTML5)
onseeking	Seeking is initiated on the audio or video (HTML5)
onstalled	An attempt to retrieve data for the video or audio is not forthcoming (HTML5)
ontimeupdate	The current playback position of the video or audio element changes (HTML5)
onvolumechange	The volume of the video or audio element changes (HTML5)
onwaiting	Playback of the video or audio stops because the next frame is unavailable (HTML5)

HTML Elements and Attributes

The following table contains an alphabetic listing of the elements and attributes supported by HTML. Some attributes are not listed in this table, but are described instead in the general attributes tables presented in the previous section of this appendix.

Element/Attribute	Description
`<!-- text -->`	Inserts a comment into the document (comments are not displayed in the rendered page)
`<!doctype>`	Specifies the Document Type Definition for a document
`<a> </a>`	Marks the beginning and end of a link
`charset="text"`	Specifies the character encoding of the linked document (obsolete)
`coords="value list"`	Specifies the coordinates of a hotspot in a client-side image map; the value list depends on the shape of the hotspot: shape="rect" "*left, right, top, bottom*"shape="circle" "*x_center, y_center, radius*"shape="poly" "*x1, y1, x2, y2, x3, y3, ...*" (obsolete)
`href="url"`	Specifies the URL of the link
`hreflang="text"`	Specifies the language of the linked document
`name="text"`	Specifies a name for the enclosed text, allowing it to be a link target (obsolete)
`rel="text"`	Specifies the relationship between the current page and the link specified by the href attribute
`rev="text"`	Specifies the reverse relationship between the current page and the link specified by the href attribute (obsolete)
`shape="rect|circle|polygon"`	Specifies the shape of the hotspot (obsolete)
`title="text"`	Specifies the pop-up text for the link
`target="text"`	Specifies the target window or frame for the link
`type="mime-type"`	Specifies the data type of the linked document
`<abbr> </abbr>`	Marks abbreviated text

Element/Attribute	Description
`<acronym> </acronym>`	Marks acronym text (deprecated)
`<address> </address>`	Marks address text
`<applet> </applet>`	Embeds an applet into the browser (deprecated)
`align="align"`	Specifies the alignment of the applet with the surrounding text where *align* is absmiddle, absbottom, baseline, bottom, center, left, middle, right, texttop, or top.
`alt="text"`	Specifies alternate text for the applet (deprecated)
`archive="url"`	Specifies the URL of an archive containing classes and other resources to be used with the applet (deprecated)
`code="url"`	Specifies the URL of the applet's code/class (deprecated)
`codebase="url"`	Specifies the URL of all class files for the applet (deprecated)
`datafld="text"`	Specifies the data source that supplies bound data for use with
`datasrc="text"`	Specifies the ID or URL of the applet's data source
`height="integer"`	Specifies the height of the applet in pixels
`hspace="integer"`	Specifies the horizontal space around the applet in pixels (deprecated)
`mayscript="mayscript"`	Permits access to the applet by programs embedded in the document
`name="text"`	Specifies the name assigned to the applet (deprecated)
`object="text"`	Specifies the name of the resource that contains a serialized representation of the applet (deprecated)
`src="url"`	Specifies an external URL reference to the applet
`vspace="integer"`	Specifies the vertical space around the applet in pixels (deprecated)
`width="integer"`	Specifies the width of the applet in pixels (deprecated)
`<area />`	Marks an image map hotspot
`alt="text"`	Specifies alternate text for the hotspot
`coords="value list"`	Specifies the coordinates of the hotspot; the value list depends on the shape of the hotspot: shape="rect" "*left, right, top, bottom*" shape="circle" "*x_center, y_center, radius*" shape="poly" "*x1, y1, x2, y2, x3, y3, …*"
`href="url"`	Specifies the URL of the document to which the hotspot points
`hreflang="lang"`	Language of the hyperlink destination
`media="media"`	The media for which the destination of the hyperlink was designed
`rel="text"`	Specifies the relationship between the current page and the destination of the link
`nohref="nohref"`	Specifies that the hotspot does not point to a link
`shape="rect|circle|polygon"`	Specifies the shape of the hotspot
`target="text"`	Specifies the target window or frame for the link
`<article> </article>`	Structural element marking a page article (HTML5)
`<aside> </aside>`	Structural element marking a sidebar that is tangentially related to the main page content (HTML5)
`<audio> </audio>`	Marks embedded audio content (HTML5)
`autoplay="autoplay"`	Automatically begins playback of the audio stream
`preload="none|metadata|auto"`	Specifies whether to preload data to the browser
`controls="controls"`	Specifies whether to display audio controls

Element/Attribute	Description
loop="loop"	Specifies whether to automatically loop back to the beginning of the audio clip
src="url"	Provides the source of the audio clip
<b> </b>	Mark text offset from its surrounding content without conveying any extra emphasis or importance
<base />	Specifies global reference information for the document
href="url"	Specifies the URL from which all relative links in the document are based
target="text"	Specifies the target window or frame for links in the document
<basefont />	Specifies the font setting for the document text (deprecated)
color="color"	Specifies the text color (deprecated)
face="text list"	Specifies a list of fonts to be applied to the text (deprecated)
size="integer"	Specifies the size of the font range from 1 (smallest) to 7 (largest) (deprecated)
<bdi> </bdi>	Marks text that is isolated from its surroundings for the purposes of bidirectional text formatting (HTML5)
<bdo> </bdo>	Indicates that the enclosed text should be rendered with the direction specified by the dir attribute
<big> </big>	Increases the size of the enclosed text relative to the default font size (deprecated)
<blockquote> </blockquote>	Marks content as quoted from another source
cite="url"	Provides the source URL of the quoted content
<body> </body>	Marks the page content to be rendered by the browser
alink="color"	Specifies the color of activated links in the document (obsolete)
background="url"	Specifies the background image file used for the page (obsolete)
bgcolor="color"	Specifies the background color of the page (obsolete)
link="color"	Specifies the color of unvisited links (obsolete)
marginheight="integer"	Specifies the size of the margin above and below the page (obsolete)
marginwidth="integer"	Specifies the size of the margin to the left and right of the page (obsolete)
text="color"	Specifies the color of page text (obsolete)
vlink="color"	Specifies the color of previously visited links (obsolete)
 	Inserts a line break into the page
clear="none|left|right|all"	Displays the line break only when the specified margin is clear (obsolete)
<button> </button>	Creates a form button
autofocus="autofocus"	Gives the button the focus when the page is loaded (HTML5)
disabled="disabled"	Disables the button
form="text"	Specifies the form to which the button belongs (HTML5)
formaction="url"	Specifies the URL to which the form data is sent (HTML5)
formenctype="mime-type"	Specifies the encoding of the form data before it is sent (HTML5)
formmethod="get|post"	Specifies the HTTP method with which the form data is submitted
formnovalidate="formnovalidate"	Specifies that the form should not be validated during submission (HTML5)
formtarget="text"	Provides a name for the target of the button (HTML5)
name="text"	Provides the name assigned to the form button
type="submit|reset|button"	Specifies the type of form button
value="text"	Provides the value associated with the form button

Element/Attribute	Description
`<canvas> </canvas>`	Marks a resolution-dependent bitmapped region that can be used for dynamic rendering of images, graphs, and games (HTML5)
`height="integer"`	Height of canvas in pixels
`width="integer"`	Width of canvas in pixels
`<caption> </caption>`	Creates a table caption
`align="align"`	Specifies the alignment of the caption where *align* is bottom, center, left, right, or top (deprecated)
`valign="top|bottom"`	Specifies the vertical alignment of the caption
`<center> </center>`	Centers content horizontally on the page (obsolete)
`<cite> </cite>`	Marks citation text
`<code> </code>`	Marks text used for code samples
`<col> </col>`	Defines the settings for a column or group of columns (obsolete)
`align="align"`	Specifies the alignment of the content of the column(s) where *align* is left, right, or center
`char="char"`	Specifies a character in the column used to align column values (obsolete)
`charoff="integer"`	Specifies the offset in pixels from the alignment character specified in the char attribute (obsolete)
`span="integer"`	Specifies the number of columns in the group
`valign="align"`	Specifies the vertical alignment of the content in the column(s) where *align* is top, middle, bottom, or baseline
`width="integer"`	Specifies the width of the column(s) in pixels (obsolete)
`<colgroup> </colgroup>`	Creates a container for a group of columns
`align="align"`	Specifies the alignment of the content of the column group where *align* is left, right, or center (obsolete)
`char="char"`	Specifies a character in the column used to align column group values (obsolete)
`charoff="integer"`	Specifies the offset in pixels from the alignment character specified in the char attribute (obsolete)
`span="integer"`	Specifies the number of columns in the group
`valign="align"`	Specifies the vertical alignment of the content in the column group where *align* is top, middle, bottom, or baseline (obsolete)
`width="integer"`	Specifies the width of the columns in the group in pixels (obsolete)
`<command> </command>`	Defines a command button (HTML5)
`checked="checked"`	Selects the command
`disabled="disabled"`	Disables the command
`icon="url"`	Provides the URL for the image that represents the command
`label="text"`	Specifies the text of the command button
`radiogroup="text"`	Specifies the name of the group of commands toggled when the command itself is toggled
`type="command|radio|checkbox"`	Specifies the type of command button
`<datalist> </datalist>`	Encloses a set of option elements that can act as a dropdown list (HTML5)
`<dd> </dd>`	Marks text as a definition within a definition list

Element/Attribute	Description
`<del> </del>`	Marks text as deleted from the document
`cite="url"`	Provides the URL for the document that has additional information about the deleted text
`datetime="date"`	Specifies the date and time of the text deletion
`<details> </details>`	Represents a form control from which the user can obtain additional information or controls (HTML5)
`open="open"`	Specifies that the contents of the details element should be shown to the user
`<dfn> </dfn>`	Marks the defining instance of a term
`<dir> </dir>`	Contains a directory listing (deprecated)
`compact="compact"`	Permits use of compact rendering, if available (deprecated)
`<div> </div>`	Creates a generic block-level element
`align="left|center right|justify"`	Specifies the horizontal alignment of the content (obsolete)
`datafld="text"`	Indicates the column from a data source that supplies bound data for the block (IE only)
`dataformatas="html|plaintext|text"`	Specifies the format of the data in the data source bound with the the button (IE only)
`datasrc="url"`	Provides the URL or ID of the data source bound with the block (IE only)
`<dl> </dl>`	Encloses a definition list using the dd and dt elements
`compact="compact"`	Permits use of compact rendering, if available (obsolete)
`<dt> </dt>`	Marks a definition term in a definition list
`nowrap="nowrap"`	Specifies whether the content wraps using normal HTML line-wrapping conventions
`<em> </em>`	Marks emphasized text
`<embed> </embed>`	Defines external multimedia content or a plugin (HTML5)
`align="align"`	Specifies the alignment of the object with the surrounding content where *align* is bottom, left, right, or top (obsolete)
`height="integer"`	Specifies the height of the object in pixels
`hspace="integer"`	Specifies the horizontal space around the object in pixels (obsolete)
`name="text"`	Provides the name of the embedded object (obsolete)
`src="url"`	Provides the location of the file containing the object
`type="mime-type"`	Specifies the mime-type of the embedded object
`vspace="integer"`	Specifies the vertical space around the object in pixels (obsolete)
`width="integer"`	Specifies the width of the object in pixels
`<fieldset> </fieldset>`	Places form fields in a common group
`disabled="disabled"`	Disables the fieldset
`form="id"`	The id of the form associated with the fieldset
`name="text"`	The name part of the name/value pair associated with this element
`<figcaption> </figcaption>`	Represents the caption of a figure (HTML5)
`<figure> </figure>`	A structural element that represents a group of media content that is self-contained along with a caption (HTML5)
`<font> </font>`	Formats the enclosed text (deprecated)
`color="color"`	Specifies the color of the enclosed text (deprecated)
`face="text list"`	Specifies the font face(s) of the enclosed text (deprecated)
`size="integer"`	Specifies the size of the enclosed text, with values ranging from 1 (smallest) to 7 (largest); a value of +integer increases the font size relative to the font size specified in the basefont element (deprecated)

Element/Attribute	Description
`<footer> </footer>`	A structural element that represents the footer of a section or page (HTML5)
`<form> </form>`	Encloses the contents of a Web form
`accept="mime-type list"`	Lists mime-types that the server processing the form will handle (deprecated)
`accept-charset= "char code"`	Specifies the character encoding that the server processing the form will handle
`action="url"`	Provides the URL to which the form values are to be sent
`autocomplete="on|off"`	Enables automatic insertion of information in fields in which the user has previously entered data (HTML5)
`enctype="mime-type"`	Specifies the mime-type of the data to be sent to the server for processing; the default is "application/x-www-form-urlencoded"
`method="get|post"`	Specifies the method of accessing the URL specified in the action attribute
`name="text"`	Specifies the name of the form
`novalidate="novalidate"`	Specifies that the form is not meant to be validated during submission (HTML5)
`target="text"`	Specifies the frame or window in which output from the form should appear
`<frame> </frame>`	Marks a single frame within a set of frames (deprecated)
`bordercolor="color"`	Specifies the color of the frame border
`frameborder="1|0"`	Determines whether the frame border is visible (1) or invisible (0); Netscape also supports values of yes or no
`longdesc="url"`	Provides the URL of a document containing a long description of the frame's contents
`marginheight= "integer"`	Specifies the space above and below the frame object and the frame's borders, in pixels
`marginwidth="integer"`	Specifies the space to the left and right of the frame object and the frame's borders, in pixels
`name="text"`	Specifies the name of the frame
`noresize="noresize"`	Prevents users from resizing the frame
`scrolling="auto| yes|no"`	Specifies whether the browser will display a scroll bar with the frame
`src="url"`	Provides the URL of the document to be displayed in the frame
`<frameset> </frameset>`	Creates a collection of frames (deprecated)
`border="integer"`	Specifies the thickness of the frame borders in the frameset in pixels (not part of the W3C specifications, but supported by most browsers)
`bordercolor="color"`	Specifies the color of the frame borders
`cols="value list"`	Arranges the frames in columns with the width of each column expressed either in pixels, as a percentage, or using an asterisk (to allow the browser to choose the width)
`frameborder="1|0"`	Determines whether frame borders are visible (1) or invisible (0); (not part of the W3C specifications, but supported by most browsers)
`framespacing="integer"`	Specifies the amount of space between frames in pixels (IE only)
`rows="value list"`	Arranges the frames in rows with the height of each column expressed either in pixels, as a percentage, or using an asterisk (to allow the browser to choose the height)

Element/Attribute	Description
`<hi> </hi>`	Marks the enclosed text as a heading, where *i* is an integer from 1 (the largest heading) to 6 (the smallest heading)
`align="align"`	Specifies the alignment of the heading text where *align* is left, center, right, or justify (obsolete)
`<head> </head>`	Encloses the document head, containing information about the document
`profile="url"`	Provides the location of metadata about the document
`<header> </header>`	Structural element that represents the header of a section or the page (HTML5)
`<hgroup> </hgroup>`	Structural element that groups content headings (HTML5)
`<hr />`	Draws a horizontal line (rule) in the rendered page
`align="align"`	Specifies the horizontal alignment of the line where *align* left, center, or right (obsolete)
`color="color"`	Specifies the color of the line (obsolete)
`noshade="noshade"`	Removes 3-D shading from the line (obsolete)
`size="integer"`	Specifies the height of the line in pixels or as a percentage of the enclosing element's height (obsolete)
`width="integer"`	Specifies the width of the line in pixels or as a percentage of the enclosing element's width (obsolete)
`<html> </html>`	Encloses the entire content of the HTML document
`manifest="url"`	Provides the address of the document's application cache manifest (HTML5)
`xmlns="text"`	Specifies the namespace prefix for the document
`<i> </i>`	Represents a span of text offset from its surrounding content without conveying any extra importance or emphasis
`<iframe> </iframe>`	Creates an inline frame in the document
`align="align"`	Specifies the horizontal alignment of the frame with the surrounding content where *align* is bottom, left, middle, top, or right (obsolete)
`datafld="text"`	Indicates the column from a data source that supplies bound data for the inline frame (IE only)
`dataformatas="html|plaintext|text"`	Specifies the format of the data in the data source bound with the inline frame (IE only)
`datasrc="url"`	Provides the URL or ID of the data source bound with the inline frame (IE only)
`frameborder="1|0"`	Specifies whether to display a frame border (1) or not (0) (obsolete)
`height="integer"`	Specifies the height of the frame in pixels
`longdesc="url"`	Indicates the document containing a long description of the frame's content (obsolete)
`marginheight="integer"`	Specifies the space above and below the frame object and the frame's borders, in pixels (obsolete)
`marginwidth="integer"`	Specifies the space to the left and right of the frame object and the frame's borders, in pixels (obsolete)
`name="text"`	Specifies the name of the frame
`sandbox="allow-forms|allow-scripts|allow-top-navigation|allow-same-origin"`	Defines restrictions to the frame content (HTML5)
`seamless="seamless"`	Displays the inline frame as part of the document (HTML5)
`scrolling="auto|yes|no"`	Determines whether the browser displays a scroll bar with the frame (obsolete)

Element/Attribute	Description
src="*url*"	Indicates the document displayed within the frame
srcdoc="*text*"	Provides the HTML code shown in the inline frame (HTML5)
width="*integer*"	Specifies the width of the frame in pixels
<img> </img>	Inserts an inline image into the document
align="*align*"	Specifies the alignment of the image with the surrounding content where *align* is left, right, top, text textop, middle, absmiddle, baseline, bottom, absbottom (obsolete)
alt="*text*"	Specifies alternate text to be displayed in place of the image
border="*integer*"	Specifies the width of the image border (obsolete)
datafld="*text*"	Names the column from a data source that supplies bound data for the image (IE only)
dataformatas="html|plaintext|text"	Specifies the format of the data in the data source bound with the image (IE only)
datasrc="*url*"	Provides the URL or ID of the data source bound with the image (IE only)
dynsrc="*url*"	Provides the URL of a video or VRML file (IE and Opera only)
height="*integer*"	Specifies the height of the image in pixels
hspace="*integer*"	Specifies the horizontal space around the image in pixels (deprecated)
ismap="ismap"	Indicates that the image can be used as a server-side image map
longdesc="*url*"	Provides the URL of a document containing a long description of the image (obsolete)
name="*text*"	Specifies the image name (obsolete)
src="*url*"	Specifies the image source file
usemap="*url*"	Provides the location of a client-side image associated with the image (not well-supported when the URL points to an external file)
vspace="*integer*"	Specifies the vertical space around the image in pixels (obsolete)
width="*integer*"	Specifies the width of the image in pixels
<input> </input>	Marks an input field in a Web form
align="*align*"	Specifies the alignment of the input field with the surrounding content where *align* is left, right, top, texttop, middle, absmiddle, baseline, bottom, or absbottom (obsolete)
alt="*text*"	Specifies alternate text for image buttons and image input fields
checked="checked"	Specifies that the input check box or input radio button is selected
datafld="*text*"	Indicates the column from a data source that supplies bound data for the input field (IE only)
dataformatas="html|plaintext|text"	Specifies the format of the data in the data source bound with the input field (IE only)
datasrc="*url*"	Provides the URL or ID of the data source bound with the input field (IE only)
disabled="disabled"	Disables the input control
form="*text*"	Specifies the form to which the button belongs (HTML5)
formaction="*url*"	Specifies the URL to which the form data is sent (HTML5)
formenctype="*mime-type*"	Specifies the encoding of the form data before it is sent (HTML5)
formmethod="get|post"	Specifies the HTTP method with which the form data is submitted
formnovalidate="formnovalidate"	Specifies that the form should not be validated during submission (HTML5)

Element/Attribute	Description
formtarget="*text*"	Provides a name for the target of the button (HTML5)
height="*integer*"	Specifies the height of the image input field in pixels (HTML5)
list="*id*"	Specifies the id of a data list associated with the input field (HTML5)
max="*value*"	Specifies the maximum value of the field (HTML5)
maxlength="*integer*"	Specifies the maximum number of characters that can be inserted into a text input field
min="*value*"	Specifies the minimum value of the field (HTML5)
multiple="multiple"	Specifies that the user is allowed to specify more than one input value (HTML5)
name="text"	Specifies the name of the input field
pattern="*text*"	Specifies the required regular expression pattern of the input field value (HTML5)
placeholder="*text*"	Specifies placeholder text for the input field (HTML5)
readonly="readonly"	Prevents the value of the input field from being modified
size="*integer*"	Specifies the number of characters that can be displayed at one time in an input text field
src="*url*"	Indicates the source file of an input image field
step="any|*value*"	Specifies the value granularity of the field value (HTML5)
type="*text*"	Specifies the input type where *text* is button, checkbox, color, date, datetime, datetime-local, email, file, hidden, image, month, number, password, radio, range, reset, search, submit, tel, text, time, url, or week (HTML5)
value="*text*"	Specifies the default value of the input field
width="*integer*"	Specifies the width of an image input field in pixels (HTML5)
<ins> </ins>	Marks inserted text
cite="*url*"	Provides the URL for the document that has additional information about the inserted text
datetime="*date*"	Specifies the date and time of the text insertion
<kbd> </kbd>	Marks keyboard-style text
<keygen> </keygen>	Defines a generate key within a form (HTML5)
autofocus="autofocus"	Specifies that the element is to be given the focus when the form is loaded
challenge="*text*"	Provides the challenge string that is submitted along with the key
disabled="disabled"	Disables the element
form="*id*"	Specifies the id of the form associated with the element
keytype="rsa"	Specifies the type of key generated
name="*text*"	Specifies the name part of the name/value pair associated with the element
<label> </label>	Associates the enclosed content with a form field
datafld="text"	Indicates the column from a data source that supplies bound data for the label (IE only)
dataformatas="html|plaintext|text"	Specifies the format of the data in the data source bound with the label (IE only)
datasrc="*url*"	Provides the URL or ID of the data source bound with the label (IE only)
for="text"	Provides the ID of the field associated with the label
form="*id*"	Specifies the id of the form associated with the label (HTML5)

Element/Attribute	Description
`<legend> </legend>`	Marks the enclosed text as a caption for a field set
`align="bottom|left |top|right"`	Specifies the alignment of the legend with the field set; Internet Explorer also supports the center option (deprecated)
`<li> </li>`	Marks an item in an ordered (ol), unordered (ul), menu (menu), or directory (dir) list
`value="integer"`	Sets the value for the current list item in an ordered list; subsequent list items are numbered from that value
`<link />`	Creates an element in the document head that establishes the relationship between the current document and external documents or objects
`charset="char code"`	Specifies the character encoding of the external document (obsolete)
`href="url"`	Provides the URL of the external document
`hreflang="text"`	Indicates the language of the external document
`media="media"`	Indicates the media in which the external document is presented
`rel="text"`	Specifies the relationship between the current page and the link specified by the href attribute
`rev="text"`	Specifies the reverse relationship between the current page and the link specified by the href attribute (obsolete)
`sizes="any|value"`	Specifies the sizes of icons used for visual media (HTML5)
`target="text"`	Specifies the target window or frame for the link (obsolete)
`type="mime-type"`	Specifies the mime-type of the external document
`<map> </map>`	Creates an element that contains client-side image map hotspots
`name="text"`	Specifies the name of the image map
`<mark> </mark>`	Defines marked text (HTML5)
`<menu> </menu>`	Represents a list of commands
`compact="compact"`	Reduces the space between menu items (obsolete)
`label="text"`	Defines a visible label for the menu (HTML5)
`type="context|list| toolbar"`	Defines which type of list to display
`<meta />`	Creates an element in the document's head section that contains information and special instructions for processing the document
`charset="char code"`	Defines the character encoding for the document (HTML5)
`content="text"`	Provides information associated with the name or http-equiv attributes
`http-equiv="text"`	Provides instructions to the browser to request the server to perform different http operations
`name="text"`	Specifies the type of information specified in the content attribute
`scheme="text"`	Supplies additional information about the scheme used to interpret the content attribute (obsolete)
`<meter> </meter>`	Defines a measurement within a predefined range (HTML5)
`high="value"`	Defines the high value of the range
`low="value"`	Defines the low value of the range
`max="value"`	Defines the maximum value
`min="value"`	Defines the minimum value
`optimum="value"`	Defines the optimum value from the range
`value="value"`	Defines the meter's value
`<nav> </nav>`	Structural element defining a navigation list (HTML5)

Element/Attribute	Description
`<nobr> </nobr>`	Disables line wrapping for the enclosed content (not part of the W3C specifications, but supported by most browsers)
`<noembed> </noembed>`	Encloses alternate content for browsers that do not support the embed element (not part of the W3C specifications, but supported by most browsers)
`<noframe> </noframe>`	Encloses alternate content for browsers that do not support frames (obsolete)
`<noscript> </noscript>`	Encloses alternate content for browsers that do not support client-side scripts
`<object> </object>`	Places an embedded object (image, applet, sound clip, video clip, etc.) into the page
`archive="url"`	Specifies the URL of an archive containing classes and other resources pre-loaded for use with the object (obsolete)
`align="align"`	Aligns the object with the surrounding content where *align* is absbottom, absmiddle, baseline, bottom, left, middle, right, texttop, or top (obsolete)
`border="integer"`	Specifies the width of the border around the object (obsolete)
`classid="url"`	Provides the URL of the object (obsolete)
`codebase="url"`	Specifies the base path used to resolve relative references within the embedded object (obsolete)
`codetype="mime-type"`	Indicates the mime-type of the embedded object's code (obsolete)
`data="url"`	Provides the URL of the object's data file
`datafld="text"`	Identifies the column from a data source that supplies bound data for the embedded object (IE only)
`dataformatas="html|plaintext|text"`	Specifies the format of the data in the data source bound with the embedded object (IE only)
`datasrc="url"`	Provides the URL or ID of the data source bound with the embedded object (IE only)
`declare="declare"`	Declares the object without embedding it on the page (obsolete)
`form="id"`	Specifies the id of the form associated with the object (HTML5)
`height="integer"`	Specifies the height of the object in pixels
`hspace="integer"`	Specifies the horizontal space around the image in pixels (obsolete)
`name="text"`	Specifies the name of the embedded object
`standby="text"`	Specifies the message displayed by the browser while loading the embedded object (obsolete)
`type="mime-type"`	Indicates the mime-type of the embedded object
`vspace="integer"`	Specifies the vertical space around the embedded object (obsolete)
`width="integer"`	Specifies the width of the object in pixels
`<ol> </ol>`	Contains an ordered list of items
`reversed="reversed"`	Specifies that the list markers are to be displayed in descending order (HTML5)
`start="integer"`	Specifies the starting value in the list
`type="A|a|I|i|1"`	Specifies the bullet type associated with the list items (deprecated)
`<optgroup> </optgroup>`	Contains a group of option elements in a selection field
`disabled="disabled"`	Disables the option group control
`label="text"`	Specifies the label for the option group
`<option> </option>`	Formats an option within a selection field
`disabled="disabled"`	Disables the option control
`label="text"`	Supplies the text label associated with the option
`selected="selected"`	Selects the option by default
`value="text"`	Specifies the value associated with the option

Element/Attribute	Description
`<output> </output>`	Form control representing the result of a calculation (HTML5)
`name="text"`	Specifies the name part of the name/value pair associated with the field
`form="id"`	Specifies the id of the form associated with the field
`for="text list"`	Lists the id references associated with the calculation
`<p> </p>`	Marks the enclosed content as a paragraph
`align="align"`	Horizontally aligns the contents of the paragraph where *align* is left, center, right, or justify (obsolete)
`<param> </param>`	Marks parameter values sent to an object element or an applet element
`name="text"`	Specifies the parameter name
`type="mime-type"`	Specifies the mime-type of the resource indicated by the value attribute (obsolete)
`value="text"`	Specifies the parameter value
`valuetype="data|ref|object"`	Specifies the data type of the value attribute (obsolete)
`<pre> </pre>`	Marks the enclosed text as preformatted text, retaining white space from the document
`<progress> </progress>`	Represents the progress of completion of a task (HTML5)
`value="value"`	Specifies how much of the task has been completed
`max="value"`	Specifies how much work the task requires in total
`<q> </q>`	Marks the enclosed text as a quotation
`cite="url"`	Provides the source URL of the quoted content
`<rp> </rp>`	Used in ruby annotations to define what to show browsers that do not support the ruby element (HTML5)
`<rt> </rt>`	Defines explanation to ruby annotations (HTML5)
`<ruby> </ruby>`	Defines ruby annotations (HTML5)
`<s> </s>`	Marks the enclosed text as strikethrough text
`<samp> </samp>`	Marks the enclosed text as a sequence of literal characters
`<script> </script>`	Encloses client-side scripts within the document; this element can be placed within the head or the body element or it can refer to an external script file
`async="async"`	Specifies that the script should be executed asynchronously as soon as it becomes available (HTML5)
`charset="char code"`	Specifies the character encoding of the script
`defer="defer"`	Defers execution of the script
`language="text"`	Specifies the language of the script (obsolete)
`src="url"`	Provides the URL of an external script file
`type="mime-type"`	Specifies the mime-type of the script
`<section> </section>`	Structural element representing a section of the document (HTML5)
`<select> </select>`	Creates a selection field (drop-down list box) in a Web form
`autofocus="autofocus"`	Specifies that the browser should give focus to the selection field as soon as the page loads (HTML5)
`datafld="text"`	Identifies the column from a data source that supplies bound data for the selection field (IE only)

Element/Attribute	Description
`dataformatas="html|` `plaintext|text"`	Specifies the format of the data in the data source bound with the selection field (IE only)
`datasrc="url"`	Provides the URL or ID of the data source bound with the selection field (IE only)
`disabled="disabled"`	Disables the selection field
`form="id"`	Provides the id of the form associated with the selection field (HTML5)
`multiple="multiple"`	Allows multiple sections from the field
`name="text"`	Specifies the selection field name
`size="integer"`	Specifies the number of visible items in the selection list
`<small> </small>`	Represents "final print" or "small print" in legal disclaimers and caveats
`<source />`	Enables multiple media sources to be specified for audio and video elements (HTML5)
`media="media"`	Specifies the intended media type of the media source
`src="url"`	Specifies the location of the media source
`type="mime-type"`	Specifies the MIME type of the media source
`<span> </span>`	Creates a generic inline element
`datafld="text"`	Identifies the column from a data source that supplies bound data for the inline element (IE only)
`dataformatas="html|` `plaintext|text"`	Specifies the format of the data in the data source bound with the inline element (IE only)
`datasrc="url"`	Provides the URL or ID of the data source bound with the inline element (IE only)
`<strong> </strong>`	Marks the enclosed text as strongly emphasized text
`<style> </style>`	Encloses global style declarations for the document
`media="media"`	Indicates the media of the enclosed style definitions
`scoped="scoped"`	Indicates that the specified style information is meant to apply only to the style element's parent element (HTML5)
`type="mime-type"`	Specifies the mime-type of the style definitions
`<sub> </sub>`	Marks the enclosed text as subscript text
`<summary> </summary>`	Defines the header of a detail element (HTML5)
`<sup> </sup>`	Marks the enclosed text as superscript text
`<table> </table>`	Encloses the contents of a Web table
`align="align"`	Aligns the table with the surrounding content where *align* is left, center, or right (obsolete)
`bgcolor="color"`	Specifies the background color of the table (obsolete)
`border="integer"`	Specifies the width of the table border in pixels (obsolete)
`cellpadding=` `"integer"`	Specifies the space between the table data and the cell borders in pixels (obsolete)
`cellspacing=` `"integer"`	Specifies the space between table cells in pixels (obsolete)
`datafld="text"`	Indicates the column from a data source that supplies bound data for the table (IE only)
`dataformatas="html|` `plaintext|text"`	Specifies the format of the data in the data source bound with the table (IE only)

Element/Attribute	Description
datapagesize= "*integer*"	Sets the number of records displayed within the table (IE only)
datasrc="*url*"	Provides the URL or ID of the data source bound with the table (IE only)
frame="*frame*"	Specifies the format of the borders around the table where *frame* is above, below, border, box, hsides, lhs, rhs, void, or vside (obsolete)
rules="*rules*"	Specifies the format of the table's internal borders or gridlines where *rules* is all, cols, groups, none, or rows (obsolete)
summary="*text*"	Supplies a text summary of the table's content
width="*integer*"	Specifies the width of the table in pixels (obsolete)
<tbody> </tbody>	Encloses the content of the Web table body
align="*align*"	Specifies the alignment of the contents in the cells of the table body where *align* is left, center, right, justify, or char (obsolete)
char="*char*"	Specifies the character used for aligning the table body contents when the align attribute is set to "char" (obsolete)
charoff="*integer*"	Specifies the offset in pixels from the alignment character specified in the char attribute (obsolete)
valign="*align*"	Specifies the vertical alignment of the contents in the cells of the table body where *align* is baseline, bottom, middle, or top (obsolete)
<td> </td>	Encloses the data of a table cell
abbr="*text*"	Supplies an abbreviated version of the contents of the table cell (obsolete)
align="*align*"	Specifies the horizontal alignment of the table cell data where *align* is left, center, or right (obsolete)
bgcolor="*color*"	Specifies the background color of the table cell (obsolete)
char="*char*"	Specifies the character used for aligning the table cell contents when the align attribute is set to "char" (obsolete)
charoff="*integer*"	Specifies the offset in pixels from the alignment character specified in the char attribute (obsolete)
colspan="*integer*"	Specifies the number of columns the table cell spans
headers="*text*"	Supplies a space-separated list of table headers associated with the table cell
height="*integer*"	Specifies the height of the table cell in pixels (obsolete)
nowrap="nowrap"	Disables line-wrapping within the table cell (obsolete)
rowspan="*integer*"	Specifies the number of rows the table cell spans
scope="col|colgroup |row|rowgroup"	Specifies the scope of the table for which the cell provides data (obsolete)
valign="*align*"	Specifies the vertical alignment of the contents of the table cell where *align* is top, middle, or bottom (obsolete)
width="*integer*"	Specifies the width of the cell in pixels (obsolete)
<textarea> </textarea>	Marks the enclosed text as a text area input box in a Web form
autofocus="autofocus"	Specifies that the text area is to receive the focus when the page is loaded (HTML5)
datafld="*text*"	Specifies the column from a data source that supplies bound data for the text area box (IE only)
dataformatas="html| plaintext|text"	Specifies the format of the data in the data source bound with the text area box (IE only)

Element/Attribute	Description
datasrc="*url*"	Provides the URL or ID of the data source bound with the text area box (IE only)
cols="*integer*"	Specifies the width of the text area box in characters
disable="disable"	Disables the text area field
form="*id*"	Associates the text area with the form identified by *id* (HTML5)
maxlength="*integer*"	Specifies the maximum allowed value length for the text area
name="*text*"	Specifies the name of the text area box
placeholder="*text*"	Provides a short hint intended to aid the user when entering data (HTML5)
readonly="readonly"	Specifies the value of the text area box, cannot be modified
required="required"	Indicates whether the text area is required for validation (HTML5)
rows="*integer*"	Specifies the number of visible rows in the text area box
wrap="**soft**|hard"	Specifies how text is wrapped within the text area box and how that text-wrapping information is sent to the server-side program
<tfoot> </tfoot>	Encloses the content of the Web table footer
align="*align*"	Specifies the alignment of the contents in the cells of the table footer where *align* is left, center, right, justify, or char (obsolete)
char="*char*"	Specifies the character used for aligning the table footer contents when the align attribute is set to "char" (obsolete)
charoff="*integer*"	Specifies the offset in pixels from the alignment character specified in the char attribute (obsolete)
valign="*align*"	Specifies the vertical alignment of the contents in the cells of the table footer where *align* is baseline, bottom, middle, or top (obsolete)
<th> </th>	Encloses the data of a table header cell
abbr="*text*"	Supplies an abbreviated version of the contents of the table cell (obsolete)
align="*align*"	Specifies the horizontal alignment of the table cell data where *align* is left, center, or right (obsolete)
axis="*text list*"	Provides a list of table categories that can be mapped to a table hierarchy (obsolete)
bgcolor="*color*"	Specifies the background color of the table cell (obsolete)
char="*char*"	Specifies the character used for aligning the table cell contents when the align attribute is set to "char" (obsolete)
charoff="*integer*"	Specifies the offset in pixels from the alignment character specified in the char attribute (obsolete)
colspan="*integer*"	Specifies the number of columns the table cell spans
headers="*text*"	A space-separated list of table headers associated with the table cell
height="*integer*"	Specifies the height of the table cell in pixels (obsolete)
nowrap="nowrap"	Disables line-wrapping within the table cell (obsolete)
rowspan="*integer*"	Specifies the number of rows the table cell spans
scope="col|colgroup|row|rowgroup"	Specifies the scope of the table for which the cell provides data
valign="*align*"	Specifies the vertical alignment of the contents of the table cell where *align* is top, middle, or bottom (obsolete)
width="*integer*"	Specifies the width of the cell in pixels (obsolete)

Element/Attribute	Description
`<thead> </thead>`	Encloses the content of the Web table header
`align="align"`	Specifies the alignment of the contents in the cells of the table header where *align* is left, center, right, justify, or char (obsolete)
`char="char"`	Specifies the character used for aligning the table header contents when the align attribute is set to "char" (obsolete)
`charoff="integer"`	Specifies the offset in pixels from the alignment character specified in the char attribute (obsolete)
`valign="align"`	Specifies the vertical alignment of the contents in the cells of the table header where *align* is baseline, bottom, middle, or top (obsolete)
`<time> </time>`	Represents a date and/or time (HTML5)
`<title> </title>`	Specifies the title of the document, placed in the head section of the document
`<tr> </tr>`	Encloses the content of a row within a Web table
`align="align"`	Specifies the horizontal alignment of the data in the row's cells where *align* is left, center, or right (obsolete)
`char="char"`	Specifies the character used for aligning the table row contents when the align attribute is set to "char" (obsolete)
`charoff="integer"`	Specifies the offset in pixels from the alignment character specified in the char attribute (obsolete)
`valign="align"`	Specifies the vertical alignment of the contents of the table row where *align* is baseline, bottom, middle, or top (obsolete)
`<track> </track>`	Enables supplementary media tracks such as subtitles and captions (HTML5)
`default="default"`	Enables the track if the user's preferences do not indicate that another track would be more appropriate
`kind="kind"`	Specifies the kind of track, where *kind* is subtitles, captions, descriptions, chapters, or metadata
`label="text"`	Provides a user-readable title for the track
`src="url"`	Provides the address of the track
`srclang="lang"`	Provides the language of the track
`<tt> </tt>`	Marks the enclosed text as teletype or monospaced text (deprecated)
`<u> </u>`	Marks the enclosed text as underlined text (deprecated)
`<ul> </ul>`	Contains an unordered list of items
`compact="compact"`	Reduces the space between unordered list items (obsolete)
`type="disc|square| circle"`	Specifies the bullet type associated with the list items (obsolete)
`<var> </var>`	Marks the enclosed text as containing a variable name
`<video> </video>`	Defines an embedded video clip (HTML5)
`audio="text"`	Defines the default audio state; currently only "muted" is supported
`autoplay="autoplay"`	Specifies that the video should begin playing automatically when the page is loaded
`controls="controls"`	Instructs the browser to display the video controls
`height="value"`	Provides the height of the video clip in pixels
`loop="loop"`	Instructs the browser to loop the clip back to the beginning
`preload="auto| metadata|none"`	Indicates whether to preload the video clip data
`poster="url"`	Specifies the location of an image file to act as a poster for the video clip
`width="value"`	Provides the width of the video clip in pixels

Element/Attribute	Description
`<wbr />`	Indicates a line-break opportunity (HTML5)
`<xml> </xml>`	Encloses XML content (also referred to as a "data island") or references an external XML document (IE only)
`ns="url"`	Provides the URL of the XML data island (IE only)
`prefix="text"`	Specifies the namespace prefix of the XML content (IE only)
`src="url"`	Provides the URL of an external XML document (IE only)
`<xmp> </xmp>`	Marks the enclosed text as preformatted text, preserving the white space of the source document; replaced by the pre element (deprecated)

Cascading Styles and Selectors

This appendix describes the selectors, units, and attributes supported by Cascading Style Sheets (CSS). Features from CSS3 are indicated in parenthesis. Note that not all CSS3 features are supported by all browsers and all browser versions, so you should always check your code against different browsers and browser versions to ensure that your page is being rendered correctly. Also many CSS3 styles are still in the draft stage and will undergo continuing revisions and additions. Additional information about CSS can be found at the World Wide Web Consortium Web site at *www.w3.org*.

STARTING DATA FILES

There are no starting Data Files needed for this appendix.

Selectors

The general form of a style declaration is:

```
selector {attribute1:value1; attribute2:value2; ...}
```

where *selector* is the selection of elements within the document to which the style will be applied; *attribute1*, *attribute2*, etc. are the different style attributes; and *value1*, *value2*, etc. are values associated with those styles. The following table shows some of the different forms that a selector can take.

Selector	Matches
*	All elements in the document
e	An element, *e*, in the document
e1, e2, e3, …	A group of elements, *e1*, *e2*, *e3*, in the document
e1 e2	An element *e2* nested within the parent element, *e1*
e1 > e2	An element *e2* that is a child of the parent element, *e1*
e1+e2	An element, *e2*, that is adjacent to element *e1*
e1.class	An element, *e1*, belonging to the *class* class
.class	Any element belonging to the *class* class
#id	An element with the id value *id*
[att]	The element contains the *att* attribute
[att="val"]	The element's *att* attribute equals "*val*"
[att~="val"]	The element's *att* attribute value is a space-separated list of "words," one of which is exactly "*val*"
[att|="val"]	The element's *att* attribute value is a hyphen-separated list of "words" beginning with "val"
[att^="val"]	The element's *att* attribute begins with "*val*" (CSS3)
[att$="val"]	The element's *att* attribute ends with "*val*" (CSS3)
[att*="val"]	The element's *att* attribute contains the value "*val*" (CSS3)
[ns|att]	References all *att* attributes in the *ns* namespace (CSS3)

Pseudo-Elements and Pseudo-Classes

Pseudo-elements are elements that do not exist in HTML code but whose attributes can be set with CSS. Many pseudo-elements were introduced in CSS2.

Pseudo-Element	Matches
e:after {content: "text"}	Text content, *text*, that is inserted at the end of an element, *e*
e:before {content: "text"}	Text content, *text*, that is inserted at the beginning of an element, *e*
e:first-letter	The first letter in the element *e*
e:first-line	The first line in the element *e*
::selection	A part of the document that has been highlighted by the user (CSS3)

Pseudo-classes are classes of HTML elements that define the condition or state of the element in the Web page. Many pseudo-classes were introduced in CSS2.

Pseudo-Class	Matches
`:canvas`	The rendering canvas of the document
`:first`	The first printed page of the document (used only with print styles created with the @print rule)
`:last`	The last printed page of the document (used only with print styles created with the @print rule)
`:left`	The left side of a two-sided printout (used only with print styles created with the @print rule)
`:right`	The right side of a two-sided printout (used only with print styles created with the @print rule)
`:root`	The root element of the document
`e:active`	The element, *e*, that is being activated by the user (usually applies only to hyperlinks)
`e:checked`	The checkbox or radio button, *e*, that has been checked (CSS3)
`e:disabled`	The element, *e*, that has been disabled in the document (CSS3)
`e:empty`	The element, *e*, that has no children
`e:enabled`	The element, *e*, that has been enabled in the document (CSS3)
`e:first-child`	The element, *e*, which is the first child of its parent element
`e:first-node`	The first occurrence of the element, *e*, in the document tree
`e:first-of-type`	The first element of type *e* (CSS3)
`e:focus`	The element, *e*, that has received the focus of the cursor
`e:hover`	The mouse pointer is hovering over the element, *e*
`e:lang(text)`	Sets the language, *text*, associated with the element, *e*
`e:last-child`	The element, *e*, that is the last child of its parent element (CSS3)
`e:last-of-type`	The last element of type *e* (CSS3)
`e:link`	The element, *e*, has not been visited yet by the user (applies only to hyperlinks)
`e:not`	Negate the selector rule for the element, *e*, applying the style to all *e* elements that do not match the selector rules
`e:nth-child(n)`	Matches n^{th} child of the element, *e*; *n* can also be the keywords odd or even (CSS3)
`e:nth-last-child(n)`	Matches n^{th} child of the element, *e*, counting up from the last child; *n* can also be the keywords odd or even (CSS3)
`e:nth-of-type(n)`	Matches n^{th} element of type *e*; *n* can also be the keywords odd or even (CSS3)
`e:nth-last-of-type(n)`	Matches n^{th} element of type *e*, counting up from the last child; *n* can also be the keywords odd or even (CSS3)
`e:only-child`	Matches element *e* only if it is the only child of its parent (CSS3)
`e:only-of-type`	Matches element *e* only if it is the only element of its type nested within its parent (CSS3)
`e:target`	Matches an element, *e*, that's the target of the identifier in the document's URL (CSS3)
`e:visited`	The element, *e*, has been already visited by the user (to only the hyperlinks)

@ Rules

CSS supports different "@ rules" designed to run commands within a style sheet. These commands can be used to import other styles, download font definitions, or define the format of printed output.

@ Rule	Description
`@charset "encoding"`	Defines the character set encoding used in the style sheet (this must be the very first line in the style sheet document)
`@font-face {font descriptors}`	Defines custom fonts that are available for automatic download when needed (CSS3)
`@import url(url) media`	Imports an external style sheet document into the current style sheet, where *url* is the location of the external stylesheet and *media* is a comma-separated list of media types (optional)
`@media media {style declaration}`	Defines the media for the styles in the *style declaration* block, where *media* is a comma-separated list of media types
`@namespace prefix url(url)`	Defines the namespace used by selectors in the style sheet, where *prefix* is the local namespace prefix (optional) and *url* is the unique namespace identifier; the @namespace rule must come before all CSS selectors (CSS3)
`@page label pseudo-class {styles}`	Defines the properties of a printed page, where *label* is a label given to the page (optional), *pseudo-class* is one of the CSS pseudo-classes designed for printed pages, and *styles* are the styles associated with the page

Miscellaneous Syntax

The following syntax elements do not fit into the previous categories but are useful in constructing CSS style sheets.

Item	Description
`style !important`	Places high importance on the preceding *style*, overriding the usual rules for inheritance and cascading
`/* comment */`	Attaches a *comment* to the style sheet

Units

Many style attribute values use units of measurement to indicate color, length, angles, time, and frequencies. The following table describes the measuring units used in CSS.

Units	Description
Color	**Units of color**
currentColor	The computed value of the color property (CSS3)
flavor	An accent color chosen by the user to customize the user interface of the browser (CSS3)
name	A color name; all browsers recognize 16 base color names: aqua, black, blue, fuchsia, gray, green, lime, maroon, navy, olive, purple, red, silver, teal, white, and yellow
#rrggbb	A hexadecimal color value, where rr is the red value, gg is the green value, and bb is the blue value
#rgb	A compressed hexadecimal value, where the r, g, and b values are doubled so that, for example, #A2F = #AA22FF
hsl(hue, sat, light)	Color value based on hue, saturation, and lightness, where hue is the degree measure on the color wheel ranging from 0° (red) up to 360°, sat is the saturation range from 0% to 100%, and light is the lightness range from 0% to 100% (CSS3)
hsla(hue, sat, light, alpha)	Semi-transparent color based on the HSL model with alpha representing the opacity of the color ranging from 0 (transparent) up to 1 (completely opaque) (CSS3)
rgb(red, green, blue)	The decimal color value, where red is the red value, green is the green value, and blue is the blue value
rgb(red%, green%, blue%)	The color value percentage, where red% is the percent of maximum red, green% is the percent of maximum green, and blue% is the percent of maximum blue
rgba(red, green, blue, alpha)	Semi-transparent color based on the RGB model with alpha representing the opacity of the color ranging from 0 (transparent) up to 1 (completely opaque) (CSS3)
Length	**Units of length**
auto	Keyword which allows the browser to automatically determine the size of the length
ch	Width of the "0" glyph found in the font (CSS3)
em	A relative unit indicating the width and the height of the capital "M" character for the browser's default font
ex	A relative unit indicating the height of the small "x" character for the browser's default font
px	A pixel, representing the smallest unit of length on the output device
in	An inch
cm	A centimeter
mm	A millimeter
pt	A point, approximately 1/72 inch
pc	A pica, approximately 1/12 inch
%	A percent of the width or height of the parent element
xx-small	Keyword representing an extremely small font size
x-small	Keyword representing a very small font size
small	Keyword representing a small font size

Units	Description
medium	Keyword representing a medium-sized font
large	Keyword representing a large font
x-large	Keyword representing a very large font
xx-large	Keyword representing an extremely large font
Angle	**Units of angles**
deg	The angle in degrees
grad	The angle in gradients
rad	The angle in radians
turns	Number of complete turns (CSS3)
Time	**Units of time**
ms	Time in milliseconds
s	Time in seconds
Frequency	**Units of frequency**
hz	The frequency in hertz
khz	The frequency in kilohertz

Attributes and Values

The following table describes the attributes and values for different types of elements. The attributes are grouped into categories to help you locate the features relevant to your particular design task.

Attribute	Description
Aural	**Styles for Aural Browsers**
cue: url(*url1*) url(*url2*)	Adds a sound to an element: if a single value is present, the sound is played before and after the element; if two values are present, the first is played before and the second is played after
cue-after: url(*url*)	Specifies a sound to be played immediately after an element
cue-before: url(*url*)	Specifies a sound to be played immediately before an element
elevation: *location*	Defines the vertical location of the sound, where *location* is below, level, above, lower, higher, or an angle value
mark: *before after*	Adds a marker to an audio stream (CSS3)
mark-before: *text*	Marks an audio stream with the text *string* (CSS3)
mark-after: *text*	Marks an audio stream afterwards with the text *string* (CSS3)
pause: *time1 time2*	Adds a pause to an element: if a single value is present, the pause occurs before and after the element; if two values are present, the first pause occurs before and the second occurs after
pause-after: *time*	Adds a pause after an element
pause-before: *time*	Adds a pause before an element
phonemes: *text*	Specifies the phonetic pronunciation for the audio stream (CSS3)
pitch: *value*	Defines the pitch of a speaking voice, where *value* is x-low, low, medium, high, x-high, or a frequency value
pitch-range: *value*	Defines the pitch range for a speaking voice, where *value* ranges from 0 to 100; a low pitch range results in a monotone voice, whereas a high pitch range sounds very animated

Attribute	Description
`play-during: url(url) mix repeat type`	Defines a sound to be played behind an element, where *url* is the URL of the sound file; mix overlays the sound file with the sound of the parent element; repeat causes the sound to be repeated, filling up the available time; and *type* is auto to play the sound only once, none to play nothing but the sound file, or inherit
`rest: before after`	Specifies the rest-before and rest-after values for the audio (CSS3)
`rest-before: type`	Specifies a rest to be observed before speaking the content, where *type* is none, x-weak, weak, medium, strong, x-strong, or inherit (CSS3)
`rest-after: type`	Specifies a rest to be observed after speaking the content, where *type* is none, x-weak, weak, medium, strong, x-strong, or inherit (CSS3)
`richness: value`	Specifies the richness of the speaking voice, where *value* ranges from 0 to 100; a low value indicates a softer voice, whereas a high value indicates a brighter voice
`speak: type`	Defines how element content is to be spoken, where *type* is normal (for normal punctuation rules), spell-out (to pronounce one character at a time), none (to suppress the aural rendering),or inherit
`voice-balance: type`	Specifies the voice balance, where *type* is left, center, right, left-wards, rightwards, inherit, or a *number* (CSS3)
`voice-duration: time`	Specifies the duration of the voice (CSS3)
`voice-family: text`	Defines the name of the speaking voice, where *text* is male, female, child, or a text string indicating a specific speaking voice
`voice-rate: type`	Specifies the voice rate, where *type* is x-slow, slow, medium, fast, x-fast, inherit, or a *percentage* (CSS3)
`voice-pitch: type`	Specifies the voice pitch, where *type* is x-low, low, medium, high, x-high, inherit, a *number*, or a *percentage* (CSS3)
`voice-pitch-range: type`	Specifies the voice pitch range, where *type* is x-low, low, medium, high, x-high, inherit, or a *number* (CSS3)
`voice-stress: type`	Specifies the voice stress, where *type* is strong, moderate, none, reduced, or inherit (CSS3)
`voice-volume: type`	Specifies the voice volume, where*type* is silent, x-soft, soft, medium, loud, x-loud, inherit, a *number*, or a *percentage* (CSS3)
Backgrounds	**Styles applied to an element's background**
`background: color url(url) repeat attachment position`	Defines the background of the element, where *color* is a CSS color name or value, *url* is the location of an image file, *repeat* defines how the background image should be repeated, *attachment* defines how the background image should be attached,and *position* defines the position of the background image
`background: url(url) position size repeat attachment origin clip color`	Defines the background of the element, where *url* is the location of the image file, *position* is the position of the image, *size* is the size of the image, *repeat* defines how the image should be repeated, *attachment* defines how the image should be attached, *origin* defines the origin of the image, *clip* defines the location of the clipping box, and *color* defines the background color (CSS3)
`background-attachment: type`	Specifies how the background image is attached, where *type* is inherit, scroll (move the image with the page content), or fixed (fix the image and not scroll)
`background-clip: location`	Specifies the location of the background box, where *location* is border-box, padding-box, content-box, no-clip, a unit of *length*, or a *percentage* (CSS3)

Attribute	Description
background-color: color	Defines the color of the background, where color is a CSS color name or value; the keyword "inherit" can be used to inherit the background color of the parent element, or "transparent"can be used to allow the parent element background image to show through
background-image: url(url)	Specifies the image file used for the element's background, where url is the URL of the image file
background-origin: box	Specifies the origin of the background image, where box is border-box, padding-box, or content-box (CSS3)
background-position: x y	Sets the position of a background image, where x is the horizontal location in pixels, as a percentage of the width of the parent element, or the keyword "left", "center", or "right", y is the vertical location in pixels, as a percentage of the height and of the parent element, or the keyword, "top", "center", or "bottom"
background-repeat: type	Defines the method for repeating the background image, where type is no-repeat, repeat (to tile the image in both directions),repeat-x (to tile the image in the horizontal direction only), or repeat-y (to tile the image in the vertical direction only)
background-size: size	Sets the size of the background image, where size is auto, cover, contain, a length, or a percentage (CSS3)
Block-Level Styles	**Styles applied to block-level elements**
border: length style color	Defines the border style of the element, where length is the border width, style is the border design, and color is the border color
border-bottom: length style color	Defines the border style of the bottom edge of the element
border-left: length style color	Defines the border style of the left edge of the element
border-right: length style color	Defines the border style of the right edge of the element
border-top: length style color	Defines the border style of the top edge of the element
border-color: color	Defines the color applied to the element's border using a CSS color unit
border-bottom-color: color	Defines the color applied to the bottom edge of the element
border-left-color: color	Defines the color applied to the left edge of the element
border-right-color: color	Defines the color applied to the right edge of the element
border-top-color: color	Defines the color applied to the top edge of the element
border-image: url(url) size	Sets an image file for the border, where url is the location of the image file and size is stretch, repeat, round, none, a length, or a percentage (CSS3)
border-style: style	Specifies the design of the element's border (dashed, dotted double, groove, inset, none, outset, ridge, or solid)
border-style-bottom: style	Specifies the design of the element's bottom edge
border-style-left: style	Specifies the design of the element's left edge
border-style-right: style	Specifies the design of the element's right edge
border-style-top: style	Specifies the design of the element's top edge
border-radius: tr br bl tl	Specifies the radius of the border corners in pixels, where tr is the top-right corner, br is the bottom-right corner, bl is the bottom-left corner, and tl is the top-left corner (CSS3)

Attribute	Description
`border-top-right-radius:` *`horiz vert`*	Specifies the horizontal and vertical radius for the top-right corner (CSS3)
`border-bottom-right-radius:` *`horiz vert`*	Specifies the horizontal and vertical radius for the bottom-right corner (CSS3)
`border-bottom-left-radius:` *`horiz vert`*	Specifies the horizontal and vertical radius for the bottom-left corner (CSS3)
`border-top-left-radius:` *`horiz vert`*	Specifies the horizontal and vertical radius for the top-left corner (CSS3)
`border-width:` *`length`*	Defines the width of the element's border, in a unit of measure or using the keyword "thick", "medium", or "thin"
`border-width-bottom:` *`length`*	Defines the width of the element's bottom edge
`border-width-left:` *`length`*	Defines the width of the element's left edge
`border-width-right:` *`length`*	Defines the width of the element's right edge
`border-width-top:` *`length`*	Defines the width of the element's top edge
`box-shadow:` *`top right bottom left color`*	Adds a box shadow, where *top*, *right*, *bottom*, and *left* set the width of the shadow and *color* sets the shadow color (CSS3)
`margin:` *`top right bottom left`*	Defines the size of the margins around the top, right, bottom, and left edges of the element, in one of the CSS units of length
`margin-bottom:` *`length`*	Defines the size of the element's bottom margin
`margin-left:` *`length`*	Defines the size of the element's left margin
`margin-right:` *`length`*	Defines the size of the element's right margin
`margin-top:` *`length`*	Defines the size of the element's top margin
`padding:` *`top right bottom left`*	Defines the size of the padding space within the top, right, bottom, and left edges of the element, in one of the CSS units of length
`padding-bottom:` *`length`*	Defines the size of the element's bottom padding
`padding-left:` *`length`*	Defines the size of the element's left padding
`padding-right:` *`length`*	Defines the size of the element's right padding
`padding-top:` *`length`*	Defines the size of the element's top padding
Browser	**Styles to affect the appearance of the browser**
`appearance:` *`type`*	Specifies that an element should be displayed like a standard browser object, where *type* is normal, button, push-button, hyperlink, radio-button, checkbox, pop-up-menu, list-menu, radio-group, checkbox-group, field, or password (CSS3)
`cursor:` *`type`*	Defines the cursor image used, where *type* is n-resize, ne-resize, e-resize, se-resize, s-resize, sw-resize, w-resize, nw-resize, cross-hair, pointer, move, text, wait, help, auto, default, inherit, or a URL pointing to an image file
`icon:` *`value`*	Specifies that an element should be styled with with an iconic equivalent, where *value* is auto, a *url*, or inherit (CSS3)
`nav-down:` *`position`*	Specifies where to navigate using the arrow-down and arrow-up navigation keys, where *position* is auto, a *target-name*, or an element *id* (CSS3)
`nav-index:` *`value`*	Specifies the tabbing order, where *value* is auto, inherit, or a *number* (CSS3)
`nav-left:` *`position`*	Specifies where to navigate using the arrow-left and arrow-right navigation keys, where *position* is auto, a *target-name*, or an element *id* (CSS3)

Attribute	Description
nav-right: *position*	Specifies where to navigate using the arrow-left and arrow-right navigation keys, where *position* is auto, a *target-name*, or an element *id* (CSS3)
nav-up: *position*	Specifies where to navigate using the arrow-down and arrow-up navigation keys, where *position* is auto, a *target-name*, or an element *id* (CSS3)
resize: *type*	Specifies whether an element is resizable and in what direction, where *type* is none, both, horizontal, vertical, or inherit (CSS3)
Column	**Styles for Multi-column Layouts**
column-count: *value*	Specifies the number of columns, where *value* is the column number or auto (CSS3)
column-fill: *type*	Specifies whether to balance the content of the columns, where *type* is auto or balance (CSS3)
column-gap: *value*	Sets the size of the gap between the columns, where *value* is the width of the gap or auto (CSS3)
column-rule: *width style color*	Adds a dividing line between the columns, where *width*, *style*, and *color* define the style of the line (CSS3)
column-rule-color: *color*	Defines the color of the dividing line (CSS3)
column-rule-style: *style*	Defines the border style of the dividing line (CSS3)
column-rule-width: *width*	Sets the width of the dividing line (CSS3)
columns: *width count*	Sets the width and number of columns in the multi-column layout (CSS3)
column-span: *value*	Sets the element to span across the columns, where *span* is 1 or all (CSS3)
column-width: *value*	Sets the width of the columns (CSS3)
Content	**Styles to generate content**
bookmark-label: *value*	Specifies the label of a bookmark, where *value* is content, an *attribute*, or a text *string* (CSS3)
bookmark-level: *value*	Specifies the bookmark level, where *value* is an *integer* or none (CSS3)
bookmark-target: *value*	Specifies the target of a bookmark link, where *value* is self, a *url*, or an *attribute* (CSS3)
border-length: *value*	Describes a way of separating footnotes from other content, where *value* is a *length* or auto (CSS3)
content: *text*	Generates a text string to attach to the content of the element
content: attr(*attr*)	Returns the value of the *attr* attribute from the element
content: close-quote	Attaches a close quote using the characters specified in the quotes style
content: counter(*text*)	Generates a counter using the text string *text* attached to the content (most often used with list items)
content: counters(*text*)	Generates a string of counters using the comma-separated text string *text* attached to the content (most often used with list items)
content: no-close-quote	Prevents the attachment of a close quote to an element
content: no-open-quote	Prevents the attachment of an open quote to an element
content: open-quote	Attaches an open quote using the characters specified in the quotes style

Attribute	Description
`content: url(url)`	Attaches the content of an external file indicated in the *url* to the element
`counter-increment: id integer`	Defines the element to be automatically incremented and the amount by which it is to be incremented, where *id* is an identifier of the element and *integer* defines by how much
`counter-reset: id integer`	Defines the element whose counter is to be reset and the amount by which it is to be reset, where *id* is an identifier of the element and *integer* defines by how much
`crop: value`	Allows a replaced element to be a rectangular area of an object instead of the whole object, where *value* is a shape or auto (CSS3)
`hyphenate-after: value`	Specifies the minimum number of characters after the hyphenation character, where *value* is an *integer* or auto (CSS3)
`hyphenate-before: value`	Specifies the minimum number of characters before the hyphenation character, where *value* is an *integer* or auto (CSS3)
`hyphenate-character: string`	Specifies the hyphenation character, *string* (CSS3)
`hyphenate-line: value`	Specifies the maximum number of hyphenated lines, where *value* is an *integer* or no-limit (CSS3)
`hyphenate-resource: url(url)`	Provides an external resource at *url* that defines hyphenation points (CSS3)
`hyphens: type`	Defines the hyphenation property, where *type* is none, manual, or auto (CSS3)
`image-resolution: value`	Defines the image resolution, where *value* is normal, auto, or the dpi of the image (CSS3)
`marks: type`	Defines an editor's mark, where *type* is crop, cross, or none (CSS3)
`quotes: text1 text2`	Defines the text strings for the open quotes (*text1*) and the close quotes (*text2*)
`string-set: values`	Accepts a comma-separated list of named strings, where *values* is the list of text strings (CSS3)
`text-replace: string1 string2`	Replaces *string1* with *string2* in the element content (CSS3)
Display Styles	**Styles that control the display of the element's content**
`clip: rect(top, right, bottom, left)`	Defines what portion of the content is displayed, where *top*, *right*, *bottom*, and *left* are distances of the top, right, bottom, and left edges from the element's top-left corner; use a value of auto to allow the browser to determine the clipping region
`display: type`	Specifies the display type of the element, where *type* is one of the following: block, inline, inline-block, inherit, list-item, none, run-in, table, inline-table, table-caption, table-column, table-cell, table-column-group, table-header-group, table-footer-group, table-row, or table-row-group
`height: length`	Specifies the height of the element in one of the CSS units of length
`min-height: length`	Specifies the minimum height of the element
`min-width: length`	Specifies the minimum width of the element
`max-height: length`	Specifies the maximum height of the element
`max-width: length`	Specifies the maximum width of the element
`overflow: type`	Instructs the browser how to handle content that overflows the dimensions of the element, where *type* is auto, inherit, visible, hidden, or scroll

Attribute	Description
`overflow-style: type`	Specifies the preferred scrolling method for overflow content, where *type* is auto, marquee-line, or marquee-block (CSS3)
`overflow-x: type`	Instructs the browser how to handle content that overflows the element's width, where *type* is auto, inherit, visible, hidden, or scroll (IE only)
`overflow-y: type`	Instructs the browser on how to handle content that overflows the element's height, where *type* is auto, inherit, visible, hidden, or scroll (IE only)
`text-overflow: type`	Instructs the browser on how to handle text overflow, where *type* is clip (to hide the overflow text) or ellipsis (to display the ... text string) (IE only)
`visibility: type`	Defines the element's visibility, where *type* is hidden, visible, or inherit
`width: length`	Specifies the width of the element in one of the CSS units of length
Fonts and Text	**Styles that format the appearance of fonts and text**
`color: color`	Specifies the color of the element's foreground (usually the font color)
`direction: type`	Specifies the direction of the text flow, where *type* equals ltr, rtl, or inherit (CSS3)
`font: style variant weight size/line-height family`	Defines the appearance of the font, where *style* is the font's style, *variant* is the font variant, *weight* is the weight of the font, *size* is the size of the font, *line-height* is the height of the lines, and *family* is the font face; the only required attributes are *size* and *family*
`font-effect: type`	Controls the special effect applied to glyphs where *type* is none, emboss, engrave, or outline (CSS3)
`font-emphasize: emphasize position`	Sets the style of the font emphasis and decoration (CSS3)
`font-emphasize-position: position`	Sets the font emphasis position, where *position* is before or after (CSS3)
`font-emphasize-style: style`	Sets the emphasis style, where *style* is none, accent, dot, circle, or disc (CSS3)
`font-family: family`	Specifies the font face used to display text, where *family* is sans-serif, serif, fantasy, monospace, cursive, or the name of an installed font
`font-size: value`	Specifies the size of the font in one of the CSS units of length
`font-size-adjust: value`	Specifies the aspect *value* (which is the ratio of the font size to the font's ex unit height) (CSS3)
`font-smooth: type`	Specifies the type of font smoothing, where *type* is auto, never, always, or a specified size (CSS3)
`font-stretch: type`	Expands or contracts the font, where *type* is narrower, wider, ultra-condensed, extra-condensed, condensed, semi-condensed, normal, semi-expanded, extra-expanded, or ultra-expanded (CSS3)
`font-style: type`	Specifies a style applied to the font, where *type* is normal, italic, or oblique
`font-variant: type`	Specifies a variant of the font, where *type* is inherit, normal, or small-caps
`font-weight: value`	Defines the weight of the font, where *value* is 100, 200, 300, 400, 500, 600, 700, 800, 900, normal, lighter, bolder, or bold

Attribute	Description
`hanging-punctuation: type`	Determines whether a punctuation mark may be placed outside the text box, where *type* is none, start, end, or end-edge (CSS3)
`letter-spacing: value`	Specifies the space between letters, where *value* is a unit of length or the keyword "normal"
`line-height: value`	Specifies the height of the lines, where *value* is a unit of length or the keyword, "normal"
`punctuation-trim: type`	Determines whether or not a full-width punctuation character should be trimmed if it appears at the start or end of a line, where *type* is none, start, end, or adjacent (CSS3)
`text-align: type`	Specifies the horizontal alignment of text within the element, where *type* is inherit, left, right, center, or justify
`text-align-last: type`	Specifies how the last line of a block is aligned for fully justified text, where *type* is start, end, left, right, center, or justify (CSS3)
`text-decoration: type`	Specifies the decoration applied to the text, where *type* is blink, line-through, none, overline, or underline
`text-emphasis: type location`	Specifies the emphasis applied to the text, where *type* is none, accent, dot, circle, or disk and *location* is before or after (CSS3)
`text-indent: length`	Specifies the amount of indentation in the first line of the text, where *length* is a CSS unit of length
`text-justify: type`	Specifies the justification method applied to the text, where *type* is auto, inter-word, inter-ideograph, inter-cluster, distribute, kashida, or tibetan (CSS3)
`text-outline: value1 value2`	Specifies a text outline, where *value1* represents the outline thickness and *value2* represents the optional blur radius (CSS3)
`text-shadow: color x y blur`	Applies a shadow effect to the text, where *color* is the color of the shadow, *x* is the horizontal offset in pixels, *y* is the vertical offset in pixels, and *blur* is the size of the blur radius (optional); multiple shadows can be added with shadow effects separated by commas (CSS3)
`text-transform: type`	Defines a transformation applied to the text, where *type* is capitalize, lowercase, none, or uppercase
`text-wrap: type`	Specifies the type of text wrapping, where *type* is normal, unrestricted, none, or suppress (CSS3)
`unicode-bibi: type`	Allows text that flows left-to-right to be mixed with text that flows right-to-left, where *type* is normal, embed, bibi-override, or inherit (CSS3)
`vertical-align: type`	Specifies how to vertically align the text with the surrounding content, where *type* is baseline, middle, top, bottom, text-top, text-bottom, super, sub, or one of the CSS units of length
`white-space: type`	Specifies the handling of white space (blank spaces, tabs, and new lines), where *type* is inherit, normal, pre (to treat the text as preformatted text), or nowrap (to prevent line-wrapping)
`white-space-collapse: type`	Defines how white space inside the element is collapsed, where *type* is preserve, collapse, preserve-breaks, or discard (CSS3)
`word-break: type`	Controls line-breaks within words, where *type* is normal, keep-all, loose, break-strict, or break-all (CSS3)
`word-spacing: length`	Specifies the amount of space between words in the text, where *length* is either a CSS unit of length or the keyword "normal" to use normal word spacing

Attribute	Description
Layout	**Styles that define the layout of elements**
bottom: *y*	Defines the vertical offset of the element's bottom edge, where *y* is either a CSS unit of length or the keyword "auto" or "inherit"
clear: *type*	Places the element only after the specified margin is clear of floating elements, where *type* is inherit, none, left, right, or both
float: *type*	Floats the element on the specified margin with subsequent content wrapping around the element, where *type* is inherit, none, left, right, or both
float-offset: *horiz vert*	Pushes floated elements in the opposite direction of where they would have been, where *horiz* is the horizontal displacement and *vertical* is the vertical displacement (CSS3)
left: *x*	Defines the horizontal offset of the element's left edge, where *x* is either a CSS unit of length or the keyword "auto" or "inherit"
move-to: *type*	Causes the element to be removed from the page flow and reinserted at later point in the document, where *type* is normal, here, or an *id* value (CSS3)
position: *type*	Defines how the element is positioned on the page, where *type* is absolute, relative, fixed, static, and inherit
right: *x*	Defines the horizontal offset of the element's right edge, where *x* is either a CSS unit of length or the keyword "auto" or "inherit"
top: *y*	Defines the vertical offset of the element's top edge, where *y* is a CSS unit of length or the keyword "auto" or "inherit"
z-index: *value*	Defines how overlapping elements are stacked, where *value* is either the stacking number (elements with higher stacking numbers are placed on top) or the keyword "auto" to allow the browser to determine the stacking order
Lists	**Styles that format lists**
list-style: *type image position*	Defines the appearance of a list item, where *type* is the marker type, *image* is the URL of the location of an image file used for the marker, and *position* is the position of the marker
list-style-image: url(*url*)	Defines image used for the list marker, where *url* is the location of the image file
list-style-type: *type*	Defines the marker type used in the list, where *type* is disc, circle, square, decimal, decimal-leading-zero, lower-roman, upper-roman, lower-alpha, upper-alpha, or none
list-style-position: *type*	Defines the location of the list marker, where *type* is inside or outside
marker-offset: *length*	Defines the distance between the marker and the enclosing list box, where *length* is either a CSS unit of length or the keyword "auto" or "inherit" (CSS3)
Outlines	**Styles to create and format outlines**
outline: *color style width*	Creates an outline around the element content, where *color* is the color of the outline, *style* is the outline style, and *width* is the width of the outline
outline-color: *color*	Defines the color of the outline
outline-offset: *value*	Offsets the outline from the element border, where *value* is the length of the offset (CSS3)
outline-style: *type*	Defines the style of the outline, where *type* is dashed, dotted, double, groove, inset, none, outset, ridge, solid, or inherit

Attribute	Description
`outline-width: length`	Defines the width of the outline, where *length* is expressed in a CSS unit of length
Printing	**Styles for printed output**
`fit: type`	Indicates how to scale an element to fit on the page, where *type* is fill, hidden, meet, or slice (CSS3)
`fit-position: vertical horizontal`	Sets the position of the element in the page, where *vertical* is top, center, or bottom; *horizontal* is left or right; or either or both positions are auto, a *value*, or a *percentage* (CSS3)
`page: label`	Specifies the page design to apply, where *label* is a page design created with the @page rule
`page-break-after: type`	Defines how to control page breaks after the element, where *type* is avoid (to avoid page breaks), left (to insert a page break until a left page is displayed), right (to insert a page break until a right page is displayed), always (to always insert a page break), auto, or inherit
`page-break-before: type`	Defines how to control page breaks before the element, where *type* is avoid left, always, auto, or inherit
`page-break-inside: type`	Defines how to control page breaks within the element, where *type* is avoid, auto, or inherit
`marks: type`	Defines how to display crop marks, where *type* is crop, cross, none, or inherit
`size: width height orientation`	Defines the size of the page, where *width* and *height* are the width and the height of the page and *orientation* is the orientation of the page (portrait or landscape)
`orphans: value`	Defines how to handle orphaned text, where *value* is the number of lines that must appear within the element before a page break is inserted
`widows: value`	Defines how to handle widowed text, where *value* is the number of lines that must appear within the element after a page break is inserted
Special Effects	**Styles to create special visual effects**
`animation: name duration timing delay iteration direction`	Applies an animation with the specified *duration*, *timing*, *delay*, *iteration*, and *direction* (CSS3)
`animation-delay: time`	Specifies the animation delay *time* in milliseconds (CSS3)
`animation-direction: direction`	Specifies the animation direction, where *direction* is normal or alternate (CSS3)
`animation-duration: time`	Specifies the duration of the animation *time* in milliseconds (CSS3)
`animation-iteration-count: value`	Specifies the number of iterations in the animation (CSS3)
`animation-name: text`	Provides a name for the animation (CSS3)
`animation-play-state: type`	Specifies the playing state of the animation, where *type* is running or paused
`animation-timing-function: function`	Provides the timing function of the animation, where *function* is ease, linear, ease-in, ease-out, ease-in-out, cubic-Bezier, or a *number* (CSS3)
`backface-visibility: visible`	Specifies whether the back side of an element is visible during a transformation, where *visible* is hidden or visible (CSS3)

Attribute	Description
`filter: type parameters`	Applies transition and filter effects to elements, where *type* is the type of filter and *parameters* are parameter values specific to the filter (IE only)
`image-orientation: angle`	Rotates the image by the specified *angle* (CSS3)
`marquee-direction: direction`	Specifies the direction of a marquee, where *direction* is forward or reverse (CSS3)
`marquee-play-count: value`	Specifies how often to loop through the marquee (CSS3)
`marquee-speed: speed`	Specifies the speed of the marquee, where *speed* is slow, normal, or fast (CSS3)
`marquee-style: type`	Specifies the marquee style, where *type* scroll, slide, or alternate (CSS3)
`opacity: alpha`	Sets opacity of the element, ranging from 0 (transparent) to 1 (opaque) (CSS3)
`perspective: value`	Applies a perspective transformation to the element, where *value* is the perspective length (CSS3)
`perspective-origin: origin`	Establishes the origin of the perspective property, where *origin* is left, center, right, top, bottom, or a *position* value (CSS3)
`rotation: angle`	Rotates the element by *angle* (CSS3)
`rotation-point: position`	Sets the location of the rotation point for the element (CSS3)
`transform: function`	Applies a 2-D or a 3-D transformation, where *function* provides the transformation parameters (CSS3)
`transform-origin: position`	Establishes the origin of the transformation of an element, where *position* is the position within the element (CSS3)
`transform-style: type`	Defines how nested elements are rendered in 3-D space, where *type* is flat or preserve-3d (CSS3)
`transition: property duration timing delay`	Defines a timed transition of an element, where *property*, *duration*, *timing*, and *delay* define the appearance and timing of the transition (CSS3)
`transition-delay: time`	Sets the delay time of the transition in milliseconds (CSS3)
`transition-duration: time`	Sets the duration time of the transition in milliseconds (CSS3)
`transition-property: type`	Defines the name of the CSS property modified by the transition, where *type* is all or none (CSS3)
`transition-timing-function: type`	Sets the timing function of the transition, where *type* is ease, linear, ease-in, ease-out, ease-in-out, cubic-Bezier, or a *number* (CSS3)
Tables	**Styles to format the appearance of tables**
`border-collapse: type`	Determines whether table cell borders are separate or collapsed into a single border, where *type* is separate, collapse, or inherit
`border-spacing: length`	If separate borders are used for table cells, defines the distance between borders, where *length* is a CSS unit of length or inherit
`caption-side: type`	Defines the position of the caption element, where *type* is bottom, left, right, top, or inherit
`empty-cells: type`	If separate borders are used for table cells, defines whether to display borders for empty cells, where *type* is hide, show, or inherit
`table-layout: type`	Defines the algorithm used for the table layout, where *type* is auto (to define the layout once all table cells have been read), fixed (to define the layout after the first table row has been read), or inherit

APPENDIX **E**

Frames and Framesets

OBJECTIVES

- Understand how to create Web frames and inline frames
- Understand how to create framed Web sites
- Learn how to specify a frame source
- Format the appearance of a Web frame
- Direct hypertext links to a target frame
- Create an inline frame

This appendix provides an overview of the HTML elements and attributes used in creating framed Web sites. While frames are not as prevalent on the Web as they once were, you can still find legacy Web sites centered around the use of frames. Knowing how to create and edit framed content is an important part of the Web designer's toolbox.

STARTING DATA FILES

There are no starting Data Files needed for this appendix.

Working with Frames

Typically, as a Web site grows in size and complexity, each page is dedicated to a particular topic or group of topics: one page might contain a list of links, another page might display contact information for the company or organization, and another page might describe the business philosophy. As more pages are added to the site, the designer might want a way to display information from several pages at the same time.

One solution is to duplicate that information across the Web site, but this strategy presents problems. It requires a great deal of time and effort to repeat (or copy and paste) the same information over and over again. Also, each time a change is required, you need to repeat your edit for each page in the site—a process that could easily result in errors.

Such considerations contributed to the development of frames. A **frame** is a section of the browser window capable of displaying the content of an entire Web page. Figure E-1 shows an example of a browser window containing three frames. The frame on the left displays the content of a Web page containing a list of links; the frame on the right displays a second Web page showing the site's home page; the top frame displays the site's logo.

Figure E-1	Frame example

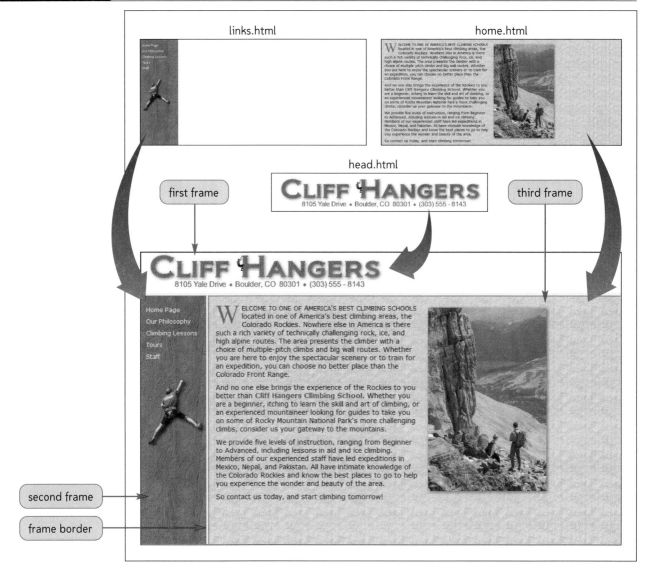

This example illustrates a common use of frames: displaying a list of links in one frame while showing individual pages from the site in another. Figure E-2 illustrates how a list of links can remain on the screen while the user navigates through the content of the site. Using this layout, a designer can easily update the list of links because it is stored on only one page rather than having to update the link list through every page in the Web site.

| Figure E-2 | Activating a link within a frame |

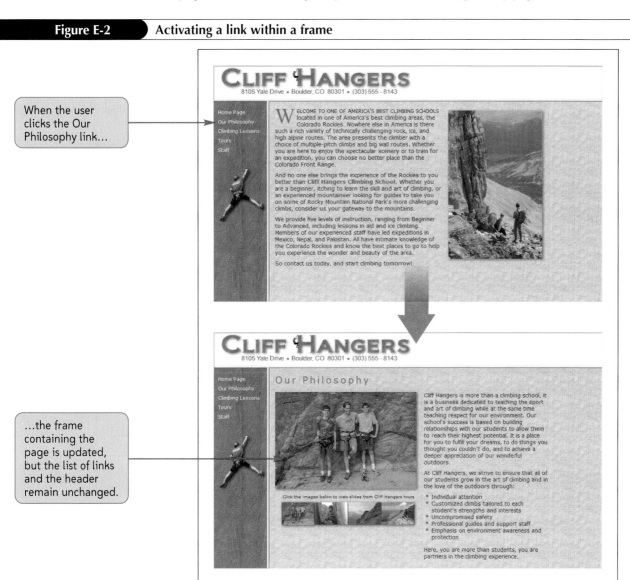

When the user clicks the Our Philosophy link...

...the frame containing the page is updated, but the list of links and the header remain unchanged.

Creating a Frameset

Within the browser window, frames are arranged in a **frameset**. The general syntax for creating a frameset is

```
<html>
<head>
<title>title</title>
</head>
<frameset>
    frames
</frameset>
</html>
```

where *frames* is the individual frames within the frameset. You'll explore how to create these frames shortly.

Note that the frameset element replaces the body element in this HTML document. Because this HTML file displays the content of other Web pages, it is not technically a Web page and, therefore, does not include a page body. A frameset is laid out in either rows or columns, but not both. Figure E-3 shows two framesets: one in which the frames are laid out in three columns and another in which they are placed in three rows.

| Figure E-3 | Frame layouts in rows and columns |

frames laid out in columns

The first frame | The second frame | The third frame

frames laid out in rows

The first frame

The second frame

The third frame

The syntax for defining the row or column frame layout is

```
<frameset rows="row1,row2,row3,..."> ... </frameset>
```

or

```
<frameset cols="column1,column2,column3,..."> ... </frameset>
```

where *row1*, *row2*, *row3*, and so on are the heights of the frame rows, and *column1*, *column2*, *column3*, and so on are the widths of the frame columns. There is no limit to the number of rows or columns you can specify for a frameset.

The row and column sizes can be specified in three ways: in pixels, as a percentage of the total size of the frameset, or by an asterisk (*). The asterisk instructs the browser to allocate any unclaimed space in the frameset to the given row or column. For example, the tag `<frameset rows="160,*">` creates two rows of frames. The first row has a height of 160 pixels, and the height of the second row is equal to whatever space remains in the browser window. You can also combine the three methods within a single frameset. The tag `<frameset cols="160,25%,*">` lays out the frames in the columns shown in Figure E-4. The first column is 160 pixels wide, the second column is 25% of the width of the display area, and the third column covers whatever space is left.

Figure E-4   **Sizing frames**

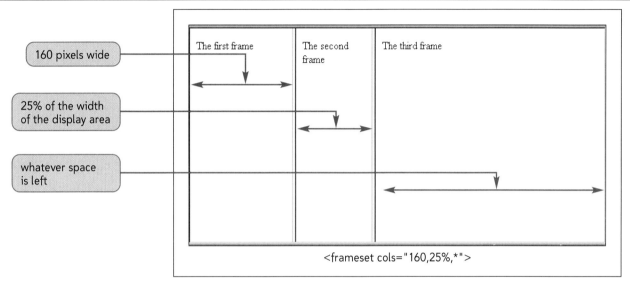

It is a good idea to specify at least one of the rows or columns of your frameset with an asterisk to ensure that the frames fill up the screen regardless of the size of the browser window. You can also use multiple asterisks, which cause browsers to allocate the remaining display space equally among the frames with no defined size. For example, the tag `<frameset rows="*,*,*">` creates three rows of frames of equal height.

A frameset places frames in either rows or columns, but not both. So, if you want to create a layout containing frames in rows and columns, you must nest one frameset within a frame in another frameset. When you use this technique, the interpretation of the rows and cols attributes changes slightly. For the nested frameset, a row height of 25% does not mean 25% of the browser window but rather 25% of the height of the frame in which that frameset has been placed.

Specifying a Frame Source

Frames are marked using the one-sided `<frame />` tag. Within the frame element, you use the `src` attribute to define which document that frame should display. The syntax is

```
<frame src="url" />
```

where `url` is the URL of the document. The following code creates three rows of frames displaying the documents *home.htm, main.htm,* and *footer.htm*:

```
<frameset rows="100, *, 100">
   <frame src="home.htm" />
   <frame src="main.htm" />
   <frame src="footer.htm" />
</frameset>
```

Note that `frame` elements can be placed only within a frameset.

Formatting Frames

You can control several attributes of your frames: the appearance of scroll bars, the size of the margin between the source document and the frame border, and whether or not users are allowed to change the frame size. By default, a scroll bar is displayed when the content of the source page does not fit within a frame. You can override this setting using the scrolling attribute. The syntax for this attribute is

```
scrolling="type"
```

where *type* can be either yes (to always display a scroll bar) or no (to never display a scroll bar). If you don't specify a setting for the scrolling attribute, the browser displays a scroll bar when necessary. When working with frames, keep in mind that you should remove scroll bars from a frame only when you are convinced that the entire Web page will be visible in the frame. To do this, you should view your Web page using several different monitor settings. Few things are more irritating to Web site visitors than to discover that some content is missing from a frame and no scroll bars are available to reveal the missing content.

When a user's browser retrieves a frame's Web page, it determines the amount of space between the content of the page and the frame border. Occasionally, the browser sets the margin between the border and the content too large. Generally, you want the margin to be big enough to keep the source's text or images from running into the frame's borders. However, you do not want the margin to take up too much space because you typically want to display as much of the source as possible. The attributes for specifying margin sizes for a frame are

```
marginheight="value" marginwidth="value"
```

where marginheight specifies the amount of space, in pixels, above and below the frame source, and marginwidth specifies the amount of space to the left and right of the frame source. You do not have to specify both the margin height and the margin width. However, if you specify only one, the browser assumes that you want to use the same value for both. Setting margin values is a process of trial and error as you determine what combination of margin sizes looks best. By default, users can resize frame borders in a browser by simply dragging a frame border. However, some Web designers prefer to freeze, or lock, frames so that users cannot resize them. The attribute for preventing frame resizing is

```
noresize="noresize"
```

Working with Frames and Links

Clicking a link within a frame opens the linked file inside the same frame; however, you can specify a different location by assigning a name to each frame and then pointing the link to one of the other named frames. To assign a name to a frame, add the name attribute to the frame element. The syntax for this attribute is

```
<frame src="url" name="name" />
```

where *name* is the name assigned to the frame. Case is important in assigning names: information is considered a different name than INFORMATION. Also, frame names cannot include spaces. To point the link to a specific frame, add the following attribute to the link tag:

```
target="name"
```

where *name* is the name you've assigned to a frame in your Web page. For example, you can name a frame main using the following code:

```
<frame src="home.htm" name="main" />
```

If you want a link's target to appear within the main frame, apply the target attribute as follows:

```
<a href="gloss.htm" target="main">Display the glossary</a>
```

In addition to frame names, you can also specify **reserved target names**, which cause a linked document to appear within a specific location in the browser. Figure E-5 lists the reserved target names supported by HTML.

Figure E-5 **Reserved target names**

Reserved Target Name	Function in a Frameset
_blank	Loads the target document into a new browser window
_self	Loads the target document into the frame containing the link
_parent	Loads the target document into the parent of the frame containing the link
_top	Loads the document into the full display area, replacing the current frame layout

For example, if you want a link target to appear in a new browser window, you could enter the following code:

```
<a href="gloss.htm" target="_blank">Display the glossary</a>
```

All reserved target names begin with the underscore character (_) to distinguish them from other target names. Note that reserved target names are case-sensitive, so you must enter them in lowercase.

Using the `noframes` Element

To make your Web site viewable with browsers that do not support frames (known as **frame-blind browsers**) as well as by those that do, you can use the `noframes` element to mark a section of your HTML file for code that browsers incapable of displaying frames can use. The `noframes` element is nested within the `frameset` element as follows, and it uses the syntax shown:

```
<html>
<head>
<title>title</title>
</head>
<frameset>
    frames
    <noframes>
        <body>
            page content
        </body>
    </noframes>
</frameset>
</html>
```

where *page content* is the content that you want the browser to display in place of the frames. A document can contain only one `noframes` element. When a browser that supports frames processes this code, it ignores everything within the `<noframes>` tag and concentrates solely on the code to create the frames. When a browser that doesn't support frames processes this HTML code, however, it doesn't know what to do with the `<frameset>` and `<noframes>` tags, so it ignores them. It does know how to render whatever appears within the `<body>` tags, though. Using this setup, both types of browsers are supported within a single HTML file. Note that when you use the `<noframes>` tag, you must enclose the page content within a `body` element.

Creating Inline Frames

Another way of using frames is to create a floating frame. Introduced by Internet Explorer 3.0 and added to the HTML 4.0 specifications, a **floating frame**, or **inline frame**, is displayed as a separate box or window within a Web page in much the same way as inline images are placed within a page. The syntax for creating an inline frame is

```
<iframe src="url">
   alternate content
</iframe>
```

where *url* is the URL of the document you want displayed in the inline frame, and *alternate content* is the content you want displayed by browsers that don't support inline frames. The following code displays the content of the *bio.htm* file within an inline frame; for browsers that don't support inline frames, it displays a paragraph containing a link to the file:

```
<iframe src="bio.htm">
   <p>
   View the online <a href="bio.htm">bio</a> of Jeff Bester
   </p>
</iframe>
```

Figure E-6 shows an example of how such an inline frame might be rendered by a Web browser.

Figure E-6	Example of an inline frame

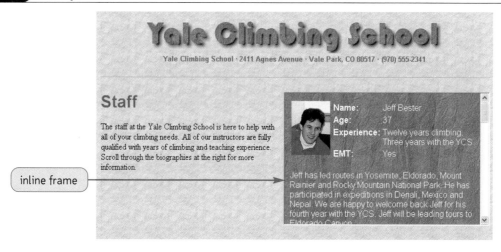

inline frame

Frame-based Web sites have drawbacks that have led many Web sites to discontinue their use. A browser that opens a framed site has to load multiple HTML files before the user can view any of them, resulting in increased waiting time for potential customers. It is also very difficult to bookmark pages within a frame-based Web site or to make their content available to Internet search engines that create content-based catalogs. (In other words, if you want your content to be easily found, don't use frames.) Some browsers also have difficulty printing the pages within individual frames, although this is less of a problem than it once was. Finally, some users simply prefer layouts where the entire browser window is devoted to a single page. For these reasons, many Web designers suggest that if you still want to use frames, you should create both framed and nonframed versions for a Web site and give users the option of which one to use.

GLOSSARY/INDEX

Note: Boldface entries include definitions.

Special Characters
\ (backslash), HTML 984
> (right angle bracket), HTML 783, HTML 810
! (exclamation point), HTML 13
(pound symbol), HTML 93
& (ampersand), HTML 848
* (asterisk), HTML 811, HTML 824, HTML 827
+ (plus sign), HTML 811, HTML 824
? (question mark), HTML 811, HTML 824
. (period), HTML 88, HTML 924
; semicolon, HTML 848

A

a element, HTML 45
    attributes, HTML 84–85

<a> tag An HTML tag used to mark hyperlinks to external documents or to locations within the current document. HTML 72, HTML 117
    interpreting in different versions of HTML, HTML 84

abbr element, HTML 45

absolute path A folder path that specifies a file's precise location within the entire folder structure of a computer. HTML 87
    element widths, HTML 295

absolute positioning A method of positioning that places objects a specified coordinates on the page. HTML 284–287

absolute unit A unit of measurement that is fixed in size regardless of the device rendering the Web page. HTML 174

access key A single key on the keyboard that, when typed in conjunction with the Alt or Control key, allows users to jump to a spot within a Web page. HTML 408

accessibility, HTML B1–B17
    checking for, HTML B17
    multimedia content, HTML 536
    navigation lists, HTML 81

Section 508 guidelines, HTML B3–B13
    WAI, HTML B13–B16

achromatopsia A form of color blindness resulting in the absence of any color sensitivity. HTML B4, HTML B5

active pseudo-class, HTML 201

ActiveX A Microsoft technology that can be used to play embedded media from within a variety of Windows programs. HTML 518–519
    classid attribute, HTML 518
    codebase attribute, HTML 519

adaptive technology Technology designed to make the Web more accessible to impaired users. HTML B2

add-on A stand-alone program run within Web browsers. HTML 475

address element An HTML element used to mark address or contact information. HTML 24, HTML 26, HTML 33–34

Adobe Device Central, HTML 610

Adobe Flash Player A video player that plays Flash Video files. HTML 510

aggregator. *See* feed reader

alert dialog box In JavaScript, a dialog box that displays a text message with an OK button. HTML 727

align attribute, HTML 351

aligning
    cell contents, with HTML, HTML 351
    vertical alignment in HTML, HTML 351–352

all A compositor that allows any of the child elements to appear in the instance document; each may appear only once, or not at all. HTML 892

Alpha filter, HTML 588

alternate content Content nested within the object element to be displayed by browsers that do not support Java. HTML 523

alternate text Text nested within an object to be displayed by browsers that cannot display the object. HTML 503

American Standard Code for Information Exchange (ASCII) A character set used for the alphabet of English characters. HTML 54

ampersand (&), entity references, HTML 848

amplitude A measure of the height of a sound wave that is related to the sound's volume. HTML 488

anchor An element marked with the <a> tag used to mark a specific location within the Web page. HTML 95

Android SDK, HTML 610

animation, Section 508 guidelines, HTML B10

anonymous simple type A simple type without a name. HTML 914

ANY content model The most general type of content model, which allows an element to store any type of content. HTML 820

Apple, Flash compatibility, HTML 511

applet. *See* Java applet

applet element, HTML 532

application
    XML. *See* XML vocabulary
    XML with, HTML 747

article element An HTML structural element used to mark articles or content about a specific area of interest. HTML 2

ASCII. *See* American Standard Code for Information Exchange

aside element An HTML structural element that marks extra or side content on the Web page. HTML 3

aspect ratio The width-to-height ratio of video frames. HTML 504

assistive technology. *See* adaptive technology

formatting tables with HTML attributes, HTML 346–352
  aligning cell contents, HTML 351
  borders, HTML 349–350
  cell padding, HTML 346–348
  cell spacing, HTML 346, HTML 347–348
  row heights, HTML 349
  table widths and heights, HTML 348–349
  vertical alignment, HTML 351–352

frame (video) A single image within a video file that is played in rapid succession with other frames to create the illusion of motion. HTML 504

frame (Web page) In HTML, a section of the browser window capable of displaying the content of an entire Web document. HTML E2–E8
  formatting, HTML E6
  frameset, HTML E3–E5
  inline (floating), HTML E8
  links, HTML E6–7
  noframes element, HTML E7
  specifying frame source, HTML E5

frame attribute, HTML 348–349

frame rate The speed at which one frame in a video is replaced by the next frame. HTML 504

frame site, Section 508 guidelines, HTML B10

frame-blind browser A Web browser incapable of displaying HTML frames. HTML E7

frameset A collection of HTML frames arranged within the browser window. HTML E3–5

frameset DTD, HTML 653

frequency A measure of the rate at which a sound wave moves that is related to the sound's pitch. HTML 488

FTP. *See* File Transfer Protocol

FTP client A program that communicates with an FTP server to exchange data files. HTML 115

FTP server A file server using the FTP protocol from which users can store and retrieve data files. HTML 114
  linking to, HTML 114–115

function, JavaScript. *See* JavaScript function

G

Garden of Eden design, HTML 951

general entity Entity that is declared in a DTD and can be referenced anywhere within the body of an XML document. HTML 848, HTML 850–857
  referencing, HTML 852–857

generic font A font name that describes the general appearance of a font. HTML 162

get method A method of submitting Web form data to a server by appending it to the end of the URL specified in the action attribute. HTML 400

global scope The type of scope that enables an object to be referenced throughout a schema document; applies to an object that is a direct child of the root schema element. HTML 717, HTML 942

global variable A variable with global scope. HTML 717

graphics, Section 508 guidelines, HTML B2–B4

grouping element HTML element that contains content that is viewed as a distinct block within the Web page. HTML 26–34
  grouping headings, HTML 29–30
  marking block quotes, HTML 32–34
  marking content headings, HTML 26–29
  marking paragraph elements, HTML 30–32

H

h2 element, HTML 24

hanging indent A negative text indentation in which the first line extends to the left of the text block. HTML 178

head element Element in an HTML document containing general information about the document. HTML 2, HTML 10–11
  adding comments, HTML 15
  marking, HTML 13–16

header element An HTML structural element that marks the introduction or header of the Web page. HTML 3

heading, tables, HTML 323–325

heading element Element used for marking page headings. HTML 26–29

hearing disability, HTML B1

height attribute, HTML 348–349

height property A CSS property that defines the height of an element. HTML 282, HTML 365–366

hexadecimal A number expressed in the base 16 numbering system. HTML 153
  color values, HTML 153–154

hgroup element An HTML element used to group page headings. HTML 25, HTML 29–30

hidden field, HTML 429

hidden input box, HTML 405

hierarchical structure A structure in which the home page links to pages dedicated to specific topics and those pages, in turn, can be linked to even more specific topic. HTML 76

hn element, HTML 26

home page A Web page that acts as a focal point for a Web site and is usually the first page that users see. HTML 75
  background, HTML 235–236

horizontal rule, HTML 51

host Device on a network that can be used to share information and services. HTML 4

hotspot A zone within an image map linked to a specific document. HTML 101, HTML 103–107

hover pseudo-class, HTML 201

HP webOS SDK, HTML 610

href The attribute in the <a> tag that contains the reference or address of the linked document. HTML 25, HTML 72

HSL model A color model in which colors are selected from a color wheel at varying levels of saturation and lightness. HTML 139, HTML 158–159

hsla value, HTML 159

HTML. *See* Hypertext Markup Language

HTML5 The latest version of HTML, which supplanted XHTML 2 as the future Web document language. HTML 6, HTML 7
  audio element, HTML 484, HTML 492–495
  audio formats, HTML 491–492

initial cap An effect in which the first letter of the first line of a text block appears larger than the surrounding text. HTML 193

inline element A text-level element in which the content is placed in line or alongside other element content. HTML 45–46, HTML 225

inline frame An HTML frame that displayed as a separate box or window within a Web document. HTML E8

inline image, HTML 52–54, HTML 101
    embedding, HTML 534

inline style A style created using the style attribute within an HTML file. HTML 149

inline validation A Web form validation process in which data errors are highlighted as they occur during data entry. HTML 442, HTML 466–470
    focus pseudo-class, HTML 466–468
    pseudo-classes for valid and invalid data, HTML 468–470

input box A Web form control used for entering text and numeric data. HTML B11, HTML 397, HTML 404–408
    types, HTML 404–405

input control, styles, HTML 413–414

input element A Web form control used to mark elements in which data can be entered. HTML 394

in-range pseudo-class, HTML 467

ins element, HTML 45

instance document An XML document to which a schema is applied; an instance document represents a specific instance of the rules defined in a schema. HTML 877
    applying namespaces, HTML 959–964, HTML 965
    applying schemas, HTML 901–904

interactive form element A form element that allows the user to enter or modify the element content. HTML B11

internal entity An entity whose content is found within the DTD. HTML 848

internal style sheet A style sheet built into a Web browser. HTML 7

internal subset, The part of the DOCTYPE that contains the rules and declarations of the DTD placed directly into the document. HTML 815, HTML 817–818

Internet The largest WAN in existence incorporating an almost uncountable number of networks and hosts involving computers, mobile phones, PDAs, MP3 players, gaming systems, and television stations. HTML 4

Internet Explorer
    conditional comments, HTML 533
    filters. *See* Internet Explorer filter

Internet Explorer filter, HTML 558–561
    combining, HTML 561
    DropShadow filter, HTML 559–560
    Shadow filter, HTML 559–560

Internet service provider (ISP) A company that provides Internet access and usually space on a Web server. HTML 60

interpreted language A programming language in which the code is executed directly without compiling. HTML 692

invalid pseudo-class, HTML 467, HTML 468–470

invalid pseudo-element A CSS pseudo-element that selects a form control storing an invalid data value. HTML 442

iPad Emulator, HTML 610

iPhone SDK, HTML 610

iPhoney, HTML 610

ISO 8859-1 (Latin-1) A character set character set that supports 255 characters and can be used by most languages that employ the Latin alphabet, including English, French, Spanish, and Italian. HTML 54

ISO/IEC character set An international numbering system for referencing characters from virtually any language. HTML 780

ISP. *See* Internet service provider

iTunes Podcast, HTML 971

J

Java A programming language used for applications on the Internet. HTML 524
    JavaScript compared, HTML 693

Java applet A program embedded within a Web page, written in the Java programming language. HTML 522–535, HTML 692
    embedding, HTML 525–526
    embedding applet element, HTML 532
    embedding HTML files, HTML 534–535
    inserting inline images, HTML 534
    inserting parameters, HTML 526–532
    Section 508 guidelines, HTML B10–B11

Java Virtual Machine A software program that runs a class file and returns the results to the user's computer. HTML 524

JavaScript A client-side programing language used on the Web. HTML 43, HTML 692–730
    accessing external JavaScript files, HTML 717–722
    commenting code, HTML 722–724
    debugging programs. *See* debugging
    development, HTML 692–693
    Java compared, HTML 693
    writing better code, HTML 706
    XML parsers, HTML 695

JavaScript function, HTML 708–717
    calling, HTML 711–716
    to return a value, HTML 716–717
    variable scope, HTML 717

JavaScript library, form controls, HTML 453

K

kbd element, HTML 45

kerning The space between letters. HTML 163, HTML 176–177

L

label Text associated with an input control on a Web form. HTML B11
    fields, HTML 408–411
    styles, HTML 413

label element An HTML element that marks a text description for a Web form control. HTML 395

LAN. *See* local area network

landscape orientation, mobile style sheet, HTML 624–626

lang pseudo-class, HTML 203

last-child pseudo-class, HTML 203

last-of-type pseudo-class, HTML 203

Latin-I. *See* ISO 8859-1

layout
    lists, HTML 198–200
    pages. *See* page layout
    tables. *See* table layout

layout viewport A mobile device viewport that displays, virtually, the entire content of the Web page. HTML 610

leading The height of a text line. HTML 163, HTML 178

legend, field sets, HTML 403–404

legend element An HTML element that marks a legend for a Web form field set. HTML 394

lexical space The set of textual representations of a value space. HTML 915

li element An HTML element used to mark a list item within an ordered or unordered list. HTML 24, HTML 26

lightness The brightness of a color ranging from 0% (black) up to 100% (white). HTML 158

line break, HTML 49–51

linear gradient A color gradient in which the color blending occurs in a straight line across an object's background. HTML 567–570

linear structure A structure in which each page is linked with the pages that follow and precede it. HTML 75

linear-gradient() function A CSS function that creates a background color consisting of two or more colors blending into one another. HTML 549

linearizing A process used to make Web tables accessible to visually impaired users. HTML B7–B8

link
    Flash, HTML 515–516
    frames, HTML E6–E7
    hypertext. *See* hypertext link
    Section 508 guidelines, HTML B12

link element An HTML element that links the document to an external style sheet file. HTML 25, HTML 121

link pseudo-class, HTML 201

liquid layout. *See* fluid layout

list, HTML 34–40
    description, HTML 38–40
    designing, HTML 195
    nesting, HTML 37–38
    ordered, HTML 35–36
    unordered, HTML 36–37

list data type A derived data type consisting of a list of values separated by white space in which each item in the list is derived from an established data type. HTML 916

list style, HTML 194–200
    changing list layout, HTML 198–200
    choosing, HTML 194–196
    images as list markers, HTML 196–197

load-time error A programming error that occurs when a script is first loaded by a browser. HTML 724–725

local area network (LAN) A network confined to a small geographic area, such as within a building or department. HTML 4

local name The part of a qualified name that identifies the element or attribute within its namespace. Also called local part. HTML 952

local namespace The namespace used for elements and attributes that don't belong to the default namespace; indicated by a namespace prefix. HTML 660

local part. *See* local name

local scope A condition in which a variable can be referenced only within the function in which it was created or which limits an object to being referenced only within the object in which it is defined. HTML 717, HTML 943

local variable A variable with local scope. HTML 717

logical error A programming error that is free of syntax and structural errors but results in incorrect answers. HTML 725–726

M

manual column break, HTML 376

margin The space that separates an element from other elements on the page. HTML 222
    setting in box model, HTML 254
    styles, HTML 252–255

margin property The CSS property used to set the margin space around an element. HTML 250

mark element, HTML 45

markup language A language that describes the content and structure of a document by identifying, or tagging, different elements in the document. HTML 5

Mathematical Markup Language (MathML), HTML 752, HTML 971

MathML. *See* Mathematical Markup Language

max attribute An attribute that specifies the maximum value of a Web form spin box or range slider. HTML 448

media attribute An attribute that specifies the device(s) associated with a style sheet. HTML 613–615

media device, HTML 588–595
    @import rule, HTML 589–590
    media groups, HTML 590–595
    @media rule, HTML 589–590

media group A CSS category that describes how different media devices render content; the four media groups are continuous or paged; visual, audio, or tactile; grid or bitmap; and interactive or static. HTML 590–595

@media *media* rule, HTML 189

media query An HTML5 and CSS3 statement that specifies the media device for a style sheet as well as the properties of that device. HTML 606, HTML 613–618
    choosing, HTML 616–618
    feature expressions, HTML 615–616
    media attribute, HTML 613–615

@media rule, HTML 589–590

member data type One of the base data types in a union data type. HTML 916

meta element, HTML 58–59, HTML 121–123, HTML 612–613
    reloading a Web page, HTML 124

metadata Information within a Web page that contains information about the Web site itself. HTML 121–124
> meta element, HTML 121–123
> reloading a Web page, HTML 124

method In JavaScript, an action that manipulates or acts upon an object. HTML 696–697

MIDI. *See* Musical Instrument Digital Interface

MIME type. *See* Multipurpose Internal Mail Extensions type

min attribute An attribute that specifies the minimum value of a Web form spin box or range slider. HTML 448

mixed content An element that contains both parsed character data and child elements. HTML 827, HTML 896

mixed structure, HTML 76–78

MML. *See* Music Markup Language

mobile device, XML with, HTML 748–749

mobile style sheet, HTML 619–627
> landscape orientation, HTML 624–626
> portrait orientation, HTML 621–623

mobile Web, HTML 606–627
> configuring the viewport, HTML 610–613
> designing for, HTML 608–609
> media queries. *See* media query
> optimizing sites for, HTML 626
> style sheet. *See* mobile style sheet
> testing mobile designs, HTML 609–610

MobiOne Studio, HTML 610

Modernizr A free, open-source, MIT-licensed JavaScript library of functions that provides support for many HTML5 elements and for the newest CSS styles. HTML 43–44

modifying symbol A symbol that specifies the number of occurrences of a child element; there are three modifying symbols: the question mark (?), the plus sign (+), and the asterisk (*). HTML 811, HTML 824–826, HTML 827

modular code Code created using a programming technique in which the code is broken

nto smaller, more manageable chunks. HTML 727

module Separate chunk of a DTD that is joined using parameter entities. HTML 857

month data type, HTML 444

motor disability, HTML B1

MP3 format, HTML 491, HTML 497

MP4 format, HTML 505

multimedia, Section 508 guidelines, HTML B4

multimedia Web site, HTML 483–536
> accessibility, HTML 536
> applets. *See* Java applet
> bandwidth, HTML 487
> digital audio. *See* digital audio
> digital video. *See* digital video; Flash Video file
> plug-ins, HTML 487

multiple attribute In a Web form selection list, an attribute that allows a user to make multiple selections. HTML 420

Multipurpose Internal Mail Extensions (MIME) type A data type that identifies the format of the information contained within a file and provides instructions about how it should be interpreted. HTML 497–498

Music Markup Language (MML), HTML 752

Musical Instrument Digital Interface (MIDI) A popular music format that synthesizes musical sounds through the use of mathematical functions that describe the pitch, length, and volume of each note. HTML 492, HTML 497

N

n regular expression quantifier, HTML 925

n, regular expression quantifier, HTML 925

name, qualified and unqualified, HTML 952, HTML 962

name attribute A Web form control attribute that provides the name of the data field. HTML 95, HTML 394

name collision A duplication of element names within the same document, which occurs when the same element name from

different XML vocabularies is used within a compound document. HTML 952, HTML 958

named attribute group A collection, or group, of attributes that is assigned a name to facilitate repeated use within a schema. HTML 915

named model group A collection, or group, of elements that is assigned a name to facilitate repeated use within a schema. HTML 915

namespace The memory space that contains each element or attribute from a particular XML vocabulary. HTML 658, HTML 767, HTML 959–971
> adding to a style sheet, HTML 976–985
> applying to elements, HTML 961–963
> associating with schemas, HTML 965–971
> attributes, HTML 963–964
> deciding whether to use, HTML 971
> declaring, HTML 793, HTML 794
> declaring and applying to a document, HTML 959–960
> declaring in style sheets, HTML 978–980
> default. *See* default namespace
> defining with escape character, HTML 984
> including and importing schemas, HTML 968–969
> local, HTML 660
> reconciling with DTDs, HTML 846
> referencing objects from other schemas, HTML 969–970
> setting, HTML 658–660
> targeting, HTML 965–967

namespace declaration A statement in an XML document that indicates the default language used in the document. HTML 16

namespace prefix The part of a qualified name that identifies the namespace vocabulary the element is associated with. HTML 952

@namespace *prefix* rule, HTML 189

nav element The HTML element used to mark navigation lists. HTML 72

navigation list A list containing links to the main topical areas of the Web site. HTML 79–81
> accessibility, HTML 81

nested A element which is enclosed within another element. HTML 8, HTML 769–770
defining elements containing nested elements and attributes, HTML 893–895
defining elements with nested children, HTML 891–893
nesting lists, HTML 37–38

network A structure that allows devices known as nodes or hosts to be linked together to share information and services. HTML 4
locating information, HTML 4

n, m regular expression quantifier, HTML 925

NMTOKEN A data type used with character data whose values must meet almost all the qualifications for valid XML names. Also called name token. HTML 838–839

node Device on a network that can be used to share information and services. HTML 4

noframes element, HTML E7

notation An enumerated type that associates the value of an attribute with a <!NOTATION> declaration that is inserted elsewhere in the DTD. HTML 836, HTML 861

not(s) pseudo-class, HTML 203

nth-last-of-type pseudo-class, HTML 203

nth-of-type pseudo-class, HTML 203

null value A data type for variables in which no value has been assigned. HTML 703

number data type An attribute value used with the input element to create a spin box. HTML 442, HTML 444, HTML 447–450

numeric character reference The numeric value of a character symbol. HTML 55, HTML 767, HTML 779–782

numeric data type, HTML 910–911

numeric value In JavaScript, any number that can be stored within a variable. HTML 703

O

object In JavaScript, any item from the browser window itself to a document displayed in the browser to an element displayed in the document. HTML 696

object element An HTML element used to embed objects within Web pages. HTML 503, HTML 509–510, HTML 518–519, HTML 523

Ogg Theora format, HTML 505

Ogg Vorbis format, HTML 491, HTML 497

ol element An HTML element used to mark an ordered list. HTML 26

OMF. *See* Weather Observation Definition Format

one-sided tag A tag used with an empty element. HTML 3, HTML 9

only-child pseudo-class, HTML 203

only-of-type pseudo-class, HTML 203

opacity value, CSS3, HTML 159

opening secondary windows or tabs, HTML 117–119

opening tag A tag that marks that beginning of a two-sided tag. HTML 8

Opera Mini Simulator, HTML 610

option button A Web form control used for selecting a single option from a predefined list of options. HTML 397, HTML 429–434

option element An HTML element that marks an option from a selection list. HTML 421

option text The text associated with a selection list option. HTML 421

optional pseudo-class, HTML 467

ordered list A list in which the items follow a sequential order. HTML 35–36

orphan The beginning lines of a page element when they appear at the bottom of a printed page. HTML 599–603

outline property The CSS property used to create an outline around an element. HTML 250

outline style, HTML 271–273

out-of-range pseudo-class, HTML 467

overflow, HTML 296–300
horizontal, HTML 299

overflow property A CSS property that defines how browsers should handle content that exceeds an element's allotted height and width. HTML 282

overflow-x property, HTML 296

overflow-y property, HTML 296

P

p element An HTML element used to mark a paragraph. HTML 24, HTML 26

padding box In the CSS box model, the box that contains the space around the content box. HTML 222

padding property The CSS property that sets the padding space around element content. HTML 251

padding space, HTML 255–262
setting in box model, HTML 254

page box A CSS model of printed page content; the content of a document is contained within the page area and surrounded by the margin area, which contains the space between the printed content and the page edges. HTML 595–596

page break, HTML 598–604
automatic, HTML 600
preventing, HTML 599
setting, HTML 601
widows and orphans, HTML 599–603

page content, generating, HTML 207

page height, HTML 240–241

page layout, HTML 237–242
fixed, HTML 239–240
fluid (liquid), HTML 239–240
managing, HTML 270–280
page width and height, HTML 240–241
tables for, HTML 341

@page *location* rule, HTML 189, HTML 597–598

page name A named style for printed pages other than the first, left, or right pages. HTML 596

page property, HTML 596

page pseudo-class, HTML 596

protocol A set of rules defining how information is passed between two devices. HTML 109

pseudo-class A classification of an element based on its current status, position, or use in the document. HTML 200–204
  inline validation, HTML 466–470
  structural, HTML 203–204

pseudo-element An element that does not exist in the document hierarchy, but rather is based on objects that exist in the rendered Web page. HTML 204–209

public identifier An identifier that specifies a name for the DTD file, which includes the owner or author of the DTD and the language used to write the DTD. Also called formal public identifier. HTML 816–817

publishing a Web page, HTML 60

pull-down menu A menu whose contents are unrolled vertically when the user clicks or activates the menu heading. HTML B11

push button A form button that can be clicked by the user. HTML B11

Q

q element, HTML 45

qualified name (qname) An element name consisting of a namespace prefix and the local name. HTML 952, HTML 962

quantifier Within a regular expression, a character or string that specifies the number of occurrences for a particular character or group of characters. HTML 925

question mark (?)
  modifying symbol, HTML 811, HTML 824
  regular expression quantifier, HTML 925

quirks mode Mode in which the browser renders the Web page in accordance with practices followed in the 1990's. HTML 11

R

radial gradient A gradient in which color blending starts from a single point within an object and proceeds outward in a circular or elliptical shape. HTML 570–571

radio button. See option button

radio data type An attribute value used with the input element to create a Web form option button control. HTML 421

radio input box, HTML 405

range data type An attribute value used with the input element to create a range slider. HTML 443, HTML 444, HTML 450–453

range slider, HTML 448

RealAudio format One of the first audio formats that allowed for streaming over low- to high-bandwidth connections. HTML 492, HTML 497

Really Simple Syndication (RSS) The language used for distributing news articles and any content that changes on a regular basis. HTML 751–752

regex. See regular expression

regular expression A concise description of a character pattern used in data validation. HTML 464–466
  deriving data types using, HTML 923–928

Regular Language description for XML (RELAX), HTML 881

Regular Language for XML Next Generation (RELAX NG), HTML 881

relative path A folder path that specifies a file's location in relation to the location of the current document. HTML 87–88

relative positioning A method of positioning that places elements relative to where the browser would have placed them by default. HTML 287–289

relative unit A unit of measurement that is expressed relative to the sizes of other objects within the Web page. HTML 174

RELAX. See Regular Language description for XML

RELAX NG. See Regular Language for XML Next Generation

reloading a Web page, HTML 124

#REQUIRED The attribute default value that indicates that an attribute is required. HTML 829, HTML 839, HTML 840

required data type A data type for a field in a Web form that indicates that a value is required for the field, and that the form will be rejected without it. HTML 442

required element, indicating, HTML 896–897

required field A Web form field that requires that a user specify a value before submitting the form. HTML 397

required pseudo-class, HTML 467

reserved target name An HTML attribute value that causes linked documents to be displayed within a specific location in the browser window. HTML E7

reset button A Web form button that resets the form, changing all field values to their default values, when clicked. HTML 457–459

reset data type An attribute value used with the input element to create a Web form reset button. HTML 443

reset input box, HTML 405

reset style sheet A style sheet that removes many of the browser-specific style rules. HTML 227–229

resolution The size of the output device, typically expressed in pixels. HTML 175

restricted data type A type of derived data type in which a restriction is placed on the facets of a preexisting data type. HTML 907, HTML 917–923

RGB model A color model in which colors are defined by varying intensities of red, blue, and green. HTML 139

RGB triplet A set of numbers representing intensities of red, green, and blue. HTML 153

rgba value, HTML 159

rhythm A design principle based on the repetition or alternating of elements in order to provide a sense of movement, flow, and progress. HTML 296

right angle bracket (>)
  character data, HTML 783
  DOCTYPEs, HTML 810

rollover, hypertext, HTML 201

Uniform Resource Name A URI that provides a persistent name for a resource, independent of that resource's location. HTML 767

union data type A derived data type based on the value and/or lexical spaces from two or more preexisting data types. HTML 916–917

unity A design principle based on combining different design elements into a cohesive whole. HTML 296

unordered list A list in which the items do not follow a sequential order. HTML 36–37

unparsed character data (CDATA) Text that is not processed by a browser or parser. HTML 675–676
    cans and cannots, HTML 787
    creating a CDATA section, HTML 784–788

unparsed entity An entity that references content that either is nontextual or cannot be interpreted by an XML parser. HTML 850, HTML 861–863

unqualified name An element name without a namespace prefix. HTML 952, HTML 962

URL. See Uniform Resource Locator

url data type, HTML 444, HTML 445

user-defined style, HTML 145

user-derived data type A data type defined by a schema's author. HTML 906

UTF-8 The commonly used character set on the Web stored as a compressed version of Unicode. HTML 54

V

valid document A well-formed XML document that also obeys the features for the XML vocabulary it uses. HTML 652–658, HTML 745, HTML 753
    creating, HTML 812–819
    declaring DTDs, HTML 815–818
    validating documents, HTML 841–846
    writing DTDs, HTML 818–819

valid pseudo-class, HTML 467, HTML 468–470

valid pseudo-element A CSS pseudo-element that selects a form control storing a valid data value. HTML 442

validating an XHTML document, HTML 664–677
    embedded style sheets, HTML 6750676
    XHTML strict, HTML 670–675
    XHTML transitional, HTML 666–670

validation The process by which the field values from a Web form are tested before they can be used. HTML 460–466
    based on data type, HTML 463–464
    with built-in data types, HTML 908–914
    client-side, HTML 460
    compound XML documents, HTML 964
    forms, constraining facets vs. HTML 918
    indicating required values, HTML 461–463
    inline. See inline validation
    schema documents, HTML 899–900
    server-side, HTML 460
    standard vocabularies, HTML 863–864
    testing for valid patterns, HTML 464–466
    XHTML documents. See validating an XHTML document

validator Program that examines document code to ensure that it meets all the syntax requirements of the specified language. HTML 11

valign attribute, HTML 351–352

value attribute A Web form control attribute that provides the default value of a data field. HTML 421

value space The set of values that correspond to a data type. HTML 915

var element, HTML 45

var keyword A JavaScript keyword used to declare a variable. HTML 686, HTML 700

variable A named item in a program that stores a value or an object. HTML 700–705
    assigning values, HTML 701–702
    data types, HTML 703–705
    declaring, HTML 700–701, HTML 702
    global, HTML 717
    local, HTML 717

vendor extension Extension to the CSS language created and supported by specific browser manufacturers. HTML 236–237

Venetian Blind design A schema design that creates named types and references those types within a single global element. HTML 943, HTML 948–951, HTML 950

vertical-align property, HTML 366–367

video, digital. See digital video; Flash Video file

video bit rate The amount of data in a video that has to be processed by a video player each second. HTML 504

video element An HTML5 element used for displaying a movie clip within the Web page body. HTML 506–509

viewport The window in which the contents of a Web page are displayed. HTML 606, HTML 610
    configuring, HTML 610–613
    layout, HTML 610
    meta element, HTML 612–613
    visual, HTML 610

viewport meta tag A meta tag that sets the size of the viewport on a mobile device. HTML 606

visited pseudo-class, HTML 201

visual disability, HTML B1

visual effect, HTML 578

visual viewport The Web content that appears on the screen of a mobile device. HTML 610

VoiceML, HTML 971

W

\W character type, HTML 924

\w character type, HTML 924

WAI. See Web Accessibility Initiative

WAN. See wide area network

watermark A semi-transparent background image resembling a printer's logo woven into the fabric of specialized paper. HTML 231

WAV format, HTML 491, HTML 497

W3C. See World Wide Web Consortium